COLLINS
COMPLETE
DO·IT·YOURSELF
MANUAL

COLLINS

COMPLETE

DO·IT·YOURSELF

MANUAL

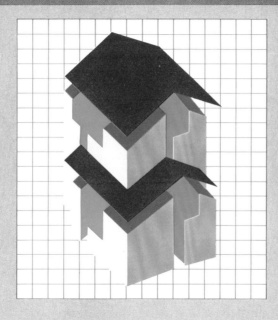

ALBERT JACKSON · DAVID DAY

**GUILD PUBLISHING
LONDON**

This edition published 1987
by Book Club Associates
by arrangement with
William Collins Sons & Co. Ltd.

**Collins Complete
Do It Yourself Manual**
was created exclusively for
William Collins Sons & Co. Ltd.
by Jackson Day Jennings Ltd.

Conceived, edited and designed
by Jackson Day Jennings Ltd.
trading as Inklink.

**Design, art direction
and project management**
Simon Jennings

Text
Albert Jackson
David Day

**Text
and editorial direction**
Albert Jackson

Illustrations editor
David Day

**Designer
and production assistant**
Alan Marshall

Illustrators
David Day
Robin Harris

Additional illustrations
Brian Craker
Michael Parr
Brian Sayers

Text editors
Sonya Mills
Ernest Roth
Geraldine Christy

Photographers
Paul Chave
Peter Higgins
Simon Jennings
Albert Jackson

Picture researchers
Anne-Marie Ehrlich
Hugh Olliff

Indexer
Jill Ford

For Collins
Executive editor
Robin Wood

Copyright © 1986
William Collins Sons & Co. Ltd.

Please note
*Great care has been taken to
ensure that the information
contained in COLLINS
COMPLETE DO IT YOURSELF
MANUAL is accurate. However,
the law concerning Building
Regulations, planning, local
by-laws and related matters is
neither static nor simple. A book of
this nature cannot replace
specialist advice in appropriate
cases and therefore no
responsibility can be accepted by
the publishers or by the authors for
any loss or damage caused by
reliance upon the accuracy of such
information.*

Colour origination
by Bright Arts (HK) Ltd, Hong Kong
Swaingrove Ltd, Bury St Edmunds

Photosetting
by FCS Ltd, London

**Printed and bound
in Great Britain**
by William Collins Sons & Co. Ltd, Glasgow

HOW TO USE THIS BOOK

The home improver of today enjoys the benefits of a highly sophisticated market that recognizes the way 'do it yourself' has developed over the years. He or she has become used to a ready supply of well-designed products and materials that are easy to use and produce first-class results which many a professional would be proud of. Any work of reference for this generation of home improvers must reflect the same high standards in its presentation, depth of information and simplicity of use. No-one reads a book of this kind from start to finish like a novel in the hope of absorbing all the information in one go. Instead, every reader wants to refer to his or her particular interest or problem without having to extract it from page after page of continuous text. This book has been written and designed to make the location of specific information as easy as possible by dividing the subject matter into clearly defined, colour-coded chapters for easy reference. Every chapter has its own contents list so that you can find the pages you are looking for, and every page is divided by specially designed features into digestible sections. The book has a detailed index, but to guide you from chapter to chapter, each page has a list of cross-references to refer you to other information related to the task in hand.

Running heads
As a guide to the number of pages devoted to a particular subject, a running head identifies the broad outline of subject matter to be found on each page.

Tinted boxes
Tinted boxes are used to separate certain information from the main text. Your attention is drawn to special safety precautions by red-tinted boxes.

Numbers in text
A bold number in the text draws your attention to a particular illustration which will help to clarify the instructions at that point.

Headings
The main text is divided into sections by clearly identifiable headings so that you can locate specific information or a single stage in the work. It is a useful feature when you want to refresh your memory without having to reread the whole page.

Colour coding
Colour-coded bands and margin tabs designate the extent of each chapter for easy identification.

Cross-references
There are few DIY projects that do not require a combination of skills. Decorating a single room, for instance, might also involve modifying the plumbing or electrical wiring, installing ventilation or insulation, repairing the structure of the building and so on. As a result, you might have to refer to more than one section of this book. To help you locate the relevant sections, a symbol (▷) in the text refers you to a list of cross-references in the page margin. Those references printed in bold type are directly related to the task in hand. Other references which will broaden your understanding of the subject are printed in light-weight type.

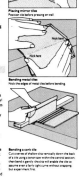

APPLICATION
TILING

CUTTING CERAMIC TILES

Having finished the main field of tiles you will have to cut the ceramic tiles to fill the border and to fit around obstructions such as window frames,

electrical fittings, pipes and the basin. Making straight cuts is easy using a purpose-made cutter but shaping tiles to fit curves takes practice.

SEE ALSO
Details for:
Slipstone
Preparing plaster
Ceramic tiles
Tiling tools

Cutting thin strips
A cutting jig is the most accurate way to cut a thin strip cleanly from the edge of a tile. If you do not want to use the strip itself, nibble away the waste a little at a time with pincers or special tile nibblers.

Tile cutting jig
A worthwhile investment if you're cutting a lot of tiles, a proprietary jig incorporates a device for measuring and scoring tiles. The cutter is drawn down the channel of the adjustable guide. The tile is snapped with a special pincer-action tool.

Tiling around a window
Tile up to the edges of a window, then stick RE tiles to the reveal so that they lap the edges of surrounding tiles. Fill in behind the edging tiles with cut tiles.

Cutting a curve
To fit a tile against a curved shape, cut a template from thin card to the exact size of a tile. Cut fingers along one edge and press them against the curve to reproduce the shape. Transfer the curve onto the face of the tile and score the line freehand. Nibble away the waste a little at a time using pincers or a tile nibbler and smooth the edge with a slipstone.

Cutting thin strips (illustration captions)
Cutting thin strips

Two edges
Make two edges
Cut and fit tile

Fitting around a pipe
Mark the centre of the pipe on the top and side edges of tile and draw lines across the tile from these points. Where they cross, draw round a coin or something slightly larger than the diameter of the pipe.
Make one straight cut through the centre of the circle and either nibble out the waste, having scored the curve, or clamp it in a vice, protected with softening, and cut it out with a saw file – a thin rod coated with hard, abrasive particles which will cut in any direction. Stick one half of the tile on each side of the pipe.

Fitting around a socket or switch
In order to fit around a socket or switch you may have to cut the corner out of a tile. Mark it from the socket then clamp the tile in a vice, protected with softening. Score then use a saw file to make one diagonal cut from the corner of the tile to where the lines meet. Snap out both triangles.
If you have to cut a notch out of a large tile, cut down both sides with a hacksaw then score between them and snap the piece out of the middle.

CUTTING BORDER TILES

It's necessary to cut border tiles one at a time to fit the gap between the field tiles and the adjacent wall: walls are rarely truly square and the margin is bound to be uneven.

Making straight cuts
Mark a border tile by placing it face down over its neighbour with one edge against the adjacent wall **[1]**. Make an allowance for normal spacing between the tiles. Transfer the marks to the edge of the tiles using a felt-tip pen.
Use a proprietary tile cutter held against a straightedge to score across the face with one firm stroke to cut through the glaze **[2]**. You may have to score the edge of thick tiles.
Stretch a length of thin wire across a panel of chipboard, place the scored line directly over the wire and press down on both sides to snap the tile **[3]**.
Alternatively use a tile cutter, which has a wheel to score the tile and jaws to snap it along the line. If you're doing a lot of tiling, invest in a purpose-made jig. The jig will hold the tile square with a cutting edge; pressing down on the guide snaps the tile cleanly. Some jigs include a device for measuring border tiles, too.
Smooth the cut edges of the tile with a tile sander or small slipstone (◁).

1 Mark the edge tile

2 Score the marked line

3 Snap the tile over a wire

104

HANGING OTHER WALL TILES

Mosaic tiles
Ceramic mosaic tiles are applied to a wall in a similar way to large square tiles. Set out the wall (▷) and use the same adhesive and grout.
The mesh backing on some sheets is pressed into the adhesive. The facing paper on other sheets is left intact on the surface until the adhesive sets.
Fill the main area of the wall, spacing the sheets to equal the gaps between individual tiles. Place a carpet-covered board over the sheets and tap it with a mallet to bed the tiles into the adhesive.
Fill borders by cutting strips from the sheet. Cut individual tiles to fit into awkward shapes and around fittings. If necessary, soak off the facing paper with a damp sponge and grout the tiles (▷).

Mirror tiles
Set out the wall with battens (▷) but avoid using mirror tiles in an area which would entail complicated fitting, as it is difficult to cut glass except in straight lines. Mirror tiles are fixed, close-butted, with self-adhesive pads. No grout is necessary.
Peel the protective paper from the pads and lightly position each tile. Check its alignment with a spirit level then press it firmly into place with a soft cloth.

Metal tiles
Set out metallic tiles as for ceramic ones. No adhesive or grout is required. Don't fit metal tiles behind electrical fittings – there's a risk that they could conduct the current.
Remove the protective paper from the adhesive pads on the back and press each tile onto the wall. Check the alignment of the tiles regularly: they are not always perfectly true.
Cut border tiles with scissors or tinsnips, but nick the edges before cutting across the face or the surface is likely to distort.
To round over a cut edge, cut a wooden block to fit inside the tile, and align it with the edge. Tap and rub along the edge with another block.
To fit into a corner, file a V-shape into the opposite edges then bend the tile over the angle of the table.
When the wall is complete, peel off any protective film, which may be covering the tiles.

Cork tiles
Set up a horizontal guide batten (▷) to make sure you lay the tiles accurately. It isn't necessary to fix a vertical batten, however: the large tiles are easy to align without one. Simply mark a vertical line centrally on the wall and hang the tiles in both directions from it.
Use a rubber-based contact adhesive to fix cork tiles, if possible the type that allows a degree of movement when positioning them. If any adhesive gets onto the surface of a tile, clean it off immediately with a suitable solvent (▷) on a cloth.
Spread adhesive thinly and evenly onto the wall and back of the tiles and leave it to dry. Lay each tile by placing one edge only against the batten or its neighbour then gradually press the rest of the tile onto the wall. Smooth it down with your palms.
Cut cork tiles with a sharp trimming knife. Because the edges are butted tightly, you'll need to be very accurate when marking out border tiles. Use the same method as for laying cork and vinyl floor tiles (▷). Cut and fit curved shapes using a template.
Unless the tiles are pre-coated, apply two coats of varnish after 24 hours.

Tiling around curves
In many older houses some walls might be rounded at the external corners. Flexible tiles such as vinyl, rubber and carpet types are easy to bend into quite tight radiuses, but cork will snap if bent too far.
Cut a series of shallow slits vertically down the tile using a tenon saw, within the central section of the tile, then bend it gently to the curve required.

APPLICATION
TILING

SEE ALSO
Details for:
Setting out
Grouting
Cork/vinyl tiles
Adhesive
solvents
Preparing plaster
Files

Bedding mosaics
Bed tiles by tapping a carpet-covered board.

Placing mirror tiles
Position tile before pressing on wall.

Nick here

Bending metal tiles
Nick the edges of metal tiles before bending.

Bending a cork tile
Cut a series of shallow slits vertically down the back of a tile using a tenon saw within the central section, then bend it gently: the slits will enable the tile to assume even a fairly tight curve without snapping but experiment first.

105

Dimensions
Although many trade suppliers use the metric system, some people are more familiar with imperial measurements. In this book, exact dimensions are given in metric followed by an approximate conversion to imperial for comparison. Do not mix imperial and metric dimensions when you are making a calculation.

CONTENTS

1

PLANNING AHEAD

Forward planning	12
Assessing a property	**12**
Room by room	14
Outbuildings & gardens	16
Using professionals	**17**
Planning permission	18
Building Regulations	18
Employing a builder	20
Employing specialists	21
Doing it yourself	**22**
Work sequence	22
Colour selection	**24**
Tone	26
Texture	28
Pattern	29
Manipulating space	30
Interior schemes	**32**
Lighting	37

2

DECORATING

Access	40
Preparation & priming	**43**
Primers/sealers	43
Masonry	44
Plaster	50
Wallcoverings	52
Woodwork	53
Metalwork	60
Tiling	62
Applying finishes	**63**
Paints	63
Exterior masonry	64
Walls & ceilings	67
Decorative effects	70
Woodwork	74
Finishes	75
Doors	77
Window frames	78
Graining	79
Staining	80
Varnishing	82
French polishing	83
Cold cure lacquer	84
Metalwork	85
Panelling	87
Wallcoverings	90
Tiling	99
Wall tiles	102
Floor tiles	107
Ceiling tiles	112
Flooring	113
Parquet	113
Sheet flooring	115
Carpets	116
Sheet vinyl	118

REPAIRS & IMPROVEMENTS

House construction	120
Walls	**122**
External	122
Internal	123
Openings	124
Closing	127
Removing	128
Constructing	135
Ceilings	**142**
Lowering	142
Loft access	147
Plasterwork	**148**
Interior	148
Types of plaster	149
Techniques of plasterwork	150
Repairing plasterwork	153
Plasterboard	158
Coving	167
Exterior rendering	**168**
Floors	**172**
Suspended	172
Solid	173
Fitting	174
Boarded	175
Flooring	176
Maintenance	177
Laying floorboards	178
Laying concrete floors	182
Doors	**184**
Types/construction	184
Fitting	186
Repairs	188
Furniture	189
Frames	190
Dividing doors	192
Sliding & folding doors	193
Fire-resisting doors	194
Garage doors	194
Windows	**196**
Types/construction	196
Fitting	198
Glass	199
Repairing glass	202
Double glazing	204
Repairing frames	205
Replacement	209
Roof windows	211
Stairs	**212**
Types/construction	212
Repairs	215
Balustrades	218
Roofs	**221**
Types/construction	221
Maintenance	226
Sheet roofing	227
Flat roofs	228
Flashings	232
Guttering	234

HOME SECURITY

Basics	238
Precautions	239
Securing doors	240
Securing windows	242
Burglar alarms	243
Fire protection	244

INFESTATION, ROT & DAMP

Infestation	**246**
Insect infestation	246
Animal infestation	248
Rot	**249**
Wet and dry rot	249
Damp	**251**
Causes of damp	251
Penetrating damp	252
Rising damp	253
Condensation	254
Damp-proof courses	256
Cellars	258

INSULATION & VENTILATION

Insulation	**260**
Insulating plumbing	261
Draughtproofing	262
Roof and loft insulation	265
Walls	268
Floors	270
Double glazing	271
Ventilation	**275**
Ventilating floors	276
Ventilating roof space	277
Extractor fans	279
Cooker hoods	281
Heat exchanging ventilators	282
Air conditioners	284

CONTENTS

7

ELECTRICITY

Economics	286
Basics	288
Safety	**289**
Bathroom safety	290
Electric shock	291
Replacements & repairs	**292**
Flex	293
Plugs and lampholders	295
Main switch equipment	**296**
Fuse boards	296
Consumer units	298
Fuses	299
Circuits	301
Cables	**302**
Cable types	302
Installing cables	303
Checklists	306
Power circuits	**308**
Mounting sockets	308
Replacing socket outlets	310
Adapting circuits	311
Fixed appliances	**314**
Fused connection units	314
Heaters	315
Small appliances	316
Larger appliances	**317**
Cookers	317
Immersion heaters	318
Storage heaters	320
Doorbells, buzzers & chimes	322
Showers	323
Lighting	**323**
Circuits	323
Fittings	325
Switches	327
Installing	330
Exterior electrics	**332**
Complete rewiring	336

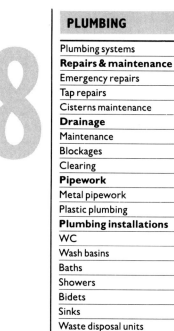

8

PLUMBING

Plumbing systems	338
Repairs & maintenance	**341**
Emergency repairs	341
Tap repairs	342
Cisterns maintenance	344
Drainage	**347**
Maintenance	347
Blockages	348
Clearing	350
Pipework	**351**
Metal pipework	351
Plastic plumbing	356
Plumbing installations	**360**
WC	360
Wash basins	363
Baths	367
Showers	369
Bidets	373
Sinks	374
Waste disposal units	375
Washing machines	376
Water softeners	378
Storage cisterns	379
Cylinders	380

9

HEATING

Open fires	**382**
Fireplaces	384
Closed fires	**386**
Log-burning stoves	387
Lining flues	388
Maintaining fire surrounds	389
Central heating	**390**
Boilers	392
Radiators	393
Controls	395
Fault finding	396
Maintenance	397
Circulating pumps	402
Control valves	403
Storage heaters	**404**

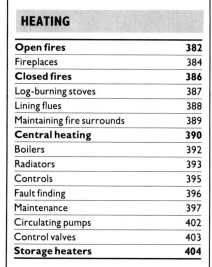

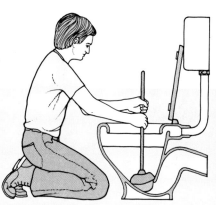

WORKING OUTDOORS

Garden planning	406
Fences	**410**
Types	410
Supporting	412
Erecting	414
Gates	**418**
Types	418
Posts	419
Walls	**420**
Masonry types and materials	420
Brickwork	426
Blockwork	434
Stonework	436
Retaining walls	437
Paths/Drives/Patios	**438**
Concrete	438
Paving slabs	446
Crazy paving	448
Brick paving	449
Cobblestones/Gravel	451
Tarmac	452
Garden steps	**453**
Concrete steps	453
Curved steps/Log steps	454
Water gardens	**455**
Ponds	455
Rockery/Waterfall	459
Swimming pools	460

TOOLS & SKILLS

Woodworker's tools	462
Basic woodworking joints	475
Builder's tools	478
Decorator's tools	481
Plumber's/Metalworker's tools	486
Electrician's tools	492

REFERENCE & INDEX

Timber & boards	494
Adhesives	495
Fixings	496
Blinds & curtain rails	499
Shelving	500
Glossary of terms	501
Index	504

Consultants
The authors are grateful to the following consultants for their contributions and assistance.

James Clark
Repairs and improvements

John Dees – LEB
Electricity

Noel Dunne
Electricity

Ian McIver
Repairs and improvements

Trevor Peake
Plumbing
Heating

Ian Penberthy
Heating

C. Tobitt
Repairs and improvements
Working outdoors

The authors and publishers wish to thank the following individuals and organizations for their help in the preparation of this book.

A. Bell & Co Ltd
Acoustics & Envirometrics Ltd
Aidelle (Airflow Developments Ltd)
All Swim Ltd
Alumasc Ltd
Amtico (National Plastics) Ltd
ARC Concrete Ltd
Aristocast Ltd
Armstrong World Industries Ltd
Artex Ltd
Arthur Sanderson and Sons Ltd
Asbestos Information Centre
Association of Builders' Hardware
    Manufacturers
The Atlas Stone Co
The Beamhanger Co
Belco Manufacturing Co Ltd
Bituminous Roofing Council
Blue Circle Industries PLC
Blue Hawk Ltd
Blundell-Permoglaze Ltd
BP Aquaseal Ltd
Bradstone Garden Products
British Carpet Manufacturers Association
British Chemical Dampcourse Association
British Gypsum Ltd
British Ivy Society
Bruce Starke & Co Ltd
Catnic Components Ltd
Cavity Trays Ltd
Cement and Concrete Association
Colas Building Products Ltd
Consculpt Ltd
Cranleigh Clark Ltd
Crescent of Cambridge Ltd
Crown Decorative Products Ltd
Cuprinol Ltd
Delta Trading
Dimplex Heating Ltd
DIY Plastics Ltd
Doulton Glass Industries
Draught Proofing Advisory Association
    Ltd
The Electricity Council
Evode Ltd
External Wall Insulation Association
GKN Crompton Ltd
GKN Kwikform Ltd
Glass and Glazing Federation
Denis Gray
H. Burbidge Ltd
Hackman U. K. Ltd
Lesley Harris
Heritage Swimming Pools Ltd
Phil Hind
Hormann (U. K.) Ltd
Hunter Building Products Ltd
Imperial Chemical Industries Ltd
Insulgard Ltd
International Paint
James Clark & Eaton Ltd
James White Swimming Pools Ltd
Lancashire Fittings
Leyland Paint & Wallpaper PLC
Loctite U. K.
London Electricity Board
London Fire Brigade
Lotus Water Garden Products Ltd
Magnet & Southerns
Manders Paints Ltd
Marley Building Products Ltd
Marley Extrusions Ltd
Marshalls Mono Ltd
Marley Waterproofing Ltd
M. G. A. Industries Ltd
Ministry of Agriculture, Fisheries and Food
MK Electric Ltd
National Association of Loft Insulation
    Contractors
National Cavity Insulation Association
Nature Conservancy Council
Neve Industries & Technical Services
Jean O'Grady
P. C. Henderson Ltd
Penguin Swimming Pools Ltd
Pilkington Glass Ltd
John Pinder
Polycell Products Ltd
Practical Householder Magazine
Producta Ltd

Qualitair (Air-conditioning) Ltd
Rainbow Pools Ltd
Reckitt & Colman Products Ltd
Redland Bricks Ltd
Redland Roof Tiles Ltd
Renubath Services Ltd
Rentokil Ltd
Royal Institution of Chartered Surveyors
Ruberoid Building Products Ltd
Rustins Ltd
Ryton's Ventilation Equipment Ltd
SEAC Ltd
Sigma Coatings Ltd
Solignum Ltd
Sommer Allibert (U. K.) Ltd
Stairways Ltd
Stapely Water Gardens Ltd
Sterling Roncraft
Swimming Pool and Allied Trades
    Association
Bob Tattersall
Therm-a-stor
Thoro London
TI Creda Ltd
Timber Research and Development
    Association
Toshiba (U. K.) Ltd
Triton Aquatherm Ltd
Truline Building Products
Turner & Newall PLC
Turner Wallcoverings
Unibond Ltd
The Velux Company Ltd
Visijar Tuckers
Wailes Dove Bitumastic PLC
Waterways Leisure Industries Ltd
Westland Engineers Ltd
W. H. Colt (London) Ltd
W. H. Hewson & Sons Ltd
Wicanders (G. B.) Ltd
Willan Building Services

The authors are indebted to the companies listed below who generously supplied samples of the materials and products featured throughout the book.

Allders Department Stores
Amtico (National Plastics) Ltd
Armstrong World Industries Ltd
Arthur Sanderson and Sons Ltd
The Atlas Stone Co
Barbee Ceramics Ltd
Bradstone Garden Products
Bruce Starke & Co Ltd
Carl Freudenberg & Co (UK) Ltd
C. F. Anderson & Son Ltd
Crown Decorative Products Ltd
Decarte
Delta Trading
E. Parkinson (London) Ltd
Magnet & Southerns
M. A. Ray & Sons Ltd
Marley Building Products Ltd
Marshalls Mono Ltd
MK Electric Ltd
Petit Roque
Ravenscroft Ltd
Redland Bricks Ltd
Redland Roof Tiles Ltd
R. V. Avery Ltd
Tile Mates
Weston Hyde Products Ltd
Wicanders (G. B.) Ltd

Picture sources

Key to photographic credits
L = Left, R = Right, T = Top, TL = Top left, TR = Top right, C = Centre, UC = Upper centre, LC = Lower centre, CL = Centre left, CR = Centre right, B = Bottom, BL = Bottom left, BR = Bottom right

Acquisitions Fireplaces Ltd. Page 389B
Albert Jackson. Pages 25BR; 406TR, BL, BR; 420T; 424TR, CL, CR; 450UC, B; 453
allmilmö Ltd. Page 34TR
Arthur Sanderson and Sons Ltd. Pages 29BL; 32TR; 33BL; BR
B. C. Sanitan. Page 35BR
Behr Furniture. Page 36C

Berger Decorative Paints. Page 32TL; 33TR; 72B
Blue Circle Industries PLC. Pages 47B; 48T, B; 49; 73
Cement & Concrete Association. Pages 171; 445
Clive Helm/EWA. Pages 31C; 32BL; 34BR; 35TR
Crown Decorative Products Ltd. Pages 27BL; 38BR; 72UC, C, LC
Dimplex Heating Ltd. Page 404T
Faber Blinds (GB) Ltd. Pages 25CR; 34BL; 36T
Frank Herholdt/EWA. Page 31T
Harry Smith Collection. Pages 407T, CR; 448B; 451B; 455; 458
Howard Ceilings. Page 146
Jerry Tubby/EWA. Page 34TR
Magnet & Southerns. Pages 189; 194; 210; 211
Michael Dunne/EWA. Pages 25BL; 35TL; 36B; 37; 38TR
Michael Nicholson/EWA. Page 38BL
Minsterstone (Wharf Lane)Ltd. Page 389T
Neil Lorimer/EWA. Pages 28BR; 38TL
Pat Brindley. Pages 406TL; 407CL, B; 451T
Patrick Fireplaces. Page 389C
Paul Chave. Pages 26; 28T; 30; 63; 67; 74; 80; 82; 90; 91; 99; 100; 101; 113; 115; 250; 289; 292; 293; 294; 295; 297L; 298; 299; 300; 302R; 303; 307L, R; 308; 309; 314; 315; 316; 317; 318; 319; 320; 321; 324; 327; 332; 393; 395; 421; 422L; 424B; 428; 446; 449
Peter Higgins. Pages 54L; 70; 71; 72T; 159; 176; 181; 223
Rentokil Ltd. Pages 246; 248T, UC, LC; 249R
Robin Harris. Pages 297R; 302L; 307C
Rodney Hyett/EWA. Pages 32BR; 35BL
Sheppard Day Designs. Page 31BR
Simon Jennings. Pages 44; 46; 47T, C; 48C 52; 53; 54R; 56; 58; 60; 65; 240; 248B; 249L; 254; 263; 409; 410; 411; 418; 419; 420UC, LC, B; 422R; 424TL; 435; 438; 448; 450T, LC
Smallbone. Pages 29BR; 31BL; 33TL
Spike Powell/EWA. Pages 25TL; 27T
The Bisque Radiator Shop. Page 25TR
TI Creda Ltd. Page 404C, B
Tim Street-Porter/EWA. Page 27BR
Waterways Ltd./Dr. D. W. Davison. Page 460
Wrighton International Ltd. Page 28BL

1

FORWARD PLANNING — 12
ASSESSING PROPERTY:ROOM BY ROOM — 14
USING PROFESSIONALS — 17
PLANNING PERMISSION/BUILDING REGULATIONS — 18
EMPLOYING A BUILDER — 20
DOING IT YOURSELF — 22
A BASIS FOR SELECTING COLOUR — 24
USING TONE — 26
USING TEXTURE — 28
USING PATTERN — 29
MANIPULATING SPACE — 30
INTERIOR SCHEMES — 32
PLANNING YOUR LIGHTING — 37

PLANNING AHEAD

FORWARD PLANNING: ASSESSING A PROPERTY

SEE ALSO

◁ Details for:
What is involved?   13

Embarking on a substantial scheme of home improvement can be an enjoyable and rewarding experience or a nightmare. Much depends on getting off on the right foot. If you plan each step in advance you are more likely to spend your money on real improvements which will benefit you and your family while adding to the value of your property. On the other hand, if you buy a property which proves to be unsuitable for your present or future needs, or launch into an ambitious project without thinking through the consequences, you could be disillusioned and waste time and money.

Check lists

Buying a house or an apartment is an exciting event, and when you find just what you have been searching for, it can be such a heady moment that it becomes all too easy to get carried away without checking the essential requirements. Your first impressions can be totally misleading so that the disadvantages and shortcomings of a particular dwelling begin to emerge only after you have moved in. If you carry with you a check list of salient points when you visit a prospective house you are less likely to be disappointed later when it can cost a great deal to bring the building up to the required standard.

In some ways, assessing the potential of your present home can be even more difficult. Everything fits like an old glove and it is hard to be objective about possible improvements. Try to step back from the familiarity by using the same sort of check list as if you were considering it as a new house.

No single property is ever absolutely ideal but forward planning will provide you with the means to make the best of what any house has to offer.

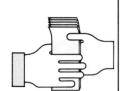

Before you buy
Buying a home will probably be your largest single investment: don't be misled by first impressions. Check your list of essential points carefully so that you can fully consider the property before investing in professional surveys.

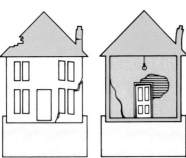

STRUCTURAL CONDITION

Before you make up your mind to buy a house or apartment the building should be inspected by a professional surveyor to make sure it is structurally sound, but make some spot checks yourself before spending money on a survey. A pair of binoculars will help you inspect the building from ground level.

Look out for cracks in the walls, both inside and out. Cracked plaster may simply be the result of shrinkage, but if the fault is visible on the outside, it may indicate deformation of the foundations.

Inspect chimney stacks for faults. A loose stack could cause considerable damage if it were to collapse.

Check the condition of the roof. A few loose slates can be repaired easily, but if a whole section appears to be misplaced it could mean a new roof.

Ask if the house has been inspected or treated for rot or insect infestation. If so, is there a guarantee available? Don't rely entirely upon your own inspection, but if the skirting boards look distorted, or a floor feels unduly springy, expect trouble.

Look for signs of damp. In hot weather the worst effects may have disappeared, but stained wallpapers, even poor pointing of the brickwork, should make you suspicious.

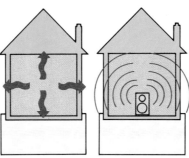

INSULATION

Ask what form of insulation, if any, has been installed. Extensive cavity or external wall insulation should carry a guarantee. You may not want to inspect loft insulation yourself, but study any surveyor's report to be certain that it is adequate by current standards.

HOME SECURITY

Look to see whether all doors and windows are secured with good-quality locks and catches. You will probably want to change the front-door lock anyway. A burglar alarm is an advantage only if it is reliable and intelligently installed. If you are buying an apartment, make sure there is adequate provision for escape during a fire.

SERVICES

An estate agent's written details of the property will describe recent re-wiring, but in the absence of such assurance, try to determine the likely condition of the installation. The presence of old-fashioned switches and sockets may indicate out-of-date wiring but new equipment is no guarantee at all that the cables themselves have been replaced. If light fittings hang from old, fabric-covered flex, be very suspicious. The age of the wiring around the consumer unit will be your best indication. Check that there are enough sockets in every room for your needs. Is the lighting well planned? Pay particular attention to safe lighting over stairs.

Is the plumbing of an age and type that can be extended easily to take new fittings? Extensive lead pipework will need to be replaced. Take note of the size of the hot water cylinder to make sure it can supply enough hot water, and check that it is insulated.

If the house is partly centrally heated, check that the boiler is large enough to cope with additional radiators or you will have to buy a new one. Is the heating system fitted with proper thermostatic controls to keep down running costs? Ask whether fireplaces and flues are in working order.

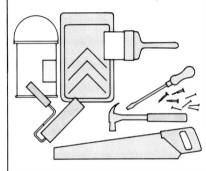

● **Apartments**
When buying an apartment, make additional checks on the type of access, whether it is by stairs or lift. Ask about shared facilities like laundry and waste disposal, and joint responsibilities such as maintenance of public areas and drainage problems.

DECOR/IMPROVEMENT

Decorative condition
Is the house decorated to a high standard both inside and out, to protect the structure and enhance the appearance of the building? The decorative condition of the house is reflected in the price and the chances are that you will be expected to pay the same whether the work is up to a good professional standard or shoddily applied. It is up to you to point out the difference to the vendor.

Improvements
Make up your own mind whether 'improvements' have been carried out tastefully. Ask yourself if you can live in a house where the original doors and windows have been replaced with alternatives that no longer suit the style of the architecture. A neighbouring house may give you some idea of its intended appearance.

There is considerable doubt about the advantages claimed for certain types of stone cladding, and painted brickwork can never be stripped back to the original successfully.

There is an understandable desire for personalizing one's home, but a small terraced house masquerading as a Tudor cottage may be a doubtful investment.

WHAT IS INVOLVED?

Having checked the condition of the building, refer to other sections of this book to ascertain how much work is involved to correct any faults you have noticed. It will help you to decide whether to do the work yourself, hire a professional or to look elsewhere.

Structural condition

Repointing	45
Spalled masonry	46
Cracked walls	46-47
Damaged concrete	49, 182
Damaged plaster	50-51, 153-157
Foundation problems	121, 409
Replacing floors	178-181
Rotten doors	188, 190-191
Broken windows	200-203
Rotten windows	205-206
Repairing staircases	214-220
Major roof problems	222
Roof repairs	226-233
New guttering	236
Treating woodworm	246-247
Wet and dry rot	249-250
Treating damp	251-258

Insulation

Roof insulation	265-268
Wall insulation	269-270
Floor insulation	270

Home security

Fitting locks and catches	240-243
Burglar alarms	243
Fire precautions	244

Services

Electrical installations	286-336
Plumbing	338-380
Shared drainage	347
Fireplaces and flues	383-389
Boilers	392-393
Heating controls	395
Replacing radiators	401

Decoration

Preparation	43-62
Application	63-118

Improvements

Replacing doors	186
Replacing windows	209-210
Double glazing	271-274

PLANNING FOR PEOPLE

Function, comfort and appearance should take equal priority when planning your home, but the best designers build their concepts around the human frame using statistics gleaned from research into the way people use their home and working environments.

Ergonomics
Although human stature varies a great deal, the study of ergonomics, as it is called, has determined the optimum dimensions of furniture and the spaces that surround it to accommodate people of average build. These conclusions have been adopted by manufacturers and designers so that most shop-bought fittings for kitchens, bathrooms, living and dining areas are built to standardized dimensions.

This is especially true of kitchen units which are designed for compatibility with appliances such as cookers and fridges to make a scheme which fits together as an integrated, functional whole. The standard worktop height allows a dishwasher or washing machine to fit neatly beneath it, while a cooker is designed to fit flush with countertops and base units. Designers adopt the same criteria for other items of furniture. Standard-size chairs, tables and desks are matched to allow most people to work and eat comfortably.

An appreciation of ergonomics avoids accidents as well. Correctly positioned shelves and worktops avoid unnecessary stretching or climbing onto a chair to reach the top shelf. Low-level easy chairs or soft beds that offer no support are bad for back sufferers, and high stools are not suitable for young children. Understanding ergonomics will help you choose appropriate furniture.

Using available space
As well as the size and function of the furniture itself, its positioning within the room falls within the province of ergonomics. An efficient use of floor area is an essential ingredient of good planning, providing people with a freedom of action and the room to make use of furniture and appliances.

When you are buying furniture or planning the furnishings and fittings for your own home, it is worthwhile familiarizing yourself with the dimensions shown on the following pages. They will help you buy wisely and make the best use of available space.

SEE ALSO

Details for: ▷

Hallway access	14
Seating arrangements	14
Dining rooms	15
Bedroom access	15
Bathrooms	15
Kitchen planning	16
Storage	16

ASSESSING A PROPERTY: ROOM BY ROOM

SEE ALSO

◁ Details for:

Moving a door	126-127
Removing walls	128-134
Dividing a room	135-141
Staggered wall for storage	138
Installing dividing doors	192-193
Installing door viewer	240
Fitting a porch light	332

Assuming the structural condition of the house is such that you are quite willing to take on the work involved, begin to check out those points which a structural surveyor won't be looking for. Is it the right home for you and your family? It takes a bit of imagination to see how a room might look when it has been divided in two or when a wall has been removed, but it is even more difficult to predict what your lifestyle might be in five or ten years' time. Unless you intend to live in a property for a couple of years only before moving on, you must try to assess whether the house will be able to evolve with you.

You will need to take measurements before you can make some decisions so carry a tape measure with you.

MEASURING A ROOM

If you think there is a possibility that you might want to change the shape of a room, or you suspect there may be a problem with fitting certain items of furniture into it, measure the floor area and the ceiling height so that you can make a scale drawing later to clarify your thoughts. Take the main dimensions, including alcoves, the chimney breast and so on. Make a note of which way the doors swing and the positions of windows, radiators and fixed furniture. Transfer the measurements to squared paper with each square representing a set dimension.

When you have drawn your plan of the room, cut out pieces of paper to represent your furniture using the same scale measurements. Rearrange them until you arrive at a satisfactory solution.

Draw a measured plan on squared paper

The hallway

When you are invited into the house, you will be able to gauge whether the entrance hall is large enough to receive visitors. Is the staircase wide enough to allow you to carry large pieces of furniture to the bedrooms?

Will there be room to store top-coats, hats, boots, umbrellas and so on?

It is an advantage if there is some facility for deliveries to be stored outside but under cover when the house is unoccupied.

Check whether it is possible to identify a visitor before opening the door, especially after dark.

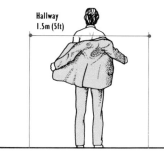

Hallway
1.5m (5ft)

Removing a coat
When planning a hallway, allow 1.5m (5ft) to remove a topcoat or a jacket.

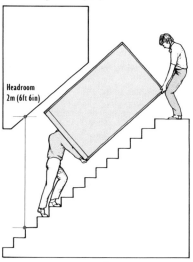

Headroom
2m (6ft 6in)

▲ **Staircase headroom**
A headroom of 2m (6ft 6in) above a staircase will allow you to carry a wardrobe to the next floor.

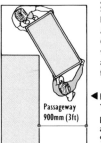

Passageway
900mm (3ft)

◁ **Negotiating a bend**
You can turn a large piece of furniture around a bend in a 900mm (3ft) wide passageway.

Living rooms

How many reception rooms are there in the house? More than one living room provides an opportunity for members of the family to engage in different pursuits without inconveniencing each other.

If there is one living room only, make sure there are facilities elsewhere for private study, music practice or hobbies.

Is the living room large enough to accommodate the seating arrangement you have in mind, or will you have to remove a wall to incorporate extra space? If you do, it is worth considering folding doors so that you can divide the area again when it suits you.

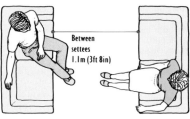

Between settees
1.1m (3ft 8in)

Arranging two settees
Allow a minimum of 1.1m (3ft 8in) between two settees facing each other.

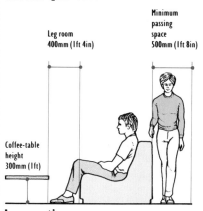

Leg room
400mm (1ft 4in)

Minimum passing space
500mm (1ft 8in)

Coffee-table height
300mm (1ft)

Low seating

The density of upholstery and the dimensions of the seat and back vary so much that it is impossible to suggest a standard, but make certain your back is supported properly and you can get out of a chair without help. If you place a coffee table in front of a settee, try to position the seating so that people can get into it from each end to avoid treading on the toes of someone seated.

ASSESSING A PROPERTY: ROOM BY ROOM

Dining room

Is there a separate dining room for formal dinner parties? Estimate whether there will be space for table and chairs with enough room to circulate freely.

A dining room should be positioned conveniently close to the kitchen so that meals are still warm when they get to the table. You may have to install a serving hatch.

If the dining area is part of the kitchen, efficient ventilation will be necessary to extract the odours of cooking and steam. Some cooks prefer a kitchen screened from visitors. Are the present arrangements suitable?

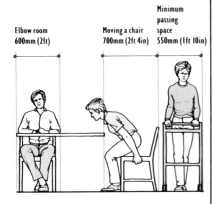

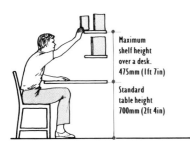

Sitting at a table
Sitting at a dining table, desk or dressing table requires the same area. Arrange the furniture for people to get in and out of a chair while leaving enough room for moving about with a trolley.

Breakfast bar
A 900mm (3ft) high breakfast bar aligns with a worktop.

Bedrooms

The number of rooms may be adequate for your present needs but what about the future? There may be additions to the family, and although young children can share a room, individual accommodation will be required eventually. You may want to put up a guest from time to time or even have an elderly relative to stay for extended periods, in which case, can they cope with stairs? It might be possible to divide a large room with a simple partition, or perhaps a room on the ground floor can double as a bedroom. As a long-term solution, you could plan for an extension or loft conversion.

Are all the bedrooms of an adequate size? As well as a bed or bunks, a bedroom must accommodate clothes storage and in some cases, books, toys and facilities for homework or pastimes. A guest room may have to function as a private sitting room, possibly with the provision for preparing snacks and hot drinks. You could dismantle or move a dividing wall, or possibly incorporate part of a large landing providing it does not interfere with access to other rooms or present obstructions in an escape route in case of fire. Try not to rely on using a bedroom which can be reached only by passing through another. This arrangement is fine when you want to be close to a young child, but a connected room could be used as a dressing room or en-suite bathroom.

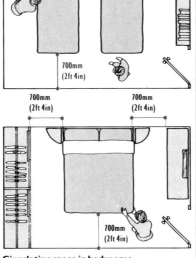

Circulating space in bedrooms

The bathroom

If the bathroom does not provide the amenities you require, estimate whether there is space to incorporate extra appliances, even if it means rearranging the existing layout, or incorporating an adjacent toilet.

Is there a separate toilet for use when the bathroom is occupied?

You should investigate the possibility of installing a second bathroom or shower cubicle elsewhere if the present bathroom is not accessible to all the bedrooms. Alternatively, consider plumbing a basin in some bedrooms.

Make a note of electrical installations in a bathroom. They must comply with accepted recommendations or be replaced with new units.

SEE ALSO

Details for: ▷	
Official permission	19
Moving a door	126-127
Removing walls	128-134
Dividing a room	135-141
Fire precautions	244
Extractor fans	279-280, 282-283
Cooker hoods	281
Plumbing a WC	360-362
Plumbing a basin	363-366
Plumbing a bath	367-368
Plumbing a shower	369-372
Plumbing a bidet	373

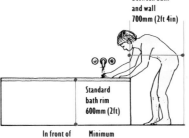

Between bath and wall
Allow sufficient room between bath and wall to dry yourself with a towel. You can bend in the same amount of space in order to clean the bath.

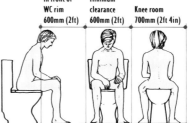

WC and bidet
Allow for the same space in front of a WC or bidet but provide extra leg room on each side of a bidet. The same spaces provide room to maintain and clean an appliance.

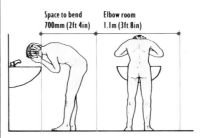

Using a basin
The generous space allows you to bend over a basin even when there is a wall behind you and provides plenty of elbow room when washing hair. You can also wash a child in the same space.

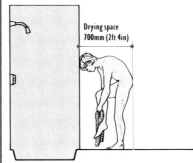

Drying after a shower
This is the minimum space required to dry yourself in front of an open cubicle. If the cubicle is screened, allow an extra 300mm (1ft).

ASSESSING A PROPERTY: ROOM BY ROOM

SEE ALSO

◁ Details for:

Wiring appliances	316
Wiring a cooker	317-318
Plumbing a sink	374-375
Waste disposal unit	375
Washing machines	376-377
Plumbing dishwasher	376-377
Water softeners	378
Garden planning	406-408
Walls/fences	410-437
Shelving	500

The Kitchen
The quality of kitchen furniture and fittings varies enormously, but every well-designed kitchen should incorporate the following features.

A labour-saving layout
Preparing meals becomes tiresome unless the facilities for cooking, the preparation of food and washing up are grouped in a layout which avoids unnecessary movement. To use designer's parlance, the kitchen must form an efficient work triangle. In ideal conditions, the sides of the triangle combined should not exceed 6 to 7m (20 to 22ft) in length.

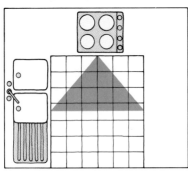

Work triangle
A typical work triangle links washing, cooking and preparation areas.

Storage
Whether you are building storage into a kitchen, workshop, bedroom or lounge, make sure every item is within easy reach and ensure there is room to open drawers and doors without backing into a wall or injuring others.

Maximum shelf height over worktop
1.05m (3ft 6in)

Optimum shelf height
900mm (3ft)

Lowest shelf height
450mm (1ft 6in)

Standard worktop height
900mm (3ft)

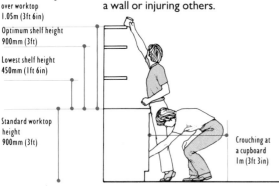

Crouching at a cupboard
1m (3ft 3in)

Kitchen storage
Plan your kitchen storage for safe and efficient access.

Access to drawers
Crouching at a drawer unit
1.25m (4ft 2in)

Storage and appliances
If the work triangle is to be effective, a kitchen must incorporate enough storage space in each area. The refrigerator and foodstuffs should be close to where meals are prepared, and adequate work surfaces must be provided. A freezer could be housed elsewhere but should be somewhere close to the kitchen.

The hob and oven should be grouped together with heat-proof surfaces nearby to receive hot dishes. Cooking equipment should be stored within easy reach.

Appliances that require plumbing are best grouped together with the sink on an outside wall. In a small house, this area will contain a washing machine and tumble dryer, although a separate laundry room is an ideal solution.

KITCHEN SAFETY

How safe is the layout of the kitchen? A cramped kitchen can lead to accidents, so ensure that more than one person at a time can circulate in safety.
- **Where possible, avoid an arrangement that encourages people to use the working part of the kitchen as a through passage to other parts of the house or garden.**
- **Make sure children cannot reach the hob and construct a barrier that will keep small children out of the work triangle.**
- **Placing the hob or cooker in a corner or at the end of a run of cupboards is not advisable. Try to plan for a clear worktop on each side. Don't place it under a window either. Eventually, someone will get burned trying to open the window, and a draught could extinguish a gas pilot light.**

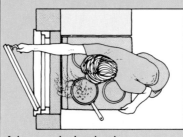

A dangerously placed cooker
Do not position cookers under windows

OUTBUILDINGS AND GARDENS

Garage and workshop
Is the garage large enough for your car, or one you aspire to, or will you need to garage two cars?

If the garage is too small to use as a workshop, you could possibly fit out a cellar so long as there is storage space for materials and you can deliver them without disruption or damaging the decorations and furniture.

A new shed or outbuilding is another solution providing there is room in the garden or beside the house, and a utilitarian building will not spoil the outlook of the property.

Long-term storage is always a problem. Every household accumulates bulky items like camping or sports equipment, which have to be stored for much of the year. Once again, a garage or outbuilding is ideal, but if necessary, can you use the loft for storage? Check the size of the hatchway, and decide whether you need to board over the joists or reposition insulation.

The garden
If you are not a keen gardener, you will want to avoid a large garden requiring a lot of attention. Does it receive enough sunlight for the type of plants you want to grow or simply for sunbathing?

Check the outlook. When foliage has dropped, you may be confronted with an eyesore that is screened during the summer months.

Make sure the fences or walls are high enough to provide privacy. If you view a house at the weekend, ask whether there are any factories, workshops or playgrounds nearby which may disturb your peace and quiet during the week.

It is an advantage if the garden has access for building materials and equipment to avoid carrying them through the house.

Can children play safely in the garden without supervision? Make sure that gates are secure and high enough to prevent them wandering out of the garden and out of sight.

USING PROFESSIONALS

Why pay someone to do a job when you can do it perfectly well yourself? There are plenty of skilled amateurs who can tackle just about any job to a high standard but it usually takes them longer than a professional specialist, and to most of us time is the enemy.

In some circumstances it is worth paying to have a job done quickly and efficiently because it is holding up a whole series of other projects. Or perhaps you do not feel sufficiently confident to handle a certain type of work. You may prefer to ask an electrician to do major wiring or a plumber to install a new bathroom, although you would carry out all the peripheral labouring and finishing yourself. Then there are certain skills such as plastering which require time and practice before you become really proficient at them. In the average-size house, you might just about develop the knack as the work is coming to an end but you probably won't plaster another wall until you buy another house.

Essential professional advice

You must seek professional advice to obtain planning permission and Building Regulation approval, and if you need a mortgage, the bank or building society will insist on the building being professionally surveyed. If the surveyor's report highlights a serious defect the mortgage company will also want the fault rectified by a specialist firm who will guarantee the work.

The Surveyor

When you apply for a mortgage the bank or building society will appoint a surveyor who is trained to evaluate a property in order to protect the mortgage company's investment. His or her job is to check that the building is structurally sound and to pinpoint anything that needs attention. You will have to pay for the service but the surveyor will report directly to the mortgage company. There was a time when the bank or building society were not obliged to show you the report but simply told you what work had to be carried out in order to secure your mortgage. Many mortgage companies are now more lenient, however, and will probably give you a copy of the surveyor's report.

Unless you are buying a fairly new property, a surveyor's report usually makes depressing reading. If the

surveyor has done a thorough job the report will list everything that is in need of attention, from peeling paintwork to dry rot in the basement. No surveyor will take the responsibility for guaranteeing the condition of areas of the house which were inaccessible at the time of inspection. For example, if the house is occupied, fitted carpets will make it very difficult to examine thoroughly the condition of the floors. The report will point out that these areas cannot be guaranteed as sound but that does not necessarily imply that there is likely to be a problem.

Study the report for specific references to serious faults which may be expensive to put right, such as damage to the foundations, dry or wet rot, woodworm, severe damp or a badly deteriorating roof. Also take note of points which could lead to trouble in the future even if there is no evidence of it at the moment. If the survey points out leaking guttering which is soaking a wall, for instance, it will have to be repaired urgently to avoid penetrating damp.

If you are not given a copy of the report you should consider having your own private survey before committing yourself to a purchase. Use a qualified surveyor. Contact the Royal Institution of Chartered Surveyors or the Incorporated Association of Architects and Surveyors for a recommendation.

> **Royal Institution of Chartered Surveyors,**
> 12 Great George Street,
> London, SW1P 3AD
> Telephone 01-222 7000
>
> **Incorporated Association of Architects and Surveyors,**
> Jubilee House,
> Billing Brook Road,
> Weston Favell,
> Northampton,
> NN3 4NW
> Telephone 0604-404121

The Architect

If you are planning ambitious home improvements, especially involving major structural alterations or extensions, you should consult a qualified architect. He or she is trained to design buildings and interiors which are not only structurally sound but aesthetically pleasing. An architect will prepare scale drawings of the development for submission to the

authorities for planning permission and Building Regulation approval. You can even employ the same architect to supervise the construction of the building to ensure that it meets the required specifications. You and your architect must work as a partnership. Brief him or her by discussing the type of development you have in mind, how you plan to use it, how much you want to spend and so on.

You can contact the Royal Institute of British Architects for a list of professionals working in your area but a personal recommendation from a friend or colleague is far more valuable. Arrange to meet the architect and to see some recent work before you commit yourself to engaging him or her.

> **Royal Institute of British Architects,**
> 66 Portland Place,
> London, WIN 4AD
> Telephone 01-580 5533

OFFICIAL PERMISSION

Before you undertake certain developments, you are obliged to obtain the approval of local-government authorities. Many people are reluctant to cooperate, fearing that the authorities are likely to be obstructive but, in fact, their purpose is to protect all of us from irresponsible builders or developers, and they are most sympathetic and helpful to any householder who seeks their advice and attempts to comply with the statutory requirements. People confuse the two main controls that exist – **planning permission** and **Building Regulation approval** . Receiving planning permission does not automatically confer Building Regulation approval and vice versa. You may require both before you can proceed. There may be variation in the planning requirements, and to some extent the Building Regulations, from one area of the country to another. Consequently, the information given on the following pages should be considered as a guide only and not as an authoritative statement of the law. If you live in a listed building of historical or architectural interest, or your house is in a conservation area, seek advice before considering any alterations.

SEE ALSO

Details for: ▷	
Planning permission	18-19
Building regulations	18-19
Plastering	157
Roofs	222-233
Guttering	234-236
Woodworm	246-247
Dry and wet rot	249
Damp	251-258
Foundation damage	121, 409

17

PLANNING PERMISSION AND BUILDING REGULATIONS

Planning permission

Planning controls exist primarily to regulate the use and siting of buildings or constructions as well as their appearance. What might seem to be a minor development in itself could have far-reaching implications you had not considered. A structure which obscured drivers' vision at a junction, for instance, might constitute a danger to traffic. Equally, the authority might refuse planning permission on the grounds that the scheme does not blend sympathetically with its surroundings.

The actual details of planning requirements are complex, but in broad terms with regard to domestic developments, the authority is concerned with construction work such as an extension to the house or the provision of new outbuildings such as a garage. Structures like walls and fences fall into the same category because their height or siting might infringe the rights of other members of the community. The planning authority will also want to approve any change of use such as converting a house into apartments or running a business from premises previously occupied as a dwelling only.

Your land or property may be affected by legal restrictions such as a right of way which might prejudice planning permission. Examine the deeds of your house or consult a solicitor.

Applying for planning permission

Obtain the necessary application form from the planning department of your local council. It is laid out simply with guidance notes to help you fill it in, but you can ask a builder or architect to apply on your behalf. This is sensible if the development you are planning is in any way complicated, because you will have to include measured drawings with the application form. In all probability, you will have to prepare a plan showing the position of the site in question (site plan) so that the authority can determine where the building is located. You must submit another plan in a larger scale to show the relationship of the building to other premises and highways (block plan). In addition, you should supply drawings which give a clear idea of what the new proposal will look like together with notes on the colour and kind of materials you intend to use. However, you are at liberty to prepare the drawings yourself so long as they are sufficiently accurate.

Under normal circumstances, you will have to pay a modest fee in order to seek planning permission but there are exceptions. The planning department will advise you.

Before preparing detailed plans, you can make an outline application furnishing information on the size and form of the development. Assuming permission is granted under these circumstances, you will then have to submit a further application in greater detail. In the main, this applies to large-scale developments only and you will be better off making a full application in the first place.

Don't be afraid to discuss the proposal with a representative of the planning department before you submit your application. He will do his very best to help you comply with the requirements, and will always grant planning permission unless there are very sound reasons for refusal, in which case, the department must explain the decision to you so that you can amend your plans accordingly and re-submit them for further consideration. A second application is normally exempt from a fee. As a last resort, however, you can appeal against a decision to the Secretary of State for the Environment. The planning authority will supply you with the necessary appeal forms. If you were to proceed with the development without approval, you might be obliged to restore the property to its original condition.

You can expect to receive a decision from the planning department within eight weeks, and once granted, planning permission is valid for five years. If the work is not begun within that time, you will have to apply for planning permission again.

Building Regulations

Even when planning permission is not required, most building works, including alterations to existing structures, are subject to minimum standards of construction to safeguard public health and safety. The Building Regulations are designed to ensure structural stability of any work, and to promote the use of suitable materials to provide adequate durability, fire and weather resistance, and the prevention of damp. The Regulations also stipulate the minimum amount of ventilation and natural light that must be provided for habitable rooms of a house or apartment.

Building standards are enforced by your local Building Control Officer (District Surveyor) but for matters concerning drainage or sanitary installations, consult the Environmental Health Officer.

Obtaining approval

You, as the builder, are required to fill in a form known as a Building Notice and return it, along with the necessary information, to the Building Control Office (District Surveyor's Office) at least two days before work commences. Alternatively, you may submit detailed plans for approval. You should check with your local council. It may save time and trouble if you make an appointment to discuss your scheme with the Building Control Officer well before you intend to carry out the work. He will want to see drawings of the proposed work, including the structural details and dimensions, together with notes on the materials you intend to use so that he can point out any obvious contravention of the regulations before you make an official application for approval. At the same time he can suggest whether it is necessary to approach other authorities to discuss planning, sanitation, fire escapes and so on. He will ask you to inform the office when crucial stages of the work are ready for inspection by a surveyor to make sure the work is carried out according to your original specification. Should the surveyor be dissatisfied with any aspect, he may suggest ways to remedy the situation.

If you wish, you can appoint a builder, but preferably an architect, to handle everything for you, but don't be bullied into ignoring the surveyor's request to inspect the site or you could incur the cost and inconvenience of exposing covered work at a later stage. Failure to serve a Building Notice or detailed plans could result in a substantial fine as well as wasted time. You will be expected to pay certain fees to the local council for the services you have received from the surveyor. These fees are not extortionate and you can obtain an estimate of the amount before building begins.

When the building is finished, you must notify the council, and it would be to your advantage to ask for written confirmation that the work was satisfactory. It will help to reassure a prospective buyer when you come to sell the property.

SEE ALSO

◁ Details for:
Listed buildings   17
Conservation area   17

WILL YOU NEED APPROVAL?

If you live in a single-family house, you are allowed to undertake certain developments without planning permission. The chart below is intended to help you decide whether you need to seek planning permission or Building Regulation approval. Always check with the relevant authority for confirmation. If your dwelling has been converted to apartments, all external alterations will require planning permission.

TYPE OF WORK	●	PLANNING PERMISSION		BUILDING REGULATION APPROVAL	
Decorations or repairs inside and outside	119 39	NO	Unless it is a listed building.	NO	
Replacing windows and doors	184 196	NO	Unless they project beyond the foremost wall of the house facing a highway.	Possibly	Consult your Building Control Officer.
Electrical work	285	NO		NO	But it must comply with IEE regulations (▷).
Plumbing	337	NO		NO	Provided it is straightforward replacement but consult the Environmental Health Officer for any installation which alters present internal or external drainage (▷).
Central heating	390	NO		NO	
Central heating oil storage tank		NO	Provided: It is in the garden and has a capacity of not more than 3,500 litres (778 gallons). And: No point is more than 3m (9ft 9in) high And: No part projects beyond the foremost wall of the house facing a highway.	NO	
Structural alterations inside	119	NO	As long as the use of the house is unchanged.	YES	
Loft conversion	147 267	NO	Provided the volume of the house remains unchanged, and the highest part of the roof is not raised.	YES	
Building a garden wall or fence	410 420	YES	If it is more than 1m (3ft 3in) high and is a boundary enclosure adjoining a highway. —or— If it is more than 2m (6ft 6in) high elsewhere.	NO	
Planting a Hedge	406	NO		NO	
Laying a path or driveway	444	NO	Unless it provides access to a main road.	NO	
Felling or lopping trees	406	NO	Unless the trees are protected or you live in a conservation area.	NO	
Installing a swimming pool	460	Possibly	Consult your planning department.	Possibly	Yes for an indoor pool.
Constructing a small outbuilding	119 420	NO	SEE MARGIN NOTE (RIGHT)	Possibly	Consult your Building Control Officer.
Building a porch	119 420	NO	Unless: The floor area exceeds 2 sq m (2.4 sq yd). —or— Any part is more than 3m (9ft 9in) high. —or— Any part is less than 2m (6ft 6in) from a boundary adjoining a highway or public footpath.	NO	
Building a conservatory	119 420	YES	Treat as an extension	NO	
Building a garage	119 420	YES	If within 5m (16ft 6in) of house, treat like an extension, otherwise treat as an outbuilding.	Possibly	Consult your Building Control Officer.
Hardstanding for a car	442	NO	Provided it is within your boundary and is not used for a commercial vehicle.	NO	
Building an extension	119 420	YES	SEE MARGIN NOTE (RIGHT)	YES	
Demolition		NO	Unless the building is listed or in a conservation area.	NO YES	No for a complete, detached house. Yes for a partial demolition to ensure that the remaining part or adjoining buildings are structurally sound.
Converting a house to apartments		YES	Including bedsitters.	YES	
Converting a house to business premises		YES		YES	

● Refer to these pages for further information.

SEE ALSO

Details for: ▷
IEE Regulations 288
Drainage systems 347

● **OUTBUILDINGS**
You can build a small outbuilding without planning permission if: It is within the boundary of your property, it is for the benefit of the household only, no part projects beyond the foremost wall of the house facing a highway and no part is more than 3m (9ft 9in) high. A ridged roof can be 4m (13ft) high.

● **EXTENSIONS**
Planning permission is required if:
Volume
The extension results in an increase in volume of the original house by whichever is the greater of the following amounts.
For terraced houses
50cu m (65.5cu yd) or 10 per cent up to a maximum of 115cu m (150.4cu yd).
Other houses
70cu m (91.5cu yd) or 15 per cent up to a maximum of 115cu m (150.4cu yd).
In Scotland
50cu m (65.5cu yd) or 20 per cent.
Height
Any part is higher than the highest part of the house roof.
Projections
Any part projects beyond the foremost wall of the house facing a highway.
Boundary
Any part within 2m (6ft 6in) of a boundary is more than 4m (13ft) high.
Area
It will cover more than half the original area of the garden.
Dwelling
It is to be an independent dwelling.

19

EMPLOYING A BUILDER

SEE ALSO

◁ Details for:
Architects   17

Finding a builder who is reliable and proficient can be frustrating. You will hear many stories of clients being overcharged for shoddy work or being left with a half-completed job for months on end. It's not that good builders don't exist but there are unscrupulous individuals who masquerade as professional tradesmen and give the whole industry a bad name.

One of the problems in finding a reputable builder is a matter of timing. A good builder will be booked up for months, so allow plenty of time to find someone who will be free when you need him or her. A builder might come so highly recommended that you won't want to look elsewhere, but unless you get two or three firms to estimate for the same job you won't know whether the price is fair. A builder who is in demand might suggest a high price because he really doesn't need the work. An inexperienced builder could submit a tempting price but might cut corners or ask for more money later because he had not anticipated all the problems.

- **Estimates and quotations**
A builder's estimate is an approximate price only. Before you engage him or her, ask for a written quotation which is a firm statement of the current market price.

Choosing a builder

Recommendation is the only safe way to find a builder. If someone whose opinion you respect has found a professional who is skilful, reliable and easy to communicate with, then the chances are you will enjoy the same experience. Even so, you should inspect the builder's work yourself before you make up your mind. If a recommendation is hard to come by, choose a builder who is a member of a reputable association such as the Federation of Master Builders. To be represented by the Federation, a builder must have a good reputation and supply bank and insurance references.

Federation of Master Builders
33 John Street,
London, WC1N 2BB
01-242 7583

SUB-CONTRACTORS

Unless a builder is a 'jack of all trades' he will have to employ electricians, plumbers, plasterers or whatever. The builder is responsible for the quality of the sub-contracted work unless you agree beforehand that you will appoint the specialists yourself. Agree to discuss anything concerning sub-contracted work with the builder himself. A sub-contractor must receive clear instructions from one person only or there is bound to be confusion.

Writing a specification

Many of the disagreements that arise between builder and client are as a result of insufficient briefing before the work was started. Do not give a builder vague instructions. He may do his best to provide the kind of work he thinks you want but it might be wide of the mark, and he can't possibly quote an accurate price unless he knows exactly what you require. You don't have to write a legal document, nor do you have to tell the builder how to do his job. Just write a detailed list of the work you want him to carry out and, as far as possible, the materials you want him to use. If you have not made up your mind about the wallcovering you want to use or the exact make of bathroom fitting, then at least say so in the specification. You can always discuss it with the builder before he submits a quotation. Read the relevant sections in this book to find out what is involved in a particular job, or, if the work is complicated, ask an architect to write a specification for you.

The specification should include a date for starting the work and an estimate of how long it will take to complete. You will have to obtain that information from the builder when he submits his estimate but make sure it is added to the specification before you both agree to the terms and price. There may be legitimate reasons why a job doesn't start and finish on time but at least the builder will be aware that you expect him to behave in a professional manner.

Getting an estimate

When you ask several builders to tender for the work you will receive their estimates of costs. They will be based on current prices and the amount of information you have supplied at the time. If you take a long time to make up your mind, or alter the specification in the meantime, prices may have changed. Before you officially engage a builder, ask him for a firm quotation with a detailed breakdown of his costs. Part of that quotation may still be estimated. If you still haven't decided on certain items, you can both agree on a provisional sum to cover them, but make it clear that you are to be consulted before that money is spent. Also, a builder might have to employ a specialist for some of the work, and that

fee might be estimated. Try to get the builder to firm up on the price before you employ him and certainly before the work begins.

Agree on a method of payment. Many builders will complete the work before any money changes hands. Some firms will ask for stage payments to cover the cost of materials. If you agree to stage payments it must be on the understanding that you will pay for work completed or that at least the materials will have been delivered to the site. Never agree to an advance payment. If you make it clear to the builder before he accepts the contract, you can retain a figure for an agreed period after the work is completed to cover the cost of faulty workmanship. Between 5 and 10 per cent of the overall cost is reasonable.

Neither you nor the builder can anticipate all the problems that might arise. If something unexpected occurs which affects the price for the job, ask the builder for an estimate of costs before you decide on a course of action. Similarly, if you change your mind or ask for work extra to the specification you must expect to pay for any resulting increase in costs – but have it agreed at the time, not at the end of the job.

Working with your builder

Most people find they get a better job from a builder if they create a friendly working atmosphere. You must provide access to electricity and water if they are required for the job, and somewhere to store materials and tools. Some mess is inevitable but a builder should leave the site fairly tidy at the end of a working day, and you should not have to put up with mud in areas of the house that are not part of the building site.

Unless you have an architect to supervise the job, keep your eye on the progress of the work. Disagreements will occur if you constantly interrupt the builder, but inspect the job when the workers have left the site to satisfy yourself on the standard of the workmanship and that it is keeping up to schedule. If you have to go out before the builder arrives, leave a note if you want to discuss something.

EMPLOYING SPECIALISTS YOURSELF

Employing a specialist tradesperson is no different from contracting a builder. Provide a detailed specification, then obtain several estimates and a firm quotation. Personal recommendation is the best guarantee of finding a reliable professional, but there are a number of organizations you can approach.

DECORATORS

British Decorators Federation,
6 Haywra Street, Harrogate,
North Yorkshire, HG1 5BL
0423 57473

Scottish Decorators Association,
249 West George Street,
Glasgow, G2 4RB 041-221 7090

PLASTERERS

Federation of Master Builders,
33 John Street, London, WC1N 2BB
01-242 7583

ROOFERS

Builders' Merchants Federation
15 Soho Square, London, W1V 5FB
01-439 1753

National Federation of Roofing Contractors,
15 Soho Square, London, W1V 5FB
01-734 9164

ASBESTOS SPECIALISTS

Asbestos Information Centre,
St Andrew's House, 22-24 High Street,
Epsom, Surrey, KT19 8AH
03727-42055

CONCRETE SPECIALISTS

British Ready Mixed Concrete Association,
Shepperton House, Green Lane,
Shepperton, Middlesex, TW17 8DN
0932-243232

HOME SECURITY

Local Crime Prevention Officer
Refer to your local directory

Local Fire Prevention Officer
Refer to your local directory

National Supervisory Council for Intruder Alarms,
St Ives House, St Ives Road,
Maidenhead, Berkshire, SL6 1QS
0628-37512

Master Locksmiths Association,
13 Parkfield Road,
Northolt, Middlesex, UB5 5NN
01-845 1676

British Security Industry Association,
Scorpio House, 102 Sydney Street,
London, SW3 6NL 01-352 8219

DAMP, ROT, INFESTATION

British Chemical Dampcourse Association,
16A Whitchurch Road,
Pangbourne, Reading,
Berkshire, RG8 7BP
073-57-3799

British Wood Preserving Association,
150 Southampton Row,
London, WC1B 5AL
01-837 8217

Nature Conservancy Council,
Northminster House, Northminster,
Peterborough, PE1 1UA 0733-40345

Local Department of Environmental Health
Refer to your local directory

GLAZING SPECIALISTS

Glass and Glazing Federation,
6 Mount Row, London, W1Y 6DY
01-409 0545

INSULATION INSTALLERS

Draught Proofing Advisory Association Ltd.,
External Wall Insulation Association,
National Cavity Insulation Association,
National Association of Loft Insulation Contractors,
PO Box 12, Haslemere,
Surrey, GU27 3AN
0428-54011

Association of Noise Consultants,
6 Long Lane, London, EC1A 9DP
01-606 1461

VENTILATION

Heating and Ventilating Contractors Association,
Esca House, 34 Palace Court,
London, W2 4JG 01-727 5556

ELECTRICIANS

National Inspection Council for Electrical Installation Contracting,
237 Kennington Lane,
London, SE11 5QJ 01-582 7746

PLUMBERS

Institute of Plumbing,
64 Station Lane,
Hornchurch, Essex, RM12 6NB
04024-72791

National Association of Plumbing, Heating and Mechanical Services Contractors,
6 Gate Street, London, WC2A 3HX
01-405 2678

HEATING INSTALLERS

Local Gas Board
Refer to local directory

Local Electricity Board,
Refer to local directory

Solid Fuel Advisory Service
Hobart House, Grosvenor Place,
London, SW1X 7AE 01-235 2020

Heating and Ventilating Contractors Association,
Esca House, 34 Palace Court,
London, W2 4JG 01-727 5556

National Association of Plumbing, Heating and Mechanical Services Contractors,
6 Gate Street, London, WC2A 3HX
01-405 2678

FENCING ERECTORS

Fencing Contractors Association,
St John's House, 23 St John's Road,
Watford, WD1 1PY 0923-27236

SPECIALIST CRAFTSMEN

Guild of Master Craftsmen,
166 High Street, Lewes,
East Sussex, BN7 1YE 0273-478449

SEE ALSO

Details for: ▷
Crime prevention officer	238
Fire prevention officer	238

21

DOING IT YOURSELF

In the majority of cases you will save money by doing most of the work yourself. You will probably have to pay more for materials than a tradesperson who benefits from discounts and can buy in greater quantities, but you will save the labour costs that account for a large part of the professional's bill. You will also gain satisfaction from producing good-quality work yourself especially as a tradesperson must equate the time he or she spends with the price for the job and may not be able to spend as much time attending to details.

SEE ALSO

◁ Details for:
Sealing to contain dust   130

Planning work priorities

Although forward planning might not be so important when you are doing all the work yourself, careful forethought will reduce disruption to the household to a minimum and will avoid spoiling finished decor and carpets with dust generated in other parts of the building. Work out a schedule for yourself listing the jobs in order of priority. Some work should be carried out urgently to safeguard the structure of the house or because the prospect of bad weather dictates the order of work. However, it is mostly dictated by what appears to be the most logical sequence to ensure that you won't have to backtrack because you forgot to complete an earlier stage.

Planning your time

Another important aspect to consider is the amount of time you can devote to the work, because that can determine how you tackle a long-term project. Unless you can work full-time for periods of weeks or even months on end, it will take several years to completely renovate even a small house. Therefore you have to decide whether you and your family are prepared to put up with the inconvenience caused by tackling the entire house in one go or whether you would be better off to divide up the work so that part of the house is still relatively comfortable. Just how you plan the work will depend on the layout of the building. If you have more than one entrance it may be possible to seal off one section completely while you work on it. If the house is built on several floors, then work out a sequence whereby you are not treading dust and dirt from a work site on an upper level through finished carpeted areas below. Leave linking areas such as stairs, landings and hallways undecorated until the last moment.

WORKING TO A SEQUENCE

PRIORITY WORK

URGENT REPAIRS

Attend to faults mentioned in a professional survey (these repairs are often insisted upon by a mortgage company). Repair anything in a dangerous condition or which is damaging to the structure of the building and getting rapidly worse. This may include:

● Dry rot, rising damp, penetrating damp.
See pages 249, 251-258.

● Seriously cracked or loose masonry.
See pages 46-47, 49, 409.

● Woodworm infestation.
See pages 246-247.

● Faulty plumbing, downpipes and drains.
See pages 338-380, 234-236.

● Faulty electrical wiring.
See pages 286-336.

● Unstable garden walls.
See pages 420-437.

● Roofwork.
See next column and pages 222-236.

SECURITY

● Fit locks to all vulnerable doors and windows.
See pages 240-243.

● Change front door lock if you have just moved in to a new house. You cannot know who has a key.
See pages 240-241.

● Install fire extinguisher and fire blanket.
See page 244.

APPROVAL

● Seek planning permission and Building Regulation approval from your local authority for any work likely to require official permission.
See pages 17-19.

No two homes or family circumstances are identical but the chart will help you plan your own sequence of events. You should always tackle first those measures which will arrest deterioration, and it is usually best to repair and decorate the exterior before the interior to make sure the house is weatherproof. In practice, you will find

ROOF WORK

ROOF COVERING

● Repair or replace damaged or missing slates or tiles.
See pages 223-227.

● Repair faulty flashings.
See pages 232-233.

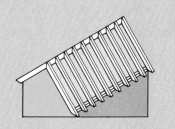

ROOF TIMBERS

● Treat or replace rotten or damaged roof timbers. You may have to hire a professional.
See pages 20-21, 222, 246, 249.

ROOF INSULATION

● Insulate and ventilate the roof space.
See pages 265-267, 277-278.

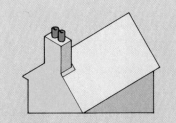

CHIMNEY STACK

● Repoint chimney stack.
See pages 45, 232, 430.

● Repair cracked flaunching.
See page 388.

● Secure loose chimney pots.
See pages 385, 388.

that it is very difficult to stick rigidly to your schedule. Unexpected problems will dictate a change of plan, and family pressures or financial restraints often demand that a task be given priority or left to a later stage even though logic would suggest another solution.

INDOOR WORK

 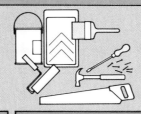

SEE ALSO

Details for: ▷
Assessing a property   12-16
Using professionals   17-21

ALTERATIONS

Undertake major interior structural changes such as:

● Building or removing dividing walls.
See pages 123, 128-134, 135-141, 434.

● Lowering ceilings.
See pages 142-146.

● Opening up or closing off doors and hatches.
See pages 124-127.

● Replacing or removing fire surrounds.
See pages 384-387.

SERVICES

PLUMBING

● Undertake new plumbing and heating work.
See pages 338-380, 382-404.

ELECTRICS

● Wire new electrical sockets and appliances.
See pages 286-336.

INSULATION

FLOOR INSULATION

● Insulate below groundfloor level.
See page 270.

DOUBLE GLAZING

● Install double glazing.
See pages 271-274.

VENTILATION

● Provide adequate ventilation.
See pages 275-284.

REPAIRS AND RENOVATIONS

FLOORS
● Repair or replace floors.
See pages 172-183.

PLASTERWORK
● Repair or replace plasterwork.
See pages 50-51, 148-167.

WOODWORK
● Fit new skirtings.
See page 181.
● Fit new door architraves.
See page 185.

FURNITURE
● Build in cupboards and fitted storage.
See page 16.

DECORATION

CEILINGS
● Paint or paper ceilings.
See pages 67-69, 98.

WALLS
● Paint walls at this stage.
See pages 67-73.

FINISH WOODWORK
● Paint or varnish woodwork.
See pages 74-84.

WALL-COVERINGS
● Hang wallpapers and wallcoverings.
See pages 90-97.

FLOOR-COVERINGS
● Lay carpets and floorcoverings.
See pages 57, 62, 107-118.

OUTDOOR WORK

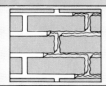 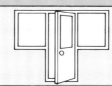

OUTSIDE WALLS

REPAIRING WALLS
● Repoint brickwork.
See pages 45, 430.
● Patch damaged rendering.
See pages 47, 168-171.
● Repair damaged masonry.
See page 46.

INSULATING WALLS
● Consider installing external or cavity-wall insulation at this stage.
See pages 269-270.

WEATHER-PROOF WALLS
● Waterproof or paint masonry walls.
See pages 46, 48, 64-66.

WINDOWS, DOORS, WOOD AND METAL

● Repair or replace doors and windows.
See pages 184-211.
● Refit locks and catches.
See pages 240-243.

● Paint or varnish all wood and metalwork.
See pages 53, 74-82, 85-86.

 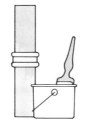

GARDEN WORK

WALLS AND FENCES
● Repair or build garden walls and fences.
See pages 410-419, 420-437.

PAVING AND STEPS
● Lay paving.
See pages 444-452.
● Build steps.
See pages 453-454.

PONDS AND WATERGARDENS
● Construct garden ponds and waterfalls.
See pages 455-459.

ROCKERY
● Build a rockery before planting.
See page 459.

A BASIS FOR SELECTING COLOUR

SEE ALSO

◁ Details for:

Tone	26-27
Texture	28
Pattern	29
Manipulating space	30-31
Decorating	40-118

Developing a sense of the 'right' colour is not the same as learning to paint a door or hang wallpaper. There are no 'rules' as such but there are simple guidelines which will help. In magazine articles on interior design or colour selection you will come across terms such as harmony and contrast. Colours are described as being cool or warm, or as tints or shades. These specialized terms form a basis for developing a colour scheme. By considering colours as the spokes of a wheel, you will see how one colour relates to another and how such relationships create a particular mood or effect.

Primary colours

All colours are derived from three basic 'pure' colours – red, blue and yellow. They are known as the primary colours.

Secondary colours

When you mix two primary colours in equal proportions, a secondary colour is produced. Red plus blue makes violet, blue with yellow makes green and red plus yellow makes orange. When a secondary colour is placed between its constituents on the wheel, it sits opposite its complementary colour – the one primary not used in its make-up. Complementary colours are the most contrasting colours in the spectrum and are used in colour schemes for dramatic effects.

Tertiary colours

When a primary is mixed equally with one of its neighbouring secondaries, it produces a tertiary colour. The complete wheel illustrates a simplified version of all colour groupings. Colours on opposite sides of the wheel are used in combination to produce vibrant, contrasting colour schemes, while those colours grouped together on one side of the wheel form the basis of a harmonious scheme.

Warm and cool colours

The wheel also groups colours with similar characteristics. On one side are the warm red and yellow combinations, colours we associate with fire and sunlight. A room decorated with warm colours feels cosy or exciting depending on the intensity of the colours used. Cool colours are grouped on the opposite side of the wheel. Blues and greens suggest vegetation, water and sky, and create a relaxed airy feeling when used together.

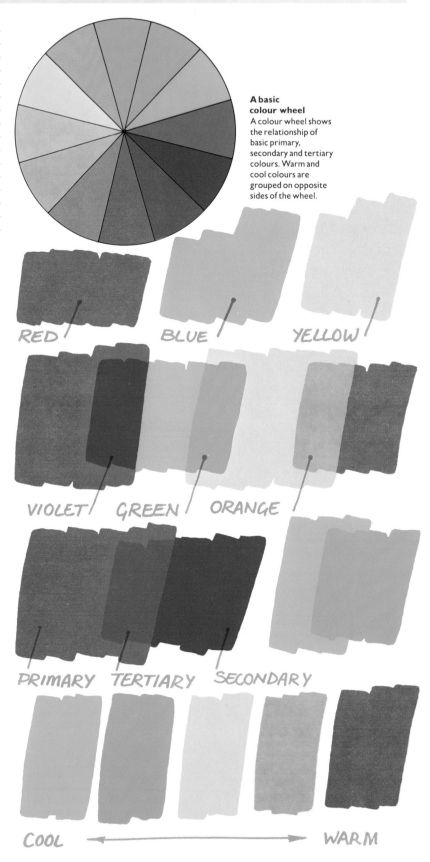

A basic colour wheel
A colour wheel shows the relationship of basic primary, secondary and tertiary colours. Warm and cool colours are grouped on opposite sides of the wheel.

RED   BLUE   YELLOW

VIOLET   GREEN   ORANGE

PRIMARY   TERTIARY   SECONDARY

COOL ⟵——————⟶ WARM

SELECTING COLOUR

1△

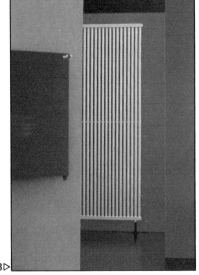

3▷

4▷

2▽

5▷

SEE ALSO	
Details for: ▷	
Tone	26-27
Texture	28
Pattern	29
Manipulating space	30-31
Decorating	40-118

**1 Bold treatment
for a living room**
A bold red treatment
always creates a warm
atmosphere. In this
interior, obvious brush
strokes add the extra
element of texture.

2 A child's playroom
Primary colours make
a lively, invigorating
playroom. The grey
floor and expanse of
white accentuate the
bright colours.

**3 Coloured
equipment**
Basic appliances such as
baths, sinks or storage
heaters were
invariably produced in
neutral colours so that
they blended into any
interior. Now it is
possible to order
equipment like these
wall-mounted
radiators which
become important
elements of a colour
scheme.

**4 Adding colour
with window blinds**
Coloured or patterned
curtains are fairly
commonplace but
fewer people choose
from the available
range of brightly
coloured venetian
blinds. Strong sunlight
contributes to the
colourful effect.

**5 Using colour
outside**
Most buildings do not
lend themselves to
being painted in bright
colours. In areas of the
country where colour
is traditionally
acceptable, a bold
treatment can be very
exciting.

25

USING TONE FOR SUBTLETY

Pure colours are used to great effect for exterior colour schemes and interior decor but a more subtle combination of colours is called for in the majority of situations. Subtle colours are made by mixing different percentages of pure colour, or simply by changing the tone of a colour by adding a neutral.

SEE ALSO

◁ Details for:

Colour theory	24-25
Texture	28
Pattern	29
Manipulating space	30-31
Decorating	40-118

Neutrals

The purest form of neutral is the complete absence of 'colour' – black or white. By mixing the two together, the range of neutrals is extended almost indefinitely as varying tones of grey. Neutrals are used extensively by decorators because they do not clash with any other colour, but in their simplest forms neutrals can be either stark or rather bland. Consequently, a touch of colour is normally added to a grey to give it a warm or cool bias so that it can pick up the character of another colour in harmony, or provide an almost imperceptible contrast within a range of colours.

Tints

Changing the tone of pure colours by adding white creates pastel colours or tints. Used in combination, tints are safe colours. It is difficult to produce anything but a harmonious scheme whatever colours you use together. The effect can be very different, however, if a pale tint is contrasted with dark tones to produce a dramatic result.

Shades

The shades of a colour are produced by adding black to it. Shades are rich dramatic colours which are used for bold yet sophisticated schemes. It is within this range of colours that browns appear – the interior designer's stock in trade. Brown blends so harmoniously into almost any colour scheme that it is tantamount to a neutral.

1 Neutrals

2 Tints

3 Shades

1 Neutrals
A range of neutral tones introduces all manner of subtle colours.

2 Tints
A composition of pale tints is always harmonious and attractive.

3 Shades
Use darker tones, or shades, for rich dramatic effects.

USING TONE

1△

◁2

3▷

SEE ALSO

Details for: ▷	
Colour theory	24-25
Texture	28
Pattern	29
Manipulating space	30-31
Decorating	40-118

1 White makes a room spacious
White paint, fabric and carpet take full advantage of available natural light to create a fresh airy interior. In this bedroom, the crisp black frames accentuate the beautifully proportioned windows.

2 Using tints creatively
Pale colours are often used when a safe harmonious scheme is required but you can create vibrant effects by juxtaposing cool and warm tints.

3 Dark dramatic tones
The very dark tone used for walls, ceiling and floors in this room is relieved by a carefully painted frieze and white accessories. Gloss paint will reflect some light even when such a dark colour is used.

27

TAKING TEXTURE INTO ACCOUNT

Colour is an abstraction, merely the way we perceive different wavelengths of light, and yet we are far more aware of the colour of a surface than its more tangible texture which we almost take for granted. Texture is a vital ingredient of any decorative scheme and merits careful thought.

SEE ALSO

◁ Details for:

Colour theory	24-25
Tone	26-27
Manipulating space	30-31
Decorating	40-118

Natural and man-made textures
(Far right)
Many people are not conscious of the actual texture of materials. This selection ranges from the warmth of wood and coarsely woven materials to the smooth coolness of marble, ceramics, plastic and metal.

Textural variety
(Below)
It's relatively simple to achieve interesting textural variety with almost any group of objects. Here, a few stylish kitchen artefacts contrast beautifully with a patterned tile splashback and warm oak cupboards.

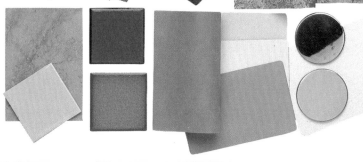

The visual effect of texture is also created by light. A smooth surface reflects more light than one that is rough. Coarse textures absorb light, even creating shadows if the light falls at a shallow angle. Consequently, when you paint a coarse texture, the colour will look entirely different from the same colour applied to a smooth one.

Even without applied colour, texture adds interest to a scheme. You can contrast bare brickwork with smooth paintwork, for instance, or use the reflective qualities of glass, metal or glazed ceramics to produce some stunning decorative effects.

Just as colour is used to create an atmosphere, texture will produce an almost instinctive impression – it's as if we could feel texture with our eyes. Cork, wood, coarsely woven fabrics or rugs add warmth, even a sense of luxury, to an interior, while smooth hard materials such as polished stone, stainless steel, vinyl, or even a black lacquered surface, give a clean, almost clinical feeling to a room.

Carefully chosen textures *(Right)*
Soft and hard textures have been selected with care for this cool sophisticated environment.

USING PATTERN FOR EFFECT

Recent, purist approaches to design have made us afraid to use pattern boldly, and yet our less-inhibited forefathers felt free to cover their homes with pattern and applied decoration with spectacular results, creating a sense of gaiety, excitement – 'punch', if you like – which is difficult to evoke in any other way.

A well-designed patterned wallpaper, fabric or rug can provide the basis for the entire colour scheme and a professional designer will have chosen the colours to form a pleasing combination. There is no reason why the same colours shouldn't look equally attractive when applied to the other surfaces of a room but perhaps the safest way to incorporate a pattern is to use it on one surface only to contrast with plain colours elsewhere.

Combining different patterns can be tricky, but a small regular pattern normally works well with large, bold decoration. Also, different patterns with a similar dominating colour can coordinate well even if you experiment with contrasting tones. Another approach is to use the same pattern in different colourways, one for the walls perhaps and the other for curtains. You should also select patterns according to the atmosphere you want to create. Simple geometric shapes are likely to be more restful than bold swirling motifs.

SEE ALSO

Details for: ▷	
Colour theory	24-25
Tone	26-27
Manipulating space	30-31
Decorating	40-118

Be bold with pattern
There is no reason to be afraid of using pattern when you consider that manufacturers have done most of the thinking for you. Well-designed materials are available to clad just about any surface in your home.

1 Coordinated pattern
The colours used for the striped curtain and furniture fabrics are the basis of this coordinated colour scheme.

2 A profusion of pattern
This bedroom combines a wealth of pattern with the rich colour of natural mahogany furniture. It shows what can be achieved if one has the courage to opt for the bold approach.

MANIPULATING SPACE

SEE ALSO

◁ Details for:
Colour theory	24-25
Tone	26-27
Pattern	29
Texture	28
Decorating	40-118
Removing walls	128-134
Lowering ceilings	142-146

There are nearly always areas of a house that feel uncomfortably small or, conversely, so spacious that one feels isolated, almost vulnerable. Perhaps the first reaction is to consider structural alterations like knocking down a wall or installing a false ceiling. In some cases, such measures will prove to be the most effective solution, but there is no doubt that they will be more expensive and disruptive than the alternative measures of manipulating space – using colour, tone and pattern.

Our eyes perceive colours and tones in such a way that it is possible to create optical illusions that apparently change the dimensions of a room. Warm colours appear to advance, so that a room painted overall with brown or red, for instance, will feel smaller than the same room decorated in cool colours such as blue or green which have a tendency to recede.

Tone can be used to modify or reinforce the desired illusion. Dark tones, even when you are using cool colours, will advance, while pale tones will open up a space visually.

The same qualities of colour and tone will change the proportion of a space. Adjusting the height of a ceiling is an obvious example. If you paint a ceiling a darker tone than the walls it will appear lower. If you treated the floor in a similar way, you could almost squeeze the room between the two. A long narrow passageway will feel less claustrophobic if you push out the walls by decorating them with pale, cool colours which will, incidentally, reflect more light as well.

Using linear pattern is another way to alter our perception of space. A vertically striped wallpaper or woodstrip panelling on the walls counteracts the effect of a low ceiling. Venetian blinds make windows seem wider, and stripped wooden floors are stretched in the direction of the boards. Any large-scale pattern draws attention to itself and will advance like warm, dark colours, but small patterns appear as an overall texture from a distance so have less effect.

Practical experiments *(Right)*
A model will help to determine whether an optical illusion will have the desired effect.

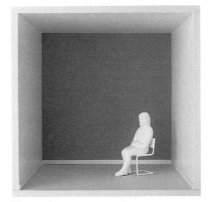

Warm colours appear to advance

A cool colour or pale tone will recede

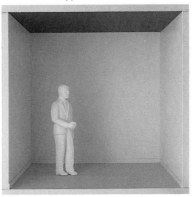

A dark ceiling will appear lower

A dark floor and ceiling make a room smaller

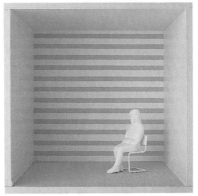

Horizontal stripes make a wall seem wider

Vertical stripes increase the height

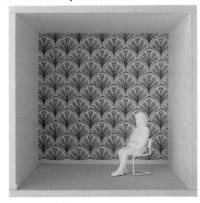

Large-scale patterns advance

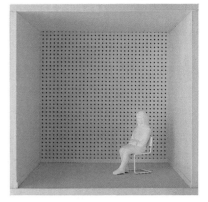

A small regular pattern recedes

1 Using mirrors
Floor to ceiling mirrors appear to double the size of a room.

2 Lowering a ceiling
A dark-tone carpet and deep-blue ceiling reduce the height of a room.

3 Incorporating an alcove
Disguise a small kitchen alcove by using colours or pattern which make it feel like part of the living room.

4 Creating space with pattern
A three-dimensional pattern can make a small space seem larger.

1△

2△

◁3

4▷

VERIFYING YOUR SCHEME

Before you spend money on paint, carpet or wallcoverings, collect samples of the materials you propose to use in order to gauge the effect of one colour or texture on another.

Collecting samples
Make your first selection from the limited choice of furniture fabrics or carpets. Collect offcuts of the other materials you are considering or borrow sample books or display samples from the suppliers to compare them at home. As paint charts are printed you can never be absolutely confident they will match the actual paint. Consequently, some manufacturers produce small sample pots of paint to try on the wall or woodwork.

Making a sample board
Professional designers make sample boards to check the relative proportions of materials as they will appear in the room. Usually a patch of floor- or wallcovering will be the largest dominating area of colour, painted woodwork will be proportionally smaller and accessories might be represented by small spots of colour. Make your own board by gluing your assembly of materials to stiff card, butting one piece against another to avoid leaving a white border around each sample which would change the combined effect.

Incorporating existing features
Most schemes will have to incorporate existing features such as a bathroom suite or kitchen units. Use these items as starting points, building the colour scheme around them. Cut a hole in your sample board to use as a window for viewing existing materials or borrowed examples against those on the card.

SEE ALSO

Details for: ▷	
Colour theory	24-25
Tone	26-27
Pattern	29
Texture	28
Decorating	40-118
Removing walls	128-134
Lowering ceilings	142-146

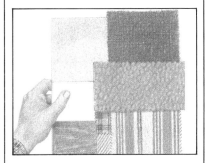

Checking your colour selection
View your completed sample board in natural and artificial light to check your colour selection.

31

SCHEMES FOR LIVING ROOMS

In most homes the living room is the largest area in the house. It's where you spend most of your leisure time and entertain your friends. It's the room upon which most money is spent on furnishings, curtains and carpets, not to mention expensive hi-fi units, the television set and so on. For all these reasons, you will want to make sure that the living room decor has lasting appeal. After all, you are unlikely to replace costly furniture and materials frequently.

Unless you are lucky enough to have more than one reception or living room, it is an area that must feel comfortable during the day, relaxing in the evening and lively enough for the occasional party. Unless the room receives an unusual amount of sunlight, a warm colour scheme is often the best, to create a cosy atmosphere. Dark cool tones will produce a similar result under artificial light, but very deep tones can have the opposite effect by creating dark shadowy areas. Predominantly neutral schemes or a range of browns and beiges lend themselves to change in the future by simply swapping the

accessories without having to spend a lot of money on replacing the essentials. Natural textures are equally versatile.

Patterned carpets or rugs are less likely to be ruined by the inevitable spillages than plain colours, but very dark tones are almost as difficult to keep clean as pale colours.

Curtains or blinds provide the perfect solution to a change of mood. During the day, they are pulled aside or withdrawn and therefore contribute very little to the general appearance of the room, but in the evening they can become a wall of colour or pattern which can transform the scheme.

SEE ALSO

◁ Details for:

Colour theory	24-25
Neutrals	26
Tone	26-27
Texture	28
Pattern	29
Manipulating space	30-31
Decorating	40-118
Interior wall paints	67
Wood finishes	74-75
Metal finishes	86
Wallcoverings	90-91
Tiles	99-101
Parquet flooring	113
Vinyl flooring	115
Carpet	116

An adaptable scheme
(Right)
A safe yet comfortable scheme lends itself to change by swapping the accessories.

Typically traditional
(Far right)
Pink-washed walls and floral pattens suit a typical country cottage.

Sympathetic style
(Below)
A surviving period living room deserves appropriate styling.

Simple styling suits a modern house *(Right)*
A modern home can be treated successfully with restrained colours and natural textures.

SCHEMES FOR BEDROOMS

A bedroom is first and foremost a personal room. Its decor should reflect the character of its occupant and the functions to which the room is put. At night, a bedroom should be relaxing, even romantic. Much depends on the lighting, but pattern and colour can create a luxurious and seductive mood.

Strangely, very few people ever use pattern on a ceiling, and yet a bedroom provides the ideal opportunity, especially as you are unlikely to spend much of your waking life there so can afford to be adventurous with the decor. Bedroom carpet is invariably of inferior quality because it need not be hardwearing but you could give the colour scheme a real lift by investing in an expensive rug or deep-pile carpet knowing that it will come to no harm.

If a bedroom faces south, early sunlight will provide the necessary stimulus to wake you up, but a north-facing room will benefit from bright invigorating colours.

Some bedrooms may serve a dual function. A teenager's bedroom may have to double as a study or a private sitting room so needs to be stimulating rather than restful. A child's room will almost certainly function as a playroom. The obvious choice would be for strong, even primary colours, but as most children accumulate brightly coloured toys, books and pictures you might select a neutral background to the colourful accessories. The smallest bedrooms are usually reserved for guests, but they can be made to appear larger and more inviting by the judicious manipulation of the proportions with colour or tone.

SEE ALSO

Details for: ▷	
Colour theory	24-25
Tone	26-27
Texture	28
Pattern	29
Manipulating space	30-31
Planning lighting	37-38
Decorating	40-118
Interior wall paints	67
Wood finishes	74-75
Metal finishes	86
Wallcoverings	90-91
Tiles	99-101
Parquet flooring	113
Vinyl flooring	115
Carpet	116

◁1

2▷

1 An elegant master bedroom
The peaceful character of this elegant bedroom is a result of a basically neutral scheme which is warmed very slightly by a hint of cream and pale yellow.

2 Bright and refreshing
The combination of bright yellow and white makes for a cheerful start to the day.

◁3

4▷

3 Dual-purpose room
When a bedroom doubles as a sitting room it needs to be stimulating during the day and cosy at night.

4 A guest room
A guest room should make a visitor feel at home immediately. The warmth of stripped pine makes this room very inviting.

DECOR FOR COOKING AND EATING

SEE ALSO

◁ Details for:

Colour theory	24-25
Tone	26-27
Texture	28
Pattern	29
Manipulating space	30-31
Decorating	40-118
Interior wall paints	67
Wood finishes	74-75
Metal finishes	86
Wallcoverings	90-91
Tiles	99-101
Parquet flooring	113
Vinyl flooring	115
Carpet	116

Kitchens need to be functional areas capable of taking a great deal of wear and tear, so the materials you choose will be dictated largely by practicalities. But that doesn't mean you have to restrict your use of colour in any way. Kitchen sinks and appliances are made in bright colours as well as the standard stainless steel and white enamel. Tiled worktops and splashbacks, vinyl floorcoverings and melamine surfaces offer further opportunity to introduce a range of colours.

Textures are an important consideration with a range of possibilities. Natural timber is still a popular material for kitchen cupboards, and wherever wood is employed, it will provide a warm element which you can choose to contrast with cool colours and textures, or pick up the warm theme with paint, paper or floor-covering. Some people prefer to rely entirely on metallic, ceramic and plastic surfaces which impose a clean, purposeful and practical character.

If the kitchen incorporates a dining area, you may decide to create within the same room a separate space that is more conducive to relaxation and conversation. Softer textures such as carpet tiles, cork flooring and fabric upholstery absorb some of the sound generated by appliances and the clatter of kitchen utensils. You could also decorate the walls in a different way to change the mood, perhaps using darker tones or a patterned wallcovering to define the dining area.

I A functional kitchen
This simple kitchen, laid out to form a perfect work triangle, looks extremely functional without feeling clinical.

2 A family kitchen
Some people like the kitchen to be part of an informal sitting and dining area where the family can relax.

3 A breakfast room
A sunny alcove linked to the kitchen makes an ideal breakfast room.

4 A kitchen extension
Colourful fabric blinds shade this kitchen extension from direct sunlight.

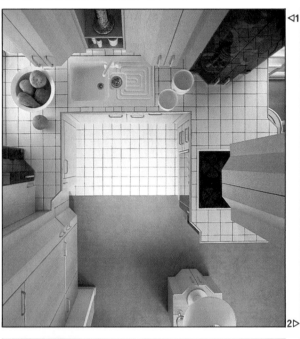

BATHROOMS

Bathrooms like kitchens must fulfil quite definite functions efficiently but they should never look clinical. Even when a bathroom is centrally heated, a cold uninviting colour scheme would not be a wise choice as enamelled and tiled surfaces are inevitable. Coloured bathroom appliances are commonplace but choose carefully as they are likely to remain the dominating influence on any future colour schemes.

A bathroom is another area where you can afford to be inventive with your use of colour or pattern. A bold treatment which might become tiresome with overexposure can be highly successful in a room used at intervals only. Try to introduce some sound-absorbing materials like ceiling tiles, carpet or cork flooring to avoid the hollow acoustics associated with old-fashioned tiled bathrooms. If you want to use delicate materials that might be affected by steam, make sure the bathroom is

properly ventilated. Bathrooms are usually small rooms with relatively high ceilings, but painting a ceiling a dark tone which might improve the proportion of a larger room can make a bathroom feel like a box. A more successful way to counter the effect of a high ceiling is to divide the walls with a dado rail, using a different colour or material above and below the line.

If you live in a hard-water area, avoid dark-coloured bathroom suites which will emphasize lime-scale deposits.

SEE ALSO

Details for: ▷	
Colour theory	24-25
Tone	26-27
Texture	28
Pattern	29
Manipulating space	30-31
Decorating	40-118
Interior wall paints	67
Wood finishes	74-75
Metal finishes	86
Wallcoverings	90-91
Tiles	99-101
Parquet flooring	113
Vinyl flooring	115
Carpet	116
Extractor fans	279-280
Water softeners	378

1 Warm and luxurious
There is no reason why a bathroom cannot be warm and inviting when there is such a choice of luxurious wallcoverings and ceramic tiles.

2 Changing the proportion
Improve the proportion of a bathroom with a high ceiling by a change of colour at dado height.

3 Fashionable styling
A clever combination of colour and shape changes a simple bathroom into a room with distinctive character.

4 A period bathroom
Reproduction fittings and marbled paintwork re-create a period bathroom.

SINGLE ROOMS OR SMALL APARTMENTS

SEE ALSO

◁ Details for:

Colour theory	24-25
Tone	26-27
Texture	28
Pattern	29
Manipulating space	30-31
Decorating	40-118
Interior wall paints	67
Wood finishes	74-75
Metal finishes	86
Wallcoverings	90-91
Tiles	99-101
Parquet flooring	113
Vinyl flooring	115
Carpet	116

1 An open-plan apartment
Create an impression of space with a fitted carpet and white walls. Vertical louvred blinds can be used to screen one area from another.

2 One large room
A warm colour scheme makes a large room feel cosier. Fold-away furniture is an advantage when you live in one room.

3 Dividing a single room
Custom-built furniture and different floor levels can be used to relieve the monotony of four walls.

When you live in one room, every activity takes place in the same area so its decor must be versatile. But much depends on your lifestyle. If you are out at work during the day you may decide to concentrate on creating a mood for the evening. On the other hand, if you work at home, your priority will be to provide a stimulating daytime environment, but not one that is too distracting.

Ideally, you should attempt to design an interior that can be changed at will to suit the time of day or your disposition. We have mentioned the fact that curtains or blinds can be used to greater effect after dark, but more positive measures are required to make the room as adaptable as possible.

Some means of screening off a sleeping alcove is always an advantage. Floor-length curtains hung from a ceiling-mounted track can form a soft wall of colour or texture. Or use vertical louvred blinds – with the flick of a pull cord, you can let in the sunlight. A concertina-folding wall of panels or louvred shutters gives the impression of a permanent screen during the day, and provides the opportunity to introduce natural or stained timber to a scheme. Alternatively, construct a portable screen from flat panels which you can decorate to suit yourself.

Dividing the floor area will define areas of activity: soft rugs for seating, polished boards or tiling for cooking or eating. You can even change the floor level with a simple wooden dais covered in carpet. Areas of wall can be sharply defined to pick up the theme using different finishes.

A small, open-plan apartment suggests other options. Prevailing natural light might persuade you to treat areas differently, either to freshen up a dark corner or to cool down an area that is constantly sunlit. You can create the impression of greater space by running the same flooring throughout the apartment, and white or pastel-painted walls will have a similar effect. Picking out some walls with strong colour or pattern will lead the eye into another area. You could play with ceiling levels using colour or tone, possibly pulling it down over a cosy sitting area or bedroom while apparently increasing the volume of another space by painting the ceiling with a pale neutral or pastel tint.

1△

2▽

3▽

PLANNING YOUR LIGHTING

Successful lighting must be functional to enable you to work efficiently and read or study without eyestrain. It must define areas of potential danger and provide general background illumination. But the decorative element of lighting is equally important. It can create an atmosphere of warmth and wellbeing, highlight objects of beauty or interest and transform an interior with areas of light and shadow.

Living areas

For the living areas of the house, the accent should be one of versatility, creating areas of light where they are needed most, both for function and dramatic effect. Seating areas are best served by lighting placed at a low level so that naked bulbs are not directed straight into the eyes, and in such a position that the pages of a book or newspaper are illuminated from beside the reader. Choose lighting which is not so harsh that it would cause glare from white paper, and supplement it with additional low-powered lighting to reduce the effects of contrast between the page and darker areas beyond.

Working at a desk demands similar conditions but the light source must be situated in front of you to avoid throwing your own shadow across the work. Choose a properly shaded desk lamp, or conceal lighting under wall storage or bookshelves above the desk.

Similar concealed lighting is ideal for a wall-hung hi-fi system but you may require extra lighting in the form of ceiling-mounted downlighters to illuminate the shelves themselves. Alternatively, use fittings designed to clip onto the shelves or wall uprights.

Concealed lighting in other areas of the living room can be very attractive. Strip lights placed on top and at the back of high cupboards will bounce light off the ceiling into the room. Hide lighting behind pelmets to accentuate curtains, or along a wall to light pictures. Individual artworks can be picked out with specially designed strip lights placed above them, or use a ceiling spot light which is adjustable to place the pool of light exactly where it is required. Take care with pictures protected by glass as reflections will destroy the desired effect. Use lighting in an alcove or recess to give maximum impact to an attractive display of collected items.

SEE ALSO

Details for: ▷	
Lighting circuits	323-331
Light fittings	325

Concealed lighting
Interesting effects are created by concealing the actual source of artificial light and allowing it to bounce off adjacent surfaces to illuminate areas of the room.

Atmospheric lighting
Carefully placed light fittings produce an atmosphere of warmth and wellbeing.

PLANNING YOUR LIGHTING

SEE ALSO

◁ Details for:
Double insulation	**288**
Two-way switching	**300**
Desk lighting	37
Bathroom safety	290
Lighting circuits	323–331
Light fittings	325
Cupboard strip lights	327
Dimmer switches	327, 328

Bedside lamps
(Below)
You can expend a great deal of thought on planning the lighting in your bedroom only to find that two simple bedside lamps are the perfect solution.

Sleeping areas

Bedside lamps are essential requirements in any bedroom, or better still, use concealed lighting above the bedhead. Position the fitting low enough to prevent light falling on your face as you lie in bed. Install two lights behind the baffle over a double bed, each controlled individually so that your partner can sleep undisturbed if you want to read into the early hours. A dressing table needs its own light source placed so that it cannot be seen in the mirror but illuminates the person using it. Wall lights or downlighters in the ceiling will provide atmospheric lighting but install two-way switching (◁) so that you can control them from the bed and the door. Make sure bedside light fittings in a child's room are completely tamper-proof and, preferably, double-insulated (◁). A dimmer switch controlling the main room lighting will provide enough light to comfort a child at night but can be turned to full brightness when he or she is playing in the evening.

Dining areas/kitchens

A rise-and-fall unit is the ideal fitting to light a dining table because its height can be adjusted exactly. If you eat in the kitchen, have separate controls for the table lighting and work areas so that you can create a cosy dining area without having to illuminate the rest of the room. In addition to a good background light, illuminate kitchen worktops with strip lights placed under the wall cupboards but hidden from view by baffles along the front edges. Place a track light or downlighters over the sink to eliminate your own shadow.

Bathrooms

Safety must be your first priority when lighting a bathroom. Fittings must be designed to protect electrical connections from moisture and steam, and they must be controlled from outside the room or by a ceiling-mounted switch. It can be difficult to create atmospheric lighting in a bathroom, but concealed light directed onto the ceiling is one solution as long as you provide another source of light over the basin mirror.

Stairways

Light staircases from above so that treads are illuminated clearly, throwing the risers into shadow. This will define the steps clearly for anyone with poor eyesight. Place a light over each landing or turn of the staircase. Two- or even three-way switching is essential to be certain that no-one has to negotiate the stairs in darkness.

Workshops

Plan workshop lighting with efficiency and safety in mind. Light a workbench like a desk and provide individual, adjustable fittings for machine tools.

Bathroom lighting
(Right)
Light fittings concealed behind a translucent screen produce an original and safe form of lighting for a bathroom.

Concentrating areas of illumination
(Above)
Spotlights will concentrate pools of light to illuminate the functional area of a kitchen and a dining table.

An improvised lampshade
(Left)
This Oriental sunshade will throw a diffused light on the dining table while bouncing extra light off the ceiling.

2

ACCESS	**40**
PREPARATION AND PRIMING	**43**
PREPARING MASONRY	44
PREPARING PLASTER	50
PREPARING WALLCOVERINGS	52
PREPARING WOODWORK	53
PREPARING METALWORK	60
PREPARING TILES	62
APPLYING FINISHES	**63**
MASONRY	64
WALLS/CEILINGS	67
WOODWORK	74
METALWORK	85
PANELLING	87
WALLCOVERINGS	90
TILING	99
FLOORCOVERINGS	113

DECORATING

BEFORE YOU BEGIN

Timing, weather and the condition of the site are important factors to consider before you decorate outside. Indoors, you have the problem of what to do with a room full of furniture and furnishings while you work.

SEE ALSO
◁ Details for:
Work platforms   42

OUTSIDE THE HOUSE

Plan your work so that you can begin the actual decoration of the house exterior in late summer and autumn so that the previous warm weather will have dried out the fabric of the building sufficiently.

The best weather for decorating is a warm but overcast day. Avoid painting on rainy days or in direct sunlight, as both can ruin new paintwork. You should follow the sun around the house, however, so that its warmth dries out the night's dew before you get there.

Don't work on windy days either, or dust will be deposited on the fresh paint. Sprinkle water around doorways or spray with a houseplant spray before you paint as this settles dust, which you would churn up with your feet.

Clear away any rubbish from around the house, which will slow down your progress or even cause accidents. Cut back overhanging foliage from trees or shrubs. Protect plants and paving with dust sheets in the work area.

INSIDE THE HOUSE

Before you decorate a room inside, carry out all repairs necessary and have the chimney swept if you use an open fire: a soot fall would ruin your decorations. Clear as much furniture from the room as possible, and group what is left under dust sheets.

Lift any rugs or carpets then spray water on the floor and sweep it to collect loose dust before you begin to paint. Protect finished wood or tiled floors with dust sheets.

Remove all furnishings such as pictures and lampshades and unscrew door handles and fingerplates. Keep the knob handy in the room with you, in case you get shut in accidentally.

WHAT TO WEAR

Naturally, you will wear old clothes when decorating, but avoid woollen garments, which tend to leave hairs sticking to paintwork. Dungarees with loops and large pockets for tools are ideal for decorating and other work.

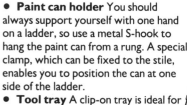

Ladder accessories
Kit out your ladder with a range of helpful devices to make working easier and safer. This ladder features adjustable feet (1) for uneven ground, a foot rest for comfort (2), a clamp for a paint can (3), a tool tray (4), and a stay (5), to hold the top away from eaves or gutters.

MEANS OF ACCESS

Whether you are decorating inside or outside, you must provide adequate means of reaching the area you are working on. Using inefficient equipment and makeshift structures is dangerous; but even if you don't want to buy your own ladders, you can hire them quite cheaply. Safety and comfort while working are other important considerations, and there's a range of devices and accessories to make the job that much easier.

Types of ladders and access equipment

Stepladders are essential for interior decoration. Traditional wooden stepladders are still available, but they have been largely superseded by lightweight aluminium alloy types. You should have at least one pair which stand about 2m (6ft 6in) high to reach a ceiling, without having to stand on the top step. Another, shorter ladder might be more convenient for other jobs and you can use them both, with scaffold boards, to build a platform.

Outdoors you'll need ladders to reach up to eaves height. Double and triple wooden extension ladders are very heavy, so consider a metal one.

Some doubles and most triples are operated by a rope and pulley so that they can be extended single-handed.

To estimate the length of ladder you need, add together the ceiling heights of your house. Add at least one metre (about 3ft) to the length to allow for the angle and access to a platform.

There are many versions of dual- or even multi-purpose ladders, which convert from stepladder to straight ladder. A well-designed, versatile ladder is a good compromise.

Sectional scaffold frames can be built up to form towers at any convenient height for decorating inside and outside. Wide feet prevent the tower sinking into the ground, and adjustable versions allow you to level it. Some models have locking castors, which enable you to move the tower.

Towers are ideal for painting a large expanse of wall outdoors. Indoors, smaller platforms made from the same scaffold components bring high ceilings within easy reach.

Accessories for ladders

• **Ladder stay** A stay holds the ladder away from the wall. It is an essential piece of equipment when painting overhanging eaves and gutters: you would otherwise be forced to lean back and possibly overbalance.
• **Clip-on platform** A wide flat board, which clamps to the rungs, provides a comfortable platform to stand on while working for long periods.
• **Adjustable legs** Bolt-on accessories, which enable you to level the foot of a ladder on uneven ground.

• **Paint can holder** You should always support yourself with one hand on a ladder, so use a metal S-hook to hang the paint can from a rung. A special clamp, which can be fixed to the stile, enables you to position the can at one side of the ladder.
• **Tool tray** A clip-on tray is ideal for holding a small selection of tools.

Alloy stepladder   **Dual-purpose ladder**   **Scaffold tower**   **Extending ladder**

WORKING WITH LADDERS

When you buy or hire a ladder, wooden or metal, bear in mind that:
- Wooden ladders should be made from straight-grained, knot-free timber.
- Good-quality wooden ladders have hardwood rungs tenoned through the upright stiles and secured with wedges.
- Wooden rungs with reinforcing metal rods stretched under them are safer than ones without.
- End caps or foot pads are an advantage to prevent the ladder from slipping on hard ground.
- Adjustability is a prime consideration. Choose a ladder that enables you to gain access to various parts of the building and which converts to a compact unit for storage.
- The rungs of overlapping sections of an extension ladder should align or the gap between the rungs might be too small to secure a good foothold.
- Choose an extension ladder with a rope, pulley and an automatic latch, which locks the extension to its rung.
- Check that you can buy or hire a range of accessories (see opposite) to fit your make of ladder.
- Choose a stepladder with a platform at the top to take cans and trays.
- Treads should be comfortable to stand on. Stepladders with wide, flat treads are the best choice.
- Stepladders with extended stiles give you a handhold at the top of the steps.
- Wooden stepladders often have a rope to stop the two halves sliding apart. A better solution used on most metal stepladders is a folding stay, which locks in the open position.

Is the ladder safe to use?

Check ladders regularly and before you use them after a winter's break. Inspect a hired ladder before use.

Look for splits opening along the stiles, check that there are no missing or broken rungs and that the joints are tight. Sight along the stiles to make sure they are aligned, or the ladder could rock when leant against a wall.

Inspect wooden ladders for signs of woodworm or rot. Even a few holes or sponginess could signify serious damage below the surface. Test that the wood is sound before using the ladder and treat it with a woodworm fluid or preservative. If in doubt, scrap the ladder for safety's sake.

Check that fixings for hinges and pulleys are secure and lubricate them. Inspect the pulley rope for fraying and renew if necessary.

Oil or varnish wooden ladders regularly to stop them drying out. Apply extra coats to the rungs (which take most wear). Don't paint a ladder as this may hide serious defects.

How to handle a ladder

Ladders are heavy and unwieldy; handle them properly so you don't damage property or injure yourself.

Carry a ladder upright, not slung across your shoulder. Hold the ladder vertically, bend your knees slightly then rock the ladder back against your shoulder. Grip one rung lower down while you support the ladder at head height with your other hand, then straighten your knees.

To erect a ladder, lay it on the ground with its feet against the wall. Gradually raise it to vertical as you walk towards the wall. Pull the feet out from the wall so that the ladder is resting at an angle of about 70 degrees – if the ladder extends to 8m (26ft) for example, its feet should be 2m (6ft 6in), or one quarter of its height, from the wall.

Raise an extending ladder to the required height while holding it upright. If it is a heavy ladder, get someone to hold it while you operate the pulley.

Handling a ladder
Carry the ladder upright, leaning back against your shoulder; grip one rung low down, another at head height. When erected, the base of the ladder should be one quarter of its height away from the wall so that it is correctly balanced.

HOW TO USE A LADDER SAFELY

More accidents are caused by using ladders unwisely than as a result of faulty equipment. Erect the ladder safely before you ascend and move it when the work is out of reach – never lean out to the side or you'll overbalance. Follow these simple, common-sense rules:

Securing the ladder
If the ground is soft, spread the load of the ladder by placing a wide board under the feet; screw a batten across the board to wedge the ladder in place.

On hard ground, make sure the ladder has anti-slip end caps and lay a sandbag (or a tough polythene bag filled with earth) at the base.

Secure the stiles near the base with rope tied to timber stakes driven into the ground at each side and just behind the ladder (1). When extending a ladder, the sections should overlap by at least one quarter of their length – but don't lean the top against the gutters, soil pipes and drainpipes, and especially glass, as they may give way.

Anchor the ladder near the top by tying it to a stout timber rail, held across the inside of the window frame. Make sure the rail extends about 300mm (1ft) on each side of the window and pad the ends to protect the wall (2).

It's a good idea to fix ring bolts at regular intervals into the masonry just below the fascia board: this is an excellent way to secure the top of a ladder as you have equally good anchor points wherever you position it. Alternatively, fix screw eyes to the masonry or a sound fascia board and attach the ladder to them.

Safety aloft
Never climb higher than four rungs from the top of the ladder or you will not be able to balance properly, and handholds will be out of reach. Don't lean sideways from a ladder either. Keep both feet on a rung and your hips centred between the stiles.

Avoid a slippery foothold by placing a sack or old doormat at the foot of the ladder to dry your boots and wipe off any mud before you ascend.

Unless the manufacturer states otherwise, do not use a ladder to form a horizontal walkway, even with a scaffold board lying on it.

Stepladders are prone to topple sideways. Clamp a strut to the ladder on uneven floors (3).

SEE ALSO

Details for: ▷	
Work platforms	42
Varnishing	82
Oiling wood	84
Woodworm	246-247
Dealing with rot	249-250

1 Staking a ladder
Secure the base of the ladder by lashing it to stakes in the ground.

2 Securing the top
Anchor the ladder to a batten held inside the window frame.

3 Supporting a stepladder
Clamp a strut to the stile to prop up a pair of stepladders.

ERECTING WORK PLATFORMS INDOORS

SEE ALSO

◁ Details for:	
Ladders	40
Scaffold tower	40

A lot of work can be carried out by moving a ladder little by little as the work progresses, but it can become tedious, perhaps leading to an accident as you try to reach just a bit further before having to move along, and then overbalance.

It's more convenient to build a work platform which allows you to tackle a large area without moving the structure. You can hire decorators' trestles and bridge a pair with a scaffold board, or make a similar structure with two pairs of stepladders (1).

Clamp or tie the board to the rungs and use two boards, one on top of the other, if two people need to use the platform at once.

An even better arrangement is to use scaffold tower components to make a mobile platform (2). Choose one with locking castors for the ideal solution for painting or papering ceilings.

2 Mobile platform
An efficient structure made from scaffold tower frames.

1 Improvised platform
A simple yet safe platform made from stepladders and a scaffold board.

Gaining access to a stairwell

Stairwells present particular problems when building work platforms. The simplest method is to use a dual-purpose staircase ladder, which can be adjusted to stand evenly on a flight (3). Anchor the steps with rope through a couple of screw eyes fixed to the stair treads; the holes will be concealed by carpet later. Rest a scaffold board between the ladder and the landing to form a bridge. Screw the board to the landing and tie the other end.

Alternatively, construct a tailor-made platform from ladders and boards to suit your staircase (4). Make sure the boards and ladders are clamped or lashed together, and that ladders can't slip on the treads. If necessary, screw wooden battens to the stairs to prevent the foot of the ladder moving.

Stair scaffold
Erect a platform to compensate for the slope of a staircase with scaffold frames.

3 Dual-purpose ladder
Use a stair ladder to straddle the flight with a scaffold board to give a level work platform.

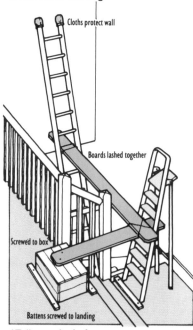

Cloths protect wall

Boards lashed together

Screwed to box

Battens screwed to landing

4 Tailor-made platform
Build a network of scaffold boards, stepladders, ladders and boxes to suit your stairwell layout.

ERECTING PLATFORMS OUTSIDE

Scaffolding is by far the best method of building a work platform to decorate the outside of a house. Towers made from slot-together frames are available for hire. Heights up to about 9m (30ft) are possible; the tallest ones require supporting 'outriggers'.

Build the lower section of the frame first and level it with adjustable feet before erecting a tower on top. As you build, climb and stand on the inside of the tower.

Erect a proper platform at the top with toe boards all round to prevent tools and materials being knocked off the tower, and extend the framework to provide hand rails all round.

Secure the tower to the house by tying it to ring bolts fixed into the masonry, as with ladders.

Some towers incorporate a staircase inside the scaffold frame; floors with a trapdoor enable you to ascend to the top of the tower. If you cannot find such a tower, the safest access is via a ladder. Make sure it extends at least 1m (about 3ft) above the staging so that you can step on and off safely.

It is difficult to reach windows and walls above an extension with just a ladder. With a scaffold tower, however, you can construct a cantilevered section fixed to the main tower, which rests on the roof of the extension.

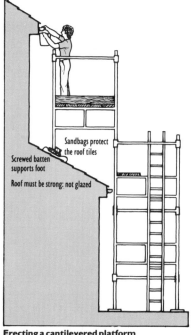

Sandbags protect the roof tiles

Screwed batten supports foot

Roof must be strong: not glazed

Erecting a cantilevered platform
The cantilever section rests on a board to spread load.

PREPARATION AND PRIMING

Thorough preparation of all surfaces is the vital first step in redecorating. If you neglect this stage, subsequent finishes will be rejected. Preparation means removing dirt, grease and loose or flaky previous finishes, as well as repairing serious deterioration such as cracks, holes, corrosion and decay. It's not just old surfaces that need attention: new masonry, timber and metalwork must be sealed against attack and priming is called for to ensure a surface is in a suitable condition to accept its finish. Consult the charts on this page for details of primers and sealers for all the materials you're likely to encounter in and around the home, then read the following sections, which examine each material in detail.

TYPES OF PRIMERS AND SEALERS

There are numerous primers and sealers to suit a variety of materials.

Stabilizing primer
Used to bind powdery or flaky materials. A clear or white liquid.
Wood primer
Standard pink or white primer prevents other coats of paint soaking in.
Aluminium wood primer
Used to seal oily hardwoods, it will also cover creosote.
General-purpose primer
Seals porous building materials and covers patchy walls and ceilings.
Metal primers
Essential to prevent corrosion in metals and to provide a key for paint.

PVA bonding agent
A general-purpose liquid adhesive for many building materials. An excellent primer and sealer when diluted, even for bituminous paints.
Water repellent
A liquid which dries colourless to seal masonry against water penetration.
Alkali-resistant primer
Used to prevent the alkali content of some materials attacking oil paints.
Aluminium spirit-based sealer
Formulated to obliterate materials likely to 'bleed' through subsequent coatings. Effective over bituminous paints, creosote, metallic paints and nicotine.

SEE ALSO
Details for: ▷
Priming brickwork	46
Waterproofing masonry	46
Priming flaky paint	48
Priming plaster	50
Priming wood	53
Priming man-made boards	54
Priming metal	60

PRIMERS AND SEALERS   SUITABILITY: DRYING TIME: COVERAGE

●Black dot denotes that primer and surface are compatible.

●Red dot denotes metal primers.

SUITABLE FOR	Stabilizing primer	Wood primer	Aluminium wood primer	General-purpose primer	Zinc phosphate	Red oxide	Calcium plumbate	Red lead	Chromate primer	PVA bonding agent	Water repellent	Alkali-resistant primer	Aluminium spirit-based sealer
Brick	●			●						●	●	●	
Stone	●			●						●	●	●	
Cement rendering	●			●						●	●	●	
Concrete	●			●						●	●	●	
Plaster	●			●						●		●	
Plasterboard	●			●								●	
Distemper	●												
Limewash	●												
Cement paint	●												
Bituminous paints										●			●
Asbestos cement	●			●						●		●	
Softwood		●	●	●					●				
Hardwood			●				●		●				
Chipboard		●	●	●					●				
Hardboard		●	●	●					●				
Plywood		●	●	●					●				
Creosoted timber			●										●
Absorbent fibre boards	●											●	
Ferrous metals (inside)					●	●							
Ferrous metals (outside)					●		●	●					
Galvanized metal							●						
Aluminium					●				●				
DRYING TIME: HOURS													
Touch dry	3	6	6	4	4	4	8	10	10	3	1	4	¼
Recoatable	16	16	16	16	10	16	24	24	24	16	12	16	1
COVERAGE (Sq. metre per litre)													
Smooth surface	9	13	15	12	13	13	13	13	13	9	3-4	10	4
Rough/Absorbent surface	7	10	11	9	10	10	10	10	10	7	2-3	7	3

• **Lead content in paint**
Lead, which is a poison, was widely used in the past as a drier in solvent-based paints including primers. (Emulsions, which are water-based, have never contained lead). Many solvent-based paints are now made without lead. If possible, choose one labelled 'no lead added' or similar. Don't let children chew old painted surfaces, which may have a high lead content.

CLEANING BRICK AND STONE

Before you decorate the outside of your house, check the condition of the brick and stonework, and carry out any necessary repairs. There's no reason why you can't paint brick or stone walls – indeed, in some areas it is traditional to do so – but if you consider masonry most attractive in its natural state, you could be faced with a problem: once masonry is painted, it is not possible to restore it to its original condition. There will always be particles of paint left in the texture of brickwork, and even smooth stone, which can be stripped successfully, may be stained by the paint.

SEE ALSO

◁ Details for:
Spirit-thinned	
masonry paint	65
Curing damp	251-258
Banister brush	482
Painting masonry	64-66

Stained brickwork

Organic growth

Efflorescence

Treating new masonry

New brickwork or stonework should be left for about three months until it is completely dry before any further treatment is considered. White powdery deposits called efflorescence may come to the surface over this period, but you can simply brush it off with a stiff-bristled brush or a piece of dry sacking (◁). After that, bricks and mortar should be weatherproof and therefore require no further protection or treatment.

Cleaning organic growth from masonry

There are innumerable species of mould growth or lichens which appear as tiny coloured specks or patches on masonry. They gradually merge until the surface is covered with colours ranging from bright orange to yellow or green, grey and black.

Moulds and lichen will only flourish in damp conditions, so try to cure the source of the problem before treating the growth (◁). If one side of the house always faces away from the sun, it will have little chance to dry out. Relieve the situation by cutting back overhanging trees or shrubs to increase ventilation to the wall.

Make sure the damp-proof course (DPC) is working adequately and is not being bridged by piled earth or debris.

Cracked or corroded rainwater pipes leaking onto the wall are another common cause of organic growth. Feel behind the pipe with your fingers or use a hand mirror to locate the leak.

Removing the growth
Brush the wall vigorously with a stiff-bristled brush. This can be an unpleasant, dusty job, so wear a gauze facemask. Brush away from you to avoid debris being flicked into your eyes.

Microscopic spores will remain even after brushing. Kill these with a solution of bleach or, if the wall suffers persistently from fungal growth, use a proprietary fungicide, available from most DIY stores.

Using a bleach solution
Mix one part household bleach with four parts water. Paint the solution onto the wall using an old paintbrush, then 48 hours later wash the surface with clean water, using a scrubbing brush. Brush on a second application of bleach solution if the original fungal growth was severe.

Using a fungicidal solution
Dilute the fungicide with water according to the manufacturer's instructions and apply it liberally to the wall with an old paintbrush. Leave it for 24 hours then rinse the wall with clean water. In extreme cases, give the wall two washes of fungicide, allowing 24 hours between applications and a further 24 hours before washing it down with water.

Removing efflorescence from masonry

Soluble salts within building materials such as cement, brick, stone and plaster gradually migrate to the surface along with the water as a wall dries out. The result is a white crystalline deposit called efflorescence.

The same condition can occur on old masonry if it is subjected to more than average moisture. Efflorescence itself is not harmful but the source of the damp causing it must be identified and cured before decoration proceeds.

Regularly brush the deposit from the wall with a dry stiff-bristled brush or coarse sacking until the crystals cease to form – don't attempt to wash off the crystals; they'll merely dissolve in the water and soak back into the wall. Above all, don't attempt to decorate a wall which is still efflorescing, and therefore damp.

When the wall is completely dry, paint the surface with an alkali-resistant primer to neutralize the effect of the crystals before you paint with oil paint; water-thinned paints or clear sealants let the wall breathe, so are not affected by the alkali content of the masonry. Some specially formulated masonry paint can be used without primer (◁).

CLEANING OLD MASONRY

Whatever type of finish you intend to apply to a wall, all loose debris and dirt must be brushed off with a stiff-bristled brush. Don't use a wire brush unless the masonry is badly soiled as it may leave scratch marks.

Brush along the mortar joints to dislodge loose pointing. Defective mortar can be repaired easily at this stage (see right), but if you fail to disturb it now by being too cautious, it will fall out as you paint, creating far more work in the long run.

Removing unsightly stains

Improve the appearance of stone or brick left in its natural state by washing it with clean water. Play a hose gently onto the masonry while you scrub it with a stiff-bristled brush (1). Scrub heavy deposits with half a cup of ammonia added to a bucketful of water, then rinse again.

Abrade small cement stains or other marks from brickwork with a piece of similar-coloured brick, or scrub the area with a household kitchen cleanser.

Remove spilled oil paint from masonry with a proprietary paint stripper (▷). Put on gloves and protective goggles, then paint on the stripper, stippling it into the rough texture (2). After about ten minutes, remove it with a scraper and a soft wire brush. If paint remains in crevices, dip the brush in stripper and gently scrub it with small circular strokes. When the wall is clean, rinse with water.

1 Remove dirt and dust by washing

2 Stipple paint stripper onto spilled oil paint

REPOINTING MASONRY

The mortar joints between bricks and stone can become porous with age, allowing rainwater to penetrate to the inside, causing damp patches to appear, ruining decorations. Replacing the mortar pointing, which deflects the water, is quite straightforward but time consuming. Tackle only a small, manageable area at a time, using a ready-mixed mortar or your own mix.

Applying the pointing mortar

Rake out the old mortar pointing with a thin wooden lath to a depth of about 12mm (½in). Use a cold chisel or a special plugging chisel and a club hammer to dislodge firmly embedded sections, then brush out the joints with a stiff-bristled brush.

Flick water into the joints using an old paintbrush, making sure the bricks or stones are soaked so they will not absorb too much water from the fresh mortar. Mix up some mortar in a bucket and transfer it to a hawk. If you're mixing your own mortar, use the proportions 1 part cement: 1 part lime: 6 parts builders' sand.

Pick up a little sausage of mortar on the back of a small pointing trowel and push it firmly into the upright joints. This can be difficult to do without the mortar dropping off, so hold the hawk under each joint to catch it.

Try not to smear the face of the bricks with mortar, or it will stain. Repeat the process for the horizontal joints. The actual shape of the pointing is not vital at this stage.

Once the mortar is firm enough to retain a thumb print, it is ready for shaping. Match the style of pointing used on the rest of the house (see below). When the pointing has almost hardened, brush the wall to remove traces of surplus mortar.

Shaping the mortar joints

The joints shown here are commonly used for brickwork but they are also suitable for stonework. Additionally, stone may have raised mortar joints.

Flush joints

The easiest profile to produce, a flush joint is used where the wall is sheltered or painted. Rub each joint with sacking; start with the verticals.

Rubbed (rounded) joints

Bricklayers make a rubbed or rounded joint with a tool shaped like a sled runner with a handle: the semi-circular blade is run along the joints.

Improvise by bending a short length of metal tube or rod. Use the curved section only or you'll gouge the mortar. Alternatively, use a length of 9mm (⅜in) diameter plastic tube.

Raked joints

A raked joint is used to emphasize the type of bonding pattern of a brick wall. It's not suitable for soft bricks or for a wall that takes a lot of weathering. Scrape out a little of the mortar then tidy up the joints by running a 9mm (⅜in) lath along them.

Weatherstruck joints

The sloping profile is intended to shed rainwater from the wall. Shape the mortar with the edge of a pointing trowel. Start with the vertical joints, and slope them in either direction but be consistent. During the process, mortar will tend to spill from the bottom of a joint, as surplus is cut off. Bricklayers use a tool called a 'frenchman' to neaten the work: it has a narrow blade with the tip bent at right-angles. Make your own by bending a thin metal strip then bind insulating tape round the other end to form a handle, or bend the tip of an old kitchen knife after heating it in the flame of a blowtorch or cooker burner.

You will find it easiest to use a wooden batten to guide the blade of the frenchman along the joints, but nail scraps of plywood at each end of the batten to hold it off the wall.

Align the batten with the bottom of the horizontal joints, then draw the tool along it, cutting off the excess mortar, which drops to the ground.

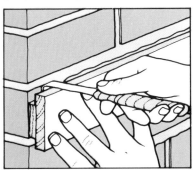
Use a frenchman to trim weatherstruck joints

SEE ALSO

Details for: ▷

Paint stripper	59
Penetrating damp	251-252
Mixing mortar	425
Pointing tools	478
Plugging chisel	480
Banister brush	482

● **Mortar dyes**
Liquid or powder additives are available for changing the colour of mortar to match existing pointing. Colour matching is difficult and smears can stain the bricks permanently.

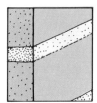
Flush joint

Rubbed joint

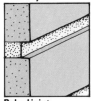
Raked joint

Weatherstruck joint

45

REPAIRING MASONRY

Cracks in external walls can be either the source of penetrating damp (◁), which ruins your decorations inside, or the result of a much more serious *problem: subsidence in the foundations. Whatever the cause, it's obvious that you shouldn't just ignore the danger signs, but effect immediate cures.*

SEE ALSO

◁ Details for:

Work platform	42
Efflorescence	44
Organic growth	46
Reinforced emulsion	65
Penetrating	
damp	251-252
Building	
Control Officer	18
Primers	43
Paint brushes	482
Spray equipment	484

Filling cracked masonry

If substantial cracks are apparent in a brick or stone wall, consult a builder or your local Building Control Officer to ascertain the cause.

If the crack seems to be stable, it can be filled. Where the crack follows the line of the mortar joints, rake out those affected and repoint in the normal way, as previously described. A crack that splits one or more bricks or stones cannot be repaired, and the damaged area should be removed and replaced, unless you are painting the wall.

Use a ready-mixed mortar with a little PVA bonding agent added to help it to stick. Soak the cracked masonry with a hose to encourage the mortar to flow deeply into the crack.

Crack may follow pointing only

Cracked bricks could signify serious faults

Priming brickwork

Brickwork will only need to be primed in certain circumstances. An alkali-resistant primer will guard against efflorescence (◁) and a stabilizing solution will bind crumbling masonry and help to seal it at the same time.

If you are planning to paint the wall for the first time with an exterior emulsion, you may find that the first coat is difficult to apply due to the suction of the dry, porous brick. Thin the first coat slightly with water.

To economize when using a reinforced emulsion (◁) prime the wall with a cement paint with a little fine sand mixed in thoroughly.

Waterproofing masonry

Colourless water-repellent fluids are intended to make masonry impervious to water without colouring it or stopping it from breathing (important to allow moisture within the walls to dry out).

Prepare the surface thoroughly before applying the fluid: make good any cracks in bricks or pointing and remove organic growth (◁) and allow the wall to dry out thoroughly.

Apply the fluid generously with a large paintbrush and stipple it into the joints. Apply a second coat as soon as the first has been absorbed to ensure that there are no bare patches where water could seep in. To be sure that you're covering the wall properly, use a sealant containing a fugitive dye, which disappears gradually after a few weeks.

Carefully paint up to surrounding woodwork; if you accidentally splash sealant onto it, wash it down immediately with a cloth dampened with white spirit.

If the area you need to treat is large, consider spraying on the fluid, using a hired spray gun. You'll need to rig up a substantial work platform (◁) and mask off all timber and metalwork that adjoins the wall. The fumes from the fluid can be dangerous if inhaled, so be sure to wear a proper respirator, which you can also hire.

I Replacing a spalled brick
Having mortared top and one end, slip the new brick into the hole you have cut.

REPAIRING SPALLED MASONRY

Moisture penetrating soft masonry will expand in icy weather, flaking off the outer face of brickwork and stonework. The process, known as spalling, not only looks unattractive but also allows water to seep into the surface. Repairs to spalled bricks or stones can be made, although the treatment depends on the severity of the problem.

If spalling is localized, it is possible to cut out individual bricks or stones and replace them with matching ones. The sequence below describes how it's tackled with brickwork, but the process is similar for a stone wall.

Spalling bricks caused by frost damage

Where the spalling is extensive, it's likely that the whole wall is porous and your best remedy is to paint on a stabilizing solution to bind the loose material together, then apply a textured wall finish, as used to patch pebbledash, which will disguise the faults and waterproof the wall at the same time.

Replacing a spalled brick
Use a cold chisel and club hammer to rake out the pointing surrounding the brick then chop out the brick itself. If the brick is difficult to prise out, drill into it many times with a large-diameter masonry bit, then attack the brick with a cold chisel and hammer: it should crumble, enabling you to remove the pieces easily.

To fit the replacement brick, first dampen the opening and spread mortar on the base and one side. Butter the dampened replacement brick on the top and one end and slot it into the hole (**I**).

Shape the pointing to match the surrounding brickwork then, once it is dry, apply a clear water repellent.

REPAIRING RENDER

Brickwork may be clad with a smooth or roughcast cement-based render for improved weatherproofing and to give a decorative finish; often the render is susceptible to the effects of damp and frost, which can cause cracking, bulging and staining. Before you redecorate a rendered wall, make good any damage, clean off surface dirt, mould growth and flaky material to achieve a long-lasting finish.

Cracked render allows moisture to penetrate

Blown pebbledash parts from the masonry

Rust staining due to leaky guttering

Repairing defective render

Before you repair cracked render, correct any structural faults which may have contributed to it. Brush to remove loose particles. Apply a stabilizing solution if the wall is dusty.

Ignore fine hair cracks if you paint the wall with reinforced emulsion, which covers minor faults. Rake out larger cracks using a cold chisel, dampen with water and fill flush with the surface with exterior filler. Fill major cracks with a mortar mix comprising 1 part cement: 4 parts builders' sand, with a little PVA

Reinforcing a crack in render

To prevent a crack in render opening up again, reinforce the repair with a fine scrim embedded in a bitumen base coat. Rake out the crack to remove any loose material, then wet it. Fill the crack just proud of the surface with a mortar mix of 1 part cement: 4 parts builders' sand. When this has stiffened scrape it flush with the render.

When the mortar has hardened, brush on a generous coat of bitumen base coat, making sure it extends at

Patching pebbledash

Pebbledash comprises small stones stuck to a thin coat of render over a thicker base coat. If damp gets behind pebbledashing, one or both layers may separate. Hack off any loose render to a sound base and seal it with stabilizer. If necessary, repair the first 'scratchcoat' of render. Restore the texture of the top 'buttercoat' with a thick paste made from PVA bonding agent. Mix one part of cement paint powder with three parts clean, sharp (plastering) sand. Stir in one measure of bonding agent diluted with three parts water to form a thick, creamy paste. Load a banister brush and scrub the paste onto the bare surface.

Apply a second generous coat of

Removing rust stains

Faulty plumbing will often leave rusty streaks on a rendered wall. Before decorating, prime the stains with an aluminium spirit-based sealer or they will bleed through. Rust marks may also appear on a pebbledashed wall, well away from any metalwork: these are caused by iron pyrites in the aggregate. Chip out the pyrites with a cold chisel, then seal the stain.

bonding agent added to help it stick to the masonry.

Bulges in render can indicate that the cladding has parted from the masonry. Tap gently with a hammer to find the extent of these hollow areas; hack off the material to sound edges. Undercut the perimeter of the hole to give a grip for the filler material.

Brush out debris then apply a coat of PVA bonding agent. When PVA is tacky, trowel on a mortar mix as for filling cracks then smooth with a wet trowel.

least 75mm (3in) on both sides of the crack. Embed strips of open weave scrim (sold with the base coat) into the bitumen, using a stippling and brushing action (1). While it is still wet, feather the edges of the bitumen with a foam roller (2), bedding the scrim into it. After 24 hours, the bitumen will be hard, black and shiny. Apply a second coat, feather with a roller and, when it has dried, apply two full coats of a compatible reinforced emulsion (▷).

paste, stippling it to form a coarse texture (1). Leave for about 15 minutes to firm up then, with a loaded brush, stipple it to match the texture of the pebbles. Let the paste harden fully before painting.

To leave the pebbledash unpainted, make a patch using replacement pebbles. The result will not be a perfect match but could save you painting the entire wall. Cut back the blown area and apply a scratchcoat followed by a buttercoat. While this is still wet, fling pebbles onto the surface from a dustpan; they should stick to the soft render but you'll have to repeat until the coverage is even.

SEE ALSO

Details for: ▷	
Reinforced emulsion	65
Masonry paints	65
Structural faults	121
Rendering	168-171

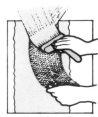
1 Embed the scrim

2 Feather with roller

1 Stipple the texture

PAINTED MASONRY

Painted masonry inside the house is usually in fairly good order, and apart from a good wash down to remove dust and grease, and a light sanding to give a key for the new finish, there's little else you need to do. Outside, however, it's a different matter: subjected to extremes of heat, cold and rain, the surface is likely to be detrimentally affected by stains, flaking and chalkiness.

SEE ALSO

◁ Details for:

Spalled brick	46
Flue liners	388-389
Primers	43
Bitumen basecoat	47
Curing damp	251-258

Chalky surface needs stabilizing

Strip flaky paintwork to a sound surface

Curing a chalky surface

Rub the palm of your hand lightly over the surface of the wall to see if it is chalky. If the paint rubs off as a powdery deposit, treat the wall before you redecorate. Brush the surface with a stiff-bristled brush then liberally paint the whole wall with a stabilizing primer, which binds the chalky surface so that paint will adhere to it. Use a white stabilizing primer, which can act as an undercoat. Clean splashes of the fluid from surrounding woodwork with white spirit. If the wall is very dusty, apply a second coat of stabilizer after about 12 hours. Wait a further 12 hours before painting over.

Dealing with flaky paintwork

Flaking is commonly due to poor surface preparation or because the paint and preparatory treatments were incompatible. Damp walls will cause flaking, so remedy this and let the wall dry out before further treatment. Another cause could be too many previous coats of paint, which makes the top layers flake off.

Subsequent coats of paint will not bind to a flaky surface, so this must be removed. Use a paint scraper and stiff-bristled brush to remove all loose material. Coarse glasspaper should finish the job or at least feather the edges of any stubborn patches. Stabilize the surface as for chalky walls before repainting.

If the flaking is as a result of spalling brickwork (◁), stabilize the affected bricks with a bitumen base coat. Feather the edges with a foam roller, leave the bitumen to harden for 24 hours then paint the wall with two coats of reinforced emulsion.

Treating a stained chimney

A painted brick chimney stack with the outline of courses showing clearly through the paint as brown staining is caused by a breakdown of the internal rendering or 'pargeting' of the chimney; this allows tar deposits to migrate through the mortar to the outer paintwork. To solve the problem, fit a flue liner in the chimney (◁), then treat the stains with an aluminium spirit-based sealer before applying a new coat of paint.

ASBESTOS CEMENT

Asbestos cement is used to make various items in and around the home, typically wallboards, corrugated lightweight roof cladding, gutters and downpipes. Nowadays, asbestos is regarded as an unnecessary danger – the dust is a real health hazard if inhaled – and it's consequently not recommended where an alternative is available. But if your home already contains the material, there's a safe way to treat it and keep it looking good.

Whenever you are working with any material containing asbestos, take the precaution of wearing a gauze facemask and of damping the surface with water whenever rubbing down. If asbestos sheets or boards are in a friable (crumbly) condition, seek professional advice.

Dealing with new asbestos
Asbestos cement boards or sheets vary in their alkali content but oil paints are likely to be attacked if the boards become damp, unless they are primed with an alkali-resistant primer. Where possible, prime both sides and edges of asbestos sheets, particularly where condensation might occur.

Before you fill fixing nails or screws, treat them with a metal primer to prevent rust stains.

Normally no primer is needed for emulsion paint, except perhaps a coat of stabilizing solution. Apply a thinned coat of paint or seal with cement paint then reinforced emulsion.

If you want to decorate over asbestos sheets with wallcovering, prime and fill all fixings and treat with one coat of white spirit-thinned stabilizing primer. Follow with one coat of size and allow it to dry before you hang the paper.

Previously painted asbestos
Wash down paintwork that's in good condition with a sugar soap or detergent solution, then rinse with clean water. Lightly key gloss paint with wet and dry abrasive paper dipped in water. Avoid rubbing through to the surface of the asbestos.

Use a stiff-bristled brush to remove flaky paint then wash down as previously described. Let the surface dry then bind it with a stabilizing primer, before painting. Build up low patches with undercoat, rubbing down with wet and dry abrasive paper.

Chimney stained by tar deposits from the flue

REPAIRING CONCRETE

Concrete is used in and around the house as a surface for solid floors, drives, paths and walls. In common with other building materials, it suffers from the effects of damp – spalling and efflorescence – and related defects such as cracking and crumbling. Repairs can usually be made in much the same way as for brickwork and render, although there are some special considerations you should be aware of. If the damage is widespread, however, it's quite straightforward to resurface it prior to decorating.

Sealing concrete

New concrete has a high alkali content and efflorescence can develop on the surface as it dries out. Do not use any finish other than a water-thinned paint until the concrete is completely dry. Treat efflorescence on concrete as for brickwork (▷).

A porous concrete wall should be water-proofed with a clear sealant on the exterior. Some reinforced emulsions will cover bitumen satisfactorily but it will bleed through most paints unless you prime it with a PVA bonding agent diluted 50 per cent with water. Alternatively, use an aluminium spirit-based sealer.

Cleaning dirty concrete

Clean dirty concrete as you would brickwork. Where a concrete drive or garage floor, for instance, is stained with patches of oil or grease, soak up fresh spillages immediately to prevent them becoming permanent stains. Sprinkle dry sand onto patches of oil to absorb any liquid deposits, collect it up and wash the area with white spirit or degreasing solution.

Binding dusty concrete

Concrete is trowelled when it is laid to give a flat finish; if this is overdone, cement is brought to the surface and when the concrete dries out, this thin layer begins to break up within a short time, producing a loose, dusty surface. You must not apply a decorative finish to concrete in this condition.

Treat a concrete wall with stabilizing primer but paint a dusty floor with one or two coats of PVA bonding agent mixed with five parts of water. Use the same solution to prime a particularly porous surface.

Making good cracks and holes

Rake out and brush away loose debris from cracks or holes in concrete. If the crack is less than about 6mm (¼in) wide, open it up a little with a cold chisel so that it will accept a filling. Undercut the edges to form a lip so the filler will grip.

To fill a hole in concrete, add a fine aggregate such as gravel to the sand and cement mix. Make sure the fresh concrete sticks in shallow depressions by priming the damaged surface with 3 parts bonding agent: 1 part water. When the primed surface becomes tacky, trowel in the concrete and smooth it.

Treating spalled concrete

When concrete breaks up or spalls due to the action of frost, the process is accelerated when steel reinforcement is exposed and begins to corrode. Fill the concrete as described above but prepare and prime the metalwork first (▷). If spalling recurs, particularly in exposed conditions, protect the wall with a bitumen base coat and a compatible reinforced emulsion paint.

Spalling concrete ▷
Rusting metalwork causes concrete to spall

REPAIRING A CONCRETE FLOOR

An uneven or pitted concrete floor must be made flat and level before you apply any form of floorcovering. You can do this fairly easily using a proprietary self-levelling screed. But first of all you must ensure the surface is free from dampness.

Testing for dampness
Do not lay any tiles or sheet floorcoverings (or apply a levelling screed) to a floor that's damp. A new floor should incorporate a damp-proof membrane (DPM) but must be left to dry out for six weeks before any covering is added.

If you suspect an existing floor is damp, make a simple test by laying a small piece of polythene on the concrete then seal it all round with adhesive tape. After one or two days, look to see if there are any traces of moisture on the underside.

For a more accurate assessment, hire a moisture meter. This device has contact pins or deep wall probes, which, when stuck into the suspect surface, gives a moisture saturation percentage: if the moisture reading does not exceed 6 per cent proceed with covering or levelling the floor.

If either test indicates treatment is necessary, paint the floor with a waterproofing compound. Prime the surface first with a slightly diluted coat, then brush on two full-strength coats, allowing each to dry between applications. If necessary you can then lay a self-levelling screed over the waterproofing compound.

Applying a self-levelling compound
Fill holes and cracks deeper than about 3mm (⅛in) by first raking out and undercutting the edges (1), then spreading self-levelling compound over the entire floor surface. This material is supplied as a powder, which you mix with water.

Make sure the floor is clean and free from damp, then pour some of the compound in a corner furthest from the door. Spread the compound with a trowel (2) until it is about 3mm (⅛in) thick, then leave it to seek its own level.

Continue across the floor, joining the area of compound until the entire surface is covered. You can walk on the floor after about one hour, but leave the compound to harden for a few days before laying permanent floorcovering.

SEE ALSO

Details for: ▷

Efflorescence	44
Priming metal	60
Primers	43
Repairing brickwork	46
Repairing render	47
Masonry paints	65
Damp-proof membrane	182
Curing damp	251-258
Mixing concrete	439

1 Rake out cracks

2 Apply compound
Spread levelling compound with a trowel.

49

PLASTERWORK: MAKING GOOD

SEE ALSO

◁ Details for:
Lining paper   94
Plasterboard
joints   164-165
Primers   43
Decorator's tools   481

Plaster is used to finish the inner surfaces of the walls and ceilings in most houses. Ceilings are traditionally clad with slim wood laths which are then plastered over: the plaster grips between the laths. Walls are usually covered directly with a backing (floating) coat of plaster and a smooth finish coat – various grades of plaster are used to suit the condition and quality of the masonry.

In very old houses, the walls might be lath-and-plaster covered. In modern houses, plasterboard is used instead for convenience. A plastered or boarded surface can be decorated with paint, paper or cladding such as tiles; the preparation is similar for each. Whatever you intend to use as a decorative finish, the plastered wall or ceiling must be made good by filling cracks or holes.

Smooth finish
Smooth the surface of small repairs with a wet brush or knife to reduce the amount of sanding required later.

PREPARING TO DECORATE

NEW PLASTER

New plaster must dry out thoroughly before it can be decorated with paint or paper. Allow efflorescence to form on the surface then wipe off with coarse sacking; repeat periodically until the crystals cease to appear.

Use an alkali-resistant primer if you are applying oil paint. Priming isn't necessary for emulsion, but apply a thinned coat on absorbent plaster.

Size new, absorbent plaster before wallpapering, or the water will be sucked too quickly from the paste, resulting in poor adhesion. Use a proprietary size or heavy-duty wallpaper paste. If you are hanging vinyl wallcovering, make sure the size contains fungicide as the covering can't breathe like a plain paper can.

For tiling, no further preparation is needed, once the plaster is dry.

OLD PLASTER

Apart from filling minor defects and dusting down, old dry plaster needs no further preparation. If the wall is patchy, apply a general purpose primer. If the surface is friable apply a stabilizing solution before you decorate.

Don't decorate damp plaster; cure, then let the plaster dry out first.

PLASTERBOARD

Fill all joints between newly fixed plasterboard (◁) then, whether you're painting or papering the board, daub all nail heads with zinc phosphate primer.

Before you paint plasterboard with oil paint, prime it with one coat of general-purpose primer. One coat of thinned emulsion may be needed on an absorbent board before the normal full-strength coats are applied.

Prior to hanging wallcovering on plasterboard, seal the surface with a general-purpose primer thinned with white spirit. After 48 hours, apply a coat of size. This allows wet-stripping without disturbing the board's paper facing.

PAINTED PLASTER

Wash any paintwork in good condition with sugar soap or detergent solution to remove dirt and grease. Use water and medium-grade wet and dry abrasive paper to key the surface of gloss paint, particularly if covering with emulsion. Prime and allow to dry.

If the ceiling is severely stained by smoke and nicotine, prime it with an alkali-resistant primer or an aluminium spirit-based sealer.

If you want to hang wallcovering on oil paint, key then size the wall. Add dry plaster or cellulose filler to the size to provide an additional key. Cross-line the wall with lining paper (◁) before hanging a heavy embossed paper on oil paint.

Remove flaky materials with a scraper or stiff-bristled brush. Feather off the edges of the paintwork with wet and dry abrasive paper. Treat bare plaster patches with a general-purpose-primer. Should the edges of old paintwork continue to show, prime those areas again, rubbing down afterwards. Apply stabilizing primer if the paint is friable.

Apply tiles over sound paintwork after you have removed any loose material.

Cracks in solid plaster

Rake loose material from a crack with the blade of a scraper or filling knife (1). Undercut the edges of larger cracks to provide a key for the filling. Mix up interior-grade cellulose filler to a stiff consistency or use a pre-mixed filler.

Dampen the crack with a paintbrush, then press the filler in with a filling knife. Drag the blade across the crack to force the filler in then draw it along the crack (2) to smooth the filler. Leave the filler standing slightly proud of the surface ready for rubbing down smooth and flush with abrasive paper.

Fill shallow cracks with one application, but for deep ones, build up the filler in stages, letting each set before adding more.

Cracks sometimes appear in the corner between walls or a wall and ceiling; fill these by running your finger dipped in filler along the crack. When the filler has hardened, rub it down with medium-grade abrasive paper.

Fill and rub down small holes and dents in solid plasterwork in the same way as for filling cracks.

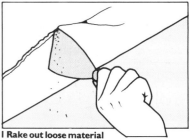

1 Rake out loose material

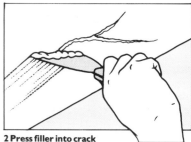

2 Press filler into crack

PATCHING HOLES IN PLASTER

A lath-and-plaster wall

If the laths are intact, plaster up the holes as for solid plasterwork. A hole under 75mm (3in) wide can simply be packed out with a ball of wet newspaper dipped in plaster. Fill flush to the surface with cellulose filler.

If some laths are broken, reinforce the repair with a piece of fine expanded metal mesh. Rake out loose plaster and undercut the edge of the hole with a bolster chisel. Use tinsnips to cut the metal to the shape of the hole but a little larger (1).

The mesh is flexible so you can bend it in order to tuck the edge behind the sound plaster all round (2). Flatten it against the laths with light taps from a hammer and if possible staple the mesh to a wall stud to hold it (3).

Gently apply one thin coat of backing plaster (4) and let it dry for about one hour before you continue patching.

1 Cut with tinsnips

2 Tuck mesh into hole

3 Staple mesh to stud

4 Trowel on plaster

A plasterboard wall or ceiling

A large hole punched through a plasterboard wall or ceiling cannot be patched with wet plaster only. Cut back the damaged board to the nearest studs or joists at each side using a sharp trimming knife against a straightedge. Keep the cut-out slim to avoid having to fit braces at the long sides (1).

Cut a new panel of plasterboard to fit snugly within the hole and nail it to the joists or studs using galvanized plasterboard nails. Use a steel trowel to spread finish plaster over the panel, forcing it well into the edges (2). Allow the plaster to stiffen then smooth over it with a dry trowel. You may have to add another layer to bring the patch to the level of the wall or ceiling.

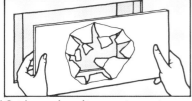
1 Cut damaged panel to nearest supports

2 Nail on the new panel and coat with plaster

A small hole in plasterboard

For very small holes in plasterboard use cellulose filler instead of plaster. Use a glass-fibre patching tape for holes up to about 90mm (3½in) across. Stick on the self-adhesive strips in a star shape over the hole then apply filler (1).

Alternatively, use an offcut of plasterboard just larger than the hole yet narrow enough to slot through. Bore a hole in the middle and thread a length of string through. Tie a galvanized nail to one end of the string (2). Butter the ends of the offcut with filler then feed it into the hole (3). Pull on the string to force it against the back of the cladding then press more filler into the hole so it's not quite flush with the surface. When the filler is hard, cut off the string then apply a thin coat of filler for a flush finish.

1 Fill and feather the patch

2 Fix string to offcut

3 Pull on string

DEALING WITH DISTEMPER

Distemper was once a popular finish, so you may have to deal with it if your house is old. Distemper is basically powdered chalk or whiting, mixed with glue size and water. It makes a poor base for decorating: when wet it redissolves and comes away from the surface along with the new decorations.

To remove it, brush away all loose material and wash off what you can. A little wallpaper stripper in the water will help. Apply a stabilizing primer to bind any traces left on the surface.

Many delicate plaster mouldings have been obliterated over the years with successive coats of distemper. Being water-soluble, you can remove it with a lot of care and patience. Work on a small area at a time, wetting it through with water. Remove the distemper with an old toothbrush until the detail of the moulding becomes clear, then scrape out the softened paint with pointed sticks such as wooden skewers. Wash over the moulding finally and apply a stabilizing primer.

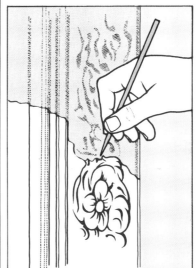
How to remove distemper
Scrub with a toothbrush, then scrape out the softened paint with a pointed stick.

Limewash and cement paints
Other water-thinned paints such as limewash and cement paints are less likely to cause problems when they're overpainted, unless they are in poor condition. Scrape and brush down with a stiff-bristled brush, then wipe the surface with white spirit to remove grease (it is best not to use water on these paints). Ensure the surface is sound by applying a stabilizing primer.

SEE ALSO

Details for: ▷	
Finish plaster	157
Primers	43
Plaster repairs	153-156
Floats and trowels	478

External corners
Dampen the chipped corner then use a filling knife to scrape the filler onto the damaged edge, working from both sides of the angle (1). Let the filler stiffen then shape it with a wet finger to closely resemble the original profile (2).

1 Use filler knife

2 Shape with finger

● **Lath-and-plaster ceiling**
If the laths are sound, plaster over as for solid plasterwork. If the laths are broken, cut back to the nearest joist and secure with galvanized nails. Fit a panel of plasterboard and spread on a coat of bonding plaster followed by a coat of finish plaster (▷).

51

ERADICATING MOULD GROWTH

When provided with damp conditions, mould can develop, usually in the form of black specks. The cause of the damp should be remedied before you treat the walls or ceiling.

Sterilize the mould growth before you carry out any other preparatory work to avoid distributing spores into the atmosphere. Apply a liberal wash of a solution made from 1 part household bleach: 16 parts water. Don't make the solution any stronger as it may damage the wall decoration. Leave the solution for at least four hours then carefully scrape off the mould, wipe it onto newspaper and burn it outside.

Wash the wall again with the solution but leave it for three days to sterilize the wall completely. When the wall is dry, paint it with a stabilizing primer thinned with white spirit. If you plan to hang wallpaper, size the wall using a size containing a fungicide solution.

Where mould growth is affecting wallpaper, soak the area in a warm water and bleach solution, then scrape off the contaminated paper and burn it. Wash the wall with a fresh bleach solution to remove paste residue.

Apply a liberal wash of similar solution to sterilize the wall and leave it for at least three days, but preferably one week, to make sure no further growth occurs. When the wall is completely dry, apply a stabilizing primer thinned with white spirit, followed by a coat of size if you plan to re-paper the wall.

SEE ALSO

◁ Details for:
Painted plaster	50
Repairing plaster	50-51
Blown vinyl	90
Consumer unit	296
Primers	43
Wallcoverings	90-98
Scrapers	481

2 Steam stripper
To remove painted and washable wallpapers, use a steam stripper – little more than a water boiler which exudes steam from a sole plate. To use the machine, hold the plate against the wall until the steam penetrates, soaks and softens the paper, then remove it with a scraper. Wash the wall to remove traces of paste.

Mould growth ▷
Mould, typified by black specks, will grow on damp plaster or paper.

52

PREPARING WALLCOVERINGS

Faced with a previously papered surface the best solution is to strip it completely before hanging new wallcoverings. However, if the paper is perfectly sound, you can paint it with emulsion or oil paints (but be warned: it will be difficult to remove in the future). Don't paint vinyl wallcovering except blown vinyl (◁). If the paper has strong reds, greens or blues, the colours may show through the finished paint; metallic inks have a similar tendency. You can mask strong colours by applying knotting thinned by 25 per cent with methylated spirit, but over a large area, use an aluminium spirit-based sealer. If you opt for stripping off the old covering, the method you use depends on the material and how it's been treated.

Stripping wallpaper

Soak the paper with warm water with a little washing-up liquid or proprietary stripping powder or liquid added to soften the adhesive. Apply the liquid with a sponge or houseplant sprayer. Repeat and leave the water to penetrate for 15 to 20 minutes.

Use a wide metal-bladed scraper to lift the softened paper, starting at the seams. Take care not to dig the points of the blade into the plaster. Re-soak stubborn areas of paper and return to strip them later.

Electricity and water are a lethal combination: where possible, dry-strip around switches and sockets. If the paper cannot be stripped dry, switch off the power at the consumer unit (◁) when you come to strip around electrical fittings. Unscrew the faceplates so that you can get at the paper trapped behind. Don't use the sprayer near electrical accessories.

Collect all the stripped paper in plastic sacks, then wash the wall with warm water containing a little detergent. From then on, treat the wall as for plaster (◁).

Scoring washable wallpaper

Washable wallpaper has an impervious plastic surface film, which you must break through to allow the water to penetrate to the adhesive.

Use a wire brush, coarse abrasive paper or a serrated scraper to score the surface, then soak it with warm water and stripper. It may take several applications of the liquid before the paper begins to lift.

Peeling off vinyl wallcovering

Vinyl wallcovering consists of a thin vinyl layer, which is fused with the pattern, on a paper backing. It is possible to peel off the film, leaving the backing paper on the wall; this can then be painted or used as a lining for a new wallcovering.

To remove the top layer, lift both bottom corners, then pull firmly but steadily away from the wall. Either soak and scrape off the backing paper or, if you want to leave it as a lining paper, smooth the seams with medium-grade abrasive paper, but use very light pressure or you'll wear a hole.

Stripping painted wallcoverings

Wallcoverings which have been painted previously can be difficult to remove, especially if a heavy embossed paper was used. If the paper is sound, prepare in the same way as painted plaster (◁) and decorate over it.

Use a wire brush or home-made scraper (1) to score the surface then soak with warm water plus a little paper stripper. Painted papers (and washables) can easily be stripped using a hired steam stripper. Hold the stripper plate against the paper until the steam penetrates, then remove the soaked paper with a wide-bladed scraper (2).

1 Wallpaper scorer
Drive some nails through a block of softwood measuring about 150mm x 125mm x 25mm (6in x 5in x 1in), so that the points just protrude.

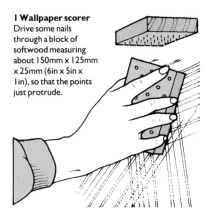

The wooden joinery in our homes needs redecorating long before any other part of the house, particularly on the exterior of windows and doors, bargeboards and fascias. The cause is the nature of the wood itself, which swells when it becomes moist, then shrinks again when the sun or central heating dries it out. Paint will not adhere for long under these conditions, nor will any other finish. Wood is also vulnerable to woodworm and various forms of rot caused primarily by damp, so it is not surprising that careful preparation is essential to preserve most types of timber.

SEE ALSO

Details for: ▷	
Primers	43
Finishing woodwork	74-84
Wood stains	80
Timber preservatives	250

Treating new timber

A lot of new joinery is primed at the factory but check that the primer is in good condition before it is installed: there may have been a long delay before it was delivered. Don't leave it uncovered outside, either, as primer itself is not sufficient protection against prolonged exposure to the weather. If the primer seems to be satisfactory, rub it down lightly with fine-grade abrasive paper, dust it off, then apply a second coat of wood primer to the areas that will be inaccessible after installation.

To prepare bare timber, first make sure it is dry, then sand the surface in the direction of the grain only, using a fine-grade glasspaper (wrap it round a wood block for flat surfaces; roll it round a pencil or piece of dowel for moulded sections).

Once you have removed all raised grain and lightly rounded sharp edges, dust the wood down. Rub it over finally with a tack rag – an impregnated cloth to which dust will stick; they're sold in many DIY stores.

Seal resinous knots with shellac knotting

Knots and other resinous areas of the wood must be treated to prevent them staining subsequent paint layers. Pick off any hardened resin, then seal the knots by painting them with two coats of shellac knotting. This is the best material to use when you plan to paint with pale finishing colours; for darker paints, seal the knots and prime the timber in one operation using aluminium primer.

Alternatively, paint bare timber with a standard resin-based primer or use a quick-drying water-thinned acrylic primer. Apply either liberally, taking care to work it well into the joints and particularly the end grain (which will require at least two coats to give it adequate protection).

Wash oily hardwoods with white spirit immediately prior to priming with an aluminium primer. For other hardwoods, use oil- or water-thinned wood primers, thinned slightly to encourage penetration into the grain.

When the primer is dry, fill open-grained timber with a fine surface filler. Use a piece of coarse cloth to rub it well into the wood. Use circular strokes followed by parallel strokes in the direction of the grain. When the filler is dry, rub it down with a fine abrasive paper to a smooth finish.

Fill larger holes, open joints, cracks and similar imperfections with interior or exterior wood filler. Press it into holes with a filling knife, leaving it slightly proud of the surface so that it can be sanded flush with fine-grade abrasive paper once it has set. Dust down ready for painting. If you find a hole you have missed just before you start applying the undercoat, fill it with putty; unlike other fillers, you can paint straight over putty without having to wait for it to dry, although you should wait until it forms a skin.

Filling the grain

If you plan to clear-finish an open-grained timber, apply a proprietary grain filler after sanding. Use a natural filler for pale timbers: for darker wood, buy a filler that matches the timber. Rub the filler across the grain with a coarse rag, leave to harden for several hours, then rub off the excess along the grain with a clean coarse rag.

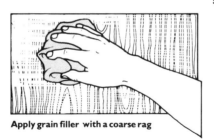

Apply grain filler with a coarse rag

Preparing for a clear finish

There's no need to apply knotting when you intend to finish the timber with a clear varnish or lacquer. Sand the wood in the direction of the grain using progressively finer grades of abrasive paper, then seal it with a slightly thinned coat of the intended finish.

If the wood is in contact with the ground or in proximity to previous outbreaks of dry rot, treat it first with a liberal wash of clear timber preservative. Check with the maker's recommendations that the liquid is compatible with the finish. This treatment is equally well suited to a painted finish.

Cellulose filler would show through a clear finish, so use a proprietary stopper to fill imperfections: these are thick pastes made in a range of colours to suit the type of timber. You can adjust the colour further by mixing it with wood stains. As stoppers can be oil- or water-based, make sure you use a similarly-based stain. Where possible, use an oil-based stopper outside. Fill the blemishes as before and rub down when the stopper hardens.

Sand along the grain with abrasive paper

MAN-MADE BOARDS

Versatile and relatively inexpensive, man-made boards are used extensively in the home, typically for cladding walls, levelling floors, shelving – even for *building units for the kitchen or bedroom. Preparation for decoration depends on whether you plan to paint the surface or hang wallcovering.*

SEE ALSO

◁ Details for:
Stripping paper	52
Taping joints	165
Man-made boards	494-495
Primers	43
Panelling	87-88
Wallcoverings	90-98

Preparing man-made boards for decoration

Wallboards such as plywood, chipboard, blockboard, hardboard and softboard (◁) are all made from timber, but they must be prepared for decoration in a different way to natural timber. Their surface finish, for instance, varies according to the quality of the board: some are compact and smooth and may even be pre-sealed ready for painting; others must be filled and sanded before a smooth finish is achieved.

As a rough guide, no primer will be required when using emulsion other than a sealing coat of the paint itself, slightly thinned with water. However, any nail or screw heads must be driven below the surface and coated with zinc phosphate primer to prevent rust stains.

If you are using oil paint, prime the boards first with a general-purpose primer (stabilizing primer for porous softboard). Where possible, you should prime both sides of the board. If the boards are pre-sealed, apply undercoat directly to the surface.

1 Hardboard face
2 Hardboard back
3 Blockboard
4 Chipboard
5 Plywood
6 Softboard

Wallpapering man-made boards

If you want to fix a wallcovering to a boarded wall, careful preparation is required to ensure that the boards will not contract and split the paper. If the wall is insufficiently battened, water absorbed from the paste could make untreated boards buckle and warp. Unless the boards are primed, the same could happen if the wall is wet-stripped later (◁). The surface must be clean and dry prior to priming. Sand it down and dust off. Treat nail and screw heads with metal primer.

Fill joints with cellulose filler, using scrim as reinforcement (◁). Fill any holes, too. Rub down the filler, dust off and treat the boards with a stabilizing primer thinned slightly with white spirit. When the paint is dry, size the wall or use a heavy wallpaper paste.

BLEACHING STAINS FROM TIMBER

Discoloured or stained timber can be bleached in preparation for colour-staining and polishing. If possible, try to bleach the entire area rather than an isolated part, to avoid a light patch in place of the stain.

Traditionally, oxalic acid in the form of white crystals (available from chemists) is used to bleach the wood. Make a solution with warm water: add water until no more crystals will dissolve. Oxalic acid is poisonous, so handle only when wearing protective gloves, and do not use where it could contaminate food. Keep it out of reach of children and pets.

To use the bleaching solution, apply a liberal wash to the wood, using an old paintbrush (or a wad of cloth). Watch carefully until the stain has disappeared, then rinse the wood thoroughly with clean water and allow to dry.

Two-part bleach
An alternative to the oxalic acid solution is to use a proprietary two-part wood bleach. One part is brushed onto the wood and ten to twenty minutes later the second part is applied over the first. The bleach is then left to work on the stain.

After three to four hours, the bleach should have removed the discoloration from the wood and can be washed off with an acid such as white vinegar (but follow the manufacturer's instructions).

Bleaching timber
Apply a solution of bleach to stained wood using a paintbrush and leave until the discoloration has disappeared, then wash off with water or vinegar.

SANDING A WOODEN FLOOR

A sanded wooden floor sealed with a clear finish that highlights its grain is a most attractive feature for many rooms. Although straightforward, the job is laborious, dusty and extremely noisy. Considerable patience is also required in order to achieve an even, scratch-free and long-lasting finish.

Repairing the floorboards

There's no point in spending time and money sanding floorboards which are in poor condition, so examine them first. Look for any boards with signs of woodworm infestation. If the beetle is still active, treat the remaining boards and joists below with a proprietary woodworm fluid (▷). Even if the beetle has been eradicated, replace any boards with more than a few holes in them: beneath the surface there may be a honeycomb of tunnels made by the woodworm larvae. As the sanding process will remove a lot of timber, these tunnels may be revealed on the surface of the boards.

If you find signs of dry or wet rot when you lift a floorboard, have it treated straightaway before you continue with the sanding (▷).

Examine the floor for boards which have been lifted previously by electricians and plumbers. Replace any that are split, too short or badly jointed (▷). Try to find secondhand boards to match the rest of the floor, but if you have to use new wood, stain it after the floor is sanded to match the colour of the old boards. Drive all nail heads below the surface with a punch and hammer: a raised head will rip the abrasive paper on the sander's drum.

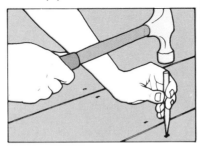

Sink nail heads below the surface

Filling gaps between floorboards

What you do about gaps between boards depends on how much they bother you. Many people simply ignore them, but you will end up with a superior job as well as improved draughtproofing if you make the effort to fill them invisibly or close them up.

Closing up
Over a large area, the quickest and most satisfactory solution is to lift the boards a few at a time and re-lay them butted side by side, filling in the final gap with a new board (▷).

Filling with papier mâché
If there are a few gaps only, make up a stiff papier mâché paste with white newsprint and wallpaper paste, plus a little water-based wood dye to colour it to match the sanded floor. Scrape out dirt and wax from between the boards and press the paste into the gap with a filling knife. Press it well below the level likely to be reached by the sander, and fill flush with the floor surface. Run the blade along the gap to smooth it.

Inserting a wooden lath
Large gaps can be filled by a thin wood lath planed to fit tightly between the boards. Apply a little PVA adhesive to the gap and tap the lath in with a hammer until it is flush with the surface. Skim it with a plane if necessary. Don't bother to fill several gaps this way: it is easier to close up the boards and fill one gap only with a new floorboard (▷).

Force papier mâché between boards

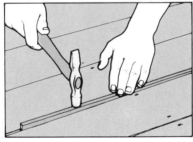

Wedge a wooden lath into a wide gap

CHOOSING A SANDING MACHINE

The area of a floor is far too large to contemplate sanding with anything but an industrial sanding machine. You can obtain such equipment from the usual tool hire outlets, which also supply the abrasive papers. You will need three grades of paper: coarse, to level the boards initially, medium and fine to achieve a smooth finish.

It's best to hire a large upright drum sander for the main floor area and a smaller rotary sander for tackling the edges. For small rooms such as bathrooms and WCs, you can use the rotary sander only.

Some companies also supply a scraper for cleaning out the inaccessible corners, but do make sure it is fitted with a new blade when you hire.

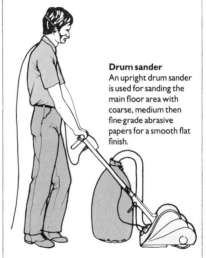

Drum sander
An upright drum sander is used for sanding the main floor area with coarse, medium then fine-grade abrasive papers for a smooth flat finish.

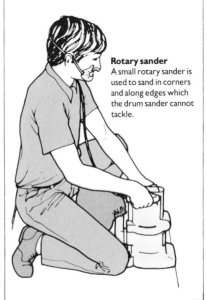

Rotary sander
A small rotary sander is used to sand in corners and along edges which the drum sander cannot tackle.

SEE ALSO

Details for: ▷	
Replacing boards	177-178
Woodworm	246-247
Dry and wet rot	249-250
Wood stains	80

Hook scraper
Use a small hook scraper for removing paint spots from the floor, and for reaching into spaces that are inaccessible to the rotary sander. The tool cuts on the backward stroke; various sizes and blade shapes are available to deal with most situations.

USING SANDING MACHINES

SEE ALSO

◁ Details for:
Repairing boards   55
Sanding machines   55
Varnish and lacquer   75
Wood scrapers   470

Fitting the abrasive sheet

Precise instructions for fitting the abrasive paper to the sanding machine should be included with the hire kit, or the hirer will demonstrate what you need to do. Never attempt to change abrasive papers while the machine is plugged into a socket.

With most machines the paper is wrapped round the drum and secured with a screw-down bar (**1**). Ensure that the paper is wrapped tightly around the drum: if it is slack it may slip from its clamp and will be torn to pieces.

Edging sanders take a disc of abrasive, usually clamped to the sole plate by a central nut (**2**).

1 Drum sander   **2 Rotary sander**

Operating a drum sander

Stand at the beginning of a run with the drum sander tilted back so that the drum itself is clear of the floor. Drape the electric lead over one shoulder to make sure it cannot become caught in the sander.

Switch on the machine then gently lower the drum onto the floor. To hold the machine still for even a short time will sand a deep hollow in the floor. There is no need to push a drum sander: it will move forward under its own power. Hold the machine in check so that it proceeds at a slow but steady walking pace along a straight line.

When you reach the other side of the room, tilt the machine back, switch off and wait for it to stop before lowering it to the floor.

If the paper rips, tilt the machine onto its back castors and switch off. Wait for the drum to stop revolving, disconnect the power then change the paper: if you let go of the machine it will run across the room on its own, almost certainly damaging the floor in the process.

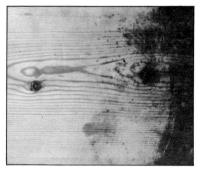

Sanding cleans and rejuvenates wooden floors

Using an edging sander

Hold the handles on top of the machine and drape the flex over your shoulder. Tilt the sander onto its back castors to lift the disc off the floor. Switch on and lower the machine. As soon as you contact the boards, sweep the machine in any direction but keep it moving. As soon as it comes to rest the disc will score deep, scorched swirl marks in the wood, which are difficult to remove. There is no need to press down on the machine. When you have finished, tilt back the machine and switch off, leaving the motor to run down.

Sanding procedure

A great deal of dust is produced by sanding a floor, so before you begin, empty the room of furniture and take down curtains, lampshades and pictures. Seal around the room door with masking tape and stuff folded newspaper under it. Open all windows. Wear old clothes and a gauze facemask.

Sweep the floor to remove grit and other debris. Old floorboards will most likely be curved across their width, or cupped, so the first task is to level the floor across its entire area.

With coarse paper fitted in the drum sander, sand diagonally across the room (**1**). At the end of the run, tilt the machine, pull it back and make a second run parallel to the first. Allow each pass to slightly overlap the last.

When you have covered the floor once, sand it again in the same way, but this time across the opposite diagonal of the room (**2**). Sweep the sawdust from the floor after each run is completed.

Once the floor is flat, so that the boards are clean all over, change to a medium grade paper and sand parallel to the boards (**3**). Overlap each pass as before. Finally, switch to the fine grade paper to remove all obvious scratches and give a smooth finish.

Sand the edges of the room with the rotary machine. As soon as you change the grade of paper on the drum sander, put the same grade on the edging sander. In this way, the edges of the room are finished to the same standard as the main area (**4**).

Even the edging sander cannot clean right up to the skirting or into the corners; finish these small areas with a scraper, or fit a flexible abrasive disc in a power drill.

Vacuum the floor and wipe it over with a cloth dampened with white spirit ready for finishing.

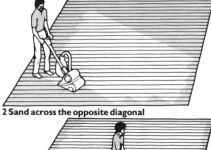

1 Sand diagonally across the floorboards

2 Sand across the opposite diagonal

3 Sand parallel to the floorboards

4 Finish the edges with the rotary sander

LEVELLING A WOODEN FLOOR

Tiles, sheet vinyl or carpet must not be layed directly onto an uneven suspended timber floor. The undulations would cause the tiles or covering to lift or even crack. The solution is to panel over the floorboards with 3mm (⅛in) thick hardboard or, preferably, 6mm (¼in) plywood. The method is identical whichever board you use.

Priming and conditioning boards

Before you seal your floor with plywood or hardboard, make sure that underfloor ventilation is efficient to prevent problems from damp or dry rot. Bear in mind, too, that once the floor is sealed you will not have ready access to underfloor pipework and electric cables, which could be a problem should you need to make repairs at some time in the future.

If the house is not regularly heated,

condition the hardboard to prevent buckling after it has been layed by soaking its textured back with warm water, then leave the sheets stacked back-to-back for 24 hours.

If central heating has been in use for some time, there is no need for such treatment: just stack the plywood or hardboard sheets on edge in the room for 48 hours so that they can adjust to the atmosphere.

SEE ALSO

Details for: ▷

Laying floor tiles	107-111
Laying parquet	113-114
Laying carpet	117
Laying sheet vinyl	118
Ventilation	276
Coping saw	464

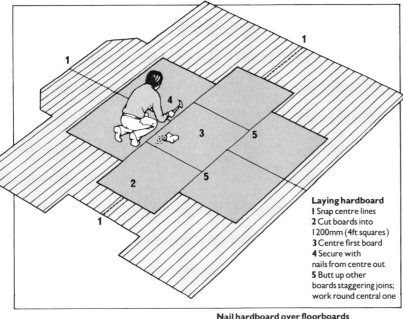

Laying hardboard
1 Snap centre lines
2 Cut boards into 1200mm (4ft squares)
3 Centre first board
4 Secure with nails from centre out
5 Butt up other boards staggering joins; work round central one

Nail hardboard over floorboards
Secure from centre outwards then fill margin

Fill the margin

1 Butt to skirting

2 Scribe to fit

3 Nail to floor

Fit to a doorway

4 Scribe to skirting

5 Trace frame shape

6 Cut and nail down

LAYING A BASE FOR CERAMIC TILES

A concrete platform is the most suitable base for ceramic floor tiles, but you can lay them on a suspended wooden floor so long as the joists are perfectly rigid so that the floor cannot flex. The space below must be adequately ventilated with air bricks to prevent the formation of rot. Level the floor using 12mm (½in) plywood and screw it down every 300mm (1ft) for a firm fixing.

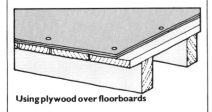

Using plywood over floorboards

Laying the boards

Unless flooring manufacturers suggest otherwise, fix the boards rough side up, as a key for the adhesive. Cut boards to form 1200mm (4ft) squares. Nail loose floorboards and plane off high points, then sink the nail heads.

Use chalked string to snap two centre lines across the room, crossing at right-angles. Lay the first board on the centre; adjust it so that its edges do not align with the gaps between floorboards. Loose-lay the boards in both directions: if you'll be left with narrow margins, reposition them.

Nail the first board to the floor with 20mm (¾in) hardboard pins. Start near the centre of the board and fix it every 150mm (6in) until you get within 25mm (1in) of the edge, then nail around the edge every 100mm (4in). Nail other boards butted up to the first (see

above). Scribe the narrow edge strips to fit the margin. Lay the board on the floor touching the skirting but square to the edges of the nailed boards (1). Hold the board firmly and scribe along it to fit the skirting (2). Cut the scribed line and butt it up to the skirting then mark the position of the nailed boards on both edges. Join the marks then cut along this line. Nail the board to the floor (3).

To fit into a doorway, butt a board up to the frame; measure to the door stop. Cut a block of wood to this size and scribe to the skirting (4). Use the same block to transfer the key points of reference for the shape of the door frame (5). Cut out the shape with a coping saw. Slide the board into the doorway, mark and cut the other edge to meet the nailed boards then fix it to the floor (6).

● **Shortening a door**
If you level a floor with hardboard or ply, you may have to plane the bottom of the door to provide a new clearance. Take it off its hinges and plane towards the centre from each end.

57

PAINTED AND VARNISHED WOODWORK

Most of the joinery in and around your house will have been painted or varnished at some time and so long as it is in good condition, it will form a sound base for new paintwork. But when too many coats of paint have been applied, mouldings around door and window frames begin to look poorly defined and the paintwork has an unattractive, lumpy appearance; it's best to strip off all the old paint to bare wood and start again. Stripping off is also essential where the paintwork has deteriorated and is blistering, crazing or flaking.

SEE ALSO

◁ Details for:
Painting	74-78
Sealing frames	254
Scraper	470
Soldering and brazing	488
Primers	43

Dry, flaky paintwork

Liquid sander
You can chemically prepare paintwork in good condition using a liquid sander: wipe it onto the surface with a cloth or sponge and leave it to slightly soften the top layer of paint, leaving a matt finish. It is an ideal surface for applying the new top coat of paint. The chemical cleans and degreases the paintwork, too.

Heavily overpainted woodwork

Badly weathered varnish

Preparing paintwork in good condition

Wash the paintwork from the bottom upwards with a solution of warm water and sugar soap or detergent. Pay particular attention to the areas around door handles and window catches, where dirt and grease will be heaviest. Rinse with fresh water from top to bottom to prevent runs of dirty liquid on a newly cleaned surface.

Use fine grade wet and dry abrasive paper dipped in water to rub down gloss paintwork, providing a key for the new finish coat, and remove any blemishes. Prime bare patches of wood. Build up these low spots gradually with undercoat, rubbing down between each application.

Fill any open joints or holes with filler and rub down when set. Renew old and crumbling window putty and seal around window and door frames with mastic (◁). Proceed with your chosen undercoat and top coat, following the basic paint system (◁).

Preparing unsound paintwork or varnish

Unsound paintwork or varnish such as the examples pictured left must be stripped to bare wood. There are several methods you can use but always scrape off loose material first.

In some cases, where the paint is particularly dry and flaky, dry-scraping may be all that is required, using a proprietary hook scraper (◁), plus a light rub down with abrasive paper. Where most of the paint is stuck firmly to the woodwork, remove it using one of the methods described below and on the facing page.

Stripping paint and varnish with a blowtorch

The traditional method for stripping old paint is to burn it off with a flame. The paraffin-fuelled blowlamp has now been largely superseded by the more convenient, safer blowtorch, which is fuelled by liquid gas in a replaceable pressurized canister.

More sophisticated tools are designed so that the torch itself is connected by a hose to a metal gas bottle, the type used for camping or in caravans. This type of gas torch is finely adjustable, so is useful for other jobs such as brazing and soldering (◁).

To reduce the risk of fire, take down curtains and pelmets and, outside, rake out old bird's nests from behind your roof fascia board and soffit.

It's only necessary to soften the paint with a flame, but it is all too easy to heat the paint so that it is actually burning when you scrape it off. Deposit these scrapings in a paint kettle or metal bucket as you remove them.

Start by stripping mouldings from the bottom upwards. Never direct the flame at one spot but keep it moving all the time, so that you do not scorch the wood. As soon as the paint has softened, use a shavehook to scrape it off easily. If it is sticky or hard, heat it a little more then try scraping again.

Having dealt with the mouldings, strip flat areas of woodwork, using a wide-bladed stripping knife. When you have finished stripping, sand the wood with medium-grade abrasive paper to remove hardened specks of paint and any accidental light scorching.

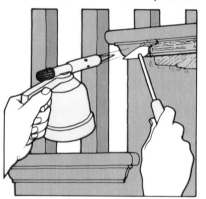
Shavehook, used for mouldings

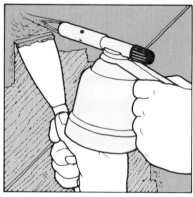
Scraper, used for flat surfaces

SELECTING AND USING CHEMICAL STRIPPERS

An old finish can be removed using a stripper which reacts chemically with paint or varnish. There are basically two types: those with a liquid or gel consistency based on methylene chloride; and strippers in the form of a thick paste, which are caustic based.

All chemical strippers can be dangerous if splashed on your skin or eyes, so take proper precautions:
● Wear vinyl work gloves and safety spectacles. If you have a respiratory problem, wear a face mask, too.
● Work in a well-ventilated area and never smoke near the chemicals: some give off fumes which are toxic when inhaled through a cigarette.
● If you get stripper on your skin, wash it off immediately with copious amounts of cold water. If it gets in your eyes, wash it out under running water and seek medical advice.
● Keep pets and small children out of the way when using chemical strippers.

GEL OR LIQUID STRIPPERS

Liquid strippers are only suitable when you can lay an object horizontal. For stripping household joinery, use a gel stripper, which is stiff enough to cling to vertical surfaces.

Lay polythene sheet or plenty of newspaper on the floor, then apply a liberal coat of stripper to the paint, working well into the mouldings.

Leave it for about 10 minutes then try scraping a patch to see if the paint has softened through to the wood. If not, don't waste time removing the top layers only, but apply more stripper and stipple the softened paint back down with a brush. Leave for five minutes.

Once the chemicals have completed their work, use a stripping knife to scrape the paint from flat surfaces and a shavehook to remove it from mouldings.

Wipe the paint from deep carvings with fine wire wool; use small pieces of coarse sacking when stripping oak as particles of metal can stain the wood.

When you have removed the bulk of the paint, clean off residual patches with a wad of wire wool dipped in fresh stripper. Rub with the grain, turning the wad inside out to present a clean face as it becomes clogged with paint.

Neutralize the stripper by washing the wood with white spirit or water (depending on the manufacturer's advice). It is cheaper to use water when washing large areas but it will raise the grain and can cause joints to swell. Let the wood dry out thoroughly then treat as new timber (▷).

PASTE STRIPPERS

Spread a paste stripper onto wood in a thick layer, working it well into crevices and mouldings and making sure all air bubbles are expelled.

The paste must be kept moist long enough for the chemicals to work – it may dry out too quickly in direct sunlight or a heated room – so cover it with a thin polythene sheet. Some manufacturers supply a blanket which seals the moisture in. Leave the stripper in place for several hours, then lift the leathery substance at the edge with a scraper and peel it off, complete with paint, in one layer. If it has become too hard to peel, soften it by soaking.

Discard the paste wrapped in newspaper, then wash the wood with water and a scrubbing brush. Leave it to dry before priming and finishing.

INDUSTRIAL STRIPPING

Any portable woodwork can be taken to a professional stripper, who will immerse the whole thing in a tank of stripping solution. Many companies use a solution of hot caustic soda, which must be washed out of the wood by hosing down with water. It is an efficient process (which incidentally kills woodworm at the same time) but there is a risk of splitting the panels, warping the wood and of opening up joints. At best, you can expect a reasonable amount of raised grain, which you will have to sand before refinishing.

Some companies use a cold chemical dip, which does little harm to solid timber and raises the grain less. This process is likely to be more expensive than the caustic soda method.

Most stripping companies will collect, many will rehang a door for you, and some offer a finishing service, too.

Never submit veneered items to either treatment: it may peel off.

Using a hot air stripper

Although stripping paint with a flame is fast and efficient, there is always the risk that you will burn the wood. Scorching can be covered by paint, but if you want to varnish the stripped wood, scorch marks will mar the finish.

Electrically-heated guns – like powerful hair dryers – work almost as quickly as a torch with less risk of scorching or fire. They do operate at an extremely high temperature: under no circumstances test the stripper by holding your hand over the nozzle.

Some guns come with variable heat settings and a selection of nozzles for various uses (see below). Hold the gun about 50mm (2in) from the surface of the paintwork and move it slowly backwards and forwards until the paint blisters and bubbles. Immediately remove the paint with a shavehook or scraper. Aim to heat the paint just ahead of the scraper so you develop a continuous work action.

Fit a shaped nozzle onto the gun when stripping glazing bars to concentrate the jet of hot air and reduce the risk of cracking the glass.

Old primer can sometimes be difficult to remove with a hot air stripper. If you are repainting the timber this is no problem; just rub the surface down with abrasive paper. For a clear finish remove residues of paint from the grain with wads of wire wool dipped in chemical stripper (see left).

SEE ALSO

Details for: ▷
Preparing timber	53
Primers	43
Finishing wood	74-84
Scrapers	470

Nozzles for hot air guns
Hot air strippers come with a standard wide mouth for general usage but most offer optional extras, typically a push-on nozzle for stripping thin glazing bars (1) and a conical nozzle to concentrate the heat on a small area (2). Some offer nozzles for a wide spread of heat (3).

With a hot air gun there's less risk of scorching

METALWORK: IRON AND STEEL

Metal is a strong, hardwearing material that's used extensively throughout the home — for window frames, railings, gutters, pipework and radiators, to name but a few. Oddly, they're areas that are in close proximity to water, and consequently particularly prone to attack by metal's worst enemy: rust. Paint alone won't guard against this corrosive menace, so special treatments are necessary to ensure the long life of metal.

SEE ALSO

◁ Details for:
Industrial stripping   59
Primers   43
Finishing metal   85-86
Wire brushes   481

Cast iron railings deeply pitted with rust

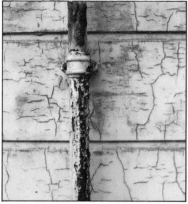

Flaking casement window as a result of rust

Severely corroded cast iron drainpipe

What is rust?

Rust is a form of corrosion that affects only the ferrous metals — notably iron and steel — due to the combination of water, oxygen and carbon dioxide. Although paint slows down the rate at which moisture penetrates, it doesn't stop it altogether; inhibitors and primers are needed to complete the protection, and the type you use depends on the condition of the metal and how you plan to decorate it. Prepare thoroughly or the job will be ruined.

Treating bare metal

Remove light deposits of rust by rubbing with wire wool or wet and dry abrasive paper dipped in white spirit. If the rust is heavy and the surface of the metal pitted, use a wire brush or, for extensive corrosion, a wire wheel or cup brush in a power drill. Wear goggles while wire brushing to protect your eyes from flying particles.

Paint a proprietary rust inhibitor onto the cleaned metal, following the manufacturer's instructions: some inhibitors remain on the surface to protect the metal, others must be washed off after a few minutes. Some car accessory shops carry a range of suitable inhibitors.

Wash off deposits of grease with white spirit and wire wool. As soon as the metal is clean and dry, apply a primer. For general inside use, choose a zinc phosphate or red oxide primer. For exterior paintwork, use calcium plumbate, red lead or zinc phosphate primers. Work the primer into crevices and fixings, and make sure sharp edges and corners where corrosion often begins are coated generously.

Preparing previously painted metal

If the paint is perfectly sound, wash it with sugar soap or a detergent solution, rinse and dry. Key gloss paint with fine wet and dry abrasive.

If the paint film is blistered or flaking where water has penetrated and corrosion has set in, remove all loose paint and rust with a wire brush or rotary attachment to an electric drill. Apply rust inhibitor to bare patches, working it well into joints, bolt heads and other fixings. Prime bare metal immediately: rust can reform rapidly.

When you're preparing cast iron guttering, brush out dead leaves and other debris and wash it clean. Paint the inside with a bitumen paint. If you want to paint over old bitumen paint, use an aluminium primer first to prevent it bleeding to the surface.

Stripping painted metal

Delicately moulded sections — on fire surrounds, garden furniture and other cast or wrought ironwork — can't easily be rubbed down with a wire brush, and will often benefit from stripping off old paint and rust which is masking fine detail. A hot air stripper cannot be used here as the metal dissipates the heat before the paint softens. A gas blowtorch can be used to strip wrought ironwork, but cast iron might crack if it becomes distorted by localized heating.

Chemical stripping is the safest method but before you begin, check that what appears to be a metal fire surround is not in fact made from plaster mouldings on a wooden background: the stripping process can play havoc with soft plasterwork. Tap the surround to see if it is metallic, or scrape an inconspicuous section.

Apply a proprietary rust-killing jelly or liquid, chemicals which will remove and neutralize rust: usually based on phosphoric acid, they combine with the rust to leave it quite inert in the form of iron phosphate. Some rust killers will deal with minute particles invisible to the naked eye, and are self-priming, so no additional primer is required.

Alternatively, if the metalwork is portable, you can take it to a sandblaster or an industrial stripper (◁). None of the disadvantages of industrial stripping apply to metal.

Clean the stripped metal with a wire brush then wash with white spirit before finishing it.

TREATING OTHER METALS

Corrosion in aluminium

Aluminium does not corrode to the same extent as ferrous metals. Indeed, modern aluminium alloy window and door frames, for example, are designed to withstand weathering without a coat of protective paint. Nevertheless, in adverse conditions, aluminium may corrode to a dull grey and even produce white crystals on the surface.

To remove the corrosion, rub the aluminium with fine wet and dry abrasive paper using white spirit as a lubricant until you get back to bright, but not gleaming, metal. Wipe the metal with a cloth dampened with white spirit to remove particles and traces of grease. When dry, prime the surface with a chromate primer. Never use a primer containing lead on aluminium, as there is likely to be an adverse chemical reaction between the metals in the presence of moisture.

Painting galvanized metal

Galvanized iron and steel has a coating of zinc applied by hot dipping; when new, it provides a poor key for most paints. Leaving the galvanizing to weather for six months will remedy this, but in many cases the manufacturer of galvanized metalwork will prepare it chemically for instant priming. If possible, check when you purchase it.

Treating chipped galvanizing

Any small rust spots caused by accidental chipping of the zinc coating should be removed by gentle abrasion with wire wool but take care not to damage the surrounding coating. Wash the area with white spirit then allow the surface to dry. Prime with calcium plumbate primer.

Protecting corrugated iron

For long-term protection of corrugated iron, first remove rust deposits then prime with a bitumen basecoat before finishing with a compatible reinforced emulsion paint.

Maintaining brass and copper

Ornamental brassware – typically door knobs, fingerplates and other door furniture – should not be painted, especially as there are clear lacquers which protect it from the elements. Strip painted brass with a chemical stripper; deal with corroded brass as described right.

Copper – mainly plumbing pipework and fittings – doesn't require painting for protection but visible pipe runs are usually painted so they blend in with the room decor (it is possible to make a feature of them by polishing, but it's a chore to keep them looking pristine).

Don't just paint onto the bare pipes: degrease and key the surface with fine wire wool lubricated with white spirit. Wipe away metal particles with a cloth dampened with white spirit. Apply undercoat and top coats direct: no primer is needed.

Painting over lead

In order to decorate old lead pipework, scour the surface with wire wool dipped in white spirit; no further preparation is required before you apply paint.

Advanced lead corrosion

The cames (grooved retaining strips) of stained glass windows can become corroded, producing white stains.

Mix some mild white vinegar in a little water and rub the cames thoroughly with the solution until the corrosion disappears. Next, apply a solution of washing soda and water to neutralize the acid content of the vinegar, then rinse several times with clean water and cloths.

Key lead pipes for painting with wire wool

REMOVING CORROSION FROM BRASS FITTINGS

Brass corrodes to a dull brown colour but corrosion is normally easy to remove with a standard metal polish. However, if exterior brass door fittings have been left unprotected, deposits build up until they are difficult to polish off.

Mix one level tablespoonful of salt plus the same amount of vinegar in 275 ml (½ pint) of hot water. Soften the corrosion by applying liberal washes of the solution to the brass using very fine wire wool.

Wash the metal in hot water containing a little detergent, then rinse and dry it before polishing.

Clean brass with salt and vinegar solution

Removing verdigris

Badly weathered brass can develop green deposits called verdigris. This heavy corrosion may leave the metal pitted, so clean it as soon as possible.

Line a plastic bowl with ordinary aluminium cooking foil. Attach a piece of string to each item of brassware then place in the bowl on top of the foil. Dissolve a cup of washing soda in four pints of hot water and pour it into the bowl to cover the metalware.

Leave the solution to fizz and bubble for a couple of minutes, then lift out the brass items with the string. Replace any that are still corroded. If necessary, the process can be repeated using fresh solution and new foil.

Rinse the brass with hot water, dry it with a soft cloth, then·polish.

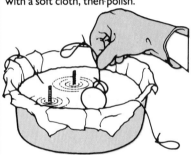

Remove verdigris with a washing soda dip

SEE ALSO

Details for: ▷	
Primers	43
Finishing metal	85-86
Polishing metal	491

61

TILED SURFACES

Tiles are used to clad walls, floors and ceilings, and are made in a vast range of materials – ceramic, cork, vinyl and polystyrene are popular – and in a host of different surface textures and finishes. If they're looking shabby it's possible to either revive their existing finish or decorate them with paint or wallcoverings – with some it's even possible to stick new tiles on top for a completely new look.

SEE ALSO

◁ Details for:
Levelling compound	49
Glass-fibre wallcovering	91,97
Lining paper	94
Tiling	99-112
Replacing tiles	384

CLEANING AN OLD QUARRY TILED FLOOR

Old quarry tiles are absorbent and dirt and grease become ingrained in the surface. If normal washing with detergent fails to revitalize their colour and finish, clean the tiles with a diluted hydrochloric acid (available from a chemist as spirits of salts).

Add a drop or two of acid to some warm water in a plastic bucket. Stir it gently with a wooden stick and try it on a small patch of floor. Don't make the solution any stronger than is necessary: the solution attacks the grouting, so work quickly in small sections. Wash the floor with the solution, rinsing off the diluted acid with clean, warm water.

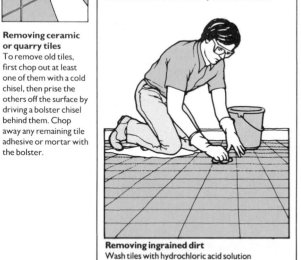

Removing ingrained dirt
Wash tiles with hydrochloric acid solution

WHEN USING ACID

● **Wear PVC gloves, old clothes and goggles.**
● **Add acid to water, never the other way around.**
● **Keep acid out of reach of children and animals.**

Removing ceramic or quarry tiles
To remove old tiles, first chop out at least one of them with a cold chisel, then prise the others off the surface by driving a bolster chisel behind them. Chop away any remaining tile adhesive or mortar with the bolster.

Ceramic wall and floor tiles

Ceramic tiles are stuck to the wall or floor with a special adhesive or, in the case of quarry tiles, mortar. Removing them in their entirety in order to redecorate the wall is messy and time-consuming, but is often the most satisfactory longterm solution.

So long as a ceramic tiled wall is sound, you can paint it with oil-based paint. Wash the surface thoroughly with sugar soap or detergent solution. The problem with this treatment is that glazed tiles do not provide a good key for paintwork and you'd find that the new surface would chip easily. You can lay new tiles directly over old ones but make sure the surface is perfectly flat – check by holding a long spirit level or straight-edged batten across the surface. Tap the tiles to locate any loose ones and either glue them firmly in place or chop them out with a cold chisel and club hammer and fill the space with mortar. Wash the wall to remove grease and dirt.

It's also possible to tile over old quarry or ceramic floor tiles in the same way. Treat an uneven floor with a self-levelling compound (◁).

It is not practicable to paper over old ceramic wall tiles, as the adhesive would not be able to grip on the shiny surface. Instead, you could hang a woven glass-fibre wallcovering, which is designed to be painted afterwards (◁). The tiles must be perfectly sound and free from dirt and grease, or this rather coarse material might peel off.

Polystyrene ceiling tiles

Polystyrene tiles are stuck directly onto the surface with a water- or solvent-based adhesive that can be difficult to remove. The adhesive was commonly applied in five small dabs: this method is now unapproved due to the risk of fire. Manufacturers recommend a complete bed of adhesive, which makes removal even worse.

Remove tiles by prising them off with a wide-bladed scraper then prise off the adhesive dabs. On stubborn patches, try to soften the adhesive with warm water, wallpaper stripper or even paint stripper (but wear goggles and PVC gloves: it's difficult to avoid splashes). For larger areas of adhesive try a solution of ammonia (see below). One way to give the tiles a facelift is to paint them. These tiles should never be painted with an oil paint, which increases the risk of fire spreading across the tiles. Brush the tiles to remove dust, then apply emulsion paint.

Vinyl floor tiles

Vinyl floor tiles are not a good foundation so resurface them or remove them completely. Soften the tiles and their adhesive with a domestic iron, then use a scraper to prise them up. Remove the old adhesive by applying a solution of half a cupful of household ammonia and a drop of liquid detergent in a bucketful of cold water. When the floor is clean, rinse it with water.

If vinyl tiles are firmly glued to the floor, you can clean them then resurface them with a latex self-levelling screed (◁). Before you apply this method, however, check the recommendations of your floorcovering manufacturer: it may not be suitable for laying after this treatment.

Cork floor and wall tiles

It's possible to decorate over cork tiles, although absorbent types will need priming first. The advice given for vinyl floor tiles applies for cork tiles also. Hard, sound wall tiles can be painted so long as they are clean. Prime absorbent cork first with a general-purpose primer before painting over it.

Unless the tiles are textured or pierced, they can be papered over but size the surface with commercial size or heavy-duty wallpaper paste, then line them horizontally (◁) to prevent joins showing through.

Fibre ceiling tiles

Acoustic fibre tiles can be painted with water-based paints. Wash them with a mild detergent but do not soak the tiles as they're quite absorbent.

APPLYING FINISHES

A finish in decorating terms means a liquid or semi-liquid substance which sets, dries or cures to protect and sometimes colour materials such as wood or masonry. Apart from paint, other finishes for wood include stains, varnishes, oil, wax and French polish, all of which are used specifically where you want to display the grain of the timber for its natural beauty.

The make-up of paint

Paint is basically made from solid particles of pigment suspended in a liquid binder or medium. The pigment provides the colour and body of the paint, the medium allows the material to be brushed, rolled or sprayed and, once applied, forms a solid film binding the pigment together and adhering to the surface. Binder and pigment vary from paint to paint, but the commonest two families are solvent- (sometimes known as oil) and water-based.

COMMON PAINT FINISHES AND ADDITIVES

The type of paint you choose depends on the finish you want and the material you're decorating. Various additives adapt the paint's qualities.

SOLVENT-BASED (OIL) PAINT

The medium for solvent-based paints (commonly called oil paints) is a mixture of oils and resin. A paint made from a natural resin is slow-drying, but modern paints contain synthetic resins such as alkyd, urea, epoxy, acrylic and vinyl, which all make for fast-drying paints. A white pigment, titanium dioxide, is added, plus other pigments to alter the colour.

WATER-BASED PAINT

Emulsion is the commonest water-based paint. It has a binder made from synthetic resins similar to those used for oil paints, but it is dispersed in a solution of water. Titanium is the white pigment used for good-quality paints. It is also used with additional pigments for a wide range of colours.

ADDITIVES IN PAINT

No paint is made from simply binder and pigment. Certain additives are included during manufacture to give the paint qualities such as faster drying, high gloss, easy flow, longer pot life, or to make the paint non-drip.
• **Thixotropic** paints are the typical non-drip types; they are thick, almost jelly-like in the can, enabling you to pick up a brush load without dripping.
• **Extenders** are added as fillers to strengthen the paint film. Cheap paint contains too much filler, reducing its covering power.

PAINT THINNERS

If a paint is too thick it cannot be applied properly and must be thinned before it is used. Some finishes require special thinners provided by the manufacturer, but most oil paints can be thinned with white spirit, and emulsions with water.
  Turpentine will thin oil paint but has no advantages over white spirit for household paints and it is much more expensive.

GLOSS OR MATT FINISH?

The proportion of pigment to resin affects the way the paint sets. A gloss (shiny) paint contains approximately equal amounts of resin and pigment, whereas a higher proportion of pigment produces a matt (dull) paint. By adjusting the proportions, it is possible to make satin or eggshell paints. Matt paints tend to cover best due to their high pigment content, but the greater proportion of resin in gloss paints is responsible for their strength.

Applying a paint system

No paint will provide protection for long if you apply one coat only. It is necessary to apply successive layers to build up a paint system.
• Paint for walls requires a simple system comprising two or three coats of the same paint.
• Paint intended for woodwork and metalwork needs a more complex system using paints with different qualities. A typical paint system for woodwork is illustrated below.

SEE ALSO

Details for:	▷
Choosing colours	24-25
Primers	43
Lead content	43
Preparing paint	64

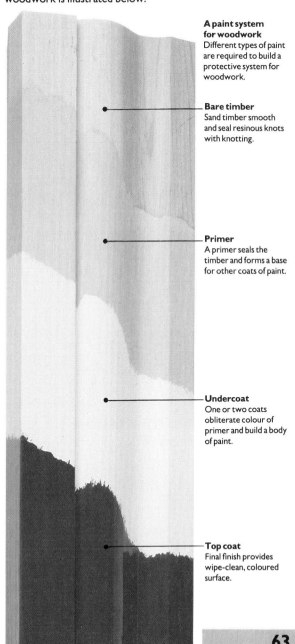

A paint system for woodwork
Different types of paint are required to build a protective system for woodwork.

Bare timber
Sand timber smooth and seal resinous knots with knotting.

Primer
A primer seals the timber and forms a base for other coats of paint.

Undercoat
One or two coats obliterate colour of primer and build a body of paint.

Top coat
Final finish provides wipe-clean, coloured surface.

SEE ALSO

◁ Details for:
Planning priorities   22-23
Ladders and towers   40-42
Preparing masonry   44-49

Strain old paint
If you're using leftover paint, filter it through a piece of muslin or old tights stretched over the rim of a container.

Resealing the lid
Wipe the rim of the can clean before you replace the lid, then tap it down all round with a hammer over a softwood block.

SAFETY WHEN PAINTING

Decorating isn't dangerous so long as you take sensible precautions to protect your health.

- **Ensure good ventilation indoors while applying a finish and when it is drying. Wear a facemask if you have respiratory problems.**
- **Do not smoke while painting or in the vicinity of drying paint.**
- **Contain paint spillages outside with sand or earth and don't allow it to enter a drain.**
- **If you splash paint in your eyes, flush them with copious amounts of water with your lids held open; if symptoms persist, visit a doctor.**
- **Wear barrier cream or gloves on sensitive hands. Use a proprietary skin cleanser to remove paint from the skin or wash it off with warm soapy water. Do not use paint thinners to clean your skin.**
- **Keep any finish and thinners out of reach of children. If a child swallows a substance, do not attempt to make it vomit but seek medical treatment.**

PREPARING THE PAINT

Whether you're using newly purchased paint or leftovers from previous jobs, there are some basic rules to observe before you apply it.

- Wipe dust from the paint can, then prise off the lid with the side of a knife blade. Don't use a screwdriver: it only buckles the edge of the lid, preventing an airtight seal and making subsequent removal difficult.
- Gently stir liquid paints with a wooden stick to blend the pigment and medium. There's no need to stir thixotropic paints unless the medium has separated; if you have to stir it, leave it to gel again before using.
- If a skin has formed on paint, cut round the edge with a knife and lift out in one piece with a stick. It's a good idea to store the can on its lid, so that a skin cannot form on top of the paint.
- Whether the paint is old or new, transfer a small amount into a paint kettle or plastic bucket. Old paint should be filtered at the same time, tying a piece of muslin or old nylon tights across the rim of the kettle.

PAINTING EXTERIOR MASONRY

The outside walls of your house need painting for two major reasons: to give a clean, bright appearance and to protect the surface from the rigours of the climate. What you use as a finish and how you apply it depends on what the walls are made of, their condition and the degree of protection they need. Bricks are traditionally left bare, but may require a coat of paint if they're in bad condition or previous attempts to decorate have resulted in a poor finish. Rendered walls are normally painted to brighten the naturally dull grey colour of the cement; pebbledashed surfaces may need a colourful coat to disguise previous conspicuous patches. On the other hand, you may just want to change the present colour of your walls for a fresh appearance.

Working to a plan

Before you start painting the outside walls of your house, plan your time carefully. Depending on the preparation even a small house will take a few weeks to complete.

It's not necessary to tackle the whole job at once, although it is preferable – the weather may change to the detriment of your timetable. You can split the work into separate stages with days (even weeks) in between, so long as you divide the walls into manageable sections. Use window and door frames, bays, downpipes and corners of walls to form break lines that will disguise joins.

Start at the top of the house, working right to left if you are right-handed (vice versa if you are left-handed).

FINISHES FOR MASONRY

● Black dot denotes compatibility. All surfaces must be clean, sound, dry and free from organic growth.

	Cement paint	Exterior emulsion paint	Reinforced emulsion paint	Spirit-thinned masonry paint	Textured coating	Floor paint
SUITABLE TO COVER						
Brick	●	●	●	●	●	●
Stone	●	●	●	●	●	●
Concrete	●	●	●	●	●	●
Cement rendering	●	●	●	●	●	●
Pebbledash	●	●	●	●	●	●
Asbestos cement	●	●	●	●	●	●
Emulsion paint		●	●	●	●	●
Oil-based paint		●	●	●	●	●
Cement paint	●	●	●	●	●	●
DRYING TIME: HOURS						
Touch dry	1-2	1-2	2-3	1-2	6	2-3
Re-coatable	24	4	24	24	24-48	12-24
THINNERS: SOLVENTS						
Water-thinned	●	●	●		●	
White spirit-thinned				●		●
NUMBER OF COATS						
Normal conditions	2	2	1-2	2	1	1-2
COVERAGE: DEPENDING ON WALL TEXTURE						
Sq.metres per litre		4-10	3-6.5	3-6		5-15
Sq.metres per kg	1.5-3.5				1-2	
METHOD OF APPLICATION						
Brush	●	●	●	●	●	●
Roller	●	●	●	●	●	●
Spray gun	●	●	●		●	●

SUITABLE PAINTS FOR EXTERIOR MASONRY

There are various grades of paint suitable for decorating and protecting exterior masonry, which take into account economy, standard of finish, durability and coverage. Use the chart opposite for quick reference.

CEMENT PAINT

Cement paint is supplied as a dry powder, to which water is added. It is based on white cement but pigments are added to produce a range of colours. Cement paint is the cheapest of the paints suitable for exterior use, although it is not as weatherproof as some others. Spray new or porous surfaces with water before you apply two coats.

Mixing cement paint
Shake or roll the container to loosen the powder, then add two volumes of powder to one of water in a clean bucket. Stir it to a smooth paste then add a little more water until you achieve a full-bodied, creamy consistency. Mix up no more than you can use in one hour, or it will start to dry.

Adding an aggregate
When you're painting a dense wall or one treated with a stabilizing solution so that its porosity is substantially reduced, it is advisable to add clean sand to the mix. It also provides added protection for an exposed wall and helps to cover dark colours. If the sand changes the colour of the paint, add it to the first coat only. Use one volume of sand to four of powder, but stir it in when the paint is still in its paste-like consistency.

EXTERIOR-GRADE EMULSION

Exterior-grade emulsion resembles the interior type; it is water-thinnable and dries to a similar smooth, matt finish. However, it is formulated to make it weatherproof and includes an additive to prevent mould growth; so apart from reinforced emulsions, it is the only emulsion paint recommended for use on outside walls.

The paint is ready for use but thin the first coat on porous walls with 20 per cent water. Follow up with one or two full-strength coats (depending on the colour of the paint).

REINFORCED EMULSION

Reinforced emulsion is a water-thinnable, resin-based paint to which has been added powdered mica or a similar fine aggregate. It dries with a textured finish that is extremely weatherproof, even in coastal districts or industrial areas where darker colours are especially suitable.

Although cracks and holes must be filled prior to painting, reinforced emulsion will cover hair cracks and crazing. Apply two coats of paint in normal conditions but you can economize by using sanded cement paint for the first coat.

SPIRIT-THINNED MASONRY PAINT

A few masonry paints suitable for exterior walls are thinned with white spirit but they are based on special resins so that, unlike most oil-based paints, they can be used on new walls without priming first with an alkali-resistant primer (▷). Check with manufacturer's recommendations. However, it is advisable to thin the first coat with 15 per cent white spirit.

TEXTURED COATING

A thick textured coating can be applied to exterior walls. It is a thoroughly weatherproof, self-coloured coating, but it can be overpainted to match other colours. The usual preparation is necessary and brickwork should be pointed flush. Large cracks should be filled, but a textured coating will cover fine cracks. The paste is brushed or rolled onto the wall, then left to harden, forming an even texture. On the other hand, you can produce a texture of your choice using a variety of simple tools (▷). It's an easy process, but practise on a small section first.

Concrete floor paints

Floor paints are specially prepared to withstand hard wear. They are especially suitable for concrete garage or workshop floors, but they are also used for stone paving, steps and other concrete structures. They can be used inside for playroom floors.

The floor must be clean and dry and free from oil or grease. If the concrete is freshly laid, allow it to mature for at least three months before painting. Thin the first coat of paint with 10 per cent white spirit.

Don't use floor paint over a surface sealed with a proprietary concrete sealer, but you can cover other paints so long as they are keyed first.

The best way to paint a large area is to use a paintbrush around the edges, then fit an extension to a paint roller for the bulk of the floor.

SEE ALSO

Details for: ▷	
Primers	43
Textured coating	73
Preparing masonry	44-49
Paint rollers	483

Apply paint with a roller on an extension

Paint in manageable sections
You can't hope to paint an entire house in one session, so divide each elevation into manageable sections to disguise the joins. The horizontal moulding divides the wall neatly into two sections, and the raised door and window surrounds are convenient break lines.

TECHNIQUES FOR PAINTING MASONRY

SEE ALSO

◁ Details for:
Work platforms 40-42
Preparing masonry 44-49
Brushes and rollers 482-483
Paint sprayers 484

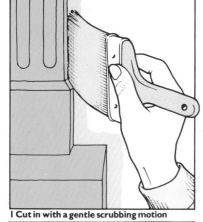

1 Cut in with a gentle scrubbing motion

3 Use a banister brush
Tackle deeply textured wall surfaces with a banister brush, using a scrubbing action.

2 Protect downpipes with newspaper

4 Use a roller
For speed in application, use a paint roller with a deep pile for heavy textures, a medium pile for light textures and smooth wall surfaces.

5 Spray onto the apex of external corners

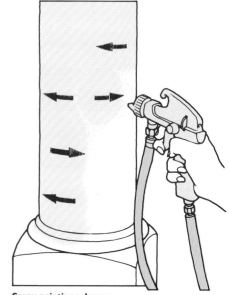

6 Spray internal corners as separate surfaces

Using paintbrushes

Choose a 100 to 150mm (4 to 6in) wide paintbrush for walls; larger ones are heavy and tiring to use. A good-quality brush with coarse bristles will last longer on rough walls. For a good coverage, apply the paint with vertical strokes, criss-crossed with horizontal ones. You will find it necessary to stipple paint into textured surfaces.

Cutting in

Painting up to a feature such as a door or window frame is known as cutting in. On a smooth surface, you should be able to paint a reasonably straight edge following the line of the feature, but it's difficult to apply the paint to a heavily textured wall with a normal brush stroke. Don't just apply more paint to overcome the problem; instead, touch the tip of the brush only to the wall, using a gentle scrubbing action (1), then brush excess paint away from the feature once the texture is filled.

Wipe splashed paint from window and door frames with a cloth dampened with the appropriate thinner.

Painting behind pipes

To protect rainwater downpipes, tape a roll of newspaper around them. Stipple behind the pipe with a brush then slide the paper tube down the pipe to mask the next section (2).

Painting with a banister brush

Use a banister brush (3) to paint deep textures such as pebbledash. Pour some paint into a roller tray and dab the brush in to load it. Scrub the paint onto the wall using circular strokes to work it well into the uneven surface.

Using a paint roller

A roller (4) will apply paint three times faster than a brush. Use a deep-pile roller for heavy textures or a medium-pile for lightly textured or smooth walls. Rollers wear quickly on rough walls, so have a spare sleeve handy. Vary the angle of the stroke when using a roller to ensure an even coverage and use a brush to cut into angles and obstructions.

A paint tray is difficult to use at the top of a ladder, unless you fit a tool support, or better still erect a flat platform to work from (◁).

Using a spray gun

Spraying is the quickest and most efficient way to apply paint to a large expanse of wall. But you will have to mask all the parts you do not want to paint, using newspaper and masking tape. The paint must be thinned by about 10 per cent for spraying: set the spray gun according to the manufacturer's instructions to suit the particular paint. It is advisable to wear a respirator when spraying.

Hold the gun about 225mm (9in) away from the wall and keep it moving with even, parallel passes. Slightly overlap each pass and try to keep the gun pointing directly at the surface – tricky while standing on a ladder. Trigger the gun just before each pass and release it at the end of the stroke.

When spraying a large, blank wall, paint it into vertical bands overlapping each band by 100mm (4in).

Spray external corners by aiming the gun directly at the apex so that paint falls evenly on both surfaces (5). When two walls meet at an internal angle, treat each surface separately (6).

Spray-painting columns
Columns, part of a front door portico, for instance, should be painted in a series of overlapping vertical bands. Apply the bands by running the spray gun from side to side as you work down the column.

Most interior walls and ceilings will be plastered and most probably papered or painted, unless the house has been recently built. Apart from their preparation, the methods for painting them are identical and they can be considered smooth surfaces in terms of paint coverage. Although a flat, matt finish is usually preferred indoors for walls and ceilings, there's no reason why you shouldn't use a gloss or even a textured paint in your scheme.

Finishes for bare masonry

Some interior walls are left unplastered – and some may even have been stripped on purpose – either for their decorative appearance or because it was considered unnecessary to clad the walls of certain rooms such as the basement, workshop or garage. A stripped brick or stone chimney breast makes an attractive focal point in a room, and an entire wall of bare masonry can create a dramatic effect or suggest a country cottage style.

If you want to finish brick, concrete or stone walls, follow the methods described for exterior walls. However, because they will not have to withstand weathering, you can use paint designed for interior use. Newly stripped masonry will require sealing to bind the surface (▷).

SEE ALSO

Details for: ▷	
Primers and sealers	43
Cement paint	65
Preparation	44-51
Stripping wallcoverings	52

SELECTING PAINTS FOR INTERIOR SURFACES

Although you really only have a choice of two finishes for interior walls and ceilings – emulsion or oil paint – there are various qualities which offer depth of sheen, texture, one-coat coverage and good obliteration.

EMULSION PAINT

The most popular and practical finish for walls and ceilings, emulsions are available in liquid or thixotropic consistencies with matt or satin (semi-gloss) finishes.

A satin finish emulsion is less likely to show fingerprints or scuffs. A non-drip, thixotropic paint has obvious advantages when painting ceilings, and covers in one coat. But apply a thinned coat on new, porous plaster, followed by a full-strength coat to achieve the required finish.

Emulsion is also available in a solid form, which comes in its own roller tray. It paints out well with minimal spatter and no drips.

REINFORCED EMULSION

Emulsion paints, reinforced with fine aggregate, are primarily for use on exterior walls but their fine textured finish is just as attractive inside and will cover minor imperfections, which would show through standard emulsions.

OIL PAINT

Oil paints dry to a hard, durable finish. Although these paints are mainly intended for woodwork, they can be used on walls that require an extra degree of protection: they were once popular in bathrooms and kitchens, where you might expect condensation, but this is unnecessary with the development of modern water-thinned emulsions, which resist moisture.

High-gloss paints accentuate uneven wall surfaces, so most people prefer a satin finish. Both types are available in liquid or thixotropic form. Most gloss paints should be preceded by one or two undercoats, but satin finishes, which have a very fine texture, form their own undercoats.

UNDERCOAT

Undercoat is a relatively cheap paint used to build up the full system of protective paintwork. It will obliterate underlying colours and fill minor irregularities. If speed is essential, choose a quick-drying primer/undercoat – a three-coat system of two undercoats and a top coat can be built up in one day.

CEMENT PAINT

Cement paint is an inexpensive exterior finish which is ideal for a utilitarian area indoors, such as a cellar, workshop or garage. Sold in dry powder form, it must be made up with water and dries to a matt finish (▷).

Paints for walls and ceilings
Emulsion paint, in its many forms, is the most practical finish for interior walls and ceilings, but use oil paints on wall-fixed joinery like skirtings and picture rails. The example above illustrates the advantage of contrasting textures: matt emulsion for the cornice up to the ceiling; gloss oil paint for the picture rail; satin emulsion for the woodchip covered walls.

USING BRUSHES, PADS AND ROLLERS

SEE ALSO

◁ Details for:
Work platforms	42
Radiator roller	483
Spraying	66
Cleaning brushes	482
Cleaning pads	483
Cleaning rollers	483
Spray equipment	484

Applying paint by brush

Choose a good-quality brush for painting walls and ceilings. Cheap brushes tend to shed bristles – infuriating and less economical in the long run. Buy a brush about 200mm (8in) wide for quickest coverage: if you're not used to handling a brush your wrist will soon tire and you may find a 150mm (6in) brush, plus a 50mm (2in) brush for the edges and corners, more comfortable to use, although take into account that the job will take longer.

Loading the brush

Don't overload a brush with paint; it leads to messy work and ruins the bristles if it is allowed to dry in the roots. Dip no more than the first third of the brush into the paint, wiping off excess on the side of the container to prevent drips (**1**). When using thixotropic paint, load the brush and apply paint without removing excess.

Using a brush

You can hold the brush whichever way feels comfortable to you, but the 'pen' grip is the most versatile, enabling your wrist to move the brush freely in any direction. Hold the brush handle between your thumb and forefinger, with your fingers on the ferrule (metal band) and your thumb supporting it from the other side (**2**).

Apply the paint in vertical strokes then spread it at right angles to even out the coverage. Emulsion paint will not show brush marks when it dries but finish oil paints with light upward vertical strokes for the best results.

1 Dip only the first third of bristles in paint

2 Place fingers on ferrule, thumb behind

Applying paint by roller

A paint roller with interchangeable sleeves is an excellent tool for applying paint to large areas. Choose a roller about 300mm (1ft) long for painting walls and ceilings.

There are a number of different sleeves to suit the type of paint and texture of the surface. Long-haired sheepskin and woven wool sleeves are excellent on texture surfaces, especially with emulsion paint. Choose a short-pile for smooth surfaces, and with oil paints.

Disposable plastic foam rollers can be used to apply any paint to a smooth surface but they soon lose their resilience and have a greater tendency to skid across the wall.

Special rollers

Rollers with long extension handles are designed for painting ceilings without having to erect a work platform (◁).

Some have a built-in paint reservoir for automatic reloading.

Narrow rollers are available for painting behind radiators, if you are unable to remove them (◁).

Loading a roller

You will need a special paint tray to load a standard roller. Having dipped the sleeve lightly into the paint reservoir, roll it gently onto the ribbed part of the tray to coat the roller evenly (**1**).

Using a roller

Use zig-zag strokes with a roller (**2**), covering the surface in all directions. Keep it on the surface at all times. If you let it spin at the end of a stroke it will spray paint onto the floor or adjacent surface. When applying oil paint, finish in one direction, preferably towards prevailing light.

1 Dip roller in paint, roll onto ribbed tray

2 Apply in zig-zags, finish in one direction

● **Spraying**
It is possible to spray paint onto interior walls and ceilings, but it is only practical for large rooms: you'll have to mask everything you don't want to paint; and the sprayed paint would be forced through even the narrowest gaps between doors and frames. Adequate ventilation is vital when spraying indoors.

Applying paint by pad

Paint pads for large surfaces have flat rectangular faces covered with a short mohair pile. A plastic foam backing gives the pad flexibility so that the pile will always be in contact with the wall, even on a rough surface.

The exact size of the pad will be determined by the brand you choose but one about 200mm (8in) long is best for applying paint evenly and smoothly to walls and ceilings. You will also need a small pad or paintbrush for cutting in at corners and ceilings.

Loading a pad

Load a pad from its own special tray, drawing the pad across the captive roller so that you pick up an even amount of paint (**1**).

Using a pad

To apply the paint consistently, keep the pad flat on the wall and sweep it gently and evenly in any direction (**2**). Use criss-cross strokes for emulsion, but finish with vertical strokes with oil paints to prevent streaking.

1 Loading a paint pad
Load the pad evenly by drawing it across the integral roller on the tray without squeezing.

2 Sweep pad gently in any direction

APPLYING PAINT TO WALLS AND CEILINGS

Even the most experienced painter can't help dripping a little paint, so always paint a ceiling before the wall, especially if they are to be different colours. Erect a work platform so that you can cover as much of the surface as possible without having to change position: you will achieve a better finish and will be able to work in safety. When you start to paint, follow a strict working routine to ensure a faultless finish. Choose your tools wisely so you can work efficiently. Refer to the chart below for professional results.

● Black dot denotes compatibility. All surfaces must be clean, sound, dry and free from organic growth.

FINISHES FOR INTERIOR WALLS & CEILINGS

	Emulsion paint	Reinforced emulsion paint	Oil-based paints	Undercoat	Primer/ undercoat	Cement paint	Textured coating
SUITABLE TO COVER							
Plaster	●	●	●	●	●	●	●
Wallpaper	●		●	●	●		
Brick	●	●	●	●	●	●	●
Stone	●	●	●	●	●	●	●
Concrete	●	●	●	●	●	●	●
Previously painted surface	●	●	●	●	●		●
DRYING TIME: HOURS							
Touch dry	1-2	2-3	4	4	½	1-2	6
Re-coatable	4	24	16	16	2	24	24-48
THINNERS: SOLVENTS							
Water	●	●				●	
White spirit			●	●	●		
NUMBER OF COATS							
Normal conditions	2	1-2	1-2	1-2	1-2	2	1
COVERAGE: APPROXIMATE							
Sq. metres per litre	9-15	3-6.5	12-17	15-18	15		
Sq. metres per kg						1.5-3.5	1-2
METHOD OF APPLICATION							
Brush	●	●	●	●	●	●	●
Roller	●	●	●	●	●	●	●
Paint pad	●		●	●	●	●	
Spray	●	●	●	●	●	●	

Painting the ceiling

Start in a corner near the window and carefully paint along the edges with a small paintbrush.

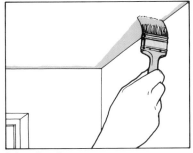

Paint edges first

Working from the wet edges, paint in 600mm (2ft) wide bands, working away from the light. Whether you use a brush, a pad or a roller, apply each fresh load of paint just clear of the previous application, blending in the junctions for even coverage.

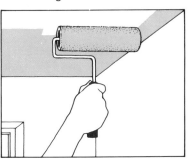

Work from wet edges

Electrical fittings

Unscrew a ceiling rose cover so that you can paint right up to the backplate with a small brush. Loosen the faceplate or mounting box of sockets and switches to paint behind them.

Remember: switch off at the mains before exposing electrical connections (▷).

SEE ALSO

Details for: ▷
Consumer unit	296
Work platforms	42
Primers	43
Preparing masonry	44-46
Preparing paint surfaces	48,50
Preparing concrete	49
Preparing plaster	50-51
Stripping wallpaper	52
Pressurized roller	483

Paint reservoir
Use a special roller with a pressurized paint reservoir to avoid having to constantly reload a roller; it's an excellent boon for painting ceilings and high walls, when frequent returns to the tray would be tiresome.

Painting the walls

Use a small brush to paint the edges starting at a top corner of the room. If you are right-handed, work right to left. Paint an area of about 600mm (2ft) square at a time. If you are left-handed, paint the wall in the opposite direction. When using emulsion, paint in horizontal bands (1), but, with oil paints, use vertical strips (2) as the junctions are more likely to show unless you blend in the wet edges quickly. Always finish a complete wall before you take a break or a change of tone will show between separate painted sections.

1 Paint emulsion in horizontal bands

2 Apply oil paints in vertical strips

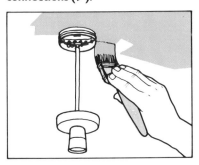

Unscrew rose cover to keep it clean

DECORATIVE EFFECTS: SPATTERING AND STIPPLING

SEE ALSO

◁ Details for:
Colour schemes   24-35
Preparing plaster   50-51
Paints   67
Painting walls   67-69

Decorative effects with paint, once common practice, can be applied to walls, ceilings, furniture and joinery to give an individual look to a scheme. Some of the more complex effects – traditionally the domain of the skilled craftsman – are made easier to achieve using easily workable modern materials and improvised equipment.

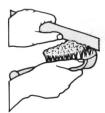

1 Spatter paint
Produce a speckled effect by drawing a ruler across a banister brush.

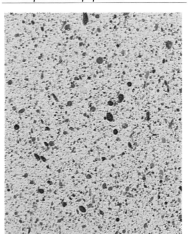

The speckled effect of spattering

2 Sponge stipple
Apply delicate stipple textures by patting a paint-dampened natural sponge on the wall.

Subtle textures with sponge stippling

3 Rag stipple
Create vivid stipple textures using a crumpled cotton rag.

70

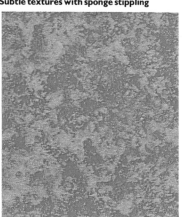

More vivid effects of rag stippling

The importance of practice

Although some of the techniques are easy, it is worth practising them on a piece of flat board before you tackle a whole room. The texture of the actual wall might influence the finished effect, but at least you will be familiar with the basic techniques. If the result is not to your satisfaction, don't worry – you can always paint or paper over it.

Spattering

Achieve a speckled effect by spattering two or three contrasting colours onto an emulsion background. When planning your colour scheme, consider the background as your dominant colour. Cover the floor with dust sheets and mask door and window frames (plus the panes) unless you want to cover them with the same effect. Use masking tape to cover electrical fittings.

Use oil paint for the spatter colours, reduced to the required consistency with a little white spirit; this is best achieved by trial and error on your practice board. Avoid making the paint too liquid or your speckled effect will become a mass of runs. If an accident occurs, blot the paint immediately with an absorbent rag or paper tissue and allow it to dry. Obliterate the mistake by dabbing with a sponge dipped in the base colour.

Choose any stiff-bristled brush, such as a banister brush. Dip the tips of the bristles only into the paint then, holding the brush about 100mm (4in) from the wall, drag an old ruler towards you, across the bristles: this flicks tiny drops of paint onto the wall (**1**). Produce an even or random coverage as you prefer, but avoid concentrating the effect in one place. When the first spatter coat is dry, apply other colours in turn, if required, in the same way.

Sponge stippling

Stipple simple textures onto an emulsioned background with a natural sponge. Use a dark-toned emulsion paint to stipple over a lighter base colour for a two-tone effect. When choosing, remember that the base colour will be the dominant colour in the room.

Dampen a natural sponge with water until it swells to its full size. Squeeze out excess water to leave it moist. Pour a tablespoonful of paint into a shallow tray and dip the sponge into it. Touch off excess paint onto a piece of plain scrap paper until it leaves a mottled effect, then apply it lightly to the wall (**2**).

Do not press hard or the sponge will leave a patch of almost solid paint. Group the impressions closely to form an even texture across the wall. If any area appears too dark when dry, stipple base colour over it to tone it down.

When the first stipple coat has dried, sponge another tone or colour over it.

Rag stippling

Using a ball of cotton rag instead of a sponge produces a more vivid stippled effect, although the technique is similar. Crumple a piece of cotton rag about the size of a large handkerchief into a ball and dip it into the paint until it is saturated. Squeeze it out and try stippling onto scrap paper. Use a wrinkled part of the ball rather than a flat section to achieve the most interesting patterns. When you achieve the effect you like on the paper, apply the rag lightly to the wall (**3**).

Use different parts of the ball as you work across the wall and re-fold it to vary the pattern. Stipple out mistakes using a clean rag dipped in base colour once the first stipple coat is dry.

Applying a basecoat

Although decorative effects can be applied successfully to woodwork, nevertheless they are best when applied to a flat plaster surface, and thorough preparation is essential as with any decoration. Any of the following finishes require a flat basecoat in your choice of colour. This initial coat can be applied by brush, roller or paint pad. Leave to dry.

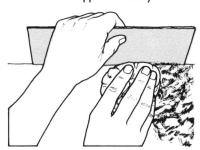

Mask adjoining areas with card

Bag graining

Bag graining involves a stippling action but it is used to remove paint from the wall instead of applying it. Use a darker graining paint over a pale emulsion background. The graining colour is likely to be the most dominant of the two. It is more convenient if two people work together, one to apply the paint while the other patterns it.

Dilute emulsion paint with about 50 per cent water and stir it to an even consistency. Make up enough paint to cover at least one complete wall at a time in case a fresh batch differs slightly in tone. Before you start, mask off areas you don't want to treat with newspaper and masking tape.

Use a wide brush to paint it over the base colour with vertical strokes (1). Take care to avoid runs. After you have applied a band of paint about 600mm (2ft) wide, take a plastic bag half-filled with rags and use it to stipple the wet paint (2). Overlap each impression to produce an overall crinkled effect. When paint builds up on the bag, wipe it off onto a piece of absorbent rag.

Your helper should work just ahead of you, applying fresh paint so that you can texture it before it dries.

SEE ALSO

Details for: ▷

| Paints | 67 |
| Brushes | 482 |

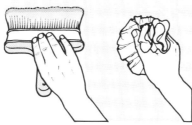

I Apply by brush 2 Stipple off

Two-tone patterns with bag graining

Marbling

Producing a marble-like effect with paint is not an easy technique to master, so be prepared to experiment on a practice board until you achieve a convincing result. Study some examples of marble, taking note of the basic colours and tones involved. Choose a limited colour range, which you can mix to produce a variety of hues.

Artist's student oil paints are the best materials to use for veining and mottling – characteristic patterns in marble – as they take longer to dry (it's necessary to work the whole effect with wet paint) and they blend extremely well. They are relatively expensive, however, so you may prefer to use ordinary oil paints in satin finish instead.

Starting with an oil glaze

A transparent oil glaze, obtainable from a professional paint supplier, is the best material to use as a basecoat and as a medium for the mottling and veining paints. Dip a lint-free rag into the glaze and rub it evenly over the wall surface. A light coating is usually quite sufficient to achieve the best surface.

Mottled effects typical of marbling

Applying a mottled pattern

Mix up one or two colour washes using oil paints and glaze. Use a 25mm (1in) paintbrush to paint uneven patches onto the wet glazed surface. Space them randomly and you can then overlap colour and tones.

Take the rag used to apply the glaze and stipple the patches to blend them and lose the distinct edges. Complete the effect using a clean, soft-bristled paintbrush; sweep it very gently back and forth across the paintwork to produce a delicately softened effect.

Adjust the tone of any dark areas by applying small patches of lighter paint on top, then soften them in again.

Forming the veining

Use an artist's paintbrush to draw on the veins using colour washes, mixed as for mottling. Veins are best freely painted with varying thicknesses of line. Note carefully the branching lines typical of marble veining. Blot any thick paint carefully with a tissue, then blur the veins by brushing back and forth with a soft paintbrush until they appear as subtle, soft-edged lines.

Sealing with varnish

Allow the paintwork to dry thoroughly, then paint on a coat of semi-gloss polyurethane varnish. When the varnish is hard, burnish the wall with a soft cloth to give a delicate sheen. Apply a little wax polish if necessary.

Veining characteristic of marbling

RAG ROLLING, LINEAR AND STENCILLED EFFECTS

1 Rag rolling
Roll off a dark finish to reveal a paler basecoat.

SEE ALSO

◁ Details for:

Colour schemes	24-35
Preparing plaster	50-51
Paints	67
Painting walls	67-69
Bag graining	71

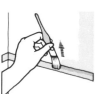

2 Paint a clean edge
Use masking tape to define a line; brush paint away from the tape to avoid a thick edge forming.

3 Striping tape
Paint bands of colour with striping tape.

4 Cutting a stencil

5 Stipple on colour

Define areas with linear effects

Stripes for a geometric design

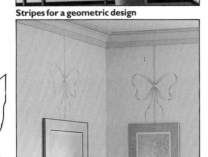

Decorative motifs using stencils

Rag rolling

Also known as scumbling, rag rolling is a technique similar to bag graining. You will need a helper to paint vertical bands of diluted colour ahead of you. The best results are achieved with a flat basecoat of pale satin finish oil paint overlaid with a darker satin finish oil paint mixed with 50 per cent white spirit. The top coat will be the dominant colour.

Take a piece of rag about the size of a tea cloth, fold it into quarters then twist it into a roll. Start at the bottom of the wall and roll the rag upwards to remove wet paint, producing a texture resembling watered silk (**1**).

As you reach the ceiling, use the roll to stipple the margin. If you touch the ceiling accidentally, wipe off the paint immediately with a clean rag dampened with white spirit.

Start the next band of texturing at the bottom again, but don't attempt to produce straight strips of pattern. Change direction constantly to overlap and blend with previous impressions. Remake the rolled rag each time it becomes impregnated with paint, or use a clean rag.

Masking straight edges

Use low-tack masking tape when you want to paint two areas of colour, or even a coloured band, perhaps, to finish off a painted dado. This tape can be peeled off without removing the painted surface below. Don't use transparent PVC tape for this reason.

Marking the line
Draw straight horizontal lines with a batten and a spirit level. Vertical lines can be marked by snapping a chalked plumbline on the wall.

Painting the edge
Run masking tape along one side of the marked line, taking care not to stretch or curve the tape. Using a small brush, paint away from the tape so that you do not build a thick edge of paint against it, which could peel off with the tape (**2**). Paint the rest of the wall with a roller or brush. When the paint is touch-dry peel off the tape. Pull back and away from the edge to leave a clean line. If you happen to pull away specks of paint, touch in with an artist's paintbrush.

Painting a band of colour
To paint a band of colour, complete the background then mask top and bottom of the band. Apply the paint and when touch-dry, remove both tapes.

Alternatively, use striping tape designed to paint lines on car bodies. Once the tape is applied to the wall, the centre section is peeled away, leaving a gap between two masked edges, which you fill in with paint (**3**).

Stencilling

Ready-made paper stencils for painting patterns or motifs onto a wall are available from artists' shops. If you cannot find a stencil which suits your purpose, buy blank sheets of stencil paper from the same outlets and cut your own design with a sharp scalpel (**4**). Design your stencil with thin strips to hold the shapes together.

Ordinary emulsion paint is ideal for stencilling. You will need a stencil brush. It has short stiff bristles and is used with a stippling action (**5**).

Mark out the wall lightly to position the stencil horizontally and vertically. At the same time, make small marks to indicate the position of repeat patterns. Use small pieces of masking tape to hold the stencil on the wall. Spoon a little paint onto a flat board. Take a stencil brush and touch the tips of the bristles into the paint. Stipple excess paint onto waste paper until it deposits paint evenly, then transfer it to the wall.

Hold the stencil flat against the wall. Stipple the edges of the motif first, then fill in the centre. If necessary, apply a second coat immediately to build up the required depth of colour.

When the motif is complete, hold the stencil perfectly still while you slowly peel it away from the wall. Make sure paint has not crept under the stencil before repositioning it to repeat the motif next to the painted area.

If paint has crept under the stencil, try to dab it off with a piece of absorbent paper rolled into a thin taper. Alternatively, allow the paint to become touch-dry then scrape it carefully away with a scalpel blade. Touch in the scraped area with background paint.

APPLYING TEXTURED COATING

You can apply the coating with either a roller or a broad wall brush: finer textures are possible using the latter. Buy a special roller if recommended by the coating manufacturer.

With a well-loaded roller, apply a generous coat in a 600mm (2ft) wide band across the ceiling or down a wall. Do not press too hard and vary the angle of the stroke.

If you decide to brush on the coating, do not spread it out like paint. Lay it on with one stroke and spread it back again with one or two strokes only.

Clean up any splashes then apply a second band and texture it, blending both bands together. Continue in this way until the wall or ceiling is complete. Keep the room ventilated until the coating has hardened.

Painting around fittings
Use a small paintbrush to fill in around electrical fittings and along edges, trying to copy the texture used on the surrounding wall or ceiling. Some people prefer to form a distinct margin around fittings by drawing a small paintbrush along the perimeter to give a smooth finish.

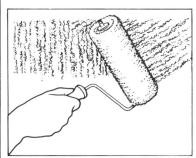

Creating a texture
You can experiment with a variety of tools to make any number of textures. You can use a standard roller, or use ones made with special surfaces to produce diagonal or diamond patterns, or you can apply a swirling, ripple or stipple finish with improvized equipment, as shown right.

TEXTURED COATINGS

Textured coatings can be obtained as a dry powder for mixing with warm water, or in a ready-mixed form for direct application from the tub. Most manufacturers supply a fine or a thick mix; if you want a heavy texture, choose the thicker mix. Where you're likely to rub against the wall – in a narrow hall, small bathroom or children's room, a fine texture is preferable: the coating dries very hard and could graze your skin.

Textured coatings are suitable for exterior walls as well as indoors. They are also available in a range of colours – you can cover the texture with emulsion paint if a standard colour does not fit your decorative scheme.

Preparing for textured coatings

New surfaces will need virtually no preparation, but joints between plasterboard must be reinforced with tape (▷). Strip any wallcoverings and key gloss paint with glasspaper. Old walls and ceilings must be clean, dry, sound and free from organic growth. Treat friable surfaces with stabilizing solution (▷).

Although large cracks and holes must be filled, a textured coating will conceal minor defects in walls and ceilings by filling small cracks and bridging shallow bumps and hollows.

Masking joinery and fittings
Use 50mm (2in) wide masking tape to cover door and window frames, electrical socket outlets, switches and ceiling roses, plumbing pipework, picture rails and skirting boards. Lay dust sheets over the floor.

I Diamond pattern

3 Swirl design

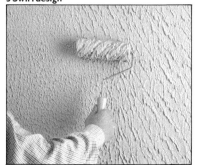

5 Tree bark simulation

2 Stipple effect

4 Combed arcs

6 Stucco finish

SEE ALSO

Details for: ▷

Friable surfaces	48
Plasterboard tapes	164
Using texture	28
Preparing plaster	50-51
Stripping wallpaper	52

I Geometric patterns
Use a roller with diamond or diagonal grooves: load the roller and draw lightly across the textured surface.

2 Stippled finish
Pat the coating with a damp sponge to create a pitted profile. Rinse out frequently. Alter your wrist angle and overlap sections.

3 Random swirls
Twist a damp sponge on the textured surface, then pull away to make a swirling design. Overlap swirls for a layered effect.

4 Combed arcs
A toothed spatula sold with the finish is used to create combed patterns: arcs, criss-cross patterns or wavy scrolls.

5 Imitation tree bark
Produce a bark texture by applying parallel strokes with a roller then lightly drawing the straight edge of a spatula over it.

6 Stucco finish
Apply parallel roller strokes, then run the rounded corner of a spatula over it in short straight strokes.

73

FINISHING WOODWORK

Paint is the usual finish for woodwork in and around the house – it gives a protective, decorative coating and there's a vast choice of colours and surface finishes. But stains, varnishes or polishes can also be used not just for furniture but as an attractive, durable finish for joinery. They enable

you to add colour to woodwork without obliterating the natural beauty of its grain; transparent finishes are also a good alternative where you don't want to alter the natural wood colour. Bear in mind the location of the woodwork and the amount of wear it is likely to get when choosing a finish.

Left to right
1 Wax polish
2 Coloured preserver
3 Satin oil paint
4 Cold cure lacquer
5 Gloss oil paint
6 Oil finish

7 Unsealed wood stain
8 Opaque microporous wood stain
9 Clear microporous wood stain
10 Polyurethane varnish

SEE ALSO

◁ Details for:
Colour and texture	24-28
Painting wood	76-79
Staining wood	80-81
Varnishing wood	82,84
Polishing wood	83,84
Oiling wood	84
Preservers	250

THE CHOICE OF FINISHES FOR WOOD

The list below comprises a comprehensive range of finishes available for decorating and protecting woodwork in and around the house. Each finish has qualities particular to its intended usage, although many can be used simply for their attractive appearance rather than for any practical considerations – this, however, depends on the location of timberwork, as some finishes are much more durable than others.

OIL PAINT

Oil (solvent-based) paints are still the most popular finish, primarily for the range of colours offered by all paint manufacturers, secondarily because they last for many years with only the occasional wash down to remove finger marks. Outside, their durability is reduced considerably due to the combined action of sun and rain: consider redecoration every two or three years. They are available as a gloss or satin finish with both liquid and thixotropic consistencies.

One or two undercoats are essential, especially for outside.

GLOSS EMULSION PAINT

Emulsion-based gloss paint was introduced by several manufacturers but is still quite rare. Beneficially, it dries much faster than oil paint and without the strong smell associated with such paint. It is suitable for both interior and exterior use. It allows moisture to escape from the wood while protecting it from rainwater – which oil paint does not – so reduces the risk of flaking and blistering. Gloss emulsion requires its own compatible primer/undercoat. The usual system of two undercoats and one top coat can be applied in one day.

WOOD STAIN

Unlike paint, which after the initial priming coat rests on the surface of timber, stain penetrates the wood. Its main advantage is to enhance the natural colour of the woodwork or to unify the slight variation in colour found in even the same species.

Water- or oil-based stains are available ready for use but powdered pigments are available for mixing with

methylated spirit. None of these stains will actually protect the timber and you will have to seal them with a clear varnish or polish.

There are protective wood stains (often sold as *microporous paints* or *breathing paints*) specially made for use on exterior joinery. The microporous nature of the coating allows water to escape from the wood, yet provides a weather-resistant satin finish. Being a stain, it does not crack, peel or flake. Choose a semi-transparent stain when you want the grain to show, or an opaque one for less attractive timbers.

COLOURED PRESERVERS

Sawn timber fencing, wall cladding and outbuildings look particularly unattractive when painted, yet they need protection. Use a wood preserver, which penetrates deeply into the timber to prevent rot and insect attack (▷). There are clear preservers, plus a range of browns and greens, and usually one for red cedar.

Traditional preservers such as creosote have a strong, unpleasant smell and are harmful to plants, but there are several organic solvent preservers, which are perfectly safe – even for greenhouses and propagators.

VARNISH

Varnish is a clear protective coating for timber. Most modern varnishes are made with polyurethane resins to provide a waterproof scratch- and heat-resistant finish. The majority are ready to apply, although some are supplied with a catalyst, which must be added before the varnish is used. These two-component varnishes are even tougher than standard polyurethanes and are especially suitable for treating wooden floors (▷): you can choose from high gloss, satin or matt.

An exterior grade of varnish is more weather-resistant. Yacht varnish, which is formulated to withstand even salt water, would be an ideal finish for exterior woodwork in a coastal climate.

Coloured varnishes are designed to provide a stain and clear finish at the same time. They are available in the normal wood shades and some strong primary colours. Unlike a true stain, a coloured varnish does not sink into the timber, so there is a possibility of a local loss of colour in areas of heavy wear or abrasion unless you apply additional coats of clear varnish.

COLD CURE LACQUER

Cold cure lacquer is a plastic coating, which is mixed with a hardener just before it is used. It is extremely durable, even on floors, and is heat- and alcohol-resistant. The standard type dries to a high gloss, which can be burnished to a lacquer-like finish if required. There is also a matt finish grade but a smoother matt surface can be obtained by rubbing down the gloss coating with fine steel wool and wax. It is available in clear, black or white.

OIL

Oil is a subtle finish which soaks into the wood, leaving a mellow sheen on the surface. Traditional linseed oils remain sticky for hours but a modern oil will dry in about one hour and provides a tougher, more durable finish. Oil can be used on softwood as well as open-grained oily hardwoods, such as teak or afromosia (▷). It's suitable for interior and exterior woodwork.

WAX POLISH

Wax can be used as a dressing to preserve and maintain another finish, or it can be used as a finish itself. A good wax should be a blend of beeswax and a hard polishing wax such as carnauba. Some contain silicones to make it easier to achieve a high gloss.

Polishes are white or tinted to various shades of brown to darken the wood. Although it is attractive, wax polish is not a durable finish and should be used indoors only.

FRENCH POLISH

French polish is made by dissolving shellac in alcohol and if properly applied, can be burnished to a mirror-like finish. It is easily scratched and alcohol, or even water, will etch the surface, leaving white stains. Consequently, it can be used only on furniture unlikely to receive normal wear and tear.

There are several varieties of shellac polish. Button polish is the best quality standard polish and is reddish brown in colour. It is bleached to make white polish for light coloured woods and if the natural wax is removed from the shellac, a clear, transparent polish is produced. For mahogany, choose a darker red garnet polish.

SEE ALSO

Details for: ▷
Wood flooring	113
Preservers	250
Hardwood	494-495
Primers	43

PAINTING WOODWORK

When you're painting wood, take into account that it's a fibrous material, which has a definite grain pattern, different rates of absorbency, knots that may ooze resin – all qualities that influence the type of paint you use and the techniques and tools you'll need to apply it.

Basic application

Prepare and prime all new woodwork thoroughly (◁) before applying the final finish. If you are using gloss paint, apply one or two undercoats, depending on the covering power of the paint. As each coat hardens, rub down with fine wet and dry paper to remove blemishes and wipe the surface with a cloth dampened with white spirit.

Best quality paintbrushes are the most efficient tools for painting woodwork. You will need 25mm (1in) and 50mm (2in) brushes for general work and a 12mm (½in) paintbrush for painting narrow glazing bars. Apply the paint with vertical strokes then spread sideways to even out the coverage. Finish with light strokes – called laying off – in the direction of the grain. Blend the edges of the next application while the paint is still wet, or a hard edge will show. Don't go back over a painted surface that has started to dry, or it will leave a blemish in the surface.

It is not necessary to spread thixotropic paint in the same way. Simply lay on the paint in almost parallel strokes leaving the brush strokes to settle out naturally.

THE ORDER OF WORK

Follow the sequences recommended below for painting interior and exterior woodwork successfully:

INSIDE

Start painting windows early in the day, so you can close them at night without the new film sticking. Paint doors, then picture rails; finish with skirting boards so that any specks of dust picked up on the brush won't be transferred to other areas.

OUTSIDE

Choose the order of painting according to the position of the sun. Avoid painting in direct sunlight as this will cause glare with light colours and results in runs or blistering. Never paint on wet or windy days: rain specks will pit the finish and airborne dust will ruin the surface. Paint windows and exterior doors early, so that they are touch-dry by the evening.

SEE ALSO

◁ Details for:
Primers	43-54
Preparing wood	53
Preparing paintwork	58-59
Paint system	63
Paint brushes	482
Cleaning brushes	482
Pads	483
Spray guns	484

● **Removing a blemish**
If you find specks of fluff or a brush bristle embedded in fresh paintwork, don't attempt to remove them once a skin has begun to form on the paint. Let it harden then rub down with wet and dry paper. The same applies if you discover runs.

Painting a panel
When painting up to the edge of a panel, brush from the centre out: if you flex the bristles against the edge, the paint will run.

Similarly, moulding flexes the bristles unevenly and too much paint flows: spread it well, taking care at corners of moulded panels.

Making a straight edge
To finish an area with a straight edge, use one of the smaller brushes and place it a few millimetres from the edge. As you flex the bristles, they'll spread to the required width, laying on an even coat of paint.

● Black dot denotes compatibility. All surfaces must be clean, sound, dry and free from organic growth.

FINISHES FOR WOODWORK

	Oil Paint	Gloss emulsion	Wood stain	Protective wood stain	Coloured preserver	Varnish	Coloured varnish	Cold cure lacquer	Oil	Wax polish	French polish
SUITABLE FOR											
Softwoods	●	●	●	●	●	●	●	●	●	●	
Hardwoods	●	●	●	●	●	●	●	●	●	●	●
Oily hardwoods	●	●	●			●	●	●	●	●	●
Planed wood	●	●	●	●		●	●	●	●	●	●
Sawn wood				●	●						
Interior use	●	●	●	●		●	●	●	●	●	●
Exterior use	●	●		●	●	●	●		●		
DRYING TIME: HOURS											
Touch-dry	4	1	½	4	1-2	4	4	1	1		½
Re-coatable	14	3	6	6-8	2-4	14	14	2	6	1	24
THINNERS: SOLVENTS											
Water		●			●						
White spirit	●		●	●	●	●	●		●	●	
Methylated spirit											●
Special thinner								●			
NUMBER OF COATS											
Interior use	1-2	1-2	2-3	2		2-3	2-3	2-3	3•	2	10-15
Exterior use	2-3	1-2		2	2	3-4	3-4	3			
COVERAGE											
Sq metres per litre	12-16	10-15	16-30	10-25	4-12	15-16	15-16	16-17	10-15	VARIABLE	VARIABLE
METHOD OF APPLICATION											
Brush	●	●	●	●	●	●	●	●	●	●	●
Paint pad	●	●	●	●	●		●	●			
Cloth pad (rubber)			●				●	●		●	●
Spray gun	●	●		●				●			●

PAINTING DOORS

Doors have a variety of faces and conflicting grain patterns that need to be painted separately – yet the end result must look even in colour without ugly brush marks or heavily painted edges. There's a strict system for painting panel, flush or glazed doors.

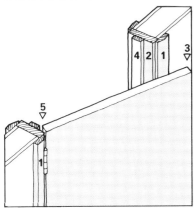

Painting each side a different colour
Make sure all the surfaces that face you when the door is open are painted the same colour.

Opening side: paint the architrave (1) and door frame up to and including the edge of the door stop (2) one colour. Paint the face of the door and its opening edge (3) the same colour.

Opposite side: paint the architrave and frame up to and over the door stop (4) the second colour. Paint the opposite face of the door and its hinged edge (5) with the second colour.

Preparation and technique

Remove the door handles and wedge the door open so that it cannot be closed accidentally, locking you in the room. Keep the handle in the room with you, just in case.

Aim to paint the door and its frame separately so that there is less chance of touching wet paintwork when passing through a freshly painted doorway. Paint the door first and when it is dry finish the framework.

If you want to use a different colour for each side of the door, paint the hinged edge the colour of the closing face (the one that comes to rest against the frame). Paint the outer edge of the door the same colour as the opening face. This means that there won't be any difference in colour when viewed from either side.

Each side of the frame should match the corresponding face of the door. When painting in the room into which the door swings, paint that side of the frame, including the edge of the stop bead against which the door closes, to match the opening face. Paint the rest of the frame the colour of the closing face.

System for a flush door

To paint a flush door, start at the top and work down in sections, blending each one into the other. Lay on the paint, then finish each section with light vertical brush strokes. Finally, paint the edges. Brush from edges, never onto them, or the paint will build up, run and a ridge will form.

System for a panel door

The different parts of a panelled door must be painted in logical order. Finish each part with parallel strokes in the direction of the grain.

Whatever the style of panelled door you are painting, start with the mouldings (1) followed by the panels (2). Paint the centre verticals – muntins (3) next, then the cross rails (4).

Finish the face by painting the outer verticals – stiles (5). Paint the edge of the door (6).

To achieve a superior finish, paint the muntins, rails and stiles together, picking up the wet edges of paint before they begin to dry, show brush strokes and pull out bristles. To get the best results you must work quickly.

SEE ALSO

Details for: ▷	
Glazing bars	78
Primers	43
Preparing wood	53
Preparing paintwork	58
Staining a door	81
Doors	184

Glazed doors
To paint a glazed door, begin with the glazing bars (▷) then follow the sequence as described for panel doors.

Flush door
Apply square sections of paint, working down from the top, and pick up the wet edges for a good blend. Lay off with light vertical brush strokes.

Panel door: basic painting method
Follow the numbered sequence for painting the various parts of the door, each finished with strokes along the grain to prevent streaking.

Panel door: advanced painting method
Working rapidly, follow the alternative sequence to produce a finish free from joins between sections.

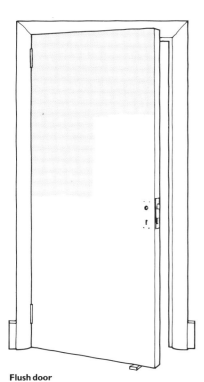

Flush door

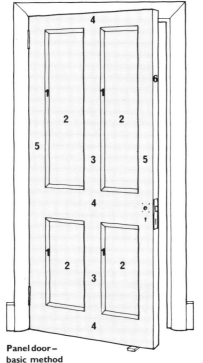

Panel door – basic method

Panel door – advanced method

SEE ALSO

◁ Details for:
Primers	43
Preparing wood	53
Preparing paintwork	58
Windows	196

● **Clean windows first**
Clean the glass in your windows before decorating to avoid picking up particles of dust in the paint.

Cutting-in brush
Paint glazing bars with a cutting-in brush, which has its bristles cut at an angle to enable you to work right up to the glass with a thin line of paint.

● **Painting French windows**
Although French windows are really glazed doors, treat them like large casement windows.

PROTECTING THE GLASS

When painting the edge of glazing bars, overlap the glass by about 2mm (¹/₁₆in) to prevent rain or condensation seeping between the glass and woodwork.

If you find it difficult to achieve a satisfactory straight edge, use a proprietary plastic or metal paint shield held against the edge of the frame to protect the glass.

Alternatively, run masking tape around the edges of the window pane, leaving a slight gap so that the paint will seal the join between glass and frame. When the paint is touch-dry, carefully peel off the tape. Don't wait until the paint is completely dry or the film may peel off with the tape.

Scrape off any paint accidentally dripped onto the glass using a razor blade, once it has set. Plastic handles to hold blades are sold by many DIY stores for this purpose.

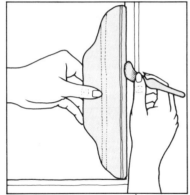

Using a paint shield
A plastic or metal paint shield enables you to paint a straight edge up to glass.

KEEPING THE WINDOW OPEN

With the catch and stay removed there's nothing to stop the frame closing. Make a stay with a length of stiff wire, hook the other end and slot it into one of the screw holes in the frame.

Temporary stay
Wind wire around a nail driven in the underside of the frame and use as a stay.

PAINTING WINDOW FRAMES

Window frames need to be painted in strict order, like doors, so that the various components will be evenly treated and so that you can close them at night. You also need to take care not to splash panes with paint or apply a crooked line around the glazing bars – the mark of poor workmanship.

Painting a casement window

A casement window hinges like a door, so if you plan to paint each side a different colour, follow a similar procedure to that described for painting doors and frames.

Remove the stay and catch before you paint the window. So that you can still operate the window during decorating without touching wet paint, drive a nail into the underside of the bottom rail as a makeshift handle.

Painting sequence
First paint the glazing bars (1), cutting into the glass on both sides. Carry on with the top and bottom horizontal rails (2) followed by the vertical stiles (3). Finish the casement by painting the edges (4) then paint the frame (5).

Painting sequence for casement window ▷

Painting a sash window

Sash windows are the most difficult type to paint, as the two panes slide vertically, overlapping each other.

The following sequence describes the painting of a sash window from the inside. To paint the outside face, use a similar procedure but start with the lower sash. When using different colours for each side, the demarcation lines are fairly obvious. When the window is closed, all the visible surfaces from one side should be the same.

Painting sequence
Raise the bottom sash and pull down the top one. Paint the bottom meeting rail of the top sash (1) and the accessible parts of the vertical members (2). Reverse the position of the sashes, leaving a gap top and bottom and complete the painting of the top sash (3). Paint the bottom sash (4) then the frame (5) except for the runners in which the sashes slide.

Leave the paint to dry then paint the inner runners (6) plus a short section of the outer runners (7). When painting the runners, pull the cords aside to avoid splashing paint on them, as this will make them brittle, shortening their working life. Make sure the window slides before the paint dries.

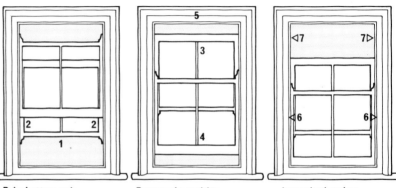

Raise bottom sash and pull down top

Reverse the position of the sashes

Lower both sashes for access to runners

PAINTING FIXED JOINERY

Staircase

Paint banisters first, making sure that you do not precipitate runs by stroking the brush against the edges or mouldings. Start at the top of the stairs, painting the treads, risers and strings (▷) together to keep the edges of the paintwork fresh.

If there is any chance that the paint will not dry before the staircase is used again, paint all risers but alternate treads only. The next day, paint the remainder.

Skirting boards

The only problem with painting a skirting board is to protect the floor from paint and at the same time avoid picking up dust on the wet paintbrush.

Slide strips of thin card under the skirting as a paint shield (don't use newspaper; it will tear and remain stuck to the skirting).

PAINTING EXTERIOR WEATHERBOARDING

Start at the top of the wall and apply paint to one or two boards at a time. Paint the under-edge first, then the face of the boards; finish parallel with the edge. Make sure you coat exposed end grain well, as it is more absorbent and requires extra protection.

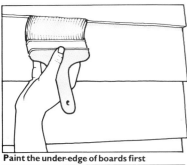

Paint the under-edge of boards first

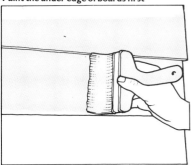

Paint the face of boards next

GRAINING TIMBER

Graining is a technique for simulating natural wood with paint. It was used extensively on cheap softwood joinery to imitate expensive hardwoods. Doors and panels can look attractive treated in this way. The basic method is simple to describe but practice on a flat board is essential before you can achieve convincing results. A skilled grainer can simulate actual species of timber, but just try to suggest ordinary wood grain rather than attempt to produce a perfect copy.

Equipment and preparation for graining

The simplest graining effects can be achieved by removing dark paint to reveal a paler basecoat below. The traditional way to carry out this effect is to use a special hog's- or squirrel's-hair brush called a mottler or grainer. To compromise, try any soft-bristled paintbrush or even a dusting brush. You can also buy steel, rubber or leather combs from decorator's suppliers to achieve similar effects.

Applying a basecoat (ground)

Prepare the basecoat as normal paintwork, finishing with a satin oil paint. It should represent the lightest colour of the timber you want to reproduce and is normally beige or olive green. The basecoat will look more convincing if it is slightly dull rather than being too bright.

Choosing the graining colour

Translucent, flat-drying paints are produced especially for graining in a range of appropriate colours. These paints must be thinned with a mixture comprising 2 parts white spirit: 1 part raw linseed oil to make a graining glaze. The quantity of thinners controls the colour of the graining, so add it to the paint sparingly until you achieve the required result. Try the method on a practice panel first.

Producing the effect

Paint an even coat of glaze onto the ground with a 50 mm (2 in) paintbrush. After only two or three minutes, lightly drag the tip of the mottler or comb along the line of the rail or panel, leaving faint streaks in the glaze.

When two rails meet at right-angles, mask the joint with a piece of card to prevent the simulated grain being disturbed on one rail while you paint a rail next to it.

The grain does not have to be exactly parallel with the rail. You can vary the pattern by allowing the comb or mottler to streak out the glaze at a slight angle and over the edge of some of the rails.

Leave the graining to dry overnight then apply one or two coats of clear varnish to protect and seal the effects.

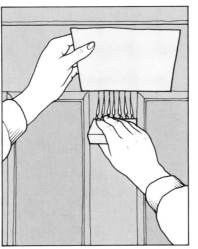

Masking meeting rails
Hold a piece of card over the joint between two meeting rails – on a panel door, for instance, where muntins meet cross rails – to prevent spoiling the graining effect on one while you treat the other.

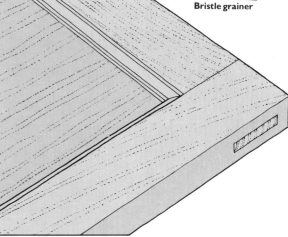

Applying graining patterns
Produce graining patterns that are as authentic as possible. Don't just run the streaks in one direction, or parallel to the timber: simulate actual wood grain by running the pattern at an angle.

SEE ALSO

Details for: ▷
Staircases	213
Preparing wood	53
Painting wood	76
Varnishing wood	82

Steel graining comb

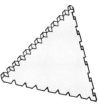

Rubber or leather comb

Bristle grainer

STAINING WOODWORK

Unless the wood is perfectly clean and free from grease, the stain will be rejected, producing an uneven, patchy appearance. Strip any previous finish and sand the wood with progressively finer abrasive papers, always in the direction of the grain. Scratches made across the grain will tend to be emphasized by the stain.

SEE ALSO

◁ Details for:

Making a rubber	83
Preparing wood	53
Filling grain	53
Stains	74-75
Stripping wood	58-59
Paintbrushes	482
Paint pads	483

Testing the stain
Make a test strip (far right) to assess the depth of colour of various stains before embarking on the final job. Apply a band of varnish along the bottom half of the strip to see how the colours are affected.

Paint pad

Paintbrush

Rubber

Making a test strip

The final colour is affected by the nature of the timber, the number of coats and the overlying clear finish. You can also mix compatible stains to alter the colour or dilute them with the appropriate thinner.

Make a test strip so that you will have an accurate guide from which you can choose the depth of stain to suit your purpose. Use a piece of timber from the same batch you are staining, or one that resembles it closely.

Paint the whole strip with one coat of stain. Allow the stain to be absorbed then apply a second coat, leaving a strip of the first application showing. It is rarely necessary to apply more than two coats of stain, but for the experiment add a third and even a fourth coat, always leaving a strip of the previous application for comparison.

When the stain has dried completely, paint a band of clear varnish along the strip: some polyurethane varnishes react unfavourably with oil-based stains, so it is advisable to use products made by the same manufacturer.

USING A RUBBER

Wear gloves to protect your skin and pour some stain into a shallow dish. Saturate the rubber with stain then squeeze some out so that it is not dripping but still wet enough to apply a liberal coat of stain to the surface.

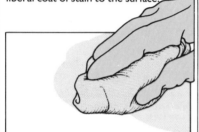

Apply stain by rubber

If you wet a piece of timber, water is absorbed by the wood, raising a mass of tiny fibres across the surface. A water-based stain will produce the same result and the final finish will be ruined. Solve the problem by sanding the wood until it is perfectly smooth, then dampen the whole surface with a wet rag. Leave it to dry out then sand the raised grain with very fine abrasive paper before you apply the stain. If you are using an

oil-based stain, this preliminary process is unnecessary.

If you want to fill the grain, first apply a seal coat of clear finish over the stain. Choose a grain filler that matches the stain closely, adjusting the colour by adding a little stain to it, but make sure that the stain and filler are compatible. An oil-based stain will not mix with a water-based filler and vice versa, so check before you buy either.

How to apply wood stain

Use a 100mm (4in) paintbrush to apply stains over a wide, flat surface. Do not brush out a stain like paint, but apply it liberally and evenly, always in the direction of the grain.

It is essential to blend wet edges of stain, so work fairly quickly and don't take a break until you have completed the job. If you have brushed a water-based stain onto the wood it is sometimes advantageous to wipe over the wet surface with a soft cloth and remove excess stain.

A paint pad is one of the best applicators for achieving an even coverage of wood stain over a flat surface. However, you may find that you will still need a paintbrush to get the stain into awkward corners and for tackling mouldings.

Because stains are so fluid, it's often easier to apply them with a wad of soft, lint-free rag called a rubber (◁). You'll be able to control runs on a vertical panel and it's the best way to stain turned wood and rails.

STAINING PANELS, FLOORS AND DOORS

Staining a flat panel

Whenever possible, set up a panel horizontally for staining, either on trestles or raised on softwood blocks. Shake the container before use and pour the stain into a flat dish so that you can load your applicator properly.

Apply the stain, working swiftly and evenly along the grain. Stain the edges at the same time as the top surface. The first application may have a slightly patchy appearance as it dries because some parts of the wood will absorb more stain than others. The second coat normally evens out the colour without difficulty. If powdery deposits are left on the surface of the dry stain, wipe them off with a coarse, dry cloth, before applying the second coat in the same way as the first.

Leave the stain to dry overnight then proceed with the clear finish of your choice to seal the colourant.

Staining floors

Because a wooden floor is such a large area it is more difficult to blend the wet edges of the stain. Work along two or three boards at a time, using a paintbrush, so that you can finish at the edge of a board each time.

Wood block floors are even trickier, so try to complete one panel at a time, and use a soft cloth to blend in any overlapping areas.

Staining a door

Stain a new or stripped door before it is hung so that it can be layed horizontally. A flush door is stained just like any other panel but use a rubber to carefully colour the edges so that stain does not run under to spoil the other side.

When staining a panelled door, it is essential to follow a sequence which will allow you to pick up the edges of stain before they dry. Use a combination of brush and rubber to apply the stain.

Follow the numbered sequence below and note that, unlike painting a panel door, the mouldings are stained last – this is to prevent any overlapping showing on the finished door. Stain the mouldings carefully with a narrow brush and blend in the colour with a rubber.

Method for staining a panel door
Follow this practical sequence, using a combination of paintbrush or paint pad and rubber to apply the stain evenly to the various sections. Start with the inset panels first (1), then continue with half of the centre vertical rail (2), the bottom cross rail (3) and half the stiles (4). Pick up the wet edges with the other half of the centre vertical (5) and the stiles (6). Stain the centre cross rail (7), then repeat the procedure for the second half of the door (8-12), finishing with the mouldings (13) using a narrow brush and rubber.

• **Pads for mouldings**
Although paint pads are excellent for laying on flat areas of stain, they can be awkward to use on moulded woodwork, particularly when staining glazed bars. However, small pads are made specifically for this purpose.

USING WOOD STAINS OUTSIDE

Standard wood stains are not suitable for exterior use. They have no protective properties of their own and they have a tendency to fade in direct sunlight. For planed joinery and weatherboarding, use a microporous protective wood stain (▷). For sawn timber use a coloured wood preserver. Both materials are much thinner than paint, so take care to avoid splashing.

Protective wood stain
Make sure the surface is clean, dry and sanded. All previous paint or varnish must be stripped. For blemished timber, use an opaque wood stain so that you can fill cracks and holes. For extra protection treat the timber with a clear wood preserver before staining.

Apply two coats with a paintbrush, making sure that the coating is even, and avoid any overlaps.

Stain wall cladding one board at a time (treating the under-edge first).

Wood preserver
Before you apply wood preserver, remove surface dirt with a stiff-bristled brush. Paint or varnish must be stripped completely, but previously preserved or creosoted timber can be treated, so long as it has weathered.

For additional protection against insect and fungal attack, treat the timber first with a clear wood preserver, either by immersion or by full brush coats (▷).

Paint a full coat of coloured preserver onto the wood followed by a second coat as soon as the first has soaked in. Brush out sufficiently to achieve an even colour and avoid overlaps by following immediately with the edges of boards, rails and posts.

Replacing putty
Stain will not colour putty. In any case, microporous stains allow the wood to breathe, so there's likely to be some movement, which puts greater strain on the glass. For both reasons, remove the old putty (▷) and stain the frame. Seal the rebate with mastic (1).

Set lengths of stained wooden beading into the mastic and secure them with panel pins (2). You'll find it easiest to fix the beading if you tap in the pins beforehand, so they just protrude through the other side. Remove excess mastic squeezed from beneath the beading with a putty knife (3).

SEE ALSO

Details for: ▷

Protective stains	75
Removing putty	202
Wood preservers	250
Preparing wood	53
Sanding floors	55-56
Stripping wood	58-59
Painting a door	77

1 Apply mastic

2 Fix beading

3 Trim mastic

VARNISHING WOODWORK

Varnish serves two main purposes: to protect the wood from knocks, stains and other marks, and to give it a sheen that accentuates the beautiful grain pattern. In some cases, it can even be used to change the colour of the wood to that of another species – or to give it a fresh, new look with a choice of bright primary colours.

SEE ALSO

◁ Details for:

Linseed oil	75
Using a rubber	80
Test strip	80
Preparing wood	53
Stripping wood	58-59
Varnishes	75
Wax polish	75

The effect of varnish
The example below demonstrates how different varnishes affect the same species of wood. From top to bottom: untreated birch plywood; matt clear varnish; gloss clear varnish; wood shade coloured varnish; pure coloured varnish.

How to apply varnish

Use paintbrushes to apply varnish in the same way as paint. You will need a range of sizes for general work: 12mm (½in), 25mm (1in) and 50mm (2in) are useful widths. For varnishing floors use a 100mm (4in) brush for quick coverage. With any brush, make sure it's spotlessly clean; any previous traces of paint may mar the finish.

Load a brush with varnish by dipping the first third of the bristles into the liquid, then touch off the excess on the side of the container. Don't scrape the brush across the rim of the container as it causes bubbles in the varnish, which can spoil the finish if transferred to the woodwork.

A soft cloth pad, or rubber (◁) can be used to apply the first thinned coat of varnish into the grain. It is not essential to use a rubber – even for the sealing coat – but it is a convenient method, especially for coating shaped or turned pieces of wood.

Applying the varnish

Thin the first coat of varnish with 10 per cent white spirit and rub it well into the wood with a cloth pad in the direction of the grain. Brush on the sealer coat where the rubber is difficult to use.

Apply the second coat of varnish not less than six hours later. If more than 24 hours have elapsed, key the surface of gloss varnish lightly with fine abrasive paper. Wipe it over with a cloth dampened with white spirit to remove dust and grease, then brush on a full coat of varnish as for paint.

Apply a third coat if the surface is likely to take hard wear.

Using coloured varnish

A wood stain can only be used on bare timber, but you can use a coloured varnish to darken or alter the colour of woodwork that has been varnished previously without having to strip the finish. Clean the surface with wire wool and white spirit mixed with a little linseed oil (◁). Dry the surface with a clean cloth then apply the varnish.

Apply tinted varnish in the same way as the clear type. It might be worth making a test strip to see how many coats you will need to achieve the depth of colour you want (◁).

Varnishing floors

Varnishing a floor is no different to finishing any other woodwork but the greater area can produce an unpleasant concentration of fumes in a confined space. Open all windows for ventilation and wear a gauze facemask.

Start in the corner furthest from the door and work back towards it. Brush the varnish out well to make sure it does not collect in pools.

DEALING WITH DUST PARTICLES

Minor imperfections and particles of dust stuck to the varnished surface can be rubbed down with fine abrasive paper between coats. If your top coat is to be a high-gloss finish, take even more care to ensure that your brush is perfectly clean.

If you are not satisfied with your final finish, dip very fine wire wool in wax polish and rub the varnish with parallel strokes in the direction of the grain. Buff the surface with a soft duster. This will remove the high gloss but it leaves a pleasant sheen on the surface with no obvious imperfections.

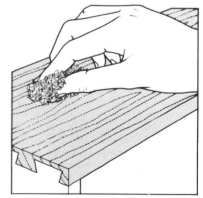

Produce a soft sheen with wire wool and wax

FRENCH POLISHING

The art of French polishing has always been considered the province of the expert, which a wise amateur would leave well alone. It is true that an expert will make a better job of the polishing and can work much faster than an amateur, but there's no reason why anyone cannot produce a satisfactory finish with a little practice.

Basic French polishing

Try out French polishing using one of the prepared proprietary kits available from DIY stores. A kit typically contains a bottle of thin shellac for building up the body of polish and a separate clear burnishing liquid.

Brush coating

Pour some shellac into a shallow dish so that you can use a brush to paint the polish onto the wood. Keep the coating even and work quickly to pick up the moist edges. Don't go over an area more than once.

Half an hour later, brush coat the work again then leave it for another hour. Next, lightly sand the polish with a silicon carbide paper (grey with a dry lubricant embedded in its surface) to remove any blemishes.

Building up the polish

With the workpiece set up at a comfortable working height and in good light, distribute the polish along the surface of the wood with continuous, circular strokes of the rubber.

There's no need to press too hard at first as a fully charged rubber flows easily. As the rubber gradually dries out, increase the pressure.

Never bring the pad to rest on the surface of the polish. As you reach the edge of the workpiece, sweep the rubber off the surface and sweep it back on again for the next pass. If you pull the

Woodwork must be prepared immaculately before polishing, as every blemish will be mirrored in the finish. The grain should be filled, either with a proprietary filler ($\triangleright$) or by layers of polish, which are rubbed down and repeated until the pores of the wood are filled flush with polish.

Work in a warm, dust-free room:

rubber off the workpiece it will leave a blemish in the polish.

Cover the surface, perhaps ten or twelve times. As you feel the rubber drying out, open it up and pour a little more shellac onto the back of the cotton wool filling. Occasionally change the rag for a spare one, leaving the used one to soak in a jar of methylated spirit to wash out the polish ready for the next exchange.

Seal the rubber in an empty glass jar and leave the surface to harden for about one hour, then if necessary, lightly flatten the polish with silicon carbide paper using fingertip pressure.

Build up another layer of polish with the rubber. Vary the size and shape of your strokes so that every part of the surface is covered (see below). In between each coat, make straight parallel strokes along the grain.

Repeat the process for a third time, more if you want a deeper colour. Make your final coat with slightly less polish; allow it to harden overnight.

Burnishing the polished surface

Take a handful of clean cotton wool and dampen the sole with burnishing liquid. Use it to burnish a small section at a time, rubbing forcefully along the grain. As the sole of the pad becomes dirty, pull it off to reveal a clean surface. Buff each section with a soft duster before burnishing the next.

dust's effect is obvious, but a low temperature will make the polish go cloudy (bloom).

Work in a good light so that you can glance across the surface to gauge the quality of the finish you are applying.

TRADITIONAL FRENCH POLISHING

With traditional polishing, the shellac is thicker, therefore do not soak the rag with meths. Charge the rubber and dab linseed oil on the sole.

Apply all the shellac with a rubber, using a combination of strokes (see below). Recharge the rubber and add a touch of oil to the sole when it starts to drag or catch. Leave to dry for twenty minutes. Repeat four or five times.

Leave to harden overnight then build up more layers – ten may be enough but continue until you're happy with the depth of colour. To remove surface marks, rub down the hard polish with silicon carbide paper. The top layer may be streaked due to the linseed oil: add meths to the rubber's cotton wool. Burnish with straight strokes parallel with the grain, sweeping the rubber on and off at each end. As the rubber drags, recharge. Leave for a few minutes to see if the streaking disappears. If not, repeat with more meths. Polish with a duster and leave to harden.

SEE ALSO

Details for: $\triangleright$

Grain filler	53
Preparing wood	53
Stripping wood	58-59
French polish	75

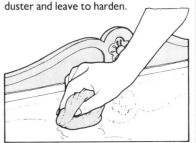
Apply French polish with a rubber

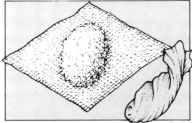
Making a rubber for basic polishing
Saturate a 300mm (1ft) square of white cotton rag with meths, wring out until damp, dip a handful of cotton wool into the shellac and squeeze out excess. Wrap in rag, twist excess into a handgrip; smooth sole of rubber.

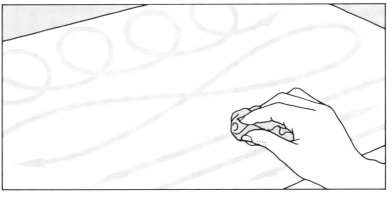

Using the rubber
Apply the polish with a combination of circular and figure-of-eight strokes so that every part of the surface is covered. When you finish each coat, run the rubber in long straight strokes, parallel to the wood grain. Keep the pad moving constantly and smoothly: if you lift it from the surface a scar will form.

COLD CURE LACQUER

SEE ALSO

◁ Details for:

Using a rubber	80
Preparing wood	53
Stripping wood	58-59
Cold cure lacquer	75
Oil	75
Wax polish	75

Due to its chemical composition, careful preparation is essential or plastic coating will take days to cure instead of only two hours. It must be applied to a clean, grease-free surface, which has been sanded smooth. Strip the old finish but do not use a caustic stripper, as this will react against the coating.

Clean old wax polish from the wood. You must remove every trace, even from the pores of the timber. Wash it with white spirit, using a ball of fine wire wool in the direction of the grain. When the wood is dry, scrub it with water and detergent, then rinse the surface with clean water with a little white vinegar added.

If you use wood stain, make sure it is made by the manufacturer of the lacquer, otherwise it might change colour. Use the same manufacturer's stopping to fill cracks and holes and never use plaster or plastic fillers.

Mixing cold cure lacquer

In most cases, it's best to use a paintbrush to apply plastic coating, although you can use a plastic foam roller instead, especially for large areas of woodwork.

When you are ready to apply the lacquer, mix the coating and hardener in a glass, polythene or enamel container.

Use the proportions recommended by the manufacturer. Mix just enough for your immediate needs, as it will set in two to three days in an open dish. Don't be tempted to economize by pouring mixed lacquer back into its original container: the hardener will ruin any remaining substance.

Applying the lacquer

Plastic coating must be applied in a warm atmosphere. Use a well-loaded applicator and spread the lacquer onto the wood. There is no need to over-brush the liquid as it will flow unaided and even a thick coat will cure thoroughly and smoothly. Plastic coating dries quickly and will begin to show brush marks if disturbed after 10 to 15 minutes, so you should work swiftly to pick up the wet edges.

After two hours, apply the second coat. If necessary, rub down the hardened lacquer with fine abrasive paper to remove blemishes, then add a third coat. You will achieve better adhesion between the layers if you can apply all the coats in one day, so long as each has time to dry.

Burnishing lacquer

If you want a mirror finish, wait for 24 hours then use a proprietary burnishing cream. Rub down the lacquer with very fine abrasive paper or wire wool, then rub the cream onto the surface with a soft cloth. Burnish it vigorously with a clean soft duster to achieve the required depth of sheen.

Matting lacquer

To produce a subtle satin coat, rub the hardened lacquer along the grain with fine wire wool dipped in wax polish. The grade of the wire wool will effect the degree of matting. Use very fine 000 grade for a satin finish and a coarse 0 grade for a fully-matted surface. Polish with a clean, soft duster.

● **Spontaneous combustion**
It is essential to dispose of oily rags immediately you have finished with them as they have been known to burst into flames.

SAFETY WHEN USING LACQUER

Although cold cure lacquer is safe to use, you should take care when applying it to a large surface such as a floor, due to the concentration of fumes.

Open all windows and doors if possible for ventilation – but remember the necessity for a warm atmosphere, too – and take the extra precaution of wearing a simple gauze facemask to prevent you breathing in the fumes. You can buy cheap masks and spare lint filters, which you should renew frequently, from chemists and DIY stores.

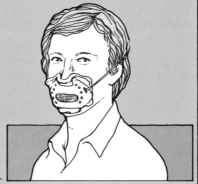

OILING AND WAXING WOODWORK

Applying the oil

Clean and prepare the wood for oiling. Remove previous finishes carefully so that oil can penetrate the grain.

The most efficient way to apply a finishing oil is to rub it into the wood with a soft, lint-free rag in the form of a rubber (◁). Don't store oily rags: keep them in a sealed tin while the job is in progress then unfold them and leave them outside to dry before throwing them away.

A brush is a convenient way to spread oil liberally over large surfaces and into carvings or deep mouldings.

Rub or brush a generous coating of oil into the wood grain. Leave it to soak in for a few minutes, then rub off excess oil with a clean cloth. After about six hours, coat the wood with oil once more. The next day, apply a third and final coat; raise a faint sheen by burnishing with a soft duster.

Wax polishing timber

If you want to wax-polish new timber, seal the wood first with one coat of clear varnish (or French polish on fine furniture). This will stop the wax being absorbed too deeply into the wood and provides a slightly more durable finish. Before waxing an old clear finish, clean it first to remove deposits of dirt and possibly an old wax dressing.

To remove dirty wax, mix up white spirit with 25 per cent linseed oil. Use the liquid to clean the surface quite hard with a coarse cloth. If there is no obvious improvement, try dipping very fine wire wool into the cleaner and rub in the direction of the grain. Don't press too hard as you want to remove wax and dirt only without damaging the finish below. Wash the cleaned surface with a cloth dipped in white spirit and leave to dry before refinishing.

You can use a soft cloth to apply wax polish but use a paintbrush to spread liquid wax over a wide area. Pour liquid wax polish onto a cloth pad and rub it into the sealed wood with a circular motion followed by strokes parallel with the grain. Make this first coat a generous one.

Buff up the wax after one hour then apply a second, thinner coat in the direction of the grain only. Burnish this coat lightly and leave it for several hours to harden. Bring the surface to a high gloss by burnishing vigorously with a soft duster.

FINISHING METALWORK

Ferrous metals that are rusty will shed any paint film rapidly, so the most important aspect of finishing metalwork is thorough preparation and priming to prevent this corrosion from returning; then applying the finish is virtually the same as painting woodwork.

When you are choosing a finish for metalwork in and around the house (see chart below and table overleaf for suitable types) make sure it fulfils your requirements. Many of the finishes listed are easy to apply to metal, but the ability of some to withstand heavy wear is likely to be poor (▷)

Methods of application

Most of the finishes suggested for use on metalwork can be applied with a paintbrush. The exception is black lead (▷). In the main, use the standard techniques for painting woodwork (▷), but bitumen-based paints should be laid on only and not brushed out like conventional coatings.

Remove metal door and window fittings for painting, suspending them on wire hooks to dry. Make sure that sharp or hard edges are coated properly, as the finish can wear thin quickly.

Some paints can be sprayed but there are few situations where it is advantageous, except perhaps for intricately moulded ironwork such as garden furniture, which you can paint outside – otherwise ventilation is a necessity indoors.

A roller is suitable on large flat surfaces and pipework requires its own special V-section roller (▷), which is designed to coat curved surfaces.

SEE ALSO

Details for: ▷	
Preparing metal	60-61
Painting wood	76
Metal finishes	86
Pipe roller	483
Primers	43
Removing radiators	399

● Black dot denotes compatibility. Thorough preparation is essential before applying any finish to metals (▷).

FINISHES FOR METALWORK

	Oil paint	Emulsion paint	Metallic paint	Bituminous based paint	Security paint	Radiator enamel	Black lead	Varnish	Bath paint	Non-slip paint
DRYING TIME: HOURS										
Touch-dry	4	1-2	4	1-2		2-6		0-3	6-10	4-6
Re-coatable	14	4	8	6-24		7-14		1	16-24	12
THINNERS: SOLVENTS										
Water		●		●						
White spirit	●		●	●	●		●	●	●	●
Special						●				
Cellulose thinners								●		
NUMBER OF COATS										
Normal conditions	1-2	2	1-2	1-3	1	1-2	VARIABLE	1-2	2	2
COVERAGE										
Sq metres per litre	12-16	9-15	10-14	6-15	2½	13	VARIABLE	13	13-14	3-5
METHOD OF APPLICATION										
Brush	●	●	●	●	●	●	●	●	●	●
Roller	●	●		●						
Spray gun	●	●		●				●		
Cloth pad (Rubber)							●			

PAINTING RADIATORS AND PIPES

Leave radiators and hot water pipes to cool before you paint them. The only problem with decorating a radiator is how to paint the back: the best solution is to remove it completely or, if possible, swing it away from the wall, paint the back, reposition the radiator then paint the front.

If this is inconvenient, use a special radiator brush with a long metal handle (see right). Use the same tool to paint in between the leaves of a double radiator. It is difficult to achieve a perfect finish even with the brush, so aim at covering areas you are likely to see when the radiator is fixed in position rather than a complete application.

Don't paint over radiator valves or fittings or you will not be able to operate them afterwards.

Paint pipework lengthwise rather than across, or runs are likely to form. The first coat on metal piping will be streaky, so be prepared to apply two or three coats. Unless you are using radiator enamel, allow the paint to harden thoroughly before turning on the heat, or it may blister.

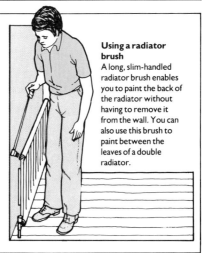

Using a radiator brush
A long, slim-handled radiator brush enables you to paint the back of the radiator without having to remove it from the wall. You can also use this brush to paint between the leaves of a double radiator.

METALWORK

SUITABLE FINISHES FOR METALWORK

Gutters and downpipes

It is best to coat the inside of gutters with a bituminous paint for thorough protection against moisture, but you can finish the outer surfaces with oil paint or security paint.

To protect the wall behind a downpipe, slip a scrap of card between while painting the back of the pipe (1).

Metal casement windows

Paint metal casement windows using the sequence described for wooden casements (◁), which allows you to close the frame at night without spoiling a freshly-painted surface.

Varnishing metalwork

Polish the metal to a high gloss then use a nail brush to scrub it with warm water containing some liquid detergent. Rinse the metal in clean water then dry it thoroughly with an absorbent cloth.

Use a large, soft artist's brush to paint on acrylic lacquer (2), working swiftly from the top. Let the lacquer flow naturally, working all round the object to keep the wet edge moving.

If you do leave a brush stroke in partially-set varnish, do not try to overpaint it but finish the job then warm the metal (by standing it on a radiator if possible). As soon as the blemish disappears, remove the object from the heat and allow it to cool gradually in a dust-free atmosphere.

Blacking cast iron

Black lead produces an attractive finish for cast iron. It is not a permanent or durable finish and will have to be renewed periodically. It may transfer if rubbed hard.

The material is supplied in a toothpaste-like tube. Squeeze some of the black cream onto a soft cloth and spread it onto the metal. Use an old toothbrush (3) to scrub it into decorative ironwork for best coverage.

When you have covered the surface, buff the black lead to a satin sheen with a clean, dry cloth. Build up a patina with several applications of black lead for a moisture-proof finish.

OIL PAINT

Standard oil paints are perfectly suitable for metal. Having primed the surface, interior metalwork will need at least one undercoat plus a top coat. Add an extra undercoat for greater protection of exterior metalwork.

EMULSION PAINT

Strictly, emulsion paint is not suitable for finishing metal. Being water-based, it may promote corrosion on ferrous metals if applied directly; it can be used to paint radiators to match the wall colour if the metal has been factory-painted.

METALLIC PAINT

For a metallic-like finish, choose a paint containing aluminium, copper, gold or bronze powders: these paints are water-resistant and are able to withstand very high temperatures – up to about 100°C (212° F).

BITUMINOUS PAINT

Bitumen-based paints give economical protection for exterior storage tanks and piping. Standard bituminous paint is black but there is also a limited range of colours, plus 'modified' bituminous paint, which contains aluminium.

Before coating the inside of drinking water tanks, make sure the paint is non-contaminating. Don't apply over other types of paint.

SECURITY PAINT

Non-setting security paint, primarily for rainwater and waste downpipes, remains slippery to prevent intruders from scaling the wall via the pipe. Restrict it to pipework over about 1.8m (6ft) above the ground, out of reach.

RADIATOR ENAMEL

A heat-stoving acrylic paint which is applied in two thin coats. It can be used over emulsion or oil paints so long as these have not been recently applied (don't rub them down first).

Apply a compatible metal primer over new paint or factory priming to prevent strong solvents in the enamel reacting with the previous coating. A special thinner is required for brush cleaning. A choice of satin and gloss finishes is available.

Finish the radiator in position then turn the heating on (boiler set to maximum) for a minimum of two hours to bake the enamel onto the metal. Apply a second coat six to eight hours later.

Also use to repaint central heating boiler cabinets, refrigerators, cookers and washing machines.

BLACK LEAD

A cream used to colour cast ironwork, it is a mixture of graphite and waxes. After several coats it is moisture-proof, but it is not suitable for exterior use.

VARNISHES

Virtually any clear lacquer can be used on polished metalwork without spoiling its appearance, but many polyurethanes yellow with age. An acrylic lacquer is clear and will protect chrome-plating, brass and copper – even outside.

NON-SLIP PAINT

Designed to provide good foot-holding on a wide range of surfaces, including metal, non-slip paint is ideal for painting metal spiral staircase treads and exterior fire escapes. The surface must be primed before application.

SEE ALSO

◁ Details for:
Painting casements	78
Primers	43
Preparing metal	60-61
Painting radiators	85
Home security	238-239
Polishing metal	491

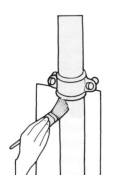

1 Protect wall
Use card behind a downpipe when painting behind it.

2 Apply lacquer
Use a large, soft artist's paintbrush.

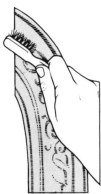

3 Apply black lead
Scrub cream into intricate surfaces using an old toothbrush.

INTERIOR PANELLING

Walls that are in poor condition – except those that are damp – can be covered with panelling to conceal them and to provide a decorative surface. Panelling can be practical in other ways, too, if used in conjunction with insulation. There are various types of decorative panelling for walls, notably solid wood planking and decorative wallboards faced with various patterns.

Tongued-and-grooved boards

Solid wooden panelling is made from planks with a tongue along one edge and a matching groove on the other. This provides a way to fix the planks to the wall and allows movement in the timber – due to the atmosphere – to prevent splitting. The meeting edges of some planks – called tongued, grooved and V-jointed (TGV) boards – are machined to produce a decorative V-shaped profile, accentuating the shape of each board. Other types have more decorative profiles. Shiplap has a rebate on the back face, which holds down the coved front edge of the next board.

A few hardwoods are available as panelling but the majority is made from softwood, typically knotty pine, which is unsuitable for joinery because of the large amounts of knots it contains.

Buy boards in one batch
Make sure you buy enough TGV boards to complete the work. If you have to use a few boards from another batch, the machine used to shape the tongues and grooves may not be set to exactly the same tolerances, and the joints won't fit.

Wallboards

A wider choice of panelling exists in the form of manufactured sheet wallboards. They are made to various standard sizes and in thicknesses ranging from 4 to 6mm (3/16 to 1/4 in).

Plywood or hardboard panels are faced with real timber veneers or paper printed to simulate wood grain, and there are plastic-faced boards in various colours. Typical surfaces include embossed brick, stone, plaster or tiled effects as well as a random V-grooved panel like timber TGV boards.

Wall panels made from wood fibre board are 12mm (1/2in) thick and can be bought with cork, grass and fabric surfaces; they are sound- and heat-insulating.

CONSTRUCTING A FRAMEWORK FOR PANELLING

If a wall is flat you can glue thick wallboards directly to the surface, but as most walls are fairly uneven, it is best to construct a frame from softwood battens, called furring strips. For TGV boarding and thin wallboards, this is the only practical solution. You can pin any type of panelling directly to the studs and noggings of a stud partition wall (▷).

Before you start, carefully prise off the skirting boards, picture rails and coving, so that you can refix these on the panelling, if required. If you are fixing to a solid wall, erect the framework using 50mm x 25mm (2in x 1in) planed or sawn softwood. Treat the timber with a proprietary woodworm eradicating fluid (▷).

Line an external wall with a polythene vapour barrier before attaching the furring strips, to prevent condensation. The simplest way to do this is to tack the polythene sheets to the wall using masonry nails, then secure them with the battens.

You can also insulate the wall by sandwiching a layer of glass fibre insulation material or polystyrene sheets between it and the panelling. If you do this, fix the polythene vapour barrier over the furring strips.

The battens should be fixed 400mm (1ft 4in) apart with 50mm (2in) masonry nails or screws and wallplugs. Use a builder's spirit level to align each batten with its neighbour to produce a vertical, flat plane. Pack out hollows with card or thin strips of hardboard.

Wallboards are fixed vertically to the framework but TGV boards can be arranged in a variety of patterns – vertically, horizontally, diagonally, or even in a zig-zag fashion for a really individual effect.

To fix vertical TGV panelling, run the furring strips horizontally. The lowest strip should be level with the top of the skirting, with short vertical strips below it for fixing the skirting to. For horizontal boards, run the furring strips from floor to ceiling. Nail offcuts of panelling to the bottom of the strips as spacers to support the skirting board at the new level. Stagger the joints between boards on alternate rows. Fix diagonal boards to strips running horizontally and stagger the joints also.

To fix wallboards, centre vertical furring strips on the edges of each wallboard. Fill in with horizontal strips every 400mm (1ft 4in).

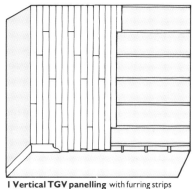

1 Vertical TGV panelling with furring strips running horizontally and short strips for skirting.

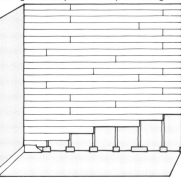

2 Horizontal TGV panelling with furring strips fixed vertically and panel offcuts for skirting.

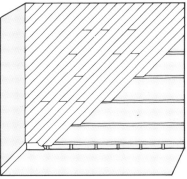

3 Diagonal TGV panelling with furring strips fixed horizontally. Stagger joints on alternate rows.

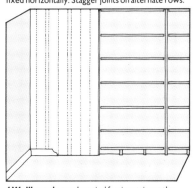

4 Wallboards need vertical furring strips at the edges and horizontal strips between.

SEE ALSO

Details for: ▷

Stud partition	120-121
Woodworm	246-247
Insulant	265

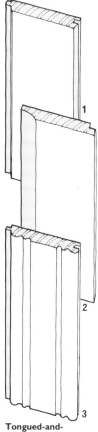

Tongued-and-grooved boarding
Solid wood tongued-and-grooved planks are sold by timber merchants in various lengths up to 3m (10ft); nominal dimensions are 100 x 12mm (4 x 1/2in). Pre-packed kits of TGV boards are available from specialists. Packs contain six 2.4 or 2.7m (8 or 9ft) lengths. Various profiles are made: tongued, grooved and V-jointed (**1**), rebated shiplap (**2**), moulded TGV (**3**).

ATTACHING STRIP WOOD PANELLING

SEE ALSO

◁ Details for:
Locating joists   112
Turning off power   296
Mounting boxes   308-309
Wiring   310,328

Internal corners
Scribe a butt joint using
a block of wood and a
pencil, then plane a
chamfer on one board.
Pin the chamfered
board to the furring
strips through its face.
The detailing is identical
for either vertical or
horizontal boards.

I Vertical panels

2 Horizontal panels

External corners
To join vertical panels,
lap one board with
another and pin
together. Plane a bevel
on the outer corner (1).
For horizontal panels,
pin on a bevelled
moulding to cover the
end grain (2).

88

Fixing vertical panelling

Mark out and cut the boards to length,
using a tenon saw. Sand all the boards
before fixing them (unless they're in a
kit). With the grooved edge against the
left-hand wall, plumb the first board
with a spirit level. Nail it to the battens
through the centre of the face, using
25mm (1in) panel pins. Use 36mm
(1½in) pins when fixing to a
timber-framed wall.

Slide the next board onto the
tongue – protect the edge while you tap
it in place with a hammer. Fix the board
to the battens using the secret nailing
technique: drive a pin through the inner
corner of the tongue, at an angle (1).
Sink the head below the surface with a
nail punch. Slide on the next board to
hide the fixing, and repeat to cover wall.

Use up short lengths of boarding by
butting them end to end over a furring
strip, but stagger such joints across the
wall to avoid a continuous line.

When you reach the other end of the
wall, cut the last board down its length
(using a jigsaw or circular saw for
accuracy) to fit the gap. Nail it through
the face. If it is a tight fit, spring the last
two boards in at the same time: slot
them together, slot the penultimate
board's groove onto the exposed
tongue then push both into the wall. Pin
a small quadrant cover strip down the
edges, nail the skirting board in place
and fit a ceiling coving to conceal the
edges of the boards.

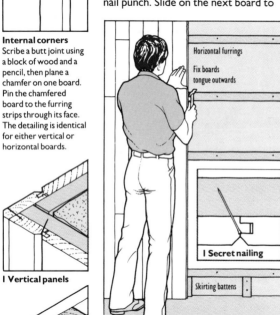

Horizontal furrings

Fix boards
tongue outwards

I Secret nailing

Skirting battens

Fixing vertical TGV boards

Fixing horizontal panelling

Follow the same procedure as for
vertical cladding but position the first

board just below skirting level, with its
groove at the bottom.

Panelling around doors and windows

Remove the architrave and sill
mouldings and nail furring strips (1)
close to the frame. Fix the panelling (2)
and cover the edge with a thin wooden
strip (3) so that it is flush with the inner
face of the frame. Refit the mouldings
(4) on top of the panelling.

Adapting the mouldings ▷
Follow the numbered sequence to adapt mouldings
around doors and windows.

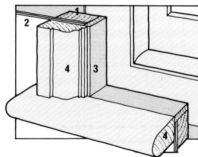

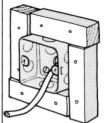

Metal clip flange
slots into groove

An alternative method of fixing boards

Metal clips

Some prepacked boards are attached to
the battens with metal clips, which
locate in the groove of a board, leaving a
tab which takes the pin. With this type
of fixing, plane the tongue from the first
board and place that edge against the
left-hand side wall (or the ceiling). The
clips are concealed by the next board.

DEALING WITH ELECTRICAL FITTINGS

Socket outlets and light switches must
be brought forward to the new wall
surface. If they are surface-mounted,
simply panel around the fitting, when
they'll become flush-mounted. If they're
flush-mounted already, you'll either
have to convert them to
surface-mounted types or bring them
forward and set them flush with the
new wall surface.

Flush-mounted fittings
Turn off the power at the mains (◁),
then unscrew the faceplate and draw it
away from the wall. Remove the screws
that attach the metal mounting box to
the wall. There should be enough slack
in the cable for you to refix the box
flush with the new wall surface (1), or
fix it to the cladding using metal box
mounting flanges intended for use on
partition walls (◁).

To do this, batten around the fitting
but allow for a narrow margin of
panelling all round. Fit the flanges then
screw on the faceplate: the flanges pull
it against the margin.

You can also buy mounting boxes for
fixing in this situation, which don't need
separate flanges (◁).

Surface-mounted fittings
Nail short battens on each side of the
cable to take the screws holding the
fitting to the wall (2). Drill a hole in the
panelling, pass the cable through and
screw the mounting box over it. Wire
and fit the faceplate (◁).

If you don't want to surface-mount
the fitting, frame it with short battens
nailed to the wall then cut the panelling
to fit around it.

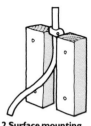

I Flush mounting   **2 Surface mounting**

Panelling a ceiling

It is relatively straightforward to panel a
ceiling with TGV boards, following the
methods described for cladding a wall.
First locate the joists (◁) then nail or
screw the furring strips across them.

ATTACHING SHEET PANELLING

Pinning wallboards

Scribe the first board to the left-hand side wall and ceiling. Cut the boards with a panel saw, face side uppermost to avoid splitting the grain.

Use a footlifter to hold the panel off the floor (▷) and pin it through the grooves. Tap the pins just below the surface with a fine nail punch ready for filling later.

Butt-join subsequent panels. The edges are bevelled to make a matching V-groove. Cut the last board to fit against the opposite wall, then fit cover strip and moulding.

Gluing on wallboards

Wood fibre boards can be pinned to the furring strips but nail heads may spoil the appearance. For a better result, use a proprietary wallboard adhesive to glue the boards to the framework. If the panels are narrower than standard wallboards, reduce the spacing of the furring strips accordingly.

Fit the first board to the wall and ceiling. Use a sharp knife to cut the panel as a saw tends to fray the edges. Follow the manufacturer's instructions to apply the glue. Some recommend applying it in patches or continuous bands, before pressing the panels in place. Strike the edges with the side of your fist to spread the glue.

Contact adhesive can also be used to fix the boards. Apply the adhesive to the strips, then press the board against the framework; peel it off again to leave glue on both surfaces. Wedge a batten under the bottom edge to maintain its position relative to the wall. When the glue is touch-dry, press the panel in place again for an immediate bond.

Pin external corners
Nail softwood blocks to one furring strip to support the edges of the board. Add adhesive to the blocks, then pin the boards along a groove. Bevel the boards at the corner and stain the core.

Pin internal corners
Butt-join the wallboards at an internal corner. For neatness, you can conceal the join by gluing a matching cover strip into the angle.

Using contact adhesive
Glue strips, press on board then peel off; refit when touch-dry.

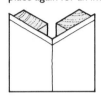

Glue external corners
Cut a V-shaped groove in the back of the board, leaving the facing intact. Fold it around to make a mitred joint, then glue to the furring strips.

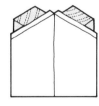

Glue internal corners
Cut through the wallboard as far down as the face material then fold it – face to face – to fit the corner and glue to the furring strips.

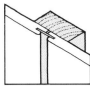

Joining grooved boards
Some boards are grooved along the vertical edges to accept a fillet joint strip. Nail or staple along the joint covering the fixing with the fillet.

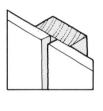

Butt-jointing boards
Square-edged boards can be butt-jointed or left with a slight gap between; stain or paint the furring strip behind as a decorative feature of the panels.

Fitting a cover strip
The third method of concealing the joins between wallboards is to leave a slight gap between butted boards and glue on a rounded cover strip.

REPRODUCTION PANELLING

Period solid-timber panelling was an important part of older houses' decorative character and unless it's in poor condition is worth preserving (▷). If you don't have any existing panelling, but feel that it would enhance your room's decor, reproduction versions are available. There are two basic types: one comprises panels moulded from originals in rigid urethane foam; the other consists of ply-faced panels which you attach to the wall with moulded urethane foam battens.

Fitting urethane panelling
Reproduction panelling in rigid foam usually comprises standard components:
● **Panels** moulded from rigid urethane foam come in various sizes, from about 165 × 95 to 495 × 292mm (6½ × 3¾in to 1ft 6½ × 11½in), with many intermediate sizes. Face designs are typically linenfold (resembling a fold of fabric) or floral. Panels can be stuck directly to the wall with contact adhesive. Some have tongued-and-grooved edges.
● **Rails and stiles** come in lengths of about 3m (10ft); they're used to frame doors and windows or to finish the edge of panelling. Some panels require cover strips, which may be grooved to take a tongued panel, to conceal joins.

With some urethane panelling it's necessary to frame the wall with rebated edging strips, then stick on the panels within them, covering the joins with cover strips.

Veneered timber panelling
Oak-faced plywood, 4mm (3/16in) thick, is available from many timber merchants and gives a more realistic appearance and texture. Cut into panels to suit the size and proportions of your walls, it is fixed with rigid foam rails and stiles: these are cut from the same section supplied in 2.4m (8ft) lengths, and have a rebate moulded on each side to hold a panel against the wall.

When a rail is needed to surround a door or window or to finish an edge of panelling, the beaded rebate is sawn off to leave a square edge.

Ply panels are fixed from one end of the room by fixing stiles, rails and panels in sequence using wallboard adhesive. The stiles must be notched to take the ends of the rails, which must be mitred, and a jig is sold with the battens.

SEE ALSO

Details for: ▷
Footlifter	159
Preserving wood	246-247,250
Varnishing	75,82
Furring strips	87
Adhesives	496-497

● **Shiplap cladding**
Shiplap boards are normally used outside but there is no reason why you cannot use them to panel an interior. To attach them, start at skirting level with the rebate at the bottom (or left-hand side wall). Position the next board and nail it through the face just about the rebate.

WALLCOVERINGS

Although wallcoverings are often called 'wallpaper', only a proportion of the wide range available is made solely from wood pulp. There is a huge range of paper-backed fabrics from exotic silks to coarse hessians; other types include natural textures such as cork or woven grass on a paper backing. Plastics have widened the choice of wallcoverings still further: there are paper- or cotton-backed vinyls, and plain or patterned foamed plastics. Before wallpaper became popular, fabric wall hangings were used to decorate interiors and this is still possible today, using unbacked fabrics glued or stretched across walls.

SEE ALSO

◁ Details for:
Sizing wall	50
Choosing colour/pattern	24-25,29
Preparing plaster	50-51
Mould growth	52
Stripping wallpaper	52
Preparing boards	54

Top right
1 Expanded polystyrene
2 Lining paper
3 Woodchip

Bottom left
4 Hand-printed
5 Machine-printed

Bottom right
6 Anaglypta
7 Supaglypta
8 Lincrustas
9 Vinaglypta

Ensuring a suitable surface

Although many wallcoverings will cover minor blemishes, walls and ceilings should be clean, sound and smooth. Eradicate damp and organic growth before hanging any wallcovering. Consider whether you should size the walls to reduce paste absorption (◁).

COVERINGS THAT CAMOUFLAGE

Although a poor surface should be repaired, some coverings hide minor blemishes as well as providing a foundation for other finishes.

Expanded polystyrene sheet
Thin polystyrene sheet is used for lining a wall before papering. It reduces condensation but will also bridge hairline cracks and small holes. Polystyrene dents easily, so don't use where it will take a lot of punishment. A patterned ceiling version is made.

Lining paper
A cheap, buff coloured wallpaper for lining uneven or impervious walls prior to hanging a heavy or expensive wallcovering. Can also provide an even surface for emulsion paint.

Woodchip paper
Woodchip or ingrain paper is a relief covering made by sandwiching particles of wood between two layers of paper. It's inexpensive, easy to hang (but a problem to cut), and must be painted.

Relief papers ▷
'Whites', or relief papers, with a deeply embossed pattern, are for hiding minor imperfections and for over-painting.

Anaglypta is made by bonding two sheets of paper together, which then pass between embossing rollers. A stronger version, *Supaglypta,* is made using cotton fibres instead of wood pulp, and withstands deeper embossing.

The raised pattern on *Lincrusta* is a solid film of linseed oil and fillers fused onto a backing paper before the pattern is applied by an engraved steel roller. Deep relief wallcoverings are made from vinyl – notably *Vinaglypta* – either as solid plastic, or it is heated in an oven, which 'blows' or expands the vinyl, embossing it. Relief vinyls are intended to be painted over.

◁ Printed wallpapers
One advantage of ordinary wallpaper is the superb range of printed colours and patterns, which is much wider than for any other covering. Most papers – the cheapest – are machine-printed.

Hand-printed papers are more costly. Inks have a tendency to run if you smear paste on the surface, are prone to tearing when wet, and are not really suitable for walls exposed to wear or condensation. Pattern matching can be awkward, because hand-printing isn't as accurate as machine printing.

WALLCOVERINGS

Washable papers
Ordinary printed papers with a thin, impervious glaze of PVA to make a spongeable surface, washables are suitable for bathrooms and kitchens. The surface must not be scrubbed or the plastic coating will be worn away.

Vinyl wallcoverings
A base paper, or sometimes a cotton backing, is coated with a layer of vinyl upon which the design is printed. Heat is used to fuse the colours and vinyl. The result is a durable, washable wallcovering ideally suited to bathrooms and kitchens. Many vinyls are sold ready-pasted for easy application.

Foamed polyethylene coverings
A lightweight wallcovering, called *Novamura,* made solely of foamed plastic with no backing paper. It is printed with a wide range of patterns, colours and designs. You paste the wall instead of the covering. It is best used on walls that are not exposed to wear.

Flock wallcoverings
Flock papers have the major pattern elements picked out with a fine pile produced by gluing synthetic or natural fibres (such as silk or wool) to the backing paper, so that it stands out in relief, with a velvet-like texture.

Standard flocks are difficult to hang as paste will ruin the pile. Vinyl flocks are less delicate, can be hung anywhere, and may even be ready-pasted.

You can sponge flock paper to remove stains, but brush to remove dust from the pile. Vinyl flocks can be washed without risk of damage.

Foil wallcoverings
Paper-backed foils are coated with a metallized plastic film to give a shiny finish. They are expensive but come in a range of beautiful contrasting textures (over-printed designs allow the foil to show through). Foils should not be used on uneven walls, as the shine will highlight imperfections.

Glass fibre wallcovering
Woven glass fibre fabric is a durable fire-resistant wallcovering that will bridge minor irregularities. After 24 hours, the fabric can be painted.

Grass cloth
Natural grasses are woven into a mat, which is glued to a paper backing. These wallcoverings are very attractive but fragile and difficult to hang.

Cork-faced paper
A wallpaper surfaced with thin sheets of coloured or natural cork, which is not as easily spoiled as other special papers.

Paper-backed fabrics
Finely woven cotton, linen or silk on a paper backing must be applied to a flat surface. They are expensive, not easy to hang, and you must avoid smearing the fabric with adhesive. Most fabrics are delicate but some are plastic-coated to make them scuff-resistant.

Unbacked fabrics
Upholstery width fabric – typically hessian – can be wrapped around panels, glued to the wall.

SEE ALSO

Details for: ▷	
Sizing wall	50
Choosing colour/pattern	24-25,29
Preparing plaster	50-51
Mould growth	52
Stripping wallpaper	52
Preparing boards	54
Preparing tiles	62

Left to right
1 Washable papers
2 Vinyls
3 Foamed polyethylene
4 Flock papers
5 Foil papers
6 Glass fibre
7 Cork faced papers
8 Paper-backed fabrics
9 Unbacked fabrics
10 Grass cloth mats

WALLCOVERINGS: ESTIMATING QUANTITIES

Calculating the number of rolls of wallcovering you will need to cover your walls and ceiling depends on the size of the roll – both length and width - the pattern repeat and the obstructions you have to avoid. Because of variations in colour between batches, you must take into account all these points – and allow for wastage, too. A standard roll of wallcovering measures 530mm (1ft 9in) wide and 10.05 metres (33ft) long. Use the two charts on this page to estimate how many rolls you will need for walls and ceilings.

SEE ALSO

◁ Details for:
Wallcoverings   90-91
Papering walls   94-97
Papering ceilings   98

Estimating non-standard rolls

If the wallcovering is not cut to a standard size, calculate the amount you need in this way:

Walls

Measure the height of the walls from skirting to ceiling. Divide the length of the roll by this figure to find the number of wall lengths you can cut from a roll.

Measure around the room, excluding windows and doors, to work out how many widths fit into the total length of the walls. Divide this number by the number of wall lengths you can get from one roll to find how many rolls you need.

Make an allowance for short lengths above doors and under windows.

Ceilings

Measure the length of the room to determine one strip of paper. Work out how many roll widths fit across the room. Multiply the two figures. Divide the answer by the length of a roll to find out how many rolls you need. Check for waste and allow for it.

Checking for shading

If rolls of wallcovering are printed in one batch, there should be no problem with colour matching one roll to another. When you buy, look for the batch number printed on the wrapping.

Make a visual check before hanging the covering, especially for hand-printed papers or fabrics. Unroll a short length of each roll and lay them side by side. You may get a better colour match by changing the rolls around, but if colour difference is obvious, ask for a replacement roll.

Some wallcoverings are marked 'reverse alternate lengths' in order to even out any colour variations. Take this into account when checking.

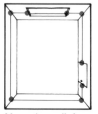

Measuring walls for standard rolls
You can include windows and doors in your estimate.

Measuring walls for non-standard rolls
Do not include doors and windows when estimating for expensive materials. Allow for short lengths afterwards.

Walls:
Standard rolls
Measure your room, then look down height column and across wall column to assess number of standard rolls required.

WALLS	NUMBER OF ROLLS REQUIRED FOR WALLS							
	2.0-2.25m	2.25-2.50m	2.50-2.75m	2.75-3.0m	3.0-3.25m	3.25-3.50m	3.50-3.75m	3.75-4.0m
10.0m	5	5	6	6	7	7	8	8
10.5m	5	6	6	7	7	8	8	9
11.0m	5	6	7	7	8	8	9	9
11.5m	6	6	7	7	8	8	9	9
12.0m	6	6	7	8	8	9	9	10
12.5m	6	7	7	8	9	9	10	10
13.0m	6	7	8	8	9	10	10	10
13.5m	7	7	8	9	9	10	10	11
14.0m	7	7	8	9	10	10	11	11
14.5m	7	8	8	9	10	10	11	12
15.0m	7	8	9	9	10	11	12	12
15.5m	7	8	9	9	10	11	12	13
16.0m	8	8	9	10	11	11	12	13
16.5m	8	9	9	10	11	12	13	13
17.0m	8	9	10	10	11	12	13	14
17.5m	8	9	10	11	12	13	14	14
18.0m	9	9	10	11	12	13	14	15
18.5m	9	10	11	12	12	13	14	15
19.0m	9	10	11	12	13	14	15	16
19.5m	9	10	11	12	13	14	15	16
20.0m	9	10	11	12	13	14	15	16
20.5m	10	11	12	13	14	15	16	17
21.0m	10	11	12	13	14	15	16	17
21.5m	10	11	12	13	14	15	17	18
22.0m	10	11	13	14	15	16	17	18
22.5m	11	12	13	14	15	16	17	18
23.0m	11	12	13	14	15	17	18	19
23.5m	11	12	13	15	16	17	18	19
24.0m	11	12	14	15	16	17	18	20
24.5m	11	13	14	15	16	18	19	20
25.0m	12	13	14	15	17	18	19	20
25.5m	12	13	14	16	17	18	20	21
26.0m	12	13	15	16	17	19	20	21
26.5m	12	14	15	16	18	19	20	22
27.0m	13	14	15	17	18	19	21	22
27.5m	13	14	16	17	18	20	21	23
28.0m	13	14	16	17	19	20	21	23
28.5m	13	15	16	18	19	20	22	23
29.0m	13	15	16	18	19	21	22	24
29.5m	14	15	17	18	20	21	23	24
30.0m	14	15	17	18	20	21	23	24

MEASUREMENT IN METRES AROUND WALLS INCLUDING DOORS AND WINDOWS

HEIGHT OF ROOM IN METRES FROM SKIRTING

Ceilings:
Standard rolls
Number of standard rolls required are shown next to overall room dimensions.

Dimensions
All dimensions are shown in metres.
(1m = 39in)

CEILINGS: NUMBER OF ROLLS REQUIRED							
Measurement around room (m)	Number of rolls	Measurement around room (m)	Number of rolls	Measurement around room (m)	Number of rolls	Measurement around room (m)	Number of rolls
11.0	2	16.0	4	21.0	6	26.0	9
12.0	2	17.0	4	22.0	7	27.0	10
13.0	3	18.0	5	23.0	7	28.0	10
14.0	3	19.0	5	24.0	8	29.0	11
15.0	4	20.0	5	25.0	8	30.0	11

TRIMMING AND CUTTING TECHNIQUES

Most wallcoverings are already machine-trimmed to width so that you can butt-join adjacent lengths accurately. Some hand-printed papers and speciality coverings are left untrimmed. These are usually expensive, so don't attempt to trim them yourself: ask the supplier to do this for you – it's worth the slight additional cost.

Cutting plain wallcoverings

To cut a plain paper to length, measure the height of the wall at the point where you will hang the first 'drop'. Add an extra 100mm (4in) for trimming top and bottom. Cut several pieces from your first roll to the same length and mark the top of each one.

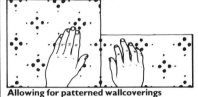

Allowing for patterned wallcoverings
You may have to allow extra on alternate lengths of patterned wallcoverings to match patterns. Check before you cut your second length.

CHOOSING PASTE

Most wallpaper pastes are supplied as powder or flakes for mixing with water. There are several specific types:

All-purpose paste
Standard wallpaper paste is suitable for most light- to medium-weight papers. By adding less water, it can be used to hang heavyweight papers.

Heavy-duty paste
Specially prepared to hang embossed papers, paper-backed fabrics and other heavyweight wallcoverings.

Fungicidal paste
Most pastes contain a fungicide to prevent mould growth under certain impervious wallcoverings, which slow down the drying rate of the paste. It is essential to use a fungicidal paste when hanging vinyls, washable papers, foils and foamed plastic coverings.

Ready-mixed paste
Tubs of ready-mixed, thixotropic paste are specially made to give the high adhesion required for heavyweight luxury wallcoverings such as fabric.

PASTING WALLCOVERINGS

You can use any wipe-clean table for pasting, but a narrow fold-up pasting table is a good investment if you are doing a lot of decorating. Lay several cut lengths of paper on top of each other face down on the table to keep it clean. Tuck the ends under a length of string tied loosely round the table legs to stop the paper rolling up while you paste it.

Applying the paste

Use a large, soft wall brush or pasting brush to apply the paste. Mix the paste in a plastic bucket and tie string across the rim to support the brush, keeping its handle clean while you paperhang.

Align the covering with the far edge of the table (so you don't get paste on the table, then transfer it to the face of the wall covering). Apply the paste by brushing away from the centre. Paste the edges and remove any lumps.

If you prefer, apply the paste with a short-piled paint roller; pour the paste into a roller tray. Roll in one direction only towards the end of the paper.

Pull the covering to the front edge of the table and paste the other half. Fold the pasted end over – don't press it down – and slide the length along the table to expose an unpasted part.

Paste the other end then fold it over to almost meet the first cut end: the second fold is invariably deeper than the first, a good way to denote the bottom of patterned wallcoverings. Fold long drops concertina-fashion.

Leave the pasted covering to soak, draped over a broom handle spanning two chair backs. Some heavy or embossed coverings may need to soak for 15 minutes: let one length soak while you hang another. Vinyls and lightweight papers can be hung immediately.

Pasting the wall

Hang exotic wallcoverings by pasting the wall, to reduce the risk of marking their delicate faces. Apply a band of paste just wider than the length of covering, so that you will not have to paste right up to its edge for the next length. Use a brush or roller.

Ready-pasted wallcoverings

Many wallcoverings come pre-coated with adhesive, activated by soaking a cut length in a trough of cold water (▷). Mix ordinary paste to recoat dry edges.

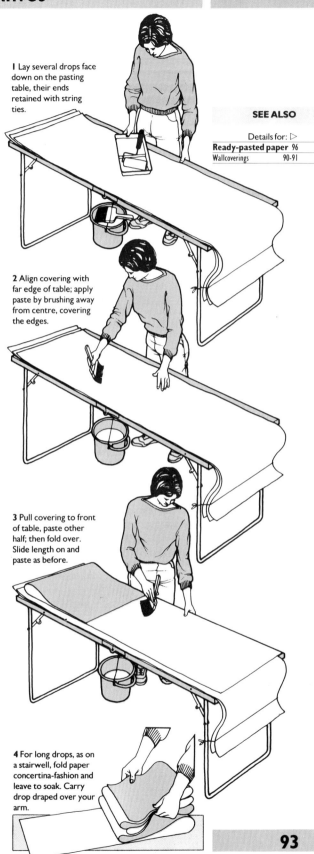

1 Lay several drops face down on the pasting table, their ends retained with string ties.

SEE ALSO

Details for: ▷
Ready-pasted paper 96
Wallcoverings 90-91

2 Align covering with far edge of table; apply paste by brushing away from centre, covering the edges.

3 Pull covering to front of table, paste other half; then fold over. Slide length on and paste as before.

4 For long drops, as on a stairwell, fold paper concertina-fashion and leave to soak. Carry drop draped over your arm.

LINING A WALL

Lining a wall prior to decorating is only necessary if you are hanging embossed or luxury wallcoverings, or if the wall is uneven and imperfections might show through a thin paper. Lining paper is hung horizontally so that the joins cannot align with those in the top layer. Work from right to left if you are right-handed, vice versa if you are left-handed.

Mark a horizontal line near the top of the wall, one roll width from the ceiling. Holding the concertina-folded length in one hand, start at the top right-hand corner of the wall, aligning the bottom edge with the marked line. Smooth the paper onto the wall with a paperhanger's brush, working from the centre towards the edges.

Work along the wall gradually, unfolding the length as you do so. Take care not to stretch or tear the wet paper. Use the brush to gently stipple the edge into the corner at each end.

Use the point of a pair of scissors to lightly mark the corner, peel back the paper and trim to the line. Brush the paper back in place. You may have to perform a similar operation along the ceiling if the paper overlaps slightly. Work down the wall butting each strip against the last, or leave a tiny gap between the lengths.

Trim the bottom length to the skirting. Leave the lining paper to dry out for 24 hours before covering.

Lining prior to painting
If you line a wall for emulsion painting, hang the paper vertically as for other wallcoverings as the joins will be minimally visible.

SEE ALSO

◁ Details for:
Painting ceiling	69
Painting wood	76-78
Varnishing	82
Papering ceiling	98
Preparing plaster	50-51
Wallcoverings	90-91
Papering tools	484-485

● **Hide a join in a corner**
When you are using a wallcovering with a large pattern, try to finish in a corner where you will not notice if the pattern does not match.

Sticking down the edges
Ensure that the edges of the paper adhere firmly by running a seam roller along the butt join.

Losing air bubbles
Slight blistering usually flattens out as wet paper dries and shrinks slightly. If you find that a blister remains, either inject a little paste through it and roll it flat, or cut across it in two directions, peel back the triangular flaps and paste them down.

Hanging lining paper horizontally
Hold the concertina-folded paper in one hand and smooth onto the wall from top right, butting strips.

PAPERING A WALL

Where to start

Don't apply wallcovering until all the woodwork has been painted or varnished (◁) and start by painting or papering the ceiling (◁).

The traditional method for papering a room is to hang the first length next to a window close to a corner, then work in both directions away from the light, but you may find it easier to paper the longest uninterrupted wall to get used to the basic techniques before tackling corners or obstructions.

If your wallcovering has a large regular motif, centre the first length over the fireplace for symmetry. You could centre this first length between two windows, unless you will be left with narrow strips each side, in which case it's best to butt two lengths on the centre line.

Centre a large motif over fireplace

Or butt two lengths between windows

Hanging on a straight wall

The walls of an average room are rarely truly square, so use a plumb line to mark a vertical guide against which to set the first length of wallcovering. Start at one end of the wall and mark the vertical line one roll width away from the corner, minus 12mm (½in) so the first length will overlap the adjacent wall.

Allowing enough wallcovering for trimming at the ceiling, unfold the top section of the pasted length and hold it against the plumbed line. Using a paperhanger's brush, work gently out from the centre in all directions to squeeze out any trapped air.

When you are sure the paper is positioned accurately, mark the ceiling line with outer edge of your scissors blade, peel back the top edge and cut along the crease. Smooth the paper back and stipple it down carefully with the brush. Unpeel the lower fold of the paper, smooth it onto the wall with the brush then stipple it firmly into the corner. Trim the bottom edge against the skirting, peel away, trim and brush back against the wall.

Hang the next length in the same way. Slide it with your fingertips to align the pattern and produce a perfect butt joint. Wipe any paste from the surface with a damp cloth. Continue to the other side of the wall, allowing the last drop to overlap the adjoining wall by 12mm (½in).

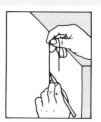
I Mark first length
Use a roll of paper to mark the wall one width away from the corner – less 12mm (½in) for an overlap onto the return wall – then draw a line from ceiling to skirting using a plumb line.

2 Hang first drop
Cut the first drop of paper, allowing about 50mm (2in) at each end for trimming, paste and allow to soak. Hang the top fold against the plumbed line and brush out from the centre, working down.

3 Trim at ceiling
When the paper is smoothly brushed on, run the outer edge of your scissors along the ceiling angle, peel away the paper, cut off the excess then brush back onto the wall.

4 Trim at skirting
Hang the lower fold of paper. At the skirting, tap your brush gently into the top edge, peel away the paper and cut along the folded line with scissors, then brush back.

PAPERING PROBLEM AREAS

Papering around doors and windows

Hang the length next to a door frame, brushing down the butt joint to align the pattern, but allow the other edge to loosely overlap the door.

Make a diagonal cut in the excess towards the top corner of the frame (**1**). Crease the waste along the frame with scissors, peel it back, trim it off then brush it back. Leave a 12mm (½in) strip for turning onto the top of the frame. Fill in over the door.

Butt the next full length over the door and cut the excess diagonally into the frame so that you can paste the rest of the strip down the side of the door. Mark and cut off the waste.

When papering up to flush window frames, treat them like a door. Where a window is set into a reveal, hang the length of wallcovering next to the window and allow it to overhang the opening. Make a horizontal cut just above the edge of the window reveal. Make a similar cut near the bottom then fold the paper around to cover the side of the reveal. Crease and trim along the window frame and sill.

Cut a strip of paper to match the width and pattern of the overhang above the window reveal. Paste it, slip it under the overhang and fold it around the top of the reveal (**2**). Cut through the overlap with a smooth, wavy stroke, remove the excess paper and roll down the join (**3**).

To continue, hang short lengths on the wall below and above the window, wrapping top lengths into the reveal.

1 Cut the overlap diagonally into the frame

SEE ALSO

Details for: ▷
Turning off power	296
Radiator roller	483
Preparing plaster	50-51
Wallcoverings	90-91

Papering around a fireplace

Paper around a fireplace as for a door. Make a diagonal cut in the waste overlapping the fireplace, up to the edge of the mantel shelf, so that you can tuck the paper in all round for creasing and trimming to the surround.

To cut to an ornate surround, paper the wall above the surround; cut strips to fit under the mantel at each side, turning them around the corners of the chimney breast. Gently press the wallcovering into the moulding, peel it away and cut round the impression using nail scissors. Brush the paper back.

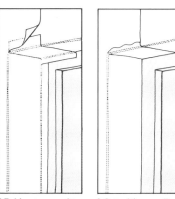

2 Fold onto reveal top   3 Cut with wavy line

Papering internal and external corners

Turn an internal corner by marking another plumbed line so that the next length of paper covers the overlap from the first wall. If the piece you trimmed off at the corner is wide enough, use it as your first length on the new wall.

To turn an external corner, trim the last length so that it wraps around it, lapping the next wall by about 25mm (1in). Plumb and hang the remaining strip with its edge about 12mm (½in) from the corner.

12mm (½in) overlap ▷

Internal corner

Papering behind radiators

If you can't remove a radiator, turn off the heating and allow it to cool. Use a steel tape to measure the positions of the brackets holding the radiator to the wall. Transfer these measurements to a length of wallcovering, slit it from the bottom up to the top of the bracket. Feed the pasted paper behind the radiator, down both sides of the brackets. Use a radiator roller to press it to the wall (▷). Crease and trim to the skirting board.

25mm (1in) overlap ▷

12mm (½in) from corner

External corner

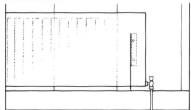

Slit to top of bracket behind radiator

Papering around switches and sockets

Turn off the electricity at the mains (▷). Hang the wallcovering over the switch or socket. Make diagonal cuts from the centre of the fitting to each corner. Trim off the waste leaving 6mm (¼in) all round. Loosen the faceplate, tuck the margin behind and retighten it. Don't switch the power back on until the paste is dry. Don't use for foils: the metallic surface can conduct electricity.

- **Papering archways**
  Arrange strips to leave even gaps between arch sides and the next full-length strips. Hang strips over face of arch, cut curve leaving 25mm (1in) margin. Fold it onto underside snipping into margin to prevent creasing. Fit a strip on the underside to reach from floor to top of arch. Repeat on opposite side of arch.

- **Trimming foils around electrical fittings**
  Make diagonal cuts (See left), but crease the waste against the fitting and trim off with a sharp knife when the paste has dried.

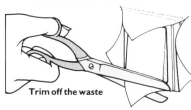

Trim off the waste

95

STAIRWELLS

SPECIAL TECHNIQUES FOR WALLPAPERING

The only real problem with papering a stairwell is the extra long drops on the side walls. You will need to build a safe work platform over the stairs (◁). Plumb and hang the longest drop first, lapping the head wall above the stairs by 12mm (½in).

Carrying the long drops of wallcovering – sometimes as much as 4.5m (15ft) long – is awkward: paste the covering liberally so it's not likely to dry out while you hang it, then fold it concertina-fashion. Drape it over your arm while you climb the platform. You'll need a helper to support the weight of the pasted length while you apply it. Unfold the flaps as you work down.

SEE ALSO

◁ Details for:
Work platforms	42
Preparing plaster	50-51
Wallcoverings	90-91

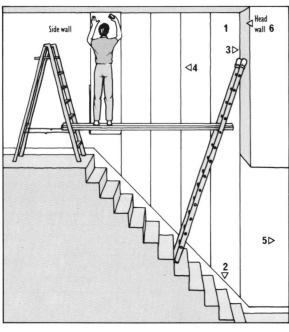

Papering sequence
Follow this sequence for papering a stairwell.
1 Hang the longest drop
2 Crease it into the angled skirting and cut
3 Lap the paper onto the head wall
4, 5 Work away from the first drop in both directions
6 Paper the head wall

Crease and cut the bottom of the paper against the angled skirting. Don't forget – when first you cut the length – to allow for this angle; work to the longest edge measurement. Work away from this first length in both directions, then hang the head wall.

Where the banister rail is let into the stairwell wall, try to arrange the rolls so that the rail falls between the two butted drops. Hang the drops to the rail and cut horizontally into the edge of the last strip at the centre of the rail, then make radial cuts so the paper can be moulded around the rail. Crease the flaps, peel away the wallcovering and cut them off. Smooth the covering back.

Hang the next drop at the other side of the rail, butting it to the previous piece and make similar radial cuts.

Whatever you are using as a wallcovering, follow the standard wallpapering techniques as explained previously. However, there are some additional considerations and special techniques involved in using certain types of wallcovering, as explained below and opposite.

RELIEF WALLCOVERINGS

When hanging *Anaglypta*, line the wall first and use a heavy-duty paste. Apply the paste liberally and evenly but try not to leave too much paste in the depressions. Allow it to soak for 10 minutes. *Supaglypta* will need 15 minutes soaking time.

Don't use a seam roller on the joins: tap the paper gently with a paperhanger's brush to avoid flattening the embossing.

Don't turn a relief wallcovering around corners. Measure the distance from the last drop to the corner and cut your next length to fit. Trim and hang the offcut to meet at the corner. Fill external corners with cellulose filler once the paper has dried thoroughly.

To use *Lincrusta*, sponge the back with hot water until it is thoroughly soaked. Apply the paste and hang the length, rubbing it down with a felt or rubber roller.

Use a sharp knife and straightedge to trim *Lincrusta*. Treat the corners with filler as for *Anaglypta*.

VINYL WALLCOVERINGS

Paste paper-backed vinyls in the normal way, but cotton-backed vinyl hangs better if you paste the wall and leave it to become tacky before applying the wallcovering. Use fungicidal paste.

Hang and butt join lengths of vinyl using a sponge to smooth them onto the wall rather than a brush. Crease a length top and bottom, then trim it to size with a sharp knife.

Vinyl will not stick to itself, so when you turn a corner, use a knife to cut through both pieces of paper where they overlap. Peel away the excess and rub down the vinyl to produce a perfect butt join.

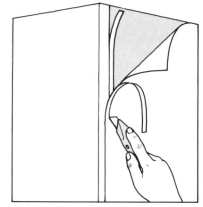

Cut through overlap and remove excess

READY-PASTED WALLCOVERINGS

Place the trough of cold water next to the skirting at the position of the first drop. Roll a cut length loosely from the bottom with the pattern on the outside. Immerse the roll in the trough for the prescribed time, according to the manufacturer's instructions.

Take hold of the cut end and lift the paper, allowing it to unroll naturally, draining the surface water back into the trough at the same time.

Hang and butt join the coverings in the usual way — use a sponge to apply vinyls but use a paperhanger's brush for other coverings.

Hanging a long wet length can be difficult if you follow the standard procedure. Instead, roll the length from the top with the pattern outermost. Place it in the trough and immediately re-roll it through the water. Take it from the trough in roll form and drain excess water. Hang it by feeding from the roll as you proceed.

Pull paper from trough and hang on the wall

SPECIAL TECHNIQUES FOR WALLPAPERING

METALLIC FOILS

The acid content of old paste may discolour metallic foil papers, so coat either the paper or the wall with fresh fungicidal paste.

FLOCK PAPER

Protect the flocking with a piece of lining paper and remove air bubbles with a paperhanger's brush. Cut through both

FABRICS AND SPECIAL COVERINGS

Try to keep paste off the face of paper-backed fabrics and any other special wallcoverings. There are so many different coverings, so check with the supplier which paste to use.

So you don't damage a delicate surface, use a felt or rubber roller to press in place or stipple with a brush.

Most fabric coverings will be machine-trimmed but if the edges are

FOAMED POLYETHYLENE

Novamura (foamed polyethylene) can be hung straight from the roll onto a pasted wall. Sponge in place and trim it top and bottom with scissors.

thicknesses of overlapped joins and remove the surplus; press back the edges to make a neat butt join.

frayed, overlap the joints and cut through both thicknesses then peel off the waste to make a butt join. Make a similar join at a corner.

Many fabrics are sold in wide rolls: even one cut length will be heavy and awkward to handle. Paste the wall, then support the rolled length on a batten between two stepladders. Work from the bottom upwards.

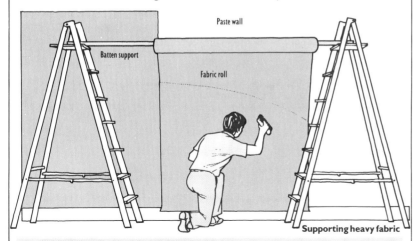
Paste wall
Batten support
Fabric roll
Supporting heavy fabric

GLASS FIBRE WALLCOVERINGS

Hang glass fibre coverings by applying the special adhesive to the wall with a roller. Hang and butt the lengths, then use a spatula to smooth the covering from the centre outwards (or use a felt or rubber roller).

Crease and trim glass fibre as for ordinary wallcoverings, or use a knife and straightedge. Leave the glue to set for 24 hours, then paint. When the first coat has dried, lightly rub down to remove raised fibres, then recoat.

EXPANDED POLYSTYRENE

Paint or roll special adhesive onto the wall. Hang the covering straight from the roll, smooth gently with the flat of your hand, then roll over it lightly with a dry paint roller.

If the edge is square, butt adjacent drops. If it is crushed or crumbled, overlap the join and cut through both

thicknesses with a sharp trimming knife, peel away the offcuts and rub the edges down. Unless the edges are generously glued, they will curl apart. Trim top and bottom with a knife and straightedge. Allow the adhesive to dry for 72 hours then hang the wallcovering using a thick fungicidal paste.

UNBACKED FABRICS

If you want to apply a plain coloured medium-weight fabric, you can glue it directly to the wall. However, it is easy to stretch an unbacked fabric so that aligning a pattern is difficult.

For more control, stretch the fabric onto 12mm (½in) thick panels of lightweight insulation board (you'll then have the added advantage of insulation and a pin-board). Stick the boards directly onto the wall.

Using paste

Test an offcut of the fabric first to make sure that the adhesive will not stain it. Use a ready-mixed paste and roll it onto the wall.

Wrap a cut length of fabric around a cardboard tube (from a carpet supplier) and gradually unroll it on the surface, smoothing it down with a dry paint roller. Take care not to distort the weave. Overlap the joins but do not cut through them until the paste has dried, in case the fabric shrinks. Re-paste and close the seam.

Press the fabric into the ceiling line and skirting and trim away the excess with a sharp trimming knife when the paste has set.

Making wall panels

Cut the insulation board to suit the width of the fabric and the height of the wall. Stretch the fabric across the panel, wrap it around the edges, then use latex adhesive to stick it to the back. Hold it temporarily with drawing pins, while the adhesive dries.

Either use wallboard adhesive to glue the panels to the wall or pin them, tapping the nail heads through the weave of the fabric to conceal them.

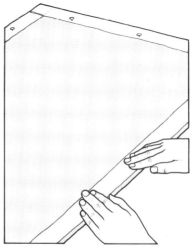
Stretch unbacked fabric over insulation board

SEE ALSO

Details for: ▷

Preparing plaster	50-51
Preparing tiles	62
Wallcoverings	90-91
Felt/rubber roller	485

PAPERING A CEILING

SEE ALSO
◁ Details for:
Work platforms   42
Pasting paper   93
Preparing plaster   50-51
Wallcoverings   90-91
Papering tools   484-485

Papering a ceiling isn't as difficult as you may think: the techniques are basically the same as for papering a wall, except that the drops are usually longer and more unwieldy to hold while you brush the paper into place. Set up a sensible work platform - it's virtually impossible to work by moving a single stepladder along – and enlist a helper to support the pasted, folded paper while you position one end, and progress backwards across the room. If you've marked out the ceiling first, the result should be faultless.

Setting out the ceiling

Arrange your work platform (◁) before you begin to plan out the papering sequence for the ceiling. The best type of platform to use is a purpose-made decorator's trestle, but you can manage with a scaffold board spanning between two pairs of stepladders.

Now mark the ceiling to give a visual guide to positioning the strips of paper. Aim to work parallel with the window wall and away from the light, so you can see what you are doing and so that the light will not highlight the joins between strips. If the distance is shorter the other way, hang the strips in that direction for ease.

Mark a guide line along the ceiling, one roll-width minus 12mm (½in) from the side wall, so that the first strip of paper will lap onto the wall.

Putting up the paper

Paste and fold the paper as for wallcovering, concertina fashion (◁), drape it over a spare roll and carry it to the work platform. You'll certainly find it easier to get a helper to hold the folded paper, giving you both hands free for brushing into place.

Hold the strip against the guideline, using a brush to stroke it onto the ceiling. Tap it into the wall angle then gradually work backwards along the scaffold board, brushing on the paper as your helper unfolds it.

If the ceiling has a cornice, crease and trim the paper at the ends. Otherwise, leave it to lap the walls by 12mm (½in) so that it will be covered by the wallcovering. Work across the ceiling in the same way, butting the lengths of paper together. Cut the final strip to roughly the width, and trim into the wall angle.

Working from a ladder
If you have to work from a stepladder, an assistant can support the paper on a cardboard tube taped to a broom.

Papering a ceiling
The job is so much easier if two people work together.
1 Mark guide line on ceiling
2 Support folded paper on tube
3 Brush on paper, from centre outwards
4 Overlap covered by wallpaper
5 Use two boards to support two people

LIGHTING FITTINGS AND CENTREPIECES

There are usually few obstructions on a ceiling to make papering difficult – unlike walls, which have doors, windows and radiators to contend with. The only problem areas occur where there's a pendant light fitting or a decorative plaster centrepiece.

Cutting around a pendant light
Where the paper passes over a ceiling rose, cut several triangular flaps so that you can pass the light fitting through the hole. Tap the paper all round the rose with a paperhanging brush and continue to the end of the strip. Return to the rose and cut off the flaps with a knife.

Papering around a centrepiece
If you have a decorative plaster centrepiece, work out the position of the strips so that a joint will pass through the middle. Cut long flaps from the side of each piece of paper so that you can tuck it in all round the plaster moulding.

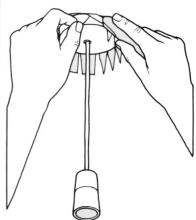

Cut off triangular flaps when paste is dry

Cut long strips to fit around moulding

CHOOSING TILES

Tiling is a universally popular method of decorating a surface, with an almost inexhaustible range of colours, textures and patterns to choose from depending on the degree of durability required. Tiling provides the facility of finishing a surface with small, regular units which can be cut and fitted into an awkward shape far easier than sheet materials.

Glazed ceramic tiles

Hard ceramic tiles, usually glazed and fired, are made for walls and floors. Unglazed tiles are available but only to provide a surer grip for flooring. A textured surface reduces the risk of accidents where a floor might become wet. All ceramic tiles are durable and waterproof, but be sure to use special heat- and frost-resistant tiles where appropriate. Do not use wall tiles on the floor as they cannot take the weight of traffic or furniture.

The majority of tiles are square but dimensions vary according to use and the manufacturer's preference. Rectangular and more irregular shaped tiles are available. Typical shapes include hexagons, octagons, diamonds and interlocking units with curved elaborate edges. Other units include slim rectangles with pointed (pic) or slanted (cane) ends. Use them in combination to produce patterned floors and walls.

Mosaic tiles

Mosaic tiles are small versions of the standard ceramic tiles. To lay them individually would be time consuming and lead to inaccuracy, so they are usually joined by a paper covering, or a mesh background, into larger panels. Square tiles are common but rectangular, hexagonal and round mosaics are also available. Because they are small, mosaics can be used on curved surfaces, and will fit irregular shapes better than large ceramic tiles.

Quarry tiles

Quarry tiles are thick, unglazed ceramic tiles used for floors which need a hardwearing, waterproof surface. Colours are limited to browns, reds, black and white. Machine-made tiles are regular in size and even in colour but hand-made tiles are variable, producing a beautiful mottled effect. Quarry tiles are difficult to cut so do not use them where you will have to fit them against a complicated shape. Rounded-edge quarry tiles can be used as treads for steps, and a floor can be finished with skirting tiles.

Stone and slate flooring

A floor laid with real stone or slate tiles will be exquisite but expensive. Sizes and thicknesses will vary according to the manufacturer – some will even cut to measure. A few materials are so costly that you should consider hiring a professional to lay them, otherwise treat cheaper ones like quarry tiles.

SEE ALSO

Details for: ▷	
Choosing colour/pattern	24-25,29
Levelling concrete	49
Preparing plaster	50-51
Levelling floors	57
Wall tiling	102-104
Floor tiling	110-111

Standard tile sections
A range of sections is produced for specific functions:

Field tile for general tiling with spacing lugs moulded onto them.

Rounded-edge (RE) tile for edging the field.

REX tile with two adjacent rounded edges.

Universal tile with two glazed, square edges for use in any position.

Tile selection
The examples shown left are a typical cross-section of commercially available ceramic tiles.
1 Glazed ceramic
2 Shape and size variation
3 Mosaic tiles
4 Quarry tiles
5 Slate and stone

CHOOSING TILES

SEE ALSO

◁ Details for:
Choosing colour/pattern	24-25,29
Levelling concrete	49
Preparing plaster	50-51
Levelling floors	57
Brick tiling	106
Floor tiling	107-109

Stone and brick tiles

Thin masonry facing tiles can be used to simulate a stone or brick wall as a feature area for a chimney breast, for example, or to clad a whole wall. Stone tiles are typically made from reconstituted stone in moulds, and most look unconvincing as an imitation of the real thing. Colour choice is intended to reflect local stone types, and is typically white, grey or buff. Some 'weathered' versions are also made.

Brick tiles look much more authentic. The best ones are actually brick 'slips' – slivers cut from kiln-produced bricks. A very wide range of traditional brick colours is available.

Left to right
1 Brick tiles
2 Vinyl floor tiles

2

Vinyl tiles

Vinyl tiles are among the cheapest and easiest floorcoverings to use. Vinyl can be cut easily, and so long as the tiles are firmly glued, with good joints, the floor will be waterproof. However, it will still be susceptible to scorching. A standard coated tile has a printed pattern between a vinyl backing and a harder, clear vinyl surface. Solid vinyl tiles are made entirely of the hardwearing plastic. Some vinyl tiles have a high proportion of mineral filler. As a result they are stiff and must be laid on a perfectly flat base. Unlike standard vinyl tiles, they will resist some rising damp in a concrete sub-floor. Most tiles are square or rectangular but there are interlocking shapes and hexagons. There are many patterns and colours to choose from, including embossed vinyl which represents ceramic, brick or stone tiling.

CARPET TILES

Carpet tiles have advantages over wall-to-wall carpeting. There is less to fear when cutting a single tile to fit, and, being loose-laid, a worn, burnt or stained tile can be replaced instantly. However, you can't substitute a brand new tile several years later, as the colour will not match. Buy several spares initially and swap them around regularly to even out the wear and colour change. Most types of carpet are available as tiles, including cord, loop and twist piles in wool as well as a range of man-made fibres. Tiles are normally plain in colour but some are patterned to give a striking grid effect. Some tiles have an integral rubber underlay.

A selection of carpet tiles
Tiles are used extensively for contract carpeting but they are equally suitable as a hard-wearing floor covering in the home.

1

CHOOSING TILES

Polystyrene tiles

Although expanded polystyrene tiles will not reduce heat loss from a room by any significant amount, they will deter condensation as well as mask a ceiling in poor condition. Polystyrene cuts easily so long as the trimming knife is very sharp. For safety in case of fire, choose a self-extinguishing type and do not overpaint with an oil paint. Wall tiles are made but they will crush easily and aren't suitable for use in a vulnerable area. There are flat or decoratively-embossed tiles.

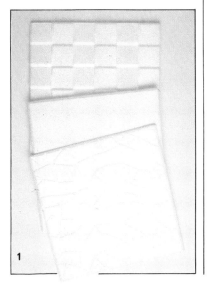

1

Mirror tiles

Square and rectangular mirror tiles can be attached to walls with self-adhesive pads in each corner. There is a choice of silver, bronze or smoke grey finish. Don't expect tiles to produce a perfect reflection unless they are mounted on a really flat surface.

Mineral fibre tiles

Ceiling tiles made from compressed mineral fibre are dense enough to be sound and heat insulating. They often have tongued-and-grooved edges so that, once stapled to the ceiling, the next interlocking tile covers the fixings. Fibre tiles can also be glued directly to a flat ceiling. A range of textured surfaces is available.

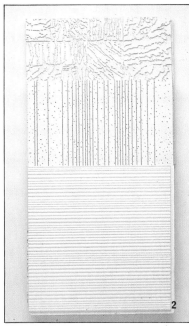

2

Metal tiles

Lightweight pressed metal tiles are fixed in the same way as mirror tiles. Choose from aluminium, bronze and gold coloured tiles with satin or bright finishes. These tiles are not grouted so do not use them where food particles can gather in the crevices.

Rubber tiles

Soft rubber tiles were originally made for use in shops and offices, but they are equally suitable for the home, being hardwearing yet soft and quiet to walk on. The surface is usually studded or textured to improve the grip. Choice is limited to a few plain colours.

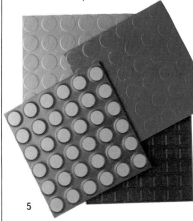

5

Cork tiles

Cork is a popular covering for walls and floors. It is easy to lay with contact adhesive and can be cut to size and shape with a knife. There's a wide range of textures and warm colours to choose from. Pre-sanded but unfinished cork will darken in tone when you varnish it. Alternatively, you can buy ready-finished tiles with various plastic and wax coatings. Soft, granular insulating cork is suitable as a decorative finish for walls only. It crumbles easily, so should not be used where it will be exposed on external corners.

SEE ALSO

Details for: ▷	
Choosing colour/pattern	24-25,29
Levelling concrete	49
Preparing plaster	50-51
Levelling floors	57
Wall tiling	105
Floor tiling	107-109
Tiling a ceiling	112

3

4

6

Left to right
1 Polystyrene tiles
2 Mineral fibre tiles
3 Mirror tiles
4 Metal wall tiles
5 Rubber tiles
6 Cork floor tiles

Setting out
The setting out procedure described on this page is applicable to the following tiles: cork, mosaics, ceramic, mirror, metal.

SEE ALSO

◁ Details for:
Flaky paint	48
Preparing plaster	50-51
Stripping wallpaper	52
Tiles	99-101

SETTING OUT FOR WALL TILES

Whatever tiles you plan to use, the walls must be clean, sound and dry. You cannot tile over wallpaper, and flaking or powdery paint must be treated first to give a suitably stable base for the tiles. It's important that you make the surface as flat as possible so the tiles will stick firmly. Setting out the prepared surface accurately is a vital aid to hanging the tiles properly.

MAKING A GAUGE STICK

First make a gauge stick (a tool for plotting the position of tiles on the wall) from a length of 50 x 12mm (2 x ½in) softwood. Lay several tiles along it, butting together those with lugs, or add spacers for square-edged tiles, unless they're intended to be close-butted. Mark the position of each tile on the softwood batten.

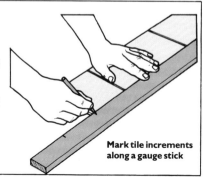

Mark tile increments along a gauge stick

Using a gauge stick
Hold a home-made gauge stick firmly against the wall and mark the positions of the tiles on the surface.

Setting out for tiling
Plan out the tiling arrangement on the walls as shown right, but first plot the symmetry of the tile field with a gauge stick to ensure a wide margin all round.
1 Temporarily fix a horizontal batten at the base of the field
2 Mark the centre of the wall
3 Gauge from the mark then fix a vertical batten to indicate the side of the field
4 Start under a dado rail with whole tiles
5 Use a row of whole tiles at sill level
6 Place cut tiles at back of a reveal
7 Support tiles over window while they set

Setting out a plain wall

On a plain uninterrupted wall, use the gauge stick to plan horizontal rows starting at skirting level. If you are left with a narrow strip at the top, move the rows up half a tile-width to create a wider margin. Mark the bottom of the lowest row of whole tiles. Temporarily nail a thin guide batten to the wall aligned with the mark (**1**). Make sure it is horizontal by placing a level on top.

Mark the centre of the wall (**2**), then use the gauge stick to set out the vertical rows at each side of it. If the border tiles are less than half a width, reposition the rows sideways by half a tile. Use a spirit level to position a guide batten against the last vertical line and nail it (**3**).

Plotting a half-tiled wall

If you are tiling part of a wall only, up to a dado rail for instance, set out the tiles with a row of whole tiles at the top (**4**).

This is even more important if you are using RE or REX tiles which are used for the top row of a half-tiled wall.

Arranging tiles around a window

Use a window as your starting point so that the tiles surrounding it are equal and not too narrow. If possible, begin a row of whole tiles at sill level (**5**), and position cut tiles at the back of a window reveal (**6**). Fix a guide batten over a window to support the rows of tiles temporarily (**7**).

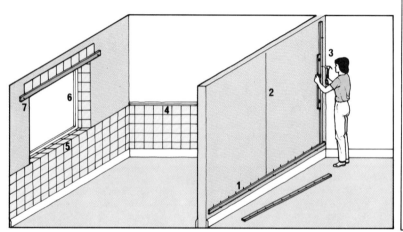

RENOVATING TILES

A properly tiled surface should last for many years but the appearance is often spoiled by one or two damaged tiles, by discoloured grouting on ceramic tiles, lifting or curling of cork, vinyl or polystyrene tiles. There is usually no need to redecorate – most problems can be solved fairly easily.

Renewing the grouting
It's not necessary to rake out old, drab grouting: use a renovation kit to brighten up the existing grout.

Brush on the liquid colourant (supplied in red, white, blue, green, beige or brown), following the lines of the grout which must be clean and dry. After about an hour, wet the area with a sponge, leave it for three minutes, then wipe excess colourant from the tiles. The liquid forms a strong bond with the grout and provides a water-resistant finish which can be polished with a dry cloth if required.

Replacing a cracked ceramic tile
Scrape the grout from around the damaged tiles then use a fine cold chisel to carefully chip out the tile, working from the centre. Take care not to dislodge its neighbours.

Scrape out the remains of the adhesive and vacuum the recess. Butter the back of the replacement tile with adhesive then press it firmly in place. Wipe off excess adhesive, allow it to set, then renew the grouting.

Lifting a cork or vinyl floor tile
Try to remove a single tile by chopping it out from the centre with a wood chisel. If the adhesive is firm, try warming the tile with a domestic iron.

Scrape the floor clean of old adhesive and try the new tile for fit. Trim the edges if necessary. Spread adhesive on the floor, then place one corner of the tile in position. Gradually lower it into the recess. Spread the tile with your finger tips to squeeze out any air bubbles, place a heavy weight on it and leave overnight.

Removing a ceiling tile
Loosen a polystyrene tile by picking it out from the centre with a sharp knife and paint scraper. Don't lever it out or you will crush the adjoining tile. Stick the replacement tile back on a complete bed of special adhesive. Remove a stapled ceiling tile by cutting through the tongues all round.

TILING A WALL: CERAMIC TILES

Choosing the correct adhesive

Most ceramic tile adhesives are sold ready-mixed, although a few need to be mixed with water. Tubs or packets will state the coverage.

A standard adhesive is suitable for most applications but use a waterproof type in areas likely to be subjected to running water or splashing. If the tiles are to be laid on a wallboard, use a flexible adhesive and make sure it is heat resistant for worktops or around a fireplace. Some adhesives can also be used for grouting the finished wall.

A notched plastic spreader is usually supplied with each tub, or you can use a serrated trowel.

Hanging the tiles

Spread enough adhesive on the wall to cover about one metre square (about 3ft square). Press the teeth of the spreader against the surface and drag it through the adhesive so that it forms horizontal ridges (1).

Press the first tile into the angle formed by the setting-out battens (2) until it is firmly fixed, then butt up tiles on each side. Build up three or four rows at a time. If the tiles do not have lugs, place matchsticks, thick card or proprietary plastic spacers between them to form the grout lines. Wipe away adhesive from the surface with a damp sponge.

Spread more adhesive and tile along the batten until the first rows of whole tiles are complete. From time to time, check that your tiling is accurate by holding a batten and spirit level across the faces and along the top and edge. When you have completed the entire field, scrape adhesive from the border and allow it to set before removing the setting-out battens.

Grouting tiles and sealing joins

Use a ready-mixed paste called grout to fill the gaps between the tiles. Standard grout is white, grey or brown, but there is also a range of coloured grouts to match or contrast with the tiles. Alternatively, mix pigments with dry, powdered grout before adding water to match any colour.

Waterproof grout is essential for showers and bath surrounds, and you should use an epoxy-based grout for worktops to keep them germ-free.

Leave the adhesive to harden for 24 hours, then use a rubber-bladed squeegee or plastic scraper to press the grout into the joins (3). Spread it in all directions to make sure all joins are well filled.

Wipe grout from the surface of the tiles with a sponge before it sets and smooth the joins with a blunt-ended stick – a dowel will do.

When the grout has dried, polish the tiles with a dry cloth. Do not use a tiled shower for about seven days to let the grout harden thoroughly.

Sealing around bathroom fittings

Don't use grout or ordinary filler to seal the gap between a tiled wall and shower tray, bath or basin: the fittings can flex enough to crack a rigid seal, and frequent soakings will allow water to seep in, create stains and damage the floor and wall. Use a silicone rubber caulking compound to fill the gaps; it remains flexible enough to accommodate any movement.

Sealants are sold in a choice of colours to match popular tile and sanitaryware colourways. They come in tubes or cartridges and can cope with gaps up to 3mm (⅛in) wide: over that, pack out with soft rope or twists of soaked newspaper.

If you're using a tube, trim the end off the plastic nozzle and press the tip into the joint at an angle of 45 degrees. Push forward at a steady rate while squeezing the tube to apply a bead of sealant. Smooth any ripples with the back of a wetted teaspoon.

If you're using a cartridge, again, snip the end off the angled nozzle – the amount you cut off dictates the thickness of the bead – and use the container's finger-action dispenser to squirt out the sealant (4).

Alternatively, use ceramic coving or quadrant tiles to edge a bath or shower unit, or glue on a plastic coving strip which you cut to length.

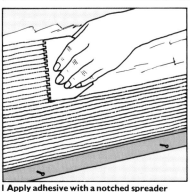

1 Apply adhesive with a notched spreader

2 Stick first tile in angle of 'setting-out' battens

3 Press grout into joins with rubber squeegee

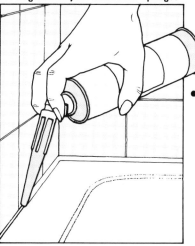

4 Seal between tiles and fittings with sealant

SEE ALSO

Details for: ▷	
Preparing plaster	50-51
Ceramic tiles	99
Tiling tools	485

Ceramic coving tiles

Quadrant
Used to fill the joint between bath and wall

Mitred tile
Use at the end if you want to turn a corner

Bullnose tile
Use this tile to finish the end of a straight run

● **Tiling around pipes and fittings**
Check with the gauge stick how the tiles will fit round socket outlets and switches, pipes and other obstructions. Make slight adjustments to the position of the main field to avoid difficult shaping around these features.

103

CUTTING CERAMIC TILES

SEE ALSO

◁ Details for:
Slipstone	469
Preparing plaster	50-51
Ceramic tiles	99
Tiling tools	485

Having finished the main field of tiles you will have to cut the ceramic tiles to fill the border and to fit around obstructions such as window frames, *electrical fittings, pipes and the basin. Making straight cuts is easy using a purpose-made cutter but shaping tiles to fit curves takes practice.*

Cutting thin strips
A cutting jig is the most accurate way to cut a thin strip cleanly from the edge of a tile. If you do not want to use the strip itself, nibble away the waste a little at a time with pincers or special tile nibblers.

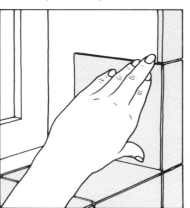

Tiling around a window
Tile up to the edges of a window, then stick RE tiles to the reveal so that they lap the edges of surrounding tiles. Fill in behind the edging tiles with cut tiles.

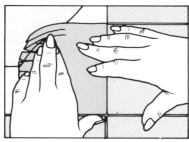

Cutting a curve
To fit a tile against a curved shape, cut a template from thin card to the exact size of a tile. Cut 'fingers' along one edge; press them against the curve to reproduce the shape. Transfer the curve onto the face of the tile and score the line freehand. Nibble away the waste a little at a time using pincers or a tile nibbler and smooth the edge with a slipstone.

Tile cutting jig
A worthwhile investment if you're cutting a lot of tiles, a proprietary jig incorporates a device for measuring and scoring tiles. The cutter is drawn down the channel of the adjustable guide. The tile is snapped with a special pincer-action tool.

Mark two edges

Cut and fit tile

Fitting around a pipe
Mark the centre of the pipe on the top and side edges of a tile and draw lines across the tile from these points. Where they cross, draw round a coin or something slightly larger than the diameter of the pipe.

Make one straight cut through the centre of the circle and either nibble out the waste, having scored the curve, or clamp it in a vice, protected with softening, and cut it out with a saw file – a thin rod coated with hard, abrasive particles which will cut in any direction. Stick one half of the tile on each side of the pipe.

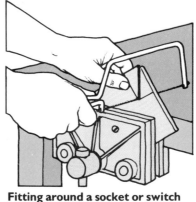

Fitting around a socket or switch
In order to fit around a socket or switch you may have to cut the corner out of a tile. Mark it from the socket then clamp the tile in a vice, protected with softening. Score both lines then use a saw file to make one diagonal cut from the corner of the tile to where the lines meet. Snap out both triangles.

If you have to cut a notch out of a large tile, cut down both sides with a hacksaw then score between them and snap the piece out of the middle.

CUTTING BORDER TILES

It's necessary to cut border tiles one at a time to fit the gap between the field tiles and the adjacent wall: walls are rarely truly square and the margin is bound to be uneven.

Making straight cuts
Mark a border tile by placing it face down over its neighbour with one edge against the adjacent wall (1). Make an allowance for normal spacing between the tiles. Transfer the marks to the edge of the tiles using a felt-tip pen.

Use a proprietary tile cutter held against a straightedge to score across the face with one firm stroke to cut through the glaze (2). You may have to score the edge of thick tiles.

Stretch a length of thin wire across a panel of chipboard, place the scored line directly over the wire and press down on both sides to snap the tile (3).

Alternatively use a tile cutter, which has a wheel to score the tile and jaws to snap it along the line. If you're doing a lot of tiling, invest in a purpose-made jig. The jig will hold the tile square with a cutting edge; pressing down on the guide snaps the tile cleanly. Some jigs include a device for measuring border tiles, too.

Smooth the cut edges of the tile with a tile sander or small slipstone (◁).

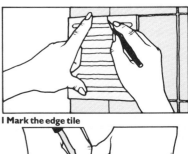

1 Mark the edge tile

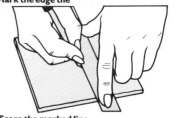

2 Score the marked line

3 Snap the tile over a wire

Mosaic tiles

Ceramic mosaic tiles are applied to a wall in a similar way to large square tiles. Set out the wall (▷) and use the same adhesive and grout.

The mesh backing on some sheets is pressed into the adhesive. The facing paper on other sheets is left intact on the surface until the adhesive sets.

Fill the main area of the wall, spacing the sheets to equal the gaps between individual tiles. Place a carpet-covered board over the sheets and tap it with a mallet to bed the tiles into the adhesive.

Fill borders by cutting strips from the sheet. Cut individual tiles to fit into awkward shapes and around fittings. If necessary, soak off the facing paper with a damp sponge and grout the tiles (▷).

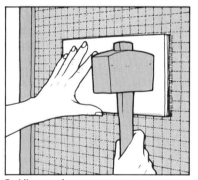

Bedding mosaics
Bed tiles by tapping a carpet-covered board.

SEE ALSO

Details for: ▷	
Setting out	102
Grouting	103
Cork/vinyl tiles	108
Adhesive solvents	496-497
Preparing plaster	50-51
Tiles	99, 101

Mirror tiles

Set out the wall with battens (▷) but avoid using mirror tiles in an area which would entail complicated fitting, as it is difficult to cut glass except in straight lines. Mirror tiles are fixed, close-butted, with self-adhesive pads. No grout is necessary.

Peel the protective paper from the pads and lightly position each tile. Check its aligment with a spirit level then press it firmly into place with a soft cloth.

Use a wooden straightedge and a wheel glass cutter to score a line across a tile. Make one firm stroke. Lay the tile over a stretched wire and press down on both sides. Remove the sharp cut edge with an oiled slipstone.

Add spare pads and fix the tile in place. Finally, polish the tiles to remove any unsightly fingermarks.

Placing mirror tiles
Position tile before pressing on wall.

Metal tiles

Set out metallic tiles as for ceramic ones. No adhesive or grout is required. Don't fit metal tiles behind electrical fittings – there's a risk that they could conduct the current.

Remove the protective paper from the adhesive pads on the back and press each tile onto the wall. Check the alignment of the tiles regularly: they are not always perfectly made.

Cut border tiles with scissors or tinsnips, but nick the edges before cutting across the face or the surface is likely to distort.

To round over a cut edge, cut a wooden block to fit inside the tile, and align it with the edge. Tap and rub along the edge with another block.

To fit into a corner, file a V-shape into the opposite edges then bend the tile over the edge of the table.

When the wall is complete, peel off any protective film, which may be covering the tiles.

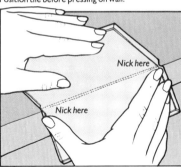

Bending metal tiles
Nick the edges of metal tiles before bending.

Cork tiles

Set up a horizontal guide batten (▷) to make sure you lay the tiles accurately. It isn't necessary to fix a vertical batten, however; the large tiles are easy to align without one. Simply mark a vertical line centrally on the wall and hang the tiles in both directions from it.

Use a rubber-based contact adhesive to fix cork tiles, if possible the type that allows a degree of movement when positioning them. If any adhesive gets onto the surface of a tile, clean it off immediately with a suitable solvent (▷) on a cloth.

Spread adhesive thinly and evenly onto the wall and back of the tiles and leave it to dry. Lay each tile by placing one edge only against the batten or its neighbour then gradually press the rest of the tile onto the wall. Smooth it down with your palms.

Cut cork tiles with a sharp trimming knife. Because the edges are butted tightly, you'll need to be very accurate when marking out border tiles. Use the same method as for laying cork and vinyl floor tiles (▷). Cut and fit curved shapes using a template.

Unless the tiles are pre-coated, apply two coats of varnish after 24 hours.

Tiling around curves
In many older houses some walls might be rounded at the external corners. Flexible tiles such as vinyl, rubber and carpet types are easy to bend into quite tight radiuses, but cork will snap if bent too far.

Cut a series of shallow slits vertically down the back of a tile within its central section, using a tenon saw, then bend it gently to the curve required.

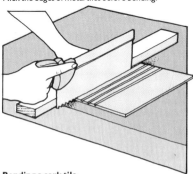

Bending a cork tile
Cut a series of shallow slits vertically down the back of a tile using a tenon saw within the central section, then bend it gently: the slits will enable the tile to assume even a fairly tight curve without snapping, but experiment first.

FIXING BRICK TILES

SEE ALSO

◁ Details for:
Pointing bricks	45
Headers/stretchers	425
Bonding bricks	426
Brick tiles	100

Applying adhesive
Butter the tile back using a notched spreader.

Corner tiles
Start with three corner tiles at each end of a run.

Fixing brick tiles
Follow this procedure when fixing brick tiles to your wall.
1 Plot the tile courses vertically and horizontally with two gauge sticks. Allow joint spaces between each tile
2 Use pre-formed tiles at external corners
3 Set a course of tiles on end above a window as a brick lintel
4 Set the bottom row of tiles on the skirting on the new wall suface or substitute with a row of brick tiles on end
5 Leave a gap for ventilating the flue in a blocked off fireplace
6 Fix tiles from the bottom up, staggering the vertical joints

Brick tiles can look quite authentic if laid in a standard running bond (◁), although you need not be hampered by structural requirements: you can hang them vertically, horizontally, diagonally or even in zig-zag fashion to achieve a dramatic effect.

You can either leave the skirting in place and start the first course of tiles just above it, or remove the skirting and replace it just lapping over the bottom course of tiles. Alternatively, remove the skirting and set a row of brick tiles on end.

Setting out the wall

Make two gauge sticks, one for the vertical coursing and another to space the tiles sideways. Allow 10mm (⅜in) spacing between each tile for the mortar joints, but adjust this slightly so there will be a full-width tile top and bottom.

Work out your spacing side to side so that, if possible, you have one course of whole tiles, alternating with courses containing a half tile at each end.

If you are using corner tiles at each end, work out your spacing from them towards the middle of a wall, and place cut tiles centrally.

Gluing on the tiles

You can use mortar to stick brick tiles to the wall but most types are sold with a compatible adhesive. Use a notched spreader to coat the back of each tile (left), then press it on the wall. Some manufacturers recommend spreading the adhesive onto the wall, instead of the tile.

If you are using pre-formed corner tiles, fix them first, three at a time, alternating headers and stretchers (◁). Check that they are level at each side of the wall with a batten and spirit level

Fitting around a window
Lay tiles vertically above a window in a 'soldier course' to simulate a brick lintel. Use prefabricated corner tiles to take the brickwork into a window reveal for the most realistic effect.

Cutting brick tiles
Most brick tiles can be cut with a hacksaw, but if a cut edge looks too sharp, round it over by rubbing with a scrap piece of tile. You can also cut tiles using a club hammer and bolster chisel, and the thinnest type can even be cut with scissors.

then fill in between.
Start filling in by tiling the bottom course, using small 10mm (⅜in) wooden offcuts to space the tiles: some tiles come with polystyrene packing, which you should cut into pieces to use as spacers. Every third course, use a spirit level to check the alignment of the tiles, and adjust if necessary.

STONE TILES

Stone tiles are laid in the same way as brick tiles. Coursed stones should be arranged with a selection of small and large tiles for the most authentic look: lay the tiles on the floor to plan the setting out, then transfer them to the wall one by one.

Irregularly-shaped stones can be laid in any pattern you want, but again, it's best to set them out on the floor to achieve a good balance of large and small sizes for realism.

With some stone tiles you have to coat the wall with a special mortar-coloured adhesive, which gives an overall background, then stick the individual tiles on by buttering their backs with adhesive.

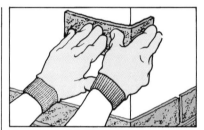

Bending brick tiles
Most brick tiles are made from rigid ceramic but some plastic tiles can be hand bent around a corner or even a curved column. Heat the tile gently with a hot air stripper or hair dryer until it is pliable. Wearing thick gloves, grasp the tile and bend it round the angle.

Pointing the joints
After 24 hours, use a ready-mixed mortar to point the wall as for real brickwork (◁). Brush smears of mortar from the face of the tiles with a stiff-bristled brush.

If you don't want to point the joints, simply leave them as they are: the adhesive is coloured to resemble mortar and the joints will resemble raked joints (◁).

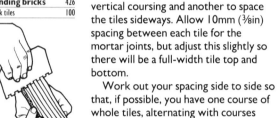

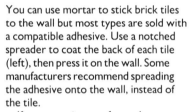

SETTING OUT FOR DIAGONAL TILING

Arranging the tiles diagonally can create an unusual decorative effect, especially if your choice of tiles enables you to mix colours. Setting out and laying the tiles off centre isn't complicated – it's virtually the same as fixing them at right-angles, except that you'll be working into a corner instead of a wall. Mark a centre line, and bisect it at right-angles using an improvised compass (right). Draw a line from opposite diagonal corners of the room through the centre point. Dry lay a row of tiles to plot the margins (See below). Mark a right-angle to the diagonal. Fix a batten along one diagonal as a guide to laying the first row of tiles.

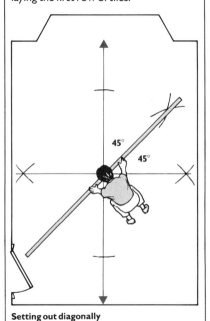

Setting out diagonally
Bisect the quartered room at 45 degrees

Plotting margin width (near right)
Lay loose tiles to make sure there is a reasonable gap at the margins. If not, move the line half a tile-width to the left.

Plotting an odd-shaped room (far right)
When a room is not a single rectangle, set out the lines using the fireplace and door as focal points.

SETTING OUT FOR SOFT FLOOR TILES

Vinyl, rubber, cork and carpet tiles are relatively large, so you can complete the floor fairly quickly. Some vinyl tiles are self-adhesive, and carpet tiles are loose-laid, both of which speed up the process still further. Soft tiles such as these can be cut easily with a sharp trimming knife or even scissors, so fitting to irregular shapes is easier.

Marking out the floor

You can lay tiles onto a solid concrete or suspended wooden floor, so long as the surface is level, clean and dry. Most soft tiles can be set out in a similar way: find the centre of two opposite walls, snap a chalked string between them to mark a line across the floor (**1**). Lay loose tiles at right-angles to the line up to one wall (see below left). If there is a gap of less than half a tile-width, move the line sideways by half a tile to give a wider margin.

To draw a line at right-angles to the first, use string and a pencil as an improvised compass to scribe arcs on the marked line, at equal distances each side of the centre (**2**).

From each point, scribe arcs on both sides of the line (**3**), which bisect each other. Join the points to form a line across the room (**4**). As before, lay tiles at right-angles to the new line to make sure border tiles are at least half width. Nail a guide batten against one line to align the first row of tiles.

If the room is noticeably irregular in shape, centre the first line on the fireplace or the door opening (see below right).

SEE ALSO

Details for: ▷	
Levelling concrete	49
Levelling floors	57
Floor tiles	100-101

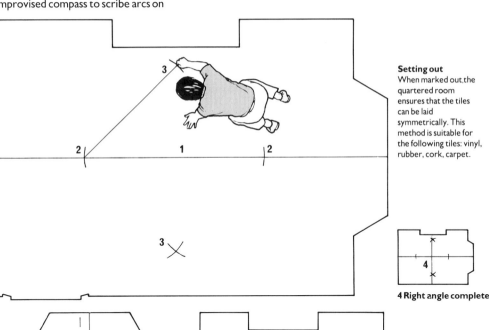

Setting out
When marked out, the quartered room ensures that the tiles can be laid symmetrically. This method is suitable for the following tiles: vinyl, rubber, cork, carpet.

4 Right angle complete

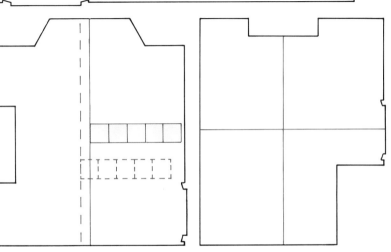

LAYING VINYL FLOOR TILES

Tiles pre-coated with adhesive can be laid quickly and simply, plus there is no risk of squeezing glue onto the surface. If you're not using *self-adhesive tiles, however, follow the tile manufacturer's instructions concerning the type of adhesive to use.*

SEE ALSO

◁ Details for:
Threshold bars	117
Levelling concrete	49
Levelling floors	57
Vinyl tiles	100

Fixing self-adhesive tiles

Stack the tiles in the room for 24 hours before you lay them so they become properly acclimatized.

If the tiles have a directional pattern – some have arrows printed on the back to indicate this – make sure you lay them the correct way.

Remove the protective paper backing from the first tile prior to laying (**1**), then press the edge against the guide batten. Align one corner with the centre line (**2**). Gradually lower the tile onto the floor and press it down.

Lay the next tile on the other side of the line, butting against the first one (**3**). Form a square with two more tiles. Lay tiles around the square to form a pyramid (**4**). Continue in this way to fill one half of the room, remove the batten and tile the other half.

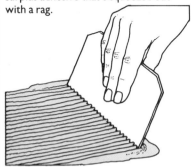

I Peel off paper backing from adhesive tiles

GLUING VINYL TILES

Spread adhesive thinly but evenly across the floor, using a notched spreader, to stick about two or three tiles only. Lay the tiles carefully and wipe off surplus adhesive that's squeezed out with a rag.

Apply bed of adhesive with notched spreader

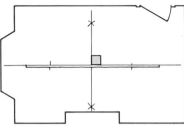

2 Place first tile in angle of intersecting lines

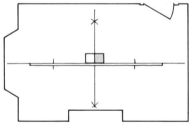

3 Butt up next tile on other side of line

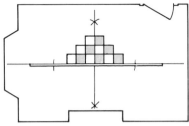

4 Lay tiles in a pyramid then fill in half room

Finishing off the floor

As soon as you have laid all the floor tiles, wash over the surface with a damp cloth to remove any finger marks. It is not often necessary to polish vinyl tiles, but you can apply an emulsion floor polish if you wish.

Fit a straight metal strip (available from carpet suppliers) over the edge of the tiles when you finish at a doorway. When the tiles butt up to an area of carpet, fit a single threshold bar onto the edge of the carpeting. (▷)

CUTTING TILES TO FIT

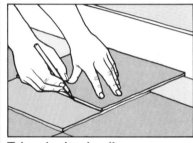

Trimming border tiles

Edges are rarely square, so cut border tiles to the skirting profile. To make a border tile, lay a loose one exactly on top of the last full tile. Place another tile on top but with its edge touching the wall. Draw along the edge of this tile with a pencil to mark the tile below. Remove the marked tile and cut along the line, then fit the cut off portion of the tile into the border.

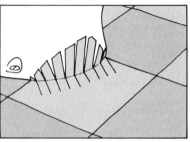

Cutting irregular shapes

To fit curves and mouldings, make a template for each tile out of thin card. Cut fingers which can be pressed against the object to reproduce its shape. Transfer the template to a tile and cut it out. You can also use a profile gauge to mark tiles for cutting complex curves.

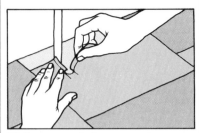

Fitting around pipes

Mark the position of the pipe on the tile using a compass. Draw parallel lines to the edge of the tile, taken from the perimeter of the circle. Measure halfway between the lines and cut a straight slit to the edge of the tile. Fold back the slit and slide the tile in place.

LAYING OTHER TYPES OF SOFT FLOOR TILES

Carpet tiles

Carpet tiles are laid as for vinyl tiles, except that they are not usually glued down. Set out centre lines on the floor (▷) but don't fit a guide batten: simply aligning the row of tiles with the marked lines is sufficient.

Carpet tiles have a pile which must be laid in the correct direction, sometimes indicated by arrows on the back face. One problem with loose-laid carpet tiles is preventing them from slipping – particularly noticeable in a large room.

Some tiles have ridges of rubber on the back which mean they will slip easily in one direction but not in another. The non-slip direction is typically denoted by an arrow on the back of the tile. It's usual to lay the tiles in pairs so that one prevents the other from moving.

Stick down every third row of tiles using double-sided carpet tape to make sure the tiles don't slide.

Cut and fit carpet tiles as described for vinyl tiles.

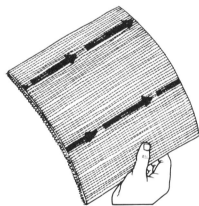

Checking direction of pile
Some carpet tiles have arrows on their back to indicate laying direction.

Using pile for decoration
Two typical arrangements of tiles using the pile to make decorative textures.

Cork tiles

Use the methods described for laying vinyl tiles to cut and fit cork tiles, but use a contact adhesive: thixotropic types allow a degree of movement as you position the tiles.

Make sure the tiles are level by tapping down the edges with a block of wood. Unfinished tiles can be sanded lightly to remove minor irregularities.

Vacuum then seal unfinished tiles with three or four coats of clear polyurethane varnish.

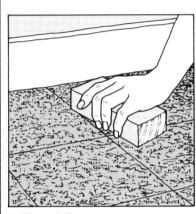

Bedding cork tiles
Bed the edges of cork tiles with a wood block.

Rubber tiles

Use the same methods for laying rubber tiles as for vinyl types. Use a latex flooring adhesive.

Laying rubber tiles
Lay large rubber tiles by placing one edge and corner against neighbouring tiles before lowering it onto a bed of adhesive.

NEAT DETAILING FOR SOFT FLOOR TILES

Covering a plinth

Create the impression of a floating bath panel or kitchen base units by running floor tiles up the face of the plinth. Hold carpet tiles into a tight bend with gripper strip (**1**) or glue other tiles in place for a similar detail. Glue a plastic moulding, normally used to seal around the edge of a bath, behind the floor covering to produce a curved detail which makes cleaning the floor a lot easier (**2**).

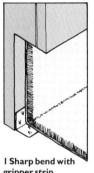

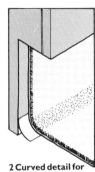

1 Sharp bend with gripper strip　　**2 Curved detail for easy cleaning**

Cutting holes for pipes

With most soft floor tiles you can cut neat holes for central heating pipes using a home-made punch: cut a 150mm (6in) length of the same diameter pipe and sharpen the rim on the inside at one end with a metalworking file. Plot the position for the hole on the tile then place the punching tool on top. Hit the other end of the punch with a hammer to cut through the tile cleanly. With some carpet tiles you may have to cut round the backing to release the cut-out and prevent fraying with tape.

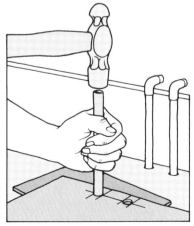

Punch holes for pipes with sharpened offcut

SEE ALSO

Details for: ▷	
Setting out	107
Levelling concrete	49
Levelling floors	57
Carpet tiles	100
Cork tiles	101
Rubber tiles	101

● **Access to plumbing**
If you are covering completely a bath panel with tiles, remember to make a lift-off section in the panel to gain access to pipes and taps around the bath.

LAYING CERAMIC FLOOR TILES

Ceramic floor tiles make a durable, hard surface that can also be extremely decorative. Laying the tiles on a floor is similar to hanging them on a wall, *although being somewhat thicker than wall tiles, you have to be especially careful when cutting them to fit for neat and accurate results.*

SEE ALSO

◁ Details for:
Levelling concrete	49
Levelling floors	57
Border wall tiles	104
Sawing tiles	104
Marking out	107
Ceramic tiles	99
Grouting tiles	103
Tiling tools	485

• **Battens on concrete**
Use masonry nails to hold battens onto a concrete floor.

Spacing the tiles
Use offcuts of thick card to set ceramic floor tiles apart consistently to allow for grouting.

• **Grouting the joins**
Grout the tiles as for walls, but fill the joins flush rather than indenting them, so that dirt will not clog them. A dark grout is less likely to show up dirt.

Setting out for tiling
Mark out the floor as for soft floor tiles then set out the field with battens.
1 Fix temporary guide battens at the edge of the field on two adjacent walls farthest from the door
2 Ensure that the battens are at true right-angles by measuring the diagonal
3 Dry-lay a square of 16 tiles in the angle as a final check

Setting out

You cannot lay ceramic tiles on a suspended wooden floor without constructing a solid, level surface that will not flex (◁). A flat, dry concrete floor is an ideal base (◁).

Mark out the floor as for soft floor tiles (◁) and work out the spacing to achieve even, fairly wide border tiles. Nail two softwood guide battens to the floor, aligned with the last row of whole tiles on two adjacent walls farthest from the door. Set the battens at a right-angle — even a small error will become obvious by the time you reach the other end of the room. Check the angle by measuring three units from one corner along one batten and four units along the other. Measure the diagonal between the marks: it should measure five units if the battens form an angle of 90 degrees. Make a final check by dry-laying a square of tiles in the angle.

Laying the tiles

Use a proprietary floor tile adhesive that is waterproof and slightly flexible when set. Spread it on using a plain or notched trowel, according to the manufacturer's recommendations. The normal procedure is to apply adhesive to the floor for the main area of tiling but to butter the back of individual cut tiles as well.

Spread enough adhesive on the floor for about sixteen tiles. Press the tiles into the adhesive, starting in the corner. Work along both battens then fill in between, to form the square. Few floor tiles have spacing lugs, so use plastic spacers or card.

Check the alignment of the tiles with a straightedge and make sure they're lying flat by spanning them with a spirit level. Work along one batten laying squares of sixteen tiles each time. Tile the rest of the floor in the same way, working back towards the door. Leave the floor for 24 hours before you walk on it to remove the guide battens and fit the border tiles.

Cutting ceramic floor tiles

Measure and cut the tiles to fit the border as described for wall tiles (◁). Because they are thicker, floor tiles will not snap quite so easily, so if you have a large area to fill, buy or hire a tile cutting jig.

Alternatively, make your own device by nailing two scraps of 12mm (½in) thick plywood to 50 × 25mm (2 × 1in) softwood battens, leaving a parallel gap between them which is just wide enough to take a tile. Hold the device on edge, insert a scored tile into the gap, up to the scored line — which should be uppermost — and press down on the free end (see below right). Snap thin strips from the edge in this way. Saw or nibble curved shapes (◁).

LAYING MOSAIC FLOOR TILES

Set out mosaic tiles on a floor as for ceramic floor tiles. Spread on the adhesive then lay the tiles, paper facing uppermost, with spacers that match the gaps between individual pieces. Press the sheets into the adhesive, using a block of wood to tamp them level. Remove the spacers and soak then peel off the facing with warm water 24 hours later. Grout as normal.

If you have to fit a sheet of mosaic tiles around an obstruction remove individual mosaic pieces as close to the profile as possible. Fit the sheet (**1**) then cut and replace the pieces to fit around the shapes.

If you're using mosaics in areas of heavy traffic — a step on the patio, for example — protect vulnerable edges with a nosing of ordinary ceramic floor tiles to match or contrast (**2**).

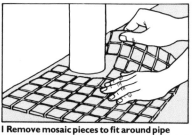

1 Remove mosaic pieces to fit around pipe

2 Lay a nosing of ceramic tiles on step treads

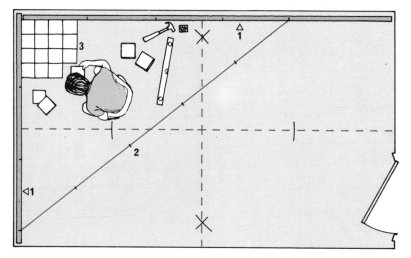

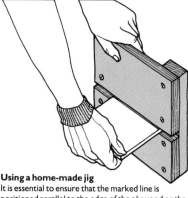

Using a home-made jig
It is essential to ensure that the marked line is positioned parallel to the edge of the plywood or the tile will not snap accurately.

LAYING QUARRY TILES

Quarry tiles are the best choice for a tough, hardwearing flooring that will receive a lot of heavy foot traffic. But beware: they're fairly thick and making even a straight cut is not easy. Reserve them for areas that don't require a lot of complex shaping.

Don't lay quarry tiles on a suspended wooden floor; replace the floorboards with 18 or 22mm (¾ or 1in) exterior-grade plywood to provide a sufficiently flat and rigid base (▷). A concrete floor presents no problems, providing it is free from damp. So long as the floor is reasonably flat, the mortar bed on which the tiles are laid will take care of the fine levelling.

Setting out for tiling

Set out two guide battens in a corner of the room at right-angles to each other, as described for ceramic floor tiles, opposite. The depth of the battens should measure about twice the thickness of the tiles to allow for the mortar bed. Fix them temporarily to a concrete floor with long masonry nails. The level of the battens is essential, so check with a spirit level; pack out under the battens with scraps of hardboard or card where necessary. Mark tile widths along each batten, leaving 3mm (⅛in) gaps between for grouting, as a guide to positioning.

Dry-lay a square of sixteen tiles in the angle, then nail a third batten to the floor, butting the tiles and parallel with one of the other battens. Level and mark it as before.

Bedding down the tiles

Quarry tiles are laid on a bed of mortar mixed from 1 part cement: 3 parts builder's sand. When water is added, the mortar should be stiff enough to hold an impression when squeezed in your hand.

Soak quarry tiles in water prior to laying to prevent them sucking water from the mortar too rapidly, when a poor bond could result. Cut a stout board to span the parallel battens: this will be used to level the mortar bed and tiles. Cut a notch in each end to fit between the battens, and the thickness of a tile less 3mm (⅛in).

Spread the mortar to a depth of about 12mm (½in) to cover the area of sixteen tiles. Level it by dragging the notched side of the board across.

Dust dry cement on the mortar to provide a good key for the tiles, then lay the tiles along three sides of the square against the battens. Fill in the square, spacing the tiles equally by adjusting them with a trowel.

Tamp down the tiles gently with the un-notched side of the board until they are level with the battens. If the mortar is too stiff, brush water into the joins. Wipe mortar from the faces of the tiles before it hardens, or it will stain.

Fill in between the battens then move one batten back to form another bay of the same dimension. Level it with the first section of tiles. Tile section-by-section until the main floor is complete. When the floor is hard enough to walk on, lift the battens and fill in the border tiles.

CUTTING QUARRY TILES

Because quarry tiles are difficult to cut you may think it worthwhile having them cut by a specialist tile supplier. Measure border tiles as described for wall tiles then, having scored the line, number each one on the bottom and mark the waste with a felt-tip pen.

If you want to cut the tiles yourself, scribe them with a tile cutter, then make a shallow cut down each edge with a saw file (▷). With the face side of the tile held in a gloved hand, strike behind the scored line with the cross pein of a hammer.

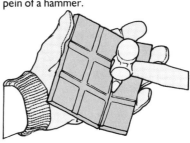

Score tile face: tap the back with a hammer

SEE ALSO

Details for: ▷	
Levelling floors	57
Saw file	485
Levelling concrete	49
Damp floors	49
Mixing mortar	170

Levelling the mortar
With a notch located over each guide batten, drag the levelling board towards you.

Notching the levelling board
Cut the same notch at each end of the board for levelling the mortar.

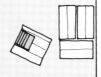

The set-up for a quarry tiled floor
The arrangement for quarry tiles is similar to glazed tiles.
1 Fix two guide battens – about twice the tile thickness – at right-angles to each other
2 Fix a third batten, parallel with one of the others
3 Dry-lay sixteen tiles between the battens so check their accuracy then proceed with tiling

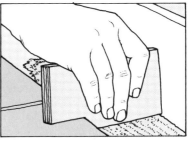

Levelling border tiles
Use a notched piece of plywood to level the mortar in the margin and tamp down the tiles with a block.

● **Finishing off the quarry tiling**
Grout quarry tiles as for ceramic floor tiles, using cement or proprietary waterproof grout. Clean it off the surface by sprinkling sawdust onto it and wiping off with a cloth. Wash the finished floor with a soapless detergent.

FITTING CEILING TILES

SEE ALSO

◁ Details for:
Preparing plaster	50-51
Marking out	107
Gluing tiles	108
Border tiles	108
Using template	108
Turning off power	296
Connecting a rose	324

There are basically two types of tiles which you can use on a ceiling: the most popular, polystyrene tiles, are easy to cut and – because they're so lightweight – they can be stuck to the ceiling without any difficulty. For a more luxurious finish, consider using mineral fibre ceiling tiles. They, too, can be glued directly to a ceiling, although some have tongued-and-grooved edges which are best stapled to a timber framework nailed to the ceiling.

Installing stapled tiles

Mineral fibre tiles are stapled to a batten framework nailed to the ceiling joists. The first job is to locate the joists and arrange the battens to suit the tile size.

Locating the joists
Start by marking out two bisecting lines across the ceiling (◁), so that you can work out the spacing of the tiles with even borders. Mark the edges of the last whole tile on the ceiling.

Check the direction of the joists by examining the floor above if you're in a downstairs room, or by looking in the loft if you're upstairs.

To locate the joists on the ceiling, poke a bradawl through the plaster at each side of a few joists (if you can gain access via the loft). Don't go to the trouble of lifting floorboards in a room above: floorboards run at right-angles to joists, so to locate them, try tapping the ceiling with your knuckles. Listen for the dull thud when you're over a joist. Use the bradawl – or a small-diameter drill bit – to locate the approximate centre of the joists.

Measure from these points to the next joists – they'll be anything from 300 to 450mm (1 to 1ft 8in) apart – and mark their centres. Nail parallel strips of 50 × 25mm (2 × 1in) sawn timber to

the joists, at right-angles to them. Space them so the distance between the centre of each strip is a tile width. Fitting the strips is easier with a spacer – two softwood battens nailed together **(1)** to set the spacing. Finish by nailing the last strip against the far wall. Transfer the line marking the edge of the border tiles to the battens along both sides of the ceiling.

Fitting stapled tiles
Unlike any other form of tiling, you must start by fixing stapled tiles at the borders. Mark and cut off the tongued edges of two adjacent rows of border tiles, starting with the one in the corner. Staple them through the grooved edge to the furring strips but secure the cut edges with panel pins driven through their faces.

Proceed diagonally across the ceiling by fixing whole tiles into the angle formed by the border tiles. Slide the tongues of the loose tile into the groove of its neighbours, then staple it through its own grooved edge **(2)**.

To fit the remaining border tiles, cut off the tongues and nail them through their face.

1 Make a spacing gauge
Set out the furring strips at the correct spacing using a gauge made from two battens nailed together.

2 Securing the tiles
Fix the tiles groove outwards and staple through the grooved edge. Slot the tongues of butting tiles into them.

How stapled ceiling tiles are fixed
Mineral fibre tiles require a set-up of battens attached to the ceiling surface.
1 Nail battens to the joists at right-angles, a tile-width apart. Arrange substantial borders by altering the starting point
2 Fix the border tiles first on two adjacent rows, starting with the corner tile
3 Staple the remaining tiles to the battens through their grooves, working diagonally across the ceiling

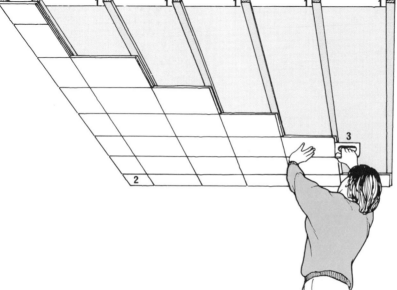

FIXING POLYSTYRENE CEILING TILES

Where to use the tiles
Polystyrene tiles can be used in virtually any room in the house except the kitchen, where they would be directly over a source of heat – the cooker or a gas-fired water heater.

Setting out the ceiling
Remove any friable material and make sure the ceiling is clean and free from grease (◁). Snap two chalked lines which cross each other at right-angles in the centre of the ceiling (◁). Hang the tiles to the chalked lines, checking their alignment frequently (◁).

Sticking up the tiles
Use a proprietary polystyrene adhesive or a heavy-duty wallpaper paste. Spread the adhesive across the back of the tile to cover all but the very edge.

Press the first tile into one of the angles formed by the marked lines. Use the flat of your hand: fingertip pressure can crush polystyrene. Proceed with subsequent tiles to complete one half of the ceiling, then the other.

Cutting the tiles
Mark the border tiles (◁) then use a sharp trimming knife with a blade long enough to cut through a tile with one stroke. Cut the tiles on a flat piece of scrap board. Clean up the edges but don't rub too hard or the polystyrene granules will crumble.

Mark out curves with a card template (◁), then follow the marked line freehand with a trimming knife.

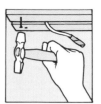

1 Fix battens to joists   **2 Replace ceiling rose**

Dealing with electrical fittings
Turn off the power at the mains (◁) unscrew the ceiling rose cover, and release the flex conductors.

Nail battens to the ceiling joists to correspond with the screw fixings of the rose **(1)**. Cut a hole through the covering tile for the cable, replace the rose **(2)**, screwing it through the tile to the battens. Reconnect the conductors (◁), replace the rose cover then restore the power.

PARQUET FLOORING

Parquet flooring is a relatively thin covering of decorative timber laid in the form of panels or narrow strips. A range of hardwoods such as oak, birch, cherry, mahogany and teak are used for their beautiful grain patterns and rich colouring, which can be highlighted with waxes, polishes and varnishes.

PREPARING THE SUB-FLOOR

Whether the sub-floor is concrete or wooden, it must be clean, dry and flat before parquet flooring is laid. Level wooden floors with hardboard panels (▷) and screed a concrete base (▷).

Some manufacturers recommend that a building paper or thin plastic foam underlay is laid for floating parquetry. Leave any parquet panels or strips in the room where they will be laid for several days to adjust to the atmosphere which will make them less likely to warp.

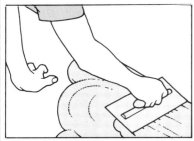

Preparation for solid floors
When laying parquet flooring on a solid concrete base, ensure the floor is completely dry and damp-proof (impervious to rising damp), make good, and screed the surface with a proprietary self levelling compound.

Types of parquet flooring

The type of flooring you choose will be determined by the range of timbers offered by the manufacturer and of course, the price, but consider also the method of laying to suit the type of sub-floor you have as well as your own preference. All types compare in ease of application, being no more difficult than tiling a floor.

Tongued-and-grooved wood strip

Wooden floors can also be constructed from tongued-and-grooved (T&G) strips or tiles, either machined from solid timber or made from veneered plywood. They can be nailed to a wooden floor or left as floating parquetry by gluing just the jointed edges together.

Tiles and strips range in thickness from 9 to 14mm (⅜ to ⅝in). Fix them either as parallel strips or arrange them in various combinations to make herringbone or woven patterns. Manufacturers supply patterns.

Hardwood panels

Perhaps the most common form of hardwood flooring is a 450mm (1ft 6in) square panel made by gluing 8mm (⅜in) solid wooden fingers into herringbone or basketweave patterns. Panels are pre-sanded and are fitted with a bitumen-impregnated backing to protect them from rising damp (although the floor itself must include a damp-proof membrane). Panels can be glued to wooden or concrete floors, their edges butted like floor tiles.

SEE ALSO

Details for: ▷	
Levelling concrete	49
Levelling floors	57
Vinyl and cork tiling	107-109
Choosing colour/ texture	24-28

Hardwood parquet panels
Solid wood strips make up flat panels for gluing to the floor.

Timber-faced cork

This is not a true parquet flooring, being simply a composite tile made from a layer of cork backed with vinyl and surfaced with a hardwood veneer. The timber is protected by a clear vinyl coating. The tiles are available in 900mm × 150mm (3ft × 6in) strips.

For setting out, fitting and cutting timber-faced cork, see the section on vinyl and cork tiles (▷).

Timber-faced cork
This type of flooring is very easy to lay and is cut to fit with a sharp knife.

Tongued and grooved flooring
These short sections of woodstrip flooring illustrate a few of the beautiful hardwoods available for this type of parquet. Remember to allow for the additional cost of varnish when budgeting for wooden floors.

LAYING PARQUET FLOORING

SEE ALSO

◁ Details for:
Finishing wood	82,84
Setting out	107
Border panels	108
Using templates	108
Levelling concrete	49
Levelling floors	57
Parquet flooring	113
Profile gauge	485

1 Edge detail
An expansion gap is necessary around a parquet tiled floor, but you can conceal it for neatness by nailing a strip of quadrant moulding to the skirting.

● **Floating parquetry**
Instead of nailing the strips to the floor, floating parquetry is glued edge-to-edge by applying a little PVA adhesive to each groove, as it is tapped in place. Place wedges between the parquetry and the skirting to maintain the 12mm (1/2in) expansion gap until the moulding is fixed.

2 Fitting the last strip
Lever in the last strip using a crowbar with an offcut of board to protect the paintwork.

Laying hardwood panels

Set out the floor to calculate the position of panels as described for vinyl tiles (◁), but instead of fixing a guide batten, drive a nail into each end of a line marking the edge of the last whole panels along the wall furthest from the door. Stretch a length of string between the nails.

Use a notched trowel to spread the recommended adhesive onto the floor to cover a strip next the string. Align the first row of hardwood panels with the string, levelling the panels with a softwood block and hammer. Check the alignment with a straightedge. Lay subsequent panels butted against the preceding row, working from the centre in both directions.

Cutting border panels

Measure and mark border panels as described for vinyl (◁) but deduct 12mm (1/2in) to provide an expansion gap along the skirting. Cut the panels with a tenon saw.

Glue the border panels in place then cover the gap with quadrant moulding pinned to the skirting (**1**). Don't pin the moulding to the flooring, as it would part from the skirting and serve no useful purpose.

Finishing the flooring

Sand any slight irregularities between tiles, then vacuum the floor. Seal the parquetry with three or four coats of clear finish (◁).

How panels are fitted
1 Mark out the floor as for vinyl tiles
2 Stretch a stringline between nails to mark the edge of field
3 Lay the first row from the centre out, butting panels
4 Lay subsequent rows, checking alignment with a spirit level
5 Fit border panels

Laying strip flooring

Decide on the direction of the strip flooring then snap a chalked line about 12mm (1/2in) from a skirting which runs parallel with it.

Place the grooved edge of the first strip against the line and nail it through the face with panel pins. Tap the next strip onto the tongue using a scrap strip to protect the edge.

Nail through the inner angle of the tongue every 200mm (8in) up to 35mm

(1 1/2in) from the ends. Use a nail punch and hammer to drive the nail heads below the surface.

Proceed across the floor cutting each strip 12mm (1/2in) short of the skirting board. At the far end the gap will allow you to lever the last strip in place and nail it through the face (**2**). Nail a cover moulding all round.

Finish strip flooring with clear varnish in the same way as panel flooring.

How strips are fixed
Flooring strips are fixed across the floor from the skirting.
1 Snap a chalked stringline parallel with the skirting
2 Nail a strip through its face, tongue outwards, against the chalk guideline
3 Slot on subsequent strips and nail through the tongues
4 Stagger joins

CUTTING WOOD STRIP & PANEL FLOORING

Cutting curves
Mark out curved shapes with a cardboard template (◁), transfer to the strip or panel, then cut along the line with a coping saw.

Fitting into a doorway
If the parquetry is to run through two rooms, use a piece of the flooring to guide the blade of a panel saw to cut off the bottom of the door frame, rather than trying to cut the panel to the moulded architrave. The parquetry will fit neatly under the frame.

If the flooring is to change at the door, fit a hardwood threshold the same thickness as the panels and the full depth of the frame. Cut the bottom of the frame to take the threshold then screw or nail it to the floor.

Fitting around a pipe
Measure and mark the position of a pipe projecting from the floor, or use a profile gauge. Drill a hole slightly larger than the pipe diameter then cut out a tapered section of tile to accommodate the pipe; retain the offcut. Glue the tile to the floor and fit the wedge-shaped offcut behind the pipe.

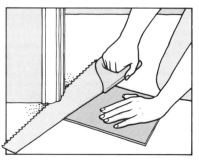

Cutting away a door frame
Professional fitters cut away the bottom of the frame to the thickness of the flooring.

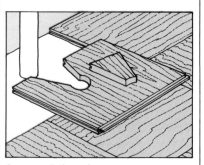

Accommodating a pipe
Fit the notch over the pipe, locate the tongue then lower the panel into place.

ESTIMATING SHEET VINYL AND CARPET

Measure the floor area carefully and draw a freehand plan, including the position of doors, window bay, alcoves and so on, plus the full width of the door frame. Make a note of the dimensions on the plan and take it to the supplier, who will advise you on the most economical way to cover the floor.

The ideal solution is to achieve a seamless wall-to-wall covering, but this is often impossible, either because a particular width is unobtainable or because the room is such an irregular shape that there would be an unacceptable amount of wastage if it was cut from one piece. Carpet or sheet vinyl widths have to be butted together in these circumstances, but try to avoid seams in the main walkways. You will also have to consider matching the pattern and the direction of carpet pile. Pile must run in the same direction or each piece of carpet will look different. Remember to order about 75mm (3in) extra all round for fitting.

Standard widths

Most manufacturers produce carpet or vinyl to standard widths. Some can be cut to fit any shape of room but the average wastage factor is reflected in the price. Not all carpets are available in the full range of widths and you may have some difficulty in matching a colour exactly from one width to another, so ask the supplier to check. Carpet and vinyl are made to metric sizes but the imperial equivalent is normally quoted.

Available Widths	
Carpet	**Vinyl**
*0.69m (2ft 3in)	2m (6ft 6in)
0.91m (3ft)	3m (9ft 10in)
2.74m (9ft)	4m (13ft)
3.66m (12ft)	
*4m (13ft)	
*4.57m (15ft)	

*rare

Carpet widths of 2.74m (9ft) and over are called Broadlooms; narrower widths are called Body or Strip carpets.

Carpet squares

Carpet squares, not to be confused with tiles (▷), are large rectangular loose-laid rugs. Simply order whichever size suits the proportion of your room. Carpet squares should be turned from time to time to even out wear.

SHEET VINYL AND CARPET

Sheet flooring fits wall-to-wall. The coverings most often used today are sheet vinyl (the modern equivalent of linoleum) and carpet in all its forms. Included in the cost of an expensive floorcovering should be an allowance for having it professionally laid – and even if there's an additional charge, you'd be well advised to spend that little extra to avoid the risk of spoiling costly carpet or vinyl. On the other hand, there's no reason why you shouldn't lay the cheaper ranges, where cost-saving makes more sense.

Types of sheet floorcovering

There are many types of carpet and vinyl flooring: choose according to durability, colour and pattern.

Unbacked vinyl

Sheet vinyl is made by sandwiching the printed pattern between a base of PVC and a clear protective PVC covering. All vinyl is relatively hardwearing but some have a thicker, reinforced protective layer to increase their durability. Discuss with the supplier the best quality to suit your needs and choose from the vast range of colours, patterns and embossed textures available.

Backed vinyl

Backed vinyl has similar properties to the unbacked type, with the addition of a resilient underlay to make them softer and warmer to walk on. The backing may be felt or, more often, a cushion of foamed PVC.

Vinyl carpet

Vinyl carpet is a cross between carpet and sheet vinyl originally developed for contract use but now available for domestic installation. It has a velvet-like pile of fine nylon fibres embedded in a waterproof, expanded PVC base. It's popular for kitchens as spillages are washed off easily with water and a mild detergent. Rolls are 1.5m (5ft) wide.

Carpet

Originally, piled carpets were made by knotting strands of wool or other natural fibres into a woven foundation but gradually, with the introduction of machine-made carpets and synthetic fibres, a very wide variety of different types has been developed. There is a good choice available for virtually every situation – whether the need is for something luxurious or practical and hardwearing.

SEE ALSO

Details for: ▷	
Levelling concrete	49
Levelling floors	57
Carpet tiles	100
Choosing colour/ pattern/texture	24-29
Laying sheet vinyl	118

Vinyl flooring
Being hardwearing and waterproof, sheet vinyl is one of the most popular floorcoverings for bathrooms and kitchens. Vinyl carpet (6th from right) has a pile but is equally suitable in those areas.

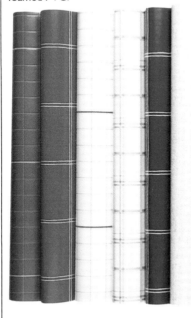

Preparing the floor for floorcovering

Before you lay a sheet covering make sure the floor is flat and dry. Take out any unevenness by screeding or hardboarding the floor (▷). A concrete floor must have a DPM and a wooden floor must be ventilated below. Don't lay vinyl over timber recently treated with preservative.

CHOOSING CARPET

There are various factors to consider when you're shopping for carpeting, such as fibre content, type of pile and durability to wear. Although wool is luxurious, don't be put off by the synthetic version widely available – they have a lot to offer in terms of comfort underfoot, finish and texture.

SEE ALSO
◁ Details for:
Choosing colour/
texture/pattern   24-29
Levelling concrete   49
Levelling floors   57
Carpet tiles   100

How fibre content affects the carpet

The best carpets are made from wool or a mixture of wool plus a percentage of man-made fibre. Wool carpets are expensive, so manufacturers have experimented with a variety of fibres to produce cheaper but still durable and attractive carpets. Materials such as nylon, polypropylene, acrylic, rayon and polyester are all used for carpet-making – singly or combined.

Synthetic fibre carpets were once inferior substitutes, often with an unattractive shiny pile and a reputation for building up a charge of static electricity that produced mild shocks when anyone touched a metal doorknob. Nowadays, manufacturers have largely solved the problem of static but you can seek the advice of the supplier before you buy.

So far as appearance is concerned, a modern carpet made from good quality blended fibres is hard to distinguish from one made from wool. Certain combinations produce carpets that are so stain-resistant that they virtually shrug off spilled liquids. To their disadvantage, synthetic fibres tend to react badly to burns, shrivelling rapidly from the heat, whereas wool tends only to smoulder.

Rush, sisal, coir and jute are natural vegetable fibres used to make coarsely-woven rugs or strips.

Which type of pile?

The nature of the pile is even more important to the feel and appearance of a carpet than the fibre content. Piled carpets are woven or tufted. Axminster and Wilton are names used to describe two traditional methods of weaving the pile simultaneously with the foundation so that the strands are wrapped around and through the warp and weft threads.

With tufted carpets, continuous strands are pushed between the threads of a pre-woven foundation. Although it is secured with an adhesive backing, tufted pile is not as permanent as woven pile. Consult the box, right, for the various ways tufted and woven piles are created. Where durability is important, see below.

The importance of underlay

It is false economy to try to save on the cost of underlay. Without it, carpet wears faster and is not as comfortable underfoot. Eventually, the lines of floorboards will begin to show as dirty lines on a pale carpet as dust from the gaps begins to emerge.

An underlay can be a thick felt or foamed rubber and plastic. Rubber or foam-backed carpets need no underlay.

As an extra precaution, it is worth laying rolls of brown paper over the floor to stop dust and grit working its way into the underlay and to prevent rubber-backed carpet sticking to the floor, and tearing when lifted.

HOW CARPETS ARE MADE

Tufted and woven carpet pile is treated in a number of ways to give some different qualities of finish: with some types the strands are left long and uncut; with others the looped pile is twisted together to give a coarser texture; very hardwearing types have their looped pile pulled tight against the foundation; cut, velvety and shaggy types have the top of their loops removed to leave single fibre strands.

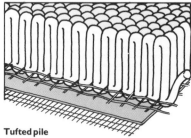

Tufted pile
Continuous strands pushed into a woven foundation secured on an adhesive backing.

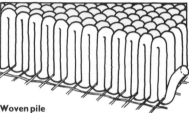

Woven pile
Continuous strands woven onto the warp and weft threads of the foundation.

1 Looped pile
Ordinary looped pile gives a smooth feel

2 Twisted pile
Looped pile twisted for a coarser texture

3 Cord pile
Loops are pulled tight against the foundation

4 Cut pile
Loops are cut, giving a velvety textured pile

5 Velvet pile
Loops are cut short for a close-stranded pile

6 Shag pile
A long cut pile up to 100mm (4in) long

Fibre-bonded pile
The most modern method of carpet production, fibre-bonded pile consists of synthetic fibres, packed tightly together, and bonded to an impregnated backing. It produces a texture much like coarse felt.

CHOOSING A DURABLE CARPET

Whether it is woven, tufted or bonded, a hardwearing carpet must have a dense pile. When you fold the carpet and part the pile you should not be able to see the backing to which it is attached.

Fortunately, the British Carpet Classification Scheme categorizes floorcoverings according to their ability to withstand wear. If the classification is not stated on the carpet, ask the supplier how it is categorized.

● **Light domestic**	Bedrooms
● **Medium domestic**	Light traffic only, dining room, well-used bedroom
● **General domestic**	Living rooms
● **Heavy domestic**	Hallways and stairs

Some people prefer to loose-lay carpet, relying on the weight of furniture to stop it moving around. However, a properly stretched and fixed carpet looks much better, and isn't difficult to accomplish. There are three main methods of fixing, as detailed right.

Laying a standard width

The only special tool required for laying carpet is a knee kicker for stretching the covering. It has a toothed head, which is pressed into the carpet while you nudge the padded end with your knee. You can hire a knee kicker from a supplier.

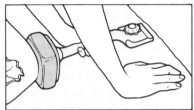

A knee kicker, used to stretch carpet to fit

Join the underlay with short strips of carpet tape or secure it with a few tacks to stop it moving. Roll out the carpet butting one machine-cut edge against a wall and fix that edge. (If the carpet is patterned, it should run parallel to the main axis of the room.)

Stretch the carpet to the wall directly opposite and temporarily fix it with tacks, or slip it onto gripper strips, but do not cut it yet. Work from the centre towards each corner, stretching and fixing. Do the same along the other sides of the room.

Cut the corners like sheet vinyl (▷) to allow the carpet to lie flat. Adjust it until it is stretched evenly then fix it permanently. When you are using tape or strips, press the carpet into the angle between skirting and floor with a bolster chisel; trim with a knife held at 45° to the skirting. Tuck the cut edge behind the strip with the bolster.

Cutting to fit

Cut and fit carpet into doorways and around obstacles like sheet vinyl (▷). Join carpets at a doorway with a single- or double-sided threshold bar.

Joining carpet

Don't join expensive woven carpets; they should be sewn by a professional. Glue straight seams with latex adhesive or use adhesive tape for rubber-backed carpet. Use as described for vinyl (▷).

Methods of fixing

Tacks

A 50mm (2in) strip of carpet is folded under and nailed to a wooden floor with improved cut tacks about every 200mm (8in). Lose the head in the pile by rubbing the pile with your fingertips. Underlay should be laid 50mm (2in) short of the skirting to allow the carpet to lie flat along the edge.

Double-sided tape

For rubber-backed carpets only. Stick 50mm (2in) tape around the perimeter of the room. When you are ready to fix

Carpeting a staircase

If possible use one of the narrow standard widths of carpet for a staircase. Order an extra 450mm (1ft 6in) to the required length so that the carpet can be moved at a later date to even out the wear. This allowance is turned under onto the bottom step.

You can fit stair carpeting across the entire width of the treads or stop short to reveal a border of polished or painted staircase. If you adopt the latter style of carpeting, you can use the traditional metal or wooden stair rods to hold the carpet against the risers. Fixing is simply a matter of screwing brackets on each side.

Alternatively, you can tack the carpet to the stairs every 75mm (3in) across the treads. Push the carpet firmly into the angle between riser and tread with a bolster chisel while you tack the centre, then work outwards to each side.

So long as the carpet is not rubber-backed, you can use angled gripper strip to fix the run in place.

Fitting the underlay

Cut underlay into separate pads for each tread. Secure each pad next to the riser with tacks or gripper strip, and tack the front edge under the nosing.

the carpet, peel off the protective paper layer from the adhesive tape to expose the sticky surface.

Gripper strip

Wooden or metal strips with fine metal teeth which grip the woven foundation. Not really suitable for rubber-backed carpets, although it is used. Nail strips to the floor, 6mm (¼in) from the skirting with the teeth angled towards the wall. Cut short strips to fit doorways and alcoves. Glue the strips to a concrete floor. Cut underlay up to the edge.

Laying a straight run

The pile of a carpet should face down the stairs. Rub the palm of your hand along the carpet in both directions. It will feel smoother in the direction of the pile.

Start at the bottom of the staircase with the carpet laid face down on the first tread. Fix the back edge with tacks or nail a strip over it. Stretch the carpet over the nosing and fix it to the bottom of the riser by nailing through a straight strip. Run the carpet up the staircase, pushing it firmly into each gripper strip with a bolster. Nail the end of the carpet against the riser on the last tread. Bring the landing carpet over the top step to meet it.

Carpeting winding stairs

To carpet the winding section of a staircase, keep the carpet in a continuous length but fold the excess under and secure it to the riser with a stair rod or straight gripper strip.

Alternatively, fold the slack against the riser and tack through the three thicknesses of carpet.

To install fitted carpet on winding stairs, cut a pattern for each step and carpet it individually.

SEE ALSO

Details for: ▷	
Fitting vinyl	118
Joining vinyl	118
Levelling concrete	49
Levelling floors	57
Staircases	212-214

Fixing carpet
Use one of three ways:

Fold tacked to floor

Double-sided tape

Gripper strip

Joining at a doorway
Use one of the bars below:

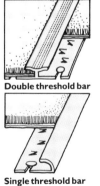

Double threshold bar

Single threshold bar

Carpeting stairs
1 Tack underlay pads
2 Tack carpet face down on first tread
3 Pull over nosing and tack to base of riser
4 Run carpet up stairs, fixing to grippers

Carpeting winding stairs
1 Don't cut the carpet but fold the excess under and fix to riser with stair rod or straight strip

Straight run

Winding stairs

LAYING SHEET VINYL

SEE ALSO

◁ Details for:
Levelling concrete	49
Levelling floors	57
Sheet flooring	115

Vinyl floorcovering makes a durable, wall-to-wall surface for floors subject to likely spillages of water, such as the kitchen, utility room and bathroom.

There are numerous colours, patterns and embossed effects available, and you will find most types straightforward to lay if you follow a systematic routine.

Leave the vinyl in a room for 24 to 48 hours before laying, preferably opened flat or at least stood on end, loosely rolled. Assuming there are no seams, start by fitting the longest wall first. Drive a nail through a wooden lath about 50mm (2in) from one end.

Pull the vinyl away from the wall by approximately 35mm (1½in). Make sure it is parallel with the wall or the main axis of the room. Use the nailed strip to scribe a line following the skirting (**1**). Cut along the vinyl with a sharp knife or scissors and slide the sheet up against the wall.

To get the rest of the sheet to lie as flat as possible, cut a triangular notch out of each corner. Make a straight cut down to the floor at external corners. Remove as much waste as possible leaving 50 to 75mm (2 to 3in) turned up all round.

Press the vinyl into the angle between skirting and floor with a bolster. Align a metal straightedge with the crease and run along it with a sharp knife held at a slight angle to the skirting (**2**). If your trimming is less than perfect, nail a cover strip of quadrant moulding to the skirting.

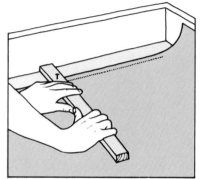
1 Fit to first wall by scribing with a nailed strip

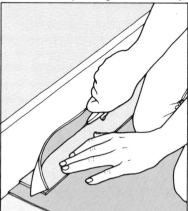
2 Press the edge to the skirting and cut

Trimming and gluing vinyl sheet

Trimming to fit a doorway
Work around the door frame moulding making straight cuts and removing triangular notches at each change of angle as if they were miniature corners. Crease the vinyl against the floor and trim the waste. Make a straight cut across the opening and fit a threshold bar over the edge of the sheet.

Cutting around an obstruction
To fit around a WC pan or basin pedestal, fold back the sheet and pierce it with a knife just above floor level. Draw the blade up towards the edge. Make triangular cuts around the base, gradually working around the curve until the sheet can lie flat on the floor (**3**). Crease and cut off the waste.

Sticking the sheet
Modern vinyls can be loose-laid, but you may prefer to glue the edges and especially along a door opening. Peel back the edge and spread a band of the recommended flooring adhesive with a toothed spreader (**4**) or use a 50mm (2in) wide double-sided tape.

Making a join
If you have to join widths of vinyl, scribe one edge as described above, then overlap the free edge with the second sheet until the pattern matches exactly. Cut through both pieces with a knife, then remove the waste strips.

Without moving the sheets, fold back both cut edges, apply tape or adhesive and press the join together.

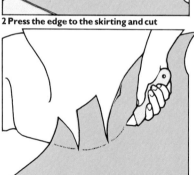
3 Make triangular cuts around a curve

Positioning the vinyl
Aligning the vinyl sheet squarely on the floor is essential.
1 Fit the longest, uninterrupted wall
2 Cut triangular notches at each external and internal corner so the sheet will lie flat
3 Allow folds of about 75mm (3in) all round for scribing to fit accurately
4 Make a straight cut against the door opening so a threshold bar can be fixed

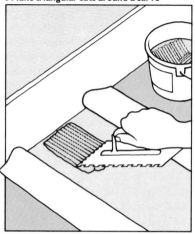
4 Secure butting edges on a bed of adhesive

3

HOUSE CONSTRUCTION	120
WALLS	122
CEILINGS	142
INTERIOR PLASTERWORK	148
EXTERIOR RENDERING	168
FLOORS	172
DOORS	184
WINDOWS	196
STAIRS	212
ROOFS	221

REPAIRS & IMPROVEMENTS

BRICK HOUSE CONSTRUCTION

Brick-built houses follow a long tradition of styles and methods of construction. The brickwork gives the building character and is the main load-bearing element. If you have to repair and renovate your home it is useful to understand the basic principles of its construction.

SEE ALSO

◁ Details for:
Solid walls	122
Cavity walls	122
Internal walls	122,123
Lintels	124,198
Floors	172-175
Brick bonding	426
Damp-proof membrane	182,251
Pitched roofs	221
Roof coverings	223
Damp-proof course	251

Foundations
The foundations carry the whole weight of the house. The type, size and depth are determined largely by the loadbearing properties of the subsoil.

Strip foundation
A continuous strip of concrete set well below ground.

Trench foundation
Similar to the strip type but concrete fills the trench.

Raft foundation
A concrete slab covers the whole ground area.

Support for the house

To support the weight of the structure, most brick-built buildings are supported on a solid base called foundations (See diagrams left).

Wall formation

External walls are loadbearing, supporting roof, floors and internal walls. Cavity walls (◁) comprise two leaves braced with metal ties. Older houses have solid walls (◁) at least 225mm (9in) thick. Bricks are laid with mortar in overlapping bonding patterns (◁) to give the wall rigidity. A damp-proof course (DPC) just above ground level prevents moisture rising.

Window and door openings are spanned above with rigid supporting beams called lintels (◁).

Internal walls (◁) are either non-loadbearing divisions made from lightweight blocks, manufactured boards, or timber studding; or loadbearing structures of brick or block.

Solid and timber floors

Ground floors are either solid concrete or suspended timber types (◁). A damp-proof membrane (DPM) is laid between walls where a floor is concrete. With timber floors, sleeper walls of honeycomb brickwork are built on oversite concrete between the base brickwork; a timber sleeper plate rests on each wall and timber joists are supported on them. Their ends may be similarly supported, let into the brickwork or suspended on metal hangers. Floorboards are laid at right angles to joists. First floor joists are supported by the masonry or hangers.

Pitched roof construction

Pitched (sloping) roofs comprise angled rafters fixed to a ridge board, braced by purlins, struts and ties, fixed to wallplates bedded on top of the walls. Roofs are usually clad with slates or tiles to keep the weather out.

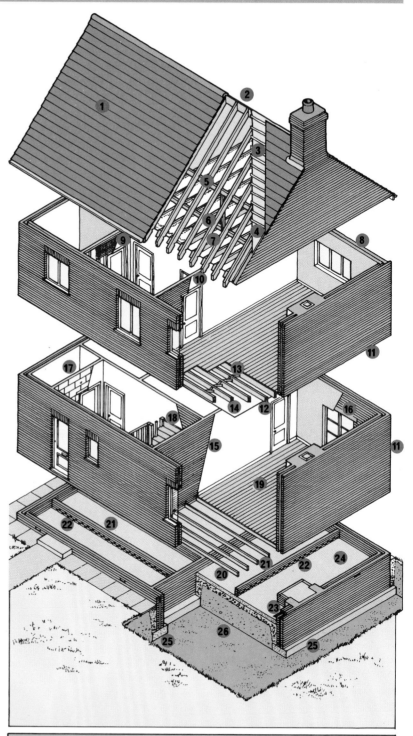

TYPICAL COMPONENTS OF A BRICK-BUILT HOUSE

1 Tiles or slates	8 Wall plate	14 Plaster ceiling	20 Ground floor joists
2 Ridge board	9 Lath-and-plaster stud	15 Brick loadbearing	21 Timber sleeper plate
3 Tile battens	partition	internal wall	22 Sleeper wall
4 Roofing felt	10 Internal brick wall	16 Lintel	23 Damp-proof course
5 Purlin	11 Brick cavity wall	17 Block partition wall	24 Oversite concrete
6 Rafters	12 Suspended joists	18 Staircase	25 Strip foundation
7 Ceiling joist	13 Herringbone bracing	19 Floorboards	26 Ground

TIMBER-FRAMED HOUSE CONSTRUCTION

Timber is an excellent all-purpose material for building and has been used in house construction for centuries. Modern timber-framed houses differ from their brick-built counterparts in that the main structural elements are timber frames, irrespective of whether the walls of the building are clad with brickwork, timber boarding or tiles.

Foundations

As with a brick house, a timber one is built on sound concrete foundations, usually 'strip' or 'raft' types, to spread weight to firm ground.

Wall assembly

Modern timber-framed house walls are constructed with vertical timber studs with horizontal top and bottom plates nailed to them. The frames – which are erected on a concrete slab or a suspended timber platform supported by cavity brick walls – are faced on the outside with plywood sheathing, which stiffens the structure. Breather paper – a moisture barrier – is fixed over the top. Insulation quilt is used between studs.

Stiff timber lintels at openings carry the weight of the upper floor and roof.

Brick cladding is typically used to cover the exterior of the frame, giving the house the appearance of one built from bricks. The cladding is attached to the timber frame with metal ties. Weatherboarding often replaces the brick cladding on upper floors.

Floor construction

Floors in a timber-framed house are either solid concrete or suspended timber, as with a masonry house. In some cases, a concrete floor may be screeded or surfaced with timber or chipboard flooring. Suspended timber floor joists are supported on wallplates and surfaced with chipboard.

Prefabricated roof

Timber-framed houses usually have trussed roofs – prefabricated triangulated frames which combine the rafters and ceiling joists – which are lifted into place and supported by the walls. The trusses are joined together with horizontal and diagonal ties. A ridge board is not fitted, nor are purlins required. Roofing felt, battens and tiling are applied in the usual way.

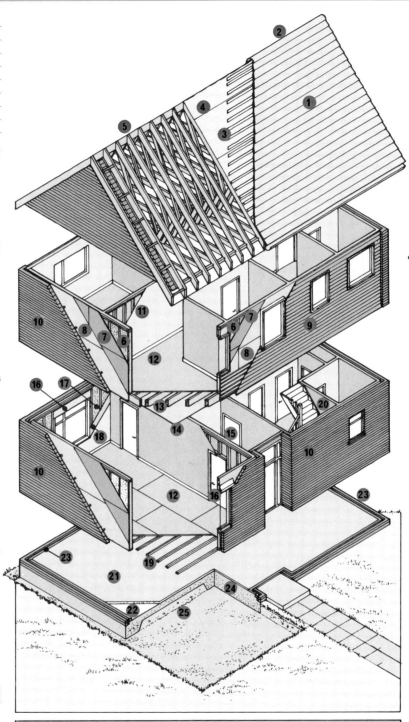

SEE ALSO

Details for: ▷	
Subsidence	409
Cavity walls	122
Floors	172-175
Pitched roofs	221
Roof coverings	223
Insulation	265

● **Foundation problems**
Consult your Building Control Officer when dealing with problems or new work involving foundations.

Settlement
Settlement cracks in walls are not uncommon, and if not too wide and have stablized they are not a serious problem.

Subsidence
Subsidence caused by weak or shallow foundations or excessive moisture-loss from the ground (▷) can be more serious. Widening cracks from window or door openings indicate this.

Heave
Weak foundations can also be damaged by ground swell, or 'heave'.

Light foundations
The walls of extensions or bays with lighter or shallower foundations than the house may show cracks where the two meet due to differential movement.

TYPICAL COMPONENTS OF A TIMBER-FRAMED HOUSE

1 Tiles or slates	8 Breather paper	15 Loadbearing internal stud wall	22 Damp-proof membrane
2 Ridge tiles	9 Weatherboarding	16 Lintel	23 Timber sole plate
3 Tile battens	10 Brick cladding tied to timber frame	17 Insulation	24 Concrete slab
4 Roofing felt	11 Stud partition	18 Vapour barrier	25 Ground
5 Trussed rafters	12 Chipboard floor	19 Floor battens	
6 Timber-framed loadbearing wall	13 First floor platform	20 Staircase	
7 Plywood sheathing	14 Plasterboard ceiling	21 Concrete screed	

WALLS: EXTERNAL WALLS

Solid walls provide good sound insulation, but poor thermal insulation. There are three basic types: made from brick, block or natural stone. Cavity walls, a relatively modern form of construction, are more effective in preventing moisture penetration and heat loss than solid walls.

SEE ALSO

◁ Details for:
Damp-proof course	251
Brick bonding	426
Rendering walls	168-171
Cavity insulation	269
Brick types	422-423
Concrete blocks	423

How solid walls are made

Solid walls are mainly constructed from bonded brickwork or concrete blocks, although local natural stone is also used in certain areas. They're usually at least 225mm (9in) thick – the length of a standard brick – but if they're exposed to severe weather conditions, are frequently a brick and a half thick.

Moisture resistance
Moisture is prevented from penetrating to the inside surface of the wall by evaporation. Rainwater absorbed by the bricks is normally drawn out before it reaches the inner surface. Moisture is prevented from being absorbed from the ground by an impervious damp-proof course (DPC), usually of bituminous felt, set in a bed joint of the brickwork at least 150mm (6in) – two brick courses – from ground level (◁).

Weatherproofing qualities
Many solid walls are cement-rendered or otherwise clad to weatherproof the brickwork. Exterior-grade concrete blocks 225mm (9in) thick can be left exposed but their appearance is improved by rendering. Natural stone walls are usually left bare and weatherproofing relies solely on thickness and density of the material.

Solid walls
Traditional brick and stone walls will vary in thickness according to the age and size of the building. Concrete blocks are now common.

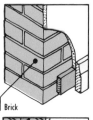
Brick

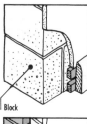
Block

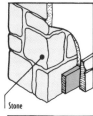
Stone

Cavity walls
This type has replaced solid walls in modern houses. A combination of brick, block and timber frame may be used to construct a cavity wall where brick is usually used for the outer leaf.

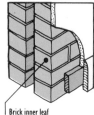
Brick inner leaf

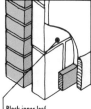
Block inner leaf

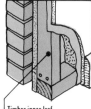
Timber inner leaf

How cavity walls are made

Cavity walls consist of two 100mm (4in) thick walls or 'leaves', separated by a 50mm (2in) gap. They may be constructed from bricks, concrete blocks, hollow clay bricks or timber framing, or a combination of these. The stretcher-bonded (◁) leaves must be tied together to make them stable with metal wall ties (See left).

For the cavity to work as a moisture barrier, it is essential that the gap is not bridged. This can happen if mortar collects on the ties during construction.

Where openings occur at a door or window the cavity is closed and a DPC provided to stop moisture seeping in. Weep holes – unmortared vertical joints between every third or fourth brick – are usually provided in the outer leaf above lintels and below the main DPC. Their function is to drain any moisture from the cavity that penetrates the outer leaf.

Cavity walls may be given improved thermal insulation by installing insulating panels as the wall is built, or filling with an insulating material later on (◁).

Cavity ties
Cavity wall ties are laid in the bed joints at 900mm (3ft) spacings horizontally and 450mm (1ft 6in) vertically and staggered on alternate rows.

Wire butterfly tie

Sheet metal tie

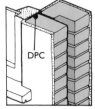
Vertical DPC at window opening in cavity wall.

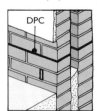
Weep holes are formed below main DPC.

IDENTIFYING LOADBEARING AND NON-LOADBEARING WALLS

The external walls of the house transmit the loads of suspended timber floors, most of the roof and other structures to the foundations. Usually all the external walls are loadbearing. The floor and ceiling joists and other internal walls might also be carried on loadbearing internal walls.

Not all internal walls are loadbearing or 'structural', however: loadbearing walls can be identified by their position in the structure, and the materials used in their construction.

A wall which carries the floor joists will have the floorboards running parallel with it. Check at each floor level as a wall which passes through the centre of the house may carry the first floor but not the ground floor. Floor joists are usually run in the direction of the shortest span. Check roof braces, which may bear on an internal wall.

Loadbearing walls are usually made of brick or loadbearing concrete blocks. Occasionally, wooden stud walls are used to carry some weight. A wall may also be termed loadbearing or structural where it is not carrying a load but is adding to the stability of the structure, perhaps stiffening an adjacent wall.

Non-loadbearing walls
Walls which divide the floor space into rooms, and not intended to support the structure, are known as non-loadbearing. They may be made of brick, lightweight concrete blocks, timber studding or cellular core wallboard, and are usually only a single storey in height. If the floorboards run under the wall you can safely assume that the wall is non-loadbearing.

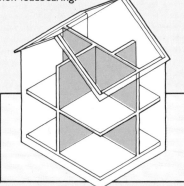
Non-loadbearing walls
These walls divide the internal space into smaller rooms and are relatively lightweight.

INTERNAL WALLS

There are basically two types of internal wall: party walls, which divide houses built side by side, and partition walls, which divide up the space within the house. The former are structural, the latter load or non-loadbearing.

Party wall construction

Party walls, or separating walls, are shared solid walls which divide houses built side by side. Party walls separate the properties over the entire height of the building to prevent the spread of fire and provide good sound insulation.

Partition walls

Internal partition walls can be loadbearing or non-loadbearing, but are usually relatively lightweight and not more than one brick thick. Partition walls for houses may be made from brick, concrete blocks, hollow clay blocks, timber framing or cellular core wallboard (See below). A plaster finish is usually applied to brick or block walls for a smooth surface.

Stud-partition walls
Timber-framed partitions called stud walls are common in new and old houses. They are usually made from 100m (4in) wide sawn softwood. The vertical timbers, called studs, may be placed 350mm (1ft 2in), 400mm (1ft 4in) or 600mm (2ft) apart. Diagonal braces may be included for strength.
Laths – thin strips of wood nailed horizontally to the studs – are used as a key for plaster in old houses; plasterboard has now replaced lath-and-plaster on this type of wall. Although stud walls are usually non-loadbearing, they can carry a lateral load.
Stud walls offer a convenient duct for running services such as wiring but because of their hollow construction, special fixings are required when attaching anything to the surface (▷).

Lightweight concrete blocks
Blocks are widely used for modern partition walls. They're made to course with bricks and are nominally 150 to 225mm (6 to 9in) high and 450 or 600mm (1ft 6in or 2ft) long.
The most common size is 450 x 225mm (1ft 6in x 9in) and a range of thicknesses from 50 to 300mm (2 to 12in) is available – use the 100mm (4in) wide block for a partition wall. This size corresponds to standard brick bonding, being equal to three courses high and two bricks long. Blocks are grey in colour, made from cement and lightweight aggregate. Their large size makes building a wall quick and simple. They provide good sound and thermal insulation and are fireproof. Fixings can be made at any point on the wall using special plugs, and services can be channelled into the surface. Blocks are cut easily with a bolster chisel.

Hollow clay blocks
Clay blocks are red in colour, may be smooth-faced or horizontally grooved as a key for a plaster coating, and are hollow for a lightweight wall that has good sound and thermal insulation properties and is fireproof. Hollow clay blocks do not take nails well; fixings should be made with screws and suitable cavity fixings. Where nailing is required – for fixing skirtings or door linings, for example – solid blocks would be incorporated.

Cellular-core wallboard
This manufactured wall panel is made from two sheets of plasterboard with a gridded cardboard core bonded between them. It is available in similar sizes to standard plasterboard sheets, and 50, 56 or 63mm (2, 2¼ or 2½in) thick. The cell structure makes a light but rigid partitioning that is simple to install and can be decorated directly or finished with plaster. All fixings to this type of wall require a screwed cavity device unless wooden plugs are fitted during erection. The plugs are short lengths of the battening used to fix the panels together. It is necessary to pre-plan the placing of the fixtures before the plugs are driven into the core from the edge. The face of the board is marked to indicate the positions of the plugs before the partition is assembled. Clear channels for cable or pipe runs before assembly.

SEE ALSO

Details for: ▷
Cavity fixings	499
Fitting services	139
Cellular-core partitions	140-141
Traditional plastering	148
Plasterboard	158
Concrete blocks	423
Building a block wall	434
Cutting blocks	434

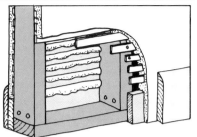

Lath-and-plaster stud partition

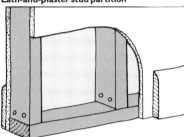

Plasterboarded stud partition

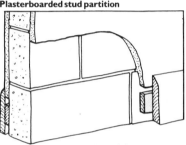

Plastered concrete block partition

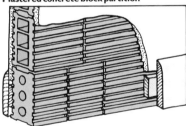

Plastered hollow clay-block partition

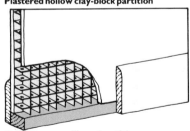

Cellular-core wallboard partition

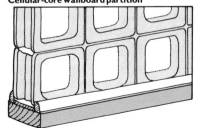

Glass-block partition

Glass blocks
Hollow glass blocks can be used for non-loadbearing feature walls. Made in square and rectangular shapes and a range of colours they can be laid in mortar or dry-fixed with plastic jointing strips in a frame.

TYPES OF LINTEL

A lintel bridges the gap above an opening. The type used will depend on the size of the opening and availability.

WOOD

Wooden lintels were commonly built into the brick walls of older houses, often in exterior walls, behind a stone lintel or brick arch. They can suffer from rot due to penetrating damp, but are still used in timber-framed houses.

BRICK

Brick lintels are used with wood, steel or concrete lintels over external openings but are not strong. Some are supported by a flat or angled metal bar.

STONE

A feature of the exterior of older houses, stone is not strong in tension and cannot be used for wide spans. The stone block does not usually support the full thickness of the wall – a timber lintel is often used behind it.

CONCRETE

Concrete lintels are used for interior and exterior openings. Concrete is good in compression but not in tension. To overcome this, metal rods are embedded in the lower portion of the beam to reinforce it. Prestressed concrete lintels, reinforced with wire strands set in the concrete under tension, are lighter than other concrete lintels. Concrete lintels are made in a range of sizes to match brick and block courses and to suit various wall thickness. Though capable of spanning large openings, their weight can make handling awkward.

STEEL

Galvanized pressed steel lintels are widely used for internal and external openings. They are designed for cavity and solid walls of brick and block or timber-framed construction. Versions for cavity walls include a tray to channel moisture to the outside. Standard sections and lengths are available and are fairly lightweight. Some are perforated for plastering direct.

Heavyweight rolled steel joists (RSJs) are mainly used when making two rooms into one (◁). The supplier will cut the I-section beam to length.

SEE ALSO

◁ Details for:
Building	
Regulations	18-19
Adjustable props	125
Rolled steel joists	128
Choosing a beam	129
Calculating a beam	129
Steel lintels	198

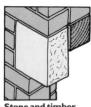
Stone and timber

Brick and steel

Reinforced concrete

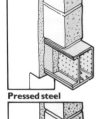
Pressed steel

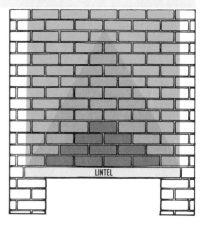
Rolled steel

SPANNING OPENINGS IN WALLS

A doorway, window or hatchway requires an opening to be created in the wall. In a loadbearing wall, the top of the opening must be built to carry the structure above – even cutting a hole in a partition means propping the masonry.

Where supports are needed

Door or window frames aren't designed to carry superimposed loads, so the load from floors above – even the brickwork above the opening – must be supported by a rigid beam called a lintel, which transmits the weight to the sides where the bearings are firm. Wider openings call for stronger beams, such as rolled steel joists (RSJs). There are numerous beams, but all work in the same way.

The forces on a beam

When a load is placed at the centre of a beam supported at each end, the beam will bend. The lower portion is being stretched and is in 'tension'; the top portion is being squeezed and is in 'compression'. The beam is also subjected to 'shear' forces where the vertical load is trying to sever the beam at the points of support. A beam must be able to resist these forces. This is achieved by the correct choice of material and the depth of the beam in relation to the imposed load and the span of the opening.

Calculating lintel size

The purpose of a lintel is to form a straight bridge across an opening, which can carry the load of the structure above it. The load may be relatively light, being no more than a number of brick or block courses. It is more likely that other loads from upper floors and the roof will also bear on the lintel.

The size of the lintel must be suitable for the job it has to do. The size should be derived from calculations based on the weight of the materials used in the construction of the building. Calculation for specifying a beam is a job for an architect or structural engineer. Tables relating to the weight of the materials are used on which to base the figures.

In practice, for typical situations, a builder can help you decide on the required size of lintel based on his experience. A Building Control Officer will be happy to accept this type of specification but he can insist that proper calculations are submitted with your application for Building Regulations approval (◁).

When to support a wall

If you are creating a door, window or hatchway which is no wider than 1m (3ft) across in a non-loadbearing wall you can cut the hole without having to support the walling above providing the wall is properly bonded and sound. The only area of brickwork that is likely to collapse is roughly in the shape of a 45 degree triangle directly above the opening leaving a self-supporting stepped arch of brickwork. This effect is known as self-corbelling. Do not rely on the self-corbelling effect to support the wall if you plan to make an opening which is more than 1m (3ft) wide. In that case, temporarily support the wall as if it were loadbearing.

Before you make any opening in a loadbearing wall you will need to erect adjustable props (◁) as temporary supports, not only for the weight of the masonry but also for the loads that bear on it from floors, walls and roof above.

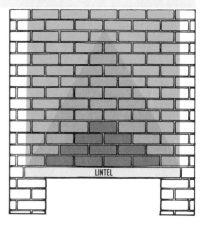

Self-corbelling
The shaded bricks are the only ones at risk of falling out before the lintel is installed because of the self-corbelling effect of the bricks above. Theoretically the lintel supports the weight of the materials within the 60 degree triangle plus any superimposed floor or roof loading, but when the side walls (piers) are narrow, the load on the lintel is increased to encompass the area of the rectangle.

RIGGING UP ADJUSTABLE PROPS

To remove part of a loadbearing wall it's necessary to temporarily support the wall above the opening. Hire adjustable steel props (▷) and scaffold boards to spread the load across the floor. Where the brickwork will remain below the ceiling level, you will also need 'needles' to spread the load. Needles must be of sawn timber at least 150 x 100mm (6 x 4in) in section and about 1.8m (6ft) long.

For a hatchway or door opening, probably only one needle and two props will suffice: place the needle centrally over the opening about 150mm (6in) above the lintel position. For wider openings, or where a load is great, two needles and four props will be needed, spaced no more than 1m (3ft) apart across the width of the opening.

Chop a hole in the wall for each needle and slot them through. Support each end with a prop, which works like a car jack. Stand the props on scaffold boards no more than 600mm (2ft) from each side of the wall.

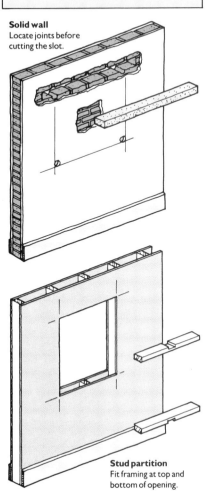

Solid wall
Locate joints before cutting the slot.

Stud partition
Fit framing at top and bottom of opening.

MAKING A HATCHWAY

A serving hatch is a convenient opening in a wall, usually between a kitchen and dining area, through which you can pass food, drinks and equipment. If you are blocking off a doorway, or making a stud wall, it may be advantageous to allow for a hatch. You may want to make a hatchway in an existing wall.

Planning the size and shape

Ideally the bottom of the opening should be an extension of the kitchen worktop or at least flush with a work surface: 900mm (3ft) is a comfortable working height (▷) and the standard height for kitchen worktops. For practicality – passing through a tray and serving dishes, for instance – it should not be narrower than 750mm (2ft 6in).

Hatches should be fitted with some means of closing the opening for privacy, preventing cooking smells from drifting and, in some cases, as a fire-check (See right).

Creating the opening

You can make a hatchway in either a loadbearing or a solid non-loadbearing wall in much the same way: the main requirement with the former is temporarily supporting the masonry above and the load imposed on the wall. Mark the position for the hatch on one side of the wall. Align the hole with the vertical and horizontal mortar courses between bricks or blocks to save having to cut too many bricks – hack off a square of plaster at the centre to locate the joints.

Mark out the shape and position of the opening on the other side of the wall using adjacent walls, the ceiling and floor as references, or drill through at the corners. Make the hole about 25mm (1in) oversize to allow for fitting a lining frame. Mark the lintel position.

Set up adjustable props and needles if you're working on a loadbearing wall (See left), then chop a slot for the lintel with a club hammer and bolster chisel – on a brick wall this will probably be a single course of bricks deep; on a block wall, remove a whole course of blocks and fill the gap with bricks. Trowel mortar onto the bearings and lift on the lintel. Use a spirit level to check that the lintel is perfectly horizontal – pack under it with pieces of slate if necessary. Replace any bricks above the lintel that have dropped. Leave for 24 hours to set, then remove props and needles and hack away the masonry below.

Making a hatchway in a stud wall

Cutting an opening in a stud partition wall is simpler than making one in a solid wall, but if the wall bears some weight you'll need to support the floor or ceiling above with props using planks to spread the load.

Mark out, then cut away the plasterboard or lath-and-plaster covering from each side to expose the studs. For a hatch the width between studs (about 450mm/1ft 6in), just skew-nail a nogging between them at the top and bottom of the opening. If it's to be wider, make the opening span three studs. Cut away part of the middle stud at the height you want the hatch, allowing for the thickness of a horizontal frame member above and below the opening. Make the framing from studding timber and cut them to fit between the two studs on each side of the cut one. Fit and check for level.

Fitting a lining frame

Line the four sides of the hatch opening with 25mm (1in) thick planed softwood joined at the corners with butt joints or bare-faced tongued and grooved joints (▷) for a neater result. The frame can either finish flush with the plaster wall surface and be covered with an architrave, or it can project beyond the plaster to form a lip or shelf.

The sides of the opening in a masonry wall are likely to be rough – it's not easy to chop a clean line. Make and fit the frame, then pack out the gap between masonry and lining with offcuts of wood – the frame must be truly square within the opening; check this with a spirit level. Screw the frame to the masonry using fixing plugs, fitted when the frame is positioned. Make good with mortar all round it. Rake back the surface of the mortar and when set finish flush with plaster.

SEE ALSO

Details for: ▷	
Kitchen work height	16
Adjustable props	130
T&G joint	190

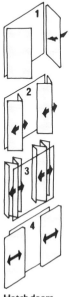

Hatch doors
1 Double-hinged
2 Twin bi-fold
3 Concertina
4 Horizontal-sliding

Finishing the frame
Use an architrave to cover the joint between the lining and wall or let the frame project to mask it.

Fit an architrave

Let frame project

CUTTING AN INTERNAL DOORWAY

INSTALLING THE LINTEL

Making a doorway in an existing wall may be necessary if you're changing the use of the room or improving its layout: this is typical when converting a kitchen, where fitted units dictate the positions of access and exit doors. As with fitting a hatchway (◁), it's necessary to install a lintel to ensure the stability of the wall itself and any other load which bears on it.

SEE ALSO

◁ Details for:
Loadbearing walls	122
Partition walls	123
Making a hatchway	125
Adjustable props	125
Closing floor gap	133
Locating studs	137
Plastering	152, 164
Door casings	185
Fixing a casing	190
Masonry saw	479

I Fix galvanized ties

2 Nail to wedges

Preparing a brick or block wall

First check whether the wall is non-loadbearing or loadbearing (◁). If the former, seek approval from the Building Control Officer (BCO). Mark the opening on one side of the wall, then examine the coursing of the bricks or blocks by exposing a small area; move the opening if necessary to align the perimeter with the vertical joints.

The height should allow for the height of the door plus 10mm (⅜in) tolerance, the thickness of the soffit lining and a new concrete or steel lintel. The width of the opening should be the width of the door plus 6mm (¼in) tolerance and twice the thickness of the door jamb lining. Allow a further 12mm (½in) for fitting the lining.

Carefully prise off the skirtings from both sides of the wall. They can be cut and reused later. Prop the wall and fit the lintel (See right) before cutting out the bulk of the masonry. Leave overnight for the bearings to set hard. The next day, starting from the top just below the lintel, chop out the individual bricks using a club hammer and bolster chisel. At the sides of the opening cut

the half or three-quarter bricks protruding into the doorway. Chop downwards where you can. If the wall is built from lightweight blocks, use a universal hand saw or a masonry saw (◁) to slice through the bonding.

Bag up the rubble frequently in stout polythene sacks and stack whole bricks out of the way for re-use. Spray the area with water from a plant sprayer to settle the dust.

At the bottom, chop out the brickwork to just below floor level so that you can continue the flooring(◁).

Fitting the door lining

You'll have to fit a timber frame within the new doorway to which you can attach the stop-bead, door and decorative architrave (◁). Make the frame from planed timber 25mm (1in) thick and the width of the wall. Fit the lining (◁) to the sides of the opening with galvanized metal frame cramps (**I**) mortared into slots cut in the brickwork, or fit wooden wedges in the mortar joints and nail the frame to them (See diagram (**2**) left).

Draw in the position for the lintel, allowing a margin for fitting tolerance. Chop a groove around the perimeter of the opening with a club hammer and bolster chisel, then hack off the plaster. Fit adjustable metal props and needles (◁), then cut a slot for the lintel. Bed a concrete lintel in a mortar mix of 1 part cement: 3 parts sand on bearings no narrower than 150mm (6in) at each side of the slot, and set level. Pack underneath with pieces of slate to wedge it horizontal. Replace loose bricks and fill any gaps with the same mortar mix.

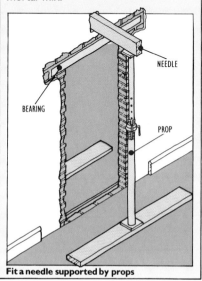

NEEDLE

BEARING

PROP

Fit a needle supported by props

Dealing with a stud wall

First locate the positions of the studs (◁), then prise off the skirting. Mark out the position for the opening on the wall then remove the plasterwork. For lath-and-plaster walls, chop through to the laths with a bolster chisel, then saw the strips off. For a plasterboard wall, saw through the cladding or use a sharp trimming knife. If there are studs on each side of the opening, cut the laths or plasterboard flush with these timbers. The hole position often won't correspond with the studs, so cut back to the centre of the nearest stud on each side. Cut one or two studs to the required height—door plus 10mm (⅜in) tolerance and the lining thickness plus a 50mm (2in) head member.

Level up and skew-nail the head member to the remaining studs at each end. Also dovetail-nail it to the ends of the cut studs. Saw through and remove the floor plate to the width of the door, plus 6mm (¼in) tolerance and twice the

thickness of the door lining. Cut and nail the new studs, which will form the door jambs, to fit between the head and sill. Fit noggings between the new and original stud or studs. Cut and nail plasterboard to fill the gaps between the original wall surface and the new studs. Make and fit the door lining (◁). Finish the surfaces with plaster (◁), fit the architraves and replace the skirting.

Alternatively, cut the cladding from floor to ceiling and refit the studding flush with the cut edge. Mark the width of the opening, saw through the plaster from both sides of the wall then strip the plasterwork and knock out the exposed studs and noggings. Cut the floor sill level with the plaster and remove. Drive the studs into the cut edges until flush. Nail them at top and bottom. Fit a door head member between them and a short vertical stud above it. Cover the space above the doorway with plasterboard.

Door aligns with studs   **Door is misaligned**

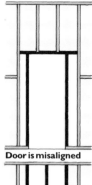

Making the frame
The method you adopt for the frame will depend on the positions of the studs. The diagrams illustrate typical solutions.

Studs repositioned

FILLING AN OPENING IN A STUD PARTITION

Strip the door lining as described (See right). Trim the lath-and-plaster or plasterboard back to the centre line of the door jamb studs and head member, with a sharp trimming knife. Lever out the old nails with a claw hammer. Nail the new cut edge all round.

Nail a matching sill to the floor between the studs. Cut and nail a new stud centrally between head and sill. Cut and nail noggings between the studs across the opening. Fix plasterboard to each face of the opening. Cut the board 3mm (⅛in) less all round. Fill and tape the joints (▷), then finish as required with wallcovering or tiles (▷).

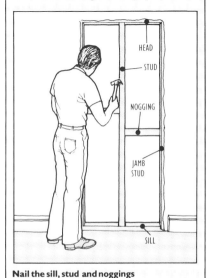

Nail the sill, stud and noggings

BLOCKING OFF A DOORWAY

If you are making a new opening in a wall, it's possible that you will also have to block off the original one.

Obviously, you'll want the patch to be invisible, which takes careful plastering or joint filling of plasterboard.

Choosing the right materials

It is generally better to fill in the opening with the same materials used in the construction of the wall – although you can consider bricks and blocks as the same – to prevent cracks forming due to movement in the structure. You could use a wooden stud frame with a plasterboard lining and plaster finish to fill an opening in a brick wall, but it would not have the same acoustic properties as a solid infill and cracks are difficult to prevent or disguise.

Removing the woodwork

Saw through the door jamb linings close to the top and prise them away from the brickwork with a wrecking bar. Start levering at the bottom. If the linings were fitted before the flooring, the ends could be trapped: cut them flush with the floor. Next, prise the soffit board away from the top.

Bricking up the opening

Cut back the plaster about 150mm (6in) all round the opening. It need not be an even line; unevenness helps to disguise the outline of the doorway.

To bond the new brickwork into the old, cut out a half-brick on each side of the opening at every fourth course, using a club hammer and bolster chisel. For a block wall, remove a quarter of a block from alternate courses.

It's not vital to tooth-in the infill if you're using blocks (which are easy and quick to lay) as it will require more cutting to fit. Instead, 100mm (4in) cut clasp nails driven dovetail fashion into the bed joints of the side brickwork (1) can be used to tie the masonry together. Galvanized metal frame cramps can also be used to save cutting into the bricks (2) – screw them to the wall, resting on every fourth brick.

Lay the bricks or blocks in mortar, following the original courses. If a wooden suspended floor runs through the opening, lay the bricks on a timber sole plate nailed across the opening. When the mortar has set, spread on a base coat of plaster, followed by a finishing coat (▷). Fit two complete lengths of new matching skirting, or add to the original. When making up the skirting from old pieces, make sure the joints do not occur in the same place as the original opening.

SEE ALSO	
Details for: ▷	
Papering walls	93-97
Tiling	99-106
Plasterwork	148-153
Taping joints	164
Fitting skirting	181
Door casings	185

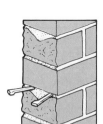

1 Nail ties

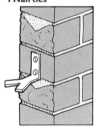

2 Frame cramp

Lay bricks into the courses

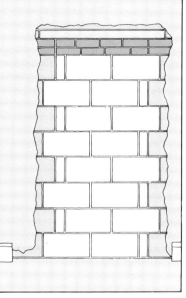

Cut blocks to match bonding

Cut out half-bricks

CONVERTING TWO ROOMS TO ONE

Making a through room is the best way to improve access between areas frequently used – the dining and living rooms, for instance – and of course expands your living space considerably. The job uses similar principles to making a hatchway or a new doorway, although on a much larger scale. Removing a dividing wall – whether it's structural or simply a non-loadbearing partition – is a major undertaking, but it needn't be daunting. If you follow some basic safety and rigid structural rules, much of the job is straightforward, if messy and disruptive. Before you start, plan out your requirements and consult the at-a-glance flow chart, right, for a break-down of just what's involved.

SEE ALSO

◁ Details for:

Planning for people	13-16
Obtaining approval	17-19
Removing walls	130-133

WHY DO YOU WANT A THROUGH ROOM?

Before you go ahead and demolish the wall between two rooms, consider just how the new space might function, its appearance, the time it will take you to carry out the work, and the cost.

Ask yourself the following questions:
● Will the shape and size of the new room suit your needs? Remember, if you have a young family, your needs are likely to change as they grow up.
● Will most of the family activities be carried out in the same room (eating, watching TV, playing music, reading, conversation, playing with toys, hobbies, homework)?
● Will removing the wall deprive you of privacy within the family, or from passers-by in the street?
● Will the new room feel like one unit and not a conversion? For example, do the skirtings and mouldings match? Are the fireplaces acceptable when seen together, or should one be removed? Should one of the doorways, if close together, be blocked off?
● Will the loss of a wall make the furniture arrangements difficult – particularly if central heating radiators are in use and take up valuable wall space elsewhere?
● Will the heating and lighting need to be modified?
● Will the proposed shape of the opening be in character with the room and the right proportion?

●**Hiring professionals**
If you're in doubt, hire a professional builder: to save costs, you may be able to work as a labourer or do preparation and clearing work .

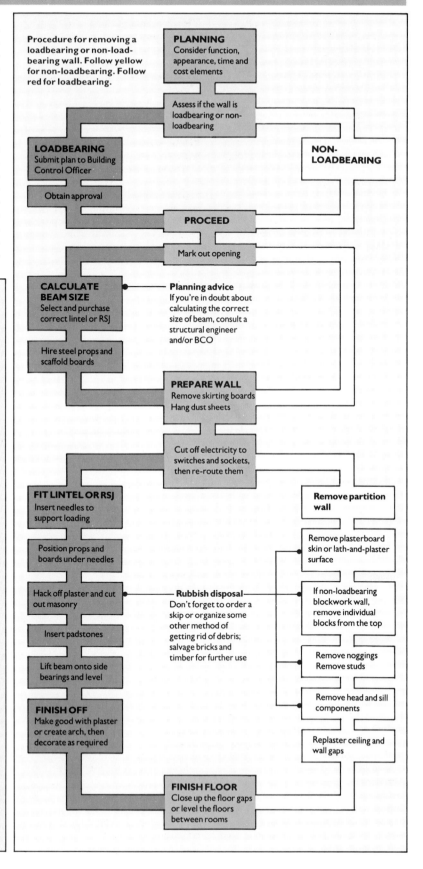

Procedure for removing a loadbearing or non-load-bearing wall. Follow yellow for non-loadbearing. Follow red for loadbearing.

PLANNING
Consider function, appearance, time and cost elements

Assess if the wall is loadbearing or non-loadbearing

LOADBEARING
Submit plan to Building Control Officer

Obtain approval

NON-LOADBEARING

PROCEED

Mark out opening

CALCULATE BEAM SIZE
Select and purchase correct lintel or RSJ

Hire steel props and scaffold boards

Planning advice
If you're in doubt about calculating the correct size of beam, consult a structural engineer and/or BCO

PREPARE WALL
Remove skirting boards
Hang dust sheets

Cut off electricity to switches and sockets, then re-route them

FIT LINTEL OR RSJ
Insert needles to support loading

Position props and boards under needles

Hack off plaster and cut out masonry

Insert padstones

Lift beam onto side bearings and level

FINISH OFF
Make good with plaster or create arch, then decorate as required

Rubbish disposal
Don't forget to order a skip or organize some other method of getting rid of debris; salvage bricks and timber for further use

Remove partition wall

Remove plasterboard skin or lath-and-plaster surface

If non-loadbearing blockwork wall, remove individual blocks from the top

Remove noggings
Remove studs

Remove head and sill components

Replaster ceiling and wall gaps

FINISH FLOOR
Close up the floor gaps or level the floors between rooms

SUPPORTING THE STRUCTURAL WALL

Once you have satisfied yourself that the opening will be an improvement to your home's layout, consider the practical problems: first determine whether or not the wall is loadbearing or a non-loadbearing partition (▷).

Choosing a beam

The most suitable beam for a through room is usually a rolled-steel joist (RSJ), although this type of beam will require special preparation before it can be plastered over. Reinforced and pre-stressed concrete lintels can also be used for openings up to about 3m (10ft), but, over a wide span, their considerable weight makes them difficult to handle; pre-stressed types are lighter but best suited to single door or hatch openings (▷) rather than wide spans. Pressed steel box lintels – available in lengths up to 5.4m (about 18ft) – are much lighter and can be plastered directly.

Mark out the proposed opening on the wall with chalk to help you visualise its size and proportion. Bear in mind that a loadbearing wall will need a beam spanning the opening with at least 150mm (6in) bearings at each end.

What size beam?
For specifying an RSJ the following rule of thumb can be employed, although exact details depend on the particular location and the result must be approved by the Building Control Officer. For pressed steel lintels, refer to the manufacturer for sizes:

CALCULATING THE SIZE OF A BEAM
A rule-of-thumb guide used by builders
Make beam 25mm (1in) deep for every 300mm (1ft) span.

Height of opening

The height of the opening is to some extent determined by the height of the ceiling and the depth of the beam. The depth of the beam is determined by the width of the opening it has to span, and the load it must carry. Consult an architect or structural engineer who, for a fee, can calculate this for you. The beam can be positioned directly under the ceiling joists of a low ceiling.

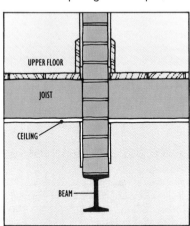

Brickwork supported below ceiling level

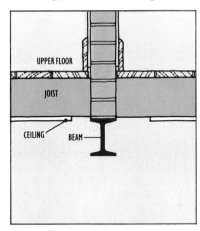

Brickwork supported directly under ceiling

Applying for permission

Before any work is started on a loadbearing wall you must seek approval from your local authority's Building Control Officer. He will require a drawing showing the proposed opening, its overall height and width and how the structure above the opening is to be supported. This need not be drawn up by a professional, but it should be clear. Approval is unlikely to be withheld providing the work complies with the Building Regulations (▷). The BCO must be satisfied that the removal of the wall will not weaken the structure of the house, or any buildings attached to it, and that it does not encourage the spread of fire. Where a party wall is involved, it will be necessary to get written approval from your neighbour. The BCO will advise you.

HOW A BEAM IS SUPPORTED

The supports are usually brick piers, which are in effect columns attached to the side walls and formed from the remainder of the old wall. Concrete padstones are required on which to sit the beam. The BCO may want the piers increased in thickness to give sufficient support to the beam and the side flanking wall.

Ideally, it would be better if no piers were used as they interrupt the line of the side walls running through. It might be possible to run the ends of the beam into the walls, eliminating the need for piers, but this must be subject to local approval. It would require a horizontal concrete beam called a spreader set in the wall to distribute the load across more of the wall.

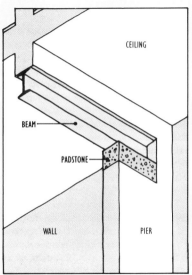

Pier capped by padstone supports the beam

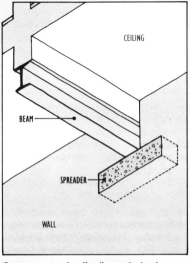

Concrete spreader distributes the load

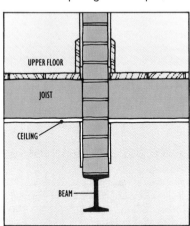

SEE ALSO

Details for: ▷

Building Regulations	18-19
Loadbearing walls	122
Partition walls	123
Types of lintel	124

SEE ALSO

◁ Details for:
Adjustable props 125
Removing skirting 181
Measuring tools 478
Hammers 479
Chisels 480

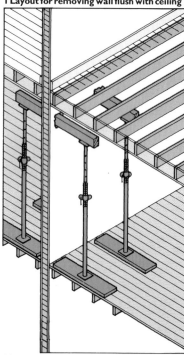

1 Layout for removing wall flush with ceiling

Supporting the wall
1 When removing a wall up to ceiling level, support the upper floor with scaffold boards and props alone when the joists pass through the brickwork to support the wall. Otherwise, in addition, use needles on jacks placed directly above the props.
2 Normally brickwork projects below the ceiling level and is supported on needles passing through holes in the wall.

2 Layout for removing wall below ceiling

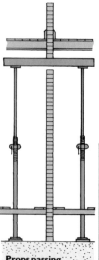

Props passing through the suspended floor

130

TRANSFER THE LOAD TO THE SUBFLOOR

If the floor appears to spring when you jump on it, consult a builder to make sure the floor can carry the weight imposed. It may be necessary to lift some of the floorboards and support the props on the foundations. In older houses, where there is no concrete below the floor, scaffold boards must be placed under the props to spread the load over the ground.

REMOVING THE WALL

To remove part of a loadbearing wall you must temporarily support the walling above the opening. You will need to hire adjustable steel props (◁), and scaffold boards on which to support them. Where the beam is to be placed at ceiling level, hire extra boards to support the ceiling (**1**). Generally you will have to fit needles through the wall to transfer the load to the props (**2**). The needles must be at least 150 × 100mm (6 × 4in) in section.

Hire sufficient props to be spaced not more than 1m (3ft) apart across the width of the opening. If possible, buy the beam after the Building Control Officer's inspection. It can then be cut to your exact requirements.

Preparation and marking out
Remove the skirting boards from both sides of the wall (◁). Working from one side, mark out the position of the beam on the wall in pencil. Use a steel tape measure, spirit level and straightedge for accuracy.

Hang dust sheets around the work area on the opposite face of the wall to help contain much of the inevitable airborne dust; attach them with battens nailed over them at the top. Seal gaps around all doors with masking tape to prevent the dust from travelling throughout the house. Open windows in the rooms you're working in.

Inserting the needles
Mark the positions for the needles on the wall, then cut away the plaster locally and chisel a hole through the brickwork at each point. Finish level with the bottom of one course of bricks. Make the holes slightly oversize so you can easily pass the needles through. Position a pair of adjustable props under each needle not more than 600mm (2ft) from each side of the wall. Stand the props on scaffold boards to spread the load over the floor.

Adjust the props to take the weight of the structure and nail their base plates to the supporting boards to prevent them being dislodged.

Supporting the ceiling
If the ceiling needs supporting, stand the props on scaffold boards at each side of the wall and adjust so they're virtually to ceiling height – they should be placed 600mm (2ft) from the wall. Place another plank on top of the pairs of props and adjust simultaneously until the ceiling joists are supported.

Removing the wall
Hack off the plaster using a club hammer and bolster chisel, then start to cut out the brickwork, working from the top. Once you've removed four or five courses, cut the bricks at the side of the opening. Chop downwards with the bolster pointing in towards the wall to cut the bricks cleanly. Remove all the brickwork down to one course below the floorboards. Clear the rubble as you work into stout polythene sacks – it may be worth hiring a skip. The job is slow and extremely laborious, but you can make it easier and quicker using a power brick-cutting saw (See below).

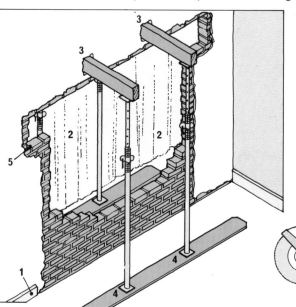

Cutting the opening
1 Remove or cut back the skirting and mark the beam's position.
2 Hang dust sheets around the work area.
3 Cut openings and insert needles.
4 Stand props on scaffold boards and adjust them to support the needles.
5 Cut away the plaster, then chisel out the bricks starting from the top of the opening.

Brick-cutting saw

PLACING THE BEAM

Building piers

If the wall you're removing is deemed unsuitable as a basis for the supporting piers, you have two other choices. Where the adjacent wall is double thickness, you may be able to cut a hole to take the end of the beam allowing the weight to be distributed to the existing foundations. If this isn't possible, you'll have to build new piers with their own foundations. The piers must be built below the floor on concrete padstones cast on hardcore; they must include a DPC – engineering bricks may suffice – and must themselves be bonded in single – or double – brick thickness and toothed at every fourth course into the brickwork of the adjoining wall. The BCO will tell you the size for the piers.

Installing the beam

Make two wooden forms or boxes from thick plywood or softwood and cast concrete padstones (on which to bed the RSJ) to the size required by the BCO. Mix the concrete to the proportions 1 part cement: 2 parts sand: 4 parts aggregate. When set, bed the padstones in mortar at the top of each pier. When a large padstone is required, it may be better to cast it in situ: set up formwork at the required height on each side and check the level between the two.

Build a work platform by placing doubled-up scaffold boards between steady stepladders, or hire scaffold tower sections. You'll need help to lift the beam into position.

Apply mortar to the padstones, then lift and set the RSJ in place. Pack pieces of slate between the beam and the brickwork above to fill out the gap. Alternatively, 'dry-pack' the gap with a mortar mix of 1 part cement: 3 parts sand, which is just wet enough to bind it together. Work it well into the gap with a bricklaying trowel and compact it with a wooden batten and a hammer. Where the gap can take a whole brick or more, apply a bed of mortar and rebuild the brickwork on top of the beam. Work the course between the needles so that when the timbers are removed the holes can be filled in to continue the bonding. Allow two days for the mortar to set, then remove the props and the needles and fill in the holes.

When the beam is fitted against ceiling joists you can use a different method. Support the ceiling with props and a board to spread the load (See left), on each side of the wall. Cut away the wall, then lift the beam into position and fit a pair of adjustable props under it. Apply mortar to the top of the beam and screw up the props to push it against the joists and brickwork above. Bed padstones in mortar or build formwork at each end and cast them.

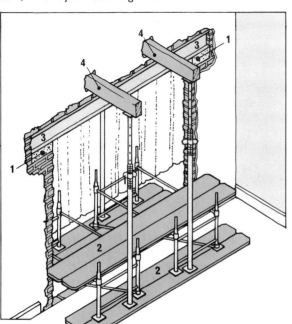

Installing the beam
1 Cast concrete padstones and set them on the brickwork piers.
2 Set up a secure platform to enable two people to work safely.
3 Place the beam on the mortared padstones and check level. Fill the gaps between the beam and the brickwork.
4 When set remove the props and needles and fill the holes.

FINISHING THE BEAM

A steel beam should be enclosed to provide protection from fire (which would cause it to distort) and to give a flat surface that can be decorated. Wet plaster, plasterboard or a specially made fireproof board can be used.

Cladding with plaster

Box in an RSJ with expanded galvanized metal mesh to provide a key for the plaster. Fold the mesh around the beam, then lap it up onto the brickwork above and secure with galvanized nails.

Alternatively, wedge shaped wooden blocks (soldiers) into the recessed sides of the beam and nail the expanded metal to these. It's a good idea to prime the cut edges of the mesh to prevent corrosion which can stain the plaster.

Making good with plasterboard

To box in the beam with plasterboard, you will need to fit shaped wooden blocks, wedged into the sides. To these fix wooden battens nailed together to make fixings for the plasterboard panels (if you plan to install a folding door system in the opening, you can nail the door lining directly to these same fixings (▷). Set the plasterboard about 3mm (⅛in) below plaster level to allow for a skim coat to finish flush with the surrounding wall. Fill and seal the joints with tape (▷).

Plaster the piers, then finish the beam and pier together.

Disguising the beam

You can conceal the angular RSJ by fitting a simulated oak beam, moulded from rigid urethane foam plastic, which can be simply glued or nailed over the beam, to give a country cottage effect to the room.

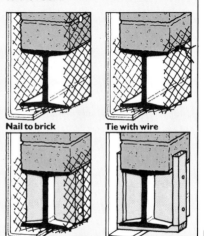

Nail to brick   Tie with wire

Or nail to blocks   Or use plasterboard

SEE ALSO

Details for: ▷	
Plasterboard	164-165
Door casings	185, 190
Obtaining approval	18
Supporting a beam	129
Plasterwork	148-153
Mixing concrete	439

• **Finishing a pressed-steel beam**
Pressed-steel box-profile beams are made with perforated faces to provide a key for the plaster.

FITTING ARCHES

MAKING A CUSTOMIZED ARCH

Removing a dividing wall – to create a through living-and-dining room, for instance – leaves you with a boxy break formed by the RSJ and its piers. The angularity might suit your decor and furnishings, but for a softer look, an arch is the answer: you can buy ready-made arch formers, which you fix in the opening and plaster over; for an individual profile, however, it's quite straightforward to make your own arch using wet plaster or plasterboard.

SEE ALSO

◁ Details for:
Mixing plaster	151
Plastering techniques	152
Power jigsaw	465
Plasterer's trowel	478
Spirit level	478

Arch formers
Expanded-metal arch formers are made in standard shapes and are easy to install. The shapes can be modified by adding a soffit strip.

Semi-circular

Oriental

Tudor

Spanish

Deciding on the arch profile

It's advisable to plan for the installation of an arch before you make your opening. Choose the style of arch carefully: the shape will effectively lower the height of the opening at the sides, which may be impracticable and poorly proportioned for the room.

Corner arches simply round off the angle and don't encroach on headroom; semi-circular types give a full, rounded shape but eat into headroom at the sides; pointed arches make a distinctive shape without taking up headroom at the middle of the opening.

Metal mesh arch formers

Expanded metal mesh arch formers are available from builders' merchants to give quick and easy installation. Various profiles are made, typically semi-circles, corner quadrants and ellipses, although Spanish, Oriental and Tudor styles are also available.

One-piece mesh frames are also sold, but they're suitable only for use on 112mm (4½in) thick walls. Segmented formers – half the face and half the soffit (underside) – are more versatile; some offer a separate soffit strip to cope with any wall thickness.

Fitting the former
You'll need to wedge a batten at the top of the opening, to which you can attach the mesh with nails. Hold the former in position, and set it squarely using a spirit level (1). Secure the mesh to the piers with galvanized masonry nails – you may have to hack off a margin of plaster at the sides so the mesh can be fixed flat against the bricks. Hold a

spirit level diagonally against the fold of mesh at the curves and the hard plaster surface on the pier, to check that it's set at the correct depth (2).

If you're fitting mesh segments, fit one half, then the other (3) and tie the soffit strips together with galvanized or copper wire to prevent the mesh sagging under the weight of the plaster. On a thick wall, insert a soffit strip and tie it to the side pieces.

Mix up some metal lathing plaster (◁) and spread a rough key coat onto the soffit with a plasterer's steel trowel, working from bottom to top from both sides (4). Don't press too hard or the plaster will be forced through the mesh. Apply plaster to the face of the arch, scraping it off level with the hard plaster edge on the pier and the rigid mesh fold on the arch curve. When the plaster has stiffened, after about 15 minutes, apply a thin coat of ordinary finish plaster. Apply a second coat immediately after the first and trowel smooth.

1 Set former square   2 Check it is level   3 Tie former soffits   4 Apply plaster

Fibrous plaster arches

Prefabricated decorative archways are available made from fibrous plaster. They are usually fixed with screws to wooden battens at the top and sides of the opening. The joints between the fibrous plaster mouldings and the wall

plaster are filled after installation.

To complete an authentic period look, ornate fibrous plaster accessories such as corbels (supporting brackets) or pillars and pilasters are also available with which to clad the piers.

When you cannot find the arch profile you require as a pre-made former, make your own in one of two ways.

Using wet plaster
The arch may be a single curve, or may incorporate intricate curves and points. Cut 12mm (½in) plywood ribs to the contour of the arch shape but make them 12mm (½in) less than the finished size. Nail or screw them to the beam fixings and piers. Nail softwood spacer battens between the ribs.

Cut and fix expanded metal mesh sheeting across the faces and edge of the shape, moulding it around the curves (1). You may have to snip the mesh with tinsnips to enable you to fold it around tight shapes.

Make up plastering guides from hardboard. Cut these to the finished shape you require. Temporarily nail them, smooth side inwards, over the mesh, with packing pieces behind. The packing should equal the finished thickness of the plaster. Set the edges of the guide to overlap the underside of the arch by 12mm (½in), the required thickness of plaster. Spread plaster onto the underside of the arch, between the overlapping edges. When this has set, remove the guides and plaster the wall faces using the hard plaster edge as a level. Finally apply finish plaster.

 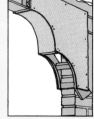
1 Fix mesh to ribs   2 Fit plasterboard

Using plasterboard
You can use plasterboard to make an arch to your own design. Cut the sheet to the required profile and nail it over the framework (2). Cut a thin strip of hardboard or thin plywood for the soffit and pin it to the frame to form the underside of the arch. Fix the hardboard textured side out. Bed paper scrim in plaster over the joins to prevent cracking due to slight movement. Apply a skim coat of finish plaster to all the surfaces. Alternatively, pin a strip of metal mesh to the soffit and apply a base coat and finish coat of plaster.

REMOVING A NON-LOADBEARING WALL

Lightweight partition walls which are not loadbearing can be removed safely without consulting the authorities for approval, and without the need to add temporary supports. You must, however, be certain that the wall is in fact not structural before doing so, as some partitions do offer partial support.

Dismantling a stud partition

Remove the skirting boards from both sides of the wall, plus any picture rail mouldings: it's a good idea to save these for re-use or repairs in the future. If any electrical switches or socket outlets are attached to the wall, they must be disconnected and re-routed before work begins (▷).

Removing the plasterwork
Use a claw hammer or wrecking bar to hack off the plaster and laths or plasterboard cladding covering the wall frame. Once stripped to the framework, remove the vertical studs. Bag up the debris during stripping and remove.

Removing the framework
First knock away any nailed noggings from between the studs. If the studs are nailed to the head and sill, they can be knocked apart. If they are housed or mortised in place, saw through them (at an angle to prevent the saw jamming). If you make the cut close to the joint, you will be left with a useful length of re-usable timber.

Prise off the head and sill members from the ceiling joists and floor. If the end studs are fixed to the walls, prise them away with a wrecking bar.

Finishing off
Replaster the gap in the ceiling and walls, fitting a narrow strip of plasterboard if necessary (▷). Fit floorboarding to close the gap if the boards are not continuous.

Dismantling a blockwork wall

Partition walls are sometimes made using lightweight concrete blocks (▷). To remove the wall, start to cut away the individual units with a bolster chisel and club hammer from the top. Work from the middle out to the sides.

Chop off an area of plaster first, so that you can locate the joints between blocks, then drive your chisel into these to lever them out.

METHODS OF CLOSING A FLOOR GAP

When you remove a dividing wall that penetrates the floor, you are left with a gap between the floors on each side. The floorboards may run parallel with, or at right-angles to, the line of the wall. Filling the gap with new floorboards is straightforward.

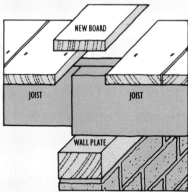

Boards running parallel
When the boards are parallel with the wall the supporting joists may rest on a wall plate (▷) built into the lower wall. Cut a board matching the thickness of the floorboards to fill the gap. Nail the board to the joists.

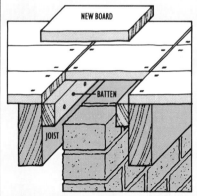

Boards at right-angles
When the boards are at right-angles to the gap, the ends will be supported on joists running parallel with the wall and about 50mm (2in) from it.

Cut the ends of the board flush with the joists. Nail 50 x 25mm (2 x 1in) sawn softwood battens to the sides of the joists level with the underside of the boards. Cut short lengths of matching floorboards to bridge the gap and nail them to the battens.

SEE ALSO

Details for: ▷	
Wall plate	120,172
Switching off	296,300
Running cable	303-305
Power circuits	308-313
Lighting circuits	323-331
Concrete blocks	423
Removing skirting	181
Bolster chisel	480

● **Making a room divider in an old house**
Create a room divider by stripping the plasterwork from the studding to reveal the timber framework. Once it is clean, paint or stain the frame to suit your interior decorative scheme.

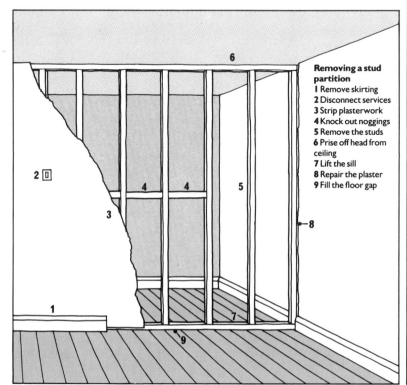

Removing a stud partition
1 Remove skirting
2 Disconnect services
3 Strip plasterwork
4 Knock out noggings
5 Remove the studs
6 Prise off head from ceiling
7 Lift the sill
8 Repair the plaster
9 Fill the floor gap

ALIGNING FLOORS

When the joists run parallel with a wall that's been removed (◁), you may find that one floor is out of level with the other. This may have been caused by slight movement in parts of the building or they may have been built that way; the floors were never intended to be aligned. Depending on the difference between floors, you can make a slope or step to deal with the unevenness satisfactorily.

SEE ALSO

◁ Details for:
Removing a wall	130
Parallel boards	133
Fitting doors	186
Stair going	212, 502
Lifting floorboards	177
Removing skirting	181
Adjustable bevel	462
Power saws	465

Packing and trimming

When the joists of the two floors are supported on the same wall plate (◁), the chances are that both floors will be at the same level. Because wood can shrink or warp, however, it may be necessary to pack or trim the top of one or two joists slightly to allow for the infill board to sit properly.

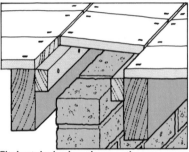

Fit short sloping boards across the gap

Dealing with misalignment

A misalignment up to 18mm (¾in) can be accommodated by the short lengths of floorboards cut to span the gap. Although probably acceptable, the slope will be apparent. Where the difference in level is large, it may be necessary to create a single step or make a gradual slope. A gradual slope should be less noticeable, but cannot satisfactorily run across a door opening.

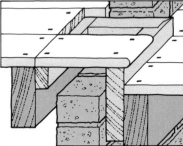

Make a step if difference in level is large

Making a step

Trim the ends of the floorboards on the high side flush with the joists and nail a batten to it. Trim the boards on the low side in the same way, but screw a 38mm (1½in) thick planed softwood riser to the side of the joist to finish level with the batten on the higher floor (See left).

If the floors are to be covered, cut and nail short lengths of floorboards to form the step tread. Where you want a bare wood floor, a single board running the width of the step would look better. In this case, skew-nail noggings flush with and between the riser and adjacent joists at approximately 750mm (2ft 6in) centres – necessary for a wide board that is weak across its width.

Where a floor has been raised, make a shallow threshold step at a doorway. Prepare a hardwood threshold board to fit between the door linings and finish flush with the raised floor. Nail it to the lower floor. Trim the bottom of the door to clear the step and refit it on its hinges (◁).

Fit a threshold at a doorway

MAKING A GRADUAL SLOPE

Cut the floorboards flush with the joist on the high side and nail a batten to it as before. Remove the skirting boards from the side walls and lift the floorboards of the room with the lower floor. Rest the edge of a straight-edged board on the nailed batten of the high floor and one of the joists of the lower floor to give a gradual slope. **(1)**

Take measurements between each joist and the underside of the straight-edged board. Set an adjustable bevel to the angle between the side of the joist and the board. Cut with a power saw lengths of 50mm (2in) wide softwood to these dimensions at the required angle. Nail the prepared packing to the top of the joists in descending order.

Re-lay the floorboards, butting their ends against the cut board of the higher floor. Adjust the lengths of the boards for extension pieces to be laid into the floor at their other ends. **(2)** For a finished wood floor, re-lay and stagger the boards of both floors to break up the straight joint line.

Replace the skirting following the line of the floor and re-nail to the wall.

Setting the slope
Measure gap between a straight-edged board and each joist and set an adjustable bevel to the angle. Cut packing strips to fit and nail in place, followed by the floorboard.

1 Use a straight-edged board to assess the slope

2 Nail packing to joists and relay floor

MAKING ONE ROOM INTO TWO

Building a partition to divide a large area into two smaller ones – to improve storage facilities, or simply because the house layout isn't as you'd like it – is quite straightforward using a frame of timber studs. You can clad the wall and plaster it so the new addition looks an integral part of the design. Before you can go ahead, however, you may need to seek approval.

Complying with the Regulations

Before you build a partition wall, check with your local council beforehand in order that the space you are creating complies with the Regulations.
These state that if a new room is to be 'habitable' – a living room, dining room, bedroom (but not a WC, bathroom or kitchen) – it must meet requirements, relating to ventilation.

The Regulations stipulate that an open space must be available on the outside of the window to provide sufficient ventilation to the room. The openable area of the windows to each room must be not less than a twentieth of the room's floor area. To check this, divide the area of the floor by the area of the window's sash or top vent. If the openable part is too small you may need to change the window.

Alternative and additional means of ventilation may be provided by a mechanical ventilator direct to the open air. It may be permissible for a fanlight to connect to a vented lobby.

If you plan to partition a large bedroom to make an en-suite shower or WC on an internal wall, natural light will not be required, but ventilation will. Consider the positioning of the new room in relation to the existing plumbing and the means of ventilation.

Should you plan to make a large bedroom into two smaller units, for example, bear in mind the size and shape of the rooms in relation to the furniture. Provide space around the bed to allow it to be made comfortably. You'll also need a corridor to make the two rooms self-contained.

Constructing a stud partition

Timber-framed non-loadbearing walls can be built relatively easily. The frame is usually made from 100 x 50mm (4 x 2in) or 75 x 50mm (3 x 2in) sawn softwood. The partition comprises: a head or ceiling plate, which forms the top of the wall and is fixed to the ceiling joists; a matching length, nailed to the floor, which forms the sill, or sole plate; studs which fit between the plates, equally spaced – about 400mm (1ft 4in) apart – and fixed with nails; short noggings which are nailed between the studs to make the structure rigid. Noggings will be needed where horizontal joints occur in the panelling.

Positioning the partition

If the new partition is run at right-angles to the floor and ceiling joists, it can be fitted at any point. Each joist will share the load and provide a solid fixing.

If the wall is to run parallel with the joists, it must stand directly over one of them: this may mean altering the overall dimensions of your planned rooms. Locate the floor joist in question and check whether stiffening is required. If so, reinforce it as described, which will require considerable work (▷).

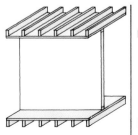

Right-angle
A partition set at right-angles to joists is well supported.

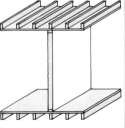

Parallel
A partition parallel with the joists must be supported by one of them.

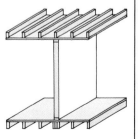

Reinforcing
The floor joist may need stiffening to bear the extra weight of the partition (See right).

REINFORCING A JOIST

Remove the skirting and lift the floorboards. Temporarily lay some of the boards to walk on while working. Screw metal joist hangers (▷) to the walls at each end, using 50mm (2in) long screws, to support the reinforcing joists flush with the original joist. Cut two reinforcing joists to fit between the hangers. Allow not more than 6mm (¼in) for tolerance.

Use 12mm (½in) diameter coachbolts to clamp the joists together. Drill the holes for them slightly larger than their diameter and spaced not more than 900mm (3ft) apart, working from the centre. Place large plain washers under the head and nut.

You can alternatively use 75mm (3in) diameter double-sided timber connectors between the meeting faces instead of joist hangers. If you have room, and a drill bit long enough, drill through all three joists while they are held together with cramps. If not, cramp one in place and drill through the two. Remove the reinforcing joist and cramp the other on the opposite side. Drill through it using the hole in the original joist as a guide. Bolt the reinforcing joists together.

Replace the floorboards on which to erect the partition (See below).

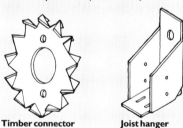

Timber connector   **Joist hanger**

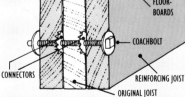

Stiffening the joist
Bolt a joist to each side of the original using coachbolts and timber connectors.

SEE ALSO

Details for: ▷	
Suspended floors	172
Joist hangers	174
Planning a room	15
Building Regulations	18-19
Ventilation	275-276
Plumbing	338-373

Parts of a stud partition
1 Head plate
2 Sole plate (sill)
3 Wall stud
4 Studs
5 Noggings

Fitting a partition between joists
Fit timber bearers between the floor joists and ceiling joists to support the stud partition.

135

BUILDING A STUD PARTITION

Making a stud partition wall is the easiest way to divide a room into two: you can construct a plain wall, or add a doorway, serving hatch or glazed area to 'borrow' light from an existing window. You can build the partition directly onto the floorboards, or the joists below, so that the flooring can be independent of the partition, should you need to lift boards later. The sides of the partition can be set against the plaster surface or set in channels to provide a better fixing to the masonry and make any unevenness easier to fill.

SEE ALSO

◁ Details for:

Dovetail-nailing	472
Door casings	185
Try square	462
Housing joints	476
Plumb line	478, 484
Chalk line	484

Marking out and spacing the studs

Mark the width of the sill for the new wall on the floor in chalk. Use the sill member – a length of 100 x 50mm (4 x 2in) sawn softwood – as a guide to draw the line. Continue the guidelines up the walls at each side, using a spirit level and straight-edged plank or a plumbline and bob. Continue the guidelines onto the ceiling, by snapping a distinct chalk line onto the surface with a taut string (1).

Spacing the studs
Lay the sill and head members together with their face sides uppermost. Mark the position of the studs at 400mm (1ft 4in) or 600mm (2ft) centres, working from the middle. Square the lines across both members against a try square (2). Use the 400mm (1ft 4in) spacing to support thin board materials and 9.5mm (⅜in) thick plasterboard.

If you are fixing 12.7mm (½in) plasterboard or tongued-and-grooved (T&G) boarding the 600mm (2ft) spacing should be used.

Marking out a doorway
If you are including a doorway in the wall, make an allowance for the width of the opening. The studs that form the sides of the opening must be spaced apart by the width of the door plus a 6mm (¼in) tolerance gap and the thickness of both door linings. Mark the width of the opening on the head plate at the required positions, then mark the positions for the studs working from the opening. Take the dimensions for the sill from the head and cut both plates to length (3). The door studs overlap the ends of the sills, which must be cut back to allow for them.

Fixing the framework

Secure the sill to the floor on each side of the door opening using 100mm (4in) long nails or 75mm (3in) long No. 10 countersunk woodscrews. Use the head plate as a guide to keep both parts of the sill in line.

Prop the head plate against the ceiling on its line and check the stud marks are true with the sill, using a plumbline. Nail or screw it to the joists (4).

Measure the distance between the head and sill at each end and cut the outer wall studs to length: they should be a tight fit between the sill and head plate. Drill and plug the walls if you're fixing the studs with screws, or use 75mm (3in) long masonry nails.

Fixing door studs
Cut the door studs to fit between the head plate and floor. Wedge them in place but do not fix them yet. Add together the door height and the thickness of the head lining, plus 10mm (⅜in) for tolerance, then mark the position of the underside of the door head on the edge of one stud. Hold a spirit level on this mark and transfer it accurately to the other door stud.

Fixing the door head
Remove the studs, then mark and cut a 12mm (½in) deep housing to receive the 50mm (2in) door head. Reposition and skew-nail the door studs to the head plate and dovetail-nail into the ends of the sills (◁). Locate the door head member in its housing and dovetail-nail it through the studs (5). Fit a short stud between the head plate and door head.

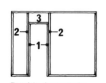

Double door studs
1 Door-height studs
2 Full-height studs
3 Door head

Alternative fixing for door studs

An alternative method for fixing the door studs is to cut the door studs to the required door height and double up with a stud between the sill and head plate. Support the door head and nail it to the top of the door studs. Cut a short length of studding to fit vertically between the centre of the head plate and door head. Secure in place by dovetail-nailing. Make sure when nailing all the parts together that their faces are flush.

1 Snap a chalk line onto the ceiling

2 Mark the sill and head plate together

3 Mark a door opening on the head plate first

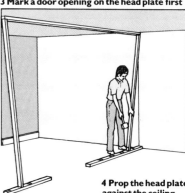

4 Prop the head plate against the ceiling

5 Nail the studs to the door head

STUD PARTITIONS

Fixing studs and noggings

Measure and cut each full length stud and fix in turn (See right). Cut the noggings to fit between the studs and, working from the wall, skew-nail the first end to the wall stud then dovetail-nail through the next stud into the end of the nogging. One or two rows of noggings may be required: if you are going to fit plasterboard horizontally, place the centre of the noggings at 1.2m (4ft), working from the ceiling. When the boards are to be fitted vertically, space the line of noggings evenly, staggering them to make the fixing easier.

Space studs equally and nail top and bottom

Nail noggings between studs to stiffen them

Fixing to an existing stud wall

Stud partitions are commonly used for internal walls of rooms on the first floor level. If your new partition meets a timber-framed wall, align it with the existing solid frame members.

Fix the wall stud of the new partition to a stud in the existing wall, where possible. Locate the stud by tapping, then drill a series of closely spaced holes through the plaster to find its centre.

When the new partition wall falls between the studs of the original one, fix its studs to the noggings, head and sill of the original wall. Construct the new wall as above but, in this instance, cut the wall stud to fit between the floor and the ceiling and fix it before the sill and head plate are nailed into place.

Fixing plasterboard vertically

Start at the doorway with the edge of the first board flush with the stud face. Before fixing, cut a 25mm (1in) wide strip, from the edge, down to the bottom edge of the door head member. Fix the board with 30mm (1¼in) or 40mm (1½in) plasterboard nails not more than 150mm (6in) apart. Fit the boards on both sides of the doorway then cut and fit a section over the opening. Allow a 3mm (⅛in) gap at the cut joint. Fit the remaining boards.

Fixing plasterboard horizontally

Plasterboard can be fitted horizontally where it is more economical or convenient to do so. First nail the top line of boards in place, so that, should it be necessary to cut the bottom run of boards, the cut edge will fall behind the skirting. Cut a strip from the edge of the boards on each side of the doorway to allow for the boarding over the door to be fixed to the studs.

Temporarily nail a horizontal support batten to the studs 3mm (⅛in) below the centre line of the noggings. Sit a board on the batten and nail it to the studs. Fit the remainder of the top boards in this way; then fit the bottom row. Stagger the vertical joints.

A second person should assist you by holding the plasterboard steady. If you have to work alone use a length of timber to prop the board while you work. Nail from the centre of the board.

NAILING TECHNIQUES

Use two 100mm (4in) round wire nails to skew-nail each butt joint, one through each side. Temporarily nail a batten behind the stud to prevent it moving sideways when driving in the first nail. Battens cut to fit between each stud can be permanently nailed in place to form housings for extra support.

Alternative stud fixing method
For a really rigid fixing, set the studs into 12mm (½in) deep housings notched into the head and sill plates before nailing.

Skew-nailing
Skew-nail the butt joints with two nails.

Nailing technique
Support the stud with a block while driving the first nail.

Supporting joint
Battens fixed to each side brace the joint.

Housing joints
Housing joints ensure a true and rigid frame.

SEE ALSO

Details for: ▷	
Plasterboard	158
Plasterboarding a wall	159
Nail fixing	159
Scribing plasterboard	160
Finishing plasterboard	164-165

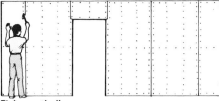

Fixing vertically
Work away from a doorway or start at one end.

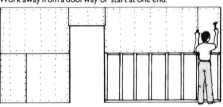

Fixing horizontally
Fix the top row first, stagger the joints on the next.

BUILDING A STAGGERED PARTITION

A stud wall can be built to divide a room into two and provide alcoves for storage at the same time. The method of construction is the same as described for the straight partition (◁) but also includes right-angle junctions. Constructing a staggered partition with a door at one end and a spacious alcove, as shown below, makes sensible use of available space.

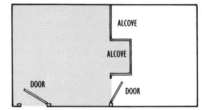

A staggered partition will form storage alcoves on each side, one for each room.

SEE ALSO

◁ Details for:
Stud partition	136-137
Plasterboarding a wall	159
Nail fixing	159
Scribing plasterboard	160
Finishing plasterboard	164-165

Building the wall
1 Mark out partitions
2 Transfer the marks to the ceiling
3 Cut and fix the sills to the floor
4 Fix the head plates to the ceiling
5 Make corners from three studs
6 Fix the other studs at required spacing
7 Fit noggings, then fix the boarding
8 Fit door frame and complete the boarding
9 Fit door lining, door and mouldings

Positioning the wall

Mark out the thickness of the main partition across the floor. Mark the position of the 'recessed' partition parallel with it. For clothes storage set them apart by 600mm (2ft).

Calculate the length of the partitions by setting them out on the floor. Starting from the wall adjacent to the doorway measure off the thickness of a stud, the door lining, the width of the

door, a second door lining and a second stud. Also add 6mm (¼in) for clearance around the door. This takes you to the face of the first short partition that runs parallel to the wall. Measure from this point to the other wall and divide the dimension in two. This gives you the line for the other short partition. Set out their thicknesses at right angles to the main partitions.

Fixing the sill and head plates

Mark the positions for the head plates on the ceiling. Use a straight edge and spirit level or a plumbline to ensure that the marks exactly correspond with those marked on the floor.

Cut and fix the sill and head plates to the floor and ceiling respectively, as for erecting a straight partition. Cut and fit the studs at the required spacing to suit the thickness of the cladding.

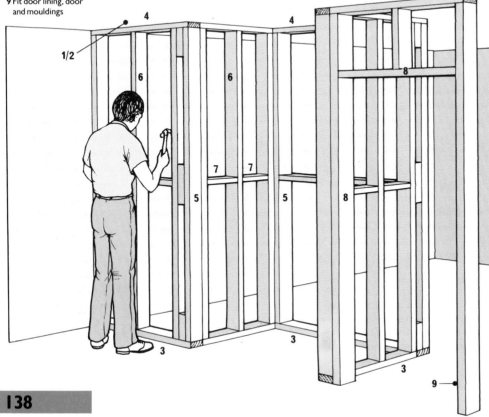

CONSTRUCTING THE CORNERS

The right-angled corners and the end of the short partition, which supports the door frame, need extra studs to provide a fixing for the plasterboard.

Make up a corner from three studs arranged and nailed in place. Fit short off-cuts of studding to pack out the gap. Fix the offcuts level with the noggings. Fit the boards with one edge overlapping the end of the adjoining panel. For the end of the short partition fit two studs spaced 50mm (2in) apart with nailed offcuts between. Nail the board to the two faces of the partition. Leave the end exposed until the door frame is fitted.

Measure and cut the door studs, ceiling and door head plates to length. Nail the ceiling head in place and fix one stud to the room wall and one to the stud wall. Ensure they are square and flush with the end of the partition. Fit the door head plate and a short vertical stud above it. Plasterboard over the doorway and to the side faces of the studs, including the end of the wall.

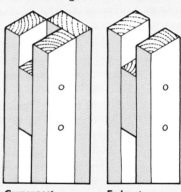

Corner post
Use three studs at the partition corners.

End post
Use two studs at the end of the partition.

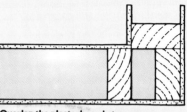

Overlap the plasterboard at corners

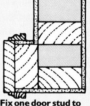

Fix one door stud to the partition

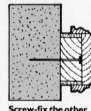

Screw-fix the other stud to wall

Unlike solid walls of brick or block, stud walls are mainly hollow, presenting problems when wall fixtures are to be hung. Wherever possible these should be fixed directly to the structural stud members for maximum support, but if the positions of fixtures are pre-planned, extra studding, noggings or mounting boards can be incorporated before the wall lining is applied.

Mounting a hand basin

A wall-mounted hand basin will need a sound enough fixing to carry its own weight and that of someone leaning on it when it is in use.

Buy the basin before building the wall – or work from the manufacturer's literature, which usually specifies the distance between centres for fixing the brackets – and position two studs to take the fixing screws. Mark the centre lines of the studs on the floor before applying the wall lining, then draw plumbed lines from the marks up the face of the lining. Measure the height from the floor for the brackets and fix them securely with wood screws.

If you plan wall-mounted taps above the basin make a plywood mounting board to fit between a pair of standard spaced studs to carry both the basin and the taps. Use exterior grade plywood at least 18mm (¾in) thick. Plywood is tougher and more stable than softwood and chipboard doesn't hold screws well.

Screw 50 x 50mm (2 x 2in) battens to the inside faces of the studs, set back from their front edges by the thickness of the board. Cut the board to size with enough height to support basin and taps, then screw it to the battens to lie flush with the two studs.

Apply the lining to the side of the wall that will carry the basin, leaving the other side open for plumbing in the appliances. Drill clearance holes and fit the taps; fix the basin support brackets, preferably with bolts.

To hide the plumbing within the wall pass the waste downpipe through a hole drilled in the wall sill member and run it under the floor. If the waste pipe must run sideways in the wall, notch the studs (See below).

Fitting a wall cupboard

It is not always possible to fix in the studding because walls tend to be put up well before furnishings are considered. If there are no studs just where you want them you will have to use cavity fixings instead. Choose a type that will adequately support the cabinet (▷).

Hanging shelving

Wall-mounted bookshelves have to carry a considerable weight and must be fixed securely, especially to stud partitions. Use a shelving which has strong metal uprights into which adjustable brackets are slotted. The uprights spread the load across all the wall fixings. Screw into studs if you can; otherwise use suitable cavity fixings (See below right).

Hanging small fixtures

Load-carrying fixtures with a small contact area can crush the plaster and strain the fixings. Mount coat hooks, for instance, on a board to spread the load and screw the boards to studs. Hang small pictures on picture hooks secured with steel pins, larger ones on a double pin type, preferably fixed to a stud. Put mirror plates on the frame of a heavy mirror or picture for screw fixing. Use stranded wire if hanging them on a hook fixed to a stud or a cavity fixing.

SEE ALSO

Details for: ▷	
Plumbing a basin	365
Cavity fixings	499
Dry-wall fixing flanges	309
Hole saw	465
Drills	471,472
Shelving	500

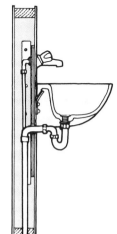

Mounting a basin ▶
Fix a wall-mounted hand basin and taps to an exterior-grade plywood board.

FITTING SERVICES IN STUD PARTITIONS

It is easy to plan and fit services in a stud partition wall before lining it. To guard against future occupants drilling into service runs set horizontal cables or pipes no more than 300mm (12in) above floor level.

Plumbing

Plan the runs of supply or waste pipes by marking the faces of the vertical studs or the noggings that brace them. Remember that a waste pipe must have a slight fall (▷). When you are satisfied with the layout cut notches in the timbers for the pipework (See right).

Transfer the marked lines to the sides of the studs or noggings and drill holes for the pipes close to their front edges. Cut in to the holes to make notches. If cut at a slight angle they will hold the pipes while they are being fitted.

Notches cut for waste pipes must be reinforced to prevent them weakening the studs. Drill the holes in the centres of the studs, following the pipe run.

Before cutting in to the holes cut housings for 300mm (12in) lengths of 50 x 25mm (2 x 1in) softwood to bridge the notches. Make the notches, set the waste pipe in place, then screw the bridging pieces into their housings flush with the fronts of the studs.

Noggings need not be braced, but fit one under a pipe bend as a support.

Running electric cable

Drill 12 to 18mm (½ to ¾in) holes at the centres of the studs for level runs of cable and in noggings for vertical runs. Fit extra noggings to carry mounting boxes for sockets and switches. For a flush-mounted fitting inset the board to the depth of the box so that its front edge lies flush with the lining. Run the cable. With the lining in place mark and cut an opening for the box and pull the cable through. If you have omitted a mounting board during construction, you can use dry-wall fixing flanges to hold the metal box to the lining.

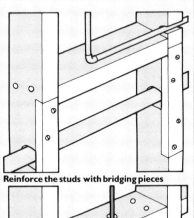

Reinforce the studs with bridging pieces

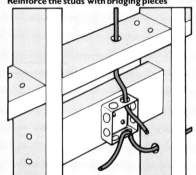

Fit metal boxes to a mounting board

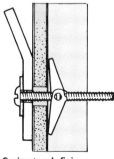

Spring-toggle fixing

Cavity fixings
Various cavity fixings may be had for insertion into holes and securing with screws or bolts. Some expand to grip the lining as a screw is tightened; some are held in place by a toggle that springs out behind the lining.

BUILDING A DRY PARTITION WALL

SEE ALSO

◁ Details for:
**Cellular-core
wallboard**   123
Nail fixing   159
Marking out   136
Cutting plasterboard   158
Finishing plasterboard 164-165

*For a lightweight non-loadbearing
partition, cellular-core dry
partitioning is easy to construct. Made
from two sheets of plasterboard with a
cardboard core (◁), it makes a rigid wall
when installed. The panels can be
purchased from larger builders'
merchants but would probably need to
be ordered. Tapered-edged panels for
decorating and square-edged panels for
plastering are available. The panels
provide a reasonable level of sound
insulation, but as air gaps can reduce
their performance an acoustic sealant
can be applied to all the jointing
surfaces during erection.*

Fixing the framing

The panels are fixed to a lightweight
timber frame. Mark out the floor, walls
and ceiling in the same way as for a stud
partition. Nail to the floor a 50mm (2in)
planed (PAR) softwood sill, which
matches the thickness of the
partitioning. Plane 18mm (¾in) thick
softwood ceiling and perimeter wall
battens to make a snug fit in the gap
between the plasterboard sheets.
Remove the arris from the outside long
edges of the battening and then nail or
screw it to the wall. To locate the
bottom of the partition cut a point on a
150mm (6in) length of the ceiling/wall
batten and nail it to the sill with its
square end against the wall batten. Use
50mm (2in) wall nails.

Fixing the panels

Cut the panels to fit between the sill
and the ceiling with a 3mm (⅛in)
tolerance using a saw. Rip out the
cardboard core with the claw of a
hammer to the depth of the battens —
about 18mm (¾in) — along the top and
two long edges. Also remove 150mm
(6in) of the core from each end of the
bottom edge. Use a wood chisel to trim
away any lumps of glue.

Drive a 150mm (6in) length of
battening into the core at the bottom of
the partitioning. This plug is used to fix
skirtings — add more approximately
400mm (1ft 4in) apart. Mark the
position of each on the surface of the
partition for reference later.

Lift and locate the top of the first
panel over the ceiling batten about
200mm (8in) from the wall. Swing the
panel into the vertical position and
locate it on the floor sill. Slide the panel
carefully along the sill to locate over the
locating block and wall batten. Cut an
intermediate locating block 300mm
(1ft) long and taper each end. Tap half of
its length into the bottom corner of the
panel's core and nail it to the sill.

Cut a length of square-section
vertical joint batten to fit between the
ceiling batten and intermediate block.
Tap the batten half way into the edge of
the panel. Skew-nail it at the top and
bottom. Fix the boards to the
framework with galvanized nails at
225mm (9in) centres (◁).

Prepare the other panels and secure
them in the same way. Butt the edges of
the tapered panels, but leave a 3mm
(⅛in) gap when they are square-edged.

**Partition
components**
1 Softwood sill at base
of panel
2 Wall batten (hidden
inside long edge of
panel)
3 Ceiling batten
4 Locating block
(hidden)
5 Cellular-core panel
6 Intermediate locating
block
7 Vertical joint batten

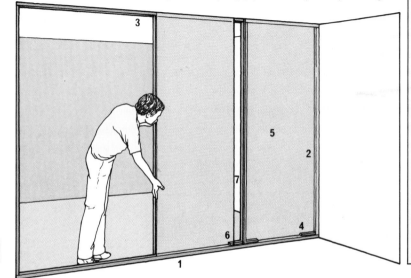

JOINTS AND JUNCTIONS

Joints
To make a T-joint, nail a vertical wall
batten to one of the joint battens or to
plugs cut from the joint battening and
driven into the core of the
corresponding partition. Fit the 150mm
(6in) long plugs horizontally, spaced
about 600mm (2ft) apart, before
erecting the partition. Hammer them
into the edge, following a line of cells.
Use a spare length of battening to drive
the plugs further in from the edge if
required. Always mark the position of
the plugs on the surface.

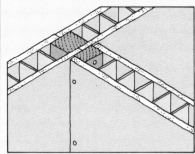
Fixing to joint batten

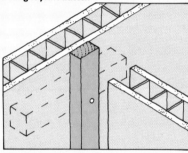
Fixing to batten plugs

Junctions
Right–angle corners are made by cutting
away the inside face of the plasterboard
and core to form a rebate for the full
width of the adjoining panel. A batten
must be fitted into each panel for
nailing.

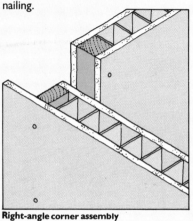
Right-angle corner assembly

DRY PARTITIONS

Making a door opening

Mark the position of the doorway on the floor. Make allowances for the width of the door and door linings (▷). Mark out the width of the panels, working from the opening to each wall. Fit the ceiling and wall battens. Cut the sill to stop at the opening and fix it to the floor. Fit the panels working from the wall towards the opening, starting with any cut panels. At the opening, remove the core from the vertical edges of the panels and insert vertical battens flush wih the edges. Skew-nail them at top and bottom and fix the plasterboard with galvanized nails at 225mm (9in) intervals.

Measure and cut a panel to fit over the door opening. Nail a length of wall batten with one end tapered to the side of the vertical batten on each side of the

opening. The battens should be about 75mm (3in) shorter than the depth of the cut panel: Ensure they are set true.

Clear the core from all round the panel, allowing enough room at the bottom to accommodate a length of joint battening. Slide the panel over the side battens and nail it in place with a 3mm (¹⁄₈in) gap at the top.

Fit the horizontal head batten into the core flush with the bottom edge and nail it to the vertical battens at each end, then nail the door linings to the stud framework.

If you fit a made-up door frame, treat it as a panel and build it in as the other partitions are erected. When assembling the partition, don't forget to omit a section of the sill at the doorway.

Slide the panel over the side battens

SEE ALSO

Details for: ▷
Door casings ... 185,190
Dry-wall fixings ... 309

Fitting a partition between walls

Working from one wall mark out the width of the full panels across the floor. Inevitably, you will have to cut the last panel to fit. Measure and cut it to the required width, less 6mm (¹⁄₄in). Fix the framing to the floor, ceiling and both walls. Fit the bottom locating batten.

Prepare and fit the cut panel at one end and then proceed from each end towards the centre. Clean out the core from the panels on each side of the opening to allow the jointing batten to be set in flush. Make three equally spaced

wide saw cuts in the edge of the panels. Cut the vertical battens so that they fit loosely between the ceiling batten and sill. Set them flush into the prepared edges of the panel. Fit 50mm (2in) screws part way into the centre of the battens at each of the saw cuts. Lift the last panel into position, then tap the screws sideways to drive half the vertical batten into the edge of the last panel. Skew-nail the vertical batten to the top and bottom frames through the board. Fix the panels along the vertical edges.

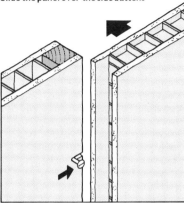
Insert last panel then tap batten sideways

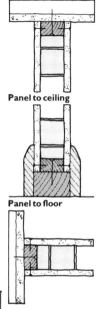
Fixing details
Panel to ceiling
Panel to floor
Panel to wall

FITTING FIXTURES AND INSTALLING SERVICES

Fixtures
Lightweight loads such as pictures, clocks and display shelving may be fitted with cavity wall fixings. Heavy loads such as shelving or storage units should be screwed to wooden plugs installed into

the core before assembly. Shelving systems with metal uprights can be screwed to the plugs. A surface-mounted board screwed to a pair of plugs will help to spread the load of a heavy cabinet.

Services
Electric cable can be passed horizontally through the centre of the core as the panels are erected. Use a 25mm (1in) diameter pipe to clear a path for the cable. A permanent length of plastic conduit running through the core may help you to feed the cable through as the panels are fitted. Vertical cable runs can be made providing they occur next to a joint in the panel.

Accurately cut an opening in the face of the partitioning for a switch or socket mounting box, and fit them with partition wall flanges (▷).

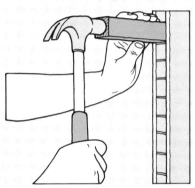
Drive wooden plugs in from the edge

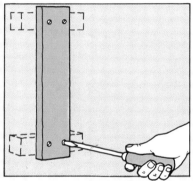
Fix mounting boards for heavy loads

◀ Mounting boxes
Plugs can also be employed for fixing mounting boxes in the core cavity.

CEILINGS: LOWERING A CEILING

SEE ALSO

◁ Details for:
Use of colour	30
Lighting	37-38
Cornice mouldings	156
Craft knife	485

From a practical point of view, a high ceiling can be a liability. It incurs greater heating bills, and decorating costs will be higher as more material is required to cover the walls. Lowering the ceiling can help solve these problems as well as providing a distinctive feature in a room.

High ceilings are generally found in older types of house. Some are decorative moulded ceilings, while many others have simpler but attractive cornice mouldings and these should be preserved to maintain the character of the house. But where a room is plain and the ceiling needs attention, or where the proportions of the room would benefit from alteration, a lowered ceiling can be an improvement. It can be used to hide ducting, improve sound and heat insulation and provide a space for flush or concealed lights.

Changing the character of a room

A room's character is largely determined by the relation of its area to its ceiling height. Low cottage ceilings are considered charming and cosy, while tall rooms are felt to be very imposing, though they are usually larger all round. Other high-ceilinged rooms feel somehow rather 'uncomfortable'.

The sense of cosiness or emptiness may be based on practical experience. For example, the volume of a cottage room is less than that of a high-ceilinged room of the same floor area, so it would be easier to heat evenly, and a room with an even temperature feels more comfortable than one where the temperature varies due to rising air currents. The acoustics in a small room may also be better, inducing a relaxed feeling. Yet the qualities of light and space in a room may be due to its high ceiling, and if it were lowered, changing the room's proportions, the tall windows might look awkward and the sense of space be lost.

Making a model

Making a simple card model of a room's interior is a good way to check that a planned project will suit the room before spending time and money on the real thing.

Measure the length, width and height of the room and the height, width and positions of the windows and doors. Mark out and cut pieces of stiff card for the floor and walls to a scale of 1:10 (1mm = 1cm) or, in the imperial

measure, 1:12 (1in = 1ft).

Mark the positions of the doors and windows on the cardboard walls and cut out the openings with a craft knife. The openings will allow light into the finished model. You can hinge the 'door' in place with self-adhesive tape. Draw lines on the walls to represent the skirting and the architraves round the doors and windows. You can colour these details to make them more realistic. Also mark in the fireplace to the same scale. A projecting chimney breast can be easily formed in card and glued on.

Punch a small peep-hole in each wall at a height scaled to your eye level and assemble the floor and walls, using adhesive or sticky tape.

Cut a cardboard panel, representing the ceiling, to fit closely between the walls. If the real ceiling is to be the suspended type, with lighting round its edges, cut the panel smaller to provide the gap at the sides.

Cut two strips of card about 50mm (2in) wide and as long as the width of the ceiling piece and glue them on edge across the back of the 'ceiling'. Cut two more strips, the same width but a little longer, and use clips to attach these to the shorter ones. The longer strips will rest across the walls and the clips are adjusted to set the card ceiling at various heights. Check the effect of this on the room by viewing the interior space through the peepholes and the door and window openings.

To simulate a grid-system illuminated ceiling make a framework with strips of balsa wood to the same scale as the room and covered with tracing paper.

RECOMMENDED DIMENSIONS

The height of a new ceiling should be no less than 2.3m (7ft 6in). In some cases 2m (6ft 6in) is acceptable under beams or bay windows.

You can construct a slightly lower ceiling in a kitchen, provided at least half of it is at, or above, 2.3m (7ft 6in).

In a roof space the ceiling height must be a minimum of 2.3m (7ft 6in) for at least half the area of the room. However, this area might not represent the whole floor. Mark all the sloping ceilings 1m (3ft 3in) or 1.5m (5ft) above the floor, then use a plumbline to mark the floor directly below. The area of the floor within the marked lines represents the actual area used to calculate the ceiling height.

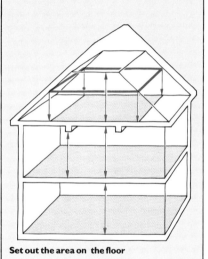

Set out the area on the floor

Cardboard model parts
1 Walls
2 Chimney breast
3 Floor
4 Ceiling panel
5 Fixed card strip
6 Adjustable card strip
7 Clips

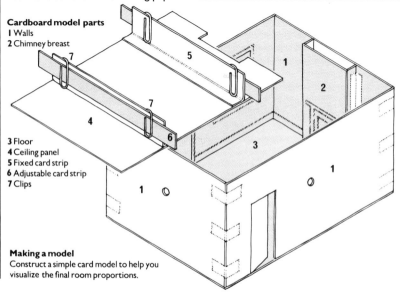

Making a model
Construct a simple card model to help you visualize the final room proportions.

LOWERING A CEILING: OPTIONS

You might decide to lower a ceiling for practical reasons or simply to change the style of the interior, but whatever the reason, you should consider your options carefully because a ceiling is a large area which can be costly to cover.

Timber-framed ceilings are heavy but they can be tailor-made to suit the style and shape of a room using basic woodworking skills.

Manufactured suspended ceiling systems are relatively lightweight, easy to install and offer a wide choice of materials for the panelling, but a strong grid pattern is unavoidable.

Use the chart to help you consider the project in advance and to compare one system with another.

PROJECT CONSIDERATIONS

Advantages of a lowered ceiling
- Improves room proportions.
- Provides a feature.
- Conceals poor lighting.
- Offers various lighting options.
- Conceals ducting.
- Reduces heating bills.
- Saves on decorating material costs.

Disadvantages of a lowered ceiling
- Spoils proportions of a room.
- Covers decorative features.
- Large area can be costly.
- Systems will require periodic cleaning.
- Some materials can be a fire hazard.

Points to check
- Recommended dimensions
- Consult local Fire Officer for kitchens.
- Style of proposed ceiling/interior.
- Ease of making.
- Cost of materials.
- Alternative systems.

Services
- New light fittings required. Surface, recessed and concealed types are options.
- Lighting circuit will need extending.
- Provide access for extractor ducting, electricity consumer unit, meter and water valves.

OPTIONS (See right) ▷

LOWERED CEILING

Design features	Planning the scheme	Type of construction	Covering/finishes
Will change the room proportions. Will hide old ceiling or services. Least likely to appear a conversion. Can be fitted with cornice mouldings. Without a hatch, prevents access to the void above.	Make initial sketches of the proposed interior, then draw scale plans on graph paper to detail and cost the scheme. Make a scale model to visualize the effect of the ceiling.	This type of construction uses new ceiling joists to span room in shortest direction. The joists are notched over battens fixed to the walls. Ties and hangers are used for spans over 2.4m (8ft).	Materials: Plasterboard. Fire-resistant building board. Veneered board. Tongued and grooved boarding. Mineral-fibre tiles. Finishes; papered, painted, varnished or ready-finished

PART-LOWERED CEILING

Design features	Planning the scheme	Type of construction	Covering/finishes
Similar to the full lowered ceiling above but has added interest of the split-level. The end 'drop' can be vertical or sloped, the latter being preferable when parallel with a window.	As for lowered ceiling (See above). Consider the line of the 'drop' in relation to the window. It should not cut across the window when viewed from the opposite side of the room.	Timber-frame construction as for lowered ceiling (See above). The end framework is formed from ties and hangers. The hangers are set at an angle for a sloped end.	As for lowered ceiling (See above).

SLATTED CEILING

Design features	Planning the scheme	Type of construction	Covering/finishes
Not a true ceiling but a framework which appears to be continuous. Most effective in hallways or passage. It does not seal off the old ceiling. Can be dismantled for access to services.	As for lowered ceiling (See above). The spacing and depth of the slats can be varied: you should not be able to see between the slats when looking straight ahead.	Edge-on plank construction using no sub-structure. Perimeter planks are housed and fixed to the wall; the slats are slotted into them.	No covering is used. The ceiling and walls above the slats are painted a dark colour. Finish for woodwork: Light-coloured stain, clear varnish or paint.

SUSPENDED CEILING

Design features	Planning the scheme	Type of construction	Covering/finishes
Appears to be suspended away from the walls and appears to float: concealed lighting enhances this illusion. Has modern character. Will mask old ceiling or services. Not demountable.	As for lowered ceiling (See above). Locate original ceiling joists and set out their position on your plan drawing: design the structure around them.	Timber-frame construction using ties fixed across ceiling joists and carrying hangers from which the new frame is suspended. The main components are assembled with bolts.	As for lowered ceiling (See above).

SUSPENDED CEILING SYSTEMS

Design features	Planning the scheme	Type of construction	Covering/finishes
A grid system manufactured from lightweight materials for self-assembly. Individual translucent or opaque panels sit in the grid framework. The system is demountable.	As for lowered ceiling (See above). Draw a plan of the room on graph paper and set out a symmetrical grid.	Lightweight aluminium T-sectioned bearers suspended from angle sections screwed to the walls. Bearers are loose fitted.	Metal: anodized. Panel materials: plain, textured and coloured translucent plastic; opaque plastic; mineral fibre.

SEE ALSO

Details for: ▷
Drawing a plan	14
T&G boarding	87-88
Decorating ceilings	98
Mineral-fibre tiles	112
Making a hatch	147
Lighting circuits	323-331
Wood joints	475

Vapour checks
Provide a vapour check to prevent condensation problems in an unventilated space above a lowered ceiling. Use a vapour-check plasterboard, an impervious sealer or polythene sheeting. The gaps between the boards or the polythene must be sealed effectively.

Plasterboard
Bed joints in mastic

Polythene sheeting
Fold and staple edges

CONSTRUCTING A LOWERED CEILING

You can build the new ceiling at any height providing it complies with the regulations. However, the height of window openings may limit your choice. About 2.4m (8ft) is a useful height for a lowered ceiling. It is a common room height for modern houses and relates to standard wallboard sheet sizes. Most manufacturers of built-in furniture adopt it as a standard height for ceilings.

SEE ALSO

◁ Details for:
Plasterboard	158
Noggings	166, 502
T&G boarding	87-88
Height regulations	142
Plasterboarding a ceiling	166

Planning the layout

Making a lowered ceiling requires a considerable amount of timber for the framework and boarding to cover it. Work out your material requirements by drawing a plan to establish the most economical way to construct it. If you intend to use plasterboard choose a vapour-check type. Arrange the panels with the paper-covered edges set at right angles to the timber supports. Stagger the end joints between each row of boards and arrange them so as to fall on a joist.

If you plan to use tongued and grooved boarding, buy it in lengths that can be economically cut to suit your joist arrangement, as short off-cuts are wasteful. Avoid butt joints coinciding on adjacent boards.

Materials for the framework

Make a cutting list of the materials you will need to make up the structure. Use 75 x 50mm (3 x 2in) sawn softwood for the ceiling joists. These should span the room in the shortest direction. Calculate the number of joists you will need. These should be spaced at 400mm (1ft 4in) or 600mm (2ft) centres according to the thickness of the plasterboard. (◁). These dimensions will also suit other types of boarding.

You will need extra joist timber for the noggings fitted between the joists (◁). In addition 50 x 25mm (2 x 1in) sawn softwood is used for wall battens to run round the perimeter of the room.

Spans of over 2.4m (8ft) should be supported by hangers and ties, made from timber not less than 50 x 50mm (2 x 2in) which are fixed to the ceiling above. Place the hangers about the middle of the joists' span.

It is possible to use more hangers and reduce the section of the joists from 75 x 50mm (3 x 2in) to 50 x 50mm (2 x 2in). In this case place the hangers about 1m (3ft) apart.

Cutting list
A cutting list is your shopping guide. It will enable you to establish your requirements and help your supplier in making up your order. List the individual parts of the structure, and, under separate columns, fill in the quantity, length, width, thickness and material, required.

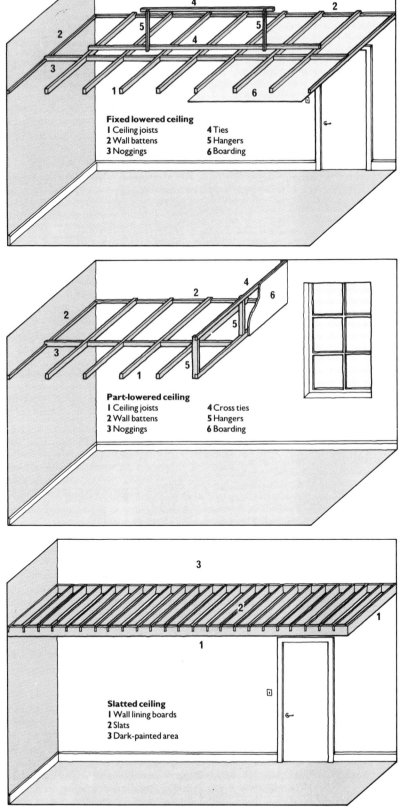

Fixed lowered ceiling
1 Ceiling joists	4 Ties
2 Wall battens	5 Hangers
3 Noggings	6 Boarding

Part-lowered ceiling
1 Ceiling joists	4 Cross ties
2 Wall battens	5 Hangers
3 Noggings	6 Boarding

Slatted ceiling
1 Wall lining boards
2 Slats
3 Dark-painted area

Constructing the ceiling

Mark the height of the new ceiling, including the thickness of the boarding, on one wall. At this level draw a horizontal line across the wall using a straightedge and spirit level for accuracy. Continue the line around the room at this height. Cut the 50 x 25mm (2 x 1in) wall battens to length. Nail or screw them to the walls at 400mm (1ft 4in) intervals, with the bottom edge level with the line.

Cut the 75 x 50mm (3 x 2in) ceiling joists to length. Notch the ends to sit over the wall battens to bring the bottom edges flush. Skew-nail the joists to the wall battens. Cut and fit hangers and ties to prevent long joists sagging (See left). These supports also stiffen the structure.

Cut and nail noggings between the joists to support the edges of the plasterboard. Nail tapered-edge plasterboard to the joists, noggings and wall battening. Fill and tape the joints between boards and walls (▷).

Lowering part of a ceiling

You can lower part of a ceiling to overcome problems around tall window openings or to create a split-level effect. Follow the method for constructing a ceiling as described above but enclose the end drop with plasterboard nailed to hangers fixed in a line to a cross-tie member set above the last joist.

Making a slatted ceiling

Planed softwood planks 150 x 25mm (6 x 1in) in size, set on edge and spaced apart can create a simple yet effective slatted ceiling. Smaller sections can be used where the span is short, as with a narrow hallway.

Cut four lengths of planking to line the walls all round. Before nailing or screwing them at the required height, mark and cut housings in two of the planks opposite one another. Space the housings 225mm (9in) apart. For boards less than 150mm (6in) wide, space them about 100 to 150mm (4 to 6in) apart. Cut notches in the ends of the 'slat' boards to sit in the housings so that the bottom edges finish flush.

Before fitting the slats, paint walls and ceilings above the lining boards with a dark emulsion paint. Also paint ducting or plumbing to disguise it. Finish the slats with varnish, stain or paint.

MAKING A SUSPENDED CEILING

A suspended ceiling is a framed panel which appears to float away from the walls. Fluorescent lights can be placed around the edge of the panel to enhance the floating effect and provide wall-washing illumination (▷). The panel can be covered with plasterboard, decorative veneered ply or mineral-fibre ceiling tiles.

Locate the position of the ceiling joists by noting the direction of the floorboards of the room above; the joists will run at right angles to them (▷). Pinpoint the joists from below by drilling or boring pilot holes through the ceiling (▷). Mark the centre of each joist.

Setting out the grid

Measure the lengths of the walls and draw a scaled plan of the room on graph paper. Set out the shape of the ceiling panel on the drawing with its edges approximately 200mm (8in) from each wall. Then set out the position of the 50 x 50mm (2 x 2in) softwood ceiling ties. The ties should run at right angles to the joists of the ceiling above. The ends of the ties and sides of the two outer ones should be about 300mm (1ft) from the walls. The number of ties you'll need will depend on the size of the ceiling, but three should be a minimum. They should be spaced not more than 1m (3ft) apart for adequate support.

Constructing the ceiling

Counterbore and securely screw the ties in position to each of the joists they cross. Cut 50 x 50mm (2 x 2in) softwood hangers to the required length and fix

them to the ties with coach bolts not more than 1m (3ft) apart.

Cut additional ties to the same length as the planned ceiling panel. Bolt them across the ends of the hangers with an equal space at each end.

Cut the required number of 50 x 50mm (2 x 2in) planed softwood furring battens to suit the spacings necessary to support the boardings or tiles used as a covering. The length of the furring battens should be equal to the width of the ceiling panel less two 50 x 25mm (2 x 1in) capping battens. Equally space and screw the furring battens to the tie members. Countersink the screw heads.

Mark off the positions of the furring battens along the sides of each capping batten. Drive 75mm (3in) nails into, but not quite through, the cappings at these points. Apply woodworking adhesive and nail the cappings to the ends of the furring battens.

Finishing the assembly

Run electrical wiring in readiness for the fluorescent lights to be fitted (▷). Cover the underside of the frame with plasterboard, decorative veneered boarding or ceiling tiles (▷). Fill and finish the surface and edges of a plasterboard ceiling panel. Finish the exposed edges of the frame to match other materials as required.

Wire up and fit slim fluorescent light fittings to loose boards, which sit on top of the projecting frame. The fittings can then be easily removed for servicing at any time. Leave enough spare flex to allow the lights to be lifted clear.

SEE ALSO

Details for: ▷	
Lighting	37-38
Suspended floors	120
Locating joist	147
Plasterboard	164-165
Lighting circuits	323
Man-made boards	494-495
Skew-nailing	472
Housing joint	476

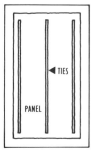

Setting out
Set out the panel on graph paper with a 200mm (8in) gap all round. Inset the ties about 300mm (1ft).

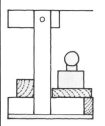

Light fitting
Fix a fluorescent light to a removable board for servicing.

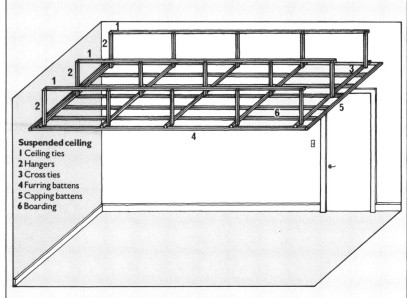

Suspended ceiling
1 Ceiling ties
2 Hangers
3 Cross ties
4 Furring battens
5 Capping battens
6 Boarding

SUSPENDED CEILING SYSTEMS

◁ Details for:
Repairing plaster 50-51
Applying paint 69
Fluorescent lights 327
Sawing metal 487

Manufactured suspended ceiling systems are made from slim metal sections, which provide a fairly lightweight structure for acoustic or translucent panels. They're quick and easy to fit using no specialist tools.

Panel layouts

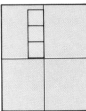
1 Main bearer on centre

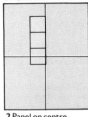
2 Panel on centre

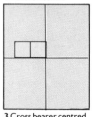
3 Cross bearer centred

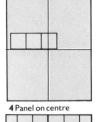
4 Panel on centre

5 Best grid arrangement

Manufactured systems
Manufacturers offer a choice of coloured framing as well as coloured translucent and opaque panels.

The lightweight alloy framework is made from three basic elements: an angle section, which is fixed to the walls; a main bearer section, which spans the room, usually in the shortest direction; and a lighter T-sectioned cross bearer, which bridges the space between the main bearers.

The loose panels sit on the flanges provided by the bearers. They can be easily lifted out for access to ducting or to service light fittings, which can be concealed behind them. You need at least 200mm (4in) above the framework to fit the panels.

Setting out the grid

Normally, 600mm (2ft) square panels are used for suspended ceiling systems. Before fitting the framework, draw a plan of the ceiling on squared graph paper to ensure that the borders are symmetrical. Draw a plan of the room with two lines taken from the halfway point on each wall to bisect at the centre. Lay out the grid on your plan with a main bearer centred on the short bisecting line (1), then lay it out again with a line of panels centred on the same line (2). Use the grid that provides the widest border panels.

Plot the position of the cross bearers in the same way, using the other line (3,4). Try to get the border panels even on opposite sides of the room (5).

Fitting the framework

Before building a suspended ceiling with translucent panels, remove flaking materials and make good any cracks in the plaster ceiling above. Paint the ceiling with white emulsion to improve reflectivity if concealed fluorescent lighting is to be used.

Fix fluorescent light fittings to the joists spaced evenly across the ceiling: 16 watts per square metre is recommended for a suitable level of light in most rooms.

Mark the height of the suspended ceiling on the walls with a continuous levelled line. Hacksaw two lengths of wall angle section to fit the longest walls. Remove burrs from the ends with a file. Drill screw holes at 600mm (2ft) intervals. Drill and plug the walls using the angle as a guide and screw the components in place (1).

Next cut lengths of wall angle to fit the shorter walls. Their ends should fit on the angles already fitted. Screw-fix them in the same way.

Mark the positions of the bearers along two adjacent walls, as set out on the graph paper. Cut the main bearers to span the room. Sit them on the wall angles (2). Use a ceiling panel to check they are parallel and at right angles to the wall and each other.

Cut the border cross bearers to fit between the end main bearers and wall angles. Set them in line with the points marked on the wall. Position the remainder of the cross bearers following the same line.

Working from the centre, drop in the full-sized panels. Measure and cut the border panels to fit and then drop them into place.

Spanning wide rooms
If the size of the room exceeds the maximum length of the main bearer, join two or more pieces together. A joint bridging piece is provided if the ends of the bearers are not made to lock together.

For spans exceeding 3m (10ft) support the main bearers with wire hangers. Fix each wire, spaced not more than 1.5m (5ft) apart, through a hole in the bearer and hang it from a screw eye in a furring strip or joist in the ceiling.

Lightweight suspended ceiling
1 Angle section
2 Main bearer
3 Cross bearer
4 Drop-in panels
5 Wire hangers

1 Screw the angle to the wall

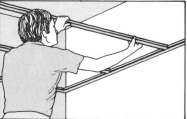
2 Position the main bearers

INSTALLING A FOLDING LOFT LADDER

Access to the roof space is more convenient and safer if you install a folding loft ladder. Some are complete with built-in hatch cover, frame and fittings ready to install in a new opening. Normally, the length of the ladders suits ceiling heights 2.3 and 2.5m (7ft 6in and 8ft 3in). Some can extend to 2.9 to 3m (9ft 6in to 10ft).

Concertina ladder
To fit a concertina ladder, securely screw the fixing brackets of the aluminium ladder to the framework of the opening. Fit the retaining hook to the framework to support the ladder in the stowed position. Operate the ladder with a pole, which hooks over the bottom rail. Fit the hatch door to the frame with a continuous hinge, followed by a push-to-release latch fixed to the edge of the hatch door.

Ready-to-install folding ladder
Cut the opening and trim the joists to the size specified by the manufacturer. Insert the casing with built-in frame in the opening and screw it to the joists.

A concertina ladder is simple to install.

Folding ladders are easy to deploy.

CEILINGS
LOFT ACCESS

MAKING A LOFT ACCESS HATCH

Many houses are provided with a hatch in the ceiling to give access to the roof space for servicing water tanks and maintaining the roof structure. Should your house have a large roof space without access, installing a hatch could provide you with extra room for storage. Although the job is basically straightforward, it does entail cutting into the roof structure.

In older houses this is not a problem as the timbers are substantial. In modern houses, however, lightweight timber is used to make strong triangulated trussed-roof structures (▷). These are designed to carry the weight of the roof with each member playing an important part, so any alteration may dangerously weaken the structure. If your house is relatively new you should check with the company that built it, or with a local builder, whether it is safe to proceed.

If you have a choice, site the hatchway over a landing, but not close to a stair, rather than in a room. In this way a ladder used for access will not interfere with the occupants or function of the room, and furniture arrangements are not affected. Allow for the pitch of the roof, as you will need headroom above the hatch.

Making the opening
If you are planning to fit a special folding loft ladder, the size of the new opening will be specified by the manufacturer. Generally aim to cut away no more than one of the ceiling joists: these are usually spaced 400mm (1ft 4in) apart.

Locate three of the joists by drilling or boring pilot holes in the ceiling. Mark out a square for the opening between the two outer joists. Cut an inspection hole inside the marked area to check no obstacles are in the way of the cutting line (▷). Saw through the ceiling plasterwork and strip it away.

Pass a light into the roof space and climb up into it between the joists. Lay a board across the joists to support yourself. Saw through the middle joist, cutting it back 50mm (2in) from each edge of the opening. Cut two new lengths of joist timber – called trimmers – to fit between the joists. Allow for a 12mm (½in) deep square housing at each end (1). Nail the housed joints and the butt joints between the trimmer joists. Use two 100mm (4in) round wire nails to secure each joist.

Nail the ceiling laths or plasterboard to the underside of the trimmer joists. Cut timber linings to cover the joists and the edges of the plaster. Make good the damaged edges of the plaster with filler. When set, nail mitred architrave moulding around the opening. Make a drop-in or hinged panel of 18mm (¾in) plywood or blockboard. If you plan to use the loft space mainly for storage, fix chipboard panels over the joists (▷). Cut them to fit through the opening.

SEE ALSO

Details for: ▷	
Patching a ceiling	154
Chipboard-flooring	176
Laying chipboard	179
Pitched roofs	221
Repairing plaster	50-51

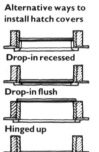
Alternative ways to install hatch covers

Drop-in recessed

Drop-in flush

Hinged up

Hinged down

Housing joints
A housing joint will give better support to the trimmer joist than nails alone.

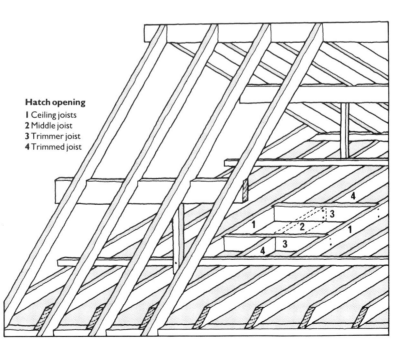
Hatch opening
1 Ceiling joists
2 Middle joist
3 Trimmer joist
4 Trimmed joist

INTERIOR PLASTERWORK

SEE ALSO

◁ Details for:
Plaster coverage	151
Types of plasterboard	158
Fixing plasterboard	158-163
Builder's tools	478-479

Storing plaster
Keep an open bag of
plaster in a plastic sack
sealed with adhesive
tape.

Plasterwork is used to provide internal walls and ceilings with a smooth, flat surface suitable for decorating with paint or paper. The plaster also provides sound and thermal insulation as well as protection from fire. Decorative mouldings – a feature of walls and ceilings in many older houses – are also made of plaster; they're still available for renovations. There are basically two methods for providing a plaster finish: the traditional way is wet plastering; the modern one uses plasterboard, and is known as 'dry lining'.

Traditional plastering techniques

Traditional plastering uses a mix of plastering materials and water, which is spread over the rough background in one, two or even three layers. Each layer is applied with a trowel and levelled accordingly; when set, the plaster forms an integral part of the wall or ceiling. The background may be solid masonry for walls, or timber-framed walls and ceilings finished with lath-and-plaster. Laths are thin strips of wood nailed to the timber framework to support plaster, which, forced between the laths, spreads to form nibs that grip on the other side. With traditional plastering, it takes practice to achieve a smooth, flat surface over a large area. With care, an amateur can produce satisfactory results, provided the right tools and plaster are employed and the work is divided into manageable sections. All-purpose one-coat plasters are now available to make traditional plastering easier for amateurs.

Dry lining with plasterboard

Manufactured boards of paper-covered plaster are widely used to dry-line the walls and ceilings in modern homes and during renovations. Its use overcomes the drying out period required for wet plasters and requires less skill to apply.

The large flat boards are nailed or bonded to walls and ceilings to provide a separate finishing layer. The surface may be decorated directly once the boards are sealed, or covered with a thin coat of finish plaster.

BUYING AND STORING PLASTER

Plaster powder is normally sold in 50kg (1cwt) paper sacks. Smaller sizes, including 2.5kg (5½lb) bags are available from DIY stores for repair work. It's generally more economical to buy the larger sacks, but this depends on the scale of the work. Try to buy only as much plaster as you need. It's better to overestimate, however, to allow for wastage and prevent running short (◁).

Store plaster in dry conditions: if it is to be kept in an outbuilding for some time, cover it with plastic sheeting to protect it from moisture. Keep the paper bags off a concrete floor by placing them on boards or plastic sheeting. Open bags are more likely to absorb moisture, which can shorten the setting time and weaken the plaster. Keep an opened bag in a sealed plastic sack. Use self-adhesive tape to seal it. Discard plaster which contains lumps.

Ready-to-use plaster is also available in plastic tubs. It can be more expensive to buy it this way but it is easier for amateurs to use and it will keep for a long time, provided the airtight lid is well sealed.

**Traditional
Plastering**
(Right)
The construction of a
lath-and-plaster ceiling
and plastered masonry
wall.
1 Brick background
2 Ceiling joists
3 Lath background
4 Rendering coat
5 Floating coat
6 Finishing coat
7 Cornice moulding

Dry lining
(Far right)
The construction of a
modern dry-lined wall
and ceiling.
1 Block background
2 Batten fixing
3 Ceiling joists
4 Noggings
5 Plasterboard
6 Coving
7 Tape
8 Filler

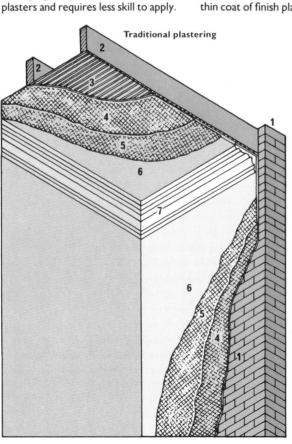

Traditional plastering

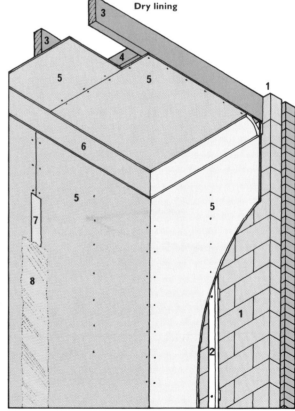

Dry lining

Plastering is carried out using modern gypsum plasters or mixes based on cement, lime and sand. By varying the process and introducing additives, a range of plasters can be produced within a given type to suit different background materials.

Plasters are basically produced in two grades—one as a base or 'floating' coat, the other for finishing coats. Base coat gypsum plasters are pre-mixed types, which contain lightweight aggregates. Base coat sanded plasters which are based on cement or cement/lime have to be mixed on site with a suitable grade of clean, sharp sand (although finish plasters are ready to use with the addition of water).

The following information deals only with those materials suitable for domestic work.

SEE ALSO

Details for: ▷
| Rendering mixes | 169 |
| Applications | 151 |

CHOOSING PLASTERS FOR DOMESTIC WORK

GYPSUM PLASTERS

Most plasters in common use are produced from ground gypsum rock by a process which removes most of the moisture from the rock to produce a powder that sets hard when mixed with water. Setting times are controlled by the use of retarding additives which give each of the several types of plaster a setting time suitable to its use.

Gypsum plasters are intended for interior work only, they should not be used on permanently damp walls. They must not be remixed with water once they start to set.

PLASTER OF PARIS

This quick-setting non-retarded gypsum plaster gives off heat as it sets. It is white or pinkish, and is mixed to a creamy consistency with clean water. It is unsuitable for general plastering but good for casting, and can be used for repairs to decorative mouldings.

CARLITE PLASTER

Carlite refers to a range of retarded gypsum plasters which are premixed with a lightweight aggregate and need only water to prepare them for use. The undercoat bonds well to most backgrounds, and this, coupled with their light weight – about half that of plasters mixed with sand – makes Carlite plasters fairly easy to use. The lightweight aggregate also gives improved thermal insulation. Setting time for Carlite plasters is about 1 to 2 hours.

Three types of Carlite undercoat plasters – 'browning', 'bonding' and 'metal lathing' – are available, each formulated to suit a background of a particular surface texture and suction. Browning is generally used for backgrounds with average suction, such as brickwork. For low-suction surfaces like dense brick and concrete blocks the bonding undercoat is preferred. The metal lathing is less commonly used and is primarily for metal lath backgrounds.

When more than one undercoat layer is needed to build up a thickness the same plaster should be used for all layers to ensure compatibility.

There is only one Carlite finishing plaster and it can be used over all the undercoats, being applied as soon as the undercoat has set.

THISTLE PLASTERS

Thistle is the brand name of a range of building plasters used for a variety of conditions and backgrounds.

Two types of finishing plaster are made, both mixed with water only: the finish plaster, for use over sanded undercoats, and the board finish plaster, used for finishing plasterboard surfaces.

Two special 'renovating' plasters are for use on walls with residual dampness. The undercoat is a pre-mixed gypsum plaster with special additives and the finish, formulated specially for use with the undercoat, contains a fungicide. The plaster is for use on damp walls which are slow to dry out, as in new, exposed building work or in old houses with new damp-proof courses installed. The plaster is not itself a damp-proofing material, but it allows the background material to breathe and dry out without letting the moisture show on the surface.

The cause of the problem must be dealt with before the plaster is applied.

SIRAPITE B

Sirapite B is a finish coat gypsum plaster for use over undercoats which contain sand, including cement rendering. It is not suitable for application to plasterboard. Only water is needed to prepare it. It contains additives which improve its workability, it has a gradual, progressive set and it can be brought to a high standard of finish.

Sirapite B is widely used by skilled professional plasterers.

SANDED PLASTERS

Before the advent of modern gypsums, lime and sand for undercoats and neat lime for finishes were used in traditional wet plastering, often with animal hair added to the undercoat mix as a binder. Lime plasters are generally less strong than gypsum and cement-based plasters.

Lime is still used, but mainly as an additive to improve the workability of a sand and cement plaster or rendering (▷). Cement-based sanded plaster undercoats may be required by some authorities for kitchen and bathroom walls constructed on timber and expanded-metal lathing. These undercoats can also be used on old brickwork or where a strong impact-resistant covering is required.

SINGLE-COAT PLASTERS

A universal one-coat plaster can, as its name implies, be used in a single application on a variety of backgrounds and trowelled to a normal finish.

The plaster is available in 40kg (88lb) bags and only water is added to prepare it for use. It will stay workable for up to an hour and can be built up to a thickness of 50mm (2in) in one coat.

One-coat plaster is also available in small packs contained in mixing tubs, and these are ideal for such small repair jobs as making good where a fireplace has been removed. For larger areas than this it is more economical to buy bigger bags and mix on a board in the usual way.

FILLERS

Fillers are fine plaster powders used for repairs. Some, reinforced with cellulose resin, are sold in small packs and need only mixing with clean water for use. They are non-shrinking, adhere well and are ideal for filling cracks and holes in plaster and wood. Extra-fine fillers are also available ready-mixed in small tubs for levelling dents in woodwork.

- **Avoiding old plaster**
Plaster may deteriorate if stored for more than two months so suppliers try to ensure it is sold in rotation. The paper sacks in which plaster is supplied are usually date-stamped by the manufacturer. If you are buying from a self-service supplier, choose a sack with the latest date.

TYPES OF SURFACE

SEE ALSO

◁ Details for:
Efflorescence	44
Concrete blocks	423
Workmate bench	474
Builder's tools	478-479

● **Providing a 'key'**
Rake out mortar joints to help plaster and cement renderings grip.

A well-prepared background is the first step to successful plastering. New surfaces of block or brickwork may need only dampening or priming with a bonding agent, depending on their *absorbency. Old plastered surfaces needing repair should be thoroughly checked. If the plaster has 'blown', hack it off back to sound material, then treat the surface and replaster the area.*

Background preparation and absorbency

Brush down the surface of a masonry background to remove loose particles, dust and efflorescent salts (◁). Test the absorption of the background by splashing on water; if it stays wet, consider the surface 'normal' – this means that it will only require light dampening with clean water prior to applying the plaster.

A dry background which absorbs the water immediately takes too much water from the plaster, making it difficult to work, prevents it from setting properly and can result in cracking. Soak the masonry with clean water applied with a brush.

High-absorbency surfaces

For very absorbent surfaces, such as aerated concrete blocks (◁), prime the background with 1 part PVA bonding agent: 3 to 5 parts clean water. When dry, apply a bonding coat of 3 parts bonding agent: 1 part water. Apply the plaster when the bonding coat is tacky.

Low-absorbency surfaces

Prime low-absorption smooth brickwork or concrete with a solution of 1 part bonding agent: 3 to 5 parts water. Allow to dry. Apply a second coat of 3 to 5 parts bonding agent: 1 part water, and apply the plaster when tacky or allow it to dry for no more than 24 hours before plastering.

Non-absorbent surfaces

Glazed tiles and painted walls are considered non-absorbent and will require a coating of neat bonding agent to enable the plaster to stick. The plaster is applied while the agent is still wet. An alternative for glazed tiles is to apply a slurry of 2 parts sharp sand: 1 part cement mixed with a solution of 1 part bonding agent: 1 part water. Apply the slurry with a stiff-bristled brush to form a stippled coating. Allow to dry for 24 hours then apply the plaster.

Another option is to chip off the old tiles. Always remove loose tiles.

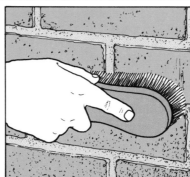
Remove loose particles with a stiff brush

Prime porous surfaces to control the suction

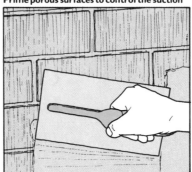
A bonding agent improves adhesion

Smooth tiles can be 'keyed' with a slurry

MAKING FILLER AND MORTAR BOARDS

Filler board
You can make a useful board for mixing and working with filler from 6mm (¼in) marine plywood. Cut out a 300mm (1ft) square with a projecting handle on one side, or make a thumb hole like an artist's palette. Seal the surface with a polyurethane varnish or apply a plastic laminate for a smooth finish.

Mortar board
Cut a piece of 12mm (½in) or 18mm (¾in) marine plywood approximately 900mm (3ft) square. Round off the corners and chamfer the edges all round. Screw three lengths of 50 x 25mm (2 x 1in) softwood across the underside, spread equally apart. A smaller board, known as a 'spotboard', 600mm (2ft) square, can be made in a similar way.

Using a stand ▶
You will find it easier to handle plaster with the mix at table height.

Using a stand
A stand is used to support the mortar board at table height, about 700mm (2ft 4in) from the ground. This enables the plaster to be picked up on a hawk by placing it under the edge of the board and drawing the plaster onto it (◁).

Make a folding stand using 50 x 38mm (2 x 1½in) softwood for the legs and 75 x 25mm (3 x 1in) softwood for the rails. Make one leg frame fit inside the other and bolt them securely together at the centre.

A portable Workmate bench can be used to support the board instead of making a stand: grip the centre batten in the vice jaws.

MIXING PLASTER

With the background prepared, the next step for the amateur plasterer is to make a good mix. It is best to mix your plaster close to the working place, as it can be messy. Also cover the floor with old newspapers and remember to wipe your feet when leaving the room.

A plaster that is well mixed to the right consistency will be easier to apply. Use a plastic bucket to acccurately measure the cement, lime and sand, or plaster. For large quantities of plaster, multiply the number of bucket measures. For small quantities, just use half-bucket measures or less.

Old hard plaster stuck to your equipment can shorten the setting time and reduce the strength of the newly mixed plaster. Do not try to re-work plaster that has begun to set by adding more water: discard it and make a fresh batch. Mix only as much plaster as you will need. For larger areas, mix as much as you can apply in about twenty minutes – judge this by practice.

Base coat plasters

Mix base coat plasters on a mortar board (see opposite). For sanded plasters, measure out each of the materials and thoroughly dry-mix them with a shovel or trowel for small quantities (▷). Make a well in the heaped plaster and pour in some clean water. Turn in the plaster, adding water to produce a thick, creamy consistency.

Just add water to pre-mixed gypsum plaster (which already contains an aggregate). Mix them on the board in the same way. Always wash down the board after use.

You can mix small quantities of pre-mixed plaster in a bucket. Pour the plaster into the water and stir to a creamy consistency; 1kg (2lb 4oz) of plaster will need about 0.75 of a litre (1 1/3 pints) of water.

Finish plaster

Mix finish plaster in a clean plastic bucket. Add the powder to the water. Pour not more than 2 litres (4 pints) of water into the bucket. Sprinkle the plaster into the water and stir it with a stout length of wood to a thick, creamy consistency. Tip the plaster out onto a clean, damp mortar board ready for use. Wash the bucket out with clean water before the plaster sets in it.

SEE ALSO

Details for: ▷
Builder's tools	478
Repairing plaster	50-51

BONDING AGENTS

Bonding agents modify the suction of the background or improve the adhesion of the plastering. When used, the base coat plaster should not exceed 10mm (3/8in) in thickness. If you need to build up the thickness, scratch the surface to provide an extra key, and allow at least 24 hours between coats.

Bonding agents can be mixed with plaster or sand and cement to fill cracks. First brush away any loose particles and then apply a solution of 1 part agent: 3 to 5 parts water with a brush.

Mix the plaster or sand and cement with 1 part bonding agent: 3 parts water to a stiff mix. Apply the filler with a trowel pressing it well into the crack.

Wash tools and brushes thoroughly in clean water when you are finished. It may be necessary to rinse out the brushes as the work progresses on a large job.

Wash agent from brushes before it sets

PLASTER TYPES, APPLICATION AND COVERAGE.

Type	Background	Type of coat	Coat thickness	Average ● coverage
CARLITE				
Browning *Normal suction*	Brick walls	Undercoat	10mm (3/8in)	6.5-7.5 sq.m. (7¾-9 sq yd)
	Block walls	Undercoat	10mm (3/8in)	6.5-7.5 sq.m. (7¾-9 sq yd)
	Concrete bricks	Undercoat	10mm (3/8in)	6.5-7.5 sq.m. (7¾-9 sq yd)
	Coarse concrete	Undercoat	10mm (3/8in)	6.5-7.5 sq.m. (7¾-9 sq yd)
Bonding *Low suction*	Brick walls	Undercoat	10mm (3/8in)	5.0-8.25 sq.m. (6-9¾ sq yd)
	Block walls	Undercoat	10mm (3/8in)	5.0-8.25 sq.m. (6-9¾ sq yd)
	Concrete bricks	Undercoat	10mm (3/8in)	5.0-8.25 sq.m. (6-9¾ sq yd)
	Smooth pre-cast concrete	Undercoat	8mm (5/16in)	5.0-8.25 sq.m. (6-9¾ sq yd)
	Plasterboards (Greyface)	Undercoat	8mm (5/16in)	5.0-8.25 sq.m. (6-9¾ sq yd)
	Polystyrene	Undercoat	10mm (3/8in)	5.0-8.25 sq.m. (6-9¾ sq yd)
Metal lathing	Expanded metal	Undercoat	10mm (3/8in)	3.0-3.5 sq.m. (3½-4 sq yd)
Finish	Carlite plaster Undercoats	Finish top coat	2mm (1/16in)	20.5-25.0 sq.m. (24½-30 sq yd)
THISTLE				
Finish	Sanded undercoats	Finish top coat	2mm (1/16in)	175-22.5 sq.m. (21-27 sq yd)
Board Finish	Plasterboards (Greyface)	Finish top coat	5mm (3/16in)	8.0-8.5 sq.m. (9½-10 sq yd)
Renovating *Normal suction*	Brick walls	Undercoat	10mm (3/8in)	6.0 sq.m. (7 sq yd)
	Block walls	Undercoat	10mm (3/8in)	6.0 sq.m. (7 sq yd)
	Concrete bricks	Undercoat	10mm (3/8in)	6.0 sq.m. (7 sq yd)
Renovating finish	Renovating plaster	Finish top coat	2mm (1/16in)	19.0-21.0 sq.m. (22¾-25 sq yd)
SIRAPITE				
	Sanded undercoats	Finish top coat	3mm (1/8in)	12.5-13.5 sq.m. (15-16 sq yd)
ONE COAT				
	All types	Undercoat/finish	12mm (1/2in)	4.5 sq.m. (5½ sq yd)

● m² per 50kg (sq yd per 50kg)

Plaster fillers

Pour out a small heap of the powder on to a small board, make a hollow in its centre and pour in water. Stir the mix to a creamy thickness; if it seems too runny add more powder. Use a rather drier mix for filling deeper holes.

APPLYING PLASTER

To the beginner plastering can seem a daunting business, yet it has only two basic requirements: that the plaster should stick well to its background and that it should be brought to a smooth, flat finish. Good preparation, the careful choice of plaster and working with the right tools should ensure good adhesion of the material, but the ability to achieve the smooth, flat surface will come only after some practice. Most of the plasterer's tools (◁) are rather specialized and unlikely to be found in the ordinary jobbing toolkit, but their cost may prove economical in the long term if you are planning several jobs.

SEE ALSO

◁ Details for:
Builder's tools	478
Plasterer's rule	479
Wall coverings	90-98
Using screeds	157
Finishing plasterboard	165

Problems to avoid

Uneven surfaces
Many amateurs tackle plastering jobs, large or small, planning to rub the surface down level when it has set. This approach is very dust-creating and laborious, and invariably produces a poor result. If a power sander is used the dust is unpleasant to work in and permeates other parts of the house, making more work. Far better to try for a good surface as you put the plaster on, using wide-bladed tools to spread the material evenly. Ridges left by the corners of trowel or knife can be carefully shaved down afterwards with the knife – not with abrasive paper.

When covering a large area with finishing plaster it is not always easy to see if the surface is flat as well as smooth. Look obliquely across the wall or shine a light across it from one side to detect any irregularities.

Crazing
Fine cracks in finished plaster may be due to a sand-and-cement undercoat still drying out, and therefore shrinking. Such an undercoat must be fully dry before the plaster goes on, though if the plaster surface is sound the fine cracks can be wallpapered over.

Top coat and undercoat plaster can also crack if made to dry out too fast. Never heat plaster to dry it out.

Loss of strength
Gypsum and cement set chemically when mixed with water. If they dry out before the chemical set takes place they do not develop their full strength, and become friable. Should this happen it may be necessary to strip the wall and replaster it.

PLASTERING TECHNIQUES

Picking up
Hold the edge of the hawk below the mortar board and scrape a manageable amount of plaster onto the hawk, using the trowel (1). Take no more than a trowelful to start with.

Tip the hawk towards you and in one movement cut away about half of the plaster with the trowel, scraping and lifting it off the hawk and onto the face of the trowel (2).

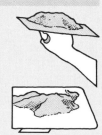

1 Load the hawk   2 Lift off the plaster

Application
Hold the loaded trowel horizontally but tilted at an angle to the face of the wall (1). Apply the plaster with a vertical upward stroke, pressing firmly so that plaster is fed to the wall. Flatten the angle of the trowel as you go (2) but never let its whole face come into contact with the plaster as suction can pull it off the wall again.

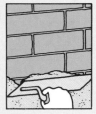

1 Tilt the trowel   2 Apply the plaster

Levelling up
Build a slight extra thickness of plaster with the trowel, applying it as evenly as possible. Use the rule (◁) to level the surface, starting at the bottom of the wall, the rule held against original plaster or wooden screeds nailed on at either side. Work the rule upwards while moving it from side to side , then lift it carefully away and the surplus plaster with it. Fill in any hollows with more plaster from the trowel, then level again. Let the plaster stiffen before a final smoothing with the trowel.

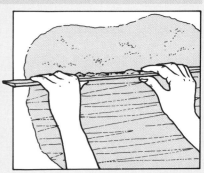

Work the rule up the wall to level the surface

Finishing
You can apply the finishing coat to a gypsum plaster undercoat as soon as it is set. A cement-based sanded plaster must dry thoroughly, but dampen its surface to adjust suction before finish-plastering. The grey face of plasterboard is finished immediately and is not wetted.

Apply the finish with a plasterer's trowel as described above, spreading it evenly, no more than 2 to 3mm (1/16 to 1/8in) judging this by eye, as screeds are not used. To plasterboard apply two coats to build a 5mm (3/16in) thickness.

As the plaster stiffens, brush or lightly spray it with water, then trowel the surface to consolidate it and produce a smooth matt finish. Avoid pressing hard and overworking the surface. Lastly remove surplus water with a sponge.

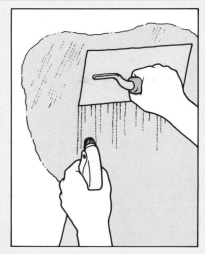

Spray plaster occasionally as you smooth it

REINFORCING A CORNER

When damage to a corner extends along most of the edge you can reinforce the repair plasterwork with a metal corner beading (1). As well as strengthening and protecting the new corner it will considerably speed up the repair work because it cuts out the need to use a board as a guide. You can obtain the beading from a good builders' merchant or DIY store.

Cut the beading to the required length with snips and a hacksaw. It has a galvanized protective coating, and the cut ends must be sealed with a metal primer or bituminous paint.

Cut back the old plaster from the damaged edge, wet the brickwork and apply patches of undercoat plaster at each side of the corner. Press the expanded metal wings of the beading into the plaster patches (2), using your straightedge to align its outer nose with both original plaster surfaces or checking the beading for plumb with a builder's level. Allow the plaster to set.

Build up the undercoat as before (3), but this time scrape it back to 2mm (^{1}/16in) below the old finished level.

Apply the finishing coat, using the beading as a level to achieve flush surfaces. Take care not to damage the beading's galvanized coating with your trowel; rust can come through later and stain wallcoverings. To be on the safe side you can brush metal primer over the new corner before decorating.

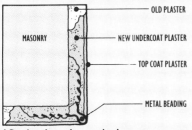

OLD PLASTER
MASONRY
NEW UNDERCOAT PLASTER
TOP COAT PLASTER
METAL BEADING

1 Section through a repaired corner

2 Set in plaster   **3 Trim undercoat back**

REPAIRING PLASTERWORK

Every decorator will at some time have to fill small holes and cracks with plaster or filler as part of normal preparations (▷), and these should present few problems. But once you start tackling more ambitious jobs, like removing fireplaces and taking down walls, you will need to develop some of the professional plasterer's skills in order to handle larger areas.

Plastering over a fireplace

A bricked-in fireplace provides an area large enough to give the amateur good practice without the work becoming unmanageable. Jobs of this kind can be done with a one-coat plaster, or you can apply an undercoat plaster followed by a top coat of finishing plaster.

Using a one-coat plaster
Prepare the background by cutting away any loose plaster above and around the brickwork. Remove dust and loose particles with a stiff brush.

Mix the plaster in a tub according to the maker's instructions.

Dampen the background with clean water and place a strip of hardboard below the work area to help you to pick up dropped plaster cleanly.

Tip the mixed plaster onto a dampened mortar board, then scoop some onto a hawk, and with a trowel (or the spreader provided) apply the plaster to the brickwork.

Work in the sequence shown (1), starting at the bottom of each section and spreading the plaster vertically. Work each area in turn, blending the edge of one into the next to build up a slight extra thickness, then level with a rule (▷). Fill any hollows and level again.

Leave the plaster to stiffen for about 45 minutes, when firm finger pressure should leave no impression, and lightly dampen the surface with a close-textured plastic sponge.

Wet the trowel or spreader and give the plaster a smooth finish, using firm pressure vertically and horizontally and keeping the tool wet.

Let the plaster dry thoroughly, for about six weeks, before decorating.

Two-coat plastering
Apply undercoat and finishing coat plasters as described above, scraping the undercoat back to allow for the thickness of the finishing coat.

Repairing a chipped corner

When part of the external corner of a plastered wall has broken away to show the brickwork behind, you can rebuild it with either one- or two-coat plaster. Use a 100mm (4in) wide board as a guide to get the corner straight.

With a bolster (▷), cut the plaster back from the damaged edge and reveal about 100mm (4in) of the brickwork.

For two-coat plaster, place the guide board against the old plaster work, set back about 3mm (^{1}/8in) from the surface of the plaster on the other side of the corner (1). Fix the board to the brickwork temporarily with masonry nails through the mortar joints, placing them well away from the corner.

Mix up the undercoat plaster, wet the brickwork and edge of the old plaster, then fill the one side of the corner flush with the edge of the board but not the wall (2). Scratch-key the new plaster with the trowel.

When the plaster is stiff remove the board, pulling it straight from the wall to prevent the new plaster breaking away. The exposed edge represents the finished surface, so scrape it back about 3mm (^{1}/8in) with the trowel and straight edge (3) to allow for the top coat.

For such a job a professional would simply hold the board over the new repair and fill the second side of the corner immediately. But this leaves only one hand to lift and apply the plaster, a difficult trick for the amateur. An easier, though slower, method is to let the new plaster harden, then nail the board through it before applying and keying fresh plaster as before (4). Or, if the new plaster is set hard, you can use the scraped edge as a guide.

Let the undercoat set, then nail the board to the wall as before, but this time set it flush with the corner and level off with finishing plaster. Dampen the undercoat if necessary, to help the top coat to stick.

When both sides are firm, polish the new plaster with a wet trowel, rounding over the sharp edge slightly, then leave it to dry out.

If you choose to carry out the repair with a one-coat plaster you must set the board flush with the corner before applying the material.

SEE ALSO

Details for: ▷
Repairing plaster 50-51
Builder's tools 478-479
Preparing the background 150
Removing a fireplace 384

1 Plastering sequence
Divide the area into manageable portions and apply the plaster in the sequence shown.

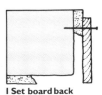

1 Set board back

2 Fill flush with board

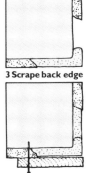

3 Scrape back edge

4 Fill second side

153

SEE ALSO

◁ Details for:
Repairing plaster 50-51
Types of plaster 149
Taping joints 164
Switching off 296

PATCHING A PLASTERBOARD CEILING

A misplaced foot in the attic, a roof leak not attended to, a leaking water pipe – any of these can cause damage to a ceiling. Fortunately the damage is usually of a localized kind that can be simply patch-repaired.

Before starting work turn off the electricity supply at the mains (◁). The next job is to check the direction in which the ceiling joists run and whether there is any electrical wiring close by the damaged area. If the damaged ceiling is below a floor such an inspection can usually be carried out from above, by raising a floorboard. Alternatively knock an inspection hole through the centre of the damage with a hammer. You will find that it is possible to look along the void with the help of a torch and a mirror (1).

1 Use a mirror and torch to inspect a void

Close round the damaged area, mark out a square or rectangle on the ceiling. Cut away an area of the plasterboard slightly larger than the damage, working up to the sides of the nearest joists (2). Use a padsaw or, if there is wiring nearby, a craft knife which will just penetrate the thickness of the plasterboard.

Cut and skew-nail 50mm (2in) noggings between the joists at the ends of the cut-out, with half of their thickness projecting beyond the cut edges of the plasterboard (3).

Nail 50 x 25mm (2 x 1in) softwood battens to the sides of the joists flush with their bottom edges (4).

Cut your plasterboard patch to fit the opening with a 3mm (⅛in) gap all round, and nail it to the noggings and battens. Fill and tape over the joints to give a flush surface (◁).

Minor damage
Repair minor damage to plasterboard as when preparing to decorate (◁).

2 Cut an opening

3 Nail in noggings

4 Nail in battens

REPAIRING LATH AND PLASTER

When the plaster of a lath and plaster wall deteriorates with age it can lose its grip on the laths because its key has gone. This may show itself as a swelling, *perhaps with some cracking. It will give a hollow sound if tapped and will yield when it is pressed. The loose plaster should be replaced.*

Repairing a wall

Cut out the plaster with a bolster and hammer (1). If the laths are sound you can replaster over them. Dampen the wooden laths and plaster edges (2) round the hole and apply a one-coat plaster with a plasterer's trowel, pressing it firmly between the laths as you coat them (3). Build up the coating flush with the surrounding plaster and level it with a rule. Let the plaster stiffen and smooth it with a damp sponge and a trowel. Alternatively, apply it in two coats. Scratch-key the first coat and let it set (4), then apply the second and finish as before.

For large repairs use two coats of pre-mixed lightweight bonding undercoat or metal-lathing plaster followed by a finishing plaster. For a small patch repair use a cellulose filler, pressing it on and between the laths (◁).

If laths are damaged cut them out and replace them, or cover the studs with plasterboard and finish with plaster. When using plasterboard nail it in the opening with the grey side towards you.

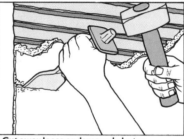

1 Cut away loose or damaged plaster

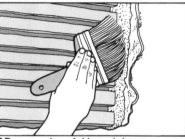

2 Dampen edges of old sound plaster

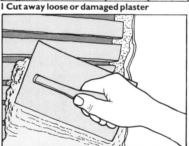

3 Apply plaster pressing it well between laths

4 Scratch key the undercoat

Repairing a ceiling

A water leak above a lath and plaster ceiling will cause localized damage to the plaster. Repair the ceiling with metal-lathing plaster, finishing with a top-coat gypsum plaster (◁).

Carefully cut back the plaster to sound material. Dampen the background and apply the undercoat (1). Don't build up a full thickness. Key the surface and let it set. Give the ceiling a second coat, scrape it back 3mm (⅛in) below the surface and lightly key it. When set, finish-coat the ceiling using a plasterer's trowel (2).

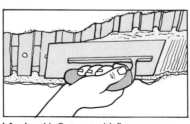

1 Apply a thin first coat with firm pressure

2 Level top coat over keyed undercoat

CEILING CENTRE PIECES

Most Victorian and Edwardian houses of any quality had moulded cornices and centre pieces in at least some of their rooms. Though many of these disappeared in the modernism of recent decades, appreciation of them has now revived, and where they cannot be restored they are often replaced with reproductions.

Restoring originals

A ceiling centre piece, or 'rose', is a decorative plaster moulding placed at the centre of a ceiling and usually has a pendant light fitting hung from it. Old mouldings of this kind are often caked in accretions of ancient distemper that mask their fine detail. Restore them whenever possible by cleaning away the old paint build-up (▷) and repairing any cracks and chipped details with filler.

Fitting a reproduction moulding

To replace original ceiling mouldings that are past repair or have been removed, there are some excellent reproduction mouldings made from fibrous plaster and available in a range of styles and sizes.

Prepare to fit such a reproduction by first carefully chipping away the old moulding, if present, with a hammer and chisel back to the ceiling plaster. Make good the surface with plaster.

If there is already a light fitting in place on the ceiling, turn off the power supply at the mains (▷) and remove the whole fitting. If the ceiling is bare, find its centre by means of strings stretched across between diagonally opposite corners. The point where the strings cross is the centre. Mark the point and drill a hole there for the lighting cable.

If the new moulding itself lacks a hole for the lighting cable, drill one through its centre.

Apply a commercial plaster adhesive to the back of the moulding and press it firmly into place after first passing the cable through both holes. On a flat ceiling the suction of the adhesive should be enough, but if you are in any doubt use hired screw props.

The larger types of moulding should have the additional support of brass screws driven into the joists, the screw heads then being covered with filler.

Wipe away surplus adhesive from round the edges of the moulding with a damp brush or sponge.

When the adhesive is set, attach the light fitting. Longer screws will now be needed to secure it.

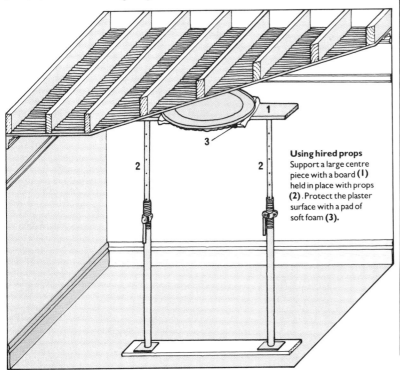

Using hired props
Support a large centre piece with a board (**1**) held in place with props (**2**). Protect the plaster surface with a pad of soft foam (**3**).

REPAIRING MOULDED CEILINGS

SEE ALSO

Details for: ▷	
Cleaning moulding	51
Switching off	296
Lighting	324-325
Screws	498

Sagging plaster on a traditional moulded ceiling can, if it is left unchecked, develop into an expensive repair job requiring the services of a professional. But if part of the plaster has broken away from its lath background, yet is otherwise intact, it can be re-fixed and prevented from collapsing.

Screw repair

Lift and support the sagging portion of the ceiling with wide boards propped in place with lengths of timber or hired screw props.

Drive countersunk plated screws fitted with galvanized or plated washers through the plaster and into the ceiling joists. The washers should be about 25mm (1in) in diameter and the fixings should be spaced about 300mm (12in) apart. They will bed themselves down into the plaster and can then be concealed with filler.

Plaster repair

A laborious but more substantial repair to a sagging ceiling can be made by using plaster of Paris to bond the plaster back to the laths.

Prop up the ceiling as for the screw repair, then lift the floorboards in the room above – this is not usually necessary in an attic – so that you can get at the back of the ceiling.

Thoroughly brush and vacuum-clean all loose material, dust and dirt away. If the groundwork is not clean the plaster of Paris will not hold.

Liberally soak the back of the ceiling with clean water, then mix the plaster of Paris to a creamy consistency and spread it quickly over the whole of the damaged area, covering both the laths and the plaster (**1**).

Plaster of Paris dries very quickly, but leave the props in place until it has set quite hard.

I Spread plaster over laths and old plaster

REPAIRING CORNICE MOULDINGS

MAKING A NEW LENGTH OF MOULDING

SEE ALSO

◁ Details for:
Cleaning moulding	51
Scrim	165
Profile gauge	485
Files	490
Gluing laminates	495

Cornice mouldings are decorative plaster features running round the perimeter of a room in the angles between the walls and the ceiling, and they can often be damaged by the 'settling down' of a house over a long period of time. Cracks can easily be made good with filler, while missing sections of mouldings have to be re-created. Small pieces of straight mouldings can be formed in situ, but longer sections should be made on a bench and then fixed in place with plaster adhesive. In either case, clean all the old paint off the remaining moulding before starting, so as to regain the sharp modelling of the shape and make a better repair (◁).

In situ repair

First, temporarily nail a straight guide batten to the wall, tucked up against the lower edge of the moulding (1) and spanning the missing section.

Now make a template of the moulding profile, including the guide batten (2) . Use a needle template tool to 'take' the profile shape, then transfer it to a piece of stiff aluminium sheet or plastic laminate. Cut the shape out with a saw file blade fitted to a hacksaw and finish off the profile with shaped files, regularly checking its fit against a good section of the moulding.

Contact glue and screw the template to a backing board and cut the board to the same shape but with the contoured edge also cut back to an angle of about 45 degrees from the template (3) .

Screw a straight-edged base board to the template so that it just touches the wall when the template is in position. Be sure that the template is at 90 degrees to the edge of the base board. Screw a triangular brace to the back edge of the template and to the base board to make the whole assembly rigid. Finally, fix a 'fence' batten to the base board on each side of the template and level with the shaped edge. When the template is in use the fence runs along the face of the wall guide batten (4) .

Clear away any loose material and dampen the area to be restored. Mix plaster of Paris to a creamy consistency and spread it over the damage. Build the thickness up gradually with progressive layers of plaster, running the template along the guide batten to form the shape as the plaster stiffens. Include pieces of jute scrim in the thick sections to reinforce the plaster.

Long sections of cornice moulding can be made up on the bench in a former constructed by screwing two lengths of board together to represent the angle between the wall and the ceiling, then gluing a triangular batten into the angle between them. Measure the height of the existing cornice and fix a guide batten to the board representing the wall at that distance from the 'ceiling' board. Next paint and wax all of the interior surfaces of the former.

Take the profile of the cornice and make up template assembly (See left). Mix up the plaster and spread it onto the faces of the former while working the template carefully along the guide batten to form the shape as layers of plaster are added and the cornice is built up in stages. Reinforce the thick parts of the moulding with pieces of jute scrim. When the moulding is hard and dry remove it from the former. Cut back the old damaged cornice to sound material, making square cuts with a fine-toothed saw and cleaning out any broken pieces from the angle with a hammer and chisel. Cut the new section of moulding to fit into the cut-out stretch, apply a proprietary plaster adhesive to its back and top, and press it into place. A very large section should have the extra support of brass screws driven into the ceiling joists.

Scrape away any surplus adhesive and fill the joints where the section butt together, then wipe down with a damp brush or sponge.

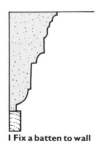
1 Fix a batten to wall

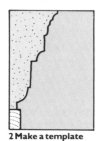
2 Make a template

3 Bevel backing board

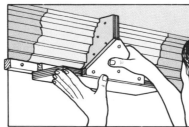
4 Run the fence along the wall batten

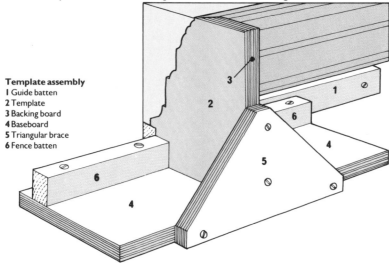
Template assembly
1 Guide batten
2 Template
3 Backing board
4 Baseboard
5 Triangular brace
6 Fence batten

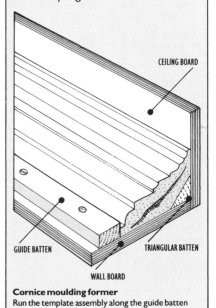
CEILING BOARD
GUIDE BATTEN
TRIANGULAR BATTEN
WALL BOARD

Cornice moulding former
Run the template assembly along the guide batten

PLASTERING A WALL

The plastering of a complete wall is not likely to be required in many households. Any new work is much more easily carried out with plasterboard (▷), but there are times when repairs arising out of damp problems, or alterations such as moving doorways, *will leave large areas to be plastered, and this can be done by the non-professional. The key to success is to divide the wall into manageable areas (See below) though some previous practice, for example when patching up decayed plaster, would be of help.*

Applying the plaster

Using the face of the plasterer's trowel, scrape a couple of trowel-loads of plaster onto the hawk and start undercoat plastering at the top of the wall, holding the trowel at an angle to the face of the wall and applying the plaster with vertical strokes. Work from right to left if you are right handed and from left to right if you are left handed (See below).

Using firm pressure to ensure good adhesion, apply a first thin layer and then follow this with more plaster, building up the required thickness. If the final thickness of the plaster needs to be more than 10mm (⅜in), key the surface with a scratcher and let it set, then apply a second or 'floating' coat.

Fill in the area between two screed battens. It is not necessary to work tight up against them. Level the surface by running the rule upwards, laid across the battens, and working it from side to side as you go. Fill in any hollows and then level the plaster again. Scratch the surface lightly to provide a key for the finishing coat and let the plaster set. Work along the wall in this way, then remove the battens, and fill the gaps they have left between the plastered areas, again levelling with the rule.

With gypsum plasters the finishing coat can be applied as soon as the undercoat is set. Cement undercoats must be left to dry for at least 24 hours because of shrinkage (▷), then wetted when the top coat is applied.

PREPARING TO PLASTER

In addition to the plastering tools you need a spirit level and some lengths of 10mm (⅜in) thick planed softwood battening. The battens – known as screeds – are for nailing to the wall to act as guides when it comes to levelling the plaster. Professional plasterers form 'plaster screeds' by applying bands of undercoat plaster to the required thickness. These may be vertical or horizontal.

Prepare the background (▷) and fix the wooden screeds vertically to the wall with masonry nails. Driving the nails fully home will make it easier for you to work the trowel, but it can also make it more difficult to remove the screeds afterwards. The screeds should be spaced no more than 600mm (2ft) apart. Use the spirit level to get them truly plumb, packing them out with strips of hardboard or wood as necessary.

Mix the undercoat plaster to a thick, creamy consistency and measure out two bucketfuls to begin with, though you can increase this to larger amounts when you become a little more proficient at working with the material.

Finishing

Cover the undercoat with a thin layer of finishing plaster, working from top to bottom and from left to right (See left) using even, vertical strokes. Work with the trowel held at a slight angle so that only its one edge is touching.

Make sweeping horizontal strokes to level the surface further. You can try using the rule in getting the initial surface even, but you may risk dragging the finish coat off. Use the trowel to smooth out any slight ripples.

Wet the trowel and work over the surface with firm pressure to consolidate the plaster, and as it sets trowel it to produce a smooth matt finish. Don't over work it, and wipe away any plaster slurry which appears with a damp sponge.

The wall should be left to dry out for some weeks before decorating (▷).

SEE ALSO

Details for: ▷	
Painting walls	67-73
Papering walls	91-97
Preparing the walls	150
Plasterboard	158-165
Rendering mixes	169
Plastering techniques	152
Builder's tools	478-479

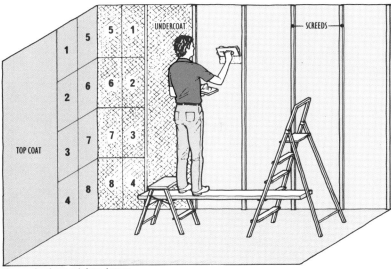

The order for applying plaster

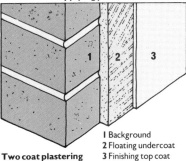

Two coat plastering
1 Background
2 Floating undercoat
3 Finishing top coat

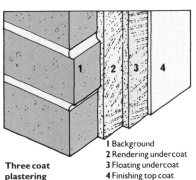

Three coat plastering
1 Background
2 Rendering undercoat
3 Floating undercoat
4 Finishing top coat

Plumb the screeds
Pack out the screed battens at the fixing points as required.

◄**Plaster layers**
Plaster is applied in layers to build up a smooth level surface. Two or three coats may be used.

PLASTERBOARD

STORING AND CUTTING PLASTERBOARD

SEE ALSO

◁ Details for:
Tools	464, 465, 485
Surface preparation	50, 165
Vapour check	87, 143, 503
Filling edges	164-165
Insulation	269

Plasterboard provides a relatively quick and simple method of smooth-covering the rough structural materials of walls and ceilings. It is easy to cut and to fix in place, either by bonding or nailing.

A range of dry-lining plasterboards is available from builders' merchants. The boards are all based on a core of aerated gypsum plaster covered on both sides with a strong paper liner. They may have a grey paper facing for finishing with plaster or an ivory-coloured paper for direct decorating with wallpaper or paint. As well as coming in a range of thicknesses and sheet sizes the boards can also have tapered or bevelled edges on the ivory-coloured sides (See below), though boards with square edges are used for most work. The edge on the grey side is always square.

Plasterboard provides good sound insulation and fire protection.

Plasterboard is fragile, having very little structural strength, and the sheets are quite heavy, so always get someone to help you carry a sheet, and hold it on its edge. To carry it flat is to run a serious risk of breaking it.

Manufacturers and suppliers of the material store it flat in stacks, but this is usually inconvenient at home and is anyway not necessary for a small number of sheets. Instead store them on edge, leaning them slightly against a wall, their ivory-coloured faces together to protect them.

Place the sheets down carefully to avoid damaging their edges.

Cutting plasterboard
Plasterboard can be cut with a saw or with a stiff-bladed craft knife.

The sheet must be supported, face side up, on lengths of wood laid across trestles and the cutting line marked on it with the aid of a straightedge. When sawing, the saw should be held at a shallow angle to the surface of the plasterboard, and if the off-cut is a large one an assistant should support it to prevent it breaking away towards the end of the cut.

When cutting plasterboard with a knife, cut well into the material following a straight edge, snap the board along the cutting line over a length of wood and cut through the paper liner on the other side to separate the pieces.

To make openings in plasterboard for electrical and other fittings you can use a keyhole saw, a power jigsaw or a craft knife (◁).

Remove any ragged paper after the cutting by rubbing down the cut edges with an abrasive paper.

Tapered edge

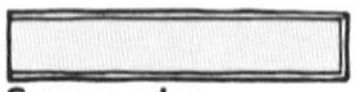

Square edge

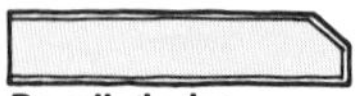

Bevelled edge

Types of edge
Tapered and square-edged boards are most common and the joints of both are filled flush. Bevelled-edge boards are used for walls where the joints are featured.

PLASTERBOARD SPECIFICATIONS

	WIDTHS	LENGTHS	THICKNESS	EDGE FINISH
PLASTERBOARD: TYPES, USAGE				
Standard plasterboard				
This material is generally used for the dry lining of walls and ceilings. It is produced in as many as nine lengths, and though most suppliers stock only a limited range other sizes can be ordered. One side is ivory-coloured for direct decoration and the other is grey for plastering.	600mm (2ft) 900mm (3ft) 1.2m (4ft)	1.8m (6ft) to 3.6m (12ft) *Commonly stocked in 2.43m (8ft) and 3.0m (10ft) lengths*	9.5mm (⅜in) 12.7mm (½in) 12.7mm (½in)	Tapered or square Bevelled
Baseboard				
Baseboard is a square-edged plasterboard that is lined with grey paper and is produced as a backing for a plaster finish. It is used mainly for plastered ceilings.	914mm (3ft)	1.2m (4ft) 1.22m (4ft) 1.35m (4ft 5in) 1.37m (4ft 6in)	9.5mm (⅜in)	Square
Lath board				
Lath board is used similarly to baseboard but has its long edges rounded.	406mm (1ft 4in)	1.2m (4ft) 1.22m (4ft) 1.35m (4ft 5in) 1.37m (4ft 6in)	9.5mm (⅜in) 12.7mm (½in)	Round
Thermal insulation board				
Thermal insulation boards are standard sheets of plasterboard with a backing of expanded polystyrene or urethane laminate. The paper surface may be ivory-coloured for direct decoration or grey for plastering.	1.2m (4ft)	2.4m (7ft 10½in) 2.43m (8ft) 2.7m (8ft 10¼in)	25mm (1in) 32mm (1¼in) 40mm (1⅝in) 50mm (2in) *thickness only available for polystyrene backed*	Tapered or square
Vapour-check plasterboard				
These boards have a tough metallized polyester film backing which is vapour resistant and provides reflective thermal insulation. They are used as an internal lining to prevent warm moist air condensing on or inside structural wall or ceiling materials.	406mm (1ft 4in) 900mm (3ft) 914mm (3ft) 1.2m (4ft)	*Stocked in same lengths as standard board, baseboard, and lath*	*Stocked in same thicknesses as standard board, baseboard and lath*	Tapered, square or round

N.B. Metric sizes actual, imperial size approximate

PLASTERBOARDING A WALL

Plasterboard can be nailed directly on to the timber framework of a stud partition or on to wooden battens that are fixed to a solid masonry wall. It can also be bonded straight onto solid walls with plaster or an adhesive.

The boards may be fitted horizontally if it is more economical to do so, but generally they are placed vertically. All of the edges should be supported.

When plasterboarding a ceiling and walls, cover the ceiling first.

Methods of fixing plasterboard

Nailing to a stud partition

Timber-framed partition walls may be simply plain room-dividers or they may include doorways. When you are plasterboarding a plain wall you should work from one corner when you start fixing the boards, but where there is a doorway you should work away from it towards the corners.

Starting from a corner

Using the footlifter, try the first board in position. Mark and scribe the edge that meets the adjacent wall if this is necessary (▷), then nail the board into position, securing it to all the frame members (See right).

Fix the rest of the boards in place, working across the partition. Butt the edges of tapered-edged boards, but leave a gap of 3mm (⅛in) between boards that are going to be coated with a board-finishing plaster.

If necessary, scribe the edge of the last board to fit the end corner before nailing it into place.

Cut a skirting board, mitring the joints at the corners or scribing the ends of the new board to the original (▷). Fit the skirting board.

Starting from a doorway

Using the footlifter, position the first board flush with the door stud and mark the position of the underside of the door's head member on the edge of the board. Between the mark on the board's edge and its top edge cut out a strip 25mm (1in) wide. Reposition the board and fix it in place, nailing it to all frame members (See right).

Fix the rest of the boards in place, working towards the corner. Butt the edges of tapered-edge boards but leave a 3mm (⅛in) gap all round boards which are to be coated afterwards with a board-finishing plaster.

If necessary, scribe the last board to fit any irregularities in the corner (▷) before fixing it in place.

Cover the rest of the wall on the other side of the doorway in the same way, starting by cutting a 25mm (1in) strip from the first board between its top edge and a mark indicating the lower side of the door's head member.

Cut a plasterboard panel to go above the doorway, butting into the cutouts in the boards on each side of the door. Sandpaper away the ragged edges of paper before fitting the panel.

When all of the plasterboard is in place fill and finish the joints (▷). Cut and fit door linings (▷) and cover the edges with an architrave moulding.

Cut and fit skirtings (▷), nailing through the plasterboard into alternate studs underneath.

NAIL FIXING

Use special galvanized plasterboard nails of lengths appropriate to the thickness of the plasterboard, as shown in the table below.

Space the nails 150mm (6in) apart and place them not less than 10mm (⅜in) from the paper-covered edge and 12mm (½in) from the cut ends. Drive the nails in straight so that they sink just below the surface without tearing through the paper lining.

Board thickness	Nail length
9.5mm (⅜in)	32mm (1¼in)
12.7mm (½in)	40mm (1⅝in)
19mm (¾in)	50mm (2in)
25mm (1in)	50mm (2in)
32mm (1¼in)	63mm (2½in)
40mm (1⅝in)	63mm (2½in)
50mm (2in)	75mm (3in)

Plasterboard nails
1 Galvanized nails
2 Double-headed nail
3 Nailable plug
4 Jagged nail

Types of nail used with plasterboard

SEE ALSO

Details for: ▷
Scribing to fit	160
Finishing joints	164
Skirtings	181
Door casings	185,190
Filling nails	165

● **Distances between stud centres**
When providing new supports it is cheaper to use 12.7mm (½in) thick board on studs set 600mm (2ft) apart. Maximum distance between stud centres: for 9.5mm (⅜in) board –450mm (1ft 6in), for 12.7mm to 50mm (½ to 2in) thick board – 600mm (2ft).

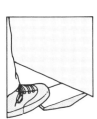

Using a footlifter
Cut the board about 16mm (⅝in) below room height to clear the footlifter, a simple tool that holds the board against the ceiling leaving both hands free for nailing. You can make one from a 75mm (3in) wide wood block.

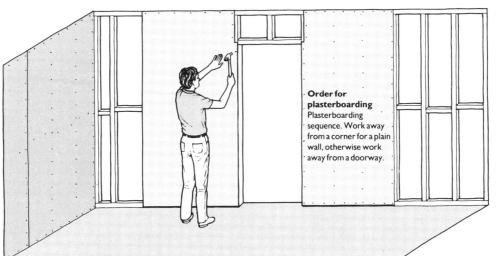

Order for plasterboarding
Plasterboarding sequence. Work away from a corner for a plain wall, otherwise work away from a doorway.

SCRIBING PLASTERBOARD

If the inner edge of the first sheet of plasterboard butts against an uneven wall, or its other edge does not fall on the centre of the stud, the board must be scribed to fit.

SEE ALSO

◁ Details for:
Stud partitions	136-137
Cutting plasterboard	158
Fixing plasterboard	159
Finishing plasterboard	164-165

Scribing the first board

Try the first board in position (**1**). The case shown is of an uneven wall pushing the plasterboard beyond the stud at the other edge of the plasterboard, and of the problem encountered when the end stud in a partition is not set at the normal spacing.

Move and reposition the board (**2**) so that its inner edge lies on the centre of the stud and tack it into place with plasterboard nails driven part way into the intermediate studs. Before temporarily fixing the board make sure it is set at the right height by using the foot lifter. With a pencil and a batten (cut to the width of the board) trace a line down the face of the board, echoing the contour of the wall. It is essential to keep the batten level while doing this.

Trim the waste away from the scribed edge, following the line, replace the board in the corner and fix it with plasterboard nails (**3**).

Scribing the last board

Temporarily nail the board to be scribed over the last fixed board (**4**), ensuring that their edges lie flush.

Using a batten and a pencil as above, trace a pencil line down the face of the board, using the batten as a guide and carefully keeping it level.

Remove the marked board, cut away the scribed area to cut it to size and nail it into place (**5**).

1 Try the first board in the corner

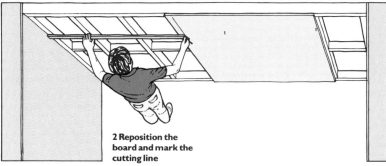

2 Reposition the board and mark the cutting line

3 Cut the board to size and nail in place

4 Temporarily nail and mark out the last board to fit

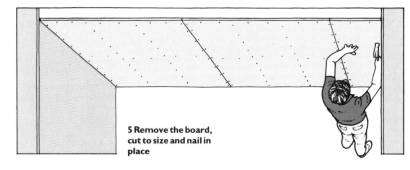

5 Remove the board, cut to size and nail in place

SOLID WALL FURRING

Plasterboard cannot be nailed directly to solid masonry walls. Battens of sawn timber known as furring strips are used to provide a good fixing for the nails and to counter any unevenness of the wall surface. These should be treated with a wood preservative.

You can cover sound old plaster but if it is in poor condition strip it back to the brickwork. If the failure of the original plaster was caused by damp, it must be treated (▷) and if possible allowed to dry out before lining.

Fit any plumbing pipe runs, electrical conduit or cable to the wall before the battens are fixed to conceal them.

Marking out

Use a straightedge to mark the position of the strips on the wall with vertical chalk lines. The lines should be placed at 400mm (1ft 4in), 450mm (1ft 6in) or 600mm (2ft) centres according to the width and thickness of the plasterboard being used, bearing in mind that sheets of plasterboard must meet on the centre lines of the battens. Work away from any door or window opening and allow for the thickness of the battens and plasterboard at the reveals (▷).

Fixing the battens

Cut the required number of furring battens from 50 x 25mm (2 x 1in) sawn softwood. The vertical battens should be cut 155mm (6¼in) less than the height of the wall. The horizontal battens should be cut to run along the tops and bottoms of the vertical ones and any short vertical infill battens above and below openings (See below).

Nail the vertical furring battens on first, setting their bottom ends 100mm (4in) above the floor. Fix them with masonry nails or cut nails, with the face of each batten level with the guide line (See right), and check with the straightedge and spirit level that they are also flat and plumb, packing them out if and as necessary.

Now nail the horizontal battens across the tops and bottoms of the vertical members, packing them to the same level if necessary.

Fixing the plasterboard

To fix plasterboard to furring strips follow the same procedure as described for nailing to a stud partition (▷), except that in this case the boards at the sides of doors and windows do not need to be notched to receive panels above or below the openings.

The procedure for filling and finishing the joints between the sheets of plasterboard is also identical.

Cut the skirting board to length and nail it through the plasterboard to the bottom horizontal furring strip, though if it is a high skirting of the type used in old high-ceilinged houses it can be nailed to the vertical battens.

LEVELLING THE FURRING BATTENS

Masonry walls are often uneven and this must be taken into account when fixing the battens if the lining is to finish straight and flat.

To check if the wall is flat hold a long straightedge horizontally against it at different levels. If it proves to be uneven, mark the vertical chalk line already drawn on the wall which is the closest to the highest point (**1**).

Hold a straight furring batten vertically on the marked chalk line keeping it plumb with a straightedge and spirit level, then mark the floor (**2**) where the face of the batten falls. Draw a straight guide line across the floor (**3**), passing through this mark and meeting the walls on each end at right angles.

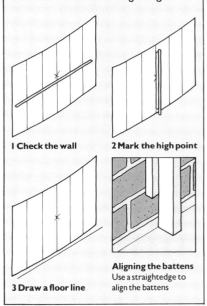

1 Check the wall

2 Mark the high point

3 Draw a floor line

Aligning the battens
Use a straightedge to align the battens

SEE ALSO

Details for: ▷
Fixing plasterboard	159
Angles and openings	163
Treating damp	251-254
Finishing plasterboard	164-165
Vapour-check plasterboard	158
Fitting skirting	181
Spirit level	478
Straightedge	479
Nails	497

Using furring strips
Order of working
1 Mark batten positions
2 Fix vertical battens
3 Fix horizontal battens
4 Fix short pieces over doors and windows and offset the short vertical ones.
5 Nail boards in place working away from a door or window

BONDING TO A SOLID WALL

SEE ALSO

◁ Details for:
Preparation	52, 150
Scribing to fit	160
Finishing joints	164
Double-headed nail	159
Insulation	269
Plasterer's trowel	478

As an alternative to using batten fixing for dry-lining a solid wall, tapered-edged plasterboard can be bonded directly to the wall with dabs of plaster or an adhesive. Special pads are produced for levelling up the wall, but squares cut from remnants of the plasterboard itself can be used.

The pads are first bonded to the wall in lines that substitute for battens, then dabs of plaster are applied between the lines of pads and the plasterboard is temporarily nailed to the pads while the plaster sets. The special double-headed nails are then removed.

Boards 900mm (3ft) wide are usually used with this technique. The wall must first be prepared in the usual way (◁).

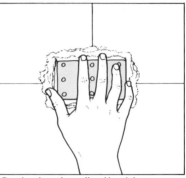

I Bond pads to the wall and level them

Fixing the pads

Set out vertical chalk lines on the wall 450mm (1ft 6in) apart, working from one corner or from a doorway or window opening (See below).

Draw a horizontal line 225mm (9in) from the ceiling, one 100mm (4in) from the floor and another centred between them. If the wall is more than 2.4m (8ft) high divide the space between the top and bottom equally with two lines. The pads are placed where the horizontal and vertical lines intersect.

Using a spirit level and a straightedge almost the height of the wall, check the wall at each vertical line, noting high spots at the intersections of the lines.

Bond a pad on the most prominent intersection point, using a bonding-coat plaster or a proprietary plaster adhesive, and press it in place to leave not less than 3mm (⅛in) of adhesive behind it **(I)**. All the rest of the pads are levelled up to this first one with plaster or adhesive.

Bond and plumb the other pads on the same vertical line, then complete a second vertical row two lines from the first. Check these pads for level vertically, then diagonally with the first row. Work across the wall in this way, then fix the remaining pads on the other intersections. Allow two hours to set.

2 Apply thick dabs of plaster between the pads

Fixing the plasterboard

Double-headed nails
Use these special nails to temporarily hold the board while the plaster adhesive sets.

Apply thick dabs of adhesive or bonding plaster to the wall with a trowel **(2)** over an area for one board at a time. Space them 75mm (3in) apart vertically and do not overlap the area of the next board. Press the board firmly against the pads so that the plaster spreads out behind it. Use the straightedge to press it evenly and the footlifter to position it.

Check the alignment, then fix the board with double-headed nails driven through it into the pads round the edge. Fix the next board in the same way, butting it to the first, and work on across the wall, scribing the last board into the internal angle (◁). When the plaster has set remove the nails with pincers or a claw hammer, protecting the plasterboard surface **(3)**.

Work round angles and openings (See opposite) and when all surfaces are covered fill and finish the joints (◁).

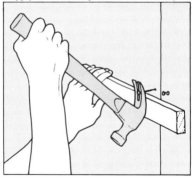

3 Pull out the nails when plaster is set

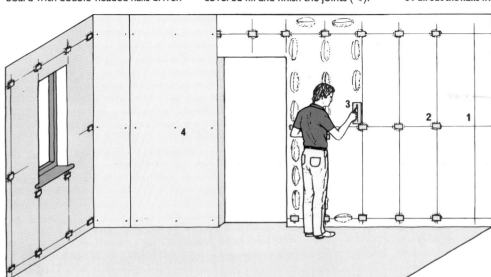

The bonding method order of working
1 Mark pad positions
2 Stick the pads to the wall
3 Apply dabs of plaster
4 Place plasterboard and temporarily nail. Remove nails when plaster is set

WINDOW OPENINGS

Cut the plasterboard linings for the window reveals and soffit to length and width. These are put into place before the wall linings. Their front edges should line up with the faces of the wall pads or furring strips.

Apply evenly spaced dabs of plaster adhesive to the back of the soffit lining, press it into place (1) and prop it there while the plaster adhesive sets. If the lining covers a wide span also use a wooden board to support it. Fit the reveal linings in the same way (2).

Working away from the window, fix the wall linings so that the paper-covered edge of the board laps the cut edge of the reveal lining.

The panels for above and below the window are cut and fitted last. Sandpaper off any rough edges of paper and leave a 3mm (⅛in) gap for filling.

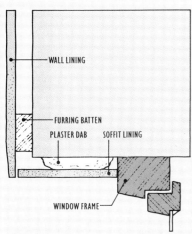

1 Soffit lining
Fix a soffit lining with dabs of plaster and prop in place until set

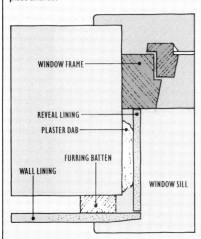

2 Reveal lining
Like the soffit lining, cut and fix the reveal so the wall lining overlaps its cut edge.

ANGLES AND OPENINGS

Internal angle

Fix wooden furring battens or bonded fibreboard pads close to the corner. Whenever possible always place the cut edges of the plasterboard into an internal corner.

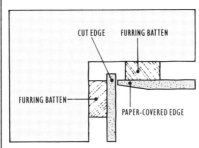

Internal corner
Set cut edges into the angle

External angle

Attach furring battens or fibreboard pads as close to the corner as possible. Use screws and wall plugs to fix the battens so as to prevent the corner breaking away. At least one board should have a paper-covered edge, which should lap the other.

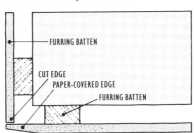

External corner
A paper-covered edge should lap the other edge

Door openings

The reveals of doorways in exterior walls should be treated in the same way as is described for window openings (See left).

In the case of interior door openings screw-fix timber furring strips or bond fibreboard pads level with the edge of the blockwork, then nail or bond the plasterboard wall linings into place.

Fit a new door lining or modify the old one if necessary and cover the joint with an architrave moulding.

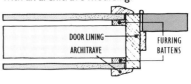

Electrical outlets

Depending on the type of fitting, chase the wall or pack out the mounting box for an electrical switch or socket outlet so that it finishes flush with the face of the plasterboard lining. Screw-fix short lengths of furring batten at each side of the box, or apply dabs of adhesive or plaster for pads if using the bonding method (See opposite).

Cut the opening for the box before fixing the board. If you find it difficult to mark the opening accurately by transferring measurements to the board, remove the fitting from the box and take an impression of it by placing the board in position and pressing it against the box.

Fix the plasterboard panel in place and replace the electrical fitting.

SEE ALSO

Details for: ▷	
Electrical fittings	88
Cutting plasterboard	158
Finishing corners	165
Wall plugs	498

Interior door opening
Fit a new lining or widen the old one and cover the joint between the lining and plasterboard with an architrave.

Electrical outlets
Chase the wall or pack out the mounting box to set it flush with the plasterboard.

Angle treatments
Order of working
1 Fit soffit lining
2 Fit reveal lining
3 Fit boarding working away from window
4 Fit panels over and under window
5 Fit boarding working away from doorway
6 Cut and fit panel over doorway
7 Cut openings for electrical fittings as they occur

FINISHING PLASTERBOARD

All of the joints between boards and the indentations left by nailing must be filled and smoothed before the ivory-coloured surface of the *plasterboard is ready for direct decoration. You will need filler, finish and jointing tape.*

SEE ALSO

◁ Details for:
Metal beading   165
Tools   478, 481

Tools and materials

The filler and finish are prepared for use by being mixed with water. The paper jointing tape is 53mm (2⅛in) wide with feathered edges, and is creased along its centre. It is used for reinforcing flat joints and internal angles. A special paper jointing tape is available for covering and reinforcing external angles. This tape has thin metal strips on each side of its central crease which strengthens the corners.

Skilled plasterers use purpose-made tools for finishing joints, but you can use medium and wide filling knives, a plaster's trowel and a close-textured plastic sponge.

Covering nails

Fill the indentations left by the nailing, using a filling knife to apply the filler and smooth it out.

When the filler has set apply a thin coating of finish and feather it off with a damp sponge.

Filling tapered-edge board joints

Mix the joint filler to a creamy consistency and apply a continuous band of it about 60mm (2½in) wide down the length of the joint.

Press the paper tape into the filler, using the medium size filling knife, bedding it in well and excluding air bubbles (1). Follow this with another layer of filler applied over the tape to level the surface, this time using the wide filling knife. When the filler has stiffened slightly, smooth its edges with the damp sponge, then let it set completely before filling any remaining small hollows.

When all the filler has set coat it with a thin layer of the joint finish. Mix the finish thoroughly to the consistency of thick cream and apply it in a wide band down the joint with a plasterer's trowel (2). Before it sets feather off its edges with the dampened sponge, and after it has set apply another thin but wider band over it, again feathering the edges with the sponge, working in a circular motion (3).

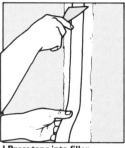
1 Press tape into filler

2 Apply finish in a wide band

3 Feather edge with a sponge

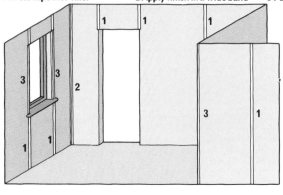

Filling the joints
1 Use the tape flat for flush jointing
2 Fold the tape for internal corners
3 Use metal-reinforced tape or metal beading on external corners (◁).

CUT EDGES

Treat a butt joint between a tapered edge and a cut edge of plasterboard in a way similar to that described for joints between two tapered edges (See left), but build up the tapered edge with filler, level with the cut edge, before applying the tape.

When two cut edges meet press the filler into the 3mm (⅛in) gap to finish flush. When the filler is set apply a thin band of finish to it and press the paper tape tight against the board. Cover this with a wide but thin coat of finish and feather the edges, then finish off as before.

▽ FILLER		
TAPERED EDGE	/	CUT EDGE
TAPE		

▽ FILLER		
CUT EDGE	/	CUT EDGE
TAPE		

GLASS–FIBRE TAPE

A self-adhesive glass–fibre mesh tape can be used instead of traditional paper tape for jointing new plasterboard or for making patch repairs. The 50mm (2in) wide tape is a strong binder and does not need prior application of filler to bond it in place. The tape is put on first, then the filler is pressed through the mesh afterwards.

Applying the tape
Ensure that the jointing edges of the plasterboard are dust-free. If the edges of boards have been cut, burnish them with the handle of your filling knife to remove all traces of rough paper.

Starting at the top, centre the tape over the joint, unroll and press it into place as your work down the wall. Cut it off to length at the bottom. Do not overlap ends if you have to make a join in the tape; butt them.

Mix the filler and press it through the tape into the joint with the filling knife, then level off the surface so that the mesh of the tape is visible and let the filler set.

Finish the joint with finishing compound, as with paper tape.

Applying the filler
Press the filler through the tape with a filling knife.

FINISHING PLASTERBOARD

Internal corners

The internal corners of dry-lined walls are finished in a way similar to the method used for flat joints. Any gaps are first filled flush with filler and if necessary a band of PVA bonding agent is applied to the original ceiling or wall plaster to reduce its suction.

Cut the paper tape to length and fold it down its centre. Brush a thin band of finish on to each side of the corner and press the paper into it while it is wet. You can use a square section length of wood to press down both sides at once to remove air bubbles (1).

With a filling knife apply a 75mm (3in) wide band of finish to both sides of the corner immediately and feather the edges with a damp sponge (2).

When the finish is set apply a second, wider coat and feather the edges again.

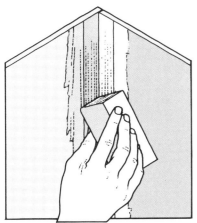

I Press into the corner with a wooden block

2 Apply a wide band of finish and feather edge

External corners

When finishing an external corner joint of plasterboard use the metal-reinforced corner tape. Cut it to length, fold it down its centre, apply a 50mm (2in) wide band of filler down both sides of the corner and bond the tape on it using a wide filling knife to keep the corner straight. Press the tape down well so that the metal strips are bedded firmly against the plasterboard, except when tapered edged board is used and the corner tape is filled out flush with the surface. Apply two coats of finish, feathering the edges as for internal corners (1).

For a very vulnerable corner use a length of metal angle bead. Apply a coating of filler to each side of the corner, then bed the angle bead in it, flushing it off with a knife before leaving it to set (2).

Apply a second coat of filler to both sides in a wide band and feather it off with a damp sponge.

When the filler is set apply two coats of finish, feathering off as before.

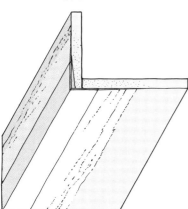

I Fill out a tapered-edge board then bed tape

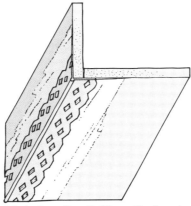

2 Embed metal bead in filler and feather edge

PREPARING FOR DECORATION

Finishing with plaster
The alternative to direct decoration of the ivory-coloured side of plasterboard is to precede decoration by applying a thin finishing coat of actual plaster to the grey face. The plastering is not easy for the inexperienced but with some practice you could tackle your walls. Ceilings should be left to professionals though you can prepare the plasterboard and have it ready for the tradesman to plaster.

Preparing the background
First fill the gaps between the board joints and at the angles, bringing them flush with the boards. Use board-finish plaster for one-coat plastering, an undercoat first for two-coat plastering.

Reinforce all of the joints and angles with jute scrim pressed into a thin band of the plaster. Let the plaster set, but not dry out, before applying the finishing plaster.

Rolls of jute scrim 90mm (3½in) wide are available from builders' merchants.

If you intend to plaster the walls yourself, first study the section on plastering thoroughly (▷).

Reinforce joints with scrim before plastering

Decorating direct
Before the ivory side of plasterboard can be directly decorated it must be given a uniform surface by the application of a sealer.

Brush or sponge-apply a thin coating of finish mixed to a thin consistency. If applying it by brush, follow it up with the sponge worked in a light circular motion over the entire surface. Alternatively, use a proprietary ready-mixed top coat which can be applied with a brush or roller and is suitable for all decorative treatments. Two coats will also provide a vapour barrier.

SEE ALSO	
Details for: ▷	
Plasterwork	148-157
Bonding agent	151
Plasterboarding ceilings	166
Vapour barrier	503

PLASTERBOARDING A CEILING

SEE ALSO

◁ Details for:
Finishing joints   164
Woodworm
treatment   246
Noggings   137,502
Types of plasterboard   158
Fixing plasterboard   159

A new ceiling may be made with plasterboard which can also be used to replace on old lath and plaster ceiling which is beyond repair.

Fixing the plasterboard in place and finishing its surface ready for direct decoration can be tackled by the non-professional, but wet plastering over a boarded ceiling should be left to the skilled tradesman as it is hard work and difficult to do well.

Preparing an old ceiling

Start by stripping away all the old damaged plaster and laths, and pull out all the nails.

This is a messy job, so wear protective clothing, a pair of goggles and a face mask while working. It's also a good idea to seal the gaps round doors in the room to prevent dust escaping through the rest of the house.

If necessary, trim back the top edge of the wall plaster so that the edge of the ceiling plasterboard can be tucked in.

Inspect and treat the exposed joists for any signs of woodworm (◁).

FITTING NEW BOARDING

Measure the area of ceiling and select the most economical size of boards to cover it.

The boards should be fitted with their long paper-covered edges running at right angles to the joists. The butting joints between the ends of boards should be staggered on each row and supported by a joist in every case.

Fit perimeter noggings between the joists against the walls and other intermediate ones in lines across the ceilings to support the long edges of the boards. It is not always necessary to fit intermediate supports if the boards are finally to be plastered, but they will ensure a sound ceiling. The intermediate noggings should be at least 50mm (2in) thick and should be fitted so that the edges of the boards will fall along their centre lines.

If necessary trim the length of the boards to ensure that their ends fall on the centre lines of the joists.

Start fixing the boards working from one corner of the room. It takes two people to support a large sheet of plasterboard while it is being fixed. Smaller sizes may be fixed single-handed, but even then a temporary wooden prop to hold them in place during nailing will be useful.

Using galvanized plasterboard nails, fix the first board, working from the joist nearest its centre and nailing at 150mm (6in) centres. This is to prevent the boards sagging in the middle, which can happen if their edges are nailed first.

Fix all the remaining boards in the same way.

If the boards are to be plastered leave 3mm (1/8in) gaps between the cut ends and the paper-covered edges. For direct decoration butt the paper-covered edges but leave 3mm (1/8in) gaps at the ends of the boards.

Finish the joints by the method described for plasterboard walls (◁).

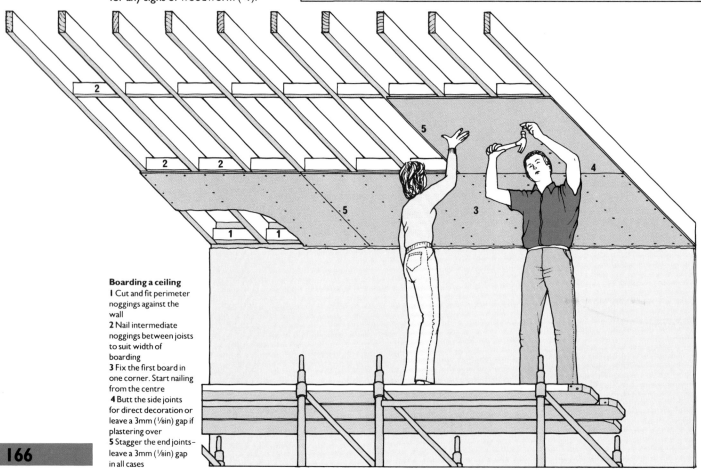

Boarding a ceiling
1 Cut and fit perimeter noggings against the wall
2 Nail intermediate noggings between joists to suit width of boarding
3 Fix the first board in one corner. Start nailing from the centre
4 Butt the side joints for direct decoration or leave a 3mm (1/8in) gap if plastering over
5 Stagger the end joints – leave a 3mm (1/8in) gap in all cases

JOINTS BETWEEN WALLS AND CEILINGS

Coving

Plaster coving is used to cover cracks in the angles between ceilings and walls, and to provide a decorative finish to plastering. It has a gypsum plaster core, moulded into a curved section, and is covered with a thick paper. Two sizes are commonly available in various lengths, with girths (widths) of 127mm (5in) and 100mm (4in).

Templates are provided by the makers to be used as guides for cutting the internal and external mitre joints.

Fitting coving

Start by marking parallel lines along the wall and ceiling, setting them off from the angle at the distance specified in the manufacturer's instructions, then scratch the plastered surfaces within the lines in order to provide a good key for the adhesive (1).

Take the measurements of the wall, then measure out the coving and cut it to fit, using the template to cut the mitres (See right). Remember that when you are cutting mitres for outside corners the coving must be longer than the wall, and must extend up to the line of the return angle drawn on the ceiling. Cut the coving with a fine-toothed saw, sawing from the face side, then lightly sandpaper the cut edges of the paper lining until smooth.

Prepare the adhesive by mixing the powder with clean water and stirring it to a creamy consistency. The adhesive should remain usable for about 30 minutes, but it's best to aim at making just enough for one length of coving.

With a filling knife apply the adhesive liberally to the back faces of the coving which will be in contact with the wall and ceiling.

Dry, bare plaster must be dampened just before the coving is put in place. Press it into the angle and level it with the guide lines (2). If a piece of coving is more than about 2m (6ft 6in) long two people should fit it. Should it tend to sag when in place support it with a couple of nails driven temporarily into the wall under its bottom edge and remove them when the adhesive has set.

Scrape away any squeezed-out beads of surplus adhesive before it sets and use it to fill the mitre joints as the work progresses. Use your finger to apply the adhesive to internal mitres if you find it easier, but finish off with a filling knife to leave a good sharp corner (3).

Wipe along the edges of the coving with a damp brush or sponge to remove any traces of adhesive. When it dries prime the coving for painting.

CUTTING THE MITRES

Using a template

The makers of plaster coving supply a cardboard template with their product which enables you to cut mitred corners more easily.

Mark the coving to length on one edge, bearing in mind whether you are mitring for an external corner or an internal one. Trim and fold the template and place it over the coving in line with the measured mark, then press it down so that it moulds itself to the curve of the material. Use the appropriate edge of the template – for an external or an internal mitre – and with a soft pencil draw the cutting line along it on the face and edges of the coving, tracing the template's edge.

Cut the mitre with a fine-toothed saw, following the marked angle.

Using a jig

If you plan to use plaster coving right through the house it will be worthwhile to make a mitre block as a jig for cutting the joints accurately.

Cut a baseboard from 18mm (¾in) plywood or chipboard about 200mm (8in) wide and 450mm (1ft 6in) long. Cut a piece of 100 x 50mm (4 x 2in) planed softwood to the same length for a fence.

Glue the fence to the baseboard flush with one long edge. When the adhesive has set mark out and make three saw cuts, one at right angles to the face of the fence and two at 45 degrees in opposite directions. Nail a stop batten to the baseboard at a distance from the fence which will allow the coving to fit snugly between them for cutting.

The baseboard of the mitre block represents the ceiling and the fence represents the wall. Lay the coving in the jig with the end to be cut in the right direction for either an external or an internal mitre (See right).

SEE ALSO

Details for: ▷	
Working platforms	40-42
Primers	43
Combination square	462
Mitre box	464
Filing knife	481
Adhesives	495-496

External mitre
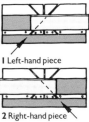

1 Left-hand piece

2 Right-hand piece

Internal mitre
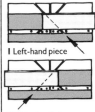

1 Left-hand piece

2 Right-hand piece

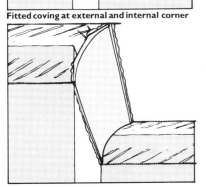

Fitted coving at external and internal corner

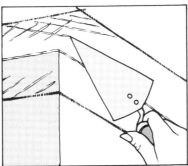

1 Scratch surface between marked lines

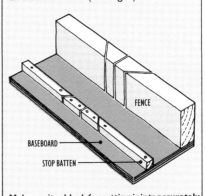

FENCE

BASEBOARD

STOP BATTEN

Make a mitre block for cutting joints accurately

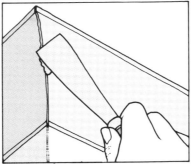

2 Press the coving into angle, level with the lines   3 Finish off with a filling knife

EXTERIOR RENDERING

SEE ALSO

◁ Details for:
Sealing brickwork	**46**
Screeds	**157**
Render	47
Mixing mortar	170
Textured renderings	171
Builder's tools	478-480

Rendering is the application of a relatively thin layer of cement or cement-and-lime mortar to the surfaces of exterior walls to provide a decorative and weather-resistant finish.

Any such treatment of exterior walls should be carefully considered beforehand, because the finished outer surface should always harmonize with the character of a building and not look ill at ease with those of its neighbours. This is particularly important in the case of terraced housing, where the fronts of the houses form an unbroken run of wall.

Planning ahead

There are no regulations controlling the change of colour or texture of outer walls except those of listed buildings and consequently one often sees houses made conspicuous by their individualistic decorative treatment.

Rerendering a wall would always be acceptable as it is merely a case of renewing what is already there.

Rendering old brickwork might improve its weather-resistance, but at the cost of destroying the appearance of the building. Here it would be better to rake out the mortar joints, repoint them and, if necessary, treat the brickwork with a clear sealant (◁).

Rendering techniques

The technique used in rendering is virtually the same as in plastering, for which cement and lime are also sometimes used, and it generally involves using the same tools, though a wooden float is better than a plasterer's trowel for finishing the cement rendering. The wood leaves a finely textured surface that looks better than the very smooth one produced with a metal trowel.

Rendering the walls of a house is really a job for the professional, as it involves covering a large area and colour-matching the batches of mortar, which is critical if the finished job is not to look patchy.

While a non-professional can undertake repairs to rendering it is very difficult to match the colour of the new work to the old. You might consider finishing the complete wall with paint.

New work can be approached by dividing the wall into manageable panels, using screed battens as in plastering (◁). But colour matching the mortar will still be a problem, and 'losing' the joints can be difficult. It might pay to concentrate on getting the rendering flat and then disguising any patchiness with paint – here again arises the question of the character of the house.

Before attempting to render a large wall, practise if possible on a smaller project, such as a garden wall.

BINDERS FOR EXTERIOR RENDERING

MORTAR

Mortar is a mixture of sand, cement and clean water. The sand gives the mix bulk and the cement binds the particles. A cement mix will bond to any ordinary masonry material and to metal. Mortars of various strengths are produced by adjusting the proportions of sand and cement, or by adding lime.

A mortar must not be stronger than the materials onto which it is being applied. In a wall of dense, hard bricks a cement-and-sand mix can be used. For soft bricks or blocks a weaker mix of cement, sand and lime is appropriate.

Cement sets by a chemical reaction with water known as hydration, and begins as soon as the water is added. Cement does not need to dry out in order to set, and the more slowly it dries out the stronger it will be.

Normally an average mix will stay workable for at least two hours. It will continue to gain strength for a few days after its initial set, reaching full strength in about a month.

Hot weather will reduce the workable time and can affect the set of the mortar by making it dry out too fast. In these conditions the work should be kept damp by being lightly sprayed with water or by being covered with polythene sheeting to retain the moisture and slow the drying time.

CEMENT

Cement made from limestone or chalk and clay is generally called Portland cement. Various types are made by adding other materials or by modifying the production methods.

Ordinary Portland cement (OPC)

This common light grey cement is mixed with aggregates for concrete and mortars. It is available in 50kg (110lb) bags but can be had in smaller amounts.

White Portland cement

This is similar to ordinary Portland but is white and more expensive. It makes light-coloured mixes for bricklaying, rendering and concrete.

Coloured cement

Some coloured cements are available and also pigments for colouring mortar mixes. The materials must be carefully proportioned for the batches to match.

Quick-setting cement

This cement is mixed with water and sets hard in 30 minutes. It is non-shrinking and waterproof; useful for small repair jobs.

Masonry cement

Specially made for rendering and bricklaying, this grey cement is not suitable for concrete. Add no lime to it.

LIME

Lime is made from limestone or chalk. When it leaves the kiln it is called quicklime, and may be non-hydraulic or hydraulic. Non-hydraulic lime, in use generally, sets by combining with carbon dioxide from the air as the water mixed with it dries out. Hydraulic lime has similar properties to cement; it sets when water is added and so can be used under water. When quicklime is 'slaked' – mixed with water – it expands and gives off heat. This is particularly strong with non-hydraulic quicklime.

Lime must be properly slaked before use, and at one time a batch would be soaked in a tub weeks beforehand. This soaked lime was called lime putty.

Pre-slaked non-hydraulic lime powder, or hydrated lime, is sold by builders' merchants. It can be used at once, but is often soaked 24 hours before use to make lime putty. The lime is mixed with water to a creamy consistency or with sand and water and left to stand as lime mortar called 'coarse stuff'. This can be kept for some days without setting if it is heaped up and covered with polythene sheet to prevent the water evaporating.

The less active hydraulic lime is dry-mixed with the sand like cement powder and the slaking process takes place when the water is added.

AGGREGATES

Mortars are mixed with the finest aggregate, sand, and sand is graded by the size and shape of its particles. A well-graded sand will have particles of different sizes, not ones which are uniformly large or small.

Types of sand

'Sharp' sand is used with other, coarse aggregates for making concrete and floor screeds. Plasterers' sharp sand is of a finer grade, and is used for rendering. 'Soft', 'builders' or 'bricklayers' sand has smoother particles and is used for masonry work.

Use well-washed sand, as impurities can weaken a mortar and affect the set. A good sand should not stain your hand if you squeeze it.

Most aggregates may be bought from builders' merchants by the cubic metre; some suppliers sell it in small packs.

Stone chippings

Specially prepared crushed stone in various colours is used for pebble-dash rendering. Buy enough for the whole job in hand (check this with your supplier) as additional stones from another batch may not match the colour of those you have.

If you do start running short, stop work at a corner rather than part way across a wall. The extra stones can be mixed with the remaining ones and a subtle change of colour is less likely to show on the adjacent wall.

Dry-mixed mortar

Pre-packed sand-and-cement mortar mixes are sold by builders' merchants and DIY shops in large and small packs. They are ready-proportioned for different kinds of application and require only water to be added. As sand and cement 'settle out', a whole bag should be used and mixed well, before adding the water.

This way of buying sand and cement is more expensive than buying loose material but the convenience and low wastage are great advantages, especially for small jobs.

STORING SAND AND CEMENT

Storing the materials should not normally be necessary because it is best that they should be bought as required and used up by the end of the job.

However, if you are held up for a time after taking delivery, you should store powder or pre-mixed materials as recommended for plaster (▷). Sand should be stored in a neat heap on a board or a plastic sheet and protected from windblown dirt and rain with plastic sheeting.

Storing sand ▶
Dirty sand can affect the set of the cement. Keep it covered with plastic sheeting.

ADDITIVES

Proprietary additives which modify the properties of mortar are added to the mix in precise proportions according to manufacturers' instructions. Their functions vary. Waterproofers, which make mortar impervious by sealing its pores, may be used when rendering on exposed walls. Plasticisers, additives which make a mortar easier to work, can be used instead of lime.

SEE ALSO

Details for: ▷	
Storing plaster	148
Mixing mortar	170

MORTAR MIXES FOR RENDERING

The mix for a mortar will depend on the strength of the material being rendered and the degree of its exposure. The undercoat mix should not be stronger than the background, and the top coat should be no stronger than the undercoat.

Though these considerations are not critical in most DIY work with mortar, where a situation does dictate that a precise mix is required, the proportions of the materials must be measured quite accurately.

The material is measured by volume, using a bucket. Loose cement and damp sand tend to 'bulk up' when loaded. Cement powder can be made to settle by tapping the bucket, and it is then topped up. Damp sand will not settle, so the measure is usually increased by 25 per cent. Dry sand and saturated sand will settle to a normal measure.

TYPE OF BACKGROUND	TYPE OF MIX	PARTS BY VOLUME			
		AVERAGE EXPOSURE		**SEVERE EXPOSURE**	
		UNDERCOAT	TOP COAT	UNDERCOAT	TOP COAT
Low suction backgrounds: Hard dense clay bricks Dense concrete blocks Stone masonry Normal ballast concrete	Cement: lime: sand	1-½-4½	1-1-6*	1-½-4½	1-1-6
	Cement: sand & plasticiser	1-4	1-6*	1-4	1-6
	Masonry cement: sand	1-3½	1-5*	1-3½	1-5
Normal absorption backgrounds: Most average strength bricks Clay blocks Normal concrete blocks Aerated concrete blocks	Cement: lime: sand	1-1-6	1-2-9*	1-1-6	1-1-6
	Cement: sand & plasticiser	1-6	1-8*	1-6	1-6
	Masonry cement: sand	1-5	1-6½*	1-5	1-5

*Suitable mixes for interior plastering undercoats

MIXING MORTAR FOR RENDERING

SEE ALSO

◁ Details for:	
Mortar board	150
Lime	168
Builder's tools	478-480

1 Shovel dry mix from one heap to another

2 Form a well in the heap and pour in water

3 Shovel dry material into water and mix

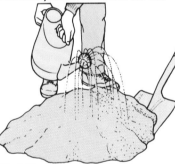

4 Sprinkle mix with water if too dry

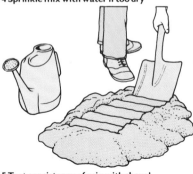

5 Test consistency of mix with shovel

Mix only as much mortar as you can use in an hour, and if the weather is very hot and dry shorten this to half an hour. Keep all your mixing tools and equipment thoroughly washed so that no mortar sets on them.

Measure the required level bucketfuls of sand onto the mortar board (◁) or – for larger quantities – onto a smooth, level base such as a concrete drive.

Using a second dry bucket and shovel, kept exclusively for cement powder, measure out the cement, tapping the bucket to settle the loose powder and topping it up as needed. Tip the cement over the heaped-up sand and mix sand and cement together by shovelling them from one heap to another and back again (**1**), and continue to turn this dry mix – the sand will actually be damp – until it takes on a uniform grey colour.

Form a well in the centre of the heap and pour in some water (**2**) – but not too much at this stage.

Shovel the dry mix from the sides of the heap into the water until the water is absorbed (**3**). If you are left with dry material add more water as you go until you achieve the right firm, plastic consistency in the mortar, turning it repeatedly to mix it thoroughly to an even colour. It is quite likely that you will misjudge the amount of water at first so if after turning the mix it is still relatively dry sprinkle it with water (**4**). But remember that too much water will weaken the mix.

Draw the back of your shovel across the mortar with a sawing action to test its consistency (**5**). The ribs formed in the mixture by this action should not slump back or crumble, which would indicate respectively that it is either too wet or too dry. The back of the shovel should leave a smooth texture on the surface of the mortar.

Make a note of the amount of water used in proportion to the dry materials so that further mixes will be consistent.

For cement-lime-sand mixes the lime powder can be added with the cement and dry-mixed as described above. Otherwise lime putty can be mixed with the sand before the cement is added, or the cement can be added to prepared 'coarse stuff' (◁). When you have finished, hose down and sweep clean the work area particularly if it is a driveway as any remaining cement slurry will stain the surface.

MIXING MORTAR BY MACHINE

You can hire a small-capacity electric or petrol-driven cement mixer. Such a mixer can save you much time and effort, especially on big jobs, and is quite easy to use.

Set the machine as close as possible to the work area and place a board under the drum to catch any spilt materials. If it is an electric-powered machine take all due precautions with the power supply and keep the cables well clear of the work.

Load the drum with half the measure of sand and add a similar proportion of cement, and lime if required. Dry-mix them by running the mixer, then add some water.

Load the remainder of the materials in the same sequence, adding a little water in between.

Run the mixer for a couple of minutes to mix the materials thoroughly, then stop the machine and test some of the mix for consistency, as it may appear stiffer than it is.

A rendering mix should be less workable than a mix for bricklaying, and for rendering blockwork it is usually stiffer than for brickwork, but this will depend on the absorbency of the wall.

It is advisable to wash out the drum of the mixer after each mix and to scour it out with water and some coarse aggregate at the end of the working day.

If you return the machine with dry or drying mortar in its drum you may be charged extra.

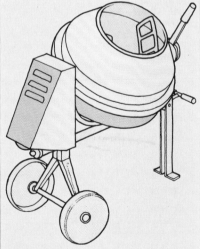

Cement mixer
Hire an electric or petrol-driven mixer when a large batch of mortar is required

TEXTURED RENDERINGS

Renderings may be textured by tooling while damp to make patterns or by applying a coarse aggregate, which is a fairly skilled procedure (See below for details). Reproduce a texture when patch repairing.

Roughcast rendering
For this rendering, mix aggregate no more than 10mm (⅜in) in size with the top coat mortar. Use about half as much as the sand used with enough water for a sticky mix. Flick it on the wall to build up an even coat.

Pebbledash rendering
Crushed stone aggregate gives pebbledash its colour, and an even distribution of the chippings is required to avoid patchiness.
A 10 to 12mm (⅜ to ½in) top coat is applied and the stones thrown at it while soft, then pressed with a float to bed them in.

Tyrolean finish
A fine cement mix is sprayed from a hand-cranked 'Tyrolean machine' to build up a decorative honeycomb texture over a dry undercoat rendering. Doors, windows, gutters etc., must be masked beforehand. Tyrolean machines may be hired.

APPLYING RENDERINGS

Preparing the surface

Neatly chop away the old loose coating on areas of cracked or blistered rendering, using a hammer and chisel. Rake out the mortar joints in the exposed brickwork if necessary and brush the area down. Clean off any organic growth like lichen or algae and apply a fungicide (▷).

Working platform

Set up a safe working platform from which to do rendering. You will need both hands free to use the tools, so it cannot be done from a ladder. Pairs of steps with a scaffold board between them can be used for working on ground floor walls, but for upper walls you will need a scaffold tower (▷).

New work

Set up 10mm (⅜in) vertical screed battens spaced no more than 900mm (3ft) apart, fixing them with masonry nails into the mortar joints of the brickwork. Check them for level and pack them out where necessary.
Between two battens apply undercoat rendering with a firm pressure to make it bond well onto the background, building it up to the thickness of the screed battens.
Level the mortar off with a straight-edge laid across the battens and worked upward with a side-to-side movement, then scratch the surface of the mortar to provide a key for the top coat and leave it to set for a week.

You can fill in the panels between the battens in sequence or fill alternate ones. Whichever you do, let them set before removing the screeds. The former method will leave narrow strips to be filled in where the screeds have been removed, whereas in the second method the newly set alternate panels of rendering will provide a levelling surface for those to be done.
Apply top coat rendering about 6mm (¼in) thick, either freehand or with the aid of screed battens as before. In any case use a straightedge for levelling it off, then finish it with a wooden float, which will produce a finely textured surface on the rendering.

SEE ALSO

Details for: ▷	
Work platform	40-42
Organic growth	44
Render	47
Plastering techniques	152
Spraying equipment	484

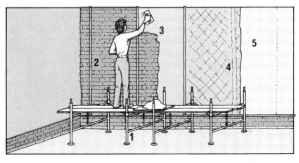

Applying rendering
Order of working
1 Set up a safe work platform
2 Divide the wall with vertical screeds
3 Apply the undercoat rendering between the screeds or alternate panels
4 Remove screeds and fill in gaps or panels
5 Apply top coat over keyed undercoat

PATCH REPAIRS

The rendering should be applied with a metal plasterer's trowel and the top coat finished with a wooden float.
Take a trowelful of mortar from your hawk and spread it on the wall with a firm pressure and applying it with an upward stroke (**1**).
Build up the undercoat layer no more than two thirds the thickness of the original rendering or 10mm (⅜in), whichever is the thinner.
Level the mortar with a straight-edged batten that fits within the cut-out of the area being patched, then scratch a key in the surface for the top coat (**2**). Leave the undercoat to set and strengthen for a few days.

The top coat
Before applying the top coat dampen the undercoat rendering if necessary to even out the suction. When the coat is on, level it with a straightedge laid across the surfaces of the surrounding rendering and worked upward with a side-to-side motion.

1 Use firm pressure

2 Key the surface

FLOORS: SUSPENDED FLOORS

SEE ALSO

◁ Details for:

Lifting floorboards	177
Fitting services	180
Repairing joists	180
Woodworm treatment	246
Damp-proof course	251

Floor construction in most buildings is based on timber beams known as joists. These are rectangular in section, placed on edge for maximum strength, usually about 400mm (1ft 4in) apart, and supported at the ends by the walls.

Such 'suspended floors' contrast with the concrete 'solid floors' – supported over their whole area by the ground –

which are usually to be found in basements, and commonly at ground level in modern houses.

Traditional suspended floors are usually boarded with tongued and grooved or plain-edged planks, though in modern houses flooring-grade chipboard is now being used on both types of floor.

Ground floors

The joists of a suspended ground floor are usually made from 100 x 50mm (4 x 2in) sawn softwood. Their ends and centre portions are nailed on to supporting lengths of 100 x 75mm (4 x 3in) softwood called wall plates, and these distribute the load from the joists to the walls, which, in turn, support them.

In traditional houses various methods have been used for supporting the wall plates. At one time it was common for the ends of the joists to be slotted into the walls and set on wall plates that were built into the brickwork. Alternatively the brickwork was formed to provide ledges – called offsets – to support the wall plates. But despite damp-proof courses being laid under the wall plates of these mortar bed joists the wood was vulnerable to timber

decay caused by rising and penetrating damp in the brickwork.

The relatively lightweight joists tend to sag in the middle and are therefore generally supported by further wall plates set on three or four courses of honeycombed brickwork known as sleeper walls. The spaces in the brickwork are left so that air can circulate under the floor. Sleeper walls are usually spaced at intervals of about 2m (6ft), and are now also used to support the ends of the joists.

Beneath a fireplace in a room with a suspended floor will be found a solid brick wall, built to the same height as the sleeper walls, for retaining and supporting the concrete hearth. This fender wall carries a wall plate along its top edge to support the ends of the floor joists that run up to it.

UPPER FLOORS

Obviously the first-floor joists and those of other upper floors can be supported only at their ends, so they are usually laid in the direction of the shortest span. Also, as they can have no intermediate support, such joists are cut deeper to give them greater rigidity. These 'bridging joists' are usually 50mm (2in) thick, but their depth will be determined by the distance they must span. The joists supporting the floor of an average-size upper room would be about 225mm (9in) deep.

Where floor joists cannot run right through – as around a fireplace or at a stairway opening – a thicker joist is used to bear the extra load of the short joists. This load is transferred to the thicker joist by crosspieces jointed at right angles (See left). The thicker joists are 'trimming joists', the short ones parallel to them are 'trimmed joists' and the crosspieces joining them together are 'trimmer joists'.

In older properties the upstairs joists may be supported on wall plates which are built into solid walls; the problem of damp is less critical here. With modern cavity wall construction the ends of the joists may also be built in, but in this case they rest directly on the blockwork inner skin. The joist-ends must not project into the cavity itself, and they must be treated with a preservative to guard against the risk of timber decay (See opposite).

Suspended ground and first floors
The floor joists of a traditionally built floor are supported by wall plates and are tenon and housing jointed where one member meets another.

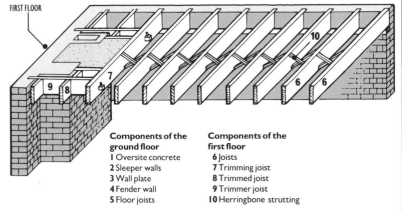

FIRST FLOOR

Components of the ground floor
1 Oversite concrete
2 Sleeper walls
3 Wall plate
4 Fender wall
5 Floor joists

Components of the first floor
6 Joists
7 Trimming joist
8 Trimmed joist
9 Trimmer joist
10 Herringbone strutting

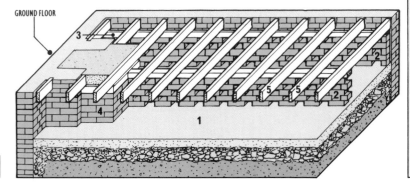

GROUND FLOOR

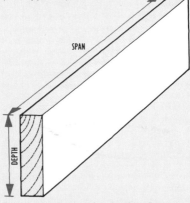

SPAN

DEPTH

To estimate the size of timber for a floor joist use the following rule of thumb as a guide.

Depth in units of 25mm (1in) =
$$\frac{\text{Span of joist in units of 300mm (1ft)}}{2} + 2$$

Examples:
● **Metric.**
Joists span 3m divided by 300mm = <u>10 units</u>

$\frac{10 \text{ units}}{2} + 2 = 5 + 2 = 7$ units x 25mm = <u>175mm</u>

● **Imperial.**
$\frac{\text{Joist span 10ft}}{2} + 2 = 5 + 2 = $ <u>7 inches</u>

BRACING FLOORS

For extra stiffness the joists of an upper floor are braced with 'solid strutting', solid sections of timber nailed between them (1), or with 'herringbone strutting', diagonal wooden braces (2).

The traditional herringbone strutting, of 50 x 25mm (2 x 1in) softwood, is preferable because it can compensate for timber shrinkage. Folded wedges or packing blocks are placed in line with the strutting between the outer joists and the walls to keep the joints tight.

In modern floor construction herringbone strutting is carried out with ready-made metal units (3), usually equipped with a drilled flange at each end for nailing between joists set at 400, 450 or 600mm (1ft 4in, 1ft 8in or 2ft) centres.

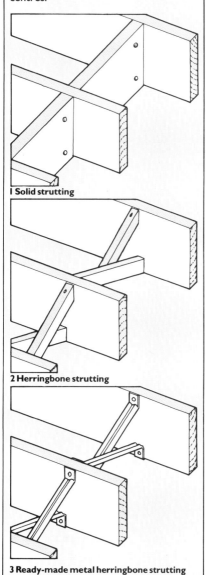

1 Solid strutting

2 Herringbone strutting

3 Ready-made metal herringbone strutting

SOLID GROUND FLOORS

Though solid floors are to be seen at all levels in large industrial buildings, in domestic houses they are normally ground floors or basements.

A solid ground floor is essentially a concrete slab laid on a sub-stratum of coarse rubble, or hardcore. To lay such a floor the topsoil is first removed and the hardcore then laid to consolidate the ground and level up the site. The rough surface of the hardcore is filled (blinded) with a thin layer of sand which is rolled flat. This sand layer prevents the cement draining out of the concrete and into the hardcore, which would cause the concrete to be weakened.

The concrete slab is usually about 100-150mm (4 to 6in) thick and is either laid over or covered by a continuous layer of moisture-resistant material, the damp-proof membrane, or DPM. The membrane may be a sheet of heavy-weight polythene – this is commonly used in modern houses – or the more traditional liquid coating of bituminous or asphalt material. The DPM, whether it is laid under or over the concrete slab, or sandwiched within it, is joined to the damp-proof course (DPC) set in the walls.

A concrete raft foundation can form a solid floor on which the walls are built, or, where strip or trench foundations are used, the slab can be laid over the ground contained within the brickwork walls.

If a floor covering is to be laid directly onto a concrete floor the floor must first be covered with a screed of sand and cement, and the screed brought to a good smooth finish. No screed is needed before laying quarry tiles if the tiles are laid with mortar rather than a proprietory tile adhesive.

Where the DPM is below the concrete slab the screed can be 45mm (1¾in) thick, but where a membrane is laid over the slab the screed should be at least 63mm (2½in) in thickness.

SEE ALSO

Details for: ▷	
Quarry tiles	111
Metal fittings	174
Solid floors	175
Concrete floors	182-183
Damp-proof membrane	182, 251

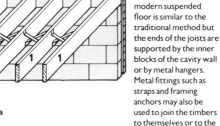

FIRST FLOOR

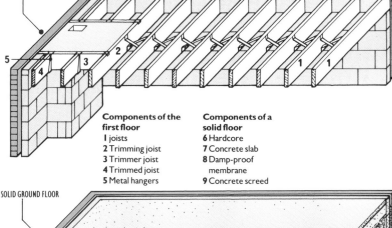

Components of the first floor
1 Joists
2 Trimming joist
3 Trimmer joist
4 Trimmed joist
5 Metal hangers

Components of a solid floor
6 Hardcore
7 Concrete slab
8 Damp-proof membrane
9 Concrete screed

SOLID GROUND FLOOR

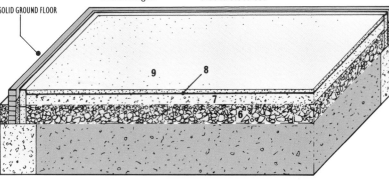

REINFORCED-CONCRETE RAFT

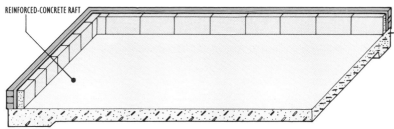

Suspended floor
The construction of a modern suspended floor is similar to the traditional method but the ends of the joists are supported by the inner blocks of the cavity wall or by metal hangers. Metal fittings such as straps and framing anchors may also be used to join the timbers to themselves or to the walls.

Solid floors
A solid floor is often used in preference to a suspended floor as it can be cheaper to construct. A concrete floor can be laid after the foundations and first courses of brickwork are built above ground level or be an integral part of a reinforced concrete foundation (See below).

METAL FITTINGS FOR FLOORS

Floor construction is one of the many areas in which modern builders have been able to substitute the use of factory-made fittings for traditional methods of construction.

SEE ALSO

◁ Details for:
Reinforcing a joist	135
Trimmed joists	172
Repairing joists	180
Nails	497

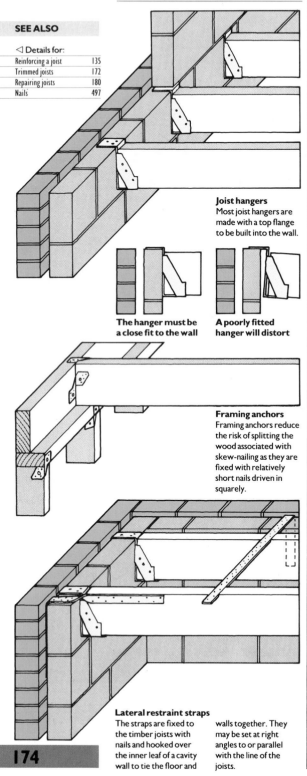

Joist hangers
Most joist hangers are made with a top flange to be built into the wall.

The hanger must be a close fit to the wall

A poorly fitted hanger will distort

Framing anchors
Framing anchors reduce the risk of splitting the wood associated with skew-nailing as they are fixed with relatively short nails driven in squarely.

Lateral restraint straps
The straps are fixed to the timber joists with nails and hooked over the inner leaf of a cavity wall to tie the floor and walls together. They may be set at right angles to or parallel with the line of the joists.

Joist hangers

Galvanized steel joist hangers are now in wide use in the construction of upper timber floors. These are brackets which are fastened to walls to support the ends of the joists. There are various versions for securing to solid or cavity walls and for constructing timber-to-timber joints.

The use of metal joist hangers allows brickwork or blockwork to be completely built up before the joists are fitted. It also saves the awkward infilling between joists that is necessary when the ends of the joists are built into the inner leaf of the walls.

The hangers must be fitted properly, with the top flange sitting squarely on the surface of the brickwork. Any packing that is used must cover the whole bearing surface and must be as strong in compression as the masonry. The rear face of the bracket must fully meet the face of the brickwork.

The ends of the joists are fixed into hangers with 32mm (1¼in) sherardized twisted nails or plasterboard nails, one or two being driven through the holes in the side gussets.

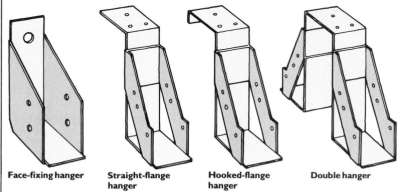

Face-fixing hanger   Straight-flange hanger   Hooked-flange hanger   Double hanger

Framing anchors

Framing anchors are steel brackets which are used to make butt joints with timbers. They are in growing use among builders to fix trimmed joists instead of the traditional – and time-consuming – tenon and housing joints.

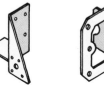

Framing anchors are made left- and right-handed

Lateral restraint straps

While the walls carry the weight of the floor, the floor adds to the lateral stiffness of the walls. In areas where the force of the wind can threaten the stability of modern lightweight walls, lateral restraint straps are used to provide ties between the walls and the floor. They are simply stiff strips of galvanized steel, perforated for nail fixing and bent in various ways to suit the direction of the joists.

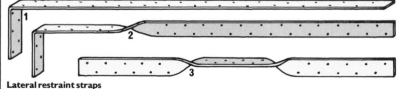

Lateral restraint straps
1 For tying joists parallel to an external wall
2 For tying joists at right angles to an external wall
3 For tying joists on either side of an internal wall

BOARDED SOLID FLOORS

Most floor coverings, including wooden block flooring, can be bonded directly to a dry, smooth screeded floor (▷), but floor boards cannot be directly bonded, and so must be fixed by other means.

The boards are nailed down to 50 x 50mm (2 x 2in) softwood battens, or bearers. The battens are embedded in the concrete while it is wet or are later fixed to clips which have been embedded. In either case the timber must be treated with a wood preservative. A damp-proof membrane (DPM) must be incorporated, usually in the form of a continuous coat of bituminous material sandwiched within the slab. A smooth finished screed is unnecessary under a boarded floor.

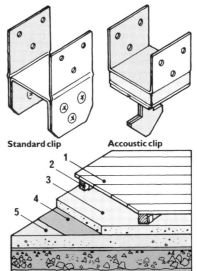

Standard clip   **Accoustic clip**

SEE ALSO

Details for: ▷	
Floor covering	113-118
Flooring	176
Insulation	265
Concrete floor	182-183

The clip method

This means of fixing requires the slab to be level and relatively smooth. The flanges of the clips are pressed into the surface of the concrete before it sets, while a marked guide batten is used to space the clips and align them in rows. The rows are normally set 400mm (1ft 4in) apart to centres starting 50mm (2in) from one wall. When the concrete is completely dry the 'ears' of the clips are raised from their folded position with a claw hammer. The battens, having been cut to length and their ends treated with a preservative, are nailed in place through the holes in the clips. The boards are nailed to the battens.

1 Clip method
Composition of floor
1 Floorboards
2 Clipped battens
3 Concrete screed
4 DPM
5 Concrete slab

Embedded battens

These are splayed in section so as to key into the concrete slab. Again, the slab is built up in two layers with the damp-proof membrane sandwiched between them. Before the top layer is laid the treated battens are positioned at 400mm (1ft 4in) centres and levelled on dabs of concrete. Strips of wood are nailed across them temporarily to hold them in position. When the dabs of concrete are set and the battens firmly held, the wood strips are removed and the top layer of concrete is poured and compacted. It is levelled with a rule, notched to fit over the battens, which is drawn along them and finishes the concrete 12mm (½in) below their tops. When the concrete layer is fully dry the boards are nailed on the battens in the conventional way.

2 Embedded battens
Composition of floor
1 Floorboards
2 Embedded battens
3 Concrete screed
4 DPM
5 Concrete slab

Chipboard floating floors

Flooring grade chipboard is a relatively recent innovation as a material for boarding over a solid floor. It is quicker and cheaper to lay a chipboard floor than one made of boards. It is also more stable and it can be laid without being fixed to the concrete slab.

It produces a floor of the type known as a 'floating floor'. The simplest floor of this kind is laid with 18mm (¾in) tongued and grooved chipboard, either the standard grade or the moisture-resistant type (▷).

First a sheet of insulating material such as rigid polystyrene or fibre board is laid on the concrete slab (▷); then, normally, a vapour barrier of polythene sheet is laid above the polystyrene. The vapour barrier must be a continuous sheet, with its edges turned up and trapped behind the skirting boards. The chipboard, its edges glued, is then laid on the vapour barrier.

The chipboard flooring is held in place by its own weight, but is also trapped by the skirting boards, which are nailed to the walls round its edges. The skirting boards also cover a 10mm (⅜in) gap between the chipboard and the walls, allowing for expansion across the floor.

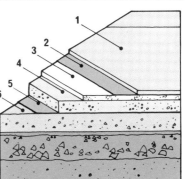

3 Chipboard floating floor
Composition of floor
1 Chipboard flooring
2 Vapour check
3 Polystyrene insulation
4 Concrete screed
5 DPM
6 Concrete Slab

Battened floating floor

Battens can be incorporated in a floating floor. Lengths of 50 x 50mm (2 x 2in) softwood, treated with a preservative, are used. They are spaced at 400mm (1ft 4in) intervals for the 18mm (¾in) chipboard; for the heavier gauge 22mm (⅞in) material they are spaced 600mm (2ft) apart.

A quilt-type sheet of insulating material is laid on the concrete slab, then covered with a polythene vapour barrier. The battens are positioned on the insulation, held together temporarily with strips of wood nailed across them. Tongued and grooved chipboard flooring is laid at right angles to the battens, the edges being glued before it is nailed down.

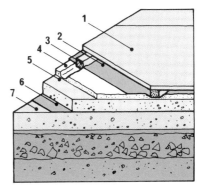

4 Battened floating floor
Composition of floor
1 Chipboard flooring
2 Vapour check
3 Battens
4 Insulation
5 Concrete screed
6 DPM
7 Concrete slab

175

FLOORING

Flooring is the general term used to describe the boarding which is laid over the floor's structural elements – the timber floor joists or the concrete slab.

This boarding can consist of hardwood or softwood planks, or it can be constructed with manufactured boards of plywood or chipboard.

SEE ALSO

◁ Details for:
Timber sizes	494
Laying floorboards	178
Laying chipboard	179

1 Quarter-sawn boards
Shrinkage does not distort these boards

2 Tangentially-sawn boards
Shrinkage can cause these boards to 'cup'

Floorboards

Softwoods are generally used for making floorboards. The standard sizes are 125 x 25mm (5 x 1in) or 150 x 25mm (6 x 1in) nominal (◁). They are sold planed all round (PAR) with square edges or tongued and grooved ones. Their thicknesses range between 22mm (⅞in) and less commonly 32mm (1¼in).

However, boards as narrow as 90mm (3½in) and others as wide as 280mm (11in) may be found in some houses. The narrow boards produce superior floors because they make any movement due to shrinkage less noticeable. But installing them is costly in labour, and they are used only in expensive houses. Hardwoods, such as oak or maple, are also used for high-grade floor construction but are not common due to their high cost.

The best floorboards are quarter sawn (1) from the log, a method that diminishes distortion from shrinkage. But as this method is wasteful of timber, boards are more often cut tangentially (2) for reasons of economy. Boards cut in this way tend to bow, or 'cup' across their width and they should be fixed with the cupped side facing upwards, as there is a tendency for the grain of the other side to splinter. The cut of a board – tangential or quarter cut – can be checked by looking at the annual growth rings on the end grain.

The joint of tongued and grooved boards is not at the centre of their edges but closer to one face, and these boards should be laid with the offset joint nearer to the joist. Though tongued and grooved boards are nominally the same sizes as square edged boards the edge joint reduces their floor coverage by about 12mm (½in) per board.

In some old buildings you may find floorboards bearing the marks left by an adze on their undersides. Such old boards have usually been trimmed to a required thickness only where they sit over the joists, while their top faces and edges are planed smooth.

SHEET FLOORING

Softwood and hardwood boards not only provide a tough flooring; when sealed and polished they will also take on an attractive colour. But sheet materials such as flooring grade plywood or chipboard are merely functional, and are used as a sub-base for other floor surfaces.

Plywood

Any exterior grade plywood – known in the trade as WPB bonded plywood – can be used for flooring. Those sold as flooring grade plywoods are tongued and grooved on two or all four edges.

Plywood flooring laid directly over the joists should be 16 to 18mm (⅝ to ¾in) thick, though boards laid over an existing floor surface, to level it or to provide an underlay for tiles, can be 6 to 12mm (¼ to ½in) in thickness. Plywood floors are laid in the same way as chipboard ones.

Chipboard

Only proper flooring grade chipboard, which is compressed to a higher density than the standard material, should be used for flooring. It is available in square-edged and tongued and grooved boards. The square-edged boards measure 2.4 x 1.22m (8 x 4ft) and are 18mm (¾in) thick. Tongued and grooved boards are available in two grades: the standard Type II and the moisture-resistant Type II/III. Both grades come in sheets measuring 2.4m x 600mm (8 x 2ft) and 22mm (⅞in) thick. The moisture-resistant type should always be used where damp conditions may occur, such as in bathrooms or kitchens.

The 18mm (¾in) thick boards are suitable for laying on joists spaced no more than 400mm (1ft 4in) apart. Where the joists are at 600mm (2ft) intervals the 22mm (⅞in) boarding must be used.

Types of flooring
1 Square-edged chipboard
2 T and G chipboard
3 T and G plywood
4 T and G softwood boards
5 Square-edged softwood boards
6 T and G hardwood boards

TONGUED AND GROOVED BOARDING

You can detect whether your floorboards are tongued and grooved by trying to push a knife blade into the gap between them.

To lift a tongued and grooved board it is necessary first to cut through the tongue on each side of the board. Saw carefully along the line of the joint with a dovetail or tenon saw (1) held at a shallow angle. A straight batten temporarily nailed along the edge of the board may help you to keep the saw on a straight line.

With the tongue cut through, saw across the board and lift it as you would a plain-edged one.

If the original flooring has been 'secret nailed' (2), use lost head nails (3) to fix the boards back in place and conceal the recesses with a matching wood filler.

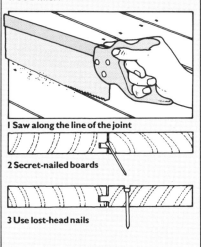

1 Saw along the line of the joint

2 Secret-nailed boards

3 Use lost-head nails

REFITTING A CUT BOARD

The butted ends of floorboards normally meet and rest on a joist (1) and a board which has been cut flush with the side of a joist must be given a new means of support when replaced (2).

Cut a piece of 50 x 50mm (2 x 2in) softwood and screw it to the side of the joists flush with the top. Screw the end of the floorboard to the support.

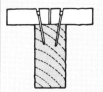

1 Boards share a joist   2 Support a cut board

LIFTING FLOORBOARDS

Floorboarding is produced in lengths that are intended to run from wall to wall. In practice this is rarely carried out entirely because odd, shorter lengths are often laid to save on materials.

When lifting floorboards it is these shorter pieces that you should start with if possible. In many older homes one or two boards will probably have been lifted already for access to services.

Square-edged boards

Tap the blade of a bolster (▷) into the gap between the boards close to the cut end (1). Lever up the edge of the board but try not to crush the edge of the one next to it. Fit the bolster into the gap at the other side of the board and repeat the procedure. Ease the end of the

board up in this way, then work the claw of a hammer under it until you can lift it enough to slip a cold chisel (▷) under it (2). Move along the board to the next set of nails and proceed in the same way, continuing until the board comes away.

1 Lever up board with bolster chisel

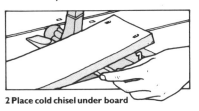

2 Place cold chisel under board

Lifting a continuous board

Floorboards are nailed in place before the skirting boards are fixed, so the ends of a continuous board are trapped under them. If you need to lift such a board it will have to be cut.

Ease up the centre of the board with the bolster so that its full thickness is clear of the adjacent boards, then slip the cold chisel under it to keep it bowed (1). Remove the nails, and with a tenon saw cut through the board over the centre of the joist. You can then lift the two halves of the board using the same method as for a short one.

Boards that are too stiff to be bowed upwards, or are tongued and grooved, will have to be cut across in situ. This means cutting flush with the side of the joist instead of over its centre.

Locate the side of the joist by passing the blade of a padsaw (2) vertically into the gaps on both sides of the board (the joints of tongued and grooved boards will also have to be cut (See left). Mark the edges of the board where the blade stops, and draw a line between these points representing the side of the joist. Make a starting hole for the saw blade by drilling three or four 3mm (⅛in) holes close together at one end of the line marked across the surface.

Work the tip of the blade into the hole and start making the cut with short strokes. Gradually tip the blade to a shallow angle to avoid cutting into any cables or pipes that may be hidden below. Lever up the board with a bolster chisel as described above.

SEE ALSO

Details for: ▷
Bolster	480
Cold chisel	480
Saws	463-464
Nails	497

1 Saw across the board

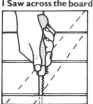

2 Find the joist's side

Freeing the end of a board

The end of the board trapped under the skirting can usually be freed by being lifted to a steep angle, when the 50mm (2in) gap between the joists and the wall should allow the board to clear the nails and be pulled free (1).

To raise a floorboard that runs beneath a partition wall, the board must also be cut close to the wall. Drill a starting hole and then cut the board as close to the wall as possible (2).

There is a special saw (3) that can be used for cutting floorboards. It has a curved cutting edge that allows you to cut a board without fully lifting it.

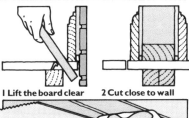

1 Lift the board clear   2 Cut close to wall

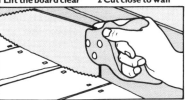

3 Hire a floorboard saw if necessary

177

RE-LAYING A FLOOR

SEE ALSO

◁ Details for:
Lifting floorboards   177
Repairing joists   180
Removing skirting   181
Woodworm   246
Nails   497
Secret nailing   177

Though floors probably take more wear and tear than any other interior surface this is not usually the reason why re-laying boarding becomes necessary. Fire damage or timber decay – which would also affect the joists – or simply large gaps in the boarding caused by shrinkage may require the floor to be re-laid, or even entirely renewed.

If the floor is to be renewed, measure the room and buy your materials in advance. Leave floorboards or sheets of chipboard to acclimatise – ideally in the room where they are to be laid – for at least a week before fixing.

Removing the flooring

To lift the complete flooring you must first remove the skirting boards from the walls (◁). If you intend to re-lay the boards, number them with chalk before starting to raise them. Lift the first few boards as described (◁), starting from one side of the room, then prise up the remainder by working a cold chisel or crowbar between the joists and the undersides of the boards. In the case of tongued and grooved boards, two or three should be eased up simultaneously, to avoid breaking the joints, and progressively pulled away.

Pull all the nails out of the boards and joists, and scrape any accumulated dirt from the tops of the joists. Clean the edges of the boards similarly if they are to be re-used. Check all timbers for rot or insect infestation and treat or repair them as required (◁).

Laying new floorboards

Though the following deals with fixing tongued and grooved floorboarding, the basic method described applies equally to square-edged boarding.

Lay a few loose boards together to form a work platform. Measure the width or length of the room – whichever is at right angles to the joists – and cut your boards to stop 10mm (⅜in) short of the walls at each end. Where two shorter boards are to be butted end to end, cut them so that the joint will be centred on a joist and set the boards out so as to avoid such joins occurring on the same joist with adjacent boards. Any two butt joints must be separated by at least one whole board. Lay four to six boards at a time.

Fix the first board with its grooved edge no more than 10mm (⅜in) from the wall and nail it in place with cut floor brads or lost head nails (◁) that are at least twice as long as the thickness of the board.

Place the nails in pairs, one about 25mm (1in) from each edge of the board and centred on the joists. Punch them in about 2mm (¹⁄₁₆in). Place one

nail in the tongued edge if secret nailing.

Lay the other cut boards in place and cramp them up to the fixed one so as to close the edge joints. Special floorboard cramps can be hired for this, but wedges cut from 400mm (1ft 4in) off-cuts of board will work just as well (**1**). To cramp the boards with wedges, temporarily nail another board just less than a board's width away from them. Insert the pairs of wedges in the gap, resting on every fourth or fifth joist, and with two hammers tap the wedges' broad ends toward each other. Nail the cramped-up boards in place as before, then remove the wedges and temporary board and repeat the operation with the next group of boards, continuing in this way across the room.

At the far wall place the remaining boards, cutting the last one to width, its tongue on the 'waste' side. It should be cut to leave a gap equal to the width of the tongue or 12mm (½in), whichever is less. If you cannot get the last board to slot in, cut away the bottom section of the grooved edge so that it will drop into place (**2**).

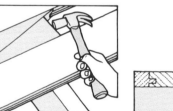
1 Make wedges to cramp boards

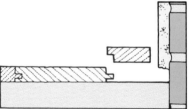
2 Cut away part of last board's grooved edge

● **Closing gaps**
You can re-lay floorboards without removing all the boards at once. Lift and re-nail about six boards at a time as you work across the floor. Finally cut and fit a new board to fill the last gap.

Laying the boards
Working from a platform of loose boards, proceed in the following order
1 Fix first board parallel to the wall
2 Cut and lay up to six boards, cramp them together and nail
3 Lay the next group of boards in the same way, continue across the floor and cut the last board to fit

FLOORBOARD CRAMP

This special tool automatically grips the joist over which it is placed by means of two toothed cams. A screw-operated ram applies pressure to the floorboards when the tommy bar is turned.

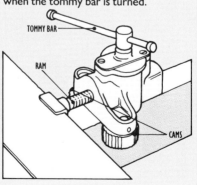

TOMMY BAR

RAM

CAMS

LAYING CHIPBOARD FLOORING

For a floor that is going to be invisible beneath some kind of covering – vinyl, cork, fitted carpet or whatever – chipboard is an excellent material. It is laid relatively quickly and is much cheaper than an equivalent amount of timber flooring. It comes square-edged or tongued and grooved. Each has its own laying technique.

CUTTING TO FIT

Square-edge boards
The widths of the boards may have to be cut down (1) so that their long edges will butt on the joists' centre lines.

Tongued and grooved boards
Only the last boards need be cut in their width (2) to fit against the wall.

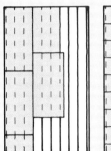

1 Square-edged boards

2 T&G boards

Square-edged boards

All the edges of square-edged chipboard flooring must be supported. Lay the boards with their long edges along the joists and nail 75 x 50mm (3 x 2in) softwood noggings between the joists to support the boards' ends. The noggings against the wall can be placed in advance; those supporting joints between boards must be nailed into place as the boards are laid.

Start with a full-length board in one corner and lay a row of boards the length of the room, cutting the last one to fit as required. Leave an expansion gap of about 10mm (⅜in) between the outer edges of the boards and the walls. If the boards' inner edges do not fall on the centre line of a joist, cut them down so that they do so on the nearest one, but cut the surplus off the outer edge, near the wall.

Nail the boards down close together, using 50mm (2in) or 56mm (2¼in) annular ring nails spaced about 300mm (1ft) apart along the joists and noggings. Place the nails about 18mm (¾in) from the edges.

Cut and lay the remainder of the boards with the end joints staggered on alternate rows.

Tongued and grooved boards

Tongued and grooved boards are laid with their long edges running across the joists. Noggings are needed only against the walls, to support the outer edges. The ends of the boards are supported by joists.

Working from one corner, lay the first board with its grooved edges about 10mm (⅜in) from the walls and nail it into place.

Apply PVA wood adhesive to the joint along the end of the first board, then lay the next one in the row. Knock it up to the first board with a hammer for a good close joint, protecting the edge with a piece of scrap wood. Nail the board down as before, then wipe any surplus adhesive from the surface before it sets, using a damp rag. Continue in this way across the floor, gluing all of the joints as you go. Cut boards to fit at the ends of rows or to fall on the centre of a joist as and stagger these end joints on alternate rows.

Finally fit the skirting, which will cover the expansion gaps.

You can seal the surface of the chipboard with two coats of clear polyurethane varnish if you wish, to protect it from dirt.

SEE ALSO

Details for: ▷	
Floor covering	115
Chipboard flooring	176
Fitting skirting	181
Nails	497

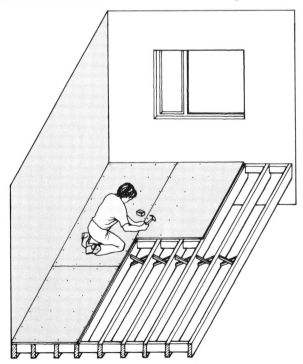

1 Arrangement for laying square-edged boards

2 Arrangement for laying T&G boards

1 Square-edged boards
Lay the boards with their long edges on a joist and the ends supported with noggings.

2 Tongued and grooved boards
Lay the boards across the joists with the ends falling on a joist.

FLOOR JOISTS

SEE ALSO

◁ Details for:

Size guide	172
Joist hangers	174
Lifting floorboards	177
Fitting skirting	181
Curing damp	249-257

Fitting services
1 Make holes within the shaded line
2 Place notches within shaded area

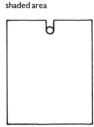

Drill and saw notches to accommodate pipe

Repairing a joist
The stages for replacing a joist are combined in the illustration.

Order of working
1 Cut away old joist
2 Cut out wall plate
3 Fit new wall plate
4 Cut and fit new joist and brace the joint with bolted joist timbers

Floor joists are important structural elements of a house. Being load-bearing, their size and spacing in new structures is strictly specified by the Building Regulations and they must satisfy a Building Control Officer. But for most domestic repairs or replacements the rule of thumb guide (◁) is adequate. Usually calculations are not necessary; matching new timber for old in size should suffice.

Use 'structurally graded' timber; it has been expertly examined or machine tested. Two common grades are marked with coloured code letters. A purple SS is the grade mark of 'special structural timber', used for joists. A green GS indicates 'general structural timber', for general framing but also joists. MSS and MGS denote machine-graded timber to the same specification.

Fitting services

Service runs like heating pipes and electric cables can run in the void below a suspended ground floor, but those running at right angles to the joists in upper floors must pass through the joists, which are covered by flooring above and a ceiling below.

So as not to weaken joists the holes for cables should centre on the joist's depth, in any event at least 50mm (2in) below the top surface to clear floor nails, and always within the middle two thirds of the joist's length (1).

Notches for pipe runs in the top edge should be no deeper than one eighth the depth of the joist and within a quarter of the joist's length at each end (2). Make notches by drilling through the joist, then sawing down to the hole.

Repairing joists

Floor joists which have been seriously attacked by wet rot, dry rot or insect infestation have to be cut out and replaced. Such attack usually occurs at ground floor level because of its closeness to the damp soil. If the damage is extensive, or if the upper floors are also affected, you should really call in an expert, but if it is localised and not too serious you can deal with it yourself.

Remove the skirtings and lift the floorboards over the infected area until you reach a sleeper wall (◁). Test the condition of the wood – joists, floorboards and skirting boards – by spiking it with a sharp knife. If the blade penetrates easily the wood will have to be replaced. Sound wood can be chemically treated to kill rot spores or wood-boring insect larvae (◁).

Preparation
The damp conditions which have caused the outbreak of wet or dry rot must themselves be identified and corrected before any remedial work on the timbers is carried out (◁).

All infected timbers must be removed in an area extending at least 450mm (1ft 6in) beyond the last visible signs of attack, and all surrounding masonry must be treated with a fungicide (◁). Burn all the infected timber. The following assumes that the end of a joist and perhaps also the wall plate are affected.

Saw through and remove the infected end of the joist, cutting it back to the centre of the nearest sleeper wall. If the wall plate which has been supporting

the joist is also affected, cut it away. If the wall plate is built into the brickwork, drill a series of holes into its edge and finish cutting it away with a wood chisel and mallet, trimming the remaining ends square. Wall plates on sleeper walls are simply cut with a saw.

Replacement
Cut a new length of wall plate timber to fill the gap and treat it thoroughly with wood preservative.

If the original mortar bed joint and damp-proof course are undamaged, apply a coating of liquid bituminous damp-proofing over it and put the new section of wall plate into place.

If necessary, re-lay the bed joint and insert a new length of DPC, making sure that its ends overlap the ends of the old one, if present, by at least 150mm (6in). Then reseat the wall plate.

Now cut a length of new joist to sit on the repaired wall plate and meet the cut end of the old joist on the sleeper wall. Treat it well with the timber preservative. To ensure that it is level with the other joists, trim its underside or pack it with DPC felt.

Brace the joint with two 1m (3ft) lengths of joist timber – also treated – on each side and bolt through with four coach bolts and two timber connectors for each bolt.

Finally replace the floorboards and skirtings (◁).

FITTING JOIST HANGERS

Sections of infected wall plate which have had to be removed can be replaced with metal joist hangers (◁) to support the ends of the repaired joists.

Having removed the damaged joist and section of wall plate (See above), lay bricks in the resulting slot. But before laying the cement check on the condition of the DPC and reinforce it with an extra layer of DPC felt or a liquid damp-proofing material if you think it necessary.

Set the flange of the joist hanger in mortar at the required level, then allow the mortar to harden before fitting the new section of joist as indicated above.

SKIRTINGS

Skirtings are protective 'kick boards', but are usually also moulded to form a decorative border between the floor and walls. Modern skirtings are relatively small and simply formed, with either a rounded or bevelled top edge.

Skirtings found in older houses can be as much as 300mm (1ft) wide and quite elaborately moulded, but those in most homes are about 175mm (7in)

wide and of 'ovolo' or 'torus' design. These can still be bought from timber merchants. Some will supply more elaborate designs to special order.

Skirtings can be nailed directly on to plastered brickwork or to battens, known as 'grounds', which have been fixed during the plastering stage. Skirting boards on partition walls are nailed to timber studs.

SKIRTING MOULDINGS

Most standard skirting mouldings are made in softwood ready for painting. Hardwood is not so common and is reserved for special decorative skirting. Hardwoods are coated with a clear finish (▷). 'Moulded-reverse' skirtings have a different profile machined on each side of the board – providing two skirtings in one.

SEE ALSO

Details for: ▷	
Finishing wood	74-79
Try square	462
Panel saw	463
Coping saw	464
Nails	497

Removing skirting

Remove skirting by levering it away from the wall with a crowbar or bolster chisel. Where a skirting butts against a door architrave or an external corner it can be levered off easily enough, but a continuous length whose ends are mitred into internal corners will have to be cut before it can be removed.

Tap the blade of the bolster between the skirting and the wall, and lever the top edge away sufficiently to insert the chisel end of the crowbar behind it. Place a thin strip of wood behind the crowbar to protect the wall, tap the bolster in again a little further on, and work along the skirting in this way as

the nails loosen.

With the board removed, pull the nails out through the back to avoid splitting the face.

Cutting a long skirting

A long stretch of skirting will bend out sufficiently for you to cut it in place if you lever it away at its centre and insert blocks of wood (1), one on each side of the proposed cut, to hold the board about 25mm (1in) from the wall.

Make a vertical cut with a panel saw held at about 45 degrees to the face of the board (2) and work with short strokes, using the tip of the saw.

Selection of skirting mouldings
(From top to bottom) Bevelled hardwood. Bevelled/rounded reverse. Ovolo/bevelled reverse. Torus/bevelled reverse. Ovolo/torus reverse. Hard wood skirting.

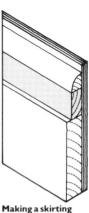

Making a skirting
If you are unable to buy a length of skirting to match your original, and the cost of having it specially machined is too high, make it up from various sections of wood.

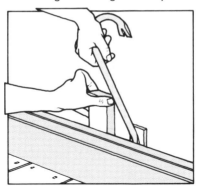

1 Prise skirting away from wall and pack out

2 Cut through skirting with tip of saw

Fitting new skirting

A skirting board can be damaged by timber decay or woodworm, or it can suffer in the process of being removed when a repair to a floor is being made. Restore the skirting if you can, especially if it is a special moulding; otherwise try to make it up from various moulded sections (See right). Standard mouldings are easily available.

Measure the length of the wall. Most skirtings are mitred at the corners, so take this into account when you are measuring between internal and external corners.

Mark the length on the plain bottom edge of the board, then mark a 45

degree angle on the edge and square it across the face of the board (▷). Fix the board on edge in a vice and carefully cut down the line at that angle.

Sometimes moulded skirtings are scribed and butt-jointed at internal corners. To achieve the profile, cut the end off one board at 45 degrees as you would for a mitre joint (1), and with a coping saw cut along the contour line on the moulded face so that it will 'jig-saw' with its neighbour (2).

Fix skirting boards with cut clasp nails when nailing to brickwork and with lost head nails when attaching them to wooden grounds.

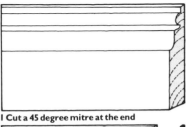

1 Cut a 45 degree mitre at the end

2 Cut the shape following the contour line

SEE ALSO

◁ Details for:
Rot treatment	249
Running cable	303-305
Plumbing	351-359
Solid ground floor	173
Damp-proofing	251-258
Sledghammer	479

REPAIRING A CONCRETE FLOOR

Concrete floors can be subject to cracking caused by shrinkage. Usually the cracks are only in the screed and can be easily repaired, but a cracked floor that is also uneven may be a sign of settlement in the sub-base, and you should have it checked by a surveyor or by the Building Control Officer, who will advise you on what steps to take.

Filling a crack

Clean all dirt and loose material out of the crack and, if necessary, open up narrow parts with a cold chisel to allow better penetration of the filler.

Prime the crack with a solution of 1 part bonding agent : 5 parts water and let it dry. Make a filler of 3 parts sand : 1 part cement mixed with equal parts of bonding agent and water; or use a ready-mixed quick-setting cement. Apply the filler with a trowel, pressing it well into the crack.

Laying a pipe in a concrete floor

Installations like central heating call for pipework to run across a room. If the floor is solid that means either running it round the walls or setting it into the floor. The latter looks better, though it involves more work.

Cut a 100mm (4in) wide channel with a cold chisel and club hammer. It should be deep enough for the pipe to be set about 25mm (1in) below the surface while also having a clearance under it.

You may damage the damp-proof membrane while cutting the channel, in which case it must be repaired. Bitumen-based liquid damp-proofing can be used to restore a bitumen or polythene DPM. For a polythene one carefully cut back the screed about 100mm (4in) all round the channel to expose the polythene surface.

Remove all loose material and apply a primer coat of diluted damp-proofer according to the maker's instructions and allow it to dry.

With the pipework installed, apply two or three coats to the bottom and sides of the channel, stopping about 12mm (½in) from the surface. Allow each coat to dry before applying the next. The coatings must overlap the original DPM to form a continuous skin.

Test the pipework before filling the channel with a mix of 3 parts sand : 1 part cement and trowel it level.

LAYING A CONCRETE FLOOR

A suspended timber floor which has been seriously damaged by rot or insect infestation can be replaced with a solid concrete floor provided that the space below it needs no more than 600mm (24in) of infill material. (If this were the case a concrete floor would be liable to damage through settlement of the infill, so a new suspended floor would have to be fitted.)

Before taking any action consult your local Building Control Officer, because the converting of one floor can affect the ventilation of another.

If the work involves the electrical supply main or the supply pipes for gas or water you should check with the appropriate authority.

Wiring and heating pipes should be re-run before the infill is laid (◁).

Preparing the ground

Remove and burn all of the old infected timbers and take off the door of the room. Treat the ground and all the surrounding masonry thoroughly with a good fungicide (◁). With bricks and mortar fill in any recesses in the walls left by the timbers. Demolish the sleeper walls and combine the fragments with the infill material.

Mark the walls with a levelled chalk line to indicate the finished floor level, at the same time making allowance for the floor covering if you intend to use a thick material such as quarry tiles or wood blocks. About 50mm (2in) below this line mark another one, the space between them representing the thickness of the screed. Then mark a third line a further 100mm (4in) down, indicating the thickness of the slab.

The infill

Lay the infill material to the required depth in layers of no more than 225mm (9in) at a time, compacting each layer thoroughly and breaking up the larger pieces with a sledgehammer (1). You can use brick and tile rubble or, better still, gravel rejects, which are coarse stones from quarry waste. If you are using secondhand rubble you should remove from it any fragments of plaster, which can react unfavourably with cement, and any pieces of wood.

Bring the surface of finely broken rubble up to within 25mm (1in) of the chalk line for the concrete and 'blind' the surface with a layer of sand, tamped or rolled flat.

The damp-proofing

Spread a sheet polythene damp-proof membrane of 1000-gauge (0.010in) minimum thickness over the surface of the sand turning its edges up all round and lapping it up the walls to form a tray. Make neat folds at the corners and hold them temporarily in place with paper clips. If the floor needs more than one sheet to cover it the sheets must overlap by at least 200mm (8in) and the joints be sealed with a special waterproof tape available from builders' merchants.

1 Preparing the ground
Mark the walls with chalk lines for the finished floor level, thickness of the screed and thickness of the concrete slab. Fill the floor area with hardcore within 25mm (1in) of the first line, compacting it well with a sledgehammer. Cover the hardcore with sand up to the line and lay a damp-proof membrane over it.

CONCRETE FLOORS

Laying the concrete

Mix a medium-strength concrete of 1 part cement: 2½ parts sand: 4 parts aggregate. Do not add too much water; the mix should be a relatively stiff one.

Lay the concrete progressively in bands about 600mm (2ft) wide. The direction of the bands will depend on the door because you will have to work in such a way as to finish at the doorway. Tamp the concrete with a length of 100 x 50mm (4 x 2in) timber to compact it and finish level with the chalked line **(2)**. As you go along, check the overall surface with a spirit level and straight edge, and fill in any hollows, though slight unevennesses will be taken up by the screed.

When the concrete has set firmly enough to support a board to walk on, brush the surface with a stiff broom to make a key for the screed. Leave it to cure for at least three days under a sheet of polythene to prevent shrinkage caused by rapid drying.

Laying the screed

Mix the screed material from 3 parts sharp sand : 1 part portland cement. Dampen the floor and prime it with a cement grout mixed to a creamy consistency with water and bonding agent in equal parts. Working from one wall, apply a 600mm (2ft) band of grout with a stiff brush.

Apply a bedding of mortar at each end of the grouted area to take 38 x 38mm (1½ x 1½in) 'screed battens'. True them with a spirit level and straight edge so that they are flush with the surface-level line on the walls.

Lay mortar between the battens, tamp it well down **(3)**, level it with the straight edge laid across the battens and smooth it with a wooden float. Lift the battens out carefully, fill the hollows left with mortar and level with the float.

Repeat the procedure, working across the floor in bands 600mm (2ft) wide. Cover the finished floor with a sheet of polythene and leave it to cure for about a week.

The floor will be hard enough to walk on in two weeks, but not fully dry for about six months. Allow a month for every 25mm (1in) of thickness and meanwhile do not lay an impermeable floor covering.

Trim the damp-proof membrane to within 25mm (1in) of the floor and fit the skirtings to cover its edges **(4)**.

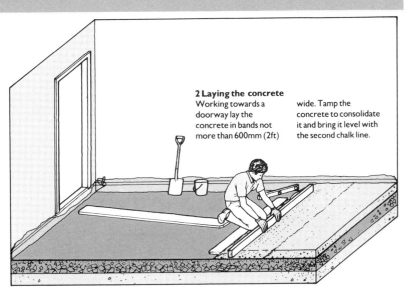

2 Laying the concrete
Working towards a doorway lay the concrete in bands not more than 600mm (2ft) wide. Tamp the concrete to consolidate it and bring it level with the second chalk line.

SEE ALSO

Details for: ▷	
Bonding agent	151
Fitting skirting	181
Mixing concrete	439
Builder's tools	478-480

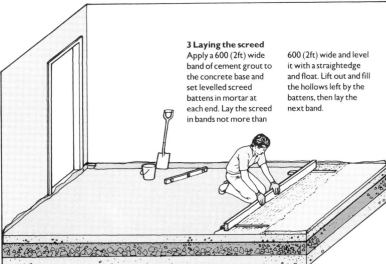

3 Laying the screed
Apply a 600 (2ft) wide band of cement grout to the concrete base and set levelled screed battens in mortar at each end. Lay the screed in bands not more than 600 (2ft) wide and level it with a straightedge and float. Lift out and fill the hollows left by the battens, then lay the next band.

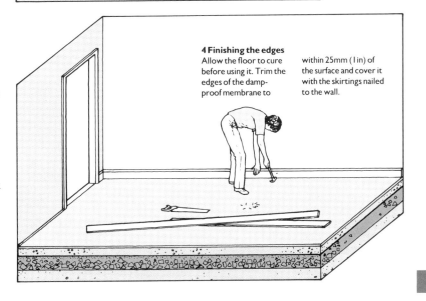

4 Finishing the edges
Allow the floor to cure before using it. Trim the edges of the damp-proof membrane to within 25mm (1in) of the surface and cover it with the skirtings nailed to the wall.

DOORS: TYPES AND CONSTRUCTION

At first glance there appears to be a great variety of doors to choose from, but in fact most of the differences are simply stylistic. They are all based on a small number of construction methods.

The wide range of styles can sometimes tempt householders into buying doors that are inappropriate to the houses they live in. When replacing a front door you should be careful to choose one that is not incongruous with the architectural style of your house.

SEE ALSO

◁ Details for:

Painting a door	77
Fitting a door	186
Weather bar	187
Door furniture	189
Firecheck doors	194
Fitting locks	240-241

Buying a door

Doors in softwood and hardwood are available, the latter being the more expensive and normally used for a special interior or an entrance where the natural features of the wood can be exploited to the best effect.

Softwood doors are for more general workaday use and are intended to be painted as opposed to clear finished.

Glazed doors are becoming common features in the front and rear entrances of today's houses. They are traditionally of wooden frame construction, though modern aluminium-framed doors can be bought in the standard sizes, complete with double glazing and fitments.

Wooden framed and panel doors are supplied in unfinished wood, and these require trimming, glazing and fitting out with hinges, locks and letter plates (◁).

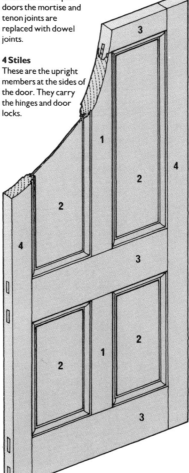

External flush door
A central rail is fitted to take a letter plate.

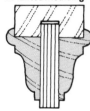

1 Planted moulding

2 Bolection moulding

DOOR SIZES

Doors are made in several standard sizes to meet most domestic needs.

The range of heights is usually 2m (6ft 6in), 2.03m (6ft 8in) and occasionally 2.17m (7ft). The widths range from 600mm (2ft) to 900mm (3ft) in steps of about 75mm (3in). Thicknesses vary from 35mm (1⅜in) to 45mm (1¾in).

In older houses it is common to find that larger doors have been used for the main room on the ground floor than for others, but modern homes tend to have standard-size joinery and all internal doors the same size. The standard is usually 2m x 762mm (6ft 6in x 2ft 6in), though front entrance doors are always larger than internal ones to suit the proportions of the building.

When replacing doors in an old house, where the openings may well be non-standard sizes, buy one of the nearest size and cut it down, removing an equal amount from each edge to preserve the frame's symmetry (◁).

Panel doors

Panel doors are stronger and more attractive than flush doors but are also more expensive. They have hardwood or softwood frames, mortise-and-tenon jointed, with grooves that house the panels, which can be of solid wood, plywood or glass.

1 Muntins
These are the central vertical members of the door. They are jointed into the three cross rails.

2 Panels
These may be of solid wood or of plywood. They are held loosely in grooves in the frame to allow for shrinkage without splitting. They stiffen the door.

3 Cross rails
Top, centre and bottom rails are tenoned into the stiles. In cheaper doors the mortise and tenon joints are replaced with dowel joints.

4 Stiles
These are the upright members at the sides of the door. They carry the hinges and door locks.

Panel door mouldings
The frame's inner edges may be plain or moulded as a decorative border. Small mouldings can be machined on the frame before assembly or pinned to the inside edge. Ordinary planted moulding (**1**) can shrink from the frame, making cracks in the paintwork. Bolection moulding (**2**) laps the frame to overcome this. It is decorative but more vulnerable.

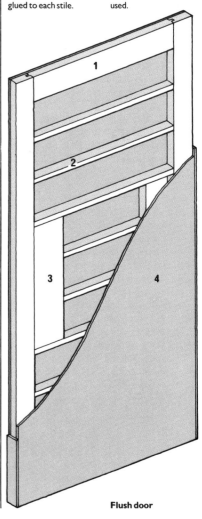

Panel door

Flush doors

Flush doors are softwood frames with plywood or hardboard covering both sides and packed with a core material. Used mainly internally, they are lightweight, cheap, simple and rather lacking in character. External ones have a central rail to take a letter plate. Firecheck doors are a special fire-retardant grade.

1 Top and bottom rails
These are tenoned into the stiles (side pieces).

2 Intermediate rails
These lighter rails, jointed to the stiles, are notched to allow passage of air and prevent the panels sinking.

3 Lock blocks
A softwood block to take a mortise lock is glued to each stile.

4 Panels
the plywood or hardboard panels are left plain for painting or finished with a wood veneer. Metal skinned doors may be had to special order.

Core material
Paper or cardboard honeycomb is sometimes sandwiched between the panels. In firecheck doors a fire-retardant material is used.

Flush door

DOOR FRAMES AND CASINGS

Ledged and braced doors

These doors have a rustic, cottagey look and are often found in old houses, out-buildings and garden walls. They are weather-resistant, strong, secure and cheap, but a little crude. A superior framed version is tenon-jointed instead of being merely nailed.

1 Battens
Tongue-and-groove boards are nailed to the ledges.

2 T-hinges
Butt hinges will not hold in the end-grain of the ledges, so long T-hinges take the weight.

3 Braces
These diagonals, notched into the ledges, transmit the weight to the hinges and stop the door sagging.

4 Ledges
These are the cross rails to which the battens are nailed.

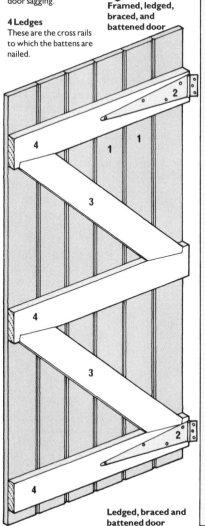

Framed, ledged, braced, and battened door

Ledged, braced and battened door

External frames

An exterior door is fitted into a stout wooden frame consisting of the head (**1**) at the top, the sill (**2**) below, with a water-repellent weather bar, and – mortised and tenoned between them – two rebated side posts (**3**).

The horns, 50mm (2in) projections (**4**) of the head on each side, support the joints and are built into the brickwork to hold the frame in place. The pallets (**5**) are wooden plates, also built into the brickwork, for nail-fixing the frame.

Metal brackets (**6**) can provide an alternative way of fixing the door frame.

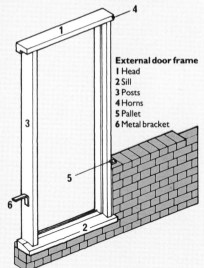

External door frame
1 Head
2 Sill
3 Posts
4 Horns
5 Pallet
6 Metal bracket

Internal casings

Internal doors are hung in a timber lining frame (See below) made up from three members: the soffit casing (**1**) at the top and jamb casings (**2**) on both sides of the opening. They are jointed together at the corners with bare-faced tongue-and-groove joints (**3**) as well as being nailed to pallets, wooden plugs (**4**) in the brickwork at 600mm (2ft) intervals. Casings may also be nail-fixed directly to block walls.

The architrave (**5**), plain or moulded, covers the joints and gives the casing a finish. The door closes against applied door stops (**6**) which form a rebate.

In better-quality buildings hardwood casings are often nailed to softwood grounds (See below). These are rough-sawn lengths of timber which are nailed in place to form a frame on each side of the door opening.

The soffit grounds (**7**) are nailed to the front of the lintel and the jamb grounds (**8**) to wooden plugs in the brickwork. They provide a level for the wall plaster and a good fixing for the architrave moulding.

Internal door casing
1 Soffit casing
2 Jamb casing
3 Bare-faced T&G joint
4 Pallet
5 Architrave
6 Door stop

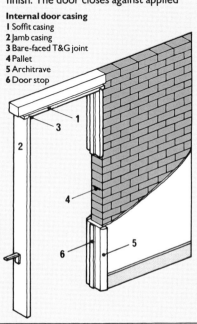

Internal hardwood casing
7 Soffit grounds
8 Jamb grounds

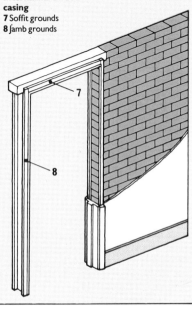

SEE ALSO

Details for: ▷

Painting a frame	77
Renewing a frame	190
Fixing a casing	190
Fire-resistant frame	194
Gate fittings	419

FITTING AND HANGING DOORS

Whatever the style of door you wish to fit, the procedure is the same, though minor differences between some external doors may show themselves. Two good-quality 100mm (4in) butt hinges are enough to support a standard door, but if you are hanging a heavy hardwood one you should add a third, central hinge.

All doors are fairly heavy, and as it is necessary to try a door in its frame several times to get the fit right you will find that the job goes much more quickly and easily if you have a helper working with you.

SEE ALSO

◁ Details for:
Marking gauge	**463**
Fitting locks	240-241
Draught excluders	262-263
Chisels	468-469
Mallet	473
Workmate bench	474

Fitting a door

Before attaching the hinges to a new door make sure that it fits nicely into its frame. It should have a clearance of 2mm (1/16in) at the top and sides and should clear the floor by at least 6mm (1/4in). As much as 12mm (1/2in) may be required for a carpeted floor.

Measure the height and width of the door opening and the depth of the rebate in the door frame into which the door must fit. Choose a door of the right thickness and, if you cannot get one that will fit the opening exactly, one which is large enough to be cut down.

Cutting to size
Some doors are supplied with 'horns', extensions to their stiles which protect the corners while the doors are in storage. Cut these off with a saw **(1)** before starting to trim the door to size.

Transfer the measurements from the frame to the door, making necessary allowance for the clearances all round. To reduce the width of the door stand it on edge with its latch stile upwards while it is steadied in a portable vice. Plane the stile down to the marked line, working only on the one side if a small amount is to be taken off. If a lot is to be removed, take some off each side. This is especially important with panel doors to preserve the symmetry.

If you need to take off more than 6mm (1/4in) to reduce the height of the door, remove it with a saw and finish off with a plane. Otherwise plane the waste off **(2)** . The plane must be sharp to deal with the end grain of the stiles. Work from each corner towards the centre to avoid 'chipping out' the corners.

Try the door in the frame, supporting it on shallow wedges **(3)** . If it still doesn't fit take it down and remove more wood where appropriate.

1 Saw off horns

2 Plane to size

3 Wedge the door

Fitting hinges

The upper hinge is set about 175mm (7in) from the door's top edge and the lower one about 250mm (10in) from the bottom. They are cut equally into the stile and door frame. Wedge the door in its opening and, with the wedges tapped in to raise it to the right floor clearance, mark the positions of the hinges on both the door and frame.

Stand the door on edge, the hinge stile uppermost, open a hinge and, with its knuckle projecting from the edge of the door, align it with the marks and draw round the flap with a pencil **(1)** . Set a marking gauge (◁) to the thickness of the flap and mark the depth of the housing. With a chisel make a series of shallow cuts across the grain **(2)** and pare out the waste to the scored line. Repeat the procedure with the second hinge, then, using the flaps as guides, drill pilot holes for the screws and fix both hinges into their housings.

Wedge the door in the open position, aligning the free hinge flaps with the marks on the door frame. Make sure that the knuckles of the hinges are parallel with the frame, then trace the housings on the frame **(3)** and cut them out as you did the others.

Adjusting and aligning
Hang the door with one screw holding each hinge and see if it closes smoothly. If the latch stile rubs on the frame you may have to make one or both housings slightly deeper. If the door strains against the hinges it is what is called 'hinge bound'. In this case insert thin cardboard beneath the hinge flaps to pack them out. When the door finally opens and closes properly drive in the rest of the screws.

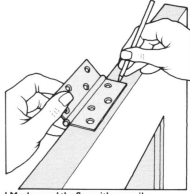

1 Mark round the flap with a pencil

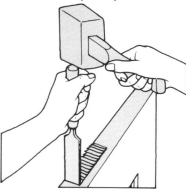

2 Cut across the grain with a chisel

3 Mark the size of the flap on the frame

MEASUREMENTS

A door that fits well will open and close freely and look symmetrical in the frame. Use the figures given as a guide for trimming the door and setting out the position of the hinges.

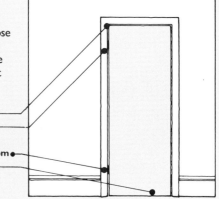

3mm (1/8in) clearance at top and sides ●

Upper hinge 175mm (7in) from the top ●

Lower hinge 250mm (10in) from the bottom ●

6 to 12mm (1/4 to 1/2in) gap at the bottom ●

Rising butt hinges

Rising butt hinges lift a door as it is opened and are fitted to prevent it dragging on thick pile carpet.

They are made in two parts: a flap, with a fixed pin, which is screwed to the door frame, and another, with a single knuckle, which is fixed to the door, the knuckle sliding over the pin.

Rising butt hinges can be fixed only one way up, and are therefore made specifically for left- or right-hand opening. The countersunk screwholes in the fixed pin flap indicate the side to which it is made to be fitted.

Fitting

Trim the door and mark the hinge positions (See opposite), but before fitting the hinges plane a shallow bevel at the top outer corner of the hinge stile so that it will clear the frame as it opens. As the stile (▷) runs through to the top of the door, plane from the outer corner towards the centre to avoid splitting the wood. The top strip of the door stop will mask the bevel when the door is closed.

Fit the hinges to the door and the frame, then lower the door on to the hinge pins, taking care not to damage the architrave above the opening.

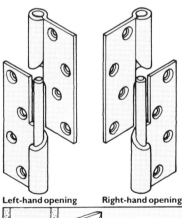

Left-hand opening   Right-hand opening

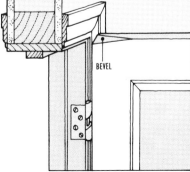

Plane a shallow bevel to clear the door frame

Weatherproofing a door

Fitting a weatherboard

A weatherboard is a special moulding fitted to the bottom of an outer door to shed rainwater away from the threshold. To fit one measure the width of the opening between the door stops and cut the moulding to fit, cutting one end at a slight angle where it meets the door frame on the latch side. This will allow it to clear the frame as the door swings open.

Make a weatherproof seal between the moulding and the door. On an unfinished door use screws and a waterproof adhesive to attach the moulding. On a pre-painted one apply a thick coat of primer to the back surface of the moulding and screw it into place while the primer is still wet. Fill or plug all screwholes and thoroughly prime and finish the surfaces.

Allowing for a weather bar

Though a rebate cut into the head and side posts of an outer door frame provides a seal round an inward opening door, a rebate cut into the sill at the foot of the door would merely encourage water to flow into the house.

Unless protected by a porch, a door in an exposed position needs to be fitted with a weather bar to prevent rainwater running underneath.

This is a metal or plastic strip which is set into the step or sill. If you are putting in a new door and wish to fit a weather bar, use a router or power saw to cut a rebate across the bottom of the door in order to clear the bar.

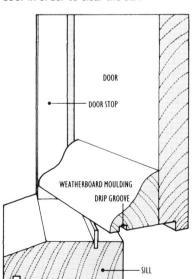

DOOR
DOOR STOP
WEATHERBOARD MOULDING
DRIP GROOVE
SILL

Door fitted with a weather board

ADJUSTING BUTT HINGES

Perhaps you have a door catching on a bump in the floor as it opens. You can, of course, fit rising butt hinges, but the problem can be overcome by resetting the lower hinge so that its knuckle projects slightly more than the top one. The door will still hang vertically when closed, but as it opens the out-of-line pins will throw it upwards so that the bottom edge will clear the bump.

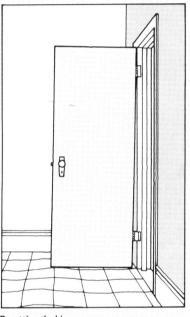

Resetting the hinge
You may have to reset both hinges to the new angle to prevent binding.

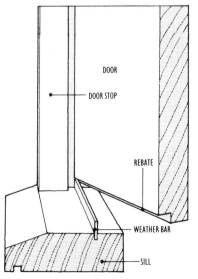

DOOR
DOOR STOP
REBATE
WEATHER BAR
SILL

Sill fitted with weather bar

SEE ALSO

Details for: ▷	
Door construction	184
Power saw	465
Router	468
Plug cutter	472
Adhesives	495-496

REPAIRS AND IMPROVEMENTS

SEE ALSO

◁ Details for:
Wood preservative	250
Painting doors	77
Wood stains	80-82
Door construction	184
Saws	463
Man-made boards	494
Adhesives	495-496

Repairing a battened door

The battens, or tongue-and-groove jointed boards, of a ledged and braced cottage or garage door can rot at the bottom because of the end grain absorbing moisture. The damage can be patch-repaired. Nailing a board across the bottom of the door is not the easy solution it may appear because moisture will be trapped behind the board and will increase the rot.

Remove the door and cut back the damaged boards to sound material. Where a batten falls on a rail, use the tip of a tenon saw, held at a shallow angle, to cut through most of it, then finish off the cut with a chisel. Use a padsaw or a power jigsaw where the blade can pass clear of the rail.

When replacing the end of a single batten make the cut at right angles (1). When a group of battens is to be replaced make 45 degree cuts across them (2). In this way the interlocking of the tongued and grooved edges between old and new sections is better maintained.

When cutting new pieces of boarding to fit, leave them over length. Apply an exterior woodworking adhesive to the butting ends of the battens but take care not to get any on the tongue-and-groove joints. Tap the pieces into place and nail each to the rail with two staggered lost head nails. Cut off the ends in line with the door's bottom edge and treat the wood with a good preservative (◁) to prevent any further rot damage.

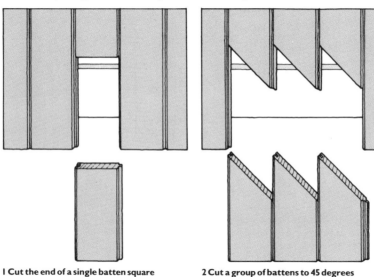

1 Cut the end of a single batten square

2 Cut a group of battens to 45 degrees

Easing a sticking door

If the bottom corner of a door is rubbing on the frame it is probably swollen. Take it off its hinges and shave the corner down with a plane. If the top corner is rubbing check the hinges before doing any planing. After years of use, hinges become worn so that the pins are slack and the door drops. In this case fit new hinges, or, as a cheaper alternative, swap the old hinges, the top with the bottom, which will reverse the wear on the pins.

Swopping hinges ▶
Swop worn hinges, top with bottom, for a cheap and convenient repair.

FLUSH-PANELLING A DOOR

An old framed and panelled door can be given a new lease of life by flush-panelling it with a sheet of hardboard or wood-veneered panelling on each side.

Using hardboard
The easiest way is to cut and fit a hardboard panel 25mm (1in) smaller all round than the door. This can be done without removing the door.

Sandpaper the surface of the frame to provide a key, then apply contact adhesive to the frame members and to the corresponding areas on the back of the hardboard. Position the panels carefully and fix the edges with hardboard nails at 150mm (6in) intervals. Tap all over the glued areas with a wood block and a hammer.

Fill the nail recesses, prime the surfaces and paint as required.

Using a wood-veneered panel
This should extend to all four edges of the door, so the door must first be removed from the frame and the hinges and latch taken off.

Remove any paint from the long edges, scrape them back to bare wood and sandpaper them smooth.

Cut the panels slightly larger than the door, key the surface of the frame with abrasive paper and bond the panels to it with a contact adhesive.

When the adhesive is set plane the panel edges flush with the door all round. With a chisel trim away the edge of the panel where it overlaps the hinge housing. Stain the stripped edges of the door and edges of the panel to match the colour of the veneer.

Before rehanging the door remove the door stop strips. Fit the hinges and latch, rehang the door and replace the door stops against the door while it is in the closed position.

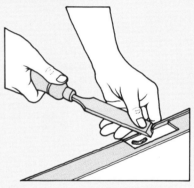

Trim the panelling at the hinge housings.

Fitting a centre pull

A period brass door knob, kept well polished, or one of black iron, can be an attractive feature on a panelled door. Such knobs are now being reproduced in many traditional styles and patterns.

Feature door knobs are usually fitted on the centre line of a panelled door. If a letter plate is occupying the middle rail place the knob above it on the muntin, the central vertical member.

Drill a counterbore on the inside of the door to take the head of the screw that's used for fixing the knob, then a clearance hole for the thread that goes through the door (1).

The back plate of the knob usually has a locating peg on its back which stops the knob turning when the screw is tightened. To mark its position press the back plate on to the door so that the peg leaves an indentation, then drill a shallow recess there for the peg. Fit the assembly and tighten up the screw.

For a neat finish plug the counterbored hole on the inside to conceal the screw head.

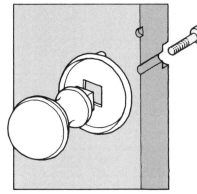

1 Counterbore the hole for the fixing bolt

SEE ALSO

	Details for: ▷
Metalwork	60-61, 85-86
Door construction	184
Doorbells	322
Padsaw	464
Power jigsaw	465

Fitting a letter plate

Letter plates, for fitting horizontally or vertically, in a variety of styles and materials – solid brass, stainless steel, plated, cast iron and aluminium – are readily available. Horizontal plates are the more common and are usually fitted in the centre rail of the door. Occasionally, in a fully glazed door, they are placed on the bottom rail, but this makes them awkward to reach. The problem can be overcome by fitting a plate vertically in one of the door's stiles (vertical side members), but this can weaken a door.

Fitting a horizontal letter plate is dealt with below, but the method described applies to both types. Postal knockers, which incorporate a knocker with the letter plate, are fitted in a similar manner. Measure the width of the door and mark its centre. From this mark out the opening, which must be only slightly larger than the hinged flap on the letter plate in the middle of the rail on the centre line.

Drill a 12mm (½in) clearance hole in each corner of the marked rectangle and cut the opening with a padsaw or power jigsaw, working from the holes. Trim the corners square with a chisel and clean up the cut edges.

Mark the centres for the fixing screw holes. These are usually close to the edge, so take care when drilling them.

Drill counterbores on the outside of the door to take the threaded bosses on the back of the letter plate, and on the inside to take the heads of the machine screws, then drill clearance holes for the screw threads through the centres of the counterbores (2).

Fix the letter plate in place. You may have to shorten the screws to suit a thin door. Plug or fill the counterbores that house the screw heads.

Better still, fit an internal flap cover. These are made in metal or plastic and held with small wood screws. They will cut down draughts, look better and allow the letter plate to be removed easily if it is to be machine polished from time to time.

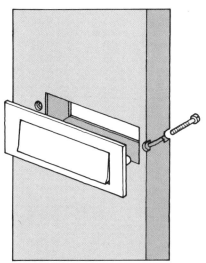

2 Counterbore the door for the plate and bolts

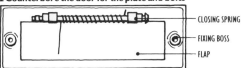

CLOSING SPRING
FIXING BOSS
FLAP

Sizing the opening
Take dimensions from the flap and make the opening slightly larger

Fitting a door knocker

A complete set of brass reproduction exterior door furniture in the traditional manner comprises a letterplate, a door knob and a knocker. Such sets are available in various patterns in Regency, Georgian and Victorian styles. Manufacturers all have their own interpretations of these styles, so if you plan to fit a set you should buy all of the items together.

You can, of course fit items individually, and perhaps the one most widely used is the knocker, which can also be used as an alternative to a centre pull. Being the most ornate item in a door set, a knocker is often used as a decorative feature rather than for its original function. Electric door bells have made knockers obsolete.

On a panelled door fit a feature knocker to the muntin at about shoulder height. Mark a vertical centre line on the muntin at the required height and drill a counterbore and clearance hole for the fixing screw as described for fixing a centre pull (See above). Plug the counterbored hole on the inside after fixing the backplate.

Reproduction brass fittings are finished with a clear lacquer to prevent tarnishing. When this wears through regular polishing maintains the shine.

Victorian   **Georgian**

Knocker Styles

Fitting finger plates
Finger plates, used to protect the paintwork on interior doors, are screwed to each side of the lock stile just above the centre rail.

SEE ALSO

◁ Details for:
Fitting a door   186
Patching rendering   47, 171
Patching plaster   50-51, 152
Vertical DPC   122, 198
Sealing gaps   254
Universal saw   479
Wall plugs   498

FIXING A DOOR CASING

A new internal door opening will need a casing to finish it. These are usually of board 25mm (1in) thick where the applied door stop is used, or 38mm (1½in) when they are rebated to take the door. The width of the casing should equal the thickness of the finished wall.

Door casings are available from joinery suppliers in unassembled kits for standard door sizes. If your door is not standard you can make a lining, using a bare faced tongue-and-groove joint (1).

Wedge the assembled and braced frame in position in the opening (2) and place hardboard or plywood packing between the lintel and the soffit casing at each end if necessary. Check that the edges project equally from both faces of the wall and nail the soffit casing with two 75mm (3in) oval or cut clasp nails.

Plumb one jamb casing with a straight edge and spirit level and pack it in place (3). Start nailing about 75mm (3in) from the bottom and work up, checking the casing for true as you go. Place the nails in pairs 450mm (1ft 6in) apart.

Cut a 'pinch rod' to fit closely between the jamb casings at the top of the frame, then place it across the bottom and pack out the unfixed jamb to fit (4). Check that the jamb is plumb. Nail the casing in place and use the pinch rod to check the distance between the jamb casings at all levels.

Finish the wall surface round the opening and cover the joint with a mitred architrave moulding.

Hang the door and fit the door stop battens to the inside of the casing.

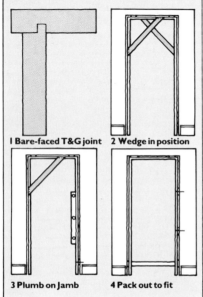

1 Bare-faced T&G joint   2 Wedge in position

3 Plumb on Jamb   4 Pack out to fit

RENEWING A DOOR FRAME

External door frames are built into the brickwork as it is erected, so replacing an old one means some damage to the plaster or the outside rendering.

In older houses the frames are recessed into the brickwork, the inside face of the frame flush with the plaster work and the architrave covering the joint. Modern houses may have frames close to or flush with the outer face of the brickwork. Work from the side the frame is closest to.

Measure the door and buy a standard frame to fit, or make one from standard frame sections.

Removing the old frame

Chop back the plaster or rendering with a chisel to expose the back face of the door frame (1).

With a general-purpose saw (2) cut through the three metal fixings holding the frame in the brickwork on each side, two about 225mm (9in) from the top and bottom and one half-way up.

Saw through the jambs half way up (3), and if necessary cut the head member and the sill. Lever the frame members out with a crowbar.

Clear any loose material from the opening and repair a vertical DPC in a cavity wall with gun-applied mastic to keep moisture out of the gap between inner and outer layers of brickwork.

Fitting the new frame

Fitting a frame is easier with its horns removed, but this weakens it. If possible fit the frame with horns shaped like the old ones (See right).

Wedge the frame in position, checking that it is central, square and plumb. Drill three counterbored clearance holes in each jamb for the fixing screws, positioned about 300mm (1ft) from the top and bottom with one half way, but avoid drilling in mortar joints. Run a masonry drill through the clearance holes to mark their position on the brickwork.

Remove the frame, drill the holes in the brickwork and insert No 12 wall plugs. Replace the frame and fix it with 100mm (4in) No 12 steel screws. Plug the counterbores.

Pack any gap under the sill with mortar. Make good the brickwork, rendering or plasterwork and apply mastic sealant round the outer edge of the frame to seal any small gaps. Fit the door as described (◁).

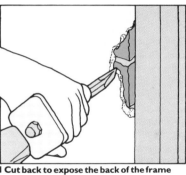

1 Cut back to expose the back of the frame

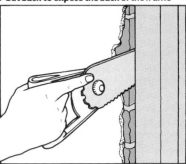

2 Cut through the frame fixings

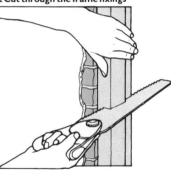

3 Saw through the frame to remove it

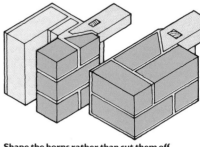

Shape the horns rather than cut them off

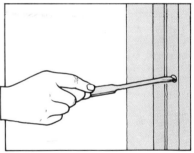

Screw the frame to the plugged wall

REPAIRING A ROTTEN FRAME

REPAIRING DOOR POSTS

The great majority of external door frames are constructed of softwood, and this, if it is regularly maintained with a good paint system (▷), will give years of excellent service. However, the ends of door sills and the frame posts are vulnerable to wet rot if they are subject to continual wetting. This can happen when the frame has moved because of shrinkage of the timber, or where old pointing has fallen out and left a gap where water can get in. Alternatively, old and porous brickwork or an ineffective damp-proof course (▷) can be the cause of wet rot damage.

Prevention is always better than any cure, so check round the frame for any shrinkage gaps and apply a mastic sealant where necessary. Keep all pointing in good order. A slight outbreak of rot can be treated with the aid of a proprietary repair kit and preservative (▷).

It is possible for the sill to rot without the frame posts being affected. In this case just replace the sill. If the posts are also affected, repair them (See right). In some cases the post ends can be tenoned into the sill and fitted as a unit.

Replacing a sill

You can buy 150 x 50mm (6 x 2in) softwood or hardwood door sill sections which can be cut to the required length. If your sill is not of a standard-shaped section the replacement can be made to order. It is more economical in the longer run to specify a hardwood such as oak or utile, as it will last much longer.

Taking out the old
First measure and note down the width of the door opening, then remove the door. The posts are usually tenoned into the sill, so to separate the sill from them split it lengthwise with a wood chisel. A saw cut across the centre of the sill can make the job easier.

The ends of the sill are set into the brickwork on either side, so cut away the bricks to make the removal of the old sill and insertion of the new one easier. Use a plugging chisel (▷) to cut carefully through the mortar round the bricks and try to preserve them for reuse after fitting the sill.

The new sill has to be inserted from the front so that it can be tucked under the posts and into the brickwork. Cut the tenons off level with the shoulders of the posts (1). Mark and cut shallow housings for the ends of the posts in the top of the new sill, spaced apart as previously noted. The housings must be deep enough to take the full width of the posts (2), which may mean the sill being slightly higher than the original one, so that you will have to trim a little off the bottom of the door.

Fitting the new
Try the new sill for fit and check that it is level. Before fixing it apply a wood preservative to its underside and ends,

and, as a measure against rising or penetrating damp, apply two or three coats of bitumen latex emulsion to the brickwork (▷).

When both treatments are dry, glue the sill to the posts, using an exterior woodworking adhesive. Wedge the underside of the sill with slate to push it up against the ends of the posts, skew-nail the posts to it and leave it for the adhesive to set.

Pack the gap between the underside of the sill and the masonry with a stiff mortar of 3 parts sand: 1 part cement, and rebond and point the bricks. Finish by treating the wood with preservative and applying a mastic sealant round the door frame.

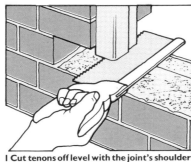

1 Cut tenons off level with the joint's shoulder

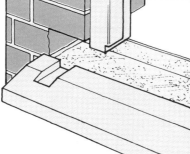

2 Cut a housing to receive the post

Rot can attack the ends of door posts, particularly in exposed positions where they meet stone steps or are set into concrete, as is found in some garages. The posts may be located on metal dowels set into the step.

If the damage is not too extensive the rotten end can be cut away and replaced with a new piece, either scarf jointed or half lap jointed into place. If your situation involves a wooden sill combine the following information with that given for replacing a sill (See left).

First remove the door, then saw off the end of the affected post back to sound timber. For a scarf joint make the cut at 45 degrees to the face of the post (1). For a lap joint cut it square. Chip any metal dowel out of the step with a cold chisel.

Measure and cut a matching section of post to the required length, allowing for the overlap of the joint, then cut the end to 45 degrees or mark and cut a half lap joint in both parts of the post (2).

Drill a hole in the end of the new section for the metal dowel if it is still usable. If it is not, make a new one from a piece of galvanized steel gas pipe, priming the metal to prevent corrosion (▷). Treat the new wood with a preservative and insert the dowel. Set the dowel in mortar, at the same time gluing and screwing the joint (3).

If a dowel is not used, fix the post to the wall with counterbored screws. Place hardboard or plywood packing behind it if necessary and plug the counterbores of the screw holes.

Apply a mastic sealant to the joints between the door post, wall and base.

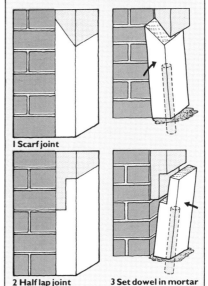

1 Scarf joint

2 Half lap joint   **3 Set dowel in mortar**

SEE ALSO

Details for: ▷

Metal primer	43, 60-61
Painting wood	74-79
Plugging chisel	480
Wood preservative	250
Damp-proof course	251
Bitumen emulsion	258
Housing joint	476

FITTING ROOM DIVIDING DOORS

SEE ALSO

◁ Details for:
| Door casing | 185, 190 |
| Tape measure | 462 |

1 Sliding doors
Sliding doors are hung from a track and are most useful where floor space is limited, but they will require clear wall space on one or both sides of the opening.

2 Bi-fold doors
Tracked systems are easy to operate and offer an attractive means of dividing a room while not requiring as much clear floor space as conventional hinged doors.

3 Multi-fold doors
Like the bi-fold doors these operate on a tracked system but have narrow door panels which enable the door to be stowed within the thickness of the wall.

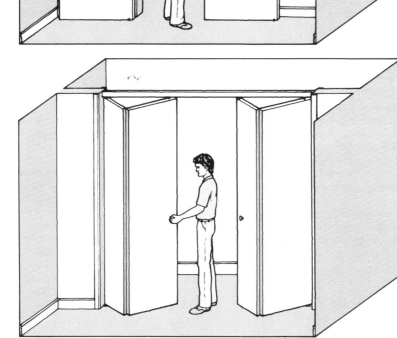

It is now fashionable for houses to be built with large through rooms in the 'open plan' style, and many owners of older properties have adopted the style by having two rooms knocked into one. But there are occasions when two rooms would be preferable in the interests of greater privacy within the family group.

A reasonable compromise is to install a door system which allows the living space to be used either way. It is a compromise because any door system will in some way intrude into an otherwise uncluttered room and when closed it is not as sound-proof as a solid wall. Sliding (**1**), bi-fold (**2**) or multi-fold (**3**) doors are the most suitable for this kind of installation.

Complete door systems, ready for fitting, are available, or you can buy the door mechanism only and fit doors of your choice.

MEASURING THE OPENING

Before ordering a made-to-measure door system, measure the opening carefully. Then double check, for your money may not be refunded in case of error. If you use a steel tape measure, get a helper to keep it taut and avoid a false reading. Measure the width at the top *and* bottom of the opening and the height at both ends. Take the smaller dimension in each case.

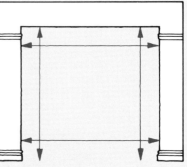

Checking the opening
If you are fitting a system in an old house check the opening is square – the house may have settled unevenly – by measuring across both the diagonals. If they are not the same you may have to true-up the frame or pack out the new system.

Sliding doors

A sliding door system is a good space saver. Whereas a hinged door needs clear floor space, an arc at least as wide as the door itself, a sliding door takes up no floor space, though it does require a clear stretch of wall at the side of the opening. Apart from such fixtures as radiators this need not be a major problem. Furniture can be placed a little away from the wall, leaving a gap behind it to accomodate the thickness of the sliding door.

A range of standard door track sets is available for light, medium and heavy doors. The doors themselves can range in size from 330mm (1ft 1in) to 2m (6ft 6in) in width, and from 16mm (⅝in) to 50mm (2in) in thickness, depending on the type chosen. For a double sliding door two sets of gear are necessary.

Though designs may vary, all track systems for sliding doors have adjustable hanger brackets which are fixed to the top edge of the door and attached to the rollers. A track screwed to the wall above the opening carries and guides the rollers. When the door is closed it should overlap the opening by about 50mm (2in) at each side.

Fitting the system

Following the manufacturer's instructions, set out the hangers and screw them to the top edge of the door. Plug and screw a packing batten for the track to the wall over the doorway. The batten must be as long as the track and equal in thickness to the skirting boards and the architrave. Sometimes it is possible to replace the top section of the architrave with the packing batten.

Screw the track to the packing batten, at the same time levelling it.

Assemble the hangers and rollers and suspend the door from the track, then adjust the hangers to level if and as necessary. Fit the door guide to the floor, and then the stops to the track.

Make a pelmet twice as long as the door's width to cover the whole track system and fix it to the top edge of the packing batten or with metal brackets.

Bi-fold doors

Bi-fold doors offer a reasonable way of closing a door opening without intruding too much on the room space when open. The opening should be lined (▷) in the normal way and fitted with an architrave. The top section of the architrave can be lowered to cover packing pieces on each side of the track.

The pivot hinge and track door gear is available in standard sets for two or four doors of equal width, but up to six doors can be hung from one track, and in this case a bottom guide track is also used. For extra-wide openings more than one door set can be used. The doors range in thickness between 18mm (¾in) and 38mm (1⅝in), and in height up to 2.4m (8ft). Maximum width is 600mm (2ft) per door.

Multi-fold doors

Multi-fold or concertina folding doors are designed to fold up and stack within the depth of the door opening. They are made up from narrow panels, hinged to each other and hung by sliders from a track in the top of the opening. No bottom track is necessary.

The panels are quite slim so that they will stack in the opening with a minimum of bulk. For this reason they do not provide much in the way of sound insulation.

The doors are available for fitting in standard single door openings or can be made to measure to fit larger openings, as, for example, where two rooms have been knocked into one. They are supplied in kits, ready for fitting.

Fitting the system

Following the manufacturer's instructions, fit the pivot hinges into the top and bottom edges of the end door, also the pivoting hangers in the top edges of alternate doors, working away from the pivoted end door.

Hinge the doors together. They will swing to one side of the wall or the other according to which way the knuckles of the hinges face. Set them out as you want them.

Locate the top pivot plate on the track, then fit the doors on the track and screw it to the underside of the opening. Fix the bottom pivot to the floor so that it is exactly plumb with the top one. Fit the door pivots in their plates and adjust them for level.

Fitting the system

Screw the lightweight track to the underside of the wall opening between two rooms or, where the opening is to full room height, fix it to the ceiling. It is possible to inset the track in a plastered ceiling but much easier to face-mount it and add a cover moulding on each side.

Fit the track over the rollers of the stacked panels (**1**), then screw it into place. Screw the cover moulding in place (**2**) to fill the gap between the soffit and the top of the door. Screw the end fixing panel of the door to the jamb (**3**) and the latch plate moulding on the opposite side (**4**) to complete the installation of the system.

SEE ALSO

Details for: ▷	
Door casing	185, 190
Door types	184
Plumb line	478, 484
Wall plugs	498
Screws	498

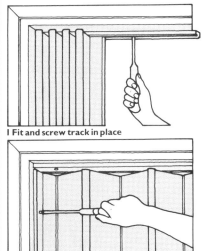

1 Fit and screw track in place

3 Screw the door to the jamb

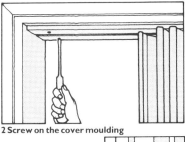

2 Screw on the cover moulding

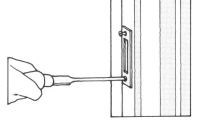

4 Fix the door latch on opposite jamb

FIRE-RESISTING DOORS

GARAGE DOORS

Fire-resisting doors and door sets – doors with frames – are constructed to resist fire for a certain minimum length of time. They are commonly referred to as half-hour or one-hour fire-check doors, but under a modified system their ratings are now expressed in minutes. For example, a 30/20 door is one that has 30 minutes' stability (resistance to collapse) and 20 minutes of integrity (resistance to penetration by flame or smoke through splits or gaps).

SEE ALSO

◁ Details for:
Door types	185
Fitting a door	186
Rising butt hinges	187
Door repairs	188
Fitting locks	240-241
Hinges	419

Fire-resisting doors: types and construction

Fire-resistant doors are generally of the flush panel type, made of wood with a core of solid board material. They are available in standard sizes and in thicknesses of 45mm (1¾in) for the 30/30 grade or 56mm (2¼in) for the 60/60 type. A simulated panelled door, faced with moulded hardboard, is available.

Doors with window openings must be glazed with wired glass.

Fire-resistant door frames have an integral stop in the form of a deep rebate whose inside face is fitted with an intumescent strip (1) that swells when heated and seals the gap round the top and sides of the door.

Flush door

Framed glazed door

Flush glazed door

Moulded panel door

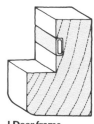

1 Door frame
A fire-resistant door frame member is machined from one piece of wood and has an intumescent strip set in the rebate.

Fitting a door

2 Extend frame lining

A fire-resistant interior door can be fitted in place of a standard door to help prevent the spread of fire, but if it is to be effective the frame must be upgraded. The simplest way to do this is to strip off the old oil paint and finish the frame with a flame-retardant paint. The addition of a band of intumescent paste in a groove cut round the edge of the door will also help. This can be applied with a gun, then planed and sanded smooth when it is dry.

Alternatively remove the old lining altogether and replace it with a new fire-resistant frame with an integral intumescent strip. This framing is not usually as wide as standard door lining and will need an extra section of lining glued to it (2). Fill the gap between the new woodwork and the walling with plaster or with fire-resistant mineral wool packing under the architrave.

Trim the new door to be a good fit in the opening (◁) and hang it on steel rising butt hinges to make it self-closing (◁). Alternatively use steel butt hinges and fit a door closer. Fit the smallest mortise-type lock and latch available, as a large mortice cut in the stile will reduce the door's fire-resistance.

BUILDING REGULATIONS

The Building Regulations require that some doors in domestic buildings meet the 30/20 level of fire-resistance and are self-closing.

This requirement normally concerns those dwellings of three or more storeys which have protected staircases or doors that separate alternative escape routes. It can also apply to the entrance door of a flat or a maisonette that leads from a common area. A door between a house and an attached garage must also meet the required standard.

Before installing a new door in any of these situations you should consult your local Fire Authority.

The traditional garage doors are pairs of wide timber ones fitted with heavy-weight hinges of the kind known as 'bands and hooks'. The doors are constructed on the ledged, braced and battened principle (◁) and may be plain or fitted with windows. Two standard sizes are available 2.13m (7ft) wide x 1.98m (6ft 6in) high; and 2.13m (7ft) wide x 2.13m (7ft) high.

Traditional hinged garage doors

These doors give long service if their softwood timbers are regularly painted, but they have a tendency to weaken after a time because of their weight, which makes the frame drop so that the doors begin to bind. If the battens rub on the ground they can absorb moisture which will lead to rot.

The modern approach is to use up-and-over doors. These are manufactured as single panels in a wide range of styles.

The up-and-over door is counter-balanced, usually by springs, and is lifted upwards to clear the opening. A system of tracks and levers at each side guides the door up and back into the garage. Depending on the design of the mechanism, the door may retract fully into the garage when it is opened or remain partly projecting out of the door frame. The latter type is known as a canopy up-and-over door. The vertically tracked canopy-type door is usually the simplest to install as it involves no horizontal guide tracks, but it has a serious limitation in that it cannot be used where the garage opening is level with the boundary line.

A third type is the sectional overhead door. This is made up of horizontal sections, hinged together, which run on wheels on a continuous track from the vertical closed position to horizontal. These doors lift vertically and so are suitable for situations where the door must not swing out. The door can be opened even when a car is parked close in front of it.

SIZES AND FIXING

Door sizes

The makers of up-and-over doors produce them in a range of standard sizes which are specified in terms of the size of the garage opening – the distance between the frame posts and the height measurement between the floor and the head member. These dimensions always include a tolerance for fitting.

Most doors require a wooden frame to provide a solid fixing, and clearance enough for the mechanism at the sides and top. These dimensions are given by the manufacturers. Some companies also produce doors complete with a metal frame that simply needs screwing to the brickwork. When a frame is included the opening's and the overall frame dimensions are specified.

If you are replacing old timber doors with an up-and-over door your frame may not be a standard size, but most firms can supply made-to-measure doors.

Fixing arrangements

Most types of up-and-over garage doors can have their frame posts, or jambs, fitted between the walls or set behind them (**1**). In the same way the head member of the frame can be fitted behind the lintel or underneath it (**2**).

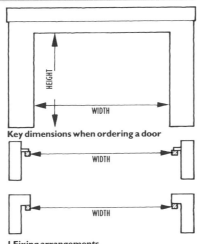

Key dimensions when ordering a door

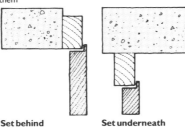

1 Fixing arrangements
Doors may be set between the walls or set behind them

Set behind   **Set underneath**

2 Head fixing
There is more headroom if the frame is set behind the opening than underneath it.

AUTOMATIC DOOR OPENING

An automatic door-opening system is now available for most types of up-and-over garage doors. The systems allow the electrically operated mechanism to be worked by remote control, from inside the car, by means of a hand-held push-button transmitter.

Automatic doors should not be regarded as merely a novel luxury. They can save you time and provide easier access to a garage that faces a busy or narrow road. The electric motor housing, which is installed inside the garage, incorporates a light that is automatically switched on as the door opens and that, in most types, turns itself off after three minutes. The door mechanism has a frequency coding system that enables it to be set to different combinations, and the transmitter, which emits an infra-red beam, is set to the same code as this mechanism. When the infra-red beam is directed towards a receiver head, fitted in a clear space above or beside the opening, the door is operated.

The system also incorporates an automatic safety device which will stop the action immediately if the door should come into contact with an obstacle left in the doorway.

SEE ALSO

Details for: ▷	
Outdoor electricity	332-335
Tape measure	462
Drilling masonry	479
Wall fixings	498

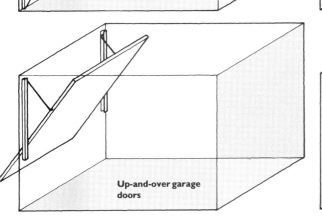

Hinged garage doors

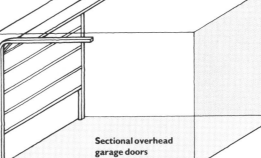

Sectional overhead garage doors

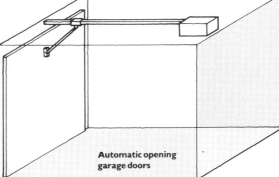

Up-and-over garage doors

Automatic opening garage doors

Hinged doors
Traditional hinged doors require considerable floor space in which to open.

Sectional overhead door
A sectional overhead door retracts within its own space and can be used on a boundary where a door must not swing out.

Up-and-over door
These counterweighted doors may be tracked or non-tracked and be fully or partially retracting.

Automatic opening door
Remote-controlled automatic door opening mechanisms can be attached to most up-and-over garage doors.

195

WINDOWS: TYPES AND CONSTRUCTION

SEE ALSO

◁ Details for:
Security	242-243
Painting windows	78
Repairing windows	200-207
Insulation	271-274

The function of any window is to allow natural light into the house and to provide ventilation. Traditionally windows have been referred to as 'lights', and the term 'fixed light' is still used to describe a window or part of a window frame that doesn't open. A section that opens for ventilation, the 'sash', is a separate frame that slides vertically or is hinged at its side, top or bottom edge. Windows of the hinged type are commonly referred to as casement windows.

A pane of glass can also be pivoted horizontally as a single sash, or several panes can be grouped together to make up a louvre window.

Most window frames and sashes are made up from moulded sections of solid wood. Mild steel and, more recently, aluminium or rigid plastic are also used, though frames of these materials are usually fixed to the brickwork by means of wooden sub-frames.

Casement windows

Window frames with hinged sashes – casement windows – are the most common and are now produced in the widest range of materials and styles.

A traditional wooden window frame and its hinged sash are constructed in much the same way as a door and its frame. A jamb at each side is mortice-and-tenon jointed into the head member at the top and into a sill at the bottom (See below). The frame may be divided vertically by a 'mullion', or horizontally by a 'transom' (**1**).

The sash, which is carried by the frame, has its top and bottom rails jointed into its side stiles. Glazing bars, relatively light moulded sections, are used to sub-divide the glazed area for smaller panes (**2**).

Side-hung sashes are fitted on butt hinges or sometimes, for better access to the outside of the glass, on 'easy

clean' extension hinges. A lever fastener, or 'cockspur', for securing the sash is screwed to the middle of the stile on the opening side. A casement stay on the bottom rail holds the sash in various open positions and acts as a locking device when the sash is closed. Top-hung sashes, or vents, are secured with a stay only (◁).

Galvanized mild steel casement windows (**3**) were once popular for domestic use. They are made in the same format as wooden hinged windows but have a slimmer framework. The joints of the metal sections are welded.

Mild steel windows are strong and long-lasting but vulnerable to rust unless protected by galvanized plating or a good paint system. The rusting can be caused by weathering outside or by condensation on the inside.

I Casement window

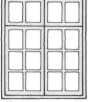

2 Glazing-bars

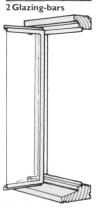

3 Steel casement type

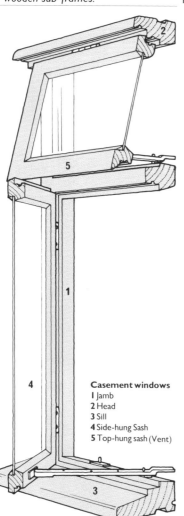

Casement windows
1 Jamb
2 Head
3 Sill
4 Side-hung Sash
5 Top-hung sash (Vent)

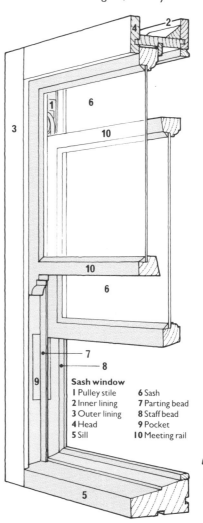

Sash window

1 Pulley stile	6 Sash
2 Inner lining	7 Parting bead
3 Outer lining	8 Staff bead
4 Head	9 Pocket
5 Sill	10 Meeting rail

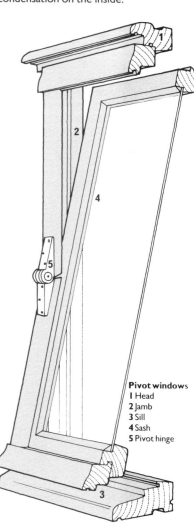

Pivot windows
1 Head
2 Jamb
3 Sill
4 Sash
5 Pivot hinge

WINDOWS: TYPES AND CONSTRUCTION

Sash windows

Vertically sliding windows are commonly known as sash windows and when both top and bottom sashes can be opened they are referred to as 'double hung' sash windows.

The traditional wooden type (See opposite) is constructed with a 'box frame' in which the jambs are made up from three boards: the pulley stile, the inner lining and the outer lining. A back completes the box that houses the sash counterweights. The head is made up in a similar way but without the back lining, and the sill is of solid wood. The pulley stiles are jointed into the sill and the linings are set in a rebate.

The sashes of a double hung window are held in tracks formed by the outer lining, a parting bead and an inner staff bead. The beads can be removed for servicing the sash mechanism. Each sash is counterbalanced by two cast-iron weights – one at each side – which are attached by strong cords or chains that pass over pulleys in the stiles. Access to the weights is through 'pockets' – removable pieces of wood – set in the lower part of the stiles.

The top sash slides in the outer track and overlaps the inner bottom sash at their horizontal 'meeting rails'. The closing faces of the meeting rails are bevelled, and their wedging action helps to prevent the sashes rattling. It also provides better clearance when the window is opened, and improves security when it is locked. The sashes are secured by two-part fasteners of various types fitted on the meeting rails.

Spiral balances

Modern wooden or aluminium vertically sliding sashes have spring-assisted spiral balances which do not need a deep box construction. Rather than being concealed, the slim balances are fitted on the faces of the stiles.

Spiral balances
The balances are usually fixed to the faces of the frame stiles and set in grooves in the sash stiles.

Pivot windows

Wooden-framed pivot windows (See opposite) are constructed in a similar way to casement windows, but the sash is held on a pair of strong pivot hinges which allow the window to be tilted right over for easy cleaning from inside. A safety roller arm can be fitted to the frame and set to prevent the window opening more than 115mm (4½in).

Pivoting roof windows are available for pitched roofs with slopes from 15 to 85 degrees. Like the standard pivoting windows, they can be fully reversed for cleaning. The windows are supplied double glazed with sealed units, and ventilators are incorporated in the frame or sash. The timbers are protected on the outside by a metal covering, and flashing kits are supplied for fitting to tile or slate roofs (▷).

Louvre windows

A louvre window is another form of pivot window. The louvres are unframed 'blades' of glass, 4mm (5/32in) or 6mm (¼in) thick, which have their long edges ground and polished. The louvres are held at each end in light alloy carriers which pivot on an upright member, and this is screwed to a wooden frame. One side is fitted with an opening and locking mechanism which links all of the louvres so that they operate together as one.

Louvre windows are effective as ventilators but they do not provide good security. They are also difficult to draught-proof.

Where an opening is more than 1.07m (3ft 6in) in width two sets of louvres are best used, with the centre pair of uprights set back to back in order to form a mullion.

Use two sets of louvres for a wide opening

ALUMINIUM AND PLASTIC WINDOW FRAMES

Aluminium windows

These are now replacing old wooden and metal-framed windows. The aluminium is extruded into complex sections (1) to hold double-glazed sealed units and draught strips and – ready finished in white, satin silver, black or bronze – is maintenance free. These windows are highly engineered and complete with concealed projection hinges and lockable fasteners. They need no stays to hold them open.

To combat condensation the latest designs incorporate a 'thermal break' of insulating material in the hollow sections of the frame.

Most aluminium windows designed for replacement work are purpose-made and fitted by specialist companies. They need wooden sub-frames.

Plastic windows

Rigid plastic windows (2) are rather similar to aluminium ones but are thicker through their sections. They are manufactured in white plastic and once installed they require no maintenance.

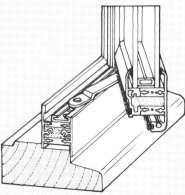

1 Extruded aluminium window set in wooden frame

2 Metal tube-reinforced extruded-plastic window

SEE ALSO

Details for: ▷	
Roof windows	211
Painting windows	78
Repairing windows	200-207
Spiral balances	208
Security	242-243
Insulation	271-274

HOW WINDOWS ARE FITTED

SEE ALSO

◁ Details for:
Sash windows   197, 207, 210
Sills   206
Replacing windows   209-210

Solid walls

In older houses it is usual to find the window frame jambs set in recesses on the inside of the brickwork. The openings were formed before the windows were fitted and the frames were nailed or screwed into wooden plugs in the brickwork. No vertical damp-proof courses were fitted. Evaporation was relied on to keep the walls dry.

The frames in a 225mm (9in) thick wall were set flush with the inside. In a 340mm (1ft 1½in) wall they had inner reveals. All required sub-sills, usually stone ones, outside.

Brickwork above the opening in a traditional brick wall may be supported by a brick arch or a stone lintel. Flat or shallow curved arches were generally used, their thickness being the width of one brick. Wooden lintels were placed behind such arches to support the rest of the wall's thickness. Semi-circular arches were usually as thick as the wall.

Many stone lintels were carved to make decorative features. As with arches, an inner lintel shared the weight. Openings like this were never wide because of the relative weakness of the materials. The wide windows of main rooms had several openings divided by brick or stone columns.

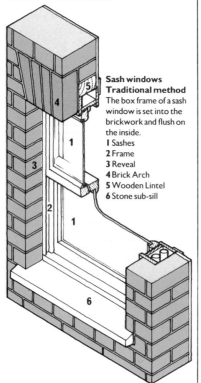

**Sash windows
Traditional method**
The box frame of a sash window is set into the brickwork and flush on the inside.
1 Sashes
2 Frame
3 Reveal
4 Brick Arch
5 Wooden Lintel
6 Stone sub-sill

Cavity walls

The window frames in modern houses are usually installed while the brickwork is being erected. They are fixed into place with metal brackets – 'frame cramps' – which are screwed to the frame's jambs and set in the mortar bed joints. There are three such cramps on each side of the frame.

Cavity walls must have a vertical damp-proof course. This is sandwiched between the brick outer leaf of the wall and the cavity-closing bricks of the inner leaf. The window frame is set forward in the opening and covers the joint. Some frames have the damp-proof courses fastened to them.

With the window frame in this position a good deal of the wall's thickness is exposed on the inside. The sides, or 'reveals' of the opening are finished off with plaster, as is the top, while the ledge at the bottom is finished with a window board which is tongued into a groove along the back of the frame sill.

The window board is also screwed or nailed down to the brickwork. Quarry tiles are sometimes used to form the inner sill.

**Sash windows
Modern method**
The brickwork is built around the window frame and includes a vertical DPC.
1 Frame
2 DPC
3 Concrete lintel
4 Wooden sill
5 Frame cramp

CONCRETE AND STEEL LINTELS

Modern lintels are made from reinforced concrete or galvanized steel or a combination of both. These extremely strong lintels can support brickwork over a considerable span, enabling large picture windows to be installed without additional support.

A damp-proof course must be provided above the window opening to prevent any moisture in the cavity permeating the inner leaf and the window frame, though some metal lintels can be installed without additional damp-proof material.

The front face of a concrete 'through-the-wall' or 'boot' lintel can be seen above the opening. Where a brick facing is required a steel lintel is used and the bricks can be laid on the relatively thin metal edge in bonded courses or on their ends to simulate a brick arch.

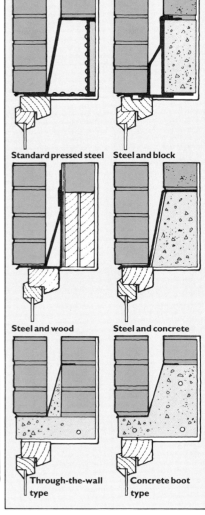

Standard pressed steel   **Steel and block**

Steel and wood   **Steel and concrete**

Through-the-wall type   **Concrete boot type**

TYPES OF GLASS

Glass is made from silica sand which, with such additives as soda, lime and magnesia, is heated until it is molten to produce the raw material. The type and quality of the glass produced for windows is determined by the method by which it is processed in the molten stage. Ordinary window glass is known as annealed glass. Special treatments during manufacture give glass particular properties, such as heat-resistance or extra strength.

SEE ALSO

Details for: ▷

Cutting glass	200
Buying glass	200
Drilling glass	201
Double-glazed units	204

SHEET GLASS

Clear sheet glass is made for general glazing and was once the most common type used in windows. It is produced by a drawn process and can sometimes be recognised by its slight distorting effect, which is a result of the manufacturing process. Though the surfaces are given a smooth 'fire-finish' they are not always quite flat or quite parallel.

Two qualities of clear glass are produced – the ordinary standard grade for general glazing and a 'selected' one for better glazing work – in thicknesses from 2mm to 4mm ($\frac{1}{16}$ to $\frac{5}{32}$in).

Horticultural glass is a poorer category produced by the same method and made in 3mm ($\frac{1}{8}$in) and 4mm ($\frac{5}{32}$in) thicknesses for use in greenhouses only.

FLOAT GLASS

Float glass is now generally used for glazing windows. It is made by floating the molten glass on a bath of liquid tin to produce a sheet with flat, parallel and distortion-free surfaces. It has virtually replaced plate glass, which was a rolled glass ground and polished on both sides.

Clear float glass is made in thicknesses from 3mm ($\frac{1}{8}$in) up to 25mm (1in), but it is generally stocked in only three: 3mm ($\frac{1}{8}$in), 4mm ($\frac{5}{32}$in) and 6mm ($\frac{1}{4}$in).

PATTERNED GLASS

Patterned glass is glass which has one surface embossed with a texture or a decorative design. It is available in clear or tinted sheets in thicknesses of 3mm ($\frac{1}{8}$in), 4mm ($\frac{5}{32}$in), 5mm ($\frac{3}{16}$in) and 6mm ($\frac{1}{4}$in).

The transparency of the glass depends on the density of the patterning. Such 'obscured' glass is used where maximum light is required while maintaining privacy, such as in bathroom windows.

Textured glass, commonly known as rough-cast glass, is another form of patterned glass. It is made in a thicker range than patterned glass, 6mm ($\frac{1}{4}$in) being the most common thickness. It is used mostly for commercial buildings.

SOLAR CONTROL GLASS

There is now special glass available which cuts down the heat received from the sun, and this is often used in roof lights. This tinted glass, which can be of the float, sheet, laminated or rough-cast type, also reduces glare, though at the expense of some illumination. It is available in thicknesses ranging from 3mm ($\frac{1}{8}$in) to 12mm ($\frac{1}{2}$in), depending on the type.

NON-REFLECTIVE GLASS

Diffuse reflection glass is a 2mm ($\frac{1}{16}$in) glass sheet with slightly textured surfaces, and is much used for glazing picture frames. When placed within 12mm ($\frac{1}{2}$in) of the picture surface the glass appears completely transparent while eliminating the surface reflections associated with ordinary polished glass.

SAFETY GLASS

Glass which has been strengthened by means of reinforcement or a toughening process is known as safety glass. It should be used whenever the glazed area is relatively large or where its position makes it vulnerable to accidental breakage. Such hazardous areas common in domestic situations are glazed doors, low-level windows and shower screens.

WIRED GLASS

Wired glass is a 6mm ($\frac{1}{4}$in) thick rough-cast or clear annealed glass with a fine steel wire mesh incorporated in it during its manufacture. Glass with a 13mm ($\frac{1}{2}$in) square mesh is known as Georgian wired glass. The mesh supports the glass and prevent it disintegrating in the event of breakage. The glass itself is not special and is no stronger than ordinary glass of the same thickness.

Wired glass is regarded as a fire-resistant material with a one-hour rating. Though the glass may break, its wire reinforcement helps to maintain its integrity and prevent the spread of fire.

TOUGHENED GLASS

Toughened glass is ordinary glass that has been heat-treated to improve its strength, and is sometimes referred to as tempered glass. The process of treatment renders the glass about four to five times stronger than an untreated glass of similar thickness. In the event of its breaking it merely shatters into relatively harmless granules.

Toughened glass cannot be cut. Any work required, such as holes to be drilled for screws, must be done before the toughening process. Joinery suppliers of doors and windows usually stock standard sizes of toughened glass to fit standard frames.

LAMINATED GLASS

Laminated glass is made by bonding together two or more layers of glass with a clear tear-resistant plastic film sandwiched between. This safety glass will absorb the energy of an object hitting it, so preventing the object penetrating the pane. The plastic interlayer also binds broken glass fragments together and reduces the risk of injury from fragments of flying glass.

It is made in a range of thicknesses from 4mm ($\frac{5}{32}$in) up to 8mm ($\frac{5}{16}$in), depending on the type of glass used. Clear, tinted and patterned versions are all available.

BUYING GLASS

You can buy most types of glass from your local stockists. They will advise you on thickness, will cut the glass to your measurements and will also deliver larger sizes and amounts.

The thickness of glass, once expressed by weight, is now measured in millimetres. If you are replacing old glass, measure its thickness to the nearest millimetre, and, if it is slightly less than any available size, buy the next one up for the sake of safety.

Though there are no regulations about the thickness of glass, for safety reasons you should comply with the recommendations set out in the British Standard Code of Practice. The required thickness of glass depends on the area of the pane, its exposure to wind pressure and the vulnerability of its situation – e.g., in a window overlooking a play area. Tell your supplier what the glass is needed for – a door, a window, a shower screen etc. – to ensure that you get the right type.

Measuring up

Measure the height and width of the opening to the inside of the frame rebate, taking the measurement from two points for each dimension. Also check that the diagonals are the same length. If they differ markedly and show that the frame is out of square, or if it is otherwise awkwardly shaped, make a cardboard template of it. In any case deduct 3mm (⅛in) from the height and width to allow for a fitting tolerance. When making a template allow for the thickness of the glass cutter.

When you order patterned glass, specify the height before the width. This will ensure that the glass is cut with the pattern running in the right direction. (Alternatively take a piece of the old glass with you, which you may need to do in any case to match the pattern.)

For an asymmetrically shaped pane of patterned glass supply a template, and mark the surface that represents the outside face of the pane. This ensures that the glass will be cut with its smooth surface outside and will be easier to keep clean.

SEE ALSO

◁ Details for:
Tape measure	462
Glass cutter	480
Pliers	491

WORKING WITH GLASS

You should always carry glass on its edge. You can hold it with pads of folded rag or paper when gripping the top and bottom edge, though it is always better to wear stout work gloves.

Protect your hands with gloves and your eyes with goggles when removing broken glass from a frame. Wrap up the broken pieces in thick layers of newspaper if you have to dispose of it in your dustbin, but before doing so check with your local glazier, who may be willing to take the pieces from you and add them to his off-cuts, which are usually sent back to the manufacturers for recycling.

Basic glass-cutting

It is usually unnecessary to cut one's own glass as glass merchants are willing to do it, but you may have some surplus glass and wish to cut it yourself. Diamond-tipped cutters are available, but the type with a steel wheel is cheaper and quite adequate for normal use.

Cutting glass successfully is largely a matter of practice and confidence. If you have not done it before, you should make a few practice cuts on waste pieces of glass and get used to the 'feel' before doing a real job.

Lay the glass on a flat surface covered with a blanket. Patterned glass is placed patterned side downwards and cut on its smooth side. Clean the surface with methylated spirit.

Set a T-square the required distance from one edge, using a steel measuring tape (1). If you are working on a small piece of glass or do not have a T-square, mark the glass on opposing edges with a felt-tipped pen or wax pencil and use a straight edge to join up the marks and guide the cutter.

Lubricate the steel wheel of the glass cutter by dipping it in thin oil or paraffin. Hold the cutter between middle finger and forefinger (2) and draw it along the guide in one continuous stroke. Use even pressure throughout and run the cut off the end. Slide the glass forward over the edge of the table (3) and tap the underside of the scored line with the back of the cutter to initiate the cut. Grip the glass on each side of the score line with gloved hands (4), lift the glass and snap it in two. Alternatively, place a pencil under each end of the scored line and apply even pressure on both sides until the glass snaps.

1 Measure the glass with a tape and T-square

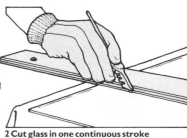

2 Cut glass in one continuous stroke

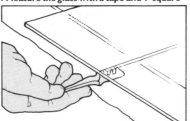

3 Tap the edge of glass to initiate the cut

4 Snap glass in two

Cutting a thin strip of glass

A pane of glass may be slightly oversize due to inaccurate measuring or cutting or if the frame is distorted.

Remove a very thin strip of glass with the aid of a pair of pliers. Nibble away the edge by gripping the waste with the tip of the jaws close to the scored line.

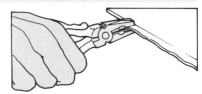

Nibble away a thin strip with pliers

Fitting items such as an extractor fan may involve cutting a circular hole in a pane of glass. This can be done with a beam compass glass cutter.

Cutting a circle in glass

Locate the suction pad of the central pivot on the glass, set the cutting head at the required distance from it and score the circle round the pivot with even pressure (**1**). Now score another smaller circle inside the first one. Remove the cutter and score across the inner circle with straight cuts, then make radial cuts about 25mm (1in) apart in the outer rim. Tap the centre of the scored area from underneath to open up the cuts (**2**) and remove the inner area. Next tap the outer rim and nibble away the waste with pliers if necessary.

To cut a disc of glass, scribe a circle with the beam compass cutter, then score tangential lines from the circle to the edges of the glass (**3**). Tap the underside of each cut, starting close to the edge of the glass.

1 Score the circle with even pressure

SEE ALSO

Details for: ▷

Removing glass	202
Fret saw	464
Hand drill	471
Glass cutter	480

Smoothing the edges of cut glass

You can grind down the cut edges of glass to a smooth finish using wet-and-dry paper wrapped round a wooden block. It is fairly slow work, though just how slow will depend on the degree of finish you require.

Start off with medium-grit paper wrapped tightly round the wood block. Dip the block complete with paper in water and begin by removing the 'arris' or sharp angle of the edge with the block held at 45 degrees to the edge. Keep the abrasive paper wet.

Follow this by rubbing down the vertical edge to remove any nibs and go on to smooth it to a uniform finish. Repeat the process with progressively finer grit papers. A final polish can be given with a wet wooden block coated with pumice powder.

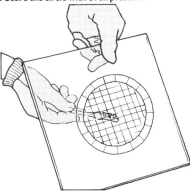

2 Tap the centre of the scored area

3 Cutting a disc
Scribe the circle then make tangential cuts from it to the edge of the glass.

Using a glass cutting template

Semi-circular windows and glazed openings in Georgian-style doors are formed with segments of glass set between radiating glazing-bars.

Windows with semi-circular openings and modern reproductions of period doors can be glazed with ready-shaped panes available from joinery suppliers, but for an old glazed door you will probably have to cut your own. The pieces are segments of a large circle, beyond the scope of the beam compass glass cutter (See above), so you will have to make a card template.

Remove the broken glass, clean up the rebate, then tape a sheet of paper over the opening and, using a wax crayon, take a rubbing of the shape (**1**). Remove the paper pattern and tape it to a sheet of thick cardboard. Following the lines on the paper pattern, cut the card to shape with a sharp knife, but make the template about 2mm (1/16in) smaller all round, also allowing for the thickness of the glass cutter. The straight cuts can be aided by a straightedge, but you will have to make curved ones freehand. A slightly wavy line will be hidden by the frame's rebate.

Fix the template to the glass with double-sided tape, score round it with the glass cutter (**2**), running all cuts to the edge, and snap the glass in the normal way.

1 Take a rubbing of the shape with a crayon

2 Cut round the template with even pressure

● **Plastic glazing**
As an alternative to glass for awkward shapes you can use acrylic plastic, cutting it with a fret saw.

Drilling a hole in glass

There are special spear-point drilling bits available for drilling holes in glass. As glass should not be drilled at high speed, use a hand-held wheel brace.

Mark the position for the hole, no closer than 25mm (1in) to the edge of the glass, using a felt-tipped pen or a wax pencil. On mirror glass work from the back, or coated surface.

Place the tip of the bit on the marked centre and, with light pressure, twist it back and forth so that it grinds a small pit and no longer slides off the centre. Form a small ring with putty round the pit and fill the inner well with a lubricant such as white spirit, paraffin or water.

Work the drill at a steady speed and with even pressure. Too much pressure can chip the glass.

When the tip of the drill just breaks through, turn the glass over and drill from the other side. If you try to drill straight through from one side you risk breaking out the surface round the hole.

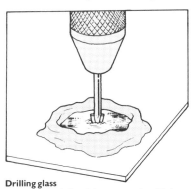

Drilling glass
Always run the drill in a lubricant to reduce friction.

REPAIRING A BROKEN WINDOW

A cracked window pane, even when no glass is missing from it, is a safety hazard and a security risk. If the window *is actually lacking some of its glass, it is no longer weatherproof and should be repaired promptly.*

SEE ALSO

◁ Details for:
Scaffold tower	40
Buying glass	200
Painting windows	78
Firmer chisel	468
Pincers	473
Glass cutter	480
Hacking knife	480
Putty knife	480
Sprigs	497

Temporary repairs

For temporary protection from the weather a sheet of polythene can be taped or pinned with battens over the outside of the window frame, and a merely cracked window can be temporarily repaired with a special clear self-adhesive waterproof tape. Applied to the outside, the tape gives an almost invisible repair.

Safety with glass

The method you use to remove the glass from a broken window will to some extent depend on conditions. If the window is not at ground level, it may be safest to take out the complete sash to do the job. But a fixed window will have to be repaired on the spot, wherever it is.

Large pieces of glass should be handled by two people and the work done from a tower rather than ladders (◁). Avoid working in windy weather and always wear protective gloves for this work.

Repairing glass in wooden frames

In wooden window frames the glass is set into a rebate cut in the frame's moulding and bedded in linseed oil putty. Small wedge-shaped nails known as sprigs are also used to hold the glass in place. In some wooden-framed windows a screwed-on beading is used to hold the pane instead of the 'weathered' (outer) putty; this type of frame may have its rebate cut on the inside instead of the outside.

Removing the glass

If the glass in a window pane has shattered, leaving jagged pieces set in the putty, grip each piece separately (wearing gloves) and try to work it loose (**1**). It is safest always to start working from the top of the frame.

Old dry putty will usually give way, but if it is strong it will have to be cut away with a glazier's hacking knife and a hammer (**2**). Alternatively, the job can be done with a blunt wood chisel. Work along the rebate to remove the putty and glass. Pull out the sprigs with pincers (**3**).

If the glass is cracked but not holed, run a glass cutter round the perimeter of the pane about 25mm (1in) from the frame, scoring the glass (**4**). Fasten strips of self-adhesive tape across the cracks and the scored lines (**5**) and tap each piece of glass so that it breaks free and is held only by the tape. Carefully peel the inner pieces away, then remove the pieces round the edges and the putty as described above.

Clean out the rebate and seal it with a wood primer. Measure the height and width of the opening to the inside of the rebates and have your new glass cut 3mm (1/8in) smaller on each dimension (◁) to give a fitting tolerance.

Fitting new glass

Purchase new sprigs and enough putty for the frame. Your glass supplier should be able to advise you on this but, as a guide, 500g (1lb) of putty will fill an average-sized rebate of about 4m (13ft) in length.

Knead a palm-sized ball of putty to an even consistency. Very sticky putty is difficult to work with so wrap it briefly in newspaper to absorb some of the oil. You can soften putty that is too stiff by adding linseed oil to it.

Press a fairly thin, continuous band of putty into the rebate all round with your thumb. This is the bedding putty. Lower the edge of the new pane on to the bottom rebate, then press it into the putty. Press close to the edges only, squeezing the putty to leave a bed about 2mm (1/16in) behind the glass, then secure the glass with sprigs about 200mm (8in) apart. Tap them into the frame with the edge of a firmer chisel so that they lie flat with the surface of the glass (**1**). Trim the surplus putty from the back of the glass with a putty knife.

Apply more putty to the rebate all round, outside the glass. With a putty knife (**2**), work the putty to a smooth finish at an angle of 45 degrees. Wet the knife with water to prevent it dragging and make neat mitres in the putty at the corners. Let the putty set and stiffen for about three weeks, then apply an oil-based undercoat paint. Before painting, clean any putty smears from the glass with methylated spirit. Let the paint lap the glass slightly to form a weather seal.

A self-adhesive plastic foam can be used instead of the bedding putty. Run it round the back of the rebate in a continuous strip, starting from a top corner, press the glass into place on the foam and secure it with sprigs. Then apply the weathered putty in the same way described above.

Alternatively, apply a strip of foam round the outside of the glass and cover it with a wooden beading, then paint.

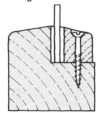

Weathered putty fixing

Wooden bead fixing
Unscrew beading and scrape out mastic. Bed new glass in fresh mastic and replace beading.

1 Work loose the broken glass

2 Cut away the old putty

3 Pull out the old sprigs

4 Score glass before removing a cracked pane

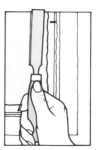

5 Tap the glass to break it free

1 Tap in new sprigs   2 Shape the putty

LEADED LIGHT WINDOWS

Leaded lights are windows glazed with small pieces of glass joined together with strips of lead known as cames. The glass may be coloured and cut to form a decorative design, as in churches, or it may be clear and set in a diamond-shaped or rectangular grid of cames.

SUPPORTING A LEADED LIGHT

Leaded lights are relatively weak and can sag with age. If you have such a window and it is bowing you can support it with the help of a 6mm (¼in) mild steel rod.

Drill a 6mm (¼in) hole on each side of the window frame. Place the holes about half-way up the sides and close to the lead strips. Drill one twice as deep as the other. Carefully flatten the window with the palm of a gloved hand or a board to spread the load.

To the back of the came(s) soft solder a few short lengths of tinned copper wire, stripped from ring main cable, or some small tinplate strips cut from a food can. Set them in line with the line of the rod.

The length of the rod should equal the distance between the window frame sides plus the depth of the two holes, but *not* the extra depth of the one hole.

Locate the rod in the holes, inserting it in the deeper hole first. Twist the wires – or crimp the tinplate straps – round the rod so that the window is tied to it for support. Finish the rod with black lead paint and wipe putty cement (See right) into the cames on the outside if necessary.

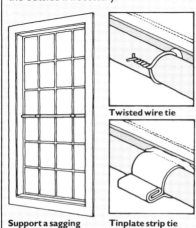

Support a sagging leaded light with a metal rod

Twisted wire tie

Tinplate strip tie

Replacing broken glass in leaded lights

It is always easier to replace a piece of glass with the window out of its frame, but leaded lights are rather fragile, so it is usually safer to carry out the repair with the window in place. If the complete unit must be removed, carefully hack out the putty and support the whole of the panel on a board as it is taken out.

Cut the cames round the broken pane at each joint, using a sharp knife **(1)**. Make the cuts on the outside if you are working with the window in place at ground floor level. The repair will then be less noticeable from inside. On the windows of an upper room the cames will have to be cut on the inside.

With a putty knife lift the edges of the cames holding the glass and prise the lead up until it is at right angles to the face of the glass **(2)**. Lift or tap out the broken pieces and scrape away the old putty cement. During this, if you are working with the leaded light in place, support it from behind with your hand or with a board fixed across the window frame.

Take a paper rubbing of the open cames to give you the shape and size of the glass needed. Lay the new glass over the rubbing and follow the shape with a glass cutter and straight edge, keeping the cut a little inside the line **(3)**. Try the glass for fit and rub down corners and edges on wetted wet-and-dry paper if necessary.

Mix a little gold size with linseed oil putty to make a putty cement, apply it to the open cames and bed the glass into it with even pressure.

Fold the edges of the cames over to secure the glass and burnish them flat with a piece of wood. Scrape away any surplus putty and gently wipe the glass and cames absolutely clean with methylated spirit.

Thoroughly clean the cut joints in the cames with fine wire wool and resolder them **(4)**, using an electric soldering iron and resin-cored solder.

SEE ALSO

Details for: ▷

Cutting glass	200
Smoothing edges	201
Putty knife	480
Soldering	488

Came styles

Round came

Flat came

Beaded came

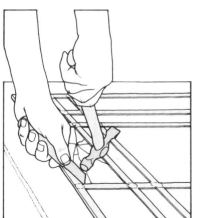

1 Cut the cames with a sharp knife

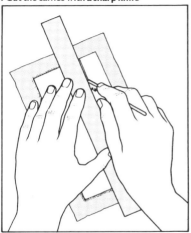

3 Cut the glass following a paper rubbing

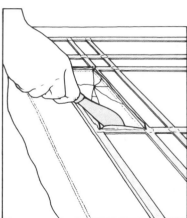

2 Prise the lead up with a putty knife

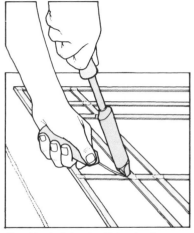

4 Resolder the joint after fitting the glass

DOUBLE GLAZING UNITS

Using putty

Set stepped sealed units (◁) in putty in the same way as for fitting new glass (◁) but place packing pieces of resilient material (supplied with the units) in the putty to support the greater weight of the double glazing.

◁ Details for:
Painting windows	78
Sash windows	196, 207
Fitting new glass	202
Double glazing	271

Using Putty
Follow the sequence when fitting stepped double glazing.
1 Set the packing in bedding putty
2 Fit the glazing and secure with sprigs
3 Weatherproof the glass with putty

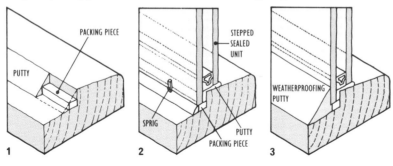

Using beading

Square-edged units (◁) are set in a non-setting glazing compound and held in place with wooden beading, a type of fixing that is normally used for hardwood or metal window frames which are meant to be maintenance-free, i.e. not painted.

Apply two coats of sealer to the rebate of a hardwood frame, and when it is dry lay a bed of the non-setting compound. Place the packing pieces on the bottom of the rebate and the spacers, or distance pieces, against the back of it to prevent the glass moving in the compound. Set the spacers about 50mm (2in) from the corners and 300mm (1ft) apart opposite a bead fixing point.

Set the sealed unit into the rebate and press it in firmly. Apply an outer layer of the non-setting compound and another set of spacers against the glass positioned as before.

Cut the beading to length, making mitred ends, press it tight against the spacers and screw it into place with countersunk brass or plated screws. Countersunk screw cups are sometimes used instead of countersinking the holes in the beading. These give a neat finish.

Using beading
Set square-edged units in a non-setting compound.
1 Set the packing and spacers in compound
2 Fit the unit, apply more compound and place spacers at the bead fixing points
3 Press the beads tight against the spacers and fix in place with screws

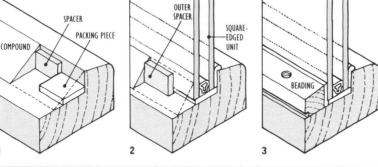

Metal-framed windows

Mild steel window frames are made with metal sections that form a rebate for the glass. This type of window is glazed in much the same way as a wooden-framed window, but a special metal quality putty is required. The putty is available from glass merchants. The glass is secured in the frame with spring clips (1) which are set in putty and locate in holes in frame. Replace glass in a metal frame following the sequence described for wooden frames but use clips instead of the sprigs mentioned. Treat any rust before fitting the glass and apply a metal primer (◁).

Modern aluminium double-glazed frames use a dry-glazing system which involves synthetic rubber gaskets. These are factory installed and should be free of the need for maintenance. If you break a pane in a window of this type you should consult the manufacturers, as they usually have their own patent repair system.

RELIEVING STICKING WINDOWS

The sashes of wooden casement windows are liable to swell in wet weather, and this causes them to bind in the frame. If the windows have not been painted properly it may be sufficient to wait for a period of dry weather, allowing the wood to shrink, and then apply a good paint system (◁).

The persistent sticking of a casement window in all weathers may be due to a too-heavy build-up of paint. In this case strip the old paint from the meeting edges of the sash and/or the frame rebate and apply fresh paint. You may also have to plane the edge a little.

A window that was not opened when the frame was painted is likely to be glued shut by the paint. Free it by working a wallpaper scraper or thin knife between the sash and the frame.

The tolerances on wooden vertically sliding sashes are such that they do not stick unless they have been painted while shut, or the staff or parting beads have been badly positioned (◁).

CURING RATTLING WINDOWS

The rattling of a casement window is usually caused by an ill-fitting lever fastener. If the fastener is worn you should either replace it with a new one or reset the plate on the frame into which the fastener locates.

Old wooden sash windows are notorious for rattling. The cause is usually a sash, generally the bottom one, being a loose fit in its stile tracks. Remove and replace the inner staff bead with a new length so that it makes a close fit against the sash. Rub candle grease on both sliding surfaces.

A rattling top sash will have to be packed out, as there is no way of adjusting its track.

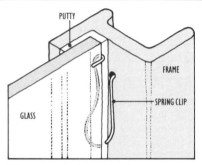

I Use spring clips to hold the glass

REPAIRING ROTTEN FRAMES

Softwood is the traditional material for making wooden window frames, and providing it is of sound quality and is well cared for, it will last the life of the building. New frames or frames which have been stripped should always be treated with a clear wood preservative before painting.

Regular maintenance

It is the bottom rail of a softwood window frame that is most vulnerable to rot if it is not protected. The water may be absorbed by the wood through a poor paint finish or by penetrating behind old shrunken putty. An annual check of all window frames should be carried out and any faults should be dealt with. Old putty that has shrunk away from the glass should be cut out and replaced with new (▷).

Remove old flaking paint, make good any cracks in the wood with a flexible filler and repaint (▷), ensuring that the underside of the sash is well painted.

Replacing a sash rail

Where rot is well advanced and the rail is beyond repair it should be cut out and replaced. This should be done before the rot spreads to the stiles of the frame. Otherwise you will eventually have to replace the whole sash frame.

Remove the sash either by unscrewing the hinges or – if it is a double-hung sash window – by removing the beading (▷).

With a little care the repair can be carried out without the glass being removed from the sash frame, though if the window is large it would be safer to take out the glass. In any event, cut away the putty from the damaged rail.

The bottom rail is tenoned into the stiles (1), but it can be replaced by using bridle joints. Saw down the shoulder lines of the tenon joints (2) from both faces of the frame and remove the rail.

Make a new rail, or buy a piece if it is a standard section, and mark and cut it to length with a full-width tenon at each end. Set the positions of the tenons to line up with the mortises of the stiles. Cut the shoulders to match the rebated sections of the stiles (3) or, if it has a decorative moulding, pare the moulding away to leave a flat shoulder (4).

Cut slots in the ends of the stiles to receive the tenons.

Glue the new rail into place with a waterproof resin adhesive and reinforce the two joints with pairs of 6mm (1/4in) stopped dowels (▷). Drill the stopped holes from the inside of the frame and stagger them.

When the adhesive is dry, plane the surface as required and treat the new wood with a clear preservative. Re-putty the glass and paint the new rail within three weeks.

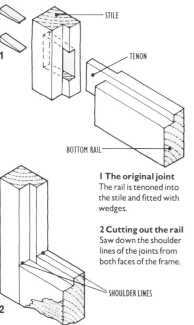

1 The original joint
The rail is tenoned into the stile and fitted with wedges.

2 Cutting out the rail
Saw down the shoulder lines of the joints from both faces of the frame.

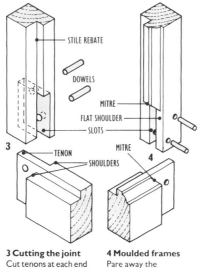

3 Cutting the joint
Cut tenons at each end of the rail with the shoulders matching the sections of the stiles.

4 Moulded frames
Pare away the moulding of the stile to receive the square shoulder of the rail. Mitre the moulding.

REPLACING A FIXED-LIGHT RAIL

The frames of some fixed lights are made like sashes but are screwed to the main frame jamb and mullion. Such a frame can be repaired in the same way as a sash (See left) after its glass is removed and it is unscrewed from the window frame. Where this proves too difficult you will have to carry out the repair in situ.

First remove the putty and the glass, then saw through the rail at each end. With a chisel trim the rebated edge of the jamb(s) and/or mullion to a clean surface at the joint (1) and chop out the old tenons. Cut a new length of rail to fit between the prepared edges and cut housings in its top edge at both ends to take loose tenons. Place the housings so that they line up with the mortises and make them twice as long as the depth of the mortises.

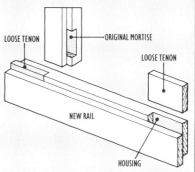

1 Chop out the tenons and cut a new rail to fit

Cut two loose tenons to fit the housings, and two packing pieces. The latter should have one sloping edge (2).

Apply an exterior woodworking adhesive to all of the jointing surfaces, place the rail between the frame members, insert the loose tenons and push them sideways into the mortises. Drive the packing pieces behind the tenons to lock them in place. When the adhesive has set, trim the top edges, treat the new wood with clear preservative, replace the glass and re-putty. Paint within three weeks.

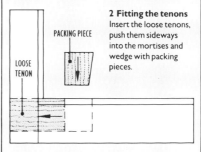

2 Fitting the tenons
Insert the loose tenons, push them sideways into the mortises and wedge with packing pieces.

SEE ALSO

Details for: ▷

Painting windows	78
Sash windows	196, 207
Removing glass	202
Fitting glass	202
Dowel joints	476, 477
Adhesives	496

● **Removing glass**
Removing glass from a window frame in one piece is not easy so be prepared for it to break. Apply adhesive tape across the glass to bind the pieces together if it should break. Chisel away the putty to leave a clean rebate, then pull out the sprigs (▷). Work the blade of a putty knife into the bedding joint on the inside of the frame to break the grip of the putty. Steady the glass and lift it out when it becomes free.

REPAIRING ROTTEN SILLS

The sill is a fundamental part of a window frame, and one attacked by rot can mean major repair work.

A casement window frame is constructed in the same way as a door frame and can be repaired in a similar way (◁). All the glass should be removed first. The window board may also have to be removed, then refitted level with the replacement sill.

Make sure that the damp-proofing of the joint between the underside of the sill and the wall is maintained. Modern gun-applied mastics have made this particular problem easier to overcome. Some traditional frames have a galvanized-iron water bar between the sill and sub-sill. When replacing a sill of this type without removing the whole frame it may be necessary to remove the bar and rely on mastic sealants alone to keep the water out.

SEE ALSO

◁ Details for:
Painting masonry 64-66
Door frame 191
Casement window 209
Sash window 210
Mixing concrete 439

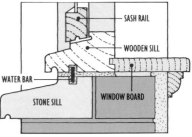

Traditional frame with stone sub-sill

Replacing a wooden sill

If you simply replace a sill by cutting through it and fitting a new section between the jambs you may not have solved your problem. Even when mastic sealants are used, any breakdown of the seal will allow water a direct path to the brickwork and the end grain of the wood, and you may find yourself doing the job all over again.

Serious rot in the sill of a sash window may require the whole frame to be taken out (◁). Make and fit a new sill using the old one as a pattern. Treat the new wood with a preservative and take the opportunity to treat the old

wood which is normally hidden by the brickwork. Apply a bead of mastic sealant to the sill, then replace the complete frame in the opening from inside. Make good the plaster.

It is possible to replace the sill from the inside with the frame in place. Saw through the sill close to the jambs and remove the cut centre portion. Cut away the bottom ends of the inner lining level with the pulley stiles and remove the ends of the old sill. Cut the ends of the new sill to fit round the outer lining and under the stiles and inner lining. Fit the sill and nail or screw the stiles to it.

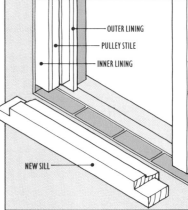

Cut the new sill to fit the frame

Repairing a stone sub-sill

The traditional stone sills that feature in older houses may become eroded by the weather if they are not protected with paint. They may also suffer cracking due to subsidence in part of the wall.

Repair any cracks and eroded surfaces with a quick-setting waterproof cement. Rake the cracks out to clean and enlarge them, then dampen the stone with clean water and work the cement well into the cracks, finishing off flush with the top surface.

Depressions caused by erosion should be undercut to provide the cement with

a good hold. A thin layer of cement simply applied to a shallow depression in the surface will not last. Use a cold chisel to cut away the surface of the sill at least 25mm (1in) below the finished level and remove all traces of dust.

Make a wooden former to the shape of the sill and temporarily nail it to the brickwork. Dampen the stone, pour in the cement and tamp it level with the former, then smooth it with a trowel. Leave it to set for a couple of days before removing the former. Let it dry thoroughly before painting (◁).

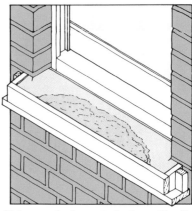

Make a wooden former to the shape of the sill

CASTING A NEW SUB-SILL

Cut out the remains of the old stone sill with a hammer and cold chisel. Make a wooden mould with its end pieces shaped to the same section as the old sill. The mould must be made upside down, its open top representing the underside of the sill.

Fill two thirds of the mould with fine ballast concrete, tamped down well, and then add two lengths of mild steel reinforcing rod, judiciously spaced to share the volume of the sill, then fill the

remainder of the mould. Set a narrow piece of wood such as a dowel into notches previously cut in the ends of the mould. This is to form a 'throat' or drip groove in the underside of the sill.

Cover the concrete with polythene sheeting or dampen it regularly for two or three days to prevent rapid drying. When the concrete is set (allow about seven days) remove it from the mould and re-lay the sill in the wall on a bed of mortar to meet the wooden sill.

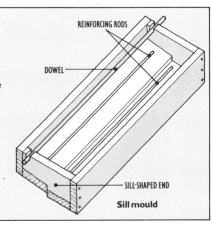

Sill mould

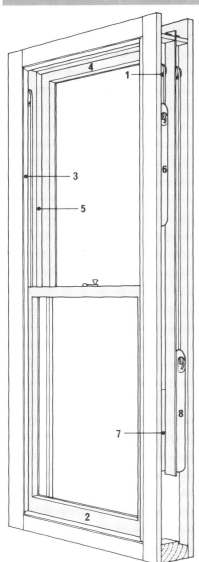

The workings of a double-hung sash window

1 Pulleys	5 Parting bead
2 Bottom sash	6 Bottom sash weight
3 Staff bead	7 Pocket
4 Top sash	8 Top sash weight

The sash cording from which the sashes are suspended will wear and in time will break. You should replace both cords even when only one has broken.

Waxed sash cording is normally sold in standard hanks, though some suppliers sell it by the metre. Each sash will require two lengths about three quarters the height of the window. Do not cut it to length beforehand.

Removing the sashes

Lower the sashes and cut through the cords with a knife to release the weights. Hold on to the cords and lower the weights as far as possible before letting them drop. Prise off the side staff beads from inside the frame, starting in the middle and bowing them to make their mitred ends spring out and avoid breakage.

Lean the inner sash forward and mark the ends of the cord grooves on the face of the sash stiles. Reposition the sash and carry the marks on to the pulley stiles (1). The sash can now be pulled clear of the frame.

Carefully prise out the two parting beads from their grooves in the stiles. The top sash can then be removed, after marking the ends of the grooves as before. Place sashes safely aside.

To gain access to the weights take out the pocket pieces which were trapped by the parting bead and lift the weights out through the openings. Hanging pieces of thin wood known as parting strips may be fitted inside the box stiles to keep the pairs of weights apart. Push these aside to reach the outer weights.

Remove the old cording from the weights and sashes and clean them up ready for the new sash cords.

Fitting the sashes

The top sash is fitted first, but not before all of the sash cords and weights are in place. Clean away any build-up of paint from the pulleys. Tie a length of fine string to one end of the sash cord. Weight the other end of the string with small nuts or a piece of chain. Thread the weight – known as a mouse – over a pulley (2) and pull the string through the pocket opening until the cord is pulled through. Attach the end of the cord to a weight with a special knot (See below left).

Use the sash marks to measure the length of cord required. Pull on the cord to hoist the weight up to the pulley. Then let it drop back about 100mm (4in). Hold it temporarily in this position with a nail driven into the stile just below the pulley. Cut the cord level with the mark on the pulley stile (3).

Repeat this procedure for the cord on the other side, and then for the bottom sash.

Replace the top sash on the sill, removing the temporary nails in turn. Lean the sash forward, locate the cords into the grooves in the stiles and nail them in place using three or four 25mm (1in) round wire nails. Nail only the bottom 150mm (6in), not all the way up (4). Lift the sash to check that the weights do not touch bottom.

Replace the pocket pieces and pin the parting beads in their grooves. Fit the bottom sash in the same way. Finally replace the staff beads; take care to position them accurately.

SEE ALSO

Details for: ▷

Craft knife	485
Nails	496-497

HOW TO TIE A SASH WEIGHT KNOT

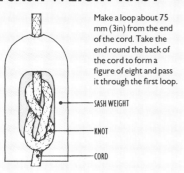

Make a loop about 75 mm (3in) from the end of the cord. Take the end round the back of the cord to form a figure of eight and pass it through the first loop.

SASH WEIGHT
KNOT
CORD

1 Mark cord grooves

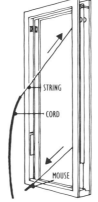

2 Pull cord through

3 Cut cords at mark

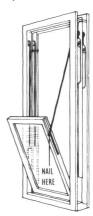

4 Nail cord to sash

SPIRAL BALANCES

SEE ALSO

◁ Details for:

Parting bead	196, 207
Spiral balances	197
Removing sashes	207

Instead of cords and counterweights, modern sash windows use spiral balances which are mounted on the faces of the frame stiles, eliminating the need for traditional box sections. The balances are made to order to match the size and weight of individual glazed sashes and can be ordered through builders' merchants or by post from the makers using an order form.

Spiral balance components

Each balance consists of a torsion spring and a spiral rod housed in a tube. The top end is fixed to the stile and the inner spiral to the bottom of the sash. The complete unit can be housed in a groove in the sash stile or in the jamb of the frame.

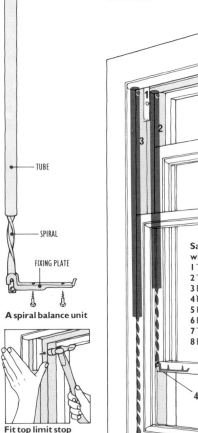

TUBE

SPIRAL

FIXING PLATE

A spiral balance unit

Fit top limit stop

Fit bottom limit stop

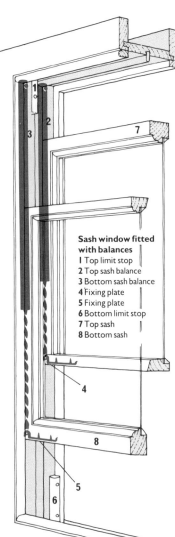

Sash window fitted with balances
1 Top limit stop
2 Top sash balance
3 Bottom sash balance
4 Fixing plate
5 Fixing plate
6 Bottom limit stop
7 Top sash
8 Bottom sash

Fitting the balances

You can fit spiral sash balances to replace the weights in a traditionally constructed sash window.

Remove the sashes and weigh them on your bathroom scales. Place your order, giving the weight of each sash and its height and width, also the height of the frame. Refit the sashes temporarily until the balances arrive, then take them out again and remove the pulleys.

Plug the holes and paint the stiles. Cut grooves, as specified by the manufacturers, in the stiles of each sash, to take the balances (**1**) . Also cut a housing at each end of their bottom edges to receive the spiral rod fixing plates. Fit the plates with screws (**2**) .

Sit the top sash in place, resting it on the sill, and fit the parting bead. Take the top pair of balances, which are shorter than those for the bottom sash, and locate each in its groove (**3**) . Fix the top ends of the balance tubes to the frame stiles with the screw nails provided (**4**) and set the ends tight against the head.

Lift the sash to its full height and prop it with a length of wood. Hook the wire 'key', provided by the makers, into the hole in the end of each spiral rod and pull each one down about 150mm (6in). Keeping the tension on the spring, add three to five turns anti-clockwise (**5**) . Locate the ends of the rods in the fixing plate and test the balance of the sash. If it drops add another turn on the springs until it is just held in position. Take care not to overwind the balances.

Fit the bottom sash in the same way, refitting the staff bead to hold it in place. Fit the stops that limit the full travel of the sashes in their respective tracks (See left).

RENOVATING SPIRAL BALANCES

In time the springs of spiral balances may weaken. Re-tension them by unhooking the spiral rods from the fixing plates, then turning the rods anti-clockwise once or twice.

The mechanisms can be serviced by releasing the tension and unwinding the rods from the tubes. Wipe them clean and apply a little thin oil, then rewind the rods back into the tubes and tension them as described above.

1 Cut a groove in the sash stiles

2 Fix the plates in their housings with screws

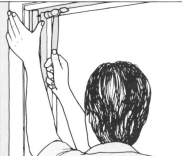

3 Fit the sash and locate the tube in its groove

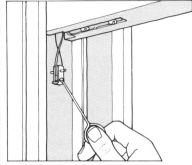

4 Nail the top end of the tube to the stile

5 Tension the springs with the key provided

READY-MADE WINDOWS

Joinery suppliers offer a range of ready-made window frames in both hardwood and softwood, and some typical examples are shown below.

Unfortunately the range of sizes is rather limited, but where a ready-made frame is fairly close to one's requirements it is possible to either cut back the brickwork or fill the gap between the frame and the wall with masonry, though this is really acceptable only for windows in rendered walls. In a wall of exposed brickwork the window frame should be made to measure.

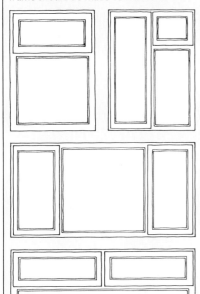

Casement windows

Vertical sliding sash windows

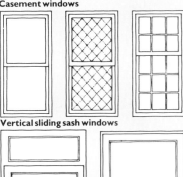

Pivot windows

REPLACEMENT WINDOWS

The style of the windows is an important element in the appearance of any house. Should you be thinking of replacing windows in an older dwelling you might find it better – and not necessarily more expensive – to have new wooden frames made rather than changing to modern windows of aluminium or plastic.

Planning and building regulations

Window conversions do not normally need planning permission as they come under the heading of house improvement or home maintenance, but if you plan to alter your windows significantly – for example, by bricking one up or making a new window opening, or both – you should consult your local Building Control Officer.

All authorities require minimum levels of ventilation to be provided in the habitable rooms of a house, and this normally means that the openable part of windows must have an area at least one twentieth that of the room.

You should also check with your local authority if you live in a listed building or in a conservation area, which could mean some limitation on your choice.

Buying replacement windows

Specialist joinery firms will make up wooden window frames to your size. Specify hardwood or, for a painted finish, softwood impregnated with a timber preservative.

Alternatively you can approach one of the replacement window companies, though this is likely to limit your choice to aluminium or plastic frames. The ready-glazed units can be fitted to your old timber sub-frames or to new hardwood ones supplied by the installer. Most of the replacement window companies operate on the basis of supplying and also fitting the windows, and their service includes disposing of the old windows and of the rubbish.

This method is saving of time and labour, but you should carefully compare the various offerings of these companies and their compatibility with the style of your house before opting for one. Choose a frame that reproduces, as closely as possible, the proportions of the original window.

Replacing a casement window

Measure the width and height of the window opening. If the replacement window will need a timber sub-frame and the existing one is in good condition, take your measurements from inside the frame. Otherwise take them from the brickwork. You may have to cut away some of the rendering or plaster first so as to get accurate measurements. Order the replacement window accordingly.

Remove the old window by first taking out the sashes and then the panes of glass in any fixed part. Unscrew the exposed fixings, such as may be found in a metal frame, or chisel away the plaster or rendering and cut through them with a hacksaw. It should be possible to knock the frame out in one piece, but if not saw through it in several places and lever the pieces out with a crowbar (1). Clean up the exposed brickwork with a bolster chisel to make a neat opening.

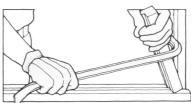

I Lever out the pieces of the old frame

Cut the horns off the new frame if present, then plumb the frame in the window opening and wedge it (2). Drill screw holes through the stiles into the brickwork (3), then remove the frame and plug the holes. Attach a bituminous felt damp-proof course to the stiles and sill and refit the frame, checking again that it is plumb before screwing it into home.

Make good the wall with mortar and plaster. Gaps of 6mm (¼in) or less can be filled with mastic. Glaze the new frame as required.

2 Fit the new frame   **3 Drill fixing holes**

SEE ALSO

Details for: ▷	
Types of windows	196-197
Fitting glass	202
Bituminous felt	431
Builder's tools	478-480
Hacksaw	486

REPLACEMENT WINDOWS

Bay windows

A bay window is a combination of window frames which are built out from the face of the building. The side frames may be set at 90, 60 or 45 degree angles to the front of the house. Curved bays are also made with equal-sized frames set at a very slight angle to each other to form a faceted curve.

The frames of a bay window are set on brickwork which is built to the shape of the bay, which may be at ground level only, with a flat or pitched roof, or may be continued up through all storeys and finished with a gabled roof.

Bay windows can break away from the main wall through subsidence caused by poor foundations or differential ground movements. Damage from slight movement can be repaired once it has stabilised. Repoint the brickwork and apply mastic sealant to gaps round the woodwork. Damage from extensive or persistent movement should be dealt with by a builder. Consult your local Building Control Officer and inform your house insurance company.

Fitting the frame

Where the height of the original window permits it, standard window frames can be used to make up a replacement bay window. Using gasket seals (◁), various combinations of frames can be arranged. Shaped hardwood corner posts are available to give a 90, 60 or 45 degree angle to the side frames. The gasket is used for providing a weatherproof seal between the posts and the frames.

SEE ALSO

◁ Details for:
Removing sashes   207
Flashing   232-233
Sealer   254
Pointing brickwork   45
Vertical DPC   198
Sash window   198
Gabled roof   223

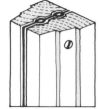
Joining frames
A flexible gasket, which is sold by the metre, is available for joining standard frames. The frames are screwed together to fit the opening.

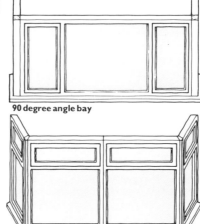
90 degree angle bay

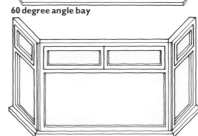
60 degree angle bay

45 degree angle bay

Hardwood bay window (Detail)

Bow windows

These are windows constructed on a shallow curve, and they normally project from a flat wall. Complete hardwood bow window frames are available from joinery suppliers, ready for installation in a brickwork opening. A flat-topped canopy of moulded plastic is made for finishing the top of the window. Bow windows can be substituted for conventional ones.

Fitting the frame

Tack a damp-proof course material to the sides of the frame and the underside of the sill, then fit the frame and the canopy into the wall opening together, the outer edges of the frame set flush with the wall finish. Screw the frame to the brickwork. The vertical damp-proofing should overlap the one in the wall if one is present.

Weatherproof the canopy with a lead flashing cut into the wall and dressed over the canopy upstand (◁). Use mastic to seal the joints between the frame's sides and sill and the brickwork.

Bow window (Detail) with leaded lights

REPLACING A SASH WINDOW

An old vertically sliding sash window with cords and counterweights can be replaced with a new frame fitted with spiral balance sashes.

Remove the sashes (◁), then take out the old frame from inside the room. Prise off the architrave, then the window boards, and chop away the plaster as necessary. Most frames make a wedge fit, and you can loosen one by hitting the sill on the outside with a heavy hammer and a wood block. Lift the frame out of the opening when it is loose (1) and remove any debris from the opening once it is clear.

Set the new frame centrally in the opening so that its stiles are showing equal amounts on each side of the exterior brickwork reveals. Check the frame for plumb and wedge the corners at the head and the sill. Make up the space left by the old box stiles with mortared brickwork (2).

Metal brackets screwed to the frame's stiles can also be set in the mortar bed joints to secure the frame.

When the mortar is set, replaster the inner wall and replace the architrave. In the meantime glaze the sashes. Finally apply a mastic sealant to the joints between the outside brickwork and the frame to keep the weather out.

1 Lift out old frame   **2 Fill gaps with brick**

ROOF WINDOWS

Double-glazed roof windows are becoming increasingly popular for the modernizing of old attic skylights and as part of loft conversions. They are supplied ready-glazed and fully-equipped with catches and ventilators. Flashing kits to fit the window frame and to suit high or low profile roofing materials are also available.

Centre-pivoting sashes can be used on roofs with pitches between 15 and 85 degrees, and special emergency exit types may be installed. These can be converted to top-hung or side-hung sashes at the turn of a handle. The former are for roof pitches of 20-60 degrees, and the latter for those of 60-85 degrees.

Roof windows are relatively easy to install using only ordinary woodworking tools and often working only from the inside. Once they are fitted the glass can be cleaned comfortably from the inside. Such accessories as blinds and remote opening devices are also available.

Roof windows reverse for easy maintenance

Blinds which fit the inside frame are available

Choosing the size

The manufacturers of roof windows offer a standard range of sizes and, apart from consideration of cost, the overall size should take account of the area of glass necessary to provide a suitable level of daylight in the room.

The height of the window is also quite important. It should be determined by the pitch of the roof in relation to how the window is going to be used. The manufacturers produce charts which give the recommended dimensions according to roof pitch. Ideally, if the window is to provide a good outlook, the bottom rails should not obstruct the view at normal seat height, nor should it cut across the line of sight of someone standing. Broadly this means that the shallower the pitch of the roof, the taller the window needs to be. The top of the window should remain within comfortable reach.

Fitting a window

Start by stripping off the roof-covering material over the area which is to be occupied by the window. The final placing of the frame will be determined by the position of the rafters and the roofing. Start by setting the bottom of the window frame at the specified distance above the nearest full course of slates and try to position it so as to have half or whole slates at each side.

Cut through the slating battens, roofing felt and rafters to make the opening, following the dimensions given by the manufacturer. Cut and nail horizontal trimmers between the rafters to set the height of the opening, and a vertical trimmer or trimmers to set the width.

With the glazed sash removed, screw

Standard-sized windows can be arranged side-by-side or one above the other to create a larger window. The widest single window available measures 1.34m (4ft 4¾in). When deciding on the size of a window bear in mind its proportions and its position in relation to the appearance of the building.

You will probably not need planning permission to install this type of window but check if you live in a listed building or in a conservation area. However, the structural alterations will have to have Building Regulations approval just as a complete loft conversion does.

The manufacturers of roof windows supply comprehensive fixing instructions to suit installation in all situations. Below is a summary of one type of window fitted into a slate-covered roof. The frame for a tiled roof has a different flashing kit.

the window frame in place with the brackets provided. A guide line is clearly marked round the frame, and this must be set level with the surface of the roofing battens. Check that the frame is square by measuring across its diagonals to be sure they are equal.

Complete the outside work by fitting the slates and flashing kit, working up from the bottom of the frame. Replace the glazed sash.

Cut and nail plasterboard to the sides of the rafters on the inside and close the top and bottom of the opening with plasterboard nailed in the groove provided in the frame and to the timbers of the roof structure.

Finish off the joints with filler and tape, ready for decoration (▷).

SEE ALSO

Details for: ▷
Plasterboard   158-159
Roofs   221-226, 232-233

Height of window
The height should enable someone sitting or standing to see out of the window with ease.

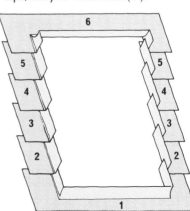

FRAME GROOVE

RAFTER
PLASTERBOARD

Lining the opening with plasterboard
Section through window seen from the inside showing the lining on the side, top and bottom of the opening.

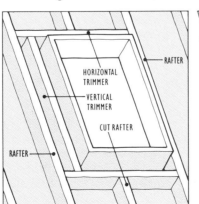

RAFTER

HORIZONTAL TRIMMER

VERTICAL TRIMMER

CUT RAFTER

RAFTER

Cut the opening and fit the trimmers

Flashing kit showing order of assembly

STAIRS

In simple functional terms a stair is a series of steps that link one floor with another, but a staircase – traditionally the stair combined with that part of the building which surrounds it – can also be a powerful expression of the style of the house itself. By its location, invariably in the entrance hall, its sometimes impressive scale and its interesting shape or decorative features, the stair is an important element in the character of a domestic interior.

SEE ALSO

◁ Details for:
Work platforms	40-42
Decorating stairwells	96
Carpeting stairs	117

In the staircases of some older houses elaborate examples of the joiner's art can be found, but unfortunately joinery nowadays has lost much of the character of earlier periods. However, the spacious and airy quality of modern open-tread stairways, although simply constructed, makes them attractive in their own right.

An old, worn or creaking stair can be repaired, and though its decorative elements may be laborious to restore the end result is worth the effort.

Types of stair

The simplest stair is a straight flight of steps. This type of stair requires the greatest 'going', that is the horizontal distance between the face of the bottom step riser and the riser of the top step (**1**). In houses where space is limited shorter flights may be used, an intermediate landing making a turn and linking one flight with another. Various more elaborate arrangements – the dog-leg, the open-well, the quarter-turn and the half-turn staircase – are also used (See right).

Most domestic stairs use newel posts for their support and are known as newel stairs. The posts are a prominent feature, the newel at the foot of the stair often being larger and rather more decorative than those above. Stairs of this type usually have straight treads, though tapered treads known as winders are used at the top or bottom of a stair where the going is restricted.

Winders may be used exclusively, forming a sweeping curved or helical stair. This type, known as a geometric stair, does not include newel posts in its construction. A spiral staircase is a helical stair constructed round a central column. Unlike the sweeping curved stair, it can be used in small houses where space is limited. Reproductions of old spiral stairs and modern styles in wood, steel and concrete are made.

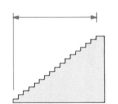

1 The going
The going of the stair is the horizontal measurement between the bottom and top riser.

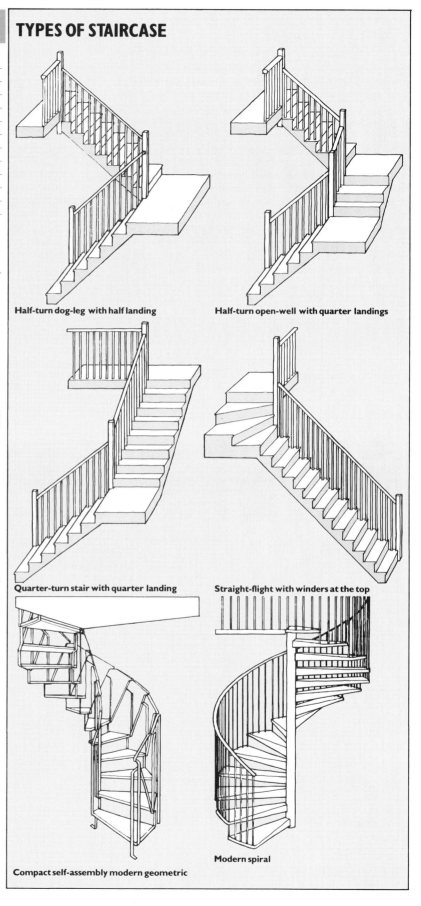

TYPES OF STAIRCASE

Half-turn dog-leg with half landing

Half-turn open-well with quarter landings

Quarter-turn stair with quarter landing

Straight-flight with winders at the top

Compact self-assembly modern geometric

Modern spiral

STAIR CONSTRUCTION

Softwood is most commonly used for the construction of traditional stairs, and expensive hardwoods such as oak, teak and mahogany are usually reserved for better-quality houses, though some hardwood is sometimes combined with *softwood in stairs for such features as newel posts and handrails.*

Stone and metal are also used for stairs, though they are rarely found in ordinary domestic contexts other than in spiral staircases.

Steps

Each step of an ordinary straight flight of stairs is made from two boards, the vertical riser that forms the front of the step and the horizontal tread, the board on which you walk. The riser is a stiffening member and is fixed between two treads, giving support to the front edge of one and the rear of the other.

Treads and risers may be jointed in a number of ways (See below right), but always there are triangular blocks glued into the angles between risers and treads to give greater stiffness.

Open tread stairs have thick treads and no risers. To comply with the Building Regulations metal tie rods must be fitted across the stair in the gaps between the treads.

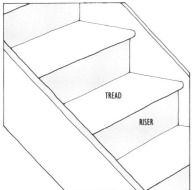

Each step of the common stair has a tread and riser

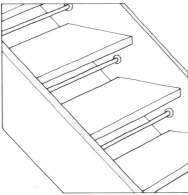

Open-tread stairs have no risers but use tie rods

Strings

Steps are carried at their ends by wide boards, set on edge, known as strings, and these are the main structural members than run from one floor level to another. A wall string is an inner one that is fixed to the wall, while the string on the open side of the stair is called the outer string.

The appearance of the stair is affected by the style of the strings, of which there are two types. The closed string has parallel long edges, while the cut or open string has its top edge cut away to the shape of the steps. The closed version is used for the wall string of a stair to pick up the line of the skirting. The outer string can be either the simple closed type, preferred in modern houses, or the cut type that is generally found in older dwellings.

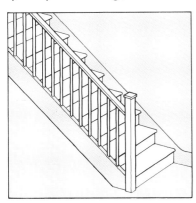

The closed string has parallel long edges

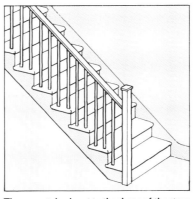

The open string is cut to the shape of the steps

Step/string joints

The treads and risers of stairs are set in housings cut into the face of a closed string and secured with glued wedges. The wedges are driven in from the underside to make a tight joint.

In the case of an open string the outer ends of the risers are mitred into the vertical cut edges and the treads are nailed down onto the horizontal edges. The nosing – the projecting rounded edge – of this type of tread, which usually has a scotia moulding underneath it, is 'returned' by a matching moulding that covers the tread's end grain.

Additional decorative features of fretted wood may be pinned and glued to the side of the string underneath the tread mouldings.

SEE ALSO

Details for: ▷

Removing a tread	216-217
Removing a riser	217
Cutting grooves	466-467, 468

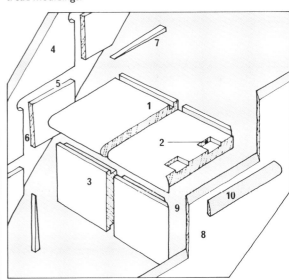

Step assembly showing typical stair joints
1 Grooved tread
2 Baluster housing
3 Tongued riser
4 Wall string
5 Tread housing
6 Riser housing
7 Wedge
8 Open string
9 Mitred butt joint
10 Moulding

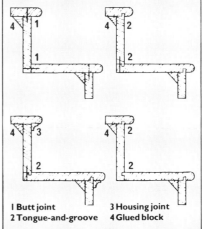

JOINTS BETWEEN TREAD AND RISER

1 Butt joint
2 Tongue-and-groove
3 Housing joint
4 Glued block

STAIRS: CONSTRUCTION

SEE ALSO

◁ Details for:
Baluster repairs	218
Fitting a handrail	219
Replacing a balustrade	220

Newels

The wall string is screwed to the wall at points underneath the treads and the outer string is tenoned into the newels at each end. Newel posts are at least 100 x 100mm (4 x 4in) in section. They give support to the stair while securing it to the floor at the bottom and to the structural trimmer of the floor or landing above. The newel at the top of a stair, or the central newel on a stair with a landing, is usually continued down to the floor. The newels also carry the handrail, which is tenoned into them.

The balustrade

The space between the handrail and the outer string may be filled with traditional balusters, modern balustrade rails or framed panelling. The assembly is known as the balustrade, or banisters. There are some fairly rigorous stipulations about balustrades under the Building Regulations (See right).

Storage space

The space underneath a stair is often enclosed to make a cupboard and provide extra storage space. The triangular infilling between the outer string of the stair and the floor is known as the spandrel. It may be a plastered surface or one of wood panelling. It is not structural and can be removed if and when required. You might think twice before opening up this area as the understair cupboard is a sensible use of a space that is otherwise of little value. Many families find it a good place for keeping such things as vacuum cleaners and folded pushchairs.

Storage space
The area below a stair is usually enclosed to provide storage space.

The central bearer

Traditional stairs 900mm (3ft) in width should be supported on their underside by a central bearer or 'carriage piece'. This is a length of 100 x 50mm (4 x 2in) timber which is birdsmouth jointed onto a 100 x 50mm (4 x 2in) floorplate at the bottom and the floor trimmer at the top. Short lengths of 25mm (1in) thick board known as rough brackets are nailed to alternate sides of the bearer to make a tight fit under each tread and riser.

If the finished underside of the stair, or soffit, is of lath and plaster, the central bearer also provides an intermediate support for the laths. The ends of the laths may be nailed to the edges of the strings or to additional bearers that run down inside them.

When central bearers are used, wider strings are fitted to clear them. Such a string may be a single wider board or made up with two boards. In the latter case the extra bottom board is tongued and grooved into the lower edge of the actual step-bearing string.

In some cases, where no bearer is used and the underside of the stair is of lath and plaster, the laths are nailed longitudinally to the under-edges of the treads, following the angle of the stair.

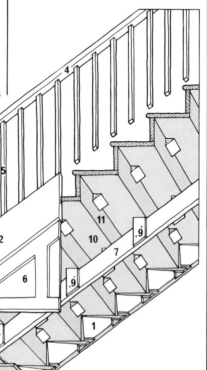

Stair components
1 Wall string
2 Outer string
3 Newel
4 Handrail
5 Balusters
6 Spandrel
7 Carriage piece
8 Floor plate
9 Rough brackets
10 Tread
11 Riser

BALUSTRADE BUILDING REGULATIONS

Current Building Regulations relating to balustrades require that the height of a stair balustrade be not less than 840mm (2ft 9in) and not more than 1m (3ft 3in), the measurement being taken vertically (1) from the pitch line, the line of the stair nosings (2). A balustrade protecting a landing or floor (3) must be no less than 900mm (2ft 11in) in height.

Balustrade with balusters
The pitch line (2) is shown dotted.

The spaces between balusters or balustrade rails must not be so wide as to allow a 100mm (4in) sphere to pass between them (4), though an exception to this rule is used in conjunction with a cut string (5), providing the rail is no more than 50mm (2in) above the pitch line.

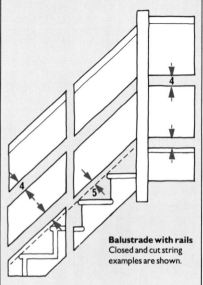

Balustrade with rails
Closed and cut string examples are shown.

Creaking in stairs begins when joints become loose and start rubbing. The slight gaps that allow this movement are often the result of the timber having shrunk, though general wear and tear will also contribute to the problem.

The method you choose for dealing with it will depend on whether you have access to the backs of the treads. A better repair can be carried out from underneath, but if that means cutting into the plaster of a soffit it will be more convenient to work from above.

Working from underneath

If it is possible to get to the underside of the stairs, have someone walk slowly up the steps, counting them out loud, and from your position under the stair follow the counting, noting any loose steps and marking them with chalk. Have your assistant work the loose treads while you inspect them to discover the source of the creaking.

Loose housing joint
If the tread or the riser is loose in its housing in the string it may be because the original wedge has become loose. Remove the wedge **(1)**, clean it up, apply PVA woodworking adhesive and re-wedge the joint **(2)**. If the wedge has got damaged while being removed make a new one out of hardwood.

Loose blocks
Check the triangular blocks that fit in the angle between the tread and the riser. If the adhesive has failed on one face remove the blocks, clean off the old adhesive and reglue them in place. Before replacing the blocks slightly prise open the shoulder of the tongue-and-groove joint with a chisel and apply new adhesive to it **(3)**, then pull the joint up tight using 38mm (1½in) countersunk screws set below the surface.

Rub-joint (▷) the blocks into the angle **(4)**. You can use panel pins to hold them while the adhesive sets.

Try to avoid treading on the repaired steps before the adhesive has set.

If some of the blocks are missing you can make new ones from lengths of 50 x 50mm (2 x 2in) softwood. Set the wood upright in a vice and, sawing across the diagonal of the end, cut down the grain for about 175mm (7in). Remove the wood from the vice and holding it on a bench hook (▷), or by repositioning it if you are using a Workmate bench, saw off 75mm (3in) long triangular blocks.

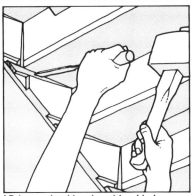

1 Prise out the old wedge with a chisel

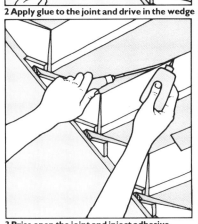

2 Apply glue to the joint and drive in the wedge

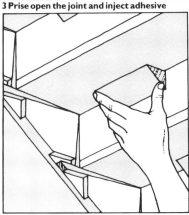

3 Prise open the joint and inject adhesive

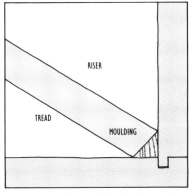

4 Rub-joint the glued blocks into the angle

Working from the top

To identify the problem areas walk slowly up the stairs – which should first be stripped of any covering – and stop at the creaking step, then shift your weight to and fro on the offending tread to discover which part is moving. It is best to do this late at night or early in the morning, when the house is quiet and small noises will not be missed.

Nosing – loose joint
To cure looseness in a tongue-and-groove joint between the riser and the nosing of a tread drill clearance holes for 38mm (1½in) countersunk screws in the tread, centring on the thickness of the riser **(1)**. Inject fresh PVA woodworking adhesive into the holes and work the joint a little so as to encourage the adhesive to spread into it, then pull the joint up tight with the screws. If the screws are not to be concealed by stair carpet you should counterbore the screw heads and plug the holes with matching wood.

Riser – loose joint
A loose joint at the back of the tread cannot be easily repaired from above. You can try working water-thinned PVA woodworking adhesive into the joint but you cannot use screws.

One form of reinforcement which may be of help is made by gluing a section of 12 x 12mm (½ x ½in) triangular moulding into the angle between the tread and the riser **(2)**, but this is possible only if it does not leave the remaining width of the tread below the Building Regulation specification for treads of 220mm (8¾in). Cut the moulding slightly shorter than the width of the stair carpet, unless the carpet is of full stair width or a similar moulding is fitted on all of the steps.

SEE ALSO

Details for: ▷	
Bench hook	463
Rub-joint	503
Carpeting stairs	117
Stair joints	213
Plug cutter	472
Workmate bench	474
Hardwood	494

1 Screw joint tight

RISER

TREAD

MOULDING

2 Glue a triangular moulding into the angle

215

REPAIRING WORN STAIRS

SEE ALSO

◁ Details for:

Fixings	496-498
Stair construction	214
Saws	463-465
Cutting grooves	466-467, 468

Old softwood stairs which have not had the protection of a floor covering will eventually become very worn. Worn treads and nosings are dangerous, and should be repaired promptly. If all the treads are badly worn you should have the stair replaced by a builder.

Treads fitted between closed strings can be replaced only from below. If the soffit of the stair is enclosed with lath and plaster, or with plasterboard, you will have to cut an opening to reach the worn-out tread. Where a central bearer has been used in the construction of the stair the work involved in the repair can be extensive, and in such a case you should seek the advice of a professional builder.

Renewing a nosing

Wear on the nosing of a tread is usually concentrated round the centre, and you can repair it without having to renew the whole tread.

Mark three cutting lines just outside the worn area, one set parallel with the edge of the nosing and the other two at right angles to it **(1)**.

Adjust the blade depth of a portable powered circular saw to the thickness of the tread. Pin a batten the required distance from, and parallel to, the long cutting line to guide the edge of the saw's baseplate.

Cutting out
Position the saw, switch it on, then make the cut by lowering the blade into the wood **(2)**. Try not to overrun the short end lines. The cut made, remove the guide batten. Hand saw the end lines, making cuts at 45 degrees to the face of the tread and taking care not to go beyond the first saw cut. Make these cuts with a tenon saw **(3)**.

You will be left with uncut waste in the corners. Remove most of the cut waste with a chisel, working with the grain and taking care to avoid damaging the riser tongue and triangular reinforcing blocks. Pare away the waste from the uncut corners **(4)**.

Replacement
In the underside of a new section of nosing plane a groove to receive the tongue of the riser and cut its ends to 45 degrees. Check its fit in the opening, then apply PVA wood adhesive to all of the meeting surfaces and fix it in place. Cramp it down with a batten screwed at each end to the tread **(5)**. Place a packing strip of hardboard under the batten to concentrate the pressure, and a piece of polythene to prevent the hardboard sticking. Drill and insert 6mm (¼in) dowels into the edge of the nosing to reinforce the butt joint and, when the adhesive is set, plane and sand the repair flush. Refix any blocks that may have fallen off.

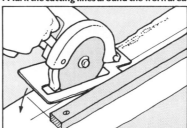
1 Mark the cutting lines around the worn area

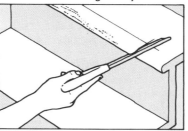
2 Make the cut with saw guided by batten

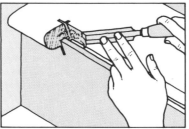
3 Make 45 degree cuts at each end

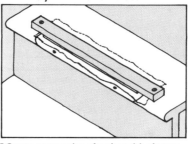
4 Pare away the waste from the corners

5 Cramp new section of nosing with a batten

REPLACING TREADS

Most stairs have tongue-and-groove joints between their risers and treads, though in some cases the tops of the risers are housed into the undersides of the treads and in other stairs simple butt joints are used and secured with nails or screws (◁).

You can determine which type of joint you are faced with by trying to pass a thin knife blade between the shoulders of the joint. It will help if you first remove any nails or screws. A butt joint will let the blade pass through, while a housed or a tongued and grooved one will not do so.

As the joints effectively lock the treads and risers together, those in contact with the damaged tread must be freed before the tread can be removed. A butt joint is relatively easy to take apart, whereas a housed or a tongue-and-groove joint will have to be cut.

Dismantling a butt joint
To take a butt joint apart first take out the nails or screws and, if adhesive has been used, give the tread a sharp tap to break the hardened adhesive, or prise it up with a chisel. In the same way remove the triangular glued blocks.

Cutting a tongue
Where the tongue of a riser is jointed into the underside of a tread you cut it working from the front of the stair, and where the riser's tongue is jointed into the top of the tread it must be cut from the rear **(1)**. If there is a scotia moulding fitted under the nosing try to prise it away first with a chisel.

Before cutting a tongue remove any screws, nails and glued reinforcement blocks, then drill a line of 3mm (⅛in) holes on the shoulders of the joint in which you can insert the blade of a padsaw **(2)**. Make a saw cut; when it is long enough, continue with a panel saw.

The method you will now use to remove the tread will depend on whether it is fitted between closed strings or has an open string at one end (See opposite).

1 Cut the tongue from the front or rear

2 Initiate the cut with a padsaw

Closed string stair

Working from the underside of the stair, chisel out the tread-retaining wedges from the string housings at the ends of the tread **(1)**, then free the joints by giving the tread a sharp tap from above with a hammer and block.

Next drive the tread backwards and out of its two housings, alternately tapping one end and then the other **(2)**.

Make a tread to fit, shaping its front edge to match the nosings of the other steps, and cut a new pair of wedges. Slide the new tread and wedges into place from underneath, measure the gaps left by the sawcuts at its front and back **(3)** and cut wooden packing strips or pieces of veneer to fill them.

Remove the tread, apply PVA wood adhesive and replace it, with the wedges and packing pieces. Secure the tread with 38mm (1½in) countersunk wood screws into the risers.

1 Remove the wedges

2 Drive out the tread

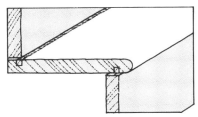
3 Pack out the saw cuts at front and back

Open string stairs

Prise off the moulding that covers the end grain of the tread, taking care not to split it **(1)**, and remove the two balusters (▷).

Chisel the wedge out of the wall string housing to free the inner end of the tread and drive the tread out from the rear of the stair, using a hammer and a wood block on the outer end of its back edge **(2)**. In this way the end of the tread fitted to the outer string is released while the inner end is still partly engaged in its housing.

You will have to cut through or extract any nails that fix the tread to the outer string before it can be pulled completely clear.

Use the original tread as a template and mark its shape out on a new board, then cut the board accurately to size. Take care to preserve the shape of the nosing which must follow that of the return moulding.

Mark out and cut the housings for the balusters **(3)** and make a new wedge for the inner tread housing.

Fit the tread from the front, packing out and gluing and screwing it following the method described for a closed string tread (See above).

Apply adhesive to the balusters and replace them. Finally pin and glue the return moulding to the end of the tread and replace any scotia moulding.

1 Prise off the return cover moulding

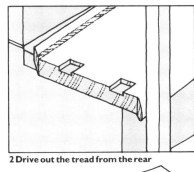
2 Drive out the tread from the rear

3 Cut the baluster housings in the new tread

REPAIRING A RISER

Risers take much less wear and tear than treads and will not ordinarily have to be replaced. Should a riser become weak through woodworm infestation it can be reinforced from behind by having a piece of new board screwed and glued to it, but the old and the new wood should both be thoroughly treated to eradicate the insects (▷). A riser which is seriously affected by woodworm should be replaced.

Closed string stair

In the case of a closed string stair remove the tread below the damaged riser using the method described (See left) but also saw through the tongue at the top of the riser. Knock the wedges out of the riser housings, then knock or prise out the riser **(1)**.

Measure the distance between the strings and between the underside of one tread to the top of the other, then cut a new riser to fit. Though you could make tongue-and-groove joints on the new riser it is easier simply to butt-joint its top and bottom edges with the treads **(2)**.

Glue and wedge the new riser into the housings and to its top edge glue and screw the upper tread **(3)**.

If yours is a 'show-wood' staircase – one whose steps are not to be covered – counterbore the screw holes and use wood plugs to conceal the screws. Another way to secure a glued butt joint is by screwing and gluing blocks to both parts underneath.

Refit the tread as previously described (See left), but note that you need pack out only the front saw cut as the new riser has been made to fit.

Open string stair

First remove any scotia moulding that is fitted under the nosing, then saw through the tongues at the top and bottom of the infected riser and remove the wedge from its wall string housing.

Knock apart the mitred joint between the end of the riser and the outer string by hammering it from behind. Once the mitred joint is free, pull the inner end of the riser out of its housing, working from the front.

Make a new riser to fit between the treads, mitring its outer end to match the joint in the string. Apply adhesive and fit the riser from the front. Re-wedge the inner housing joint, screw the treads to the riser, nail the mitred end and replace the scotia moulding.

SEE ALSO

Details for: ▷

Balusters	218
Woodworm treatment	246
Stair joints	213
Screw joints	215

1 Prise out the riser

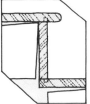
2 Cut riser to fit

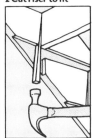
3 Wedge the riser

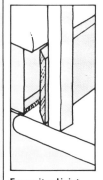
Free mitred joint

REPAIRING BALUSTERS

A broken baluster is potentially dangerous and it should be repaired or replaced promptly. If the baluster is a decorative one it should be preserved, and if the damage is not too extensive it can be repaired in situ. Otherwise, if the damage is beyond repair, a new baluster can be made to replace it.

SEE ALSO

◁ Details for:

Adjustable bevel	**462**
Strings	213
Open string	217
Joints	475-477

Buying balusters

Ready-turned balusters of various patterns are available from joinery suppliers and they can be used for replacing all the old and damaged ones where this would be more economical than having them made to order. They can also be used to replace old square balusters – perhaps originally fitted for economy reasons – and give added character to a staircase.

How balusters are fixed

Balusters are usually housed or stub-tenoned into the underside of the handrail and into the edge of a closed string or the treads of an open-stringed stair. Sometimes they are simply butt-jointed and secured with nails, or are housed at the bottom but nailed at the top (See below). You can detect a nail fixing by examining or feeling the surface of the baluster at the back. You will find a slight bump or hollow. If the wood is stripped the fixing will be obvious. A light shone across the joint can also reveal a nail fixing.

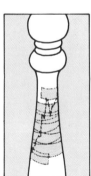

Typical examples of ready-made balusters/newels

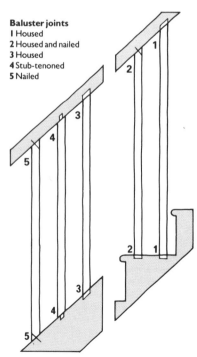

Mending a baluster
Apply glue, and tape the split

Baluster joints
1 Housed
2 Housed and nailed
3 Housed
4 Stub-tenoned
5 Nailed

Replacing a baluster

A damaged baluster that is butt-jointed and nailed can be knocked out by driving its top end backwards and its bottom end forwards. If it is housed at the bottom it can be pulled out of the housing once the top has been freed.

A baluster housed at both ends can be removed only by first cutting through the shoulder line of the joint on the underside of the handrail. It can then be pulled out of the lower housing.

When the baluster is fitted into an open string, remove the moulding that covers the end of the tread and knock the bottom end of the baluster sideways out of its housing, then pull it down to disengage it from the handrail housing.

Fitting a baluster

Measure and mark out the required length on the new baluster, then mark out and cut the ends, using the old one as a pattern. If this cannot be done, take the angle of the handrail and string by setting an adjustable bevel (◁) on an adjacent baluster, then use the bevel to mark the new baluster for cutting. Fit and fix the new baluster in the reverse order to the way in which the old one was taken out.

To replace a baluster which is housed at both ends in a closed string stair, first trim off the back corner of the top tenon **(1)**, place the bottom tenon in its housing and then swing the top end of the baluster into position **(2)**.

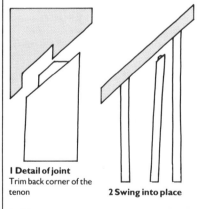

1 Detail of joint
Trim back corner of the tenon

2 Swing into place

Mending a baluster

A baluster that has split along the grain can be repaired in situ. Work PVA glue into the split and bind it with waxed string or self-adhesive tape until it dries (See far left). Before binding squeeze the parts together and wipe any surplus glue from the surface with a damp rag.

HANDRAIL REGULATIONS

Current Building Regulations require a stair in a private residential dwelling to have two handrails, one at each side, if the stair is 1m (3ft 3in) or more in width. If the stair is less than a metre wide and has tapered treads (winders) a handrail must be provided on the side of the stair where the treads are widest. This usually means the wall string side, in which case two handrails are still required because the outer string balustrade must always have a handrail.

Though these requirements concern new building work there is good reason to apply them also to existing buildings wherever possible. Tapered stairs can be hazardous, and it makes good sense to follow the guidelines for your own and your family's safety.

Handrails in hardwood and softwood, including vertical and horizontal curved sections, are available from joinery suppliers. Their various parts are bolted together with special steel handrail screws and fixed to the wall with metal handrail brackets. The size of the bracket is given as the distance of its projection from the wall to the centre of the rail fixing plate.

For safety and comfort the distance between the handrail and the wall should be no less than 50mm (2in), and the width of the stairway itself should be at least 800mm (2ft 7½in), this measurement being taken between the new handrail and the newel post opposite.

In the special situation where a staircase gives access to one room only the width of the stair may be 600mm (2ft), but no less. In such a case consult your local Building Control Officer, because the use to which the room is put can determine whether this rule applies or not.

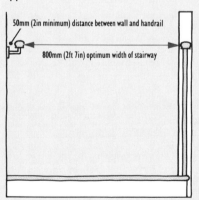

50mm (2in minimum) distance between wall and handrail

800mm (2ft 7in) optimum width of stairway

Handrail spacing for safety and comfort

FITTING A HANDRAIL

Measuring and marking out

Mark a line on the wall to represent the top of the handrail, setting the height in accordance with the Builiding Regulations (▷). Where there are tapered treads some relaxation of the rules may be necessary, but you should check with your local Building Control Officer.

Set out the line by marking a series of points measured vertically from the nosing of each tread in a straight flight. Where tapered treads occur take the same measurement from the central 'kite winder' tread and landing (1).

Marking tips and techniques
Marking the points can be greatly simplified by first cutting a straight piece of batten to the right height and then using it as a guide. Ring the points with your pencil as you make them so that you can find them easily later.

Marking out procedure
Using a straightedge, join up the marks to produce the line of the handrail, then draw a second line below and parallel to it at a distance equal to the thickness of the handrail. Where the rail changes direction draw lines across the intersections **(A)** to find the angles at which the components must be cut **(2)**.

Measure the run of the handrail and buy the required lengths, including such special sections as turns, ramps and the opening rise (See right). Also buy enough handrail brackets for them to be spaced at about 1m (3ft 3in) intervals.

Assembling and fitting

Cut the components to the correct lengths and angles, then dowel and glue short sections together, or use special handrail screws. These require clearance holes in the ends of each part and housings cut in the undersides for the nuts. When using handrail screws you must also fit locating dowels **(3)** to stop the sections rotating as they are pulled together. Assemble the rail in manageable sections.

Screw the brackets to the rail and hold it against the wall while a helper marks the fixing holes. Drill and plug the wall and screw the rail in place with No 10 or No 12 screws at least 63mm (2½in) long to take a good hold in the brickwork and not just the plaster **(4)**.

Rub the handrail down and finish it with clear varnish or paint.

1 Setting out
Mark the wall above each tread and join the marks with a straightedge

2 Changing angles
The junction of a sloping handrail with horizontal one can be made with a ramp or left as a reflex angle.

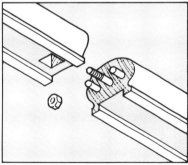

3 Handrails are joined with special screws

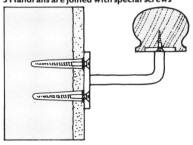

4 Securely fix handrail brackets to the wall

FIXING A LOOSE BALUSTRADE

When the whole balustrade, including the handrail and newel post, feels loose it indicates a breakdown of the joints between the steps and the outer string. You should attend to it immediately, before the whole structure becomes dangerous, and liable to collapse completely if someone were to fall against it.

Refix a loose string and newel to the steps by first removing the wedges from the tread and riser housings and then, working along the face of the string with a hammer and wood block, knocking it back into place to reseat the joints **(1)**. If it tends to spring away hold it in place with lengths of timber braced between it and the opposite wall **(2)**. Make new hardwood wedges, apply adhesive to the joints and drive the wedges in to make tight joints.

Reinforce the joint between the bottom step and the newel post with glued blocks rubbed (▷) into the angle on the underside of the stair. Alternatively screw metal angle plates into the corners **(3)**.

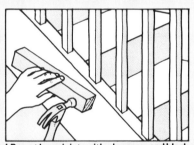

1 Reseat loose joints with a hammer and block

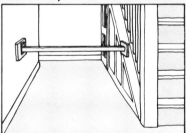

2 Brace the string against the opposite wall

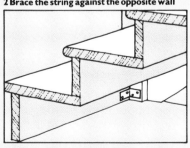

3 Reinforce the bottom joint

SEE ALSO

Details for: ▷	
Regulations	214
Rub joint	503
Wood finishes	75
Stair construction	213
Loose housing	215
Adjustable bevel	462
Dowel joints	476-477
Wall plugs	498

Handrail components
In addition to the normal handrail run, special matched components are available, such as turns, ramps and the open rise. These are joined with special handrail screws or dowels.

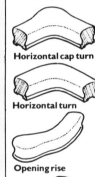

Horizontal cap turn

Horizontal turn

Opening rise

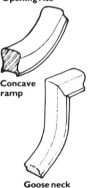

Concave ramp

Goose neck

REPLACING A BALUSTRADE

While the staircase of a house is a strong element in its interior character, the character of the staircase itself is very largely determined by the design of its balustrade.

SEE ALSO

◁ Details for:

Stair construction	214
Hole saw	465
Drill bit	471
Wood finishes	75
Building Regulations	214
Pitch line	214
Adjustable bevel	462
Adhesives	496

Older houses, including those in mass-produced terraces, were often fitted with such attractive decorative features as turned newel posts and balusters, but over the years, with changes in fashion, many of these old balustrades have been 'modernised'. Sometimes this has been done simply by panelling over the open balusters, sometimes by replacing turned ones with straight ones, and sometimes even by cutting away the whole assembly to achieve an 'open plan' appearance (which, aesthetics apart, does not comply with the Building Regulations; a new balustrade should be fitted for your own safety).

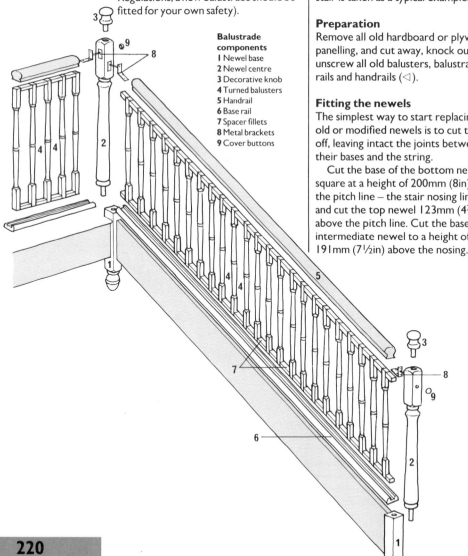

Balustrade components
1 Newel base
2 Newel centre
3 Decorative knob
4 Turned balusters
5 Handrail
6 Base rail
7 Spacer fillets
8 Metal brackets
9 Cover buttons

Using a kit to replace a balustrade

A kit of parts is available which enables you to reinstate a traditionally designed balustrade. The kit consists of: newel posts made up of three parts – a base section (**1**), a turned centre section in a choice of two styles (**2**) and decorative knobs in a choice of three styles (**3**) – plus turned balusters in many styles (**4**) with a handrail (**5**) and machine-grooved base rail (**6**) in which to fit them. Spacer fillets (**7**) are also provided to make fitting and finishing of the balusters a straightforward job, and there are special metal brackets (**8**) for joining the ends of the handrails to the posts. You can use all or any of the parts to meet the demands of most types of wooden staircase, but below a straight-flight stair is taken as a typical example.

Preparation

Remove all old hardboard or plywood panelling, and cut away, knock out or unscrew all old balusters, balustrade rails and handrails (◁).

Fitting the newels

The simplest way to start replacing the old or modified newels is to cut them off, leaving intact the joints between their bases and the string.

Cut the base of the bottom newel off square at a height of 200mm (8in) above the pitch line – the stair nosing line – and cut the top newel 123mm (4⅞in) above the pitch line. Cut the base of an intermediate newel to a height of 191mm (7½in) above the nosing.

Mark diagonal lines across the cut ends to find their centres, then drill out 50mm (2in) diameter holes centrally to receive the centre spigots of the new newel posts. You can do this with a tank cutter in a power tool or an expansion bit in a hand brace (◁).

After drilling, finish the cut ends of the posts to a slightly convex contour and set the post centres in position but do not glue them.

Fitting the rails

With an adjustable bevel take the angle of the stair string where it meets the newel base. Hold the balustrade base rail against the stair, following the angle of the string exactly, and make a mark at each end where it meets the newels, then mark the cutting lines at these points, using the bevel and a try square, and cut the rail to length.

Mark and cut the handrail in the same way, or use the base rail as a guide if it happens to be the same length. Screw the base rail to the string, then fix the special bolted handrail brackets into the posts and hand-tighten them with a spanner. Check that the posts are upright and that the rails fit properly, then glue the posts into place. Use a gap-filling powder-resin glue, or for a tight joint PVA woodworking adhesive. Tighten up the bolts fully, and when the adhesive has set fit the cover buttons (**9**) to conceal the nuts.

Fitting the balusters

Calculate the number of balusters you will need, allowing the equivalent of two per tread and one for the tread that is adjacent to the newel. In any event they should not be spaced any more than 100mm (4in) apart.

To find out how many infill fillets will be needed double the number of the balusters and add four.

Measure the vertical distance between the groove in the handrail and that in the base rail, then transfer this dimension to a baluster and mark it out, using the adjustable bevel to give the correct angle. Cut the baluster to size and check it for fit, then cut the others to suit. Space the balusters equally, using the pre-cut fillets to even out the spacing over the total run.

Pin and glue the balusters and fillets in place, and when the adhesive has set rub them down and finish the bare wood with clear varnish or paint as required.

Most pitched roofs were once built on site from individual lengths of timber, but nowadays, for economy of time and materials, many builders use prefabricated frames called trussed rafters. These are specifically designed to meet the loading needs of a given house and, unlike traditional roofs, are usually not suitable for conversion because to remove any part of the structure can cause it to collapse.

Close couple roof
A roof structure which has its rafters joined by a tie member. A variation is the collar roof where the ties (collars) are set at a higher level.

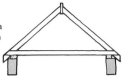

Basic construction

The framework of an ordinary pitched roof is based on a triangle, the most rigid and economical form for a load-bearing structure. The weight of the roof covering is carried by the sloping members, the 'common rafters', which are set in opposing pairs whose heads meet against a central 'ridge board'. The lower ends, or feet, of the rafters are fixed to timber wall plates which are bedded on the exterior walls and distribute the weight uniformly.

To stop the roof's weight pushing the walls out, horizontal 'ties' are fixed to the ends of each pair of rafters and the wall plates, forming a simple structure called a 'close couple' roof. The ties (ceiling joists) also usually support the ceiling plaster. The rafters are also linked by the roofing battens.

SEE ALSO

Details for: ▷	
Walls	122
Hipped roof	222
Roofing battens	224

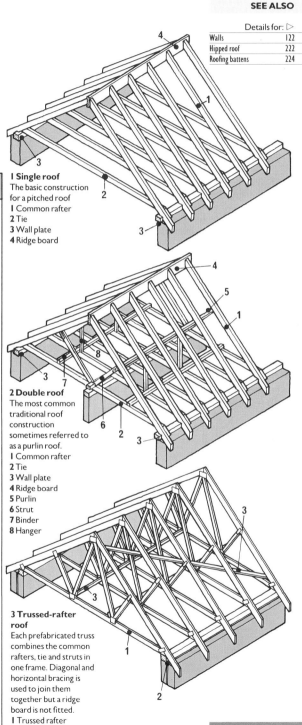

1 Single roof
The basic construction for a pitched roof
1 Common rafter
2 Tie
3 Wall plate
4 Ridge board

2 Double roof
The most common traditional roof construction sometimes referred to as a purlin roof.
1 Common rafter
2 Tie
3 Wall plate
4 Ridge board
5 Purlin
6 Strut
7 Binder
8 Hanger

3 Trussed-rafter roof
Each prefabricated truss combines the common rafters, tie and struts in one frame. Diagonal and horizontal bracing is used to join them together but a ridge board is not fitted.
1 Trussed rafter
2 Wall plate
3 Bracing

PITCHED ROOF TYPES

SINGLE ROOFS

Any roof, pitched or flat, with unbraced rafters – except the pitched roof's ties – is called a single roof (**1**), and is only suitable for light coverings and short spans. For a wide span or heavy covering the design would need unduly large roof timbers.

DOUBLE ROOFS

In double roofs horizontal beams called 'purlins' support the rafters (**2**), linking them either midway between foot and ridge or 2.5m (8ft) apart. This reduces the span of the rafters and allows lighter timber to be used, 100 × 50mm (4 × 2in) being common. The purlins' section depends on the weight of the roof covering, but it usually exceeds that of the rafters; 200 × 50mm (8 × 2in) is normal. The purlins' ends are supported on the brickwork of a gable wall or, in a hipped roof, by the hip rafters.

To keep the purlins' size down, struts may be set in opposing pairs to brace them diagonally at every fourth or fifth pair of rafters. Struts transfer some weight back to the centre of the ceiling joists, which are supported there by a load-bearing dividing wall at right angles to them.

The ends of the struts may be jointed over a horizontal 'binder' fixed to the joists right above the supporting wall.

Where ceiling joists are fairly light and the span could make them sag, vertical timber 'hangers' are fixed at the top to every third or fourth rafter or to adjacent purlins at like intervals, and at the bottom to a 'binder' fixed at right angles across the joists.

TRUSSED ROOFS

Some traditional roofs embody trusses, rigid triangular frames that replace load-bearing partition walls to give a wider span. Trusses carry the purlins, which in turn support the rafters and form a 'triple' or 'framed' roof. The trusses are spaced at 1.8m (6ft) or more depending on the purlins' section or the roof covering's weight. As main bearers for the roof they transmit weight to the exterior walls. Few trussed roofs can be converted and you should not try to cut into them.

'Trussed rafters' are now used in all new housing (**3**). Computer-designed for economy plus rigidity, the trusses are prefabricated of planed softwood 38mm (1½in) thick and up to 150mm (6in) wide, depending on roof loading. Each truss combines common rafters, tie and strut bracing in one frame; the members are butt jointed and fixed with special nailed plate connectors.

The trusses are spaced a maximum 600mm (2ft) apart, linked horizontally with bracing members nailed to the struts. Such roofs are quite light, and usually fixed to the walls with steel anchor straps to resist wind pressure.

ROOF ELEMENTS

Hips and valleys

All the components mentioned earlier (◁) are found in ordinary gable roofs. One with a hipped end or valleys has other parts, but all follow the same principles. Here a double roof shows the parts and their names.

SEE ALSO

◁ Details for:
Pitched roofs	221
Flashings	232–233
Woodworm treatment	246
Wood rot	249
Ventilation	277–278
Soffit vents	277

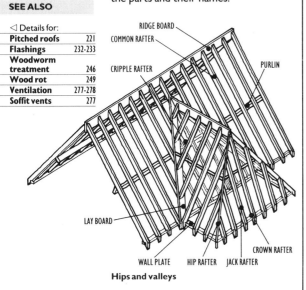

RIDGE BOARD
COMMON RAFTER
CRIPPLE RAFTER
PURLIN
LAY BOARD
WALL PLATE
HIP RAFTER
JACK RAFTER
CROWN RAFTER

Hips and valleys

Eaves

The overhang of rafters past the outer walls is called the eaves, but sometimes rafters are cut flush with the walls and a fascia board along their ends protects them and supports the guttering (1). Projecting rafters can be left open, the ends exposed (2), and gutter brackets screwed to their sides or top edge.

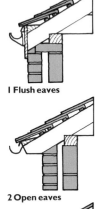

1 Flush eaves

2 Open eaves

Closed eaves

The back of a fascia is usually grooved to take a soffit board, which closes the eaves (3). The board can be at 90 degrees to the wall or slope with the rafters, and it can be of various weatherproof materials. If loft insulation is laid, a roof with closed eaves must be ventilated by a small gap between soffit board and wall or by fitted vents (◁).

3 Closed eaves

The verge

The verge is the sloping edge of the roofing and can end flush with the wall or project past it. A flush verge means a roof structure that stops at the wall, end rafters placed close to it and the roofing overlying it (4). A projecting verge means timbers extending beyond the wall and short lengths of rafter set in the brick to carry an outer rafter with a 'barge board' fixed to it. Behind the barge board may be a soffit board to conceal the outer rafters (5).

ROOF STRUCTURE PROBLEMS

A roof structure can fail when timbers decay through inadequate weatherproofing, condensation or insect attack. It can also result from overloading caused by too-light original timbers, a new roof covering of heavier material or the cutting of a window opening that is not properly braced. You can detect any movement of a roof structure from outside. From ground level any sagging of the roof will be seen in the lines of the roof covering.

INSPECTION

The roof should also be inspected from inside. In any case, this should be done annually to check the weathering and for freedom from woodworm infestation.

Work in a good light. If your loft has no lighting use a mains-powered lead light. In an unboarded attic place strong boards across the joists to walk on.

ROT AND INFESTATION

Rot in roof timbers is a serious problem which should be put right by experts, but its cause should also be identified and promptly dealt with.

Rot is caused by damp conditions that encourage wood-rotting fungi (◁) to grow. Inspect the roof covering closely for loose or damaged elements in the general area of the rot, though on a pitched roof water may be penetrating the covering at a higher level and so not be immediately obvious. If the rot is close to a gable wall you should suspect the flashing (◁). Rot can also be caused by condensation, the remedy for which is usually better ventilation (◁).

If you bring in contractors to treat the rot it is better to have them make all the repairs. Their work is covered by a guarantee which may be invalidated if you attempt to deal with the cause yourself to save money.

Wood-boring beetle infestation should also be dealt with by professionals if it is serious. Severely infected wood may have to be cut out and replaced, and anyway the whole structure will have to be spray treated (◁).

STRENGTHENING THE ROOF

A roof that shows signs of sagging may have to be braced, though it may not be necessary if a sound structure has stabilised and the roof is weatherproof. In some old buildings a slightly sagging roof line is considered attractive.

Consult a surveyor if you suspect a roof is weak. Apart from a sagging roof line, the walls under the eaves should be inspected for bulging and checked with a plumb line. Bulging may occur where window openings are close to the eaves, making a wall relatively weak. It may be due to the roof spreading because of inadequate fixing of the ties and rafters. If this is so, call in a builder or roofing contractor to do the repair work.

A lightly structured roof can be made stronger by adding extra timbers. The method chosen will depend on the type of roof, its span, its loading and its condition. Where the lengths or section of new timbers are not too large the repair may be possible from inside. If not, at least some of the roof covering may have to be stripped off. Any given roof must be surveyed and the most economical solution adopted.

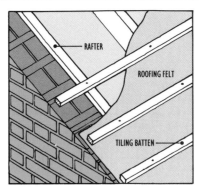

RAFTER
ROOFING FELT
TILING BATTEN

4 Flush verge

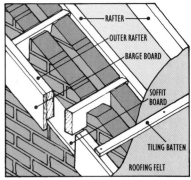

RAFTER
OUTER RAFTER
BARGE BOARD
SOFFIT BOARD
TILING BATTEN
ROOFING FELT

5 Projecting verge

TYPES OF ROOFING

Roof coverings are manufactured by moulding clay or concrete into various profiles or by cutting natural materials such as slate into flat sheets.

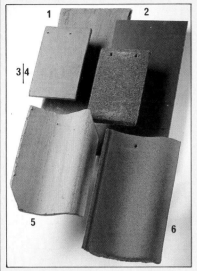

Selection of roof covering materials
1 Natural slate. 2 Machine-made slate. 3 Plain tile (clay). 4 Plain tile (concrete). 5 Plain pantile (clay). 6 Interlocking pantile (concrete).

PITCHED ROOF COVERINGS

Coverings for domestic pitched roofs follow a long tradition, and despite the developments in new materials the older ones and the ways of using them have not changed radically.

Like most early building materials, those used for roofing were generally of local origin, which led to a diversity of roof coverings, including tiles, slates and timber shingles. For centuries they were hand-made, and had their own characteristics, to be seen in various regional styles.

During the last century the more durable roof coverings, such as tiles and slates, became more widely adopted.

Most roofing materials are laid across the roof in rows called courses so that the bottom edge of each overlaps the top of the one below. This means that they are laid working from the eaves up the slope of the roof to the ridge.

Specially shaped tiles are used for capping the ridge or hips so as to weatherproof the junctions of the slopes. Where the covering meets a chimney or a wall it is protected with flashing, usually made of lead or mortar.

Roof-covering components for a pitched roof.
1 Tile or slate covering
2 Ridge tile
3 Gable end
4 Projecting verge
5 Barge board
6 Eaves
7 Fascia
8 Soffit
9 Hipped end
10 Hip tile
11 Valley
12 Flush verge
13 Lead stepped flashing
14 Back gutter
15 Apron

SEE ALSO

Details for: ▷	
Nails	224
Covering methods	224-225
Maintenance	226-227
Flashings	232-233

TYPICAL COVERINGS FOR PITCHED ROOFS

TYPE OF COVERING	Material	Common sizes	Finish	Colour	Fixing	Weight* Kg/M² (1lb/sq yd)	Minimum pitch Degrees
SLATE	Split metamorphic sedimentary rock	Lengths: 300 to 600 mm (1 ft to 2 ft) Widths: 180 to 350 mm (7 in to 1 ft 2 in)	Natural	Natural Blue Grey Green	Two nails	27.5 to 70 (50.69 to 129)	17½°
MACHINE-MADE SLATE	Non-asbestos cement Asbestos cement	Lengths: 400, 500, 600 mm (1 ft 4 in, 1 ft 8 in, 2 ft) Widths: 200, 250, 300, 350 mm (8in, 10in, 1ft, 1ft 2in)	Acrylic coating	Grey Blue Brown	Two nails plus copper disc rivet in tail	18.5 to 20.8 (34.10 to 38.34)	17½°
STONE	Split sandstone or limestone sedimentary rock	Random and as natural slate	Natural	Natural Yellow Grey Green	Two nails	90 (165.9)	17½°
SHINGLES	Split or sawn red cedar	Length: 400 mm (1 ft 4 in) Widths: 75 to 300 mm (3 in to 1 ft)	Natural	Natural Brown Grey	Two nails	7 (12.83)	20°
PLAIN TILES	Hand- or machine-moulded clay or machine-made concrete	Length: 265 mm (10½ in) Width: 165 mm (6½ in)	Sanded Smooth	Red Brown Grey Blue Green	Two nails or loose laid on nibs	65 (119.8)	40° clay 35° concrete
INTERLOCKING TILES	Hand- or machine-moulded clay or machine-made concrete	Lengths: 380, 410, 430 mm (1ft 3in, 1ft 4½in, 1ft 5in) Widths: 220, 330, 380 mm (9in, 1ft 1in, 1ft 3in)	Sanded Smooth Glazed	Red Brown Grey Blue Green	Loose laid on nibs, nailed or clipped	40 to 57 (73.73 to 105.07)	35° clay 17½° to 30° concrete

*Approx

SEE ALSO

◁ Details for:
Types of roofing   223
Maintenance   226

Tile clip

Nailed tile clip

Eave clip (flat)

Eave clip (contoured)

Verge clip (flat)

Copper rivet

TYPES OF ROOF COVERING

All roof coverings built up with small overlapping units fall broadly into two classifications: 'double-lap' and 'single-lap', categories indicating the units' profiles and how they are laid.

Double-lap coverings

Plain tiles, slates, stone 'slates' and wooden shingles are all double-lap coverings. They are basically flat – with the exception of plain tiles, which have a slight camber and nibs – and are laid with their side edges butting together, not overlapping. To prevent water penetrating the joints each course is lapped in part by the two courses above it. The joints are staggered, or 'broken jointed', on alternate courses like courses of bricks in a wall.

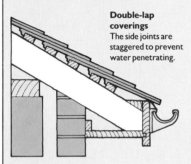

Double-lap coverings
The side joints are staggered to prevent water penetrating.

Single-lap coverings

Nearly all tiles of moulded clay and concrete are single-lap coverings, which means that each tile is profiled so as to interlock with the next one by means of a single lap on its side, and each course is laid with only a single lap at the head.

Early single-lap examples, such as clay pantiles, simply used the curved shape of the tile to form the overlap, but modern machine-made tiles of clay or concrete incorporate systems of grooves and water bars which prevent water penetrating the lap. These moulded tiles have nibs at their top back edges which hook on to the battens. They may stay in place by their own weight or be fixed with nails or clips.

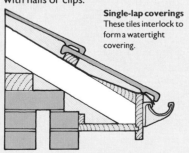

Single-lap coverings
These tiles interlock to form a watertight covering.

GENERAL CONSTRUCTION

If you intend to make repairs yourself you will need some knowledge of the roof-covering system used on a common pitched roof. It will also help you if you have to commission contractors, either for repairs or re-roofing work, as you will benefit from a better understanding of the work being done.

Underlay

To comply with current building standards new and re-covered pitched roofs must have a weather-resistant underlay of some kind.

This underlay, sometimes called sarking, should be a reinforced bituminous felt, Type 1F, or a suitable tear-resistant plastic material like polythene, which are sold in rolls to be cut to length as required.

The sheet material provides a barrier to any moisture that may penetrate the outer covering. It also improves the insulation value of the roof.

Like the tiles themselves, the sarking is laid horizontally, working upwards from the eaves, each strip overlapped by the one above it.

Battens

The roof covering is supported on sawn softwood battens which are nailed across the rafters, over the sarking (1). They are pre-treated with a preservative. When the roof is close-boarded there should be vertical counter-battens under the horizontal battens (2) to provide some ventilation under the tiles and allow any moisture to drain down freely.

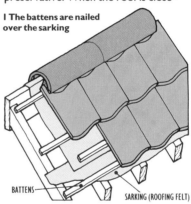

1 The battens are nailed over the sarking

BATTENS
SARKING (ROOFING FELT)

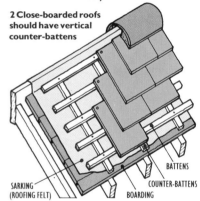

2 Close-boarded roofs should have vertical counter-battens

SARKING (ROOFING FELT)
BATTENS
COUNTER-BATTENS
BOARDING

Fixings

Most roof coverings are fixed with nails or clips. Slates and shingles are fixed individually with nails, normally two placed halfway up, though some are nailed at the top. Asbestos cement slates are centre-nailed with copper rivets to hold down the tails (See left).

Tiles have nibs that hook over the battens, keeping them in place, and some types of tile need nothing more, Those that do may be held with nails or clips.

The fixings are determined by the type and size of tile, the roof's pitch and the building's exposure.

	TYPE OF ROOF COVERING					
● Black dot denotes that nail type and roof covering are compatible	Slate	Asbestos cement slate	Clay tiles	Concrete tiles	Shingles	Felt
TYPE OF NAIL						
COPPER	●	●			●	
ALUMINIUM ALLOY	●		●	●	●	
SILICON BRONZE	●	●	●	●	●	
GALVANIZED IRON					●	●
GALVANIZED STEEL					●	●

ROOF SAFETY

Working on a roof can be hazardous, and if you are unsure of yourself on heights you should call in a contractor to do the work. If you do decide to do it yourself, do not use ladders alone for roof work. Hire a sectional scaffold tower and scaffold board to provide a safe working platform complete with toe boards (▷).

Roof coverings are fairly fragile and should not be walked on. Hire crawl boards or special roof ladders to gain access. A roof ladder should reach from the scaffold tower to the roof's ridge and hook over it. Wheel the ladder up the slope and then turn it over to engage the hook (1) .

Roof ladders are made with rails that keep the treads clear of the roof surface and spread the load (2) , but if you think it necessary you can place additional padding of paper-stuffed or sand-filled sacks to help spread the load further.

Never leave tools on the roof when they are not being used, and keep those that are needed safely contained inside the ladder framework.

1 Engage the hook of the ladder over the ridge

2 Roof ladders spread the load

GENERAL CONSTRUCTION

It is important for the overall appearance and performance of the roof that the covering is well finished at the verge, eaves and valley edges.

Verges

In the interest of neatness the verge is normally formed by first laying an undercloak of plain tile or slate bedded on the brickwork or – in the case of an overhanging verge – nailed to the timber frame. The roof covering is then bedded in mortar on top of the undercloak and finished flush. The verge of a slate or plain tiled roof is set to slope inwards slightly to prevent rainwater running down the walls, but single lap tiles are laid flat.

Special dry-fixed verge tiles and metal extrusions are available for use with single-lap concrete tiles.

Eaves

The detail of the roof covering at the eaves depends on the type of covering. Plain tiles should have a course of under-tiles, nailed to a batten and projecting 38 to 50mm (1½ to 2in) over the gutter. The first course of tiles is laid with staggered joints over the under-tiles with their tail edges flush (1) .

Some single-lap tiles, such as pantiles, also use an undercloak of plain tiles, the first course being bedded in mortar that fills up the hollow rolls. As an alternative there are also special eaves tiles with blocked ends or overhangs.

Single-lap low-profile tiles are normally laid directly over and supported by the fascia board (2) .

When the roof covering is natural slate a double course is laid at the eaves. A course of short slates is nailed to the first batten and covered by a course of full slates with their tails flush and their joints staggered.

Three courses are used for asbestos cement slates to support the tail rivets used with this type of covering.

Valleys

Traditional double-lap roof coverings of plain tiles may embody special valley tiles, or, as with slate, may be formed into 'swept' or 'laced' valleys. The latter call for great skill and are expensive to make. Most valleys are formed as open gutters using sheet metal (▷).

Single-lap roofing may use sheet valleys or special trough units.

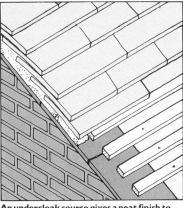

An undercloak course gives a neat finish to the verge

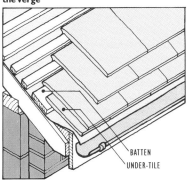

BATTEN
UNDER-TILE

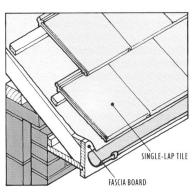

SINGLE-LAP TILE

FASCIA BOARD

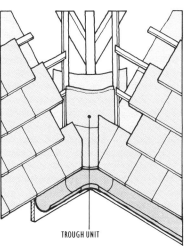

TROUGH UNIT

SEE ALSO

Details for: ▷	
Work platforms	40-42
Flashings	232
Verge types	222
Types of roofing	223

Verge detail at ridge
The ridge tile is set flush with the verge and filled with bedding mortar

1 Plain tiles
The eaves under-tiles are nailed to a batten. The joints between them are covered with full tiles.

2 Single-lap low-profile
Not all interlocking tiles need an under-tile at the eaves but the fascia must support the eaves course at the correct angle.

Valley tiles
Modern roofs may have trough units instead of the traditional lead sheeting.

ROOF MAINTENANCE

SEE ALSO

◁ Details for:
Flashings	232-233
Roofing nails	224
Roof safety	225
Roof ventilator	277-278
Bricklayer's trowel	478
Masonry drill	479
Universal saw	479

The roof and upper parts of a building, such as chimneys and parapet walls, must be kept in sound condition if they are to remain weatherproof. Failure of the roof covering can cause an expensive deterioration of the underlying timber structure, the interior plaster fabric and the decorative finishes.

All roof coverings have a limited life, *the length depending on the quality of materials used, the workmanship and the exposure of the house. An average roof covering might be expected to give good service for 40 to 60 years, and some materials can last for a hundred years or more, though some deterioration of the fixings and the flashings may take place. Reuse the old materials if you can.*

Patch repairs may prove to be of only temporary value and can look unsightly. If they become a recurrent chore it is time for the roof to be re-covered. This will mean stripping off the original old material and possibly reusing it, or perhaps replacing it with a new covering similar to the old.

Major roof work is not something you should tackle yourself. A contractor will do it more quickly and will guarantee the work.

Reroofing work may qualify for a discretionary improvement grant from your local authority, depending on the age and rateable value of the house. You will not require planning approval unless you live in a listed building or a conservation area.

Inspecting the roof

The roofs of older houses are likely to show their age and should be checked at least once a year.

Start by taking a general look at the whole roof from ground level. Slipped or disjointed tiles or slates should be easily spotted against the regular lines of the undisturbed covering. The colour of any newly exposed and unweathered slate will also pinpoint a fault. Look at the ridge against the sky to check for misalignment and gaps in the mortar jointing. Follow this with a closer inspection through binoculars, checking the state of the flashings at abutments and around the chimney brickwork (◁).

From inside an unlined roof you can easily spot chinks of daylight that indicate breaks in the covering, and with a light you can inspect the roof timbers for water stains, which may show as dark or white streaks. Trace the stain to find the source.

Removing and replacing a slate

A slate may slip out of place because of its nails becoming corroded or because of a breakdown of the material of the slate itself. Whatever the cause, slipped or broken slates must be replaced as soon as possible.

Use a slater's ripper to remove the trapped part of a broken slate. Slip the tool under the slate and locate its hooked end over one of the fixing nails **(1)**, then pull down hard on the tool to extract or cut through the nail. Remove the second nail in the same way. Even

where an aged slate has already slipped out completely you may have to remove the nails in the same way to allow the replacement slate to be slipped in.

You will not be able to nail the new slate in place. Instead cut a 25mm (1in) wide strip of lead or zinc to the length of the slate lap plus 25mm (1in) and nail the strip to the batten, nailing between the slates of the lower course **(2)**. Then slide the new slate into position and turn back the end of the lead strip to secure it **(3)**.

1 Pull out nails

2 Nail strip to batten

3 Fold strip over edge

Cutting slate

Cut from each edge

With a sharp point mark out the right size on the back of the slate, either by measuring it out or scribing round another slate of that size. Place the slate, bevelled side down, on a bench, the cutting line level with the bench's edge, then chop the slate with the edge of a bricklayer's trowel. Work from both edges towards the middle, using the edge of the bench as a guide. Mark the nail holes and punch them out with a nail or drill them with a bit the size of

the nails. Support the slate well while making the holes.

Asbestos cement slates

These can be cut by scribing the lines, then breaking the slates over a straight edge or sawing with a general-purpose saw. If you saw them wear a mask, keep dust damped down well and sweep it into a plastic bag for disposal.

REPLACING A TILE

Individual tiles can be difficult to remove for two reasons: the retaining nibs on their back edges and their interlocking shape which holds them together.

You can remove a broken plain tile by simply lifting it so that the nibs clear the batten on which they rest, then drawing it out. This is made easier if the overlapping tiles are first lifted with wooden wedges inserted at both sides of the tile to be removed **(1)**.

If the tile is also nailed try rocking it loose. If this fails you will have to break it out carefully. You may then have to use a slater's ripper to extract or cut any remaining nails.

Use a similar technique for single-lap interlocking tiles, but in this case you will also have to wedge up the tile to the left of the one being removed **(2)**. If the tile is of a deep profile you will have to ease up a number of the surrounding tiles to get the required clearance.

If you are taking out a tile to put in a roof ventilator unit you can afford to smash it with a hammer. But take care not to damage any of the adjacent tiles. The remaining tiles should be easier to remove once the first is out.

1 Lift the overlapping tiles with wedges

2 Lift interlocking tiles above and to the left

CUTTING TILES

To cut tiles use an abrasive cutting disc in a power saw or hire an angle grinder for the purpose. Always wear protective goggles and a mask when cutting with a power tool.

For small work use a tungsten grit blade in a hacksaw frame or, if trimming only, pincers but score the cutting line first with a tile cutter.

REBEDDING RIDGE TILES

Ridge tiles on old roofs often become loose because of a breakdown of the old lime mortar.

To rebed ridge tiles first lift them off and clear all the old crumbling mortar from the roof, and from the undersides of the tiles.

Give the tiles a good soaking in water before starting to fix them. Mix a new bedding mortar of 1 part cement to 3 parts sand. It should be a stiff mix and not at all runny. Load about half a bucketful and carry it on to the roof.

Dampen the top courses of the roof tiles and throw the mortar from the trowel to form a continuous edge bedding about 50mm (2in) wide and 75mm (3in) high, following the line left behind by the old mortar.

Where the ridge tiles butt together, or come against a wall, place a solid bedding of mortar, inserting pieces of slate in it to reduce shrinkage. Place the mortar for all the tiles in turn, setting each tile into place and pressing it firmly into the mortar. Strike off any squeezed-out mortar cleanly with the trowel, without smearing the tile. Ridge tiles should not be pointed.

Apply bands of bedding mortar on each side

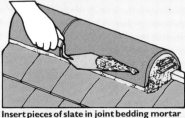

Insert pieces of slate in joint bedding mortar

HALF-ROUND   HOG-BACK   ANGLE

Typical ridge tile shapes

SHEET ROOFING

The commonest sheeting materials for roofing are corrugated asbestos cement and rigid PVC plastic. Aluminium and steel corrugated sheeting are made for roofing but are not generally used for domestic work.

Sheet roofings are used mainly for outbuildings such as garages and garden sheds, and the plastic types may be used for lean-to extensions.

Consult your local Building Control Officer when considering a plastic roofing to ensure that it complies with the fire regulations.

Corrugated sheet roofing

Corrugated sheeting is produced in standard profiles of 32mm (1¼in) for plastic, and 75mm (3in) and 150mm (6in) for plastic and asbestos cement. When calculating the number of sheets you need you must make an allowance for the side overlap. Small-profile sheeting should overlap at least two corrugations **(1)**, while larger ones can be used with only one **(2)**. The end overlap should be at least 150mm (6in) in sheltered locations for roofs with pitches of about 22 degrees or more. For pitches of less than this a 300mm (1ft) overlap should be allowed.

Corrugated sheeting is carried by purlins (▷). They are of wood in most domestic buildings, though some system-built garages embody steel sections. Wood screws or drive screws fix the roofing to wooden purlins **(3)** and hooked bolts are used with metal ones **(4)**. There are special plastic washers and caps for sealing the heads of the screws or bolts.

Cutting corrugated plastic

On thin plastic sheet mark the cutting lines with a felt-tipped pen, then cut it with a fine-toothed tenon saw. Support the sheeting between two boards on trestles and use the top board as a guide for your saw.

When cutting to length saw across the peaks of the corrugations with the saw held at a very shallow angle. Cut halfway through, then turn the sheet over and cut from the other side.

When cutting to width make the cut along the peak of a corrugation, again working with the saw at a shallow angle. For a cut near the middle of the sheet support the sheet on both sides of the cutting line from below.

Cutting corrugated asbestos

Lay the sheet on boards supported by trestles. As the material is fairly thick you will not need a top supporting board and you can saw the sheet without turning it over. Use a sheet saw or general-purpose saw, damping down the dust and sweeping it into a plastic bag, to be sealed with adhesive tape and put in a dustbin. Damp newspaper under the trestles will help contain the dust.

Laying corrugated sheet

You can work from stepladders inside the structure or from above on boards, depending on the pitch of the roof.

Start at the eaves and work from left to right or vice versa.

Asbestos cement sheet is laid smooth side up.

Plastic sheet

Position the first sheet and drill oversized clearance holes for the fixing screws on the centre lines of the wooden purlins. Drill the holes in the crowns of the corrugations and space them at about every third or fourth corrugation. Never place fixings in the troughs of the sheeting.

Don't make holes where the next sheet will overlap the first. Instead lay the second sheet with two corrugations overlapping and drill through both sheets. Lay and fix the rest of the row of sheets in the same way.

Start the next row on the same side as the first one **(1)**, overlapping the ends by at least 150mm (6in), and drill and fix through both layers.

Finally fit the protective plastic caps over the fixing washers.

Laying asbestos sheet

Corrugated asbestos sheet is fairly thick material, and to deal with the bulk of four thickness at the end laps you should cut some of the corners away to form mitres **(2)**. The angle of the mitre is drawn between two points representing the length of the end lap and the width of the side lap.

Fix the sheets as for plastic sheet (See above). For the large profile sheeting use only two fixings to each purlin, placed adjacent to the side laps. The end laps are fixed through both layers.

SEE ALSO

Details for: ▷	
Trussed roof	221, 502
Ladders	40-41
Roof safety	225
Sealing roofs	233
Saws	463, 479
Drills	471-472

1 Small-profile lap

2 Large-profile lap

3 Wood purlin fixing

4 Metal purlin fixing

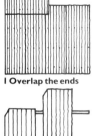

1 Overlap the ends

2 Mitre the corners

FLAT ROOFS

Timber-framed flat roofs are used for the main roof and rear extensions and for outbuildings. Most have joists carrying stiff wooden decking, and these usually cross the shorter span, spaced at 400mm (1ft 4in), 450mm (1ft 6in) or 600mm (2ft) between centres. Herringbone or solid strutting is needed for a span of more than 2.5m (8ft) to prevent the joists buckling. Their ends may be fixed to wall plates on load-bearing walls or, as on an extension, they are set in metal hangers or into the brickwork of the wall. Metal restraint straps tie the ends of the timbers down to the walls.

SEE ALSO

◁ Details for:

Strutting	173
Floors	179
Nails	224
Felt roof	230
Roof repairs	231
Man-made boards	494-495

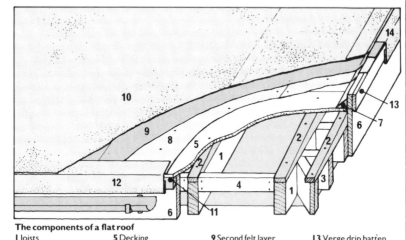

The components of a flat roof

1 Joists	5 Decking	9 Second felt layer	13 Verge drip batten
2 Furring	6 Fascia board	10 Third felt layer	14 Felt verge drip
3 Return-joist	7 Angle fillet	11 Eaves drip batten	
4 Nogging	8 First felt layer	12 Felt eaves drip	

Fall

The fall of a flat roof should be at least 1:80 for smooth surfaces like metal or plastic, and 1:60 for rougher materials. It is meant to shed water, but if too shallow will allow puddles to form. These, aided by sun or frost, can break some roof coverings down and let the standing water get through.

To give the fall the joists may be sloped, but this means that any ceiling will also slope. Where a flat ceiling is wanted tapered 'furrings' are nailed to the tops of the joists. Otherwise joists may be set across the line of the fall with parallel furring pieces of decreasing thickness nailed to them or tapered furrings fixed across them. The latter gives better cross ventilation.

Furring methods

1 Tapered furrings fixed in line with joists

2 Tapered furrings fixed across joists

3 Furrings of decreasing size fitted across fall

Decking

A decking in the form of boards — square-edged or tongued and grooved — or of such sheet materials as plywood or chipboard, is fixed to the joists to make a flat support for the final covering.

Solid boarding of the kind found in older flat roofs should be laid with its joints running with the fall for most efficient water-shedding.

Plywood and chipboard, normally 18mm (¾in) thick, are laid with their long edges across the joists and their ends centred over supporting joists. Noggings may be fitted between the joists to give extra support to the long edges of the board, depending on its thickness and the joist spacing.

If you wish to have a felted roof you might consider using the pre-felted chipboard now available. This material is laid with 3mm (⅛in) gaps between the boards to allow for thermal expansion, and fixed down with nails or screws. The gaps between the boards are filled with a cold bonding mastic and then sealed with tape.

Pre-felted chipboard provides a weatherproof decking that does not need the built-up roof covering to be applied immediately as do others.

Finishing

The decking is waterproofed with either mastic asphalt or roofing felt (See right). In addition, a felted roof may be covered with a layer of 12mm (½in) light-coloured chippings which reflect some of the sun's heat from the roof.

FLAT ROOF COVERINGS

Bitumen-based coverings fall into two types: asphalt and bituminous felt. They are much better than they once were and are now generally used on domestic buildings instead of the expensive lead, zinc or copper seen on older houses.

MASTIC ASPHALT

This waterproof material, made from either natural or synthetic bitumen, weathers very well. It is melted in a cauldron and spread over the roof hot, to set in an impervious layer. Two layers are applied with a float to a combined thickness of 18mm (¾in) on a separating layer of sheathing felt that covers the decking. The felt is loose-laid with 50mm (2in) lapped joints. It allows movement in the substrate without affecting the asphalt. If the substrate has a pre-felted or other surface likely to adhere, a non-bituminous building paper is placed beneath the felt layer.

Laying hot asphalt is a skilled job.

ROOFING FELTS

These bitumen-impregnated sheet materials are applied in layers to produce 'built-up' roofing, bonded with hot or cold bitumen. Making such a roof with hot bitumen is a professional job.

Several felts are available, and the choice can affect a roof's cost and its long-term performance. Traditional British Standard felts are classified by their reinforcing base material and finish, indicated by a number and letter. A colour strip identifies the base material (See opposite). These cheaper felts are well tried but less tough than modern high-performance ones. The latter are based on glass tissue reinforced with polyester or polyester fabric, some with modified bitumen for greater flexibility.

BONDING FELTS

Plywood, chipboard, wood-wool and concrete decks need partial bonding of the first layer, using a perforated underlay either applied loose or bonded with bands of bitumen about 500mm (1ft 8in) wide around the edges. The first layer is then only partially bonded by the hot bitumen penetrating through the holes. On solid timber the first layer is secured with clout nails. Subsequent layers are fully bonded by applying hot or cold bitumen with a trowel or notched spreader over the whole surface.

ABUTMENTS AND PARAPETS

Wherever a flat roof abuts a house or parapet wall leaks can occur, so the covering is usually turned up the wall – called a 'skirting' – and tucked into the mortar bed of the brickwork, or covered by flashing (▷).

Parapet walls are prone to damp, being exposed on both sides. Their top edges are usually finished with brick, stone or tile coping which should overhang the wall faces to throw off rainwater. Damp-proof courses of lead, bituminous felt or asphalt must underlie copings **(1)**.

Parapet walls of no more than 350mm (1ft 2in) may have the skirting taken up their face and continued under the full width of the coping **(2)**.

When a parapet wall's inside face has no impervious layer a second damp-proof course is needed directly above the skirting. A solid wall may have asphalt roof covering taken up two courses of bricks, then continued across the wall to form a DPC **(3)**. Or a flexible DPC like bituminous felt or lead may be set in the bed joint before the roofing is laid and dressed down to form a flashing over the skirting **(4)**.

Cavity parapet walls also need a DPC where the roof abuts. Water penetrating from the roof side must be prevented from running down the cavity to damage the interior walls below roof level **(5)**. The DPC is stepped up from the inside leaf across the cavity to the outer leaf to form a cavity tray. Cement rendering is not a satisfactory solution as the inevitable movement of the wall can cause cracks that will let in water.

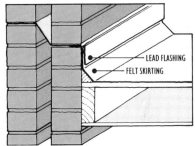
LEAD FLASHING
FELT SKIRTING
A dressed flashing normally laps the skirting

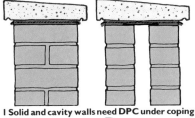
1 Solid and cavity walls need DPC under coping

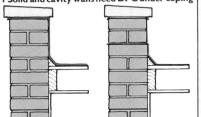
2 Full-height skirting   **3 Continuous covering**

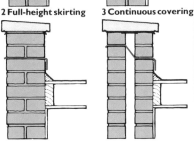
4 DPC flashing   **5 DPC cavity tray**

FITTING A NEW CAVITY TRAY

A cavity wall abutted by an extension roof needs a cavity tray to protect it from damp. Normally it would be built-in, but in existing buildings with new extensions special trays – moulded units of polypropylene – can be inserted from outside by removing a course of bricks. A tray equals two brick-lengths and can also be used singly where a cavity is bridged by an extractor.

Inserting the tray

Two courses above the proposed roof level remove three bricks, whole if possible, and without letting rubble fall into the cavity. On the cleaned bricks lay a length of flashing wide enough to project 50mm (2in) into the wall and cover the roof skirting by 75mm (3in) when dressed down. Trap the flashing with the first tray unit, pushing it into one end of the opening **(1)**. Place two bricks in the tray and bed and joint them in mortar **(2)**. Pack out the top joint with slate pieces and fill it with mortar pushed well home but not out at the back. Rake out a weep hole at the base of the middle joint with a wire.

Cut out two more bricks, again leaving a three-brick opening **(3)**, roll out the flashing and insert a second tray. Join the trays with the clip provided, fitting it over the meeting ends to make a water tight joint **(4)**, and lay two more bricks in the opening. Continue in this way until the tray is the required length. Only one brick need be removed at the end to make a two-brick opening for the last unit.

SEE ALSO

Details for: ▷
Flashings	232-233
Ventilators	276, 279, 283
Builder's tools	478-480

Moulded cavity tray
Straight and angled sections are available from most builders' merchants.

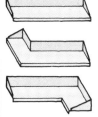

1 Trap the flashing

2 Lay two bricks

3 Cut out two bricks

4 Insert second tray

TYPES OF FELTS FOR FLAT ROOFS

Felt type British Standard Ref.	Base	Surface Finish	Colour code	Weight Kg/per roll	Properties and uses
BS 747 **1B**	Fibre	Sand	White	36 Kg (79lb)	Least expensive type. Relatively weak. Good for roofing outbuildings.
BS 747 **1E**	Fibre	Mineral	White	38 Kg (84lb)	
BS 747 **2B**	Asbestos	Sand	Green	36 Kg (79lb)	Good fire-resistance. More expensive than glass-fibre base felts. Can be nailed on sloping roofs. Use for underlays, vapour checks or complete systems.
BS 747 **2E**	Asbestos	Mineral	Green	38 Kg (84lb)	
BS 747 **3B**	Glass fibre	Sand	Red	36 Kg (79lb)	Rot proof, inexpensive, unsuitable for nailing. Good for 2 or 3 layer systems.
BS 747 **3E**	Glass fibre	Mineral	Red	28 Kg (62lb)	
BS 747 **3G**	Glass fibre	Grit underside Sand topside	Red	32 Kg (70lb)	Perforated first layer for partial bonding systems.
HIGH PERFORMANCE FELTS					
NO BS NUMBERS	Glass/polyester	Sand	Black	36 Kg (79lb)	Rot proof, tough, good weathering, can be nailed. Use for 2 or 3 layer systems.
	Glass/Polyester	Mineral	Blue/grey. Green	28 Kg (62lb)	
BS 747 **5U,5B** BS 747 **5E**	Polyester	Sand	Blue	18,42Kg (40,93lb)	More expensive than glass polyester but better performance. Use for 2 or 3 layer systems. The best type for house extensions.
	Polyester	Mineral	Blue	47Kg (104lb)	

RENEWING A FELT ROOF

SEE ALSO

◁ Details for:

Nails	224
Felt types	229
Flashings	232-233
Guttering	234-236
Insulation	265, 268

Covering flat roofs, or stripping and re-covering them, should usually be left to professionals. A built-up felt system using hot bitumen or torching — using a gas-powered torch to soften bitumen coated felt — is beyond the amateur.

Yet a competent person can confidently replace perished felt on a garage roof, using a cold bitumen adhesive. The following example assumes a detached garage with a solid timber decking covered with three layers of felt.

Replacing perished felt

Wait for dry weather, then strip the old felt. Pull out any clout nails and check the deck for distorted or rotten boards. Lift and replace unsound ones with new ones, using galvanized wire nails and punching them below the surface.

Cutting to stagger joints
For a three-layer build-up start at one edge with a strip about one third of the roll width. The second layer starts with two-thirds width, the top layer with a full width. A two-layer roof starts with half a roll width, then with a full one. You can modify this to suit your roof and avoid a too-narrow strip at the other edge. If, for economy or ease of handling, you use short lengths the end should overlap at least 100mm (4in), the lower piece always lapped by the higher one as you work up the slope.

First layer
Cut the strips for the first felt layer slightly longer than the slope of the roof, and allow for an overlap of at least 50mm (2in) at the long edges. Cut one narrow side length so that successive lapped joints will be staggered.

Nail the felt down with 18mm (¾in) clout nails 50mm (2in) apart down the centres of the laps and 150mm (6in) apart overall (**1**). Tuck and trim the felt into the corners of the verge upstand to get mitred butt joints. Trim the felt

flush at eaves and verges and form and fit the drip at the eaves (See right).

Second layer
Cut lengths for the second layer, put the side piece in place, then roll it back halfway from the eaves end. Brush or trowel cold bitumen adhesive on the felt below but not on the verge upstand. Re-lay the felt, press it down, then roll up the other half and repeat, ensuring that the adhesive is continuous (**2**).

Fold and tuck the felt into the corner of the verge upstand and trim it to a mitred butt joint. Turn it back from the verge, apply adhesive and press it into place against the upstand. Trim the end to butt against the edge of felt for the eaves drip (See below) and trim the other edges flush with the verge. Place the next length, overlapping the first by at least 50mm (2in), and again roll back each half in turn, applying the adhesive. Repeat this across the roof, and cut and tuck the felt at the other verge corner.

Third layer
Cut and lay the mineral felt top layer or 'capsheet' in the same way as the second layer but lap the eaves drip and not the verge upstands (**3**).

Cut strips of the felt to form verge drips (See right) and nail and bond them into place around the side and near edges.

Built-up felt system
Lap the edges of the felt strips and stagger the joints in alternate layers.

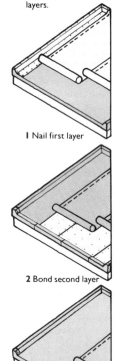

1 Nail first layer

2 Bond second layer

3 Lap eaves drip

MAINTAINING A FLAT ROOF

Whatever the material used for covering your flat roof it is sensible to carry out a routine inspection of its current condition at least once a year.

Climb on to the roof to inspect it, wearing soft-soled shoes, and make the check in two parts: once on a dry day and again shortly after there has been rain, when standing water can be seen.

Remove any old leaves, twigs or other matter that may have found its way there and brush off any silt deposits that may have built up. Note the positions of puddles because, although

they may not present an immediate problem, leaks occurring later in the life of the roof will be more easily traced. In an asphalt or felted roof you should also note any blisters or ripples.

On a felted roof test the overlapping joints to see that they are still well bonded. Also make a close inspection of the vulnerable edges of the roof. Check the soundness of the coving at the verges and eaves and the flashings at abutments. You should also inspect the condition of the gutterings and outlets and remove any blockages.

MAKING DRIPS

Eaves
Cut 1m (3ft 3in) long strips from the length of a roll of felt. Calculate the width of the strips by measuring the depth of the drip batten and adding 25mm (1in), then doubling this figure and adding at least 100mm (4in). Cut away 50mm (2in) from one corner to enable the ends to be overlapped and make folds in the strips, using a straight edge. Nail the drip sections to the drip batten with galvanized clout nails and fold each strip back on itself and bond it over the first layer of felt (**1**).

Cutting the corners
Where the drip meets the verge, cut the corners to cover the end of the upstand (**2**). If necessary, make a paper pattern before cutting the felt. You may need an extra wide strip to allow for a tall upstand. Fold the tabs and bond into place, except the end one, which is left free to be tucked into the verge drip.

Verge drips
Cut and fix the verge drips in place after the top layer of roofing. Cut the strips 1m (3ft 3in) long and calculate their width as with the eaves drip, but allow extra for the top edge and slope of the upstand. Working from the eaves, notch the ends of the strips where they overlap, as described for eaves.

Cut and fold the end of the first strip where it meets the eaves (**3**), nail the strip to the batten and bond the remainder into place (**4**).

At the rear corners cut and fold the end strip covering the side verge (**5**). Cover the rear verge last, cutting and folding the corners to lap the side pieces and finishing with neat mitres (**6**).

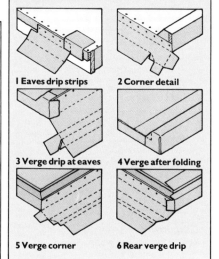

1 Eaves drip strips   2 Corner detail

3 Verge drip at eaves   4 Verge after folding

5 Verge corner   6 Rear verge drip

FAULT-FINDING

Damp patches
Damp patches on a ceiling are a clear sign that the roof needs attention, but the source of the problem is not always obvious. If they are near an internal wall you should suspect a breakdown of the flashing details.

Locating the leak
A leak anywhere else in the roof may be hard to find, as the water can run downhill from its entry point before dripping on to the ceiling. Measure the distance between the patch and the edges of the ceiling, then locate the point on the roof surface and work from it up the slope seeking the source.

Splits and blisters
Splits and blisters on the smooth surface of an asphalt or bitumen felt covering may be obvious, but chippings on a covering can be troublesome and must be cleared away. This is not easy, and the attempt can obliterate the cause of the leak. Use a blowtorch or hot-air paint stripper to soften the bitumen and scrape the chippings away. The surface must be made smooth if it is to be patch-repaired.

Splits in the covering caused by some movement of the substrate can be recognised by the lines they follow. Blisters formed by trapped moisture or air should be pressed to locate any weaknesses in the covering, which will show as moisture is expelled. These must be sealed with patches. Their cause may be moisture permeating the substrate from below and, heated by the sun, expanding under the covering. If this is undamaged the blister can be left, but its cause must be dealt with.

Damp and condensation
Damp near a wall may be caused by porous brickwork above the flat roof, lack of pointing or DPC, slipped or inadequate coping on parapet walls and/or a breakdown of flashings, which should be made good as required. Condensation may also cause dampness, and is potentially a more serious problem. If warm moist air permeates the ceiling the vapour can condense under the cold roof and start rot in the structural timbers. In such a case upgrade the ceiling with a moisture check and fit some type of ventilation (▷). If the problem is not solved so easily, have the roof recovered and also include better insulation.

FLAT ROOF REPAIRS

Just how a flat roof is to be repaired will depend on its general condition and age, and the extent of the damage. If inspection shows that the surface of the covering has decayed, as may happen to some traditional bitumen felts, it may be better to call in a contractor and have the roof re-covered.

Patch repairs

Such localised damage as splits and blisters can be patch-repaired with the aid of proprietary repair kits, but, as their effectiveness is only as good as their adhesion to the background, take care when cleaning the surface. Kill any lichen or moss spores with a good fungicide or bleach before starting the repair work.

A patched roof, if visible from above, can be rather an eyesore. This can be corrected with a finishing coat of bitumen and chippings or reflective paint to unify the surface area. Work on a warm day, preferably after a spell of dry weather.

Dealing with splits

You can use most self-adhesive repair tapes to patch-repair splits in all types of roof coverings.

First remove any chippings (See left), then clean the split and its surrounding surface thoroughly. Fill a wide split with a mastic compound before taping. Apply the primer supplied over the area to be covered and leave it for an hour.

Where a short split has occurred along a joint in the board substrate prepare the whole line of the joint for covering with tape.

Peel back the protective backing of the tape and apply it to the primed surface(**1**). If you are working on short splits cut the tape to length first. Otherwise work from the roll, unrolling the tape as you work along the repair.

Press it down firmly and, holding it in place with your foot, roll it out and tread it into place as you go, then cut it off at the end of the run. Go back and ensure that the edges are sealed (**2**).

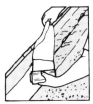
1 Apply the tape

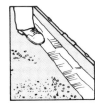
2 Press tape firmly

Dealing with blisters

Any blisters in asphalt or felted roofs should be left alone unless they have caused the covering to leak or they contain water.

To repair a blister in an asphalt roof first heat the area with a blow torch or hot-air stripper and, when the asphalt is soft, try to press the blister flat with a block of wood. If water is present cut into the asphalt to open the blister up and let the moisture dry out. This can be encouraged by careful use of the heat before pressing the asphalt back into place. Work mastic into the opening before closing it, then cover the repair with a patch of repair tape.

In a blister on a felted roof, make two crossed cuts and peel back the covering. Heating the felt will make this easier. Dry and clean out the opening, apply bitumen adhesive, and when it is tacky nail the covering back into place with galvanized clout nails (**3**).

Cover the repair with a patch of roofing felt, bonded on with the bitumen adhesive. Cut the patch so as to lap at least 75mm (3in) all round. Alternatively you can use repair tape.

Treating the whole surface

A roof which has already been patch-repaired and is showing general signs of wear and tear can be given an extra lease of life by means of a liquid waterproofing treatment.

The treatment consists of a thick layer of cold-applied bitumen and latex rubber waterproofer which can also be reinforced with an open-weave glass fibre membrane.

First sweep the roof free of all dirt and loose material and treat the surface with a fungicide to kill off any traces of lichen and moss.

Following the maker's instructions, apply the first coat of waterproofer with a brush or broom (**4**), then lay the glass fibre fabric into the wet material and stipple it with a loaded brush. Overlap the edges of the fabric strips by at least 50mm (2in) and bed them down well with the waterproofer. Clean the brush with soapy water.

Let the first coat dry thoroughly before laying the second and allow that one to dry before applying the third and last coat. When the last coat becomes tacky cover it with fine chippings or clean sharp sand to provide it with a protective layer.

SEE ALSO

Details for: ▷	
Ventilation	277
Organic growth	44
Parapets	229
Flashings	232-233
Condensation	254-255
Hot-air stripper	481
Gas torch	488

3 Nail cut edges
Use bitumen adhesive to glue a felt patch over the repair.

4 Brush on first coat

FLASHINGS

Flashings are used to weatherproof the junctions between a roof and the other parts of the building, which are usually at the abutments with walls and chimneys and where one roof meets another.

SEE ALSO

◁ Details for:

Roof coverings	223-224
Valley tiles	225
Sheet roofing	227
Pointing	430

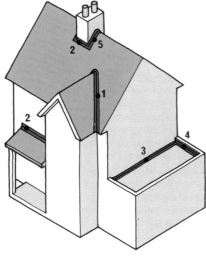

Where flashing is used
Typical types of flashing for pitched and flat roofs ▶
1 Valley
2 Apron
3 Wall abutment
4 Parapet abutment
5 Chimney abutment

Flashing materials

The most common flashing materials are lead, zinc, roofing felt and mortar fillets. Of all these lead is by far the best because it weathers well, is easily worked – though shaping it is generally a craft skill – and can be applied to any situation and roof covering.

Zinc is a cheaper substitute for lead and is not so long-lasting or so easy to work into shape. Where zinc flashings need to be replaced the extra cost of using lead would be easily repaid because of lead's much longer life.

Bitumen felt may be used for flashings on felted roofs, but this material cannot be easily manipulated and is used normally for the more simple cover flashings that overlap the upturned skirtings of the felt roofing.

Flashings of mortar fillets are common on the pitched roofs of older terraced houses, but are prone to shrinkage. They are still used for reasons of economy or for re-roofing work, sometimes with inset cut tiles.

Flashing construction

The design of a given flashing will be determined by the particular details at the junction and to some extent by the materials being used.

Typical situations are generally treated in a standard way, and these are shown here, using lead for the flashings.

Abutments
Where the inclined edge of a typical pitched roof abuts a wall the type of flashing used is determined by the nature of the roof covering and the pitch of the roof.

Double-lap tiles
Slate or plain tiled roofs with a pitch of 30 degrees or more, normally use soakers and a cover flashing. Soakers are lead or zinc pieces, equal in length to the tile's gauge plus the lap, folded into right angles lengthwise. The part that lies on the tiles should be at least 100mm (4in) wide and the upstand 75mm (3in). The back edge turns down over the tile's top edge, so 12 to 25mm (½ to 1in) extra in length is added.

A soaker is laid over the end tile or slate as a course is laid, the upstands flat against the brickwork and protected by a stepped cover flashing dressed down over them. The flashing's top edges are turned into the bed joints, held by lead wedges and pointed with mortar (**1**).

Single-lap tiles
Contoured single-lap tiles can be treated at abutments with one-piece flashing. The lead is tucked into the brick wall by the stepped or chased method and dressed down over the tile, the amount of overlap depending on tile contour and roof pitch. On a shallow pitch it should be at least 150mm (6in). The lead is dressed to the tile's shape and the step at each course and its free edge carried over the nearest raised tile contour (**2**).

Valley flashing
Some plain tiled roofs have special valley tiles that take the tiling into the angle, but most tiled and slated roofs have valley gutters of metal flashing. A valley flashing is made by laying a lead lining on boarding that runs from eaves to ridge, following the angle of the valley, and dressing it over wooden fillets nailed to the boarding to form an upstand (**3**).

Where two valleys meet at the ridge a lead saddle is formed. The edges of the tiles or slates are cut to follow the angle of the valley and to leave a gap of no less than 100mm (4in) between them. Slate coverings should overhang the supporting valley fillet by 50mm (2in) and contoured tiles should be bedded in mortar and finished flush with the edge of the tiles to form a watertight gutter.

1 Double-lap flashing

2 Single-lap flashing

3 Valley flashing

APRON FLASHING

The head of a lean-to roof is weatherproofed with a lead apron flashing, its top edge pointed into a mortar joint two courses above the roof, dressed down on to the roof. It should lap the roof covering by 150mm (6in) or more.

Special moulded flashing units are available for use with corrugated sheet roofing of plastic or asbestos cement. These are shaped to fit the contour of the roofing and have flat hinged upstands which adapt to any roof slope. The upstand can have conventional cover flashing or can be sealed with self-adhesive flashing tape.

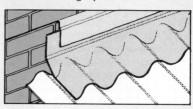

Moulded apron flashing for corrugated roofing

CHIMNEY FLASHING

The flashing where a roof meets the side of a chimney is much the same as at an abutment, but there are junctions at the front and back of the chimney.

An apron flashing is fitted in front, the upstand is returned on to the sides of the stack and its top edge set in a bed joint. The apron, extending beyond the chimney sides, is dressed to the tile contour. Side flashings are fitted, using soakers or one-piece flashing, and the back of the chimney receives a timber-supported back gutter. The lead's front edge is turned up the brick face, its ends folded on the side flashings, and a separate cover flashing is dressed over the upstand.

The back of the gutter follows the roof slope and is lapped by the tiles, which are fitted last.

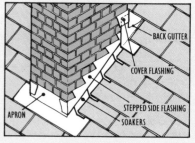

Chimney flashing for a slate roof

FLASHING REPAIRS

Many problems come about with flashings because of corrosion of the flashing material or failure of the joints between different materials due to erosion or thermal movement.

A perished flashing should be stripped out and replaced. If this will require craft skills the work should be done by a specialist contractor, but in many cases leaks may be caused by shrinkage cracks, and you can repair these with self-adhesive flashing materials.

Using caulking compound

Cement fillets often shrink away from wall abutments. If the fillets are otherwise sound – free of cracks for example – fill the gap with a gun-applied flexible caulking compound, having chosen a colour to match the fillet. Brush the surfaces to remove any loose material before injecting the compound.

Flashing tape

Prepare the surfaces by removing all loose and organic material. A broken or crumbling cement fillet should be made good with mortar.

Ensure that the surfaces are dry and if necessary apply a primer – it is supplied with some tapes – about one hour before using the tape **(1)**.

Cut the tape to length and peel away the protective backing as you press the tape into place. Work over the surface with a cloth pad, applying firm pressure to exclude any air trapped underneath the tape **(2)**.

1 Apply a primer with a 50mm (2in) paintbrush

2 Press tape with a pad to exclude air bubbles

Repointing flashing

Metal flashings which are tucked into brickwork may have worked loose where the old mortar is badly weathered. If the flashing is otherwise sound rake out the mortar joint, tuck the lead or zinc into it and wedge it there with rolled strips of lead spaced about 500mm (20in) apart. Then repoint the joint. While you have the roof ladders and scaffolding in place, rake out and repoint all of the mortar joints if in poor condition.

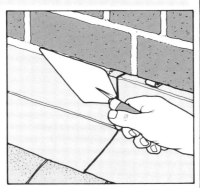

Rake out joint and repoint with fresh mortar

Patching lead

Lead will not readily corrode but splits can occur in it where it has buckled through expansion and contraction over the years.

Flashing tape can be used but it is possible to patch lead by soldering or, for a more substantial repair, cutting away a weak or damaged portion and joining on a new piece by lead 'burning' or welding. This is not a job you can easily do yourself and it should be handed over to a professional. It should be done only when it is more economical to have the old lead repaired than to have a new flashing made and fitted.

SEALING GLAZED ROOFS

Traditional timber-framed conservatories, glazed porches and greenhouses can suffer from leaks caused by a breakdown of the seal between the glass and the glazing bars. Minor leaks should be dealt with promptly because the trapped moisture could lead to timber decay and expensive repair work.

Using aluminium tape

You can waterproof glazing bars with self-adhesive aluminium tape simply cut to length and pressed in place.

Clean all old material from the glazing bars and the edges of glass on both sides of them, let the wood dry out if necessary and apply wood primer. When the primer is dry fill the rebates with putty or mastic. The width of tape must cover the upstand of the bars and lap the glass each side by 18mm (¾in).

Start at the eaves and work up the roof, peeling off its backing as you unroll the tape. Mould it to the glazing bars' contour, excluding air bubbles.

At a step in the glass cut the tape for a 50mm (2in) overlap and mould the end over the stepped edge, then start a new length lapping the stuck-down end by 50mm (2in) and so on, to the ridge.

At the ridge you may cut the tape to butt against the framework or lap on to it. A horizontal tape should cover the turned ends. Where a lean-to roof has an apron flashing tuck the tape under it.

Self-adhesive aluminium tape can be painted or left its natural colour.

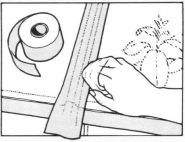

Clean the surfaces before applying the tape.

Clear tape

You can make a temporary repair to cracked glass with clear self-adhesive waterproofing tape.

Clean the glass and apply the tape over the crack on the weather side. It will make an almost invisible repair, especially if done promptly.

You can also use this tape for sealing the overlaps on translucent corrugated plastic roofing.

SEE ALSO

Details for: ▷	
Primers	43
Glazing	200-202
Pointing	430
Mastic gun	481

233

GUTTERING

Guttering collects the rainwater that runs down a roof and leads it to a downpipe through which it discharges *into a drain. Good rainwater disposal is vital in preventing damp developing in the fabric of a house.*

SEE ALSO

◁ Details for:
Valleys	232
Ladders	40-42
Painting wood	76
Painting metal	85-86
Fitting guttering	236

Roof drainage

The size and layout of a roof drainage system should enable it to discharge all the water from a given roof area. The flow load determining the guttering's capacity depends mainly on the area of the roof. Makers of rainwater goods usually specify the maximum area for a given size and profile of gutter based on a rainfall rate of 75mm/hr (3in/hr). If you replace an old gutter, perished but of the right capacity, have the size that of the original or slightly larger.

A downpipe's position can affect the system's performance. A system with a central downpipe can serve double the roof area of one with an end outlet. A right-angled bend will reduce the flow capacity by about 20 per cent if it is near the outlet.

In practice, unless you are working on a new building, the positions of drains and downpipes are already fixed.

Sizes
Gutter sizes are generally specified by their overall width in cross section and sometimes by their depth as well.

TYPICAL PROFILES AND SIZES OF GUTTERING

Half round	Ogee (OG)	Moulded OG	Box
75mm (3in)			
100mm (4in)	100mm (4in)	100 x 75mm (4 x 3in)	100 x 75mm (4 x 3in)
112mm (4½in)	112mm (4½in)		
125mm (5in)	125mm (5in)	125 x 100mm (5 x 4in)	125 x 100mm (5 x 4in)
150mm (6in)	150 x 100mm (6 x 4in)	150 x 100mm (6 x 4in)	

TYPES OF GUTTERING

The guttering on domestic buildings is used in various ways adapted to the design of the roof.

EAVES GUTTERS

The commonest types by far are the eaves gutters, which are fixed along the eaves fascia boards (See below). They are made in many materials and designs.

PARAPET GUTTERS

Parapet gutters are generally found in older houses and may serve a flat or pitched roof set between two parapet walls. This type is generally purpose-made as part of the original structure of the roof and is usually covered with a metal or bituminous roofing material.

VALLEY GUTTERS

Valley gutters are a form of flashing used at the junctions between sloping roofs. They are not gutter systems in themselves but they direct the rainwater into eaves or parapet gutters (◁).

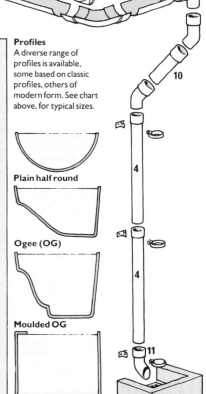

EAVES GUTTER SYSTEMS

Eaves gutter systems are fabricated in cast iron, cast and rolled sheet aluminium, asbestos cement and a uPVC rigid plastic. With the exception of the roll-formed aluminium type the systems are made up from basic lengths of gutter and downpipes with a range of fittings (See diagram).

Moulded or cast gutters have a socket at one end into which the plain spigot end of the next section is jointed.

For gutters that are not symmetrical in section, such as an OG, this means that components are left- or right-handed, and this has to be noted when replacement parts are being ordered.

Traditional cast iron and modern aluminium guttering may be compatible should you wish to renew only a part of your system, or extend it, but with the modern patented-design plastic systems you will have to stay with the same make, for, though similar in style, they are not interchangeable.

1 Stopend
Internal and external fittings for socketed or non-socketed types.

2 Gutter brackets
Normally screwed to fascia board, but some can fix to rafter bracket arms.

3 Guttering
In various profiles and lengths of 1.8 to 3m (6 to 10ft) with socket at one end or spigots both ends.

4 Downpipe
Available in 1.8 to 3m (6 to 10ft) lengths. Metal types may have integral fixing lugs.

5 Hopperhead
May be used as part of downpipe system to receive waste pipes from another source.

6 Pipe clip
Secures downpipes to wall.

7 Running outlet
May be double or single socketed.

8 Gutter angle
Available in 90, 120 and 135 degree angles in most systems for turning corners.

9 Stopend outlet
Used with downpipe at an end.

10 Offset
Used on guttering fitted to overhanging eaves. Available in standard projections or can be made up with special offset bends and a length of downpipe.

11 Shoe
Throws water clear of a wall into open gulley (◁).

Profiles
A diverse range of profiles is available, some based on classic profiles, others of modern form. See chart above, for typical sizes.

Plain half round

Ogee (OG)

Moulded OG

Box

MAINTENANCE

Cast iron, cast aluminium and asbestos cement guttering are all rigid and will support a ladder. But this is not really advisable, and it is much better to use a ladder stay (▷). Never prop a ladder against either plastic or roll-formed aluminium gutters.

Inspect and clean out the interiors of gutters regularly. Gutters concentrate the dirt, and sometimes sand washed down from the tiles by the rain. This can quickly build up if the flow of water is restricted by leaves or twigs. Birds' nests also can effectively block the guttering or downpipes.

The weight of standing water can distort plastic guttering, and if a blockage that is causing the gutter to overflow is left unchecked it can lead to problems with damp in the walls.

Removing debris
First block the gutter outlet with rag. With a shaped piece of plastic laminate scrape the silt into a heap, scoop it out of the gutter with a garden trowel and deposit it in a bucket hung from the ladder. Sweep the gutter clean with a stiff hand brush.

Remove the rag and flush the gutter down with a bucket of water.

Fit a wire or plastic 'balloon' to prevent debris falling into the downpipe or birds nesting on top of it.

Snow and ice
Plastic guttering can be badly distorted and even broken by snow and ice building up in it. Dislodge the build-up with a broom from an upstairs window if you can reach it safely. Otherwise climb a ladder to remove it.

If snow and ice become a regular seasonal problem you should screw a snow board made from 75 x 25mm (3 x 1in) planed softwood treated with a wood preservative and painted. Fix it to stand about 25mm (1in) above the eaves tiles, using 25 x 6mm (1 x ¼in) steel straps bent as required.

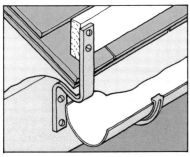
A snow board protects gutters or glazed roofs

GUTTERING MATERIALS

CAST IRON

The cast iron rainwater systems common on old houses are mostly of the OG type, fixed to the fascia board by mushroom-headed short screws through the back of the gutter above the water line and spaced about 600mm (2ft) apart.

Each 1.8m (6ft) standard length of the guttering has a socket end into which the plain spigot end of the next piece fits **(1)**. Short bolts secure the joint and a bedding of putty forms a seal when they are tightened **(2)**.

Cast iron is heavy and brittle, and installing or dismantling such a system needs two people. The iron can be cut with a hacksaw and drilled with standard twist drills in a power tool.

The guttering needs normal regular painting, and a bituminous paint applied inside makes for a longer life. If it is unprotected it will rust, usually along the back edge round the screws. Badly rusted guttering should be replaced, as it is likely to collapse.

1 A standard gutter has a socket at one end

2 The joint is sealed with putty then bolted

CAST ALUMINIUM

Cast aluminium guttering comes in a wide range of profiles, including OG, moulded OG and half round. It is assembled in a similar way to cast iron guttering, with bolted joints, but a flexible mastic is used instead of putty to make the seals. The guttering may be fitted to the fascia with screws through the back, or with gutter brackets. All of the fixings should also be of aluminium.

Cast aluminium is about one third the weight of cast iron and can be left unpainted, but in some situations it can corrode, and if it is used as part of a cast iron system all the aluminium surfaces must be protected with zinc chromate or bituminous paint. It can be worked with ordinary metal-working tools.

ASBESTOS CEMENT

Asbestos cement guttering is of the socket-and-spigot type. The joints are secured with galvanised iron bolts and the seals are made with a mastic jointing compound. The guttering is produced in half round profiles in a range of several sizes. It is fixed to the house fascia board with gutter brackets, and these should not be spaced more than 900m (3ft) apart.

Asbestos cement has good weathering properties and does not need to be painted. It can be cut with a hacksaw and drilled normally (▷).

ROLLED SHEET ALUMINIUM

Rolled sheet aluminium guttering is a moulded lightweight OG system made from thin, prepainted flat sheet aluminium which is roll-formed to the gutter shape by a portable machine. This is done on site by the suppliers, and unbroken lengths are made to measure.

The end stops and angles are supplied as separate items, crimped to the ends of the gutter sections. Outlets are formed by punching holes in the bottom.

Simple metal fixing brackets are clipped to the front and back edges of the guttering and fixed to the fascia with drive screws. The system needs no maintenance but can be painted.

UPVC

Guttering of unplasticised PVC (uPVC) is now the most widely used, for new buildings and for replacing old systems. In many profiles and sizes, it is self-coloured in brown, black, grey and white. It needs no painting.

Most uPVC systems use clip-fastened joints with synthetic rubber gaskets to form the seals. Some use a solvent cement to weld the joints. Downpipes may be a push fit, and sealed with an 'O' ring or solvent-welded. The guttering is usually supported by brackets, but some systems use screws in the back edge of the outlet and corner fittings for easier installation.

SEE ALSO

Details for: ▷

Ladders	40-42
Cutting asbestos	227
Primers	43
Painting metal	85-86

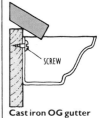
Cast iron OG gutter

Cast aluminium

RAFTER BRACKET   FASCIA BRACKET
Gutter brackets

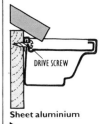
Sheet aluminium

Plastic guttering

235

FITTING NEW GUTTERING AND DOWNPIPE

When your old gutter system reaches the end of its useful life you should replace it. Try to do so with a system in the same style or, at least, one that *goes with the character of your house. If you plan to install the guttering yourself a plastic system is probably the best choice, being easy to handle.*

SEE ALSO

◁ Details for:

Fascia board	222
Builder's tools	478-480
Drilling masonry	479
Hacksaw	486-487
Wall plugs	498
Screws	498

Installing the guttering

Measure round the base of the house to find the total length of gutter needed, and note the number and type of fittings to be ordered.

Use a plumb line to mark the position of the gutter outlet – directly over the existing drain – on the fascia board (**1**). Screw the outlet or its support bracket – depending on the system – to the fascia no more than 50mm (2in) below the tile level (**2**).

Fix a gutter bracket at the opposite end of the run, close to the top of the fascia board. This is to give a fall of at least 25mm (1in) in 15m (50ft) (**3**). Run a taut string between the bracket and outlet and fix the rest of the brackets along the slope of the string, spaced no more than 1m (3ft 3in) apart (**4**). There should be a bracket at every joint unless the system uses screw-fixed outlets and angles (**5**).

Fitting the gutter

Tuck the back edge of a length of gutter under the roofing felt and into the rear lips of the brackets, then clip its front edge into all of the brackets (**6**).

Fit the second length in the same way, with its spigot end pushed into the socket of the first length. Some pressure will be needed to compress the rubber seal. Leave a gap of about 6mm (¼in) between the end of the spigot and the shoulder of the socket to allow for expansion.

Cutting the gutter

Cut the gutter squarely with a hacksaw. You can snap a clip or bracket over it first to give rigidity and guide the cut. Smooth the rough edges with a file. In some systems notches for the clips are made in the gutter's front and back edges; this can be done with a file.

Connecting to existing guttering

To renew guttering on a terrace house may mean joining your system to your neighbours'. There are left- and right-hand adaptors for this.

Remove your old guttering to the nearest joint between the houses, bolt the adaptor on, sealing the joint with mastic, and fix the new plastic gutter with the clip provided. (**7**).

Fitting the downpipe

Work downward from the gutter outlet. If the eaves overhang you will need to fit an offset.

Fit a clip to the top of a length of downpipe. Hold it against the wall and measure the distance from its centre to a plumb line dropped through the outlet's centre (**8**). You may find an offset to fit but will most likely have to make it up with offset bends and pipe. Use a solvent cement and assemble it on a table so that the bends lie in the same plane.

Fit the offset to the outlet spigot and the pipe to the offset. Adjust the pipe so that the clip's back plate falls on a mortar joint (**9**). Trim the offset spigot if necessary.

Mark the fixings, drill and plug the wall and fix the pipe and clip with plated round-head screws.

Mark and fix the lower lengths of pipe in the same way, with a 6mm (¼in) expansion gap between each pipe and the socket shoulder. Fit extra clips at the centre of any pipe longer than 2m (6ft 6in).

Cut the bottom pipe to length and fit a shoe in the same way (**10**). If the pipe is jointed into a gulley trap (**11**) or a drainsocket you may have to work from the bottom.

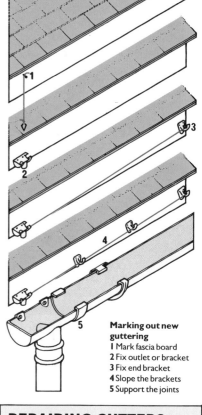

Marking out new guttering
1 Mark fascia board
2 Fix outlet or bracket
3 Fix end bracket
4 Slope the brackets
5 Support the joints

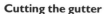

6 Clip the guttering into the brackets

7 Use an adaptor to join different systems

REPAIRING GUTTERS AND DOWNPIPES

It is always better to replace a damaged part of a gutter system than to repair it, but a neat repair that stays watertight can be regarded as permanent.

Mending a crack

Chipped or cracked guttering and downpipes of cast iron or asbestos cement can be repaired with a 'cement bandage'.

Clean the surface, cut the bandage to length and soak it in water for 15 to 20 seconds. Wearing rubber gloves position the bandage over the crack, smooth it in place and leave it to set hard. If possible cover it with polythene for 72 hours to delay the drying time.

Using epoxy putty

You can build up the chipped edge of a cast iron gutter with epoxy putty. Tape a waxed or polythene-lined piece of card across the outside of the broken edge and bent to follow the contour of the gutter. Mix the two-part putty, fill the gap with it and remove the cardboard 'former' when the putty sets.

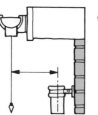
8 Drop a plumb line

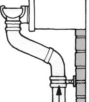
9 Fit an offset

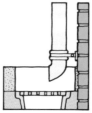
10 Finish with a shoe

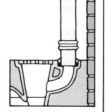
11 Fit into gulley

4

BASICS	238
PRECAUTIONS	239
SECURING DOORS	240
SECURING WINDOWS	242
BURGLAR ALARMS	243
FIRE PROTECTION	244

HOME SECURITY

HOME SECURITY

All responsible householders will want to take reasonable precautions to protect themselves, their families and their property against the risks of fire and burglary. The cost and effort involved is small by comparison with the possible expense of replacement or even rebuilding – not to mention the grief caused by personal injury and the loss of items of sentimental value.

SEE ALSO

◁ Details for:
Securing doors	240-241
Securing windows	242-243
Fire precautions	244

The vulnerable areas of a house
1 The front door
An inadequately locked door invites a forced entry
2 Darkened porch
Prevents identification of callers
3 Back or side doors
Often fitted with minimal locks
4 Burglar alarm
A useful deterrent
5 French windows
Can be sprung with one well placed blow
6 Downstairs windows
A common means of entry when unlocked

How a burglar gains entry

Many people innocently believe that they are unlikely to be burgled because they are not conspicuously wealthy. But statistics prove that most intruders are opportunists in search of one or two costly items, such as electrical hardware – typically the video, radio and television set – jewellery or cash. And the average burglar takes only a few minutes to rob a house: and often in broad daylight, too.

Consequently, no house is immune *to attack, especially those which* afford an open invitation to thieves. It's virtually impossible to prevent a determined burglar from breaking in, but you can do a great deal to make it difficult for the inexperienced criminal. The illustration below indicates the vulnerable areas of an average house and the points listed in the box opposite suggest methods for safeguarding them. Check out each point and compare them with your own home to make sure your security is up to the minimum standard recommended.

Crime Prevention Officer
Local police authorities appoint a full-time Crime Prevention Officer (CPO), who is responsible for advising commercial establishments and private individuals on ways to improve the security of their premises. Telephone your nearest police station to arrange for a confidential visit from the CPO, who will discuss any aspect of home security that may concern you.

Fire Prevention Officer
Contact the Fire Prevention Officer (FPO) at your local fire brigade headquarters for advice on how to balance your needs for security against the necessity to provide escape routes in case of fire. He will also explain the merits of simple fire-fighting equipment available to the home owner.

Insurance companies
Check with your insurance company that your home and its contents are adequately covered against fire and theft. Most policies are now index-linked, which means that the company automatically adjusts the premiums to allow for inflation.

However, they cannot allow for new items or improvements and if you are under-insured you may receive only a percentage of the true value of lost or destroyed property in the event of a claim. In some circumstances, an insurance company may insist on certain precautions but they may also be willing to reduce your premium if you provide adequate security.

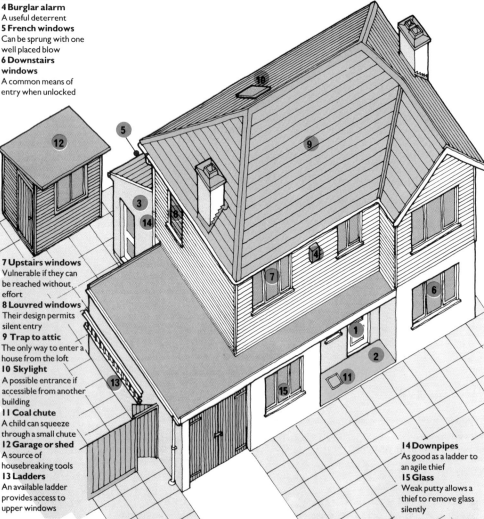

7 Upstairs windows
Vulnerable if they can be reached without effort
8 Louvred windows
Their design permits silent entry
9 Trap to attic
The only way to enter a house from the loft
10 Skylight
A possible entrance if accessible from another building
11 Coal chute
A child can squeeze through a small chute
12 Garage or shed
A source of housebreaking tools
13 Ladders
An available ladder provides access to upper windows

14 Downpipes
As good as a ladder to an agile thief
15 Glass
Weak putty allows a thief to remove glass silently

GUARDING AGAINST INTRUDERS

HOME SECURITY
PRECAUTIONS

Simple precautions

Many burglaries can be prevented by adopting security-conscious habits. Most burglaries occur during daylight hours when the home is unoccupied. Discourage opportunist burglars by closing and locking all windows and doors, even if you will be absent for a short time only.

Burglaries have occurred while the family is watching television in another room, so lock up before sitting down for the evening.

When you leave the house at night, close your curtains and leave a light on in a living room, not just in the hall. Alternatively, fit automatic time switches or random switches ($\triangleright$).

Make sure you open the curtains again in the daytime before you go out.

Bona fide officials from the gas or electricity boards always carry identification. It's best to keep a security chain attached until you are satisfied that the identification is genuine.

When you go on holiday, cancel milk and paper deliveries. If possible, ask a trusted neighbour to switch lights on and off for you, and open and close curtains. Remove a letterbox basket so that mail won't pile up. Don't advertise the fact that you will be absent but tell the police and inform them that a neighbour has a key. Deposit valuables with the bank.

Mark your possessions by engraving, etching or with an invisible marker. Such measures help the police identify your belongings if they are recovered. Photograph jewellery or paintings which are difficult to mark, and keep a record at the bank in case of fire. Small floor or wall safes are available from a locksmith to store small valuables and important documents.

SEE ALSO

Details for: $\triangleright$

Security paint	86
Time switches	240
Deadlocking bolt	240
Hinge bolts	241
Rack bolts	241
Window locks	242-243

1 FRONT DOOR

An intruder will ring the doorbell and if there's no answer he will force an entry. Fit a strong deadlocking bolt that conforms to BS 3621 ($\triangleright$).

Fit a bolt top and bottom on the inside. If there is a glass panel in the door, the bolts must be lockable.

Attach a security chain or similar fitting to prevent an intruder bursting in as you open the door a fraction. A door viewer allows you to identify a caller.

If you live in a flat or apartment where the entrance door is the only vulnerable spot, consider having a multi-point lock fitted: it throws bolts into all four sides simultaneously.

2 DARKENED PORCH

Fit a porch light so that a door viewer is usable after dark. The light should make an intruder think twice before attempting to break in.

3 BACK OR SIDE DOORS

A burglar can often work unobserved at the rear or side of a house. Fit similar mortise locks and bolts to those described for the front door. If the door opens outwards, fit hinge bolts, which will hold the door firmly in its frame, even if the hinge pins are driven out ($\triangleright$).

4 BURGLAR ALARM

An alarm is an additional deterrent but not a sufficient safeguard on its own.

5 FRENCH WINDOWS

Insecure French windows can be sprung by a heavy blow or kick. Fit rack bolts ($\triangleright$) top and bottom.

6 DOWNSTAIRS WINDOWS

Always vulnerable, particularly at the back and side of the house. Fit locks and catches to suit the material and style of the window ($\triangleright$). They must have removable keys so that a thief can't break the glass and release them.

7 UPSTAIRS WINDOWS

If they cannot be reached other than by ladder it is probably safe enough to use a standard catch, but fit a cheap key-operated catch to be absolutely sure. Windows accessible by scaling drainpipes, flat roofs or walls, must be secured as for those downstairs.

8 LOUVRED WINDOWS

Each individual pane can be removed silently simply by bending the aluminium holders. Use an epoxy adhesive to glue each one to its fitting or fix a grille.

9 TRAP TO ATTIC

Put a bolt on the trap door leading to your attic or roof space. Burglars have been known to break through the dividing walls of the adjoining house: and some terraced and semi-detached houses have common lofts.

10 SKYLIGHTS

Windows at roof level are at risk only if they can be reached easily by drainpipes, but fit a lock to deter thieves.

11 COAL CHUTE

Burglars with a child accomplice can gain access through a small coal chute. If the cellar is no longer used, seal the chute.

12 GARAGES AND SHEDS

Lock outbuildings to protect contents and prevent an intruder using your tools to break into your own house. Fit a standard lock or padlock with a close-fitting or concealed shackle, so that it cannot be cut easily. Choose a design that covers the fixing screws. If possible, substitute bolts for screws to prevent the lock being prised off.

13 LADDERS

Lock up ladders even if it means chaining them outside (to a garage wall, for instance): a loose ladder can be used to reach open windows upstairs.

14 DOWNPIPES

Paint a downpipe with security paint to dissuade a burglar from climbing it: the substance remains slippery, preventing a good grip ($\triangleright$).

15 GLASS

Most people accept the risk that glass can be broken or cut. However, you can buy toughened or wired glass, or cover ordinary glass with a metal grille. A sliding grille on the inside can be concealed by curtains or a pelmet when it is not in use.

Double glazing will deter a burglar to some extent but don't rely on it alone as a security measure.

Keep window putty in good repair so that it cannot be picked out with a penknife to expose the fixings and remove the pane.

Lead cames holding stained glass can be peeled silently and the glass removed, and the only way to prevent this is to fit a metal grille.

SECURING DOORS

Doors are vulnerable to forcing and often used by an intruder as a quick means of exit with his haul, even if he entered through a window. It makes good sense to fit strong locks and bolts: don't just rely on the old nightlatch, which offers no security at all – it is only as strong as the screws holding it to the door and a thief can easily break a pane of glass to operate it or simply slide back the bolt with a credit card. Front doors and back doors need different locking arrangements and there are various mechanisms to choose.

SEE ALSO
◁ Details for:
Fitting a
porch light   332
Outdoor lighting   333

The choice of door locks

The door by which you leave the house – usually the front door – needs a particularly strong lock because it can't be bolted top and bottom, except at night when you're at home and a break-in is less likely. Back and side doors need bolts top and bottom to prevent them being smashed in from outside, plus a lock to stop thieves making a getaway with their spoils.

The basic choice of locks is between mortise and rim types.

How a mortise lock works

A mortise lock is fitted into a slot cut in the edge of the door, where it cannot easily be tampered with. There are various patterns to suit the width of the door stile (which should be a minimum of 45mm (1³/₄in) thick – the standard for exterior-quality doors) and the location of the door: a two-bolt mortise is suitable for back and side doors. It has a handle or knob on each side, to operate a springbolt, and a key-operated deadbolt which can't be pushed back once the door is closed.

Purely key-operated mortise locks and cylinder mortise locks are best for final exit doors, where no handle is necessary. It's best to use one in tandem with a rim latch.

Choose a lock that conforms to BS 3621; this ensures that it has a minimum of 1000 key variations, is proof against 'picking' and is strong enough to resist drilling or forcing, having a deadbolt of hardened steel. Some locks are intended for right- or left-hand opening doors.

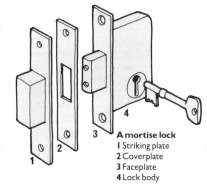

A mortise lock
1 Striking plate
2 Coverplate
3 Faceplate
4 Lock body

How a cylinder rim lock works

A cylinder rim lock is usually used on final exit doors as an alternative to a mortise lock (or as an addition for extra security): it fits on the inner face of the door and shoots a bolt into a plate fixed to the face or into the edge of the frame. A rim lock automatically holds the door closed when it is pulled shut, can be opened from inside by a knob, but needs a key so it can be opened from outside.

Choose a rim lock which has a deadlockable bolt, thrown by an extra turn of the latch key, or one that is automatically deadlocking. The best type has its staple fixed into the edge of the frame with screws or a metal stud: if it's only screwed to the face, a well-placed kick will rip out the screws.

A more secure type of rim latch incorporates a hook bolt, which is difficult to force open.

A cylinder rim lock
1 Cylinder
2 Mounting plate
3 Lock body
4 Staple

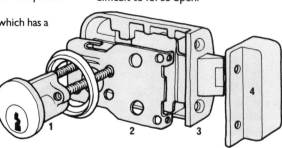

USING AUTOMATIC TIME SWITCHES

Give the impression that someone is in residence by using an automatic time switch plugged into an ordinary wall socket to control a table lamp or radio. By setting a dial you can have it switch the light on and off several times over a period of 24 hours, or buy a more sophisticated version that will control the lighting at different times for every day of the week.

A random switch can be fitted to a table lamp to control the lighting at undetermined periods.

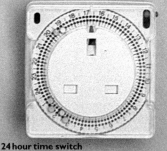

24 hour time switch

INSTALLING A DOOR VIEWER

A door viewer enables you to identify callers before admitting them. Select a viewer with as wide an angle of vision as possible: you should be able to see someone standing to the side of the door or even crouching below the viewer. Choose one that is adjustable to fit any thickness of door.

Drill the recommended size hole – usually 12mm (½in) – right through the centre of the door at a comfortable eye level, insert the barrel of the viewer into the hole from the outside then screw on the eyepiece from inside, using a coin to tighten it.

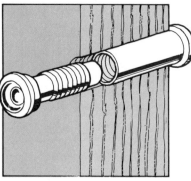

A telescopic viewer fits any size of door

FITTING LOCKS

Fitting a mortise lock

Scribe a line centrally on the edge of the door with a marking gauge and use the lock body as a template to mark the top and bottom of the mortise (**1**). Choose a drill bit that matches the lock body thickness and drill out the majority of the waste.

Square up the edges of the mortise with a bevel-edged chisel (**2**) until the lock fits snugly in the slot. Mark around the edge of the faceplate with a knife (**3**), then chop a series of shallow cuts across the waste. Pare out the recess until the faceplate is flush with the edge of the door.

Hold the lock against the face of the door and mark the centre of the keyhole with a bradawl (**4**). Clamp a block of scrap timber to the other side of the door over the keyhole position and drill right through on the centre mark: the block prevents the drill bit splintering the face of the door as it bursts through on the other side. Cut out the keyhole slot on both sides with a padsaw.

1 Mark the mortise

2 Chop out the waste

3 Mark the faceplate

4 Mark the keyhole

Screw the lock into its recess, check its operation; screw on the coverplate and then the escutcheons over each side of the hole (**5**). With the door closed, operate the bolt; it may incorporate a marking device to gauge the position of the striking plate on the door frame. If it doesn't have a marking device, shoot the bolt fully open, push the door to, and draw round the bolt on the face of the frame (**6**).

Mark out and cut the mortise and recess for the striking plate as described for the lock (**7**).

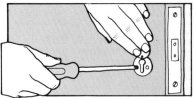
5 Screw on escutcheon to cover the keyhole

6 Mark bolt on frame

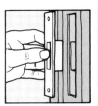
7 Fit striking plate

Fitting a cylinder rim lock

Tape the template provided with the lock to the door and mark then drill holes to accept the cylinder (**1**). They vary in size between models. Pass the cylinder into the hole from the outside and connect it to the mounting plate on the inside with machine screws (**2**).

Drill and insert the woodscrews to hold the plate to the door. Check the required length of the connecting bar, which projects through the plate and, if necessary, cut it to the correct size with a hacksaw (**3**).

Mark and cut the recess in the door edge for the lock, and attach it to the door and mounting plate with screws (**4**). Mark the position of the lock on the frame and use the template to drill for staple fixing screws or stud. Hold the staple against the frame to mark its recess. Chop and pare out the recess then screw on the staple.

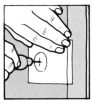
1 Mark cylinder centre

2 Fit mounting plate

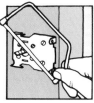
3 Cut connecting bar

4 Screw lock to door

FITTING RACK BOLTS

There are many strong bolts for securing a door from the inside, but the rack bolt can be fitted into the door edge: secure and unobtrusive. Fit them to front, back and side doors in addition to mortise and rim locks.

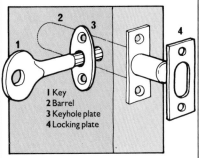

1 Key
2 Barrel
3 Keyhole plate
4 Locking plate

The components of a standard rack bolt

Drill a hole – usually 16mm (⅝in) in diameter – for the barrel of the bolt in the edge of the door. Use a try square to transfer the centre of the hole to the inside face of the door. Measure the keyhole and drill it with a 10mm (⅜in) bit. Insert the bolt (**1**).

With the key in position, mark the recess for the faceplate (**2**) then cut it out with a chisel. Screw the bolt and keyhole plate to the door. Operate the bolt to mark the frame, then drill a 16mm (⅝in) diameter hole to a depth that matches the length of the bolt. Fit the locking plate over the hole.

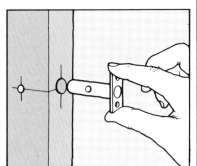
1 Drill holes for barrel and key then fit bolt

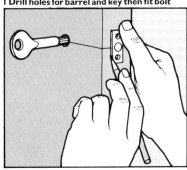
2 With the key holding bolt, mark faceplate

SEE ALSO

Details for: ▷

Woodworker's tools	462-473
Junior hacksaw	487

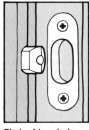

Fitting hinge bolts
Fit two bolts per door near the hinges. Drill hole in door edge for bolt and another in door frame. Recess the locking plate in frame.

Attaching a security chain
No special skills are needed to fit a chain, simply screw the fixing plates to the door and frame. Fit the chain just below the lock.

SECURING WINDOWS

Windows are a common means of entry for burglars, so take particular care to ensure they're secured, especially those in vulnerable locations. There are special locks for both timber and metal windows: the best type for wooden frames are set in mortises, whereas locks for metal frames are more limited due to the necessity to cut threads in the material for the screw fixings.

SEE ALSO

◁ Details for:
Vulnerable	
windows	238
Rack bolts	241
Sash windows	196
Casement windows	196
Repairing glass	202-203
Woodworker's tools	462-473
Metalworker's tools	486-491

How windows are locked

The way you lock a window depends on how it opens: sliding sashes, for instance, should be secured by locking the two frames together; casements, which open like doors, should be fastened to the outer frame or locked by rendering the catches and stays immovable. But whichever type of lock you choose, it makes sense to buy the best you can afford for the most vulnerable windows (◁) and to spend less on those which are difficult to reach.

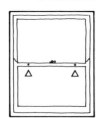

The best positions for window locks
The black dots in the illustrations above indicate where you should place bolts or locks.

Locks must be strong enough to resist forcing and they must be situated correctly for optimum security. For small windows, fit one lock as close to the centre as possible, but fit two locks spaced apart on large windows so that a thief cannot lever the opening edge and split the frame.

A window lock should be released by a removable key only. Some keys will open all locks of the same design (an advantage to some extent as you'll need to handle fewer keys – although a determined burglar may carry a range of standard keys). Other locks have several key variations.

Only fairly large windows can accommodate mortise-type locks, so many are surface-mounted. They're perfectly adequate, so long as the mechanism covers the screws, or where plugs are provided to seal them off once the lock is fixed. If neither is the case, drill out the centre of the screws once fitted so that they cannot be withdrawn.

Fitting sash window locks

Installing dual screws
Cheap but effective, dual screws comprise a bolt which passes through both meeting rails so that the sashes are immobilized. There is little to see when the window is closed and they are simple to operate with a special key.

With the window closed and the standard catch engaged, drill through the inner meeting rail into the outer one. Tape the drill bit to gauge the depth. Slide the sashes apart and tap the two bolt-receiving devices into their respective holes. Close the window and insert the threaded bolt with the key until it is flush with the window frame. If necessary, saw the bolt to length.

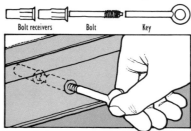

Bolt receivers   Bolt   Key

Turn a dual screw until it is flush with the frame

Using sash stops
When the bolt is withdrawn with a key, a sash stop fitted to each side of a window allows it to be opened slightly for ventilation. Apart from deterring a burglar, they will also prevent children from opening the window any further.

To fit the stop, drill a hole in the upper sash for the bolt and screw the faceplate over it. On close-fitting sashes, you will have to recess the faceplate. Screw the protective plate to the top edge of the lower sash.

Extract sash stop with key to secure window

Lock for aluminium sash windows
Secure a metal sash window with the lock described for securing fanlights.

Fitting a key-operated sash lock
A key-operated cylinder sash lock can be screwed to the outer frame at top and bottom, and drives a small bolt into a reinforced bolt hole. It's more obtrusive than other sash locks.

Locking casement windows

Fitting rack bolts
On a large casement window, fit a rack bolt as described for doors (◁).

Fitting a casement lock
A locking bolt can be attached to wooden window frames: the bolt is engaged by a simple catch but can only be released by a key.

With the lock body screwed to the opening part of the window, mark and cut a small mortise in the frame for the bolt. Screw on the coverplate.

For metal windows a similar device is a clamp which, fixed to the opening part of the casement, shoots a bolt that hooks onto the fixed frame.

Another metal casement lock fits within the metal section of the casement and a key-operated device expands the lock to secure the casement and frame together.

A good casement lock has a removable key

Locking the cockspur handle
The cockspur handle, which secures the opening edge of the casement to the fixed frame, can be locked using a device that you screw to the frame below the handle: when a key is turned, a bolt is extended to prevent the cockspur from moving. Lockable handles can be substituted for the standard handle; a key locks the handle, which can be fixed so the window is ajar for ventilation.

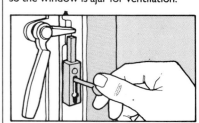

The extended bolt stops handle turning

Securing pivot windows

If a pivot window is not supplied with an integral lock, use the rack bolts or locks recommended for casement windows. Alternatively, fit the screw-mounted lock suggested for a fanlight window.

WINDOWS

Securing fanlight windows

Various types of casement and fanlight stay locks are available for securing the stay to the window frame. The simplest device is screwed below the stay arm and a key-operated bolt passes through one of the holes into it. Purpose-made key-lockable stays are also made.

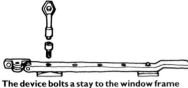

The device bolts a stay to the window frame

Fit a screw-mounted lock to wooden or metal fanlights. Attach the lock to the window then use it to position the staple on the fixed frame.

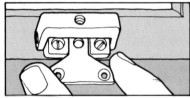

Position the staple to fit screw-mounted lock

Securing French windows

French windows or other glazed doors are vulnerable to forcing – a burglar only has to break a pane to reach the handle inside. Key-operated locks are essential to prevent a break-in.

Each door of French windows requires a rack bolt (▷) at the top and bottom, positioned so that the bolt shoots into the upper frame and the threshold below. Take each door off its hinges to fit the lower bolt.

Locking sliding doors
If you have aluminium sliding patio doors, fit additional locks at the top and bottom to prevent the sliding frame from being lifted off its track. These locks are costly, but offer at least 1000 key variations for good security.

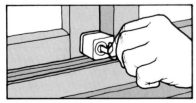

Fit a lock top and bottom of a sliding door

BURGLAR ALARM SYSTEMS

Although they are no substitute for good locks and catches, an alarm system does provide an extra sense of security and may deter an intruder if there are other less well-protected premises nearby. An alarm must be reliable but you and your family must be trained and disciplined in its use. If your neighbours are constantly subjected to false alarms, they're less likely to be vigilant and call the police in an emergency. Burglar alarm systems and installers vary in quality – the good ones are not always the most expensive.

A typical system

Alarm systems differ greatly but they fall into two basic categories: a passive system, which detects the presence of an intruder inside the house; or a perimeter system, which guards all likely means of entry. The best systems incorporate a combination of features for comprehensive security in case the perimeter detectors are by-passed.

Control unit
The control unit is the centre of the system to which all detectors are connected. From there, the signal is passed to a bell or siren. It should provide the necessary time for legitimate entry and exit from the premises. Units with separate zone monitoring allow you to set specific circuits while others are switched off. This facility provides freedom of movement upstairs, for instance, while the downstairs is fully guarded.

A control unit must be tamper-proof so that it will sound the alarm if disarming is attempted by any means other than with a key or digital code. Most systems are wired directly to the consumer unit but should be fitted with an additional battery in case of power failure.

Detectors
All entrances can be fitted with magnetic switches, which sound the alarm when broken by someone opening a door or window. Small detectors sense the vibration caused by an attempted entry, including breaking glass. They must be accurately placed and set to differentiate between an intrusion and other types of vibration from external sources.

A pressure mat activates the alarm when a person stands on it, closing two metallic strips. A mat can be placed under a carpet in the vicinity of a likely target or possible means of entry. Although efficient, pressure mats are not so popular nowadays, as experienced thieves are able to detect their presence.

Scanning devices
Sensors can be placed strategically to scan a wide area using infra red, ultrasonic or radio waves to detect movement or human presence. This type of detector is useful in a small apartment and can be self-contained, mains- or battery-operated.

The alarm
Most alarms are bells or sirens mounted on an outside wall. More sophisticated versions switch off after about twenty minutes but continue signalling with a flashing light. Some will automatically re-arm themselves. A system can transmit a warning directly to the police or a monitoring centre for swift response to a break-in.

Whatever alarm is incorporated, it must be capable of being triggered by an attempt to tamper with it by cutting wires or dismantling.

Personal attack button
Most systems provide the option of a button situated near the front door or in a bedroom, which you can operate in the event of an attack. It trips the alarm even when the rest of the system is switched off.

DIY systems

If you want to avoid the cost of professional installation, there are several DIY alarm systems on the market, which are quick and easy to install with minimal disruption to the house. Choose carefully, as many kits are inadequate for any but the smallest house.

A good system will enable you to select the type and number of detectors you require and should incorporate a reliable, tamper-proof control unit to avoid false alarms. Fitting and wiring instructions are provided with all kits but you'd be wise to discuss the procedure with the supplier so you know what the installation involves.

SEE ALSO

Details for: ▷

Rack bolts	241
Crime prevention officer	238
Consumer unit	296
Woodworker's tools	462-473
Metalworker's tools	486-491

PROTECTING YOUR HOUSE AGAINST FIRE

No one needs to be reminded about the potential risk of fire, yet nearly all domestic fires are caused by careless disregard of the dangers. Many could be prevented by simple awareness and sensible precautions.

SEE ALSO

◁ Details for:
Fire-check doors	194
Checking electrics	306-307
Fitting sockets	308-313
Bell wire	322
Fire prevention officer	238

Fire blanket and extinguisher
Fit one of each in the kitchen and garage.

Smoke detector
A detector will give you early warning of a fire when it can still be tackled easily.

Avoiding the risks

Make sure all your electrical installations and equipment are safe and in good order (◁). Remove all plugs from sockets at night, especially the one connected to the television set. Don't overload power sockets with adaptors – fit more sockets instead (◁). Don't trail long extension leads and flexes under carpets or rugs: if they become damaged they could overheat and start a serious fire.

Never leave a fire unguarded, for safety's sake. And remember: you could be prosecuted if a young child is injured as a result of an unguarded fire or heater. Don't dry clothes in front of a fire; they could easily fall onto the elements or flames.

Take particular care with smoking materials. Empty ashtrays at night, but dampen the contents first, before discarding them in a waste bin. Don't rest ashtrays on chair arms: a burning cigarette's centre of gravity shifts as it burns and could topple off and ignite carpets and upholstery. Never smoke in bed: many fires are caused by smokers falling asleep and setting light to the bedclothes.

Keep a workshop or garage clear of rubbish or shavings and dispose of oily rags – it's been known for them to ignite spontaneously. Store flammable chemicals and paints outside if possible, not under the stairs.

As a means of fighting a fire, install an all-purpose fire extinguisher and a fire blanket adjacent to the cooker, and another set in the garage. The FPO will recommend reliable equipment for domestic use. Don't buy inferior items in preference.

Providing escape routes

Your first responsibility is to the occupants of a dwelling, so ensure that your family can escape safely from a burning building. Close internal doors before you go to bed to contain a fire but don't lock them: a locked internal door rarely deters a burglar.

Although you should not leave a key in an external lock, keep it conveniently close by but out of reach of the door or window. Make sure everyone knows where the key is kept and make a habit of returning it to the same place after it has been used.

It is most important to keep stairs and hallways free from obstructions as it may be difficult to see in dense smoke. In particular, avoid using an oil heater to warm these areas in case it is knocked over during an escape and spreads the fire further.

Communal staircases to flats are especially important, so talk to your neighbours about keeping them clear. Fire-check doors are a wise precaution and may be required by law in dwellings of three stories or more (◁). Never use a lift to effect an escape.

Tackling a fire

Don't attempt to tackle a fire yourself unless you discover it early – and then only with the proper equipment. Throwing water onto an electrical fire, for instance, could be fatal.

Fat fire
When cooking fat or oil reaches a certain temperature it ignites. Unattended chip pans are one of the most common causes of domestic fires. Don't attempt to move a burning pan:
● Turn off the source of heat.
● Smother the fire with a glass fibre blanket or soak a towel in water and drop it over the pan.

● Let the pan cool for half an hour before removing the towel or blanket.
● If the fire is not extinguished immediately, call the fire brigade.

Chimney fire
If a chimney catches fire, phone the fire brigade then stand a guard in the fireplace. Remove hearth rugs in case burning material drops to the grate.

Clothes on fire
If a person's clothes catch fire, throw him to the ground and roll him in a blanket or rug. Seek medical attention in the event of burns.

You can't rely on your sense of smell to rouse you in the event of a fire – the toxic gases produced could render you unconscious before you have a chance to raise the alarm. A smoke detector will identify the presence of smoke, even before flames start, and will sound a shrill 85 decibel warning. Although you can have detectors wired into an alarm system, self-contained battery-operated units are easy to fix.

There are two types of detector. Photo-electric devices shine a beam of light into an open chamber, which just misses a photo-electric cell; if smoke fills the chamber, light is dispersed into the cell and the alarm sounds.

Ionization types have a minute radioactive source, which ionizes the air in an open chamber so it carries an electric current: smoke entering the chamber spoils the conductivity and an alarm is sounded.

Photo-electric types can detect smoke from smouldering or slow-burning fires, while ionization types are more attuned to smoke from fast flaming fires. Combination detectors are made. Choose a detector with a light which shines to guide you to an exit.

Siting a smoke detector
The best place to position a smoke detector is on the ceiling between potential sources of fire – the kitchen or garage, for instance – and a hall between the sleeping areas.

The detector should be kept out of draughts, away from shower areas (steam can trigger the alarm) and fixed either to the wall or ceiling no closer than 150mm (6in) to a wall or ceiling angle as the 'dead air space' in the corner may prevent efficient working.

Fix the device's baseplate to the wall with screws driven into wallplugs, or directly to the ceiling joists. Clip in the battery – usually a 9 volt zinc carbon or alkaline type – and test the alarm. The detector cover simply clips on.

Linking detectors
To link several smoke detectors, first fix them to the wall or ceiling then connect them with lengths of twin bell wire (◁) to the connector blocks within the devices. Run the wire by the most inconspicuous route round the house, clipping it at 300mm (1ft) intervals to the joists in the loft space or to the tops of picture rails, skirtings and around door frames.

5

INFESTATION	246
INSECT INFESTATION	246
ANIMAL INFESTATION	248
ROT	249
WET AND DRY ROT	249
DAMP	251
DAMP:CAUSES	251
PENETRATING DAMP	252
RISING DAMP	253
CONDENSATION	254
DAMP-PROOF COURSES	256
CELLARS	258

INFESTATION/ROT & DAMP

INFESTATION: INSECTS

Our homes and surroundings are often invaded by various voracious insect pests: Some of them are quite harmless, although they cause a great deal of annoyance and even alarm, but certain insects can seriously weaken the structure of a building and it is these pests which often go unnoticed until the damage is done. At the first signs of infestation, try to identify and eradicate the cause as quickly as possible, before it escalates.

SEE ALSO

◁ Details for:
Surveyor   17
Lifting boards   177

Wood-boring insects
(Not to scale)
These can destroy the timbers and furniture in your home – eradicate immediately!

Furniture beetle

Deathwatch beetle

House longhorn beetle

Weevil

Attack by woodworm

Woodworm is the term used to describe all kinds of wood-boring insects, although the most common is the furniture beetle. The adult insect is a brown beetle about 2mm (⅛in) long, but the damage is caused by its larvae, which feed on the sapwood of most household timbers.

The beetle, which is most active in early summer, lays its eggs in the crevices of bare timber. When the grubs hatch, they burrow into the wood for up to three years until they pupate just below the surface. The new adult emerges by chewing its way out, leaving the familiar round flight hole. These 1 to 2mm (about 1/16in) diameter holes are normally the first signs of infestation, but there may be several generations of woodworm active inside the timber.

The furniture beetle is said to inhabit three-quarters of British homes so most outbreaks of woodworm are almost certainly due to this particular pest – but there are other wood-boring insects which can cause even more damage. The deathwatch and house longhorn beetles bore much larger holes, from 3 to 6mm (⅛ to ¼in) in diameter. Authorities are anxious to control the spread of these rarer insects, so contact your local Environmental Health Department if you suspect their presence.

Another common insect pest is the weevil, which damages wood in two ways: both adults and grubs burrow into all types of timber, but only when it is already under attack by decay, and in an extremely moist condition.

Locating woodworm
Check the unfinished parts of your furniture, particularly plywood drawer bottoms and backs of cabinets, as woodworm has a taste for the glues used in their manufacture. The timber frames of upholstered pieces of furniture are another common habitat for the pest – likewise any form of wickerwork.

It is the structural timbers of the house where woodworm can do the most harm. Inspect the roof timbers, stairs, floorboards and joists. However, the unpainted under-edges of doors and skirtings are favourite breeding grounds, as is the top edge of a picture rail.

Where the flight holes are dark in colour, the wood may have been treated already, but clean holes, particularly when surrounded by fine dust, called 'frass', are signs of recent activity. If the signs are extensive, push a knife blade into the infected timbers. If the wood crumbles the infestation is serious and the woodwork must be cut away and replaced: seek the advice of a specialist contractor immediately. You can, nevertheless, treat basically sound timber yourself.

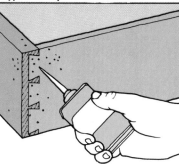

A typical example of woodworm attack

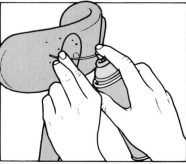

Treat a small outbreak with a can of fluid

Use aerosol to flood holes then spray wood

Treating woodworm

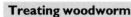

Where woodworm is located by a surveyor while inspecting a potential purchase, a mortgage company will insist that you hire a reputable specialist to eradicate the pest because their work carries a 30-year guarantee. Similarly, if you detect woodworm in your present home, you'd be wise to at least have it inspected by a similar company, who will advise you on the extent of the damage (it's not always entirely obvious to the untrained eye), and quote a price for treatment. There is normally no charge for this service.

Any but the most serious infestation can be easily treated using an insecticidal wood preserver. Most fluids are flammable, so don't smoke while applying it, and extinguish naked lights. Wear protective gloves and, when spraying timbers, a facemask and goggles. The initial smell of the fluid is unpleasant but fades gradually.

Treating house timbers ▷
Hire a spray lance and compressor to treat woodworm in the structural timbers. Lift several floorboards and use the lance to treat the joists and undersides of the boards. Don't forget to spray the boards you have removed before replacing them.

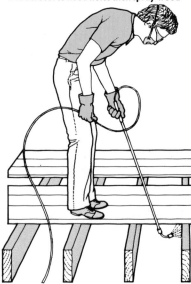

WOODWORM

Dealing with a minor outbreak

Treating woodworm in furniture is a fairly simple task: use a can with a pointed nozzle or an aerosol with a special applicator to inject woodworm fluid into holes every 75 to 100mm (3 to 4in). As the tunnels are connected, that will be enough to penetrate deeply.

Continue the treatment by painting all unfinished timber with fluid. There is no need to paint a polished surface, although the fluid will not harm it.

Use the aerosol without its injector to coat wickerwork or the inside of confined spaces.

After treatment, flight holes can be filled with cellulose filler, or for show-wood, use wax crayons melted into a tin to match the colour. Press the wax into each hole with a filling knife.

Treating structural timbers

It's possible to treat timbers by flooding on the fluid using a brush, but it's more effective to spray them. Hire a sprayer which will produce a coarse spray; you'll need an extended lance to reach under floors and up into roof timbers.

Remove insulation from between ceiling joists and vacuum the dust so that the fluid can penetrate the wood. Cover the water cistern and check that electrical wiring is sound and properly insulated. Have rubber-insulated wiring replaced before spraying (▷).

All exposed timbers must be soaked but take care not to leave puddles in an attic as they might stain the ceiling below. If this should happen, let it dry and prime the stain with aluminium sealer (▷).

To treat floors, lift every fourth floorboard so that you can spray all the joists and the underside of the boards. Spray the tops of the boards, too. It will take two to three weeks for the timber to dry out thoroughly, but you shouldn't lay impervious floorcoverings for about six months.

Preventative treatment

Any new timber can be treated with woodworm fluid to prevent attack. Once dry, it can be decorated in the normal way. Furniture can be protected with insecticidal polishes – if you buy an old piece of furniture, it's best to treat it if there are signs of infestation, in case the outbreak spreads.

If you take a door off its hinges, take the opportunity to paint the bottom edge, as woodworm doesn't attack painted timber.

ERADICATING OTHER INSECT PESTS

Insecticides can be dangerous if allowed to contaminate food and they are also harmful to honey bees, so follow the manufacturer's instructions carefully when using them to eradicate insect pests of any kind.

ANTS

The common black ant will enter a house foraging for food. Once established, the workers follow well-defined trails. In summer, great numbers of winged ants emerge from the nest to mate but the swarming is over in a matter of hours, and the ants themselves are harmless. If winged ants stray into the house, they can be overcome with an aerosol insecticidal spray.

To locate the nest, follow the trail of ants. It will be situated under a path, at the base of a wall, in the lawn or under a flat stone, perhaps 6m (20ft) from the house. Destroy the nest by pouring boiling water into the entrances. If this will damage plants, use an insecticidal dust or spray.

WASPS

Wasps are beneficial in spring and early summer as they feed on garden pests, but later in the year they destroy soft fruit. They will also kill bees and raid the hive for honey. Wasps sting when aroused or frightened.

Trap foraging wasps in open jam jars containing a mixture of jam, water and detergent. Flying wasps can be killed with an aerosol fly spray.

You can destroy wasps at the nest by depositing insecticidal powder near the entrances and areas where insects alight. Approaching a nest can be hazardous, so tie a spoon to a cane to extend your reach. Alternatively, use a smoke generator where there is no risk of fire. Light a pellet, place it in the entrance and seal the opening.

Treat a wasp sting with a cold compress soaked in witch-hazel or use an anti-histamine cream or spray.

FLIES

According to the species, flies breed in rotting vegetables, manure, decaying meat and offal. They can carry the eggs of parasitic worms and spread disease by leaving small black spots of vomit and excreta on foodstuffs.

Cover food and keep refuse sealed in newspaper or plastic bin liners. Gauze screens fitted over windows and bead curtains hung in open doorways will prevent flies entering the house.

An aerosol fly spray will deal with small numbers but for swarming flies in a roof space, for instance, use an insecticidal smoke generator from a hardware store or chemist. Large numbers in a living room can be sucked into a vacuum cleaner: suck up some insecticidal powder and wait a few hours before emptying.

COCKROACHES

It is rare to find cockroaches in domestic buildings, but they can occur where there's a supply of food and water in warm conditions. Cockroaches are unhygienic, and smell unpleasant.

Being nocturnal feeders, cockroaches hide during the day in crevices in walls, behind cupboards and especially under cookers, fridges or near central heating pipes, where it is warmest. A serious outbreak should be dealt with by professionals, but you can lay a finely dusted barrier of insecticidal powder between suspected daytime haunts and supplies of food. Don't sprinkle insecticides near food itself. Use a paintbrush to stipple powder into crevices and under skirting boards. When you have eradicated the pests, fill cracks and gaps to prevent return.

SILVER FISH

Silver fish are tapered, wingless insects about 12mm (½in) long. They like moist conditions found in kitchens, bathrooms and cellars. You may find them behind wallpaper, where they feed on the paste, or in bookshelves because they also eat paper. Use an insecticidal spray or powder in these locations.

SEE ALSO

Details for: ▷
Aluminium sealer	43
Replacing wiring	302-305
Checking electrics	306-307

Typical household pests
(Not to scale)
The insects shown below are more of a nuisance and a health hazard than a threat to the structure of your house.

Common black ant

Wasp

Housefly

Cockroach

Silver fish

INFESTATION: ANIMALS

SEE ALSO

◁ Details for:
Spraying preservatives   247

Rat damage to plug

Rat damage to electric cable

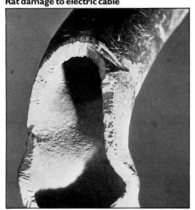

Rat damage to pipework

Domestic mouse
Not a serious threat to
health but they are
unhygienic.

Common rat
A serious health risk.
Seek expert advice.

Bat
Bats are completely
harmless and should not
be disturbed.

Insects aren't the only pests to set up home in your house: mice and rats can be a menace, especially in houses that offer plenty of underfloor runs, where they can live and prosper uninterrupted and find a plentiful supply of food by invading your living quarters. Mice are a nuisance, but rats can be a positive health hazard and eradication is vital. Even bats are known to shelter inside houses – usually occupying the roof space – and although they're harmless, you might not relish sharing your home with them; but they are protected by law.

Mice

Mice will be attracted by fallen food scraps so the best remedy is to keep the floors spotlessly clean. However, mice will move readily from house to house through the roof spaces, wall cavities and under floors, so it is sometimes difficult to eradicate them completely. Contact your local Environmental Health Department if the mice persist.

Ready-poisoned bait can be obtained, which you should sprinkle onto a piece of paper or card. In this way, uneaten bait can be removed simply. Keep pets and children away from the bait. If signs of mice are still evident after three weeks you should resort to a trap. Humane traps capture mice alive in a cage, so that you can deposit them elsewhere, or you can use the spring-loaded snap-traps.

Most people set too few traps. Ideally, place them every 2m (6ft) across mouse runs. The best place is against the skirting, facing the wall. Bait traps with flour, porridge oats or chocolate moulded onto the bait hook. Dispose of the mouse bodies by burying, burning or flushing down the WC.

Rats

Serious rat infestation occurs rarely in the average domestic situation but they can be a problem in rural areas or near rivers and docks. They can be killed with anti-coagulant poisons, but as rats are a health hazard, always contact the Environmental Health Department for expert advice.

Bats

Bats prefer to roost in uninhabited structures – farm buildings, caves, mines and tunnels – but occasionally they will inhabit domestic housing. They do not constitute a health hazard in any way; their droppings are dry insect skeletons and they do not gnaw at wood or paintwork. In fact, they are an advantage in a roof space, as they will feed on woodworm beetles.

Bats are becoming very rare and are now a protected species. It is illegal to kill or injure a bat, disturb its roosting place or block its means of access. If you are alarmed by their presence, contact the Nature Conservancy Council for advice. You must inform the same authority if you plan to spray wood preservatives in a roof space inhabited by bats in case it harms them.

If a bat should enter a living space, try to keep calm. They will avoid you if possible – and they don't become entangled in hair, as the old wives' tale suggests. Open all doors and windows and allow the bat to escape. A crawling bat can be picked up carefully in gloved hands and put outside.

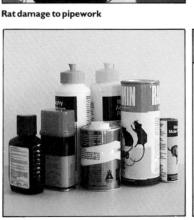

HANDLING POISONS SAFELY

Poisons designed to eradicate rodents are equally deadly to humans so it is most important to follow the manufacturer's handling and storage instructions to the letter. Make sure they are always out of the reach of children, and where pets or other animals cannot get to them. Never store them under the kitchen sink where they might be mistaken for household products, or anywhere else where food could become contaminated. In the case of accidental consumption by animals or humans, keep the container so that the poison can be readily identified by a vet or doctor. Some containers are colour-coded specially for the purpose. Wear protective gloves whenever you handle poisons and chemicals.

DRY AND WET ROT

Rot occurs in unprotected household timbers, fences and outbuildings, which are subjected to damp. Fungal spores, which are always present, multiply and develop in these conditions until eventually the timber is destroyed. Fungal attack can be serious, requiring immediate attention to avoid very costly structural repairs. There are two main scourges: wet and dry rot.

Recognizing rot

Signs of fungal attack are easy enough to detect but it is important to be able to identify certain strains which are much more damaging than others.

Mould growth

White furry deposits or black spots on timber, plaster or wallpaper are mould growths; usually these are a result of condensation. When they are wiped or scraped from the surface, the structure shows no sign of physical deterioration apart from staining. Cure the source of the damp conditions and treat the affected area with a solution of 16 parts warm water: 1 part bleach (▷).

Wet rot

Wet rot occurs in timber with a high moisture content. As soon as the cause is eliminated, further deterioration is arrested. It frequently attacks the framework of doors and windows which have been neglected enabling rainwater to penetrate joints or between brickwork and adjacent timbers. Peeling paintwork is often the first sign, which when removed, reveals timber that is spongy when wet but dark brown and crumbly when dry. In advanced stages, the grain will have split and thin, dark brown fungal strands will be in evidence on the timber. Treat wet rot as soon as practicable.

Dry rot

Once it has taken hold, dry rot is a most serious form of decay. Urgent treatment is essential. It will attack timber with a much lower moisture content than wet rot, but – unlike wet rot, which thrives outdoors as well as indoors – only in poorly ventilated, confined spaces indoors.

Dry rot exhibits various different characteristics depending on the extent of its development. It sends out fine, pale grey tubules in all directions, even through masonry, to seek out and infect other drier timbers: it actually pumps water from damp timber and can progress at an alarming rate. The strands are accompanied by white cotton wool-like growths called mycelium in very damp conditions. When established, dry rot develops wrinkled, pancake-shaped fruiting bodies, which produce rust red spores that are expelled to rapidly cover surrounding timber and masonry. Infested timbers become brown and brittle, exhibiting cracks across and along the grain until it breaks up into cube-like pieces. You may also detect a strong, musty, mushroom-like smell associated with the fungus.

Wet rot - treat it at your earliest opportunity.

Dry rot - urgent treatment is essential.

TREATING ROT

Dealing with wet rot

Having eliminated the cause of the damp, cut away and replace badly damaged wood, then paint the new and surrounding woodwork with three liberal applications of fungicidal wood preservative. Brush the liquid well into the joints and end grain.

Before decorating, you can apply a wood hardener to reinforce slightly damaged timbers, then follow six hours later with wood filler to rebuild the surface. Repaint as normal (▷).

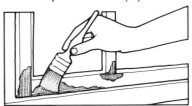

Paint rotted timbers with wood hardener

Dealing with dry rot

Dry rot requires more drastic action and should be treated by a specialist contractor unless the outbreak is minor and self-contained. Remember that dry rot can penetrate masonry: look under the floorboards in adjacent rooms before you are satisfied with the extent of the infection; check cavity walls for signs of rot.

Eliminate the source of water and ensure adequate ventilation in roof spaces or under the floors by unblocking or replacing air bricks. Cut out all infected timber up to at least 450mm (1ft 6in) beyond the last visible sign of rot. Chop plaster from nearby walls, following the strands. Continue for another 450mm (1ft 6in) beyond the extent of the growth. Collect all debris in plastic bags and burn it.

Use a fungicidal preservative fluid to kill remaining spores. Wire brush the masonry then apply three liberal brush-coats to all timber, brickwork and plaster within 1.5m (5ft) of the infected area. Alternatively, hire a coarse sprayer and go over the same area three times.

If a wall was penetrated by strands of dry rot, drill regularly spaced but staggered holes into it from both sides. Angle the holes downwards so that fluid will collect in them to saturate the wall internally. Patch holes after treatment.

Treat replacement timbers and immerse the end grain in a bucket of fluid for five to ten minutes. When you come to make good the wall, you should apply a zinc-oxychloride plaster (▷).

SEE ALSO

Details for: ▷
Mould growth	52
Painting wood	53,76
Plaster	149-152
Repairing rotten frames	190-191,205-206
Preventing damp	251-258

ROT: PREVENTATIVE TREATMENT

SEE ALSO

◁ Details for:
Painting wood	53,76
Varnishing	53,82
Fire precautions	244
Insect attack	246
Wet and dry rot	249

Fungal attack can be so damaging that it is well worth taking precautions to prevent it occurring. Regularly decorate and maintain window and door frames, where moisture can penetrate; seal around them with mastic. Provide adequate ventilation between floors and ceilings. Do the same in the loft. Check and eradicate any plumbing leaks and other sources of damp, and you'll be less likely to experience the stranglehold rot can apply.

Looking after timberwork

Existing and new timbers can be treated with a preservative. Brush and spray two or three applications to standing timbers, paying particular attention to joints and end grain.

Immersing timbers
Timber in contact with the ground would benefit from prolonged immersion in preservative. Stand fence posts on end in a bucket of fluid for 10 minutes. For other timbers, make a shallow bath from loose bricks and line it with thick polythene sheet. Pour preservative into the trough and immerse the timbers, weighing them down with bricks (**1**). To empty the bath, sink a bucket at one end of the trough, then remove the bricks adjacent to it so the fluid pours out (**2**).

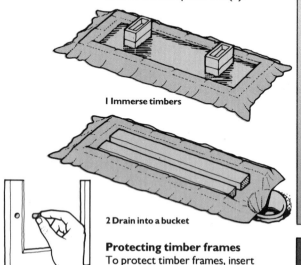

1 Immerse timbers

2 Drain into a bucket

Protecting joints
Place preservative tablets close to the joints of a frame

Protecting timber frames
To protect timber frames, insert preservative in solid tablet form into holes drilled at regular 50mm (2in) intervals in a staggered pattern. If the timber becomes wet, the tablets dissolve, placing preservative exactly where it is needed. Fill the holes with wood filler and paint as normal (◁).

WOOD PRESERVATIVES

There are numerous types of wood preservatives for use inside and out.

Choose the correct one for the timber you want to protect:

CLEAR PRESERVATIVE

Clear liquids are specially formulated to protect timber from dry or wet rot. Alternatively, use an all-purpose fluid, which also provides protection against wood-boring insects. Paint or varnish the surface when dry.

COLOURED PRESERVATIVES

Tinted preservatives protect sound timbers against fungal and insect attack and stain the wood at the same time. Some are harmful to plants, however, so check before you buy. There is a choice of brown shades intended to simulate common hardwoods and one specifically for red cedar.

GREEN PRESERVATIVE

Green preservative is normally harmless to plants when it dries, so it is used for horticultural timbers. It can be used to eradicate rot and insect attack as well as protecting sound household timbers. Its colour helps to identify treated timbers in the future. However, the colour is due to its copper content and is not a permanent colouring agent when used outdoors. Its protective properties are unaffected, even when the colour is washed out by heavy rain.

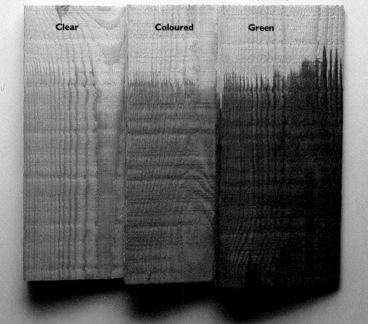

Clear   Coloured   Green

SAFETY WITH PRESERVATIVES

All preservatives are flammable so do not smoke while using, and extinguish naked lights.

Wear protective gloves at all times when applying preservatives and wear a facemask when using these liquids indoors.

Ensure good ventilation when the liquid is drying, and do not sleep in a freshly treated room for two nights to allow the fumes to dissipate fully.

Damp, or rather the symptoms of it, can be most distressing both in terms of your health and the condition of your home. Try to locate the source of the problem as quickly as possible before it promotes its even more damaging side effects – wet and dry rot. Unfortunately, this is sometimes easier said than done, as one form of damp may obscure another, or may appear in an unfamiliar guise. The two main classifications are penetrating and rising damp, although condensation may appear as one or the other.

SEE ALSO

Details for: ▷
Wet and dry rot   249-250

Principal causes of penetrating damp
1 Broken gutter
2 Leaking downpipe
3 Missing roof tile
4 Damaged flashing
5 Faulty pointing
6 Porous brick
7 Cracked masonry
8 Cracked render
9 Blocked drip groove
10 Defective seals around frames
11 Missing weatherboard
12 Bridged cavity

Principal causes of rising damp
● Missing DPC or DPM
● Damaged DPC or DPM
● DPC too low
● Bridged DPC
● Earth piled above DPC

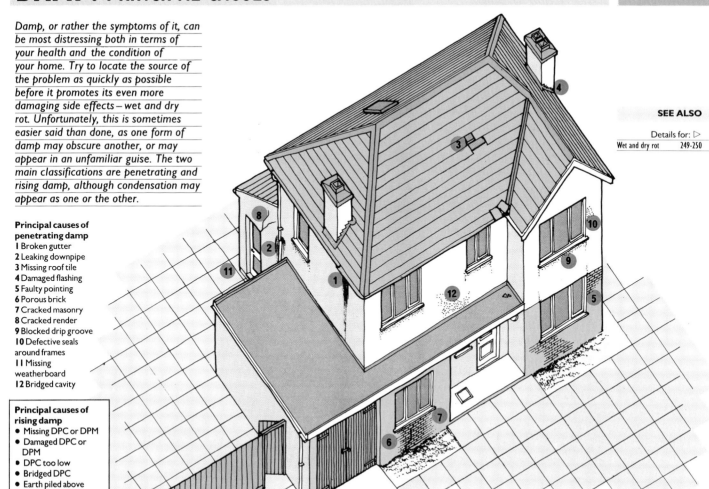

Penetrating damp

Penetrating damp is the result of water permeating the structure of the house from outside. The symptoms occur with wet weather only. After a few dry days, damp patches dry out but frequently leave stains.

Isolated patches are caused by a heavy deposit of water in one area and should pinpoint the source fairly accurately. General dampness usually indicates that the wall itself has become porous, but it could equally be caused by some other problem.

Penetrating damp occurs more often in older homes with solid walls. Relatively modern houses built with a cavity between two thinner brick skins are less likely to suffer from penetrating damp, unless the cavity is bridged in one of several ways.

Rising damp

Rising damp is caused by water soaking up from the ground into the floors and walls of the house. Most houses are protected with an impervious barrier built into the walls and under concrete floors so that water cannot permeate above a certain level.

If the damp-proof course (DPC) in the walls or the membrane (DPM) in a floor breaks down, water leaks into the upper structure. Alternatively, there may be something forming a bridge across the barrier so that water is able to flow around it. Some older houses were built without a DPC.

Rising damp is confined to solid floors and the lower sections of walls. It is a constant problem even in dry weather but becomes worse with prolonged wet weather.

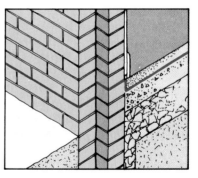

DPC in a solid wall
A layer of impervious material is built into a joint between brick courses, 150mm (6in) above the ground.

DPC and DPM in a cavity wall structure
The damp-proof membrane in a concrete floor is linked to the DPC protecting the inner leaf of the wall. The outer leaf has its own damp-proof course.

PENETRATING DAMP: PRINCIPAL CAUSES

SEE ALSO

◁ Details for:
Repointing	45
Waterproofing brick	46
Repairing bricks	46
Defective render	47
Exterior paints	64
Rendering	168-171
Replacing tiles	226-227
Parapet walls	229
Flashings	232-233
Guttering	234-236
Downpipes	234-236

CAUSE	SYMPTOMS	REMEDY
Broken or blocked gutter Rainwater overflows the gutter, typically at the joints of old metal types, and saturates the wall directly below, so that it is prevented from drying out normally.	Damp patches appearing near the ceiling in upstairs rooms. Mould forming immediately behind the leak.	Clear leaves and silt from the gutters. Repair the gutters, or replace a faulty system with a maintenance-free plastic set-up (◁).
Broken or blocked downpipes A downpipe that has cracked or rusted douses the wall immediately behind the leak. Leaves lodged behind the pipe at the fixing brackets will produce a similar effect eventually.	An isolated damp patch, often appearing halfway up the wall. Mould growth behind the pipe.	Repair or replace the defective downpipe, using a maintenance-free plastic type (◁). Clear the blockage.
Loose or broken roof tiles Defective tiles allow rainwater to penetrate the roof.	Damp patches appearing on upstairs ceilings, usually during a heavy downpour.	Replace the faulty tiles (◁), renewing any damaged roofing felt.
Damaged flashing The joins between the roof of a lean-to extension and the side wall of the house, or where a chimney stack emerges from the roof, are sealed with flashing strips, usually lead or zinc (or sometimes a mortar fillet). When the flashing cracks, peels or parts from its fixing, water trickles down the wall or down the chimney stack.	Damp patch on the ceiling extending from the wall or chimney breast; also on the chimney breast itself. Damp patch on the side wall near the join with the lean-to extension; damp patch on the lean-to ceiling itself.	Repair the existing flashing by refitting if it appears to be undamaged, or replace it with a similar material or a self-adhesive flashing strip (◁).
Faulty pointing Ageing mortar between bricks will eventually dry and fall out; water then penetrates the remaining jointing mortar to the inside of the wall.	Isolated damp patches or sometimes widespread dampness, depending on the extent of the deterioration.	Repoint the joints between bricks (◁) then treat the entire wall with water-repellent fluid or paint.
Porous bricks Bricks in good condition are weatherproof but old, soft bricks become porous and often lose their faces so that the whole wall is eventually saturated, particularly on an elevation that faces prevailing winds, or where some other drainage fault occurs.	Widespread damp on the inner face of exterior walls. A noticeable increase in damp during a downpour. Mould growth appearing on internal plaster and decorations.	Waterproof the exterior with a clear repellent fluid or exterior paint, or cement-render the surface (◁) where the deterioration is extensive.
Cracked brickwork A crack in a brick wall allows rainwater (or water from a leak) to seep inside then run to the inside face.	An isolated damp patch, which may appear on a chimney breast if the stack is cracked.	Fill the cracks and replace any damaged brickwork (◁).
Defective render Cracked or blown render encourages rainwater to seep between it and brick wall behind. The water is prevented from evaporating and so becomes absorbed by the wall.	An isolated damp patch, which may become widespread. The trouble can persist for some time after rain ceases.	Fill and reinforce the crack. Hack off the damaged or blown render, patch it with new sand-cement render, then weatherproof the wall by applying exterior paint (◁).
Damaged coping If the coping stone on top of a roof parapet wall (◁) is missing, or the joints are open, water can penetrate the wall.	Damp patches on the ceiling against the wall just below the parapet.	Bed a new stone on fresh mortar and make good the joints.

PENETRATING DAMP: PRINCIPAL CAUSES

CAUSE	SYMPTOMS	REMEDY
Blocked drip groove Exterior window sills should have a groove running longitudinally on the underside. When rainwater runs under, it falls off at the groove before reaching the wall. If the groove becomes bridged with layers of paint or moss, water will soak the wall behind.	Damp patches along the underside of a window frame. Rotting wooden sill on the inside and outside. Mould growth appearing on the inside face of the wall below the window.	Rake out the drip groove. Nail a batten to the underside of a wooden sill to form a deflection for drips (▷).
Failed seals around windows and door frames Timber frames shrink, pulling the pointing from around the edge so that rainwater can penetrate the gap.	Damp surrounding frames and rotting woodwork. Sometimes the gap itself is obvious where the mortar has fallen out.	Repair the frames (▷). Seal around the edge with mastic (▷).
No weatherboard An angled weatherboard across the bottom of a door should shed water clear of the threshold and prevent water running under the door.	Damp floorboards just inside the door. Rotting at the base of the door frame.	Fit a weatherboard even if there are no obvious signs of damage. (▷). Repair the frame (▷).
Bridged wall cavity During building, mortar inadvertently dropped onto a wall tie connecting the inner and outer leaves of a cavity wall allows water to bridge the gap.	An isolated damp patch appearing anywhere on the wall, particularly after a heavy downpour.	Open up the wall and remove the mortar droppings (▷), then waterproof the wall externally with paint or clear repellent (▷).

SEE ALSO

Details for: ▷

Waterproofing bricks	46
New DPM	182,258
Weatherboard	187
Repairing frames	190-191,205-206
Drip batten	254
Sealing frames	254
Bridged cavity	254
New DPC	256-257

RISING DAMP: PRINCIPAL CAUSES

CAUSE	SYMPTOMS	REMEDY
No DPC or DPM If a house was built without either a damp-proof course or damp-proof membrane, water is able to soak up from the ground.	Widespread damp at skirting level. Damp concrete floor surface.	Fit a new DPC or DPM (▷).
Broken DPC or DPM If either the DPC or DPM has deteriorated, water will penetrate at that isolated point.	Possibly isolated but spreading damp at skirting level.	Repair or replace the DPC or DPM (▷).
DPC too low The DPC may not be the necessary 150mm (6in) above ground level. Heavy rain is able to splash above the DPC and soak the wall surface.	Damp at skirting level but only where the ground is too high.	Lower the level of the ground outside. If it's a path or patio, cut a 150mm (6in) wide trench and fill with gravel, which drains rapidly.
Bridged DPC Exterior render taken below the DPC, or fallen mortar at the foot of a cavity wall (within the cavity), allows moisture to cross over to the inside.	Widespread damp at, and just above, skirting level.	Hack off render to expose DPC. Remove several bricks and rake out debris from the cavity (▷).
Debris piled against wall A flower bed, rockery or area of paving built against a wall bridges the DPC. Building material and garden refuse left there will do likewise.	Damp at skirting level in area of bridge only, or spreading from that point.	Remove the earth or debris and allow the wall to dry out naturally.

DPC too low

Render bridges DPC

Earth piled over DPC

253

CURING DAMP

CONDENSATION

SEE ALSO

◁ Details for:
Wallpapering	94-96
Repointing	45
Waterproofing bricks	46
Painting wood	53,76
Varnishing	53,82

Remedies for different forms of damp are suggested throughout the Principal Causes boxes on the previous pages, and you will find detailed instructions for carrying out many of them in other sections of the book, where they contribute to other factors such as heat loss, poor ventilation, and spoiled decoration. The information below supplements those instructions, by providing advice on measures solely to eradicate damp.

WATERPROOFING WALLS

Applying a water repellent to the outside of a wall not only prevents water infusion but also it improves insulation, reducing the possibility of interstitial condensation: this occurs when water vapour from inside the house penetrates the wall until it reaches the damp, colder part of the structure within the brickwork, where it condenses and eventually migrates back to the inner surface, causing stains and mould growth.

There are several damp-proofing liquids for painting on the inside of a wall, but they should be considered a temporary measure only, as they do not cure the source of the problem. Apply two full brush coats over an area appreciably larger than the present extent of the damp. Once dry, you can decorate the wall as required with paint or a wallcovering.

Alternatively, apply a waterproof laminate or paper. It is hung using standard wallpapering techniques (◁) using the manufacturer's own primer and adhesive. However, seams must be lapped by 12mm (½in) to prevent moisture penetration. Apply paint or paper over the laminate, or better still, panel it to hide the seams.

PROVIDING A DRIP MOULDING

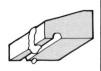

1 Water drips to ground

2 A bridged groove

3 Drip moulding

Because water cannot flow uphill, a drip moulding on the underside of an external window sill forces water to drip to the ground before it reaches the wall behind (**1**). When decorating, scrape the old paint or moss from the groove before it provides a bridge (**2**).

You can add a drip moulding to a wooden sill that does not have a pre-cut drip groove by pinning and gluing a 6mm square (¼in square) hardwood strip 35mm (1½in) from the front edge (**3**). Paint or varnish the strip along with the window sill.

SEALING AROUND WINDOW FRAMES

Apply mastic with an applicator gun

Scrape out old loose mortar from around the frame. Fill deep gaps with rolled paper or card then seal all round with a flexible mastic. Mastic is available in cartridges to fit an applicator gun, or in tubes, which you squeeze just like toothpaste. Cut the end off the nozzle, then run it down the side of the frame to form a continuous, even bead. If the gap is very wide, fill it with a second bead when the first has set. Most sealants form a skin and can be overpainted after a few hours although they are waterproof even without painting.

BRIDGED CAVITY

The simplest way to deal with a bridged wall cavity which allows water to flow to the inner leaf is to apply a water repellent to the outer surface.

However, this doesn't cure the cause, which may promote other damp conditions later. When it is convenient, when repointing perhaps, remove two or three bricks from the outside in the vicinity of the damp patch by chopping out the mortar around them. Use a small mirror and a torch to inspect the cavity. If you locate mortar lying on a wall tie, chip it off with a rod or opened metal coat hanger and replace the bricks.

Exposing a bridged wall tie
Remove a few bricks to chip mortar from a wall tie.

Air carries moisture as water vapour but its capacity depends on temperature. As it becomes warmer, air absorbs more water like a sponge. When water-laden air comes into contact with a surface that is colder than itself, it cools until it cannot any longer hold the water it has absorbed, and just like the sponge being squeezed, it condenses, depositing water in liquid form onto the surface.

Conditions for condensation

The air in a house is normally warm enough to hold water without reaching saturation point, but a great deal of moisture is also produced by using baths and showers, cooking and even breathing. In cold weather when the low temperature outside cools the external walls and windows below the temperature of the heated air inside, all that extra water runs down window panes and soaks into the wallpaper and plaster. Matters are made worse in the winter by sealing off windows and doors so that fresh air cannot replace humid air before it condenses.

Damp in a fairly new house which is in good condition is almost certainly due to condensation.

The root cause of condensation is rarely simple, as it is a result of a combination of air temperature, humidity, lack of ventilation and thermal insulation. Tackling one of them in isolation may transfer condensation elsewhere or even exaggerate the symptoms. However, the box opposite lists major contributing factors to the total problem.

Condensation appears first on cold glazing

CONDENSATION: PRINCIPAL CAUSES

CAUSE	SYMPTOMS	REMEDY
Insufficient heat The air in an unheated room may already be close to the point of saturation. (Raising the temperature increases the ability of the air to absorb moisture without condensing.)	General condensation.	Heat the room (but not with an oil heater, which produces moisture).
Oil heater An oil heater produces as much water vapour as the paraffin it burns, and condensation will form on windows, walls and ceilings.	General condensation in the room where the heater is used.	Substitute another form of heating.
Uninsulated walls and ceilings Moist air readily condenses on cold exterior walls and ceilings.	Widespread damp and mould. The line of ceiling joists is picked out as mould grows less well along these relatively 'warm' spots.	Install loft insulation (▷) and/or line the ceiling with insulating tiles or polystyrene lining (▷).
Cold bridge Even when a wall has cavity insulation, there can be a cold bridge across the lintel over windows and the solid brick down the sides.	Damp patches or mould surrounding the window frames.	Line the walls and window reveal with sheets of expanded polystyrene or foamed polyethylene.
Unlagged pipes Cold water pipes attract condensation. It is often confused with a leak when water collects and drips from the lowest point of a pipe run.	Line of damp on a ceiling or wall following the pipework. Isolated patch on a ceiling, where water drops from plumbing. Beads of moisture on the underside of a pipe.	Insulate the plumbing with proprietary foam lagging tubes or mineral-fibre wrapping (▷).
Cold windows Glass shows condensation usually before any other feature, due to the fact that it's very thin and constantly exposed to the elements.	Misted glass, or water collecting in pools at the bottom of the window pane.	Double-glaze the window (▷). If condensation occurs inside a secondary glazing system, place some silica gel crystals (which absorb moisture) in the cavity between panes (▷).
Sealed fireplace When a fireplace opening is blocked, the air trapped inside the flue cannot circulate and consequently it condenses on the inside, eventually soaking through the brickwork.	Damp patches appearing anywhere on the chimney breast.	Ventilate the chimney by inserting a grille at a low level in the blocked-up part of the fireplace (▷).
Loft insulation blocking airways If loft insulation blocks the spaces around the eaves, air cannot circulate in the roof space, and condensation is able to form.	Widespread mould affecting the timbers in the roof space.	Unblock the airways and, if possible, fit a ventilator grille in the soffit or install tile/slate vents (▷).
Condensation on recent building If you have carried out work involving new bricks, mortar and especially plaster, condensation may be the result of these materials exuding moisture as they dry out.	General condensation affecting walls, ceiling, windows and solid floors.	Wait for the new work to dry out, then review the situation, before decorating or otherwise treating.

SEE ALSO

Details for: ▷

Polystyrene lining	90
Lagging pipes	261
Loft insulation	265-266
Wall insulation	268-270
Double glazing	271-274
Secondary glazing	272-274
Chimney ventilation	275
Soffit grille	277
Tile/slate vents	277
Extractor fans	279-282
Dehumidifiers	283

INSERTING A DAMP-PROOF COURSE

When an old damp-proof course (DPC) has failed, or where none exists, the only certain remedy is to insert a new one. Of the four options available, chemical injection is the only method you should attempt yourself. Even then, consider whether it is cost-effective in the long run: rising damp can lead to other expensive repairs unless it is completely eradicated, so hiring a reputable company may prove to be a wise investment (they normally provide a 30-year guarantee). Ask for a detailed specification – known as an Agrément certificate – to ensure that the work is carried out to approved standards and check that the guarantee is covered by insurance in case the company goes out of business.

SEE ALSO

◁ Details for:
Rising damp   251

A physical DPC

A traditional DPC consists of a layer of impervious material incorporated into the wall during building at approximately 150mm (6in) – or three brick courses – above ground level. A similar DPC can be installed in an existing building by cutting out a mortar joint with a chain saw or grinding disc. Copper sheet, polythene or bituminous felt is inserted and the joint wedged and filled with fresh mortar. Considerable experience is required to avoid structurally weakening the wall, and there's always the risk of cutting through an electric cable and plumbing pipework. A physical DPC is costly to install but it is considered to be the most reliable method.

Electro-osmosis

This is a method utilizing the principle that a minute electrical charge will prevent water rising by capillary action. Copper electrodes are inserted into the wall and connected to earthing rods buried in the ground. Active systems are connected to the electrical supply but a passive system requires no power at all to operate. These are systems which can only be installed by a professional. Consider for thick walls, which may be difficult to treat by other means.

Porous tubes

Porous clay tubes are inserted into a row of closely spaced holes to increase the rate of evaporation before moisture rises to a higher level. This is a simple and cheap method.

A physical DPC: a joint is removed to insert impervious layer.

Electro-osmosis: a copper electrode is planted in the wall.

Porous tubes: the wall is drilled to receive the tubes.

INJECTING A CHEMICAL DPC

DAMP
DAMP PROOFING

The most widely practised method today is to inject a waterproofing chemical, usually silicone-based, to form a continuous barrier throughout the thickness of the wall. It is suitable for brick or stone walls up to 600mm (2ft) thick, and is straightforward to install yourself using hired equipment.

Preparing the wall for injection

If you want to carry out the injection work yourself, use a pressure injection machine, which can be hired. You will require 68 to 90 litres (15 to 20 gallons) of DPC fluid per 30m (100ft) of 225mm (9in) thick wall.

Remove skirtings and hack off plaster and render to a height of 450mm (1ft 6in) above the line of visible damp. Repair and repoint the brickwork with new mortar (▷).

Drilling the injection holes

Drill a row of holes about 150mm (6in) above external ground level, but below a suspended wooden floor or just above one of solid concrete. If the wall has an old DPC, set the new course just above it, but take care not to puncture it when drilling. Use a masonry drill of about 18 to 25mm (¾in to 1in) in diameter but not less than the injecting nozzle of the machine. If possible, drill an identical row of holes from both sides of a wall 225mm (9in) thick or greater, to provide a continuous DPC.

When drilling a 225mm (9in) solid brick wall, the holes should be at 112mm (4½in) centres, about 25mm (1in) below the upper-edge of a brick course. Angle them downwards slightly. Drill 75mm (3in) deep unless treatment is limited to one side only, when you should drill to a depth of 190mm (7½in). Treat each leaf of a cavity wall separately, drilling to a depth of 75mm (3in) in each one.

If the wall is made of impervious stone, drill into the mortar course around each stone block at the proposed DPC level, spacing the holes every 75mm (3in).

Injecting the fluid

There are various types of injection pump available, but most work in basically the same way. Usually you must insert the pump's filtered suction hose into the drum of chemical. Make sure that the valves controlling the injection nozzles are closed then connect the pump to the mains electrical supply.

Most machines have three nozzles. Connect them to the end of the hoses — if you're treating a thick wall, drill 75mm (3in) deep holes to begin with, and start with the shorter nozzles — and push them into the holes in the wall. Turn their wing nuts to secure them and form a seal (don't overtighten them or you may damage the expansion nipples at their tips). Open the control valves on the two nozzles then switch on the pump so the chemical circulates through the machine.

Bleed off some fluid through the third nozzle into a container to expel air from the system, by opening its valve. Switch it off again and insert in the wall. Re-open the valve and allow the fluid to be injected until it wets the surface of the bricks. Maintain the pressure at about 100 PSI (pounds per square inch) by adjusting the valve on the pump body.

Switch off all three valves then move them on to the next holes and repeat the procedure. When you reach the other end of the wall, switch off the pump then return to the starting point and drill the same holes to 190mm (7½in) deep. Swap the short injection nozzles for the longer 190mm (7½in) ones — you may need to wrap PTFE sealing tape round the threads (▷) — slot them into the wall, tighten their nuts, and inject the fluid.

Flush the machine through with white spirit after use to get rid of the fluid, which otherwise would 'cure' in the system, damaging the pump.

SEE ALSO

Details for: ▷	
Repointing	45
PTFE	354
Masonry drill	479

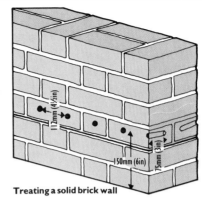

Treating a solid brick wall

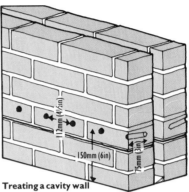

Treating a cavity wall

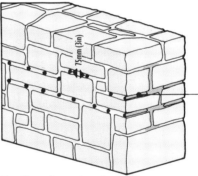

Treating an impervious stone wall

•At least one third thickness. Seek local professional advice.

◁ **Hiring the equipment**
Any tool hire specialist will supply you with all the necessary equipment and materials to inject a chemical DPC yourself. It is an economical method requiring careful work rather than experience. Flush the machine thoroughly before you return it.

DAMP-PROOFING A CELLAR

SEE ALSO

◁ Details for:
Efflorescence	44
Cleaning concrete	49
New DPM	182
Bonding agent	43
Repairing concrete	49
Rendering	168-171
Rising damp	251
Condensation	254-255
Ventilation	275-284
Cold chisel	480

Being at least partially below ground level, the walls and floors of a cellar or basement invariably suffer from damp to some extent. Because the problem cannot be tackled from the outside in the normal way, you will have to seal out the damp by treating the internal surfaces. Rising damp in concrete floors, whatever the situation, can be *treated as described below, but penetrating or rising damp in walls other than in a cellar should be cured at source: merely sealing the internal surface encourages the damp to penetrate elsewhere eventually. In addition, ensure a treated cellar is properly ventilated, and even heated to avoid condensation in the future.*

Treating the floor

If you are laying a new concrete floor, incorporate a damp-proof membrane (DPM) during its construction (◁). If the DPM was omitted or has failed in an existing floor, seal it with a heavy-duty, moisture-curing polyurethane.

Preparing the surface
The floor must be clean and grease-free (◁). Fill any cracks and small holes by priming with one coat of urethane, then one hour later apply a mortar made from 6 parts sand: 1 part cement plus enough urethane to produce a stiff paste. Although urethane can be applied to damp or dry surfaces, it will penetrate a dry floor better, so force-dry excessively damp basements with a fan heater before treatment. Remove all heaters from the room before you begin damp-proofing.

Applying urethane
Use a broom to apply the first coat of urethane using one litre to cover about 5sq m (50sq ft). If you are treating a room with a DPC in the walls, take the urethane coating up behind the skirting to meet it.

Two or three hours later, apply a second coat. Further delay may result in poor inter-coat adhesion. Apply three or four coats in all.

After three days, you can lay any conventional floorcovering or use the floor as it is.

PATCHING ACTIVE LEAKS

Before you damp-proof a cellar, patch cracks which are active water leaks (running water) with a quick-drying hydraulic cement. Supplied as a powder for mixing with water, the cement expands as it hardens, sealing out the running water.

Undercut a crack or hole with a chisel and club hammer. Mix up cement and hold it in the hand until warm then push it into the crack. Hold it in place with your hand or a trowel for three to five minutes until hard.

TREATING THE WALLS

If you want, you can continue with moisture-cured polyurethane to completely seal the walls and floor of a cellar. Decorate with emulsion or oil paints within 24 to 48 hours after treatment for maximum adhesion.

If you'd prefer to hang wallcoverings apply two coats of emulsion paint first and use a heavy-duty paste. Don't hang impervious wallcoverings such as vinyl, however, as it's important that the wall can breathe.

Bitumen latex emulsion
Where you plan to plaster or dry-line the basement walls, you can seal out the damp with a cheaper product, bitumen latex emulsion. It is not suitable as an unprotected covering to walls or floors, although it is often used as an integral DPM under the top screed of a concrete floor and as a waterproof adhesive for some tiles and wooden parquet flooring.

Hack off old plaster to expose the brickwork, then apply a skim coat of mortar to smooth the surface. Paint the wall with two coats of bitumen emulsion, joining with the DPM in the floor. Before the second coat dries, imbed clean, dry sand into it (blinding) to provide a key for the coats of plaster (See below left).

Cement-based waterproof coating
In severe conditions of damp, use a cement-based waterproof coating. Hack off old plaster or render to expose the wall then, to seal the junction between a concrete floor and the wall, cut a chase about 20mm (¾in) wide by the same depth. Brush out the debris and fill the channel with hydraulic cement (see left), finishing it off neatly as an angled fillet.

Mix the powdered cement-based coating to a butter-like consistency, according to the manufacturer's instructions, then apply two coats to the wall with a bristle brush.

However, when brick walls are damp, they bring salts to the surface in the form of white crystals known as efflorescence (◁), so before treating with waterproof coating, apply a salt-inhibiting render consisting of 1 part sulphate-resisting cement: 2 parts clean rendering sand. Add 1 part liquid bonding agent to 3 parts of the mixing water. Apply a thin trowelled coat to a rough wall or brush it onto a relatively smooth surface and allow it to set.

Treating a wall with bitumen latex emulsion
1 Skim coat of mortar
2 Coat of bitumen latex
3 Blinded coat of latex
4 Plaster or dry lining

Moisture-curing polyurethane
Damp-proof a floor with three or four coats of urethane applied with a broom.

6

INSULATION	**260**
INSULATING PLUMBING	261
DRAUGHTPROOFING	262
ROOF AND LOFT INSULATION	265
INSULATING WALLS	268
FLOOR INSULATION	270
DOUBLE GLAZING	271
VENTILATION	**275**
VENTILATING FLOORS	276
VENTILATING ROOFS	277
EXTRACTOR FANS	279
COOKER HOODS	281
HEAT EXCHANGING VENTILATORS	282
DEHUMIDIFIERS	283
AIR CONDITIONERS	284

INSULATION/VENTILATION

INSULATION

No matter what fuel you use, the cost of heating a home has, over recent years, risen dramatically – and there's no reason to suppose it won't continue to rise, perhaps at an even faster rate. What makes matters worse for many householders is the heat escaping from their draughty, uninsulated homes. Even if the expense of heating wasn't an important factor, the improved comfort and health of the occupants would more than justify the effort of installing adequate insulation.

SEE ALSO

◁ Details for:
**Double-
glazing systems**   271
Lagging pipes/cylinders   261
Radiator foil   261
Draughtproofing   262-264
Insulating roofs   265-268
Insulating walls   268-270
Insulating floors   270

Sound insulation
It is difficult to effectively insulate an existing building against sound, but attend to noisy plumbing (◁) and triple glaze your windows against airborne sound from outside (◁).

Local authority grants

The Government believe that home insulation is important to the economy of the country, so much so that they have made grants available through local authorities to encourage people to insulate their lofts, storage tanks and pipework. Everyone with less than 30mm (1¼in) of insulation is eligible for a grant of some sort. You must get local authority approval before you carry out the work or even purchase the insulation to qualify for the grant.

Specifications for insulation

When comparing thermal insulating materials, you will encounter certain technical specifications.

U-values
Elements of a house structure or the insulation itself are often given a U-value, which is a measurement of thermal transmittance. This represents the rate at which heat travels from one side to the other.

The U-value is an expression of watts of energy per square metre per °C difference ($W/m^2 °C$). If a solid brick wall is specified as having a U-value of 2.0, it means that 2 watts of heat is conducted from every square metre of the wall for every °C difference in the temperature on each side of the wall. If the temperature outside is 10 degrees lower than inside, each square metre of wall will conduct 20 watts of heat. For comparison, the lower the U-value the better the insulation.

R-values
In other cases, a material may be given an R-value, an indication of resistance to heat flow of a specified thickness. Materials with superior insulating qualities have the highest R-values.

CHOOSING INSULATION PRIORITIES

To many people, the initial outlay for total house insulation is prohibitive, even though they will concede that it is cost-effective in the long term. Nevertheless, it's important to instigate a programme for insulation as soon as possible – every measure contributes some saving.

Most authorities suggest that 35 per cent of lost heat escapes through the walls of an average house, 25 per cent through its roof, 25 per cent through draughty doors and windows and 15 per cent through the floor. At best, this can be taken as a rough guide only as it is difficult to define an 'average' home and therefore to deduce the rate of heat loss. A terraced house, for instance, will lose less than a detached house of the same size, yet both may have a roof of the same area and a similar condition. Large, ill-fitting sash windows will permit far more draughts than small, well-fitting casements, and so on.

The figures identify the major routes for heat loss, but don't necessarily indicate where you should begin your programme in order to achieve the quickest return on your investment or, for that matter, the most immediate improvement in comfort. Start with the relatively inexpensive measures.

1 HOT WATER CYLINDER AND PIPES

Begin by lagging your hot water storage cylinder and any exposed pipework running through unheated areas of the house. This treatment will constitute a considerable saving in a matter of a few months only.

2 RADIATORS

Apply metallic foil behind any radiators on an outside wall: it will reflect heat back into the room; before the wall absorbs it.

3 DRAUGHTPROOFING

Seal off the major draughts around windows and doors. For a modest outlay, draughtproofing provides a substantial return both economically and in terms of your comfort. It is also easy to accomplish.

4 ROOF

Tackle the insulation of the roof next as, in addition to the eventual reduction in fuel bills, you may be eligible for a local authority grant towards the cost of its insulation (see left). It is a very economical proposition.

5 WALLS

Depending on the construction of your house, insulating the walls may be a sound investment. However, it's likely to be relatively expensive, so it will take several years to recoup your initial expenditure.

6 FLOORS

Most of us insulate our floors to some extent by laying carpets or tiles. Taking extra measures will depend on the degree of comfort you wish to achieve and whether you can install more efficient insulation while carrying out some other improvement to the floor, such as laying new boards.

7 DOUBLE GLAZING

Contrary to typical advertisements, double glazing will produce only a slow return on your investment, especially if you choose one of the more expensive systems (◁). However, it may help to increase the value of your property – and a double-glazed room is definitely cosier and you will be less troubled by noise from outside especially if you choose to install triple glazing.

LAGGING PIPES, CYLINDER AND RADIATORS

Insulating a hot water cylinder

Many people think that an uninsulated cylinder is providing a useful source of heat in an airing cupboard, but in fact it squanders a surprising amount of energy. Even a lagged cylinder should provide ample background heat in an enclosed cupboard – but if not, an uninsulated pipe will.

Proprietary cylinder jackets are made from segments of 80 to 100mm (3¼ to 4in) thick mineral-fibre insulation material wrapped in plastic. Measure the approximate height and circumference of the cylinder to choose the right size. If necessary, buy a larger jacket rather than one that is too small. Make sure you buy a good-quality jacket by checking that it is marked with the British Standard kite mark (BS 5615).

If you should ever have to replace the cylinder, consider buying a pre-insulated version, of which there are various types on the market (▷).

Thread the tapered ends of the jacket segments onto a length of string and tie it round the pipe at the top of the cylinder. Distribute the segments evenly around the cylinder and wrap the straps or string provided around it to hold the insulation in place.

Spread out the segments to make sure the edges are butted together and tuck the insulation around the pipes and the cylinder thermostat.

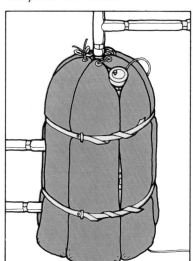

Lagging a hot water cylinder
Fit a jacket snugly around the cylinder and wrap insulating foam tubes (See above right) around the pipework, especially the vent pipe directly above the cylinder.

Lagging pipe runs

You should insulate hot water pipes where their radiant heat is not contributing to the warmth of your home, and also cold water pipe runs in unheated areas of the house, where they could freeze. You can wrap pipework in one of several lagging bandages, some of which are self-adhesive, but it is more convenient to use foamed plastic tubes designed for the purpose, especially along pipes running close and clipped to a wall, which would be awkward to wrap.

Plastic tubes are made to fit pipes of different diameters and the tube walls vary in thickness from 10mm to 20mm (½in to ¾in). More expensive tubing incorporates a metallic foil backing to reflect some of the heat back into hot water pipes.

Most tubes are pre-slit along their length so that they can be sprung over the pipe (1). Butt successive lengths of tube end-to-end and seal the joints with PVC adhesive tape.

At a bend, cut small segments out of the split edge so it bends without crimping. Fit it around the pipe (2) and seal the closed joints with tape. If pipe is joined with an elbow fitting (▷), mitre the ends of the two lengths of tube, butt them together (3) and seal with tape.

Cut lengths of tube to fit completely around a tee-joint, linking them with a wedge-shaped butt joint (4) and seal with tape as before.

| 1 Spring onto pipe | 2 Cut to fit bend | 3 Mitre over elbows | 4 Butt at tee-joint |

Reflecting heat from a radiator

Up to 25 per cent of the radiant heat from a radiator on an outside wall is lost to the wall behind. Reclaim perhaps half this wasted heat by installing a foil-faced, expanded polystyrene lining behind the radiator to reflect it back into the room.

The material is available as rolls, sheets or tiles to fit any size and shape of radiator. It is easier to stick the foil on the wall when the radiator is removed for decorating but it is not an essential requirement.

Turn off the radiator and measure it, including the position of the brackets. Use a sharp trimming knife or scissors to cut the foil to size so that it is slightly smaller than the radiator all round. Cut narrow slots to fit over the fixing brackets (1).

Apply heavy-duty fungicidal wallpaper paste to the back of the sheet and slide it behind the radiator (2). Rub it down with a radiator roller (▷) or smooth it against the wall with a wooden batten. Allow enough time for the adhesive to dry before turning the radiator on again.

1 Cut slots to align with wall brackets

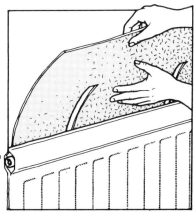

2 Slide lining behind radiator and press to wall

SEE ALSO

Details for: ▷	
Plumbing joints	352
Cylinders	380
Radiator roller	483
Wallpaper paste	93

261

DRAUGHTPROOFING DOORS

SEE ALSO

◁ Details for:
Condensation	254
Ventilating appliances	276

A certain amount of ventilation is desirable for a healthy environment and to keep water vapour at an acceptable level; it's also essential to enable certain heating appliances to operate properly and safely. But using uncontrolled draughts to ventilate a house is not the most efficient way of dealing with the problem. Draughts account for a large proportion of the heat lost from the home and are also responsible for a good deal of discomfort. Draughtproofing is easy to fit, requires no special tools, and there's a wide choice of excluders available to suit all locations.

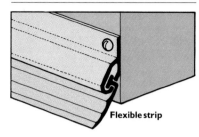

Flexible strip

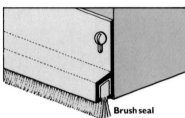

Brush seal

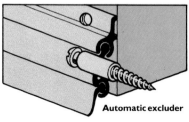

Automatic excluder

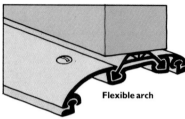

Flexible arch

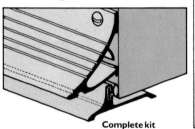

Complete kit

Locating and curing draughts

Proof exterior doors– and windows– (◁) first, and seal only those interior doors which are the worst offenders to provide 'trickle' ventilation from room to room. Check out other possible sources of draughts, such as floorboards and skirtings, fireplaces, loft hatches, and overflow pipes from sanitaryware.

Locate draughts by running the flat of your hand along the likely gaps. Dampening your skin will enhance its sensitivity to cold, or wait for a very windy day to conduct your search.

There are so many manufacturers and variations of draught excluders, it's quite impossible to describe them all, but the following examples illustrate the principles commonly employed to seal out draughts. Choose the best you can afford, but perhaps more importantly, try to decide which type of draught excluder will suit your particular requirements best.

THRESHOLD DRAUGHT EXCLUDERS

The gap between the door and floor can be very large and will admit fierce draughts. Use a threshold excluder to seal this gap. If it is to be used on an exterior door, make sure it is suitable for this purpose. Buy a device that fits the opening exactly, or cut it to fit from a larger size.

FLEXIBLE STRIP EXCLUDERS

The simplest form of threshold excluder is a flexible strip of plastic or rubber, which sweeps against the floorcovering to form a seal. The basic versions are self-adhesive strips that are simply pressed along the bottom of the door but others have a rigid plastic or aluminium extrusion screwed to the door to hold the strip in contact with the floor. This type of excluder is rarely suitable for exterior doors and quickly wears out. However, it is inexpensive and easy to fit. Most types work best over smooth flooring.

BRUSH SEALS

A nylon bristle brush set into a metal or plastic extrusion acts as a draught excluder. It is suitable for slightly uneven or textured floorcoverings; the same excluder works on both hinged and sliding doors.

AUTOMATIC EXCLUDER

A plastic strip and its extruded clip are sprung-loaded to lift from the floor as the door is opened. On closing the door, the excluder is pressed against the floor by a stop screwed to the door frame. This is a good-quality interior and exterior excluder that reduces wear on the floorcovering.

FLEXIBLE ARCH

An aluminium extrusion with a vinyl arched insert, which presses against the bottom edge of the door. The extruder has to be nailed or screwed to the floor, so it would be difficult to use on a solid concrete floor. If you fit one for an external door, make sure it is fitted with additional under-seals to prevent the rain from seeping beneath it. You may have to plane the bottom of the door.

DOOR KITS

The best solution for an outside door is a kit combining an aluminium weather trim, which sheds the rainwater, and a weather bar with a built-in tubular rubber or plastic draught excluder screwed to the threshold.

WEATHERSTRIPPING THE DOOR EDGES

Any well-fitting door requires a gap of 2mm (1/16in) at top and sides so that it can be operated smoothly. However, the combined area of a gap this large loses a great deal of heat. There are several ways to seal it, some of which are described here. The cheaper varieties have to be renewed regularly.

FOAM STRIPS

The most straightforward excluder is a self-adhesive foam plastic strip, which you stick around the rebate: it's compressed by the door, forming a seal. The cheapest polyurethane foam will be good for one or two seasons (but it's useless if painted) and is suitable for interior use only. Better-quality vinyl-coated polyurethane, rubber or PVC foams are more durable and do not perish on exposure to sunlight, as their cheaper counterparts do. Don't stretch foam excluders when applying them, as it reduces their efficiency. The door may be difficult to close at first but the excluder soon adjusts.

FLEXIBLE TUBE EXCLUDERS

A small vinyl tube held in a plastic or metal extrusion is compressed to fill the gap around the door. The cheapest versions have an integrally moulded flange, which can be stapled to the door frame, but they are not as neat.

SPRING STRIP

Thin metal or plastic strips with a sprung leaf are pinned or glued to the door frame. The top and closing edges of the door brush past the leaf, which seals the gap, while the hinged edge compresses it. It can't cope with uneven surfaces unless it incorporates a foam strip on the flexible leaf.

V-STRIP

A variation on the spring strip, the leaf is bent right back to form a V-shape. The strip can be mounted to fill the gap around the door or attached to the door stop so that the door closes against it. Most are cheap and unobtrusive.

DRAUGHTPROOFING SEALANT

With this excluder, a bead of flexible sealant is squeezed onto the door stop: a low-tack tape applied to the surface of the door acts as a release agent. When the door is closed, it flattens the bead, which fills the gap perfectly. When it is set, the parting layer of tape is peeled from the door, leaving the sealant firmly attached to the door frame. If the door warps, the seal is not so good.

SEALING KEYHOLES AND LETTERBOXES

Make sure the outer keyhole for a mortise lock is fitted with a pivoting coverplate to seal out the draughts in the winter.

Special hinged flaps are made for screwing over the inside of a letterbox. Some types contain a brush seal behind the flap, forming an even better seal.

Keyhole coverplate
The coverplate is part of the escutcheon.

Letterbox flap
A hinged flap neatens and draughtproofs a letterbox.

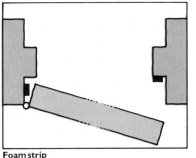

Foam strip

SEE ALSO

Details for: ▷

Doors	184-185
Letter plates	189

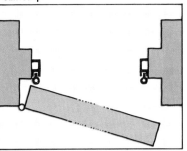
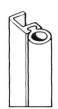

Flexible tube

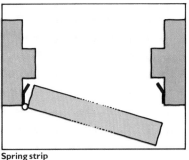

Spring strip

V-strip

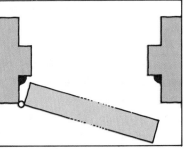
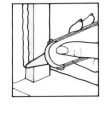

Sealant

GENERAL DRAUGHTPROOFING

Hinged casement windows can be sealed with any of the draught excluders suggested for fitting around the edge of a door, but draughtproofing a sliding sash window presents a more difficult problem.

SEE ALSO

◁ Details for:
Hardboard floor	**57**
Sealant	**263**
Flue ventilation	**275**
Sealing fireplace	**385**
Windows	196-197
Ventilating below floors	276

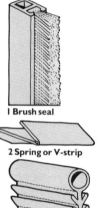

I Brush seal

2 Spring or V-strip

3 Tubular strip

Sealing a sash window

The top and bottom closing rails of a sash window can be sealed with any form of compressible excluder; the sliding edges admit fewer draughts but they can be sealed with a brush seal fixed to the frame, inside for the lower sash, outside for the top one.

A spring or V-strip could be used to seal the gap between the central meeting rails but you may not be able to reverse the sashes once it is fitted. Perhaps the simplest solution is to seal it with a reusable tubular plastic strip.

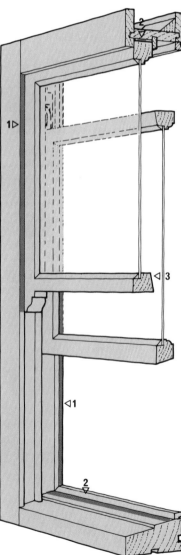

Clear liquid sealer

If you plan never to open a window during the winter, you could seal all gaps with a clear liquid draught seal, applied from a tube. It is virtually invisible when dry and can be peeled off, without damaging the paintwork, when you want to open the window again after the winter.

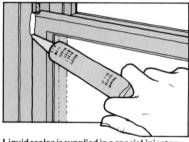

Liquid sealer is supplied in a special injector

Sealing a pivot window

As you close a pivot window, the moving frame comes to rest against fixed stops, but the stops for the top half of the window are on the outside of the house. These exterior stops, at least, must be sealed with draught excluders that are weatherproof so use spring or V-strip compressible draughtproofing, or a good-quality flexible tube strip. Alternatively, use a draughtproofing sealant (◁).

DRAUGHTY FIREPLACES

A chimney can be an annoying source of draughts. If the fireplace is unused, you can seal it off completely (◁), but be sure to fit a 'hit-and-miss' ventilator to provide ventilation for the flue (◁).

If you want to retain the appearance of an open fireplace, cut a sheet of thick polystyrene to seal the throat but leave a hole about 50mm (2in) across to provide some ventilation. Should you ever want to use the fireplace again, don't forget to remove the polystyrene, which is flammable.

DRAUGHTPROOFING FLOORS AND SKIRTINGS

The ventilated void below a suspended wooden floor is a prime source of draughts through large gaps in the floorboards and under the skirting. Fill between floorboards or cover them with hardboard panels (◁).

Seal the gap between the skirting board and the floor with mastic applied with an applicator gun or in the form of caulking strips. For a neat finish, pin a quadrant moulding to the skirting to cover the sealed gap.

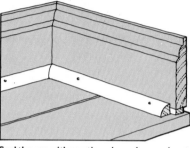

Seal the gap with mastic and wooden quadrant

DRAUGHTS FROM OVERFLOW PIPES

Overflow pipes leading directly from bath tubs, sinks and basins can be the passage for serious draughts when there's a strong wind. The problem is how to seal the pipes without interfering with their function.

Covering the opening
The simplest solution is to cut the neck off a balloon and stretch it over the end of the pipe. It hangs down to cover the opening but gushing water will pass through safely.

Fitting a coverflap
Alternatively, cut a coverflap from a lightweight metal such as zinc or aluminium, which will not rust. Make a simple pivot from the same metal and attach the flap to the end of the tube with a pipe clip. Inspect it regularly to ensure that it is working smoothly.

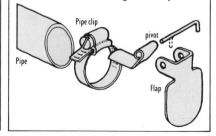

INSULATING ROOFS

About a quarter of the heat lost from an average house goes through the roof, so preventing this should be one of your priorities when it comes to insulating your home. Providing you're able to gain access to your loft floor, reducing substantial heat loss is just a matter of laying the insulation material between the joists: it's cheap, quick and effective. If you want to use the attic, insulating the sloping surface of the roof is a quite straightforward alternative.

Treating a flat roof

A flat roof – on an extension for instance – may also need insulating, but the only really practical solution for most householders is to apply a layer of insulation to the ceiling surface. It is not a particularly difficult task, providing the area is not too large, but you will have to re-locate lighting and take into consideration features such as cupboards or windows that extend to the ceiling. Fixing ceiling tiles is an alternative (▷) but their insulation value is minimal.

Preparing the loft

On inspection, you may find that the roof space has existing but inadequate insulation. At one time even 25mm (1in) of insulation was considered to be acceptable. It is worth installing extra insulation to bring it up to the recommended thickness of 100mm (4in). Check roof timbers for woodworm or signs of rot so that they can be treated first (▷). Make sure that the electrical wiring is sound; lift it clear so that you can lay insulation beneath it.

Plaster or plasterboard ceiling surfaces will not support your weight, so lay a plank or two, or a panel of chipboard, across the joists so that you can move about safely: don't allow it to overlap the joists; if you step on the edge it will tip over.

If there is no permanent lighting in the loft, rig up an inspection lamp on an extension lead, so you can move it wherever it is needed, or hang it high up for best overall light.

Most attics are very dusty, so wear old clothes and a gauze facemask. You may wish to wear protective gloves, particularly if you are handling glass-fibre batts or blanket insulation, which can irritate sensitive skin.

TYPES OF INSULATION

There's a wide range of different insulation materials available. Check out the recommended types with your local authority before you apply for a grant.

BLANKET INSULATION

Glass-fibre and mineral- or rock-fibre blanket insulation is commonly sold as rolls made to fit snugly between the joists. The same material cut to shorter lengths is also sold as 'batts'. A minimum thickness of 100mm (4in) is recommended for loft insulation. Blanket insulation may be unbacked, paper-backed to improve its tear-resistance, or it may have a foil backing as a vapour barrier (See below).

The unbacked type is normally used for laying on the loft floor. Blankets are usually 75mm (3in) or 100mm (4in) thick and typically 400mm (1ft 4in) wide – suitable for the normal joist spacing. For wider than usual joist spacing, choose the 600mm (2ft) width (cut it in half for narrow joist spaces with a panel saw before you unwrap it). Rolls are typically 6 to 8m (20 to 25ft) long.

If you want to fit blanket insulation to the sloping part of the roof, buy it with a lip of backing along each side for stapling to the rafters.

Both glass and mineral fibre are non-flammable and proofed against damp, rot and vermin.

LOOSE-FILL INSULATION

Loose-fill insulation in pellet or granular form is poured between the joists on the loft floor to a minimum depth of 100mm (4in), although a depth of 130mm (5¼in) is recommended for the same value of insulation as 100mm (4in) thick blanket – but this could rise above some joists.

Exfoliated vermiculite, made from a mineral called mica, is the most common form of loose-fill insulation but others such as mineral wool, polystyrene or cork granules may be available. Loose-fill is sold in bags containing 110 litres (4cu ft) – sufficient to cover 1.1sq m (12sq ft) at 100mm (4in) deep.

It's inadvisable to use loose-fill in a draughty, exposed loft: high winds can cause it to blow about. However, it's convenient to use if the joists are irregularly spaced.

BLOWN FIBRE INSULATION

Professional contractors can provide inter-joist loft insulation by blowing glass, mineral or cellulose fibres through a large hose. A minimum, even depth of 100mm (4in) is required. Blown fibre insulation may be unsuitable for a house in a windy location but seek the advice of the contractor.

RIGID AND SEMI-RIGID SHEET INSULATION

Sheet insulation is principally for fixing between the rafters. You can choose semi-rigid batts of glass or mineral fibre, or fibre insulation board. A minimum thickness of 25mm (1in) is required when covered with plasterboard, but install thicker insulation where possible, allowing for sufficient ventilation between it and the roof tiles or slates to avoid condensation (▷).

VAPOUR BARRIERS

Installing insulation has the effect of making the areas of the house outside that layer of insulation colder than before, so increasing the risk of condensation (▷) either on or within the structure itself. In time this could result in decreased value of the insulation and may promote a serious outbreak of dry rot in household timbers (▷).

To prevent this happening, it's necessary to provide adequate ventilation for those areas outside the insulation or to install a vapour barrier on the inner, or warm, side of the insulation to prevent moisture-laden air passing through. This is usually a plastic sheet or layer of metal foil, which is sometimes supplied along with the insulation. It is essential that a vapour barrier is continuous and undamaged or its effect is greatly reduced.

SEE ALSO

Details for: ▷	
Ceiling tiles	112
Woodworm	246
Dry and wet rot	249
Condensation	254
Roof ventilation	277-278
Extension lead	294
Checking electrics	306-307

ESTIMATING FOR BLANKET INSULATION
400mm wide rolls

Approx. loft area		
Square metres	Square feet	No. of rolls
29	314	13
31.5	339	14
34	363	15
36	387	16
38	411	17
40.5	435	18
43	460	19
45	487	20
56	605	25
67.5	726	30
79	847	35
90	968	40

Allows for average joist widths of 50mm (2in)

● **Ventilating the loft**
Laying insulation between the joists increases the risk of condensation in an unheated roof space above, but, provided there are gaps at the eaves, there will be enough air circulating to keep the loft dry (▷).

INSULATING THE LOFT

INSULATING TANKS AND PIPES

Laying blanket insulation

Seal gaps around pipes, vents or wiring entering the loft with flexible mastic. Remove the blanket wrapping in the loft (it's compressed for storage and transportation but swells to its true thickness when released) and begin by placing one end of a roll into the eaves. Make sure you don't cover the ventilation gap – trim the end of the blanket to a wedge-shape so it does not obstruct the airflow, or fit eaves vents.

Unroll the blanket between the joists, pressing it down to form a snug fit, but don't compress it. If the roll is slightly wider than the joist spacing, allow it to curl up against the timbers on each side.

Continue at the opposite side of the loft with another roll: cut it to butt up against the end of the first one, using a large kitchen knife or long-bladed pair of scissors. Continue across the loft until all the spaces are filled. Cut the insulation to fit odd spaces.

Do not cover the casing of any light fittings which protrude into the loft space. Avoid covering electrical cables, as there's a risk it may cause overheating. Instead, lay the cables on top of the blanket, or clip them to the sides of the joists above it.

Do not insulate the area directly below a cold water tank, so that heat rising from the room below will help to prevent freezing. Cut a piece of insulation to fit the hatch cover and attach it with PVA adhesive or hold it down with cloth tapes and drawing pins. Fit foam draught excluder around the edge of the hatch.

Insulating tanks

Insulate the cold water storage tanks in the loft, including the central heating expansion tank. Buy a ready-made kit to fit the tank or make one from suitable insulation.

You can construct a hardboard liner to contain loose-fill insulation, but it's easier to surround the tank with sheets of 25mm (1 in) thick expanded-polystyrene or mineral-fibre slabs. Cut slots for the pipework and make a lid to cover the tank. Fit a plastic funnel in the lid to catch drips from the expansion pipe (◁). Join the corners with sharpened wooden dowel pegs or tie with string, wire or tape.

Alternatively, lag the tank with blanket insulation but cut a rigid lid to fit and cover it with insulation; wrap with polythene to prevent fibres contaminating the water.

Insulating pipes

If cold water pipes run between the joists, lay the blanket insulation over them to ensure they will not freeze. If this is not practical, insulate all pipe runs separately (◁).

Lay a thin card bridge over cold water pipework running between the joists before pouring loose insulation, so that the pipes benefit from warmth rising from the room below. If the joists are shallow, cover the pipes with foam sleeves before pouring the insulation.

SEE ALSO

◁ Details for:
Lagging pipes	261
Expansion (vent) pipe	379,391
Draught excluders	263
Insulant	265
Roof ventilation	277-278
Electrical wiring	304

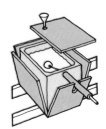

Insulating a tank
Cut slabs of insulant to fit sides: peg corners. Fit lid plus a funnel to collect drips from expansion pipe (See box right)

Laying loose-fill insulation

Take similar precautions against condensation to those described for blanket insulation. To prevent blocking the eaves, wedge strips of plywood or thick cardboard between the joists. Pour insulation between the joists and distribute it roughly with a broom. Level it with a spreader cut from hardboard to fit between the joists: notch it to fit over the joists so the central piece levels the granules accurately.

To insulate the entrance hatch, screw battens around the outer edge of the cover, fill with granules and pin on a hardboard lid to contain them.

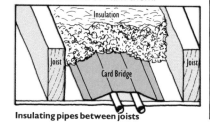

Insulating pipes between joists

Left
Seal gaps around pipes and vents (1). Place end of roll against eaves and trim ends (2) or fit eaves vents (3). Press rolls between joists (4) Insulate tank and pipes (5).

Right
Seal gaps to prevent condensation (1). Stop insulant blocking ventilation with strips of plywood (2) or eaves vents (3). Cover cold water pipes with a cardboard bridge (4) then use a spreader to level the insulant (5). Insulate and draughtproof the hatch cover (6).

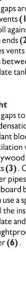

Laying blanket insulation in the loft

Spreading loose-fill insulant in the loft

INSULATING A SLOPING ROOF

Insulating between the rafters

If the attic is in use, you will need to insulate the sloping part of the roof in order to heat the living space. Repair tiles or slates first, as not only will leaks soak the insulation but also it will be difficult to spot them after insulating.

Condensation is a serious problem when you install insulation between the rafters, as the undersides of the tiles will become very cold. You must provide a 50mm (2in) gap between the tiles and the insulation to promote sufficient ventilation to keep the space dry, which in turn determines the maximum thickness of insulation you can install. The ridge and eaves must be ventilated (▷) and you should include a vapour barrier on the warm side of the insulation, either by fitting foil-backed blanket or by stapling sheets of polythene to the lower edges of the rafters to cover unbacked insulation.

Whatever insulation you decide on, you can cover the rafters with sheets of plasterboard as a final decorative layer. The sizes of the panels will be dictated by the largest boards you can pass through the hatchway. Use plasterboard nails or screws to hold the panels against the rafters, staggering the joints (▷). Alternatively, provide insulation and surface finish together by fitting insulated (thermal) plasterboard to the underside of the rafters (▷).

Fixing blanket insulant

Unfold the side flanges from a roll of foil-backed blanket and staple them to the underside of the rafters. When fitting adjacent rolls, overlap the edges of the vapour barrier to provide a continuous layer.

Attaching sheet insulant

The simplest method is to cut the sheet insulation accurately so that it will be a wedge-fit between the rafters. If necessary, screw battens to the sides of the rafters to which you can fix the insulating sheets. Treat the battens beforehand with preservative. Staple a polythene sheet vapour barrier over the rafters. Double-fold the joints over a rafter and staple in place.

INSULATING AN ATTIC ROOM

If an attic room was built as part of the original dwelling, it will be virtually impossible to insulate the pitch of the roof unless you are prepared to hack off the old plaster and proceed as left. It may be simpler to insulate from the inside as for a flat roof (▷) but your headroom may be seriously hampered.

Insulate the short vertical wall of the attic from inside the crawlspace, making sure the vapour barrier faces the inner, warm side of the partition. Insulate between the joists of the crawlspace at the same time.

Fit blankets with vapour barrier facing the room

SEE ALSO

Details for: ▷	
Plasterboarding	159
Insulating a flat roof	268
Thermal board	269
Ventilating ridge/eaves	277
Preservatives	250
Staple guns	485

Insulating a room in the attic
Surround the room itself with insulation but leave the floor uninsulated so that the room benefits from rising heat generated by the space below.

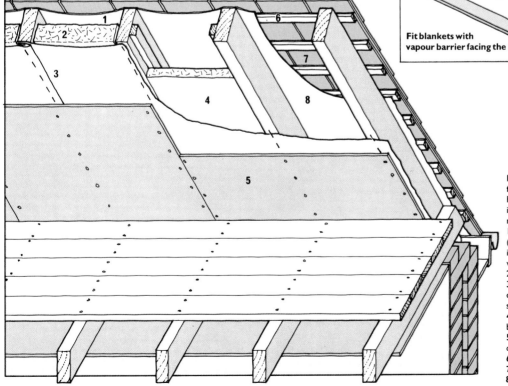

Insulating an attic from the inside
Fit blanket or sheet insulant between the rafters.
1 Minimum of 50mm (2in) between insulation and tiles for ventilation
2 Blanket or batts
3 Vapour barrier with double-folded joints stapled to rafters
4 Sheet insulant fixed to battens
5 Plasterboard nailed over vapour barrier
6 Tile battens
7 Tiles or slates
8 Roof felt

INSULATING A FLAT ROOF

Treatment from above

A flat roof can be insulated from the outside by laying rigid insulating board on the original deck and weighting it down with paving slabs or a layer of pebbles. This is a job for a professional only, but insist that the contractor checks that the roof can support the additional weight and that the insulation is waterproofed and sealed all round to prevent penetrating damp.

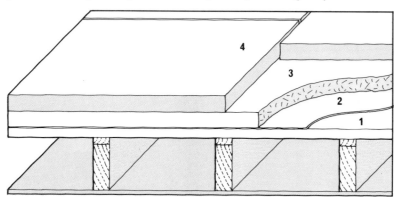

SEE ALSO

◁ Details for:
Plasterboarding	166
External	
wall insulation	270
Heating controls	395
Staple guns	485

Insulating a flat roof from outside
A professional company can insulate the roof from above.
1 Roof deck
2 Waterproof covering
3 Insulation
4 Paving slabs to hold insulant in place

Treatment from below

The only other option for insulating a flat roof is to treat the ceiling below; you can do this so long as you have sufficient headroom. You must guard against condensation in the restricted space within the roof structure, particularly as it is often insufficiently ventilated – if at all. You should include a polythene vapour barrier on the warm side of the ceiling, below the insulation.

Fire-retardant expanded polystyrene 25mm (1in) thick is normally recommended for its lightness, with softwood battens screwed to the joists between the panels of insulation every 400mm (1ft 4in) across the ceiling. Fit the first batten against the wall at right-angles to the joists, and one at each end of the room. Butt the polystyrene against the first batten, gluing it to the ceiling with special polystyrene adhesive. Coat the entire back of the material.

Continue with alternate battens and panels until you reach the opposite side of the room, finishing with a batten against the wall. Staple a polythene vapour barrier across the framework, double-folding the joins, over the nearest batten. Fix plasterboard panels to the battens with galvanized plasterboard nails. Stagger the joins between the panels then fill the joins and finish ready for decorating as required (◁). A double coat of oil paint is a vapour barrier itself.

Insulating the ceiling
Insulate a flat roof by fixing insulant to the ceiling.
1 Existing ceiling
2 Softwood battens screwed to joists
3 Insulation glued to existing ceiling
4 Polythene vapour barrier stapled to battens
5 Plasterboard nailed to battens

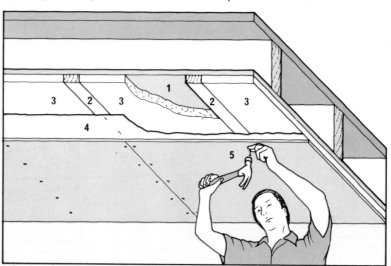

INSULATING WALLS

How you insulate the walls of your home will be determined by several factors. Firstly, the type of construction. If the house was built since 1920 and certainly after 1950, it will probably have cavity walls – two skins of brick, or one of brick and one of concrete block, with a gap between through which air circulates to reduce the likelihood of water penetration. Although heat loss is slightly slower through a cavity wall than one of solid brick, it is not sufficiently insulating to substantially reduce the cost of home heating. However, filling the cavity with insulation prevents circulation, trapping the air in millions of tiny air pockets within the material: it's a process that can cut heat loss through the wall by about 65 per cent.

Solid walls require different treatment: basically, you can either insulate the external face of the walls or line the inner surface – and either of these methods can involve considerable disruption to the joinery, electrical and plumbing supplies.

Advantages and disadvantages

With cavity filling, every exterior wall must be treated simultaneously, so it is most cost-effective for homes which are heated throughout for long periods and with a properly controlled system. Heating without controls will simply increase the temperature inside instead of saving on fuel bills. This type of insulation is impractical for flats or apartments unless the whole building is insulated at the same time.

Solid masonry walls must be insulated in some other way. It is possible to hire a contractor to clad the exterior of the house with insulation (◁) but it is expensive and alters the appearance of some buildings. The comments concerning the manner of heating and effective controls to make cavity filling worthwhile apply equally to exterior wall insulation.

Another method is to line the inner surface of either type of wall construction with insulation. It may involve a great deal of effort depending on the amount of alteration required to joinery, electrical fittings, and so on, but it provides the opportunity for selective insulation, concentrating on those rooms which would benefit most, and it is the only form of wall insulation which can be carried out by the householder.

INSULATING A CAVITY WALL

When constructing a new house, a builder will include a layer of insulation between the two masonry leaves of exterior walls: a simple measure, which greatly increases the thermal insulation of the building. To insulate an existing wall is a different matter. It requires a skilled and experienced contractor to introduce an insulant through holes cut in the outer brick leaf to fill the cavity in such a way that you achieve the savings in heat loss without the side effects of damp penetrating to the inner leaf.

Hire a contractor who is approved by the Agrément Board, registered with the British Standards Institution, or who is a member of the National Cavity Insulation Association.

You should expect the contractor to carry out a thorough survey of the building to make sure the walls are structurally fit for filling, with no evidence of frost damage or failed pointing. An approved company will also make the necessary application to the local authority before commencing installation to comply with the Building Regulations. This is particularly important if you live in an area of the country where your house is exposed to severe driving rain for prolonged periods. Not all cavity fillings are suitable for such extreme weather conditions.

Do not hire a firm which does not provide a long-term guarantee, which is transferable with home ownership. It should state that the insulant will be effective for the period of the guarantee and that it is rot- and vermin-proof. Be especially careful to check that the contractor's guarantee states that damp resulting from faulty material or installation will be cured free of charge.

More than likely you will be offered one of three insulants: urea formaldehyde foam is the cheapest and most widely used insulant, despite its reputation for releasing unpleasant odours as the foam cures. In reality, it happens in very few instances and is due to a poor survey, which did not detect that the walls were not in a fit condition for filling.

Mineral or glass fibre treated with water repellent are the next most popular cavity insulants. Both materials are completely inert and if properly installed, will form a stable insulation that will neither settle nor shrink once installed in the cavity.

Expanded-polystyrene beads form the third most commonly used insulant. Some of them are lightly coated with adhesive at the moment of injection so that the fill does not settle over a period of time. If polystyrene is treated and properly installed it does not affect the fire resistance of a masonry wall.

Whatever process you choose, it should take no more than two to three days to complete. All the work is carried on outside the house, where holes are drilled at regular intervals in the brickwork (**1**). The insulant is injected or blown through a hose (**2**) and finally the holes are plugged. If the work is done properly, the holes should be virtually invisible, except perhaps by close inspection.

1 Drilling holes in the outer leaf
A professional contractor will begin by drilling large diameter holes through the outer skin of brickwork into the cavity.

2 Introducing the insulant
A hose is inserted into each hole and the insulant is injected or blown under pressure into the cavity, filling it from the base. When the job is complete, the holes are plugged with colour-matched mortar.

DRY-LINING FROM THE INSIDE

If you are planning to dry-line an external wall with some form of panelling (▷), take the opportunity to include blanket or sheet insulation between the wall battens or furring strips (▷). Fix a polythene vapour barrier over the insulation by stapling it to the furring strips before nailing the panelling in place.

Alternatively, use a metallized plastic-backed plasterboard, which requires no additional vapour barrier.

Any form of panelling can be applied over mineral- or glass-fibre blanket but plasterboard should be used to cover expanded-polystyrene insulant.

A simpler method is to glue insulated (thermal) plasterboard directly to a sound plaster surface. This type of wall lining is standard plasterboard, backed with a layer of expanded-polystyrene or rigid-polyurethane foam. An integral vapour barrier is incorporated in both boards (see below).

Using a notched applicator, apply a 200mm (8in) wide band of the manufacturer's adhesive to the wall to coincide with the vertical edges of the panel and its centre line (**1**). Spread horizontal bands top and bottom. Press the panel against the adhesive and tamp it down with a heavy straightedge then secure it to the wall with nine nailable plugs (**2**) in three rows. Position the plugs 50mm (2in) from all edges of the panel and one in the centre. Cut a panel to fit into a corner with a fine-toothed saw. Allow for a 3mm (⅛in) gap at a cut edge for filling after the panel is fixed. Tape and fill all joints (▷).

Details for door and window mouldings are described for wall panelling (▷), but bed the skirting board into a bead of mastic sealant applied to the floor and plasterboard. Fix the skirting board through the panel to the wall behind.

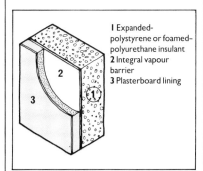

1 Expanded-polystyrene or foamed-polyurethane insulant
2 Integral vapour barrier
3 Plasterboard lining

The structure of insulated plasterboard

SEE ALSO

Details for: ▷	
Furring strips	87
Panelling	87-89
Taping joints	164

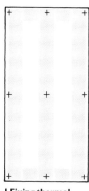

1 Fixing thermal plasterboard
Spread adhesive along the bands shown in the diagram above. The crosses indicate the centres of nailable fixing plugs

2 Nailable plug
Used to fix insulated plasterboard to the wall. Push the plug into a hole drilled through the board, then drive in the nail to expand the plug and grip the masonry.

269

SEE ALSO

◁ Details for:
Hardboard flooring	*57*
Planning permission	18-19
Penetrating damp	251-253
Rising damp	251-253
Blanket insulant	265
Batts	265
Ventilating floor void	276
Staple guns	485

EXTERNAL WALL INSULATION

External wall insulation should be undertaken only after careful consideration of the benefits – and the pitfalls. The techniques involved in the process are relatively untried, so little is known about their long-term effectiveness or durability.

As expert installation is required, choose a contractor who is a registered member of the External Wall Insulation Association, which has a vested interest in promoting a high standard of workmanship.

It may be necessary to obtain planning permission before the work is undertaken, as it may be totally unsuitable for the style of the building. In particular, the treatment of doors and windows must be sensitively detailed in order to preserve the character of the house. Downpipes, ventilators, telephone and TV cables will have to be relocated. Quite clearly, exterior cladding involves a lot of labour and the high cost reflects it.

Apart from reducing heat loss, the main advantage of exterior insulation is weatherproofing. If you are faced with the expense of tackling severe penetrating damp, it may prove economical to choose external insulation as a solution to both problems. It will have no effect on rising damp, however, which must be remedied beforehand.

One method currently available involves the application of an insulating render of cement and polystyrene beads. It is trowel-applied to a maximum thickness of 80mm (3¼in), then decorated with a suitable waterproof finish.

Alternatively, polystyrene, mineral or glass-fibre slabs are mechanically fixed or glued to the walls. The insulation is covered with a wire or glass-fibre mesh before rendering.

With a third method, timber or plastic wall cladding is applied over a wooden framework incorporating slab or blanket insulation.

INSULATING A FLOOR

It is rarely necessary to insulate a concrete floor other than by applying a normal floorcovering, but a suspended wooden floor can lose heat to the crawl space below, which must be ventilated to keep it free from rot. Lining the floor with hardboard is often sufficient insulation (◁), provided a carpet with underlay is laid on top, but in a cold climate, take extra precautions.

Methods of treatment

If you are prepared to lift the floorboards, you can lay a substantial amount of insulation between the joists. Staple plastic netting to the sides of the joists to support blanket insulation or nail battens in place to support panels cut from sheet insulant.

Where you can gain access to the joists from below, it is easier to push insulation between them before stapling netting or wire mesh across the undersides to hold it there.

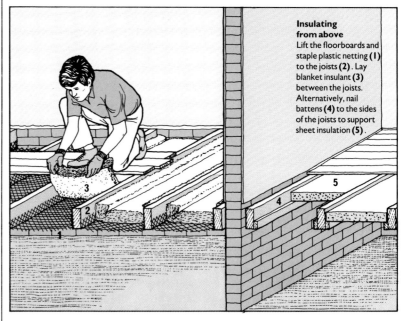

Insulating from above
Lift the floorboards and staple plastic netting (1) to the joists (2). Lay blanket insulant (3) between the joists. Alternatively, nail battens (4) to the sides of the joists to support sheet insulation (5).

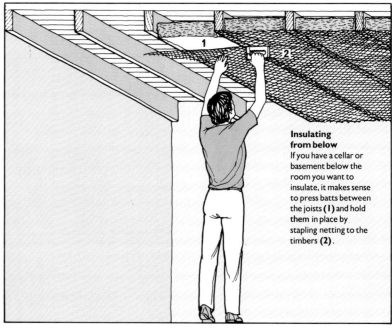

Insulating from below
If you have a cellar or basement below the room you want to insulate, it makes sense to press batts between the joists (1) and hold them in place by stapling netting to the timbers (2).

DOUBLE GLAZING

A double-glazed window consists of two sheets of glass separated by an air gap. The air gap provides an insulating layer, which reduces heat loss and sound transmission. Condensation is also reduced because the inner layer of glass remains relatively warmer than that on the outside. Factory-sealed units and secondary glazing are the two methods in common use for domestic double glazing. Both will provide good thermal insulation. Sealed units are unobtrusive, but secondary glazing can offer improved sound insulation. But which do you choose to suit your house and your lifestyle?

What size air gap?

For heat insulation a 20mm (¾in) gap provides the optimum level of efficiency. Below 12mm (½in) the air can conduct a proportion of the heat across the gap. Above 20mm (¾in), there is no appreciable extra gain in thermal insulation and air currents can occur, which transmit heat to the outside layer of glass. A larger gap of 100 to 200mm (4 to 8in) is more effective for sound insulation. A combination of a sealed unit plus secondary glazing provides the ideal solution, and is known as triple glazing.

Double glazing will help to cut fuel bills but its immediate benefit will be felt by the elimination of draughts. The cold spots associated with a larger window, particularly noticeable when sitting relatively still, will also be reduced. In terms of saving energy, the heat lost through windows is relatively small – around 10 to 12 per cent – compared to the whole house. However, the installation of double glazing can halve this amount.

Double glazing will improve security against forced entry, particularly if sealed units or toughened glass have been used. However, ensure some accessible part of the window is openable to provide emergency escape in case of fire.

SEE ALSO

Details for: ▷

Double-glazed units 204

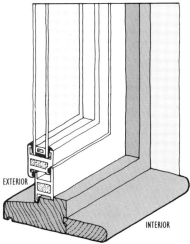

Factory-sealed unit
A complete frame system installed by a contractor.

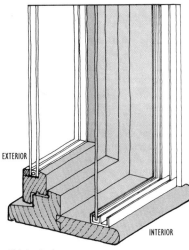

Secondary window system
Fitted in addition to the normal glazed window.

Triple glazing
A combination of secondary and sealed units.

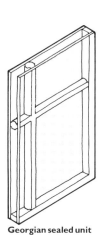

Georgian sealed unit

Double-glazed sealed units

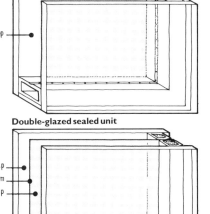

Double-glazed sealed unit

Heat-retentive sealed unit

Double-glazed sealed units are manufactured from two panes of glass separated by a spacer and hermetically sealed all round. The cavity between the glass may be 5, 9, 12 or 20mm (¼, ⅜, ½ or ¾in) wide. The gap may contain dehydrated air to eliminate condensation between the glass, or inert gases which also improve thermal and accoustic insulation.

The thickness and type of glass is determined by the size of the unit. Clear float glass or toughened glass is common. When obscured glazing is required for privacy, patterned glass is used. Special heat-retentive sealed units are also supplied by some double glazing companies, incorporating special glass or a plastic film embodied within the unit.

A leaded light and a Georgian version of the sealed unit are also produced. The former is made by bonding strips of lead to the outer pane of the glass, the latter by placing a moulded framework of glazing bars in the cavity. The improved security, lack of maintenance and ease of cleaning in some way make up for their lack of character compared with the original style of window.

Generally these special sealed units are produced and installed by suppliers of ready-made double-glazed replacement windows. Sealed units are available for self-fixing from some joinery suppliers or they can be made to order by specialists. Square-edged units are made for frames with a deep rebate, and stepped units for frames intended for single glazing (▷).

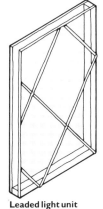

Leaded light unit

271

SECONDARY DOUBLE GLAZING

SEE ALSO

◁ Details for:
Draughtproofing   264

Secondary double glazing comprises a separate pane of glass or plastic sheet which is normally fitted to the inside of existing single-glazed windows. It *is a popular method for double glazing windows, being relatively easy for home installation – and usually at a fraction of the cost of other systems.*

How the glazing is fixed

Glazing can be fastened to the sash frames (**1**), the window frames (**2**), or across the window reveal (**3**). The choice depends on the ease of fixing, the type of glazing and personal requirements for ventilation.

Glazing fixed to the sash will cut down heat loss through the glass and provide accessible ventilation, but it will not stop draughts. That fixed to the window frame will reduce heat loss and stop draughts at the same time. Glazing fixed across the reveal will also offer

improved sound insulation as the air gap can be wider. Any system should be readily demountable or preferably openable to provide a change of air in a room without some other form of ventilation.

Rigid glazing of plastic or glass can be fitted to the exterior of the window opening if secondary glazing would spoil the appearance of the interior. In this case, windows which are set in a deep reveal, such as the vertically sliding sash type, are the most suitable (**4**).

Glazing with renewable film

Effective double glazing can be achieved using double-sided adhesive tape to stretch a thin, flexible sheet of plastic across the window frame. It can be removed at the end of the cold season without harming the paintwork.

Clean the window frame (**1**) then cut the plastic sheet roughly to size, allowing an overlap all round. Apply double-sided tape to the frame edges (**2**) and peel off its backing paper.

Attach the film to the top rail (**3**),

then tension it onto the tape on the sides and bottom of the frame (**4**). Apply light pressure only until the film is positioned then rub it down onto the tape all round.

Use a hair dryer set to a high temperature to remove all creases and wrinkles in the film (**5**). Starting at an upper corner, move the dryer slowly across the film, holding it about 6mm (¼in) from the surface. When the film is tensioned, cut off the excess plastic (**6**).

GLAZING POSITIONS

Secondary double glazing is particularly suitable for DIY installation, partly because it is so versatile. It is possible to fit a system to almost any style or shape of window.

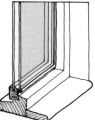
1 Sash fixed
Glazing fixed to the opening window frame

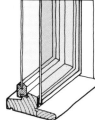
2 Frame fixed
Glazing fixed to the structural frame

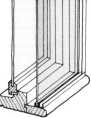
3 Reveal fixed
Glazing fixed to the reveal and interior window sill

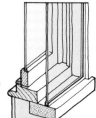
4 Exterior fitted
Glazing fixed to the reveal and exterior window sill

1 Wipe woodwork to remove dust and grease

2 Apply double-sided tape to the fixed frame

3 Stretch the film across the top of the frame

4 Pull the film tight and fix to sides and bottom

5 Use a hair dryer to shrink the film

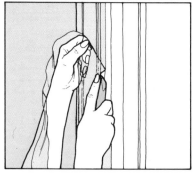
6 Trim the waste with a sharp knife

PLASTIC GLAZING

Demountable systems

A simple method for interior secondary glazing uses clear plastic film or sheet. These lightweight materials are secured by self-adhesive strips or rigid moulded sections, which form a seal. Most strip fastenings use magnetism or some form of retentive tape, which allows the secondary glazing to be removed for cleaning or ventilation. The strips and tapes usually have a flexible foam backing, which takes up slight irregularities in the woodwork. They are intended to remain in place throughout the winter and be removed for storage during the summer months.

Fitting a demountable system

Clean the windows and the surfaces of the window frame. Cut the plastic sheet to size. Place the glazing on the window frame and mark around it (**1**). Working with the plastic on a flat table, peel back the protective paper from one end of the self-adhesive strip. Tack it to the surface of the plastic, flush with one edge. Cut it to length and repeat on the other edges. Cut the mating parts of the strips and apply them to the window frame following the guidelines. Press the glazing into place (**2**).

When dealing with rigid moulded sections, cut the pieces to length with mitred corners. Fit the sections around the glazing, peel off the protective backing and press the complete unit against the frame (**3**).

1 Mark round glazing

2 Position glazed unit

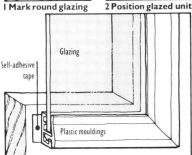

Glazing

Self-adhesive tape

Plastic mouldings

3 Rigid plastic mouldings support the glazing

PLASTIC MATERIALS FOR DOUBLE GLAZING

For economy and safety, plastic sheet materials can be used in place of glass to provide lightweight double glazing. They are available in clear thin flexible films or clear, textured and coloured rigid sheets.

Unlike glass, plastic glazing has a high impact-resistance and will not splinter when broken. Depending on thickness, plastic can be cut with scissors, drilled, sawn, planed and filed.

The clarity of new plastics is as good as glass but they will scratch. They are also liable to degrade with age and are prone to static. Plastic sheet should be washed with a liquid soap solution. Slight abrasions can be rubbed out with metal polish.

Film and semi-rigid plastics are sold by the metre or in rolls. Rigid sheets are available in a range of standard sizes or can be cut to order. Rigid plastic is covered with a protective film of paper or thin plastic on both faces which is peeled off only after cutting and shaping to keep the surface scratch-free.

POLYESTER FILM

A plastic film for inexpensive double glazing. It can be trimmed with scissors or a knife and fixed with self-adhesive tape or strip fasteners.

It is a tough, virtually tearproof film, which is very clear – ideal, in fact, for glazing living rooms. It is sold in 5, 10 and 25 metre (32, 64 and 160ft) rolls, 1143mm (3ft 9in) and 1300mm (4ft 3in) wide.

POLYSTYRENE

A relatively inexpensive clear or textured rigid plastic. Clear polystyrene does not have the clarity of glass and will degrade in strong sunlight. It should not be used for south-facing windows or where a distortion-free view is required. Depending on climatic conditions, the life of polystyrene is reckoned to be between three and five years. Its working life can be extended if the glazing is removed for storage in summer. It is available in thicknesses of 1.5mm (1/16in), 2.5mm (3/32in) and 4mm (5/32in) and sheet sizes up to 1220mm × 2440mm (4ft × 8ft).

ACRYLIC

A good-quality rigid plastic with the clarity of glass. It costs about the same as glass and about half as much again as polystyrene. Its working life is considered to be at least 10 years. Acrylic is also available in a wide range of translucent and opaque colours. The common thicknesses available for clear glazing are 1.5mm (1/16in), 2.5mm (3/32in) and 4mm (5/32in) and it is available in sheet sizes up to 1220mm × 2440mm (4ft × 8ft).

POLYCARBONATE

A relatively new plastic glazing material, which is virtually unbreakable. It provides a lightweight vandal-proof glazing with a high level of clarity. The standard grade costs about twice the price of acrylic. It is made in clear, tinted, opal and opaque grades, some with textured surfaces. Thicknesses suitable for domestic glazing are 2mm (1/16in), 3mm (1/8in) and 4mm (5/32in), although greater thicknesses are made, some in grades which are even bullet-proof. Sheet size can be up to 2050mm × 3000mm (7ft × 10ft).

PVC GLAZING

PVC is available as a flexible film or as a semi-rigid sheet. The film provides inexpensive glazing where a high degree of clarity is not required such as in a bedroom. PVC is ultraviolet-stabilized so is suitable for outside or inside use. Consequently, it is very suitable for glazing conservatories (and carport roofs). Rigid PVC is 3mm (1/8in) thick in sheet sizes up to 1220mm × 2440mm (4ft × 8ft).

SEE ALSO

Details for: ▷	
Saws	463-464
Planes	466
Drills	471
Files	490

273

OPENABLE SECONDARY GLAZING SYSTEMS

SEE ALSO

◁ Details for:

Glass	199
Cutting glass	200-201
Junior hacksaw	487
Files	490

Hinged or sliding secondary glazing systems are available in kit form for home assembly. Sliding systems are also made and installed by glazing companies – and both sliding and hinged types are intended to be permanent fixtures.

Types of glass used

Normally, 4mm ($^{5}/_{32}$in) glass is used on openable secondary glazing systems. For sliding windows no pane of glass should exceed 1.85 sq m (20 sq ft), and no more than 1.1 sq m (12 sq ft) should be used for side-hung, hinged sections.

When top-hung, each pane can be 1.65 sq m (18 sq ft). The height of each pane should not exceed 1.5m (5ft) or be greater than twice its width. Use toughened glass for low windows or those at risk from impact.

Hinged system

A hinged system incorporates an aluminium extrusion to form a frame for the glass or rigid plastic sheet. The glazing is seated in a flexible gasket. Corner joints fix the four sides together. Pivot hinges are fitted into the extrusion to make side-hung or top-hung units. A meeting rail section is also made for one frame to close against another where the window is too large to cover in one.

The hinged frames are fitted to the face of a wooden window frame and secured by turn buttons. A flexible draughtproofing strip is fixed to the back of the aluminium.

Hinged system
1 Glazing
2 Flexible gasket
3 Corner joints
4 Hinges
5 Aluminium extrusion
6 Turn button
7 Draughtproofing strip

Sliding systems

A sliding system can operate horizontally or vertically. The horizontal version is normally used for casement windows and the vertical type for tall windows, such as double-hung sashes. You can get systems made of rigid plastic or aluminium.

Each pane of glass is framed by a lightweight extrusion which is jointed at the corners. The glass is sealed into its frame with a gasket. Two or more horizontally sliding panes can be used to suit the width of the window. They are held in a tracked frame, which is screwed to the window frame or the reveal. Fibre seals are fitted to the frame members to prevent draughts between the moving parts. The glazing is opened by a catch and each pane can be lifted out for cleaning.

A vertically sliding system uses a similar form of construction but incorporates catches to hold the panes open at any height.

Sliding system
1 Glazing extrusion
2 Glazing
3 Corner joints
4 Gasket
5 Top track
6 Bottom/side track
7 Fibre draught seal
8 Catches
9 Rollers

Fixing a horizontally sliding system

Measure the width and height of your window opening. Buy the appropriate kit of parts to the nearest larger size. Cut the vertical and horizontal track members to size using a junior hacksaw (1) and fit the fibre seals in their grooves. Plug and screw them to the window reveal or the inside face of the window frame (2).

Following the manufacturer's instructions regarding tolerances, measure the opening for the glass and have it cut to size. Cut and fit the section of glazing frame, including the gasket. Join them together – usually with screw-fixed corner joints (3) but sometimes slot-together types – having inserted sliders and handles. Lift the glazing into the sliding tracks to complete the installation (4).

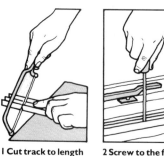

1 Cut track to length   2 Screw to the frame

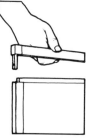

3 Assemble the frame

4 Fit into the tracks

VENTILATION

Ventilation is essential for a fresh, comfortable atmosphere but it has a more important function with regard to the structure of our homes. It wasn't a problem when houses were heated with open fires, drawing fresh air through all the natural openings in the structure. With the introduction of central heating, insulation and draughtproofing, well-designed ventilation is vital. Without a constant change of air, centrally heated rooms quickly become stuffy and before long the moisture content of the air becomes so high that water is deposited as condensation ($\triangleright$) – often with serious consequences. There are various ways to provide ventilation, some extremely simple, others much more sophisticated for total control.

Initial considerations

Whenever you undertake an improvement which involves insulation in one form or another, take into account how it is likely to affect the existing ventilation. It may change conditions sufficiently to create a problem in those areas outside the habitable rooms so that damp and its side-effects develop unnoticed under floorboards or in the loft. If there is a chance that damp conditions might occur, provide additional ventilation.

Fitting a fixed window vent

Provide continuous 'trickle' ventilation by installing a simple fixed vent in a window. A well-designed vent allows a free flow of air without draughts, normally by incorporating a wind shield on the outside. It is totally reliable as there are no moving parts to break down or produce those irritating squeaks which are a feature of wind-driven fans.

Have a glazier cut the recommended size of hole in the glass ($\triangleright$), then place one louvred grille on each side, clamping them together with the central fixing bolt. Bolt the clear plastic windshield to the outer grille.

Ventilating a fireplace

An open fire needs oxygen to burn brightly. If the supply is reduced by thorough draughtproofing or double glazing, the fire smoulders and the slightest downdraught blows smoke into the room. There may be other reasons why a fire burns poorly, such as a blocked chimney for example, but if it picks up within minutes of partially opening the door to the room, you can be sure that inadequate ventilation is the problem.

The most efficient and attractive solution is to cut holes in the floorboards on each side of the fire and cover them with a ventilator grille. Cheap plastic grilles work just as well, but you may prefer brass or aluminium for a living room. Choose a 'hit-and-miss' ventilator, which you can open and close to seal off unwelcome draughts when the fire is not in use. Cut a hole in a fully fitted carpet and screw the grille on top.

If the floor is solid, your only alternative is to fit a grille over the door to the room. An aperture at that height will not create a draught because cold air will disperse across the room and warm as it falls slowly.

Ventilating an unused fireplace

An unused fireplace that has been blocked by brickwork, blockwork or plasterboard should be ventilated to allow air to flow up the chimney to dry out penetrating damp or condensation. Some people believe a vent from a warm interior aggravates the problem by introducing moist air to condense on the cold surface of the brick flue. However, so long as the chimney is uncapped, the updraught should draw moisture-laden air to the outside. An airbrick cut into the flue from outside is a safer solution but it is more difficult to accomplish and quite impossible if you live in a terraced house. Furthermore, the airbrick would have to be blocked should you want to re-open the fireplace at a later date.

To ventilate from inside the room, leave out a single brick, form an aperture with blocks, or cut a hole in the plasterboard used to block off the fireplace ($\triangleright$). Screw a face-mounted ventilator over the hole or use one that is designed for plastering in. The thin flange for screw-fixing the ventilator to the wall is covered as you plaster up to the slightly protruding grille.

SEE ALSO

Details for: $\triangleright$
Cutting glass	201
Condensation	254-255
Sealed fireplace	385
Plastering	157
Insulation	260-274
Airbricks	276
Sweeping chimney	382

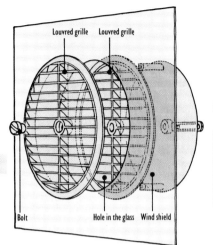
Louvred grille   Louvred grille
Bolt   Hole in the glass   Wind shield
The components of a fixed window vent

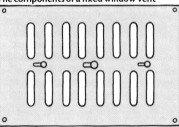
Hit-and-miss ventilator grille

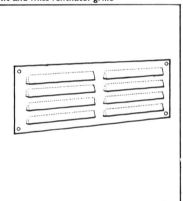
Face-mounted grille for ventilating a fireplace

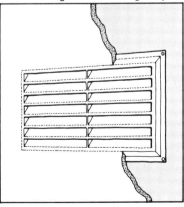
Hide the fixings of a grille with plaster

275

VENTILATING BELOW FLOORS

Perforated openings known as airbricks are built into the external walls of a house to ventilate the space below suspended wooden floors. Without them, there's a strong possibility of dry rot developing in the timbers (◁), so check their condition regularly: they

occasionally become clogged with leaves or earth piled against them, and rubble left by a builder may cover an airbrick on the inside. Clear a blocked airbrick as soon as you discover it, and if the original ones are inadequate replace them with new, larger ones.

SEE ALSO

◁ Details for:	
Repointing	45
Cavity tray	229
Dry rot	249
DPC	251
Balanced flue	392
Cutting bricks	428
Basic bricklaying	428
Masonry drill	479
Cold chisel	480

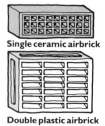

Single ceramic airbrick

Double plastic airbrick

Checking out the airbricks

Ideally there should be an airbrick every 2m (6ft) along an external wall but in many buildings there is less provision for ventilation with no ill-effects. Sufficient airflow is more important than the actual number of openings in the wall.

Floor joists that span a wide room are supported at intervals by low sleeper walls of brick. Sometimes they are perforated to facilitate an even airflow throughout the space. In other cases, the builder merely left gaps between sections of solid wall. This method of constructing sleeper walls can lead to pockets of still air in corners where draughts never reach. Even when all existing airbricks are open, dry rot can

break out in those areas which never receive an adequate change of air.

If there appears to be likely dead areas under your floor, particularly if there are signs of damp or mould growth, fit an additional airbrick in a wall nearby.

Old ceramic airbricks do get broken and are often ignored because it has no detrimental effect on the ventilation. However, even a small hole provides access for vermin. Don't be tempted to block the opening, even temporarily, but replace the broken airbrick with a similar one of the same size. Choose from single- or double-size airbricks made in ceramic or plastic.

Installing or replacing an airbrick

Use a masonry drill to remove the mortar and a cold chisel to chop out the brick you are replacing. You may have to cut some bricks to install a double-size vent. Having cut through the wall, spread mortar on the base of the hole

and along the top and both sides of the new airbrick. Push it into the opening, keeping it flush with the face of the brickwork. Repoint the mortar to match the profile used on the surrounding wall (◁).

Ventilating the space below a suspended floor
The illustration, right, is a cross-section through a typical cavity wall structure with a wooden floor suspended over a concrete base. A house with solid brick walls is ventilated in a similar way.
1 Airbrick
2 Sleeper wall built with staggered bricks to allow air to circulate
3 Joists and floorboards suffer from rot caused by poor ventilation

BRIDGING A CAVITY WALL

BRIDGING A CAVITY WALL

If you build an airbrick into a cavity wall, bridge the gap with a plastic, telescopic unit, which in turn is mortared into the hole from both sides. If necessary, a ventilator grille can be screwed to the inner end of the telescopic unit. Where an airbrick is inserted above the DPC (◁), you must fit a cavity tray over the telescopic unit to stop water running to the inner leaf of the cavity wall (◁).

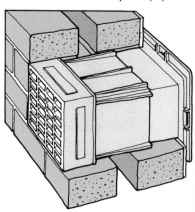

Airbrick with telescopic sleeve
Bridge a cavity wall with this type of unit.

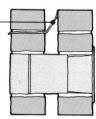

Cavity tray
A cavity tray sheds any moisture which penetrates the cavity above the unit to the outer leaf of the wall. It is necessary only when the airbrick is fitted above the DPC.

VENTILATING AN APPLIANCE

A flued, fuel-burning appliance must have an adequate supply of air to function efficiently and safely. If any alteration or improvement interferes with that supply you must provide alternative ventilation. If you plan to block a vent, change the window or even install an extractor fan in the same room as the appliance, consult a professional fitter. He will tell you whether the alteration is advisable, what type and size of vent to install, and where it should be positioned for best effect. An appliance with a balanced flue (◁) draws air directly from outside the house, so will be unaffected by internal alterations.

VENTILATING THE ROOF SPACE

When insulating the loft first became popular as an energy-saving measure, householders were recommended to tuck insulant right into the eaves to keep out draughts. What people failed to recognize was the fact that the free flow of air is necessary in the colder roof space to prevent moisture-laden air from the dwelling below condensing on the structure. Inadequate ventilation can lead to serious deterioration: wet rot develops in the roof timbers and water drops onto the insulant, eventually saturating the material and rendering it ineffective as insulation. If water builds up into pools, the ceiling below becomes stained and there is a risk of short-circuiting the electrical wiring in the loft. Efficient ventilation of the roof space, therefore, is an absolute necessity for every home.

Ventilating the eaves

Regulations for new housing insist on ventilation equivalent to continuous openings of 10mm (⅜in) along two opposite sides of a roof with a pitch (slope) of 15 degrees or more. If the pitch is less than 15 degrees, ventilation should amount to the equivalent of 25mm (1in) continuous openings. It makes sense to follow similar recommendations when refurbishing older houses.

The simplest method of ventilating a standard pitched roof is to fit round soffit vents made with integral insect screens. The spacing is determined by the size of opening provided by the particular vent. Push the vents into openings cut with a hole saw.

If the opening at the eaves is likely to be restricted by insulation, insert a plastic or cardboard eaves vent between each pair of joists. Push the vent into the angle between the rafters and the joists with the ribbed section uppermost. Vents can be cut to length with scissors for an exact fit. When installing blanket or loose-fill insulation (▷), push it up against the vent.

Slate and tile vents

Certain types of roof construction do not lend themselves to ventilation from the eaves only, but the structure can be ventilated successfully by replacing strategic tiles or slates with specially designed roof vents. A range of colours and shapes is available to blend with various roof coverings.

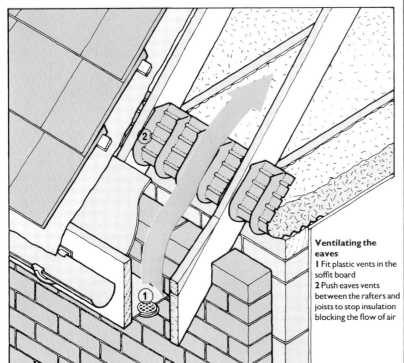

Ventilating the eaves
1 Fit plastic vents in the soffit board
2 Push eaves vents between the rafters and joists to stop insulation blocking the flow of air

WHEN ROOF VENTS ARE ESSENTIAL

Eaves-to-eaves ventilation is the standard method for keeping the roof space dry, but there are times when it is essential to fit tile or slate vents to draw air through the roof space.

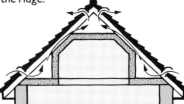

An attic space
If you insulate the slope of your roof you must provide a minimum 50mm (2in) airway between the insulant and the roof covering. It may be possible to fit eaves vents plus slate or tile vents near the ridge.

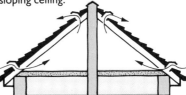

A room in the roof
Where a room is built into the attic, fit vents near the eaves and ridge to draw air through the narrow spaces over the sloping ceiling.

A fire or party wall
A solid wall built across the loft prevents eaves-to-eaves ventilation. Fit slate or tile vents to ventilate each side of the wall independently. Use the same arrangement to ventilate a mono pitch roof over an extension or lean-to (▷).

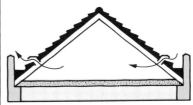

A roof with parapet
The roofs of older houses with parapets can be ventilated with vents positioned at a low level to give effective eaves-to-eaves ventilation.

SEE ALSO

Details for: ▷

Insulation	266
Mono-pitch roof	502
Wet rot	249
Insulating sloping roof	267
Insulating an attic	267
Fitting roof vents	278
Hole saw	465

Soffit vent

Slate/tile vents
Roof vents are made to resemble typical roof coverings.

Double Roman tile vent

Slate vent

Double pantile vent

FITTING ROOF VENTS

Installing a slate or tile vent

SEE ALSO

◁ Details for:
Removing tiles   226
Replacing tiles   226
Roof construction   224
Use of roof vents   277

If you are contemplating having your roof replaced, ask the roofing contractor to incorporate vents at the same time, otherwise install vents in an existing roof yourself. Fitting instructions for individual models will vary in detail but the description below for a double pantile vent demonstrates the principle.

As each vent must be placed between rafters, select the approximate position of a vent and remove enough tiles (◁) to expose the felt and to locate the heads of the nails holding the tile-support battens to the roof. The nails indicate the position of the rafters.

Centre the template supplied by the manufacturer between the rafters and mark the position of the hole on the roof felt by scratching the corners with a knife (1). Cut the diagonals of the opening and bend back the flaps (2). Cut a slit in the felt, 100mm (4in) above and centred on the opening, and insert the tail of the undercloak of the vent (3), then align the edge of the undercloak with the opening (4). Plug the extension sleeve onto the underside of the cowl (5), then insert the sleeve into the hole in the felt and nail the cowl to the support batten above the opening (6). Replace the surrounding tiles, using hook clips to hold them in position (◁).

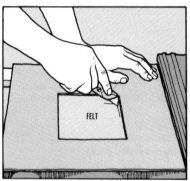

1 Scratch the corners of the hole with a knife

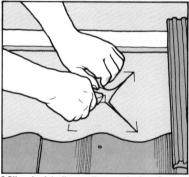

2 Slice the felt diagonally to make four flaps

The undercloak
The undercloak fits beneath the vent cowl to prevent water running through the opening cut in the roof felt.

3 Put undercloak under batten if necessary

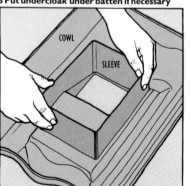

4 Position the undercloak to align with hole

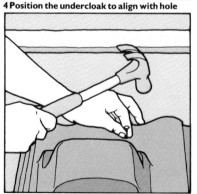

5 Plug sleeve onto the bottom of the vent cowl

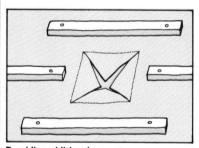

6 Nail the vent to the tile batten

CALCULATING AIR FLOW CAPACITY

All vents positioned near the eaves should provide the equivalent of 10 or 25mm (3/8 or 1in) continuous gap depending on the pitch of the roof. The ones near the ridge should provide air-flow to suit the construction of a particular roof.

Divide the specified airflow capacity of the vent you wish to use into the recommended continuous gap to calculate how many vents you will need. If in doubt, provide slightly more ventilation than is indicated.

Place eaves vents in the fourth or fifth course of slates or tiles. Position the higher vents a couple of courses below the ridge. Space all vents evenly along the roof to avoid any areas of 'dead' air.

CLEARING THE OPENING

When replacing certain tiles or slates with a vent it may be necessary to cut through a tile support batten to clear the opening. Nail a short length of batten above and below the opening to provide additional support.

Because roofing slates overlap each other by a considerable amount, you will have to cut away the top corners of the lower slates.

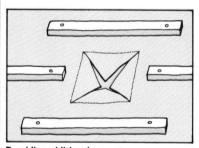

Providing additional support
Cut a tile batten that obstructs a hole, then place battens above and below to support the vent.

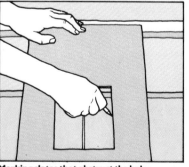

Marking slates that obstruct the hole
When slates cover the opening for a vent, use the template to mark the corners, then remove them.

FITTING AN EXTRACTOR FAN

Kitchens and bathrooms are particularly susceptible to problems of condensation so it is especially important to have a means of efficiently expelling moisture-laden air along with unpleasant odours. An electrically driven extractor fan will freshen a room faster than relying on natural ventilation and without creating uncomfortable draughts.

Positioning an extractor fan

The best place to site a fan is either in a window or on an outside wall but its exact position is more critical than that. Stale air extracted from the room must be replaced by fresh air, normally through the door leading to other areas of the house. If the fan is sited close to the source of replacement air it will promote local circulation but will have little effect on the rest of the room.

The ideal position would be directly opposite the source as high as practicable to extract the rising hot air (**1**). In a kitchen, try to locate the fan adjacent to the cooker but not directly over it. In that way, steam and cooking smells will not be drawn across the room before being expelled (**2**). If the room contains a flued, fuel-burning appliance, you must ensure there is an adequate supply of fresh air at all times or the extractor fan will draw fumes down the flue (▷). The only exception is an appliance with a balanced flue, which takes its air directly from outside (▷).

1 Fit extractor opposite replacement air source

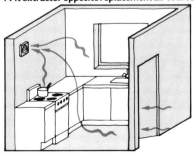

2 Place extractor near a cooker in a kitchen

Types of extractor fan

Many fans have integral switches but, if not, a switched connection unit can be wired into the circuit (▷) when you install the fan. Some models incorporate built-in controllers to regulate the speed of extraction and timers to switch off the fan automatically after a certain time. Fans can be installed in a window and some, with the addition of a duct, will extract air through a solid or cavity wall (see illustrations below). Choose a fan with external shutters that close when the fan is not in use, to prevent backdraughts.

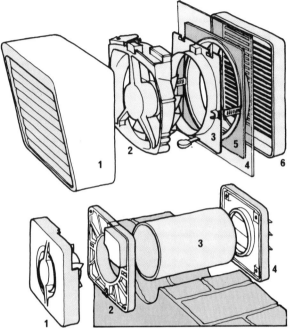

Window-mounted fan
1 Inner casing
2 Motor assembly
3 Interior clamping plate
4 Glass
5 Grille clamping plate
6 Exterior grille

Wall-mounted fan
1 Motor assembly
2 Interior backplate
3 Duct
4 Exterior grille

SEE ALSO

Details for: ▷

Switched connection unit	314
Flues	386-387,392
Balanced flues	392
Wall construction	122
Condensation	254-255
Cooker hoods	281

Choosing the size of a fan

The size of a fan, or to be accurate, its capacity, is determined by the type of room in which it is installed and the volume of air it must move.

A fan installed in a kitchen must be capable of changing the air completely ten to fifteen times per hour. A bathroom requires fifteen to twenty air changes per hour and a WC, ten to fifteen. A living room normally requires four to six changes per hour, but fit a fan with a slightly larger capacity in a smoky environment.

To calculate the capacity of the fan you require, find the volume of the room (length x width x height) then multiply that figure by the recommended number of air changes per hour. Choose a fan which is capable of the same or slightly higher capacity.

CALCULATING THE CAPACITY OF FAN FOR A KITCHEN

SIZE			
Length	**Width**	**Height**	**Volume**
3.35m (11ft)	3.05m (10ft)	2.44m (8ft)	24.93m^3 (880ft^3)

AIR CHANGES		
Per hour	**Volume**	**Fan capacity**
15	24.93m^3 (880ft^3)	374m^3 per hour (13,200ft^3)

SEE ALSO

◁ Details for:

Cutting glass	200-201
Fitting glass	202
Sash stop	242
Consumer unit	296
Masonry drills	479
Removing window glass	202
Wiring a fan	316

Metal detector
Detect buried pipes or
cables by placing a hired
electronic sensor
against the plaster

1 Hold panel with
plank

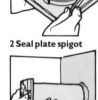

2 Seal plate spigot

3 Insert duct in hole

4 Screw-fix grille

FITTING A WALL-MOUNTED UNIT

Satisfy yourself that there is no
plumbing or wiring buried in the wall by
looking in the loft or under the
floorboards (see left). Make sure there
are no drain pipes or other obstructions.

Cutting the hole

Wall-mounted fans are supplied with a
length of plastic ducting for inserting in a
hole which you must cut through the
wall to the outside. Plot the centre of
the hole and draw its diameter on the
inside of the wall. Use a long-reach
masonry drill (◁) to bore a central hole
right through. To prevent the drill
breaking out brickwork or rendering on
the outside, hold a stout plywood panel
against the wall and wedge it with a
scaffold board supported by stakes
driven into the ground (1).

Before cutting the brick, drill holes
close together around the inner edge of
the hole. With a cold chisel, cut away
the plaster using the holes as a guide,
then continue to cut away the
brickwork (try to avoid debris falling
inside a cavity wall). When you reach
the centre of the wall, remove the panel
then use the same technique to finish
the hole from the outside face.

Fitting the fan

Most wall fans are fitted in a similar
manner, but check specific instructions
beforehand. Separate the components
of the fan, then attach a self-adhesive
foam sealing strip to the spigot on the
backplate to receive the duct (2).

Insert the duct in the hole so that the
backplate fits against the wall (3). Mark
the length of the duct on the outside,
allowing sufficient to fit the similar
spigot on the outer grille. Cut the duct
to length with a hacksaw. Reposition
the backplate and duct to mark the
fixing holes on the wall. Drill and plug
the holes then feed the electrical supply
cable into the backplate before
screwing it to the wall. Stick a foam
sealing strip inside the spigot on the
grille. Position it on the duct then mark,
drill and plug the wall fixing holes. Use a
screwdriver to stuff scraps of loft
insulation between the duct and the cut
edge of the hole, then screw on the
exterior grille (4).

If the grille does not fit flush with the
wall, seal the gap with mastic. Wire the
fan according to the manufacturer's
recommendations. Attach the motor
assembly to the backplate.

FITTING AN EXTRACTOR FAN

Installing a fan in a window

An extractor fan can only be installed in
a fixed window. If you wish to fit one in
a sash window, it's necessary to secure
the top sash in which the fan is installed
and fit a sash stop (◁) on each side of
the window to prevent the lower sash
damaging the casing of the fan should it
be raised too far.

To install an extractor fan in an
hermetically sealed double glazing
system, ask the manufacturer to supply a
special unit with a hole cut and sealed
around its edges to receive the fan.
Some manufacturers supply a kit which
adapts a fan for installing in a window
with secondary double glazing. It allows
the inner window to be opened without
dismantling the fan.

Cutting the glass

Every window-mounted fan requires a
round hole to be cut in the glass. The
size is specified by the manufacturer. It
is possible to cut a hole in an existing
window but stresses in the glass will
sometimes cause it to crack, and while
the glass is removed for cutting there is
always a security risk, especially if you
decide to take it to a glazier. All things
considered, it is advisable to fit a new
pane: it's easier to cut and can be
installed immediately the old one has
been removed.

Cutting a hole in glass is not easy (◁)
and it may be more economical in the
long run to order it from a glazier.
You'll need to supply exact dimensions,
including the size and position of the
hole. Use 3mm glass for a pane that
does not exceed 0.2 sq m (2 sq ft) in
area. Cut a larger pane from 4mm glass.

Installing the fan

The exact assembly may vary but the
following sequence is a typical example
of how a fan is installed in a window.
Take out the existing window pane and
clean up the frame, removing traces of
old putty and retaining sprigs. Fit the
new pane, with its hole pre-cut, as for
fitting window glass (◁).

From outside, fit the exterior grille
by locating its circular flange in the hole
(1). Attach the plate on the inside,
which clamps the grille to the glass.
Tighten the fixing screws in rotation to
achieve a good seal and an even
clamping force on the glass (2). Screw
the motor assembly to the clamping
plate (3). Wire up the fan following the
maker's instructions. Fit the inner casing
over the motor assembly (4).

WARNING

**Never make electrical connections
until the power is switched off at
the consumer unit (◁).**

1 Place grille in the hole from outside

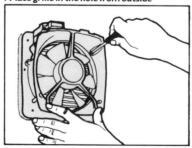

3 Screw the motor assembly to the plate

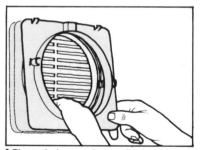

2 Clamp the inner and outer plate together

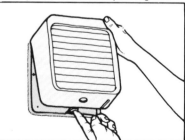

4 Attach the inner casing to cover the assembly

INSTALLING A COOKER HOOD

Window- and wall-mounted fans are designed for overall room extraction, but the ideal way to tackle steam and greasy cooking smells from a cooker is to mount a specially designed extracting hood directly over it.

Where to mount the cooker hood

Mount a cooker hood between 600mm (2ft) and 900mm (3ft) above the hob or about 400 to 600mm (1ft 4in to 2ft) above an eye-level grill. Unless the manufacturer provides specific dimensions, mount a hood as low as possible within the recommended tolerances.

Depending on the model, a cooker hood may be cantilevered from the wall or, alternatively, screwed between or beneath kitchen cupboards. Some kitchen manufacturers produce a cooker hood housing unit, which matches the style of the cupboards. Opening the unit operates the fan automatically. Most cooker hoods have two or three speed settings and an inbuilt light fitting to illuminate the hob or cooker below.

Installing trunking

When a cooker hood is mounted on an outside wall, air is extracted through the back of the unit into a straight duct passing through the masonry. If the cooker is situated against another wall, it is possible to connect the hood with the outside by means of fire-resistant plastic trunking. Straight and curved components plug into each other to form a continuous shaft running along the top of the wall cupboards.

Plug the female end of the first trunking component over the outlet spigot fitted to the top of the cooker hood. Cutting them to fit with a hacksaw or a tenon saw, run the rest of the trunking, making the same female-to-male connections along the shaft. Some trunking is printed with airflow arrows to make sure each component is orientated correctly: if you were to reverse a component somewhere along the shaft, air turbulence might be created around the joint, reducing the effectiveness of the extractor. At the outside wall, cut a hole through the masonry for a straight piece of ducting and fit an external grille (See opposite).

Fitting a cooker hood

Recycling and extracting hoods are hung from wall brackets supplied with the machines. Screw fixing points are provided for attaching them to wall cupboards. Cut a ducting hole through a wall as for a wall-mounted fan (See opposite). Wire a cooker hood following the maker's instructions.

RECIRCULATION OR EXTRACTION?

The only real difference between one cooker hood and another is the way it deals with the stale air it captures. Some hoods filter out the moisture and grease before returning the freshened air to the room. Other machines dump stale air outside through a duct in the wall, just like a conventional wall-mounted extractor fan.

Because the air is actually changed, extraction is the more efficient method but it is necessary to cut a hole through the wall and, of course, the heated air is lost – excellent in hot weather but rather a waste in winter. Cooker hoods which recycle the air are much simpler to install but never filter out all the grease and odours, even when new. It is essential to clean and change the filters regularly to keep the hood working at peak efficiency.

SEE ALSO

Details for: ▷	
Kitchen planning	16
Condensation	254-255
Wiring a cooker hood	316
Tenon saw	463
Hacksaws	486-487

Recirculation hood returns filtered air to room

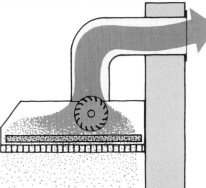

Extraction hoods suck air outside via trunking

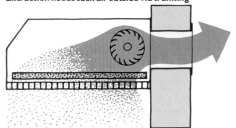

Alternatively, air is extracted through ducting

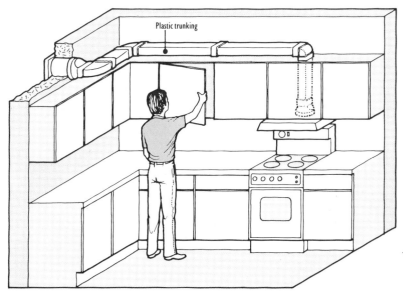

Plastic trunking

◁ **Running trunking outside**
When a cooker is placed against an inside wall, run plastic trunking from the extractor hood along the top of wall-hung cupboards.

281

HEAT EXCHANGING VENTILATORS

Most people naturally think of ventilating a room in hot weather when it is most likely to be unpleasantly stuffy. In all but the hottest of summers it can be achieved simply by opening windows or using a mechanical fan. However, ventilation is equally important in the winter – but we keep our weatherstripped windows closed against draughts, promoting an unhealthy atmosphere and a rise in condensation.

Using a conventional extractor fan solves the problem, but at the cost of throwing away heated air. A heat exchanging ventilator is the answer: two centrifugal fans operate simultaneously, one to suck in fresh air from the outside while the other extracts the same volume of foul air from inside. The system is perfectly balanced so the unit works efficiently even in a totally draughtproofed room.

SEE ALSO

◁ Details for:
Flashing tape	233
Preventing break out	280
Fused connection unit	314
Hole saw	465
Condensation	254-255
Glass-fibre insulation	265
Wiring a fan	316

The benefits of a heat exchanger

An important plus for heat exchanging ventilators is that heat loss is cut to a minimum by passing the extracted air through a series of small vents sandwiched between similar vents containing cold outside air moving in the other direction. Most of the heat is transferred to the fresh air so it is blown into the room warmed.

If you want to install a heat exchanger in a kitchen or bathroom, check that the unit is suitable for steamy atmospheres and greasy air.

Heat exchangers are either wall-mounted much like a standard extractor fan, or flush-mounted so that the cabinet housing the unit is set into the wall. A slim, grilled casing only is visible from inside. The former version is relatively simple to fit but more obtrusive. To install a flush-mounted unit, it is necessary to cut a large rectangular hole through the wall and, in some cases, line it with timber.

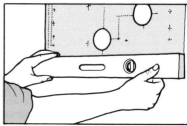
1 Position template to mark ducts and fixings

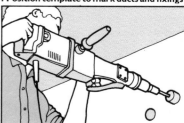
2 Bore holes for ducting with a hired core drill

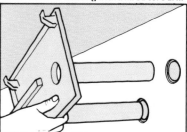
3 Pass both ducts through the wall

4 Plug gaps around ducts with insulation

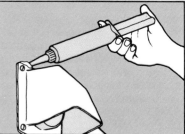
5 Seal edge of duct covers with mastic

6 Fit the ventilator unit on the inside

How the ventilator functions
Hot, stale air is drawn into the unit (1) by a centrifugal fan (2). It is passed via the heat exchanger (3) to the outside (4). Fresh air is sucked from outside (5) by fan (6) to be warmed in the heat exchanger and passed into the room (7).

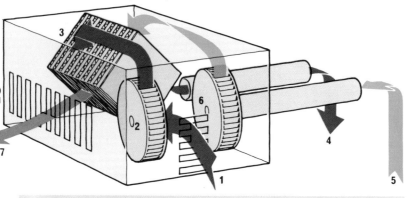

Fitting a wall-mounted ventilator

With the aid of a spirit level, use the manufacturer's template to mark the position of the ventilator on the wall, including the centre of both ducts (1). Locate the unit high on the wall but with at least 50mm (2in) clearance above and to the sides.

The ducting is likely to be narrower than that used for standard extractor fans, so it may be possible to use a hole saw or core drill to cut through the masonry (◁). Wedge a board outside to prevent the masonry breaking out (◁) then drill a pilot hole centred on each duct. Use a long-reach masonry drill to bore right through the wall. Angle the drill downwards five degrees so that the ducting will slope to drain condensation to the outside.

Locate the centre of the core drill in the pilot hole then drill halfway through the wall before removing the board from the outside to continue there towards the inside (2). Use a hacksaw to cut the plastic ducting to a length equalling the depth of the wall plus 8mm (⅜in). Use aluminium flashing tape (◁) to hold ducting to both spigots on the rear of the wall-mounting panel. Insert the ducting into the drilled holes (3), push the panel against the wall and screw-fix it.

Outside, plug the gaps round the ducting with glass-fibre insulation (4) and screw the weather covers over the ends of the ducts. Seal around the edges of both covers with mastic (5). Fit the main unit to the mounting panel on the inside wall (6) and wire up to a fused connection unit nearby (◁).

VENTILATORS

Mounting a flush ventilator

Most flush-mounted ventilators require a wooden frame to line a hole cut through the wall. Make it to the dimensions supplied by the manufacturer of the ventilator. Construct the frame with lap joints (▷) or pinned and glued butt joints, and draw round it to mark the position of the hole on the wall. Apply a timber preservative.

Use a masonry drill to bore a hole through the wall at each corner then chop along the plaster between them with a bolster chisel. Drill further holes around the perimeter of the hole and chop out the masonry with a cold chisel. Remove whole bricks by drilling out the mortar joints. After cutting halfway through the wall, finish the hole from the outside.

The ventilator must be angled downwards a few degrees towards the outside to drain away condensation. If this angle is built into the ventilator unit, the wooden lining can be set flush with the wall, otherwise tilt it fractionally within the brickwork. Wedge the lining in place and fix it with masonry nails or fit wallplugs for fixing screws. Measure the diagonals to make sure the lining is square in the hole.

Fit the main unit in the liner and screw it to the front edge of the timber. Fit the front grille onto the unit. Outside, seal the junction between the unit and the lining with mastic. Do exactly the same where the timber frame meets the brickwork.

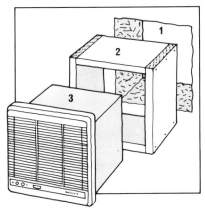

Mounting a flush ventilator
Cut a rectangular hole through the masonry (1). Construct a softwood liner using butt joints at the corners (2). Screw the ventilator (3) to the front edge of the liner.

FITTING A UNIT IN A TIMBER-FRAME WALL

Decide on the approximate position of the unit then locate the studs (▷) to align one with the side of the unit. Mark the rectangle for the wooden lining then drill through the plasterboard at the corners. Cut out the rectangle with a padsaw. Cut and remove the wall insulation. Working from outside, cut away the external cladding along the same lines. Saw off any studs obstructing the hole flush with its edges. Make and fit a timber lining as for a solid wall. Nail it to the studs and install the unit.

Mounting a ventilator liner ▷
Fit a timber liner in the wall close to the ceiling where it will be in the best position to extract hot rising air.

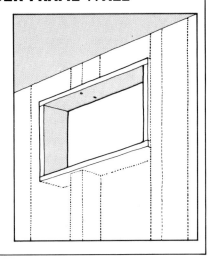

SEE ALSO

Details for: ▷	
Locating studs	137
Lap joint	475
Preservatives	250
Condensation	254-255
Padsaw	464
Masonry drill	479
Cold chisel	480

DEHUMIDIFIERS CONTROL CONDENSATION

To combat condensation you can remove the moisture-laden air by ventilation or warm it so that it can carry more water vapour before it becomes saturated. An alternative measure is to extract the water itself from the air using a dehumidifier. This is achieved by drawing air from the room into the unit and passing it over cold coils upon which water vapour condenses and drips into a reservoir. The cold, but now dry air is drawn by a fan over heated coils before being returned to the room as additional convected heat.

The process is based on the refrigeration principle that gas under pressure heats up and when the pressure drops, so does the temperature of the gas. In a dehumidifier, a compressor delivers pressurized gas to the 'hot' coils, in turn leading to the larger 'cold' coils, which allow the gas to expand. The cooled gas returns to the compressor for recycling.

A dehumidifier for domestic use is built into a cabinet which resembles a large hi-fi speaker. It contains a humidistat, which automatically switches on the unit when the moisture content of the air reaches a predetermined level. When the reservoir is full, the machine shuts down

to prevent overflow and an indicator lights up to remind you to empty the water in the container.

When installed in a damp room, a dehumidifier will extract excess moisture from the furnishings and fabric of the building in a week or two. After that it will monitor the moisture content of the air to maintain a stabilized atmosphere. A portable version can be wheeled from room to room, where it is plugged into a standard wall socket.

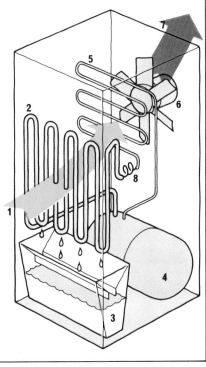

The working components of a dehumidifier ▷
The diagram illustrates the layout of a typical domestic dehumidifier.
1 Incoming damp air
2 Cold coils

3 Water reservoir
4 Compressor
5 Hot coils
6 Fan
7 Dry warm air
8 Capillary tube where gas expands

AIR CONDITIONERS

SEE ALSO

◁ Details for:
Dehumidifier 283
**Timber lining
for ventilator** 283

*Air conditioning is rarely
installed in this country because
the few weeks of uncomfortably hot
or humid weather hardly warrant
the expense of installing and
running a system. A central system
which cools an entire dwelling
would be extravagent and is not
suitable for DIY installation.*

*On the other hand, individual
units which cool the main bedroom
or lounge only are not prohibitively
expensive and are relatively simple
to fit. What's more, if you choose
a unit that can reverse the cooling
process, it works as a heat pump
in cold weather to supplement the
domestic central heating.*

How air conditioning works

An air conditioner works on the same
refrigeration principle described for a
dehumidifier (◁) and incorporates
similar gas-filled coils and a compressor.
However, airflow within the unit is
different. Individual units are divided
into separate compartments within one
cabinet. Room air is drawn into the
cooling compartment and passed over
the evaporation coils which absorb heat
before a fan returns the air to the room
at a lower temperature. As moisture
vapour condenses on the coils, the unit
also acts as a dehumidifier, a welcome
bonus in hot humid weather.
Condensed water is normally drained to
the outside of the house.

Gas in the evaporation coils moves
on, carrying absorbed heat to the
compartment facing the outside, where
it is radiated from condenser coils and
blown outside by a fan.

A thermostat operates a valve, which
reverses the flow of refrigerant when
the temperature in the room drops
below the setting. The system is
automatic, so that the unit can heat the
room if it is cold in the early morning.
As the sun rises and boosts the
temperature, the air conditioner
switches over to maintain a constant
temperature indoors.

Choose a unit with variable fan speed
and a method for directing the chilled
air where it will be most effective in
cooling the whole room. Usually this is
at ceiling level, where the cold air falls
slowly over the whole room area.

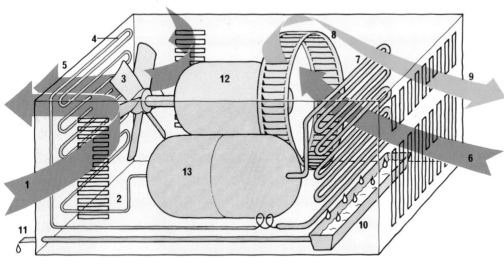

**How an air
conditioner works**
The diagram shows the
mechanism of a small
wall- or window-
mounted air
conditioner but it
illustrates the principle
employed by all air
conditioners.

Outside air (1) drawn
through the side vents
(2) by fan (3) which
blows it over the hot
coils (4). The air
extracts heat from the
coils and takes it outside
(5). Warm humid air
from the interior (6) is
drawn over the cold
coils (7) by a centrifugal
fan (8) and returned to
the room cooled and
dry (9). The condensed

water drips into a
reservoir (10) and
drains to the outside
(11). The motor (12)
powers the fans and
compressor (13) which
pumps gas around the
system.

CHOOSING THE CAPACITY

To reduce the running costs of an air
conditioner, try to match its capacity –
the amount of heat it can absorb – to
the size of the room it will be cooling. A
unit which is too small will be running
most of the time without complete
success, while one that is much too large
will chill the air so quickly that it won't
be able to remove much moisture
vapour, so the atmosphere may still feel
uncomfortable when it is humid. Ideally,
the unit should be working flat-out on
only the hottest of days.

The capacity of a conditioner is
measured in British Thermal Units
(BTU). A unit with a capacity of 9000
BTU will remove that amount of heat
every hour. As a rough guide to
capacity, find the volume of the area you
wish to cool (length x width x height)
then allow 175 BTU per cubic metre (5
BTU per cubic foot). Ask the supplier to
provide a more accurate calculation
which will take into consideration other
factors such as size and number of
windows, insulation and heat-generating
equipment in the room.

MOUNTING THE UNIT

Cut a hole through the wall and fit a
timber lining as for a heat exchanging
ventilator (◁). Being a somewhat larger
and heavier unit, an air conditioner will
have some sort of supporting cage or
metal brackets.

If the wall is more than 300mm (1ft)
thick, the vertical wall adjacent to the
side vents must be cut away to an angle
of 45 degrees to permit adequate air
circulation.

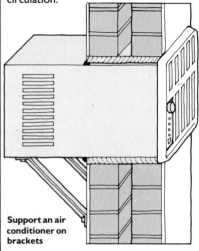

**Support an air
conditioner on
brackets**

7

ECONOMICS   286

BASICS   288

SAFETY   289

BASIC REPAIRS   292

FUSE BOARDS   296

CIRCUITS   301

CABLES   302

CHECKLISTS   306

POWER CIRCUITS   308

FIXED APPLIANCES   314

LARGER APPLIANCES   317

LIGHTING   323

EXTERIOR ELECTRICS   332

COMPLETE REWIRING   336

ELECTRICITY

REDUCING THE COST OF ELECTRICITY

SEE ALSO

◁ Details for:
Insulation	261
Time switches	240
Immersion heaters	318-319
Storage heaters	320-321
Heating controls	395

● **Insulation**
Measures taken to save energy are of little use unless you insulate the house as well as the hot water cylinder and pipework (◁). You can do most of the work yourself with very little effort or cost.

Pressures from all sides urge us to conserve energy – electricity as well as fossil fuels like coal, oil and gas – but even without such encouragement the totals on our quarterly electricity bills should be stimulus enough to make us find ways of using less power. No-one wants to live in a poorly heated, dismally lit house without the comforts of hot baths, TV, record players and other conveniences, but you may be able to identify where energy is wasted, then find ways to reduce waste without compromising your comfort or pleasure.

Avoid false economy

Whether you do your own wiring or employ a professional, don't try to economize by installing fewer sockets than you really need. When you rewire a room fit as many as you may possibly use. The inconvenience, later on, of running extra cable and disturbing decoration will far outweigh the cost of an extra socket or two.

Similarly, don't restrict your use of lighting unnecessarily. It uses relatively little power, so there is no point in risking, say, accidents on badly lit stairs. Nor need you strain your eyes in the glare from a single light hanging from the ceiling when extra lights can give comfortable and attractive background illumination where needed.

Fitting controls to save money

It will be clear from the chart (See opposite) that heating of one sort or another is the main consumer of power. One way to economize is to fit devices that are designed to regulate its use to suit your life style and keep your heating at comfortable but economic temperatures.

Thermostats
Most modern heating has some form of thermostatic control – a device that will switch power off when surroundings reach a certain temperature. Many thermostats are marked out simply to increase or decrease the temperature. In this case you have to experiment with various settings to find the one that suits you. If you can set it accurately try 18°C (65°F) for everyday use, though elderly people are more comfortable at about 21°C (70°F).

An immersion heater thermostat both saves money and prevents water becoming dangerously hot. Set it at 60°C (140°F). (For Economy 7 setting see right.)

Time switches
Even thermostatically controlled heating is expensive if run continuously but an automatic time switch can turn it on and off at pre-set times so that you get up in the morning or home in the evening to a warm house. Set it to turn off the heating a half-hour before you leave home or go to bed, as the house will take time to cool down.

A similar device will ensure water at its hottest when it is needed.

Recording consumption

Keep an accurate record of your energy saving by taking weekly readings. Note the dates of measures taken to cut consumption and compare the corresponding drop in meter readings.

Digital meters
Modern meters simply display a row of figures or digits that represent the total number of units consumed since the meter was installed. To deduce the number of units used since your last electricity bill subtract the 'present reading' shown on the bill from the number of units now shown on the meter. Make sure that the bill shows an actual reading and not an estimate, indicated by an E before the reading.

ECONOMICAL OFF-PEAK RATES

Electricity is normally sold at a general-purpose rate, every unit used costing the same, but if you warm your home with storage heaters and heat your water electrically you should consider the advantages of the economical off-peak rate. The system, called Economy 7, allows you to charge storage heaters and heat water at less than half the general-purpose rate for seven hours starting between midnight and 1 a.m. Any other appliance used in that time gets cheap power too, so more savings can be made by having a timer to turn on a dishwasher or automatic washing machine when the household has gone to bed. Economy 7 daytime rate is higher than the general-purpose one, but the cost of running 24-hour appliances like freezers and refrigerators is balanced because they too use cheap power for seven hours.

For full benefit from off-peak water heating use a 182 to 227 litre (40 to 50 gallon) cylinder to store as much cheap hot water as possible. You will need a twin-element heater or two separate units. One heater, near the base of the cylinder, heats the whole tank on cheap power; another, about half way, tops up the hot water during the day. Set the night-time heater about 5°C (10°F) higher than the upper heater.

The Electricity Board supplies those using the Economy 7 programme with a special meter to record daytime and night-time consumption separately, also a timer that switches the supply from one rate to the other.

HOW TO READ DIAL METERS

The principle of a dial meter is simple. Ignore the dial marked 1/10, which is only for testing. Start with the dial indicating single units (kWh) and, working from right to left, record the readings from 10, 100, 1000 and finally 10,000 units. Note the digits the pointers have passed. If a pointer is, say, between 5 and 6 record 5. If a pointer is right on a number, say 8, check the next dial on the right. If that point is between 9 and 0 record 7; if it is past 0 record 8.

Remember that adjacent dials revolve in opposite directions, alternating along the row.

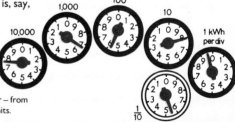

Reading a dial meter
Write down your reading in reverse order – from right to left. This meter records 76,579 units.

Apart from the standing charge or hire-purchase payments, your electricity bill is calculated from the number of units of electricity you have used in a given period. Each unit represents the amount used in one hour by a 1kW appliance. An appliance rated at 3kW uses the same amount of energy in 20 minutes.

TYPICAL RUNNING COSTS

	Appliance	Typical usage	No. of units		Appliance	Typical usage	No. of units
	Cooker	Cooks one day's meals for four people	2½		Iron	In use for 2 hours	1
	Microwave	Cooks two joints of meat	1		Vacuum cleaner	Works for 1½-2 hours	1
	Slow cooker	Cooks for 8 hours	1		Cooker hood	Runs for 24 hours continuously	2
	Storage heater (2 kW)	Provides one day's heating	8½		Extractor fan	Runs for 24 hours continuously	1
	Bar fire or fan heater (3 kW)	Gives heat for one hour	3		Hair dryer	Runs for 2 hours	1
	Immersion heater	Supplies one day's hot water for family of four	9		Shaver	Provides 1800 shaves	1
	Instant water heater	Heats 2 to 3 bowls of washing up water	1		Single overblanket	Warms the bed for one week	2
	Instant shower	Delivers 1 to 2 showers	1		Single underblanket	Warms the bed for one week	1
	Dishwasher	Washes one full load	2		Power drill	Works for 4 hours	1
	Automatic washing machine	Deals with one full load with pre-wash	2½		Hedge trimmer	Trims for 2½ hours	1
	Tumble dryer	Dries same load	2½		Cylinder lawn mower	Cuts grass for 3 hours	1
	4 cu ft refrigerator	Keeps food fresh for one week	7		Hover mower	Cuts grass for 1 hour	1
	6 cu ft freezer	Maintains required temperature for one week	9		Stereo system	Plays for 8 hours	1
	Heated towel rail	Warms continuously for 6 hours	1½		Colour TV	Provides 6 hours viewing	1
	Electric kettle	Boils 40 cups of tea	1		VCR	Records for 10 hours	1
	Coffee percolator	Makes 75 cups of coffee	1		100W bulb	Gives 10 hours illumination	1
	Toaster	Toasts 70 slices of bread	1		40W fluorescent strip	Gives 20 hours illumination	1

SEE ALSO

Details for: ▷

Electric fires	315
Heated towel rail	315
Instant water heater	316
Wiring kitchen appliances	316
Wiring cooker hood	316
Wiring extractor fan	316
Wiring a cooker	317-318
Immersion heaters	318-319
Storage heaters	320-321
Instant shower	323
Lighting	323-331

● **Typical running costs**
The table shows you how much electricity is used, on average, by common household appliances with different kW ratings. For example, a 100W light bulb can give you 10 hours of illumination before it uses up one 1 kilowatt unit, whereas a 3 kilowatt bar fire will give off heat for only 20 minutes for the same 1 kilowatt.

UNDERSTANDING THE BASICS

SEE ALSO

◁ Details for:

Earth bonding	290,297
Flex	292
Fuses	295,299
Circuits	301
Cable	302
Running cable	303-305

Though many people imagine working on the electrical circuits of their homes to be a complicated business it is, in fact, based on very simple principles.

For any electrical appliance to work, the power must have a complete circuit, flowing along a wire from its source – a battery, for instance – to the appliance – say a light bulb – then flowing back to the source along another wire. That is a circuit, and if it is broken at any point the appliance stops working – the bulb goes out.

Breaking the circuit – and restoring it as required – is what a switch is for. With the switch on, the circuit is complete and the bulb or other appliance operates. Switching off makes a gap in the circuit so that the electricity stops flowing.

Though a break in either wire will stop the power flow, in practice a

switch should be wired so that it interrupts the live wire, the one taking power to the appliance. In this way the appliance is completely dead when the switch is off. If the switch is wired so as to interrupt the neutral wire, which takes the electricity back to its source, the appliance will stop working but elements in it will still be 'live', which can be dangerous.

Though mains electricity is much more powerful than that produced by a battery it operates in exactly the same way, flowing through a live or 'phase' wire which is linked to every socket outlet, light and fixed electrical appliance in your home.

For purposes of identification when wiring is done the covering of the live wire is coloured red or brown. The covering on the neutral wire, which takes the current back out of the house after its work, is black or blue.

A basic circuit
Electricity runs from the source (battery) to the appliance (bulb) and returns to the source. A switch breaks the circuit to interrupt the flow of electricity.

Double insulation
A square within a square printed or moulded on an appliance means that it is double-insulated and its flex needs no earth wire.

Identifying conductors ▶
The insulation covering the conductors in cable and flex are colour-coded to indicate live, neutral and earth.

LIVE	NEUTRAL	EARTH
Flex	Flex	Flex
Cable	Cable	Cable

Earthing

Any material that electricity can flow through is known as a conductor. Most metals are good conductors of electricity, which is why metal – most often copper, which is probably the best – is used for electrical wiring.

However the earth itself, the ground on which we stand, is an extremely good conductor, a better one than the wiring used in the circuits, and associated with this is the fact that electricity will always flow into the earth if it can, and by the shortest available route. This means that if you were to touch a live conductor the current would divert and take the short route through you to the earth, perhaps with fatal consequences to you.

A similar thing can happen if a live wire comes accidentally into contact with any exposed metal component of an appliance, including its casing. To prevent this a third wire is incorporated in the wiring system and connected to the earth, usually via the outer casing of the Electricity Board's main service cable. This third, 'earth wire' is attached

to the metal casing of some appliances, and to special 'earth terminals' in others, providing a direct route to earth should a fault occur. This change of route by the power, called a 'short circuit', causes a fuse to blow or circuit breaker to operate, cutting off the current.

Some appliances are double-insulated, which usually means that they have non-conductive plastic casings that insulate the user from any metal part that could become live. For this reason double-insulated appliances do not have to be 'earthed' with a third wire.

The earth wire either has a green and yellow covering or is a bare copper wire sandwiched between the insulated live and neutral wires in the electrical cable. Whenever a bare earth wire is exposed for linking to socket outlets or lighting fittings it should be covered with a green or green-and-yellow sleeve.

Because of the danger of faulty wiring coming into contact with them, exposed metal water, heating and gas pipes should also be connected to the earthing system by a separate cable (◁).

DIY WIRING

Many householders have a certain reluctance to undertake any but the simplest jobs involving electricity, no matter how competent they may be in other areas of home improvement.

To some extent the attitude is quite justifiable. It is sensible to have a healthy respect for anything as potentially dangerous as electricity, and it would be very foolhardy of anyone to jump in at the deep end and undertake a major installation before gaining some experience on less ambitious jobs.

In the end, though, many of us are driven to doing our own house wiring by the prohibitive cost of hiring the professionals. No-one minds paying for expert knowledge, but the truth is that much of the expert's time is taken up lifting floorboards, chopping out and repairing plaster and drilling holes in walls and timbers to run the cable – all jobs that most people would be happy to do themselves.

The electrician's 'Bible'

What unnerves the householder is the possibility of making mistakes with the connections or with the choice of equipment. Fortunately we are guided in this country by a set of detailed rules laid down by the Instititution of Electrical Engineers in a document known as the IEE Wiring Regulations. This is the professional electrician's 'Bible', and it covers every aspect of electrical installation. If you follow its recommendations you can feel confident that your work will satisfy the Electricity Board. Indeed the Board will refuse to connect up an installation that doesn't comply with the Regulations.

You can buy a copy of the Wiring Regulations from the IEE itself or you can borrow one from your public library. Unfortunately the guide is notoriously difficult to understand, and it has even proved necessary to publish a 'guide to the guide', so that electricians can find their way through this exacting reference book.

The methods suggested in these pages comply with the Regulations, so you should have no need to refer to the originals unless you plan to undertake a job beyond the scope of this book.

Nevertheless, take the trouble to read all of the relevant information in the chapter so that you fully understand what you are doing. If at any time you become unsure of your competence don't hesitate to ask a professional electrician for help or advice.

FUSES AND CIRCUIT BREAKERS

A conductor will heat up if an unusually high current flows through it. This can damage electrical equipment and cause a serious risk of fire if it is allowed to continue in any part of a domestic wiring system. As a safeguard weak links are included in the wiring to break the circuit before the current can reach a dangerously high level.

The most common form of protection is a fuse, a thin wire designed to break the circuit by melting at a certain temperature depending on the part of the system it is protecting – an individual appliance, a single power or lighting circuit or a whole domestic wiring system.

Alternatively, a special automatic switch called a circuit breaker will trip and cut off the current as soon as it detects an overload on the wiring.

A fuse will 'blow' in the following circumstances:

- When too many appliances are operated on a circuit the excessive demand for current will blow the fuse in that circuit.
- When current reroutes to earth because of a faulty appliance the flow of current increases in the circuit and blows the fuse. This is called short circuiting.

WARNING: The original fault must be dealt with before the fuse is replaced.

Measuring Electricity

Watts measure the amount of power used by an appliance when working. The wattage of an electrical appliance should be marked on its casing. One thousand watts (1000W) equals one kilowatt (1kW).

Amps measure the flow of electric power necessary to produce the required wattage for an appliance.

Volts measure the 'pressure' provided by the generators of the Electricity Board that drives the current along the conductors to the various outlets. In Britain 240 volts is standard.

If you know two of these factors you can determine the other:

Watts = Amps Volts	Amps x Volts = Watts
A method to determine a safe fuse or flex.	Indicates how much power is needed to operate an appliance.

WITH SAFETY IN MIND

Throughout this chapter you will find many references to safety while actually working on any part of your electrical system, but it cannot be stressed too strongly that you must take every step to safeguard yourself and others who will later be using the system. Faulty wiring and appliances are dangerous. When you deal with electricity the rule is 'safety first'.

- Never inspect or work on any part of an electrical installation without first switching off the power at the consumer unit and removing the circuit fuse (▷).
- Disconnect any portable appliance or light fitting that is plugged into a socket before you work on it.
- Double-check all your work, especially connections, before you turn the power on again.

- Always use the correct tools for any electrical job, and use good-quality equipment and materials.
- Fuses are important safety devices. Never fit one that is rated too highly for the circuit it is to protect (▷). No other type of wire or metal strip should be used in place of proper fuses or fusewire.
- Wear rubber-soled shoes when working on an electrical installation.

Using professionals

Always be prepared to seek the advice and/or help of a professional electrician if you do not feel competent to handle a particular job yourself, especially if you discover, or even only suspect, that some part of an installation is out of date or dangerous for some other reason.

But make sure that any professional you hire is fully qualified. Check whether he or she is registered with the NICEIC (National Inspection Council for Electrical Installation Contracting). To be a member of this association an electrician must be fully cognizant of, and must comply with, the Regulations for Electrical Installations, the code of practice published by the Institution of Electrical Engineers (▷).

Electricity Board testing

Any significant rewiring, especially newly installed circuits, must be tested by the Electricity Board before they can be connected to the mains supply.

Contact your local Board before you start on an installation and ask for their advice. Never attempt to make connections yourself to the Board's meter or to the consumer's earth terminal. If an installation is found to be faulty when it is tested by a Board representative he will refuse to make the connections to the meter or earth terminal until all has been put right.

SEE ALSO

Details for: ▷

Employing professionals	21
Switching off	296, 298
Fuse ratings	299
Electric shock	291
Fuses	295,299
Meter	296
Consumer's earth terminal	296
Electrician's tools	492

IS THE POWER OFF?

Having turned off the power you can make doubly sure that a particular outlet is safe to work on by plugging into it some appliance that you know to be in working order – a table lamp, for instance, which you have tested before switching off.

As a further precaution you should check on whether actual terminals or wires are live before tampering with them. Use an electronic mains tester, of the kind in the form of a screwdriver. With your fingertip on its metal cap touch the terminal or wire with the tip of the blade. An indicator in the insulated handle lights up if the terminal or wire is live. Don't use one of the cheap neon testers. Their indicators are not clear in strong light.

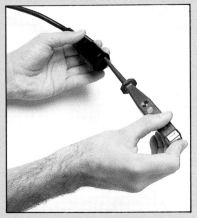

Using an electronic tester
With your finger on the metal cap, touch a terminal with the end of the blade. The terminal is live if the indicator glows.

BATHROOM SAFETY

SEE ALSO

◁ Details for:
Bonding earth	297
Protective	
multiple earthing	297
Running cable	303-305
Bathroom heaters	315
Shaver sockets	316
Cable	302
Electric shower	323
Close-mounted lights	325
Ceiling switch	327, 329

● **Supplementary bonding in a kitchen**
Supplementary bonding regulations apply to kitchens as well as bathrooms. Bond metal sink units, metallic supply and wastepipes, radiators and central heating pipework. Space and water heaters must be bonded as for bathrooms.

Water and electricity form a very dangerous combination, for water is a highly efficient conductor of electric current. For this reason bathrooms are potentially the most dangerous areas in terms of electricity. Where there are so many exposed pipes and fittings, combined with wet conditions, stringent regulations must be observed if fatal accidents are to be avoided.

GENERAL SAFETY

● No sockets should be fitted in a bathroom except special ones approved for electric shavers (◁).

● Regulations stipulate that any standard light switches in bathrooms must be out of reach of anyone using a shower, bath or washbasin. The only sure way of complying with this is to fit nothing but ceiling-mounted pull-cord switches.

● Any bathroom heater must comply with IEE Regulations (◁).

● If you have a shower unit in a bedroom it must be at least 2.5m (8ft) from any socket outlet.

● Light fittings must also be out of reach, so fit a close-mounted ceiling light, properly enclosed, rather than a pendant fitting.

● Never use portable fires or other appliances such as hair dryers in a bathroom even if they are plugged into a socket outside.

WARNING

Have supplementary bonding tested by a qualified electrician. If you have had no previous experience of wiring and making connections have supplementary bonding installed by a professional.

Supplementary bonding

In a bathroom there are many non-electrical metallic components such as metal baths and basins, supply pipes to bath and basin taps, metal wastepipes, radiators, central heating pipework and so on, all of which could become dangerous if they were to come into contact with a live electrical conductor. To ensure that such an occurrence would blow a fuse in the consumer unit, Wiring Regulations specify that all these metal components must be connected one to another by an earth conductor which itself is connected to a terminal on the earthing block in the consumer unit. This is known as supplementary bonding and is required for new bathrooms even when there is no electrical equipment installed in the room and even though the water and gas pipes are bonded to the consumer's earth terminal near the consumer unit (◁). When electrical equipment like a heater or shower is fitted in a bathroom, that too must be supplementary bonded by connecting its metalwork, such as the casing, to the non-electrical pipework even though the appliance is connected to the earthing conductor in the supply cable.

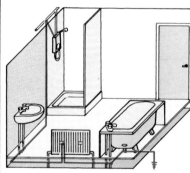

Supplementary bonding in a bathroom

Making the connections

Wiring Regulations specify the minimum size of earthing conductor that can be used for supplementary bonding in different situations so that large electrical installations can be costed economically. In a home environment use 6mm^2 single-core cable insulated with green or green/yellow PVC for all the supplementary bonding. It is large enough to be safe in any domestic situation unless your house is wired with Protective Multiple Earthing (◁) in which case you should consult a professional. For a neat appearance plan the route of the earth cable to run from point to point behind the bath panel, under floorboards and through basin pedestals. If necessary run the cable through a hollow wall or under plaster like any other electrical cable (◁).

Connecting to pipework

Use an earth clamp (**1**) to make connections to pipework. Clean the pipe locally with wire wool to make a good connection between the pipe and clamp, and scrape or strip an area of paintwork if the pipe has been painted.

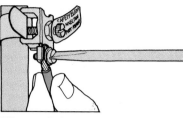

1 Fit an earth clamp to pipework

Connecting to a bath or basin

Metal baths or basins are made with an earth tag. Connect the earth cable by trapping the bared end of the conductor under a nut and bolt with metal washers (**2**). Make sure the tag has not been painted or enamelled.

If an old bath or basin has not been provided with an earth tag, drill a hole through the foot of the bath or to the rim at the back of the basin and connect the cable with a similar nut and bolt.

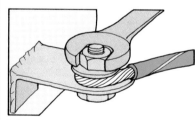

2 Connect to bath or basin earth tag

Connecting to an appliance

Connect the earth to the terminal provided in an electrical appliance (**3**) and run it to a clamp on a metal supply pipe nearby.

3 Fix to an appliance earth terminal

DEALING WITH ELECTRIC SHOCK

If someone in your presence gets an electric shock and is still in contact with its source, turn off the current at once by pulling out the plug or switching off at the socket or the consumer unit. If you cannot do this don't take hold of the person; the current may pass through you too. Pull the victim free with a dry towel, a necktie or something like that, or knock their hand free of the electrical equipment with a piece of wood. As a last resort free the victim, using their loose clothing, but without touching the body.

Don't try to move anyone who has fallen as a result of electric shock. They may have sustained other injuries. Wrap them in a blanket or coat to keep warm until they can move themselves.

Treat electrical burns by reducing the heat of the injury under slowly running cold water once the person can move and is no longer in contact with the electrical equipment. Then apply a dry dressing and seek medical advice.

Isolating the victim
If a person sustains an electric shock turn off the supply of electricity immediately, either at the consumer unit or at a socket (1). If this is not possible, pull the victim free with a dry towel, or knock their hand free of the electrical equipment (2) with a piece of wood or a broom.

ARTIFICIAL RESPIRATION

Severe electric shock can make a person stop breathing. Having freed them from the electricity supply, revive them by means of artificial respiration.

Clear the airways
Clear the victim's airways by loosening the clothing round the neck, chest and waist. Make sure that the mouth is free of food and remove any dentures (1). Lay the person on his or her back and tilt the head back while supporting the back of the neck with one hand.

I Clear the mouth of food or dentures

Restart the breathing
With your free hand close and open the jaw several times in an attempt to restart the person's breathing (2). If this does not succeed quickly, try more direct methods of artificial respiration.

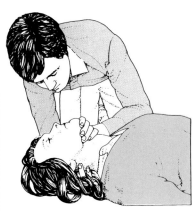

2 Open and close victim's jaw several times

Mouth to nose
Cover the victim's mouth with one hand and blow firmly into the nose (3). Look for signs of the chest rising and falling, then blow again three or four times in rapid succession. Repeat this procedure every four or five seconds until normal breathing resumes.

Mouth to mouth
Pinch shut the victim's nostrils, then cover the mouth with your own, making a seal all round (4), and proceed as in mouth to nose above.

3 Mouth to nose   4 Mouth to mouth

Reviving a child
With a baby or small child cover both the nose and the mouth at the same time with your own mouth (5), then proceed as above.

5 Cover a baby's nose and mouth

Recovery
Once breathing has started again, turn the victim face down with the head turned sideways and tilted up slightly so that the chin juts out. This will keep the airways open.

Lift one arm and one leg out from the body (6), then with blankets or coats arrange for the victim to stay warm while you summon medical help.

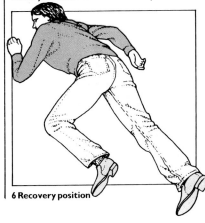

6 Recovery position

SEE ALSO
Details for: ▷
Safety tips   289

SIMPLE REPLACEMENTS

You can carry out many repairs and replacements without having to concern yourself with the wiring system installed in your home. Many light fittings and appliances are supplied with electricity through flexible cords that simply plug into the system and are easily disconnected, so there can be no risk of getting an electric shock while you are working on them.

SEE ALSO

◁ Details for:
Colour coding	288
Switching off	296
Fabric-covered flex	324

WARNING

Never attempt to carry out electrical repairs without first disconnecting the appliance or switching off the power supply at the consumer unit (◁).

Flexible cord

All portable appliances and some of the smaller fixed ones, as well as pendant and portable light fittings, are connected to the permanent wiring system by means of conductors of flexible cord, normally called 'flex'. Each conductor in any type of flex is made up of many fine wires twisted together, and each one is insulated from the others with a covering of non-conductive material to contain the current. Insulation material is usually colour-coded to identify live, neutral and earth conductors – brown = live; blue = neutral; green/yellow = earth.

Further protection is provided on some flexible cords in the form of an outer sheathing of insulating material enclosing all the inner conductors.

Heat-resistant flex is available for enclosed light fittings and appliances whose surfaces will become hot.

COILED FLEX

A coiled flex which stretches and retracts is ideal for a portable lamp or appliance.

Coiled flex is sold as a standard length

TYPES OF ELECTRICAL FLEX

PARALLEL TWIN

Parallel twin flex has two conductors, insulated with PVC (polyvinyl chloride) and running side by side. The insulation is joined between the two conductors along the length of the flex. This flex is used mostly for low-powered appliances like shavers and some light fittings. The wires are hardly ever colour-coded.

TWISTED TWIN

Twisted twin flex is similar to parallel twin, but the PVC-insulated conductors are twisted together for extra strength to support hanging light fittings and shades. However, it is better to use a two-core sheathed flex when wiring up pendant lights. Any old rubber-insulated flex with braided cotton covering still found in some homes should be replaced.

FLAT TWIN SHEATHED

Flat twin sheathed flex has colour-coded live and neutral conductors inside a PVC sheathing. This flex is used for double-insulated light fittings and small appliances.

TWO-CORE CIRCULAR SHEATHED

This has colour-coded neutral and live conductors inside a PVC sheathing that is circular in its cross section. It is used for wiring pendant lights and some double-insulated appliances.

THREE-CORE CIRCULAR SHEATHED

This is like two-core circular sheathed flex but it also contains an insulated and colour-coded earth wire. This flex is perhaps the most commonly used for all kinds of appliances.

UNKINKABLE BRAIDED

This flex is used on appliances like kettles and irons, which are of a high wattage and whose flex must stand up to movement and wear. The three rubber-insulated conductors are strengthened by textile cords running parallel with them, all contained in a rubber sheathing bound outside with braided material.

This type of flex can be wound round the handle of a cool electric iron.

STRIPPING AND CONNECTING FLEX

Though the spacing of terminals in plugs and appliances varies, the method of stripping and connecting the flex is the same.

Stripping the flex

If the flex is sheathed slit the sheath lengthwise with a sharp knife **(1)**, being careful not to cut into the insulation covering individual conductors. Divide the conductors of parallel twin flex by pulling them apart before you expose their ends.

Peel the sheathing from the conductors, fold it back over the knife blade and cut it off **(2)**.

Separate the conductors, crop them to length and with wire strippers remove about 12mm (½in) of insulation from the end of each one **(3)**.

MULTI-PURPOSE TOOL

A multi-purpose tool will crop and strip any size of cable or flex.

Stripping flex with a multi-purpose tool

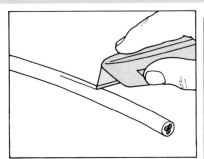

1 Slit sheathing lengthwise

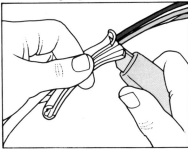

2 Fold sheathing over blade and cut it off

3 Strip insulation from conductors

Connecting the conductors

Twist together the individual filaments of each conductor to make them neat.

If the plug or appliance has the post type of terminals fold the bared end of wire **(1)** before pushing it in the hole. The insulation should butt against the post. Tighten the clamping screw, then pull gently on the wire to be sure it is held quite firmly.

SEE ALSO

Details for: ▷	
Measuring electricity	289
Wire strippers	492

1 Post terminal

When connecting to clamp-type terminals you wrap the bared wire round the post clockwise **(2)**, then screw the clamping nut down tight on the wire and check that the conductor has been securely held.

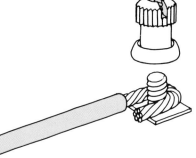

2 Clamp terminal

To attach the wire to a snap-fastening terminal swing open the back of the locking clip, insert the bared end of wire **(3)** and snap the clip back to grip the wire firmly.

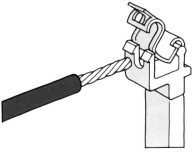

3 Snap-fastening terminal

CHOOSING A FLEX

Not only the right flex for the job is important; the size of its conductors must suit the amount of current that will be used by the appliance.

Flex is rated according to the area of the cross section of its conductors, 0.5mm^2 being the smallest for normal domestic wiring. Any required size is determined by the flow of current that it can handle safely. Excessive current will make a conductor overheat, so the size of the flex must be matched to the power (wattage) of the appliance which it is feeding.

Manufacturers often fit 1.25mm^2 flex to appliances of up to 3000W (3kW) because it is safer to use a larger conductor than necessary if a smaller flex might be easily damaged. Adopt the same procedure to replace flex.

Conductor	Current rating	Appliance
0.5 mm^2	3 amps	Light fittings up to 720W
0.75 mm^2	6 amps	Light fittings and appliances up to 1440W
1.0 mm^2	10 amps	Appliances up to 2400W
1.25 mm^2	13 amps	Appliances up to 3120W
1.5 mm^2	15 amps	Appliances up to 3600W
2.5 mm^2	20 amps	Appliances up to 4800W
4.0 mm^2	25 amps	Appliances up to 6000W

EXTENDING FLEXIBLE CORD

When you plan the positions of socket outlets (◁) make sure there will be enough, all conveniently situated, so that it is never necessary to extend the flexible cord of a table lamp or other appliance. But if you do find that a flex will not reach a socket extend it so that it cannot be pulled tight, which can cause an accident. Never join two lengths of flex by twisting the bared ends of wires together, even if you bind them with insulating tape. People do this as a temporary measure, intending to make a proper connection later, but often forget to, and this can have fatal consequences eventually.

SEE ALSO

◁ Details for:
Positioning sockets 308
Flex 292
Connecting flex 293

Below are illustrated four of the devices available for extending the flexible cords of electrical appliances (See left).

Flex connectors

Ideally you should fit a new length of flex, wiring it into the appliance itself. If you can't do this, or don't wish to dismantle the appliance, use a flex connector, a two- or three-terminal one, according to the type of flex.

Strip off just enough sheathing so that the conductors can reach the terminals and the sheathed part of each cord will be secured under the cord clamp at each end of the connector.

Cut the conductors to length with engineers' pliers and strip and connect them, the live conductor to one of the outer terminals, the neutral to the other and the earth wire (if present) to the central one. Make sure that matching conductors of the two cords are connected to the same terminals, then tighten the cord clamps and screw the cover in place.

In-line switches

You can extend flex by using an in-line switch instead of a flex connector. It is fitted in the same way but allows you to control the appliance from some distance away – a great advantage for the elderly or bed-ridden. Some in-line switches are fluorescent.

Drum-type extension lead

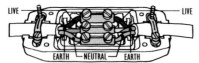
Wiring a flex conductor

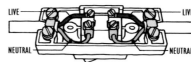
Wiring an in-line switch

13amp plug and trailing socket

Extension leads

If you fit a long flexible cord to a power tool it will inevitably become tangled and one of the conductors will eventually break, perhaps causing a short circuit. The solution is to buy or make an extension lead into which you can plug any tool or appliance you need.

The best type of extension lead to be had commercially is wound on a drum. There are 5amp ones, but it is safer to buy one rated at 13amps so that you can run a wider range of equipment with no danger of overloading it. If you use such a lead while it is wound on the drum it can overheat, so develop the habit of fully unwinding it each time.

The drums of these leads have a built-in 13amp socket to take the plug of the appliance. The plug on the lead is connected to the ordinary wall socket.

You can make an extension lead from a length of 1.5mm^2 three-core flex with a standard 13amp plug on one end and a trailing socket on the other. Use those with unbreakable rubber casings. A trailing socket is wired similarly to a 13amp plug (See opposite). Its terminals are marked to indicate which conductors connect to them.

'Multi-way' trailing sockets will take more than one plug and are ideal for hi-fi systems with individual components that must be connected to mains supply. With a multi-way socket in the cabinet the whole system is supplied from one plug in the wall socket.

Alternatively you can use a lightweight two-part flex connector. One half has three pins which the other half receives.

Unwind a lead
Always fully unwind a 13amp extension lead before you plug in an appliance rated at 1.4kW or more.

WARNING

When wiring a two-part flex connector never attach the part with the pins to the extension lead. The exposed pins will become live – and dangerous – when the lead is plugged into the socket. In fact nothing electrical should ever be wired so that a plug can become live other than when its pins are concealed in a socket.

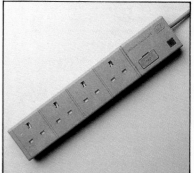
Multi-way trailing socket

Two-part flex connector

WIRING A PLUG

In the past there were many types of plug. Nowadays there are standard ones for all light fittings and portable appliances – 13amp square-pin plugs. They are available with rigid plastic or unbreakable rubber casings. Some have integral neon indicators to show when they are live, and pins insulated for part of their length now prevent the user getting a shock from a plug pulled partly from the socket.

Safety standards and fuses

Use only plugs marked BS 1363, which means conformity to British Standards and therefore safety in use. All square-pin plugs have a small cartridge fuse to protect the appliance – 3amp (red) for appliances of up to 720W or 13amp (brown) for those of from 720 to 3000W. There are 2, 5 and 10 amp fuses but they are rarely used in the home.

Wiring a 13amp plug

Loosen the large screw between the pins and remove the cover. Position the flex on the open plug to determine how much sheathing to remove, remembering that the cord clamp must grip sheathed flex, not the conductors.

Strip the sheathing and again position the flex on the plug so that you can cut the conductors to the right length.

These should take the most direct routes to their terminals and lie neatly in the channels of the plug.

Strip and prepare the ends of the wires, then secure each to its terminal. If you are using two-core flex, wire to the live and neutral terminals, leaving the earth terminal empty.

Tighten the cord clamp to grip the end of the sheathing and secure the flex. One type of plug has a sprung cord grip that tightens if the flex is pulled hard.

Check that a fuse of the correct rating is fitted.

Replace the plug's cover and tighten up the screw.

Wiring older plugs

If your home still has old round-pin sockets you must go on using round-pin plugs, which are not fused. Use the small 2amp one for lighting only, a 5amp one for appliances of up to 1000W and a 15amp one for anything between 1000W and 3000W. You should have your wiring upgraded as soon as possible so that you can use modern fused square-pin plugs.

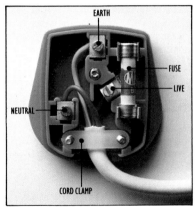

Post-terminal plug

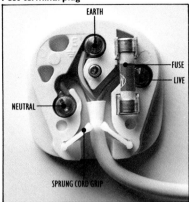

Clamp-terminal plug

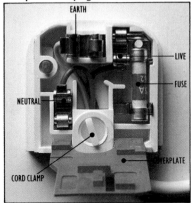

Snap-fastening terminal plug

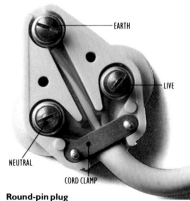

Round-pin plug

REPLACING A PENDANT LAMPHOLDER

Because they are not easy to inspect damaged lampholders can go unnoticed. You should check their condition every so often and replace any suspect ones before they become dangerous.

Pendant lampholders, which hang on flex from the ceiling, are in a stream of hot air rising from the bulb, and in time this can make plastic holders brittle and more easily cracked or broken. On a metal lampholder the earth wire can become detached or corroded so that the fitting is no longer safe.

Types of lampholder

Plastic lampholders are the most common. These have a threaded skirt that screws onto the actual holder, the part that takes the bulb, and some versions have an extended skirt for fitting in bathrooms. You should fit heat-resistant plastic holders if you use a close-fitting or badly ventilated shade.

Plastic holders are designed to take only two-core flex. Don't fit one on a three-core flex as it will have no place to attach the earth wire.

Metal lampholders are similar in their construction but they must be wired with three-core flex so that they can be connected to earth. Never fit a metal lampholder in a bathroom, and never attach one to a two-core flex, which has no earth conductor.

Fitting a lampholder

Before you start remove the fuse for the circuit or switch off the circuit breaker at the consumer unit ($\triangleright$) so that no-one can turn the power on.

Unscrew the old holder's cap – or the retaining ring if it's a metal one – and slide it up the flex to expose the terminals. Loosen their screws and pull the wires out. If some wires are broken or brittle cut back slightly to expose sound wire before fitting the holder.

Slide the cap of the new fitting up the flex and attach it temporarily with adhesive tape.

Fit the live or neutral wire into either terminal and twist the conductors round the supporting lugs of the holder to take the weight off the terminals, then screw the cap down.

On a metal holder pass the earth wire through the hole in the cap before you screw it down. Wrap the wire clockwise round the fixing screw and tighten it. Screw down the retaining ring to secure the cap.

SEE ALSO	
Details for: $\triangleright$	
Switching off	296, 300
Flex	292
Connecting flex	293

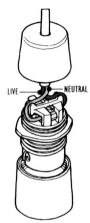

Wiring a plastic pendant lampholder

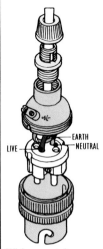

Wiring a metal pendant lampholder

MAIN SWITCH EQUIPMENT

SEE ALSO

◁ Details for:

Circuit breakers 300
Cheap electricity 286
Consumer unit 298
Fuses/circuit breakers 299
Switchfuse unit 318
Storage heaters 320

Electricity flows because of a difference in pressure between the live wire and the neutral one, and this difference in the pressures is measured in volts.

Domestic electricity is supplied at 240 volts (240V) 'alternating current' by way of the Electricity Board's service cable, which enters your house underground, though in some areas power is distributed by overhead cables.

The sealing chamber

The main cable terminates at the service head, or sealing chamber, which contains the service fuse. This fuse prevents the neighbourhood being affected if there should be a serious fault in your circuitry. A cable connects the sealing chamber to the meter, which registers how much power is used. The meter and sealing chamber belong to the Electricity Board and must not be tampered with. The meter is sealed to detect interference.

If you use the cheap night-time power for storage heaters and hot water a time switch will be mounted somewhere between the sealing chamber and the meter.

Consumer units

Electricity is fed to and from the consumer unit by 'meter leads', thick single-core cables made up of several wires twisted together. The consumer unit is a box that contains the fuseways which protect the individual circuits in the house. It also incorporates the main isolating switch with which you can cut off the supply of power to the whole of the house.

In a house where several new circuits have been installed over the years the number of circuits may exceed the number of fuseways in the consumer unit, so an individual switchfuse unit – or more than one – may have to be mounted alongside the main unit. Switchfuse units comprise a single fuseway and an isolating switch. They too are connected to the meter by means of meter leads.

If your home is heated by storage heaters you will probably have a separate consumer unit for the circuits that supply the heaters.

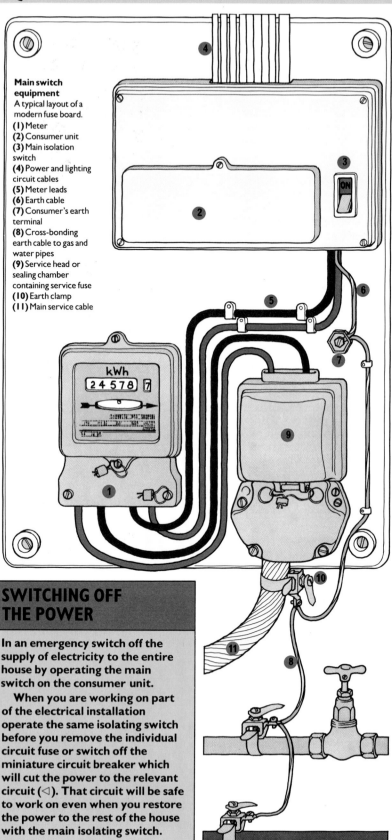

Main switch equipment
A typical layout of a modern fuse board.
(1) Meter
(2) Consumer unit
(3) Main isolation switch
(4) Power and lighting circuit cables
(5) Meter leads
(6) Earth cable
(7) Consumer's earth terminal
(8) Cross-bonding earth cable to gas and water pipes
(9) Service head or sealing chamber containing service fuse
(10) Earth clamp
(11) Main service cable

kWh
24578 7

SWITCHING OFF THE POWER

In an emergency switch off the supply of electricity to the entire house by operating the main switch on the consumer unit.

When you are working on part of the electrical installation operate the same isolating switch before you remove the individual circuit fuse or switch off the miniature circuit breaker which will cut the power to the relevant circuit (◁). That circuit will be safe to work on even when you restore the power to the rest of the house with the main isolating switch.

EARTHING SYSTEMS

The earthing system

All of the individual earth conductors of the various circuits in the house are connected to one heavy earth cable in the consumer unit. This cable is sheathed in green or green/yellow and runs from the unit to the consumer's earth terminal. In most town houses the earth cable continues from the earth terminal to a clamp on the metal sheath of the main service cable just below the sealing chamber. This is an effective path to earth. The current will pass along the sheath to the Electricity Board's substation, where it is solidly connected to earth.

Until recently most electrical installations were earthed to the cold water supply so that earth-leakage current passed out along the metal water pipes into the ground in which they were buried. But more and more water systems now use non-metallic, non-conductive pipes, so that means of earthing is no longer reliable. Despite this you will find that your pipework is connected to the earth terminal in case one of the live conductors in the house should touch a pipe at some point. The same earth cable is usually clamped to a nearby gas pipe on the house side of the meter before running on to the consumer's earth terminal. This ensures that both water and gas piping systems are cross-bonded so that earth-leakage current passing through either system will run without hindrance to the clamp on the service cable sheath and so to earth. The clamps must never be interfered with.

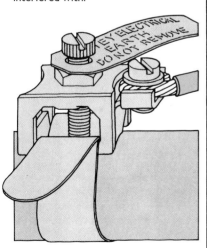

Earth clamp
The earthing system of the house finally connects to the main service cable with this type of clamp. It should not be removed under any circumstances.

PME

Sometimes, especially in country areas, the Electricity Board provides another method of earthing the system called 'protective multiple earth' (PME) by which earth-leakage current is fed back to the substation along the neutral return wire, and so to earth.

Regulations regarding the earthing of the system are particularly stringent, so if you live in a house with PME (check this with your Electricity Board) you should engage a qualified professional electrician for any but the most minor type of work.

RCCBs

Though the Electricity Board normally provides effective earthing, actually it is the consumer's responsibility. It is often achieved by installing a 'residual-current circuit breaker' or RCCB, into the house circuitry.

Under normal conditions the current flowing out through the neutral conductor is exactly the same as that flowing in through the live one. Should there be an imbalance between the two caused by an earth leakage the RCCB will detect it immediately and isolate the system.

An RCCB can be either installed as a separate unit or incorporated into the consumer unit together with the main isolating switch.

A separate unit containing an RCCB

RECOGNIZING AN OLD FUSE BOARD

Domestic wiring was once very different from a modern system. Beside lighting, water-heating and cooker circuits, each individual socket outlet had its own circuit and fuse, while further circuits would usually be installed from time to time as the needs of the household changed. Consequently an old house may have a mixture of 'fuse boxes' attached to a fuse board along with the meter. The wiring itself may be haphazard and badly labelled, with the constant risk that you have not safely isolated the circuit you wish to work on. Further, you will be unable to tell if a given fuse is correctly and safely rated unless you know what type of circuit it is protecting.

If your home still has such an old-style fuse board have it inspected and tested by a qualified electrician before you attempt to work on any part of the system. He can advise you on whether to replace the installation with a modern consumer unit or, if the system is in good working condition, he can at least label the various circuits clearly to help you in the future.

An old-fashioned fuse board
This type of installation is out of date. A professional electrician may advise you to replace at least some of the components.

SEE ALSO

Details for: ▷	
Supplementary bonding	290
RCCBs	332

● **RCCB**
An RCCB may be referred to as an RCD – residual-current device. It was formerly known as an ELCB – earth-leakage circuit breaker.

THE CONSUMER UNIT

The consumer unit is the heart of your electrical installation, for every circuit in the house must pass through it. There are several different types and styles of consumer unit but they are all based on similar principles.

SEE ALSO

◁ Details for:
RCCB	297
Ring circuit	301
Main switch equipment	296

Every unit has a large main switch that can turn off the whole installation. On some, more expensive units the switch is in the form of an RCCB (◁) which can be operated manually but will also 'trip' automatically, isolating the entire household system, should any serious fault occur, and much more quickly than the Electricity Board's fuse would take to blow in a similar emergency.

Some consumer units are designed so that it is impossible to remove the outer cover without first turning off the main switch. Even if yours is not of this type you should always switch off before exposing any of the elements within the consumer unit.

Having turned off the main switch, remove the cover or covers so that you can see how the unit is arranged. The cover must be replaced before the unit is switched on again – and remember: even when the unit is switched off the cable connecting the meter to the main switch is still live, so take care.

Take note of the cables that feed the various circuits in the house. Ideally they should all enter the consumer unit from the same direction.

The black-insulated neutral wires run to a common neutral block where they are attached to their individual terminals. Similarly the green earth wires run to a common earthing block. The red-covered live conductors are connected to terminals on individual fuseways or circuit breakers.

Some wires will be twisted together in one terminal. These are the two ends of a ring circuit (◁) and that is how they should be wired.

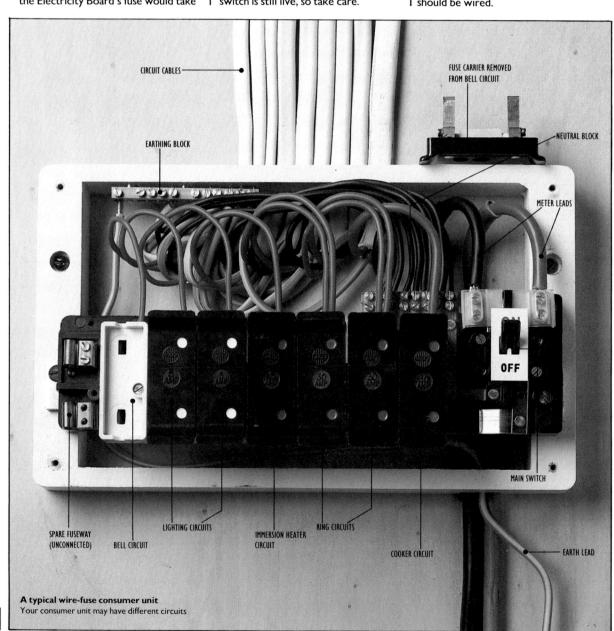

A typical wire-fuse consumer unit
Your consumer unit may have different circuits

FUSES: TYPES AND RATINGS

Into the fuseway of each circuit is plugged a fuse carrier, which is essentially a bridge between the main switch and that particular circuit. When the fuse carrier is removed from the unit current cannot pass across the gap.

Identifying a fuse

Pull any individual fuse carrier out of the unit to see what kind of fuse it contains. At each end of the carrier is a single- or double-bladed contact. A rewirable carrier will have a thin wire running from one contact to the other, held by a screw terminal at each end. The fuse wire is available in different thicknesses, carefully calculated to melt at given temperatures when a circuit is substantially overloaded, breaking the 'bridge' and isolating the circuit.

Alternatively the carrier may contain a cartridge fuse like those used in 13amp plugs, though circuit fuses are larger, varying in size according to their rating. The cartridge is a ceramic tube containing a fuse wire packed in fine sand. The wire is connected to metal caps at the ends of the cartridge which snap into spring clips on the contacts of the fuse carrier. Cartridge fuses provide better protection, as they blow faster than ordinary fuse wire.

Fuse ratings

Whatever the type of fuses used in the consumer unit they are rated in the same way. Cartridge fuses are colour-coded and marked with the appropriate amp rating for a certain type of circuit. Fuse wire is bought wrapped round a card which is clearly labelled.

Never insert fuse wire that is heavier than the gauge intended for the circuit. To do so would mean that a dangerous fault could go unnoticed because of the fuse failing to melt. It is even more dangerous to substitute any other type of wire or metal strip; these will give no protection at all.

When changing a fuse do not replace it automatically with one of the same rating without checking that it is the correct one for the circuit.

The fuse carrier should be marked and/or colour-coded. You can also check the list of circuits on the inside of the consumer unit cover to identify the carriers and their required ratings.

Keep spare fusewire or cartridge fuses in or close to the consumer unit.

FUSE RATINGS		
Circuit	**Fuse**	**Colour coding**
Doorbell	5amp	White
Lighting	5amp	White
Immersion heater	15 or 20amp	Blue or yellow
Storage heater	20amp	Yellow
Radial circuits 20m²	20amp	Yellow
50m²	30amp	Red
Ring circuits	30amp	Red
Shower unit	30amp	Red
Cooker: up to 12kW	30amp	Red
over 12kW	45amp	Green

A selection of circuit fuses and fuse wire
From left to right: fuse wire, 45amp fuse, 30amp fuse, 20amp fuse, 15amp fuse, 5amp fuse.

SEE ALSO

Details for: ▷
Circuit breakers 300

FUSE CARRIERS AND MCB'S

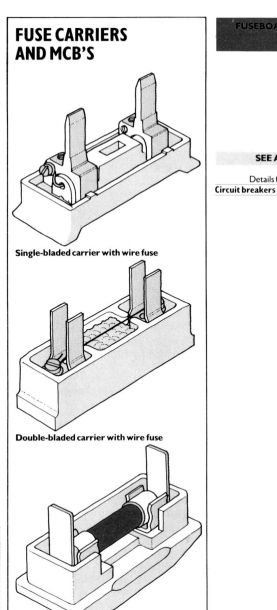

Single-bladed carrier with wire fuse

Double-bladed carrier with wire fuse

Cartridge fuse carrier

Switch-operated miniature circuit breaker (▷)

Button-operated miniature circuit breaker (▷)

299

CHANGING A FUSE

SEE ALSO

◁ Details for:
Consumer unit	298
Fuses/ratings	299
Circuit breakers	299

When everything on a circuit stops working your first step is to check the fuse on the circuit and see if it has blown. Turn off the main switch on the consumer unit, remove the cover and look for the failed fuse. The fuse will be easier to find if you know which circuit is affected, so check the list of circuits inside the unit's cover. If there is no list you will have to inspect all likely circuits. For instance, if the lights 'blew' when you switched them on you need check only the lighting circuits. These are colour-coded white.

Checking a cartridge fuse

The simple way to check a suspect cartridge fuse is to replace it with a new one and see if the circuit works. Or you can check the fuse with a metal-cased torch. Remove the bottom cap of the torch and touch one end of the fuse to the base of the battery while resting its other end against the battery's metal casing. If the battery bulb lights up the fuse is sound.

Testing a cartridge fuse
With the torch switched on, hold the fuse against the battery and the metal casing.

Checking a rewirable fuse

On a blown rewirable fuse a visual check will usually detect the broken wire and scorch marks on the fuse carrier. If the fuse is one on which you cannot see the whole length of the fuse wire you should pull gently on each end of the wire with the tip of a screwdriver to see if it is intact.

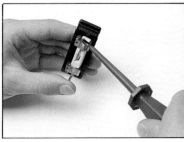

Pull the wire gently with a small screwdriver

HOW TO REPLACE FUSE WIRE

To replace a blown fuse wire loosen the two terminals holding the fuse and extract the broken pieces. Wrap one end of a new length of wire clockwise round one terminal and tighten the screw on it **(1)**, then run the wire across to the other terminal, leaving it slightly slack, attach it in the same way **(2)** and cut off any excess from the ends.

If the wire passes through a tube in the fuse carrier it has to be inserted before either terminal is tightened **(3)**.

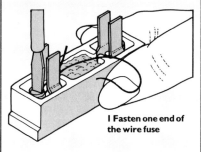

I Fasten one end of the wire fuse

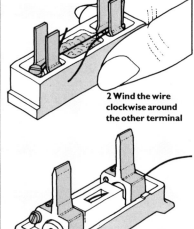

2 Wind the wire clockwise around the other terminal

3 You must pass the wire through some carriers

IF THE FUSE BLOWS AGAIN

If a replaced fuse blows again as soon as the power is switched on there is a fault or an overload – too many appliances plugged in – on that circuit and it must be detected and rectified before another fuse is inserted.

Circuit breakers

In some consumer units you will find miniature circuit breakers (MCBs) instead of the usual fuse holders. These are amp-rated just like fuses but instead of removing an MCB to isolate the circuit you merely operate a switch or a button on it to 'off'. When a fault occurs the circuit breaker switches to the 'off' position automatically, so the faulty circuit is obvious as soon as you open the consumer unit. Turn the main switch off, then simply close the switch on the MCB to reset it. There is no fuse to replace. If the switch or button will not stay in the 'on' position when power is restored there is still a fault on the circuit which must be rectified.

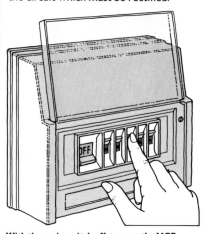

With the main switch off, turn on the MCB

Checking out a fault

An electrician can test a circuit for you with special equipment, but first carry out some simple tests yourself.

Before inspecting any part of the circuit turn off the consumer unit's main switch, remove the relevant fuse holder and keep it in your pocket so that no one can replace it while you work. If you have circuit breakers instead of fuses fix the switch at 'off' with bright adhesive tape and leave a note on the consumer unit.

Unplug all appliances on the faulty circuit to make sure that it is not simply overloaded, then switch on again. If the circuit is still faulty switch off again and inspect the socket outlets and light fittings to see if a conductor has worked loose and is touching one of the other wires, terminals or outer casing, causing a short circuit.

If none of this enables you to find the fault call in an electrician.

Running from the consumer unit are the cables which supply the various fixed wiring circuits in your home. Not only are the sizes of the cables different ($\triangleright$); the circuits themselves also differ, depending on what they are used for and also, in some cases, how old they happen to be.

RING CIRCUITS

The most common form of 'power' circuit for feeding socket outlets is the ring circuit, or 'ring main', in which a cable starts from terminals in the consumer unit and goes right round the house, connecting socket to socket, and arriving back at the same terminals. By this method power can reach any of the socket outlets or fused connection units ($\triangleright$) from both directions, which reduces the load on the cable.

Ring mains are always run in 2.5mm^2 cable and are protected by 30amp fuses. There is no limit to the number of socket outlets or fused connection units that can be fitted to one ring circuit so long as it does not serve a floor area of more than 100sq m (120sq yd), a limit based on the number of electric heaters which would be adequate to heat that space. In practice most two-storey dwellings have one ring main for the upper floor and another for downstairs.

Spurs
The number of sockets on a ring main can be increased by adding extensions, or 'spurs'. A spur can be a single 2.5mm^2 cable connected to the cables of an existing socket or fused connection unit or it can run from a junction box inserted in the ring.

Current regulations allow each spur to serve one fused connection unit for a fixed appliance or one single or double socket outlet. You can have as many spurs on a ring circuit as there were sockets on it originally, and for this calculation a double socket is counted as two. The 30amp fuse that protects the ring main is unchanged no matter how many spurs are connected to the circuit.

RADIAL CIRCUITS

A radial power circuit feeds a number of socket outlets or fused connection units but, unlike a ring circuit, its cable terminates at the last outlet. The size of cable and the fuse rating depend on size of the floor area to be supplied by the circuit. In a room of up to 20sq m (24sq yd) the cable should be 2.5mm^2, protected by a 20amp MCB or fuse of any type. For a larger area, up to 50sq m (60sq yd) you should use 4mm^2 cable with a 30amp cartridge fuse or MCB, but a rewirable fuse is not permitted.

Any number of socket outlets can be supplied by one of these circuits, and spurs can be added if required. The circuits are known as multi-outlet radial circuits, but a powerful appliance like a cooker or shower unit must have its own radial circuit ($\triangleright$).

LIGHTING CIRCUITS

Domestic lighting circuits are also of the radial kind, but there are two systems currently in use.

The loop-in system has a single cable that runs from ceiling rose to ceiling rose, terminating at the last one on the circuit while single cables run from the ceiling roses to the light switches.

The older, junction-box system incorporates a junction box for each light. The junction boxes are situated conveniently on the single supply cable. A cable runs from each junction box to the ceiling rose and another from the box to the light switch. In practice, most lighting systems are combinations of the two methods.

A single circuit of 1mm^2 cable can serve the equivalent of twelve 100W light fittings, though you might have to reduce the number if you wished to install multi-light fittings or if one of your lamps was more powerful than 100W. Once again it is more practical to have two or more separate lighting circuits running from the consumer unit.

Lighting circuits are protected by 5amp fuses.

SEE ALSO

Details for: $\triangleright$	
Cables	302
Socket outlets	308
Fused connection units	314
Cooker circuit	317
Shower circuit	323
Fuse ratings	299

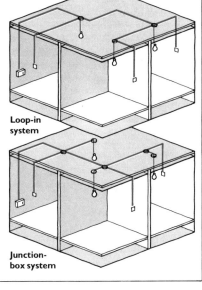

Ring circuit

Ring circuit with spurs

Radial circuit

Loop-in system

Junction-box system

CABLE: TYPES

SEE ALSO

◁ Details for:

Meter leads	296
Earth cable	296
Two-way lighting	330
Wire strippers	492

Two-core and earth

Cable for the fixed wiring of electrical systems normally has three conductors: the insulated live and neutral ones and the earth conductor lying between them, uninsulated except for the sheathing that encloses all three. Cable up to 2.5mm^2 has solid, single-core conductors, but larger sizes, up to 10mm^2, would be too stiff with solid conductors so each one is made up of seven strands. The live conductor is insulated with red PVC and the neutral one with black. When an earth conductor is exposed, as in a socket outlet, it should be covered with a green and yellow sleeve. You can buy this from any electricians' supplier. The PVC sheathing on the outside of the cable is usually white or grey.

Heat-resistant cable is available for use in a situation where extra heat may be generated, and there is heat-resistant sleeving for the conductors in enclosed light fittings.

Three-core and earth

This type of cable is used in two-way lighting systems, which can be switched on and off at different switches. It contains three insulated conductors and a bare earth wire. The conductors have red, yellow and blue coverings.

Single-core cable

Insulated single-core cable is used in buildings where the electrical wiring is run in metal or plastic conduit. This is rare in domestic buildings. The cable is colour-coded in the normal way: red for live, black for neutral and green/yellow for earth.

Single core 6mm^2 cable is used for connecting the consumer unit to the earth, and single-core 16mm^2 cable is used for connecting the unit to the meter. Meter leads are insulated and sheathed in red for the live conductor and black for the neutral one.

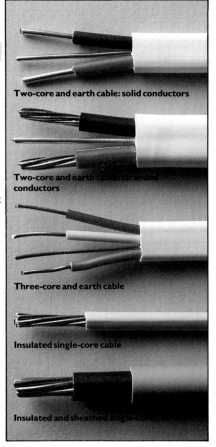

Two-core and earth cable: solid conductors

Two-core and earth cable: stranded conductors

Three-core and earth cable

Insulated single-core cable

Insulated and sheathed single-core cable

OLD CABLE

Houses which were wired before World War II may still have old rubber-sheathed and -insulated cable, and some old cable may even be sheathed in lead.

Rubber sheathing is usually a matt black. It is more flexible than the modern PVC insulation unless it has deteriorated, when it will be crumbly.

This type of cable may be dangerous

STRIPPING CABLE

When cable is wired up to an accessory some of the sheathing and insulation must be removed.

Slit the sheathing lengthwise with a sharp knife, peel it off the conductors, fold it over the blade and cut it off.

Take about 12mm (½in) of insulation off the ends of the conductors using wire strippers.

Cover the uninsulated earth wire with a green/yellow sleeve, leaving 12mm (½in) of the wire exposed for connecting to the earth terminal.

If more than one conductor is to be inserted in the same terminal twist the exposed ends together with strong pliers to ensure the maximum contact for all of the wires.

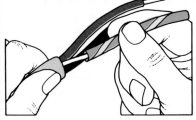

Slip colour-coded sleeving over the earth wire

CIRCUIT CABLE SIZES		
Circuit	**Size**	**Type**
Lighting	1·0mm^2	Two-core and earth
Bell or chime transformer	1·0mm^2	Two-core and earth
Immersion heater	2·5mm^2	Two-core and earth
Storage heater	2·5mm^2	Two-core and earth
Ring circuit	2·5mm^2	Two-core and earth
Spurs	2.5mm^2	Two-core and earth
Radial — 20 amp	2·5mm^2	Two-core and earth
Radial — 30 amp	4·0mm^2	Two-core and earth
Shower unit	6.0mm^2	Two-core and earth
Cooker up to 12 kW	6·0mm^2	Two-core and earth
Cooker over 12 kW	10·0mm^2	Two-core and earth
Consumer earth cable	6.0mm^2	Single core
Meter leads	16·0mm^2	Single core
	All cable sizes in square millimetres	

INSIDE A HOLLOW WALL

For a short cable run on a lath-and-plaster wall, hack the plaster away, fix the cable to the studs and then plaster over again in the normal way.

While you can run cable through the space between the two claddings of a stud partition wall there is no way of doing this without some damage to the wall and the decoration. Drill a 12mm (½in) hole through the top wall plate above the position of the switch, then tap the wall directly below the hole to locate the nogging (▷). Cut a hole in the lath and plaster to reveal the top of the nogging and drill a similar hole through it.

Pass a lead weight on a plumb line through both of the holes and down to the location of the switch. Tie the cable to the line and pull it through.

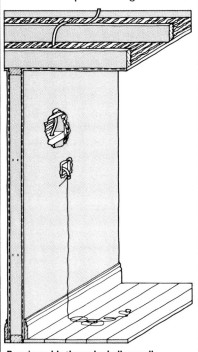

Running cable through a hollow wall
If a nogging prevents you running cable directly to a switch, cut away some laths and plaster to drill a hole through the timber.

RUNNING CABLE

Long runs of cable are necessary to take power from the consumer unit to all the sockets, light fittings and fixed appliances in the home.

The cable must be fixed securely to the structure of the house along its route except in confined spaces to which there is normally no access, such as voids between floors and inside hollow walls. There are accepted ways of running and fixing cable, depending on particular circumstances.

SEE ALSO

Details for: ▷
Nogging	135,137
Repairing plaster	51
Switching off	296

Surface fixing

PVC-insulated and -sheathed cable can be fixed directly to the surface of a wall or ceiling without any further protection. Fix it with plastic cable clips **(1)** or metal buckle clips **(2)** every 400mm (1ft 4in) on vertical runs and every 250mm (10in) on horizontal runs. Keep the runs as straight and neat as possible, and when several cables run in the same direction group them together. Avoid kinks in the cable by keeping it on the drum as long as possible, but if you do have to get any kinks out pull the cable round a thick dowel held in a vice.

If a cable seems vulnerable you can cover it with an impact-resistant plastic channel **(3)** . Having secured the cable with clips, you simply nail the channel in place over it.

1 Plastic cable clip

2 Metal buckle clip

3 Impact-resistant plastic channel

Concealed fixing

While surface-fixed cable is quite acceptable in cellars, under stairs and in workshops and garages, few people want to see it running across their living room walls or ceilings. It's better to bury it in the plaster or hide it in a wall void. Sheathed cable can be buried without further protection.

Wherever possible cable should run vertically to switches or sockets, to avoid dangerous clashes with wall fittings or fixtures installed later. Most people allow for it to run this way. If you must run horizontal cable confine it to within 150mm (6in) of the ceiling or 300mm (1ft) of the floor. Never run a buried cable diagonally across a wall.

Some people cover all buried cable with a channel, but it isn't required by the IEE Regulations.

Cable buried in light plastic conduit can be withdrawn later, if necessary, without disturbing decorations, but the need is so rare in a house as to be hardly worth considering.

Mark out your cable runs on the plaster, allowing a channel about 25mm (1in) wide for single cable. Cut both sides with a bolster and club hammer and hack out the plaster between the cuts with a cold chisel. Normally plaster is thick enough to conceal cable, but you may have to chop out some brickwork to get the depth. Clip the cable in the channel **(1)** and, when you have checked that the installation is working, plaster over it. To avoid electric shock ensure that the power to that circuit is turned off before you use wet plaster round a switch or socket outlet **(2)** .

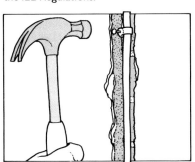

1 Nail plastic clips over the cable

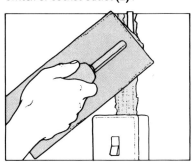

2 Repair the plaster up to the switch

RUNNING CABLE UNDER FLOORS

SEE ALSO
◁ Details for:
Removing skirting 181
Protective channel 303
Spur cables 311
Padsaw 464
Power jigsaw 465
Floorboard saw 479

Power and lighting circuits are often concealed beneath floors if access is possible. It isn't necessary to lift every floorboard to run a cable from one side of a room to the other; by lifting a board every 2m (6ft) or so you should be able to pass the cable from one gap to the next with the help of a length of stiff wire bent into a hook at one end. Look for boards that have been taken up before, as they will be fairly easy to lift and you will damage fewer boards.

Lifting floorboards

Lifting square-edged boards

Drive a wide bolster chisel between two boards about 50mm (2in) from the cut end of one of them (**1**). Lever that board up with the bolster, then do the same on its other edge, working along the board until you have raised it enough to wedge a cold chisel under it (**2**). Proceed along the board, raising it with the chisel, until the board is loose.

Full-length boards

If you have to lift a board that runs the whole length of the floor, from one skirting to the other, start somewhere near the middle of the board and close to a floor joist. The nail heads indicate the positions of joists. Lever the board up and make a saw cut through it centred on the joist, then lift the board in the normal way.

Lifting tongued and grooved boards

You cannot lift a tongued and grooved floorboard until you have cut through the tongues along both sides of the board, either with a special floorboard saw, which has a blade with a rounded tip, or with a power jigsaw.

Cutting a full-length board
Cut a full-length board in two directly over a floor joist.

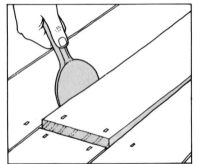

I Prise up the floorboard with a bolster

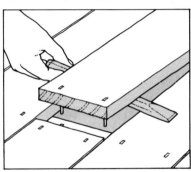

2 Wedge the raised end with a cold chisel

CUTTING A BOARD NEXT TO A SKIRTING

Should you need to cut through a board that lies close to a wall it may not be possible to lift it without damaging the bottom edge of the skirting board. In such a case drill a starting hole through the board alongside the joist nearest to the wall, insert the blade of a padsaw or power jigsaw in the hole and cut across the board flush with the side of the joist (**1**). To support the cut end afterwards nail a length of 50 x 50mm (2 x 2in) softwood to the joist. Hold it up tightly against the undersides of the adjacent floorboards while fixing it to ensure that the cut board will lie flush with the others (**2**).

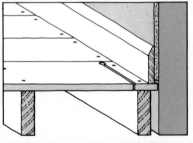

I Cut through a trapped board with a jigsaw

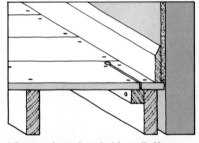

2 Support the cut board with a nailed batten

Solid floors

In a new concrete floor you can lay conduit and run cable through it before the concrete is poured.

In an existing solid floor you can cut a channel for conduit – hard work without an electric hammer and chisel bit – but if the floor is tiled you will not want to spoil it for one or two socket outlets. An alternative is to drop spur cables, buried in the wall plaster, from the ring circuit in the upper floor. Another way is to run cable through the wall from an adjacent area and channel it horizontally in the plaster just above the skirting. Yet another is to remove the skirting (◁), clip the cable to the wall and cover it with protective channel. Note the position of the cable to avoid piercing it when you nail back the skirting board.

In the roof space

In the roof space all wiring can be surface-run, but as people may enter it occasionally you must see that the cable is clipped securely to the joists or rafters. You can even run cable along the tops of joists in some areas, but run it through holes in the normal way where joists are to be boarded over or in areas of access such as round water tanks and the entrance hatch itself.

Wiring overlaid by roof insulation has a slightly higher chance of heating up. Ring mains and lighting circuits do not present a problem , but circuits to heaters, cookers or shower units are more critical. Wherever possible run cable over thermal insulation. If you cannot avoid running it under the material you should use a heavier cable to be on the safe side.

When expanded-polystyrene insulation is in contact with electric cable for a long time it affects the plasticizer in the PVC sheathing on the cable. The plasticizer moves to the surface of the sheathing, reacts with the polystyrene and forms a sticky substance on the cable. This becomes a dry crust which cracks if the cable is lifted out of the roof insulation and bent. It gives the impression that the cable insulation is cracking, but scientific testing has shown that the cracking is merely in the surface crust. On balance it is best to keep cable away from polystyrene.

Running cable through the house structure
Use the most convenient method to run cable to sockets and switches.
1 Clip cable to roof timbers in loft.
2 Junction boxes must be fixed securely.
3 Run cable through holes in the joists near the hatch.
4 Run cable over loft insulation.
5 To avoid damaging a finished floor you can run a short spur through the wall from the next room.
6 When cable runs across the line of joists drill holes 50mm (2in) below the top edges.
7 Cable running parallel to joists can lay on the ceiling below.
8 Let cable drape onto the base below a suspended floor.
9 When you cannot run cable through a concrete floor you can drop a spur from the floor above.
10 Take the opportunity to bury conduit for cable in a new concrete floor.

Running the cable

On the ground floor the cable can rest on the earth or on the concrete platform below the joists if there will not normally be access to the space. Allow enough slack so that the cable is not suspended above the platform, which might put a strain on any fixings to junction boxes or socket outlets. For the same reason secure the cable with clips to the side of the joist beside junction boxes or other accessories.

When laying cable between a floor and the ceiling below, it can rest on the ceiling without any other fixing so long as it runs parallel with the joists. If it runs at right angles to the joists drill a series of 12mm (½in) holes, one through each joist along the intended cable run. The holes must be at least 50mm (2in) below the tops of the joists so that floorboard nails cannot at some time be hammered through the cable. The space between the joists is limited but you can hire a special joist brace or you can cut down a spade bit and use it in a power drill.

When you reach the last joist against the wall, instead of drilling a hole cut a notch in its top so that you can feed the cable up behind the skirting board to reach a socket outlet. Cover the notch with a stout metal plate to protect the cable, then cut a notch in the end of the floorboard to clear it.

Never attach electrical cable to gas or water pipes, and don't run it next to heating pipes, as the heat can melt the insulation.

Having marked out the position of a socket or fused connection unit, cut a channel from it down to the skirting board and, with an extra-long masonry drill in a power tool, remove the plaster from behind the skirting board. By using the drill at a shallow angle you can loosen much of the debris, but you will probably have to finish the job with a slim cold chisel. Raking the debris out from below with the same chisel will also help to dislodge it.

Pass a stiff wire with a hook formed on its end down behind the skirting board, hook the cable and pull it through, at the same time feeding it from below with your other hand.

SEE ALSO

Details for: ▷	
Cable clips	303
Concealing cable	303
Running a spur	311
Spade bit	472
Joist brace	492

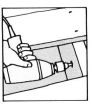

Drilling the joists
Shorten a spade bit so that your drill fits between the joists.

Notching a joist
Screw a thick metal plate over a notch in a joist close to a wall.

Drilling behind skirting
Use a long masonry drill to remove the plaster behind a skirting board.

ASSESSING YOUR INSTALLATION

Inspect your electrical system to ensure that it is safe and adequate for your future needs. But remember, you should never examine any part of it without first switching off the power at the consumer unit (◁).

If you are in doubt about some aspect of the installation you should ask a qualified electrician his opinion. If you get in touch with your Electricity Board they will arrange for someone to test the whole system for you.

SEE ALSO

◁ Details for:
Switching off	296
Earth	
connection	296-297
Old fuse boxes	297
RCCB	297
Fuse ratings	299
Old cable	302
Replacing fuses	300
Running cable	303-305
Replacing sockets	310
Converting radial circuit	313
Replacing switches	328

QUESTIONS	ANSWERS
Do you have a modern consumer unit or a mixture of old 'fuse boxes' (◁)?	Old fuse boxes can be unsafe and should be replaced with a modern unit. Seek professional advice on this.
Is the consumer unit in good condition?	Replace broken casing or cracked covers and check that all fuse carriers are intact and that they fit snugly in the fuseways.
Are the fuse carriers for the circuits clearly labelled?	If you cannot identify the various circuits, have an electrician test the system and label the fuses.
Are all your circuit fuses of the correct ratings (◁)?	Replace any fuses of the wrong rating. If an unusually large fuse is protecting one of the circuits get professional advice before changing it. It may have a special purpose. Any wire other than proper fuse wire found in a fuse should be replaced at once.
Are the cables that lead from the consumer unit in good condition?	The cables should be fixed securely, with no bare wires showing. If the cables seem to be insulated with rubber (◁) have the whole of the insulation checked as soon as possible. Rubber insulation has a limited life, so yours could already be dangerous.
Is the earth connection from the consumer unit intact and in good condition (◁)?	If the connection seems loose or corroded have the Electricity Board check on whether the earthing is sound. You can check an RCCB (◁) by pushing the test button to see if it is working mechanically.
What is the condition of the fixed wiring between floors and in the loft or roof space?	If the cables are rubber-insulated have the system checked by a professional, but first examine each of the circuits, as they may not all have been renewed at the same time. If cable is run in conduit it can be hard to check on its condition, but if it looks doubtful where it enters accessories have the circuit checked professionally. Wiring should be fixed securely and sheathing should run into all accessories, with no bare wire in sight. Junction boxes on lighting circuits should be screwed firmly to the structure and should have their covers in place.
Is the wiring discreet and orderly?	Tidy all surface-run wiring into straight properly-clipped runs. Better still, bury the cable in the wall plaster or run it under floors and inside hollow walls.
Are there any old round-pin socket outlets?	See that their wiring is adequate, though old radial circuits should be replaced with modern ring circuits and 13amp square-pin sockets.
Are the outer casings of all accessories in good condition and fixed securely to the structure?	Replace any cracked or broken components and secure any loose fittings.
Do switches on all accessories work smoothly and effectively?	Where not, replace the accessories.
Are all the wires inside accessories attached securely to their terminals?	Tighten all loose terminals and ensure that no bare wires are visible. Fit sleeves to earth wires where missing.

QUESTIONS	ANSWERS
Is the insulation round wires dry and crumbly inside any accessories?	If so it is rubber insulation in advanced decomposition. Replace the covers carefully and have a professional check the system as soon as possible.
Do any sockets, switches or plugs get warm when live? Is there a smell of burning, or scorch marks on sockets or round the bases of the pins of plugs? Do sockets spark when you remove a plug, or switches when you operate them?	These things mean loose connections in the accessory or plug, or a poor connection between plug and socket. Tighten loose connections and clean all fuse clips, fuse caps and the pins of plugs with fine wire wool. If the fault persists try a new plug; lastly replace the socket or switch.
Is it difficult to insert a plug in a socket?	The socket is worn and should be replaced.
Are your sockets in the right places?	Sockets should be placed conveniently round a room so that you need never have long flexes trailing across the floor or under carpets. Add sockets to the ring circuit by running spurs.
Do you have enough sockets?	If you have to use plug adaptors you need more sockets. Replace singles with doubles, add spurs or extend the ring circuit.
Is there old, braided, twin flex hanging from some ceiling roses?	Replace it with PVC-insulated flex (▷). Also check that the wiring inside the rose is PVC-insulated.
Are there earth wires inside your ceiling roses?	If not get professional advice on whether to replace the lighting circuits.
Is your lighting efficient (▷)?	Make sure you have two-way switching on stairs, and consider extra sockets or different light fittings to make the lighting more effective or atmospheric (▷).
Is there power in the garage or the workshop?	Outbuildings separate from the house need their own power supply (▷).

SEE ALSO

Details for: ▷

Planning lighting	38-39
Flex	292
Wiring outbuildings	334-335
Replacing fuses	300
Replacing sockets	310
Running a spur	311
Extending ring circuit	312
Replacing switches	328
Two-way switching	330

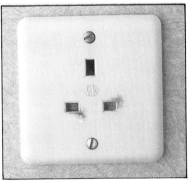

From left to right:

Scorch marks
Scorch marks on a socket or round the base of plug pins indicates poor connections.
Overloaded socket
If you have to use an adaptor to power your appliances fit extra sockets.
Unprotected connections
Make sure covers or faceplates are fitted to all accessories.

From left to right:

Incorrect fuse
Replace improper wire with fuse wire.
Round-pin socket
Replace a round-pin socket with a 13amp square-pin version.
Damaged socket
Replace cracked or broken faceplate.

POWER CIRCUITS: SURFACE-MOUNTING SOCKET OUTLETS

SEE ALSO

◁ Details for:
Wiring a socket	310
Wall fixings	497-498
Stud partitions	135
Switching off	296
Wiring kitchen appliances	316

Whatever the type of circuits in your home, use only standard 13amp square-pin sockets. All round-pin sockets are now out of date, and though they may not be actually dangerous at the moment you should have them checked and consider changing the wiring to accommodate new 13amp socket outlets.

Before you start work on any socket switch the power off at the consumer unit and remove the fuse for that circuit, then test the socket with an appliance that you know to be working so as to be sure that the socket has been properly switched off.

TYPES OF 13AMP SOCKET

Though all sockets are functionally very similar there are several variations on the basic component.

There are single and double sockets, and both are available either switched or unswitched and with or without neon indicators which tell you at a glance whether the socket is switched on. All these sockets are wired in the same way.

Another basic difference is in how sockets are mounted. They can be surface-mounted – screwed to the wall in a plastic box or pattress – or flush-mounted in a metal box buried in the wall with only its faceplate visible.

Triple sockets
Triple sockets are useful in a situation where several electrical appliances are grouped together.

Switched single   **Unswitched single**

Switched double

Single switched with indicator

Positioning sockets

Decide on the most convenient positions for television, hi-fi, table lamps and so on and position sockets accordingly. To avoid using adaptors or long leads distribute the sockets evenly round the living room and bedrooms, and wherever possible fit doubles rather than singles. Don't forget sockets for running the vacuum cleaner in hallways and on landings.

The optimum height for a socket is 225 to 300mm (9in to 1ft) above the floor. This will clear most skirting boards and leave ample room for flexible cord to hang from a plug, while being high enough to be in no danger of getting struck by the vacuum cleaner. In the kitchen fit at least four double sockets 150mm (6in) above the worktops, more if you have a lot of small appliances. In addition fit sockets for floor-standing appliances like the refrigerator and dishwasher.

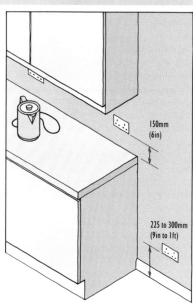

150mm (6in)

225 to 300mm (9in to 1ft)

Optimum heights for socket outlets

Fixing to masonry

First break out the thin plastic webs that cover the fixing holes in the back of the pattress. The best tool for this is an electrician's screwdriver. Two fixings should be sufficient. The fixing holes are slotted to allow for adjustment.

Hold the pattress against the wall, levelling it at the same time with a small spirit level, and mark the fixing holes on the wall with a bradawl through the holes in the pattress. Drill and plug the holes with No 8 wall plugs.

With a larger screwdriver and pliers break out the plastic web covering the most convenient cable-entry hole in the pattress. For surface-run cable this will be in the side; for buried cable it will be the one in the base.

Feed the cable into the pattress to form a loop about 75mm (3in) long **(1)**, then fix the box to the wall with 32mm (1¼in) countersunk woodscrews.

Finally wire and fit the socket (◁).

Fixing to a hollow wall

On a dry partition or lath-and-plaster wall a surface-mounted pattress is fixed with any of the standard fixings for use on hollow walls (◁), though you can use ordinary woodscrews if you can position the pattress over a stud. In the latter case be sure you can feed the cable into it past the stud **(2)**.

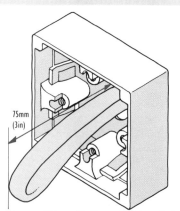

75mm (3in)

1 Leave a 75mm (3in) loop of cable at the box

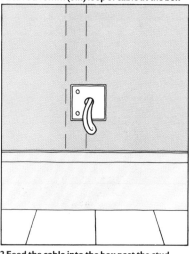

2 Feed the cable into the box past the stud

FLUSH-MOUNTING SOCKET OUTLETS

Fixing to masonry

Hold the metal box against the wall and draw round it with a pencil **(1)**, then mark a 'chase' or channel running up from the skirting to the box's outline.

With a bolster and cold chisel cut away the plaster, down to the brickwork **(2)**, within the marked area.

With a masonry drill bore several rows of holes down to the required depth **(3)** across the recess for the box, then with a cold chisel cut away the brick to the depth of the holes so that the box will lie flush with the plaster.

Try the box in the recess. If it fits in snugly mark the wall through the fixing holes in its back, then drill the wall for the screw plugs. If you have made the recess too deep, or the box rocks from side to side, apply some filler in the recess and press the box into it, flush with the wall and properly positioned. After about 10 minutes ease the box out carefully and leave the filler to harden so that you can mark, drill and plug the fixing holes through it.

Knock out one or more of the blanked-off holes in the box to accommodate the cable. Fit a grommet into each hole to protect the cable's sheathing from the metal edges **(4)**, feed the cable into the box and screw the box to the wall.

Plaster up to the box and over the cable chased into the wall, and when the plaster has hardened wire and fit the socket (▷).

Fixing to plasterboard

To fit a flush socket to a wall made of plasterboard over wooden studs trace the outline of the box in position on the wall, then drill a hole in each corner of the shape with a brace and bit and cut out the waste with a padsaw.

Punch out the blanked-off entry holes in the box, fit rubber grommets and feed the cable into the box.

Clip dry-wall fixing flanges to the sides of the box **(5)**. These will hold it in place by gripping the wall from inside. Ease one side of the box, with flange, into the recess and then, holding the screw fixing lugs so as not to lose the box, manoeuvre it until both flanges are behind the plasterboard and the box sits snugly in the hole.

Now wire and fit the socket (▷). As you tighten the fixing screws the plasterboard will be gripped between the flanges and the faceplate.

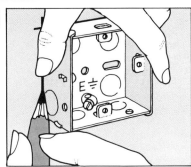
1 Draw round the mounting box

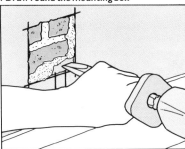
2 Chop away the plaster with a cold chisel

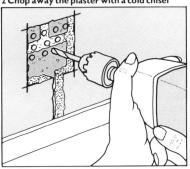
3 Drill out the brickwork with a masonry bit

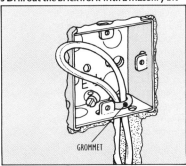
GROMMET
4 Fit a soft grommet in the cable-entry hole

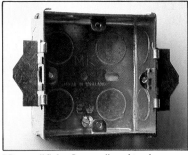
5 Dry-wall fixing flanges clipped to a box

FLUSH MOUNTING TO LATH AND PLASTER

If you wish to fit a flush socket in a lath-and-plaster wall try to locate it over a stud or nogging (▷).

Mark the position of the box, cut out the plaster and saw away the laths with a padsaw. Try the box for fit and, if necessary, chop a notch in the woodwork until the box lies flush with the wall surface **(1)**. Feed in the cable and screw the box to the stud before wiring and fitting the socket (▷).

If you cannot position the socket on a stud, cut away enough plaster and laths to make a slot in the wall running from one stud to the next. Between the studs screw or skew-nail a softwood nogging to which you can fix the box. Set the batten back from the front edges of the studs if that is necessary to make the box lie flush with the wall surface **(2)**. Feed the cable into the box and make good the surrounding plaster before you wire and fit the socket.

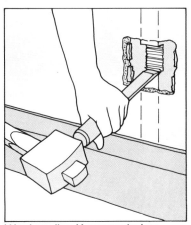
1 Notch a wall stud for a mounting box

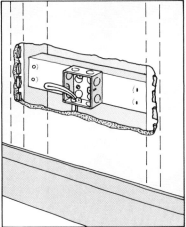
2 Nail a nogging between studs
Cut away wall plaster and laths when you have to fix a mounting box between wall studs.

SEE ALSO

Details for: ▷	
Locating studs/	
noggings	137
Wiring a socket	310
Running a cable	303–305
Padsaw	464

REPLACING SOCKET OUTLETS

If you have a socket outlet that needs to be replaced because it is faulty or broken you should consider some options before undertaking the job.

SEE ALSO

◁ Details for:
Recessing metal	
box	309
Flush-mounted box	309
Cutting brickwork	309
Mounting to a	
hollow wall	309
Switching off	296
Stripping cable	302
Types of socket	308

Simple replacement

Replacing a damaged socket with a similar one is quite straightforward. Any style will fit a flush-mounted box, but look carefully when you substitute a socket that screws to a surface-mounted pattress. Though it will fit and function perfectly well, square corners and edges on either will not suit rounded ones on the other. In such a case you may also have to buy a new, matching pattress.

An unswitched socket can be replaced with a switched one without any change to the wiring or fixing.

Switch off the power supply to the circuit, then remove the fixing screws holding the faceplate and pull the socket out of the box.

Loosen off the terminals and free the conductors. Check that all is well inside the pattress, then connect the conductors to the terminals of the new socket. Fit the faceplate, using the original screws if those supplied with the new socket don't match the thread in the pattress.

Surface to flush mounted

If you have to renew a socket for some reason you can use the occasion to replace a surface-mounted pattress with a flush box.

Turn off the power, remove the old socket and recess the metal box into the wall (◁), taking care not to damage the fixed wiring in the wall.

Replacing a single socket with a double

One way to increase the number of sockets in a room is to substitute doubles for singles. Any single socket on a ring circuit can be replaced with a double with no change to the wiring. You can similarly replace a single socket on a spur. Consider using the safer, switched sockets. The wiring is identical.

Surface to surface

Replacing a surface-mounted single unit with a surface-mounted double is quite easy. Having removed the old socket, simply fix the new, double pattress to the wall in the same place.

Flush to surface

Though flush-mounted sockets are neater, you may not want the disturbance to decor of installing a double one. Instead you can fit a double surface-mounted socket over the buried box of the single one (**1**). Turn off the power and remove the socket, leaving the metal box and the wiring in place. Knock out the cable-entry hole in the plastic double pattress and feed the

cable through it. When the pattress is centred over the old box (◁) two fixing holes will line up with the fixing lugs on the buried box. Break out the plastic webs and fix the new pattress to the lugs with the screws that held the old socket in place. Wire up the new double socket and fit it.

Flush to flush

Switch off the power to the circuit, remove the old socket at its metal box, then try the new double box over the hole. You can centre the box over the hole or align it with one end (**2**), whichever is the more convenient. Trace the outline of the box on the wall and cut out the brickwork (◁).

To substitute a double socket in a hollow wall use a similar procedure, installing the socket by whichever method is most convenient (◁).

Surface to flush

To replace a single surface-mounted socket with a flush double one proceed as described above.

CONNECTING UP TO A SOCKET

When a single cable is involved strip off the sheathing in the ordinary way and connect the wires to the terminals: the black wire to neutral – N, the red one to live – L and the earth wire, which you should insulate yourself with a sleeve, to earth – E (**1**). If necessary fold the stripped ends over so that no bare wire protrudes from a terminal.

When connecting to a ring circuit you can cut through the loop of cable, strip the sheathing from each half and twist together the bared ends of matching wires – live with live and so on – after slipping sleeves on the earth wires (**2**). Alternatively you can slit the sheathing lengthwise and peel it off, leaving the wires unbroken (**3**), bare a part of each wire by cutting away insulation, then pinch the exposed part of each wire into a tight fold with the pliers so that it will fit into its terminal. The second method ensures perfect contact, as the ring circuit is uninterrupted. You may have to cut the earth wire to slip sleeves over the halves.

Cable is stiff, and can make it hard to close the socket faceplate, so bend each conductor so that it will fold into the box or pattress. Locate both fixing screws and tighten them gradually in turns until the plate fits firmly in place against the wall or pattress.

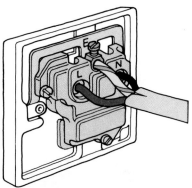

I Wiring a socket outlet

2 Twist cut wires together

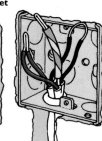

3 Crimp continuous wires with pliers

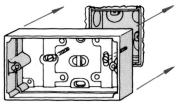

I Fixing a double pattress over a flush box

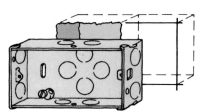

2 Cut out extra brickwork for a double box

ADDING A SPUR TO A RING CIRCUIT

If you need more sockets in convenient positions round a room you can run 2.5mm² spur cables from a ring circuit

and have as many spurs as there are sockets already on the ring, each spur feeding a single or double socket.

A spur cable can be connected to any socket – or fused connection unit – on the ring, or to a junction box inserted in the ring, whichever is the easier. If running cable from one of the present sockets would mean disturbing the plaster it is more convenient to use a junction box, and if there is no socket within easy reach of the proposed new one using a junction box will save cable.

If cable is surface-run and you want to extend a row of sockets – behind a workbench, for example – it is simpler to connect the spur to a socket.

Examine the socket. If there is one cable feeding it, it is already on a spur; if there are three cables in the socket it is already feeding a spur itself. In either case you cannot connect a new spur, so look for a socket with two cables.

Connecting to an existing socket

Fix the new socket, wire it up in the ordinary way (See opposite) and run its spur cable to the existing socket. Switch off power and remove the existing socket. You may have to enlarge the entry hole in the pattress or knock out another to take the spur cable. Feed the cable into the pattress, prepare the conductors and twist their bared ends together with those of the matching conductors of the ring circuit. Insert the wires in their terminals: red – L, black – N and green/yellow – E and replace the socket. Switch the power back on and test the new spur socket.

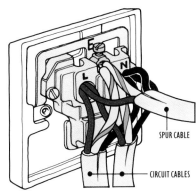

SPUR CABLE

CIRCUIT CABLES

Taking a spur from an existing socket outlet

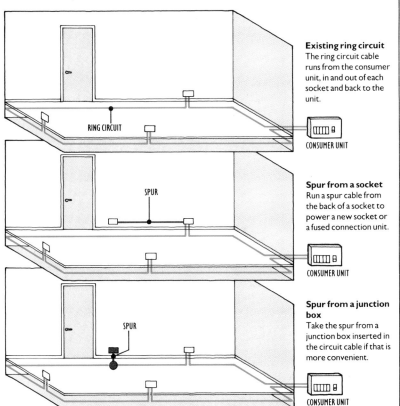

RING CIRCUIT

SPUR

SPUR

CONSUMER UNIT

CONSUMER UNIT

CONSUMER UNIT

Existing ring circuit
The ring circuit cable runs from the consumer unit, in and out of each socket and back to the unit.

Spur from a socket
Run a spur cable from the back of a socket to power a new socket or a fused connection unit.

Spur from a junction box
Take the spur from a junction box inserted in the circuit cable if that is more convenient.

CONNECTING TO A JUNCTION BOX

You will need a 30amp junction box with three terminals to connect to a ring circuit. It will have either knock-out cable-entry holes or a special cover that rotates to blank off unneeded holes. The cover must be screw-fixed.

Lift a floorboard close to the new socket and where you can connect to the ring circuit cable without having to stretch it.

Fix a platform for the box by nailing battens near the bottoms of two joists (See right) and screwing a 100 x 25mm (4 x 1in) strip of wood between the joists and resting on the battens. Loop the ring circuit cable over the platform before fixing it so that the cable need not be cut for connecting up. Remove the cover, screw the junction box to the platform and break out two cable-entry holes. If you do forget to loop the cable over the platform, just cut the cable when you come to connect it up.

Turn off the power at the consumer unit, then rest the ring circuit cable across the box and mark the amount of sheathing to remove. Slit it lengthwise and peel it off the conductors. Don't cut the live and neutral conductors, but slice away just enough insulation on each to expose a section of bare wire that will fit into the terminal (See right). Cut the earth wire and put insulating sleeves on the two ends.

Remove the screws from the terminals and lay the wires across them, the earth wire in the middle terminal and the live and neutral ones on the ends. Push the wires home with a screwdriver.

Having fitted and wired the new spur socket, run its cable to the junction box, cut and prepare the ends of the wires and break out an entry hole so that the spur wires can be fitted to the terminals of the box (See right). Take care that only colour-matched wires from both cables share terminals.

Replace the fixing screws, starting them by hand as they easily cross-thread, then tighten them with a screwdriver. Check that all the wires are secured and that the cables fit snugly in their entry holes with the sheathing running into the box, then fit the cover on the box.

Fix each cable to a nearby joist with cable clips, to take the strain off the terminals, then replace the floorboards.

Switch the power back on and test the new socket.

SEE ALSO

Details for: ▷

Switching off	296
Cables	302
Stripping cable	302
Running cable	303-305
Lifting floorboards	304

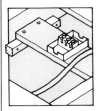

Make a wooden platform for a junction box

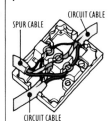

CIRCUIT CABLE

SPUR CABLE

CIRCUIT CABLE

Taking a spur from a junction box

311

EXTENDING A RING CIRCUIT

There are situations in which it is better to extend a ring circuit than to fit spurs. For instance, you may want to wire a room that was not adequately serviced before, or perhaps all of the conveniently placed sockets already have spurs running from them.

There are two ways of breaking into the ring: at an existing socket or via junction boxes. Whichever method you decide on, switch off the power to the circuit before you break into it.

SEE ALSO

◁ Details for:
Running cable	303-305
Mounting boxes	308-309
Switching off	296
Ring circuit regulations	301
Positioning sockets	308
Wiring sockets	310
Junction box	311

Using an existing socket

Disconnect one in-going cable from a socket on the ring circuit and take this to the first new socket. Do it via a junction box if the cable will not reach otherwise. Continue the extension with a new section of cable from socket to socket, finally running it from the last one back to the socket where you broke into the ring. Joining the new cable to the old one within the socket completes the circuit.

Using junction boxes

Cut the ring cable and connect each cut end to a junction box, then run a new length of cable from one box to the other, looping it into the new sockets.

Running the extension

No matter how you plan to break into the ring always install the new work first and connect it up to the circuit only at the last moment. This allows you to use power tools on the extension. Switch the power off just before connecting up.

Decide on the positions of the new sockets and plan your cable run: an easy route is better than a difficult shorter one. Allow some slack in the cable.

Cut out the plaster and brickwork for sockets and cable and fit the boxes (◁). Now run the cable, leaving enough spare for joining to the ring circuit (◁), and take it up behind the skirting to the first socket. Leave a loop hanging from the box (See right), then take the cable on to the next, and so on until all the new sockets are supplied. Take the excess cable on to the point where you plan to join the ring.

Make good the plasterwork and fit the new sockets. Switch off the power, break into the ring and connect the extension to it. Switch the power on and test the new sockets separately.

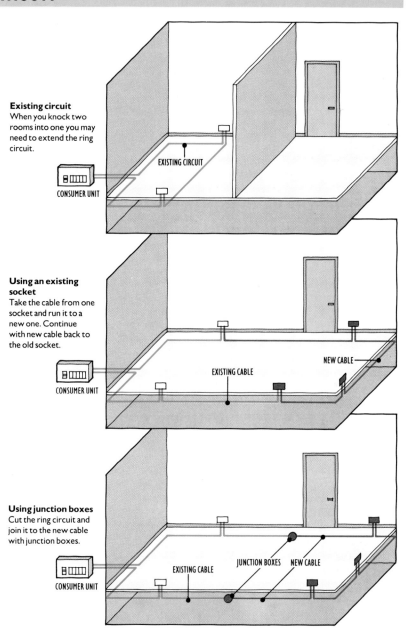

Existing circuit
When you knock two rooms into one you may need to extend the ring circuit.

Using an existing socket
Take the cable from one socket and run it to a new one. Continue with new cable back to the old socket.

Using junction boxes
Cut the ring circuit and join it to the new cable with junction boxes.

LEAVE SOME SLACK IN THE CIRCUIT

Don't pull the cable too tight when you are running a new circuit: it puts a strain on the connections and makes it difficult to modify the circuit at a later stage should it become necessary.

Leave a generous loop of cable at each new socket position until you have run the complete circuit. At that stage you can pull the loop back ready for connecting to the socket.

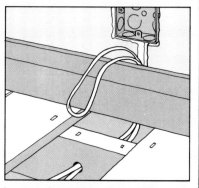

Leave ample cable above the skirting

CONVERTING A RADIAL CIRCUIT TO A RING CIRCUIT

If, when you examine your installation, you find that the power circuit is radial you may decide to convert it to a ring circuit, particularly if you wish to supply a larger area (▷).

Checking cable and fuse

If the radial circuit is wired with 2.5mm^2 cable (solid conductors) continue the circuit back to the consumer unit with the same size cable but change the 20amp circuit fuse for a 30amp fuse and fuseway. If it is wired with 4mm^2 (stranded conductors) you can complete the ring with 2.5mm^2 cable and leave the 30amp circuit fuse alone.

The additional cable is run in exactly the same way as described for extending a ring circuit (See opposite). Join the new cable at the last socket on the radial circuit and run it to all the new sockets. From the last one run it to the consumer unit. Turn off the power.

Connecting to consumer unit

You should examine your consumer unit and familiarize yourself with it (▷). Even when the unit is switched off, the cable that connects the meter to the main switch is still live – so take care.

First locate the terminals to which the radial circuit is connected. The live (red wire) terminal is on the fuseway (or MCB) from which you removed the circuit fuse before starting the work. The neutral (black wire) terminal is on the neutral block, to which all of the black wires are connected. You can usually trace the black wire you're looking for by working along from the sheathed part of the cable, and the earth terminal similarly, by tracing the green-insulated conductor.

Pass the end of the new cable into the consumer unit as closely as possible to the original radial circuit cable. Cut it to length, strip off the sheathing and prepare the ends of the conductors.

Disconnect the live (red) conductor from its terminal and twist its end together with that of the red wire from the new cable, then reconnect both wires in the same terminal. Do the same for the black wires and then the green ones, but first slip a length of insulating sleeving over the new earth wire. Replace the cover.

Check that the circuit fuse is of the correct rating and then replace the fuse carrier. Close the consumer unit, switch on the power and test the circuit.

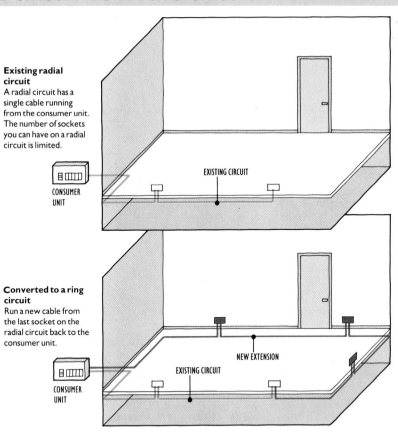

Existing radial circuit
A radial circuit has a single cable running from the consumer unit. The number of sockets you can have on a radial circuit is limited.

CONSUMER UNIT

EXISTING CIRCUIT

Converted to a ring circuit
Run a new cable from the last socket on the radial circuit back to the consumer unit.

CONSUMER UNIT

NEW EXTENSION

EXISTING CIRCUIT

SEE ALSO	
Details for: ▷	
Consumer unit	298
Radial circuit regulations	301
Switching off	296
Fuse ratings	299
Cable	302
Running cable	303-305
Positioning sockets	308
Wiring sockets	310

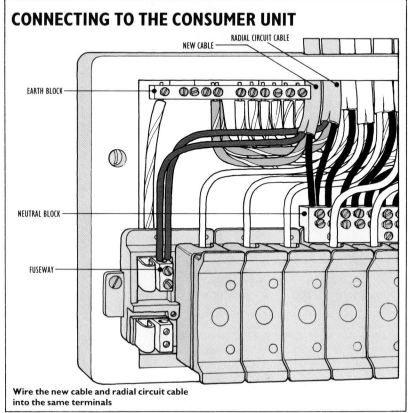

CONNECTING TO THE CONSUMER UNIT

RADIAL CIRCUIT CABLE

NEW CABLE

EARTH BLOCK

NEUTRAL BLOCK

FUSEWAY

Wire the new cable and radial circuit cable into the same terminals

FIXED APPLIANCES

A 13amp socket is designed to be flexible in use, enabling appliances to be moved from room to room and one socket to be used for different appliances at different times. But many appliances, large and small, are fixed to the structure of the house, or stand in one position permanently. Such appliances may just as well be wired permanently into the electrical installation. For some there is no alternative, and they may even require individual radial circuits direct from the consumer unit.

SEE ALSO

◁ Details for:

Mounting boxes	308-309
Stripping flex	293
Switching off	296
Power circuits	301
Stripping cable	302

FUSED CONNECTION UNITS

A fused connection unit is basically a device for joining circuit wiring to the flex – or sometimes cable – of an appliance. The junction incorporates the added protection of a cartridge fuse like that found in a 13amp plug. If the appliance is connected by a flex, choose a unit with a cord outlet in the faceplate.

Some fused connection units are also switched, with or without a neon indicator that shows when the switch is on. The switched connection unit allows you completely to isolate the appliance from the mains.

All fused connection units are single – there are no double ones – with square faceplates that fit the standard plastic surface-mounted pattresses or the metal boxes for flush mounting.

Changing a fuse
With the power off, remove the retaining screw in the face of the fuse holder. Take the holder from the unit, prise out the old fuse and fit a new one. Replace the fuse holder.

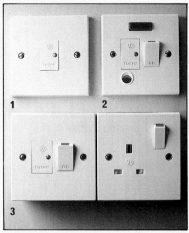

Fused connection units
1 Unswitched connection unit
2 Switched unit with cord outlet and indicator
3 Connection unit and socket in a dual box

Small appliances

All small electrical appliances with ratings of up to 3000W (3kW) – wall heaters, cooker hoods, heated towel rails and so on – can be wired into a ring or radial circuit by means of fused connection units. They could also be connected by 13amp plugs to sockets, but the electrical contact is not so good and there is some risk of fire with that type of permanent installation.

Always remember to switch off the power at the consumer unit before wiring a fused connection unit to the house circuitry.

Mounting a fused connection unit

A fused connection unit is mounted in the same type of box as an ordinary socket outlet, and the box is fixed to the wall in the same way (◁). The unit can also be mounted in a dual box which is designed to hold two single units – for example, a standard socket outlet next to a connection unit. The socket is wired to the ring circuit and the two units are linked together inside the box by a short 2.5mm² spur.

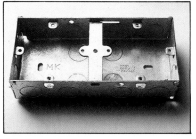

A dual mounting box

Wiring a fused connection unit

Fused connection units can be supplied by a ring circuit, a radial circuit or a spur.

Some appliances are connected to the unit by a length of flex while others are wired up with cable but the wiring arrangements inside the units are the same. Units with cord outlets have clamps to secure the connecting flex.

An unswitched connection unit has two live (L) terminals, one marked 'Load' for the brown wire of the flex, and the other marked 'Mains' for the red wire from the circuit cable. The blue wire from the flex and the black wire from the circuit cable go to similar neutral (N) terminals and both earth wires are connected to the E terminal or terminals (**1**).

A switched connection unit

A fused connection unit with a switch has two sets of terminals. Those marked 'Mains' are for the spur or ring cable that supplies the power; the terminals marked 'Load' are for the flex or cable from the appliance.

Wire up the flex side first, connecting the brown wire to the L terminal and the blue one to the N terminal, both on the Load side. Connect the green/yellow wire to the E terminal (**2**) and tighten the cord clamp.

Attach the circuit conductors to the Mains terminals – red to L and black to N, then sleeve the earth wire and take it to the E terminal (**2**).

If the fused connection unit is on a ring circuit you must fit two circuit conductors into each Mains terminal and the earth terminal.

Before securing the unit in its box with the fixing screws make sure the wires are held firmly in the terminals and that they can fold away neatly.

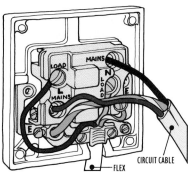

1 Wiring a fused connection unit

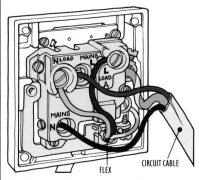

2 Wiring a switched fused connection unit

WIRING HEATERS

Skirting heaters, wall-mounted heaters and oil-filled radiators should be wired to a fused connection unit mounted nearby, between 150mm (6in) and 300mm (1ft) from the floor. Whether the connection to the unit is by flex or cable will depend on the type of heater. Follow the manufacturer's instructions, and fit a 13amp cartridge fuse in the connection unit.

In a bathroom a fused connection unit must be mounted out of reach, so any heater mounted near the floor of a bathroom must be on a cable to a connection unit installed outside the room. If the appliance is fitted with flex, mount a flexible cord outlet (1) next to the appliance, run a cable from the outlet to the fused connection unit outside and connect it to the 'Load' terminals in the unit.

The flex outlet is mounted on a standard surface-mounted pattress or flush on a metal box. At the back of the faceplate are three pairs of terminals to take the conductors from the flex and the cable (2).

Radiant wall heaters for use in bathrooms must be fixed high on the wall and out of reach from shower or bath. A fused connection unit, fitted with a 13amp fuse, must be mounted at the same level and the heater must be controlled by a pull-cord double-pole switch – the type that works by breaking both live and neutral contacts. Many heaters have built-in double-pole switches; otherwise you must fit a ceiling-mounted 15amp double-pole switch between the connection unit and the heater (▷). Switch terminals marked 'Mains' are for the cable on the circuit side of the switch; those marked 'Load' are for the heater side. The earth wires are connected to a common terminal on the switch pattress.

If it is not possible to run a spur to the fused connection unit from a socket outside the bathroom don't be tempted to connect a radiant wall heater to the lighting circuit. Instead run a separate radial circuit from the fused connection to a 5amp fuseway in the consumer unit, using 2.5mm² cable.

Heated towel rail

The Regulations covering other kinds of heater apply to a heated towel rail if it is situated in a bathroom. As it is mounted near the floor, run a flex from it to a flexible-cord outlet which is in turn wired to a fused connection unit outside the bathroom.

Fit a 13amp fuse, or, for a heater of 1kW or less, a 5amp fuse.

If a heated towel rail is installed in a bedroom the fused connection unit can be mounted alongside it.

Heat/light unit

Heat/light units, which are usually fitted in bathrooms, incorporate a radiant heater and a light fitting in the one appliance. They are ceiling-mounted, usually in the position of the ceiling rose, but these units should never be connected to lighting circuits.

To install a heat/light unit in this position turn off the power and, having identified the lighting cables (▷), remove the rose and withdraw the cables into the ceiling void. Fit a junction box to a nearby joist and terminate the lighting cables at that point (3). Don't connect the switch cable, as it won't be needed.

From an unswitched fused connection unit mounted outside the bathroom run a 1.5mm² two-core and earth spur cable to a ceiling-mounted 15amp double-pole switch, and from there to the heat/light unit. Connect up to the fused connection unit (See opposite), then wire the heat/light unit according to the maker's instructions and fit a 13amp fuse in the connection unit.

SEE ALSO

Details for: ▷

Double-pole ceiling switch	323
Ceiling-rose connections	324
Switching off	296
Running cable	303-305

1 Flexible cord outlet

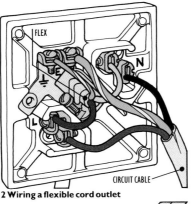

2 Wiring a flexible cord outlet

DISCONNECTED SWITCH CABLE

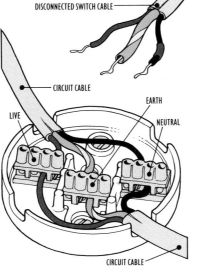

CIRCUIT CABLE
EARTH
LIVE
NEUTRAL
CIRCUIT CABLE

3 Terminating the lighting cables
Join the circuit cables in a junction box. Label the switch wire for future reference.

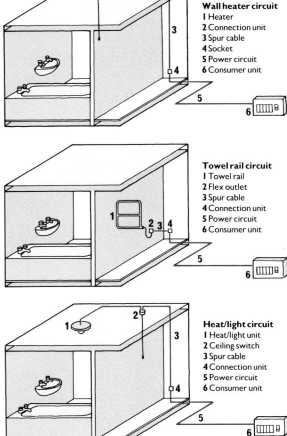

Wall heater circuit
1 Heater
2 Connection unit
3 Spur cable
4 Socket
5 Power circuit
6 Consumer unit

Towel rail circuit
1 Towel rail
2 Flex outlet
3 Spur cable
4 Connection unit
5 Power circuit
6 Consumer unit

Heat/light circuit
1 Heat/light unit
2 Ceiling switch
3 Spur cable
4 Connection unit
5 Power circuit
6 Consumer unit

WIRING SMALL APPLIANCES

SHAVER SOCKETS

SEE ALSO

◁ Details for:
Wiring a shower	323
Fitting a fan	279-280
Fitting a cooker hood	281
Running a spur	311
Fused connection unit	314
Flex outlet	315
30amp DP wall switch	319
Double-pole ceiling switch	323
Connecting to light circuit	329
Waste disposal unit	375
Plumbing a water heater	380

Extractor fan

To install an extractor fan in a kitchen mount a fused connection unit 150mm (6in) above the worktop and run a cable to the fan or to a flex outlet next to it. If the fan has no integral switch use a switched connection unit to control it. Fit a 3 or 5amp fuse as recommended by the maker.

If the fan's speed and direction are controllable it may have a separate control unit, in which case wire the connection unit to it following the manufacturer's instructions.

To fit an extractor fan in a bathroom mount the fused connection unit outside and run the cable to the fan or its flex outlet via a ceiling-mounted double-pole pull-switch.

Fridges, dishwashers and washing machines

There is no reason why you cannot plug an appliance like a fridge, dishwasher or washing machine into a standard socket outlet except that in modern kitchens such appliances fit snugly under worktops, and sockets mounted behind them are hard to reach.

To control an appliance conveniently first mount a switched fused connection unit 150mm (6in) above the worktop and connect it to the ring circuit, then run a spur, using 2.5mm² cable, from the connection unit to a socket outlet mounted behind the appliance.

Cooker hood

Mount a fused connection unit, using a 3amp fuse, close to the cooker hood itself, or mount the connection unit at worktop height, then run a 1mm² cable from the unit to a flex outlet beside the cooker hood.

Instantaneous water heater

You can install an instantaneous water heater above a sink or washbasin to provide on-the-spot hot water. Join a 3kW model by heat-resistant flex to a switched fused connection unit mounted out of reach of anyone using the water.

If the heater is used in a bathroom wire it via a flex outlet to a ceiling pull-switch, then to the connection unit outside the bathroom. Lastly fit a 13amp fuse in the connection unit.

Wire a 7kW water heater like a shower (◁). If it is in the kitchen you can use a double-pole wall switch to control it.

Waste disposal unit

The waste disposal unit is housed in the sink base unit. Mount a switched fused connection unit 150mm (6in) above a worktop near the sink but out of reach of those using it and of small children.

From the unit run a 1mm² cable to a flex outlet next to the disposal unit.

Clearly label the connection unit 'disposal' to avoid accidents.

Finally fit a 3amp fuse.

Special shaver outlets are the only sockets allowed in bathrooms. They contain transformers which isolate the user side of the units from the mains, so they cannot cause an electric shock.

A shaver unit can be wired to a spur from a ring circuit or to a junction box on an earthed lighting circuit. Connect the conductors to the shaver unit: red to L, black to N and earth to E (**1**).

This type of socket conforms to the exacting British Standard, BS 3535, but there are shaver socket outlets which do not have isolating transformers. These are quite safe to install and use in a bedroom but must not be fitted in a bathroom. Wire such an outlet from the lighting circuit or from a fused connection unit on a ring circuit spur. Fit a 3amp fuse.

Shaver unit for use in a bathroom

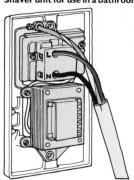

1 Wiring a shaver unit

Kitchen equipment circuits
1 Connection units
2 Flex outlets
3 Socket outlets

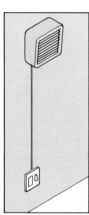

Wall-mounted fan
Run a 1.5mm² cable from a fused connection unit to a wall-mounted extractor fan.

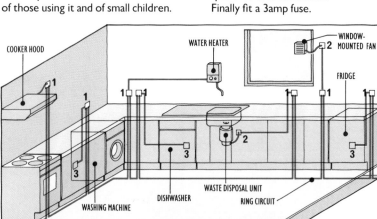

Powerful appliances such as cookers, with a power load greater than 3000W (3kW), must have their own radial circuits connected directly to the consumer unit, with separate fuses protecting them.

Cookers

Some small table cookers and separate ovens, which rate no more than 3000W (3kW), can consequently be connected to a ring circuit by a fused connection unit, or even by means of a 13amp plug and socket. But most domestic cookers are much more powerful, and must be installed on their own circuits.

The radial circuit
Cookers with a loading of up to 12000W (12kW) must be connected to a 30amp circuit. This requires a single radial circuit run in 6mm^2 two-core and earth cable protected by a 30amp circuit fuse.

For a cooker with a loading greater than 12000W you must install a 45amp circuit using 10mm^2 cable and a 45amp fuse. A separate radial circuit needs its own fuseway, and you can either use a spare fuseway in your consumer unit or fit an individual switchfuse unit, which will perform the same function as the consumer unit, but for a single appliance. Preferably choose a unit with a miniature circuit breaker; failing that, one with a cartridge fuse. As a last resort choose one that uses fuse wire.

Cooker control units
The cable from the consumer unit runs to a cooker control unit situated within 2m (6ft 6in) of the cooker.

The control unit is basically a double-pole isolating switch, but it may also incorporate a single 13amp switched socket outlet that can be used for an appliance such as an electric kettle. Now that more homes have a number of sockets installed at worktop height the additional one on the cooker control unit is not so important, and in fact it's better not to have one if it is to be situated above the cooker, from where a flex could trail across one of the hotplates.

The control unit must not only be within reach of the cooker but easily accessible, so don't install it inside a cupboard or under a worktop.

A single control unit can serve both parts of a split-level cooker, with separate cables running to the hob and the oven, provided the control unit is within 2m (6ft 6in) of both. If this is not possible in your case you will have to install a separate control unit for each part. The connecting cables must be of the same size as the cable used in the radial circuit.

Cooker control units can be surface- or flush-mounted.

Because a free-standing cooker has to be moved from time to time for cleaning round and behind it, it should be wired with enough cable to allow it to be moved well out from the wall. The cable is connected to a terminal outlet box which is screwed to the wall about 600mm (2ft) above floor level. A fixed cable runs from the outlet box to the cooker control unit.

Above ▲
1 Control unit with socket
2 Basic control unit
3 Terminal outlet box

Cooker circuit
1 Cooker
2 Terminal outlet box
3 Control unit
4 Radial circuit
5 Consumer unit

WIRING THE CONTROL UNIT

Having decided on the position for the cooker control unit knock out the cable-entry holes in the pattress and screw it to the wall. If your unit is to be flush-mounted cut a hole in the plaster and brickwork for the metal box (▷).

Running cable
Run and fix the cable, taking the most economical route to the cooker from the switchfuse unit or the consumer unit (▷). Cut a channel in the wall up to the control unit if you intend to bury the cable in the plaster, then cut similar channels for cables running to the separate hob and oven of a split-level cooker or for a single cable running to a terminal outlet box.

Connecting up the control unit
Feed the circuit cable and cooker cable into the control unit, then strip and prepare the conductors for connection. There are two sets of terminals in the control unit, one marked 'Mains' for the circuit conductors, and the other marked 'Load', for the cooker cable.

Run the red wires to the L terminals and the black ones to the terminals marked N. Put insulating sleeves on both earth conductors and connect them to the E terminals (I). Fold the wires to fit into the box and screw on the faceplate.

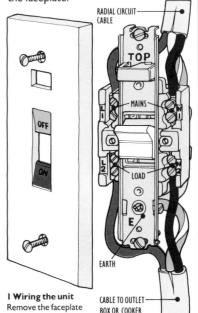

I Wiring the unit
Remove the faceplate to wire some units.

RADIAL CIRCUIT CABLE
TOP
MAINS
LOAD
E
EARTH
CABLE TO OUTLET BOX OR COOKER

SEE ALSO

Details for: ▷	
Running cable	303-305
Flush mounting	309
Circuit fuses	299
Stripping cable	302
Switchfuse unit	318

CONNECTING THE COOKER

IMMERSION HEATERS

SEE ALSO

◁ Details for:
Consumer unit	298
Switching off	296
Circuit fuses	299
Cables	302
Stripping cable	302
Running cable	303-305

Wiring to the cooker

Connect the cable to the hob and the oven following the manufacturer's instructions exactly.

For a free-standing cooker run the cable down the wall from the control unit to the terminal outlet box, which has terminals for connecting both cables. Strip and insert the wires of the control unit cable in the terminals (1), then take the cooker cable and insert its wires in the same terminals, matching colour for colour, and secure it with the clamp. Screw the plastic faceplate onto the outlet box.

Wiring the switchfuse unit

If you are wiring to a fuseway in your consumer unit simply run the red wire to the terminal on the fuseway, the black one to the neutral terminal block and – having sleeved it – the earth wire to the earth terminal block (◁). All other connections will already be made. Don't forget to switch off the power before starting this work.

Here we will assume a cooker circuit to be run from a switchfuse unit. Screw the unit to the wall close to the consumer unit, feed the cooker circuit cable into it and prepare the conductors for connection. Fix the red wire to the live terminal on the fuse carrier or MCB, the black wire to the neutral terminal and the sleeved earth wire to the earth terminal (2).

Prepare the meter leads, one black and one red, from PVC-sheathed and -insulated $16mm^2$ single-core cable. (Use $10mm^2$ cable if $16mm^2$ cable is too thick for the switchfuse unit terminals but keep the meter leads as short as possible.)

Bare about 25mm (1in) of each cable and connect them to their separate terminals on the main isolation switch, red to L and black to N (2). For an earth lead prepare a similar length of $6mm^2$ single-core cable insulated in green/yellow PVC and attach it to the earth terminal in the switchfuse unit (2). Fit the appropriate fuse, then plug in the fuse carrier. Label the carrier to indicate what circuit is run from the unit and fit the cover.

CABLE FROM CONTROL UNIT

L E ⏚ N

COOKER CABLE

1 Wiring a terminal outlet box

METER LEADS — CIRCUIT CABLE — LIVE

OFF

NEUTRAL — EARTH LEAD

2 Wiring switchfuse unit for the cooker

CONNECTING TO THE MAINS

The Electricity Board will send a qualified electrician to test your installation and connect your meter leads to their meter and the earth lead to the consumer's earth terminal. On no account should you try to make these connections yourself.

It may not be possible to attach both sets of meter leads – from consumer unit and switchfuse unit – to the meter, and the Board will have to install a service connector box with enough terminals to accommodate all the conductors. It's as well to consult the Electricity Board on these matters before starting.

Water in a storage cylinder is heated by an electric immersion heater, providing a central supply of hot water for the whole house. The heating element, rather like a larger version of the one that heats an electric kettle, is normally sheathed in copper, but more expensive sheathings of incoloy or titanium will increase the life of an element in hard water areas.

Adjusting the water temperature

A thermostat to control the maximum temperature of the water is set by adjusting a screw inside the plastic cap that covers the terminal box (1).

Types of immersion heater

An immersion heater can be installed from the top of the cylinder or from the side, and top-entry units can have single or double elements. In the single-element top-entry type of heater the element extends down almost to the bottom of the cylinder, so that the whole of its contents is heated whenever the heater is switched on (2). For economy one element in the double-element type is a short one that heats only the top half of the cylinder while the other element is a full-length one that is switched on when greater quantities of hot water are needed (3).

A double-element heater with a single thermostat is called a twin-element heater. One with a thermostat for each element is known as a dual-element heater.

Side-entry heaters are the same length, one being positioned near the bottom of the cylinder and the other a little above half way (4). This is a more efficient arrangement for heating water and controlling its temperature.

ELEMENT
TERMINAL BOX
THERMOSTAT
SETTING SCREW

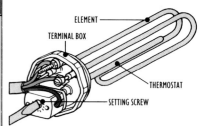

1 Adjusting the thermostat

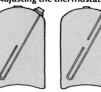

2 Single element **3 Double element** **4 Side-entry elements**

HEATING WATER ON THE NIGHT RATE

If you agree to have a special meter installed the Electricity Board will supply you with power at a cheap rate for seven hours between midnight and 8.00 a.m., the hours varying with the time of year.

The scheme is called Economy 7 (▷). Providing you have a cylinder of big enough capacity to store hot water for a day's requirements you can benefit by producing all your hot water during the Economy 7 hours. Even if you heat your water electrically only in the summer it can be worth considering the scheme. For the water to retain its heat all day you must have an efficient insulating jacket fitted to the cylinder or a cylinder already factory-insulated with a layer of heat-retaining foam (▷).

If your cylinder is already fitted with an immersion heater you can use its wiring by fitting an Economy 7 programmer, a device which will switch your immersion heater on automatically at night and heat up the whole cylinder. If you should occasionally run out of hot water during the day you can adjust the programmer's controls to boost the temperature briefly on the more expensive daytime rate.

You can make even greater savings if you have two side-entry immersion heaters or a dual-element one. The programmer will switch on the longer element – or the bottom one – at night, but should you need daytime water-heating only the upper element is used.

You can have a similar arrangement without a programmer by wiring two separate circuits for the elements. The upper element is wired to the daytime supply and the lower one is wired to its own switchfuse unit and operated by the Electricity Board's Economy 7 timeswitch during the hours of the night-time tariff only. A setting of 75°C (167°F) is recommended for the lower element and 60°C (140°F) for the upper one. If you live in a soft water area or have heater elements sheathed in incoloy or titanium you can raise the temperatures to 80°C (175°F) and 65°C (150°F) respectively without reducing lives of the elements.

To ensure that you never run short of hot water leave the upper unit switched on permanently. It will start heating up only when the thermostat detects a temperature of 60°C (140°F), which should happen only rarely if you have a large and properly insulated cylinder.

WIRING THE IMMERSION HEATER

The circuit

Most immersion heaters are rated at 3kW, but while you can usually wire a 3kW appliance to a ring circuit an immersion heater is seen as taking a continuous 3kW, even though rarely switched on continuously. A continuous 3kW load would seriously reduce a ring circuit's capacity, so immersion heaters must have their own radial circuits.

The circuit is run in 2.5mm² two-core and earth cable protected by a 15amp fuse, though a 20amp fuse can be fitted quite safely. Each element must have a two-pole isolating switch mounted near the cylinder, probably marked 'water heater' and having a neon indicator (1). From a flex outlet at the switch a 2.5mm² heat-resistant flex runs to the immersion heater.

If the cylinder is in a bathroom the switch must be inaccessible to anyone using the bath or shower. If this precludes a normal water-heater switch use a 20amp ceiling-mounted pull-switch with a mechanical ON/OFF indicator.

Wiring two side-entry heaters

For simplicity use two switches, one for each heater and marked accordingly.

Wiring the switches

Fix the mounting boxes to the wall, feed a circuit cable to each and wire them in the same way. Strip and prepare the wires, connect them to the 'Mains' terminals – red to L, black to N – sleeve the earth wire and fix it to the common earth terminal (2). Prepare a heat-resistant flex for each switch. At each take the green/yellow earth wire to the common earth terminal, the other wires to the 'Load' terminals – brown to L and blue to N (2) – tighten the flex clamps and screw on the faceplates.

Wiring the heaters

The flex from the upper switch goes to the top heater and that from the lower switch to the bottom one. At each one feed the flex through the hole in the cap and prepare the wires. Connect the brown wire to one terminal on the thermostat (the other terminal on the thermostat is already connected to the wire running to the L terminal of the heating element). Connect the blue wire to the N terminal and green/yellow wire to the E terminal (3) and replace the caps on the terminal boxes.

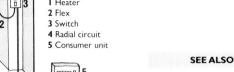

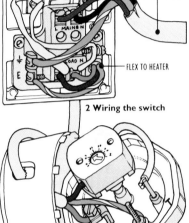

Heater circuit
1 Heater
2 Flex
3 Switch
4 Radial circuit
5 Consumer unit

CIRCUIT CABLE

FLEX TO HEATER

2 Wiring the switch

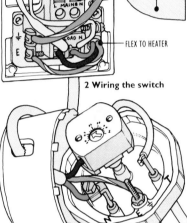

3 Wiring the heater

Running the cable

Run the circuit cables from the cylinder cupboard to the fuseboard and, with the power off, connect the cable from the upper heater to a spare fuseway in the consumer unit. Though the consumer unit is switched off the cable between main switch and meter is live, so take care. Wire the other cable to its own switchfuse unit – or storage-radiator consumer unit if you have one – ready for connecting to the Economy 7 timeswitch. Make the connections as described for a cooker circuit. (▷).

WIRING A DUAL-ELEMENT HEATER

Wire the circuit as described above but feed the flex from both switches into the cap on the terminal box of the heater. Strip and prepare the wires and connect both blue ones to the same N terminal and both earth wires to the E terminal. Connect the brown wire from the upper switch to the L1 terminal of the elements and the other brown wire to the L2 terminal (4).

SEE ALSO

Details for: ▷	
Insulation	261
Economy 7	286
Cooker circuit	317-318
Switching off	296
Consumer unit	298, 318

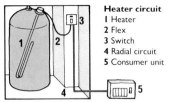

1 20amp switch for immersion heater

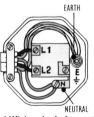

EARTH

NEUTRAL

4 Wiring dual-element

319

STORAGE HEATERS

SEE ALSO

◁ Details for:
Running a spur   311
Fused
connection unit   314
Storage heaters   390-391, 404

The heart of a storage heater is a heat-retaining core, or block, that houses heating elements which are supplied with electricity during the night-time off-peak hours to take advantage of a cheap rate for power. The storage core is insulated in such a way that it will give off heat gradually during the day. Heat-emission is controlled in various ways.

With the earliest storage heaters it was not possible to control the rate of heat-emission, and towards the end of the day emission tended to lessen. This is no longer a problem. Modern heaters have dampers to regulate the flow of air through the core and control the rate of heat-loss. Some heaters have dampers that are automatically controlled by circuits that monitor the air temperature in the room.

Research has shown that a cold day is preceded by a proportionally cold night, and the more sophisticated storage heaters use this fact to store just the right amount of heat during the night to meet the needs of the following day.

Fan-assisted storage heaters have a similar heat-retaining core, efficiently insulated to reduce heat-loss to an absolute minimum. When the fan is switched on it draws air into the unit to be warmed before flowing out into the room. Apart from a very small amount of radiant heat through the casing, heat-emission occurs only when it is required, particularly if the fan is controlled thermostatically.

Storage heaters vary in size, with ratings from 1.2kW to 3.4kW. The fan-assisted ones are rated even higher, with loadings of up to 6kW. A large area needs a heater with a big heat-retaining core, able to store enough heat to warm it. As the lower-cost electricity is supplied for only a few hours a large core will need more powerful elements to charge it completely. The rate of heat-emission is not affected by the rating of a heater.

When you install storage heaters you have to assemble them yourself. Follow the maker's instructions and handle the heating elements and insulation carefully. Make sure that slim heaters are fixed securely to the walls, but with a 75mm (3in) gap all round so that air can circulate. Use fibre wall plugs for the fixings, as plastic ones can soften with heat.

Drying clothes on a storage heater will make a fusible link in the unit melt. Don't assemble old secondhand heaters as they may contain asbestos.

Storage heater circuits

Unlike other kinds of electrical heating the storage heaters in a house are all switched on at the same time, a procedure that would overload a ring circuit, so you have to provide an individual radial circuit for each heater. A separate consumer unit is installed to cope with off-peak load.

It's wise to choose a unit that is not only large enough to take all of the heater circuits but also has spare fuseways for possible additional heaters in the future. Make sure that there is an extra fuseway to take the immersion heater circuit so that your water can be heated at the night-time rate.

The circuit for storage heaters up to 4.8kW should be wired with 2.5mm² two-core and earth cable with a 20amp circuit fuse.

Outlets for storage heaters

The circuit cable for an ordinary storage heater should terminate at a 20amp double-pole switch with a flex outlet (1) that fits into a standard plastic or metal mounting box. A three-core heat-resistant flex connects the switch to the storage heater.

A fan-assisted heater needs a more complex circuit. The heating elements are supplied from a straightforward radial circuit using 2.5mm² cable, but the fan needs its own circuit for daytime use. Take a spur from a ring circuit to a fused connection unit that has a 3amp fuse (◁) and run a 1.5mm² two-core and earth cable from the unit for the fan. The heater and fan circuits both terminate at a special dual switch (2) where fan and heater can be isolated simultaneously. Two lengths of heat-resistant flex run from the switch, one to the heater, the other to the fan. The dual switch can be surface- or flush-mounted.

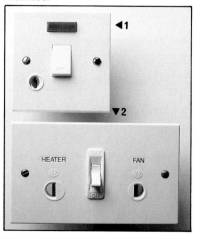

Electricity Board equipment

Because a storage heater system uses cheap-rate power to make it economical you need a special meter which calculates separately the number of units consumed during the night and those used in daytime. You also need a time switch to connect the various circuits at the appropriate time.

This equipment is supplied by the Electricity Board, which you should contact for advice as soon as possible if you plan to have storage heaters. At the same time make sure that your present electrical installation is safe, in particular the provision for earthing; otherwise the Board may be unwilling to connect the new circuits.

Storage heater circuits
1 Off-peak consumer unit
2 Day-time consumer unit
3 Radial circuits to heaters
4 20amp switch
5 Storage heater
6 Fan-assisted storage heater
7 Dual switch
8 Connection unit
9 Ring circuit

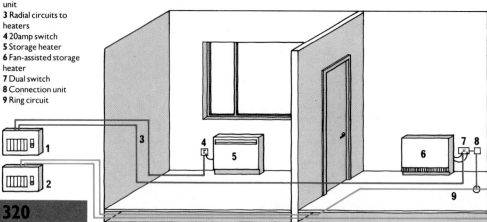

Wiring storage heaters

For ordinary storage heaters mount a 20amp switch close to where you will stand each heater. Run a single length of 2.5mm² two-core and earth cable from each switch to the site of the new consumer unit, taking the most economical route (▷).

Feed a cable into the mounting box of each switch, strip and prepare the wires and connect them to the 'Mains' terminals: red to L, black to N. Sleeve the earth wire and connect it to the E terminal (1).

Pass the flex from each heater through the outlet hole in the faceplate of its switch, strip and prepare the wires and connect them to the 'Load' terminals: brown to L, blue to N and the green/yellow earth wire to E (1). Tighten the cord clamp and fix the switch into its mounting box.

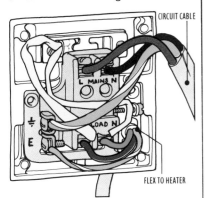

1 Wiring a 20amp switch for a storage heater

Wiring fan-assisted heaters

When you wire a fan-assisted heater mount a dual switch nearby, and from its 'heater' side (2) run a 2.5mm² two-core and earth cable to the consumer unit.

Mount a fused connection unit near the switch and run a short length of 1.5mm² two-core and earth cable between the two, connecting to the 'Load' side of the connection unit and the 'Fan' side of the dual switch (2).

Run a spur of 2.5mm² two-core and earth cable from the 'Mains' terminals on the connection unit (2) to a junction box or socket on the nearest ring circuit (▷).

Feed the fan and heater flex into the outlets in the faceplate of the dual switch and strip and prepare the wires. Connect each flex to its own part of the switch, which is clearly labelled (2).

Tighten the cord clamps and screw the switch to its box.

WIRING THE CONSUMER UNIT

When you buy a new consumer unit get one with miniature circuit breakers, or at least cartridge fuses. Install a 20amp fuse carrier or MCB for each heater circuit and a 15amp one for an immersion heater circuit if needed.

Mount the unit on an 18mm (¾in) plywood board, not on the Electricity Board's meter board even if there's room. Cut your board to size, knock out the entry holes in the back of the unit, lay it on the board and mark out the positions of the holes – for fuseways, meter leads and earth wire. Drill 18mm (¾in) holes in the board for the cables and paint or varnish both sides to damp-proof it.

Screw the board to the wall, using plastic or ceramic insulators to space it away so that damp won't penetrate it. Get the insulators when you buy the consumer unit. Position the board as close to the meter as you can so as to keep the meter leads short.

Screw the consumer unit to the board, run the circuit cables from the heaters into it, one at a time, and prepare the wires for connection.

The circuits are wired in the same way to separate fuseways: the red wire to the terminal on the fuseway, the black one to the neutral terminal block and the earth wire to the earth block after being sleeved green/yellow.

Use 16mm² single-core cable for the meter leads. They are insulated in red for the live conductor and black for the neutral. The outer sheathing may be in the same colours but it is often grey for both. Feed the leads into the consumer unit and connect them to their terminals – red to L, black to N – on the main isolating switch.

Connect a length of green 6mm² single-core cable to the earth block. Its other end will be connected by an Electricity Board representative to the consumer's earth terminal.

Fit MCBs or clip a fuse into each of the fuse carriers and insert the carriers into their fuseways. Label all of the circuits clearly so that in future you can tell which heater each one supplies.

Fit the covers on the consumer unit and arrange for the Electricity Board to test the circuits and connect the unit to the meter and earth. Don't, in any circumstances, try to make these connections yourself.

SEE ALSO

Details for: ▷

Running cable	303-305
Running a spur	311
Stripping flex	293
Fuses/MCBs	299
Cables	302
Stripping cable	302

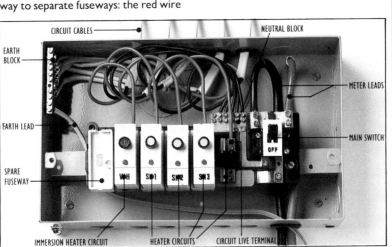

Wiring the consumer unit for storage heaters

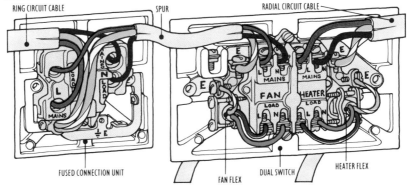

2 Wiring a dual switch
Connect a fused connection unit to the dual switch.

DOORBELLS, BUZZERS AND CHIMES

Whether you choose a doorbell, a buzzer or a set of chimes there are no practical differences to affect the business of installing them.

Bells

Most doorbells are of the 'trembler' type. When electricity is supplied to the bell – that is when someone presses the button at the door – it activates an electro-magnet which causes a striker to hit the bell. But as the striker moves to the bell it breaks a contact, cutting off power to the magnet, so the striker swings back, makes contact again and repeats the process, going on for as long as the button is depressed. This type of bell can be operated by battery or by a mains transformer. Other types of doorbells, known as AC bells, can be used only with mains power.

Buzzers

A buzzer operates on exactly the same principle as a trembler bell but in the buzzer the striker hits the magnet itself instead of a bell.

Chimes

A set of ordinary door chimes has two tubes or bars tuned to different notes. Between them is a solenoid, a wound coil that acts like a magnet when it is energized. When the button is pressed a spring-loaded plunger inside the solenoid is thrown against one tube, sounding a note. When the button is released the spring throws the plunger against the other tube, sounding the other note before returning to its point of rest. Other chimes have a programmed microprocessor that gives a choice of tunes when operated by the bell push. Most chimes can be run from a battery or a transformer.

Bell pushes

When the bell push at the door is pressed it completes the circuit that supplies power to the bell. It is a switch that is on only when held in the 'on' position. Inside it are two contacts to which the circuit wires are connected. One contact is spring-loaded, touching the other when the push is depressed, to complete the circuit, and springing back when the push is released (1).

Illuminated bell pushes incorporate a tiny bulb which enables you to see the bell push in the dark. These must be operated from mains transformers, as the power to the bulb, though only a trickle, is on continuously and would soon drain a battery. Luminous types glow at night without a power supply.

Batteries or transformer?

Some doorbells and chimes house batteries inside their casings, while others incorporate built-in transformers that reduce the 240-volt mains electricity to the very low voltages needed for this type of equipment. For many bells or chimes you can use either method. Most of them use two or four 1½ volt batteries, but some require a 4½ volt battery, housed separately. Transformers sold for use with doorbell systems have three low-voltage tappings – 3 volt, 5 volt and 8 volt – to meet various needs. Usually 3 volt and 5 volt connections are suitable for bells or buzzers, and the 8 volt tapping is enough for many sets of chimes.

Some other chimes need higher voltages, and for these you will need a transformer with 4 volt, 8 volt and 12 volt tappings. A bell transformer must be designed so that the full mains voltage cannot cross over to the low-voltage wiring.

Circuit wiring

The battery, bell and push are connected by fine insulated 'bell wire', usually two-core. Being so fine, it is often surface-run, fixed to the skirting and door frame by small staples, but it can be run under floors and in cupboards. Bell wire also connects a transformer to a bell and bell push.

The transformer itself connects to a junction box or ceiling rose on a lighting circuit with 1mm² two-core and earth cable; it must be earthed, so if your lighting system has no earth wire use another method.

Run a spur from a ring circuit in 2.5mm² two-core and earth cable to an unswitched fused connection unit fitted with a 3amp fuse, then a 1mm² two-core and earth cable from the unit to the transformer 'Mains' terminals.

Alternatively, you can run 1mm² two-core and earth cable from a spare 5amp fuseway in a consumer unit to the transformer 'Mains' terminals.

SEE ALSO

◁ Details for:
Consumer unit	298, 318
Running cable	303-305
Running a spur	311
Connecting to light circuit	329

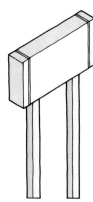

Chimes
A set of chimes has two tubes, each tuned to a different note.

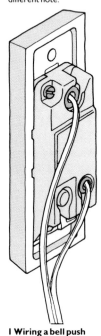

1 Wiring a bell push

INSTALLING A SYSTEM

The bell itself can be installed in any convenient position except over a source of heat. The entrance hall is usually best as a bell there can be heard in most parts of the house. Keep the bell wire runs to a minimum, especially for a battery-operated bell. With a mains-powered bell you will not want long and costly runs of cable, so place the transformer where it can be wired simply. A cupboard under the stairs is a good place, especially if it is near the consumer unit.

Drill a small hole in the door frame and pass the bell wire through to the outside. Fix the conductors to the terminals of the push, then screw it over the hole.

If the battery is in the bell casing there will be two terminals for attaching the other ends of the wires. Either wire can go to either terminal. If the battery is separate from the bell run the bell wire from the push to the bell. Separate the conductors, cut one of them and join each cut end to a bell terminal. Run the wire on to the battery and attach it to the terminals (1).

When you wire to a transformer proceed as above but connect the bell wire to whichever two of the three terminals combine to give you the required voltage (2). Some bells and chimes need separate lengths of bell wire, one from the bell push and another from the transformer. Fix the wires to terminals in the bell housing following manufacturers' instructions.

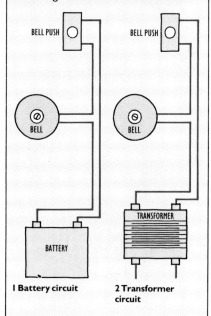

1 Battery circuit   2 Transformer circuit

WIRING A SHOWER UNIT

An electrically heated shower unit is plumbed into the mains water supply (▷). The water pressure operates a switch to energize a heater that heats the water on its way to the shower head. Because there is so little time to heat the flowing water instantaneous showers use a heavy load, from 6 to 8kW. Consequently a shower needs a separate radial circuit.

The circuit cable must be 6mm² two-core and earth, protected by a 30amp fuse in a spare fuseway at the consumer unit or in a separate 30amp switchfuse unit. The cable runs directly to the shower unit where it must be wired according to the manufacturer's instructions.

The shower has its own on/off switch, but there must also be a separate isolating switch in the circuit. This must not be accessible to anyone using the shower, so install a ceiling-mounted 30amp double-pole pull-cord switch with a contact gap of at least 3mm, and preferably one with a neon 'on' indicator. Fix the backplate of the switch to the ceiling (▷) and, having sleeved the earth conductors, connect them to the E terminal on the switch. Connect the conductors from the consumer unit to the 'Mains' terminal of the switch and those of the cable to the shower to the 'Load' terminals (**1**).

Shower unit, metallic pipes and fittings must be bonded to earth (▷).

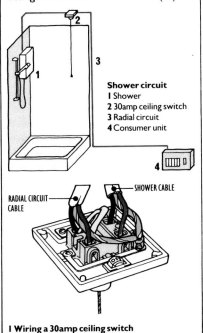

Shower circuit
1 Shower
2 30amp ceiling switch
3 Radial circuit
4 Consumer unit

RADIAL CIRCUIT CABLE

SHOWER CABLE

1 Wiring a 30amp ceiling switch

LIGHTING CIRCUITS

Every lighting system needs a feed cable to supply power to all the lighting points, and a switch that can interrupt the supply to each point. There are two ways of meeting these requirements in your home: the junction-box system and the loop-in system. Your house may be wired with either one, though it is quite likely that there will be a combination of the two systems.

The junction-box system
In the junction-box system a two-core and earth feed cable runs from a fuseway in the consumer unit to a series of junction boxes, one for each lighting point. From each junction box a separate cable runs to a light and another runs to its switch.

The loop-in system
In the loop-in system the ceiling rose takes the place of the junction box. The cable from the consumer unit runs into each rose and out again, then on to the next. The switch cable and the flex to the bulb are connected at the rose.

Combined system
The loop-in system is now the most widely used as it entails fewer connections as well as saving on the cost of junction boxes. However, lights at some distance from a loop-in circuit are often run from a junction box on the circuit to save cable, and lights added after the circuit has been installed are often wired from junction boxes.

The circuit
Both the junction-box and the loop-in systems are, in effect, multi-outlet radial circuits. The cable runs from the consumer unit, looping in and out of the ceiling roses or junction boxes and terminating at the last one. It doesn't return to the consumer unit like the cable of a ring circuit. Lighting circuits require 1mm² PVC-insulated and -sheathed two-core and earth cable. Each circuit is protected by a 5amp circuit fuse, and so up to twelve 100W bulbs or their equivalent can use the circuit. In the average house it is practical to have two separate lighting circuits, one for the ground floor and another for one upstairs.

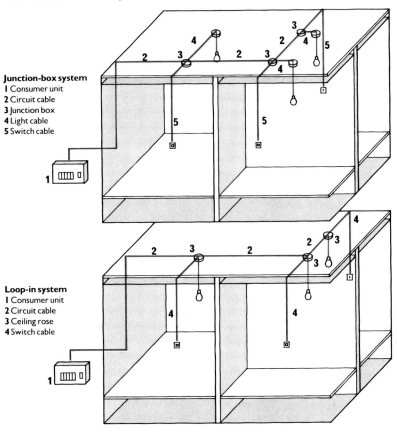

Junction-box system
1 Consumer unit
2 Circuit cable
3 Junction box
4 Light cable
5 Switch cable

Loop-in system
1 Consumer unit
2 Circuit cable
3 Ceiling rose
4 Switch cable

SEE ALSO

Details for: ▷
Bonding to earth	290
Fixing to ceiling	325
Plumbing a shower	372
Consumer unit	298, 318
Circuit fuses	299
Cables	302
Running cable	303-305
Switchfuse unit	318

IDENTIFYING THE CONNECTIONS

SEE ALSO

◁ Details for:
Lighting circuits   323

Loop-in system

A modern loop-in ceiling rose has three terminal blocks arranged in a row. The live (red) conductors from the two cut ends of the circuit-feed cable run to the central live block, and the neutral (black) conductors run to the neutral block on one side. The earth conductors run to a common earth terminal (1).

The live (red) conductor from the switch cable is connected to the remaining terminal in the central live block. Power runs through this conductor to the switch and back to the ceiling rose through the black conductor, the 'switch-return wire', and this is connected to the third terminal block in the ceiling rose, the 'switch-wire block'. When the light is 'on' the switch-return wire is live, so it should

be identified with a piece of red tape wrapped round it to distinguish it from the other black wires, which are neutral. The earth conductor in the switch cable goes to the common earth terminal (1).

The brown conductor from the pendant-light flex connects to the remaining terminal in the switch block while the blue conductor runs to the neutral block. If three-core flex is used the green/yellow earth conductor runs to the common earth terminal (1).

When the circuit-feed cable terminates at the last ceiling rose on the circuit only one set of cable conductors is connected (2). Switch cable and light flex are connected like those in a normal loop-in rose.

Junction-box system

The junction boxes on a lighting circuit normally have four unmarked terminals, for live, neutral, earth and switch connections. The live, neutral and earth conductors from the circuit feed cable go to their respective terminals (3).

The live conductor from the cable that runs to the ceiling rose is connected to the switch terminal, the black wire to the neutral terminal and the earth conductor to the earth terminal (3).

The red wire from the switch cable is connected to the live terminal, the earth conductor to the earth terminal and the black return wire from the switch goes to the switch terminal (3).

This last conductor should be identified by having a piece of red tape wrapped round it.

At the ceiling rose the live cable conductor is connected to one of the outer terminal blocks, the neutral conductor to the other and the central block left empty. The earth conductor goes to the earth terminal (4).

The flex conductors are wired up to match those from the cable. The brown wire is connected to the same terminal block as the red conductor and the blue wire goes to the block holding the black conductor. If the flex has a yellow/green earth wire it is connected to the common earth terminal (4).

Checking an old light circuit

Switch off the power at the consumer unit, remove the circuit fuse and examine ceiling roses and light switches for any signs of deterioration. Pre-World War II wiring will have been carried out in rubber-insulated and -sheathed cable. If the insulation seems dry and crumbly it is no longer safe. The circuit should be rewired. If you detect any signs at all that the circuitry is out of date, and perhaps dangerous, consult a professional electrician.

An old installation may have loop-in or junction-box lighting circuits, though the junction-box system is more likely. It may also lack any earth conductors, another good reason for renewing it.

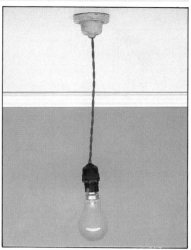

Old fabric-covered flex should be replaced

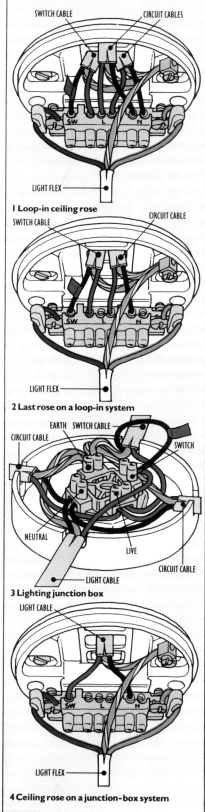

CONNECTIONS FOR LOOP-IN AND JUNCTION-BOX SYSTEMS

1 **Loop-in ceiling rose**

2 **Last rose on a loop-in system**

3 **Lighting junction box**

4 **Ceiling rose on a junction-box system**

LIGHT FITTINGS

There is now a vast range of lighting fittings that can be used in the home, and though they may differ greatly in
their appearance they can be grouped roughly in about eight basic categories according to their functions.

Types of light fitting

Pendant lights
The pendant light is probably the most common light fitting. It comprises a lamp-holder with bulb, usually with some kind of shade, suspended from a ceiling rose by a length of flex. The flex is connected to the power supply through terminals inside the ceiling rose (See opposite).

Decorative pendant lights
Most decorative pendant light fittings are designed to take several bulbs, and are consequently much heavier than standard pendant lights. Because of its weight this type of fitting is attached to the ceiling by a rigid tube. The flex that conducts the power to the bulbs passes through the tube to the lighting circuit.

Close-mounted ceiling lights
A close-mounted ceiling light is screwed directly to the ceiling, dispensing with a ceiling rose, by means of a backplate that houses the lampholder or holders. The fitting is usually enclosed by some kind of rigid light-diffuser that is also attached to the backplate.

Recessed ceiling lights
In this type of light fitting the lamp housing itself is recessed into the ceiling void and the diffuser lies flush with, or projects only slightly below, the ceiling. Lights of this type are ideal for rooms with low ceilings; they are often referred to as downlighters.

Track lights
Several individual light fittings can be attached to an aluminium track which is screwed to the ceiling or wall. Because a contact runs the length of the track, lights can be fitted anywhere along it.

Fluorescent light fittings
A fluorescent light fitting uses a glass tube containing mercury vapour. The power makes electrons flow between electrodes at the ends of the tube and bombard an internal coating, which fluoresces to produce the light. The fitting, which also contains a starter mechanism, is usually mounted directly on the ceiling, though as they produce very little heat fluorescent lights are used for under-cupboard lighting.

Wall lights
A light fitting adapted for screwing to a wall instead of a ceiling can be supplied from the lighting circuit in the ceiling void or from a spur off the ring circuit. Various kinds of close-mounted fittings or adjustable spotlights are the most popular wall lights.

Batten holders
A batten holder is a basic fitting with a lamp-holder mounted on a plate that fixes directly to wall or ceiling. Straight, angled and swivel versions are available. Batten holders are for use in areas – such as lofts or cellars – where appearance is not important.

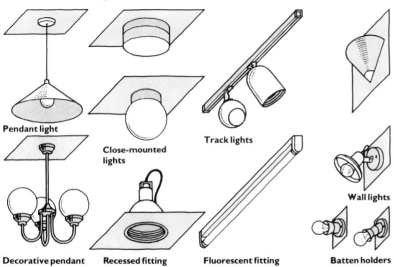

Pendant light

Close-mounted lights

Track lights

Decorative pendant

Recessed fitting

Fluorescent fitting

Wall lights

Batten holders

REPLACING A CEILING ROSE

Turn off power at the consumer unit and remove the circuit fuse. Switching off at the wall is not enough.

Unscrew the rose's cover and inspect the connections so that you can wire the new ones to work in the same way. A modern loop-in rose will be wired by one of the methods shown opposite. Identify the switch-return wire with tape if it is not already marked. If there is only one red and one black conductor the rose is on a junction-box system and will have no switch cable.

In an old rose you may have to identify the wires. If there are wires running into three terminal blocks look first for the one with all red wires and no flex wires. That is the live block, containing live circuit-feed wires and a live switch wire. The neutral terminal block contains the black neutral circuit feed wires and the blue flex wire. The third block will contain the brown flex wire plus a black conductor – the switch return wire – which should be marked with red tape, and may even be sheathed in red PVC.

All earth wires will run to one terminal on the backplate, but an old system may have no earth wires. In this case reconnect the other conductors temporarily but get expert advice on rewiring the circuit.

Fixing the new rose
Disconnect the wires from the terminals and separate any that are twisted together, but identify them with tapes. Unscrew the old backplate from the ceiling. Knock out the entry hole in the new backplate, thread the cables through it and fix the backplate to the ceiling, using the old screws and fixing points if possible. If the old fixings are not secure nail a piece of wood between the joists above the ceiling (See right) and drill a hole through it from below for cable access. Screw the new rose backplate to the wood through the ceiling.

Make sure that the ends of the conductors are clean and sound, then wire the ceiling rose, following the diagrams opposite.

Slip the new cover over the pendant flex and connect the flex wires to the terminals in the rose, looping the wires over the rose's support hooks to take the weight off the terminals. Screw the cover onto the backplate, switch on the power and test the light.

SEE ALSO

Details for: ▷	
Lampholders	295
Switching off	296
Close-mounted light	326
Track light	326
Fluorescent light	327
Wall lights	331

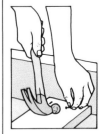

Fixing a platform
Scew-nail a board between the joists to support a ceiling rose.

FITTING A CLOSE-MOUNTED LIGHT

SEE ALSO

◁ Details for:
Junction box	324
Fixing to ceiling	325
Switching off	296
Loop-in system	323,324
Close-mounted lights	325
Track lights	325
Recessed lights	325
Padsaw	464

I BESA box
Use a BESA box to house the connections when a light fitting is supplied without a backplate.

Some close-mounted light fittings have a backplate that screws directly to the ceiling in place of a ceiling rose. To fit one, first switch off the power for the circuit at the consumer unit and take out the fuse, then remove the ceiling rose and fix the backplate to the ceiling (◁).

If only one cable feeds the light attach its conductors to the terminals of the lampholder and the earth wire to the terminal on the backplate.

As more heat will be generated in an enclosed fitting, slip heat-resistant sleeving over the conductors before attaching them to their terminals.

If the original ceiling rose was wired into a loop-in system the light fitting will not accommodate all the cables. Withdraw them into the ceiling void and wire them into a junction box (◁) screwed to a length of 100 x 25mm (4 x 1in) timber nailed between the joists, then run a short length of heat-resistant cable from the junction box to the close-mounted light fitting.

FITTING A BESA BOX

Fix a wooden platform between the ceiling joists to support the junction box and the BESA box.

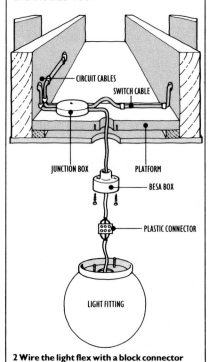

2 Wire the light flex with a block connector

Fittings without backplates

Sometimes close-mounted lights are supplied without backplates.

Wiring Regulations recommend that all unsheathed conductors and terminals must be enclosed in a non-combustible housing, so if you use a fitting with no backplate you must find a means of complying. The best way is to fit a BESA box (I), a plastic or metal box that is fixed into the ceiling void so as to lie flush with the ceiling.

Screw-fixing lugs on the box should line up with the fixing holes in the light fitting's coverplate, but check that they do so before buying the box. You will also need two machine screws of the right thread for attaching the light to the BESA box.

Check that there is no joist right above where you wish to fit the light. If there is one, move the light to one side until it fits between two joists. Hold the box against the ceiling, trace round it and with a padsaw carefully cut the traced shape out of the ceiling.

Cut a fixing board from 25mm (1in) thick timber to fit between the joists and place it directly over the hole in the ceiling while an assistant marks out the position of the hole on the board from below, then drill a cable-feed hole centrally through the marked-out shape of the ceiling aperture on the board. This hole must also be able to take any boss on the back of the BESA box. Position the box and screw it securely to the board.

Have your assistant press some kind of flat panel against the ceiling and over the aperture. Fit the BESA box into the aperture from above so that it rests on the panel, mark the level of the fixing board on both joists, then screw a batten to each joist to support the board at that level.

Fix the board to the battens and feed the cable through the hole in the centre of the BESA box. The light fitting will probably have a plastic connector for attaching the cable conductors (2), and this may have three terminals. Alternatively, a separate terminal for the earth conductor may be attached to the coverplate.

When the conductors are secured fix the coverplate to the BESA box with the machine screws.

If the original ceiling rose was fed by more than one cable, connect them to a junction box in the ceiling void as described above left.

FITTING A DOWNLIGHTER

Decide where you want the light, check from above that it falls between joists, then use the cardboard template supplied with all downlighters to mark the circle for the aperture on the ceiling. Drill a series of 12mm (½in) holes just inside the perimeter of the marked circle to remove most of the waste, then cut it out with a padsaw.

Bring a single lighting circuit cable from a junction box (◁) through the opening and attach it to the downlighter, following the manufacturer's instructions. You may have to fit another junction box into the void to connect the circuit cable to the heat-resistant flex attached to the light fitting.

Fit the downlighter into the opening and secure it there by adjusting the clamps that bear on the upper, hidden surface of the ceiling.

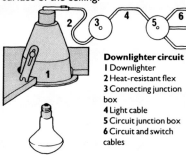

Downlighter circuit
I Downlighter
2 Heat-resistant flex
3 Connecting junction box
4 Light cable
5 Circuit junction box
6 Circuit and switch cables

FITTING TRACK LIGHTING

Ceiling fixings are supplied with all track lighting systems. Mount the track so that the terminal block housing at one end is situated where the old ceiling rose was fitted. Pass the circuit cable into the fitting and wire it to the cable-connector provided.

If the circuit is a loop-in system mount a junction box in the ceiling void (◁) to connect the cables.

Make sure that the number of lights you intend to use on the track will not overload the lighting circuit, which can supply a maximum of twelve 100W lamps or the equivalent.

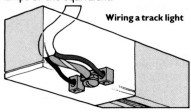

Wiring a track light

Fluorescent lights

Fluorescent light fittings are supplied with terminal blocks for connection to the mains supply.

With the ceiling rose removed screw the fitting to the ceiling, positioned so that the circuit cable can be fed into it conveniently. The terminal block will take only three conductors, so the fitting must be connected to a junction-box system, or a junction box must be installed in the ceiling void to accommodate loop-in wiring as for a close-mounted light (See opposite).

Fluorescent lights normally need earth connections, so they cannot be used on old systems that have not got earth conductors.

You can mount a fluorescent unit by screwing directly into ceiling joists or into boards nailed between joists to provide secure fixings.

Wiring a fluorescent light fitting
A simple plastic block connector is fitted inside a fluorescent light fitting for the circuit cable.

FLUORESCENTS UNDER CUPBOARDS

You can fit fluorescent lighting under kitchen cupboards to illuminate the work surfaces below, the power being supplied from a switched fused connection unit (▷) fitted with a 3amp cartridge fuse.

You can install a second fluorescent light fitting and supply its power by wiring it into the terminal block of the first one.

LIGHT SWITCHES

The commonest type of switch for controlling lighting is the plateswitch. It has a switch mechanism mounted behind a square faceplate that may have one, two or three rockers. Though these are usually quite adequate for domestic use there are also double faceplates with four or six rockers.

A one-way switch simply turns a light on and off, but two-way switches are wired in pairs so that the light can be controlled from two places – typically, the head and foot of a staircase. There is also an intermediate switch that allows a light to be controlled from three places.

Any switch can be flush-mounted in a metal box that is buried in the wall, or surface-mounted in a plastic pattress. Boxes 16 and 25mm (⅝ and 1in) deep are available to accommodate switches of different depths.

Where there is not enough room for a standard switch a narrow architrave switch can be used. There are single ones and double versions that have their rockers one above the other.

A dimmer switch is a device by which the intensity of light can be controlled as well as switching on and off. In some versions a single knob works as both switch and dimmer. Others have a separate one for switching so that the light level does not have to be adjusted each time the light is switched on.

A conventional switch cannot be mounted within reach of a bath or shower unit, and in such situations ceiling-mounted double-pole switches with pull-cords are installed.

Fixing and cable runs
Lighting cable is run underneath floorboards or within the hollow of cavity walls, or is buried in wall plaster (▷). The mounting boxes and switches are fixed to various walls by exactly the same methods as used for sockets (▷).

Light switches must be installed in relatively accessible positions, which normally means at about adult shoulder height for a wall switch and just inside the door of a room.

TYPES OF SWITCHES

Most light switches are made from white plastic but there are some more striking finishes to compliment your decorative scheme. Bright primary-coloured switches can be matched with coloured flex, plugs and socket outlets to make an unusual and attractive feature. Brass antique-reproduction switches suit traditional interiors.

Selection of light switches
1 One-gang rocker
2 Two-gang rocker
3 Switches are made in a range of colours
4 Reproduction antique switch
5 One-gang dimmer
6 Two-gang dimmer
7 Touch dimmer
8 Two-gang architrave switch
9 Ceiling switch

SEE ALSO

Details for: ▷	
Running cable	303-305
Mounting boxes	308-309
Fused	
connection unit	314
Switching off	296
Junction box	324
Fluorescent lights	325
Fixing to ceiling	325
Wiring switches	328, 330

REPLACING SWITCHES

SEE ALSO

◁ Details for:
Flush mounting	309
Switches	327
Two/three-way lighting	330
Switching off	296
Cables	302

Replacing a damaged switch is a matter of connecting the existing wiring to the new switch in exactly the same way as it was connected to the old one.

Always turn off the power and remove the fuse before you take off the faceplate to inspect the wiring.

In the case of a surface-mounted switch make sure that a new faceplate will fit the existing pattress; otherwise you will have to replace both parts. If you do use the old pattress, also use the old machine screws for fixing on the faceplate. In this way you know that you have matching threads on the screws.

To replace a surface-mounted switch with a flush-mounted one remove the old switch, then hold the metal box over the position of the original switch and trace round it. Cut away the plaster to the depth of the box and screw it to the brickwork (◁). Take great care not to damage the existing wiring while you are working.

Replacing a one-way switch

A one-way switch will be serviced by a two-core and earth cable, and the earth conductor, where there is one, will be connected to an earth terminal on the mounting box. The red and black wires will be connected to the switch itself.

A true one-way switch has only two terminals, one above the other, and the red or black conductors can be connected to either terminal **(1)** . The back of the faceplate will be marked 'top' to ensure that you mount the switch right way up, so that the rocker is depressed when the light is on. The switch would work just as well upside down but the 'up for off' convention is a good one as it tells you that a switch is on or off even when a bulb has failed.

Occasionally you will find a switch that is fed by a two-core and earth cable and operates as a one-way switch, yet has three terminals **(2)** . This is a two-way switch wired up for a one-way function, something that is fairly common and perfectly safe. With the switch mounted right way up the red and black wires should be connected to the 'Common' and 'L2' terminals.

Replacing a two-way switch

A two-way switch will have at least one conductor in each of its three terminals. Without going into the complexities of two-way wiring at this stage, the simplest method for replacing a damaged two-way switch is to write down a note of which wires run to which terminals before disconnecting them. Another way is to detach the conductors from their terminals one at a time and connect each one to the corresponding terminal on the new two-way switch before dealing with the next conductor.

Two-gang switches

A two-gang switch is two single switches mounted on one faceplate. Each switch may be wired differently. One may be working as a one-way switch and the other as a two-way **(3)** .

Use one of the methods described above, for replacing a two-way switch, to transfer the wires from the old to the new terminals, working on one switch at a time.

Replacing a rocker switch with a dimmer switch

Examine the present switch to determine the type of wiring that feeds it and buy a dimmer switch that will accommodate it. The manufacturers of dimmer switches provide instructions with them, but the connections are basically the same as for ordinary rocker switches **(4)**.

HOW SWITCHES ARE WIRED

It is very easy to replace a damaged switch or swap one for a switch of a different nature (◁). The illustrations below show four common methods of wiring switches. If your switch is wired differently it is probably part of a two- or three-way lighting system (◁). Replace the switch as described left.

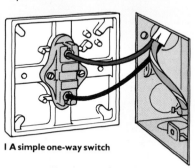

1 A simple one-way switch

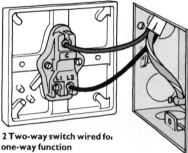

2 Two-way switch wired for one-way function

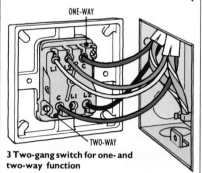

3 Two-gang switch for one- and two-way function

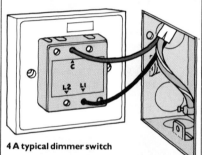

4 A typical dimmer switch

ADDING NEW SWITCHES AND CIRCUITS

When you want to move a switch or install one where none existed before you will have to modify the circuit *cables or run a new spur cable from the existing lighting circuit to take the power to where it is needed.*

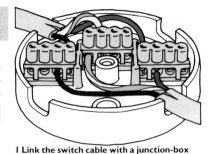

Replacing a wall switch with a ceiling switch

Light switches must be out of reach of anyone using a bath or shower. If your bathroom has a wall switch that breaks this rule replace it with a ceiling switch that operates by a pull-cord.

Turn the power off at the consumer unit and remove the old switch. If the cable running up the wall is surface-mounted or in a plastic conduit you can pull it up into the ceiling void. It should be long enough to reach the point where the new switch is to be.

If the switch cable is buried in the wall trace it in the ceiling void and cut it, then wire the part that runs to the light into a three-terminal junction box fixed to a joist or to a piece of wood nailed between two joists (▷). Connect the conductors to separate terminals (1),

and from those terminals run matching 1mm² two-core and earth cable to the site of the ceiling switch.

Bore a hole in the ceiling to pass the cable through to the switch. Screw the switch to the joist if the hole is close enough; otherwise fix a support board between joists.

Knock out the entry hole in the switch backplate, pass the cable through it and screw the plate to the ceiling.

Strip and prepare the ends of the conductors, connecting the earth to the terminal on the backplate. Connect the red and black conductors to the terminals on the switch – either wire to either terminal (2) – then attach the switch to the backplate and make good any damage done to the plasterwork.

1 Link the switch cable with a junction-box

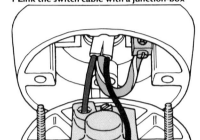

2 Wiring a ceiling switch

SEE ALSO

Details for: ▷	
Cutting a chase	303
Running a cable	303-305
Wiring a rose (last on loop-in)	324
Nail-fixed wood	325
Wiring one-way switch	328
Wiring one-way as two-way	328
Switching off	296
Connecting to junction box	311

Adding a new switch and light

Turn the power off at the consumer unit and check your lighting circuit to see if it is earthed. If there is no earth wire get expert advice before you try to install a new light.

Decide on where you want the fitting and bore a hole through the ceiling for the cable. Screw a ceiling rose to a nearby joist or nail a board between two joists to provide a strong fixing for the rose (▷).

Bore another hole in the ceiling right above the site of the new switch and as close to the wall as possible. Push twists of paper through both holes so that you can find them easily from above.

Screw the switch mounting box to the wall and cut a chase in the plaster for the cable up to the hole already bored in the ceiling (▷).

Your new light can be supplied from a nearby junction box, from a ceiling rose that is already on the lighting circuit or, if it is more convenient that way, from a new junction box wired into the lighting circuit cable.

From whichever of these sources you choose run a length of 1mm² two-core and earth cable to the new light position, but do not connect the circuit until the whole of the installation is complete. Push the end of the cable through the hole in the ceiling and identify it with tape (1). Write 'Mains' on the tape to be absolutely sure. Now

run a similar cable from the switch to the same lighting point (▷).

Strip and prepare the cable at the switch, connecting the earth wire to the terminal on the mounting box, and connect the red and black wires, either wire to either terminal (▷) if it is a one-way switch. If you can get only a two-way switch connect the wires to its 'Common' and 'L2' terminals (▷). It will work just as well. Now screw the switch to the mounting box.

Knock out the entry hole in the ceiling rose, feed both cables through it and screw the rose to the ceiling.

Take the cable marked 'Mains' and connect its red conductor to the central live block, its black one to the neutral block. Slip a green/yellow sleeve over the earth wire and connect it to the earth terminal (▷).

Connect the red wire of the switch cable to the live block and the black wire to the switch-wire block after marking the black wire with red tape. Connect the switch earth wire to the same earth terminal (▷). Screw the cover on the rose.

Make sure that the power is switched off and connect the new light circuit to the old one at the rose or junction box. The new conductors will have to share terminals already connected: red to live, black to neutral and earth to earth (2).

Switch on and test the new circuit.

1 Identify the cables

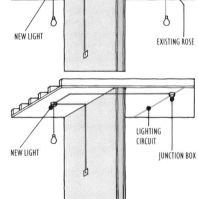

Circuit for a new light ▶
Take the power for a new light from an existing ceiling rose, or insert a new junction box into the existing lighting circuit.

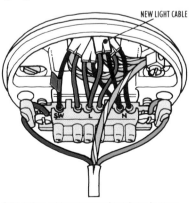

2 Lighting cable connected to a loop-in rose

ADDING TWO- OR THREE-WAY LIGHTING

Adding a two-way light

There are several situations in which a light should be controllable from two points. A hall light is best switched from both ends of the passageway, and a landing light must be controlled from top and bottom of the stairs.

Installing a new two-way light is very similar to installing a one-way, the only real difference being in the wiring of the switches.

Mount the ceiling rose and both two-way switches, then run 1mm² two-core and earth cable from the power source to the light and from the light to the nearest switch. Don't connect the new installation to the circuit until all the wiring is completed.

Run a 1mm² three-core and earth cable from the first switch to the second, strip and prepare the conductors for connecting to the switches and slip insulating sleeves over the bare ends of the earth wire.

At the first switch you have two cables to connect: the one from the light and the one linking the switches. The light cable has three conductors –

red, black and green/yellow; the linking cable has four – red, yellow, blue and green/yellow. Take the two green/yellow wires, twist their bare ends together and connect them to the earth terminal on the mounting box (1).

Connect the red wire from the linking cable to the 'Common' terminal on the switch. Twist together the ends of the yellow wire and either the red or black light cable wire, and connect them to the 'L1' terminal. Twist together the ends of the blue wire and the remaining light cable wire and connect them to the 'L2' terminal (1). Screw the switch faceplate to the mounting box.

At the second switch, connect the linking cable's green/yellow wire to the earth terminal, its red wire to the 'Common' terminal, its yellow wire to 'L1' and its blue wire to 'L2' (1). Screw the switch's faceplate to the box.

Make sure that the power is switched off and then connect the installation to the lighting circuit at a ceiling rose or a junction box (◁). Test the new installation and repair the plasterwork.

Three-way lighting

You can control a light from three places by adding an intermediate switch to the circuit described above.

The third switch interrupts the three-core and earth cable linking the other two. It has two 'L1' terminals and two 'L2' ones.

At its mounting box you will have two identical sets of wires – red, yellow, blue and green/yellow. Connect the green/yellow wires to the earth

terminal on the box (2) and join the two red wires, which play no part in the intermediate switching, with a plastic block-connector (2). Ease the block to one side so as to clear the switch when you fit it.

Connect the blue and yellow wires of either cable to the 'L1' terminals on the new switch and those of the other cable to the 'L2' terminals (2). Screw the faceplate to the mounting box.

SEE ALSO

◁ Details for:
**Connecting to
junction box**   311
Connecting to
loop-in rose   329
Adding new switch
and light   329

**Two-way lighting
Circuit** (Right)
1 Consumer unit
2 Light fitting
3 Lighting circuit cable
4 Two-way circuit cable
5 Switch
6 Linking cable
7 Junction box

**Three-way lighting
Circuit** (Far right)
1 Consumer unit
2 Light fitting
3 Lighting circuit
4 Three-way
  circuit cable
5 Switch
6 Intermediate switch
7 Linking cable
8 Junction box

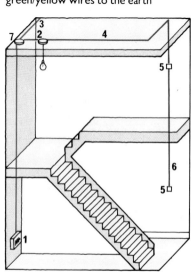

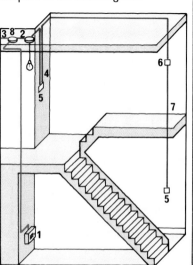

WIRING TWO- AND THREE-WAY SWITCHES

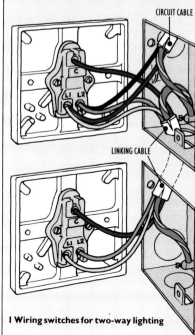

1 Wiring switches for two-way lighting

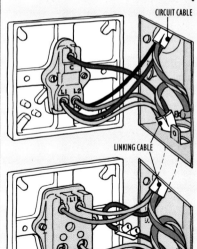

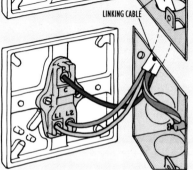

2 Wiring switches for three-way lighting

Many wall lights are supplied without integral backplates to enclose the bared wires and connections. To comply with Wiring Regulations such a fitting must be attached to a non-combustible mounting like a BESA box (▷), a round plastic or metal box which is screwed to the wall in a recess chopped out of the plaster and brickwork.

Alternatively use an architrave switch mounting box. This is a slim mounting that leaves plenty of room on each side for wall plug fixings for the light. Both mountings are fixed to the wall as described for flush socket outlet mountings (▷).

The basic circuit and connections

The simplest way of connecting wall lights to the lighting circuit is via a junction box (▷). The procedure is: complete the wall-light installation, switch off the power, then connect the new installation with the junction box.

Wire up a one-way switch (▷). All the wall lights will be controlled by this switch, though if you choose lights that have their own integral switches they can also be controlled individually.

Run a 1mm² two-core and earth cable from the junction box, looping in and out of each wall-light mounting and on to the last, where the cable ends.

Instead of cutting the cable at the light mountings strip off the outer sheathing, leaving the conductors intact, then carefully slice about 18mm (¾in) of insulation from the middle of each one and pinch the bared wire into a tight bend with pliers. At each light slip green/yellow sleeving over the doubled earth wire and connect it to the earth terminal on the mounting box (**I**).

Connect the doubled red and black wires to the block-connector inside the wall light, the black one to the terminal holding the blue wire and the red one to the terminal holding the brown wire (**I**).

The last wall-light mounting will have one end of the cable entering it, so strip and prepare the ends of the wires, then connect them as described above.

SEE ALSO

Details for: ▷	
Flush mounting	309
Fused connection unit	314
Junction-box connection	324
BESA box	326
One-way switch	328
Double-gang switch	328
Switching off	296
Running a cable	303-305
Running a spur	311

I Wiring a typical wall light

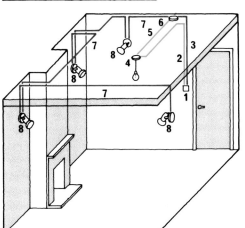

Basic wall-light circuit
The basic circuit and connections are as described above.
I Switch
2 Junction box
3 Loop-in lighting circuit cable
4 Wall-light circuit cable
5 Wall light

Replacing a ceiling light
You can dispense with a ceiling light in favour of wall lights and use the existing wiring and switch. Switch off the power, remove the rose and connect the wiring to a fixed junction-box (▷).
I Existing switch and cable
2 Junction box replaces rose
3 Loop-in lighting circuit cable
4 1mm² wall-light cable
5 Wall-light

Ceiling light plus wall lights
If you want to keep your ceiling light you can substitute a double-gang switch for the single one (▷), then wire the present ceiling-light cable to one half of the switch and the new wall-lighting cable to the other.
I Double-gang switch
2 Old switch cable
3 New switch cable
4 Ceiling light
5 Loop-in circuit
6 Junction box (▷)
7 1mm² lighting cable
8 Wall light

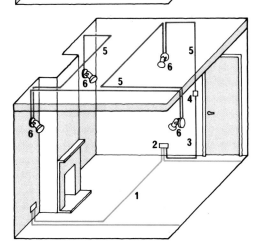

Using a spur
Wall lights can be wired to a ring circuit by means of a spur cable. Run a 2.5mm² two-core and earth spur from a nearby socket to a switched fused connection unit that has a 3amp fuse (▷).
I Ring circuit
2 Socket outlet
3 Spur cable
4 Fused connection unit
5 1mm² lighting cable
6 Wall light

USING ELECTRICITY OUTSIDE

SEE ALSO

◁ Details for:

Wiring regulations	288
RCCB	297
Running a spur	311
Junction box	324
One-way switch	328
Adding new light	329
Connecting to loop-in rose	329
Switching off	296
Running cable	303-305

There are good reasons for extending your electrical installation outside the house. First, and most important, it is safer to run electric garden tools from a convenient, properly protected socket than to trail long leads from sockets inside the house – a practice that can lead to serious accidents.

A garage or workshop is much more efficient if it is equipped with good lighting and its own circuit from which to run power tools.

Finally, well-arranged lighting and electric pumps for waterfalls and fountains can add much charm to a garden and extend its use in summertime by providing a background for barbecues and outdoor parties.

SAFETY OUTDOORS

The need for absolute safety in outdoor electrical installations is obvious. Damp conditions and the fact that users are likely to be in direct contact with the earth can lead to fatal accidents if proper installing procedures haven't been carried out originally.

- Install only proper outdoor light fittings outside.
- Use only recommended cable, following the Wiring Regulations, and check on its condition regularly.
- Protect all outside installations with residual-current circuit breakers, which provide an almost instantaneous response to earth-leakage faults.
- Make sure that the power is disconnected before servicing any equipment, particularly pool lighting and pumps.
- Wear thick rubber-soled footwear when you use electric garden tools.
- Choose double-insulated power tools for extra protection.

Fitting a porch light

A light that illuminates the front or back entrance to your home suggests a welcoming atmosphere to visitors and helps them to identify the house. It can also enable you to inspect unexpected callers before you open the door.

Fit only a light that is designed for the purpose. The fitting should be weatherproof and the lamp or bulb itself should be held in a moisture-proof rubber gasket or cup that surrounds the electrical connections.

You should try to position a porch light so that the cable to it can be run straight through a wall or ceiling of the porch and into the back of the fitting, but if you do have to run ordinary cable along an outside wall it should be protected by being passed through a length of metal or plastic conduit.

Wiring procedure

A porch light is installed by a procedure very like that for adding a new light (◁). Take your power from the nearest ceiling rose – probably in the entrance hall – and run it to a 20amp four-terminal junction box screwed to a board between ceiling joists (◁).

Run a 1mm² two-core and earth cable from the junction box to a light switch (◁) mounted near the door and another one to the light fitting itself. Using a large masonry drill, bore a hole through the wall where you plan to fix the fitting. Cement a short length of conduit into it with a plastic grommet in each end to prevent the edges cutting the cable's sheathing.

Run the cable through the tube, wire it into the fitting, following the maker's instructions, and then, with the power switched off, connect the new light up at the ceiling rose (◁).

INSTALLING A SOCKET FOR GARDEN TOOLS

Many people plug garden tools into the nearest indoor socket, which often results in long extension leads trailing across a kitchen or living room and out into the garden. A lead that will eventually cause someone to trip is dangerous, but more importantly, IEE Wiring Regulations (◁) state that a socket supplying mains power to garden tools or equipment must be protected by a residual-current circuit breaker (RCCB) with a trip rating of 30 milliamps. This device switches off the power as soon as it detects a fault and before anyone using the equipment can receive a fatal electric shock.

Sockets can be mounted outside the house as long as they are protected from the weather, though the special procedures involved are best left to a qualified electrician. But you can install a socket in a weatherproof garage, lobby or conservatory which is part of the house by running a spur from a ring circuit (◁). Mount it high enough to avoid being struck by a wheelbarrow or hidden by sacks or garden tools.

You can provide RCCB protection in several ways. The simplest is to attach a special plug with built-in RCCB to the lead of the power tool. They are relatively cheap but protect only the one tool. A better method is to install a socket that incorporates an RCCB **(1)** or plug an adaptor type RCCB **(2)** into a standard 13amp socket. Alternatively fit an RCCB near the consumer unit so that it can protect the whole ring circuit, including the new spur for garden equipment (◁).

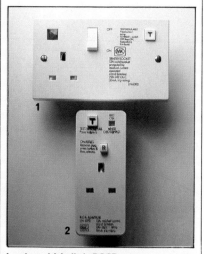

1 socket with built-in RCCB
2 Adaptor RCCB plugs into any socket outlet

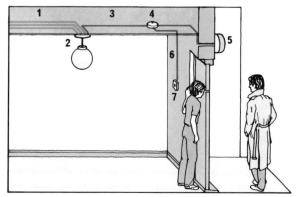

Porch-light circuit
1 Loop-in circuit and switch cables
2 Ceiling rose
3 1mm² lighting cable
4 Junction box
5 Porch light
6 Switch cable
7 Porch-light switch

GARDEN LIGHTING AND PUMPS

Just a few outdoor light fittings can transform a garden dramatically. Spot or flood lights can emphasize particularly attractive features as well as providing functional lighting for pathways and steps, while strings of coloured light bulbs woven through foliage give attractive background illumination. The most impressive effects are produced with underwater lights that make even small pools and fountains the focal points of gardens after dark.

Low-voltage lighting

A number of garden light fittings can be powered directly from mains electricity, but you should hire a professional electrician to install such equipment. However, you can install light fittings or a complete lighting kit that connects up to a low-voltage transformer. Store the transformer under cover in a garage or workshop close to a 13amp socket outlet and connect it to the socket by an ordinary square-pin plug. The flex, which is normally supplied with the light fitting, is connected to the two 12 volt outlet terminals on the transformer. Carry out the connections to the lights themselves according to the instructions supplied by the manufacturer.

Unless otherwise stated by the makers, low-voltage flex supplying garden lights can be run along the surface of the ground without further protection, but inspect it regularly and don't let it trail over stone steps or other sharp edges that may damage the PVC insulation if someone should step on it. If you have to add extra flex use a waterproof flex-connector.

Pool lighting

Pool lights are normally submerged so as to have at least 18mm (¾in) of water above their lenses. Some are designed to float unless they are held below the surface by smooth stones placed carefully on the flex.

Submerged lights can get covered by particles of the debris that floats in all ponds. Clean the lenses under water by directing a gentle stream of water from a garden hose over them. Occasionally you will have to remove a light and wash the lens thoroughly in warm soapy water. Always disconnect the power supply before handling lights or taking them out of a pond.

Run flex to pool lights under the edging stones via a drain made from corrugated plastic sheeting (▷). The whole length of flex can be protected from adverse weather conditions by being run through a length of ordinary garden hose. Take the safest route to the supply of electricity, anchoring the flex gently in convenient spots, but do not cover it with soil or grass in case someone should inadvertently cut through it with a spade or fork. Join lengths of low-voltage cable with waterproof connectors.

Pumps

Electric pumps in garden pools provide fountains and waterfalls. A combination unit sends an adjustable jet of water into the air, at the same time pumping water through a plastic tube to the top of a rockery, to trickle back into the pool.

Some pumps have to be run directly from the mains supply. To fit these consult the maker's instructions and a qualified electrician. But there are low-voltage pumps that connect to a transformer shielded from the weather (See left). In order to disconnect the pump without disturbing the low-voltage wiring to the transformer join two lengths of cable with a waterproof connector. Conceal the connector under a stone or gravel beside the pool.

Most manufacturers recommend that you take a pump from the water at the end of every season, clean it thoroughly, then return it to the water immediately. To avoid corrosion don't leave it out of the water for very long without cleaning and drying it. Never service a pump without first disconnecting it from the power supply.

During the winter you should run a pump for an hour every week to keep it in good working condition.

SEE ALSO

Details for: ▷
Pond drain   457

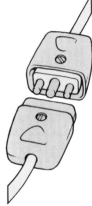

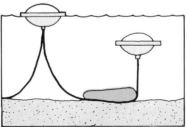
Stand underwater floodlights on a flat stone

Place a stone on the cable to submerge a light

Cable connector
A low-voltage cable connector, as supplied by pump or lighting manufacturers, should be wrapped in plastic for extra protection.

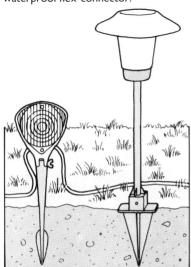
Typical low-voltage garden light fittings

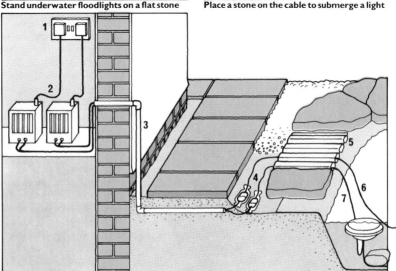

Pump and lighting circuits
1 Socket outlet
2 Low-voltage transformers
3 Plastic conduit
4 Waterproof connectors wrapped in plastic
5 Home-made drain (▷)
6 Pump cable
7 Lighting cable

333

RUNNING POWER TO OUTBUILDINGS

The power supply to a separate workshop, garage or toolshed cannot be tapped from other domestic circuits.

The cable must run from its own fuseway or switchfuse unit and pass safely underground or overhead to the outside location, where it is wired into another switchfuse unit from which the various circuits in the outbuilding can then be distributed as required.

SEE ALSO

◁ Details for:
PVC-insulated cable   302

Types of cable permitted outdoors

Three types of cable can be used outside. The one you choose will depend on how you wish to run it.

Armoured
This two- or three-core cable is insulated in the ordinary way but is also protected by a steel-wire armour which is itself insulated with an outer sheath of PVC. In the two-core cable the wire armour provides the path to earth, but some local authorities insist on the third, earth conductor.

Armoured cable is expensive, and must be terminated at a special junction box at each end of its run where it can be connected to ordinary PVC-insulated cable. It is fitted with threaded glands for attaching it to the junction boxes. This type of cable needs no further protection if it is run under the ground.

Mineral-insulated and copper-sheathed
The only other cable that can be buried without further protection is mineral-insulated, copper-sheathed (MICS) cable, whose PVC-insulated conductors are tightly packed in magnesium-oxide powder within a copper sheathing. The copper sheath can act as the earth conductor, and is itself sheathed in PVC insulation.

Because the mineral powder will absorb moisture special seals must be fitted at the ends of the cable when you order it.

MICS cable is expensive and, like armoured cable, must be terminated at junction boxes so that cheaper cable can be used in the outbuilding itself.

PVC-insulated and -sheathed
Ordinary two-core and earth PVC-insulated cable can be run underground to an outbuilding if it is protected against damage by being run through an impact-resistant plastic conduit. For turning corners elbow joints are cemented onto the ends of the straight runs of conduit. The electrical cable itself can be continuous.

This is a much cheaper way of taking power to an outbuilding than by armoured or MICS cable. PVC-insulated cable can also be run overhead quite safely under certain specified conditions (See below).

Outdoor cables
1 Armoured cable
2 Mineral-insulated, copper-sheathed cable
3 PVC-insulated and sheathed cable

Ways of running outdoor cable

Underground
Running cable underground is the best way of supplying power to an outbuilding.

You should bury the cable in a trench at least 500mm (1ft 8in) deep – deeper still if the cable has to pass under vegetable plots or other areas where digging is likely to go on. It's best to plan your cable run so as to avoid such areas as much as possible, but you can provide extra protection for the cable by laying housebricks along both sides of it to support a covering made from pieces of paving slab. Line the bottom of the trench with finely sifted soil or sand, lay the cable, then carefully fill in.

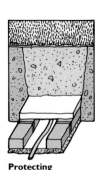

Protecting underground cable
Support paving slabs on bricks to protect a cable at the bottom of a trench.

Overhead
Ordinary PVC-insulated cable can be run from house to outbuilding as long as it is at least 3.5m (12ft) above the ground or 5.2m (17ft) above a driveway that is accessible to vehicles. The cable may not be used unsupported over a distance of more than 3m (10ft), though the same distance can also be covered by running the cable through a continuous length of rigid steel conduit suspended at least 3m (10ft) above the ground or 5.2m (17ft) above a driveway. The conduit itself must be earthed.

Over greater distances the cable must be supported by a catenary wire stretched taut between the house and outbuilding and to which the cable is clipped or hung from slings. The supporting metal wire must be earthed.

PVC-insulated cable can be run through conduit mounted on a wall.

Unsupported cable
Height above pathway:
3.5m (12ft) minimum
Height above driveway:
5.2m (17ft) minimum
Span:
3m (10ft) maximum

On catenary wire
Height above pathway:
3.5m (12ft) minimum
Height above driveway:
5.2m (17ft) minimum
Span:
Unlimited

Through steel conduit
Height above pathway:
3m (10ft) minimum
Height above driveway:
5.2m (17ft) minimum
Span:
3m (10ft) maximum

Running cable overhead

RUNNING THE CIRCUIT

Various equipment and cables can be used to run a circuit to an outbuilding. The method described here uses normal PVC-insulated cable and a switchfuse unit at each end of the circuit, but you could start in a spare fuseway in the consumer unit if one is available.

It is assumed that power sockets and lighting are required in the outbuilding, so the lighting circuit is taken from the power cable via a junction box and an unswitched fused connection unit.

Run the cable underground in impact-resistant plastic conduit, entering both buildings above the DPC but under the floorboards if possible.

House end of the circuit

Install a 30amp switchfuse unit near the meter and fit a 30amp circuit fuse. Mount a residual-current circuit breaker between the unit and the meter.

Run 6mm^2 two-core and earth cable from the 'Load' terminals of the RCCB to the 'Mains' terminals of the switchfuse unit. Connect the outgoing 2.5mm^2 cable to the 'Load' terminals **(1)** of the unit.

Prepare one red and one black 16mm^2 PVC-sheathed and -insulated cable for the meter leads and attach them to the 'Mains' terminals of the RCCB. Wire a 6mm^2 earth lead to the RCCB **(1)** ready for connecting to the consumer's earth terminal. Have the Electricity Board make the connections to the meter and earth terminal when the circuit is finished.

Outbuilding end of circuit

Run 2.5mm^2 two-core and earth cable through conduit from the house to the outbuilding, terminating at a 30amp switchfuse unit mounted on the wall.

Connect the incoming cable to the supply or 'Mains' terminals of the switchfuse unit and the outgoing 2.5mm^2 cable to its 'Load' terminals **(2)**, then run this cable to the socket outlets ($\triangleright$) in the outbuilding.

Insert a 30amp junction box at some point along the power cable **(3)** and from it run a spur to an unswitched fused connection unit ($\triangleright$). Fit a 3amp fuse in the connection unit and run 1mm^2 two-core and earth cable from the connection unit to the light fitting and switch ($\triangleright$).

SEE ALSO

Details for: $\triangleright$

Connecting sockets	310
Fused	
connection unit	314
Running cable	303-305
Lighting junction box	324
One-way switch	328

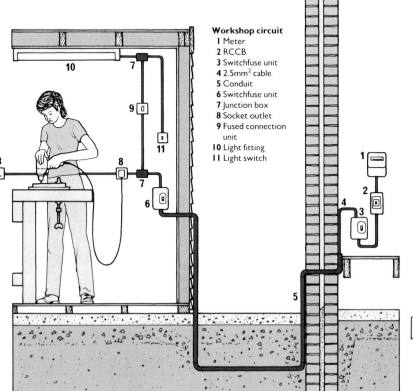

Workshop circuit
1 Meter
2 RCCB
3 Switchfuse unit
4 2.5mm^2 cable
5 Conduit
6 Switchfuse unit
7 Junction box
8 Socket outlet
9 Fused connection unit
10 Light fitting
11 Light switch

HOUSE END OF CIRCUIT

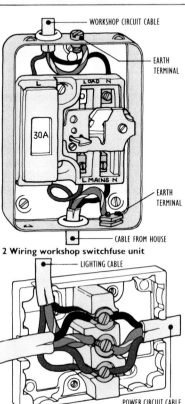

1 Wiring switchfuse unit and RCCB

2 Wiring workshop switchfuse unit

3 Wiring junction box on power circuit

335

COMPLETE REWIRING

Planning ahead

As an amateur you should carefully consider the time factor before deciding to tackle the complete rewiring of your house. When you are working on only one circuit the rest of the household can function normally, but to install whole new circuitry running to a consumer unit means that eventually every part of the house will be affected.

A full-time professional can cope with all this in such a way that the level of inconvenience to the household is held to a minimum. The amateur, perhaps obliged to work only at weekends, will have to consider a time span of several weeks, especially as it is very important

not to work hastily on such installations. Hurried work can lead to dangerous mistakes.

So unless you are very experienced, and are prepared to make the installation a full-time commitment for a week or two, you would be well advised to employ a fully qualified electrician for this time-consuming job (◁). The expert may be willing to work alongside you, so that you can save considerably on the cost by doing some of the jobs that really have nothing to do with actual electrical work – running cable under floors and channelling out plaster and brickwork, for example.

SEE ALSO

◁ Details for:

Hiring an	
electrician	21
RCCB	297
Consumer unit/fuses	298-299
Power circuits	301
Lighting circuits	301
Fixed appliances	314-316
Larger appliances	317-323

DESIGNING YOUR SYSTEM

Before meeting your professional you should form clear ideas about the kind of installation you want. Though you may decide between you to change some of the details a proper specification can help the electrician considerably and make expensive later additions and modifications unnecessary.

CHOOSING THE BEST CONSUMER UNIT

Choose the best consumer unit that you can afford. Cartridge fuses are better than the rewirable ones and are hardly any different in price, while units with miniature circuit breakers are the best of all, though they are far more costly.

Whichever type you decide to buy, be sure that it has enough spare fuseways for possible additional circuits.

RESIDUAL-CURRENT CIRCUIT BREAKERS

Ask your professional about the value of installing a residual-current circuit breaker (RCCB) (◁). You could have one built into your consumer unit.

POWER CIRCUITS

For supplying socket outlets ring circuits are better than radial ones. You can have as many sockets as you like providing the floor area in question doesn't exceed 100sq m (120 sq yd), so make sure that your plan includes enough outlets to meet your present and likely future needs. Trying now to save on the cost of a few sockets can cause you inconvenience in the future, when you may have to start adding spurs.

LIGHTING CIRCUITS

Modern domestic lighting circuits are usually designed round a loop-in system, but remember that for expediency you can supply individual lights from a junction box. You should insist in your plan on a lighting circuit for each floor so that you will never be totally without electric light if a fuse should blow.

In the interests of safety have two-way or three-way switches installed for the lights in passageways and on landings and staircases.

ADDITIONAL CIRCUITS

If you are having the whole house rewired consider extra radial circuits for such things as immersion heaters and showers.

8

PLUMBING SYSTEMS	338
EMERGENCY REPAIRS	341
TAPS:REPAIRS	342
CISTERNS:MAINTENANCE	344
DRAINAGE	347
PIPEWORK	351
WC	360
WASH BASINS	363
BATHS	367
SHOWERS	369
BIDETS	373
SINKS	374
WASTE DISPOSAL UNITS	375
WASHING MACHINES	376
WATER SOFTENERS	378
STORAGE CISTERNS	379
CYLINDERS	380

PLUMBING

PLUMBING – UNDERSTANDING THE SYSTEM

SEE ALSO
◁ Details for:
Draining rainwater 234
Earthing 290,297

Over recent years, house owners and tenants have demonstrated a willingness, indeed a preference, to tackle their own plumbing repairs. As manufacturers responded to these demands by supplying hardware specially designed for them, householders in turn became even more ambitious, stimulating a growing industry aimed directly at the DIY market. Almost every aspect of home plumbing repair and improvement has been catered for with lightweight, attractive fittings which can be plumbed in quickly and confidently with traditional metal or modern plastic pipework. As usual, the need to save money has been the main incentive for the increased interest in DIY plumbing.

Materials alone are relatively expensive but the price of professional labour constitutes the greater part of any bill you incur, especially if it is necessary to call out a plumber at weekends or at an inconveniently late hour. Furthermore, stopping a leak quickly can save the expense and disappointment of ruined decorations or even the replacement of rotted household timbers. Even if you are insured against plumbing failures, it does not compensate for the disruption caused by major refurbishment. Lastly, there is the cost of water itself. A dripping tap wastes gallons of water a day, and if it's a hot water tap, there is the additional expense of heating it literally down the drain. The few pence spent on a washer can save you pounds.

Direct and indirect systems

You should familiarize yourself with the plumbing system in your own house so that you can isolate the relevant sections and drain the water during an emergency or prior to repairs and rerouting pipework.

Direct system
In many older properties, mains pressure is supplied to all cold water taps and WCs. Hot water is fed indirectly from the storage cistern via the hot water cylinder. The only advantage with this direct system is that drinking water can be drawn from any cold water tap in the house.

Indirect system
Most homes, and certainly modern houses, are plumbed with an indirect system. Water under mains pressure enters the house through a service pipe and proceeds via the rising main directly to the cold water storage cistern, normally situated in the roof space. A branch pipe from the rising main delivers drinking water to the kitchen sink, and possibly to a garden tap

through another pipe. All other cold water taps and appliances are fed indirectly, that is, under gravity pressure only, from the storage cistern. The hot water storage cylinder is also supplied with cold water from the same cistern. There it is heated either indirectly by the central heating system, or by electric immersion heaters, then drawn off from the top of the cylinder to hot water taps in the bathroom, kitchen and some of the bedrooms.

An indirect system provides several advantages to the householder and the water authority. Firstly, there is adequate water stored in the cistern to flush sanitary ware during a temporary mains failure. Also, as the major part of the supply is under relatively low pressure, an indirect system is reasonably quiet. (High mains pressure can cause 'water hammer' as the water tries to negotiate tight bends.) As few outlets are connected to the mains, there is less likelihood of impure water being siphoned back into the mains supply – an important consideration with regard to hygiene.

Drainage

Waste water is drained from either system in one of two ways. Up until the late 1940s or 50s, water was drained from baths, sinks and basins into a wastepipe which fed into a trapped gully at ground level. Toilet waste fed separately into a large diameter soil pipe running directly to the underground main drainage network.

A single stack waste system is used on later buildings where all waste drains into a single soil pipe. The only possible exception is the kitchen sink which still drains into a gully.

Rain water always feeds into a separate drain so that the house drainage system will not be flooded in the event of a storm (◁).

PLUMBING REGULATIONS

Your local water authority insists that certain regulations are observed whenever you alter existing installations or install new plumbing. The regulations are intended to preserve the health of the community and to reduce unnecessary waste. Except for straight-forward replacements, you should seek the advice of the appropriate authority on your local council. The methods described in this chapter comply with the regulations but a telephone call to the Town Hall will put you in touch with someone who can help you with queries about local requirements.

At the same time make sure that you do not contravene electrical regulations. All metal plumbing must be bonded to the Electricity Board's earth terminal near your meter. If you replace a section of metal plumbing with plastic, you may break the path to earth. Make sure that you reinstate the link (◁). If in doubt, consult a qualified electrician.

THE DIRECT SYSTEM

1. Water authority's stopcock

2. Service pipe

3. Main stopcock

4. Rising main
Supplies water to storage cylinder as well as cold water taps and WCs.

5. Cold water storage cistern

6. Hot water cylinder

7. Wastepipe
Surmounted by hopper head collects water from basin and bath.

8. Soil pipe
Separate pipe takes toilet waste to main drains.

9. Kitchen wastepipe
Kitchen sink drains into same gully as wastepipe from upstairs.

10. Trapped gully

Indirect system

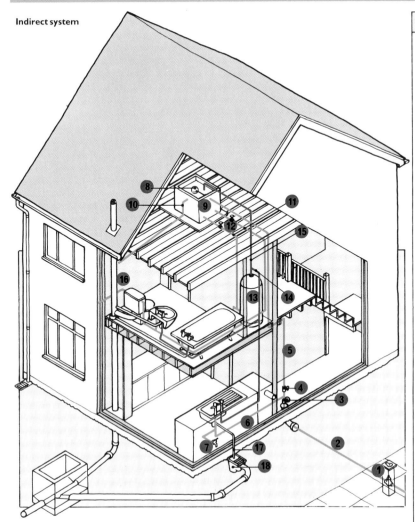

THE INDIRECT SYSTEM

1 Water authority's stopcock
Water from the public main can be turned off at this stopcock. It works like a tap but also acts as a non-return valve so that, should mains pressure drop, water will not be siphoned from the household plumbing to contaminate the public supply.

2 Service pipe
From the stopcock onwards, the plumbing becomes the responsibility of the householder. The service pipe enters the house through a drainpipe packed with insulant to prevent water freezing.

3 Main stopcock
The water supply to the whole house is shut off at this point.

4 Draincock
A draincock here allows you to drain water from the rising main.

5 Rising main
Mains pressure water passes to the cold water cistern.

6 Drinking water
Drinking water is drawn off the rising main to the kitchen sink.

7 Garden tap
The water authority allows a garden tap to be supplied with mains pressure.

8 Float valve
Shuts off the supply from the rising main when the cistern is full.

9 Cold water storage cistern
Stores 230 to 360 litres (50 to 80 gallons) of water. Positioned in the roof, it provides sufficient 'head' or pressure to feed the whole house.

10 Overflow pipe
Also known as a warning pipe, it prevents an overflow by draining water to the outside of the house should the float valve fail to operate.

11 Cold feed pipes
Water is drawn off to the bathroom and to the hot water cylinder from the base of the storage cistern.

12 Cold feed valves
Valves at these points allow you to drain the cold water in the feed pipe without having to drain the whole cistern as well. Alternatively, they may be placed in the airing cupboard.

13 Hot water cylinder
There may be a draincock in this position to empty the cylinder.

14 Hot feed pipe
All hot water is fed from this point.

15 Vent pipe
A vent pipe drains into the cistern to allow for expansion of heated water and to vent air from the system.

16 Single stack soil pipe

17 Sink waste
Drains into trapped gully.

18 Trapped gully

SEE ALSO

Details for: ▷
Wet central heating 391

Direct system

• **Central heating**
Omitted for clarity. (▷)

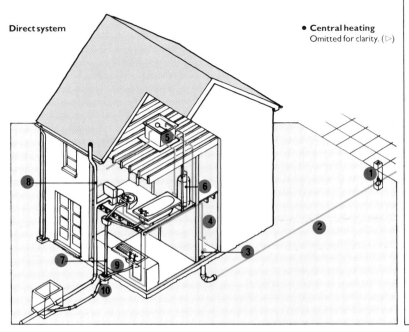

DRAINING THE SYSTEM

SEE ALSO

◁ Details for:
Cylinders   380
Cylinder vent pipe   380
Radiators   393

You will have to drain at least part of any plumbing system before you can work on it, and if you detect a leak, you will have to drain the relevant section quickly, so find out where the valves, stopcock and drain cocks are situated before you are faced with an emergency.

Draining cold water taps and pipes

• Turn off the main stopcock on the rising main to cut off the supply to the kitchen tap. (And every other cold tap on a direct system.)
• Open the tap until the water ceases to flow.
• To isolate bathroom taps, close the valve on the appropriate cold feed pipe from the storage cistern and open all taps on that section. If you can't find a valve, rest a wooden batten across the cistern and tie the arm of the float valve to it. This will shut off the supply to the cistern so you can empty it by running all the cold taps in the bathroom. If you can't get into the loft, turn off the main stopcock, then run the cold taps.

Draining hot water taps and pipes

• Turn off immersion heaters or boiler.
• Close the valve on the cold feed pipe to the cylinder and run the hot taps. Even when the water stops flowing, the cylinder will still be full.
• If there is no valve on the cold feed pipe, tie up the float valve arm, then turn on bathroom cold taps to empty the storage cistern. (If you run the hot taps first, the water stored in the cistern will flush out all your hot water from the cylinder.) When cold taps run dry, open the hot taps. In an emergency, run the hot and cold taps together to clear the pipes as quickly as possible. (With a direct system you have no choice but to drain the system via the hot taps.)

Draining a WC cistern

• To merely empty the cistern itself, tie up the float valve arm (See above) and flush the WC.
• To empty the pipe supplying the cistern, either turn off the main stopcock on a direct system, or, on an indirect system, close the valve on the cold feed from the storage cistern. Alternatively, tie up the float valve arm and empty the storage cistern through the cold taps. Flush the WC until no more water enters its cistern.

Draining the cold water storage cistern

• To drain the storage cistern in the roof, close the main stopcock on the rising main then open all the cold taps in the bathroom. (Hot taps on a direct system.) Bail out the residue of water at the bottom of the cistern.

Draining the hot water cylinder

If the cylinder springs a leak, or you intend to replace it, first turn off immersion heaters or boiler, then shut off its cold water supply or drain the cold water cistern (See above). Run hot water from taps.
• If the water is heated by immersion heaters only, there should be a draincock on the cold feed pipe just before it enters the cylinder. Attach a hose to it and drain the water still in the cylinder into the nearest drain or sink at a lower level.
• If the water is heated by a boiler which is not part of a central heating system, empty the cylinder with a hose from the draincock on the return pipe next to the boiler.
• When a boiler heats the water and the central heating system, empty the cylinder from the draincock on its cold feed pipe from the storage cistern. (The primary circuit, which heats the radiators and the heat exchanger in the cylinder (◁), is still filled with water. That circuit is drained when necessary from the draincock next to the boiler. Close both valves on radiators (◁) if you do not need to empty them.)
• If no draincocks are provided, disconnect the vent pipe (◁) and siphon the cylinder with a hosepipe.

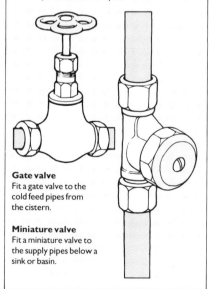

Closing a float valve
Cut off the supply of water to a storage cistern by tying the float arm to a batten.

ADDING EXTRA VALVES

You will have to drain off a substantial part of a typical plumbing installation even for a simple washer replacement unless you divide the system into relatively short pipe runs with valves.
• Install a gate valve on both cold feed pipes running from the cold water storage cistern. This will save you having to drain gallons of water in order to isolate pipes and appliances on the low-pressure cold and hot-water supply.
• When you are fitting new taps, take the opportunity to fit miniature valves on the supply pipes just below the sink or basin. In future, you will be able to isolate an individual tap in moments when you have to repair it.

Gate valve
Fit a gate valve to the cold feed pipes from the cistern.

Miniature valve
Fit a miniature valve to the supply pipes below a sink or basin.

DRAINING AND REFILLING THE WHOLE SYSTEM

Drain the complete plumbing system when you intend to leave the house unoccupied for a long period during the winter, otherwise you run the risk of a 'freeze up' which may burst pipes or force joints apart. Drain the system in the following order.

● Switch off the boiler or immersion heaters. Rake out a solid fuel boiler and allow it to cool.
● Turn off the main stopcock on the rising main, and run off the water from all cold and hot taps.
● If there is a draincock on the rising main, drain what water is left in the pipe from that point.
● Flush the WCs.
● Drain the hot water cylinder.
● Don't bother to drain the water from the central heating system but make sure it contains antifreeze (▷).
● Place a note prominently to remind yourself to fill the system before lighting the boiler or switching on the immersion heater.
● If you can expect very low temperatures where you live, pour some salt into the WC pan to stop the water freezing in the trap. Treat other traps similarly.

Refilling the system
To refill the system, close all taps and draincocks, then open the main stopcock. As the system fills, check that float valves are operating smoothly. Air trapped in the system may cause taps to splutter for a while. If it doesn't clear naturally, flush it out with mains pressure (See below).

CURING AN AIR LOCK

Air trapped in the system can cause a tap to splutter or fail completely. Force the air out using mains water pressure.

Attach a length of hosepipe between the affected tap and the cold water tap over the kitchen sink. (Any cold water tap on a direct system.) Leave both taps open for a short while and try the air-locked tap again. If necessary, repeat the procedure until water runs freely.

If you have to use a long hose, it will contain a lot of water so drain it into the kitchen sink before you move it.

EMERGENCY REPAIRS

Every householder should master the simple techniques for coping with emergency repairs in order to avoid unnecessary damage to property, and the high cost of calling out a plumber at short notice. All you need is a simple tool kit and a few spare parts.

Thawing frozen pipes

Insulate your pipework and fittings, particularly those in the loft or under the floor (▷), to stop them freezing. If you leave the house unheated for a long time during the winter, drain the system (See left). Cure dripping taps so that leaking water does not freeze in your drainage system overnight.

If water will not flow from a tap or a cistern refuses to fill in cold weather, a plug of ice may have formed in one of the supply pipes. The plug cannot be in a pipe supplying those taps or float valves which are working normally, so you should be able to trace the blockage fairly quickly. In fact, freezing usually occurs first in the roof space.

As copper pipework transmits heat readily, use a hairdryer to warm the suspect pipe, starting as close as possible to the tap or valve, then work along it. Leave the tap open so that water can flow normally as soon as the ice thaws. If you cannot heat the pipe with a hairdryer, wrap it in a hot towel or hang a rubber hot water bottle over it.

Dealing with a nailed pipe

Unless you are absolutely sure where your pipes run, it is all too easy to nail through one of them when fixing a loose floorboard. You may be able to detect a hissing sound as water escapes under pressure, but more than likely you won't notice your mistake until a wet patch appears on the ceiling below or some problem associated with damp occurs at a later date. With the nail in place, water will leak relatively slowly so don't pull it out until you have drained the pipework and can repair the leak. If you pull it out by lifting a floorboard, put it back immediately.

If you plan to lay fitted carpet, you can paint pipe runs on the floorboards to avoid a similar accident.

Patching a leak

During freezing conditions, water within a pipe will turn to ice which expands until it eventually splits the walls of the tube or forces a joint apart. Copper pipework is more likely to split than lead which can stretch to accommodate the expansion, taking a few hard winters before reaching breaking point. Patch either pipe as described right but close up a split in lead beforehand using gentle taps with a hammer. Repairing lead permanently is not easy, so hire a plumber as soon as you have contained the leak.

The only other reason for leaking plumbing is mechanical failure, either through deterioration or because the plumber failed to make a completely waterproof joint.

If you can, make a permanent repair by inserting a new section of pipe or replace a leaking joint. If it is a compression joint that has failed, try tightening it first (▷). However, you may have to make an emergency repair for the time being. Always drain the pipe first unless it is frozen, in which case make the repair before it thaws.

Using a hose and Jubilee clips
Cut a length of garden hose to cover the leak, and slit it lengthwise so that you can slip it over the pipe. Bind the hose with two or three Jubilee clips. (Normally used to attach hoses on a car engine.) If you cannot obtain clips, twist wire loops around the hose with pliers.

Patching with epoxy putty
The putty is supplied in two parts which begin to harden as soon as they are mixed, giving you about 20 minutes to complete the repair. The putty will adhere to most metals and hard plastic. Although it is better to insert a new length of pipe, epoxy putty will produce a fairly long-term repair.

Use abrasive paper or wire wool to clean a 25 to 50mm (1 to 2in) length of pipe on each side of the leak. Mix the putty thoroughly and press it into the hole or around a joint, building it to a thickness of 3 to 6mm (⅛ to ¼in). It will cure to full strength within 24 hours, but you can run low pressure water immediately if you bind the putty with self-adhesive tape.

SEE ALSO

Details for: ▷	
Insulating pipes	261
Compression joints	354
Antifreeze/inhibitor	397
Joining pipes	352-359

Thawing a frozen pipe
Play a hairdryer along a frozen pipe working away from the blocked tap or valve.

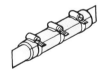

Binding a split pipe
Bind a length of hosepipe around a split pipe with hose clips.

Smoothing epoxy putty
When you have patched a hole with epoxy putty, smooth it with a damp, soapy cloth for a neat finish.

REPAIRING A LEAKING TAP

A tap may leak for a number of reasons but none of them are difficult to deal with. When water drips from a spout, for instance, it is most likely caused by a faulty washer, or if the tap is old, the seat against which the washer is compressed may be worn also. If water leaks from beneath the head of the tap when it's in use, the gland packing or 'O' ring needs replacing.

When working on taps, insert the plug and lay a towel in the bottom of the sink or bath to catch small objects.

SEE ALSO

◁ Details for:
Spanners and wrenches 489-490

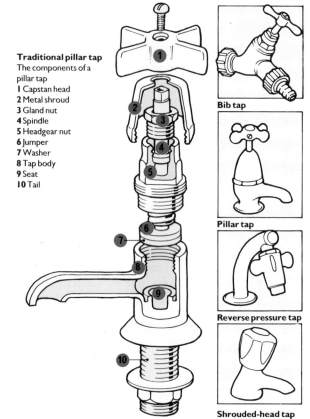

Traditional pillar tap
The components of a pillar tap
1 Capstan head
2 Metal shroud
3 Gland nut
4 Spindle
5 Headgear nut
6 Jumper
7 Washer
8 Tap body
9 Seat
10 Tail

Bib tap

Pillar tap

Reverse pressure tap

Shrouded-head tap

REMOVING A SHROUDED HEAD

On most modern taps the head and cover is in one piece. You will have to remove it to expose the headgear nut. Often a retaining screw is hidden beneath the coloured hot/cold disc in the centre of the head. Prise it out with the point of a knife. If there is no retaining screw, the head will pull off, or remove it by continuing to unscrew the head as if you were turning the tap on in the normal way.

Replacing a washer

To replace the washer in a traditional bib or pillar tap, first drain the supply pipe, then open the valve as far as possible before dismantling either of the taps.

If the tap is shrouded with a metal cover, unscrew it, by hand if possible, or tape the jaws of a wrench to protect the chrome finish.

Lift up the cover to reveal the headgear nut just above the body of the tap. Slip a narrow spanner onto the nut and unscrew it (**1**) until you can lift out the entire headgear assembly.

The jumper, to which the washer is fixed, fits into the bottom of the headgear. With some taps, the jumper is removed along with the headgear (**2**) but in other cases it will be lying inside the tap body.

The washer itself may be pressed over a small button in the centre of the jumper (**3**), in which case, prise it off with a screwdriver. If the washer is held in place by a nut, it can be difficult to remove. Allow penetrating oil to soften any corrosion, then, holding the jumper stem with pliers, unscrew the nut with a snug-fitting spanner (**4**). (If the nut will not budge, replace the whole jumper and washer.) Fit a new washer and retaining nut, then reassemble the tap.

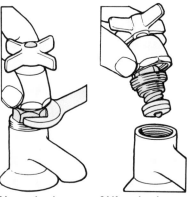

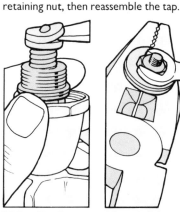
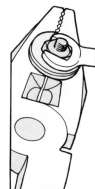

1 Loosen headgear nut   **2 Lift out headgear**   **3 Prise off washer**   **4 Or undo fixing nut**

Replacing a washer in a reverse-pressure tap

The distinctive reverse-pressure tap is like an upside down version of a conventional tap – the washer is screwed upwards against the seat. When replacing a washer, there is no need to shut off the water because an integral check valve closes automatically as the body is removed.

Loosen the retaining nut above the tap body (**1**), then unscrew the body itself as if you were opening the tap. Water will run until the check valve

operates, but continue to unscrew the body (**2**) until it drops into your hand.

Tap the nozzle on the floor (**3**), not on a ceramic basin, then turn the body upside down to tip out the finned, anti-splash device. Prise the combined jumper and washer from the end of the anti-splash device (**4**) and replace it.

Reassemble the tap in the reverse order, remembering that the body is screwed back clockwise when viewed from above.

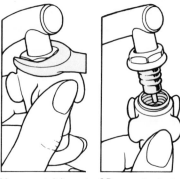

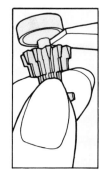

1 Loosen retaining nut   **2 Remove tap body**   **3 Tap nozzle on floor**   **4 Prise off jumper**

REPLACING 'O' RINGS ON MIXER TAPS

Each valve on a mixer tap is fitted with a washer like a conventional tap but in most mixers, the gland packing has been replaced by a rubber 'O' ring.

Having removed the shrouded head, take out the circlip holding the spindle in place (1). Remove the spindle, and slip the old 'O' ring out of its groove (2). Replace it with a new one and reassemble the tap.

1 Remove circlip   **2 Roll ring from groove**

The base of a mixer's swivel spout is sealed with a washer or 'O' ring. If water seeps from that junction, turn off both valves and unscrew the spout, or remove the retaining screw (3) on one side. Note the type of seal and buy a matching replacement.

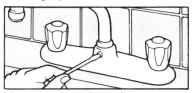

3 Remove screw to release mixer spout

MAINTAINING STOPCOCKS AND VALVES

Stopcocks and gate valves are used rarely so their maintenance is often neglected, but, if they fail to work just when you need them, you could have a serious problem on your hands.

Make sure they are operating smoothly by closing and opening them from time to time. If the spindles move stiffly, lubricate them with a little penetrating oil. Unlike a gate valve, a stopcock is fitted with a standard washer but as it is hardly ever under pressure, it is unlikely to wear. However, the gland packing on both the gate valve and stopcock may need attention (See right).

REPAIRING SEATS AND GLANDS

Regrinding the seat

If a tap continues to drip after you have replaced the washer, the seat is probably worn and water is leaking past the washer.

One way to cure it is to grind the seat flat with a specialized reseating tool rented from a hire company. Remove the headgear and jumper so that you can screw the tool into the body of the tap.

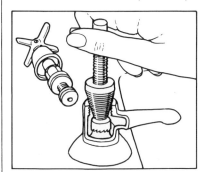

1 Revolve the tool to smooth the seat

Curing a leaking gland

The head of a tap is fixed to a shaft or spindle which is screwed up or down to control the flow of water. The spindle passes through a gland, also known as a stuffing box, on top of the headgear assembly (▷). A watertight packing is forced into the gland by a nut to prevent water leaking past the spindle when the tap is turned on. If water drips from under the head of the tap, the gland packing has failed and should be replaced.

Some taps incorporate a rubber 'O' ring which slips over the spindle to perform the same function as the packing (See left).

Replacing the gland packing

There is no need to turn off the supply of water to replace gland packing; just make sure the tap is turned off fully.

To remove a cross or capstan head,

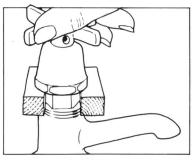

1 Jack the head off a tap with wooden packing

Adjust the cutter until it is in contact with the seat then turn the handle to smooth the seat (1). Alternatively, cover the old seat with a nylon substitute, sold with a matching jumper and washer (2). Drop the seating component over the old seat, replace the jumper and assemble the tap. Close the tap to force the seat in position.

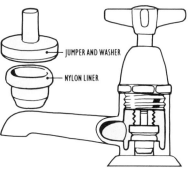

JUMPER AND WASHER
NYLON LINER

2 Repair a worn seat with a nylon liner

expose a fixing screw by picking out the plastic plug in the centre of the head, or look for a screw holding it at the side. Lift off the head by rocking it from side to side, or tap it gently from below with a hammer.

If the head is stuck firmly, open the tap as far as possible, unscrew the cover and wedge wooden packing between it and the headgear (1). Closing the tap jacks the head off the spindle.

Lift off the head and cover, then attempt to seal the leak by tightening the gland nut. If that fails, remove the nut and pick out the old packing with a small screwdriver.

To replace the packing, use special impregnated twine from a plumbers' merchant or twist a thread from PTFE (polytetrafluorethylene) tape (▷). Wind it around the spindle and pack it into the gland with a screwdriver (2).

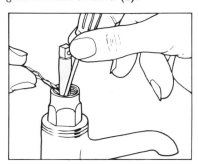

2 Stuff a thread of PTFE tape into the gland

SEE ALSO

Details for: ▷	
Tap mechanisms	342,364
PTFE tape	354
Reseating tool	491
Gate valve	352
Stopcock	356

GLAND PACKING

Gland packing
Older style taps are sealed with a watertight packing around the spindle.

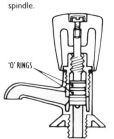

'O' RINGS

'O' ring seal
More modern taps are sealed with rubber rings in place of the gland packing.

MAINTAINING WC AND STORAGE CISTERNS

There is no reason why anyone should have to call out a plumber to service a WC cistern. Most of them are situated directly behind the WC pan so they are readily accessible, but even an old-fashioned, high-level cistern can be reached from a stepladder. The design of a cistern mechanism varies so little that components are available from the stock of any plumbers' merchant and many DIY outlets.

The water storage cistern in the loft is simply a container. Apart from a leak, which is unlikely to occur with a modern cistern, the only problems to arise are as a result of float valve failure. The float valve in a storage cistern is basically the same as that used for the WC cistern.

SEE ALSO

◁ Details for:
Float arm   346
Spanners and wrenches 489-490

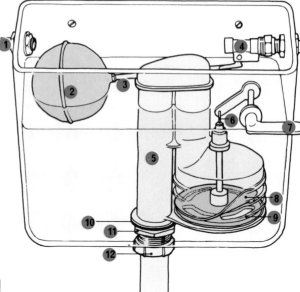

Direct action cistern
The components of a typical direct action WC cistern.
1 Overflow
2 Float
3 Float arm
4 Float valve
5 Siphon
6 Wire link
7 Flushing lever
8 Flap valve
9 Perforated plate
10 Sealing washer
11 Retaining nut
12 Flush pipe connector

DIRECT ACTION WC CISTERN

Most modern WCs are washed down with direct flushing cisterns. Water enters an empty cistern through a valve which is opened and closed by the action of a hollow float attached to one end of a rigid arm. As the water rises in the cistern, it lifts the float until the other end of the arm eventually closes the valve and shuts off the supply.

Flushing is carried out by depressing a lever which lifts a perforated metal plate at the bottom of an inverted 'U' bend tube (siphon). As the plate rises, the perforations are sealed by a flexible plastic diaphragm (flap valve) so that the plate can displace a body of water over the 'U' bend to promote a siphoning action. The resulting water pressure behind the diaphragm lifts it again so that the contents of the cistern flow up through the perforations in the plate, over the 'U' bend, and down the flush pipe. As the water level in the cistern drops, so does the float, opening the float valve to refill the cistern.

There are few problems associated with this type of cistern and all of them can be solved with regular maintenance. A faulty float valve or poorly adjusted arm allows water to leak into the cistern until it drips from the overflow pipe running to the outside of the house. Slow or noisy filling is often rectified by replacing the float valve. If the cistern will not flush until the lever is operated several times, the flap valve is probably worn and needs replacing.

Tying up a float arm
Tie the arm to a batten placed across the cistern when you need to shut off the supply of water.

Replacing the flap valve

If the WC cistern will not flush first time, take off the lid and check that the lever is actually operating the mechanism. If it is working normally, replace the flap valve in the siphon. Shut off the water by tying up the float valve arm (◁), and flush the cistern.

Use a large wrench to unscrew the nut holding the flush pipe to the underside of the cistern (1) . Move the pipe to one side.

Release the remaining nut which clamps the siphon to the base of the cistern (2) . A little water will run out as you loosen the nut so have a bucket handy. (It's just possible that the siphon is bolted to the base of the cistern instead of being clamped by one large retaining nut.)

Disconnect the flushing arm and ease the siphon out of the cistern . Lift the diaphragm off the metal plate (3) and substitute one of the same size. Reassemble the flushing mechanism in the reverse order and attach the flush pipe to the cistern.

1 Release flush pipe

2 Loosen retaining nut

3 Lift off flap valve

Making a new link

If the flushing lever feels slack and the cistern will not even attempt to flush, look to see if the wire link at the end of the flushing arm is intact.

Retrieve the broken pieces from the cistern and bend a new link from a piece of thick wire. If you have thin wire only, twist the ends together with pliers to make a temporary repair until you can buy a new link.

Curing continuous running water

If you notice water continuously trickling into the pan from the flush pipe, lift out the siphon as described above and renew the washer which seals the siphon to the base of the cistern. Make sure the replacement is identical.

DIAPHRAGM VALVES

The pivoting end of the float arm on a diaphragm valve presses against the end of a small plastic piston which moves the large rubber diaphragm to seal the water outlet.

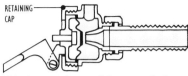

1 Diaphragm valve: retaining cap to the front

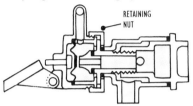

2 Diaphragm valve: retaining nut to the rear

Replacing the diaphragm

Turn off the water supply then unscrew the large retaining cap. Depending on the model, the nut may be screwed onto the end of the valve (1) or it may be behind it (2).

With the latter type of valve, slide out the cartridge inside the body (3) to find the diaphragm behind it. With the former, you will find a similar piston and diaphragm immediately behind the retaining cap (4).

Wash out the valve before assembling it along with the new diaphragm.

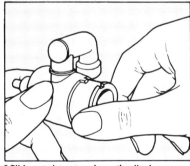

3 Slide out piston to release the diaphragm

4 Remove cap and pull float arm to find valve

RENOVATING FLOAT VALVES

A faulty float valve is responsible for most of the difficulties that arise with WC and water storage cisterns. Traditionally, the water outlet in the valve is sealed with a washer, but later patterns of valve utilize a large diaphragm instead, designed to protect the mechanism from scale deposits. Both types of valve are still widely available. If the outlet isn't sealed properly, water continues to feed into the cistern until it escapes to the outside via the overflow pipe. You may be able to solve the problem by simply adjusting the float arm, but more than likely, the washer or diaphragm is worn.

Portsmouth pattern valves

In a Portsmouth pattern valve, a piston moves horizontally inside the hollow metal body. The float arm, pivoting on a split pin, moves the piston back and forth to control the flow of water. A washer trapped in the end of the piston finally seals the outlet by pressing against the valve seat.

Replacing a washer

If you have to force the valve closed to stop water dripping, replace the washer. Cut off the supply of water to the cistern (▷), and although it is not essential, flush the cistern in case you drop a component into the water. Remove the split pin from beneath the valve and detach the float arm.

If there is a screw cap on the end of the valve body, remove it (1). You may have to apply a little penetrating oil to ease the threads, and grip the cap with slip joint pliers (▷).

Insert the tip of a screwdriver in the slot beneath the valve body and slide the piston out (2).

To remove the captive washer, unscrew the end cap of the piston with pliers. Steady the piston by holding a screwdriver in its slot (3).

Pick the old washer out of the cap (4) but before replacing it, clean the piston with fine wire wool. Some pistons do not have a removable end cap, and the washer must be dug out with a pointed knife. Take care when replacing this type of washer which is a tight fit within a groove in the piston.

Use wet and dry paper wrapped around a dowel rod to clean inside the valve body but take care not to damage the valve seat at the far end.

Reassemble the piston and smear it with a light coating of petroleum jelly. Rebuild the valve and connect the float arm. Restore the supply of water and adjust the arm to regulate the water level in the cistern (▷).

Portsmouth pattern valve

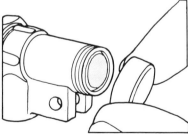

1 Take screw cap from the end of the valve

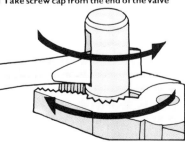

3 Split the piston into two parts

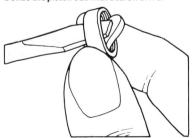

2 Slide the piston out with a screwdriver

4 Pick out the washer with a screwdriver

SEE ALSO

Details for: ▷

Turning off water	340
Adjusting float arm	346
Slip joint pliers	491

Croydon pattern valve
Only old fashioned cisterns will be fitted with this valve. The piston travels vertically to close against the seat. Replace the washer as described left.

RENOVATING VALVES AND FLOATS

Adjusting the float arm

Adjust the float to maintain the optimum level of water which is about 25mm (1in) below the outlet of the overflow pipe.

The arm on a Portsmouth valve is a solid metal rod. Bend it downward slightly to reduce the water level or straighten it to admit more water (**1**).

The arm on a diaphragm valve is fitted with an adjusting screw which presses on the end of the piston. Release the lock nut and turn the screw towards the valve to lower the water level or away from it to allow the water to rise (**2**).

SEE ALSO

◁ Details for:
Supporting pipes   355
Packaged plumbing 380

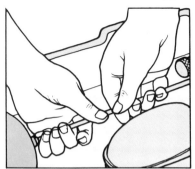

1 Straighten or bend a metal float arm

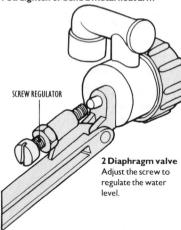

SCREW REGULATOR

2 Diaphragm valve
Adjust the screw to regulate the water level.

Replacing the float

Modern plastic floats rarely leak but old style metal floats do corrode eventually, allowing water to seep into the ball. It gradually sinks until it won't ride high enough to close the valve.

Unscrew the float and shake it to test whether there is water inside. If you can't replace it for several days, lay the ball on a bench and enlarge the leaking hole with a screwdriver, then pour out the water. Replace the float and cover it with a plastic bag, tying the neck tightly around the float arm.

Curing noisy cisterns

Cisterns that fill noisily can be a real source of annoyance, particularly if the WC is situated right next to a bedroom. It was once permitted to screw a pipe into the outlet of a valve so that it hung vertically below the level of the water. It solved the problem of water splashing into the cistern but water authorities were alarmed at the possibility of water 'back-siphoning' through the silencer tube into the mains supply. Although rigid tubes are banned nowadays, you are permitted to fit a valve with a flexible plastic silencer tube because it will seal itself by collapsing should back-siphonage occur.

A silencer tube can also prevent water hammer – a rythmic thudding that reverberates along the pipework. It is largely the result of ripples on the surface of the water in a cistern, caused by a heavy flow from the float valve. As the water rises, the float arm, bouncing on the ripples, hammers the valve and the sound is amplified and transmitted along the pipes. A flexible plastic silencer tube will eliminate ripples by introducing water below the surface.

If the water pressure through the valve is too high, the arm oscillates as it tries to close the valve – another cause of water hammer. Cure it by fitting an equilibrium valve. As water flows through the valve, some of it is introduced behind the piston or diaphragm to equalize the pressure on each side so that the valve closes smoothly and silently.

Before swapping your present valve, check that the pipework is clipped securely (◁) to cut down vibration.

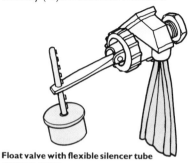

Float valve with flexible silencer tube

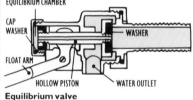
EQUILIBRIUM CHAMBER

CAP
WASHER

WASHER

FLOAT ARM

HOLLOW PISTON   WATER OUTLET

Equilibrium valve

Changing a float valve

Turn off the supply of water to the cistern and flush the pipework, then use a spanner to loosen the tap connector joining the supply pipe to the float valve stem. Remove the float arm, then unscrew the fixing nut on the outside of the cistern and pull out the valve.

Fit the new valve and, if possible, use the same tap connector to join it to the supply pipe. Adjust and tighten the fixing nuts to clamp the new valve to the cistern, then turn on the water and adjust the float arm.

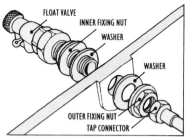
FLOAT VALVE
INNER FIXING NUT
WASHER
WASHER
OUTER FIXING NUT
TAP CONNECTOR

Replacing a float valve
Clamp a valve to the cistern with fixing nuts.

CHOOSING THE RIGHT PRESSURE

Float valves are made to suit different water pressures: low, medium and high (LP, MP, HP). It is important to choose a valve of the correct pressure or it may take a long time to fill. Conversely, the water pressure may be so high that the valve leaks continuously. Those fed direct from the mains should be HP valves, whereas most domestic WC cisterns require an LP valve. If the head (the height of the cistern above the float valve) is greater than 13.5m (45ft), fit an MP valve. In rare cases where the head exceeds 30m (100ft), fit an HP valve. In an apartment using a packaged plumbing system (a storage cistern built on top of the hot water cylinder (◁), the pressure may be so low that you will have to fit a 'full way' valve to the WC cistern to get it to fill quickly. If you live in an area where water pressure fluctuates a great deal, fit an equilibrium valve (See left).

To alter the pressure, replace the nozzle inside a modern Portsmouth or diaphragm valve. If the valve is a very old pattern, you will have to swap it for another one of a different pressure.

MAINTAINING A DRAINAGE SYSTEM

A drainage system is designed to carry dirty water and WC waste from the various appliances to underground drains leading to the main sewer. The different branches of the waste system are protected by 'U' bend traps full of water to stop drain smells fouling the house. Depending on the age of your house, it will have a two-pipe system or a single stack. Because the two-pipe system has been in use for very much longer, it is still the more common of the two. Use similar methods to maintain either system.

Two-pipe system

The wastepipes of older houses are divided into two separate systems. WC waste is fed into a large diameter, vertical soil pipe which leads directly to the underground drains. To discharge drain gases at a safe height, and to make sure that back-siphoning cannot empty the WC traps, the soil pipe is vented to the open air above the guttering.

Individual branch pipes, leading from upstairs wash basins and baths, drain into an open hopper which funnels the water into another vertical wastepipe. Instead of feeding directly into the underground drains, this wastepipe terminates over a yard gully – another trap covered by a grid. A separate wastepipe from the kitchen sink normally drains into the same gully.

The yard gully and soil pipe discharge into an underground inspection chamber, or manhole. These chambers provide access to the main drains for clearing blockages, and you will find one wherever the drain changes direction on its way to the sewer. At the last inspection chamber, just before the drain enters the sewer, there is an interceptor trap, the final barrier to drain gases, and in this case, sewer rats.

Single stack system

Since the 1960s, most houses have been drained using a single stack system. Waste from basins, baths and WCs is fed into the same vertical soil pipe or stack, which, unlike the two-pipe system, is often built inside the house. A single stack system must be designed carefully to prevent a heavy discharge of waste from one appliance siphoning the trap of another, and to avoid the possibility of WC waste blocking other branch pipes. The vent pipe of the stack terminates above the roof and is capped with an open cage to prevent birds sealing the pipe by nesting in it.

The kitchen sink can be drained through the same stack but it is still common practice to drain sink waste into a yard gully. Nowadays, wastepipes must pass through the grid, stopping short of the water in the gully trap so that even when the grid becomes blocked with leaves, the waste can discharge unobstructed into the gully. Alternatively, it will be a back-inlet gully with the waste pipe entering below ground level.

A downstairs WC is sometimes drained through its own branch drain to an inspection chamber.

RESPONSIBILITY FOR THE DRAINS

Where a house is drained individually, the whole system up to where it joins the sewer is the responsibility of the householder. Where a house is connected to a communal drainage system linking several houses, the arrangement for maintenance, including the clearance of blockages, is not so straightforward.

If the drains were constructed prior to 1937, the local council is responsible for cleansing but can reclaim the cost of repairing any part of the communal system from the householders. After that date, the entire responsibility falls upon the householders collectively, so that they are required to share the cost of both repair and cleansing of the drains up to the sewer, no matter where the problem occurs. Contact the Environmental Health Officer of your local council to find out who is responsible for your drains.

SEE ALSO

Details for: ▷	
Plumbing systems	339
Yard gully	349
Blocked soil pipe	349
Blocked drains	350

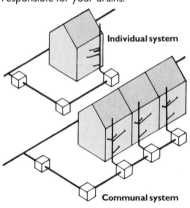

Individual system

Communal system

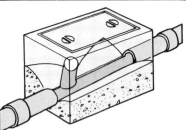

An inspection chamber where drains branch

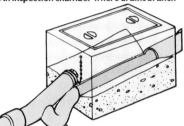

A chamber with interceptor trap

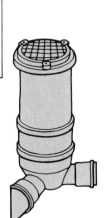

Pre-fabricated chamber
The inspection chambers of a modern drainage system may be cylindrical pre-fabricated units. There may not be an interceptor trap in the chamber before the sewer.

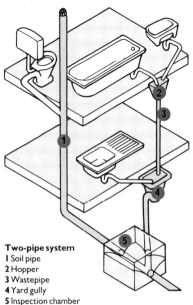

Two-pipe system
1 Soil pipe
2 Hopper
3 Wastepipe
4 Yard gully
5 Inspection chamber

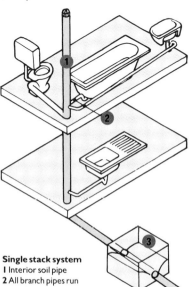

Single stack system
1 Interior soil pipe
2 All branch pipes run to stack
3 Inspection chamber

CLEARING A BLOCKED WASTE SYSTEM

SEE ALSO

◁ Details for:

Drain auger	486
Frozen pipes	341
Plungers	486

Don't ignore the early signs of an imminent blockage of the wastepipe from a sink, bath or basin. If the water drains away slowly, use a chemical cleaner to remove a partial blockage before you are faced with clearing a serious obstruction. If a wastepipe blocks without warning, try a series of measures to locate and clear the obstruction.

Cleansing the wastepipe

Grease, hair and particles of kitchen debris build up gradually within the traps and wastepipes. Regular cleaning with a proprietary chemical drain cleaner will keep the waste system clear and sweet smelling.

If water drains sluggishly, use a cleaner immediately, following the manufacturer's instructions with particular regard to safety. Always wear protective gloves when handling chemical cleaners and keep them out of the reach of children.

If unpleasant odours linger after you have cleaned the waste, pour a little disinfectant into the basin overflow.

USING COMPRESSED AIR TO CLEAR A SINK

Clear a blocked waste with compressed air using a simple hand operated tool. Three strokes of the hand pump builds a low pressure which will clear most blockages without blowing apart push-fit joints. Place the rubber nozzle of the tool into the waste outlet and squeeze the trigger. If the blockage persists, increase the pressure gradually.

Using a compressed air gun
The tool is supplied with a range of soft adaptor nozzles to fit different sizes of sink plug. Press the nozzle into the waste and squeeze the trigger to clear a blockage.

Using a plunger

If a basin fails to empty while others are functioning normally, the blockage must be somewhere along its individual branch pipe. Before you attempt to locate the blockage, try forcing it out of the pipe with a sink plunger. Smear the rim of the rubber cap with petroleum jelly, then lower it into the blocked basin to cover the waste outlet. Make sure there is enough water in the basin to cover the cup. Hold a wet cloth in the overflow with one hand while you pump the handle of the plunger up and down a few times. The waste may not clear immediately if the blockage is merely forced further along the pipe, so repeat the process until the water drains away. If it will not clear after several attempts, try clearing the trap, or use compressed air to clear the pipe (See left).

Clearing the trap

The trap, situated immediately below the waste outlet of a sink or basin, is basically a bent tube designed to hold water to seal out drain odours. Traps become blocked when debris collects at the lowest point of the bend. Place a bucket under the basin to catch the water then use a wrench to release the cleaning eye at the base of a standard trap. Alternatively, remove the large access cap on a bottle trap by hand. If there is no provision for gaining access to the trap, unscrew the connecting nuts and remove the entire trap. (Take the opportunity to scrub it out with detergent before replacing it.)

Let the contents of the trap drain into the bucket, then bend a hook on the end of a length of wire to probe the section of wastepipe beyond the trap. If the pipe is clear but the blockage is still intact, it must be in the branch running to the soil stack or outside to the hopper and vertical wastepipe.

Cleaning the branch pipe

Quite often, a vertical pipe from the trap joins a virtually horizontal section of the wastepipe. There should be an access plug built into the joint so that you can clear the horizontal pipe. Have a bowl ready to collect any trapped water then unscrew the plug by hand. Use a length of hooked wire to probe the branch pipe. If you locate a blockage which seems very firm, rent a drain auger (◁) from a tool hire company to clear the pipework.

If there is no access plug, remove the trap and probe the pipe with an auger. If the wastepipe is constructed with push-fit joints, you can dismantle it.

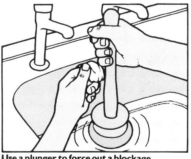
Use a plunger to force out a blockage

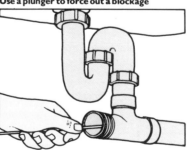
Use hooked wire to probe a branch pipe

Unscrew the access cap on a bottle trap

Tubular trap
If the access cap to the cleaning eye is stiff, remove it with a wrench.

Bottle trap
A bottle trap can be cleared easily because the whole base unscrews by hand.

CLEARING A STACK OR GULLY

If several fittings are draining poorly the vertical stack itself is probably obstructed. The hopper and downpipe as well as the yard gully are frequently blocked with leaves in the autumn. It may not be obvious when you empty a hand basin, but the contents of a bath will almost certainly cause the hopper or gully to overflow. Clear the blockage urgently to avoid penetrating damp (▷).

Cleaning out the hopper and drainpipe

Wearing protective gloves, scoop out the debris from the hopper then gently probe the drainpipe with a cane to check that it is free. Clear the bottom end of the pipe with a piece of bent wire. If an old cast iron wastepipe has been replaced with a modern plastic type, you may find cleaning eyes or access plugs at strategic points for clearing a blockage.

While you are on the ladder, scrub the inside of the hopper and disinfect it to prevent stale odours entering a nearby bathroom.

Unblocking a yard gully

Unless you decide to hire an auger, there is little option but to clear a blocked gully by hand, but by the time it overflows, the water in the gully will be quite deep so try bailing some of it out with a small disposable container. Wearing rubber gloves, scoop out the debris from the trap until the remaining water disperses.

Rinse the gully with a hose and cleanse it with disinfectant. Scrub the grid as clean as possible or alternatively, burn off accumulated grime from a metal grid with a gas torch (▷).

If a flooded gully appears to be clear, and yet the water will not drain away, try to locate the blockage at the nearest inspection chamber (▷).

Bail out the water then clear a gully by hand

Unblocking the soil pipe

Unblocking the soil pipe is an unpleasant job and it's worth hiring a professional cleaning company, especially if the pipe is made of cast iron because it will almost certainly have to be cleared via the vent above the roof.

You can clean a modern plastic stack yourself because there should be a large hinged cleaning eye or other access plugs wherever the branch pipes join the stack. If the stack is inside the house, lay large polythene sheets on the floor and be prepared to mop up trapped sewage when it spills from the pipe.

Unscrew and open the cleaning eye to insert a hired drain auger. Pass the auger into the stack until you locate the obstruction then crank the handle to engage it. Push or pull the auger until you can dislodge the obstruction to clear the trapped water, then hose out the stack. Wash and disinfect the surrounding area.

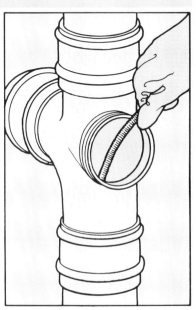
Use a hired auger to clear a soil stack

Unblocking a WC pan

If the water in a WC pan rises when you flush it, there is a blockage in the vicinity of the trap. A partial blockage allows the water level to fall slowly.

Hire a larger version of the sink plunger to force the obstruction into the soil pipe. Position the rubber cap of the plunger well down into the 'U' bend and pump the handle several times. When the blockage clears, the water level will drop suddenly accompanied by an audible gurgling.

If the trap is blocked solidly, hire a special WC auger. Pass the flexible clearing rod as far as possible into the trap, then crank the handle to dislodge the blockage. Wash the auger in hot water and disinfect it before returning the tool to the hire company.

SEE ALSO

Details for: ▷	
Penetrating damp	251
Inspection chambers	350
Gas torch	488
Guttering	234
Drain auger	486
WC plunger	486
WC auger	486

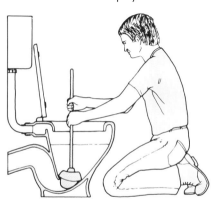
Use a special plunger to pump a blocked WC

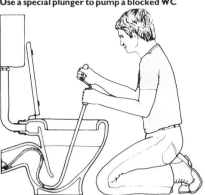
Alternatively, clear it with a WC auger

RODDING THE DRAINS

SEE ALSO

◁ Details for:
Inspection chambers   347
Drain rods   486

The first sign of a blocked underground drain could be an unpleasant smell from an inspection chamber, but a severe blockage can cause sewage to back up until it begins to overflow from a gully or from beneath the cover of an inspection chamber. Hire a set of drain rods – short, flexible components made of plastic, cane or wire, screwed end to end – to clear a blocked drain. Metal screws or a rubber plunger are threaded onto the rods.

Locating the blockage

Lift the cover from the inspection chamber nearest the house. If it is stuck firmly, or the handles have rusted away, scrape the dirt from around its edges and prise it up with a garden spade.

● If the chamber contains water, check the one nearer the road or boundary. If that chamber is dry, the blockage is between the two chambers.
● If the chamber nearest the road is full, the blockage will be in the interceptor trap or in the pipe beyond leading to the sewer.
● If both chambers are dry and yet either a yard gully or downstairs WC will not empty, check for blockages in the branch drains joining the first inspection chamber.

Rodding points
A modern drainage system could be fitted with rodding points to provide access to the drain. They are sealed with small oval or circular covers.

Rodding a drain

Screw two or three rods together and attach a corkscrew fitting to the end. Insert the rods into the drain at the bottom of the inspection chamber in the direction of the suspected blockage. If the chamber is full of water, use the end of a rod to locate an open channel running across the floor, leading to the mouth of the drain.

As you pass the rods along the drain, attach further lengths until you reach the obstruction, then twist the rods clockwise to engage the screw. (Never twist the rods anti-clockwise or they will become detached.) Pull and push the obstruction until it breaks up, allowing the water to flow away. Extract the rods, flush the chamber with a hose and replace the lid.

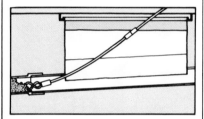
Use a corkscrew fitting to clear a drain

Clearing an interceptor trap

Screw a rubber plunger to the end of a short length of rods and locate the channel leading to the base of the trap. Push the plunger into the opening of the trap, then pump the rods a few times to expel the blockage.

If the water level does not drop after several attempts, try clearing the drain leading to the sewer. Access to this drain is through a cleaning eye above the trap. It will be sealed with a stopper which you will have to dislodge with a drain rod unless it is attached to a chain stapled to the chamber wall. Make sure the stopper doesn't fall into the channel and block the interceptor trap. Rod the drain to the sewer using the corkscrew fitting then hose out the chamber before replacing the stopper and cover.

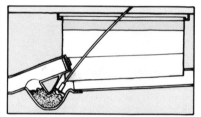
Fit a plunger to rod an interceptor trap

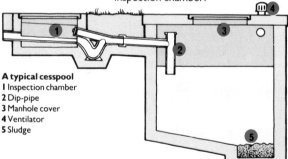

A typical cesspool
1 Inspection chamber
2 Dip-pipe
3 Manhole cover
4 Ventilator
5 Sludge

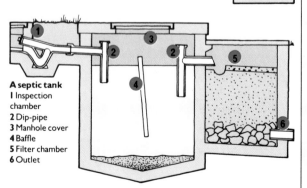

A septic tank
1 Inspection chamber
2 Dip-pipe
3 Manhole cover
4 Baffle
5 Filter chamber
6 Outlet

CESSPOOLS AND SEPTIC TANKS

Houses built in the country or on the outskirts of a town are not always connected to a public sewer. Instead, waste is drained into a cesspool or septic tank. A cesspool is simply a collection point for sewage until it can be pumped out by the local council. A septic tank is a complete waste disposal system in which sewage is broken down by bacterial action before the water is discharged into a local waterway or distributed underground.

Cesspools
Current building regulations stipulate that cesspools should have a minimum capacity of 18 cu m (4,000 gallons) but many existing cesspools accommodate far less, and require emptying perhaps once every two weeks. It would be worth checking on the capacity of a cesspool before you buy a country home to ensure it will cope with your needs. Water authorities estimate the disposal of approximately 115 litres (25 gallons) per person per day.

Most cesspools are cylindrical pits lined with brick or concrete. Modern ones are sometimes prefabricated in glass-reinforced plastic. Access is via a manhole cover.

Septic tanks
The sewage in a septic tank separates slowly, heavy sludge falling to the bottom leaving relatively clear water with a layer of scum floating on the surface. A dip-pipe discharges waste below the surface so that incoming water does not stir up the sewage. Bacterial action takes a minimum of 24 hours so the tank is divided into chambers by baffles to slow down the movement of sewage through the tank.

The partly treated waste passes out of the tank through another dip-pipe into some form of filtration system which allows further bacterial action to take place. It may be another chamber containing a deep filter bed or alternatively, the waste may flow underground through a network of drains which disperses the water over a wide area to filter through the soil.

INSTALLING PIPES

TYPES OF METAL PLUMBING

The ability to install a run of pipework, make watertight joints and connect up to fittings are the basic requirements of plumbing. Without those skills, a householder is restricted to simple maintenance. When lead piping was universal, plumbing was a trade requiring years of experience, but modern materials and technology has made it possible for anybody who is prepared to master a few techniques to upgrade and extend household plumbing without having to hire a professional.

Metric and imperial pipes

Copper and stainless steel pipes are now made in metric sizes whereas a lot of pipework already installed in a house will be of the old imperial measurements. If you compare the equivalent dimensions; 15mm – ½in, 22mm – ¾in, and 28mm – 1in; the difference seems obvious, but metric pipe is measured externally while imperial pipe is measured internally. In fact, the difference is very small, but enough to cause some problems when joining one type of pipe to the other.

An exact fit is essential when making soldered joints so imperial to metric adaptors are used for all sizes of pipe. Adaptors are not necessary when joining 15mm and 28mm pipes to their imperial equivalents with compression joints but you will have to use them for joining 22mm to ¾in pipes.

Use 22mm pipes for the main runs and 15mm for most branch pipes. 28mm pipe is for the primary flow and return pipes connected to a boiler (▷).

Electro-chemical action

If you live in a soft water area, take care when joining copper to galvanized steel (iron) pipes or storage tanks. The two metals in combination with a weak acidic solution produce the conditions of an electric cell which gradually dissolve the zinc coating on the steel.

Brass can corrode in a similar way due to the zinc content of the metal. Use corrosion-resistant brass or gunmetal fittings and special copper to steel connectors where these conditions are likely to occur. Check with your water authority for advice.

Over the years, most household plumbing systems have undergone some form of improvement or alteration. As a result you may find any of a number of metals used, perhaps in combination, depending on the availability of materials at the time it was installed, or the preference of an individual plumber.

COPPER

Half-hard tempered copper tubing is by far the most widely used material for pipework. It is lightweight, solders well and can be bent easily, even by hand with the aid of a bending spring. It is used for both hot and cold water supply as well as central heating systems. Invariably, three sizes of pipe are used for general domestic plumbing: 15mm (½in), 22mm (¾in) and 28mm (1in).

STAINLESS STEEL

Stainless steel tubing is not as common as copper but is available in the same sizes. You may have to order it from a plumbers' merchant. Stainless steel offers few advantages to a DIY plumber. It is harder than copper so cannot be bent as easily and it is difficult to solder. For both reasons, use compression joints to connect stainless steel pipes, but tighten them slightly more than you would when joining copper. Alternatively, use a special adhesive (▷). However, stainless steel does not react adversely with galvanized steel (iron) pipes which may have been installed previously. (See electro-chemical action, left)

LEAD

Lead is never used for new plumbing but thousands of houses still have a lead rising main connected to a modernized system. This is perfectly acceptable, but extensive lead plumbing still in use must be nearing the end of its useful life so replace it whenever the opportunity arises. When drinking water lies in a lead pipe for some time, it absorbs toxins from the metal. If you have a lead pipe supplying your drinking water, always run off a little water before you use any.

GALVANIZED STEEL (IRON)

Galvanized steel was used to provide strong pipework where lead might easily have been damaged. It can still be obtained but there is no longer any point in using it for general plumbing especially as the ends of straight lengths have to be threaded before you can make a joint. Take care when joining copper to existing galvanized steel pipes. (See electro-chemical action, left)

CAST IRON

All old soil pipes are made of cast iron but the metal is very prone to rusting. In fact it is only the relatively thick walls of the pipes that have preserved them for so long. Should you need to replace one, ask for one of the plastic alternatives.

BRASS

Because it machines and casts so well, brass is used to make compression joints, taps, stopcocks and other fittings. Corrosion-resistant brass is used to avoid electro-chemical action between zinc content of brass and copper pipes.

GUNMETAL

Gunmetal connectors are manufactured for joining copper pipework to galvanized steel where standard brass fittings would be corroded.

SEE ALSO

Details for: ▷	
Flow and return	380
Adhesives	495-496
Soldered joints	353
Soft water	378
Bending springs	488

METAL PIPE JOINTS

As most domestic plumbing is carried out in copper, the methods described on the next few pages are primarily for joining copper pipes. You can use the same techniques for stainless steel plumbing but, because it is harder than copper, you will find it easier to cut the metal with a hacksaw and use an active flux for soldering joints. Join copper to galvanized steel or plastic plumbing with specially designed couplings.

SEE ALSO

◁ Details for:
Metal plumbing	351
Soldering	488
Flaring tools	489

Compression & capillary joints

It would be impossible to make strong, watertight joints by simply soldering two lengths of copper pipe end to end. Instead, plumbers use capillary or compression joints.

Capillary joints

Capillary joints are made to fit snugly over the ends of the pipe. The very small space between the pipe and sleeve is filled with molten solder which solidifies on cooling to hold the joint together and make it watertight. Capillary joints are neat and inexpensive but, because you need to heat the metal with a blow torch, there is a slight risk of fire when working in confined spaces under floors and in the loft.

Compression joints

Compression joints are very easy to use but are more expensive than capillary joints. They are also more obtrusive, and you will find it impossible to manoeuvre a wrench where space is restricted. When the cap-nut is tightened with a wrench, it compresses a ring of soft metal, known as an olive, to fill the joint between fitting and pipe.

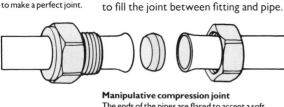

Capillary joints
Solder is introduced to the mouth of the assembled end-feed joint (top) and flows by capillary action into the fitting. The ring pressed into the sleeves of an integral ring fitting (above) contains the exact amount of solder to make a perfect joint.

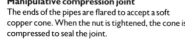

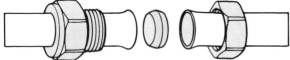

Manipulative compression joint
The ends of the pipes are flared to accept a soft copper cone. When the nut is tightened, the cone is compressed to seal the joint.

Non-manipulative compression joint
This is the simplest and most widely used compression joint. The end of each pipe is cut square before the joint is assembled.

METAL JOINTS AND FITTINGS

Capillary and compression joints are made to connect pipes at different angles and in various combinations. There are adaptors for joining metric and imperial pipes and for connecting one material to another. You will have to consult manufacturers' catalogues to see every variation, but the examples below illustrate a range of typical joints and fittings.

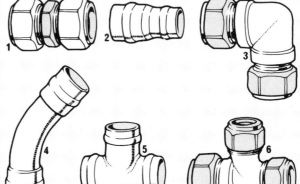

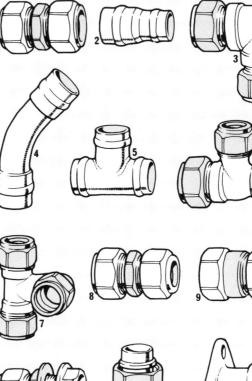

Straight connectors
To join two pipes end to end in a straight line.
1 For pipes of equal diameter – *compression joint*
2 Reducer to connect 22mm (¾in) and 15mm (½in) pipes – *capillary joint*

Bends or elbows
To join two pipes at 90 degrees or 45 degrees.
3 90 degree elbow – *compression joint*
4 45 degree elbow – *capillary joint*

Tees
To join three pipes.
5 Equal tee to join three pipes of the same diameter – *capillary joint*
6 Unequal tee to reduce size of pipe run and join a branch pipe – *compression joint*
7 Off-set tee joins branch pipe to one side of main pipe run – *compression joint*

Adaptors
To join dissimilar pipes.
8 Straight coupling to join 22mm and ¾in pipes – *compression joint*
9 Copper to galvanized steel connector – *compression joint* for copper, *threaded female coupling* for steel

Fittings
Identical jointing systems are used to connect fittings.
10 Tank connector joins pipes to cisterns – *compresson joint*
11 Tap connector with threaded nut for connecting supply pipe to tap – *capillary joint*
12 Bib tap wall plate for fixing tap on outside wall – *compression joint* for supply pipe, *threaded female connector* for tap
13 Bib tap has threaded tail to fit wall plate
14 Gate valve to fit in straight pipe run – *compression joint*
15 Drain cock to empty a pipe run – *compression joint*

MAKING SOLDERED JOINTS

Soldering pipe joints is very simple once you have had a little practice. The fittings are relatively cheap so try out the techniques before you install actual pipework. Your basic equipment is a gas torch to apply heat, some flux to clean the metal and solder to make the joint.

CUTTING METAL PIPE

Calculate the length of pipe you need, allowing enough to fit into the sleeve of the joint at each end. Whatever type of joint you use, it is essential to cut the end of every length of pipe square.

To ensure a perfectly square cut each time, use a tube cutter. Align the cutting wheel with your mark, and adjust the handle of the tool to clamp the rollers against the pipe (1). Rotate the tool around the pipe, adjusting the handle after each revolution to make the cutter bite deeper into the metal.

Use the pointed reamer on the end of the tool to clean the burr from inside the cut pipe (2). A tube cutter makes a clean cut on the outside of the pipe automatically.

If you want to use a hacksaw, make sure the cut is square by wrapping a piece of paper with a straight edge around the pipe. Align the wrapped edge and use it to guide the saw blade (3). Remove the burr, inside and out, with a file.

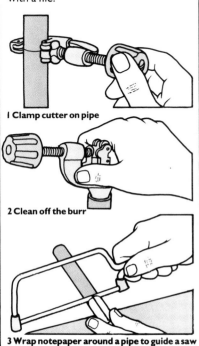

1 Clamp cutter on pipe

2 Clean off the burr

3 Wrap notepaper around a pipe to guide a saw

Gas torches

To heat the metal sufficiently to make a good soldered joint, most plumbers use a gas torch. Gas, liquefied under pressure, is contained in a disposable metal canister. When the control valve of the torch is opened, gas is vapourized to combine with air to make a highly combustible mixture. Once ignited, the flame is adjusted until it burns with a clear, blue colour.

Many professional plumbers use a propane torch connected by a hose to a metal gas bottle. The average householder does not need such expensive equipment, but if you happen to own a propane torch, perhaps for car repairs, you can use the same tool to solder plumbing joints.

Using integral ring joints

Clean the ends of each pipe and the inside of the joint sleeves with wire wool or abrasive paper until the metal is shiny. Brush flux onto the cleaned metal and push the pipes into the joint, twisting them to spread the flux evenly. Make sure each pipe is up against the integral stop in the joint. Wipe off excess flux with a cloth.

If you are using elbows or tees, mark the pipe and joint with a pencil to make sure they do not get misaligned during the soldering.

Slip a ceramic tile or plumbers' fibreglass mat behind the joint to protect any flammable materials, then apply the flame of a gas torch over the area of the joint to heat it evenly (1).

Using end-feed joints

Clean and assemble an end-feed joint like an integral ring type, then heat the area of the joint evenly. When the flux begins to bubble, remove the flame and touch the end of the solder wire to two

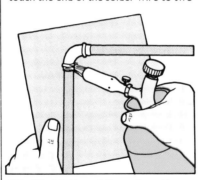

1 Heat the joint to melt the captive solder

Solder and flux

Solder is a soft alloy of tin and lead manufactured with a melting point lower than that of the metal it is joining. Plumbers' solder is sold as wound wire.

Copper must be spotlessly clean and grease-free to produce a properly soldered joint. Even when you have cleaned it mechanically with wire wool, copper begins to oxidize immediately, so a chemical cleaner known as flux is painted onto the metal to provide a barrier against oxidation until the solder is applied. A non-corrosive flux in the form of a paste is the best one to use, but for stainless steel use a highly efficient active flux but wash it off with warm water after the joint is made or the metal will corrode.

When a bright ring of solder appears at each end of the joint, remove the flame and allow the metal to cool for a couple of minutes before disturbing it.

Repairing a weeping joint
When you fill a new installation with water for the first time, check every joint to make sure it is watertight. If you notice water 'weeping' from a soldered joint, drain the pipe and allow it to dry. Heat the joint and apply some fresh solder to the edge of each mouth. If it leaks a second time, heat the joint until you can pull it apart with gloved hands. Use a new joint, or clean and flux all surfaces and reuse the same joint as an end-feed fitting.

or three points around the mouth of each sleeve (2). You will know that the joint is full of solder when a bright ring appears around each sleeve. Allow it to cool. Mend a weeping joint as above.

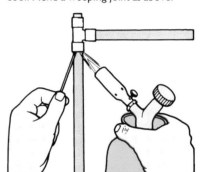

2 Introduce solder to a heated end-feed joint

SEE ALSO

Details for: ▷	
Pipe fittings	352
Tube cutter	487
Junior hacksaw	487
Cleaning metal	491

Gas torches
A gas torch is used to heat soldered joints. A simple torch (top) is available from any DIY outlet. The propane torch (above) is used by professional plumbers.

353

MAKING COMPRESSION JOINTS

MAKING COPPER TO STEEL CONNECTIONS

SEE ALSO

◁ Details for:
Plumbing adaptors	352
Flaring tools	489
Wrenches	490

Using non-manipulative joints is so straightforward that you will be able to make watertight joints without any previous experience. There is no advantage in using a manipulative joint unless it will be under tension.

Using non-manipulative joints

Cut the ends of each pipe square and clean them, along with the olives, with wire wool. Dismantle the joint and slip a cap-nut onto a pipe followed by an olive (**1**). Look carefully to see if the sloping sides of the olive are equal in length. If one is longer than the other, that side should face away from the nut.

Push the pipe firmly into the joint body (**2**), twisting it slightly to ensure it is firmly against the integral stop. Slide the olive up to the body then hand tighten the nut.

The olive must be compressed the right amount to ensure a watertight joint. As a guide, use a pencil to mark one face of the nut and the opposing face on the joint body then, holding the body steady with a spanner, use another to turn the nut one complete revolution (**3**). Assemble the other half of the joint in the same way.

To make absolutely sure the joint is watertight, some plumbers prefer to smear a little jointing compound onto the olive before tightening the nut, but a properly tightened compression joint should be watertight without it.

Repairing a weeping joint

Having filled the pipe with water, check each joint for leaks. Make one further quarter turn on any nut that appears to be weeping.

Crushing an olive by overtightening a compression joint will cause it to leak. Drain the pipe and dismantle the joint. Cut through the damaged olive with a junior hacksaw taking care not to damage the pipe. Remake the joint with a new olive, restore the supply of water and check for leaks once more.

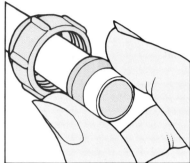

1 Slip an olive onto the pipe after a cap-nut

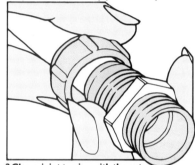

2 Clamp joint to pipe with the nut

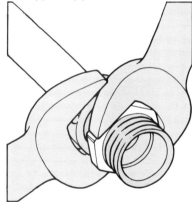

3 Tighten the joint with two spanners

Using manipulative joints

Whatever type of manipulative compression joint you use, the ends of the tubing must be shaped (manipulated) to fit the joint. There are special flaring tools to produce the effect, or drive a steel drift into the end of the pipe. Follow the manufacturer's instructions for individual joints, but the following example demonstrates the principle.

Having cut and cleaned the pipes, slip the cap-nut onto one tube and the joint body onto the other. Insert the drift into one pipe and strike it with a hammer until the cone of the drift flares the pipe (**1**). Flare the other pipe in the same way. Sandwich a copper compression ring or 'cone' between the flared pipes and smear the area with jointing compound. Hand-tighten the cap-nut then use two spanners to complete the joint.

Galvanized steel pipe is connected by threaded joints so if you plan to extend old pipework using the same material, you will need a pipe die to cut the threads on the end of each length of new pipe. You can hire the tool but it would be simpler to continue the run in copper using an adaptor to connect one system to another. One end of the adaptor has a capillary or compression joint for the copper pipework. The other end has a male or female threaded connector for the galvanized steel.

Use two stilson wrenches to unscrew the joint on the old pipework where you intend to connect up to copper. Grip the joint with one wrench and the pipe with the other, pushing and pulling in the direction the jaws face (**1**). If the joint is stiff, use penetrating oil or play the flame of a gas torch along it.

Threaded connections leak unless they are made watertight with plumbers' hemp or PTFE tape. To use hemp, smear some jointing compound (a waterproofing paste sold by plumbers' merchants) around the male thread. Tease out a short length of hemp and wrap it clockwise around the thread. Leave about one third of the thread free at the end of the pipe to engage the connector accurately before it encounters the hemp (**2**). Tighten the joint with a spanner.

PTFE tape is bound over the threads instead of the hemp. No jointing compound is required. Wrap the tape clockwise two or three times around the pipe (**3**), engage and tighten the nut.

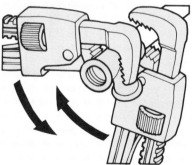

1 Unscrew a joint with two stilson wrenches

2 Wrap with hemp

3 Or use PTFE tape

1 Manipulative joint
Flare the pipe by driving a metal drift into one end.

MAKING COPPER TO LEAD CONNECTIONS

When lead plumbing is replaced with copper, the new pipework is usually connected to a short section of the original lead rising main. This is now the only time when a lead to copper joint is required, and it occurs so infrequently that it makes sense to hire a professional to make the rather specialized joint.

The joint is achieved by soldering a short length of copper pipe, to which the new rising main will be connected, into the end of the lead pipe. The lead is flared by driving a hardwood cone into it or by inserting a metal rod in the end and revolving it to force the edge of the pipe outwards (1).

A chamfer is filed around the jointing edge of the copper pipe then the tube is cleaned with wire wool. The lead is scraped, inside and out, back to clean, shiny metal.

To prevent the solder sticking to either metal outside the area of the joint, first chalk then 'plumbers' black' is applied to each pipe about 35mm (1½in) away from the joint (2).

The copper is tinned with solder before it is inserted into the pipe, then a length of dowel is passed through both tubes to align them. A nail driven through the wood stops the dowel falling into the pipe.

Heat is applied to the area of the joint with a gas torch, then tallow is smeared over the joint itself. A heavy stick of solder, composed of 2 parts lead: 1 part tin, is applied to the hot metal, and built up to a generous thickness, filling the flared end of the lead pipe (3). The soft solder is smoothed by hand with a tallow-soaked felt pad known as a 'mole' (4).

1 Flare the lead

2 Apply plumbers' black

3 Melt stick of solder

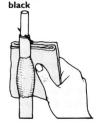
4 Smooth with a mole

BENDING PIPES

You can change the direction of a pipe run by using an elbow joint but there are occasions when bending the pipe itself will produce a neater or more accurate result. If you want to carry a pipe over a small obstruction, like another pipe for instance, a slight kink in the pipe will be less of an obstruction to the flow of water than two joints within a few centimetres of each other. It is also cheaper. You might want to run pipes into a window alcove where the walls meet at an unusual angle. Bending the pipes accurately will allow you to fit the pipes neatly against the walls of the alcove.

Using a bending spring

A bending spring is the cheapest and easiest tool for making bends in small pipe runs. It is a hardened steel coil spring which supports the walls of copper tube to stop it kinking. Most bending springs are made to fit inside the pipe but some slide over the tube.

Slide the spring into the tube to support the area you want to bend. Hold the tube against your knee and bend it to the required angle (1).

A bent tube grips the spring but if you slip a screwdriver into the ring at one end and twist it anti-clockwise, it reduces the diameter of the spring so that you can pull it out. If you make a bend some distance from the end of a tube, you can't withdraw the bending spring in the normal way. Either use an external spring, or tie a length of twine to the ring and lightly grease the spring with petroleum jelly before you insert it. Slightly overbend the tube and open it out to the correct angle to release the spring, then pull it out with the twine.

Using a pipe bender

Although you can hire bending springs to fit the larger pipes, it isn't easy to bend 22mm or 28mm (¾ or 1in) tube over your knee. It is well worth hiring a pipe bender.

Hold the pipe against the radiused former and insert the straight former to support it. Pull both levers towards each other to make the bend, then open up the bender to remove the pipe.

Getting the bends in the right place

To make sure a bend is in the right place along a pipe, bend the tube before you cut it to length.

It is difficult to position more than two bends along one length of pipe. If you want to fit an alcove for instance, bend two tubes, one to fit each side, then cut the tubes where they overlap and insert a joint.

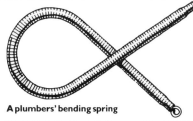
A plumbers' bending spring

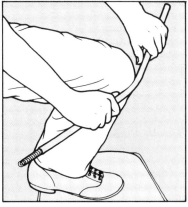
1 Bend the pipe against your knee

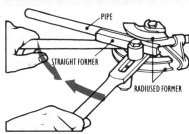
Use a pipe bender for larger tubing

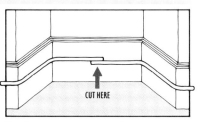
Bend two separate tubes to fit an alcove

SEE ALSO

Details for: ▷
External spring   488
Tube bender   488

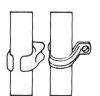
Supporting pipe runs
Place a plastic or metal clip every metre (yard) along a horizontal run of 15mm (½in) pipe, but increase the spacing to every 1.5m (4ft 6in) on a vertical run. For larger pipes, increase the spacing a little more.

Notching floorboards
When you run pipes under floorboards, notch each joist to receive the pipe. Cut the notch to align with the centre of a floorboard and drive a nail on each side when replacing the board.

PLASTIC PLUMBING

SEE ALSO

◁ Details for:

Solvent joints	358
Push-fit joints	358-359

The introduction of plastics is probably the most innovative development in plumbing since copper was first used. Plastic plumbing is cheap, lightweight and extremely easy to construct. It does not freeze, corrode or adversely affect other materials, and depending on the type of plastic, it can be used for hot and cold water including central heating pipework. It is already used universally for waste systems and is becoming increasingly popular for supply pipes.

Being a comparatively recent development, plastic plumbing is not yet standardized. As a result, it is advisable to use one manufacturer's range of equipment and materials to ensure that every component is compatible.

Some plastics are still being tested by water authorities, and may not be officially approved for certain applications. Use manufacturers' catalogues as a guide or seek the advice of your supplier.

Most plastic systems can be connected to existing metal pipe with special adaptors.

Plastic pipe: standard sizes

Plastic pipes are made to more or less standard sizes, but there may be slight variation from one manufacturer's stock to another. As with metal pipework, most metric dimensions refer to the outside diameter of the tube and imperial dimensions to the inside, but not all manufacturers specify their pipes in the same way. Check that pipes and fittings are compatible with existing plumbing before you buy them. The following list is a guide to the available sizes of plastic pipe.

PLASTIC PIPEWORK	
General pipework	15mm (½in); 22mm (¾in); 28mm (1in)
Overflow pipes	21mm (¾in)
Wash basin waste pipes	36mm (1¼in)
Bath/sink waste pipes	43mm (1½in)
Soil pipe	100mm (4in)

PLASTIC JOINTS AND FITTINGS

Most plastic joints and fittings are similar to those used for metal plumbing but in addition, there are easy-flow bends and tees for drainage systems. These joints frequently have cleaning eyes or access plugs for removing blockages in the pipe. Joints and pipes are normally made from the same material, but there are several specialized connectors with metal couplings for joining plastic plumbing to taps, valves and existing metal plumbing.

You will have to browse through different manufacturers' catalogues to see the huge variety of plastic joints for both supply and waste systems, but the selection illustrated below shows the main categories of joint with examples of the different types of coupling.

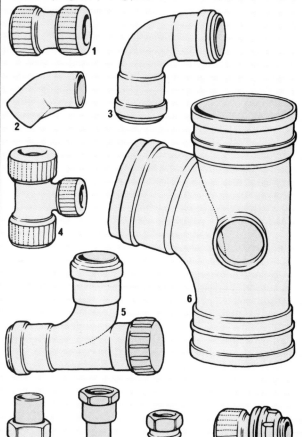

Straight connectors
To join two pipes end to end in a straight line.
1 For pipes of equal diameter – *push-fit:* supply

Bends or elbows
To join two pipes at an angle.
2 45 degree elbow – *solvent weld:* supply
3 Easy-flow bend – *push-fit:* waste

Tees
To join three pipes.
4 Unequal tee to join 15mm (½in) branch pipe to main pipe run – *push-fit:* supply
5 Swept tee with access plug – *push-fit:* waste
6 Branch tee to WC – *solvent weld:* soil pipe

Adaptors
To join dissimilar pipes.
7 Plastic to copper connector – *solvent weld* and *compression joint:* supply
8 Plastic to galvanized steel connector – *push-fit* and *threaded female coupling:* supply

Fittings
Specialized connections are available to join plastic plumbing to fittings. Each manufacturer will supply items like taps and valves to match their particular range.
9 Tap connector with threaded nut for connecting supply pipe to tail of tap – *solvent weld:* supply
10 Tank connector joins pipes to storage cisterns – *push-fit:* supply
11 Stop cock – *push-fit:* supply
12 Sink trap – *compression joint:* waste

JOINING PLASTIC PIPES

Plastics are complex materials, each with its own properties. A technique or material that is suitable for joining one plastic might be quite useless for another. To make sure joints are watertight, it is important to follow each manufacturer's instructions carefully, and to use the solvents and lubricants they recommend. The following examples illustrate the common methods used to connect plastic plumbing.

Solvent weld joints

Lengths of pipe are linked by simple socketed connectors. As they are assembled, a solvent is introduced to the joint which dissolves the surfaces of the mating components. As the solvent evaporates, the joint and pipes are literally fused together into one piece of plastic. Solvent weld joints are used for supply and waste pipes.

Push-fit joints – waste systems

Because a waste system is never under pressure, a pipe run can be constructed by simply pushing plain pipes into the sockets of the joints. A captive rubber seal in each socket holds the pipe in place and makes the joint watertight.

Push-fit joints – supply systems

Polybutylene pipes are connected with a unique push-fit joint. When the pipe is inserted, an 'O' ring seals in the water in the normal way, but a metal grab ring behind the seal has one-way barbed teeth to prevent the pipe being pulled out again. The joints can be dismantled, but only by removing the retaining cap and crushing the grab ring. The joints are more obtrusive than welded types but the speed and simplicity with which you can assemble them more than compensates.

Compression joints

So that they can be dismantled easily, sink, bath and basin traps are often connected to the pipework by compression joints incorporating a rubber ring or washer to make the joint watertight.

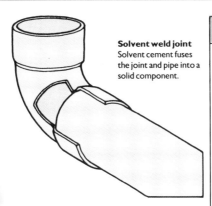

Solvent weld joint
Solvent cement fuses the joint and pipe into a solid component.

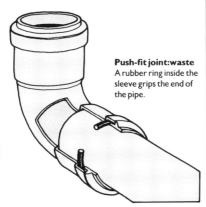

Push-fit joint: waste
A rubber ring inside the sleeve grips the end of the pipe.

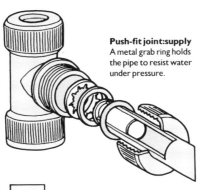

Push-fit joint: supply
A metal grab ring holds the pipe to resist water under pressure.

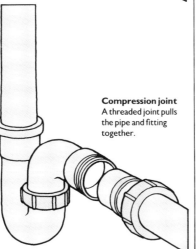

Compression joint
A threaded joint pulls the pipe and fitting together.

TYPES OF PLASTIC

The technology of plastics is such that new or modified materials are being introduced all the time, but the plastics described below are widely available.

Unplasticized polyvinyl chloride

UPVC
A hard, rigid plastic used for waste systems and cold water supply.

Modified polyvinyl chloride

PVC
A similar plastic to UPVC but it is slightly more flexible and therefore shock resistant.

Chlorinated polyvinyl chloride

CPVC
A versatile plastic suitable for hot and cold water supply. It can even withstand the temperatures required for central heating systems.

Polypropylene

PP
A slightly flexible plastic with a somewhat greasy feel. It is used for hot and cold waste systems but expands when heated. It is impossible to glue PP so it's never welded with solvent.

Acrylonitrile butadiene styrene

ABS
A very tough plastic equally suited to hot and cold waste.

Polybutylene

PB
A tough, flexible plastic used for hot and cold water supply – even central heating. Available in standard lengths or continuous coils.

SEE ALSO

Details for: ▷

Solvent joints	358
Push-fit joints	358-359

MAKING JOINTS IN PLASTIC PIPES

You should follow the detailed advice supplied with any specific make of pipe or fitting, but the instructions below and on the facing page demonstrate the basic methods used to connect plastic pipework. Do not inhale solvent fumes, and especially avoid smoking when welding joints. Some solvents give off fumes which become toxic when inhaled through a cigarette. Keep solvents away from children. Work carefully to avoid spilling solvent cement as it will etch the surface of the pipework and certain other plastics as well.

SEE ALSO

◁ Details for:
Hacksaws   486-487
Files   490

JOINING PUSH-FIT WASTE PIPES

Cut the pipe to length and chamfer the end as for solvent weld joints. Wipe the inside of the socket with the recommended cleaner and lubricate the pipe with a little of the silicone lubricant supplied with it.

Push the pipe into the joint right up to the stop and mark the edge of the socket on the pipe with a pencil (1).

Withdraw the pipe about 10mm (⅜in) (2) to allow the pipe to expand when subjected to hot water.

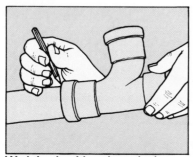

1 Mark the edge of the socket on the pipe

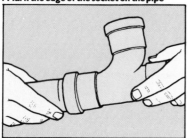

2 Withdraw the pipe about 10mm (⅜in)

Repairing a weeping joint
If a push-fit joint is leaking, the rubber seal has been pushed out of position, probably because the socket is out of line with the pipe. Dismantle the joint and check the condition of the seal.

Making solvent weld joints

Cut the pipe to length with a saw allowing for the depth of the joint socket. When working with large diameter pipes, make sure your cut is square by winding a piece of note paper around the tube, aligning the wrapped edge carefully as a guide for the saw (1).

Revolve the pipe away from you as you cut it. Smooth the cut edge with a file.

Chamfer the pipe with a file to make it easier to push into the socket (2).

Welding the joint
Push the pipe into the socket to test the fit then mark the end of the joint on the pipe with a pencil (3). This will act as a guide for applying the solvent. You must key the outside of the pipe up to this line, and the inside of the socket, with fine abrasive paper before using some solvents. Check the manufacturer's instructions.

When using elbows and tees, scratch the pipe and joint with a knife (4) before dismantling to align them correctly when you reassemble the components.

Use a clean rag to wipe the surface of pipe and fitting with the recommended spirit cleaner.

Paint solvent evenly onto both components (5) and immediately push home the socket. (Some manufacturers recommend that you twist the joint to spread the solvent.) Align the joint properly and leave it for 15 seconds.

The pipe is ready for use with cold water after one hour. Do not pass hot water through the system until at least four hours has elapsed, preferably longer, according to manufacturer's recommendations.

Allowing for expansion
Plastic pipes expand when subjected to hot water but this is only a problem over a long, straight run.
● If a waste run exceeds 1.8m (6ft), incorporate an expansion coupling with a push-fit rubber seal at one end,.
● For supply pipes over 10m (33ft) in length, form an expansion loop in the run by joining three 150mm (3in) lengths of pipe with elbows (6).

Repairing a weeping joint
If a joint leaks when the system is filled with water, drain it again and allow it to dry out. Apply a little more solvent cement to the mouth of the socket allowing it to flow into the joint by capillary action.

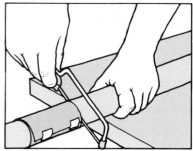

1 Use paper as a guide to keep the cut square

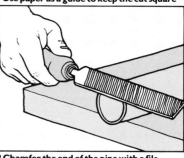

2 Chamfer the end of the pipe with a file

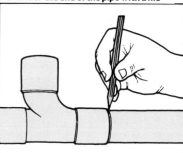

3 Assemble the joint and mark the socket

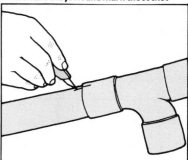

4 Scratch pipe and joint to realign them

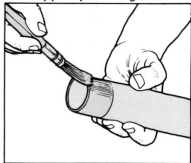

5 Paint solvent up to pencil mark

6 Expansion loop
Build a loop into a long pipe run to allow for expansion using short lengths of tube and elbows.

MAKING JOINTS IN PLASTIC PIPES

Joining push-fit supply pipes

Cut polybutylene pipe to length with special shears supplied by the manufacturer (1), or use a sharp craft knife. As long as the cut is reasonably square, the joint will be watertight.

Push a metal support sleeve into the pipe (2), then use a fingertip to smear a little silicone lubricant around the end of the pipe and inside the socket (3).

Push the prepared pipe firmly into the socket a full 25mm (1in) (4). As the joint can revolve freely around the pipe after connection without breaking the seal, there is no problem when aligning tees and elbows with other pipe runs.

1 Cut pipe to length

2 Insert metal sleeve

3 Apply lubricant

4 Push pipe into joint

Dismantling a joint

If you need to dismantle a joint to alter a system, release the cap with mole grips (▷) and unscrew it by hand. Pull out the pipe, slide the rubber ring and washer along the pipe then crush the metal grab ring with pliers (5) to remove it.

Drop a new grab ring into the socket – teeth facing into the fitting – and replace first the washer, then the rubber ring.

Screw back the cap hand-tight then use mole grips to turn it 2mm (⅛in) further. Overtightening will render the joint ineffective.

Connect to the pipe as described above. Never attempt to assemble the fitting like a compression joint or it will blow out under pressure. ·

Repairing a weeping joint
The only reason why a supply push-fit joint should leak is the failure to push home the pipe fully.

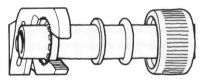

5 Crush the metal grab ring to dismantle joint

Bending plastic pipes

It isn't practical to bend plastic wastepipes especially when you can use easy-flow joints instead.

It is possible to bend a rigid supply pipe by heating it gently. Pass the flame of a gas torch over the area you wish to bend. Keep the flame moving and revolve the pipe all the time. When the pipe is soft enough, bend it by hand on a flat surface (1) and hold it still until the plastic hardens again.

Polybutylene pipe can be bent cold to a minimum radius of eight times the pipe diameter. Use a pipe clip at each side of the bend to hold the curve, or use the manufacturer's special clamp (2). Because the pipe is flexible, long gentle curves can be made by simply threading it around obstacles. Running this type of pipe under floorboards is very easy.

1 Bend the softened pipe on a flat surface

2 Hook flexible pipe into a metal clamp

MAKING COMPRESSION JOINTS TO TRAPS

With some traps, a short threaded pipe is located in the outlet of the trap and secured by a large compression nut. The other end of the pipe is connected to the rest of the waste system with a push-fit or solvent weld joint.

Other traps connect directly to a plain wastepipe. Slip the threaded nut onto the pipe followed by the washer and then the rubber ring.

Push the pipe into the socket of the trap and tighten the compression nut.

CONNECTING PLASTIC TO METAL PLUMBING

To connect most plastic pipes to copper or galvanized steel plumbing, use special adaptor couplings (▷).

To join polybutylene pipe to copper, insert the usual support sleeve then use a standard brass compression joint. Alternatively, you can joint copper to a polybutylene run using the push-fit joint. Cut and deburr the copper pipe carefully and lubricate it before pushing it into the joint.

Joining plastic pipe with compression fitting
Insert support sleeve before tightening joint.

SUPPORTING PIPE RUNS

Plastic pipework should be supported with clips or saddles similar to those used for metal pipe, but because it is more flexible, you will have to space the clips closer together. Check with manufacturers' literature for exact dimensions.

If you plan to surface-run flexible pipes, consider ducting or boxing-in because it's difficult to make a really neat installation.

SEE ALSO

Details for: ▷	
Adaptor couplings	356
Mole grips	
(plier wrench)	490
Supporting pipes	355
Push-fit joints	357
Gas torch	488
Slip-joint pliers	491

REPLACING A WC SUITE

SEE ALSO

◁ Details for:

WC cisterns	344
Bathroom planning	15
Installing a WC suite	362

When remodelling a bathroom, you may decide to relace an old-style, high-level WC cistern with one of the more compact and less obtrusive low-level versions. In many cases this can be achieved without having to renew the pan at the same time, but if that too is old and unsightly, or if the joint with the soil pipe is leaking, take the opportunity to install a completely new suite. If you connect to the existing branch of the soil pipe, it is a relatively simple operation, but if you plan to move the WC or even install a second convenience elsewhere, you will have to break into the main soil pipe itself or run the waste directly into the underground drainage system. In either case, hire a professional plumber to make the installation.

Choosing the equipment

There was a time when more or less every WC looked identical and worked in the same way, but you have now a choice of compact and colourful appliances which perform their functions more quietly and efficiently than their predecessors.

Types of cistern

Most WCs are fitted with a direct action cistern (◁) but this basic design is available in various models.

High-level cistern
If you simply want to replace an existing high-level cistern without having to modify the plumbing, comparable cisterns are still widely available.

Standard low-level cistern
Most people prefer a cistern mounted on the wall just above the WC pan. A short flush pipe from the base of the cistern connects to the flushing horn on the rear of the pan, while inlet and overflow pipes can be fitted to either side of the cistern. Most low-level cisterns are made from the same vitreous china as the pan.

Compact low-level cistern
Where space is limited, use a plastic cistern which is only 114mm (4½in)

from front to back. This type of cistern is operated by a push-down knob on top.

Concealed cistern
A low-level cistern can be concealed behind panelling. Supply and overflow connections are identical to other cisterns but the flushing lever is mounted on the face of the panel. These plastic cisterns are utilitarian in character with no concession to fashion or style, and are therefore relatively inexpensive. You must provide access for servicing.

Close-coupled cisterns
A close-coupled cistern is bolted directly to the pan forming an integral unit. Both the inlet and overflow connections are made at the base of the cistern. An internal standpipe rises vertically from the overflow connection to protrude above the level of the water in the cistern.

Types of WC pan

When you visit a showroom you are confronted with many apparently different WC pans to choose from, but in fact, there are two basic patterns, a washdown or syphonic pan.

Siphonic pans
Siphonic pans need no heavy fall of water to cleanse them and are much quieter as a result. A single trap pan has a narrow outlet immediately after the bend to slow down the flow of water from the pan. The body of water expels air from the outlet to promote the siphonic action. A double trap pan is more sophisticated and exceptionally

quiet. A small vent pipe connects the space between two traps to the inlet running between the cistern and pan. As water flows along the inlet, it sucks air from the trap system through the vent pipe. A vacuum is formed between the traps, and water in the pan is forced by atmospheric pressure into the soil pipe.

Washdown pans
If your existing pan is old enough to need replacing, it will be a standard washdown model. It is the most straightforward and least expensive pan. The contents are washed out by the water falling from the cistern.

Space for a WC
You will need a space in front of the pan of at least 600mm (2ft) square.

Floor exit trap
Use an 'S' trap when the soil pipe passes through the floor.

Wall exit trap
Use a 'P' trap when the pipe passes through the wall behind the pan.

CHOOSING A WC CISTERN

Low-level cistern
This type of cistern is very common. It is made in plastic or glazed ceramic.

Compact cistern
A very slim plastic cistern for use where space is limited.

Concealed cistern
A cheap plastic cistern which is hidden behind panelling.

Close-coupled cistern
This type of cistern is designed as part of the WC pan.

CHOOSING A WC PAN

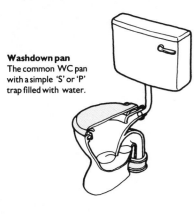

Washdown pan
The common WC pan with a simple 'S' or 'P' trap filled with water.

Single trap siphonic pan
The narrow outlet behind the trap slows down the flow of water to produce the siphonic action.

Double trap siphonic pan
Air is sucked out from between the two traps to make a vacuum.

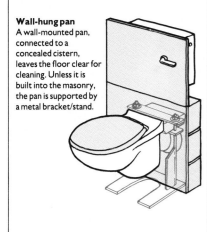

Wall-hung pan
A wall-mounted pan, connected to a concealed cistern, leaves the floor clear for cleaning. Unless it is built into the masonry, the pan is supported by a metal bracket/stand.

REMOVING THE OLD WC

Cut off the water supply (▷) then flush the cistern to empty it. If you are merely renewing a cistern, you will have to disconnect the supply and overflow pipes with a wrench and loosen the large nut connecting the flush pipe to the base of the cistern. These connections are often corroded and painted, so it is easier to hacksaw through the pipes close to the connections if you intend to replace the entire suite.

Having lifted the cistern off its support brackets, try freeing the fixing screws. In all probability, they will be corroded, so lever the brackets off the wall with a crow bar.

Cut the overflow pipe from the wall with a cold chisel. Repair the plaster when you decorate the bathroom.

If the old pan is screwed to a wooden floor, it will probably have a 'P' trap connected to a nearly horizontal branch soil pipe. Remove the floor fixing screws and scrape out the old putty around the pipe joint. Attempt to free the pan by pulling it towards you while rocking it slightly from side to side.

If the joint is fixed firmly, smash the pan outlet just in front of the soil pipe with a club hammer (1). Protect your eyes with goggles. Stuff rags into the soil pipe to prevent debris falling into it, then chip out the remains of the pan outlet with a cold chisel (2). Work carefully to preserve the soil pipe.

Smash an 'S' trap in the same way, and if the pan is cemented to a solid floor, drive a cold chisel under its base to break the seal. Chop out the broken fragments as before and clean up the floor with a cold chisel.

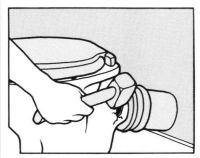

1 Break the outlet of the pan with a hammer

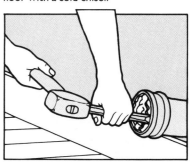

2 Use a cold chisel to cut out the remnants

Cutting the soil pipe

If you break the soil pipe while chipping out the pan outlet, cut the pipe square with a hired chain-link pipe cutter. Clamp the chain of cutters around the pipe and work the shaft back and forth to sever it. Ratchet-action cutters enable you to work in a confined space. When you buy a push-fit pan connector (see below), make sure it is long enough to reach the severed pipe.

Pan to soil pipe connection

Before you install the new suite, choose a push-fit flexible connector to join the pan to the soil pipe. Connectors of different angles are available to suit any situation, even if the two elements are slightly misaligned. You can even choose a colour to match the suite. Make a note of the following dimensions when selecting a connector: the external diameter of pan outlet; the internal diameter of soil pipe; the distance between the outlet and pipe when the pan is installed.

SEE ALSO

Details for: ▷	
Turning off water	340
WC cistern	344
Chain-link cutter	487

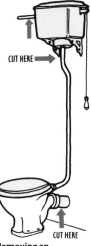

CUT HERE ➤

CUT HERE

Removing an appliance
If fittings are corroded, remove the appliance by cutting the flush pipe, overflow and pan outlet.

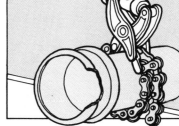

Cutting a soil pipe
Use a chain-link cutter to sever a broken soil pipe.

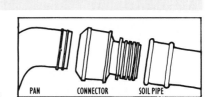

PAN   CONNECTOR   SOIL PIPE

OFF-SET   CRANKED   BENT

Push-fit flexible pan connectors

361

INSTALLING A NEW WC SUITE

SEE ALSO

◁ Details for:

Fused connection unit	314
Flex outlet	315
Float valves	345
Adjusting float valve	346
Tank connector	352,356
Running pipework	355
Waste boss	366
Overflow unit	368
Connecting pipes	352-359
WC cisterns	360
WC pans	361

To install a new WC, begin by pushing the plastic connector onto the pan outlet. Check that the inside of the soil pipe is clean and smooth. Smear a rough surface with a lubricant supplied by the manufacturer then push the pan and connector firmly into the soil pipe.

Don't fix the pan at this stage, but if the floor is made of concrete, you will have to drill holes and plug the fixing holes. Level the pan using a spirit level, adjusting it with scraps of veneer or vinyl floor covering. (Trim them with a knife when the installation is complete.)

Stand a close-coupled cistern on the pan, or connect the flush pipe and hold the cistern against the wall to mark the fixing holes. Fix the cistern to the wall with non-corroding screws and washers making sure it is level, then tighten the flush pipe connection under the cistern.

Screw the pan to the floor, tightening the screws carefully in rotation to avoid cracking the pan.

Run the new 15mm (½in) supply pipe to the float valve (◁), fit a tap connector and tighten it with a wrench.

Use a tank connector (◁) to attach the 21mm (¾in) overflow pipe. Drill a hole through the nearest outside wall where an overflow will be detected promptly. Slope the pipe a few degrees and let it project from the outer face of the wall at least 150mm (6in).

When there is no external wall nearby, you can run the WC overflow pipe to a special combined waste and overflow unit on the bath (◁).

Turn on the supply of water and adjust the float valve (◁).

Small bore waste system

The siting of a WC is normally limited by the need to use a conventional 100mm (4in) soil pipe, and to provide sufficient fall to discharge the waste into the soil stack. By using an electrically driven pump and shredder, you can discharge WC waste through a 22mm (¾in) pipe up to 50m (55yd) away from the stack. The shredder will even pump vertically to a maximum of 4m (4yd). You can run the small-bore pipework through the narrow space between a floor and ceiling (◁). Consequently, a WC can be installed as part of an en-suite bathroom, under the stairs or even in a basement providing the space is adequately ventilated.

The unit, which accepts any conventional 'P' trap WC pan, is activated automatically by flushing the cistern and switches off about 18 seconds later. It must be wired to a fused connection unit, but via a suitable flex outlet if installed in a bathroom (◁). The wastepipe is connected to the soil stack using any standard 36mm (1¼in) waste boss (◁) so long as the manufacturer supplies a 22-36mm (¾-1¼in) adaptor. A WC waste must be connected to the stack at least 200mm (8in) above other waste connections.

Check that the system is approved by your local water authority before installation.

Plumbing a WC
1 Bent plastic tank connector
2 21mm (¾in) overflow
3 Cistern
4 Float valve
5 Tap connector
6 15mm (½in) supply pipe
7 Flush pipe connector
8 Flush pipe
9 Push-fit flexible connector
10 WC pan outlet
11 Flexible outlet connector
12 Soil pipe

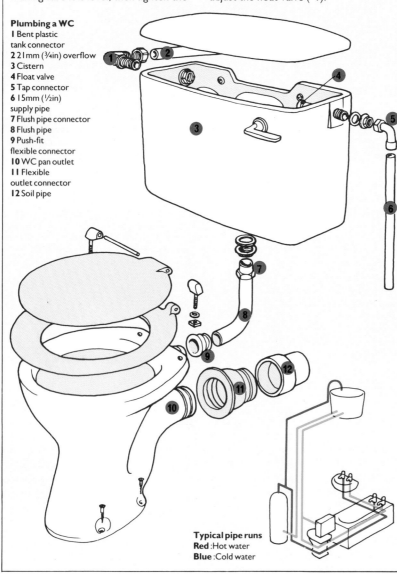

Typical pipe runs
Red : Hot water
Blue : Cold water

Small bore waste system for a WC
The shredding unit fits neatly behind a 'P' trap WC pan. When it is situated in a bathroom, the unit must be wired to a flex outlet as shown above (◁), otherwise it can be connected directly to a fused connection unit (◁).

FITTING A WASH BASIN

Whether you are modifying existing plumbing or running new pipework to a different location, fitting a wash basin in a bathroom or guest room presents few difficulties so long as you give some *thought to how you will run the waste to the vertical stack. The waste must have a minimum fall or slope of 6mm (¼in) for every 300mm (1ft) of pipe run. It should not exceed 3m (10ft) in length.*

Choosing a wash basin

Wall-hung and pedestal basins are made from vitreous china, but basins supported all round by a vanity unit counter-top are also made in pressed steel or plastic. Select the taps at the same time to ensure that the basin of your choice has holes at the required spacing to receive the taps, or no holes at all if the taps are to be wall-mounted.

Make sure the basin has sufficient space on each side or to the rear for soaps, shampoo or other toiletries otherwise you will have to provide a separate shelf or cabinet.

Pedestal basins
Although the hollow pedestal provides some additional support to the basin, its main purpose is to conceal unsightly supply pipes.

Wall-hung basin
Older wall-mounted basins are supported on large, screw-fixed brackets but a modern concealed wall mounting is just as strong and provides a far more attractive fixture.

Check that you can fix securely to the studs of a timber frame wall or hack off the plaster and install a mounting board (▷). (Use the same method to secure an existing basin with loose wall fixings.)

If you want to hide supply pipes, consider some form of panelling (▷).

Corner basin
Hand basins which fit into the corner of a room are popular because supply and wastepipes can be run conveniently through adjacent walls or concealed by boxing them in across the corner.

Recessed basin
A small hand basin can be recessed into a wall of a cloakroom or WC where space is limited.

Counter-top basins
In a large bathroom or bedroom, you can fit a wash basin into a counter-top as part of a built-in vanity unit. The cupboards below provide ample storage for towels and toiletries while hiding the plumbing at the same time.

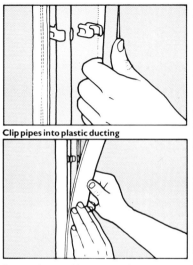

Wash basins
There are a few basic types of basin although the style will vary considerably. If it is inconvenient to fit a second basin in a bedroom, you might consider installing a counter-top in the bathroom with two basins.

Corner basin

Recessed basin

Pedestal basin

Wall-hung basin

Counter-top basin

CONCEALING PIPEWORK

The manufacturers of appliances and fittings are aware that most people find visible plumbing unattractive, and as a result, supply fitments such as sink units, panelled baths, shower cubicles, concealed cisterns, pedestal and counter-top basins, all of which are designed to hide their supply pipes and drainage. With careful selection and intelligently designed pipe runs, it should be possible to plumb your house without a single visible pipe. In practice, however, there are always situations where you have no option but to surface-run at least some pipes, especially when you cannot take them under floorboards. You can minimize the effect by taking special care to group pipes together neatly, and keep runs both straight and parallel. When painted to match the skirtings or walls, such pipes are practically invisible.

Alternatively, you can construct ducting to conceal pipes completely. Make your own ducting with softwood battens and plywood to bridge the corner of a room, or construct a false skirting deep enough to contain the pipes. It is a wise precaution to make at least part of the ducting removable to gain access to joints or other fittings in case you need to service them at a later date. For total accessibility, use proprietary ducting made from PVC. It is manufactured in a range of sizes to contain grouped or individual pipes. With right-angle and tee-piece joints, you can construct a system of ducting to cover any new or existing installation. Optional foam liners insulate hot water or central heating pipes.

Clip pipes into plastic ducting

Snap on the matching cover-strips.

SEE ALSO

Details for: ▷	
Panelling	87-88
Mounting a basin	139
Bathroom planning	15
Plasterboarding	159-160
Running pipework	355

Space for a basin
Allow extra elbow room for washing hair. A space 1100mm (3ft 8in) x 700mm (2ft 4in) should be sufficient. To suit most people, position the rim of a basin 800mm (2ft 8in) from the floor.

Most taps are made of chromium plated or enamelled brass although there is a limited range of plastic-bodied taps. Plastic taps are not as durable as metal ones but they are considerably cheaper. All basin taps have a 15mm (¹/₂in) threaded inlet known as the tail for attaching the supply pipe.

SEE ALSO

◁ Details for:
Repairing taps   342-343

Types of tap

Individual taps
The majority of wash basins are fitted with individual taps for the hot and cold water supply. Cross or capstan head taps are still manufactured for traditionally-styled bathrooms but most taps have a metal or plastic shrouded head. A lever head tap turns the tap from off to full on with one quarter turn only. They are especially convenient for the elderly or disabled.

Individual wall-mounted taps are known as bib taps while those fixed directly to the basin itself are called pillar taps.

Mixer taps
A mixer tap has a hot and cold valve linked to a common spout. Water is provided at the required temperature by adjusting the two valves simultaneously.

Basin mixer taps often incorporate a pop-up waste. A series of inter-linking rods, operated by a button on the centre of the mixer, open and close the waste plug in the basin.

Normally, the body of the tap which connects the valves and spout, rests on the upper surface of the basin. The tails only protrude through holes in the basin to meet the supply pipes. This is a two-hole mixer with tails spaced 100mm (4in) apart.

A three-hole mixer appears to have separate valves and spout but they are linked by a tube below the basin. The tube is cut to length to accommodate the distance between the holes in the basin which may be from 200 to 250mm (8 to 10in) apart.

Both inlets of a one-hole mixer pass through the same hole.

An entire mixer set can be mounted on a wall above the basin. Alternatively, the valves can be mounted on the basin yet still divert hot and cold water to a wall-mounted spout.

Shrouded-head tap

Lever-head tap

Two-hole mixer

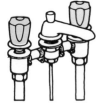
Three-hole mixer

One-hole mixer

TAP MECHANISMS

Over recent years there have been revolutionary changes in tap design, and not just in their appearance or styling. Entirely new thinking about the function of a tap has provided the consumer with taps that are easier to operate, more hard-wearing and simpler to maintain.

Rising-spindle taps
Within a traditionally designed tap, the entire spindle, jumper and washer move up and down, turning along with the head when you operate the tap.

Non-rising head taps
Outwardly, these taps resemble a rising-spindle tap but when the head turns, it does not move up and down. Instead, it causes a threaded spindle and washer unit to rise vertically without turning. Because the washer is not twisted against the seat as the valve is closed, neither the washer nor seat wear as quickly as those in a conventional tap.

Ceramic disc taps
Precision ground ceramic discs replace the traditional washer, but instead of separating, one disc rotates on the other so that waterways through them gradually align with each other allowing water to flow. There is virtually no wear as hard water scale or other debris cannot interfere with the fit of the discs. If a problem develops, the whole mechanism is replaced.

Reverse-pressure taps
An original concept in tap design. The head and spout hang from the water inlet and move as one unit forcing the washer upwards against the seat. A unique check valve inside the tap shuts off the water as the tap is dismantled to change a washer.

Electronic taps
Water flows automatically from an electronic tap as soon as an integral photo-cell detects the presence of your hands under the spout. It stops flowing when you remove your hands. The tap is powered by a transformer mounted beneath the basin or vanity unit. Water temperature is regulated by a control on the body of the tap.

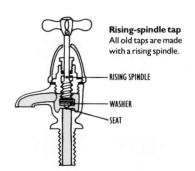
Rising-spindle tap
All old taps are made with a rising spindle.
RISING SPINDLE
WASHER
SEAT

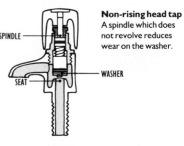
Non-rising head tap
A spindle which does not revolve reduces wear on the washer.
SPINDLE
WASHER
SEAT

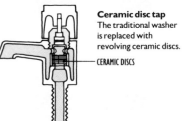
Ceramic disc tap
The traditional washer is replaced with revolving ceramic discs.
CERAMIC DISCS

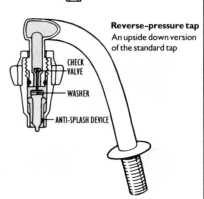
Reverse-pressure tap
An upside down version of the standard tap
CHECK VALVE
WASHER
ANTI-SPLASH DEVICE

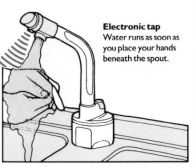
Electronic tap
Water runs as soon as you place your hands beneath the spout.

REPLACING OLD TAPS

When replacing taps, you will want to use the existing plumbing if possible but it can be difficult to disconnect old corroded fittings. Apply penetrating oil to the tap connectors and to the back-nuts clamping the tap to the basin. While the oil takes effect, shut off the cold and hot water supply.

Applying heat with a gas torch can break down corrosion by expanding metal fittings, but wrap a wet cloth around nearby soldered joints or you may melt the solder. Take care that you do not damage a plastic waste and trap, and protect flammable surfaces with a ceramic tile. Too much heat may crack a ceramic basin.

It is not always possible to engage the nuts with a standard wrench. Instead, hire a special cranked spanner designed to reach into the confined spaces below a basin or bath. You can apply extra leverage to the spanner by slipping a stout metal bar or wrench handle into the other end.

Having disconnected the pipework, tap the bottom of the tap tails with a wooden mallet to break the seal of plumbers' putty under the taps. Clean the remnants of putty from around the taps holes and fit new taps. If the tap tails are shorter than the originals, or the threads do not match the tap connectors, check a manufacturer's catalogue for various adaptors.

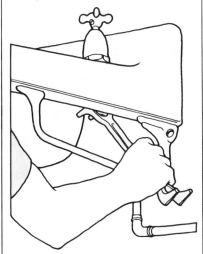

Releasing a tap connector
Use a special cranked spanner to release the fixing nut of a tap connector.

A cranked spanner fits basin and bath taps

FIXING A WALL-HUNG BASIN

Turn off the supply of water to an old basin before you disconnect it (▷). However, you can save some time by fitting the new taps to its replacement beforehand so that you are not without water in the meantime.

Removing the old basin

If you want to use existing plumbing, loosen the compression nuts on the tap tails (see left) and trap, otherwise cut through the waste and supply pipes at a point where you can most easily connect new plumbing (**1**).

Remove any fixings holding the basin to its support brackets or pedestal and lift it from the wall. Apply penetrating oil to the bracket wall fixings in an attempt to remove them without damaging the plaster, but as a last resort, lever the brackets off the wall. Take care not to break cast iron fittings as they can be quite valuable.

Fitting new taps

Fit new taps to the basin before fixing it to the wall. Slip a plastic washer supplied with the tap onto its tail, then pass the tail through the hole in the basin. If no washer is supplied, spread some plumbers' putty around the top of the tail and beneath the base of the tap.

With the basin resting on its rim, slip a second washer onto the tail then hand tighten the back-nut to clamp the tap onto the basin (**2**). Check that the spout faces into the basin then tighten the back-nut carefully with a cranked spanner (See left).

Wipe excess putty from the basin then fit the second tap.

Fixing the basin to the wall

Have an assistant hold the basin against the wall at the required height and check it is horizontal with a spirit level, then mark the fixing holes for the wall bracket (**3**). Lay the basin to one side while you drill and plug the fixing holes.

Screw the bracket securely to the wall and bolt the basin to it with whatever fixings are supplied by the manufacturer. Connect the plumbing to the taps and fit the waste system (▷).

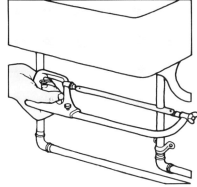

1 Cut through old supply pipes with a hacksaw

SEE ALSO

Details for: ▷	
Turning off water	340
Connecting pipes	352-359
Hacksaws	486-487
Gas torch	488
Spanners and wrenches	489-490
Wall fixings	494-495

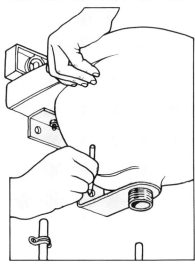

2 Slip the back-nut onto the tail of the tap

3 Mark the bracket fixing holes on the wall

CONNECTING A WALL-HUNG BASIN

SEE ALSO

◁ Details for:
Draining system	340
Connecting pipes	352-359
Fitting taps	365
Mounting a basin	365
Waste units	368
Cranked spanner	489
Guttering	234
Soil pipes	339
Pipe clips	355

A pressed-metal basin
When you fit taps to a pressed-metal basin, slip built-up 'top hat' washers onto the tails to cover the shanks. The basin itself may be supplied with a rubber strip to seal the joint with the counter-top. It will need a combined waste and overflow like a bath (◁).

• **Counter-top basin**
Manufacturers supply a template for cutting the hole in a counter-top to receive the basin. Run mastic around the edge to seal a ceramic basin, and clamp it with the fixings supplied.

Once you have fitted new taps and mounted the basin on the wall (◁), finish the installation by connecting the waste system along with the hot and cold supply pipes.

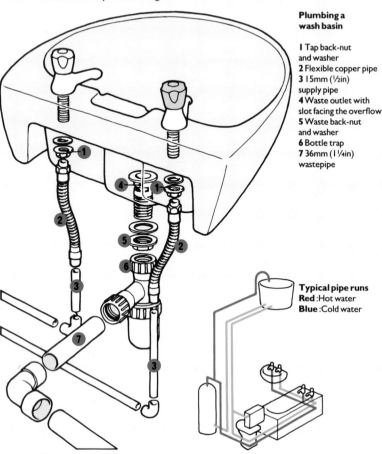

Plumbing a wash basin

1 Tap back-nut and washer
2 Flexible copper pipe
3 15mm (½in) supply pipe
4 Waste outlet with slot facing the overflow
5 Waste back-nut and washer
6 Bottle trap
7 36mm (1¼in) wastepipe

Typical pipe runs
Red : Hot water
Blue : Cold water

Fitting trap and wastepipe

Fit the waste outlet into the bottom of the basin as for taps using washers or plumbers' putty to form a watertight seal. The basin will probably have an integral overflow running to the waste, in which case ensure that the slot in the waste outlet aligns with the overflow. Tighten the back-nut under the basin while holding the outlet still by gripping its grille with pliers.

If you can utilize the existing wastepipe, connect the trap to the waste outlet and to the end of the pipe. A two-part trap provides some adjustment to align it with the old wastepipe.

If necessary, run a new 36mm (1¼in) wastepipe, cutting a hole through the wall with a masonry drill and cold chisel. Run the pipe, with sufficient fall – 6mm (¼in) per 300mm (1ft) run – to terminate over the hopper on top of the vertical wastepipe. Fix the pipe to the wall with saddle clips.

Connecting the taps

You can run standard 15mm (½in) copper or plastic pipes to the taps and join them with tap connectors, but it is easier to use short lengths of flexible, corrugated copper pipe specially designed for tap connection. They can be bent by hand to allow for any slight misalignment between the supply pipes and tap tails. Each corrugated pipe has a tap connector at one end, and at the other, a compression or capillary joint.

Connect the corrugated pipes to the tap tails but leave them hand tight only, then run new branch pipework to meet them. Make soldered or compression joints to connect the pipes (◁). Tighten the tap connectors with a cranked spanner (◁).

Turn on the water supply and check the pipes for leaks. Drain the system to repair a weeping joint (◁).

Connecting waste to soil pipe

Connect a basin wastepipe to a single stack, plastic soil pipe with a proprietary pipe boss. A boss may be connected by other methods, but is often clamped to the soil pipe with a strap.

Mark where the basin waste meets the soil pipe and cut a hole of the recommended diameter with a hole saw (1) . Smooth the edge of the hole with abrasive paper.

Wipe both contacting surfaces with the manufacturer's cleaner, then apply gap-filling solvent cement around the hole. Strap the boss over the hole and tighten the bolt (2) .

Insert the rubber lining in the boss in preparation for the wastepipe (3) .

Lubricate the end of the pipe and push it firmly into the boss (4) . Clip the pipe to the wall.

1 Cut a hole in the pipe with a hole saw

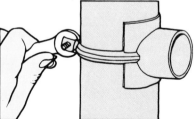

2 Strap the boss over the hole

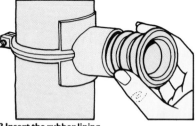

3 Insert the rubber lining

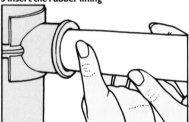

4 Push the wastepipe into the boss

INSTALLING A NEW BATH

There are companies who will re-enamel your old bath – some will even spray it in-situ. If you own an attractive, antique cast iron bath it would be worth asking for quotations before you make up your mind to discard it. Even if you don't want the bath yourself, you may be able to sell it to a company who specializes in bath restoration. On the other hand, most old baths are simply too ugly to restore, and it may prove to be more economical to replace one that is badly chipped or stained. If a bath is cracked, it is beyond repair.

Choosing a bath

You can buy reproduction or even restored Victorian baths in cast iron from specialist suppliers but they are likely to be expensive. In practical terms, a cast iron bath is far too heavy for one person to handle: even two people would have difficulty carrying one to an upstairs bathroom. A cast iron bath can look splendid when left freestanding in a room, but it can be virtually impossible to clean behind one, and panelling-in the curved and sometimes tapering shape is rarely successful.

Nowadays, the majority of baths are made from enamelled pressed steel, acrylic or glass-reinforced plastic. Two people can handle a steel bath with ease and you could carry a plastic bath on your own. Although modern plastic baths are strong and durable, some are harmed by abrasive cleaners, bleach and especially heat. It is not advisable to use a gas torch near a plastic bath.

When it comes to style and colour, there is no lack of choice in any material, although the more unconventional baths are likely to be made of plastic. Nearly every bath comes with matching panels and optional features like hand grips and dropped sides to make it easier to step in and out. Taps do not have to be mounted at the foot of the bath. Many manufacturers offer alternative corner or side mounting facilities. Some will even cut tap holes to order.

You can order a bath in any style to double as a jacuzzi, but the plumbing is somewhat complicated so you will need to have it professionally installed.

Rectangular bath
A standard, rectangular bath is still the most popular and economical design. Baths vary in size from 1.5 to 1.8m (5 to 6ft) in length, with a choice of widths from 700 to 800mm (2ft 4in to 2ft 8in)

Corner bath
A corner bath occupies more actual floor area than a rectangular bath of the same capacity, but because the tub itself is turned at an angle to the room, it may take up less wall-space. A corner bath always provides generous shelf space for essential toiletries.

Round bath
A round bath would prove to be impractical in most bathrooms, but if you are converting a spare bedroom, you may decide to make the bath a feature of interior design as well as a practical appliance.

Selecting taps for a bath

The basic design and style of bath taps are identical to basin taps (▷), but they are proportionally larger with 22mm (¾in) tails. Individual hot and cold taps or mixers are made to fit a bath with hole centres 180mm (7⅛in) apart.

Some bath mixers are designed to supply water to a shower head, either mounted telephone-style on the mixer itself, or hung from a bracket mounted on a wall above the bath (▷).

SUPPORTING A PLASTIC BATH

A metal frame is supplied to cradle a flexible plastic bath. Without it, the bath would distort and possibly crack.

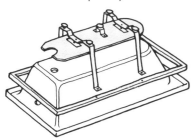

Assembling the cradle
Turn a bath on its rim to fit the cradle.

TYPES OF BATH

A rectangular bath with moulded panels

A bath shaped to fit the corner of a room

A circular bath fits flush with the floor

RENOVATING BATH ENAMEL

You can buy two-part paints prepared specifically to restore the enamel surface of an old bath, sink or basin. To achieve a first-class result, the bath must be scrupulously clean and dry, so tape plastic bags over the taps to prevent water dripping into the bath and work in a warm atmosphere where condensation will not occur. Wipe the surface with a cloth dampened with white spirit to remove traces of grease, then paint the bath from the bottom upwards in a circular direction. This type of paint is self-levelling so don't brush it out too much. Pick up runs or tears immediately and work fairly quickly to keep the wet edge fresh.

For a professional finish, hire a company which will send an operator to spray a stained bath in-situ. The whole process should take no longer than two to three hours. The bath is cleaned chemically before a grinder is used to key the surface and remove heavy stains. Chipped enamel can be repaired at the same time. Finally, surrounding areas are masked before the bath is sprayed.

SEE ALSO

Details for: ▷

Selecting taps	364
Shower mixer	370
Plumbing a bath	368
Panelling a bath	369

Access to the bath
Allow a space of 1100 x 700mm (3ft 8in x 2ft 4in) beside the bath to climb in and out safely, and for bathing younger members of the family.

PLUMBING THE BATH

Once a bath is fitted close to the walls of a bathroom, it can be difficult to make the joints and connections, so fit the taps, overflow and trap before you push the new bath into position and prior to removing the existing bath.

Fit adjustable feet to the new bath or suspend a plastic bath in its supporting cradle according to the manufacturer's instructions.

SEE ALSO

◁ Details for:
Draining system	340
Connecting pipes	352-359
Fitting taps	365
Top-hat washers	366
Stack connection	366

Waste/overflow units
A flexible tube takes overflow water to the trap.

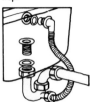

Compression unit
Runs to cleaning eye on the trap.

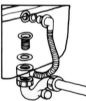

Banjo unit
Slips over tail of waste outlet.

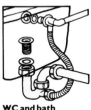

WC and bath overflow
Overflow from a WC joins the bath unit.

Shallow-seal trap
Use this type of trap when space is limited but it must discharge to a yard gully.

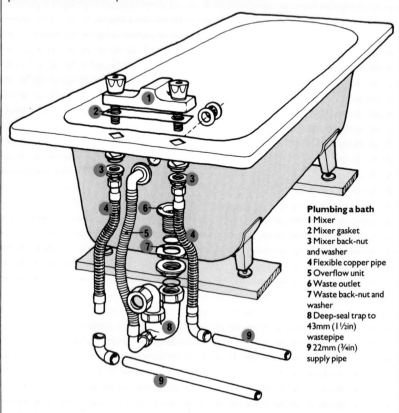

Plumbing a bath
1 Mixer
2 Mixer gasket
3 Mixer back-nut and washer
4 Flexible copper pipe
5 Overflow unit
6 Waste outlet
7 Waste back-nut and washer
8 Deep-seal trap to 43mm (1½in) wastepipe
9 22mm (¾in) supply pipe

Fitting the taps

Fit individual hot and cold taps as for a wash basin (◁). Fitting a mixer is a similar procedure, but most units are supplied with a long sealing gasket which slips over both tails. Drop the tails through the holes in the rim, slip top-hat washers onto them (◁) and tighten both back-nuts to clamp the mixer to the bath.

Fit a flexible 22mm (¾in) copper pipe (similar to those used for washbasin taps) onto each tail. As an alternative, you can attach short lengths of standard 22mm (¾in) copper or plastic pipe with tap connectors in preparation for jointing to the pipe run, but the flexible pipes allow for adjustment in case joints are slightly misaligned.

Fitting waste and overflow

Fit a combined waste and overflow unit. A flexible plastic hose takes water from the overflow outlet in the end of the bath to the waste outlet or trap. If you use a 'banjo' unit, you must fit the overflow before the trap, but the flexible pipe of a compression fitting unit connects to the trap itself. (See left)

Spread a layer of plumbers' putty under the rim of the waste outlet, or fit a circular rubber seal. Before inserting its tail into the hole in the bottom of the bath, seal the thread with PTFE tape. On the underside, add a plastic washer then tighten the large back-nut, bedding the outlet down onto the putty or rubber seal. Wipe off excess putty before it sets.

Connect the bath trap (see left) to the tail of the waste outlet with its own compression nut. (Fit a banjo overflow unit at the same time.)

Pass the threaded boss of the overflow hose through the hole in the end of the bath. Slip a washer seal over the boss, then use a pair of pliers to screw on the overflow outlet grille.

If you are using a compression fitting overflow, connect the nut on the other end of the hose to the cleaning eye of the trap.

Removing the old bath

Turn off the hot and cold water supply, then drain the system (◁).

Have a shallow bowl ready to catch any trapped water, then use a junior hacksaw to cut through the old supply and wastepipes. As the overflow from an old bath will almost certainly exit through the wall, saw through it at the same time.

If adjustable feet are fitted to the bath, lower them, pushing down on the bath to break the mastic seal between the rim and bathroom walls. Pull the bath away from the wall.

If you don't want to preserve a cast iron bath, it will be easier to break it up in the bathroom and carry it out in pieces. Wear protective goggles and ear protectors, drape a dust sheet over the bath then smash it with a heavy hammer.

Hack the old overflow from the wall with a cold chisel, fill the hole with mortar, and repair the plasterwork.

Installing the new bath

Run new 22mm (¾in) supply pipes, or attach spurs to the existing ones, ready for connection to the flexible pipes already fitted on the bath taps.

Cut two boards to support the feet of the bath and spread the point load over a wider area. Slide the bath into position and adjust the height of the feet with a spanner. Use a spirit level to check that the rim is horizontal.

Adjust the flexible tap pipes and join them to the supply pipes (◁).

Connect a 43mm (1½in) wastepipe to the trap and run it to the external hopper or soil stack as for a wash basin (◁). Restore the water supply and check for leaks before you fix the bath panels.

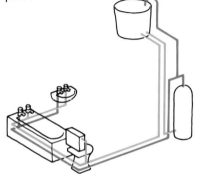

Typical bathroom pipe runs
Red:Hot water – **Blue**:Cold water.

Panelling a bath

In all probability, your bath will be supplied with moulded polystyrene panels to hide the plumbing and facilitate cleaning.

You can panel a basic rectangular bath with a softwood framework supporting a sheet of hardboard or plywood. The finish is a matter of personal choice. You can paint a standard plain hardboard or apply a wall covering to match or contrast with the bathroom decor. Alternatively, use a melamine-faced board – a practical, easy-to-clean surface – or add a texture with an embossed hardboard. You could continue the floorcovering up the panel using an adhesive to attach carpet, vinyl or cork tiles. If you want to use ceramic tiles, provide a small removable panel at the end of the bath so that you can service the plumbing. Design the panel to break between two rows of tiles.

When a bath does not fit against a wall at both ends, either continue the panelling around the exposed end, or make a fixed shelf of tiled marine plywood to fit behind the head or taps, and run the panelling from wall to wall.

Make the framework of 50mm x 25mm (2in x 1in) sawn softwood. Simple butt joints held together with timber connectors will suffice as the fixed sheet will make the frame rigid.

Scribe the sheet to fit under the rim of the bath and to fit the wall at each end, then pin and glue it to the framework. If pinning would spoil the surface, use planed timber for the frame and attach the sheet with adhesive.

Screw a vertical batten to the wall at each end of the bath to support the panelled frame and nail one or two softwood blocks to the floor for the frame to rest against. Screw the finished panel to the battens with brass screws and screw caps. Alternatively, use magnetic catches and fit small knobs or handles to the panel.

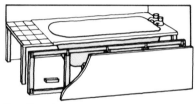

Panelling a bath
This example shows wall-to-wall panelling with a tiled shelf to fill the gap, but you can use a similar construction to fit any situation.

Soaking in a bath tub is very relaxing but taking a shower is more invigorating and hygienic while using far less hot water. A shower cubicle occupies a 750mm (2ft 6in) square of floor space so it is quite possible to locate one somewhere other than the bathroom. The corner of a bedroom is an obvious choice but you may prefer to convert a downstairs cloakroom or install a shower in a utility room along with the washing machine and tumble dryer. A separate shower can be a boon to a busy family who would otherwise queue for a single bathroom before leaving for work or school.

IMPORTANT CONSIDERATIONS

A shower must comply with certain requirements to satisfy the water authority and provide you with a facility which is both safe and comfortable.

Equal water pressure

The hot and cold water supply to a shower must be under equal pressure. You must never mix hot water from a cylinder with mains pressure cold water. The cold water must be supplied from the storage cistern. It is against water authority regulations to mix mains and stored water and, in any case, it would be difficult to maintain a comfortable temperature at the shower.

Sufficient pressure

Unless the water pressure is high enough, the performance of your shower will never be satisfactory. Apart from a mains pressure instantaneous shower, water pressure is determined by the height of the cold water storage cistern. The bottom of the cistern should be 1.5m (5ft) or more above the shower head. A shower can work satisfactorily when the shower head is only 900mm (3ft) below the cistern but only if the pipe run is short and straight.

Hot water pressure is unaffected by the position of the cylinder as it is supplied initially from the same cold water cistern and therefore its pressure is equal to the cold water supply.

When the pressure is insufficient, you can either raise the cistern on a strong wooden frame which means lengthening all the existing pipes, or you can fit a pump to boost the shower pressure.

Independent supply

If your shower is fed by branch pipes connected to the rest of the bathroom plumbing, there is a risk that water pressure will drop if someone draws water at another appliance. If it is the pressure on the hot supply that drops, then your shower will suddenly run cold which is merely unpleasant, but if pressure drops on the cold supply, the shower could become dangerously hot.

Ideally, the cold supply should be a 15mm (1/2in) pipe run independently from the storage cistern, and the hot supply should be a 15mm (1/2in) branch pipe taken directly from the vent pipe above the cylinder. Independent pipe runs are not essential if you install a thermostatic shower which can cope with slight variations in pressure.

Drainage

Because a shower tray stands on the floor, it can be difficult to obtain the minimum fall of 6mm (1/4in) per 300mm (1ft) run of wastepipe. You may be able to run the waste under floorboards, but only if the joists run in the same direction as the pipe. Sometimes it is necessary to raise the tray on a plinth.

SEE ALSO

Details for: ▷	
Finishing woodwork	74-84
Wallcoverings	90-97
Tiling	99-111
Floorcoverings	113-118
Shower units	370
Booster pumps	370
Woodworking joints	476
Man-made boards	493-494
Adhesives	495-496

SHOWER UNITS

Installing an independent shower cubicle with its own supply and waste system requires some previous experience of plumbing but if you utilize an existing bath as a shower tray, fitting a shower unit can involve little more than replacing the taps.

SEE ALSO

◁ Details for:
**Fused
connection unit**   314
Wiring a shower   323
Electricity   286-336
Fitting a mixer   368
Shower requirements   369
Plumbing showers   372

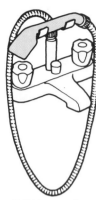

Bath/shower mixer
Fit this type of shower unit like an ordinary bath mixer.

Bath/shower mixer

This type of shower is the simplest to install. It is connected like a standard bath mixer to the existing 22mm (¾in) cold and hot water pipes, while the bath waste system takes care of the drainage. Having obtained the required temperature at the spout by adjusting the hot and cold valves, lifting a button on the mixer diverts the water, via a flexible hose, to the shower head. The shower head can be hand-held for washing hair, or hung from a wall-mounted bracket to provide a conventional shower.

You must not fit a bath/shower mixer when cold water is supplied under mains pressure to the bath tap. As the supply pipes are already part of the bathroom plumbing network, it is impossible to guard against fluctuating pressure unless the mixer is fitted with a thermostatic valve. If the pressure is insufficient, fit a booster pump.

Thermostatic shower mixer

Thermostatic mixer
This unit has separate controls for flow and temperature.

A thermostatic mixer is similar in design to a manual version but another control is incorporated to pre-set the water temperature. If the pressure drops on either the hot or cold supply, the thermostatic valve compensates by lowering the pressure on the other side. Consequently, you can supply a thermostatic shower with branch pipes from the bathroom plumbing but try to join them as near as possible to the cold cistern and hot cylinder.

The mixer cannot raise the pressure of the supply: you still need a booster pump if it is low. Neither will it compensate for the considerable difference in pressure between mains and gravity fed water.

Manual shower mixer (near right)
A unit with a single control to regulate the rate of flow and the temperature of the water.

Booster pump (far right)
The simplest type of pump is mounted to the shower wall between the mixer and shower head.

Manual shower mixer

A manual shower mixer can be mounted on the wall above a bathtub, but with its own supply of hot and cold water, or it can be situated in a separate shower cubicle. Simple mixers have individual hot and cold valves, but most manual shower mixers have a single control which regulates flow and water temperature. A manual mixer must have independent hot and cold supply.

Booster pump

If your existing shower installation is unsatisfactory due to low pressure, you can improve its performance by adding an electric booster pump. Some pumps are designed for remote installation, usually in an airing cupboard next to the hot water cylinder. Hot and cold pipes are fed to the pump, then out again to the shower mixer.

So long as you don't object to it being visible, it is simpler to mount a pump in the shower cubicle or over the bath. No extra plumbing is required as the pump is connected to the shower mixer by a flexible metal hose. A two core and earth electrical cable runs from the pump to a switched, fused connection unit (◁) which must be clearly identified and accessible, but out of reach of anyone using the shower or bath.

If you want to install a new shower where water pressure is low, buy a shower unit with an integral pump.

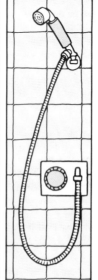
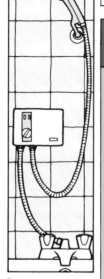

Manual shower mixer   **Booster pump**

INSTANTANEOUS SHOWER

An instantaneous shower solves many problems associated with other types of shower. It is designed specifically for connection to the mains water supply with one 15mm (½in) branch pipe from the rising main. Because the rising main passes through every floor of the house, you can install an instantaneous shower practically anywhere so long as drainage is feasible. Incoming water is heated within the unit so there is no separate hot water supply to balance. The shower is thermostatically controlled to prevent fluctuations in pressure affecting the water temperature – in fact it switches off completely if there is a serious failure of pressure.

Most instantaneous showers are electrically powered and require their own 30amp circuit from the consumer unit. A ceiling-mounted, 30 amp, double pole switch must be connected to the circuit to turn the appliance on and off (◁). Gas-heated showers are available but they should be installed by a qualified fitter.

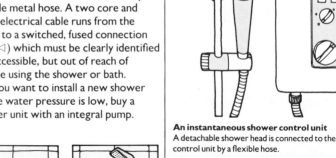

An instantaneous shower control unit
A detachable shower head is connected to the control unit by a flexible hose.

ELECTRICAL INSTALLATIONS

Electrical installations in a bathroom are dangerous unless they conform to the current Institute of Electrical Engineers wiring regulations. Read the electrical section in this book and manufacturers' instructions carefully to make sure you understand thoroughly the requirements for wiring in a bathroom before undertaking the work. If you are in any doubt, or have had no previous experience, hire a qualified electrician.

CONSTRUCTING A SHOWER CUBICLE

Without doubt, the simplest way to acquire a shower cubicle is to install a factory-assembled cabinet, complete with tray and shower mixer, together with waterproof doors or a curtain to contain the spray from the shower head. Having run supply pipes and drainage, the installation is complete. However, the cabinets are expensive. The alternative is to construct a purpose-made shower cubicle to fit exactly the space you have allocated.

SHOWER TRAYS

Shower trays are made from enamelled cast iron or steel, ceramics or glass-reinforced plastic. Metal or ceramic trays are substantial but heavy, and may require two people to move them into position. Plastic trays are lightweight and cheap but they have a tendency to flex slightly in use so it is particularly important to seal the edges carefully with a flexible mastic instead of relying on grout. Whatever material you choose, you should have no problem finding a colour to match other bathroom appliances.

Trays are between 750mm (2ft 6in) and 900mm (3ft) square. Most are designed to stand on the floor with a surrounding apron about 150mm (6in) in height. Some have adjustable feet to level the tray, or even a metal underframe to raise it off the floor to provide a fall for the waste-pipe. A plinth screwed across the front of the tray hides the underframe and plumbing while providing access to the trap for servicing. Some trays are intended to be flush with the floor.

A round waste outlet fits in the bottom of the tray much like a bath but it is not slotted to accommodate an overflow. Fit a space-saving, shallow-seal trap to the outlet.

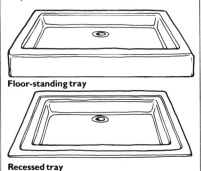

Floor-standing tray

Recessed tray

Choosing the site

When you are deciding upon the location of your shower, consider how you are going to build the walls of the cubicle. Some sites will involve more work than others.

Free-standing

You can place the shower tray against a flat wall and either construct a stud partition (▷) on each side, or surround the tray with a proprietary shower enclosure.

Corner site

If you place the tray in a corner of a room, two sides of the cubicle are ready-made. Either run a curtain around the tray or install a corner-entry enclosure with sliding doors. Alternatively, build a fixed side wall yourself and place a door or curtain across the entrance.

Built-in cupboards

Blend a shower cubicle into a bedroom by placing it into a corner as described above, then construct a built-in wardrobe unit between the shower and the opposite wall.

Concealing the plumbing

A shower with exposed pipework will work perfectly well but it spoils the appearance of the cubicle. You could install a proprietary rigid plastic pillar in the corner of the cubicle to cover the pipework and house the mixer and shower head.

If you erect a stud partition (▷) on one side, you can run the plumbing between the studs. Screw and glue exterior-grade plywood on the inside of the frame as a mounting board for the shower mixer and spray head. Connect the plumbing to the mixer before you panel the outside of the framework.

Cover the plywood panel with ceramic tiles or, alternatively, use a melamine-faced board, attaching it to the framework with metal angle-brackets. Prime the edges of the board and apply a mastic seal where it meets the wall and tray.

Running plumbing through a partition ▷
Conceal pipework in a simple timber partition covered with plywood and ceramic tiles.

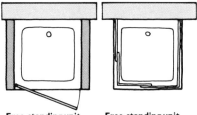

Free-standing unit
Two new partitions.

Free-standing unit
Proprietary enclosure.

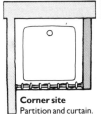

Corner site
Enclosed by a curtain.

Corner site
Proprietary enclosure.

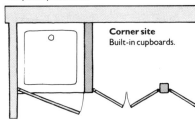

Corner site
Partition and curtain.

Corner site
Built-in cupboards.

SEE ALSO

Details for: ▷	
Stud partition	136-139
Bathroom planning	15
Primers	43
Tiling	99-104
Woodworking joints	476

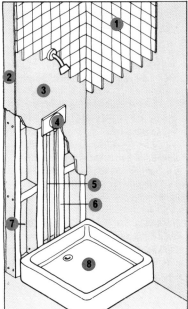

1 Ceramic tiles	5 Pipework
2 Timber cover strip	6 Timber frame
3 Exterior-grade plywood	7 Plasterboard
4 Shower mixer	8 Shower tray

Proprietary unit to conceal plumbing
The plastic corner pillar, shower set, tray and curtain are designed as a complete system.

SEE ALSO

◁ Details for:

Tiling	99-104
Wiring a shower	323
Connecting pipes	352-359
Leaking joints	353,354
Leaking joints	358,359
Strap boss	366
Waste outlet	368
Shallow-seal trap	368
Building partition	371
Panelling	87-88
Plasterboard	158-165
Turning off water	340

PROCEDURE FOR INSTALLING A SHOWER

Use the procedure below as a guide to the stage by stage installation of a shower and cubicle. Follow the instructions on fitting plastic or copper supply pipes and drainage (◁), and take note of the manufacturer's recommendations for the particular shower unit you are installing.

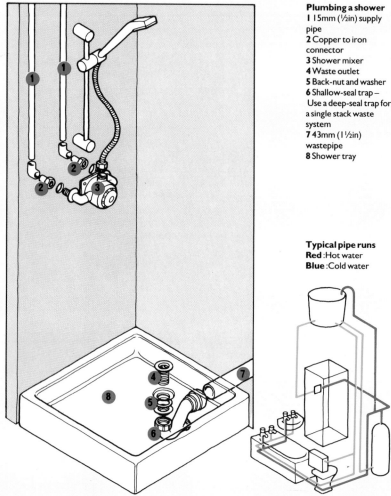

Plumbing a shower
1 15mm (½in) supply pipe
2 Copper to iron connector
3 Shower mixer
4 Waste outlet
5 Back-nut and washer
6 Shallow-seal trap – Use a deep-seal trap for a single stack waste system
7 43mm (1½in) wastepipe
8 Shower tray

Typical pipe runs
Red :Hot water
Blue :Cold water

• Fit the waste outlet in the shower tray and connect a shallow-seal trap as for a bath (◁).

• Install the tray and run a 43mm (1½in) wastepipe to the outside hopper. **To connect it to a waste stack with a strap boss** (◁), **use a deep-seal trap.**

• To enclose a shower, construct a stud partition on one side and line the inner surface with exterior-grade plywood.

• Cut a hole in the board for a flush-mounted shower mixer, or drill holes for the supply pipes to a surface-mounted version.

• Assemble the shower mixer and head according to the manufacturer's instructions.

• Connect it to 15mm (½in) pipes, running them back to the supply (◁). Turn off the water and join the pipes to the supply. Turn the water on again then test the installation for leaks (◁).

• Panel or plasterboard the outside of the stud partition and tile the inside of the cubicle using waterproof adhesive and grout (◁).

• Erect the shower enclosure or fit a shower rail and curtain.

• Seal around the edges of the tray with a flexible mastic.

Instantaneous showers

If you want to install an instanteous shower in the cubicle, run the electrical supply cable, and a single 15mm (½in) pipe from the rising main, through the stud partition (◁). Drill two holes in the wall behind the shower unit for the pipe and cable. Join a threaded or compression connector to the supply pipe, whichever is appropriate for the water inlet built into the shower unit. Make the electrical connections to the shower as recommended by the manufacturer and read the instructions for wiring a shower (◁).

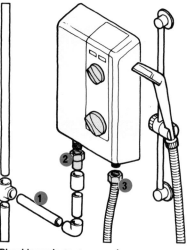

Plumbing an instantaneous shower
1 15mm (½in) pipe from rising main
2 Tap connector
3 Hose to shower head

Enclosing the shower

Showers in cubicles and over bath tubs must be provided with some means of preventing water spraying out onto the floor. Hanging a plastic curtain across the entrance is the simplest and cheapest method. Fit a ceiling-mounted curtain track or a tubular shower rail.

Even when a curtain is tucked into the shower tray, water always seems to escape around the sides of the curtain, or at least drips onto the floor when it is drawn aside. Make a more satisfactory enclosure with metal-framed glass or plastic panels. Hinged, sliding or concertina doors operate within an adjustable frame fixed to the top edge of the tray and the side walls. Bed the lower track onto mastic to make a waterproof joint with the tray and, having completed the enclosure, run a bead of mastic between the framework and the tiled walls of the cubicle.

PLUMBING A BIDET

Although a bidet is primarily for washing the lower parts of the body and genitals, it can double as a footbath for the elderly and small children. Due to the stringent requirements of the water authority, installing a bidet can be an expensive and time consuming procedure. However, if you opt for the simpler version, it is just like plumbing a wash basin.

Over-rim supply bidet

This type of bidet is simply a low level basin. It is fitted with individual hot and cold taps or a basin mixer, and has a built-in overflow running to the waste outlet in the basin. There's only one disadvantage with an over-rim bidet: it is cold when you sit astride it.

Rim supply bidet

A more sophisticated bidet delivers warm water to the basin via a hollow rim. Consequently the rim is pre-heated and comfortable to sit on. A special mixer set with a douche spray is fitted to this type of bidet. It incorporates the normal hot and cold valves but a control in the centre of the mixer diverts water from the rim to the spray head mounted in the bottom of the basin. Because the spray head is submerged when the basin is full, water authority regulations stipulate that a rim supply bidet must take its cold water directly from the storage cistern and there must be no other connections to that pipe. Similarly, the hot water supply must be completely independent and connected to the vent pipe immediately above the cylinder. Check with your water authority before you install a bidet to make sure you comply with local regulations.

INSTALLING A BIDET

When plumbing an over-rim supply bidet, use exactly the same procedures, pipes and connectors described for plumbing a washbasin (▷). Fit the taps, waste outlet and trap, then use a spirit level to position the bidet before fixing it to the floor with non-corrosive screws and washers. Supply the taps with branch pipes from the existing bathroom plumbing and take the wastepipe to the hopper or stack.

Attach the bidet set and trap to a rim supply appliance following the manufacturer's instructions. Screw the bidet to the floor before running 15mm (½in) supply pipes and a 36mm (1¼in) waste according to the water authority regulations (see left). Connect the cold supply to the cistern at the same level as the existing supply pipe (▷).

SEE ALSO

Details for: ▷	
Wash basin	365-366
Cistern supply	379
Bathroom planning	15
Connecting pipes	352-359
Taps	364
Strap boss	366

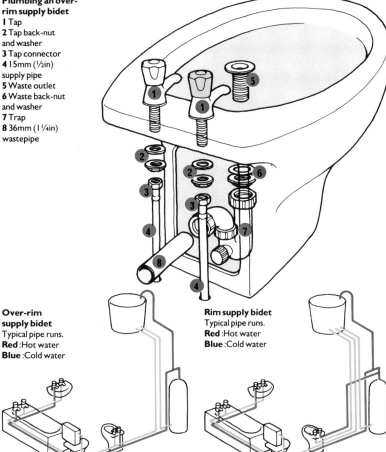

Plumbing an over-rim supply bidet
1 Tap
2 Tap back-nut and washer
3 Tap connector
4 15mm (½in) supply pipe
5 Waste outlet
6 Waste back-nut and washer
7 Trap
8 36mm (1¼in) wastepipe

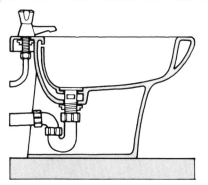

Over-rim supply bidet
Typical pipe runs.
Red : Hot water
Blue : Cold water

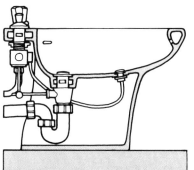

Rim supply bidet
Typical pipe runs.
Red : Hot water
Blue : Cold water

Space for a bidet
When planning the position of a bidet, allow enough knee room on each side – about 700mm (2ft 3in) overall

Over-rim supply bidet
This type of bidet is simple to install, just like any wash basin.

Rim supply bidet
The installation of this type of bidet is complicated by the submerged douche spray. Independent plumbing is essential, and you will need a special mixer set.

FITTING A NEW SINK

A house that has not been improved substantially for perhaps fifty years or more may well have an old fashioned, glazed stoneware sink in the kitchen. Even if you wanted to, it is virtually impossible to incorporate this type of sink into a modern range of kitchen fitments. As it happens, most stoneware sinks were replaced years ago by a stainless steel sinktop incorporating a bowl and drainer in a single pressing, but that too might look somewhat outdated when compared with the present-day colourful alternatives.

SEE ALSO

◁ Details for:

Kitchen planning	16
Taps	364
Kitchen decor	34

Choosing a kitchen sink

Choose the sink to make the best use of available space, to suit the style of the kitchen, and according to how many other appliances you plan to install which will relieve the sink area of certain functions. Unless your kitchen is fitted with an automatic dishwasher, for instance, the sink must be large enough to cope with a considerable volume of washing-up, and not just the obvious dishes. Don't forget to allow for larger items like baking trays, oven racks and freezer baskets. In addition, check that the bowl is deep enough to fill a bucket from the kitchen tap. If space allows, select a unit with two bowls, primarily for washing and rinsing dishes but also to ensure that one bowl is always free for washing vegetables and salads even when the second is occupied by soaking laundry. If you plan to install a waste disposal unit, one of the bowls must have a waste outlet of the appropriate size (See opposite), or choose a sink unit with a small bowl reserved especially for waste disposal. A double drainer is another useful feature, but if space is limited, allow at least some space to the side of the bowl to avoid piling soiled and clean crockery on a single drainer.

One-piece sinktops are made to modular sizes to fit standard kitchen base units, but sinks which are designed to be set into a continuous work surface offer greater flexibility in size, shape and above all, positioning. What's more, you can set individual bowls or drainers into the worktop to design the layout to suit yourself, and even add a second bowl at a later stage if the need arises. If you opt for this type of installation, choose a drainer equipped with its own waste outlet to drain surface water into the trap beneath the bowl.

Stainless and enamelled steel are still the most popular materials for sinktops, but inset sinks in particular are also made from plastics and ceramic.

Kitchen taps

Kitchen taps are similar in style to those used for wash basins (◁), and there is a kitchen version incorporating the various types of mechanism, but a kitchen mixer has an additional feature. Cold drinking water is supplied from the rising main whereas the hot water at a sink comes from the same storage cylinder that supplies all the other hot taps in the house. As it is against water authority regulations to mix mains and stored water within a fitting, a sink mixer has separate waterways to isolate one supply from the other until the water emerges from the spout. If you are fitting a double-bowl sink, choose a mixer with a swivelling spout. Some sink mixers have an additional hot rinse attachment with a lever-operated spray and detachable brush head for removing stubborn food scraps from crockery and saucepans. Alternatively, you can install an individual attachment supplied by a flexible hose plumbed into the hot water supply pipe below the sink. Make sure the sink you choose is supplied with a hole in the rim to accept the attachment holder.

Individual kitchen taps resemble basin taps in every respect except for their extended pillars to make it possible to fill a bucket in the sink. Sink taps and mixers are provided with 15mm (½in) tails for connecting to the pipes.

Accessories for a kitchen sink

There is a range of accessories designed to fit most kitchen sinks, typically a hardwood or laminated plastic chopping board which drops into the rim of the bowl or drainer; and a selection of plastic-dipped wire baskets for rinsing vegetables or draining crockery and cutlery. Pump-action dispensers for soap and washing-up liquid rid the sink of unsightly plastic bottles and soap dishes.

SINK UNITS, TAPS AND ACCESSORIES

There is a wide variety of kitchen sinks, taps and accessories for the domestic market. Steel, enamel, plastic, double, single, plain and coloured: a bewildering choice when planning your kitchen (◁). Shown below is a cross section of popular sinks, accessories and taps to assist you with your decision.

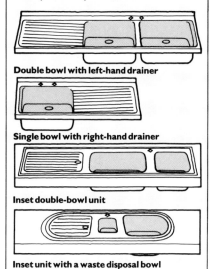

Double bowl with left-hand drainer

Single bowl with right-hand drainer

Inset double-bowl unit

Inset unit with a waste disposal bowl

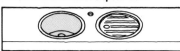

Individual sink and drainer

Swivel mixers

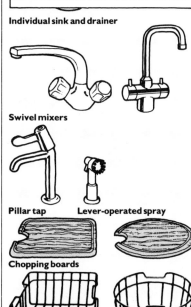

Pillar tap   **Lever-operated spray**

Chopping boards

Wire baskets

INSTALLING A SINK

The installation of a kitchen sink is essentially the same as fitting a wash basin or vanity unit (▷). All except a ceramic sink will require a combined overflow/waste outlet like a bath (▷). Fit a tubular trap to a sink because a bottle trap blocks too easily.

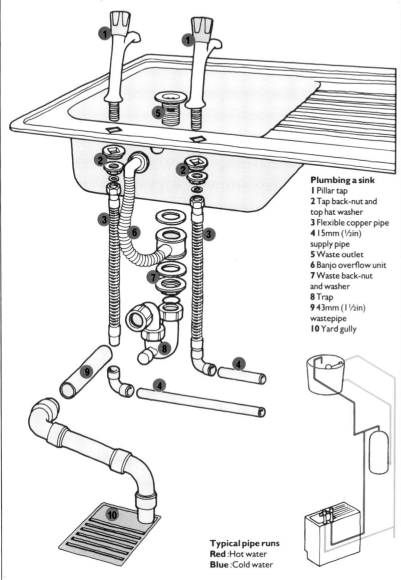

Plumbing a sink
1 Pillar tap
2 Tap back-nut and top hat washer
3 Flexible copper pipe
4 15mm (1/2in) supply pipe
5 Waste outlet
6 Banjo overflow unit
7 Waste back-nut and washer
8 Trap
9 43mm (1 1/2in) wastepipe
10 Yard gully

Typical pipe runs
Red : Hot water
Blue : Cold water

• Fit the taps, overflow and waste outlet to the sink before you place it in position.

• Turn off the hot and cold supply then remove the old sink by dismantling the plumbing. Hack the old pipes from the wall unless you plan to adapt them.

• Clamp the new sink to its base unit or worktop with the fittings provided, then run a 15mm (1/2in) cold supply from the rising main and a branch pipe of the same size from the nearest hot water pipe. Connect the pipes to the taps with flexible copper tap conectors (▷). If you prefer to use standard pipe and tap connectors, attach short spur pipes to each tap tail before you install the sink.

• Fit the trap and run a 43mm (1 1/2in) wastepipe through the wall behind the base unit to the yard gully. According to current regulations, the pipe should pass through the grid covering the gully but stop short of the water in the gully trap. Adapt an existing grid by cutting out one corner with a hacksaw.

WASTE DISPOSAL

Waste disposal units

A waste disposal unit provides an hygienic method of dealing with soft food scraps, reserving the kitchen wastebin for dry refuse and bones. The unit houses an electric motor which drives steel cutters for grinding food scraps into a fine slurry which is washed into the yard gully or soil stack. A continuous-feed disposal unit is operated by a manual switch, then, with the cold tap running, scraps are fed into it. To prevent the unit being switched on accidentally, a batch-feed model cannot be operated until a removable plug is inserted in the sink waste outlet.

Most disposal units are designed to fit an 89mm (3 1/2in) outlet in the base of the sink bowl. A special cutter can be hired to adapt a standard stainless steel or plastic sink.

With a sink waste outlet and seal in position (▷), clamp a retaining collar to the outlet from under the sink. Bolt or clip the unit housing to the collar: every unit is supplied with individual instructions.

The waste outlet from the unit itself fits a standard sink trap (not a bottle trap) and wastepipe. If the wastepipe runs to a yard gully, make sure it passes through the covering grid (see left). Wire the unit to a switched, fused connection unit (▷) mounted above the worktop where it is out of the reach of children. Identify the switch to avoid accidental operation.

SEE ALSO

Details for : ▷

Fused connection unit	314
Wash basin	365-366
Tap connectors	366
Fitting sink waste	366
Overflow/waste	368
Earthing	290
Connecting pipes	352-359

Cutting a hole for a waste disposal unit
The supplier of the waste disposal unit, or possibly a tool hire company, will rent you a special cutter to convert an existing sink. The cutter cannot be used on a ceramic sink.

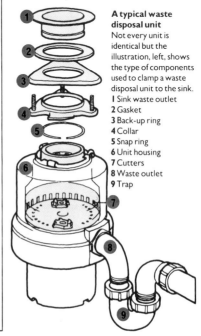

A typical waste disposal unit
Not every unit is identical but the illustration, left, shows the type of components used to clamp a waste disposal unit to the sink.
1 Sink waste outlet
2 Gasket
3 Back-up ring
4 Collar
5 Snap ring
6 Unit housing
7 Cutters
8 Waste outlet
9 Trap

375

WASHING MACHINES

PLUMBING A DISHWASHER AND WASHING MACHINE

SEE ALSO

◁ Details for:
Draining system	340
Compression joints	354
Storage cistern	369,379
Kitchen planning	16
Connecting pipes	352-359

Appliance valves
Typical valves used to connect washing machines or dishwashers to the water supply.

In-line valve

Right-angle valve

Tee-piece valve

The full potential of a dishwasher or washing machine as a labour-saving appliance is somewhat limited if you have to pull it out from under a worksurface before attaching flexible hoses to the kitchen sink. If at all possible, provide any automatic machine with permanent supply and waste systems. Dishwashers need a cold supply only whereas washing machines may be hot and cold fill. Washing machines supplied with hot water provide a faster washing cycle and may be more economical to run depending on how you heat your water. Any retailer will be happy to advise you.

Instructions supplied with the machine should state what water pressure is required. If the machine is installed upstairs, make sure the storage cistern is high enough to provide the required pressure (◁). In a downstairs kitchen or utility room, there is rarely a problem with pressure, especially if you can take the cold water from the mains supply at the sink. However, check with your water authority if you want to connect more than one machine.

Plumbing a washing machine
1 15mm (½in) supply pipe
2 Appliance valve
3 PVC inlet hose
4 Machine inlets
5 Outlet hose
6 Standpipe
7 Trap
8 43mm (1½in) wastepipe to gully

Running the supply

Washing machines and dishwashers are supplied with PVC hoses to link the water inlets at the back of each appliance to special miniature valves connected to the household plumbing. Using these valves, you can turn off the water to service a machine without disrupting the supply to the rest of the house. There are a number of valves to choose from. Select the type which provides the most practical method of connecting to the plumbing depending on the location of the machine in relation to existing pipework.

Self-bore valves

When 15mm (½in) cold and hot water pipes run conveniently behind or alongside the machine, use a valve which bores a hole in the pipe without having to turn off the water supply and drain the system. Each valve is colour coded for hot or cold, and has a threaded outlet for the standard machine hose. Self-bore valves are not approved by all water authorities because the small disc of metal they cut from the pipe may restrict the flow of water. In practice, this hardly ever happens.

To fit a valve, screw the backplate to the wall behind the pipe. Place the saddle with its rubber seal over the pipe. Ensure that the holes in the seal and saddle are aligned before screwing the saddle to the backplate (**1**).

Make sure the valve is turned off then screw it to the saddle (**2**). As you insert the valve, the integral cutter bores a hole in the pipe. With the valve in the vertical position, tighten the adjusting nut with a spanner (**3**). Connect the hose to the valve outlet (**4**).

1 Fit the saddle   **2 Insert the valve**

3 Tighten the nut   **4 Attach the hose**

Running branch pipes

If you have to extend the plumbing to reach the machine, take branch pipes from the hot and cold pipes supplying the kitchen taps. Terminate the pipes at a convenient position close to the machine and fit a small appliance valve (**See left**) with a standard compression joint (◁) for connecting to the pipework and a threaded outlet for the hose. When you are fitting this type of valve, turn off the water and drain the system in the normal way (◁). When the supply is restored, open the valve by turning the control level to align with the outlet.

SUPPLYING DRAINAGE

Washing machines and dishwashers are supplied with an outlet hose which must be connected to a waste system to discharge dirty water into a yard gully or single waste stack.

Standpipe and trap

The standard method, approved by all water authorities, employs a vertical 43mm (1½in) plastic standpipe attached to a deep-seal trap. Most plumbing suppliers stock the standpipe, trap and wall fixings as a kit. The machine hose fits loosely in the open-ended pipe to avoid the possibility of dirty water being siphoned back into the machine. Check with the machine manufacturer's instructions regarding the position of the standpipe, but in the absence of other advice, ensure that the open end is at least 600mm (2ft) above the floor.

Cut a hole through the wall to the outside and run the wastepipe to the gully, or attach it to a drainage stack with a strap boss (▷). Allow a minimum fall of 6mm (¼in) for every 300mm (1ft) of pipe run.

Anti-siphon devices

The standpipe and trap method of draining domestic appliances prevents back-siphonage by venting the pipe to the air. There are other ways of dealing with the problem, but you should check with your local water authority to ensure that such methods meet with their approval. If an existing 36 or 43mm (1¼ or 1½in) wastepipe runs behind the machine, you can attach a hose connector which incorporates a non-return valve to eliminate reverse flow. Connectors are available with short spigots (**1**) or as a standpipe. Double standpipes (**2**) permit two appliances to drain into the same connector.

Clamp the saddle over the wastepipe (**3**), then use the cutter supplied with the fitting to bore a hole in the pipe using the saddle as a guide (**4**).

You can drain a washing machine to a sink trap which has a built-in connector for the hose, but you should insert an in-line anti-siphon return valve in the appliance drain hose. It is a small plastic device with a hose connector at each end (**5**).

PREVENTING A FLOOD

Anyone who has had the misfortune of a flooded kitchen caused by a split hose or some mechanical breakdown within a machine will be only too aware of the possible extent of the damage. If the machine is unattended, water continues to flow at mains pressure, ruining floor coverings and furnishings. The consequences can be even worse if the machine is installed upstairs. Once the ceiling beneath becomes thoroughly waterlogged, it collapses, dumping the flood water into the room below.

An overflow safety valve, fitted into the supply, measures the amount of water passing through. If a fault occurs, and the volume of water exceeds a predetermined setting, the valve shuts off the supply immediately. The valve is set before installation to allow for the capacity of the machine it is monitoring plus a small safety margin to avoid excessive sensitivity. Setting instructions are provided by the manufacturer. If a flood occurs, some damage is inevitable, but the valve will avert a disaster. Once the fault is repaired, the valve is reset by pressing a button inside the outlet.

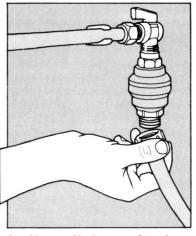

Attaching a machine hose to a safety valve

SEE ALSO	
Details for: ▷	
Strap boss	366
Cutting wall	280
Connecting pipes	352-359
Wall fixings	494-495

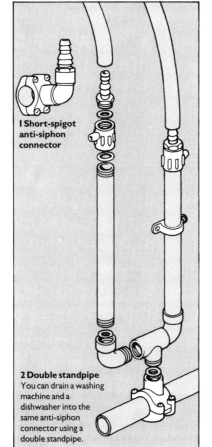

1 Short-spigot anti-siphon connector

2 Double standpipe
You can drain a washing machine and a dishwasher into the same anti-siphon connector using a double standpipe.

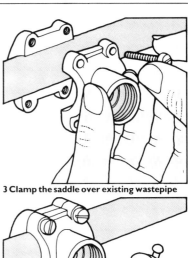

3 Clamp the saddle over existing wastepipe

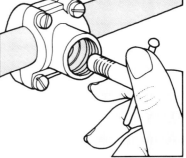

4 Bore a hole with the special cutter

5 An in-line anti-siphon hose valve

WATER SOFTENERS

Water treated at the local waterworks is rendered safe to drink in that all harmful impurities are removed before it is supplied to our houses. However, minerals absorbed from the ground before treatment are still present, and it is the concentration of these minerals which determines whether our water is hard or soft.

SEE ALSO

◁ Details for:
Fused
connection unit   314
Draining system   340
Connecting pipes 352-359
PTFE tape   354
Washing machine   376
Bib tap   352
Wall fixings   494-495

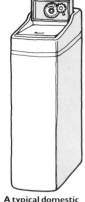

A typical domestic water softener

Rocky terrain gives rise to surface-run water which is naturally soft, but in areas of the country where water runs through the ground, rather than over it, a much higher dissolved mineral content produces slightly to very hard water. These impurities are not visible in tap water, but mineral salts are deposited in the form of hard scale on the inside of pipes, cisterns, and especially, hot water cylinders. If the concentration of minerals is very high, scale can eventually block pipework, and insulate heating elements to such an extent that their efficiency is reduced by anything from 15 to 70 per cent. The more obvious effects of hard water are the scumming and discoloration of baths and basins, blocked shower heads, blemished stainless steel surfaces and furred-up kettles. Most people learn to live with them, but all these effects can be reduced or even eliminated by installing a water softener.

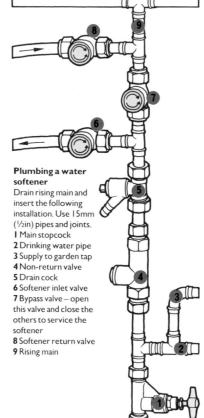

Plumbing a water softener
Drain rising main and insert the following installation. Use 15mm (½in) pipes and joints.
1 Main stopcock
2 Drinking water pipe
3 Supply to garden tap
4 Non-return valve
5 Drain cock
6 Softener inlet valve
7 Bypass valve – open this valve and close the others to service the softener
8 Softener return valve
9 Rising main

Domestic water softeners

Water softeners work on the principle of ion exchange. Incoming hard water flows through a compartment containing a synthetic resin which absorbs scale-forming calcium and magnesium ions and releases sodium ions in their place. After a period of two or three days, the resin is unable to absorb any more mineral salts at which time the softener automatically flushes the compartment with a saline solution to regenerate the resin. Topping up with granular salt is required at intervals of perhaps two to three months. Water softeners are fitted with a timer to programme regeneration for the early hours of the morning when water consumption is at its lowest.

The unit must be connected to the rising main at the point where it enters the house, which could be under the stairs, in the cellar or utility room, but more than likely in the kitchen. For this reason, softeners designed for average domestic use will fit under a standard kitchen worktop.

Installing a water softener

The installation of a water softener appears at first sight to be fairly complicated because it involves a great deal of joint making, firstly to include the valves and branch pipes to supply and bypass the softener, but also to include certain fittings to comply with water authority regulations.

The bypass assembly allows for the unit to be isolated for servicing while maintaining the supply of water to the rest of the house. In addition, you must install a branch pipe before the assembly to supply unsoftened drinking water to the kitchen sink. Supply a garden tap from the same pipe – there is no need to waste softened water on the garden.

Most water authorities will require a non-return valve in the system to prevent the reverse flow of salty water, and possibly a pressure reducing valve as well. You will also need a draincock to empty the rising main. Some manufacturers supply an installation kit which includes all the necessary equipment.

You will have to provide drainage in the form of a standpipe and trap as for a washing machine (▷).

Wire the softener to a switched, fused connection unit containing a 3 amp fuse (▷).

Typical pipe runs
A domestic system incorporating a softener.
Red:Hot water
Blue:Cold water

FITTING A GARDEN TAP

A tap situated on an outside wall is far more convenient than the kitchen sink for filling buckets or watering cans, and for attaching a hose for a lawn sprinkler or for washing the car.

Bib taps for garden installation are made with a threaded spout or push-on connector for a hose. The tap inlet screws into a wall plate.

Turn off the main stopcock and drain the rising main (◁). Fit a tee joint (**1**) in the rising main to run the supply to the tap. Connect a short length of pipe to a miniature valve (**2**). During the winter you can close this valve and run the garden tap to empty the pipe in case it should freeze. Continue with the pipework to the outside location, drilling a hole through the wall with a large masonry drill (**3**). Screw the wall plate compression joint onto the pipe (◁) but do not tighten it (**4**). Mark the wall plate fixing holes, then remove it to drill and plug the holes. Screw the plate to the wall and tighten the compression joint. Wrap PTFE tape around the tap's threaded inlet (◁) and screw it into the wall plate (**5**). Turn on the supply and check for leaks.

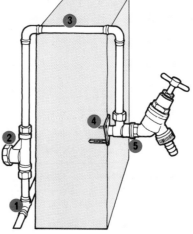

Pipes and fittings to supply a garden tap

STORAGE CISTERNS

The cold water storage cistern, normally situated in the roofspace, supplies the hot water cylinder and all the cold taps in the house other than the one used for drinking water in the kitchen. An old house may still be fitted with a heavy, galvanized steel cistern which has probably been in service since the house was built. Eventually it will corrode and although it can be patched up temporarily with an epoxy filler, it makes sense to replace it before a serious leak develops.

A circular, 227 litre (50 gallon) capacity, polythene cistern is the most popular choice as a replacement because it can be folded to pass through a narrow hatchway to the loft. It is also very much lighter and easier to handle than the old style cistern. Make sure the new cistern is supplied with a lid to keep the water clean.

Removing the old cistern

Switch off water-heating appliances, then close the stopcock on the rising main and drain the cistern by opening the bathroom cold taps.

Bail out the remaining water in the bottom of the cistern, then use a spanner to disconnect the fittings connecting the float valve, distribution pipes and overflow, to the cistern. Use a little penetrating oil if the fittings are stiff with corrosion. The cistern may have been built into the house before the roof was completed, so it is unlikely to pass through the loft hatch. In any case it is very cumbersome, so just pull it to one side.

Installing the new cistern

You may be able to use the existing fittings although the pipework is unlikely to fit the new cistern without some modification. If the fittings are badly corroded, buy new replacements.

Prepare a firm base for the cistern by nailing stout planks across the joists or build a platform with 18mm (3/4in) thick chipboard or plywood.

PLUMBING A NEW CISTERN

Connecting the float valve
A float valve shuts off the supply of water from the rising main when the cistern is full (▷). Cut a hole for the float valve, 75mm (3in) below the top of the cistern. As a float valve is relatively heavy, some cisterns are supplied with a reinforcing plate to stiffen the plastic around the hole.

Slip a plastic washer onto the tail of the float valve and pass it through the hole. Place another washer and fixing nut on the outside, then tighten the fitting with two spanners.

Screw a tap connector (▷) onto the valve ready for connecting to the 15mm (1/2in) rising main.

Connecting the distribution pipes
The 22mm (3/4in) pipes running to cylinder and cold taps are attached to the cistern with tank connectors – threaded inlets with a compression fitting (▷) for the pipework. Drill a hole for each tank connector about 50mm (2in) above the bottom of the cistern. Slip a connector, plus washer, through each hole from the inside, then tighten the fixing nut and washer on the outside to clamp the fitting to the cistern. The distribution pipes will be attached to the protruding spigots.

Take the opportunity to fit a gate valve (▷) to each distribution pipe so that you can cut off the supply of water without having to empty the cistern.

Connecting the overflow
Use a bent plastic tank connector for the overflow pipe. Drill a hole for it, 25mm (1in) below the level of the float valve inlet. Pass the connector through the hole and tighten its fixing nut on the inside of the cistern.

Attach a 21mm (3/4in) plastic overflow pipe to the connector using its compression fitting. Run the pipe to the floor, then to the outside of the house maintaining a continuous fall. The pipe must emerge in a conspicuous position so that an overflow can be detected immediately. Clip the overflow to the roof timbers.

Connecting the plumbing
Modify the rising main and distribution pipes to align with their fittings then connect them with compression fittings (▷). (Don't use soldered joints near a plastic cistern.) Clip all the pipework securely to the joists.

Open the main stopcock and check for leaks as the cistern fills. As the water level approaches the top, adjust the float arm to maintain the level 25mm (1in) below the overflow outlet (▷).

There is a hole in the lid to accommodate the vent pipe from the hot water cylinder (▷). Either adapt the pipe to pass through the hole, or drop a plastic funnel into the hole to catch the water discharged from the pipe. Finally, insulate the cistern and pipework (▷).

Plumbing a cistern.
1 Float valve
2 Reinforcing plate
3 Tap connector
4 Rising main
5 Tank connector
6 Gate valve
7 22mm (3/4in) distribution pipe
8 Pipe clip
9 21mm (3/4in) overflow pipe
10 Vent pipe

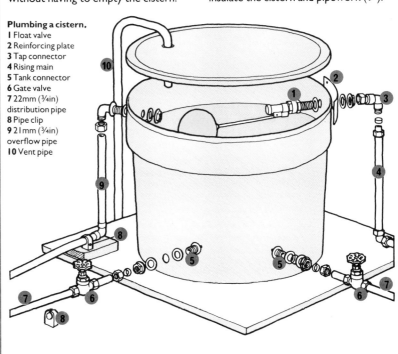

SEE ALSO

Details for: ▷	
Insulation	261,266
Float valves	345-346
Tap connector	346
Adjusting float arm	346
Gate valve	352
Compression joint	354
Cylinder	380

Tank cutters
Hire a tank cutter to bore holes in a cistern for pipework. Some cutters are adjustable to drill holes of different diameters. Alternatively, use a hole saw clamped to a drill.

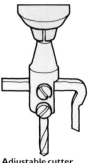

Adjustable cutter

Hole saw

REPLACING A HOT WATER CYLINDER

The hot water in most houses is heated and stored in a large copper cylinder situated in the airing cupboard. Cold water is fed to the base of the cylinder from the storage cistern in the loft. As the water is heated, it rises to the top of the cylinder where it is drawn off via the vent pipe to the hot taps.

SEE ALSO

◁ Details for:
Lagging   261
Cheap hot water   286
Fused connection   314
Side-entry heaters   318
Electrics   318-319
Ceiling switch   323
Cistern supply   339
Draining system   340
Connecting pipes 352-359
PTFE tape   354
Compression fitting 354
Boiler   391-392

Packaged plumbing
In an apartment, the cistern might be mounted in a frame over the cylinder (**1**), or both might be built into a single casing (**2**).

Direct systems
Heating may be accomplished with electric immersion heaters only. A single or double element heater is fitted into the top of the cylinder, or there may be two individual side entry heaters (◁). On the other hand, the water may be heated in a boiler with the sole purpose of providing hot water for the cylinder. A cold water pipe runs from the base of the cylinder, to the boiler where it is heated and returns to the top half of the cylinder. Both methods are known as direct systems. In reality, a boiler-heated cylinder is usually fitted with an immersion heater as well to supply hot water during the summer months when the boiler would make the kitchen or utility room uncomfortably warm.

Indirect system
When a house is centrally heated with radiators fed by a boiler (◁), the water in the cylinder is normally heated indirectly by a heat exchanger. Hot water from the boiler passes through the exchanger, a coiled tube within the cylinder, where the heat is transmitted to the stored water. The heat exchanger is part of a completely self-contained system with its own small storage cistern in the loft which tops up the system. A vent pipe terminates open-ended over the same small cistern. The whole system is known as the primary circuit, and the pipes running from and back to the boiler are known as the primary flow and return. An indirect system might be supplemented by an immersion heater.

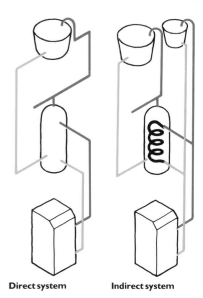

Direct system   **Indirect system**

Typical pipe runs
Red: Hot water
Blue: Cold water

CYLINDERS

The capacity of domestic cylinders ranges from 114 litres (25 gallons) to about 227 litres (50 gallons) although there are bigger cylinders to meet the requirements of large families. A cylinder with a capacity of between 182 and 227 litres (40 and 50 gallons) will store enough hot water to satisfy the needs of an average family for a whole day. Many cylinders are made from thin, uninsulated copper. They need a thick lagging jacket to reduce heat loss, but there is a growing preference for factory-insulated cylinders covered with a layer of foamed polyurethane.

1 Frame-mounted cistern

2 Cased cistern and cylinder

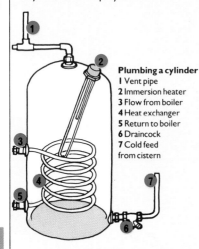

Plumbing a cylinder
1 Vent pipe
2 Immersion heater
3 Flow from boiler
4 Heat exchanger
5 Return to boiler
6 Draincock
7 Cold feed from cistern

Changing a cylinder

You may wish to replace an existing cylinder because it has sprung a leak, or because a larger one will allow you to take full advantage of economical night time electricity by storing more cheap hot water (◁). A simple replacement can be achieved without modifing the plumbing but you will have to adapt the pipework to fit a larger cylinder.

Drain the pipework and cylinder (◁). Disconnect any immersion heaters from the electrical supply (◁). Then use a special spanner available from a tool hire outlet to unscrew them. Disconnect all the pipework, springing it out of the way while you remove the cylinder.

Place the new cylinder in position and check the pipework for alignment. Modify the pipes as necessary (◁), then make the connections using PTFE tape to make sure the threaded joints are watertight (◁). Take the opportunity to fit a draincock to the supply pipe from the cistern (◁).

With the rubber sealing washer in place, wrap PTFE tape around the thread of an immersion heater and screw it into the cylinder. Reconnect it to the electrical supply (◁), then fill the system and check for leaks before attempting to heat the water. Check for leaks again when the water is up to temperature, and if all is well, lag the cylinder and pipework (◁).

INSTANTANEOUS WATER HEATERS

Instantaneous water heaters provide hot water at the point it is required – over the sink or hand basin. When you turn the tap, the flow of water activates a powerful electric heater, or ignites the burner in the case of a gas appliance. (Gas water heaters should be installed by a qualified fitter.)

Electric heaters are supplied with water from the rising main with 15mm (½in) pipework connected to the water inlet just below the tap with a standard compression fitting (◁).

A 3kW model, suitable for a basin, is wired to a fused connection unit containing a 13 amp fuse (◁). Use a 7kW heater over a sink. That requires a 30 amp circuit like a shower but in a kitchen you can use a wall-mounted double pole switch to connect it instead of a ceiling-mounted switch (◁).

Connecting a 3kW heater
1 Fused connection unit
2 15mm (½in) supply pipe

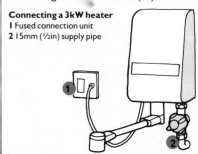

OPEN FIRES **382**

FIREPLACES 384

CLOSED FIRES **386**

LOG-BURNING STOVES 387

LINING FLUES 388

MAINTAINING FIRE SURROUNDS 389

CENTRAL HEATING **390**

BOILERS 392

RADIATORS 393

CENTRAL HEATING CONTROLS 395

FAULT FINDING 396

CENTRAL HEATING MAINTENANCE 397

PUMPS AND CONTROL VALVES 402

STORAGE HEATERS **404**

HEATING

OPEN FIRES

For centuries open fires were our only domestic heating. Inefficient and wasteful, their only benefits were the radiant heat from the burning fuel and some milder warmth from heated chimneys. They are nowadays used mainly as attractive focal points in homes heated by more modern means.

SEE ALSO

◁ Details for:

Treating stained chimney	48
Ventilating fireplace	275
Pointing trowel	478

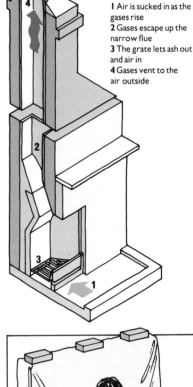

The simple workings of a traditional open fire
1 Air is sucked in as the gases rise
2 Gases escape up the narrow flue
3 The grate lets ash out and air in
4 Gases vent to the air outside

How an open fire works

To burn well any fire needs a good supply of oxygen (1) and a means for its smoke and gases to escape (2). If either of these is cut off the fire will be stifled and will eventually go out.

The domestic open fire is built on a barred grate (3) through which ash and debris fall into a removable tray and oxygen is sucked up into the base of the fire to maintain combustion.

As the fuel burns it gives off various heated gases which expand and become lighter than the surrounding air so that they rise (4). To prevent the gases and smoke drifting out and filling the room a chimney above the fire gives them an escape route, taking them above the roof level of the house to be harmlessly discharged into the atmosphere beyond.

As the hot gases rise they cause the suction at the bottom of the fire which draws in the supply of oxygen that keeps it burning. For this reason a good fire needs not only an effective chimney but also good ventilation in the room where it is burning so that the air consumed by the fire can be continually replenished. Sometimes efficient draughtproofing at doors and windows can cause problems with a fire, and prevent its burning properly by denying it the constant supply of air that it needs. In such a case the ventilation must be provided by means of an airbrick or a window vent; under floor ventilation is another possibility.

Sweeping chimneys

- **Vacuum sweeping**
You can hire a special vacuum cleaner for chimney sweeping. Its nozzle is inserted through a cover over the fire opening and sucks out the soot – a very clean method but no use for heavy soot deposits or other obstructions.

- **Chemical cleaning**
There are chemicals which remove light soot deposits and stop further sooting up. In liquid or powder form, sprinkled on the hot fire, they make a non-toxic gas which causes soot to crumble away from the chimney sides.

All solid fuels give off dust, ash, acids and tarry substances as they burn, and this material is carried up through the chimney, where a part of it collects as soot. If too much soot collects in a chimney it effectively reduces the diameter, and therefore the gas flow, and prevents the fire burning properly. It can even cause a complete blockage, particularly at a bend, or the more serious hazard of a chimney fire.

To prevent soot building up, sweep your chimneys at least twice a year, once during the heating season and once at the end to prevent acids in the soot attacking the chimney's lining and mortar joints during the summer. If a chimney is left unswept for long the fuel consumption may increase, smoke may start billowing into the room and soot may occasionally drop into the fire.

Though it's seemingly a dirty job you can sweep a chimney without making a great deal of mess to be cleaned up afterwards, providing you take some care. You can hire the brushes. The modern ones have nylon bristles and 'canes' made from polypropylene.

Remove all loose items from the fire surround and the hearth, then roll back the carpet and cover it with a dustsheet or newspapers for protection. Drape a large old sheet or blanket over the fire surround, weighting it down along the top and leaning something heavy against each side to form a seal with the edges of the fire surround.

Screw the brush to the first cane, place it in the fireplace, gather the sheet round the cane and weight down its edges on the hearth. Now screw on the next length of cane and push the brush up the chimney. Continue screwing on the lengths of cane and pushing the brush upwards until you feel the resistance to the brush from the sides of the chimney stop as the brush emerges from the top of the chimney pot. If the pot has a cowl on its top you should station someone outside, ready to shout to you when the brush appears so that you can stop pushing before you push the cowl off.

If the brush meets an obstruction in the chimney, pull it back slightly, then push upwards again, working it up and down until you clear the blockage. Don't twist the canes to and fro: this may unscrew a join and leave the brush stuck up the chimney irretrievably.

Pull the brush back down, unscrewing the canes as they appear, then finally pull out the brush and shovel the heap of soot out of the grate.

Though using a brush and canes is the most time-honoured – and the most effective – way of sweeping a chimney, in recent years some other methods have been found for doing this dirty job (See left).

Cleaning your chimney
Seal off the fireplace with an old sheet and feed the canes up under it

MENDING A CRACKED FIREBACK

Years of intense heat will damage a fireback eventually, but though large cracks may mean a replacement, fine ones can be repaired. First let the fireback cool for at least 48 hours, then brush away all soot and rake the cracks out with a trowel point, undercutting their sides to make an inverted V-shape. Brush out the dust and soak the area well with water for better cement adhesion. With a small trowel work fire cement well into the cracks, trowel away the surplus, then go over it with a paintbrush and clean water for a smooth finish. Let it dry for a few days before lighting a fire.

REPLACING A FIREBACK

You may want to remove an old fireback because it is damaged and unsightly, and the exposed brick recess can be used to make an attractive niche for

flowers, house plants and ornaments. Alternatively you can replace the fireback with a new one and have a functioning fireplace in the room again.

Removing an old fireback

If you plan to replace the old fireback, first measure the width across its mouth and order the new one. The standard sizes are 400mm (1ft 4in) and 450mm (1ft 6in), though there are larger ones.

Cover the floor with a dustsheet, protect a tiled hearth with cardboard, and remove the grate (1) . It may simply rest on the back hearth or it may be screwed down and sealed to the fireback with asbestos rope and fire cement (2) . If so, take out the screws and chip away the cement with a hammer and cold chisel to free it.

Break out the old fireback (3) with a hammer and chisel, starting at one corner. If cracks develop exploit them to remove larger pieces. Take care not to damage the fire surround when you are breaking the cement seal (4) between it and the fireback. Don't touch the asbestos braid packing (5) between the fireback and the surround unless it is in poor condition and needs replacing (See right).

With the fireback out you will find a lot of rubble in the space behind (6) . Chop this out with hammer and chisel until you have cleared the original brick-lined builder's opening.

Installing a new fireback

Though your new fireback will be supplied in one piece you will have to install it in two pieces, divided horizontally, to allow for the expansion and contraction of the lower portion because of heat from the fire.

A recessed cutting line across the fireback shows where the two halves must be separated. This is done by tapping gently along the line with a bolster chisel and a hammer.

Mix up a mortar of 4 parts vermiculite, 1 part lime or cement and trowel a layer of it round the rear edge of the back hearth (1) to make a bed for the lower portion of the fireback. Then ease that portion into position, at the same time pulling it forward so that it lightly compresses the asbestos rope packing at the edges of the fire surround. Check that the fireback is properly upright.

Now cut out two pieces of corrugated cardboard to the shape of the fireback's bottom portion and place them immediately behind it (2) . When the fire is lighted they will char away, leaving a narrow expansion gap behind the fireback.

Fill in the whole area behind the back of the fireback (3) with the same mix of mortar as was used to bed it on the hearth. To save on mortar you can add old bricks or bits of the broken old fireback to the mix as an infill (4) . Bring the mortar up level with the top edge of the fireback bottom portion (5) , tamping it well down with a piece of

wood as you go.

Trowel a layer of mortar along the top edge of the fireback lower portion and set the top portion in place on it (6), making sure that the two halves are accurately lined up. Trowel off the squeezed-out surplus mortar and finish off the joint by brushing clean water over it.

Continue filling the space behind the fireback with mortar and rubble, again tamping it down well as you work, until it reaches the top. Now form a slope with the mortar from the top of the fireback to the rear face of the chimney (7) . This slope is called the 'flaunching', and the surface of the mortar must be made parallel with the slope of the rear edge of the load-bearing lintel that runs across the top of the fire opening. The two slopes provide a narrow 'throat' be-tween them – about 100mm (4in) wide – that takes the smoke from the fire into the chimney itself. Trowel the flaunching smooth and add any mortar that may be necessary at the sides to prevent the formation of ledges that might collect soot.

Finally, seal the fireback to the fire surround with fire cement (8) (See above right) and replace the grate, taking care to cover any asbestos packing visible at the sides with a little more fire cement.

SEALING THE FIREBACK

The cement seal between fireback and surround must be renewed if a new fireback is installed or if the seal is cracked or broken. To repair the joint chip away the old cement with hammer and bolster, then rake out the debris to uncover the asbestos expansion joints. If these are sound leave them. If they are broken or crumbling cover the floor with plastic sheet, spray the asbestos with water, cut out the damp packing with a sharp knife and seal it in a plastic bag. Carefully fold the sheeting for disposal and pick up any asbestos dust with a damp sponge – not with a vacuum cleaner. Your local authority will advise you on disposal.

Repack with an asbestos-substitute, brush the joint with clean water and trowel in fire cement to finish flush with the fire surround. Smooth off with a wet paintbrush.

SEE ALSO

Details for: ▷	
Fitting fire surround	386
Cold chisel	480
Bolster	480

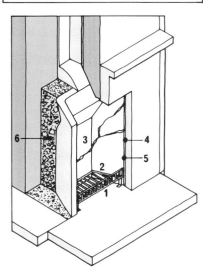

Taking out an old or damaged fireback
1 The grate may be a fixed one
2 Asbestos and cement seal a fixed grate
3 The fireback, to be broken out
4 Surround and fireback have a cement seal
5 Braided packing may need replacing
6 Rubble to be cleared from the brick-lined builder's opening

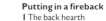
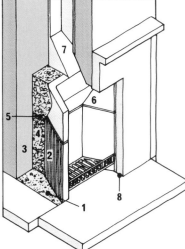

Putting in a fireback
1 The back hearth supports the fireback
2 Corrugated paper will leave an expansion gap when it burns
3 The rear space, to be filled with mortar
4 Rubble gives the mortar bulk
5 Level the mortar with the top edge of the fireback
6 The fireback top is set in place and infilled behind
7 The mortar is sloped to the chimney back
8 The fireback is sealed to the surround

REMOVING A FIREPLACE

To take out an old fire surround and hearth is easy enough but it can create much dust and debris, while any hammering may bring falls of soot down the chimney. Before you start sweep the chimney (◁), move all furniture as *far from the fireplace as possible, roll back the carpet and cover everything with dustsheets. There is a good demand for Victorian fire surrounds and some are valuable. If you remove yours undamaged you may be able to sell it.*

SEE ALSO

◁ Details for:
Applying tiles	102
Grouting tiles	103
Cutting tiles	103
Sweeping chimney	382
Bolster chisel	480
Crowbar	480

Removing the hearth

Most hearths are laid after the fire surround has been fitted and so must come out first, but check beforehand that your surround has not been installed on top of the hearth.

Wear safety goggles and heavy gloves against flying debris and use a club hammer and bolster chisel to break the mortar bond between the superimposed hearth and the constructional hearth below. Knocking in wooden wedges will help. Lever the hearth free with a crowbar or the blade of a strong garden spade and lift it clear. It will be heavy, so get someone to help.

Some older hearths are laid level with the surrounding floorboards and have a layer of tiles on top of them. Here all that's needed is to lift the tiles off carefully with a bolster chisel.

Removing the surround

Most fire surrounds are held to the wall by screws driven through metal lugs set round their edges. They will be concealed in the plaster on the chimney breast. To find the lugs chip away a 25mm (1 in) strip of plaster all round the surround, then expose them completely and take out the screws. If they are rusted and immovable soak them in penetrating oil, leave for a few hours and try again. If that fails drill out their heads. The surround will be heavy, so get some help when you lever it from the wall and lower it carefully onto the floor (See left).

Brick and stone surrounds
A brick or stone surround can be removed a piece at a time, using a bolster to break the mortar joints. There may also be metal ties holding it to the wall.

A wooden surround
A timber surround will probably be held by screws driven through its sides and top into battens fixed to the chimney breast inside the surround. The screw heads will be hidden by wooden plugs or filler. Chisel these out, remove the screws and lift away the surround.

● **Saving a fireplace**
Fire surrounds can be very heavy, especially stone or marble ones. If you wish to keep yours intact for sale lay an old mattress in front of it before you pull it from the wall so it will be less likely to break if it should fall.

Taking out a fireplace
1 The superimposed hearth chipped free
2 The constructional hearth at floor level
3 The fireback, to be broken out
4 The fire surround; a brick or stone one can be taken out in bits
5 Metal lugs hold most surrounds in place

REPLACING CRACKED TILES

Cracked or broken tiles in a hearth or fire surround should be replaced with sound ones, but you may not be able to match those in an old fireplace. One solution here is to buy some new tiles that pleasantly complement or contrast with the originals and replace more than just the damaged one or two, making a random or symmetrical pattern.

Break out the damaged tile with a hammer and cold chisel, working from the centre outwards. Wear thick gloves and safety goggles against flying bits of tile and protect nearby surfaces with dustsheets. When the tile is out remove all traces of old adhesive or mortar and vacuum up the dust.

If necessary cut the new tile to shape (◁). Spread heat-resistant tile adhesive thickly on its back and on the surface where it is to go. Don't get adhesive on its edges or the edges of surrounding tiles. Set the tile in place, taking care that the clearance is equal all round, and wipe off any excess adhesive. Leave it to set and then grout (◁).

If you are replacing only one tile it is not worth buying a tub or packet of adhesive. Instead mix a paste from cellulose filler and PVA wood adhesive, which will work just as well. If the tile is very close to the fire you can use some fire cement.

Chipping out a damaged tile
Start in the middle and work out to edges. Clean out all old mortar or adhesive.

Complete retiling
If a lot of the tiles are damaged or crazed your best course may be to retile the surround and hearth entirely. This is much less trouble than it sounds as you can simply stick the new tiles directly on top of the old ones. First make sure that the old tiles are clean and remove any loose pieces, then apply your tile adhesive and stick the tiles on in the ordinary way (◁).

MAKING GOOD AND SEALING THE OPENING

Having got your fireplace out, you can close the opening with a thin panel on a wood frame or by bricking it up. The panel will make it easier to reinstate the fireplace if you want to at some time in the future. In either case you must fit a ventilator in the centre of the opening just above skirting board level. This will provide an airflow through the chimney and prevent condensation forming and seeping through the brickwork to damage wall decorations.

Making good the floor

If the floor is solid you need only bring the constructional hearth up level with it, using cement or a self-levelling screed, and you can also do this with a boarded floor if it is to be carpeted. If you want exposed floorboards the constructional hearth will have to be broken away with hammer and cold chisel to make room for a new joist and floorboards to be fitted (▷).

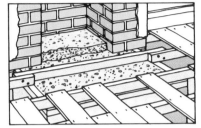
A new joist for extended floorboards

Sealing the opening with plasterboard

Make a panel from 9.5mm (⅜in) plasterboard nailed onto a timber frame fixed inside the fire opening.

Use 50 x 50mm (2 x 2in) sawn timber for the frame. Nail it into the opening with masonry nails, setting it in so that when the plasterboard is nailed on, it will lie flush with the surrounding plaster if it is to be papered. Place it 3mm (⅛in) deeper if a plaster skim is to be added. For papering fix the plasterboard with its ivory side out; for a plaster skim the grey side should be showing. After decorating or plastering the panel, fit a plastic ventilator (▷).

Panelling for a gas fire

If you are going to close off the fire opening so as to connect up the flue outlet for a gas fire you will need the same type of timber frame, but make the panel from an asbestos-free insulation board. Make a cutout in the panel for the gas fire's outlet and fix it to the frame with countersunk-head wood screws and screw cups. Make good the plaster over the top of the panel and seal the gas fire to it with a combination of asbestos-substitute packing and fire cement.

An inset frame to support plasterboard

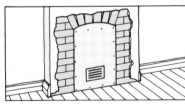
An unused chimney must be ventilated

Sealing the opening with bricks

If you wish to brick up the fire opening remove bricks from alternate courses at the edges of the opening so that the new brickwork can be 'toothed in'. Provide ventilation for the chimney by fitting an airbrick (▷) centrally in the brickwork and just above skirting board level. Plaster the brickwork and allow it to dry out thoroughly before you redecorate the wall.

Finally lever the old pieces of skirting board from the ends of the chimney breast and replace them with a full-length piece from corner to corner.

One of the bricks must be an airbrick

INSTALLING A LOG-BURNING GRATE

To install a log-burning grate you must first remove the old fireback and the rubble infill (▷) and open the fireplace out to the original builder's opening. You can leave the bricks of the opening exposed if you like their appearance or line it with fire brick, with ordinary brick or with stone.

Choose a grate that will fit into the opening with a gap of 50 to 75mm (2 to 3in) at each side. The best types have cast-iron firebacks that help to radiate more heat from the fire.

The grate must stand on a level hearth and the original back hearth will be quite suitable, but if you have taken out the old superimposed hearth you'll have to install a new one. This must be at least 50mm (2in) thick and must extend 300mm (1ft) in front of the grate and at least 225mm (9in) on each side of the fire opening – or to the width of any surround if this is greater.

The new superimposed hearth can be of brick, stone, or tiled concrete. Bed the hearth on dabs of mortar mixed with 3 parts sand: 1 part cement.

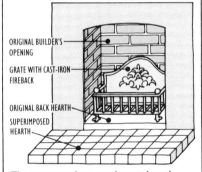
ORIGINAL BUILDER'S OPENING

GRATE WITH CAST-IRON FIREBACK

ORIGINAL BACK HEARTH
SUPERIMPOSED HEARTH

The grate must have an adequate hearth

CAPPING THE CHIMNEY

When you close off a fire opening you will have to cap its chimney in such a way as to keep rain out while allowing the air from the vent in the room to escape. Use a half-round ridge tile bedded in cement, or a proprietary cowl, either of which will do the job.

Half-round ridge tile

Commercial cowl

SEE ALSO

Details for: ▷

Laying floorboards	178
Ventilating fireplace	275
Airbricks	276
Removing fireback	383
Levelling concrete	49
Plasterboard	158-165
Fitting skirtings	181
Condensation	254-255
Laying bricks	428

SEE ALSO

◁ Details for:
Lintels	124
Plastering	148-152
Removing fireback	383
Fireplace lugs	384
Hearth dimensions	385
Black lead	86
Fitting skirtings	181

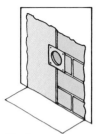

Flue box
Connecting the flue of
a log-burning stove to a
flue box set into a
bricked-up fireplace
may be preferred to
using a horizontal or
vertical closure plate.
A flue box is a
cast-iron frame with
a hole in the centre for
the flue outlet.

FITTING AN OLD-FASHIONED FIREPLACE

In the past 20 years or so traditional
fireplaces have vanished from many
older houses, swept away in the name of
modernization. But now they are being
appreciated again and even sought after.
You can reinstate an old-fashioned
fireplace as described here.

Most period fire surrounds are held in
place by lugs screwed to the wall (▷)
but some can be fixed with mortar. A
plaster surround can be held with dabs
of bonding plaster.

First remove a strip of plaster from
round the fire opening about 50mm
(2in) wider all round than the surround.

If the surround incorporates a cast-
iron centrepiece it must be fitted first.
Most of them simply stand on the back
hearth, but some have lugs for screwing
to the wall. If yours has lugs use metal
wall plugs or expanding bolts. Fit lengths
of asbestos-substitute packing as
expansion joints where the grate or
centrepiece touches the fireback.

Hold the surround in place, mark the
wall for the screw holes and drill them.
Use a spirit level to check that the
surround is upright and the mantel
horizontal, and make any needed
corrections by fitting wooden wedges
behind the surround or bending the lugs
backwards or forwards.

An alternative fixing for plaster
surrounds is to apply mortar or plaster
(◁) to the wall and prop the surround
against it with wooden battens until the
mortar or plaster sets.

Replace the superimposed hearth or
build a new one to the dimensions given
(◁). Set the hearth on dabs of mortar
and point round the edges with the
same material.

Replaster the wall and fit new skirting
boards between the hearth and the
corners of the chimney breast.

Prop a light surround while the plaster sets

CLOSED FIRES: SOLID-FUEL

*A modern solid-fuel closed fire, or room
heater, can be freestanding or inset
(built-in). Both are very efficient at
heating individual rooms and, with the
addition of back boilers, can provide
domestic hot water and central heating
too. The toughened-glass doors of solid-
fuel closed fires, which allow the glow
of the fire to be seen, open for extra
fuel to be added.*

A freestanding heater on the hearth

Freestanding room heaters are designed
to stand on the hearth forward of the
chimney breast. They radiate extra
warmth from their casings but their size
can make them obtrusive in small
rooms. You may also have to extend the
hearth to the required 300mm (1ft) in
front of the heater.

A heater of this type has a flue outlet
at its rear which must be connected to
the chimney, and the easiest way of
arranging this is to seal the outlet into a
metal backplate that closes off the fire
opening. The projecting end of the
outlet must be at least 100mm (4 in)
from the fireback. If not, take out the
fireback.

The closure plate should be of metal
at least 1mm (1/24in) thick and have its
edges turned back to form flanges
through which the fixing screws can be
driven into the edges of the fire
opening. Use metal wall plugs to hold
the screws, and seal the joint between
plate and opening with asbestos-
substitute packing and fire cement.

A backplate closes off the fire opening

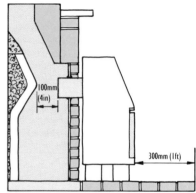

Important measurements for a closed fire

A freestanding heater in the fireplace

Some freestanding room heaters are
designed to stand in the fire opening.
Installing one means first taking out the
fireback and rubble infill (◁) to expose
the builder's brick-lined opening. This
type of heater has a flue outlet in its top
which must be connected to a closure
plate set in the base of the chimney.

The plate can be of metal or precast
concrete. For access to fit it, remove
some bricks from the chimney breast
just above the opening but below the
loadbearing lintel (◁). If the plate is of
concrete take out a course of bricks
round the bottom of the chimney to
support it properly. You can insert a
metal plate into a chased-out mortar
joint. Bed the plate on fire cement,
sealing the edges above and below,
check that the heater's outlet enters the
chimney flue, and seal the plate joint
with asbestos-substitute packing and
fire cement.

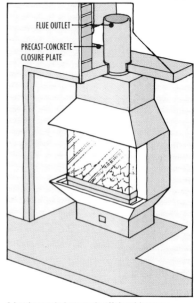

A horizontal plate seals off the chimney

An inset room heater

To install an inset room heater you must first take out the fireback and the rubble infill behind it (▷). The heater has its flue outlet mounted on top to be connected to a chimney closure plate.

This type of appliance is designed to fill and seal the fire opening completely, so to install one you may have to modify your present fire surround or, if the opening is very large, even build a new one. The sides of the surround must be exactly at right angles to the hearth as the front portion of the heater's casing has to be sealed to both. If the surround and the hearth form an odd angle a good seal with the heater casing will be impossible. The seal is made with asbestos-substitute packing material.

Most inset room heaters are screwed down to the back hearth, and some may need a vermiculite-based infill round the back of the casing which must be in place before the chimney closure plate is fitted and the flue outlet connected.

Some come supplied with their own fire surrounds, complete with drop-in closure plates designed to make their installation easier.

Finish the job by making good the brickwork of the chimney breast and replastering it.

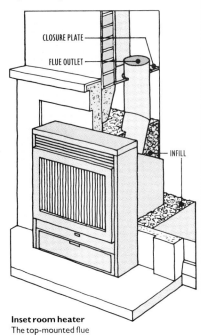

Inset room heater
The top-mounted flue outlet connects to a horizontal closure plate in the chimney base. Some versions need an infill round the rear casing.

One of the most economical ways to keep a room warm is by means of a modern slow-combustion log-burning stove – if you have access to cheap wood. Like freestanding solid-fuel room heaters they can be stood on the hearth with rear flue outlets or installed in the fireplace with top-mounted outlets. A good log-burning stove can burn all day or night on one filling of wood.

A log-burning stove is best installed forward of the chimney breast so that you'll get the full benefit of the heat that radiates from its casing. You can stand it on your present superimposed hearth provided that the hearth projects the required minimum of 300 mm (1ft) in front of the stove and at least 225mm (9in) on each side of it. Otherwise you will have to make a new and bigger hearth. The hearth must be level and constructed of stone, brick or tiles.

A log-burning stove is fitted with a vitreous-enamelled, insulated flue pipe and this can be passed through a vertical back closure plate that seals off the whole fireplace opening or through a horizontal plate that closes off the base of the chimney (▷). In either case the flue pipe is sealed to the closure plate with an asbestos-substitute packing and fire cement. The closure plates may be made of any fireproof material, the best being of metal or asbestos-free insulation board.

As an alternative to all this you can brick up the fireplace completely and install a fluebox (See opposite).

If the flue pipe is connected to a vertical closure plate its rear end must be at least 150mm (6in) short of the back wall of the chimney. If it is fixed to a horizontal plate the pipe must extend above the plate by from 100 to 150mm (4 to 6in).

As burning wood produces heavy deposits of soot the installation must incorporate good access for efficient chimney sweeping, which will be needed more often than with solid fuel.

SEE ALSO

Details for: ▷
Removing fireback 383
Closure plate 386

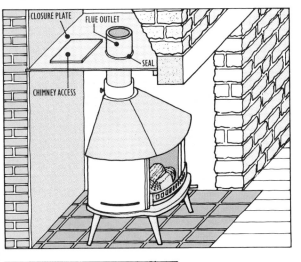

Vertical flue outlet
This type of stove has its flue sealed into the opening of a horizontal closure plate in the base of the chimney.

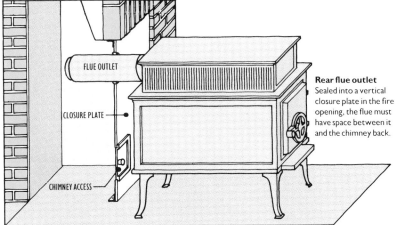

Rear flue outlet
Sealed into a vertical closure plate in the fire opening, the flue must have space between it and the chimney back.

387

INSTALLING A FLUE LINER

If your house was built before 1965 there's a good chance that its chimney is unlined and is simply a rectangular duct whose brickwork is either rendered with cement or quite exposed.

Over the years corrosive elements in the rising combustion gases eat into the *chimney's mortar and brickwork and weaken it, allowing condensation to pass through and form damp patches on the chimney breast and, in extreme cases, letting smoke seep through. This is particularly true where solid fuel or wood-burning appliances are in use.*

SEE ALSO

◁ Details for:
Sweeping chimney 382
Scaffold towers 40,42
Condensation 254-255

ROOF ACCESS

You can hire easy-to-use light alloy roof scaffolding. Two units will make a half platform for a central or side chimney; four will provide an all-round platform.

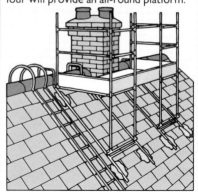

Scaffolding is essential for safe working

Choosing a flue liner

You can deal with these problems by installing a flue liner, which will prevent the corrosive elements reaching the brickwork. It will also reduce the 'bore' of the flue, and that will speed up the flow of gases and prevent their cooling and condensing. The draught of air through the fire will improve and the the fire will burn more efficiently.

It is important to fit the type of liner that's appropriate to the kind of heating appliance being used. Get advice from the appliance supplier or – in the case of an open fire – from the Solid Fuel Advisory Service.

Linings are tubes, one-piece or in sections, of metal or other rigid, non-combustible material such as pumice.

Installing a one-piece flue liner

A popular type of liner is a one-piece flexible corrugated tube of stainless steel that is easily fed into a chimney that has bends in it. Unfortunately this type of liner is not suitable for use with solid-fuel or wood-burning appliances. To install it you must get onto the roof and erect scaffolding round the chimney (See above right).

First sweep the chimney (◁), then chop away the flaunching round the base of the chimney pot with a hammer and cold chisel, remove the pot – it will be very heavy, so take care – and lower it to the ground on a rope. Clean up the top of the chimney to expose the brickwork.

The liner is fed into the chimney from the top. Drop a strong weighted line down the chimney (**1**) and attach its other end to the conical endpiece of the flue liner. Have an assistant pull gently on the line from below while you feed the liner down into the chimney (**2**). When the conical endpiece emerges below remove it and connect the liner to a closure plate set across the base of the chimney or to the flue outlet of the heating appliance, and seal the joint with an asbestos-substitute packing and some fire cement.

Return to the roof, fit the top closure plate and bed it in mortar laid on the top of the chimney, adding extra mortar to match the original flaunching (**3**). Finally fit a cowl to the top of the liner, having chosen one appropriate to the heating appliance being used (See left).

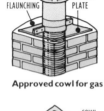

Approved cowl for gas

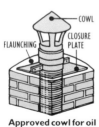

Approved cowl for oil

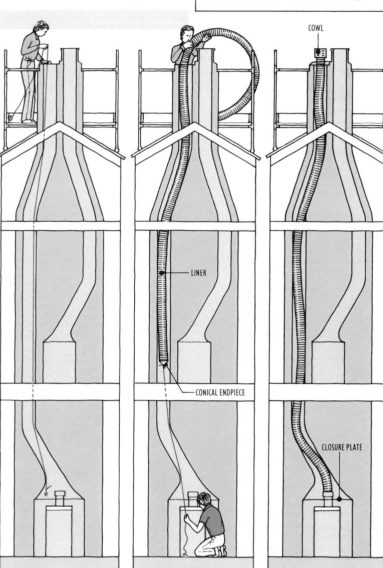

1 Lower attached line   **2 Feed liner to helper**   **3 Complete top closure**

Installing a sectional flue liner

A sectional pumice flue liner has the space round it filled with a lightweight concrete that strengthens and insulates the chimney but needs good foundations for the added weight. Like the one-piece liner (See opposite) it is inserted from the top. First cement a steel base plate across the bottom of the chimney.

Tie the first flue section to a rope and lower it into the chimney. Connect the next section to it by one of the steel collars supplied and lower the two further down. Continue adding sections and lowering the liner until it reaches the base plate, then seal it in place.

If there are any bends in the chimney you will have to break into it at those points to feed the sections in. You may think that this makes the job one for a professional builder.

For filling in the chimney round the liner use concrete made with a lightweight aggregate such as expanded clay or vermiculite. Pour this into the chimney all round the liner and finish off the flaunching at the top.

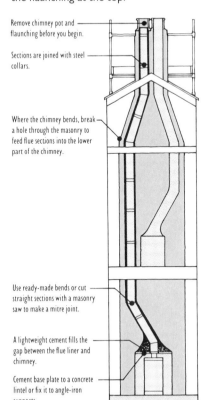

Remove chimney pot and flaunching before you begin.

Sections are joined with steel collars.

Where the chimney bends, break a hole through the masonry to feed flue sections into the lower part of the chimney.

Use ready-made bends or cut straight sections with a masonry saw to make a mitre joint.

A lightweight cement fills the gap between the flue liner and chimney.

Cement base plate to a concrete lintel or fix it to angle-iron supports.

A sectional flue liner
Installing a sectional flue liner can be such a complicated procedure that it is worth asking for professional quotes before you decide to tackle the job yourself.

MAINTAINING OPEN FIRE SURROUNDS

Though fire surrounds and hearths get a great deal of wear and tear they will keep their appearance if they're looked after and if certain elementary care is taken. For example, avoid standing cups, glasses and ashtrays on them and be especially careful with such drinks as coffee, tea, spirits and fruit juices, which can be very damaging to some surfaces, particularly marble.

Always let the hearth and surround cool down before you clean them, and avoid standing on the hearth when you clean the surround.

The different materials respond to different cleaning methods.

STONE

This can be sponged off with warm water that has a little detergent mixed into it. You can remove the more stubborn stains with a stiff brush.

MARBLE AND GRANITE

It is easy to damage the fine finish on these stones, so they should be treated with some care. Wash them regularly with warm soapy water and polish them with a chamois leather or a good-quality wax polish. Patch small chips with a putty made from kaolin powder (china clay) and epoxy glue. Rub down the hardened filler with silicon carbide paper and touch in with lacquer.

CERAMIC TILES

Wash these with warm water containing a little detergent. Never use any kind of abrasive cleaner on them.

BRICKS

Dust bricks off occasionally with a soft brush, but never use soapy water on them. If you have built your own brick surround you should treat it with a proprietary sealer to prevent 'dusting'. Broken bricks can be stuck together again with an epoxy adhesive, or you can cut them out and replace them with new ones, using fresh mortar.

SLATE

Wash this with warm water mixed with a little detergent, using a stiff brush. If the slate is unpolished remove stubborn stains with an abrasive cleaner.

METALWORK

Wash this with warm soapy water and take off stubborn tar and soot stains with methylated spirit. Clean up cast-iron surrounds with wet-and-dry abrasive paper or emery cloth, then finish with 'black lead' (▷).

WOODWORK

If the grain is exposed maintain the finish with a good wax polish (▷). Fill any cracks or gouges with a proprietary wood filler tinted to match with a little wood stain (▷). The woodwork can also be painted in the ordinary way.

Stone surround

Marble surround

Wood surround

SEE ALSO

Details for: ▷	
Wood stain	75,80
Wax polish	75,84
Black lead	86
Stabilizing primer	48
Preparing wood	53

● **Casting a flue liner**
Professional installers can cast a flue liner in-situ. A deflated tube is lowered into the chimney. It is inflated, and a lightweight infill is poured into the gap between the tube and chimney. When the infill has set, the tube is deflated and removed, leaving a smooth-bore flue.

CENTRAL HEATING SYSTEMS

SEE ALSO

◁ Details for:
Storage heaters 320-321
Running cables   303-305
Copper plumbing   351-355
Boilers   392
Radiators   393-394

More and more householders are now choosing to keep their homes warm with central heating of one kind or another.

Typically a central heating system supplies heat from a single source to selected rooms – or all the rooms – in the house. This is a much more efficient arrangement than having an individual

heater in each room as it has only one appliance to be controlled, cleaned and maintained.

All central heating systems can be broken down into two basic types: dry and wet systems. In a dry system heated air carries warmth to the rooms. In a wet system the medium heated is water.

Dry central heating systems

The heat source for most warm-air central heating systems is a large electric storage heater that contains a quantity of firebricks with electric heating elements running through them. The system takes advantage of the cheaper off-peak electricity supply available during the night to heat the bricks, and the bricks release their heat slowly during the day. A fan embodied in the unit blows the warmed air through ducts to the rooms being heated. Each duct ends in an adjustable damper that is used to regulate the temperature in the room by controlling the heat emission. Runs of ducting in this kind of system can be quite long.

The ducted warm-air system is the only dry heating system that is genuinely central–that is, with a central heat source – but there are other electric heating systems which are usually classed broadly as central heating.

Among these are the underfloor and ceiling heating systems, which use elements built into the structure of the floor or ceiling to warm their surfaces, which in turn radiate heat into the room.

A house kept warm with individual room storage heaters is also generally regarded as centrally heated, though each heater is a separate heat source. The individual heaters, like the central one in a ducted-air system, contain a number of firebricks which are heated by electric elements running on low-cost electricity during the night. They give off their heat during the daytime either by simple convection or with the aid of fans.

In recent years room storage heaters have undergone a number of improvements in terms of efficiency and control of heat emission, and are much more sophisticated than the originals.

COMPARING CENTRAL HEATING SYSTEMS

A wet system is by far the easiest kind of real central heating to install. Its small-bore copper pipes can be run through floor and ceiling voids with little trouble or they can be clipped unobtrusively along skirting boards and in corners. Panel radiators or skirting heaters take up very little room, and there is a choice of various compact boilers which can make use of a fireplace and chimney, can stand between kitchen cabinets or can even be hung on a wall. There is a much wider choice of equipment for wet central heating than for any other kind.

Most installations use small-bore 2-pipe systems (see right). Micro-bore heating also uses a 2-pipe circuit but with the radiators fed by 6-10 mm (¼ – ⅜ in) malleable copper pipes. A micro-bore system can offer less heat loss from the pipes, quicker warm-up and simpler installation compared with some small-bore systems.

Dry systems
A warm-air ducted system is really practical only if it is incorporated into the house while it is being built. The ducts that carry the air are usually some 150 x 200mm (6 x 8in) in their cross section, and installing them will entail extensive structural work on an existing building. Even then the result will probably be unsightly.

Similarly both underfloor and ceiling heating systems are best put in while a house is being built. To install either in a completed building will cause a great deal of disruption.

Of the dry heating methods room storage heaters offer the only system that can be installed in an existing house with very little fuss. They must have their own meter, consumer unit and wiring (◁) but these are easily fitted. Their cables can be run through floor and ceiling voids and in walls even more easily than the pipes used for a wet system.

Weighing rival merits
The actual installation of room storage heaters is a lot cheaper than putting in a wet system, but against this must be weighed the capacity of the wet system for providing 'heat on demand' to match sudden drops of temperature. A storage heater system must store enough heat during the night to maintain comfortable temperatures in the rooms throughout the following day.

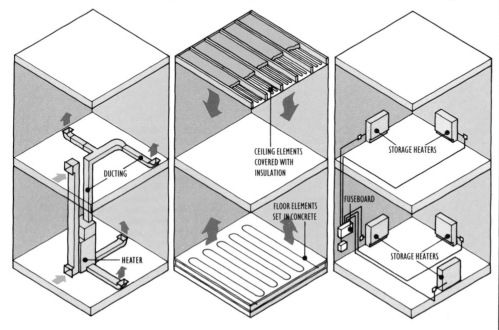

Warm-air systems
In warm-air systems air heated centrally goes via ducts to the rooms and back for reheating.

Floor and ceiling heating systems
Elements warm floor or ceiling and heat is radiated into the room.

Storage heaters
Storage heaters, run on cheap power, have special wiring, meter and consumer unit.

DUCTING

HEATER

CEILING ELEMENTS
COVERED WITH
INSULATION

FLOOR ELEMENTS
SET IN CONCRETE

STORAGE HEATERS

FUSEBOARD

STORAGE HEATERS

WET CENTRAL HEATING

The most popular form of central heating is the wet system in which water is heated by a boiler and pumped through small-bore pipes to radiators or to convector heaters, where the heat from the water is released into the rooms. The water circulates back to the boiler for reheating in a continuing cycle.

The control of such a system can be extremely flexible. Thermostats and valves allow the output of individual heat emitters to be automatically adjusted, and parts of the system can be shut down if rooms are unoccupied.

An extra advantage of the wet system is that it can be used to heat the hot water supply for the house as well as heating the house itself.

The boiler for wet central heating may be heated by gas, oil, bottled gas (propane), solid fuel such as anthracite, or electricity.

SEE ALSO

Details for: ▷	
Insulation	260-274
Off-peak electricity	286
Hot water cylinders	380

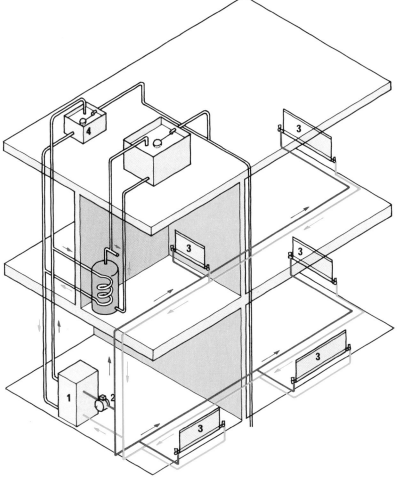

Two-pipe central heating system ▶

The water, heated by the boiler (**1**), is forced by the pump (**2**) through the pipes to the various radiators or special convector heaters (**3**) which hold it long enough for it to warm the rooms before it returns to the boiler to be reheated.

A cistern (**4**) in the roof keeps the system topped up and catches any expansion of the water due to overheating.

Red indicates the flow of water from the pump; blue shows the return flow.

One-pipe systems
A one-pipe system has a single large-bore pipe running around the perimeter of a house, forming a loop. The flow and return pipes of each radiator are connected to this large-bore pipe. The water is pumped round the loop but the radiators work by gravity circulation. Larger radiators may be used at the end of the loop to compensate for heat loss. The cistern and hot water circuits are the same as on a two-pipe system.

COMPARATIVE RUNNING COSTS

The running costs of the various central heating systems vary with local costs of fuel, the fuel chosen, the type of system, the size of the house and how well the house is insulated. Here it must be stressed that whatever kind of central heating you install you will make considerable savings if you take steps to insulate the house properly beforehand (▷). By drastically reducing the amount of heat you lose through your walls, roof, windows and doors you will also reduce the size of the heating system you need. This means substantial saving on your capital outlay as well as on subsequent running costs. A good central heating designer/installer takes account of the quality of the insulation in a house when making his calculations of the heat required.

When you're choosing your heating system you should carefully bear in mind the availability of the various fuels. Solid fuel, oil and electricity are available to every household, though note that the first two need some kind of storage facility and this may not be easy to arrange. Mains gas supply is not available everywhere, though even then, if you particularly want gas, you could opt for the bottled kind. In this case a storage facility is also needed – either a large tank or some kind of housing for several large cylinders.

The efficiency of the heat source also has an effect on overall running costs. A proportion of the heat generated by gas, oil and solid-fuel boilers is lost up the flue, only some 65 per cent getting through the system and warming the house. Off-peak electric storage heaters and boilers, whatever their drawbacks, are much more efficient, with a usable heat closer to 95 per cent of that which is generated.

When it comes to running costs there is generally little to choose between gas, solid fuel and off-peak electricity, though at the higher heat levels gas comes out marginally cheaper. Oil prices fluctuate a great deal and on average oil works out about 1 ½ times as dear as the other three. Bottled gas is even dearer, as is daytime-rate as opposed to off-peak electricity.

On balance, mains gas is probably the best fuel if it is available. It is clean, it offers infinitely controllable heat-output, it needs no storage and its supply is always secure.

CENTRAL HEATING BOILERS

The boiler is the heart of any wet central heating system, and modern ones are compact and very efficient. They can be gas- or oil-fired, can burn solid fuels like anthracite or can run on cheap off-peak electric power. Maintained properly, such a boiler will give you years of trouble-free service.

SEE ALSO

◁ Details for:

Room heaters	386
Oil-storage regulations	19
Hot water cylinders	380
Thermostats	395
Boiler maintenance	398

POSITIONING A BOILER

Modern central heating boilers are fairly easy to accommodate. Whether fired by oil, gas or solid fuel they are manufactured with neat, well-designed casings that blend in with ordinary kitchen or utility room furniture. Some gas-fired versions can be mounted high on walls, where they take up no more space than most kitchen cabinets.

Gas- and oil-fired boilers are available with a choice of conventional flues or balanced flues. Those with conventional flues are freestanding, designed for connection to an existing chimney or to a new prefabricated one. Balanced-flue boilers don't need a chimney. Their flue gases are passed along a short horizontal duct through an outside wall. The duct is split into two passages, one for the outgoing flue gases and the other for incoming combustion air drawn into the boiler from outside the house. Boilers with balanced flues are sometimes called 'room sealed' because they take no air from the room where they are sited, only from the outside.

Balanced-flue boilers can be fitted anywhere in the house so long as the site is on or next to an outside wall. Under stairs can be an ideal position.

Both gas and solid-fuel boilers offer a further choice, that of having the boiler – fitted as a back boiler behind a radiant fire or room heater (◁) – sited in the living room fireplace. In the case of gas the control of the radiant fire is independent of the boiler, and you can operate one or the other or both, as you wish according to the season.

Electrically heated boilers are completely versatile in the matter of siting. They can be placed anywhere convenient, since they have no flues and need no connection to the air outside the house.

All solid-fuel boilers must be connected to chimneys.

Gas-fired boilers

Most gas-fired boilers have pilot lights that burn constantly and light the burners when heat is required. They can work manually or by a timer set to switch the heating on and off at times you choose. You can also link the boiler to a room thermostat so that the heating is switched on and off to keep the temperatures even throughout the house. Another thermostat, in the boiler itself, prevents the water overheating at any time.

Some boilers have electronic ignition by which the pilot light ignites only when a thermostat demands heat. Once the boiler temperature is right, valves to the burner and pilot close until the next time heat is called for.

Oil-fired boilers

Oil-fired boilers, with the same efficient controls as gas-fired ones, come in two basic types: pressure jet and vaporizing. This refers to whether the oil is reduced to tiny droplets or turned into vapour to be burnt. Pressure-jet boilers are too noisy for use indoors and must be housed outside. Vaporizing boilers are much quieter. A drawback of any oil-fired boiler is the need for a large storage tank for the oil, sited outside for easy access by the delivery tanker.

Solid-fuel boilers

Solid-fuel heating also needs a suitable place for fuel storage, and as these boilers produce a considerable amount of ash it has to be removed every day.

The rate at which the solid fuel is burnt is usually controlled by a thermostatic damper, sometimes by a fan. The instant switching on and off of the heat – as with gas- and oil-fired boilers – is not possible, and the system must have some way for heat to escape in the event of the water-circulating pump failing; otherwise the water could boil in the appliance and damage it. This is usually arranged by means of a 'natural convection' pipe circuit between the boiler and the heat exchanger in the domestic hot-water cylinder, or a radiator in the bathroom, where the excess heat can be used to dry towels.

A solid-fuel boiler must be kept well stoked if it is to continue burning, and you can have one with a hopper feed that will top it up automatically while you are out of the house.

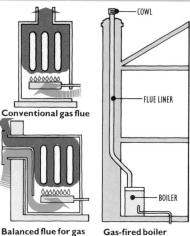

Conventional gas flue

Balanced flue for gas   **Gas-fired boiler**

Vaporizing boiler   **Pressure-jet boiler**

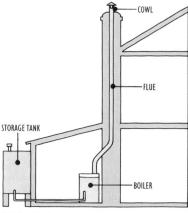

Oil-fired boiler

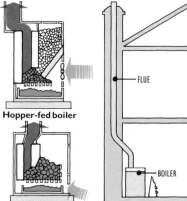

Hopper-fed boiler

Solid-fuel back boiler   **Solid-fuel boiler**

BOILER CAPACITY

Deciding what boiler capacity you'll need is not a matter of guesswork, however intelligent, but of complicated mathematical calculations that will determine accurately the total heat requirement of the house. A designer/installer of heating systems will take all the following items into account:

The size of the house; the type of house; its position; the number of rooms it has; the temperature needed in each room, based on a standard outdoor temperature; the method of its construction; the materials of the walls, floors, ceilings and roof; and the level of thermal insulation installed.

Working out your needs

From this information the designer can work out the size of the heat-emitters needed, and by adding up their outputs he will arrive at the total output needed from the boiler. Boiler outputs are quoted in British thermal units per hour (Btu/h) or kilowatts (kW); 10,000 Btu/h equals 3kW.

So many variables are involved that it is impossible to make calculations for every possible combination of them.

The best course when you consider installing a heating system is to get quotes from several designers for installing it. Each of them should produce a detailed rundown of the kind of equipment needed, and the sizes of radiators and boiler, together with an estimate of the cost of the installation. If they have done their jobs properly their figures for your heat requirements should be very similar. If the estimates show substantial differences you should ask for a further explanation of how the figures were arrived at.

If you already have central heating and wish to replace an old boiler you must get one with the same heat output as the original one, unless you plan to extend the system, in which case consult a designer/installer as you would about a new system.

Getting expert approval

When you set out to buy a boiler be sure that it has the approval of the relevant body – for gas: British Gas; for oil: Domestic Oil Burning Equipment Testing Association (DOBETA); for solid fuel: the Solid Fuel Advisory Service or the Solid Smokeless Fuels Federation; for electricity: the Electricity Board.

RADIATORS AND CONVECTORS

The hot water from a central heating boiler is pumped through the house along narrow pipes which may be connected to radiators or to special convector heaters (▷) that extract heat from the water and pass it out into their respective rooms.

You can feel radiant heat being emitted directly from the hot surface of an appliance, but convected heat warms the air that comes into contact with the hot surface. As the warmed air rises toward the ceiling it allows cooler air to flow in round the appliance, and this air in its turn is warmed and moves upwards. Eventually a steady but very gentle circulation of air takes place in the room, and the temperature gradually rises to the optimum set on the room thermostat.

SEE ALSO

Details for: ▷
Convectors   394

Radiators

An ordinary radiator is a double-skinned metal panel. Water flows into it through a manually adjustable valve at one corner and then out through a lockshield valve at the other. A bleed valve is fitted to one of the top corners to let air out and prevent airlocks, which stop the radiator heating up properly. The faces of most radiators are fluted to increase their surface area for greater heat output.

Despite the name, radiators deliver only about half of their output as radiant heat; the rest is emitted through natural convection as the surrounding air comes into contact with the hot surfaces of the radiators.

Radiators come in a wide range of sizes, and the larger they are the greater is their heat output. Heat output can be further increased by using special double- or even triple-panel radiators whose panels are mounted one behind the other. There are also some radiators with finned rear faces to step up the output of convected heat.

Single-panel radiator

Double-panel radiator

Finned radiator

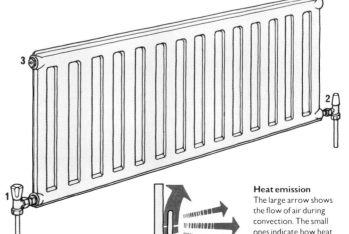

Panel radiator
1 The manual valve controls inflow
2 The lockshield valve controls outflow to keep the radiator hot
3 The bleed valve is to disperse airlocks

Heat emission
The large arrow shows the flow of air during convection. The small ones indicate how heat radiates from the radiator's surface.

CONVECTORS

You can fit convector heaters into your wet central heating system instead of the rather more conventional radiators.

Unlike radiators, convector heaters emit none of their heat in the form of direct radiation. The hot water from the boiler passes through a finned pipe inside the heater, the fins absorbing the heat and transferring it to the air surrounding them. The warmed air escapes through an opening at the top of the appliance and at the same time cool air is drawn in through the open bottom, to be warmed in its turn.

Most convector heaters have a damper that can be set to control the airflow. Some are designed for inconspicuous fixing at skirting level. An advance is a fan-assisted type in which the airflow over the heating fins is forced, making for fast room heating.

SEE ALSO

◁ Details for:
Insulation	260-274
Reflective foil	261
Double glazing	271-274
Radiators	393

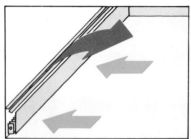
Rising warm air draws cool air in below

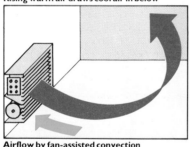
Airflow by fan-assisted convection

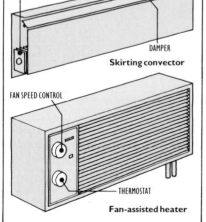

FINNED PIPE

DAMPER

Skirting convector

FAN SPEED CONTROL

THERMOSTAT

Fan-assisted heater

PLACING YOUR HEATERS

At one time central heating radiators or convectors were nearly always placed under windows to balance the chill of the panes and cut the draughts caused by warmed air cooling against them. If double glazing deals with both of these problems you can place them with an eye to maximum comfort – but keep the other on the length and consequent cost of pipe runs.

Convenience and cost

Your radiators and convector heaters can be positioned anywhere that's convenient, that suits the shape of the rooms and that keeps costly pipe runs to a reasonable minimum. Probably you'll want to take all of these considerations into account.

While double glazing means that the appliances can be sited elsewhere than under windows there is a slight drawback to placing them against walls. The warm air rising from them will tend to discolour the paint or wallpaper above. You can guard against this by fitting radiator shelves immediately above them to direct the warm air clear of the walls.

Never hang curtains or stand furniture in front of radiators or convectors. Either will absorb radiated heat and curtains will trap convected heat between themselves and the walls. While convectors radiate almost no heat you should never obstruct warm air leaving the appliance nor cool air being drawn into it.

A room's shape can affect the siting of appliances and perhaps their number. For example, you cannot heat a large L-shaped room from a radiator in its short end. A heating installer can work out a combination of appliances – and their positions – to heat the room properly.

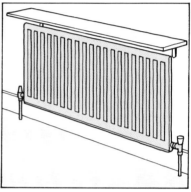
A shelf directs warm air clear of the wall

Selecting the size of heaters

A house loses heat constantly – whenever a door or window is opened; because of cold draughts; through the fabric of the doors, windows, walls, floors, ceilings and roof. To work out the heating needs of the rooms in a house the designer has to take account of the rate at which they lose heat. This varies with the materials and construction of the walls, floors and ceilings. For example, heat is lost more quickly through a solid brick wall than through a brick cavity wall with cavity insulation. Also the temperatures on the other sides of walls, floors and ceilings will come into the equation.

The designer also needs to know the temperature to which each room must be heated, and there are standard levels for particular rooms (See right). The designer's calculations will produce a heating requirement for each room, expressed in kilowatts, and the next step is to select radiators or convectors of appropriate outputs. Then all the heat output figures are totalled to give the output required from the boiler.

When you install your central heating be sure to choose radiators and convector heaters that carry the sign of approval of the Manufacturers' Association for Radiators and Convectors (MARC).

IDEAL ROOM TEMPERATURES

A central heating designer/installer aims at a system that will heat rooms to the temperatures shown here, assuming an outdoor temperature of -1°C (30°F).

ROOM	TEMPERATURE
Living room	21°C (70°F)
Dining room	21°C (70°F)
Kitchen	16°C (60°F)
Hall/landing	18°C (65°F)
Bedroom	16°C (60°F)
Bathroom	23°C (72°F)

CENTRAL HEATING CONTROLS

A range of automatic control systems and devices for wet central heating can, if used sensibly, enable you to make useful savings in running costs. They can ensure that your system never 'burns up money' by producing unwanted heat.

Three basic devices

While considerable sophistication is now available in automatic control the systems can be divided into three main types: temperature controllers (thermostats), automatic on-off switches (timers and programmers) and heating circuit controllers (zone valves).

These devices can be used individually or in combination to provide a very high level of control.

It must be added that automatic controls are really effective only with gas- or oil-fired boilers, which can be switched on and off at will. Linked to solid-fuel boilers, which take time to react to controls, the systems will be less effective and can be dangerous.

Thermostats

All boilers incorporate thermostats to prevent overheating. A gas- or oil-fired boiler will have one that can be set to alter heat output by switching the unit on and off. On a solid-fuel boiler the thermostat opens and closes a damper, allowing more or less air to the firebed to increase or reduce the rate of burning as required.

Room thermostats – 'roomstats' for short – are common forms of central heating control, often the only ones fitted. They are placed in rooms where temperatures usually remain fairly stable, and work on the assumption that any rise or drop in room temperatures will be matched by similar ones through the house. Roomstats control temperatures through simple on-off switching of the boiler – or the pump if a boiler must run constantly to provide a constant supply of domestic hot water.

The roomstat's drawback is that it can make no allowance for local temperature changes in other rooms caused, for example, by the sun shining through a window or a separate heater being switched on. Much more sophisticated temperature control is provided by thermostatic radiator valves, which can be fitted to radiators instead of the standard manually operated inlet valves. Temperature sensors open and close them, varying heat output to maintain the desired temperatures in individual rooms.

Thermostatic radiator valves need not be fitted in every room. You can use one to reduce the heat in a kitchen or reduce the temperature in a bathroom while using a roomstat to regulate the temperature in the rest of the house or upstairs and downstairs zones.

Other available thermostatic controls include devices for regulating the temperature of domestic hot water and for giving frost-protection to a boiler switched off during winter holidays.

SEE ALSO

Details for: ▷
Boilers   392

Timer

Roomstat

Programmer

ZONE CONTROL VALVES

It is not often that all the rooms in a house are in use at once. During the day it is normal for the upstairs rooms to be unused for long periods, and to heat them permanently would be very wasteful. To avoid such waste you can divide your central heating system into circuits, or zones – the usual ones being upstairs and downstairs – and heat those areas only when it's necessary.

Control is provided by motorized valves linked to a timer or programmer that directs the flow of heating water through pre-selected pipes at the pre-selected times. Alternatively zone valves can be used to provide zone temperature control by being linked to individual zone thermostats.

A motorized zone control valve

Timers and programmers

You can save a lot in running costs by ensuring that your heating system is not working when you don't need it – while you're out, for instance, or while you sleep. A timer can be set to switch the system on and off so as to suit the regular comings and goings of the family. It can switch on and warm the house just before you get up, then off again just before you leave for work, on again while you're coming home, and so on.

The simpler timers offer two 'on' and two 'off' settings which are repeated daily, though a manual override allows variations for weekends and such times. More sophisticated versions, known as programmers, offer a large number of on-off programmes – even a different one for each day of the week – as well as control of domestic hot water.

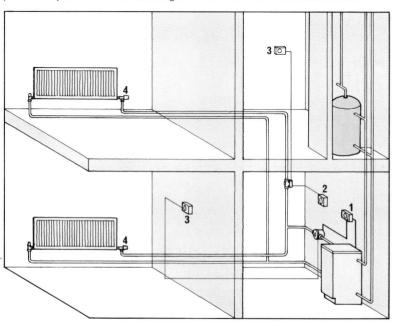

Thermostatic radiator valve

Heating controls
There are several ways to control the temperature of central heating.
1 Programmer controls boiler and pump.
2 A timer is used to control a zone valve. It can be used to regulate boiler and pump in place of a programmer.
3 Roomstat controls pump or a zone valve.
4 A non-electrical radiator valve controls an individual heater.

HEATING SYSTEM FAULTFINDER

SEE ALSO

◁ Details for:
Curing leaks	341
Ball valves	345-346
Pipework	351-359
Plumbing joints	352-355
Sweeping chimney	382
Draining system	397
Bleed valve	399
Removing/replacing radiators	399-401

SYMPTOM

Hissing or banging sounds from boiler or pipework.

Overheating caused by:

● Blocked chimney (with solid fuel).
Check flueway for substantial soot fall. Sweep chimney (◁).

● Heavy scale deposits in system due to hard water.
Shut down boiler and pump. Have a specialist treat system with a descaler, then drain, flush and refill system.

● Faulty boiler thermostat.
*Shut down boiler.
Leave pump working to circulate water round system and cool it quickly. With system cool, operate boiler thermostat control. If you do not hear a clicking sound call in an engineer.*

● Lack of water in system
*Shut down boiler.
Check feed and expansion cistern in roof. If empty, the valve may be stuck. Move ball valve float arm up and down to restore flow and fill system. If this fails, with valve in open position check whether mains water has been turned off by accident or – in winter – whether supply pipe is frozen.*

● Circulating pump not working (with solid fuel).
*Shut down boiler, then check that the pump is switched on.
If pump won't work turn off power and check wired connections to it. If pump seems to be running but outlet pipe is cool, check for airlock by using bleed screw. If pump is still not working shut it down, drain system, remove pump and check it for blockage. Clean pump or replace it if necessary.*

SYMPTOM

Continuous drip from overflow pipe of feed and expansion cistern in roof.

● Faulty ball valve or leaking float that keeps valve open.
Shut off mains water supply to cistern and bale cistern out to below level of valve. Remove valve and fit new washer (◁). Alternatively unscrew leaking float from arm and fit new one.

SYMPTOM

All radiators remain cool though boiler is operating normally.

● Pump not working
Check that pump is working by feeling for motor vibration or by listening. If pump is running check for airlock by operating bleed valve. If this has no effect the pump outlet may be blocked. Switch off boiler and pump, remove pump and clean or replace as necessary.

● Pump's thermostat or timer is set incorrectly or is faulty.
Check thermostat or timer setting and reset if necessary. If this makes no difference switch off power and check wiring connections. If connections are in good order call in an engineer.

SYMPTOM

Radiators in one part of the house do not warm up.

● Timer or thermostat which controls zone valve not set properly or faulty.
Check timer or thermostat setting and reset if necessary. If this has no effect switch off the power supply and check wired connections. If this makes no difference call in an engineer.

● Zone valve itself faulty.
Drain system and replace valve.

SYMPTOM

Single radiator does not warm up.

● Manual inlet valve closed.
Check setting of valve and open it if that is necessary.

● Thermostatic radiator valve not set properly or faulty.
Check setting of valve and reset it if necessary. If this has no effect drain system and replace valve (◁).

● Lockshield valve not set properly.
Remove lockshield cover and adjust valve setting until radiator seems as warm as those in adjacent rooms. Have lockshield valve properly balanced when system is next serviced.

● Inlet/outlet blocked by corrosion.
Close inlet and lockshield valves,

remove radiator and flush out and refit or replace as necessary.

SYMPTOM

Area at top of radiator stays cool while the bottom is warm.

● Airlock at top of radiator preventing water circulating fully.
Operate bleed valve to release the trapped air (◁).

SYMPTOM

Cool patch in centre of radiator while top and ends are warm.

● Heavy deposits of corrosion at bottom of radiator are restricting circulation of water.
Close inlet and lockshield valves, remove radiator, flush out, then refit or replace as necessary (◁).

SYMPTOM

Water leaking from system.

● Loose pipe unions at joints, pump connections, boiler connections, etc.
Switch off boiler – or close down solid-fuel appliance, raking out coals – switch off pump and tighten leaking joints. If this has no effect drain the system and remake joints completely (◁).

● Split or punctured pipes.
Wrap damage in rags temporarily, switch off boiler and pump and make a temporary repair with hose or commercial leak sealant (◁). Drain system and fit new pipe (◁).

SYMPTOM

Boiler not working

● Thermostat set too low
Check roomstat or boiler thermostat is set correctly
● Timer or programmer not working
Check the unit is switched on and set correctly. Have it replaced if the fault persists.
● Pilot light goes out
Relight a gas boiler pilot light following the manufacturer's instructions, which are usually found on the back of the boiler's front panel. If the pilot fails to ignite, have the unit replaced.

DRAINING AND FILLING A WET SYSTEM

There may be times when you will have to drain your wet central heating system completely and refill it – during routine maintenance, when dealing with a fault *(See opposite) or if you decide to extend the system or upgrade the boiler. The job can be done fairly easily if you follow the procedures outlined here.*

Draining the system

Before draining your central heating system cool the water by shutting off the boiler and leaving the pump running. The circulating water will cool quickly.

Switch off the pump and turn off the mains water supply to the feed and expansion cistern in the roof by closing the stopcock in the feedpipe or by laying a batten across the cistern and tying the float arm to it to keep the ball valve shut.

The main draincock for the system will be in the return pipe near the boiler. Push one end of a garden hose onto its outlet, lead the other end of the hose to a gully or soakaway in the garden and open the draincock. If you have no key for its square shank use an adjustable spanner.

Water will drain from the system, but some will be held in the radiators by vacuum. To release this start at the top of the house and carefully open the radiator bleed valves. Air will flow into the tops of the radiators, breaking the vacuums, and the water will drain out.

Work down through the house, allowing time for the water to drain away, until the bleed valves on all radiators are open and the water has stopped flowing. Watch out for inverted pipe loops (See below).

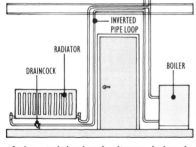

Draining procedure
Turn off the mains supply to the cistern at the feedpipe stopcock (**1**). If there's no stopcock tie the ball valve float arm to a batten laid across the cistern (**2**). With a hose on the main draincock (**3**) and its other end at a gully or soakaway outside, open the draincock and let the system empty. Release any water trapped in radiators (**4**) by opening their bleed valves (**5**), starting at the top of the house. Be sure to close all draincocks before you refill the system.

REFILLING THE SYSTEM

Before you refill the system check that you have closed all the draincocks and radiator bleed valves. Restore the water supply to the feed and expansion cistern in the roof. As the system fills up, air will be trapped in the tops of the radiators, so when the water stops running bleed each radiator in turn, starting at the bottom of the house and working upwards (▷). You may also have to bleed the circulating pump (▷).

Finally check all the draincocks and bleed valves for signs of leakage and tighten them where necessary.

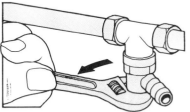

Tightening up a leaking draincock

PROTECTING THE SYSTEM

Using corrosion inhibitor

Any wet central heating system will suffer from corrosion to some extent. It is due not only to rust but also to a black sludge caused by a chemical reaction between the water, the steel radiators and the copper pipework. If it is allowed to build up it can clog the circulating pump and partially block radiators, reducing their heat output.

You can slow down corrosion by adding a proprietary corrosion inhibitor to the water. This is best done when the system is first installed, but the inhibitor can be introduced into the system at any later time. If the system has been running for some time it is better to flush it out first by draining and refilling it repeatedly until the water runs clean. Otherwise all you need to do is to drain off enough water to empty the feed and expansion cistern and a small amount of pipework – about 20 litres (4 gallons) – pour the inhibitor into the cistern and restore the water supply, which will carry the inhibitor into the pipework. About 5 litres (1 gallon) will be enough for most systems, but check the maker's instructions. Finally switch on the circulating pump to distribute the inhibitor round the system.

SEE ALSO

Details for: ▷	
Bleeding radiators	399
Bleeding pump	402
Gully	339,349
Turning off water	340

INVERTED PIPE LOOPS

When fitting a central heating system in a house with solid ground floors the installer will run the pipes from the boiler into the ceiling void and drop them down to the individual radiators. Each of these 'inverted pipe loops' has its own draincock. They must be drained separately after the main system has been emptied.

INVERTED PIPE LOOP

RADIATOR

DRAINCOCK

BOILER

An inverted pipe loop has its own draincock

BOILER MAINTENANCE

Regular cleaning and maintenance will give your central heating boiler a longer life and keep it efficient.
Gas- and oil-fired boilers should be serviced once a year by qualified engineers, but you can do a certain amount of cleaning on an oil-fired one.
Solid-fuel boilers need virtually no maintenance other than regular cleaning, which you can do yourself.

SEE ALSO

◁ Details for:
| Sweeping chimney | 382 |
| Switching off electricity | 296 |

Solid-fuel boilers

If you have a solid-fuel system it is very important to keep the chimney and flueway swept. The job, which should be done twice a year, is done in the same way as for an open fire (◁), access being through the front of a room heater with back boiler or through a soot door in the flue pipe or the chimney breast.

When you have swept the chimney, clean out the boiler with a stiff brush and take up the dust and soot particles with your vacuum cleaner.

Lift out any broken fire bars and drop new ones in place.

Oil-fired boilers

If you have an oil-fired boiler you should clean its walls and oil filter twice a year. The method you use will depend on whether the boiler is the vaporizing or pressure-jet type. Disconnect the electricity supply to the boiler and shut off the oil supply valve. Remove the boiler casing and the furnace cover plate.

Cover the burner of the vaporizing type. The side-entry pressure-jet nozzle will not usually need covering but you can block its draught tube with a rag. Clean the sides of the furnace with a wire brush, then remove the covers and extract the debris with your vacuum cleaner. Also use the vacuum cleaner to remove the dust in the casing.

Place a drip tray under the filter unit before removing the filter element. The vaporizing boiler has an oil-level control valve incorporating a filter. Unscrew the drain plug and remove the filter element (**1**). Wash it in petrol, shake dry and replace. The pressure-jet boiler has an in-line filter. Unscrew the retaining bolt (**2**) and remove the filter bowl. Clean out the bowl and wash or replace the filter before reassembly.

BURNER — FURNACE
OIL-LEVEL
CONTROL VALVE
DRAIN PLUG

Vaporizing boiler ▶

FURNACE
PRESSURE-JET
NOZZLE
DRAUGHT TUBE
FILTER UNIT

Pressure-jet boiler ▶

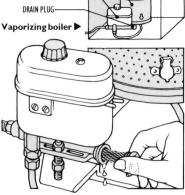

1 Unscrew drain plug and remove the filter

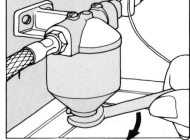

2 Slacken the bolt with a spanner

Gas-fired boilers

If your central heating system is gas-fired there is very little that you can do in the way of maintenance. The job – as for other gas appliances – is one for the professionals (See right).

But you can ensure that the interior is kept free of dust and fluff. This is important especially round the jets.

PROFESSIONAL SERVICING SCHEMES

The very high efficiency of modern gas- and oil-fired boilers largely depends on their being regularly checked and serviced. It should be done annually, and because the mechanisms involved are so complex the work should be done by qualified engineers.

For either type of boiler you can enter into a contract – with either the original installer or the fuel supplier – for regular maintenance.

Gas-fired installations

British Gas offer a choice of several servicing schemes for gas-fired boilers. These cover their own installations, but they can sometimes be arranged for systems put in by other installers on condition a British Gas inspection of the installation is carried out.

The simplest of the British Gas schemes provides for an annual check and adjustment of the boiler. If any repairs are found to be necessary, either at the time of the regular check or at other times during the year, the labour and the required parts will be charged separately. But for an extra fee it is possible to have both free labour and free parts for boiler repairs at any time of the year. British Gas will also extend the arrangement to include a check of the whole heating system at the same time as the boiler is being checked.

It may be that your own installer can offer you a similar choice of servicing schemes. The best course is to compare the charges and decide which gives the best value for money.

Oil-fired installations

The installers of oil-fired central heating systems and the suppliers of fuel oil offer servicing schemes similar to those outlined above for gas-fired systems. The choice of schemes ranges from the simple check-up each year to complete cover for new parts and labour if and when any repairs should become necessary.

Again, as with the schemes for gas, it is wisest to shop round and make a comparison of the various services on offer and the charges for them.

If a radiator feels cooler at the top than at the bottom it's likely that a pocket of air has formed in it and is stopping full circulation of the water. Getting the air out – 'bleeding' – is a simple matter.

Opening a bleed valve

Turn off the circulating pump, and preferably the boiler too, though this isn't vital.

Each radiator has a bleed valve at one of its top corners, identifiable by a square-section shank in the centre of the round blanking plug. You should have been given a key to fit these shanks by the installer, but if you weren't, or if you have inherited an old system, you can buy one at a good DIY shop or ironmonger's.

Use the key to turn the shank of the valve anti-clockwise about a quarter of a turn. It shouldn't be necessary to turn it further but have a small container handy to catch any spurting water if you do open the valve too far.

You will hear a hissing sound as the air escapes. Keep the key on the shank of the valve and when the hissing stops and the first dribble of water appears close the valve tightly.

In no circumstances must you be tempted to open the valve any more than is needed to let the air out, or to remove it completely, as this will produce a deluge of water.

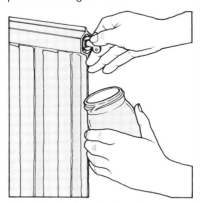

Dispersing the air pocket in a radiator

Radiator key
Keep your radiator key in a handy place where you can find it at short notice. There is no substitute for it.

Fitting an automatic bleed valve

If you find yourself having to bleed one particular radiator regularly it will save you trouble if you replace its bleed valve with an automatic one that will allow air to escape but not water.

First drain the water from the system (▷), then use your bleed-valve key to unscrew the old valve completely out of the blanking plug (**1**). Wind some PTFE tape (▷) round the threads of the automatic valve (**2**) and screw it finger tight into the blanking plug (**3**). Refill the system (▷) and if any water appears round the threads of the new valve tighten it further with a spanner (**4**).

If, when the system is going again, the radiator still feels cool on top it may be that a larger amount of air has collected than the bleed valve can cope with. In this case switch off the pump and unscrew the valve until you hear air hissing out. Tighten it again when the hissing stops and the first trickle of water appears, then restart the pump.

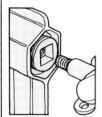  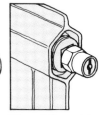 

1 Unscrew old valve   **2 Tape the new one**   **3 Screw it finger tight**   **4 Stop any leak in use**

SEE ALSO

Details for: ▷	
PTFE tape	354
Draining system	397
Filling system	397

HOW TO REMOVE A RADIATOR

You can remove an individual radiator while the wall behind it is decorated without having to drain the whole system. You simply close the valves at the ends of the radiator, drain it and then remove it.

Shut off both valves, turning the shank of the lockshield valve clockwise with a key or an adjustable spanner (**1**). Note the number of turns needed to close it so that later you can reopen it by the same amount.

Make sure that you have plenty of rag for mopping up spillage, also a jug and a large bowl. As the water in the radiator will be very dirty you should also roll back the floor covering before you start if possible.

Unscrew the cap-nut that holds one of the valves to the adaptor in the end of the radiator (**2**). Hold the jug under the joint and open the bleed valve slowly (**3**) to let the water drain out. Transfer the water from jug to bowl and keep going until no more can be drained.

Unscrew the cap-nut that holds the other valve onto the radiator, lift the radiator free from its wall brackets (**4**) and drain any remaining water into the bowl. Unscrew the wall brackets to decorate.

To replace the radiator after decorating screw the brackets back in place, hang the radiator on them and tighten the cap-nuts on both valves. Close the bleed valve and open both radiator valves, the lockshield valve by the same number of turns as you used to close it. Finally use the bleed valve to release any trapped air.

1 Close the valve   **2 Unscrew cap-nut**

3 Open bleed valve

4 Final draining
Lift radiator from brackets and drain off any remaining water.

RADIATOR VALVES

Curing a leaking radiator valve

If a manual-control valve or lockshield valve on a radiator seems to be leaking it's most likely that one of the cap-nuts that secure it to the water pipe and to the radiator's valve adaptor needs some tightening up.

Tighten the suspect cap-nut with an adjustable spanner while you hold the body of the valve with a pipe wrench to prevent it moving. If this doesn't work the valve will have to be replaced.

If the leak seems to be from the valve adaptor in the radiator the joint will have to be remade in the same way as when a new valve is fitted (See below). If the leak seems to be from the valve spindle tighten the gland nut (See left) or replace the valve.

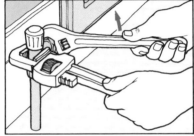

Grip leaky valve with wrench to tighten cap-nut

SEE ALSO

◁ Details for:
PTFE tape	**354**
Draining system	**397**
Adjustable spanner	489
Pipe wrench (stilson)	490

VALVE HEAD

GLAND NUT

Tightening gland nut
Tighten the gland nut with a spanner to stop a leak from a radiator valve spindle. If the leak persists, replace the valve (See right).

Replacing a worn or damaged valve

Be sure that the new valve is exactly like the old one, or it may not align with the water pipe. Drain the heating system (◁) and lay rags under the valve to catch any remaining dregs that may come out of the radiator.

Hold the body of the valve with a wrench and use an adjustable spanner to unscrew the cap-nuts that hold the valve to the water pipe and to the adaptor in the end of the radiator (**1**). Lift the valve from the end of the pipe (**2**). If the valve being replaced is a lockshield valve don't remove it before you have closed it, counting the number of turns needed so that you can open the new valve by the same number to balance the radiator.

Unscrew the adaptor from the radiator (**3**). You may manage this with an adjustable spanner or you may need a special hexagonal radiator spanner, depending on the type of adaptor.

Fitting the new one

Ensure that the threads in the end of the radiator are clean and wind PTFE tape (◁) four or five times round the thread of the new valve's adaptor, then screw it into the end of the radiator by hand and tighten it a further 1½ turns with the spanner.

Slide the valve cap-nut and a new olive over the end of the water pipe and fit the valve to the end of the pipe (**4**), but don't tighten the cap-nut at this stage. First align the valve body with the adaptor and tighten the cap-nut that holds them together (**5**). Hold the valve body firm with a wrench while you do this. Now tighten the cap-nut that holds the valve to the water pipe (**6**).

Finally refill the system, check for leaks at the joints of the new valves and tighten the cap-nuts some more if that seems necessary.

DEALING WITH A JAMMED OLIVE

If the olive is jammed onto the pipe, cut the pipe off below floorboard level and make up a new section. Join it to the old pipe by means of either a capillary or a compression joint.

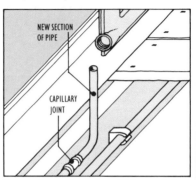

NEW SECTION OF PIPE

CAPILLARY JOINT

New section replaces pipe with jammed olive

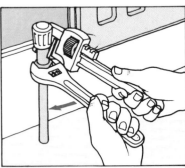

1 Hold the valve firm and loosen both cap-nuts

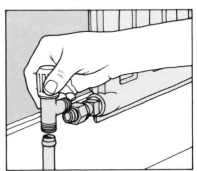

2 Unscrew the cap-nuts and lift the valve out

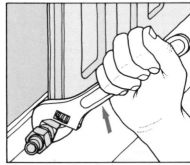

3 Remove the valve adaptor from the radiator

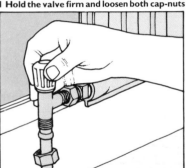

4 Fit new adaptor, then fit new valve to pipe

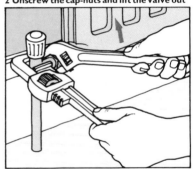

5 Connect valve to adaptor and tighten cap-nut

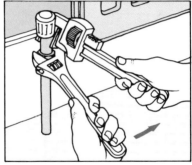

6 Tighten cap-nut holding valve to water pipe

REPLACING A CORRODED OR DAMAGED RADIATOR

Try to obtain a new radiator of exactly the same model as the one you wish to replace. This will make the job easier.

Simple replacement

Drain and remove the old radiator (▷). With it clear of the wall unscrew the valve adaptors from the bottom with an adjustable spanner or, if necessary, a hexagonal radiator spanner. Unscrew the bleed valve with its key, and then the two blanking plugs from the top of the radiator, using a square or hexagonal radiator spanner (**1**).

With wire wool clean up the threads of both adaptors and both blanking plugs (**2**), then wind four or five turns of PTFE tape (▷) round the threads (**3**). Screw them into the new radiator and the bleed valve into the blanking plug.

Hang the new radiator on its wall brackets and connect the valves to their adaptors. Open the valves and fill and bleed the radiators (▷).

Replacement with a different pattern radiator

Rather more work is involved in the replacement if you can't get a radiator of the same pattern as the old one. You'll have to fit new wall brackets and alter the water pipes.

Drain the system (▷), then take the old brackets off the wall. Lay the new radiator face down on the floor and slide one of its brackets onto the hangers welded to the back of the radiator. Measure from the top of the bracket to the bottom of the radiator, add 100 or 125mm (4 or 5in) for clearance under the radiator, then mark a horizontal line on the wall that distance from the floor. Now measure the distance between the centres of the radiator hangers and make two marks on the horizontal line that distance apart and at equal distances from the two water pipes (**1**).

Line up the brackets with the pencil marks, mark their fixing screw holes, drill and plug the holes and fix the brackets in place (**2**).

Lift up the floorboards below the radiator's position and cut off the vertical portions of the feed and return pipes. Connect the valves to the radiator and hang it on its brackets. Slip a short length of pipe into each valve as a guide for any further trimming of the pipes under the floor. Connect these lengths to the original pipes (**3**) with capillary or compression fittings (▷), then connect the new pipes to the valves (▷). Refill the system and check the connections and joints for leaks.

SEE ALSO

Details for: ▷	
Connecting	
pipes	351-359
Pipe joints	353-354
PTFE tape	354
Draining the	
system	397
Bleeding radiators	399
Removing	
radiators	399
Ajustable spanner	489
Radiator spanner	489
Wall fixings	498-499

1 Removing the plug
Use a radiator spanner to unscrew the blanking plug at each end of the radiator.

2 Cleaning the threads
Use wire wool to clean any corrosion from the threads of both blanking plugs and valve adaptors.

3 Taping the threads
Make the threaded joints watertight by wrapping PTFE tape several times around each component before screwing them into the new radiator.

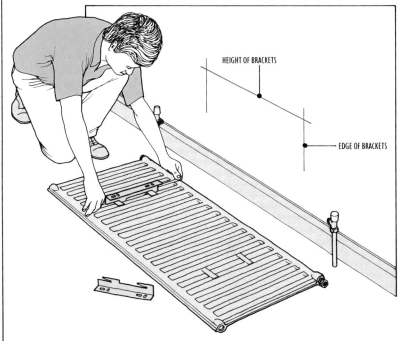

HEIGHT OF BRACKETS

EDGE OF BRACKETS

1 Taking the measurements
Measure the positions of the radiator brackets and transfer the measurements to the wall. Double-check the results to make sure the radiator is equidistant between the two pipes projecting from the floor.

2 Securing the brackets
Screw the mounting brackets to the wall
Make sure they are on the right side of the line.

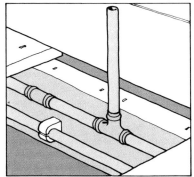

3 Connecting up
Connect the new section of pipework
The vertical pipe aligns with the radiator valve.

CIRCULATING PUMPS

Wet central heating depends on a steady cycle of hot water from boiler to radiators and back to the boiler for reheating. This is the pump's job. A faulty pump means poor circulation. A failed pump means none.

SEE ALSO

◁ Details for:
Removing a fuse 298-300
Draining system 397
Filling system 397
Connecting to terminals 293

Bleeding the pump

If your radiators don't seem to be warming up, though you can hear or feel the pump running, it's likely that an airlock has formed in the pump and its impeller is spinning in air. The air must be bled from the pump, a job that's done in the same way as bleeding a radiator. You'll find a screw-in valve for the purpose in the pump's outer casing.

The valve's position varies with the different makes but it is usually marked.

Switch off the pump, have a jug or jam jar handy to catch any water spillage and open the valve with a screwdriver or vent key. Open it only slightly, until you hear air hissing out. When the hissing stops and a drop of water appears close the valve fully.

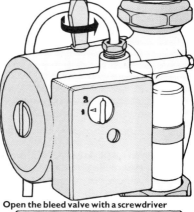

Open the bleed valve with a screwdriver

Adjusting the pump

Central heating pumps are of two kinds: fixed head and variable head. Fixed-head units run at a single speed, forcing the water round the system at a fixed rate. Variable-head pumps can be adjusted to run at different speeds, circulating the water at different rates.

When a variable-head pump is fitted as part of a central heating system the installer adjusts its speed after balancing all the radiators so that each room reaches its 'design temperature'. If you find that your rooms are not as warm as you would like, though you have opened the manual radiator valves fully, you can adjust the pump speed. But first check that all radiators show the same temperature drop between their inlets and outlets. You can get clip-on thermometers for the job from a

plumbers' merchant. You will need a pair of them.

Clip one thermometer to the feed pipe just below the radiator valve and the other to the return pipe below its valve (**1**). The difference between the temperatures registered by the two should be about 7°C (20°F). If it is not, uncover the lockshield valve and close it further (to increase the difference) or open it more (to reduce the difference).

Having balanced the radiators you can now adjust the pump. Switch it off and then turn the speed adjustment up (**2**), one step at a time, until you are getting the overall temperatures you want. You may be able to work the adjustment by hand or you may need some special tool, such as an Allen key, depending on the make and model of your pump.

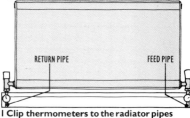

RETURN PIPE   FEED PIPE

1 Clip thermometers to the radiator pipes

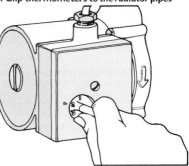

2 Adjust pump speed to increase temperature

Replacing a worn pump

If you have to replace your circulating pump be quite sure that the one you buy is of exactly the same make and model as the old one, or seek the advice of a professional installer.

Turn off the boiler and close the isolating valves on each side of the pump. If there are no isolating valves you will have to drain down the whole system (◁).

Identify the electrical circuit that controls the pump and remove the fuse of that circuit from the consumer unit (◁), then take the cover plate off the pump and disconnect its wiring (**1**).

Have a bowl or bucket at hand to catch any water left in the pump, also some old rags for any mopping up that you may have to do. Undo the nuts that hold the pump to the valves or the pipework with an adjustable spanner (**2**) and catch the water as it flows out.

Remove the pump and fit the new one in its place, taking care to fit correctly any sealing washers that are provided (**3**), then tighten up the retaining nuts.

Take the cover plate off the new pump, feed in the flex, connect the wires to the pump's terminals (**4**) and replace the cover plate. If the pump is of the variable-head type (See above) set the speed control to the speed indicated on the old pump.

Open both isolating valves – or if the system has been drained refill it (◁) – check the pump connections for leaks and tighten them if necessary, then open the pump's bleed valve to release any air that may have become trapped in it. Finally replace the fuse in the consumer unit and test the pump.

1 Remove cover plate   **2** Undo connecting nuts

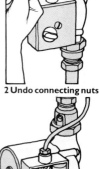

3 Attach new pump   **4** Connect power flex

CONTROL VALVES

The control valves are vital to the effective working of a modern central heating system, for it is through them that the various timers and thermostats are able to adjust the levels of heating precisely to the programmed requirements of the householder.

Worn or faulty control valves can seriously affect the reliability of the system and should be replaced promptly.

Replacing a faulty valve

First ensure that the replacement valve that you buy is of exactly the same pattern as the faulty one, or seek professional advice.

Drain down the system (▷), then identify the electrical circuit that services the central heating controls and take its fuse out of the consumer unit.

The electric flex from the valve will be connected to the terminals of a nearby junction box, which will also be linked to the heating system's other controls. Take the cover off the junction box and disconnect the wiring for the valve. As you do this you should carefully note the connections so as to make reconnection easier.

You will probably not be able to take the old valve out of the pipe run by simply unscrewing its cap-nuts, as you won't be able to pull the ends of the pipe free of their sockets in the valve. Instead cut through the pipe on each side of the valve (**1**) and take out the section, complete with valve, then make up two pieces of pipe to fit on either side of the new control valve.

Assemble the valve with its olives and cap-nuts, pipes and joints, but only loosely at first, and fit the assembly into the pipe run (**2**).

There should be enough play in the joints to allow the assembly to be sprung into place, and this may be helped if the original pipes on each side of the valve position are first freed from their clips.

When the pipes and valve are in place connect them to the original pipework with compression or capillary joints (▷), then tighten the valve cap-nuts. Hold the body of the valve with a second spanner to prevent it turning (**3**).

Reconnect the flex to the terminals of the junction box and replace its cover plate, then replace the fuse in the consumer unit.

Refill the heating system and check the working of the valve by adjusting the timer or thermostat that controls it.

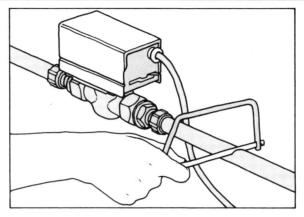

1 Removing the valve
If you cannot disconnect the valve, cut through the pipe on each side of it with a hacksaw.

SEE ALSO

Details for: ▷	
Pipe joints	353-354
Draining system	397
Removing a fuse	298-300
Junction box	311
Heating controls	395

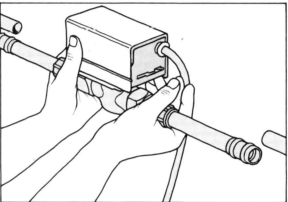

2 Fitting new valve
With the new valve connected to short sections of pipe, spring the assembly into the pipe run.

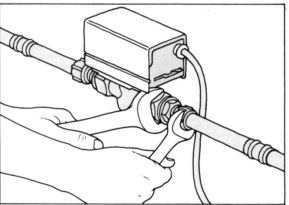

3 Closing the joints
Having connected the pipework, tighten the valve cap-nuts on each side with a pair of spanners.

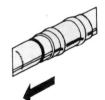

Slip coupling
If you cannot spring pipework to locate a conventional soldered joint (▷) use a slip coupling which is free to slide along the pipe to cover the junction.

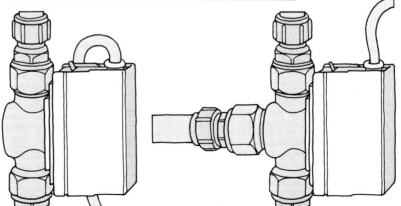

Far left
Two-port control valve
A two-port valve seals off a section of pipework when water within that section has reached the required temperature.

Left
Three-port control valve
This type of valve can independently isolate central heating or hot water circuits.

403

STORAGE HEATERS

A sound reason for the popularity of electric storage heaters is their use of cheap off-peak power during the night. The Electricity Boards' special rate for the night-time power is often only half of that charged for the daytime supply, even less. The cut-rate scheme is known as Economy 7, referring to the seven hours of the night when the cheap rate is in force.

The night-time power heats up a core of fire brick or similar material in the storage heater, and the core releases the heat next day, a process of convection in which cool air is drawn in at the bottom of the heater, to be heated as it passes over the hot core and then expelled from the top.

SEE ALSO

◁ Details for:
Heater circuits   320-321
Selecting heaters   394

Types of storage heater

The early storage heaters were bulky and space-consuming, and they emitted heat at a set rate so that the user had no control over the output. The heat stored at night could be adjusted, but this required an estimate of the next day's heating needs, and a sudden change of weather could leave the user with too much heat or too little.

Some recent advances in storage heater designs have improved the units. Modern ones are slimmer, some being only 150mm (6in) deep, and they can be wall-mounted or freestanding.

The new heaters have better insulation and allow greater control of the heat output. Adjustable dampers and fans, some thermostatically controlled, allow heaters to be run at low levels in unoccupied rooms and opened up when needed, even late in the day, when older storage heaters run out of stored heat. Some units retain a residue of the stored heat which reduces overnight charging and cuts costs further. Others can monitor room temperatures at night, assess the next day's heating needs (a cold night is normally followed by a cold day) and adjust the heat charge accordingly.

Positioning storage heaters

Like radiators, storage heaters should be placed below single-glazed windows to counter draughts and balance the room temperatures. With double glazing they can go anywhere for convenience or the best heat spread. The heaters have individual circuits, a separate consumer unit and a special off-peak meter (◁) to record their power consumption.

CHOOSING STORAGE HEATERS

To be strictly accurate when working out the size and number of storage heaters you'll need you should calculate in the same way as if you were going to install wet-system central heating radiators (◁). In that process the heat demands of each room are worked out and then heaters are chosen to meet those demands.

Since putting in storage heaters is much easier than installing a full central heating system – a common DIY job, in fact – a guide for the amateur is needed. Such a guide is provided by some manufacturers and the Electricity Boards in the form of simple charts to help you estimate each room's needs on the basis of floor area and the number of outside walls.

Charts like this are not totally accurate, but they allow you to select heaters from the three basic sizes: 1.7, 2.5 and 3.4 kW. A chart of this type is shown below left.

Low-output storage heater
Will provide ample background heat for corridors and hallways.

High-output storage heater
Runs on economical night-rate electricity and provides adequate comfort heating for living areas.

Decorative finishes
Many heaters are available with decorative panels and finishes to suit your interior scheme.

SIZING STORAGE HEATERS

Room sizes		Storage heaters required	
Dimensions	Area	Comfort heating	Background heating
2.5 × 2.75m (8′ × 9′)	0-7.4m² (0-80ft²)	1 × 2.5kW	1 × 2.5kW
3.0 × 3.4m (10′ × 11′)	7.4-11.2m² (80-120ft²)	1 × 3.4kW	1 × 2.5kW
3.0 × 4.0m (10′ × 13′)	11.2-13.0m² (120-140ft²)	1 × 1.7kW and 1 × 2.5kW	1 × 2.5kW
2.75 × 4.9m (9′ × 16′)	13.0-14.9m² (140-160ft²)	1 × 1.7kW and 1 × 2.5kW	1 × 3.4kW
4.0 × 4.0m (13′ × 13′)	14.9-16.7m² (160-180ft²)	2 × 2.5kW	1 × 3.4kW
3.7 × 4.9m (12′ × 16′)	16.7-18.6m² (180-200ft²)	2 × 2.5kW	1 × 3.4kW
3.7 × 5.5m (12′ × 18′)	18.6-20.4m² (200-220ft²)	2 × 2.5kW	1 × 1.7kW and 1 × 2.5kW
3.4 × 6.4m (11′ × 21′)	20.4-22.3m² (220-240ft²)	1 × 2.5kW and 1 × 3.4kW	1 × 1.7kW and 1 × 2.5kW
4.9 × 4.9m (16′ × 16′)	22.3-24.2m² (240-260ft²)	1 × 2.5kW and 1 × 3.4kW	1 × 1.7kW and 1 × 2.5kW
4.6 × 5.5m (15′ × 18′)	24.2-27.9m² (260-300ft²)	2 × 3.4kW	2 × 2.5kW
4.3 × 7.4m (14′ × 24′)	27.9-31.6m² (300-340ft²)	3 × 2.5kW	2 × 2.5kW
5.2 × 6.4m (17′ × 21′)	31.6-33.4m² (340-360ft²)	3 × 2.5kW	2 × 2.5kW
4.9 × 7.6m (16′ × 25′)	33.4-38.1m² (360-410ft²)	2 × 2.5kW and 1 × 3.4kW	1 × 2.5kW and 1 × 3.4kW

10

GARDEN PLANNING	406
FENCES	410
GATES	418
MASONRY	420
BRICKWORK	426
BLOCKWORK	434
STONEWORK	436
RETAINING WALLS	437
PATHS/DRIVES/PATIOS	438
CONCRETE	438
LAYING PAVING	446
COBBLESTONES/GRAVEL	451
TARMAC	452
GARDEN STEPS	453
WATER GARDENS	455
SWIMMING POOLS	460

WORKING OUTDOORS

PLANNING A GARDEN

SEE ALSO

◁ Details for:
Building regulations   18-19

Designing a garden is not an exact science. Plants may not thrive in a particular spot even though you select the right soil conditions and check the amount of daylight, and shrubs and trees may never reach the maximum size specified for them in a catalogue. Nevertheless, forward planning will produce a more satisfactory result than a haphazard approach which could involve expensive mistakes like laying a patio where it will be in shade for most of the day, building a boundary wall that is too high to meet with official council approval, or a parking space that is too small for a car. It is these permanent features of a garden which you should concentrate on planning first, always, of course, considering how they will fit into the planted and turfed areas of the garden. No-one wants to live in a concrete jungle.

Deciding on the approach

Before you even put pencil to paper, get a feel for the style of garden you would prefer and consider whether it will sit happily with the house and its immediate surroundings. Is it to be formal, laid out in straight lines or geometric patterns – a style which often marries successfully with modern architecture? Do you prefer the more relaxed style of a rambling cottage garden? Natural informality may not be as easy to achieve as you think, and it will certainly take several years to mature into the established garden you have in mind. Or, consider a blend of both, where every plant, stone and pool of water is carefully positioned. A Japanese-style garden bears all the hallmarks of a man-made landscape yet conveys a sense of natural harmony.

There is no shortage of material from which to draw inspiration – countless books and magazines are devoted to the design of gardens. Don't expect to find a total solution which fits your plot exactly – no two gardens are alike – but you may be able to adapt a particular approach or develop a small detail into a design for your own garden. Visiting other gardens is even better. Large country estates and city parks will have been designed on a much grander scale, but at least you will be able to see how a mature shrub should look, or gain a fresh idea on combining plants, stone and water in a rockery or water garden. Don't forget that your neighbours and friends may also have had to tackle problems identical to yours. If nothing else, you might learn by their mistakes!

◁1

2▷

1 Cottage-style garden
The informal character of abundant flowers planted between areas of natural-stone paving ideally complements traditional cottage architecture.

2 Consider the details
Good design does not rely on having a large garden. A successful combination of natural forms can be just as rewarding on a small scale.

3 A convincing rockery
Once plants become established, a rockery should blend into a garden without a hint of artificiality. The effect relies on the careful positioning of stones during its construction.

4 A simple layout
Simplicity is often the best approach but the proportions of the various elements must be carefully considered to avoid a boring result.

◁3

4▷

SURVEYING THE PLOT

Measuring the plot
Measure your plot of land as accurately as you can, including the diagonals, because what might appear to be square or rectangular may taper towards one end or do something equally unexpected.

Slopes and gradients
Make a note of how the ground slopes. An accurate survey is not necessary, but at least jot down the direction of the slope and plot the points where it begins and ends. You can get some idea of the differences in level by using a long straightedge and a spirit level. Place one end of the straightedge on the top of a bank, for instance, and measure the vertical distance from the other end to the foot of the slope.

Climatic conditions
Check the passage of the sun and the direction of prevailing winds. Don't forget that the angle of the sun will be higher in summer and a screen of deciduous trees will be less of a windbreak when they drop their leaves.

Soil conditions
Make a note of soil conditions. You can easily adjust soil content by adding peat or fertilizers. A peat or clay soil is not very stable, however, and will affect the type of footings and foundations you may want to lay.

Existing features
Plot the position of features you want to retain in your plan, such as existing pathways, areas of lawn, established trees and so on.

Measuring a plot
Note the overall dimensions including the diagonals to draw an accurate plan.

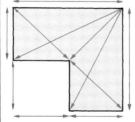

Gauging a slope
Use a straightedge and spirit level to measure the height of a bank.

1△

◁2

3▷

4▽

SEE ALSO

Details for: ▷	
Footing/foundations	427, 440
Retaining walls	437
Paving	448
Water gardens	455-459
Building a rockery	459

1 Japanese-style garden
The overall effect should be one of tranquillity.

2 Using textures
Still water punctuated with rugged stones makes for a pleasing contrast of textures.

3 A sloping site
Some of the most dramatic gardens are a result of having to contend with a sloping site. Here retaining walls are used to terrace a steep bank of colourful shrubs.

4 A formal garden
Use public parks or country estates as inspiration for planning a formal garden. These miniature hedges with selected planting outline a geometric layout of pathways.

407

GARDEN PLANNING: BASIC CONSIDERATIONS

SEE ALSO

◁ Details for:

Official approval 19
Designing a pond 456
Pumps and fountains 458

Having surveyed your plot, it is worth taking the time to plan all aspects of the design of your garden. Practical problems will need careful thought.

DRAWING A PLAN

Draw a plan of your garden on paper. It must be a properly scaled plan or you are sure to make some gross errors, but it need not be professionally perfect. Use squared paper to plot the dimensions but do the actual drawing on tracing paper laid over the graph paper so that you can try out several ideas and adapt your plan without having to redraw it every time.

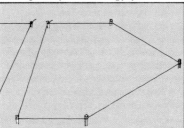
Make a garden plan on tracing paper

PLOTTING YOUR DESIGN

Planning on paper is only the first stage. Gardens are rarely seen from above so it is essential to plot the design on the ground to check your dimensions and view the features from different angles. A pond or patio which looks enormous on paper can be pathetically small in reality. Other shortcomings, such as the way a tree will block the view from your proposed patio, become obvious once you lay out the plan full-size.

Plot individual features by driving pegs into the ground and stretching string lines between them. Scribe arcs on the ground with a rope tied to a peg, and mark the curved lines with stakes or a row of bricks. Use a garden hose to mark out less regular curves and ponds. If you can scrape areas clear of weeds, it will define the shapes still further.

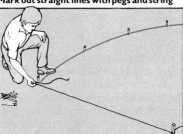
Mark out straight lines with pegs and string

PRACTICAL EXPERIMENTS

When you have marked out your design, check that it works with a few practical experiments. Will it be possible, for instance, for two people to pass each other on a footpath without stepping onto flowerbeds? Can you set down a wheelbarrow onto the path without one of its legs slipping into the pond?

Try placing some furniture on the area marked out for a patio to make sure you can sit comfortably and even take a meal when visitors arrive. Most people build a patio alongside the house, but if you have to put it elsewhere to find a sunny spot, will it become a chore to walk back and forth for drinks and snacks?

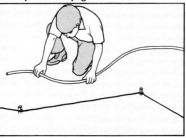
Use rope tied to a peg to scribe an arc

SITING PONDS

Site a pond to avoid overhanging trees and where it will catch at least a half-day's sunlight. Check that you can reach it with a hose for topping-up and that you can run electrical cables to power a pump or night-time lighting.

COMMON-SENSE SAFETY

Don't make your garden an obstacle course. A narrow path alongside a pond, for instance, could be intimidating to an elderly relative. Low walls or planters near the edge of a raised patio could cause someone to trip.

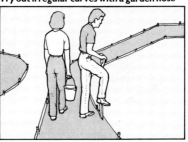
Try out irregular curves with a garden hose

DRIVEWAYS AND PARKING SPACES

Allow a minimum width of 3m (9ft 9in) for a driveway, making sure there is enough room to open the car doors if you park alongside a wall. Remember that vehicles larger than your own might need to use the drive or parking space – delivery trucks, for instance. When you drive in or out, will you be able to see? Try out the turning circle of your car in an empty car park.

Make sure two people can pass on a path

CONSIDER THE NEIGHBOURS

There may be legal restrictions on what you can erect in your garden (◁), but even if you have a free hand it is only wise to consult your neighbours if anything you plan might cause discomfort or inconvenience. A wall or even trees which are high enough to shade their favourite sunspot or block out the light to a window could be the source of argument for years to come.

TREE ROOTS AND FOUNDATIONS

As a permanent feature of your garden you will probably want to plant at least one tree. You will need to think carefully about your choice of trees and their position – they could be potentially damaging to the structure of the house if planted too near.

GROWING IVY ON WALLS

There is a widely held misconception that a climbing ivy will damage any masonry wall. If rendering or the mortar between bricks or stonework is in a poor condition then an exuberant ivy plant will undoubtedly weaken the structure as its aerial roots attempt to extract moisture from the masonry. The roots invade broken joints or rendering, and on finding a source of nourishment for the main plant, they expand and burst the weak material which accelerates deterioration by encouraging penetrating damp. If the ivy is allowed to grow unchecked, the weight of the plant can eventually topple a weakened wall.

However, with modern hard bricks and mortar, ivy can do no more than climb by the aid of training wires and its own sucker-like roots which do not provide nourishment but are for support only. So long as the structure is sound and free from damp, there is some benefit from ivy clothing a wall in that its close-growing mat of leaves, mostly with their drip tips pointing downwards, acts as insulation and a watershed against the elements. Where ivy is permitted to flourish as a climber, it must be hard-pruned to prevent it penetrating between roof tiles or slates and clogging gutters and drainpipes.

Don't allow ivy to get out of control

Cracks: subsidence and heave

Minor cracks in house plaster, rendering and even brickwork are often the result of shrinkage as the structure dries out. These sorts of cracks are not serious and can be repaired during normal maintenance, but more serious structural cracks are due to movement of foundations. Trees planted too close to a building can add to the problem by removing moisture from the site, causing subsidence of the foundations as the supporting earth collapses. The felling of trees can be just as damaging. The surrounding soil, which had become stabilized over the years, swells as it takes up the moisture which had been removed previously by the tree root system. Upward movement of the ground, known as heave, distorts the foundations until cracks appear.

Siting trees

Growing tree roots search out moisture, which can result in an expensive repair or replacement of the house drainage system. Large roots can fracture rigid pipework or penetrate joints until the drain becomes blocked.

Before you plant a tree close to a building, find out the likely spread of the mature root system. As a rough guide, make sure there is a distance of at least two-thirds the mature height of a tree between it and nearby buildings. If an existing tree is likely to cause a problem, ask your local planning department for advice – the tree may be protected by a preservation order and you could be fined if you cut it down without permission. It may be possible to prune the branches and roots to lessen the likelihood of future damage.

SEE ALSO

Details for: ▷

Repairing cracks	46
Penetrating damp	251-253

Subsidence
A mature tree planted close to a house can drain so much water from the ground that the earth collapses causing the foundations to subside.

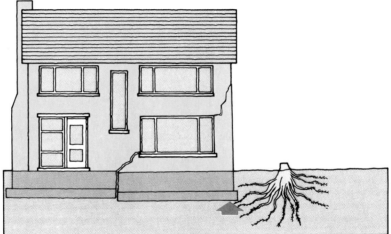

Heave
When a mature tree is felled the earth can absorb more water, causing it to swell until it displaces the foundations of a building.

FENCES: CHOOSING

A fence is the most popular form of boundary marker or garden screen because of its advantages over other methods of dividing plots of land. A fence takes very little time to erect when compared with a wall and especially with a hedge, which takes years to establish. Most fencing components are relatively lightweight and are therefore easy to transport and handle on site.

SEE ALSO

◁ Details for:
Planning permission 19
**Infestation
and rot** 246-247, 249
Preservatives 250

Economics and Maintenance

In the short term a fence is cheaper than a wall built of masonry, although one can argue that the cost of maintenance and replacement over a very long period eventually cancels out the saving in cost. Wood does have a comparatively short life because it is susceptible to insect infestation and rot (◁) when exposed to the elements, but a fence will last for many years if it is treated regularly with a chemical preservative. In any case, if you are prepared to spend a little more money on plastic or concrete components, you can erect a virtually maintenance-free fence.

Choosing your fencing

When you measure even a small garden, you will be surprised by the overall length of fencing required to surround your property, so it is worth considering the available options carefully to make sure that you invest your money in the kind of fence that will be most suitable. Unless your priority is to keep neighbourhood children or animals out of your garden, the amount of privacy afforded by a fence is likely to be your most important consideration. There are a number of 'peep-proof' options, but you may have to compromise to some extent if you plan to erect a fence on a site exposed to strong prevailing winds. In that case you will need a fence which will provide a decent windbreak without offering such resistance that the posts will have worked loose within a couple of seasons due to constant buffeting.

Planning and planning permission

You can build any fence up to 2m (6ft 6in) high without planning permission (◁) unless your boundary adjoins a highway, in which case you may not be able to erect a barrier higher than 1m (3ft 3in). In addition, there may be local restrictions on fencing if the land surrounding your house has been designed as an open-plan area. Even so, many authorities will permit low boundary markers such as a ranch-style or post and chain fence.

At least discuss your plans with your neighbours, especially as you will require their permission to enter onto their properties, and it is always an advantage to be able to work from both sides when erecting a fence. Check the line of the boundaries to make certain that you do not encroach on neighbours' land. The fence posts should run along the boundary or on your side of the line, and before you dismantle an old fence, make sure it is yours to demolish. If a neighbour is unwilling to replace an unsightly fence, or even to allow you to replace it at your expense, there is nothing to stop you erecting another fence alongside as long as it is on your property. It is an unwritten law that a good neighbour erects a fence with the post and rails facing his or her own property, but there are no legal restrictions which force you to do so.

Chain link fencing

Trellis fencing

Post and chain fence

TYPES OF FENCING

CHAIN LINK FENCING

Chain link fencing is a utilitarian form of barrier constructed from wire netting stretched between fence posts. A true chain link fence is made from strong galvanized or plastic-coated wire woven into a diamond-shape mesh, suspended from a heavy-gauge wire tensioned between the posts. A cheap fence can be made from soft wire netting or 'chicken wire'. However, it is not very durable and will stretch out of shape if a large animal leans against it. Decorative wire fencing is available at many garden centres, designed primarily for low boundary markers or to support lightweight climbing plants. In fact, any chain link fence will benefit from a screen of climbers or hedging plants.

TRELLIS FENCING

A concertina-fold trellis formed from thin softwood or cedar laths joined together is virtually useless as a fence in the true sense, relying exclusively on the posts and rails for its strength. But a similar fence made from split rustic poles nailed to stout rails and posts forms a strong and attractive barrier. Both types of trellis are ideally suited as plant supports for climbers.

POST AND CHAIN FENCING

A post and chain fence is simply a decorative feature to prevent people wandering off a path or pavement onto a lawn or flowerbed. Lengths of painted metal or plastic chain are strung between short posts sunk into the ground.

TYPES OF FENCING

FENCES

Closeboard fencing

SEE ALSO

Details for: ▷
| Wood finishes | 75 |
| Preservatives | 250 |

CLOSEBOARD FENCING

A closeboard fence is made by nailing overlapping featherboard strips to the horizontal rails. Featherboards are sawn planks which taper across their width from 16mm (⅝in) at the thicker side down to about 3mm (⅛in). The boards are 100mm (4in) or 150mm (6in) wide, and the best quality are made from cedar. However, softwood is the usual choice because of the high timber content of a closeboard fence. Although it is expensive, closeboard fencing forms a strong and attractive screen. Being fixed vertically, the boards are difficult to climb from the outside – ideal for keeping children out!

PRE-FABRICATED PANEL FENCING

Fences made from pre-fabricated panels nailed between timber posts are very common, perhaps because they are particularly easy to erect. Standard panels are 1.8m (6ft) wide, and rise in steps of 300mm (1ft) from approximately 600mm (2ft) in height to 1.8m (6ft). Most panels are made from interwoven or overlapping strips of larch sandwiched between a frame of sawn timber. The overlapping strip panels are usually designated 'larchlap', or 'rustic larchlap' if the strips have a natural wavy edge. You may also see them described as 'waney-edged', referring to where the thin strips of bark were, or may still be, attached to the planks.

A panel fence offers good value for money as a reasonably durable screen, but choose the lapped type for privacy. In the summer interwoven strips will shrink to some extent, leaving gaps.

Panel fence

INTERLAP FENCING

An interlap fence is made by nailing square-edged boards to the horizontal rails, fixing them alternately one side, then the other. Spacing is a matter of choice. For privacy, overlap the edges of the boards, or space them apart for a decorative effect.

This is the type of fence to choose for a windy site as it is substantial, yet the gaps between the boards allow the wind to pass through without exerting too much pressure. Because of its construction, an interlap fence is equally attractive from either side.

Interlap fencing

PICKET FENCING

The traditional, low picket fence is still popular as a 'cottage-style' barrier at the front of the house where a high fence is unnecessary. Narrow, vertical 'pales', with rounded or pointed tops, are spaced at 50mm (2in) centres. As they are laborious to build by hand, most picket fences are sold as ready-made panels constructed from softwood or plastic to keep down the cost.

Picket fencing

RANCH-STYLE FENCING

Low-level fences made from simple, horizontal rails fixed to short, stout posts are the modern counterpart of picket fencing. Used extensively in today's housing developments, this ranch-style fencing is often painted, although clear-finished or stained timber is just as attractive and far more durable. Softwoods and some hardwoods are used for fencing, but plastic ranch-style fences are becoming increasingly popular for their clean, crisp appearance since they do away with the chore of repainting for maintenance.

Ranch-style fence

CONCRETE FENCING

A cast concrete fence offers the security and permanence of a masonry wall and needs minimal maintenance. Interlocking, horizontal sections are built one upon the other up to the required height. Each screen is supported by grooves cast into the sides of purpose-made concrete fence posts.

Concrete fencing

FENCE POSTS

Whatever type of fence you plan to erect, its strength and durability rely on good-quality posts set solidly in the ground. Buy the best posts you can afford, and erect them carefully. It is worth taking longer over its construction to avoid having to dismantle and repair a fence in the future.

SEE ALSO

◁ Details for:
Preservatives	250
Wall fixings	**498-499**

● **Capping fence posts**
If you simply cut the end of a timber post square, the top of the post will rot relatively quickly. The solution is to cut a single or double bevel to shed the rainwater, or nail a wooden or galvanized metal cap over the end of the fence post.

TYPES OF POST

In some cases the nature of the fencing will determine the choice of post. Concrete fencing, for instance, must be supported by compatible concrete posts, but, in the main, you can choose the material and style of post which suits the appearance of the fence.

TIMBER POSTS

Most fences are supported by square-section timber posts. Standard sizes are 75mm and 100mm (3in and 4in) square, but 125mm, 150mm and even 200mm (5in, 6in, 8in) square gate posts are available. Most timber merchants supply pre-treated softwood posts unless you ask specifically for hardwood.

CONCRETE POSTS

A variety of 100mm (4in) square, reinforced-concrete posts exists to suit different styles of fence: drilled for chain link, mortised for rails and recessed or grooved for panels. Special corner and end posts are notched to accommodate bracing struts for chain link fencing.

METAL POSTS

Angle iron or plastic-coated steel posts are made to support chain link or plastic fences. Although angle iron posts are very sturdy, they do not make for a very attractive garden fence.

PLASTIC POSTS

PVC posts are supplied with plastic fencing but most have to be reinforced internally by a timber insert for fences over 750mm (2ft 6in) in height.

Preserving fence posts

Even when a timber post is pre-treated to prevent rot, provide additional protection by soaking the base of each post in a bucket of chemical preservative for at least ten minutes, and longer if possible (◁).

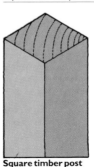
Square timber post

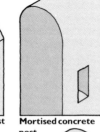
Drilled concrete post   **Mortised concrete post**

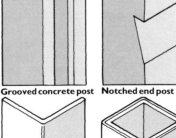
Grooved concrete post   **Notched end post**

Angle iron post   **Tubular steel post**

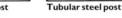
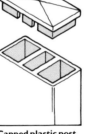
Capped plastic post

REMOVING OLD FENCE POSTS

Fixing posts in virgin soil is straightforward, but if you are replacing a fence you may want to put the new posts in the same positions as the old ones. Remove the topsoil from around each post to loosen the grip of the soil. If one is bedded firmly, or sunk into concrete, lever it out with a stout batten. Drive large nails in two opposite faces of the post, about 300mm (1ft) from the ground. Bind a length of rope around the post just below the nails, and tie the ends to the tip of the batten. Build a pile of bricks close to the post and use it as a fulcrum to lever the post out of the ground.

Levering a rotted fence post
Use a pile of bricks as a fulcrum to lift the post.

FIXING TO A WALL

If a fence runs up to the house, fix the first post to the wall with three expanding masonry bolts (◁). Place a washer under each bolt head to stop the wood being crushed. Check the post is vertical with a spirit level, driving packing between the post and wall to make slight adjustments.

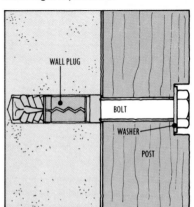
WALL PLUG
BOLT
WASHER
POST

Bolting a post to a wall
If you are fitting a pre-fabricated panel against a wall-fixed post, counter-bore the bolts so that the heads lie flush with the surface of the wood.

USING METAL SPIKES

Instead of anchoring fence posts in concrete, you can plug the base of each post into the square socket of a metal spike driven into firm ground. Use a 600mm (2ft) spike for fences up to 1.2m (4ft) high but use a 750mm (2ft 6in) spike for a 1.8m (6ft) high fence.

Place a scrap of hardwood post into the socket to protect the metal, then drive the spike partly into the ground with a sledgehammer. Hold a spirit level against the socket to make certain the spike is upright (1). Continue to hammer the spike into the ground until only the socket is visible. Insert the post and secure it by screwing through the side of the socket or by tightening clamping bolts (2), depending on the design of the spike you are using.

If you are erecting a panel fence, use the edge of a fixed panel to position the next spike (3).

Fence-post spikes

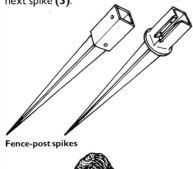

1 Check a spike is vertical with a spirit level

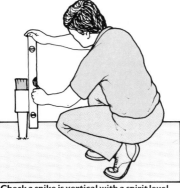

2 Fix the post

3 Position next spike

ERECTING FENCE POSTS

The type of fence often dictates whether you erect all the posts first or one at a time along with the other components. When building a pre-fabricated panel fence, for instance, fix the posts in the ground as you erect the fence, but complete the run of posts before you install chain link fencing.

Marking out

Drive a peg into the ground at each end of the fence run and stretch a line between. If possible, adjust the spacing of the posts to avoid obstructions such as large tree roots. If one or more posts have to be inserted across a paved patio, lift enough slabs to dig the necessary holes. You may have to break up a section of concrete beneath the slabs using a cold chisel and hammer.

Erecting the posts

Digging the hole
Bury one quarter of each post to provide a firm foundation. For a 1.8m (6ft) high fence, dig a 600mm (2ft) hole to take a 2.4m (8ft) post. You can hire a post hole auger to remove the central core of earth. Twist the tool to drive it into the ground (1) and pull it out after every 150mm (6in) to remove the soil. When you have reached a sufficient depth, taper the sides of the hole slightly so that you can pack hardcore and concrete around the post.

Anchoring the post
Ram a layer of hardcore (broken bricks or small stones) into the bottom of the hole to support the base of the post and provide drainage. Get someone to hold the post upright while you brace it with battens nailed to the post and to stakes driven into the ground (2). Use a spirit level to check that it is vertical. (Use guy ropes to support a concrete post.)

Ram more hardcore around the post, leaving a hole about 300mm (1ft) deep for filling with concrete. Mix some concrete to a firm consistency using the proportions 1 part cement: 2 parts sand: 3 parts aggregate (▷). Use a trowel to drop concrete into the hole all round the post and tamp it down with the end of a batten (3). Build the concrete just above the level of the soil and smooth it to slope away from the post (4). This will help shed water and prevent rot. Leave the concrete to harden for about a week before removing the struts. To support a panel fence temporarily, wedge struts against the posts.

1 Dig the post hole

2 Brace the post

3 Fill with concrete   4 Slope the concrete

Supporting end posts

Chain link fence posts must resist the tension of the straining wires (▷). Brace each end post (and some intermediate posts (▷) over a long run) with a strut made from a length of fence post. Shape the end of the strut to fit a notch cut into the post (1) and nail it in place. Order special posts and pre-cast struts for concrete components .

Anchor the post in the ground in the normal way, but dig a 450mm (1ft 6in) deep trench alongside for the strut. Wedge a brick under the end of the strut before ramming hardcore around the post and strut. Fill the trench up to ground level with concrete (2).

Support a corner post with two struts set at right angles. Where a fence adjoins a masonry wall, fix as described in the box on the opposite page.

SEE ALSO

Details for: ▷
Straining wires	414
Intermediate posts	414
Mixing concrete	438-439
Chain link fencing	414
Erecting a panel fence	416
Cold chisel	480

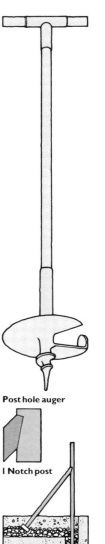

Post hole auger

1 Notch post

2 Concreting end post

413

ERECTING A CHAIN LINK FENCE

Set out a complete row of timber, concrete or angle iron posts to support chain link fencing, spacing them no more than 3m (10ft) apart. Brace the end posts with struts (◁) to resist the pull of the straining wires. A long run of fencing will need a braced intermediate post every 70m (225 ft) or so.

SEE ALSO

◁ Details for:	
Bracing struts	413
Fence posts	412-413

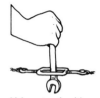

Using a turnbuckle
Apply tension by turning the turnbuckle with a metal bar.

Using timber posts

Support the chain link fencing on straining wires (See right). As it is impossible to tension this heavy-gauge wire by hand, use large straining bolts to stretch it between the posts. Mark the height of each wire on the posts: one to coincide with the top of the fencing, one about 150mm (6in) from the ground, and the third, midway between. Drill 10mm (³⁄₈in) diameter holes right through the posts, insert a bolt into each hole and fit a washer and nut, leaving enough thread to provide about 50mm (2in) of movement once you begin to apply tension to the wire (**1**).

Pass the end of the wire through the eye of a bolt and twist it around itself with pliers (**2**). Stretch the wire along the run of fencing, stapling it to each post and strut, but leave enough slack for the wire to move when tensioned (**3**). Cut the wire to length and twist it through the bolt at the other end of the fence. Tension the wire from both ends by turning the nuts with a spanner (**4**).

Standard straining bolts provide enough tension for the average garden fence, but over a long run (70m (225ft) or more) use a turnbuckle for each wire, applying tension with a metal bar (See left).

Using concrete posts

Fix straining wires to concrete posts using a special bolt and cleat (See right). Bolt a stretcher bar to the cleats when putting on the wire netting.

Tie the straining wire to intermediate posts with a length of galvanized wire passed through the pre-drilled hole.

Using angle iron posts

Winding brackets are supplied with angle iron fence posts to attach stretcher bars and to apply tension to the straining wires (See right).

As you pass the straining wire from end to end, pass it through the pre-drilled hole in every intermediate post.

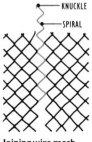

Joining wire mesh
Chain link fencing is supplied in 25m (82ft) lengths. To join one roll to another, unfold the knuckles at each end of the first wire spiral, then turn the spiral anti-clockwise to withdraw it from the mesh. Connect the two rolls by re-threading the loose spiral in a clockwise direction through each link of the mesh. Bend over the knuckle at the top and bottom.

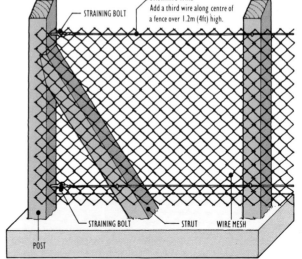

STRAINING WIRE
Add a third wire along centre of a fence over 1.2m (4ft) high.
STRAINING BOLT
STRAINING BOLT
POST
STRAINING BOLT
STRUT
WIRE MESH

Chain link fencing

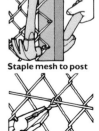

Attaching the mesh
Staple each end link to the post. Unroll the mesh and pull it taut. Tie it to straining wires every 300mm (1ft) with galvanized wire. Fix to post at other end.

Staple mesh to post

Tie with wire loops

1 Insert a straining bolt in the end post

2 Attach a straining wire to the bolt

3 Staple the wire to the post and strut

4 Tension the bolt at far end of fence

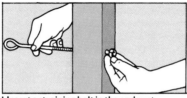

NOTCHED END POST
INTERMEDIATE POST
BOLTED CLEAT
STRETCHER BAR
STRAINING WIRES
STRUT
BOLTED CLEAT

Concrete fence posts

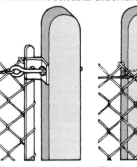

Cleat and stretcher bar   **Tie wire to post**

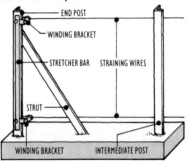

END POST
WINDING BRACKET
STRETCHER BAR
STRAINING WIRES
STRUT
WINDING BRACKET
INTERMEDIATE POST

Angle iron posts

Winding bracket

Pass wire through post

KNUCKLE
SPIRAL

ERECTING A CLOSEBOARD FENCE

The featherboards used to panel the fence are nailed to triangular-section rails known as arris rails. The arris rails are mortised into the fence posts. Concrete, and some wooden, posts are supplied ready-mortised, but if you buy standard timber posts you will have to cut the mortises. The unprotected end grain of the featherboards is liable to rot, especially if they are in contact with the ground, so fix horizontal 150 x 25mm (6 x 1in) gravel boards at the foot of the fence, and nail wooden capping strips across the tops of the featherboards. Space the fence posts no more than 3m (10ft) apart.

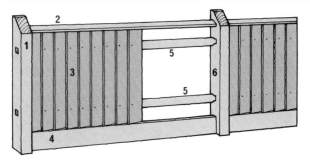

Closeboard fencing
1 End post
2 Capping strip
3 Featherboards
4 Gravel board
5 Arris rail
6 Intermediate post

REPAIRING A DAMAGED ARRIS RAIL

The arris rails take most of the strain when a closeboard fence is buffeted by high winds. Not surprisingly, they eventually crack across the middle or break where the tenon enters the mortise. You can buy galvanized metal brackets for repairing broken arris rails.

If you wish, you can use end brackets to construct a new fence instead of cutting mortises for the rails. However, it will not be as strong as a fence built with mortise and tenon joints.

SEE ALSO

Details for: ▷	
Capping posts	412
Erecting posts	413
Skew-nailing	137
Preservatives	250
Surform file	469
Cutting mortise	477

BRACKET

END BRACKET

Erecting the framework

If you are using plain wooden posts, mark and cut 50 x 22mm (2 x ⅞in) mortises for the arris rails about 150mm (6in) above and below the ends of the fixed featherboards. For fencing over 1.2m (4ft) high, cut mortises for a third rail midway between the others. Position the mortises 25mm (1in) from the front face of each post (the featherboarded side of the fence).

As you erect the fence, cut the rails to length and shape a tenon on each end with a coarse rasp or *Surform* file **(1)**. Paint preservative onto the shaped ends and into the mortises before you assemble the rails.

Erect the first fence post and pack hardcore around its base (▷). Get someone to hold the post steady while you fit the arris rails and erect the next post, tapping it onto the ends of the rails with a mallet **(2)**. Check that the rails are horizontal and the posts are vertical before packing hardcore around the second post. Construct the entire run of posts and rails in the same way. If you cannot manoeuvre the last post onto tenoned rails, cut the rails square and fix them to the post with metal brackets (See box right).

Check the whole run once more to ensure that the rails are bedded firmly in their mortises and the framework is true, then secure each rail by driving a nail through the post into the tenon **(3)**. Or drill a hole and insert a wooden dowel. Pack concrete around each post (▷). Leave to harden for about a week.

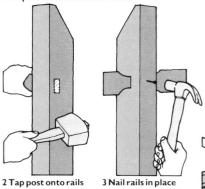

1 Shape arris rails to fit mortises

2 Tap post onto rails   3 Nail rails in place

Fitting the boards

Gravel boards
Some concrete posts are mortised to take gravel boards. In this case they must be fitted with the arris rails. To fit gravel boards to wooden posts, skew-nail treated wooden cleats at the foot of each post, then nail the gravel boards to the cleats **(4)**.

If a concrete post is not mortised for gravel boards, bed wooden cleats into the concrete filling at the base of the post, and screw the board to the cleat when the concrete is set.

Featherboards
Cut the featherboards to length and treat the end grain. Stand the first board on the gravel board with its thick edge against the post. Nail the board to the arris rails with galvanized nails positioned 18mm (¾ in) from the thick edge. Place the next board in position, overlapping the thin edge of the fixed board by 12mm (½ in). Check that it is vertical, then nail it in the same way. Don't drive a nail through both boards or they will not be able to move when they shrink. To space the other boards equally, make a spacer block from a scrap of wood **(5)**. Place the last board to fit against the next post and fix it, this time with two nails per rail **(6)**.

When the fence is completed, nail capping strips across the tops of the featherboards, cut the posts to length and cap them (▷).

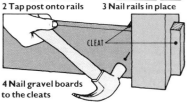

CLEAT

4 Nail gravel boards to the cleats

5 Position featherboards with a spacer block

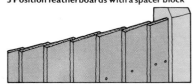

6 Fix last board with two nails

Capping the fence
Nail a wooden capping strip to the ends of the featherboards to shed rainwater.

ERECTING A PANEL FENCE

To prevent a pre-fabricated panel rotting, either fit gravel boards as for a closeboard fence, or leave a gap at the bottom by supporting a panel temporarily on two bricks while you nail it to the fence posts.

SEE ALSO

◁ Details for:

Capping posts	412
Erecting posts	413
Concrete	413
Skew-nailing	137
Preservatives	250

Using timber posts

Pack the first post into its hole with hardcore (◁), then get someone to hold a panel against the post while you skew-nail through its framework into the post (**1**). If you can work from both sides, drive three nails from each side of the fence. If the frame starts to split, blunt the nails by tapping their points with a hammer. Alternatively, use metal angle brackets to secure the panels (**2**). Construct the entire fence erecting panels and posts alternately.

Nail capping strips across the panels if they have not been fitted by the manufacturer. Finally, cut each post to length and cap it (◁).

Wedge struts made from scrap timber against each post to keep it vertical, then top up the holes with concrete (◁). If you are unable to work from both sides, you will have to fill each hole as you build the fence.

Using concrete posts

Panels are supported by grooved concrete posts without additional fixings (**3**). Recessed posts are supplied with metal brackets for screw-fixing the panels (**4**).

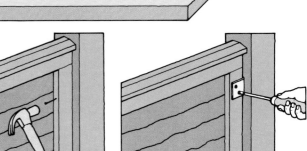

Panel fence
1 Fence posts
2 Capping strip
3 Pre-fabricated panel
4 Gravel board

1 **Nail the panel through its framework**

2 **Or use angle brackets to fix panel to posts**

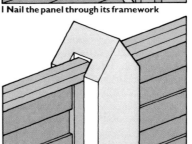

3 **A grooved concrete post for a fence panel**

4 **A recessed concrete post with fixing bracket**

Building a panel fence
Posts and panels are erected alternately. Dig a hole for the post (**1**) and hold it upright with hardcore (◁). Support a panel on bricks (**2**) and have a helper push it against the post (**3**) while you nail it (**4**). Fit gravel boards (**5**), capping strips (**6**) and cap the posts (**7**). Top up the holes with concrete (**8**) and allow it to set.

ERECTING A POST AND RAIL FENCE

A simple ranch-style fence is no more than a series of horizontal rails fixed to short posts concreted into the ground in the normal way (▷). A picket fence is made in a similar way, but with vertical pales fixed to the rails.

Fixed horizontal rails

You can simply screw the rails directly to the posts (**1**) but the fence will last longer if you cut a shallow notch in the post to locate each rail before you fix it permanently (**2**).

Join two rails by butting them over a post (**3**). Arrange to stagger these joints so that you don't end up with all the rails butted on the same post (**4**).

Fixing picket panels

When you construct a picket fence from ready-made panels, buy or make metal brackets for fixing two panels to a single post.

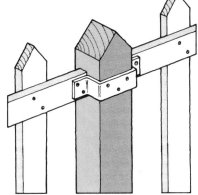

Use a metal bracket to fix picket-fence panels

Supporting a rotted post

A buried timber post will quite often rot below ground level, leaving a perfectly sound section above. To save buying a whole new post, brace the upper section with a concrete spur.

Erecting a spur
Dig the soil from around the post and remove the rotted stump. Insert the spur and pack hardcore around it (**1**), then fill with concrete (**2**). Drill pilot holes for coach screws – woodscrews with hexagonal heads (**3**). Insert the screws with a spanner to draw the post tightly against the spur.

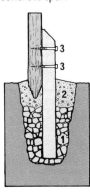

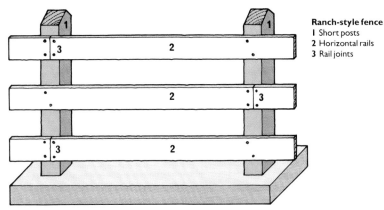

Ranch-style fence
1 Short posts
2 Horizontal rails
3 Rail joints

SEE ALSO

Details for: ▷
Erecting posts 413
Building walls 420-437

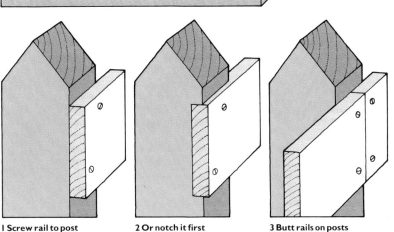

1 Screw rail to post   **2 Or notch it first**   **3 Butt rails on posts**   **4 Stagger rail joints**

ERECTING FENCES ON SLOPING GROUND

Crossways slope
If a slope runs across the garden, so that your neighbour's garden is higher than yours, build brick retaining walls between the posts or set paving stones in concrete to hold back the soil.

Downhill slope
The posts must be set vertically even when you erect a fence on a sloping site. Chain link fencing or ranch-style rails can follow the slope of the land if you wish, but fence panels should be stepped and the triangular gaps beneath filled with gravel boards or retaining walls.

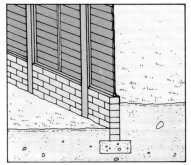

A retaining wall for a crossways slope

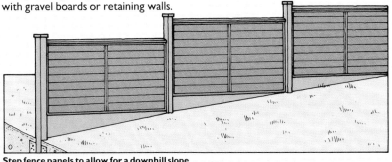

Step fence panels to allow for a downhill slope

● **Building plastic fences**
The basic construction of a plastic ranch-style fence is similar to one built from timber, but follow the manufacturer's instructions concerning the method for joining rails to posts.

417

GATES: CHOOSING

SEE ALSO

◁ Details for:

Footings	427
Painting metal	85-86
Ledged and braced doors	185
Wet rot	249
Building piers	433

There are several points to consider when choosing a gate, not the least being the cost. All gates are relatively expensive, but don't buy one merely because it is cheaper than another. A garden gate must be constructed sturdily if it is to be reasonably durable, and, perhaps even more important, it must be mounted on strong posts.

Choose a style of gate which matches the fence or complements the wall from which it is hung, with due consideration for the character of the house and its surroundings. As a guide, aim for simplicity rather than the elaborate.

Side gates

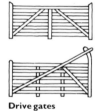
Entrance gates

Drive gates

GATES FOR DIFFERENT LOCATIONS

When you browse through suppliers' catalogues, you will find gates grouped according to their intended location, because it is where it is to be sited that has most influence on the design of a gate and dictates its function.

SIDE GATES

A side gate is designed to protect a pathway next to a house from intruders. Side gates are invariably 2m (6ft 6in) high and usually made from stout sections of timber. As a result, these gates are heavy and therefore braced with strong diagonal members to keep them rigid. With security in mind, choose a closeboarded or tongued and grooved gate – vertical boards are difficult to climb. When you hang a side gate, fit strong bolts top and bottom.

ENTRANCE GATES

An entrance gate is designed as much for its appearance as its function, but because it is in constant use, make sure it is properly braced with a diagonal strut running from the top of the latch stile down to the bottom of the hanging or hinge stile. If you hang a gate with the strut running the other way, the bracing will have no effect whatsoever.

Common fence structures are reflected in the style of entrance gates. Picket, closeboard and ranch-style gates are available, plus a simple and attractive frame and panel gate. With the latter style of gate, the solid timber or exterior-grade plywood panels keep the frame rigid. If the tops of both stiles are cut at an angle they will shed rainwater, reducing the likelihood of wet rot – a small, but important, feature to note when buying a wooden gate.

Decorative iron gates are often used for entrances but make sure the style is not too ostentatious for the building or its location. A very elaborate gate might look ridiculous in the entrance of a simple modern house or a traditional country cottage.

DRIVE GATES

First decide whether hanging a gate across a drive to a garage is such a good idea. Parking the car in a busy road in order to open the gate can be a difficult manoeuvre unless you have enough room to set the gate back from the entrance to leave enough space to pull the car off the road even when the gate is closed. Gates invariably open into the property so make certain there is enough ground clearance for a wide gate if the drive slopes up towards a garage. Or hang two smaller gates to meet in the centre. If you decide on a wide gate, choose a traditional five-bar gate for both strength and appearance.

GATE POSTS AND PIERS

Gate posts and masonry piers have to take a great deal of strain, so they must be strong in themselves and anchored securely in the ground.

Choose hardwood posts whenever possible, and select the section according to the weight of the gate. 100mm (4in) square posts are adequate for entrance gates but use 125mm (5in) posts for 2m (6ft 6in) high gates. For a wide gate across a drive, choose 150mm (6in) or even 200mm (8in) square posts.

Concrete posts are a possibility but unless you find a post pre-drilled to accept hinges and catch, you will have to screw them to a strip of timber bolted to the post, so the fittings will not be securely fixed.

Square or tubular metal posts are available with hinge pins, gate-stop and catch welded in place. Like metal gates they must be protected from rust with paint, unless they have been coated with plastic at the factory.

A pair of masonry piers is another possibility. Each pier should be a minimum of 350mm (1ft 2in) square and built on a firm concrete footing (◁). For large, heavy gates, the hinge pier at least should be reinforced with a metal rod buried in the footing and running centrally through the pier.

HARDWARE FOR GATES

Rather specialized hardware has been developed to allow for the considerable strain imposed by a garden gate on its hinges and catch.

HINGES

Strap hinges
Side gates and most wooden entrance gates are hung on strap hinges, or T-hinges. Screw the long flap horizontally to the gate rails and the vertical flap to the face of the post. Heavier gates need a stronger version which is bolted through the top rail.
Wide drive gates need a double strap hinge with a long flap bolted on each side of the top rail. These heavy-duty hinges are supported by bolts which pass through the gate post.

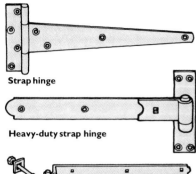

Strap hinge

Heavy-duty strap hinge

Double strap hinge

Hinge pins
Metal collars, welded to the hinge side of metal gates, drop over hinge pins attached to gate posts in a variety of ways: screw-fixed to timber posts; bolted through concrete; built into the mortar joints of masonry piers; welded to metal posts. The gate can be lifted off its hinges at any time unless you reverse the top pin or drill a hole and fit a split pin and washer.

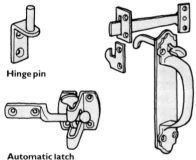

Hinge pin

LATCHES

Automatic latches
Simple wooden gates are fitted with a latch that operates automatically as the gate is closed. Screw the latch bar to the latch stile of the gate and use it to position the latch itself on the post.

Automatic latch

Thumb latch

Thumb latches
Cut a slot through a closeboard side gate for the latch lifter of a thumb or Suffolk latch. Pass the lifter bar through the slot and screw the handle to the front of the gate. Screw the latch bar to the inner face so that the lifter releases the bar from the catch plate.

Ring latches
A ring latch works in a similar way to a thumb latch but is operated from inside only, by twisting the ring handle to lift the latch bar.

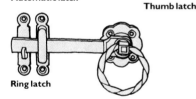

Ring latch

Chelsea catches
Bolt a Chelsea catch through a drive gate. The latch pivots on the bolt to drop into a slot in the catch plate screwed to the post.

Loop-over catches
When two wide gates are used in a drive entrance, one gate is fixed with a drop bolt located in a socket concreted into the ground. A simple 'U'-shaped metal bar, bolted through the latch stile of the other gate, drops over the stile of the fixed gate.

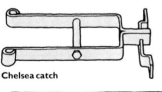

Chelsea catch

Loop-over catch

Materials for gates

Many wooden gates are made from softwood simply for economy, but a wood such as cedar or oak is a better investment. Most so-called wrought iron gates are made from mild steel bar which must be primed and painted (▷) if it is to last any time at all.

Hang a heavy drive gate on a stout post

GATE POSTS

Gate posts are set in concrete like ordinary fence posts but the post holes are linked by a concrete bridge to provide extra support.

Side and entrance gate posts

Lay the gate on the ground with a post on each side. Check that the posts are parallel and the required distance apart to accommodate hinges and catch. Nail two horizontal battens from post to post and another diagonally to keep the posts in line while you erect them (**1**).

Dig a 300mm (1ft) wide trench across the entrance and long enough to accept both posts. It need be no deeper than 300mm (1ft) in the centre but dig an adequate post hole at each end: 450mm (1ft 6in) deep for a low entrance gate; 600mm (2ft) deep for a taller gate. Set the battened gate posts in the holes with hardcore and concrete as for fence posts (▷), using temporary battens to hold them upright until the concrete sets (**2**). Fill the trench with concrete at the same time and either level it flush with the pathway, or allow for the thickness of paving slabs or blocks (▷).

SEE ALSO	
	Details for: ▷
Priming and painting metal	43, 85-86
Erecting posts	413
Paving slabs	446
Preservatives	250

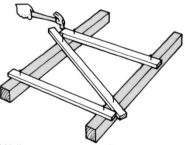

1 Nail temporary struts to the gate posts

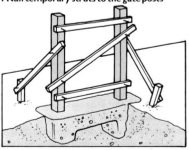

2 Support the posts until the concrete sets

Drive gate posts

Hang wide farm-style gates on posts set in 900mm (3ft) deep holes (**3**). Erect the latch post in concrete like any fence post, but bolt a stout piece of timber across the base of the hinge post before anchoring it in concrete.

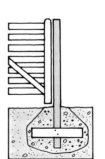

3 Drive gate post
Bolt a balk of timber to the post to help support the weight of the gate.

MASONRY: BUILDING WALLS

SEE ALSO

◁ Details for:
Local authority	
approval	18-19
Damp-proof course	251,431
Cavity wall	435

Whatever structure you build with masonry, the basic techniques for laying brick, stone or concrete blocks remain the same. On the other hand, it must be recognized that it is wise to hire a professional builder when the structure is complicated, extensive or must withstand considerable loads or stress.

A stone-built retaining wall

A boundary wall of yellow brick

Facing blocks make attractive dividing walls

A decorative pierced-block screen

Amateur bricklaying

It is difficult to suggest when a particular job is beyond the level of skill or confidence of an amateur bricklayer, clearly differing from individual to individual. It would be foolhardy for anyone to attempt to build a two-storey house, for instance, unless they had had a lot of experience and, possibly, professional tuition, but building even a high boundary wall, which in terms of pure technique is simple, would be an arduous task if it were very long or had to allow for changes in gradient. The simple answer is to begin with low retaining or dividing walls and screens until you have mastered the skills of laying bricks and blocks solidly upon one another, and the ability to build a wall both straight and vertical without danger of possible collapse.

WALLS FOR DIFFERENT LOCATIONS

RETAINING WALLS

Raised planting beds are made with low 'retaining' walls, but a true retaining wall is designed to hold back a bank of earth, usually to terrace a sloping site. As long as it is not too high, a retaining wall is easy to build although, strictly speaking, it should slope back into the bank to resist the weight of the earth. Also, you must allow for drainage, to reduce the water pressure behind the wall. Retaining walls are built with bricks, concrete blocks or stone, sometimes dry-laid with earth packed into the crevices for planting — it is a matter of personal choice.

BOUNDARY WALLS

A brick or stone wall surrounding your property provides security and privacy while forming an attractive background to trees and shrubs. New, crisp brickwork complements a formal garden or modern setting, while second-hand materials or undressed stone blend with an old, established garden. If you cannot match exactly the colour of existing masonry, encourage the growth of lichen with a wash of liquid fertilizer, or disguise the junction with a well-chosen climber. You will need local authority approval if you want to build a wall higher than 1m (3ft 3in) adjoining a highway, or 2m (6ft 6in) elsewhere (◁).

DIVIDING WALLS

Many gardeners divide a plot of land with walls to form a visual break between patio and lawn, to define the edges of pathways, or simply to add interest to an otherwise featureless site. Dividing walls are often merely 'dwarf' walls, perhaps 600 to 750mm (2 to 2ft 6in) in height. They make perfect structures upon which to practise basic techniques.

Use simple concrete block or brick walls to divide spaces inside the house – for a workshop or hobbies room.

SCREEN WALLS

Screens are also dividing walls, but they provide a degree of privacy without completely masking the garden beyond. Screens are built with decorative pierced blocks, often with solid block or brick bases and concrete piers.

STRUCTURAL WALLS

Walls of even a small building have to support the weight of a roof and, depending on the complexity of the structure, will have to incorporate door and window frames. In most cases a damp-proof course will have to be built into the walls to prevent rising damp, and some walls are constructed with a cavity between two leaves of masonry to provide insulation and weatherproofing. A brick foundation for a glazed conservatory is no more difficult to build than a simple garden wall, but make certain you are familiar with building methods before you attempt to build a garage or similar outbuilding.

CHOOSING BRICKS

The actual names given to bricks refer to their individual district of origin where a particular clay will impart a distinctive colour, or are simply chosen by the manufacturer to suggest the continuation of that tradition. Typical examples are London stocks, Pennines, Leicester reds, Blue Staffs and so on. What is important to the builder is the variety, quality and type of brick, plus its colour and texture, particularly when matching existing masonry.

The variety of brick

Facings
Facings are suitable for any type of exposed brickwork. They are water- and frost-resistant. Being visible, facings are made as much for their appearance as their structural qualities and, as such, are available in the widest range of colours and textures. Facings are graded carefully to meet standards of strength, water absorption and for their uniformity of shape.

Commons
Commons are cheap general-purpose bricks used primarily for internal brickwork which is to be plastered, or rendered if used externally. They are not colour-matched as carefully as facings but the mottled effect of a wall built with commons is not unattractive.

Although they could become damaged or cracked by frost if used on an exposed site, commons can be used for garden walling.

Engineering bricks
Engineering bricks are exceptionally dense and strong . You are unlikely to need them for the average wall, but, because they are impervious to water, they have been used to construct a damp-proof course in some houses.

The quality of brick

Internal quality
Internal-quality bricks would not be very durable if they were exposed to weathering. Most commons are of internal quality only, so check before you buy them for use in the garden.

Ordinary quality
Ordinary-quality bricks are suitable for most external uses. They may suffer, however, if used for a wall exposed to consistent driving rain and frost, or for a retaining wall which holds back earth that is poorly drained.

Special quality
Special-quality bricks will withstand extreme weathering and exposure to frost. Most types of facing bricks are available in this quality and are especially suitable for walls in coastal areas.

Seconds
Seconds are second-hand rather than second-rate bricks. They should be cheaper than new bricks but demand can inflate the price – using seconds might be the only way you can match the colour of weathered brickwork.

Types of brick

Solid bricks
The majority of bricks are solid throughout, either flat on all surfaces or with a depression known as a 'frog' on one face. When filled with mortar, the frog keys the bricks.

Cored or perforated bricks
Cored bricks are made with holes running through them, providing the same function as the frog. A wall made with cored bricks must be finished with a coping of solid bricks.

Special shapes
Specially shaped bricks are made for decorative brickwork. Master bricklayers use the full range to build arches, chamfered or rounded corners and curvilinear walls. A number of shaped bricks are made for coping garden walls.

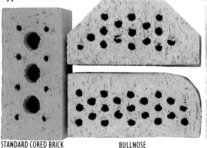

Types of brick

STANDARD CORED BRICK   DOUBLE-CANT COPING   BULLNOSE   STANDARD BRICK WITH FROG   SQUINT FOR SHAPED CORNER   HALF-ROUND COPING

BUYING BRICKS

Ordering bricks
Bricks are normally sold by the thousand but builders' merchants are usually willing to sell them in smaller quantities. It is cheaper to order them direct from the manufacturer but only if you buy a sufficient load to make the delivery charge economical.

Estimating quantities
The size of a standard brick is 215 x 102.5 x 65mm (8½ x 4 x 2½in), but because dimensions may vary by a few millimetres, even within the same batch of bricks, manufacturers normally specify a nominal size which includes an additional 10mm (⅜in) to each dimension to allow for the mortar joint.

To calculate how many bricks you need, allow about 58 bricks for every square metre (48 per sq yd) of single skin walling. Add a five per cent allowance for cutting and breakages.

Storing bricks
When bricks are delivered, have them unloaded as near as possible to the building site, and stack them carefully on a flat dry base. Cover the stack with polythene sheet or a tarpaulin until you are ready to use them to prevent them becoming saturated with rain – this could cause staining and an increased risk of frost damage to the mortar and the bricks themselves.

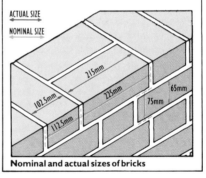

ACTUAL SIZE
NOMINAL SIZE

215mm   65mm
225mm   75mm
102.5mm
112.5mm

Nominal and actual sizes of bricks

SEE ALSO

Details for: ▷
Coloured and textured brick 422
Laying bricks   428-433

421

THE COLOUR AND TEXTURE OF BRICKS

The popularity of brick as a building material stems largely from its range of subtle colours and textures, which actually improve with weathering. Unfortunately, weathered brick can be difficult to match by using a manufacturer's catalogue. If you have spare bricks, take one to the supplier to compare with new bricks, or borrow samples from the merchant's stock.

SEE ALSO

◁ Details for:
Choosing bricks   421
Laying bricks   428-433

Colour
The colour of bricks is determined by the type of clay used in their manufacture, although it is modified by the addition of certain minerals and the temperature of the firing. Large manufacturers supply a complete range of colours from black or purple to white, plus reds, browns and yellows. There are also brindled bricks – multi-coloured or mottled – especially useful for blending with existing masonry.

Texture
Texture is as important to the appearance of a brick wall as colour. Simple rough or smooth textures are created by the choice of materials. Others are imposed upon the clay by scratching, rolling, brushing and so on. A brick may be textured all over or on the sides and ends only.

Brick colours and textures
A small selection from the extremely wide range of colours and textures.
1 Smooth blended
2 Handmade
3 Sand-faced yellow
4 Smooth blue engineering
5 Sand-faced grey
6 Smooth red stock
7 Wire-cut brindle
8 Textured multi-buff
9 Second London stock
10 Wire-cut blue
11 Red common
12 Coarse fletton
13 Moulded fletton
14 Dragwire multi-red

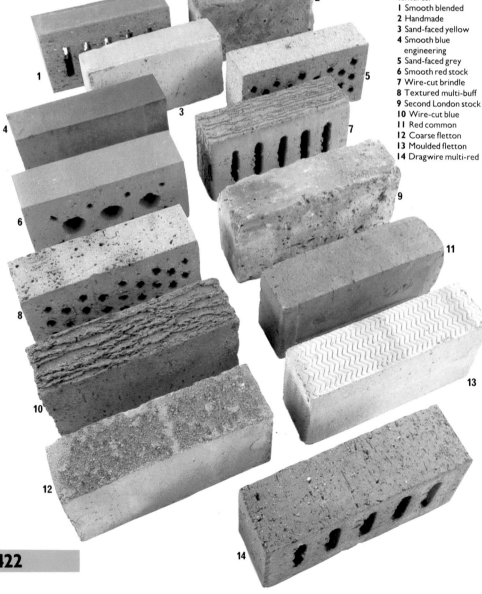

Pattern formed by projecting headers

Decorative combination of coloured bricks

Look out for second-hand moulded bricks

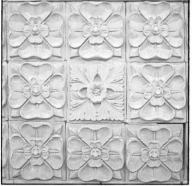
Sometimes whole panels are available

Weathered antique bricks are very attractive

CHOOSING CONCRETE BLOCKS

Cast concrete building blocks are not as standardized as clay bricks, but to describe them using the same specifications – variety, quality and type – makes for a useful comparison when choosing which to use.

Variety of block

Structural blocks
Simple rectangular blocks, cement grey or white in colour, are used as the structural core of a wall which will be rendered or plastered. Consequently, they are often made with a zig-zag key on the surface to encourage the finish to adhere. As they are not intended as visible masonry, they have no aesthetic qualities whatsoever. A wall can be constructed quickly with blocks because they are considerably larger than standard housebricks, and the wall will be relatively cheap.

Facing blocks
These are blocks with one decorative face and end for walls which are to be left exposed. They are often made to resemble natural stone by including crushed stone aggregate. There is a sufficient range of colours to blend with the local stone in most areas of the country. Facing blocks are used for the external skin of cavity walls, backed by the cheaper structural blocks. They are also used for ornamental garden walling for which matching coping slabs are available as a finishing touch.

Screen blocks
Screen blocks are pierced decorative building units for constructing a lightweight masonry trellis or screen. They are not bonded like brickwork or structural blocks and therefore require supporting piers made from matching pilaster blocks with locating channels to take the pierced blocks. Coping slabs finish the top of the screen and piers.

Quality of block

Loadbearing blocks
Structural blocks are used to construct the loadbearing walls of a building. Those made with lightweight aggregate are easier to handle, but when the loads are excessive, use stronger blocks made from dense concrete.

Non-loadbearing blocks
Non-loadbearing blocks are used to build internal, dividing partitions. They are either lightweight-aggregate blocks or low-density foamed-concrete blocks which are easy to cut to shape or chase for electrical wiring. Foamed blocks are also made in a loadbearing quality.

Decorative blocks
Pierced screen blocks should not be used in the construction of loadbearing walls. However, they are capable of supporting a lightweight structure such as a timber and plastic carport roof.

Insulating blocks
Foamed blocks are often used for constructing the inner leaf of a cavity wall. They have good insulating properties and meet the minimum Building Regulation standards without the need for secondary insulation. Use ultra-light foamed blocks when improved insulation is required.

Type of block

Solid blocks
Solid blocks are of two kinds – constructed with lightweight aggregate or foamed concrete.

Cored blocks
To reduce their weight, large dense-concrete blocks are virtually hollow with supporting ribs between the outer skins. Stretcher blocks are used for the main part of the wall, while corner blocks are used when the end of a wall is exposed. Solid-top blocks, partly hollowed out on the underside, are used to support joists.

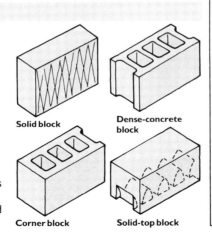

Solid block

Dense-concrete block

Corner block

Solid-top block

SEE ALSO

Details for: ▷
Blocks	424
Laying blocks	434-435

BUYING CONCRETE BLOCKS

Estimating quantities
Blocks are available in such a variety of sizes that in order to calculate the number required you must divide a given area of walling by the dimensions of a specific type. Blocks are sometimes specified in nominal sizes (also known as coordinating sizes) but with the 10mm (³⁄₈in) allowance for mortar on the length and height only. Block walls are normally constructed with one skin of masonry, so the thickness of a block remains as the actual size.

Available sizes
Structural blocks can be anything from 400 to 600mm (1ft 4in to 2ft) in length, with heights of 150 to 300mm (6in to 1ft). Actual thicknesses range from 60 to 200mm (2³⁄₈ to 8in).

Although larger sizes are available, facing blocks are normally 100mm (4in) thick, with lengths of between 225 and 450mm (9in and 1ft 6in) and heights of between 50 and 150mm (2 and 6in).

Decorative screen blocks are invariably 300mm (1ft) square and 100mm (4in) thick.

Storing blocks
When blocks are delivered have them unloaded as near as possible to the construction site to save time and reduce the possibility of damage in transit – they are quite brittle and chip easily. Stack them on a flat, dry base and protect them from rain and frost with a polythene covering or tarpaulin.

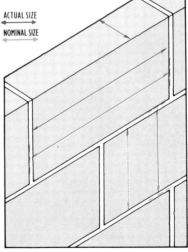

ACTUAL SIZE
NOMINAL SIZE

Sizes of structural blocks
The nominal size of a block refers to the length and height only. Thicknesses are always specified as an actual size.

BLOCKS AND STONES

Man-made blocks made from poured concrete are available in a variety of colours, shapes and sizes. Aesthetically, however, nothing can surpass quarried stone such as granite or sandstone. Hewn roughly in natural shapes and textures, or as dressed blocks, natural stone is durable and weathers well.

SEE ALSO

◁ Details for:
Choosing blocks	423
Laying blocks	434-435
Stone walling	436

Man-made concrete blocks
1 Solid dense concrete
2 Lightweight aerated
3 Lightweight aggregate
4 Pierced decorative
5 Solid decorative
6 Pitched-face reconstituted stone
7 Pilaster block
8 Pilaster coping
9 Multi-stone block
10 Screen coping
11 Split-face facing
12 Hewn-stone facing

Semi-dressed natural stone blocks

Dry stone retaining wall

Split-stone walling

Knapped-flint boundary wall

CHOOSING NATURAL STONE

Practical considerations
In practical terms, the type of natural stone you choose for walling depends almost entirely on where you happen to live. In some parts of the country there are local restrictions governing the choice of building materials, and, in any case, a structure built from stone that is indigenous to a locality is more likely to blend sympathetically into its surroundings. Furthermore, buying stone from a local quarry makes economical sense – transporting stone over long distances can be very costly.

Where to obtain stone
If you live in a large town or city, obtaining natural stone can be a real problem. You might be prepared to buy a few small boulders for a rockery from a local garden centre, but the cost of buying enough stone for even a short run of walling is likely to be prohibitive. If you don't want to use reconstituted stone – concrete facing blocks – your only alternative is to hire an open truck and drive to a quarry out of town.

Another source of materials, and possibly the cheapest way to obtain dressed stone, is to visit a demolition site. Prices vary considerably, but the cost of transport may be less than a trip to a quarry.

Estimating quantities
As most quarries sell stone by the tonne, it is difficult to estimate the quantity you need. Having worked out the approximate dimensions of the wall in question, telephone the nearest quarry for advice. Not only can you get an estimate of the cost of the stone, but you will be in a position to hire a truck of the appropriate capacity.

Types of stone
Limestone, sandstone and granite are all suitable materials for building walls. Flint and slate require specialized building methods and are often used in combination with other materials. Stone bought in its natural state is classed as undressed; it is perfect for dry stone walling in an informal garden setting. For a more regular form of masonry, ask for semi-dressed stone which is cut into reasonably uniform blocks but with uneven surfaces, or fully dressed stone with machine-cut faces. The cost of stone increases in proportion to its preparation.

MORTAR FOR MASONRY WALLS

When building a wall, mortar is used to bind together the bricks, concrete blocks or stones. The durability of a masonry structure depends on the quality of the mortar used in its construction. If it is mixed correctly to the right consistency, the mortar will become as hard and strong as the masonry itself, but if the ingredients are added in the wrong proportions, the mortar will be weak and prone to cracking. If too much water is used, the mortar will be squeezed out of the joints by the weight of the masonry, and if the mortar is too dry, adhesion will be poor.

The ingredients of mortar

The ingredients of general-purpose mortar are Portland cement, hydrated lime and sand, mixed with enough water to make a workable paste.

Cement is the hardening agent which binds the other ingredients together. The lime slows down the drying process and prevents the mortar setting too quickly. It also makes the mix flow well so that it fills gaps in the masonry and adheres to the texture of blocks or bricks. The sand acts as fine aggregate, adding body to the mortar, and reduces the possibility of shrinkage.

Use fine builders' sand for general-purpose mortar. However, use silver sand if you want a paler mortar to bond white screen blocks.

Plasticizers
If you are laying masonry in cold weather, substitute a proprietary plasticizer for the lime. Plasticizer produces aerated mortar – the tiny air bubbles in the mix allow the water to expand in freezing conditions and reduce the risk of cracking. Pre-mixed masonry cement, with an aerating agent, is ready for mixing with sand.

Ready-mix mortar
Ready-mix mortar contains all the essential ingredients mixed to the correct proportions. You simply add water. It is a more expensive way of buying mortar but convenient to use and is available in small quantities.

SEE ALSO

Details for: ▷
Cutting bricks   428

BRICKLAYERS' TERMS

Bricklayers use a number of specialized words and phrases to describe their craft and materials. Terms used frequently are listed below while others are described as they occur.

BRICK FACES *The surfaces of a brick.*
Stretcher faces The long sides of a brick.
Header faces The short ends of a brick.
Bedding faces The top and bottom surfaces.
Frog The depression in one bedding face.

COURSES *The individual, horizontal rows of bricks.*
Stretcher course A single course with stretcher faces visible.
Header course A single course with header faces visible.
Coping The top course designed to protect the wall from rainwater.
Bond Pattern produced by staggering alternate courses so that vertical joints are not aligned one above the other.
Stretcher A single brick from a stretcher course.
Header A single brick from a header course.
Closure brick The last brick laid in a course.

CUT BRICKS *Bricks cut with a bolster chisel to even up the bond.*
Bat A brick cut across its width, i.e. half-bat, three-quarter bat.
Queen closer A brick cut along its length.

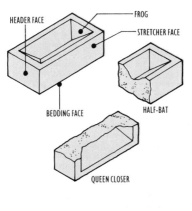

HEADER FACE — FROG
— STRETCHER FACE
BEDDING FACE   HALF-BAT
QUEEN CLOSER

Mixing mortar

Mortar must be used within two hours of mixing or be discarded, so make only as much as you can use within that time. An average of about two minutes to lay one brick is a reasonable estimate.

Choose a flat site upon which to mix the materials – a sheet of plywood will do – and dampen it slightly to prevent it absorbing water from the mortar. Make a pile of half the amount of sand to be used, then add the other ingredients. Put the rest of the sand on top, and mix the dry materials thoroughly.

Scoop a depression in the pile and add clean tap water. Never use contaminated or salty water. Push the dry mix from around the edge of the pile into the water until it has absorbed enough for you to blend the mix with a shovel, using a chopping action. Add more water, little by little, until the mortar has a butter-like consistency, slipping easily from the shovel but firm enough to hold its shape if you make a hollow in the mix. If the sides of the hollow collapse, add more dry ingredients until the mortar firms up. Make sure the mortar is not too dry or it won't form a strong bond with the masonry.

If mortar stiffens up while you are working, add just enough water to restore the consistency. Dampen the mixing board again.

Correct consistency
The mortar mix should be firm enough to hold its shape when you make a depression in the mix.

Proportions for masonry mixes

Mix the ingredients according to the prevailing conditions at the building site. Use a general-purpose mortar for moderate conditions where the wall is reasonably sheltered, but use a stronger mix for severe conditions where the wall will be exposed to wind and driving rain, or if the site is elevated or near the coast. If you are using plasticizer instead of lime, follow the manufacturer's instructions regarding the quantity you should add to the sand.

● **Estimating quantity**
As a rough guide to estimating how much mortar you will need, allow approximately 1cu m (1⅓cu yd) of sand (other ingredients in proportion) to lay: 1600 to 1650 bricks; 40 to 45sq m (69 to 70sq yd) average facing blocks; 80 to 85sq m (100 to 105sq yd) screen or structural blocks.

MORTAR MIXING PROPORTIONS			
	Cement/lime mortar	Plasticized mortar	Masonry cement mortar
General-purpose mortar (Moderate conditions)	1 part cement 1 part lime 6 parts sand	1 part cement 6 parts sand/ plasticizer	1 part cement 5 parts sand
Strong mortar (Severe conditions)	1 part cement ½ part lime 4 parts sand	1 part cement 4 parts sand/ plasticizer	1 part cement 3 parts sand

DESIGNING A WALL FOR STABILITY

It is easy enough to appreciate the loads and stresses imposed upon the walls of a house or outbuilding, and therefore the necessity for solid foundations and adequate methods of reinforcement and protection to prevent them collapsing. It is not so obvious, but even simple garden walling requires similar measures to ensure its stability. It is merely irritating if a low dividing wall or planter falls apart, but a serious injury could result from the collapse of a heavy boundary wall.

SEE ALSO

◁ Details for:

Wall ties	432
Damp-proof course	251, 431
Bricks	421-422
Copings	430
Building piers	433

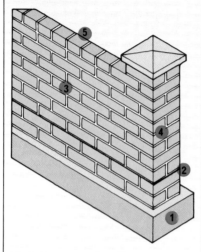

The basic structure of a wall
Unless you design and build a wall in the correct manner, it will not be strong and stable.

1 Footings
A wall must be built upon a solid concrete platform known as a strip footing. The dimensions of the footing vary according to the height and weight of the wall.

2 Damp-proof course
A layer of waterproof material 150mm (6in) above ground level stops water rising from the soil. It is not needed for most garden walling unless it abuts a building with a similar DPC. Not only does it protect the house from damp, but it reduces the likelihood of freezing water expanding and cracking the joints.

3 Bonding
The staggered pattern of bricks is not merely decorative. It is designed to spread the static load along the wall and to tie the individual units together.

4 Piers
Straight walls over a certain height and length must be buttressed at regular intervals with thick columns of brickwork known as piers. They resist the sideways pressure caused by high winds.

5 Coping
The coping prevents frost damage by shedding rainwater from the top of the wall where it could seep into the upper brick joints.

BONDING BRICKWORK

Mortar is extremely strong under compression, but its tensile strength is relatively weak. If bricks were stacked one upon the other so that the vertical joints were continuous, any movement within the wall would pull them apart and the structure would be seriously weakened. Bonding brickwork staggers the vertical joints, transmitting the load along the entire length of the wall. Try out the bond of your choice by dry-laying a few bricks before you embark on the actual building work.

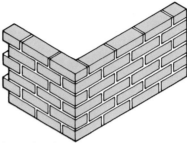

Stretcher bond
The stretcher bond is the simplest form of bonding, used for single-thickness walls, including the two individual leaves of a cavity wall found in the construction of modern buildings. Half-bats are used to make the bond at the end of a straight wall, while a corner is formed by alternating headers and stretchers.

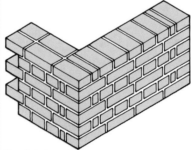

English bond
If you build a 215mm (8½ in) thick wall by laying courses of stretcher-bonded bricks side by side, there would be a weak vertical joint running centrally down the wall. An English bond strengthens the wall by using alternate courses of headers. Staggered joints are maintained at the end of a wall and at a corner by inserting a queen closer before the last header.

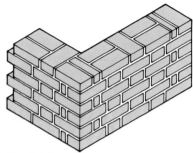

Flemish bond
The Flemish bond is an alternative method to English bond for building a solid, 215mm (8½ in) thick wall. Every course is laid with alternate headers and stretchers. Stagger the joint at the end of a course and at a corner by laying a queen closer before the header.

Decorative bonds
Stretcher, English and Flemish bonds are designed to construct strong walls – decorative qualities are incidental. Other bonds, used primarily for their visual effect, are suitable for low, non-loadbearing walls only, supported by a conventionally bonded base and piers.

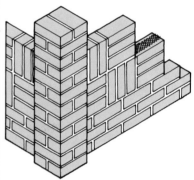

Stack bonding
A basket-weave effect is achieved by stack bonding bricks in groups of three. Strengthen the continuous vertical joints with wall ties (◁).

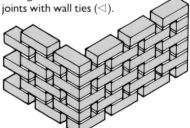

Honeycomb bond
Build an open, decorative screen using a stretcher-like bond with a quarter-bat-size space between each brick. Build the screen carefully to keep the bond regular, and cut quarter-bats to fill the gaps in the top course.

CONSTRUCTING STRIP FOOTINGS

Stringent Building Regulations govern the size and reinforcement required for the footings to support high and especially *structural walls, but most garden walls can be built upon concrete footings laid in a straight-sided trench.*

Size of footings

The footing must be sufficiently substantial to support the weight of the wall, and the soil must be firm and well drained to avoid possible subsidence. It is unwise to set footings in ground which has been filled recently, such as a new building site. Also, take care to avoid tree roots and drainpipes. If the trench begins to fill with water as you are digging, seek professional advice before proceeding.

Dig the trench deeper than the footing itself so that the first one or two courses of brick are below ground level. This will allow for an adequate depth of soil for planting right up to the wall.

If the soil is not firmly packed when you reach the required depth, dig deeper until you reach a firm level, then fill the bottom of the trench with compacted hardcore up to the lowest level of the proposed footing.

RECOMMENDED DIMENSIONS FOR FOOTINGS

Type of wall	Height of wall	Depth of footing	Width of footing
One brick thick	Up to 1m (3ft 3in)	100 to 150mm (4 to 6in)	300mm (1ft)
Two bricks thick	Up to 1m (3ft 3in)	225 to 300mm (9in to 1ft)	450mm (1ft 6in)
Two bricks thick	Over 1m up to 2m (Up to 6ft 6in)	375 to 450mm (1ft 3in to 1ft 6in)	450 to 600mm (1ft 6in to 2ft)
Retaining wall	Up to 1m (3ft 3in)	150 to 300mm (6in to 1ft)	375 to 450mm (1ft 3in to 1ft 6in)

Setting out the footings

For a straight footing, set up two profile boards made from 25mm (1in) thick timber nailed to stakes driven into the ground at each end of the proposed trench but well outside the work area.

Drive nails into the top edge of each board and stretch lines between them to mark the front and back edges of the wall. Then drive nails into the profile boards on each side of the wall line to indicate the width of the footing, and stretch more lines between them (1).

When you are satisfied that the setting out is accurate, remove the lines marking the wall but leave the nails in place so that you can replace the lines when you come to lay the bricks.

Place a spirit level against the remaining lines to mark the edge of the footing on the ground (2). Mark the ends of the footing extending beyond the line of the wall by half the wall's thickness. Mark the edge of the trench on the ground with a spade and remove the lines. Leave the boards in place.

Turning corners

If your wall will have a right-angled corner, set up two sets of profile boards as before, checking carefully that the lines form a true right angle using the 3:4:5 principle (3).

Digging the trench

Excavate the trench, keeping the sides vertical, and check that the bottom is level, using a long, straight piece of wood and a spirit level.

Drive a stake into the bottom of the trench near one end until the top of the stake represents the depth of the footing. Drive in more stakes at 1m (3ft 3in) intervals, checking that the tops are level (4).

Filling the trench

Pour a foundation mix of concrete (▷) into the trench, then tamp it down firmly with a stout piece of timber until it is exactly level with the top of the stakes. Leave the stakes in place and allow the footing to harden thoroughly before building the wall.

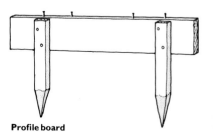

Profile board

FOOTING FOR A SLOPING SITE

When the ground slopes gently, simply ignore the gradient and make the footing perfectly level. If the site slopes noticeably, make a stepped footing by placing plywood shuttering across the trench at regular intervals. Calculate the height and length of the steps using multiples of normal brick size.

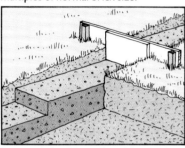

Support plywood shuttering with stakes

Section through a stepped footing
A typical stepped concrete footing with one of the plywood shuttering boards in place.

SEE ALSO

Details for: ▷	
Concrete mixes	441
Spirit level	428

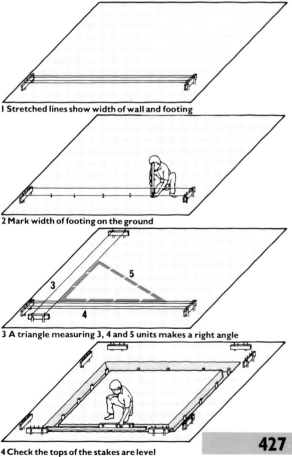

1 Stretched lines show width of wall and footing

2 Mark width of footing on the ground

3 A triangle measuring 3, 4 and 5 units makes a right angle

4 Check the tops of the stakes are level

BRICKLAYING TOOLS

You can make or improvise some builder's tools (◁) but you will have to buy some of the more-specialized bricklayer's tools.

SEE ALSO

◁ Details for:
Mixing mortar	425
Builder's tools	478-480
Bricks	421-422

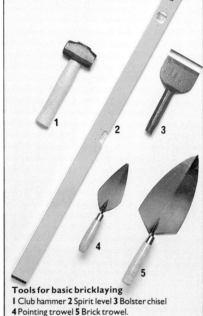

Tools for basic bricklaying
1 Club hammer 2 Spirit level 3 Bolster chisel
4 Pointing trowel 5 Brick trowel.

LAYING BRICKS

Spreading a bed of mortar— throwing a line — requires practice before you can develop speed, so concentrate at first on laying bricks neatly and accurately. Mortar mixed to the right consistency (◁) helps to keep the visible faces of the bricks clean. In hot, dry weather dampen the footings and bricks, but let any surface water evaporate before you begin to lay bricks.

Bricklaying techniques

Hold the brick trowel with your thumb in line with the handle, pointing towards the tip of the blade (**1**).

Scoop a measure of mortar out of the pile and shape it roughly to match the shape of the trowel blade. Pick up the mortar by sliding the blade under the pile, setting it onto the trowel with a slight jerk of the wrist (**2**).

Spread the mortar along the top course by aligning the edge of the trowel with the centre line of the bricks. As you tip the blade to deposit the mortar, draw the trowel back towards you to stretch the bed over at least two to three bricks (**3**).

Furrow the mortar by pressing the point of the trowel along the centre (**4**).

Pick up a brick with your other hand, but don't extend your thumb too far onto the stretcher face or it will disturb the builders' line every time you place a brick in position. Press the brick into the bed, picking up excess mortar squeezed from the joint by sliding the edge of the trowel along the wall (**5**).

With the mortar picked up on the trowel, butter the header of the next brick, making a neat 10mm (⅜in) bed for the header joint (**6**). Press the brick against its neighbour, scooping off excess mortar with the trowel.

Having laid three bricks, check they are horizontal using the spirit level. Make any adjustments by tapping them down with the trowel handle (**7**).

Hold the level along the outer edge of the bricks to check they are in line. To move a brick sideways without knocking it off its mortar bed, tap the upper edge with the trowel at about 45 degrees (**8**).

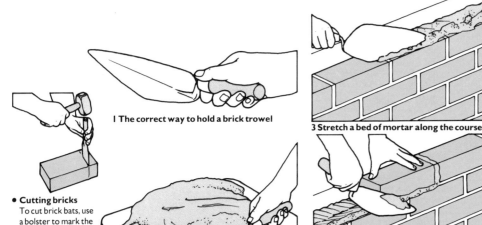

1 The correct way to hold a brick trowel

● **Cutting bricks**
To cut brick bats, use a bolster to mark the line on all faces by tapping gently with a hammer. Realign the blade on the visible stretcher face and strike the chisel firmly.

2 Scoop a measure of mortar onto the trowel

3 Stretch a bed of mortar along the course

4 Furrow the mortar with the trowel point

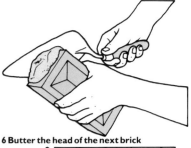

5 Push down brick and remove excess mortar

6 Butter the head of the next brick

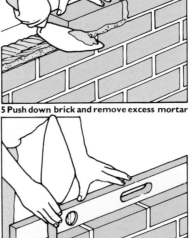

7 Level the course of bricks with the trowel

8 Tap the bricks sideways to align them

BUILDING A STRETCHER-BONDED WALL

A single-width brick wall looks visually mean and, over a certain height, is structurally weak unless it is supported with piers, or changes direction by forming right-angle corners. In any case, the ability to construct strong, accurate corners is a requirement for building most structures, including simple garden planters. Building a wall with another type of bond is a little more complicated in detail (▷) but the basic principles remain the same.

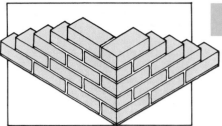

A stepped lead for a corner

Setting out the corners

Mark out the footings and face of the wall by stretching string lines between profile boards (▷). When the footings have been filled and the concrete has set, use a plumb line or hold a level lightly against the line to mark the corners and the face of the wall on the footing (1). Join the marks with a pencil and straight batten, and check the accuracy of the corners with a builder's square. Stretch a line between the corner marks to check the alignment.

1 Mark the face of the wall on the footing

SEE ALSO

Details for: ▷	
Bonding brickwork	426
Profile boards	427
Copings	430
Bricks	421-422
Footings	427

Building the corners

Build the corners first as a series of steps or 'leads' before filling between. It is essential that they form true right angles, so take your time.

Throw a bed of mortar, then lay three bricks in both directions against the marked line. Check they are level in all directions, including across the diagonal by laying a spirit level between the end bricks (2).

Build the leads to a height of five stepped courses, using a gauge stick to measure the height of each course as you proceed (3). Use alternate headers and stretchers to form the actual point of the corner.

Use a level to plumb the corner, and check the alignment of the stepped bricks by holding the level against the side of the wall (4).

2 Level the first course of bricks

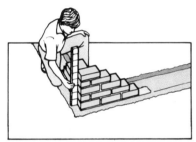

3 Check the height with a gauge stick

4 Check that the steps are in line

● **Covering the wall**
Cover finished or partly built walls overnight with sheets of polythene or tarpaulin to protect the brickwork from rain or frost. Weight the edges of the covers with bricks.

Building the straight sections

Stretch a builder's line between the corners so that it aligns perfectly with the top edge of the first course (5).

Lay the first straight course of bricks from both ends towards the middle. As you near the middle point, lay the last few bricks dry to make certain they will fit. Then mortar them in, finishing with the central or 'closure' brick. Spread mortar onto both ends of the closure brick and onto the header faces of the bricks on each side. Lay the closure brick very carefully (6), and scoop off excess mortar with the trowel.

Lay subsequent courses between the leads in the same way, raising the builder's line each time. To build the wall higher, raise the corners first by constructing leads to the required height, then fill the spaces between.

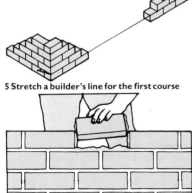

5 Stretch a builder's line for the first course

6 Carefully lay the last or closure brick

● **Building a straight wall**
To build a straight wall without a corner, follow the procedure described left, building end leads – straight stepped sections – at each end of the wall, then fill between with bricks.

Coping the wall
You could finish the wall by laying the last course frog downwards, but a coping of half-bats laid on end looks more professional. Alternatively use proprietary coping bricks or blocks (▷).

POINTING BRICKWORK

Finishing the mortar joints – pointing – compresses the materials to make a packed, watertight joint and enhances the appearance of the wall. Well-struck *joints and clean brickwork are essential if the wall is to look professionally built but the mortar must be shaped at the right time for the best results.*

SEE ALSO
◁ Details for:
DPC   251, 431
Engineering bricks   421

Mortar for pointing work

If the mortar is still too wet the joint will not be crisp and you may drag mortar out from between the bricks. On the other hand, if it is left to harden too long pointing will be hard work and you may leave dark marks on the joint.

Test the consistency of the mortar by pressing your thumb into a joint. If it holds a clear impression without sticking to your thumb the mortar is just right for pointing. Because it is so important you shape the joint at exactly the right moment you may have to point the work in stages before you can complete the wall.

Shape the joints to match existing brickwork or choose one that is suitable for the prevailing weather conditions.

How to make pointing joints

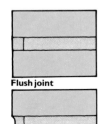

Flush joint

Concave joint

'V' joint

Raked joint

Weather joint

Shape the mortar with a jointing tool

Flush joint
Rub a piece of sacking along each joint to finish the mortar flush with the bricks. This is a utilitarian joint for a wall built with second-hand bricks which are not of a sufficiently good quality to take a crisp joint.

Concave joint
Buy a shaped jointing tool to make a concave joint, or improvise with a length of bent tubing. Flush the mortar first, then drag the tool along the joints. Finish the vertical joints, then do the long, continuous horizontal ones.

'V' joint
Produced in a similar way to the concave joint, the 'V' joint gives a very smart finish to new brickwork and sheds rainwater well.

Raked joint
Use a piece of wood or metal to rake out the joints to a depth of about 6mm (¼in), then compress them again by smoothing the mortar lightly with a piece of rounded dowel rod. Raked joints do not shed water so don't use them on an exposed site.

Coloured mortar
You can add coloured powders to your mortar mix. Make a trial batch to test the colour when dry. Rake out the joint and apply with a tray to avoid staining the bricks.

Weather joint
The angled weather joint is ideal, even in harsh conditions. Use a small pointing trowel to shape the vertical joints (**1**). They can slope to the left or right, but be consistent throughout the same section of brickwork. Shape the horizontal joints allowing the mortar to spill out slightly at the base of each joint. Professionals finish the joint by cutting off excess mortar with a tool called a Frenchman, similar to a table knife with the tip at 90 degrees. Improvise a similar tool with a strip of bent metal. Align a batten with the bottom of the joint to guide the tool and produce a neat, straight edge to the mortar. Nail two scraps of plywood to the batten to hold it away from the wall (**2**).

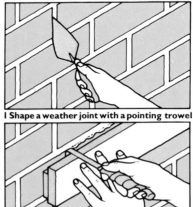

1 Shape a weather joint with a pointing trowel

2 Remove excess mortar with a Frenchman

Brushing the brickwork
Let the shaped joints harden a little before you clean scraps of mortar from the face of the wall. Use a medium-soft banister brush, sweeping lightly across the joints so as not to damage them.

COPINGS FOR BRICK WALLS

The coping, which forms the top course of the wall, protects the brickwork from weathering and gives a finished appearance to the wall. Strictly speaking, if the coping is flush with both faces of the wall it is a capping. A true coping projects from the face so that water drips clear and does not stain the brickwork.

You can lay a coping of bricks with their stretcher faces across the width of the wall. Use the same type of brick employed in the construction of the wall or specially shaped coping bricks designed to shed rainwater. Engineering bricks are sometimes used for copings. The dense water-resistant quality of the brick is an advantage and the colour makes a pleasing contrast with regular brickwork.

Stone or cast concrete slabs are popular for garden walling. They are quick to lay and are wide enough to form low, bench-type seating.

On an exposed site, consider installing a damp-proof course (◁) under the coping to reduce the risk of frost attack. Use a standard bituminous felt DPC or lay two courses of plain roof tiles with staggered joints and a brick coping above. Let the tiles project from the face of the wall but run a sloping mortar joint along the top of the projection to shed water.

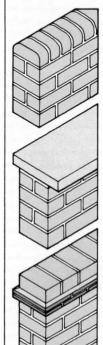

Brick coping
Specially shaped bricks are made to cope a wall.

Slab coping
Choose a concrete or stone slab that is wider than the wall itself.

Tile and brick coping
Lay flat roof tiles or specially made creasing tiles beneath a brick coping to form a weatherproof layer which allows water to drip clear of the wall.

BUILDING INTERSECTING WALLS

When building new garden walls which intersect at right-angles, either anchor them by bonding the brickwork (see below), or take the easier option to link them with wall ties at every third course (▷). If the intersecting wall is over 2m (6ft 6in) in length, make the junction a control joint by using straight metal strips as wall ties (▷).

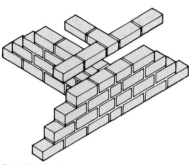
Stretcher bond

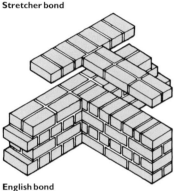
English bond

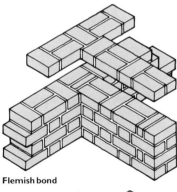
Flemish bond

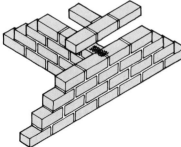
Using a wall tie

Building up to an existing wall

When you build a new wall to intersect the existing wall of a house you must include a damp-proof course to prevent water bridging the house DPC via the new masonry (▷) and you must make a positive joint between the two walls.

Inserting a DPC
Building Regulations require a damp-proof course in all habitable buildings to prevent rising damp. This consists of a layer of impervious material built into the mortar bed 150mm (6in) above ground level. When you build a new wall, its DPC must coincide with the DPC in the existing structure. Use a roll of bituminous felt chosen to match the thickness of the new wall.

Locate the house DPC and build the first few courses of the new wall up to that level. Spread a thin bed of mortar on the bricks and lay the DPC upon it with the end of the roll turned up against the existing wall (**1**). The next course of bricks will trap the DPC between the header joint and the wall. Lay more mortar on top of the DPC to produce the standard 10mm (³⁄₈in) joint ready for laying the next course in the normal way. If you have to join rolls of DPC, overlap the ends by 150mm (6in).

Tying-in the new wall
The traditional method for linking a new wall with an existing structure involves chopping recesses in the brickwork at every fourth course. End bricks of the new wall are set into the recesses, bonding the two structures together (**2**). An alternative and much simpler method, however, is to screw a special stainless metal channel to the wall, designed to accept bricks or concrete blocks and provide anchoring points for standard wire wall ties (▷). Channels are available for masonry units up to 215mm (8½in) thick.

Screw the channel to the old wall above the DPC with stainless steel coachscrews and wall plugs or use expanding bolts (**3**). Though not essential, trap 1m (3ft 3in) of DPC felt behind the channel.

Mortar the end of a brick before feeding it into the channel (**4**). As the brick is pushed home, the mortar squeezes through the perforated channel to make a firm bond.

At every third course, hook a wall tie over the pressed lugs in the channel and bed it firmly into the mortar joint (**5**).

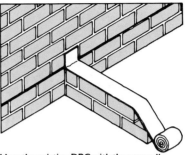
1 Lap the existing DPC with the new roll

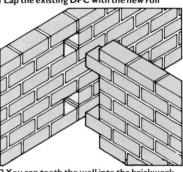
2 You can tooth the wall into the brickwork

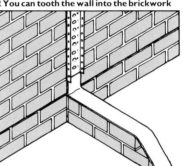
3 But it is easier to use a special channel

4 Locate the ends of the bricks in the channel

5 Hook wire wall ties over the pressed lugs

SEE ALSO

Details for: ▷	
Stepped footing	427
Wall ties	432
DPC	251
Bricks	421-422
Laying bricks	428-429
Wall fixings	498-499

DPC on a sloping site
When the site slopes noticeably, the wall footing is stepped to keep the top of the wall level (▷). If you include a DPC in the wall, that too must follow the line of the steps to keep it the required height above ground level.

431

BRICKWORK PIERS

A pier is a free-standing column of masonry used to support a porch or as an individual gatepost, for instance. When it is built as part of a wall, it is more accurately termed a pilaster. In practice, however, a column often covers either description. Columns bonded into a masonry base but extending up each side of a wooden trellis to support a pergola are typical examples. To avoid confusion, any supporting brick column will be described as a pier. Thorough planning is essential when building piers.

SEE ALSO

◁ Details for:

Footings	**427**
Bricks	421-422
Laying bricks	428-429
Reinforced piers	433

Structural considerations

Any free-standing straight wall over a certain length and height must be buttressed at regular intervals by piers. Sections of walling and piers must be tied together, either by a brick bond or by inserting metal wall ties in every third course of bricks. Any single-width brick wall, whatever its height, would benefit from supporting piers at open ends and gateways where it is most vulnerable; these will also improve the appearance of the wall. Piers over 1m (3ft 3in), and especially those supporting gates, should be built around steel reinforcing rods set in the concrete footings. Whether reinforcing is included or not, allow for the size of piers when designing the footings (◁).

Designing the piers

Piers should be placed no more than 3m (9ft 9in) apart in walls over a certain height (See chart). The wall itself can be flush with one face of a pier but the structure is stronger if it is centred on the column.

Piers should be a minimum of twice the thickness of a 102.5mm (4in) thick wall, but build 328mm (1ft 1in) square piers when reinforcement is required, including gateways, and to buttress 215mm (8½ in) thick walls.

INCORPORATING PIERS IN A BRICK WALL

Thickness of wall	Maximum height without piers	Maximum pier spacing
102.5mm (4in)	450mm (1ft 6in)	3m (9ft 9in)
215mm (8½in)	1.35m (4ft 6in)	3m (9ft 9in)

● Bonding piers
It is simpler to tie any wall to a pier with wall ties (See above right) but it is relatively easy to bond a pier into a single-brick width wall.

Colour key
You will have to cut certain bricks to bond a pier into a straight wall. Whole bricks are coloured with a light tone, three-quarter bats with a medium tone, and half-bats with a dark tone.

BONDING PIERS

If you prefer the appearance of bonded brick piers, construct them as shown below, but it is easier, especially when building walls centred on piers, to use wall ties to reinforce continuous vertical joints in the brickwork.

Various types of galvanized metal wall ties are available. Wire is bent into a butterfly shape (1). Stamped metal steel strips have forked ends and are known as fish tails (2). Expanded metal mesh is cut in straight strips (3).

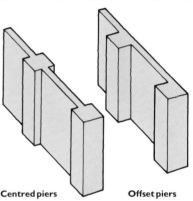

Centred piers   Offset piers

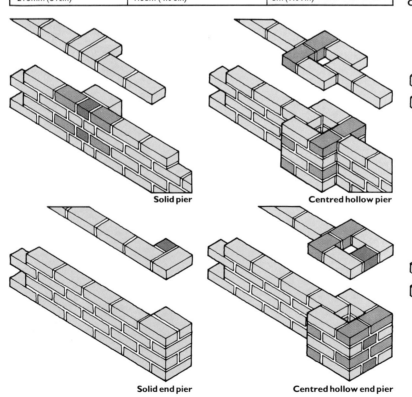

Solid pier   Centred hollow pier   Offset hollow pier

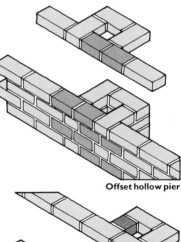

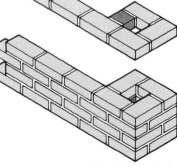

Solid end pier   Centred hollow end pier   Offset hollow end pier

BUILDING PIERS

Mark out accurately the positions of piers and the face of the wall on the concrete footing (▷). Lay the first course for the piers using a builder's line stretched between two stakes to align them (1). Adjust the position of the line if necessary, and fill in between with the first straight course working from both ends towards the middle (2). Build alternate pier and wall courses, checking the level and the vertical faces and corners of the piers. At the third course, push metal wall ties into the mortar bed to span the joint between wall and pier (3). Continue in the same way to the required height of the wall, then raise the piers to their required height (4). Lay a coping along the wall and cap the piers with concrete or stone slabs (5).

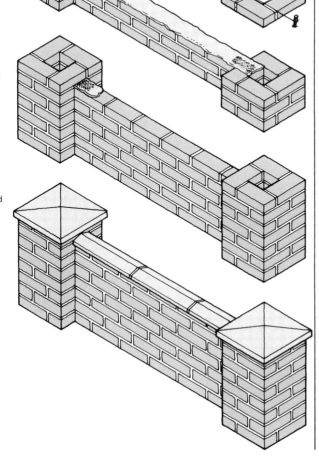

1 Lay pier bases
Stretch a builder's line to position the bases of the piers.

2 Lay first wall course
Move the line to keep the first course straight.

3 Lay pier ties
Tie the piers to the wall by inserting wall ties into every third course. Put a tie into alternate courses for a gate-supporting pier.

4 Raise the piers
Build the piers higher than the wall to allow for a decorative coping along the top course.

5 Lay the coping
Lay the coping slabs and cap the piers.

Incorporating control joints

Although you would never notice, a brick wall is constantly moving due to ground settlement as well as expansion and contraction of the materials. Over short distances, the movement is so slight that it hardly affects the brickwork, but the combined movement of masonry in a long wall can crack the structure. To compensate for this movement, build unmortared, continuous vertical joints into a wall at intervals of about 6m (19ft 6in). These control joints can be placed in a straight section of walling, but it is neater and more convenient to place them where the wall meets a pier. Build the pier and wall as normal, but omit the mortar from the header joints of the wall. Instead of inserting standard wall ties, embed a flat, 3mm (1/8in) thick galvanized strip in the mortar bed. Lightly grease one half of the strip so that it can slide lengthwise to allow for movement yet still key the wall and pier together. When the wall is complete, fill the joint from both sides with mastic.

Incorporating reinforcement

Use 16mm (5/8in) steel reinforcing bars to strengthen brick piers. If the pier is under 1m (3ft 3in) in height, use one continuous length of bar (1), but for taller piers, embed a bent 'starter' bar in the footing, projecting a minimum of 500mm (1ft 8in) above the level of the concrete (2). As the work proceeds, bind extension bars to the projection with galvanized wire up to within 50mm (2in) of the top of the pier. Fill in around the reinforcement with concrete as you build the pier but pack it carefully, trying not to disturb the brickwork.

SEE ALSO

Details for: ▷	
Marking out	429
Bricks	421-422
Laying bricks	428-429
Wall ties	432

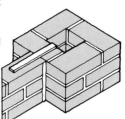

Making a control joint
Tie the pier to the wall with galvanized-metal strips when making a control joint (shown here before it's set in mortar). The mastic is squeezed into the joint between the wall and the pier.

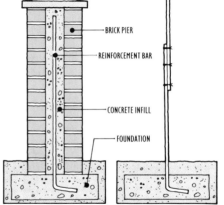

BRICK PIER

REINFORCEMENT BAR

CONCRETE INFILL

FOUNDATION

1 A reinforced pier   **2 Starter bar**

BUILDING WITH CONCRETE BLOCKS

The methods for laying concrete blocks are much the same as for building with bricks. Block walls need similar concrete footings, and the same type of mortar, although heavy blocks should be laid with a strong, firm mix (◁) to resist the additional weight of the freshly constructed wall. As blocks are made in a greater variety of sizes, you can build a wall of any thickness with a simple stretcher bond (◁). However, don't dampen concrete blocks before laying them – wet blocks can shrink and crack the mortar joints as the wall dries out. When you are building decorative walls with facing blocks use any of the pointing styles described for bricks (◁), but flush–joint a wall built with structural blocks which is to be rendered or plastered.

SEE ALSO

◁ Details for:

Door lintel	126
Stud partition	135-139
Door framing	185
Mixing mortar	425
Stretcher bond	426
Stepped leads	429
Pointing	430
Pressed-metal channel	431
Intersecting walls	431
Control joints	433
Piers	433
Blocks	423-424
Laying bricks	428-429

● **Building piers**
High, free-standing garden walls constructed from blocks must be supported by piers at 3m (9ft 9in) intervals (◁).

CONTROL JOINTS

Walls over 6m (19ft 6in) in length should be built with a continuous, vertical control joint to allow for expansion (◁). Place an unmortared joint in a straight section of wall or against a pier, and bridge the gap with galvanized-metal dowels as for brickwork (◁). Fill the gap with mastic.

It is unlikely, but if you need to insert a control joint in a dividing wall, form the joint between the door frame and wall. In this case, fill the joints with mortar in the normal way but rake them out to a depth of 18mm (¾in) around one end of the lintel and vertically to the ceiling on both sides of the wall. Fill the control joint flush with mastic.

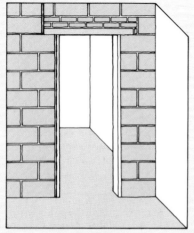

Forming a control joint next to a door opening
Take the joint around the lintel and up to the ceiling on both sides of the wall.

Building a dividing wall

Building a non-loadbearing stud partition (◁) is the usual method for dividing up a large internal space into smaller rooms, but if your house is built on a concrete pad, a practical alternative is to use concrete blocks. If you install a doorway in the dividing wall, plan its position to avoid cutting too many blocks. Allow for the wooden door frame and lining (◁) as well as a pre-cast lintel to support the masonry above the opening (◁). Fill the space above the lintel with cut blocks or bricks to level the courses.

Screw galvanized pressed-metal channels (◁) to the existing structure to support each end of the dividing wall. Plumb them accurately or the new wall will be out of true. Lay the first course of blocks without mortar across the room to check their spacing and the position of a doorway if it is to be included. Mark the positions of the blocks before building stepped leads at each end as for brickwork (◁). Check for accuracy with a spirit level. Fill between the leads with blocks.

Build another three courses, anchoring the end blocks to the channels with wall ties in every joint. Leave the mortar to harden overnight before you continue with the wall.

Building a dividing wall

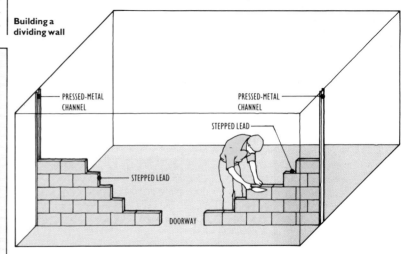

PRESSED-METAL CHANNEL

PRESSED-METAL CHANNEL

STEPPED LEAD

STEPPED LEAD

DOORWAY

Building intersecting walls

Butt intersecting garden walls together with a continuous vertical joint between them, but anchor the structure as for brickwork (◁) with wire-mesh wall ties (**1**). If you build a wall with heavy, but hollow, blocks use stout metal tie bars with a bend at each end. Fill the block cores with mortar to embed the ends of the bars (**2**). Install a tie in every course.

1 Wire-mesh wall tie for solid blocks ▶
2 Metal tie bar for hollow blocks

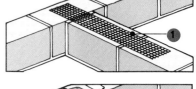

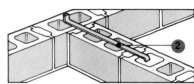

Cutting blocks

Use a bolster chisel and straightedge to score or cut a line around a block. Deepen the groove by tapping the chisel with a hammer. The chisel will ring with each blow until a crack makes its way through the block with a dull thud. One more sharp blow should split the block.

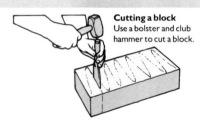

Cutting a block
Use a bolster and club hammer to cut a block.

BUILDING A DECORATIVE BLOCK SCREEN

Basic bricklaying techniques and tools (▷) are used to build a pierced concrete screen but because the blocks are stack-bonded – with continuous vertical joints – the wall must be reinforced vertically with 16mm (⅝in) steel bars, and horizontally with galvanized mesh if it is built higher than 600mm (2ft). Build the screen with supporting piers no more than 3m (9ft 9in) apart using matching pilaster blocks. Or, if you prefer the appearance of contrasting masonry, construct a base and piers from bricks or facing blocks.

Constructing the screen

Set out and fill the footings (▷) twice the width of the pilaster blocks. Embed pier reinforcing bars in the concrete (▷) and support them with guy ropes until the concrete sets.

Lower a pilaster block over the first bar, setting it onto a bed of mortar laid around the base of the bar. Check the block is perfectly vertical and level, and that its locating channel faces the next pier. Pack mortar or concrete into its core, then proceed with two more blocks so that the pier corresponds to the height of two mortared screen blocks (1). Construct each pier in the same way. Intermediate piers will have a locating channel on each side.

Allow the mortar to harden overnight, then lay a mortar bed for two screen blocks next to the first pier. Butter the vertical edge of a screen block and press it into the pier locating channel (2). Tap it into the mortar bed and check it is level. Mortar the next block and place it alongside the first.

When buttering screen blocks, take special care to keep the faces clean by making a neat, chamfered bed of mortar on each block (3).

Lay two more blocks against the next pier, stretch a builder's line to gauge the top edge of the first course, and then lay the rest of the blocks towards the centre. Lay the second course in the same way, making sure the vertical joints are aligned perfectly.

Before building any higher, embed a wire reinforcing strip running from pier to pier in the next mortar bed (4). Continue to build the piers and screen up to a maximum height of 2m (6ft 6in), inserting a wire strip into alternate courses. Finally, lay coping slabs at the top of each pier and along the top of the screen (5).

If you don't like the appearance of ordinary mortar joints, rake out some of the mortar and repoint with mortar made with silver sand. A concave joint suits decorative screening (▷).

CAVITY WALLS

Cavity walls are used in the construction of habitable buildings to prevent the passage of moisture through the wall to the interior. This is achieved by building two independent leaves of masonry with a clear gap between them. The gap provides a degree of thermal insulation but the insulation value increases appreciably if an efficient insulant is introduced to the cavity (▷). The exterior leaf of most cavity walls is constructed with facing bricks. The inner leaf is sometimes built with interior-grade bricks but more often with concrete blocks. Whatever type of masonry is used, both leaves must be tied together with wall ties spanning the gap. Cavity walls are likely to be loadbearing, so have to be built very accurately – hire a professional to construct them. Make sure the bricklayer includes a DPC in both leaves and avoids dropping mortar into the gap. If mortar collects at the base of the cavity, or even on one of the wall ties, moisture can bridge the gap leading to damp on the inside.

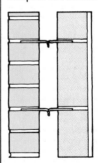

Cavity wall construction
A section through a typical cavity wall built with an exterior leaf of bricks tied to an inner leaf of plastered concrete blocks.

SEE ALSO

Details for: ▷	
Cavity insulation	269
Facing blocks	423-424
Footings	427
Laying bricks	428-429
Concave joint	430
Reinforcing piers	433
Blocks	423-424
Wall ties	432

1 Build the piers

2 Fit block to pier

3 Butter edge of block

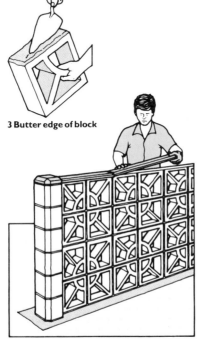

4 Lay a wire reinforcing strip into the mortar

5 Lay coping slabs along the wall

Building a brick base and piers
Build piers and a low base of bricks or facing blocks (▷), including reinforcing bars in the centre of each pier. Lay coping slabs along the wall and continue to build the piers along with the screen. Tie the screen and piers together with reinforcing strips as described left, but insert standard wall ties in alternate courses to provide additional location and support.

BUILDING WITH STONE

Constructing garden walling with natural stone requires a different approach to that needed for bricklaying or building with concrete blocks. A stone wall must be as stable as one built with

any other masonry but its visual appeal relies on less regular coursing. In fact, there is no real coursing at all in the usual sense when it is built with undressed stone or rubble.

SEE ALSO
◁ Details for:
Footings 427
Builder's line 479
Natural stone 424

Structural considerations

Stone walls don't necessarily require mortar to hold the stones together although it is often used, especially with dressed or semi-dressed stone, to provide additional stability. As a result, many stone walls taper, having a wide base of heavy, flat stones and gradually decreasing in width as the wall rises.

This traditional form of construction developed to prevent a wall of unmortared stones toppling sideways under the pressure of high winds or animals. Far from detracting from its appearance, the inherent informality of natural stone walling suits a country-style garden perfectly.

Building a dry stone wall

A true dry stone wall is built without mortar, relying instead on a selective choice of stones and careful placement to provide stability. Experience is needed for perfect results, but there is no reason why you cannot introduce mortar, particularly within the core of the wall, and still maintain the appearance of dry stone walling. You can also bed the stones in soil, packing it firmly into the crevices as you lay each course. This enables you to plant alpines or other suitable rockery plants in the wall, even during construction.

When you select the masonry, look out for flat stones in a variety of sizes, and make sure you have some large enough to run the full width of the wall, especially at the base of the structure. These 'bonding' stones, placed at regular intervals, are important components which tie the loose rubble into a cohesive structure. Even a low wall will inevitably include some heavy stones. When you lift them, keep your back straight and your feet together, using the strong muscles of your legs to take the strain.

DESIGNING THE WALL

Every dry stone wall must be 'battered'. In other words, it must have a wide base and sides that slope inwards. For a wall about 1m (3ft 3in) in height, and it is risky to build a dry stone wall any higher, the base should be no less than 450mm (1ft 6in) wide. You should aim to provide a minimum slope of 25mm (1in) for every 600mm (2ft) of height.

Traditionally, the base of this type of wall rests on a 100mm (4in) bed of sand laid on compacted soil at the bottom of a shallow trench. For a more reliable foundation, lay a 100mm (4in) concrete footing (◁), making it about 100mm (4in) wider than the wall on each side.

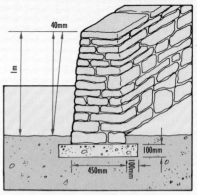

Proportions of a stone-built wall

Constructing the wall

Assuming you are using soil as a jointing material, spread a 25mm (1in) layer over the footing and place a substantial bonding stone across the width to form the bed of the first course (1). Lay other stones about the same height as the bonding stone along each side of the wall, pressing them down into the soil to make a firm base. It is worth stretching a builder's line (◁) along each side of the wall to help you make a

reasonably straight base.

Lay smaller stones between to fill out the base of the wall (2), then pack more soil into all the crevices.

Spread another layer of soil on top of the base and lay a second course of stones, bridging the joints between the stones below (3). Press them down so that they angle inwards towards the centre of the wall. Check by eye that the coursing is about level as you build

the wall and remember to include bonding stones at regular intervals.

Introduce plants into the larger crevices or hammer smaller stones into the chinks to lock the large stones in place (4).

At the top of the wall, either fill the core with soil for plants or lay large, flat coping stones, firming them with packed soil. Finally, brush loose soil from the faces of the wall.

1 Lay a bonding stone at the end of the wall

2 Fill out the base with small stones

3 Lay a second course of stones

4 Fill the chinks

BUILDING RETAINING WALLS

Retaining walls hold back a bank of earth. But don't attempt to cut into a steep bank and restrain it with a single high wall. Apart from the obvious

danger of the wall collapsing, terracing the slope with a series of low walls is a more attractive solution which offers opportunities for imaginative planting.

Choosing your materials

Bricks and concrete blocks are perfectly suitable materials to choose for constructing a retaining wall, providing they are built sturdily. It is best to support these walls with reinforcing bars buried in the concrete footing (▷). Run the bars through hollow core blocks (**1**) or build a double skin of brickwork, rather like a miniature cavity wall, using wall ties to bind each skin together (**2**).

The mass and weight of natural stone make it ideal for retaining walls. The wall should be battered to an angle of 50mm (2in) to every 300mm (1ft) of height so that it virtually leans into the bank (**3**). Keep the height below 1m (3ft 3in) for safety.

A skilful builder could construct a dry stone retaining wall perfectly safely, but use mortar for additional rigidity and support if you are an amateur.

SEE ALSO

Details for: ▷	
Footings	427
Laying bricks	428-429
Pointing	430
Reinforcing bars	433
Dry stone wall	436

Terracing with retaining walls

1 A retaining wall of hollow concrete blocks

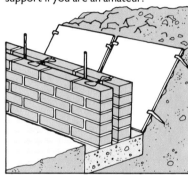
2 Use two skins of brick tied together

3 Lean a stone wall against the bank of earth

Constructing a stone wall

Excavate the soil to provide enough room to dig the footing (▷) and construct the wall. If the soil is loosely packed, restrain it temporarily with sheets of scrap plywood, corrugated iron or similar sheeting. Drive long metal pegs into the bank to hold the sheets in place (**1**). Lay the footing at the base of the bank and allow it to set before building the wall.

Lay uncut stones as if you were building a dry stone wall (▷) but set each course on mortar. If you use regular stone blocks, select stones of

different proportions to add interest to the wall, and stagger the joints. Use standard bricklaying methods (▷) to bed the stones in mortar.

It is essential to allow for drainage behind the wall to prevent the soil becoming waterlogged. When you lay the second course of stones embed 22mm (¾in) plastic pipes in the mortar bed, allowing them to slope slightly towards the front of the wall. The pipes should be placed at about 1m (3ft) intervals and pass right through the wall, projecting a little from the face (**2**).

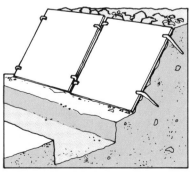
1 Hold back the earth with scrap boards

2 Set plastic pipes in the wall for drainage

FINISHING STONE WALLS

When the wall is complete, rake out the joints to give a dry wall appearance. An old paintbrush is a useful tool for smoothing the mortar in deep crevices to make firm, watertight joints. Alternatively, point regular stones as for brickwork (▷).

Allow the mortar to set for a day or two before filling behind the wall. Lay hardcore at the base to cover the drainage pipes and pack shingle against the wall as you replace the soil. Provide a generous layer of topsoil so that you can plant up to the wall.

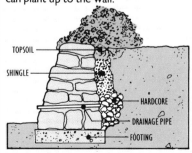

TOPSOIL

SHINGLE

HARDCORE

DRAINAGE PIPE

FOOTING

Filling behind a stone wall

PATHS, DRIVES AND PATIOS

For many people, paving of any kind is associated with the old 'back yard' environment, conjuring up an image of a concreted patch devoid of plants, trees and grass – inhuman and unattractive. In reality, introducing paving to a garden provides an opportunity to create surprising contrasts of colour and texture intensified by sunlight and deep shadows. The harshness of a hard, unyielding surface is softened by the addition of foliage, while certain sculptural plants which recede into a background of soil and grass are seen to advantage against stone and gravel.

SEE ALSO
◁ Details for:
Concrete mixes	441
Paving slabs	446
Finishing concrete	445

A paved patio
A paved area surrounded by stone or brick walls makes a perfect suntrap for swimming and relaxing.

Designing paved areas

The marriage of different materials offers numerous possibilities. It may be convenient to define areas of paving as paths, drives and patios, but they are only names to describe the function of those particular spaces in the garden. There is no reason why you cannot blend one area into another using the same material throughout, or use similar colours to link one type of paving with another. On the other hand, you could take a completely different approach and deliberately juxtapose coarse and smooth textures, or use pale and dark tones to make one space stand out from the next.

Having so many choices at your disposal does have its drawbacks. There is a strong temptation to experiment with any and every combination until the end result is a distracting mishmash. A few well-chosen materials which complement the house and its surroundings produce an environment which is not only more appealing in the short term, but actually improves as the garden matures.

Working with concrete

Concrete might not be everybody's first choice for paving a garden, but it is such a versatile material that you may not even be aware of its use. When it is cast into paving slabs (◁), for instance, it can be mistaken for natural stone, or you might be more aware of the geometric pattern created by the combination of individual units rather than the material itself. Even ordinary concrete can be finished with a surprising variety of textures, and is incomparable as a material for the foundations of outbuildings or extensions.

THE INGREDIENTS OF CONCRETE

Concrete in its simplest form consists of cement and fine particles of stone – sand and pebbles – known as aggregate. The dry ingredients are mixed with water to create a chemical reaction with the cement which binds the aggregate into a hard, dense material. The initial hardening process takes place quite quickly. The mix becomes unworkable after a couple of hours depending on the temperature and humidity, but the concrete has no real strength for three to seven days. The process continues for up to a month, or as long as there is moisture present within the concrete. Moisture is essential to the reaction and the concrete must not dry out too quickly in the first few days.

CEMENT

Standard Portland cement, sold in 50kg (110 lb) bags from builders' merchants or DIY outlets, is used in the manufacture of concrete. In its dry condition, it is a fine, grey powder.

SAND

Sharp sand, a rather coarse and gritty material, constitutes part of the aggregate of a concrete mix. Don't buy fine builders' sand used for mortar, and avoid unwashed or beach sand, both of which contain impurities that could affect the quality of the concrete. Sharp sand is sold by the cubic metre (or cubic yard) from a builders' merchant, although it is perhaps more convenient to buy it in large plastic bags if you have to transport it by car or van.

COARSE AGGREGATE

Coarse aggregate is gravel or crushed stone composed of particles large enough to be retained by a 5mm (¼in) sieve up to a maximum size of 20mm (¾in) for normal use. Once again, it can be bought loose by the cubic metre (cubic yard) or in smaller quantities packed in plastic sacks.

PIGMENTS

Special pigments can be added, but it is difficult to guarantee an even colour from one batch of concrete to another.

COMBINED AGGREGATE

Naturally occurring sand and gravel mix, known as ballast, is sold as a combined aggregate for concreting. The proportion of sand to gravel is not guaranteed unless the ballast has been reconstituted to adjust the mix, and you may have to do it yourself. In any case, make sure it has been washed to remove impurities.

DRY-PACKED CONCRETE

You can buy dry cement, sand and aggregate mixed to the required proportions for making concrete. Choose the proportion that best suits the job you have in mind (◁). Concrete mix is sold in various size bags up to 50kg (110 lb). Available from the usual outlets, it is a more expensive way of buying the ingredients, but is a simple and convenient method of ordering exactly the amount you will need. Before you add water to the mix, make sure the ingredients are mixed thoroughly.

WATER

Use ordinary tap water to mix concrete, never river or sea water.

PVA ADMIXTURE

You can buy a PVA admixture from builders' merchants to make a smoother concrete mix which is less susceptible to frost damage. Follow manufacturers' instructions for its use.

MIXING CONCRETE

You can hire small mixing machines if you have to prepare a large volume of concrete, but for the average job it is just as convenient to mix concrete by hand. It isn't necessary to weigh out the ingredients when mixing concrete. Simply mix them by volume, choosing the proportions that suit the job in hand.

Mixing by hand

Use large buckets to measure the ingredients, one for the cement and an identical one for the aggregate, in order to keep the cement perfectly dry. Different shovels are also a good idea. Measure the materials accurately, levelling them with the rim of the bucket. Tap the side of the bucket with the shovel as you load it with sand or cement to shake down the loose particles.

Mix the sand and aggregate first on a hard flat surface. Scoop a depression in the pile for the measure of cement, and mix all the ingredients until they form an even colour.

Form another depression and add some water from a watering can. Push the dry ingredients into the water from around the edge until surface water is absorbed, then mix the batch by chopping the concrete with the shovel (1). Add more water, turning concrete from the bottom of the pile and chop it as before until the whole batch has an even consistency. To test the workability of the mix, form a series of ridges by dragging the back of the shovel across the pile (2). The surface of the concrete should be flat and even in texture, and the ridges should hold their shape without slumping.

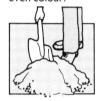

1 Mixing ingredients
Mix the ingredients by chopping the concrete mix with the shovel. Turn the mix over and chop again.

2 Testing the mix
Make ridges with the back of the shovel to text the workability of the mix.

Mixing by machine

Make sure you set up the concrete mixer on a hard, level surface and that the drum is upright before you start the motor. Use a bucket to pour half the measure of coarse aggregate into the drum and add water. This will clean the drum after each batch has been mixed. Add the sand and cement alternately in small batches, plus the rest of the aggregate. Add water little by little along with the other ingredients.

Let the batch mix for a few minutes. Then, with the drum of the mixer still rotating, turn out a little concrete into a wheelbarrow to test its consistency (See above). If necessary, return the concrete to the mixer to adjust it.

Storing materials

If you buy sand and coarse aggregate in sacks, simply use whatever you need at a time, keeping the rest bagged up until required. If you buy them loose, store sand and aggregate in piles, separated by a wooden plank if necessary, on a hard surface or thick polythene sheets. Protect the materials from prolonged rain with weighted sheets of plastic.

Storing cement is more critical. It is sold in paper sacks which will absorb moisture from the ground, so pile them on a board propped up on battens. Keep cement in a dry shed or garage if possible, but if you have to store it outdoors cover the bags with sheets of plastic weighted down with bricks. Once open, cement can absorb moisture from the air. Keep a partly used bag in a sealed plastic sack.

MACHINE SAFETY

- Make sure you understand the operating instructions before turning on the machine.
- Prop the mixer level and stable with blocks of wood.
- Never put your hands or shovel into the drum while the mixer is running.
- Don't lean over a rotating drum when you inspect the contents. It is good practice to wear goggles when mixing concrete.

READY-MIXED CONCRETE

If you need a lot of concrete for a driveway or large patio it may be worth ordering a supply of ready-mixed concrete from a local supplier. Always speak to the supplier well before you need the concrete to discuss your particular requirements. Specify the proportions of the ingredients and say whether you will require the addition of a retarding agent to slow down the setting time. Once a normal mix of concrete is delivered, you will have no more than two hours to finish the job. A retarding agent can add up to two hours to the setting time. Tell the supplier what you need the concrete for and accept his advice.

For quantities of less than 6cu m (6cu yd) you might have to shop around for a supplier who is willing to deliver without an additional charge. Discuss any problems of discharging the concrete on site. To avoid transporting the concrete too far by wheelbarrow, have it discharged as close to the site as possible, if not directly into place. The chute on a delivery truck can reach only so far, and if the truck is too large or heavy to drive onto your property you will need several helpers to move the quantity of concrete while it is still workable. A single cubic metre of concrete will fill 25 to 30 large wheelbarrows. If it takes longer than 30 to 40 minutes to discharge the load, you may have to pay extra.

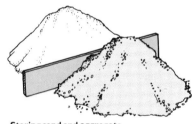

Storing sand and aggregate
Separate the piles of sand and aggregate with a wooden plank

Storing cement
Raise bags of cement off the ground and cover them with plastic sheeting.

SEE ALSO

Details for: ▷	
Calculating quantities	441
Cleaning equipment	441
Laying concrete	442-445

- **Professional mixing**
There are companies who will deliver concrete ingredients and mix them to your specification on the spot. All you have to do is barrow the concrete and pour it into place. There is no waste as you only pay for the concrete you use. Telephone a local company for details on price and minimum quantity.

DESIGNING CONCRETE PAVING

The idea of having to design simple concrete pads and pathways might seem odd, but there are important factors to consider if the concrete is to be durable. At the least, you will have to decide on the thickness of the concrete to support the weight of traffic, and determine the angle of slope required to drain off surface water. When the area of concrete is large or a complicated shape, you must incorporate control joints to allow the material to expand and contract without cracking. If a pad is for a habitable building, it must include a damp-proof membrane to prevent moisture rising from the ground (◁). Even the proportions of sand, cement and aggregate used in the concrete mix must be considered carefully to suit the function of the paving.

SEE ALSO

◁ Details for:

Damp-proof	
membrane	182,251
Control joints	444-445
Laying sub-base	443

Deciding on the slope

In theory, a free-standing pad can be laid perfectly level, especially when it is supporting a small outbuilding, but, in fact, a very slight slope or fall prevents water collecting in puddles if you have failed to get the concrete absolutely flat. When a pad is laid directly against a house, it must have a definite fall away from the building, and any parking area or drive must shed water to provide adequate traction for vehicles and to minimize the formation of ice. When concrete is laid against a building, it must be at least 150mm (6in) below the existing damp-proof course.

USE OF PAVING	ANGLE OF FALL
Pathways	Not required
Drive	1 in 40 25mm per metre 1in per yard
Patio Parking space	1 in 60 away from building 16mm per metre ⅝in per yard
Outbuildings	1 in 80 towards the door 12·5mm per metre ½in per yard

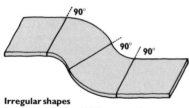

Irregular shapes
Insert control joints at 90 degrees to edges.

RECOMMENDED THICKNESSES FOR CONCRETE

The normal thicknesses recommended for concrete paving assumes it will be laid on a firm subsoil, but if the soil is clay or peat, increase the thickness by about 50 per cent. The same applies to a new site where the soil might not be compacted. Unless the concrete is for pedestrian traffic only, lay a sub-base of compacted hardcore below the paving. This will absorb ground movement without affecting the concrete itself. A sub-base is not essential for a very lightweight structure like a small wooden shed, but as you might want to increase the weight at some time, it is wise to install a sub-base at the outset.

PATHWAYS

For pedestrian traffic only
Concrete: 75mm (3in)
Sub-base: Not needed

LIGHT STRUCTURES

A support pad for a wooden shed, coal bunker and so on
Concrete: 75mm (3in)
Sub-base: 75mm (3in)

PATIOS

Any extensive area of concrete for pedestrian traffic
Concrete: 100mm (4in)
Sub-base: 100mm (4in)

PARKING SPACES

Exposed paving for parking family car
Concrete: 100mm (4in)
Sub-base: 100mm (4in)

DRIVEWAYS

A drive which is used for an average family car only
Concrete: 100mm (4in)
Sub-base: 100mm (4in)
For heavier vehicles like delivery trucks
Concrete: 150mm (6in)
Sub-base: 100mm (4in)

GARAGES

Thicken up the edges of a garage pad to support the weight of the walls
Concrete:
Floor: 100mm (4in)
Edges: 200mm (8in)
Sub-base:
Minimum 100mm (4in)

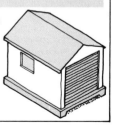

Allowing for expansion

Change in temperature causes concrete to expand and contract. If this movement is allowed to happen at random, a pad or pathway will crack at the weakest or most vulnerable point. A control joint, composed of a compressible material (◁), will absorb the movement or concentrate the force in predetermined areas where it does little harm. Joints should meet the sides of a concrete area at more or less 90 degrees. Always place a control joint between concrete and a wall, and around inspection chambers.

Positioning control joints
The position of control joints depends on the area and shape of the concrete.

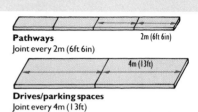

Pathways   2m (6ft 6in)
Joint every 2m (6ft 6in)

Drives/parking spaces   4m (13ft)
Joint every 4m (13ft)

          4m (13ft)

Concrete pads
Joints no more than 4m (13ft) apart and around inspection chambers.

Divide a pad into equal bays if:
● Length is more than twice the width.
● Longest dimension is more than 40 x thickness.
● Longest dimension exceeds 4m (13ft).

CALCULATING QUANTITIES OF CONCRETE

Estimate the amount of materials you require by calculating the volume of concrete in the finished pad, path or drive. Measure the surface area of the site and multiply that figure by the thickness of the concrete.

Estimating quantities of concrete

Use the gridded diagram to estimate the volume of concrete by reading off the area of the site in square metres (square yards) and trace it across horizontally to meet the angled line indicating the thickness of the concrete. Trace the line up to find the volume in cubic metres (cubic yards).

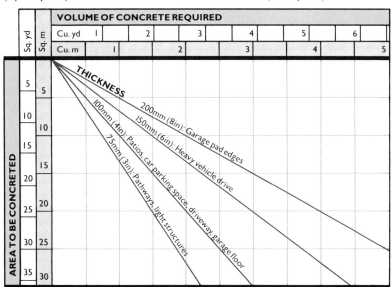

Estimating quantities of ingredients

Use the bar charts to estimate how much cement, sand and aggregate is needed to mix up the volume of concrete worked out by using the chart above.

The figures are based on the amount of ingredients used to mix one cubic metre of concrete using a particular type of mix (See below) plus about 10 per cent for wastage.

CUBIC METRES OF CONCRETE	1.00	1.50	2.00	2.50	3.00	3.50	4.00	4.50	5.00
GENERAL-PURPOSE MIX									
Cement (50kg bags)	7.00	10.50	14.00	17.50	21.00	24.50	28.00	31.50	35.00
Sand (Cubic metres)	0.50	0.75	1.00	1.25	1.50	1.75	2.00	2.25	2.50
Aggregate (Cubic metres)	0.75	1.15	1.50	1.90	2.25	2.65	3.00	3.40	3.75
Ballast (Cubic metres)	0.90	1.35	1.80	2.25	2.70	3.15	3.60	4.05	4.50
FOUNDATION MIX									
Cement (50kg bags)	6.00	9.00	12.00	15.00	18.00	21.00	24.00	27.00	30.00
Sand (Cubic metres)	0.55	0.80	1.10	1.40	1.65	1.95	2.20	2.50	2.75
Aggregate (Cubic metres)	0.75	1.15	1.50	1.90	2.25	2.65	3.00	3.40	3.75
Ballast (Cubic metres)	1.00	1.50	2.00	2.50	3.00	3.50	4.00	4.50	5.00
PAVING MIX									
Cement (50kg bags)	9.00	13.50	18.00	22.50	27.00	31.50	36.00	40.50	45.00
Sand (Cubic metres)	0.45	0.70	0.90	1.15	1.35	1.60	1.80	2.00	2.25
Aggregate (Cubic metres)	0.75	1.15	1.50	1.90	2.25	2.65	3.00	3.40	3.75
Ballast (Cubic metres)	1.00	1.50	2.00	2.50	3.00	3.50	4.00	4.50	5.00

CALCULATING AREAS

Squares and rectangles
Calculate the area of rectangular paving by multiplying width by length :

Example:
2m × 3m = 6 sq m
78in × 117in = 9126 sq in or 7 sq yd

Circles
Use the formula πr^2 to calculate the area of a circle. $\pi = 3.14$. r = radius of circle.

Example
$3.14 \times 2m^2 = 3.14 \times 4 = 12.56$ sq m
$3.14 \times 78in^2 = 3.14 \times 6084 = 19104$ sq in or 14.75 sq yd

Irregular shapes
Draw an irregular area of paving on squared paper. Count the whole squares and average out the portions to find the approximate area.

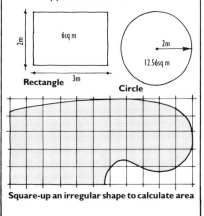

Rectangle   **Circle**

Square-up an irregular shape to calculate area

SEE ALSO

Details for: ▷
Mixing concrete	439
Shovel	480
Wheelbarrow	480

CLEANING TOOLS AND MACHINERY

Keep the shovel as clean as possible between mixing batches of concrete, and at the end of a working day wash all traces of concrete from your tools and wheelbarrow.

When you have finished using a concrete mixer, add a few shovels of coarse aggregate and a little water, then run the machine for a couple of minutes to scour the inside of the drum. Dump the aggregate, then hose out the drum with clean water.

Shovel unused concrete into sacks ready for disposal at a refuse dump and wash the mixing area with a stiff broom. Never hose concrete or any of the separate ingredients into a drain.

LAYING A CONCRETE PAD

Laying a simple pad as a base for a small shed or similar structure involves all the basic principles of concreting: building a retaining formwork, as well as the pouring, levelling and finishing of concrete. As long as the base is less than 2m (6ft 6in) square, there is no need to include control joints.

SEE ALSO

◁ Details for:

Pad thickness	440
Crossfall	440
Control joints	440
Finishing concrete	445
Spirit level	478

Mixing concrete by volume

Mixing the ingredients by volume is the easiest and most accurate way to guarantee the required proportions. Whatever container you use to measure the ingredients – shovel, bucket, wheelbarrow – the proportions remain the same.

MIXING CONCRETE BY VOLUME		
Type of mix	Proportions	For 1 cu m concrete
GENERAL PURPOSE		
Use in most situations including covered pads other than garage floors	1 part cement	6.4 bags (50kg)
	2 parts sand	0.448 cu m
	3 parts aggregate	0.672 cu m
	4 parts ballast	0.896 cu m
FOUNDATION		
Use for footings at the base of masonry walls	1 part cement	5.6 bags (50kg)
	2½ parts sand	0.49 cu m
	3½ parts aggregate	0.686 cu m
	5 parts ballast	0.98 cu m
PAVING		
Use for exposed pads such as drives, parking areas or footpaths, but also for garage floors	1 part cement	8 bags (50kg)
	1½ parts sand	0.42 cu m
	2½ parts aggregate	0.7 cu m
	3½ parts ballast	0.98 cu m

Excavating the site

Mark out the area of the pad with string lines attached to pegs driven into the ground outside the work area (1). Remove them to excavate the site but replace them later to help position the formwork which will hold the concrete in place.

Remove the topsoil and all vegetable matter within the site down to a level which allows for the combined thickness of concrete and sub-base (◁). Extend the area of excavation about 150mm (6in) outside the space allowed for the pad. Cut back any roots you encounter. Put the turf aside to cover the infill surrounding the completed pad. Level the bottom of the excavation by dragging a board across it (2), and compact the soil with a garden roller.

Erecting the formwork

Until the concrete sets hard it must be supported all round by formwork. For a straightforward rectangular pad, construct the formwork from 25mm (1in) thick softwood planks set on edge. The planks, which must be as wide as the finished depth of concrete, are held in place temporarily with stout 50 x 50mm (2 x 2in) wooden stakes. Second-hand or sawn timber is quite adequate. If it is slightly thinner than 25mm (1in), just use more stakes to brace it. If you have to join planks, butt them end to end, nailing a cleat on the outside (3).

Using the string lines as a guide, erect one board at the 'high' end of the pad, and drive stakes behind it at about 1m (3ft) intervals or less, with one for each corner. The tops of the stakes and board must be level and correspond exactly to the proposed surface of the pad. Nail the board to the stakes (4).

Set up another board opposite, but before you nail it to the stakes, establish the crossfall (◁) with a straightedge and spirit level. Work out the difference in level from one end of the pad to the other. For example, a pad which is 2m (6ft 6in) long should drop 25mm (1in) over that distance. Tape a shim of timber to one end of the straightedge, and with the shim resting on the 'low' stakes, place the other end on the opposite board (5). Drive home each low stake until the spirit level reads horizontal. Then nail the board flush with the tops of the stakes.

Erect the sides of the formwork, allowing the ends of the boards to overshoot the corners to make it easier to dismantle them when the concrete has set (6). Use the straightedge, this time without the shim, to level the boards across the formwork.

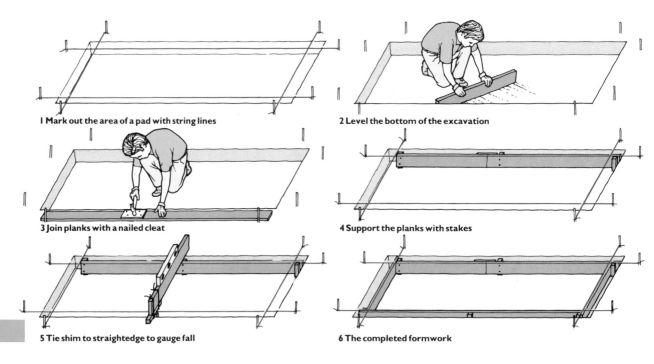

1 Mark out the area of a pad with string lines

2 Level the bottom of the excavation

3 Join planks with a nailed cleat

4 Support the planks with stakes

5 Tie shim to straightedge to gauge fall

6 The completed formwork

LAYING A CONCRETE PAD

Laying the sub-base

Hoggin, a mixture of gravel and sand, is an ideal material for a sub-base, but you can use crushed stone or brick as long as you throw out any plaster, scrap metal or similar rubbish. Also remove large lumps of masonry as they will not compact well. Pour hardcore into the formwork and rake it fairly level before tamping it down with a heavy balk of timber (7). Break up any stubborn lumps with a heavy hammer. Fill in low spots with more hardcore or sharp sand until the sub-base comes up to the underside of the formwork boards.

Filling with concrete

Mix the concrete as near to the site as is practicable and transport the fresh mix to the formwork in a wheelbarrow. Set up firm runways of scaffold boards if the ground is soft, especially around the perimeter of the formwork. Dampen the sub-base and formwork with a fine spray and let surface water evaporate before tipping the concrete in place. Start filling from one end of the site and push the concrete firmly into the corners (8). Rake it level until the concrete stands about 18mm (¾in) above the level of the boards.

Tamp down the concrete with the edge of a 50mm (2in) thick plank long enough to span across the formwork. Starting at one end of the site, compact the concrete with steady blows of the plank, moving it along by about half its thickness each time (9). Cover the whole area twice, then remove excess concrete using the plank with a sawing action (10). Fill any low spots, then compact and level once more.

Cover the pad with sheets of polythene, taped at the joints to retain the moisture and weighted down with bricks around the edge (11). Alternatively, use wet sacking which you must keep damp for three days using a fine spray. Try to avoid laying concrete in very cold weather, but if it is unavoidable, spread a layer of earth or sand on top of the sheeting to insulate the concrete from frost. You can walk on the concrete after three days but leave it for about a week before removing the formwork and erecting a shed or similar outbuilding.

SEE ALSO

Details for: ▷	
Mixing concrete	439
Digging tools	480

Extending a pad
If you want to enlarge a patio, simply butt a new section of concrete against the existing pad. The butt joint will form a control joint. To add a narrow strip, for a larger shed for instance, drill holes in the edge of the pad and use epoxy adhesive to glue in short reinforcing rods before pouring the fresh concrete.

Finishing the edges
If any of the edges are exposed, the sharp corners might cause a painful injury. Radius the corners with a home-made edging float. Bend a piece of sheet metal over an 18mm (¾in) diameter rod or tube and screw a handle in the centre. Run the float along the formwork as you finish the surface of the concrete.

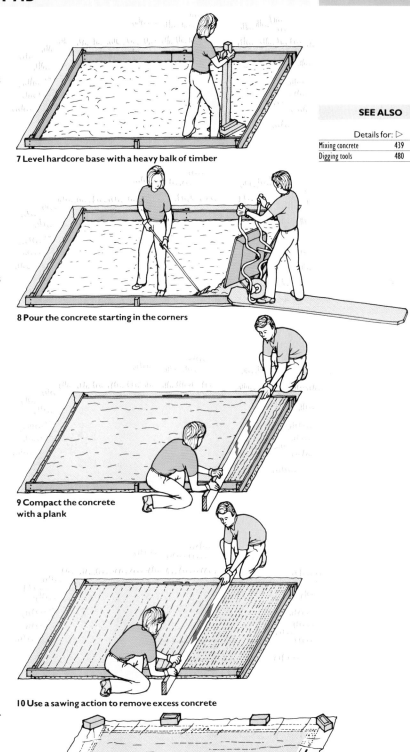

7 Level hardcore base with a heavy balk of timber

8 Pour the concrete starting in the corners

9 Compact the concrete with a plank

10 Use a sawing action to remove excess concrete

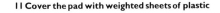

11 Cover the pad with weighted sheets of plastic

LAYING PATHS AND DRIVES

Paths and drives are laid and compacted in the same way as simple rectangular pads, using similar formwork to contain the fresh concrete, but the proportions of most paths and drives necessitate the inclusion of control joints to allow for expansion and contraction (◁). You must install a sub-base beneath a drive, but a footpath can be laid on compacted soil levelled with sharp sand. Establish a slight fall across the site to shed rainwater (◁). Don't use a vehicle on concrete for 10 days after laying.

SEE ALSO

◁ Details for:
Control joints	440
Fall across site	440
Formwork	442
Presevatives	250
Pad thickness	440
Tamping concrete	443

I A water level made from a garden hose

2 Level the formwork using a datum peg

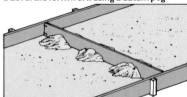
3 Curved and straight road forms

A sloping drive
If you build a drive on a sloping site, make the transition from level ground as gentle as possible. If it runs towards a garage, let the last 2m (6ft) slope up towards the door. Use a pole to impress a drain across the wet concrete at the lowest point.

5 Support board with concrete and nails

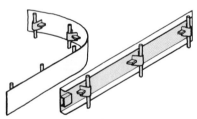
6 Make a dummy joint with T-section metal

Setting out paths and drives

Excavate the site, allowing for the thickness of sub-base and concrete. Level the bottom of the excavation as accurately as you can, using a board to scrape the surface flat.

Drive accurately levelled pegs into the ground along the site to act as datum points for the formwork. Space them about 2m (6ft 6in) apart down the centre of the pathway. Drive in the first peg until its top corresponds exactly to the proposed surface of the concrete. Use a long straightedge and spirit level to position every other peg or, better still, use a home-made water level. Push a short length of transparent plastic tubing into each end of an ordinary garden hose. Fill the hose with water until it appears in the tube at both ends. As long as the ends remain open, the water level at each end is constant so that you can establish a level over any distance, even around obstacles or corners. Tie one end of the hose to the first datum peg so that the water level aligns with the top of the peg. Use the other to establish the level of every other peg along the pathway (**1**). Cork each end of the hose to retain the water as you move it.

To set a fall with a water level, make a mark on one tube below the surface of the water and use that as a gauge for the top of the peg.

Erecting formwork

Construct formwork from 25mm (1in) thick planks as for a concrete pad (◁). To check it is level, rest a straightedge on the nearest datum peg (**2**).

If the drive or path is very long, timber formwork can be expensive. It might be cheaper to hire metal 'road forms' (**3**). Straight-sided formwork is made from rigid units, but flexible sections are available to form curves.

If you want to bend wooden formwork, make a series of parallel saw cuts across the width of the plank in the area of the curve (**4**). The timber is less likely to snap if you place the saw cuts on the inside of the bend.

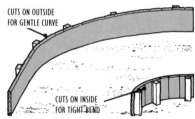
CUTS ON OUTSIDE FOR GENTLE CURVE
CUTS ON INSIDE FOR TIGHT BEND
4 Curved formwork made with wooden planks

Installing control joints

Install a permanent expansion joint every 2m (6ft 6in) for a footpath and every 4m (13ft) along a drive. Cut strips of rot-proof treated hardboard or 12mm (½in) thick softwood to fit exactly between the formwork and to match the depth of the concrete. Before pouring, hold the control joints in place with mounds of concrete and nails on each side of the board driven into the formwork (**5**). Pack more concrete carefully on each side of the joints as you fill the formwork and tamp towards them from both sides so that they are not dislodged.

As the joints are permanent fixtures, make sure they are level with the surface of the concrete. Install similar joints in a patio or use an alternate bay construction (See opposite page).

To prevent concrete cracking between joints on a narrow path, cut 18mm (¾in) deep grooves across the compacted concrete to form dummy joints alternating with the physical ones. The simplest method is to cut a length of T-section metal to fit between the formwork boards. Place it on the surface of the wet concrete and tap it down with a mallet (**6**). Carefully lift the strip out of the concrete to leave a neat impression. If the concrete should move, a crack will develop unnoticed at the bottom of the groove.

Place strips of thick bituminous felt between concrete and an adjoining wall to absorb expansion. Hold the felt in place with mounds of concrete, as described left, before pouring the full amount of concrete.

ALTERNATE BAY METHOD OF CONSTRUCTION

It is not always possible to lay all the concrete in one operation. In such cases it is easier to divide the formwork crosswise with additional planks known as stop ends to form equal-size bays. By filling alternate bays with concrete, you have plenty of time to compact and level each section and more room in which to manoeuvre. It is a convenient way to lay a large patio which would be practically impossible to compact and level in one go, and it is the only method to use for drives or paths butting against a wall which makes it impossible to work across the width. Alternate bay construction is often used for drives on a steep slope to prevent heavy, wet concrete slumping downhill.

There is no need to install physical control joints as the simple butt joint between the bays is sufficient allowance for movement within the concrete

Concreting alternate bays
Stand in the empty bays to compact concrete laid against a wall. When the first bays are set hard, remove the stop ends and fill the gaps, using the surface of the firm concrete as a level.

INSPECTION CHAMBERS

Prevent expansion damaging an inspection chamber by surrounding it with control joints. Place formwork around the chamber and fill with concrete. When set, remove the boards and place felt strips or rot-proof treated softwood boards on all sides.

Surround inspection chamber with formwork

SURFACE FINISHES FOR CONCRETE

The surface finishes produced by tamping or striking off with a sawing action are perfectly adequate for a skid-proof, workmanlike surface for a pad, drive or pathway, but you can produce a range of other finishes using simple handtools once you have compacted and levelled the concrete.

Float finishes
Smooth the tamped concrete by sweeping a wooden float across the surface, or make an even finer texture by finishing with a trowel (steel float). Let the concrete dry out a little before using a float or you will bring water to the top and weaken it, eventually resulting in a dusty residue on the hardened concrete. Bridge the formwork with a stout plank so that you can reach the centre, or hire a skip float with a long handle for large pads.

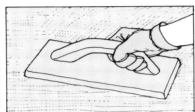

Make a smooth finish with a wooden float

Brush finishes
Make a finely textured surface by drawing a yard broom across the setting concrete. Flatten the concrete initially with a wooden float, then make parallel passes with the broom held at a low angle to avoid 'tearing' the surface.

Texture the surface with a broom

Brush-finishing concrete

Exposed-aggregate finish
Embedding small stones or pebbles in the surface makes a very attractive and practical finish but it takes a little practice to be successful.

Scatter dampened pebbles onto the freshly laid concrete and tamp them firmly with a length of timber until they are flush with the surface (1). Place a plank across the formwork and apply your full weight to make sure the surface is even. Leave the concrete to harden for a while until all surface water has evaporated, then use a very fine spray and a brush to wash away the cement from around the pebbles until they protrude (2). Cover the concrete for about 24 hours, then lightly wash the surface again to clean any sediment off the actual pebbles. Cover the concrete again and leave it to harden thoroughly.

1 Tamp pebbles into the fresh concrete

2 Wash the cement from around the pebbles

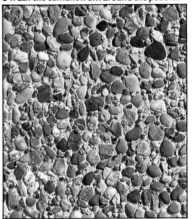

Exposed-aggregate finish

SEE ALSO

Details for: ▷	
Preservatives	250
Control joints	440
Tamping concrete	443
Floats	478

PAVING SLABS

If your only experience of paving slabs is the rather bland variety used for public footpaths, then cast concrete paving may not seem a very attractive *proposition for a garden. However, manufacturers can supply more pleasing products in a wide range of shapes, colours and finishes.*

Colours and textures

Paving slabs are made by hydraulic pressing or casting in moulds to create the desired surface finish. Pigments and selected aggregates added to the concrete mix create the illusion of natural stone or a range of muted colours. Combining two or more colours within the same area of paving can be very striking.

SEE ALSO

◁ Details for:
Brick pavers   449

1 Cobbles or sets
Large slabs resemble an area of smaller cobbles or sets. Careful laying and filling are essential. Sets are 'laid' in straight rows or as curves.

2 Planter
Four planter stones laid in a square leave a circle for a tree or shrub.

3 Exposed aggregate
Crushed stone aggregate has a very pleasing mottled appearance, either exposed to make a coarse gritstone texture or polished flat to resemble terrazzo.

4 Brushed finishes
A brush-finished slab, textured with parallel grooves as if a stiff broom had been dragged across the wet concrete, is practical and non-slip. Straight or swirling patterns are available.

5 Riven stone
The finish resembles that of natural stone. The best-quality slabs are cast from real stone originals in a wide variety of subtle textures. If the texture continues over the edge of the slabs, they can be used for steps and coping.

SHAPES AND SIZES

Although some manufacturers offer a wider choice than others, there is a fairly standard range of shapes and modular sizes. You can carry the largest slabs single-handed, but it is a good idea to have an assistant when manoeuvring them carefully into place.

Square and rectangular
One size and shape make grid-like patterns or, staggered, create a bonded brickwork effect. Rectangular slabs can form a basket-weave or herringbone pattern. Or, combine different sizes to create the impression of random paving.

Regular grid

Staggered slabs

Basket-weave pattern

Herringbone pattern

Random paving

Hexagonal
Hexagonal slabs form honeycomb patterns. Use half slabs, running across flats or from point to point, to edge areas paved in straight lines.

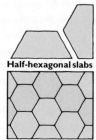

Half-hexagonal slabs

Hexagonal slab

Honeycomb pattern

Tapered slabs
Use tapered slabs to edge ponds, around trees, and for curved paths or steps. Lay them head to toe to make straight sections of paving. Use right- or left-handed half slabs at the ends.

Full and half-tapered slabs

Straight section

Circular
Circular slabs make perfect individual stepping stones across a lawn or flower bed, but for a wide area fill the spaces between with cobbles or gravel.

Butted circular slabs

LAYING PAVING SLABS

Laying heavy paving slabs involves a fair amount of physical labour, but in terms of technique it is no more complicated than tiling a wall. Accurate setting out and careful laying, especially during the early stages, will produce perfect results. Take extra care when laying hexagonal slabs to ensure that the last few slabs fit properly.

CUTTING CONCRETE SLABS

Mark a line across a slab with a soft pencil or chalk. Then, using a bolster and hammer, chisel a groove about 3mm (⅛ in) deep following the line (**1**). Continue the groove down both edges and across the underside of the slab. Place the slab on a bed of sand and put a block of wood at one end of the groove. Strike the block with a hammer while moving it along the groove until a split develops through the slab (**2**). Clean up the rough edge with a bolster.

For a perfectly clean cut each time, hire an angle grinder fitted with a stone-cutting disc. Score a deep groove on both sides of the slab and across the edges. Tap along the groove with a bolster to propagate a crack.

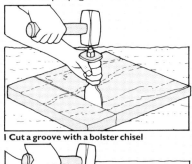

1 Cut a groove with a bolster chisel

2 Strike block over groove with a hammer

PROTECTING YOUR EYES

Whenever you cut slabs with a chisel or a grinder, always protect your eyes from flying chips of concrete by wearing plastic goggles. An angle grinder throws up a lot of dust so wear a simple gauze facemask as a safeguard.

Setting out the area of paving

Wherever possible, to eliminate the arduous task of cutting units to fit, plan an area of paving to be laid with whole slabs only. Use a straight wall as a datum line and measure away from it, or allow for a 100 to 150mm (4 to 6in) margin of gravel between the paving and wall if the location dictates that you have to lay slabs towards the house. A gravel margin not only saves time and money by using fewer slabs, but also provides an area for planting climbers and adequate drainage to keep the wall dry. Even so, establish a 16mm per metre (⅝in per yard) slope across the paving so that most surface water will drain into the garden. Any paving must be 150mm (6in) below a damp-proof course to protect the building.

As paving slabs are made to reasonably precise dimensions, marking out an area simply involves accurate measurement, allowing for a 6 to 8mm (¼in) gap between slabs. Some slabs are cast with sloping edges to provide a tapered joint (**1**) and should be butted edge to edge. Use pegs and string to mark out the perimeter of the paved area, and check your measurements before you excavate.

Preparing a base for paving

Paving slabs must be laid upon a firm, level base, but the depth and substance of that base depends on the type of soil and the proposed use of the paving.

For straightforward patios and paths, remove vegetable matter and topsoil to allow for the thickness of the slabs and a 25mm (1in) layer of sharp sand. Set the paving about 18mm (¾in) below the level of surrounding turf to avoid damaging the lawn mower when you cut the grass. Having compacted the soil using a garden roller, spread the sand with a rake and level it by scraping and tamping with a length of timber (**2**).

To support heavier loads, or if the soil is composed of clay or peat, lay a sub-base (▷) of firmly compacted hardcore – broken bricks or crushed stone – to a depth of 75 to 100mm (3 to 4in) before spreading the sand to level the surface.

If you plan to park vehicles on the paving, then increase the depth of hardcore to 150mm (6in).

Laying the paving slabs

Set up string lines again as a guide and lay the edging slabs on the sand, working in both directions from a corner. When you are satisfied with their positions, lift them one at a time and set them on a bed of mortar (1 part cement: 4 parts sand). Add just enough water to make a firm mortar. Lay a fist-size blob under each corner and one more to support the centre of the slab (**3**). If you intend to drive vehicles across the slabs, lay a continuous bed of mortar about 50mm (2in) thick.

Lay three slabs at a time with 6mm (¼in) wooden spacers between. Level each slab by tapping with a heavy hammer, using a block of wood (**4**). Check the alignment.

Gauge the slope across the paving by setting up datum pegs along the high side (▷). Drive them into the ground until the top of each corresponds to the finished surface of the paving, then use the straightedge to check the fall on the slabs (**5**). Lay the remainder of the slabs, working out from the corner each time to keep the joints square. Remove the spacers before the mortar sets.

SEE ALSO

Details for: ▷		
Paving slope		440
Sub-base	440,	443
Growing ivy on walls		409
Mixing mortar		425

1 Tapered joint

2 Level the sand base

3 Lay blobs of mortar

4 Level the slabs

5 Check the fall with a spirit level

Filling the joints

Don't walk on the paving for two to three days until the mortar has set. If you have to cross the area, lay planks across the slabs to spread the load.

To fill the gaps between the slabs, brush a dry mortar mix of 1 part cement: 3 parts sand into the open joints (**6**). Remove any surplus material from the surface of the paving, then sprinkle the area with a very fine spray of water to consolidate the mortar. Avoid dry mortaring if heavy rain is imminent; it may wash the mortar out.

6 Fill the joints

447

LAYING CRAZY PAVING

The informal nature of paths or patios laid with irregular-shaped paving stones has always been popular. The random jig-saw effect, which many people find more appealing than the geometric accuracy of neatly laid slabs, is also very easy to achieve. A good eye for shape and proportion is more important than a practised technique.

SEE ALSO

◁ Details for:
Choosing stone	424
Mixing mortar	425
Trimming slabs	447

Materials for crazy paving

You can use broken concrete slabs if you can find enough but, in terms of appearance, nothing compares with natural riven stone. Stratified rock which splits into thin layers of its own accord as it is quarried is ideal for crazy paving, and can be obtained at a very reasonable price if you can collect it yourself. Select stones which are approximately 40 to 50mm (1½ to 2in) thick in a variety of shapes and sizes.

Crazy paving made with broken concrete slabs

SETTING OUT AND LAYING A BASE

You can, if you wish, set out string lines to define straight edges to crazy paving although they will never be as precisely defined as those formed with cast concrete slabs. Or, allow the stones to form a broken irregular junction with grass or shingle, perhaps setting one or two individual stones out from the edge of the paving to blend one area into the other.

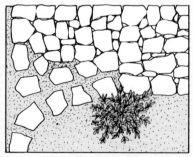

Create an irregular edge to crazy paving

Laying the stones

Arrange an area of stones, selecting them for a close fit but avoiding too many straight, continuous joints. Trim those that don't quite fit with a bolster and hammer. Reserve fairly large stones for the perimeter of the paved area as small stones tend to break away.

Use a mallet or block of wood and a hammer to bed each stone into the sand (1) until they are all perfectly stable and reasonably level. Having bedded an area of about 1sq m (1sq yd), use a straightedge and spirit level to true up the stones (2). If necessary, add or remove sand beneath individual stones until the whole area is level. When the main area is complete, fill in the larger gaps with small stones, tapping them into place with a mallet (3).

Fill the joints by spreading more sand across the paving and sweeping it into the joints from all directions (4). Alternatively, mix up a stiff, almost dry, mortar and press it into the joints with a trowel, leaving no gaps.

Use an old paintbrush to smooth the mortared joints and wipe the stones clean with a damp sponge.

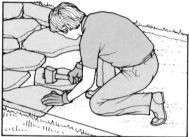

1 Bed the stones in the sand base

2 Check the level across several stones

3 Fill the gaps with small stones

4 Sweep dry sand into the joints

Laying stepping stones

Place individual stones or slabs across a lawn to form a row of stepping stones. Cut around the edge of each stone with a spade or trowel and remove the area of turf directly beneath. Scoop out the earth to allow for a 25mm (1in) bed of sharp sand plus the stone, which must be about 18mm (¾in) below the level of the surrounding turf. Tap the stone into the sand until it no longer rocks when you step on it.

Cut around a stepping stone with a trowel

Stepping stones preserve a lawn

BRICK PATTERNS

Concrete bricks have one surface face with chamfered edges all round, and spacers moulded into the sides to form accurate joints. Housebricks can be laid on edge or face down showing the wide face normally unseen in a wall.

Unlike brick walls, which must be bonded in a certain way for stability (▷), brick paths can be laid to any pattern that appeals to you.

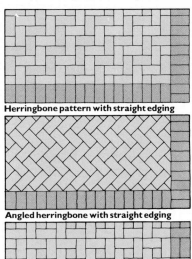

Herringbone pattern with straight edging

Angled herringbone with straight edging

Whole bricks surrounding coloured half-bats

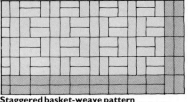

Staggered basket-weave pattern

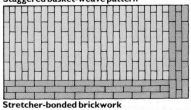

Stretcher-bonded brickwork

Cane-weave pattern

PAVING WITH BRICKS

Bricks make charming and attractive paths. The wide variety of textures and colours available gives endless possibilities of pattern, but choose the type of brick carefully, bearing in mind the sort of use your paving can expect.

Materials for brick paving

Ordinary housebricks are often selected for paths, and also small patios, even though there is the risk of spalling in freezing conditions unless they happen to be engineering bricks (▷). The slightly uneven texture and colour are the very reasons why second-hand bricks in particular are so much in demand for garden paving, so a little frost damage is usually acceptable.

Housebricks are not really suitable if the paved area is to be a parking space or drive, especially if it is to be used by heavy vehicles. For a durable surface, even under severe conditions, use concrete bricks. They are slightly smaller than standard housebricks, being 200 x 100 x 65mm (8 x 4 x 2½in). Red or grey are widely available and you can obtain other colours by special order.

Providing a base for brick paving

Lay brick footpaths and patios on a 75mm (3in) hardcore base (▷) covered with a 50mm (2in) layer of sharp sand. To lay concrete bricks for a drive, increase the depth of hardcore to 100mm (4in).

Fully compact the hardcore and fill all voids so that sand from the bedding course is not lost to the sub-base.

Provide a cross-fall on patios and drives as for concrete (▷), and ensure the surface of the paving is at least 150mm (6in) below a damp-proof course to protect the building.

Retaining edges

Unless the brick path is laid against a wall or some similar structure, the edges of the paving must be contained by a permanent restraint. Timber, treated with a chemical preservative, is one solution, constructed like the formwork for concrete (▷). The edging boards should be flush with the surface of the path, but drive the stakes below ground so that they can be covered by soil or turf **(1)**.

As an alternative, set an edging of bricks in concrete **(2)**. Dig a trench deep and wide enough to accommodate a row of bricks on end plus a 100mm (4in) concrete 'foundation'. Lay the bricks while the concrete is still wet, holding them in place temporarily with a staked board while you pack more concrete behind the edging. When the concrete has set, remove the board and lay hardcore and sand in the excavation.

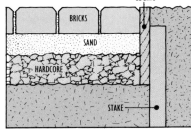

1 Wooden retaining edge

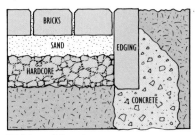

2 Brick retaining edge

SEE ALSO

Details for: ▷	
Engineering bricks	421
Brick bonding	426
Fall for patios and drives	440
Erecting formwork	442
Laying hardcore	443
Preservatives	250
Damp-proof course	251
Mixing concrete	439

Brick pavers
Clay brick pavers (top row) are made in a wide variety of colours and textures. *Concrete pavers* (bottom row) are less colourful but more shapes are available.

SEE ALSO

◁ Details for:
Cutting bricks	428
Retaining edges	449
Brick pavers	449
Providing a base	449

LAYING THE BRICKS

Having chosen your bricks, prepared the ground and set retaining edges (◁) you can start laying your paving. When bricks are first laid upon the sand they should project 10mm (⅜in) above the edging restraints to allow for bedding them in at a later stage (1). To level the sand for a path, cut a notched spreader to span the edging (2). If the paving is too wide for a spreader, lay levelling battens on the hardcore base and scrape the sand to the required depth using a straightedge (3). Remove the battens and fill the voids carefully with sand. Keep the sand bed dry at all times. If it rains before you can lay the bricks, either let the sand dry out thoroughly or replace it with dry sand.

Lay an area of bricks on the sand to your chosen pattern. Work from one end of the site, kneeling on a board placed across the bricks (4). Never stand on the bed of sand. Lay whole bricks only, leaving any gaps at the edges to be filled with cut bricks after you have laid an area of about 1 to 2sq m (1 to 2sq yd). Concrete bricks have fixed spacers, so butt them together tightly.

Fill any remaining spaces with bricks cut with a bolster (◁). If you are paving a large area you can hire an hydraulic guillotine (see left).

When the area of paving is complete, tamp the bricks into the sand bed by striking a stout batten with a heavy club hammer. The batten must be large enough to cover several bricks to maintain the level (5). For a really professional finish, hire a powered plate vibrator. Pass the vibrator over the paved area two or three times until it has worked the bricks down into the sand and flush with the outer edging (6). The act of vibrating bricks works sand up between them, but complete the job by brushing more sand across the finished paving and vibrate the sand into the open joints.

Plain concrete-brick drive and parking space

Mottled-brick garden path

Interlocking concrete pavers

Bricks laid to a herringbone pattern

Cutting bricks
Hire an hydraulic brick-cutting guillotine to cut pavers.

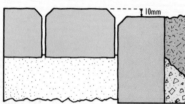
1 Start by laying bricks 10mm above edging

2 Level the sand with a notched spreader

3 Or lay levelling battens on the hardcore

4 Lay the bricks to your chosen pattern

5 Tamp the bricks with a hammer and batten

6 A vibrator levels brick paving perfectly

COBBLESTONES AND GRAVEL

Areas of cobblestones and gravel are used more for their decorative quality than as functional paving for drives or pathways. Cobbles, in particular, are most uncomfortable to walk on and, although a firmly consolidated area of gravel is fine for vehicles, walking on a gravel footpath can be rather like treading water. Both materials come into their own, however, when used as a foil for areas of flat paving slabs or bricks, and to set off plants such as dwarf conifers and heathers while keeping weed growth to a minimum.

Laying cobbles

Cobbles, large flint pebbles found on many a beach, can be laid loose, perhaps with larger rocks and plants. However, they are often set in mortar or concrete to create formal areas of texture.

Consolidate a layer of hardcore (▷) and cover it with a levelled layer of dry concrete mix about 50mm (2in) deep (▷). Press the cobbles into the dry mix, packing them tightly together and projecting well above the surface. Use a stout batten to tamp the area level (**1**). Then lightly sprinkle the whole area with water, both to set off the concrete hardening process and to clean the surfaces of the cobbles.

Large cobbles as a background to plants

1 Tamp the cobbles into a dry concrete mix

Laying gravel

If an area of gravel is to be used as a pathway or for motor vehicles, construct retaining edges of brick, concrete kerbs or wooden boards as for brick paths (▷). This will stop gravel being spread outside its allotted area.

To construct a gravel drive, the sub-base and the gravel itself must be compacted and levelled to prevent cars skidding and churning up the material. Lay a 100mm (4in) bed of firmed hardcore (▷) topped with 50mm (2in) of very coarse gravel mixed with sand. Roll it flat. Rake an 18 to 25mm (¾ to 1in) layer of fine 'pea' gravel across the sub-base and roll it down to make firm.

Making a gravel garden

To lay an area of gravel for planting, simply excavate the soil to accept a 25mm (1in) deep bed of fine gravel. Either set the gravel 18mm (¾in) below the level of the lawn or edge the gravel garden with bricks or flat stones. Scrape away a small area of gravel for planting, then sprinkle it back again to cover the soil surrounding and right up to the plant itself.

Gravel and conifer garden ▶

COARSE GRAVEL AND SAND
HARDCORE
PEA GRAVEL

Rake pea gravel across the surface of a drive

WOODEN PATHWAYS

If you live in a rural district where large logs are plentiful or perhaps a mature tree has been felled in your garden, you can use 150mm (6in) lengths of sawn timber set on end to make a practical and charming footpath. Either lay the logs together like crazy paving or use large individual pieces of wood as stepping stones. Hold wood rot at bay by soaking the sawn sections in buckets of chemical preservative.

Laying a log pathway

Excavate the area of the pathway to a depth of 200mm (8in) and spread a 50mm (2in) deep layer of gravel and sand mix across the bottom. Use concreting ballast—combined aggregate— or make up the mix yourself (▷). Level the bed by scraping and tamping with a straightedge.

Place the logs on end on the bed, arranging them to create a pleasing combination of shapes and sizes (**1**). Work them into the sand until they stand firmly and evenly, then pour more sand and gravel between them (**2**). Brush the material across the pathway in all directions until the gaps between the logs are filled flush with the surface (**3**). If any logs stand proud so that they could cause someone to trip, tap them down with a heavy hammer.

If you want to plant between the logs, scrape out some sand and gravel and replace it with the appropriate soil.

1 Arrange the logs on end

2 Shovel sand and gravel mix between the logs

3 Brush more mix into the joints

SEE ALSO

Details for: ▷

Combined aggregate	438
Concrete mixes	441
Laying hardcore	443
Path edging	449
Preservatives	250

● **Use a heavy roller**
A lightweight garden roller is fine for compacting earth or sand, but use one weighing about 100kg (2cwt) when levelling hardcore.

SEE ALSO

◁ Details for:
Edging 449

● **Laying a new path**
Although cold cure tarmac is primarily a resurfacing material, it can be applied to a new hardcore base as long as it is firmly compacted, levelled and sealed with a slightly more generous coat of bitumen emulsion.

● **Treating for heavy wear**
At entrances to drives and on bends, vehicle tyres cause more wear than normal. Treat these areas with an 18mm (¾in) rolled layer of cold cure tarmac (See far right) before applying a dressing of stone chippings.

● **Double dressing**
If the surface you are dressing is in a very poor condition or exceptionally loose, apply a first coat of bitumen emulsion at 4kg per sq m (3.3kg per sq yd). Cover with chippings and roll thoroughly. Two days later, sweep away loose chippings and apply a second coat of emulsion at 1.8kg per sq m (1.56kg per sq yd) and finish with chippings as described right.

DRESSING WITH STONE CHIPPINGS

As an alternative to tarmac, completely resurface a path or drive with natural stone chippings embedded in fresh bitumen emulsion. Chippings in various colours are available in 25kg (55lb) sacks which cover about 2.5sq m (3sq yd). Apply weedkiller and fill potholes as for tarmac (See right).

Bitumen emulsion sets by evaporation in about 12 hours, but until that time it is not completely waterproof so check the weather forecast to avoid wet conditions. You can lay emulsion on a damp surface but not on one that is icy.

Apply emulsion, available in 25 to 200kg (55 to 440lb) drums, according to the type of base you are surfacing.

SURFACE	BITUMEN EMULSION
Concrete and smooth surfaces	1.4kg per sq m (1.19kg/2.6 lb per sq yd)
Other firm, dense surfaces	1.6kg per sq m (1.56kg/3.43 lb per sq yd)
Open textured, loose surfaces	4kg per sq m (3.3kg/7.25 lb per sq yd)

Decant the emulsion into a bucket to make it easier to pour onto the surface, brushing it out, not too thinly, with a stiff broom as for laying tarmac (See right). Having brushed out one bucket of emulsion, spread the stone chippings evenly with a spade. Hold the spade horizontally just above the surface and gently shake the chippings off the edge of the blade (1). Don't pile them too thickly, but make sure the emulsion is covered completely. Cover an area of about 5sq m (5sq yd), then roll the chippings down. When the entire area is covered, roll it once more. If traces of bitumen show between the chippings, mask them with a little sharp sand and roll again. (See margin notes left for applying dressing to heavy–wear areas.)

You can walk or drive on the dressed surface immediately. One week later, gently sweep away any surplus chippings. Patch any bare areas by re-treating them with emulsion and chippings.

1 Sprinkle a layer of chippings with a spade

RESURFACING WITH TARMAC

Smarten up an old tarmac path or drive, or any basically sound but unsightly paved area, by resurfacing with cold cure tarmac. It makes a serviceable surface and is ready to lay from the sack. Roll the tarmac flat with a heavy garden roller – a light roller will do, but you will have to make extra passes.

Choosing the materials

Choose between red or black tarmac. It is available in 25kg (55lb) sacks – this will cover about 0.9sq m (10sq ft) at a thickness of 12mm (½in). Each sack contains a separate bag of decorative stone chippings for embedding in the soft tarmac as an alternative finish. Cold cure tarmac can be laid in any weather but it is much easier to level and roll flat on a warm, dry day. If you have to work in cold weather, store the materials in a warm place the night before laying. While not essential, edging the tarmac with bricks, concrete kerbs or wooden boards (◁) will improve the appearance of the finished surface.

Preparing the surface

Pull up all weeds and grass growing between the old paving, then apply a strong weedkiller to the surface two days before you lay the tarmac. Sweep the area clean, and level any potholes by first cutting the sides vertical, then remove dust and debris from the hole. Paint with bitumen emulsion, supplied by the tarmac manufacturer. Wait for it to turn black before filling the hole with 18mm (¾in) layers of tarmac, compacting each layer until the surface is level.

Apply a tack coat of bitumen emulsion to the entire surface to make a firm bond between the new tarmac and the old paving. Mask surrounding walls, kerb stones and manhole covers. Stir the emulsion with a stick before pouring it from its container, then spread it thinly with a stiff-bristled broom. Try not to splash, and avoid leaving puddles, especially at the foot of a slope. Leave the tack coat to set for about 20 minutes and, in the meantime, wash the broom in hot, soapy water. Don't apply the tack coat when it is likely to rain.

Apply a tack coat of bitumen emulsion

Applying the tarmac

Rake the tarmac to make a layer about 18mm (¾in) thick (1), using a straightedge to scrape the surface flat. Press down any stubborn lumps with your foot. Spread the contents of no more than three sacks before the initial rolling. Keep the roller wet (2) to avoid picking up specks of tarmac. Don't run the roller onto grass or gravel or you may roll particles into the tarmac.

Spread and roll tarmac over the whole area, then achieve the final compaction by rolling it thoroughly in several directions. Lightly scatter the chippings (3) prior to the final pass.

You can walk on the tarmac immediately, but avoid wearing high-heeled shoes. Don't drive on it for a day or two, and leave a note on the gate to warn the window cleaner to spread the load by placing a board under the ladder. You should always protect tarmac from oil and petrol spillage, but take special care while the surface is fresh.

1 Level the tarmac

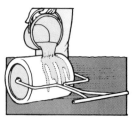
2 Keep the roller wet

3 Scatter chippings

BUILDING GARDEN STEPS

Designing a garden for a sloping site is an exciting challenge. It offers many possibilities for interesting changes of level by terracing areas of paving or with planting beds held in place with retaining walls (▷), but to move safely from one level to another requires at least one flight of steps.

Designing steps

If you are fortunate enough to own a large garden, and the slope is very gradual, a series of steps with wide treads and low risers can make an impressive feature. If the slope is steep, you can avoid a 'staircase' appearance by constructing a flight of steps composed of a few treads interposed with wide, flat landings, at which points the flight can change direction to add further interest and offer a different viewpoint of the garden. In fact, a shallow flight can be virtually a series of landings, perhaps circular in plan, gradually sweeping up the slope in a curve.

The proportion of tread, the part you stand on, to riser, the vertical part of the step, is an important factor if using the steps is to be both safe and comfortable. As a rough guide, construct steps so that the depth of the tread (from front to back), plus twice the height of the riser, equals 650mm (2ft 2in). For example, 300mm (1ft) treads should be matched with 175mm (7in) risers, 350mm (1ft 2in) treads with 150mm (6in) risers and so on. Never make treads less than 300mm (1ft) deep or risers higher than 175mm (7in).

Garden steps built with natural stone

Using concrete slabs

Concrete paving slabs in their various forms (▷) are ideal for making firm, flat treads for garden steps. Construct the risers from concrete facing blocks or bricks, allowing the treads to overhang by 25 to 50mm (1 to 2in) to cast an attractive shadow line which also defines the edge of the step.

Measure the difference in height from the top of the slope to the bottom to gauge the number of steps required. Mark the position of the risers with pegs and roughly shape the steps in the soil as confirmation **(1)**.

Either lay concrete slabs, bedded in sand (▷), flush with the ground at the foot of the slope or dig a trench to contain hardcore and a 100 to 150mm (4 to 6in) concrete base to support the first riser **(2)**. When the concrete has set, construct the riser using normal bricklaying methods (▷). Check its alignment with a spirit level **(3)**. Fill behind the riser with compacted hardcore until it is level, then lay the tread on a bed of mortar **(4)**. Using a spirit level as a guide, tap down the tread until it slopes very slightly towards its front edge to shed rainwater and so prevent ice forming in cold weather.

Measure from the front edge of the tread to mark the position of the next riser on the slabs **(5)**, and construct the step in the same way. Set the final tread flush with the area of paving, pathway or lawn at the top of the flight of steps.

Dealing with the sides

It is usually possible to landscape the slope at each side of the flight of steps, and turf or plant it to prevent the soil washing down onto the steps. Alternatively, extend the riser to edge each tread or build a wall or planter on each side of the steps. Another solution is to retain the soil with large stones, perhaps extending into a rockery on one or both sides.

1 Cut the shape of the steps in the soil

2 Dig the footing for the first riser

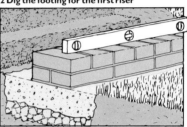

3 Build a brick riser and level it

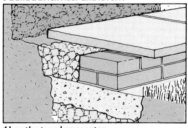

4 Lay the tread on mortar

5 Mark the position of the next riser.

SEE ALSO

Details for: ▷	
Laying bricks	428-429
Retaining walls	437
Paving slabs	446
Laying in sand	448
Mixing mortar	425
Footings	427

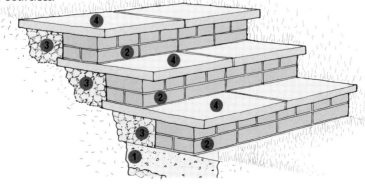

Concrete-slab steps
A section through a simple flight of garden steps built with bricks and concrete paving slabs.
1 Concrete footing
2 Brick-built riser
3 Hardcore infill
4 Concrete-slab tread

SEE ALSO

◁ Details for:
Foundation	427
Edging float	443
Laying hardcore	443
Tapered slabs	446
Crazy paving	448
Preservatives	250
Concrete mixes	441
Cold chisel	480

● **Dealing with slippery steps**
Algae will grow in damp conditions, especially under trees, and steps can become dangerously slippery if it is allowed to build up on the surfaces. Brush with a solution of 1 part household bleach: 4 parts water. After 48 hours, wash with clean water and repeat if the fungal growth is heavy. You can also use a proprietary fungicidal solution but follow manufacturers' instructions carefully.

REPAIRING CONCRETE STEPS

Casting new steps in concrete needs such complicated formwork that the end result hardly justifies the amount of effort required, especially when better-looking steps can be constructed from cast concrete slabs and blocks. Nevertheless, if you have a flight of concrete steps in your garden you will want to keep them in good condition. Like other forms of masonry, concrete suffers from spalling, where frost breaks down the surface and flakes off fragments of material. It occurs a great deal along the front edges of steps where foot traffic adds to the problem. Repair broken edges as soon as you can. Not only are they ugly, but the steps are not as safe as they might be.

Building up broken edges
Wearing safety goggles, chip away concrete around the damaged area and provide a good grip for fresh concrete. Cut a board to match the height of the riser and prop it against the step with bricks (1). Mix up a small batch of general-purpose concrete but add a little PVA bonding agent to help it stick to the damaged step. Dilute some bonding agent with water, say 3 parts water: 1 part bonding agent, and brush it onto the damaged area, stippling it into all the crevices. When the painted surface becomes tacky, fill the hole with concrete mix flush with the edge of the board (2). Radius the front edge slightly with a home-made edging float (◁), running it against the board (3).

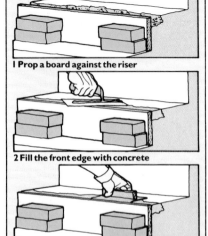
1 Prop a board against the riser

2 Fill the front edge with concrete

3 Run an edging float against the board

CURVED STEPS/LOG STEPS

Building curved steps

To build a series of curved steps, choose materials which will make the job as easy as possible. You can use tapered concrete slabs (◁) for the treads, designing the circumference of the steps to suit the proportions of the slabs. Or, you can construct the treads from crazy paving (◁), selecting fairly large stones for the front edge. Use bricks laid flat or on edge to build the risers. Set the bricks to radiate from the centre of the curve, and fill the slightly tapered joints with mortar.

Use a length of string attached to a peg driven into the ground as an improvised compass to mark out the curve of each step. Tie a batten to the string to help you gauge the front edge of the lower steps (1). Roughly shape the soil and lay a concrete foundation for the bottom riser (◁). Build risers and treads as for regular concrete slab steps, using the improvised string compass as a guide.

Building circular landings
To construct a circular landing, build the front edge with bricks and paving as for a curved step. When the mortar has set, fill the area of the landing with compacted hardcore (◁) and lay gravel up to the level of the tread (2).

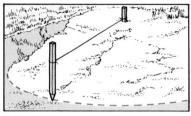
1 Mark the edge with an improvised compass

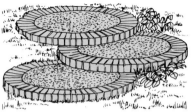
2 Circular landings made with bricks and gravel

Making log steps

For an informal garden, build steps from lengths of sawn timber soaked in a chemical preservative. Try to construct risers of a fairly regular height, otherwise someone might stumble if they are forced to break step. As it is not always possible to obtain uniform logs you may have to make up the height of the riser with two or more slimmer logs.

Cut a regular slope in the earth bank and compact the soil by treading it down. Drive stakes cut from 75mm (3in) diameter logs into the ground, one at each end of a step (1). Place one heavy log behind the stakes, bedding it down in the soil (2), and pack hardcore behind it to construct the tread of the step (3). Shovel a layer of gravel on top of the hardcore to finish the step.

If large logs are in short supply, build a step from two or three slim logs, holding them against the stakes with hardcore as you construct the riser (4).

Log-built garden steps

1 Drive a stake at each end of a step

2 Place a log behind the stakes

3 Fill behind the log with hardcore

4 Make up a riser with two slim logs

CREATING WATER GARDENS

There is nothing like still or running water to enliven a garden. Cascades and fountains have an almost mesmeric fascination – it is practically impossible to take your eyes off them – and the sound of trickling water has a charming, soothing effect. Even a small area of still water will support all manner of interesting pond life and plants, with the additional bonus of the mirrored images of trees, rocks and sky reflected in its placid surface.

Pond liners

It is not by chance that the number of garden ponds has increased over recent years. There is no doubt that their popularity is due largely to the emergence of simply installed rigid and flexible pond liners, making it possible to create a complete water garden in return for a few days' work.

In the past it was necessary to line a pond with concrete. While it is true that concrete is a very versatile material, there is always the possibility of a leak developing through cracks caused by ground movement or the force of expanding ice. There are no such worries with flexible liners. In addition to the labour and expense involved in building formers for a concrete pond, it must be left to season for about a month, during which time it must be emptied and refilled a number of times to ensure that the water will be safe for fish and plant life. But you can introduce plants to a plastic- or rubber-lined pool as soon as the water itself has matured, which takes no more than a few days.

Ordering a flexible liner

Use a simple formula to calculate the size of liner you will need. Disregard the actual plan and ignore the size and shape of planting shelves. Simply take the overall length and width of the pond and add twice the maximum depth to each dimension to arrive at the size of the liner. If possible, adapt your design to fall within the nearest stock liner size.

POND DIMENSIONS	
Length - 3m	9ft 9in
Width - 2m	6ft 6in
Depth - 450mm	1ft 6in
SIZE OF LINER	
3m + 0.900m = 3.9m	9ft 9in + 3 ft = 12ft 9in
2m + 0.900m = 2.9m	6ft 6in + 3 ft = 9ft 9in

SEE ALSO

Details for: ▷	
Installing pond liners	456-457
Building a waterfall	459

Garden pond
A well-planted water garden surrounded by flowering shrubs looks like a natural pond.

CHOOSING A POND LINER

The advantages of proprietary pond liners over concrete are fairly clear, but there are still a number of options to choose from, depending on the size and shape of the pond you wish to create and how much you propose to spend.

RIGID LINERS

Regular garden-centre visitors will be familiar with the range of pre-formed plastic pond liners. The best liners are made from rigid glass-reinforced plastic which is very strong and resistant to the effects of frost or ice. As long as they are handled with reasonable care and installed correctly, rigid plastic pools are practically puncture- and leak-proof.

Rigid pond liner
Rigid liners are moulded using glass-reinforced plastic.

SEMI-RIGID LINERS

Semi-rigid liners, made from vacuum-formed plastic, are cheaper than those made from glass fibre, but the range of sizes is very limited. However, they make ideal reservoirs or header pools for the top of a cascade or waterfall.

Rectangular or irregular-shaped liners are available in rigid or semi-rigid plastic, and a very acceptable water garden can be created with a carefully selected series of pond liners linked by watercourses.

FLEXIBLE LINERS

For complete freedom of design, choose a flexible-sheet liner designed to stretch and hug the contours of a pond of virtually any shape and size. In addition, a pond made with even the most expensive sheet liner is cheaper to construct and guaranteed to last longer than an equivalent rigid plastic liner.

Polythene liners, once the only type of flexible liner on the market, are still available but they are relatively fragile, and should be considered only for temporary pools, and even then, they should be lined with a double thickness of material. PVC liners, especially those reinforced with nylon, are guaranteed for up to 10 years of normal use, but if you want your pond to last for 50 years or more, choose a synthetic rubber membrane based on butyl. Not all butyl liners are of the same quality, so buy one from a reputable manufacturer offering a 20 year written guarantee if you want the very best product. Black and stone-coloured butyl liners are made in a wide range of stock sizes up to 6.5 x 9m (22 x 30ft) but larger liners are made to order.

Flexible liners
Best-quality flexible liners are made from butyl.

DESIGNING A POND

SEE ALSO

◁ Details for:
Rigid liners   455
Flexible liners   455
Building a rockery   459

A pond must be sited correctly if it is to have any chance of maturing into an attractive, clear stretch of water. Never place a pond under deciduous trees. Falling leaves will pollute the water as they decay, causing fish to become ill and even die. Laburnum trees are especially poisonous.

Positioning for sunlight

A pond must receive plenty of daylight. Although sunlight promotes the growth of algae, which causes ponds to turn a pea-green colour, it is also necessary to encourage the growth of other water plant life. An abundant growth of oxygenating plants will compete with the algae for the mineral salts and, with shade provided by floating and marginal plants, will keep the pond clear.

Size and shape

The proportion of the pond is important in creating harmony between plants and fish. It is difficult to maintain the right conditions for clear water in a pond less than 3.75sq m (40sq ft) in surface area, but the volume of water is even more vital. A pond up to about 9sq m (100sq ft) in area should be 450mm (1ft 6in) deep. As the area increases you will have to dig deeper to about 600mm (2ft) or more, but it is rarely necessary to go below 750mm (2ft 6in).

A flexible liner will conform better to simple curves, but the section or profile must be designed to fulfil certain requirements. To grow marginal plants, you will need a 225mm (9in) wide shelf around the edge of the pond, 225mm (9in) below the surface of the water. This will take a standard 150mm (6in) planting crate with ample water above, and you can always raise the crate on pieces of paving or bricks. The sides of the pond should slope at about 20 degrees to prevent soil collapse during construction and to allow the liner to stretch without promoting too many creases. It will also allow a sheet of ice to float upwards without damaging the liner. Judge the angle by measuring 75mm (3in) inwards for every 225mm (9in) of depth. If the soil is very sandy, increase the angle of slope slightly for extra stability.

Accommodating a sloping site

On a sloping site build up the low side with earth, turfing up to the paving surround. Cut back the higher side and build a low retaining wall, or bed stones against the earth to create a rockery.

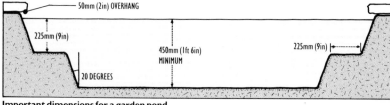

Important dimensions for a garden pond

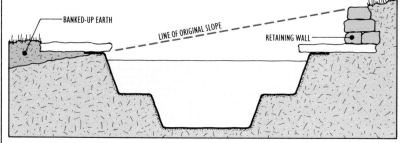

Accommodating a sloping site

Installing a rigid liner

Stand a rigid liner in position and prop it up with cardboard boxes, both to check its orientation and to mark its perimeter on the ground. Use a spirit level to plot key points on the ground **(1)** and mark them with small pegs. You will need to dig outside this line, so absolute accuracy is not required.

As you move the topsoil, either take it away in a wheelbarrow or pile it close by ready to incorporate into a rockery. Lay a straightedge across the top and measure the depth of the excavation **(2)** including marginal shelves. Keep the excavation as close as possible to the shape of the liner, but extend it by 150mm (6in) on all sides. Compact the base and cover it with a 25mm (1in) deep level of sharp sand. Lower the liner down and bed it firmly into the sand. Check that the pool stands level **(3)** and wedge it temporarily with wooden battens until the back–fill of soil or sand can hold it.

Start to fill the liner with tapwater from a hose and, at the same time, pour sifted soil or sand behind the liner **(4)**. There is no need to hurry as it will take some time to fill, but keep pace with the level of the water. Reach into the excavation and pack soil under the marginal shelves with your hands.

When the liner is firmly bedded in the soil, either finish the edge with stones as for a flexible liner (See opposite) or re-lay turf to cover the rim of the liner.

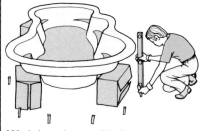

1 Mark the perimeter of the liner

2 Measure the depth of the excavation

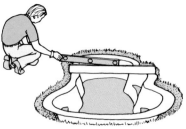

3 Make sure the liner stands level

4 Infill with sifted soil or sand

CONSTRUCTING A POND: FLEXIBLE LINER

Excavating the pond

Mark out the shape of the pond on the ground. A garden hose is useful for trying out curvilinear shapes. Excavate the pond to the level of the planting shelf, then mark and dig out the deeper sections (1). Remove sharp stones and roots from the sides and base to make sure they won't puncture the liner.

The top of the pond must be level, and the surrounding stone or concrete slabs must be 18mm (¾in) below the turf. For both reasons, cut back the turf

to accommodate the stones and then drive wooden datum pegs into the exposed surround every metre or so (3 to 4ft). Level the tops of all the pegs using a straightedge (2) and check the level across the pond as well. Remove or pack earth around the pegs until the compacted soil is level below the pegs.

When the surround is level, remove the pegs and spread 12mm (½in) of slightly damp sand over the base and sides of the excavation (3).

Installing a flexible liner

Drape the liner across the excavation with an even overlap all round, and hold it in place with bricks while you fill the pond with water from a hose (4). It will take several hours to fill a large pond, but check it regularly, moving the bricks as the liner stretches. A few creases are inevitable around sharp curves but you will lose most of them by keeping the

liner fairly taut and easing it into shape as the water rises. Turn off the water when the level reaches about 50mm (2in) below the edge of the pond. Cut off surplus liner with scissors, leaving a 150mm (6in) overlap all round (5). Push 100mm (4in) nails through the overlap into the soil so that the liner cannot slip while you place the edging stones.

Building the surround

Lay flat stones dry at first, selecting those which follow the shape of the pond with a reasonably close fit between them. Let the stones project over the water by about 50mm (2in) to cast a deep shadow line and reflection. Cut stones to fit the gaps behind the larger edging stones with a bolster (▷). Lift the stones one or two at a time and

bed them on two or three strategically placed mounds of mortar mixed with 1 part cement: 3 parts soft sand (6). Tap the stones level with a mallet and fill the joints with a trowel. Smooth the joints flush with an old paintbrush. Do not drop mortar in the water or you will have to empty and refill the pond before you introduce fish or plants.

INCORPORATING A DRAIN

The recommended water level for a pond is about 50mm (2in) below the edging stones, but in exceptional circumstances such as a heavy storm, or if you forget to turn off the water when topping up, the water can rise fast enough to spill over and flood the garden. As a precaution, build a drain beneath the edging stones to allow excess water to escape. Not only does a drain prevent a flood, it provides a means of running electric cable into the pond to power a pump or lighting. Cut corrugated plastic sheet into two strips 150mm (6in) wide and long enough to run under the edging stones. Pop-rivet the strips together to make a channel about 25mm (1in) deep (1). Scrape earth and sand from beneath the liner to accommodate the channel (2), then lay edging stones on top to hold it in place. Dig a small soakaway behind the channel and fill it with rubble topped with fine gravel or turf up to the level of the stones.

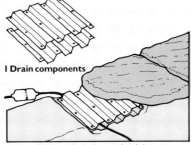

1 Drain components

2 Place finished drain beneath edging stones

SEE ALSO

Details for: ▷	
Cutting slabs	447
Running cable to pond	333
Pumps	458

1 Dig the excavation as accurately as possible

2 Level the edge using datum pegs

3 Line the excavation with damp sand

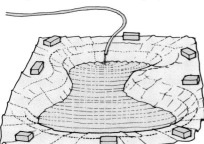

4 Stretch the liner by filling the pond

5 Cut the flexible liner to fit

6 Lay edging stones to complete the pond

MAKING A RAISED-EDGE POND

You can build a formal pond with a raised edge using bricks or concrete facing blocks. An edging about 450mm (1ft 6in) high is safer for small children while also providing seating. If you *prefer a low wall, say 225mm (9in) high, create planting shelves at ground level, digging the pond deeper in the centre. Place planting crates on blocks around the edge of a deep raised pond.*

SEE ALSO

◁ Details for:

Low-voltage wiring	333
Footings	427
Pond drain	457
Qualified electrician	289
Bricks	421-422
Concrete blocks	423-424
Laying bricks	428-429
Flexible liners	455

Building the pond

Lay 100 to 150mm (4 to 6in) concrete footings (◁) to support the walls, which are constructed from two skins of masonry set apart to match the width of flat coping stones. Allow for an overhang of 50mm (2in) over the water's edge and lap the outer wall by 12 to 18mm (½ to ¾in). To save money, build the inner wall from plain concrete blocks or cheap common bricks, reserving more expensive and decorative bricks or facing blocks for the outer skin of the wall. Raised ponds can be lined with a standard flexible liner or you can order a pre-fabricated fitted liner to reduce the amount of creasing at the corners. Trap the edge of the liner under the coping stones.

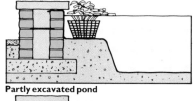
Partly excavated pond

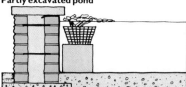
Fully raised pond built with a cavity wall

Raised-edge pond
A well-designed and constructed pond which is nicely integrated in a sloping site.

ALTERNATIVE POND EDGING

Edging a pond with flat stones provides a safe and attractive footpath for tending to water plants and fish, but a more natural setting is often required, particularly for small header pools in a rockery. Incorporate a shelf around the pond as for marginal plants, but this time for an edging of rocks. If you place them carefully there is no need to mortar them. Arrange rocks behind the edging to cover the liner (**1**).

To create a shallow, beach-like edging, slope the soil at a very shallow angle and lay large pebbles or flat rocks upon the liner. You can merge them with a rockery or let them form a natural water line (**2**).

To discourage neighbourhood cats poaching fish from a pond, create an edging of trailing plants. Without a firm foothold, no cat will attempt to reach into the water. Bed a strip of soft wire netting in the mortar below flat edging stones. Cut the strip to overhang the water by about 150mm (6in) as a support for the plants (**3**). Once the plants are established they will disguise the nature of the pool liner.

1 Rock-edged pond

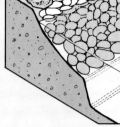
2 Pebble-strewn shelf

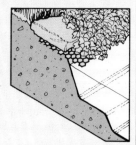
3 Wire edge holds plants

Pumps and fountains

Small submersible pumps for fountains and waterfalls are operated either directly from the mains electrical supply or through a transformer which reduces the voltage to 24 volts. Mains electricity and water can be fatal, so consult a qualified electrician if you plan to use a mains-operated pump. A low-voltage pump is perfectly safe and can be installed and wired simply (◁).

Place the pump in the water and run its electric cable beneath the edging stones, preferably via a drain (◁), to a waterproof connector attached to the extension lead of a transformer installed inside the house. This permits removal of the pump for servicing without disturbing the extension cable or transformer. Run pumps regularly, even in the winter months, to keep them in good working order, and clean both the pump and its filter according to the manufacturer's instructions.

There are so many waterfall pumps and fountain kits available that you should consult manufacturers' catalogues to find one that best suits your purpose. Place a submersible waterfall pump close to the edge of the pond so that you can reach it to disconnect the hose running to the waterfall when you need to service the pump. Stand fountain units on a flat stone or propped up on bricks so that the jet is vertical. Plant water lilies some distance away from a fountain as falling water will encourage the flowers to close up.

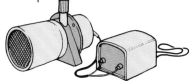
Low-voltage waterfall pump and transformer

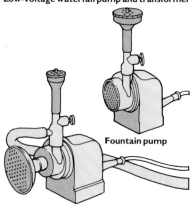
Fountain pump

Combination pump

BUILDING A ROCKERY AND WATERFALL

A waterfall, complemented by a rockery displaying clumps of alpines or graceful shrubs and trees such as Japanese maple or dwarf conifers, adds a further dimension to a water garden. The technique for building a series of watercourses is not as complicated as it may appear and, in doing so, you can also cover much of the groundwork needed for your rockery.

Materials

You will be surprised by the amount of soil produced by excavating a pond. To avoid the waste and trouble of transporting it to a local dump, use it to create your pool-side rockery. If you include a small reservoir on the higher ground you can pump water into it from the main pond to be returned via a trickling cascade or waterfall.

Soil you will have in plenty, but obtaining enough stones to give the impression of a real rocky outcrop can be very expensive, that is if you buy them from a local garden centre. A cheaper way is to use hollow, cast reproduction rocks, which surprisingly will eventually weather-in quite well. However, your best option is to buy natural stone direct from a quarry.

Real rocks can be extremely heavy, so have them delivered as close to the site as possible, and hire a strong trolley to move individual stones about the garden. A rockery and waterfall are actually built as one operation but for the sake of clarity, they are described separately here.

Creating a waterfall

So that the waterfall can discharge directly into the main pond, form a small inlet at the side of the pond by leaving a large flap of flexible liner. Build shallow banks at each side of the inlet and line it with stones (**1**). Create a stepped watercourse ascending in stages to the reservoir. Line the watercourse with off-cuts of flexible liner which must be overlapped on the face of each waterfall. Tuck the edge of each lower piece of liner under the edge of the piece above, and hold them in place with stones. To retain water in small pools along the watercourse, cut each step with a slope towards the rear (**2**), placing stones along the lip for the desired effect (**3**). A flat stone gives a sheet of water whereas a layer of pebbles produces a rippling cascade.

Test the watercourse as the construction work progresses by running water from a hose – it is difficult to adjust the angle of stones once the watercourse has been completed.

Bury the flexible hose from the waterfall pump in the rockery, making sure there are no sharp bends which would restrict the flow of water. Cut the hose so that it emerges at the edge of the reservoir and cover it with a flat stone (**4**) to hold and hide it.

A rigid plastic reservoir will have a lip moulded in an edge which will allow water to escape down the watercourse. If you construct a reservoir with flexible liner, however, shape the edge to form a low point and support a flat stone over the opening to hide the liner (**5**).

SEE ALSO

Details for: ▷	
Obtaining stone	424
Pond liners	455
Digging tools	480

Cascade or waterfall
This section shows a cascade or waterfall running from a reservoir to a pond.
1 Pond inlet.
2 Watercourse step.
3 Overhanging stone creates a sheet of water.
4 Hose from pump.
5 Reservoir outlet.
6 Reservoir

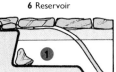

Constructing a rockery

Select and place each stone in a rockery to create an illusion of strata, or layers of rock. Stones placed haphazardly at odd angles tend to resemble a spoil heap rather than a natural outcrop. Take care not to strain yourself when lifting rocks. Keep your feet together and use your leg muscles to do the work, keeping your back as straight as possible. To move a particularly heavy rock, slip a rope around it (See left).

Lay large flat rocks to form the front edge of the rockery, placing soil behind and between them to form a flat, level platform. Compact the soil to make sure there are no air pockets which will damage the roots of plants. Lay subsequent layers of rock set back from the first, but not in a regular pattern. Place some to create steep embankments, others to form a gradual slope of wide steps. Pockets of soil for planting alpines or other small rockery plants will form naturally as you lay the stones, but plan larger areas of soil for specimen shrubs or dwarf trees.

Building a rockery
A rockery should have irregular rock 'steps' along its front edge.

AVOIDING STRAIN

Lifting stones
Keep your back straight when lifting heavy stones (Right). Use a rope to lift and place large rocks (Below)

Incorporating a bog garden

An area of wet, boggy soil where specialized waterside plants will flourish complements a pond perfectly. When you excavate the pond, make a wide planting shelf covered with the flexible liner. Place a row of stones to form the edge of the pond dividing the bog area from the deep water. Bed the stones in 50mm (2in) of mortar. When the mortar has set, its lime content must be neutralized by painting on a solution of

waterproof powder available from pond specialists. Follow manufacturers' instructions for its use.

Incorporate the bog garden into a rockery by lining the perimeter with stones, then fill the area with soil. The liner beneath the soil will retain enough moisture to keep the garden permanently damp, but make sure the planting bed is deep enough to ensure plants are not waterlogged.

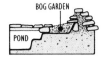

Bog garden
Construct a bog garden next to a pond for waterside plants.

CHOOSING A SWIMMING POOL

SEE ALSO
◁ Details for:
Official approval   18-19

Owning a private swimming pool is no longer the exclusive privilege of the rich and famous. Several specialist companies offer reasonably priced pool kits which you can install yourself following the manufacturer's detailed instructions. It is worth hiring professional help for deep excavations and to remove soil from the site, and anything but the most basic heating equipment should be installed by a qualified tradesperson. Most authorities do not insist on planning permission for the building of a private pool in your garden but it is required if you erect an enclosure over the pool. Once a pool is filled it requires very little water for topping up and maintenance but you may find it is advantageous to have a water meter fitted by your local water authority prior to the installation of your swimming pool.

Sunken-pool kits
Vinyl liners are used with block-built walls or a frame and panel construction.

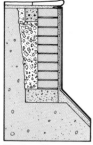

Block-wall construction

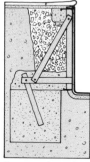

Frame and panel walling

● **Tiled concrete pools**
For a top-quality permanent pool, hire a professional contractor to install a reinforced-concrete structure. Hollow pool walls, constructed with cast-concrete sections, are filled with vibrated concrete, rendered and lined with polished marble or mosaic tiles.

A self-assembly pool
Swimming pools made from self-assembly kits are just as attractive as professionally installed pools but are a fraction of the cost.

Siting a swimming pool

The size and shape of a swimming pool is largely dictated by the area of your garden but it should be positioned away from trees so that it benefits from the sun and avoids falling leaves. Most people prefer to install a pool reasonably close to the house so that its facilities can be used to supply water, electricity and heating, and as the pool filtration plant must be housed, an existing building such as a garage can be utilized. It is normally easier to install a pool on a level site but you can partially bury one in a sloping bank and fill in the lower area with the excavated soil.

Above-ground pool kits

Above-ground pools are cheap and easy to erect. Most are circular or oval in plan, and are constructed by bolting together galvanized-steel panels and frame members. A heavy-duty vinyl liner and wide coping strips complete the basic pool. Above-ground pools are the least likely to be contaminated by wind-blown leaves and other debris, and they can be dismantled and moved when you buy another house. Young children cannot fall into the water once you have removed the steps. With some modification you can partially bury an above-ground pool and bank the excavated soil around the sides.

Sunken-pool kits

Sunken pools, in a wide range of shapes and sizes, can be built using pre-fabricated panels similar to those used for above-ground pools. The wall panels, anchored in concrete, line the perimeter of the pool to a depth of about 1m (3ft 3in). A deeper hopper-shaped excavation at one end of the pool is rendered with a sand and cement mix before a fitted vinyl liner is installed. The pool walls are back-filled with gravel to balance the water pressure, and an edging of shaped coping stones is bedded in mortar.

Similar pools are built using standard concrete blocks laid on a concrete footing to construct the walls. The walls and floor of the pool are rendered to present a smooth face to the vinyl liner. You could hire a local builder to construct and render the walls and excavation, then back-fill and line the pool yourself.

A swimming-pool liner will last for years but, should one become damaged accidentally, it can be patched without having to empty the pool.

SWIMMING-POOL ACCESSORIES

Some accessories like diving boards, water chutes and underwater lights merely add to the enjoyment of your pool. Others are absolutely essential to keep the water pure.

Skimmer and filter
A pump-operated skimmer built into the side of a swimming pool sucks lightweight floating debris into a filter housed outside the pool. The filtered water is returned to the pool via a separate inlet. The entire unit is supplied with most pool kits.

Pool vacuum cleaner
You will need a special vacuum cleaner to remove the heavier debris that sinks to the bottom of the pool. Its hose connects to the pool-side skimmer.

Leaf net
Buy a net attached to a long pole to periodically remove floating leaves which might clog the filter.

Pool cover
Lightweight woven covers are available for above-ground and sunken pools to keep leaves, twigs and other wind-blown debris out of the water during the winter months.

Test equipment
Chlorine or other chemicals must be added to the water at regular intervals to kill harmful bacteria and algae but the water must be analysed to maintain an effective chemical balance. Pool kits are supplied with simple test equipment which allows you to analyse water samples yourself.

Heating the water
Floating thermal blankets, which are removed prior to swimming, provide the cheapest method of raising the temperature of the water. They are essential to reduce the cost of heating the water by more sophisticated equipment. You can install a heat exchanger which uses heat produced by the house central-heating boiler or a separate boiler used exclusively for the pool. Both methods are expensive. Solar panels or mats provide free heat but installation costs are high. A heat pump which extracts heat from the surrounding air, even during a cloudy day, is probably the most effective way to heat a swimming pool.

11

WOODWORKER'S TOOLS   462
BASIC WOODWORKING JOINTS   475
BUILDER'S TOOLS   478
DECORATOR'S TOOLS   481
PLUMBER'S/METALWORKER'S TOOLS   486
ELECTRICIAN'S TOOLS   492

TOOLS & SKILLS

SEE ALSO

◁ Details for:
Woodworking joints   475

A TOOL KIT IS PERSONAL

If you talk to people who make a living using tools you'll find that they guard them jealously, are loath to lend them and even less likely to borrow them. Tools are very personal. The way a person uses or sharpens a tool, even his or her working stance, will shape and modify it until it works better for its owner than in other hands. This is particularly noticeable with old wooden tools. If you examine the sole of a well-used wooden jack plane, for example, you will see that it has worn unevenly to suit the style of one craftsman. Even the handle of a new plane feels unfamiliar after the feel of a plane you've used for years.

The choice of tools is equally personal. No two professionals' tool kits are identical and each might select different tools to do the same job. The tools shown and described in these pages will enable you to tackle all but the more specialized tasks involved in maintaining, repairing, extending and decorating your home and garden, but the final choice is yours.

No one buys a complete kit of tools all at once. Apart from the considerable cost it makes more sense to buy tools as you need them. You may prefer to do your own decorating but hire a professional for electrical work, in which case you are better off spending your money on good-quality brushes, rollers or scrapers than spreading it thinly on a wider range of cheaper tools. Consequently we have listed the essential tools for each 'trade' under specific headings – plumber's tool kit, decorator's tool kit and so on. But a great many tools are common to all trades, and you'll find it necessary to buy only a few extra tools as you tackle a growing range of activities.

Even hand tools are expensive, but buy the best you can afford, for top-quality tools are always a wise investment. Not only will they perform well but if they are used, stored and maintained properly they will last a lifetime. Power tools are especially expensive, so unless you plan to use them regularly it may be more economical to hire them. Make sure that hired tools are in good condition and ask for a set of written instructions or a demonstration before you leave the shop.

It is impossible to produce first-class work with blunt cutting tools, and they are more dangerous than sharp ones. Keep the blades in good condition and discard disposable ones when they no longer cut smoothly and easily. You'll find instructions for sharpening and maintaining hand tools, but have your power tools serviced professionally.

WOODWORKER'S TOOL KIT

A full tool kit for woodworking is enormous, but for general home maintenance you can make do with a fairly limited one. The most essential tools are listed in the page margin as a guide to building up a basic kit.

TOOLS FOR MEASURING AND MARKING

Take care of your measuring and marking tools. Thrown carelessly into a tool box, squares can be knocked out of true and gauges can become blunt and inaccurate.

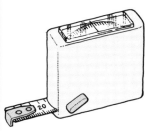

Tape measure and folding rule
A folding boxwood rule is the traditional cabinet-maker's tool for measuring, but a modern retractable steel tape measure is more versatile. Some can take measurements up to about 5m (16ft), including internal ones using the tip of the tape and the back of the case. The tape can be locked open at any point. Avoid letting the spring-loaded tape snap back into its case or the riveted hook on its end will become loose.

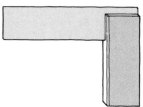

Try square
A try square is used to check the accuracy of square joints and planed timber, also for marking out timber which is to be sawn or cut 'square' to its edge. Look for a try square with its blade and stock (handle) cut from one L-shaped piece of metal. One with a straight blade riveted to the stock may lose its accuracy. Some try squares have the top of the stock cut at 45 degrees for marking out mitre joints. Buy the largest square you can afford. They come with blades up to 300mm (1ft) long.

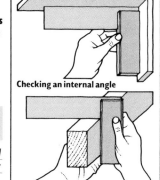

Checking an internal angle

Checking planed timber
View the work against the light to check that you are planing square.

Combination square
A combination square is a very versatile tool. Essentially a try square, but instead of a fixed blade it has a calibrated rule that slides in the stock to make a blade of any length up to 250mm (10in). This works as a useful depth and marking gauge. The head has an angled face for marking mitres and incorporates a small spirit level for checking vertical and horizontal surfaces.

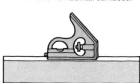

Checking horizontals
Remove the blade and place the stock face on the horizontal surface.

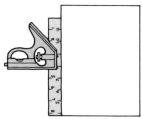

Checking verticals
Place the blade against a vertical face and read the spirit level to check its accuracy.

Sliding or adjusting bevel
A sliding bevel is used like a standard try square but its blade can be adjusted to 'take' and mark any angle.

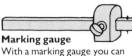

Marking knife

Before sawing timber mark the cutting lines with a knife. It is more accurate than a pencil and prevents the grain breaking out when you saw. The blade of a marking knife is ground on only one side, and its flat face is run against the square or bevel.

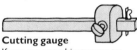

Marking gauge

With a marking gauge you can score a line parallel to an edge. Set the movable stock the required distance from the pin in the beam. Press the face of the stock against the edge of the timber, tilt the gauge to an angle, the pin touching the wood's surface, then push the tool away from you to scribe the line.

Cutting gauge

If you use a marking gauge to score a line across the grain of the wood the pin will tear the surface. A cutting gauge is designed for the purpose, and has a sharp blade in place of the pin. The blade is held in the beam with a removable wedge.

Mortise gauge

A mortise gauge has two pins, one fixed and the other movable, for marking the parallel sides of mortise and tenon joints. First set the points apart the width of the mortise chisel, then adjust the stock to place the mortise the required distance from the edge of the wood. Having marked the limits of the mortise with a try square (1), score the two lines with the gauge (2). With the same setting mark the tenon on the rail.

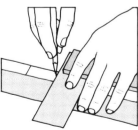

1 Mark the limits of mortise

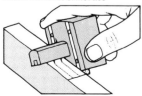

2 Score the lines

SAWS

Don't try to make do with just one or two saws in your kit. The right tool for the job will make for fast and accurate cutting.

HANDSAWS

Handsaws are a family of saws with flexible, unsupported blades. They are for converting solid timber and man-made boards. They differ mainly in the ways that their teeth are shaped and sharpened.

Ripsaw

The ripsaw is made specifically for cutting solid timber along its length ('ripping down'). Each of its teeth is like a tiny chisel that slices the timber along its grain. Alternate teeth are bent outward in opposite directions (set) so that the groove (kerf) cut in the timber is slightly wider than the thickness of the blade. Most saws are set in this way, or they would jam in the kerf.

Cross-cut saw

Unlike ripsaw teeth, which are filed square with the face of the blade, those of a cross-cut saw are filed at an angle to form points that score lines along both edges of the kerf before removing the wood between them. This allows the saw to cut across the grain of solid timber without tearing the fibres.

Panel saw

The teeth of a panel saw are set and shaped like those of a cross-cut but are smaller and closer together, and cut a finer kerf. The saw is used for cutting thin man-made boards like plywood and hardboard.

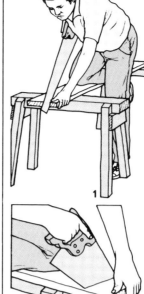

1

2

Using handsaws
Hold the saw with your forefinger extended towards the tip of the blade. This helps to keep the blade in line with your forearm and produce a straight cut.

To saw down the length of a board, support it on wooden trestles called sawhorses and start the cut at one end with short, light backward strokes only at first, to establish the kerf, while steadying the blade with the tip of your thumb against its flat face (1).

Continue cutting with slow, regular strokes, using the full length of the blade. Move the sawhorses as needed to allow the blade a clear path.

As you approach the end of the board, turn it round. Start a fresh cut at that end and saw back to meet the original kerf.

When cross-cutting, support the work with your free hand (2) and finish the cut with slow, gentle strokes to avoid breaking off the last uncut layer of wood.

STORING SAWS

Glue dowel pegs into a stout batten and screw it to the wall. Hang your saws from the pegs and protect their teeth with some plastic strip.

BACKSAWS

The blade of a backsaw is stiffened with a heavy metal strip folded over its top edge. Backsaws are for cutting narrow sections of timber to length and for cutting joints.

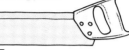

Tenon saw

A tenon saw has fine teeth shaped and set like those of a cross-cut saw. It is the perfect saw for general-purpose woodworking and is especially useful for cutting large joints.

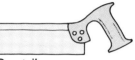

Dovetail saw

Because the tails and pins of a dovetail joint run with the grain the teeth of a dovetail saw are like miniature ripsaw teeth. Use this saw for fine cabinet work.

Gents saw

This cheap alternative to a dovetail saw has a straight wooden handle.

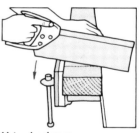

Using backsaws
Support the work in a vice or on a bench hook and hold the saw at a shallow angle to establish the kerf, gradually levelling the blade until you are sawing parallel to the face of the wood.

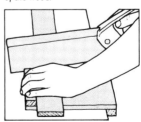

Using a bench hook
A bench hook, used in cross-cutting narrow sections of timber, hooks against the front edge of the workbench while the wood is held firmly against its top block.

SEE ALSO

Details for: ▷

Sharpening saws	464-465
Timber/man-made boards	494-495

● **Essential tools**
Tape measure
Combination square
Marking knife
Marking gauge
Cross-cut saw
Tenon saw

SEE ALSO

◁ Details for:
Handsaws   463
Backsaws   463
Flat file   490

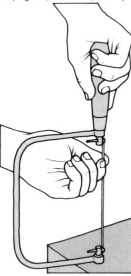

Using a mitre box
When you cut 45 degree mitre joints use a mitre box to guide your saw blade in slots set at that angle. Other slots, set at 90 degrees, can help you to cut square butt joints.

● **Essential tools**
Coping saw

464

FRAME SAWS

A frame saw is fitted with a very slim blade for cutting curves. To stop the blade bending it is held taut by the strong metal frame.

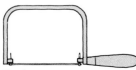

Coping saw
A coping saw is the most useful frame saw. Its teeth are coarse enough to cut fairly thick timber, yet it will cope with thin boards.

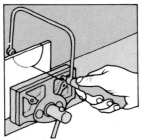

Using a coping saw
The blade is held between two pins that swivel so that you can turn it in the direction of the cut while keeping the frame out of the way.

Fitting a coping saw blade
A coping saw's blade is replaced when it gets blunt or breaks. Unscrew the handle a few turns anti-clockwise, hook the new blade into the pin furthest from the handle, press the frame down on the bench and locate the other end of the blade. Tension the blade by turning the handle clockwise. Make sure that the teeth point away from the handle and that the two pins are aligned so that the blade isn't twisted.

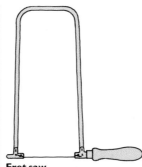

Fret saw
The blade of a fret saw is so fine that the spring of the frame alone keeps it under tension. The blade, its teeth pointing to the handle, is held at each end by a thumbscrew and plate.

Using a fret saw
Hold the work over the edge of the bench and saw with the blade upright, pulling on it from below.

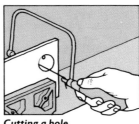

Cutting a hole
You can use a frame saw to cut a large hole in a piece of wood. Mark out the hole, drill a small one inside the outline, pass the blade through it and connect it to the saw frame. Cut out the hole, adjusting the angle of the blade to the frame as needed, then dismantle the saw to free the blade.

Padsaw or keyhole saw
A padsaw is for cutting holes in panels, but because of its relatively wide blade it is easier to use on straight cuts, in thick timber particularly. With no frame restricting its movement the saw can be used, for example, to cut the hole for a letterbox in a door. Take care not to bend the blade.

SHARPENING SAWS

A saw must be sharpened carefully with special tools if it is to cut properly, so you may prefer to have your saws sharpened by a professional, especially any that are finer than a tenon saw. If you want to keep the tools in tip-top condition yourself buy a saw file for sharpening the teeth and a saw set for bending them back to their correct angle.

Saw-sharpening tools
A saw file is double-ended and triangular in section. Its length should relate to the spacing of the saw's teeth, strictly speaking, but in practice you can use one file about 150mm (6in) long for handsaws and another 100mm (4in) long for a tenon saw. You can also buy a file guide, which locates over the saw's teeth and keeps the file at a constant angle while in use.

Closing the handles of a saw set squeezes the saw tooth between a plunger and an angled anvil which is first set to correspond with the number of tooth points per 25mm (1in) on the saw blade (**1**). To set the anvil, close the handle, release the locking screw at the end of the tool, turn the anvil until the required setting number on its edge aligns with the plunger, then tighten the locking screw.

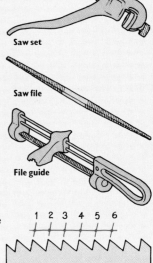

Saw set

Saw file

File guide

1 Count the points in 25mm

Topping a saw
*Topping restores all of a saw's teeth to the same height. It is not absolutely essential every time a saw is sharpened but a light topping will produce a spot of bright metal on each point that will help you to sharpen the teeth evenly. Near the top edge of a block of hardwood, plane a groove that will grip a smooth flat file (**2**). Clamp the saw, teeth up, between two battens in a vice, and with the wood block held against the flat of the blade, pass the file two or three times along the tops of the teeth (**3**) so that every one shows a tiny spot of bright metal.*

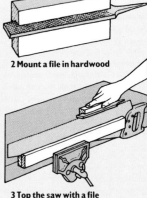

2 Mount a file in hardwood

3 Top the saw with a file

Setting the teeth
*Adjust the saw set to the right number of points (See above) and, starting at one end of the saw, place the set over the first tooth facing away from you, aligning the plunger with the centre of the tooth. Hold the set steady and squeeze the handles (**4**). Set every other tooth – those facing away – then turn the saw round and set those in between.*

Continued in next column

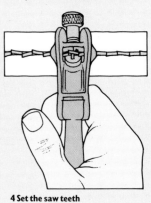

4 Set the saw teeth

SHARPENING SAWS

Sharpening the teeth
To sharpen a ripsaw, clamp the blade between the battens with its teeth projecting just above the edges of the wood. Starting next to the handle, place the saw file against the front edge of the first tooth facing away from you and settle it snugly into the space between the teeth (the gullet). With the file square to the flat of the blade (5) make two or three strokes until the edge of the tooth is shiny right up to its point and half of the bright topping spot has disappeared. File alternate teeth in this way, then turn the saw round and sharpen those in between until the bright spots are completely removed.

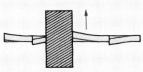

5 Filing ripsaw teeth

Sharpening a cross-cut saw
To sharpen a cross-cut saw use the same procedure but hold the file at an angle of 60 to 70 degrees to the flat of the blade (6) and with its handle slightly low.

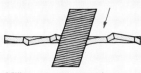

6 Filing cross-cut saw teeth

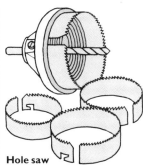

Hole saw
You can buy a set of hole saw blades for cutting perfectly round holes of different diameters. They clip into a backing plate clamped to a central twist drill which fits in the chuck of a power drill. Place the tip of the twist drill at the centre of the required hole and, with the power tool at slow speed, slowly push the revolving saw against the wood. Always place a piece of scrap timber behind the work to stop the saw breaking out the back.

POWER SAWS

Power saws are invaluable for cutting heavy structure timbers and large man-made boards. There are circular saw and jigsaw attachments for electric drills, but they are too small and low-powered for heavy work.

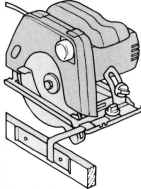

Portable circular saw
When you buy or hire a circular saw choose one with a 190mm (7½in) blade. Its motor will be powerful enough to give a blade speed that can cut thick timber and man-made boards without straining the saw or scorching the work. There are blades designed just for ripping and others for cross-cutting, but for general use choose a combination blade. This will cut efficiently both along and across the wood grain and is suitable for sawing man-made boards. There are also special blades and abrasive discs for cutting metal and stone.

On a good saw you can adjust the angle of the blade for cutting bevels.

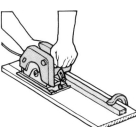

Making straight cuts
Circular saws have removable fences to guide their blades parallel to the edge of the work, but these are often too small to be of much use. You can extend the fence by screwing a length of batten to it or clamp a batten onto the work itself to guide the edge of the soleplate. By clamping the batten at various angles across the wood you can cross-cut boards or planks at these angles.

Sawing by eye
When accuracy of cut is not too important you can use the saw freehand, guiding a notch in the soleplate along a line marked on the work. Place the tip of the soleplate on the work and align the notch with the line. Switch on, let the blade get up to speed, then advance the saw steadily.

Reciprocating saw
Reciprocating saws, with powerful motors, and blades up to 300mm (1ft) long, are especially useful for such jobs as cutting openings in stud partitions.

Portable power jigsaw
A portable jigsaw is primarily for making curved cuts in timber and man-made boards. Most such saws have guide fences for straight cutting but they are rarely sturdy enough to stop the blade wandering. Discard jigsaw blades when they get blunt and keep some spares handy. As blades are fairly cheap it's worth buying some of the special ones for cutting plastics, metal, plasterboard and even ceramics.

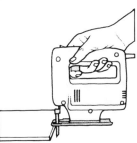

Using a jigsaw
Rest the front of the soleplate on the edge of the work, squeeze the saw's trigger and advance the moving blade into the work along the marked cutting line. Don't force or twist a blade or it will break, and let the blade come to rest before you put the saw down.

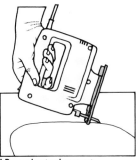

I Preparing to plunge cut

Cutting holes with a jigsaw
The simplest way to cut a large hole in a panel is first to drill a starter hole into which you then insert the jigsaw blade, but you can start the cut by 'plunge cutting'. Tilt the saw onto the front edge of its soleplate with the tip of the blade just above the surface of the work (1). Switch on the saw and gradually lower the blade into the wood until it is upright and the soleplate is flat on the surface.

POWER SAW SAFETY

A circular saw is perfectly safe to use so long as you follow the manufacturer's handling and fitting instructions carefully and observe the following safety guidelines:

- Always unplug the saw before you adjust or change the blade.
- Don't use a blunt blade. Have it sharpened professionally.
- Fit new blades according to manufacturers' instructions. The teeth at the bottom of the blade must face in the direction of the cut.
- All circular saws must have a fixed blade guard and a lower guard that swings back as the cut proceeds. Never use the saw without the guards in place, and make sure that the lower one will return to its position when the blade clears the work.
- The work must be held securely on sawhorses or a bench.
- Keep the electrical flex well behind the saw.
- Don't force the saw into a cut. If it jams, back off a little until the blade returns to full speed.
- Don't put the saw down before the blade stops revolving.
- Don't wear loose clothing, a necktie or a necklace, any of which could become entangled in the machine.

SEE ALSO

Details for: ▷

RCCBs	332
Ripsaw	463
Cross-cut saw	463

Saw bench
You can clamp a circular saw upside down under a saw bench attachment and cut wood by passing it across the blade which projects up through the flat bed.

465

SEE ALSO

◁ Details for:
Sharpening planes   467
Marking knife   463
Routers   468

PLANES AND SPOKESHAVES

Unless timber is to be used for crude framing, as in a stud partition or a bath panel, it must be planed to remove the marks of saw teeth. Planes are also used for reducing wood to size and shape. Wooden planes are still made, and many antique ones are for sale at reasonable prices, but most people find modern metal planes easier to adjust for the exact thickness of shaving they require.

BENCH PLANES

Bench planes are general-purpose tools for smoothing wood to make joints between boards or to level the surface of several boards glued together. Bench planes are all similar in design, differing only in the length of the sole.

Jointer plane
The jointer is the longest bench plane, with a sole up to 600mm (2ft) long. It is designed for truing up the long edges of boards that are to be butted and glued together, and for levelling large flat panels. Its long sole bridges minor irregularities until the blade shaves them down. A shorter plane would simply follow the uneven surface.

Jack plane
A jack plane 350 to 375mm (1ft 2in to 1ft 3in) long is a good all-purpose tool. If you can afford only one bench plane choose a jack plane, which is light enough to cope with most planing without tiring you.

Smoothing plane
A finely set smoothing plane is used for putting the final surface on a piece of timber after it has been reduced to size with a jack plane or jointer plane.

I Checking the blade angle

Adjusting a bench plane
Before you use a bench plane adjust the angle and depth of the blade. Check the angle by sighting down the sole of the plane from the toe (1) and use the lateral adjustment lever behind the blade to set the cutting edge so that it projects an equal amount across the width of the sole. Use the knurled adjusting nut in front of the handle to set the depth to take off a fine shaving.

STORING PLANES

Never put a plane sole-down on the bench during work. Lay it on its side. Similarly the plane should be stored on its side, even though the blade is withdrawn. For long-term storage dismantle and clean the plane and grease bare metal parts lightly to protect them from rust.

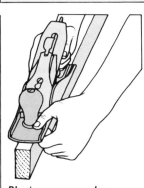

Planing a square edge
Keep the plane flat on the edge of the work by holding the toe down with the thumb of your free hand and pressing the fingers against the side of the wood to guide the tool along.

Planing a flat surface
To plane a wide surface as flat as possible work the plane diagonally across the wood but following the general direction of the grain. Finish by working parallel to the grain, taking off very fine shavings.

Block plane
The blade of a block plane is mounted at a shallow angle so that its edge can slice smoothly through the end grain of timber. Small and lightweight – it can be used in the palm of one hand – the plane is also ideal for all kinds of fine trimming and shaping.

Trimming end grain
Cut a line all round the work with a marking knife, then set it vertically in a vice. To prevent the wood splitting form a chamfer down to the line on one side by planing towards the centre. Plane the end square, working from the other side down to the marked line so that the chamfer is removed.

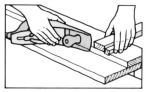

Using a shooting board
You can trim end grain with a bench plane on its side, running on a shooting board. The blade must be sharp and finely set. The work is held against the stop.

Shoulder plane
A shoulder plane is not essential for everyday use but, as its blade spans the whole width of its squarely machined body, it is ideal for trimming the square shoulders of large joints or rebates. With the body removed the exposed blade can trim a rebate right up to a stopped end.

Power plane
A power plane is useful for smoothing and shaping large structural timbers. Its revolving two- or three-cutter block can be used for planing rebates if guided by a side fence.

Spokeshaves
A spokeshave is a miniature plane for shaping curved edges in wood. Use one with a flat base to shape a convex curve, one with a bellied base for a concave curve. When you use either tool, shape the curve from two directions so as to work with the grain all the time. Sharpen a spokeshave cutter as you would a plane blade (◁).

Adjusting the blade
Use the two adjusting screws to produce a fine setting, then 'fix' the setting with the central locking screw.

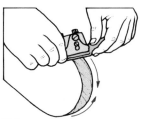

Using a spokeshave
With a handle in each hand, your thumbs on their back edges, push the tool away from you. Rock it backwards or forwards as you work to produce a continuous shaving.

MOULDING PLANES AND ROUTERS

There are many times when it's necessary to cut grooves in wood, both with and across the grain, or to plane rebates or mouldings on the edges. A multi-plane or a power router – though neither can be called an essential tool – will produce any type of groove or moulding and is extremely useful to the woodworker.

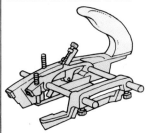

Combination plane

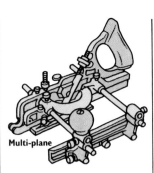
Multi-plane

Combination and multi-planes

Combination and multi-planes with variously shaped cutters can be used to plane grooves, rebates and a number of moulding profiles. Both tools have spurs – pairs of vertically adjusting blades – that cut parallel lines ahead of the cutter to prevent tearing of the wood fibres when a groove or housing is planed across the grain. Both tools can be used to cut tongue-and-groove joints along the edges of boards. The multi-plane has a larger selection of cutters than the combination plane.

Rebate plane

A rebate plane is similar to a bench plane, but its blade spans the whole width of its sole. With its depth gauge and guide fence set to the required dimensions the plane will cut any number of identical rebates.

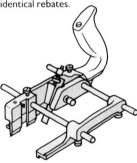

Plough plane

A plough plane has narrow blades for cutting grooves. It can be used only in the direction of the grain.

I Starting a moulding

Using moulding planes
Rebate, plough, combination and multi-planes are all used in much the same way. Follow the maker's instructions for setting the depth gauge and guide fence, which control the position of the cutter relative to the surface and edge of the wood.

Hold the guide fence against the edge of the work at the far end and make short strokes to begin the moulding (1), then move backwards, making longer and longer strokes until the depth gauge rests on the surface. Finish with one continuous pass along the length of the timber.

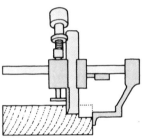

Cutting an extra-wide rebate
To cut a rebate wider than a standard cutter first plane one rebate on the outer edge, then adjust the guide fence to make a second cut that will make up the required width.

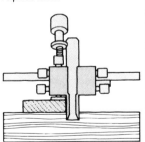

Cutting a housing
When you cut a housing – a groove across the grain – take off the guide fence and instead clamp a batten across the work to guide the body of the plane.

To keep its sharp cutting edge, a plane blade must be honed on a flat oilstone. Choose one with a medium grit on one side to remove metal quickly and a fine grit on the other for the final sharpening of the edge.

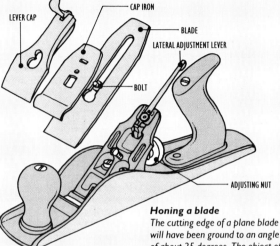
LEVER CAP
CAP IRON
BLADE
LATERAL ADJUSTMENT LEVER
BOLT
ADJUSTING NUT

Honing a blade
The cutting edge of a plane blade will have been ground to an angle of about 25 degrees. The object of sharpening on an oilstone is to hone only the leading edge to about 30 degrees.

Hold the blade against the stone at the correct angle and rub it to and fro to produce a sharp edge. A wide blade must be held at an angle across the stone so that the whole edge is in contact (1). Keep the stone lubricated with a little oil while you work.

Honing creates a burr along the cutting edge. Remove it by laying the back of the blade flat on the stone (2) and making several passes along the surface.

Removing and replacing a blade
The blade of a bench or block plane is clamped in place by a metal lever cap. Slacken the lever to remove the cap and lift the blade out of the plane. The blade of a bench plane has a cap iron bolted to it to break and curl the shavings as they are trimmed from the wood. Undo the fixing bolt with a screwdriver and remove the cap iron before you sharpen the blade.

When you replace the cap iron place it across the blade (1), then swivel it until the two are aligned (2). Don't drag the iron across the cutting edge but slide it to within 1mm (¹/₁₆in) of it (3).

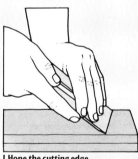
I Hone the cutting edge

2 Remove the burr

SEE ALSO
Details for: ▷
| Bench planes | 466 |

Using a honing guide
If you want to be certain that you are honing a blade to the correct angle, clamp it in a honing guide and roll the guide to and fro on the surface of the stone to sharpen the blade.

Repairing a chipped cutting edge
If you chip the cutting edge of a blade – against a nail, for example – regrind it on a bench grinder. Hold the blade against the tool rest and move the cutting edge from side to side against the revolving wheel until it is straight and clean. Use only light pressure and dip the blade in water regularly to cool it. Finally hone the ground edge on an oilstone.

● **Essential tools**
Combination oilstone

467

ROUTERS

A hand router is used for finishing the bottom of a sawn housing after most of the waste has been cut out with a chisel. A power router is a sophisticated tool that performs all the tasks of combination and multi-planes and will follow a curved edge as easily as a straight one. The cutter revolves so fast that it produces as clean a cut across the grain as with it.

SEE ALSO
◁ Details for:
Moulding planes   466-467
Oilstone   467
Mallets   473

Hand router

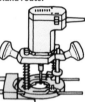

Power router

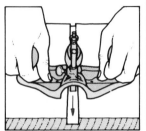

Using a hand router
To pare the bottom of a housing hold one handle of the router in each hand and push the tool away from you as you would a plane.

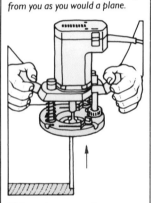

Using a power router
Always let the bit run up to full speed before you allow it to come into contact with the work, and always lift it clear of the groove or moulding before you switch off. The bit revolves clockwise; feed the machine against the rotation when moulding an edge so that the cutter pulls itself into the wood.

Router cutters and bits
Hand-router cutters have square shafts that clamp into the tool and are adjusted vertically to set the chisel-like cutting edges at the required depth.
Power-router bits fit into a chuck at the base of the tool and are adjusted until they project through the baseplate. A grooving bit has two symmetrical cutting edges that run to its bottom end. An edge-moulding bit has a cylindrical

Power-router bits
1 Grooving bit
2 Edge-moulding bit

468

pilot tip below the cutting edges that runs against the edge of the work to stop the cutter biting too deeply.
Follow the manufacturer's instructions for fitting and adjusting bits or cutters.

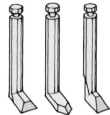

Hand-router cutters

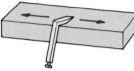

Honing a router cutter
Hone blunt hand-router cutters on an oilstone. Position the stone so that the cutter's shaft will clear the bench, then rub the cutter from side to side on the stone.

Cutting grooves and housings
To cut a groove parallel to an edge fit and set the adjustable guide fence (**1**) or run the edge of the baseplate against a batten clamped to the surface (**2**). To cut a wide housing use two parallel battens to guide the bit along both outer edges (**3**), then rout out the centre.

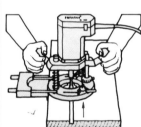

1 Using a guide fence

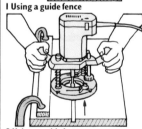

2 Using a guide batten

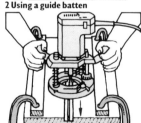

3 Cutting a wide housing

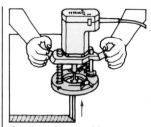

Cutting edge mouldings
Rest the baseplate on the upper surface of the work and when the bit has run up to full speed feed it against and along the edge.
When you mould all four edges of a rectangular piece of wood do the end grain first, then run the router along each side.

SHARPENING A POWER-ROUTER BIT

You can grind and hone power-router bits yourself, though as they must be symmetrical it's better to have them done by a professional.

CHISELS AND GOUGES

Chisels are general-purpose woodcutting tools but are used mostly to remove the waste from joints or to pare and trim them to size. The size of a chisel refers to the width of its cutting edge. Though chisels range from 3mm (1/8in) in width up to 50mm (2in), a selection of sizes up to 25mm (1in) is sufficient for most woodworking purposes.
Gouges are similar to wood chisels but their blades are curved in cross section for such work as cutting the shoulders of a joint to fit against a turned leg or scooping out the waste from a 'finger pull' on a drawer front or sliding door.
All wood chisels and gouges have handles of boxwood or of impact-resistant plastic.

Firmer chisel
A firmer chisel has a strong, flat, rectangular-section blade for chopping out waste wood. It is strong enough to be driven with a mallet or hammer– though hammers must not be used on wooden handles.

Bevel-edge chisel
A bevel-edge chisel is used for paring, especially in trimming undercuts like dovetail joints or housings. Its bevels enable the blade to work in tight spaces that would be inaccessible to a thick firmer chisel. It is not as strong as a firmer and may break if it is used for heavy work. If a little extra force is needed to drive the chisel forward use your shoulder or the ball of your hand.

Mortise chisel
A mortise chisel has a thick blade, rectangular in section, for chopping and levering the waste out of mortise joints. Mallets are always needed to drive mortise chisels, so many of them have a shock-absorbent leather washer between the blade and the ferrule.

Chopping out waste wood
Don't try to chop out too much waste all at once. The wood will split or the chisel will be driven over the line of the joint, resulting in a poor fit. Remove the waste a little at a time, working back to the marked line. You can use a mallet at first, but finish off by hand.

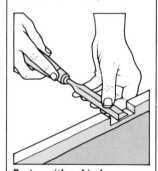

Paring with a chisel
Finish a joint by paring away very thin shavings with a bevel-edge chisel. Control the blade with finger and thumb, steadying your hand against the work, while you apply pressure to the tip of the handle with the other hand.

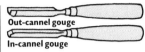

Out-cannel gouge

In-cannel gouge

Gouges

An in-cannel gouge is one whose cutting edge is formed by grinding the inside of the curved blade. It is used for trimming rounded shoulders. An out-cannel gouge is ground on the outside so that the blade will not be driven into the wood when it is scooping out shallow depressions.

STORING CHISELS

Make a wall-mounted rack for chisels and gouges by gluing spacer blocks between two strips of plywood to leave slots for the blades. Screw the rack to the wall behind your workbench so that the chisels are in easy reach.

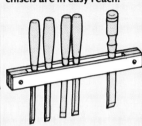

RASPS AND SURFORMS

Rasps are coarse files for shaping free curves in wood. Traditional ones have teeth formed in the solid metal to wear away the wood; modern Surform files have hollow blades pressed out to form a great many cutting edges. Surform files stay sharp for a long time, remove wood very quickly and do not get clogged up like rasps because the shavings fall through their hollow blades.

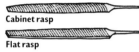

Cabinet rasp

Flat rasp

Round rasp

Rasps

Rasps are made in degrees of coarseness, designated as bastard, second-cut and smooth. Their names refer to their shapes: a cabinet rasp is half-round, with one flat and one curved face; a flat rasp has two flat faces and one cutting edge; a round rasp is circular in section, tapering towards the tip.

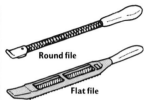

Round file

Flat file

Surform files

A round Surform file has a detachable handle and thumb-grip at the tip. A flat Surform has a disposable blade that fits into a hollow metal frame.

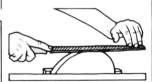

Using a rasp

A rasp cuts only on the forward stroke. Control its tip with your finger tips as you work, and never use one without first fitting a handle. Holding the bare pointed tang is very dangerous.

Cleaning a rasp

When a rasp gets clogged up with wood fibres clear them with a file card – a fine wire brush made for the purpose.

SANDERS AND ABRASIVES

Abrasive papers are used for smoothing wood after it has been shaped with rasps or Surform files. Always sand in the direction of the grain. Tiny scratches made by cross-grain sanding may not appear until the work has been clear-varnished or polished. Though flat surfaces are often sanded smooth you can get a better finish with a cabinet scraper (▷).

Sanding by hand

Abrasive papers – still sometimes called 'sandpapers' – are graded by size and the spacing of the grit. There are coarse, medium and fine grits but they are also designated by number, the higher the number the finer the grit. Particles are spaced apart on open-coat papers to reduce clogging. Tightly packed close-coat papers produce a finer finish.

TYPES OF ABRASIVE

Yellow flint or glasspaper is cheap and relatively soft. Use it for the first stages of sanding, especially on softwoods.

Garnet paper is reddish, comes in very fine grades and, being harder than glasspaper, wears more slowly. Use it on hardwoods.

Silicon-carbide paper, usually called 'wet and dry', is used mainly for smoothing paintwork, but it can be used dry for an extra-smooth finish on hardwoods.

Using abrasive papers

Tear a sheet of the paper into manageable strips over the edge of a bench. To smooth flat surfaces or square edges wrap a strip round a cork sanding block (1); on curves use your finger tips to apply the paper. To sand mouldings use a dowel (2) or a shaped block wrapped in the abrasive paper.

Use progressively finer grades of paper as you work. Before the final sanding dampen the wood with water to raise the grain. When it dries sand it with a very fine abrasive for a perfect finish.

To sand end grain, first rub the grain with your fingers. When rubbing in one direction feels less rough than in others, sand the grain in that direction only, not to and fro.

When the grit becomes clogged with wood dust tap the paper against the bench to clear it, or use a file card.

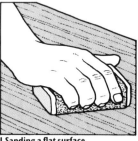

1 Sanding a flat surface

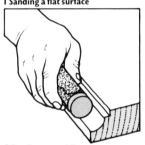

2 Sanding a moulding

SHARPENING CHISELS AND GOUGES

Sharpen a chisel as you would a plane blade (▷) but hone it across the whole surface of the oilstone in a figure 8 pattern to avoid uneven wear of the stone.

Honing an out-cannel gouge
Stand to the side of the oilstone and rub the bevel of the gouge from end to end of the stone in a figure 8 pattern (1) while you rock the blade to hone the edge evenly. Remove the burr from the inside with a slipstone (2) – a small oilstone shaped to fit different gouge sizes.

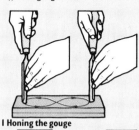

1 Honing the gouge

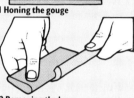

2 Removing the burr

Honing an in-cannel gouge
Hone the bevel on the inside of an in-cannel gouge with a slipstone (1), then remove the burr by holding the back of the blade flat on an oilstone and rocking it from side to side while you slide it up and down the stone (2).

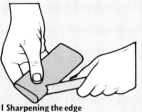

1 Sharpening the edge

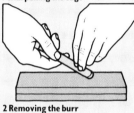

2 Removing the burr

SEE ALSO

Details for: ▷

Sharpening planes	467
Cabinet scraper	470
Preparing wood	53

● **Essential tools**
Combination oilstone
Slipstone
Sanding block
Range of abrasives
Choose a Surform in preference to a solid rasp but buy as required.

SEE ALSO

◁ Details for:
Draw filing	491
Preparing wood	53
Sanding floors	55-56
Sanding by hand	469

● **Essential tools**
Flat cabinet scraper

POWER SANDERS

Sanding machines remove wood quickly and reduce the tedium of sanding large flat surfaces. But no power sander produces a surface good enough for a clear wood finish. Always complete the work by hand.

Belt sander
A belt sander has a continuous loop of abrasive paper passing round a drum at each end. The flat plate between the revolving drums presses the moving abrasive against the wood.

Using a belt sander
Switch on the machine and lower it gently onto the work, then make forward and backward passes with it, holding it parallel to the grain. The machine's weight is enough pressure to do the work, especially when the abrasive band is fresh. Cover the surface in overlapping bands but don't let the sander ride over the edges or it will round them off. Lift the sander from the surface before you switch it off and do not put it aside before the belt comes to a stop.

Change to a finer-grade belt and remove the marks of the previous sanding. Always follow the manufacturer's instructions when fitting a belt.

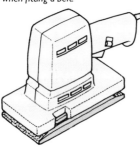

Finishing sander
The finishing sander produces a surface that needs only a light further hand finishing. On the machine, a strip of abrasive paper is stretched across a flat rubber pad which is moved by the motor in a tight, rapid orbital pattern. Use only light pressure or the paper will leave tiny swirling marks on the wood.

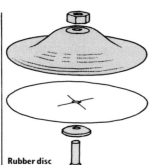

Rubber disc sander

Disc sander
Disc sanding is not suitable for fine woodwork. It inevitably leaves swirling scratches that have to be removed with a finishing sander or cabinet scraper before a clear finish can be applied. The sander removes old paint very successfully and is handy for cleaning up old floorboards that are inaccessible to a large floor-sanding machine.

The simplest disc sander has a flexible rubber pad with a central shaft that is gripped in the chuck of an electric drill. An abrasive-paper disc is bolted to the face of the pad.

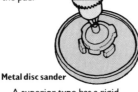

Metal disc sander

A superior type has a rigid metal plate on a ball-and-socket joint that lets the disc stay flat on the work while in use.

Using a rubber disc sander
With the drill running, flex the edge of the rubber disc against the wood. Keep the sander moving along the work to avoid deep scratching.

Foam drum sander
This is a flexible plastic-foam drum covered by an abrasive-paper band and attached to a power drill by a central shaft. The foam drum will deform against irregularly curved workpieces.

The abrasive bands are easy to take off and replace.

WOOD SCRAPERS

Scrapers give wood the smoothest finish. They take off fine shavings, whereas abrasive paper always leaves minute scratches.

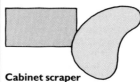

Cabinet scraper
This is a simple rectangle of thin steel used for scraping flat surfaces. Curved-edge versions are used for working mouldings and carved wood.

Using a cabinet scraper
Hold the scraper in both hands, pressing it into a slight forward curve with your thumbs, tip it away from you and scrape diagonally across the wood in two directions to keep the surface flat. Finally scrape lightly in the direction of the grain.

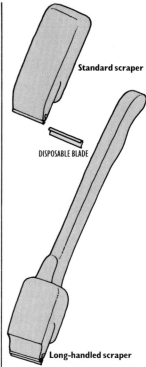

Standard scraper

DISPOSABLE BLADE

Long-handled scraper

Hook scraper
A hook scraper's disposable blade slides into a clip at the end of a wooden handle. Use the scraper by pulling it towards you along the grain of the wood, applying light pressure.

SHARPENING A CABINET SCRAPER

The scraper is sharpened by raising a burr along its edge and turning it over. Both types of scraper are sharpened in the same way, though it is harder to turn an even burr along a curved edge. Draw-file the edge of the scraper (◁) and hone it perfectly square on an oilstone (1). Raise the burr with the curved back of a gouge. Lay the scraper flat on the bench, aligned with one edge, stroke the edge of the scraper firmly several times with the gouge, holding its blade flat on the scraper (2). This stretches the metal along the edge of the scraper and forms the burr.

Turn the burr to project from the face of the scraper by holding the scraper upright against the bench and stroking the burred corner with the gouge held at an angle to the face (3).

1 Hone the edge square

2 Raise the burr

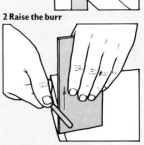

3 Turn the burr over

DRILLS AND BRACES

The versatile electric drill is the only essential power tool for a tool kit. However, it has not yet completely replaced the brace and the hand drill. These are still very useful, especially in places where it is inconvenient or impossible to run an extension lead for a power drill.

Brace
Use a brace for drilling the larger diameter holes. The bit is driven into the wood by the turning force on the handle plus pressure on the head of the tool.

A good brace will have a ratchet for turning the bit in only one direction when working in confined spaces where a full turn of the handle isn't possible.

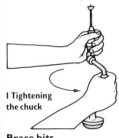

I Tightening the chuck

Brace bits
Brace bits have square-section tangs that fit into the jaws of the tool's chuck. To fit a bit, grip the chuck in one hand and turn the handle clockwise to open the jaws. Drop the bit into the chuck and tighten it on the bit by turning the handle in the anti-clockwise direction (I).

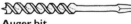

Auger bit
An auger bit has helical twists along its shank which remove the waste as the bit bores into the wood. The twisted shank, being the same diameter as the cutting tip, keeps the bit straight when you bore deep holes. A tapered lead screw helps to draw the bit into the work and knife-edge spurs cut the perimeter of the hole before the bit enters the wood.

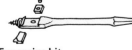

Expansive bit
This bit has an adjustable spurred cutter for making holes of up to 75mm (3in) in diameter.

Centre bit
A centre bit is fast-cutting because it has no helical twists to create friction, but it tends to wander off line. It's best for drilling man-made boards in which the holes are never very deep. Its relatively short shank makes it useful for working in confined spaces.

Using a brace
When you use a brace don't let the bit burst through and split the wood. As soon as the lead screw emerges turn the work over and complete the hole from the other side.

Hand drill
For small-diameter holes use a hand drill, also called a wheelbrace. Some have cast bodies enclosing their drive mechanisms to keep gear wheels and pinions dust-free.

Using a hand drill
Centre the drill bit on the work. This is easier if the centre for the hole has been marked with a bradawl puncture. Give the bit a start by moving the handle to and fro until the bit bites into the wood, then crank the handle to drive the bit clockwise.

Twist drills
Use standard twist drills with a hand drill. Fit a drill bit by turning the chuck anti-clockwise to open the chuck, inserting the drill bit, then turning the chuck clockwise to tighten it. Check that a very small twist drill is centred accurately between the chuck's three jaws.

SHARPENING TWIST DRILLS

You can sharpen a blunt drill on a bench grinder (▷) but it takes practice to centre the point. An electric sharpener centres the point automatically. Drop the drill tip-down into the appropriate hole in the top of the machine and switch on for a few seconds to grind one cutting edge. Rotate the drill one half turn to position the other edge and repeat the process.

SHARPENING BRACE BITS

Brace bits are sharpened with fine needle files. Put an edge on a spur by stroking its inside face with a flat file (I), then support the point of the bit on a bench and sharpen the cutting edge with a triangular file (2).

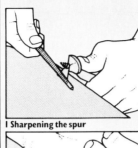

I Sharpening the spur

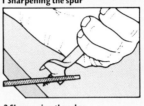

2 Sharpening the edge

Power drill
Buy a well-made drill that can cope with all the tasks you may have to tackle now and later. Choose one with a powerful motor – up to 600W – especially if you plan to use it with power-tool attachments. Continuously using a circular saw for a long time will burn out an underpowered drill. Most drills now have plastic bodies that are lighter than metal ones and will protect you from electric shock. A few drills are battery-powered and have plug-in rechargers.

SELECTING USEFUL FEATURES

Before you choose an electric drill note down the features that would be of most use to you and list them in order of priority in case you can't find a tool that has them all.

● Drill speed
A power drill with one fixed speed is too limiting for general use. Most drills have from two to four fixed speeds and a switch for selecting the one appropriate

to a given job. A slow speed uses the drill's power to produce more torque (turning force) for drilling such materials as masonry and metal; a high speed gives a clean cut when drilling wood.

Run power-tool attachments at the speeds recommended by the manufacturer.

A variable-speed drill can be operated at any speed throughout its range by varying pressure on the trigger or setting a control dial. This lets you select the ideal speeds for drilling various materials, and is essential also if you want to use a screwdriver bit in a power drill.

● Trigger lock
A trigger lock button sets the drill for continuous running when it is used to drive attachments.

● Chuck size
The chuck's size refers to the maximum diameter of drill shank or attachment spindle that it can accommodate. A 10mm (⅜in) chuck is adequate for most purposes, though there are drills with a chuck size of 16mm (⅝in). You can drill holes of greater diameter than the chuck size by using special drilling bits with cutters larger than their shanks.

● Percussion or hammer action
By operating a lever you can convert some drills from smooth rotation to a hammer action that delivers several hundred blows per second to the revolving chuck. This is required only for drilling masonry, when the hammer vibration breaks up hard particles ahead of the special toughened bit before the debris is cleared by the helical flutes on the bit.

● Reverse rotation
If you want to use a screwdriver bit with your electric drill make sure that its rotation can be reversed so that you can take screws out as well as insert them.

● Handgrips
Most power drills have a pistol-grip handle and a second handgrip for steadying the drill. Some manufacturers provide a handle that bolts onto the rear of the drill so that it can be controlled with both hands when pressure is needed directly behind the chuck.

SEE ALSO

Details for: ▷

Bench grinding	467
Power drill bits	472
Safety tips	472
Joist brace	492

● **Essential tools**
Brace
Set of auger bits
Hand drill
Set of twist drills
Power drill

471

SEE ALSO

◁ Details for:
Double insulation	288
Extension leads	294
Power drill	471

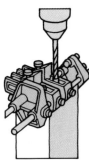

Dowelling jig
A dowelling jig
clamped to the work
ensures alignment of
the holes and keeps
the drill bit
perpendicular to the
work.

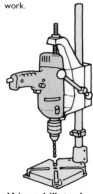

Using a drill stand
To bore holes
absolutely square to
the face of the work,
mount your electric
drill in a vertical drill
stand.

● **Essential tools**
  Set of spade or
  power-bore bits
  Countersink bit
  Claw hammer
  Cross-peen hammer
  Pin hammer
  Carpenter's mallet
  Pincers
  Nail set

472

POWER DRILL BITS

A variety of bits can be used in a power drill, depending on the kind of hole you want to bore.

Twist drill
You can use standard twist drills of any size to the maximum opening of the chuck. To bore larger holes use reduced-shank drilling bits.

Power-bore bit

Spade bit

Power-bore and spade bits
With a power-bore bit or a spade bit you can drill holes of up to 38mm (1½in) in diameter. Either bit produces minimal friction. Place the sharp lead point of the bit on the centre of the hole before pressing the trigger of the drill.

Countersink bit
To sink the head of a countersunk woodscrew flush with the surface of the work make a tapered recess in the top of the clearance hole with a 'rose' or countersink bit. These bits can be used in hand drills and braces, but a high-speed electric drill forms a neater recess.

Except with a vertical drill stand, the countersink bit 'chatters' if the hole has already been drilled, producing a rough recess. When you have to use the drill 'freehand' it's best to make the recess first, then drill the hole itself.

Screwdriver bit
With slotted-head or cross-head screwdriver bits you can use your electric drill as a power screwdriver. The drill must be capable of slow speeds.

Plug cutter
This special bit cuts cylindrical plugs of wood for concealing the heads of screws sunk below the surface of the work.

Dowel bit
This is a twist drill with a sharp lead point and cutting spurs that help to keep it on line when holes are bored for dowel joints.

Drill and countersink bit
This bit makes the pilot hole, clearance hole and countersink recess for a woodscrew in one operation. As it is matched to one specific screw size it is worth purchasing only when you plan to use a fair number of identical screws.

Fitting a power drill bit
Turn the chuck anti-clockwise to open its jaws and insert the bit. Close the jaws on the bit and tighten the chuck with the key supplied with the drill. Remove the key before you switch on.

USING A POWER DRILL SAFELY

● **Choose a drill with a plastic non-conducting body (◁).**
● **Remove the chuck key before using the drill.**
● **Don't wear loose clothing, a necktie or a necklace while using the drill.**
● **Unplug the drill before fitting bits, accessories or attachments.**
● **Don't lift the drill by its flex.**
● **Use a proper purpose-made extension lead when you want to extend the drill's flex (◁).**
● **Always fit and use attachments according to the manufacturer's safety recommendations.**

SELECTING POWER DRILL ATTACHMENTS

Most manufacturers produce a range of attachments for turning an electric drill into a circular saw, jigsaw, sander, bench grinder – even a hedgetrimmer. Most attachments fit only one make of drill, so check the quality of various attachments before you choose your drill.

HAMMERS AND MALLETS

Driving in a nail is so simple that one hammer would seem to be as effective for it as another, but having one of the right shape and weight for a given job makes for easier, trouble-free work.

Mallets have their own specific uses, and should never be used for hammering nails.

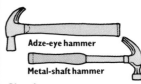

Adze-eye hammer

Metal-shaft hammer

Claw hammer
A claw hammer is a heavy-weight general-purpose tool, probably the most useful hammer to have in a tool kit. The split claw at the back of the head is for levering out nails, and to withstand the strain of this the head must be fixed firmly to a strong shaft. The traditional adze-eye head has a deep square socket driven and wedged onto a tough but flexible hickory shaft. The all-metal hammer is an even better tool. Its tubular steel shaft won't bend or break, and the head can't work loose. The rubber grip is comfortable and shock-absorbing.

Cross-peen hammer
For those jobs too delicate for a heavy claw hammer use a medium-weight cross-peen one. Its wedge-shaped peen is for setting (starting) a nail held between finger and thumb.

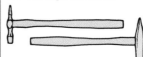

Pin hammer
A small lightweight pin hammer is perfect for tapping in fine panel pins and tacks.

Using a hammer
Set a nail in wood with one or two taps of the hammer to make it stand upright without support, then drive it home with firm steady blows, keeping your wrist straight and the hammer face square to the nail head.

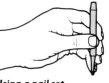

Using a nail set
A nail set is a punch with a hollow-ground tip used for sinking nails below the surface of the wood. Nail sets are made in several sizes for use with large and small nails. Hold the tool upright between thumb and fingertips and place its tip on the nailhead while it still protrudes just above the surface and tap the head of the nail set with your hammer. With a heavy hammer very little force is needed to sink the nail.

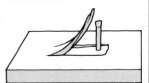

Blind nailing
To hide a nail fixing lift a flap of wood with a gouge, sink the nail with a nail set, then glue the flap and cramp it flat.

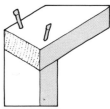

Dovetail-nailed

Skew-nailed

Making a strong nailed joint
The grip between the nails and the wood is usually enough to hold the joint together, but for stronger fixings drive the nails in at an angle. When angled nails fix wood onto the end grain of another member the technique is called dovetail-nailing. When they pass through the side of a section it's called skew-nailing.

Hammering small nails
◁ *If the nail is very small set it with the hammer peen or push it through a piece of thin card to steady it. Just before you tap the nail flush with the wood tear the card away.*

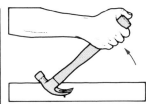

Removing a bent nail
If you bend a nail while driving it in with a claw hammer you can lever it out by sliding the claw under the nailhead and pulling back on the end of the shaft. The curved head will roll on the wood without doing too much damage but you can protect the work by placing a piece of thick card or hardboard under the hammer head. A thick packing of this kind will also give you extra leverage in removing a long nail.

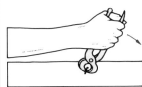

If a nailhead is too small to catch in a claw hammer, lever it out with carpenter's pincers. Grip the nail with the jaws resting on the wood, squeeze the handles together and roll the pincers away from you. Here again cardboard or hardboard packing will protect the wood.

Sanding a hammer head
You're more likely to bend nails if your hammer head gets greasy and slippery. Rub the face on fine abrasive paper for a better grip.

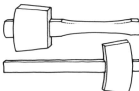

Carpenter's mallet
A carpenter's mallet is for driving a chisel or gouge into wood. Its striking faces are angled so as to deliver square blows to the end of the chisel. A loose mallet head is tightened by tapping the top of the tapered shaft on a bench.

Soft-faced mallet
Though you can use a hardwood carpenter's mallet to knock joints together or apart, a soft-faced one of rubber, plastic or leather is less likely to mark the surface of the wood.

SCREWDRIVERS
You need a number of screwdrivers of various sizes, both flat-tipped and cross-head-tipped because it's important to match the size of the driver to the screw. If the tip is a little too big or too small it can slip out of the slot while you work, damaging the screw or the surrounding woodwork, or both.

For the best grip choose screwdrivers that have large smooth handles.

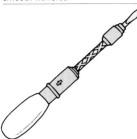

Pump-action screwdriver
The tip of a pump-action screwdriver is turned by a thrusting action on the handle. The spring-loaded shaft moves in and out of a hollow handle containing a ratchet mechanism that controls the direction of rotation. Interchangeable cross- and flat-tipped bits fit into a chuck on the end of the shaft.

Cabinet screwdriver
A cabinet screwdriver has a shaft ground on two sides to produce a flat square tip. It may have a hardwood handle, strengthened with a metal ferrule, or a plastic one moulded onto the shaft.

Cross-head screwdriver
Always use a matching cross-head screwdriver to drive screws with cruciform slots. Using a flat-tip one instead invariably damages the screw.

Ratchet screwdriver
By using a ratchet screwdriver you can insert and remove screws without having to replace the tip in the slot after each turn or shifting your grip on the handle. You can select clockwise or anti-clockwise rotation or lock the ratchet and use the tool like an ordinary fixed one.

HONING A FLAT TIP

If the tip of a screwdriver gets rounded through wear it will no longer grip screws as it should. Reshape it by honing on an oilstone, then filing the end to a good square shape.

Inserting a woodscrew
You may split timber if you drive in a screw without making a hole first. To make a starter hole for a small screw place the flat tip of a bradawl (1) across the grain of the wood and press it in and twist it. To guide a large screw, drill a pilot hole followed by a clearance hole for the shank (2). For the pilot hole use a drill bit slightly narrower than the screw's thread, but drill the clearance hole fractionally larger than the screw's shank.

Use a countersink bit to make recesses for the heads of countersunk screws.

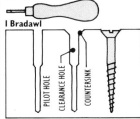

1 Bradawl

2 Drilling for screws

Lubricating a screw
If a screw is too tight a fit in its clearance hole withdraw it slightly and put a little grease on its shank.

Getting old screws out
Don't try to extract an old painted-over screw until you have cleared the slot. Scrape the paint out with the end of a hacksaw blade or by tapping the tip of a screwdriver through the slot with a hammer. For the best results, place a corner of the screwdriver tip in the slot (1) and tap it sideways into the slot until it is gripped snugly, then extract the screw.

Where a screw's slot has been completely stripped remove the head by drilling it out. Mark the middle of the head with a centre punch (▷), then use progressively larger drill bits to remove the metal in stages.

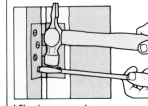

1 Clearing a screw slot

CRAMPS
Cramps are for holding glued joints together while the glue sets, for assembling structures temporarily to see if they work or fit, and for holding small workpieces on a bench while they are worked on.

Sash cramp
A sash cramp is a long metal bar with a screw-adjustable jaw at one end and another jaw, the tail slide, that can be fixed at convenient points along the bar by a metal peg inserted in any of a series of holes. Sash cramps are for clamping large glued frames, and it's worth having a couple of medium-size ones in your tool kit. Hire any additional ones as you need them.

Cramp heads
If you need a very long sash cramp hire a pair of cramp heads. Use a 75 x 25mm (3 x 1in) softwood rail as a cramp bar, locating the heads on it by plugging their pegs into holes drilled through it.

G-cramp
A G-cramp has a screw that grips the work between a shoe attached to its end and the cast metal frame. You will need at least one 150mm (6in) and one 300mm (1ft) G-cramp.

Frame and mitre cramps
The four plastic corner blocks of a simple frame cramp contain the glued corners of a mitred frame while a cord pulled taut round the blocks applies equal pressure to all four joints, holding the frame square while the glue sets.

A cast metal mitre cramp holds one joint at a time, holding the two mitred members against a right-angle fence.

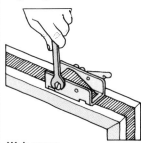

Web cramp
A web cramp acts like a frame cramp, forming a tourniquet round large frames. Its nylon webbing is tensioned by adjusting a ratchet mechanism with a spanner or screwdriver.

SEE ALSO

Details for: ▷

Centre punch	486
Oilstone	467
Nails/screws	496-498

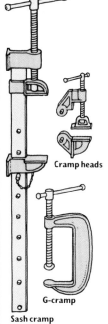

Cramp heads

G-cramp

Sash cramp

Mitre cramp

Frame cramp

● **Essential tools**
Cabinet screwdriver
Cross-head screwdriver
Bradawl

473

SEE ALSO
◁ Details for:
Sash cramps   473

Clamping a jointed frame

Prepare and adjust your sash cramps before you glue and assemble a jointed frame. If you waste time with them after the joints are glued the adhesive may begin stiffening before you can close the joints properly. Set the tail slides to accommodate the frame and make sure that the adjustable jaws will have enough movement to tighten the joints. Use softwood packing strips to protect the work from the metal jaws, place the cramps in line with the joints, then apply the pressure gradually, first with one cramp, then the other, until the joints are tightly closed (1).

Check that the frame is square by measuring both diagonals. If they are not equal set the cramps at a slight angle to the frame so as to pull it square by squeezing the long diagonal (2).

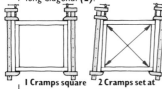

1 Cramps square to frame   **2 Cramps set at an angle**

Clamping boards together

To clamp several glued boards together edge to edge use at least three sash cramps, one on top of the assembly (1) to prevent the boards bowing under pressure from the other two. A long sash cramp will bend as it is tightened, so protect the wood with strips of hardboard packing between the sash bars and the work.

Lay a straightedge across the clamped boards to check that the panel is flat, and correct any distortion by adjusting the pressure of the cramps. To tap a misaligned board back into place put a softwood block across the joint and strike it firmly with a heavy hammer.

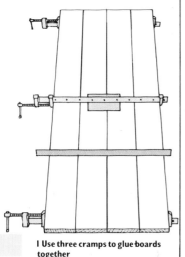

1 Use three cramps to glue boards together

BENCHES AND VICES

A woodworking bench must be strong and rigid. Heavy timbers and man-made boards put a considerable strain on a bench, and the stress imposed by sawing and hammering will eventually weaken a poorly constructed one.

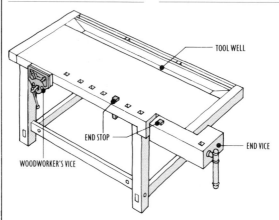

TOOL WELL
END STOP
END VICE
WOODWORKER'S VICE

Woodworker's bench

The hardwood underframe of a traditional woodworker's bench is constructed with large double-wedged mortise-and tenon joints. The longer rails are usually bolted to the rigid endframes so that the bench can be dismantled for removal. The thick worktop is normally of short-grain beech. A storage recess, or tool well, keeps the worktop free of tools for laying large boards across it. Better-quality benches have a vice built onto one end of the top for clamping long timber sections between metal pegs called bench stops.

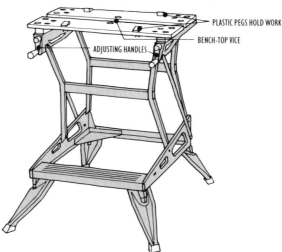

PLASTIC PEGS HOLD WORK
BENCH-TOP VICE
ADJUSTING HANDLES

Workmate bench

A Workmate is a portable bench that can be folded away between jobs. The two halves of the thick plywood worktop are, in effect, vice jaws operated by adjusting handles at the ends of the bench. As the handles work independently, the jaws can hold tapered workpieces. Plastic pegs fit into holes in the worktop and hold work laid flat on it; they can be arranged to hold very irregular shapes.

Clamp-on vice ▶

This lightweight vice can be clamped temporarily to the edge of any worktop. Though not so rigidly fixed as a proper woodworker's vice it is a lot cheaper to buy.

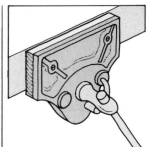

Woodworker's vice

A feature of most benches is a large woodworker's vice, screwed to the underside of the worktop, close to one leg, so that the top will not flex when you work on wood held in it. Wooden linings (pads) must be fixed inside the jaws to protect the work from the metal edges. A quick-release lever on the front of the vice lets you open and shut the jaws quickly, turning the handle only for final adjustments.

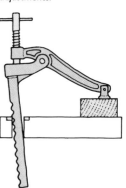

Holdfast

A holdfast is a bench-mounted cramp for holding a workpiece firmly against the worktop. The notched shaft of the tool is slipped into a metal collar which is let into the bench. When pressure is applied with the tommy bar, the shaft rocks over to lock in the collar so that the shoe at the end of the pivoting arm bears down on the workpiece. One holdfast at each end of a bench is ideal for clamping long boards.

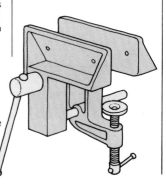

BASIC WOODWORKING JOINTS

Craftsmen have invented many ingenious ways of joining pieces of timber, some as decorative as they are practical, but for general home maintenance and joinery you need only a few basic woodworking joints.

BUTT JOINTS

When you cut a piece of wood square and simply butt it against its neighbour you need some kind of mechanical fixing to hold the joint together. The end grain of wood doesn't glue well enough for glue alone to be used.

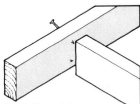

Nailed butt joints
When you nail-fix a butt joint drive the nails in at an angle (▷) to clamp the two pieces together.

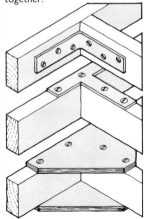

Bracket and plate fixing
Screwed-on right angle and T-shape metal brackets make strong, though not very neat-looking, butt joints. You can give similar reinforcement to a joint with a plywood plate nailed or screwed across it.

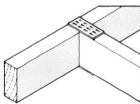

Timber connectors
The sharp-pointed teeth of metal timber connectors hammered onto a butt joint will grip the wood like a bed of nails.

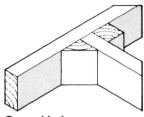

Corner blocks
Pin and glue, or screw, a square- or triangular-section block of wood into the angle between the two components.

LAP JOINTS

A lap joint can be simply one square-cut board laid across another and fixed with nails or screws, but the components of a true lap joint are cut to lie flush with each other.

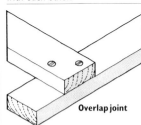

Overlap joint

Making an overlap joint
Clamp the components accurately together with a G-cramp and drill pilot holes for the screws through the top one and into the other. Make clearance holes of the necessary depth with a larger drill, and countersink if needed (▷). Remove the cramp, apply glue, and screw the two components together.

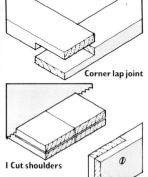

Corner lap joint

I Cut shoulders

2 Screw-fix joint

Cutting a corner lap joint
To join two pieces of wood at a right-angled corner cut identical tongues in their ends. Make each tongue as for a lap joint, but clamp the components together, side by side, and cut their shoulders simultaneously (1). Glue the joint and reinforce it with screws or with glued dowels (2).

Cutting a lap joint

Lay the crossrail on the side rail (1) and mark the width of the housing on it with a marking knife, extending the lines halfway down each edge of the rail. With a marking gauge set to exactly half the thickness of the rails, score the centre lines on both rails (2). Mark the shoulder of the tongue on the crossrail (3), allowing for a tongue slightly longer than the width of the side rail. Hold the crossrail at an angle in a vice (4) and saw down to the shoulder on one edge, keeping to the waste side of the line, then turn the rail round and saw down to the shoulder on the opposite edge. Finally saw down square to the shoulder line (5). Remove the waste by sawing across the shoulder line (6).

To cut the housing in the side rail saw down both shoulder lines to the halfway mark, then make several more saw cuts across the waste (7). With a chisel pare out the waste down to the marked lines (8), working from both sides of the rail. Glue and assemble the joint, and when the glue is set plane the end of the slightly over-long tongue flush with the side rail.

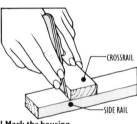
CROSSRAIL
SIDE RAIL

I Mark the housing

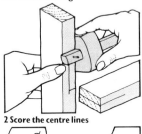

2 Score the centre lines

3 Mark the shoulder

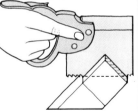

4 Saw with the rail at an angle

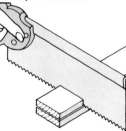

5 Saw square to shoulder

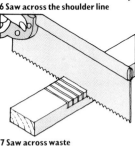

6 Saw across the shoulder line

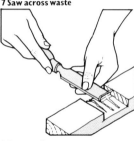

7 Saw across waste

8 Remove the waste

HALVING JOINT

When one rail must cross another cut equal housings to make a halving joint.

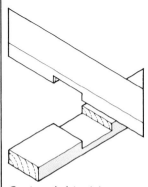

Cutting a halving joint
Cut it as described for a lap joint, but clamp the components together, side by side, and saw both sets of shoulders at the same time, then separate them and remove the waste with a chisel.

SEE ALSO

Details for: ▷

Dovetail-nailing	472
Countersink	472, 473
Marking knife	463
Marking gauge	463
Tenon saw	463
Paring	468
G-cramp	473

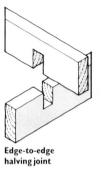

Edge-to-edge halving joint

475

SEE ALSO

◁ Details for:
Marking knife	463
Marking gauge	463
Mortise gauge	463
Tenon saw	463
Firmer chisel	468
Mortise chisel	468
Paring	468
Dovetail-nailing	472
Spade bit	472

REBATED JOINT

A rebated joint is for joining two wide boards at a corner.

Rebated joint

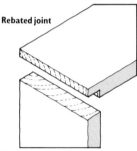

Cutting a rebated joint
Cut the square-ended board first and use it to mark out the width of the rebate on the other (1). Set a marking gauge to about a half of the timber's thickness and mark out the tongue (2). Cut out the rebate with a tenon saw, then glue and dovetail-nail the joint.

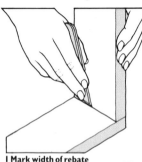

1 Mark width of rebate

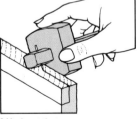

2 Mark out the tongue

BRIDLE JOINT

A bridle joint is used for making a strong joint in a frame.

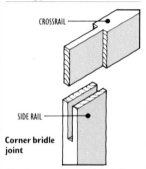

CROSSRAIL

SIDE RAIL

Corner bridle joint

Cutting a corner bridle joint
To make a corner bridle joint cut equal-size tongues, two on the side

---

rail and one centred on the crossrail. Mark the tongues out with a mortise gauge, making them slightly longer than the width of the rails. Cut the waste away from both sides of the crossrail tongue with a tenon saw, as for a lap joint. To form the side rail tongues saw down to the shoulder on both sides keeping to the waste side of the two marked lines (1), then chop out the waste with a narrow firmer chisel or mortise chisel. Glue and assemble the joint and, when the glue has set, plane the ends of the over-long tongues flush with the rails.

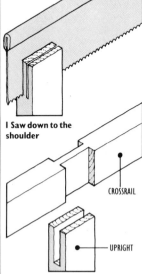

1 Saw down to the shoulder

CROSSRAIL

UPRIGHT

Through bridle joint
When a crossrail must join an upright rail to form a T, cut two tongues on the upright, as for a corner bridle joint, and a housing on each side of the crossrail, as for a lap joint. The depth of the housings must, of course, equal the thickness of the tongues.

HOUSING JOINTS

Housing joints are often used in shelving and similar constructions. A through housing can be seen from both sides of the structure while a stopped housing is not visible from the front.

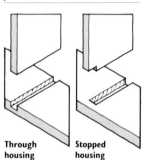

Through housing   **Stopped housing**

Cutting a through housing
Square the end of one board and use it to mark out the width of the housing on the other (1), then with a marking gauge set about a third of the board's thickness mark the depth of the housing on both edges (2). Saw along both sides of the housing (3), keeping just on the waste side of the two lines, then chisel out the waste, working from both edges of the board (4). A router is the ideal tool for levelling the bottom of the housing; failing this, pare it flat with the chisel.

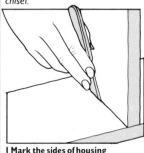

1 Mark the sides of housing

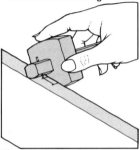

2 Mark depth of housing

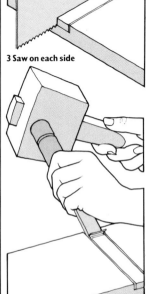

3 Saw on each side

4 Chisel out waste

Cutting a stopped housing
Mark out the housing as described before but stop about 18mm (³/₄in) short of the front edge. To give the saw clearance, cut about 38mm (1¹/₂in) of the housing at the stopped end, first with a drill and then with a chisel (1). Saw down both sides of the housing and pare out the waste to leave a level bottom. In the front corner of the other board cut a notch (2) to fit the stopped housing so that the two edges lie flush when assembled.

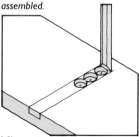

1 Chop out saw clearance

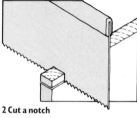

2 Cut a notch

DOWEL JOINTS

Dowel joints are strong and versatile. They can secure butt-jointed rails, mitred frames and long boards butted edge to edge. Use wooden dowels about one third the thickness of the wood to be dowel-jointed.

Dowelled butt joint

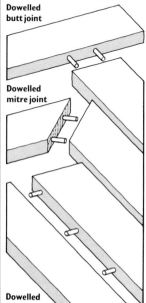

Dowelled mitre joint

Dowelled edge-to-edge joint

Cutting a dowel joint

Cut the dowels to a length equalling about two-thirds the width of the rails, but when joining boards edge to edge cut them about 38mm (1 1/2 in) long. File chamfers on both ends of each dowel and saw a groove along each (1) to allow air and surplus glue to escape as the joint is assembled. For the smaller dowelling jobs you can get ready-cut and chamfered hardwood dowels, grooved all round, in a limited range of sizes.

If you are using a dowelling jig (▷) there's no need to mark the centres of the dowel holes. Otherwise set a marking gauge to the centre line on both rails (2), drive panel pins into the edge of the side rail to mark dowel hole centres, then cut them to short sharp points with pliers (3). Line up the rails and push them together for the metal points to mark the end grain of the crossrail (4). Pull out the cut panel pins.

With the appropriate dowel bit in a power drill, bore the holes to a depth just over half the length of the dowels, then glue and assemble the joint.

Drilling accurate dowel holes is much easier with the drill mounted in a vertical drill stand (▷).

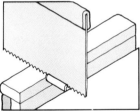

1 Saw glue escape slot

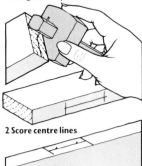

2 Score centre lines

3 Cut pins to sharp points

4 Mark hole centres on crossrail

MORTISE & TENON JOINTS

Mortise and tenon joints make a strong joint in narrow sections of timber – an essential joint for chair and table frames. A through tenon can be further strengthened with wedges but a stopped tenon is neater.

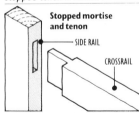

Stopped mortise and tenon

SIDE RAIL

CROSSRAIL

Cutting a mortise and tenon

Mark the width of the mortise, using the crossrail as a guide (1), and mark the shoulder of the tenon all round the crossrail (2) so that the tenon's length will be two-thirds of the side rail's width. Set a mortise gauge to one third of the crossrail's thickness and mark both mortise and tenon (3).

Cut the tenon as for the tongue of a lap joint. Remove the waste from the mortise with an electric drill – preferably mounted in a vertical stand (▷) – and square up the ends and sides with a chisel (4). Glue and assemble the joint.

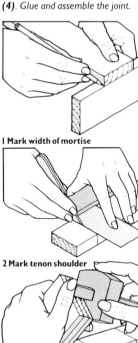

1 Mark width of mortise

2 Mark tenon shoulder

3 Mark thickness of joint

4 Chop out remaining waste

MITRE JOINT

WEDGES   SAW CUTS

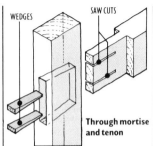

Through mortise and tenon

Cutting a through tenon

When a tenon is to pass right through a side rail cut it slightly longer than the width of the rail and make two saw cuts through it. Glue and assemble the joint, then drive two glued hardwood wedges into the saw cuts to expand the tenon in the mortise. When the glue has set plane the wedges and tenon flush with the rail.

MITRE JOINT

A mitre joint is for joining corners of frames. Especially useful for decorative moulded sections and skirting boards.

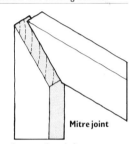

Mitre joint

Cutting a mitre joint

A right-angled mitre joint is made by sawing the ends of two rails to 45-degree angles in a mitre box (▷) and butting them together. Trim the joints with a finely set block plane and a shooting board (▷) and assemble the glued joint in a mitre cramp (▷). If the meeting faces of the rails are fairly large, glue alone will hold them together, but you can reinforce a mitre joint by sawing two slots across the corner and gluing strips of veneer into them (1), planing the veneers flush with the rails after the glue has set.

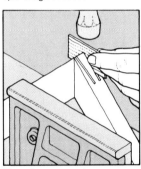

1 Inserting veneer strips

SCARF JOINT

A scarf joint is for joining two lengths of timber end to end.

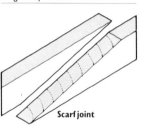

Scarf joint

Making a scarf joint

Clamp the two lengths side by side, their ends flush, and mark out the angled cut. The span of a scarf joint should be four times the width of the timber (1). Saw and plane both lengths down to the marked line simultaneously, then uncramp them. Glue the two angled faces together, securing them with battens and G-cramps while the glue sets (2).

A scarf joint that will be subject to a lot of stress can be reinforced with plywood plates screwed to both sides of the rails (3).

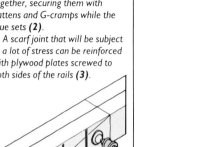

1 Proportion of a scarf joint

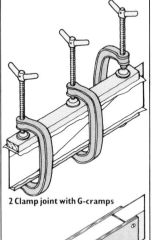

2 Clamp joint with G-cramps

3 A reinforced scarf joint

SEE ALSO

Details for: ▷

Mitre box	464
Shooting board	466
Drill stand	472
Dowelling jig	472
Mitre cramp	473
Marking gauge	463
Mortise gauge	463
Tenon saw	463
Bench planes	466
Block plane	466
Power drill	471
Twist drill	472

SEE ALSO

◁ Details for:
Try square	462
Plastering	152-157
Rendering	171
Mortar	425
Bricklaying	428-433
Using water level	444
Concrete finishing	445

Using a pointing tray
A pointing tray makes the filling of mortar joints very easy. Place the flat lip of the tray just under a horizontal joint and scrape the mortar into place with a jointer. Turn the tray round and push mortar into vertical joints through the gap between the raised sides.

Continental-pattern trowels

● **Essential tools**
Brick trowel
Pointing trowel
Plasterer's trowel
Mortar board
Hawk
Spirit level
Try square
Plumb line

BUILDER'S TOOL KIT

Bricklayers, joiners and plasterers are all specialist builders, each requiring a set of specific tools, but the amateur is more like one of the self-employed builders who must be able to tackle several areas of building work, and so need a much wider range of tools than the specialist. The builder's tool kit suggested here is for renovating and improving the structure of a house and for erecting and restoring garden structures or paving. Electrical work, decorating and plumbing call for other sets of tools.

FLOATS AND TROWELS

For professional builders, floats and trowels have specific uses, but in home maintenance the small trowel for repointing brickwork is often found ideal for patching small areas of plaster, while the plasterer's trowel is as likely to be used for smoothing concrete.

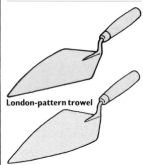

London-pattern trowel

Canadian-pattern trowel
Brick trowel
A brick trowel is for handling and placing mortar when laying bricks or concrete blocks. A professional might use one with a blade as long as 300mm (1ft), but such a trowel is too heavy and unwieldy for the amateur, so buy a good-quality brick trowel with a fairly short blade.

The blade of a *London-pattern trowel* has one curved edge for cutting bricks, a skill that needs much practice to perfect. The blade's other edge is straight, for picking up mortar. This type of trowel is made in right- and left-handed versions, so be sure to buy the right one for you. A right-handed trowel has its curved edge on the right when you point it away from you.

A Canadian-pattern trowel is symmetrical, so it's convenient when people with different left- and right-hand preferences want to share the one trowel.

Pointing trowel
The blade of a pointing trowel is no more than 75 to 100mm (3 to 4in) long, designed for repairing or shaping mortar joints between bricks.

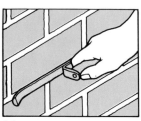

Jointer
A jointer is shaped for making 'V' or concave joints between bricks. The narrow blade is dragged along the mortar joint and the curved front end used for shaping the verticals.

Frenchman
A Frenchman is a specialized tool for cutting excess mortar away from brickwork jointing. You can make one by heating and bending an old table knife.

Wooden float
A wooden float is for applying and smoothing cement renderings and concrete to a fine attractive texture. The more expensive ones have detachable handles so that their wooden blades can be replaced when they wear, but the amateur is unlikely to use a float often enough to justify the extra cost.

Plasterer's trowel
A plasterer's trowel is a steel float for applying plaster and cement renderings to walls. It is also dampened and used for 'polishing', stroking the surface of the material when it has firmed up. Some builders prefer to apply rendering with a heavy trowel and finish it with a more flexible blade, but one has to be quite skilled to exploit such subtle differences.

BOARDS FOR CARRYING MORTAR OR PLASTER

Any convenient-sized sheet of 12 or 18mm (½ or ¾in) exterior-grade plywood can be used as a mixing board for plaster or mortar. A panel about 1m (3ft) square is ideal, and a smaller spotboard, about 600mm (2ft) square, is convenient for carrying the material to the actual work site. In either case screw some battens to the undersides of the boards to make them easier to lift and carry. Make a small lightweight hawk to carry pointing mortar or plaster by nailing a single batten underneath a plywood board so that you can plug a handle into it.

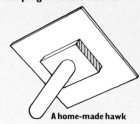

A home-made hawk

LEVELLING AND MEASURING TOOLS

You can make several specialized tools for measuring and levelling, but don't skimp on essentials like a good spirit level and a robust tape measure.

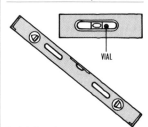

VIAL

Spirit level
A spirit level is a machine-made straightedge incorporating special glass tubes or vials that contain a liquid. In each vial an air bubble floats. When a bubble rests exactly between two lines marked on the glass the structure on which the level is held is known to be properly horizontal or vertical, depending on the vial's orientation. Buy a wooden or lightweight aluminium level 600 to 900mm (2 to 3ft) long. A well-made one is very strong, but treat it with care and always clean mortar or plaster from it before they set.

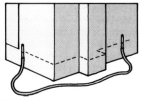

Water level
You can make a water level from a garden hose with short lengths of transparent plastic tube plugged into its ends. Fill the hose with water until it appears in both tubes. As water level is constant the levels in the tubes are always identical and so can be used for marking identical heights even over long distances and round obstacles and bends.

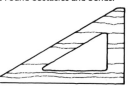

Builder's square
A large set square is useful when you set out brick or concrete-block corners. The best ones are stamped out of sheet metal, but you can make a serviceable one by cutting out a thick plywood right-angled triangle with a hypotenuse of about 750 mm (2ft 6in). Cut out the centre of the triangle to reduce the weight.

Checking a square
Accuracy is important, so check the square by placing it against a straight batten on the floor, drawing a line against the square to make a right angle with the batten, then turning the square to see if it forms the same angle from the other side.

Try square (◁)
Use a try square for marking out square cuts or joints on timber.

Making a plumb line
Any small but heavy weight hung on a length of fine string will make a suitable plumb line for judging the verticality of structures or surfaces.

Bricklayer's line

Use a bricklayer's line as a guide for laying bricks or blocks level. It is a length of nylon string stretched between two flat-bladed pins that are driven into vertical joints at the ends of a wall. There are also special line blocks that hook over the bricks at the ends of a course. As a makeshift you can stretch a string between two stakes driven into the ground outside the line of the wall.

Steel pins and line
Buy the special pins or make your own by hammering flats on 100mm (4in) nails.

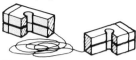

Line blocks
Blocks grip the brickwork corners; the line passes through their slots.

Plasterer's rule

A plasterer's rule is simply a straight wood batten used for scraping plaster and rendering undercoats level.

Straightedge

Any length of straight, fairly stout timber can be used to tell whether a surface is flat or, used with a spirit level, to test whether two points are at the same height.

Gauge stick

For gauging the height of brick courses, calibrate a softwood batten by making saw cuts across it at 75mm (3in) intervals – the thickness of a brick plus its mortar joint.

Tape measure

An ordinary retractable steel tape measure is adequate for most purposes but if you need to mark out or measure a large plot hire a wind-up tape up to 30m (100ft) in length.

Marking gauge (▷)

This tool has a sharp steel point for scoring a line on timber parallel to its edge. Its adjustable stock acts as a fence and keeps the point a constant distance from the edge.

HAMMERS

Very few hammers are needed on a building site.

Claw hammer (▷)

Choose a strong claw hammer for building wooden stud partitions, nailing floorboards, making door and window frames and putting up garden fencing.

Club hammer

A heavy club hammer is used for driving cold chisels and for various demolition jobs. It is also useful for driving large masonry nails into walls.

Sledgehammer

Hire a big sledgehammer if you have to break up hardcore or paving. It's also the best tool for driving stakes or fence posts into the ground, though you can make do with a club hammer if the ground is not too hard.

Mallet (▷)

A carpenter's wooden mallet is the proper tool for driving wood chisels, but you can use a hammer if the chisels have impact-resistant plastic handles.

SAWS

Every builder needs a range of handsaws, but consider hiring a power saw when you have to cut a lot of heavy structural timbers, and especially if you plan to rip floorboards down to width, a very tiring job when done by hand.

There are special power saws for cutting metal, and even for sawing through masonry.

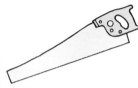

Panel saw

All kinds of man-made building boards are used in house construction, so buy a good panel saw – useful also for cutting large structural timbers to the required lengths.

Tenon saw (▷)

A good saw for accurately cutting wall studs, floorboards, panelling and joints. The metal stiffening along the top of the blade keeps it rigid and less likely to wander off line.

Padsaw (▷)

Also called a keyhole saw, this small saw has a narrow tapered blade for cutting holes in timber.

Coping saw (▷)

A coping saw has a frame that holds a fairly coarse but very narrow blade under tension for cutting curves in wood.

Floorboard saw

If you prise a floorboard above its neighbours you can cut across it with an ordinary tenon saw, but a floorboard saw's curved cutting edge makes it easier to avoid damaging the boards on either side.

Hacksaw (▷)

The hardened-steel blades of a hacksaw have fine teeth for cutting metal. Use one to cut steel concrete-reinforcing rods or small pieces of sheet metal.

Sheet saw

A hacksaw's frame prevents its use for cutting large sheets of metal. For that job bolt a hacksaw blade to the edge of the flat blade of a sheet saw, which will also cut corrugated plastic sheeting and roofing slates.

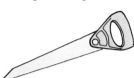

Universal saw

A universal or general-purpose saw is designed to cut wood, metal, plastics and building boards. Its short frameless blade has a low-friction coating and is stiff enough to make straight cuts without wandering. The handle can be set at various angles. The saw is particularly useful for cutting secondhand timber, which may contain nails or screws that would blunt an ordinary woodsaw.

POWER SAWS

A *circular saw* (▷) will accurately rip timber or man-made boards down to size. As well as doing away with the effort of hand-sawing large timbers a sharp power saw produces such a clean cut that there is often no need for planing afterwards.

A *power jigsaw* (▷) cuts curves in timber and boards but is also useful for cutting holes in fixed wall panels and sawing through floorboards so as to lift them.

A *reciprocating saw* (▷) is a two-handed power saw with a long pointed blade, powerful enough to cut heavy timber sections and even through a complete stud partition, panels and all.

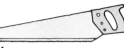

Masonry saw

A masonry saw looks very like a wood handsaw but its tungsten-carbide teeth will cut brick, concrete blocks and stone.

DRILLS

A powerful electric drill is invaluable to a builder, but a hand brace is useful when you have to bore holes outdoors or in lofts and cellars that lack convenient electric sockets.

Power drill (▷)

Buy a power drill, a range of twist drills and some spade or power-bore bits (▷) for drilling timber, and make sure that the tool has a percussion or hammer action for drilling masonry. For masonry you need special drill bits tipped with tungsten carbide. The smaller ones are matched to the size of standard wall plugs, though there are much larger ones with reduced shanks that can be used in a standard power-drill chuck. The larger bits are expensive, so hire them when you need them. Percussion bits are even tougher than masonry bits, with shatter-proof tips.

Brace and bit (▷)

A brace and bit is the ideal hand tool for drilling large holes in timber, and when fitted with a screwdriver bit it gives good leverage for driving or extracting large woodscrews.

SEE ALSO

Details for: ▷

Marking gauge	463
Tenon saw	463
Padsaw	464
Coping saw	464
Circular saw	465
Power jigsaw	465
Reciprocating saw	465
Power drill	471
Brace	471
Power-bore bit	472
Claw hammer	472
Mallet	473
Hacksaw	486

Drilling masonry for wall plugs
Set the drill for low speed and hammer action, and wrap tape round the bit to mark the depth to be drilled. Allow for slightly more depth than the length of the plug as dust will pack down into the hole when you insert it. Drill the hole in stages, partly withdrawing the bit at times to clear the debris.

Protect floor coverings and paintwork from falling dust by taping a paper bag under the position of the hole before you start drilling.

● **Essential tools**
Straightedge
Tape measure
Claw hammer
Club hammer
Panel saw
Tenon saw
Hacksaw
Padsaw
Power drill
Masonry bits
Brace and bits

SEE ALSO

◁ Details for:

Jack plane	466
Moulding and plough planes	466-467
Wood chisels	468
Cabinet screwdriver	473
Cross-head screwdriver	473
Cutting glass	200-201
Removing glass	202

ADDITIONAL BUILDER'S TOOLS
The following tools would be a useful addition to a builder's tool kit, especially when carrying out major repairs and improvements.

Crowbar
A crowbar, or wrecking bar, is for demolishing timber framework. Force the flat tip between components and use the leverage of the long shaft to prise them apart. Choose a bar that also has a claw at one end for removing large nails.

Slater's ripper
To replace individual slates you must cut their fixing nails without disturbing the slates overlapping them, and for this you need a slater's ripper. Pass the long hooked blade up between the slates, locate a hook over the fixing nail and pull down sharply to cut it.

● **Essential tools**
Glass cutter
Putty knife
Cold chisel
Bolster
Spade
Shovel
Rake
Wheelbarrow
Cabinet screwdriver
Cross-head screwdriver
Jack plane

480

GLAZIERS' TOOLS

Glass is such a hard and brittle material that it can be worked only with specialized tools.

Glass cutter
A glass cutter doesn't really cut glass but scores a line in it. The scoring is done by a tiny hardened-steel wheel or a chip of industrial diamond mounted in the pen-like holder. The glass will break along the scored line when pressure is applied to it.

Beam compass cutter
A beam compass cutter is for scoring circles on glass – when, for example, you need a round hole in a window pane to fit a ventilator. The cutting wheel is mounted at the end of an adjustable beam that turns on a centre pivot which is fixed to the glass by suction.

Spear-point glass drill
A glass drill has a flat spearhead-shaped tip of tungsten-steel shaft. The shape of the tip reduces friction that would otherwise crack the glass, but it needs lubricating with oil, paraffin or water during drilling.

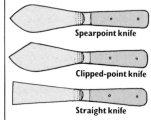

Hacking knife
A hacking knife has a heavy steel blade for chipping old putty out of window rebates so as to remove the glass. Place its point between the putty and the frame and tap its thickened back with a hammer.

Spearpoint knife

Clipped-point knife

Straight knife

Putty knife
The blunt blade of a putty knife is for shaping and smoothing fresh putty. You can choose between spearpoint, clipped-point and straight blades according to your personal preference.

CHISELS

As well as chisels for cutting and paring wood joints (◁) you will need some special ones for masonry work.

Cold chisel
Cold chisels are made from solid steel hexagonal-section rod. They are primarily for cutting metal bars and chopping the heads off rivets, but a builder will use one for cutting a chase in plaster and brickwork or chopping out old brick pointing.

Slip a plastic safety sleeve over the chisel to protect your hand from a misplaced blow with the club hammer.

Plugging chisel
A plugging chisel has a flat narrow bit (tip) for cutting out old pointing. It's worth hiring one if you have a large area of brickwork to repoint.

Bolster chisel
The wide bit of a bolster chisel is for cutting bricks and concrete blocks. It's also useful for levering up floorboards.

WORK GLOVES

Wear strong work gloves whenever you carry paving slabs, concrete blocks or rough timber. Ordinary gardening gloves are better than none but won't last long on a building site. The best work gloves have leather palms and fingers though you may prefer a pair with ventilated backs for comfort in hot weather.

DIGGING TOOLS

Much building work requires some kind of digging – for laying strip foundations and concrete pads, sinking rows of postholes and so on. You may already have the essential tools in your garden shed; others you can hire.

Pickaxe
Use a medium-weight pickaxe to break up heavily compacted soil, especially if it contains a lot of buried rubble.

Mattock
The wide blade of a mattock is ideal for breaking up heavy clay soil, and it's better than an ordinary pickaxe for ground that's riddled with tree roots.

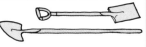

Spade
Buy a good-quality spade for excavating soil and mixing concrete. One with a stainless-steel blade is best, but alloy steel will last fairly well if it is looked after. For strength choose a D-shaped handle whose hardwood shaft has been split and riveted with metal plates to the crosspiece, and make sure that the shaft socket and blade are forged in one piece.

Square blades seem to be the most popular, though some builders prefer a round-mouth spade with a long pole handle for digging deep trenches and holes.

Shovel
You can use a spade for mixing and placing concrete or mortar, but the raised edges of a shovel retain it better.

Garden rake
Use an ordinary garden rake to spread gravel or level wet concrete, but be sure to wash it before any concrete sets on it.

Post-hole auger
Hire a post-hole auger to sink narrow holes for fence and gate posts by driving it into the ground like a corkscrew and pulling out plugs of earth.

Wheelbarrow
The average garden wheelbarrow is not really strong enough for work on building sites, which entails carrying heavy loads of wet concrete and rubble. Unless the tubular underframe is rigidly strutted the barrow's thin metal body will distort and perhaps spill its load as you cross rough ground. Check, too, that the axle is fixed securely. Cheap wheelbarrows often lose their wheels when their loads are being tipped into excavations.

SCREWDRIVERS

One's choice of screwdrivers is a personal matter, and most people accumulate a collection of types and sizes over the years.

Cabinet screwdriver (◁)
Buy at least one large flat-tip screwdriver. The fixed variety is quite adequate but a pump-action one, which drives large screws very quickly, is useful when you assemble big wooden building structures.

Cross-head screwdriver (◁)
Choose the size and type of cross-head screwdriver to suit the work in hand. There is no 'most useful size' as the driver must fit the screw slots exactly.

PLANES

Your choice of planes depends on the kind of joinery you plan to do. Sophisticated framing may call for moulding or grooving planes (◁) but most woodwork needs only skimming to leave a fairly smooth finish.

Jack plane (◁)
A medium-size bench plane, the jack plane, is the best general-purpose tool.

DECORATOR'S TOOL KIT

Most of us decorate our own houses or flats to some extent, and decorators' tools are fairly common. Though traditionalists will stick to tried and tested tools and materials of proven reliability others will prefer recent innovations aimed at making the work easier and faster for the home decorator.

TOOLS FOR PREPARATION

Whether you are painting papering or tiling, the surface to which the materials will be applied must be sound and clean.

Straight scraper

Serrated scraper

Wallpaper or paint scraper
The wide stiff blade of a scraper is for removing softened paint or soaked wallpaper. The best scrapers have high-quality steel blades and riveted rosewood handles. One with a 100 to 125mm (4 to 5in) wide blade is best for stripping wallpaper, but a narrow one, no more than 25mm (1in) wide, is useful for removing paint from window or door frames. A serrated scraper will score impervious wallcovering so that water or stripping solution can penetrate it faster. If you use one, try not to damage the wall behind the covering.

Vinyl gloves
Most people wear ordinary 'rubber' gloves to protect their hands when washing down or preparing paintwork, but tough PVC work gloves are more hardwearing and will protect you from a great many harmful chemicals.

WOODWORKING TOOLS

In addition to specialized decorating tools you will need a basic woodworking tool kit (▷) for repairing damaged framing or floorboards and for installing wall panelling or laying parquet flooring.

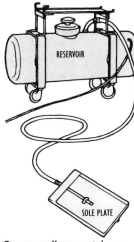

RESERVOIR

SOLE PLATE

Steam wallpaper stripper
To remove wallpaper quickly, especially thick wallcovering, hire an electric steam-generating stripper. All such strippers work on the same principle, but follow any specific safety instructions that come with the machine.

Using a steam stripper
Fill its reservoir and plug it into a socket outlet 15 minutes before starting work so as to generate a good head of steam. Hold the steaming plate against the wallpaper until it is soft enough to be removed with a scraper. The time for this will depend on the type of the wallcovering.

Straight-sided shavehook

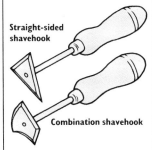

Combination shavehook

Shavehook
This is a special scraper for removing old paint and varnish. A straight-sided triangular one is fine for flat surfaces but one with a combination blade can also be used on concave and convex mouldings. You pull a shavehook towards you to remove the softened paint.

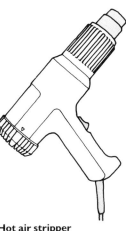

Hot air stripper
The gas blowtorch was once the professional's tool for softening old paint so as to strip it, but the modern electric hot air stripper is much easier to use. It is as efficient as a blowtorch but involves little risk of scorching woodwork. Early models were heavy and tiring to use, but today's are light enough to be used for long periods without fatigue. On some strippers the air temperature can be adjusted. Others have interchangeable nozzles shaped to concentrate the heated air or direct it away from glass panes.

Filling knife
A filling knife looks like a paint scraper but has a flexible blade for forcing filler into cracks in timber or plaster. Patch large areas of damaged wall with a plasterer's trowel (▷).

Handbrush

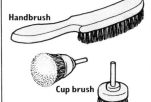

Cup brush

Wire brushes
A handbrush with steel wire 'bristles' will remove flaking paint and rust particles from metalwork before repainting. The job is easier with a rotary wire cup brush in a power drill, but wear goggles or safety glasses if you use one.

Mastic guns
Non-setting (permanently flexible) mastic is for sealing gaps between masonry and wooden frames and other joints between materials whose different rates of expansion will eventually crack and eject a rigid filler. You can buy mastic that is squeezed direct from its plastic tube like toothpaste, but it is easier to apply from a cartridge in a spring-loaded gun or an aerosol can with a special nozzle.

Tacky rag
Though you may find it hard to get one, a resin-impregnated cloth called a 'tacky rag' is ideal for picking up particles of dust and hard paint from a surface prepared for painting. Failing a tacky rag use a lint-free cloth dampened with white spirit.

Dusting brush
A dusting brush has long soft bristles for clearing dust out of mouldings and crevices just before painting woodwork. You can use an ordinary paintbrush if you keep it clean and reserve it for the job.

SEE ALSO

Details for: ▷

Woodworking tools	462-474
Plasterer's trowel	478
Stripping paper	52
Stripping wood	58-59
Preparing metal	60

WET AND DRY PAPER

Wet and dry abrasive paper is for smoothing new paintwork or varnish before applying the final coat. It is a waterproof backing paper with silicon carbide particles glued to it. Dip a piece in water and rub the paintwork until a slurry of paint and water forms. Wipe it off with a cloth before it dries, then rinse the paper clean and continue.

● **Essential tools**
Wallpaper scraper
Combination spokeshave
Filling knife
Hot air stripper
Wire brush

SEE ALSO

◁ Details for:
Paint stripper	59
Using brushes	68
Stencilling	72
Painting wood	76
Using a paint shield	78
Graining	79
Painting radiators	85

Paint kettle
To carry paint to a worksite decant a little into a cheap, lightweight plastic paint kettle.

PAINTBRUSHES

Some paintbrushes are made from natural animal hair. Hog bristle is the best, but it is often mixed with inferior horsehair or oxhair to reduce cost. Synthetic bristle brushes are usually the least expensive, and are quite adequate for the home decorator.

Bristle types
Bristle is ideal for paintbrushes because each hair tapers naturally and splits at the tip into even finer filaments that hold paint well. Bristle is also tough and resilient. Synthetic 'bristle', usually of nylon, is made to resemble the characteristics of real bristle, and a good-quality nylon brush will serve the average painter as well as a bristle one.

Choosing a brush
The bristles of a good brush – the 'filling' – are densely packed. When you fan them with your fingers they should spring back into shape immediately. Flex the tip of the brush against your hand to see if any bristles work loose. Even a good brush will shed a few individual ones at first, but never clumps. The ferrule should be fixed firmly to the handle.

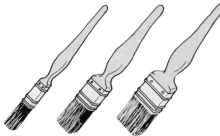

12mm (½in) 25mm (1in) 50mm (2in)

● **Essential tools**
Flat brushes
12, 25 and 50mm
(½, 1 and 2in)
Wallbrush
150mm (6in)

Flat paintbrush
The filling is set in rubber–or occasionally in pitch or resin–and bound to the wooden or plastic handle by a pressed-metal ferrule. You will need several sizes up to 50mm (2in) for painting, varnishing and staining woodwork.

One-knot paintbrush
The bristles of a one-knot paintbrush are bound to a cylindrical handle with string, wire or a metal ferrule. Their grouping makes them very resilient, but when flexed against a surface they will fan out like those of the commoner flat paintbrush.

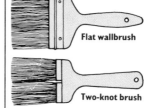

Flat wallbrush

Two-knot brush

Wallbrush
To apply emulsion paint by brush use a 150mm (6in) flat wallbrush or a two-knot brush of the kind favoured by continental painters and decorators.

Cutting-in brush
The filling of a cutting-in brush, or 'bevelled sash tool', is cut at an angle for painting moulded glazing bars right up into the corners and against the glass, though most painters make do with a 12mm (½in) flat brush.

STENCIL AND GRAIN-EFFECT TOOLS

Stencil brush
A stencil brush has short stiff bristles. The paint is stippled on with their tips and a cut-out template defines the painted shape.

Grainers
These are special brushes for reproducing the effects of natural woodgrain on paint or varnish. A 'mottler' has a dense soft filling of squirrel hair for lifting bands or streaks of colour to simulate figured hardwoods. A 'pencil grainer' has a row of fine brushes mounted in one handle for drawing patterns of parallel lines.

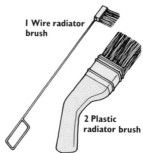

I Wire radiator brush

2 Plastic radiator brush

Radiator brush
Unless you take a radiator off the wall for decorating you need a special brush to paint the back of it and the wall behind it. There are two kinds: one with a standard flat paintbrush head at right angles to its long wire handle (**1**), the other like a conventional paintbrush but with a cranked plastic handle (**2**).

Banister brush
Use a household banister brush for painting rough or rendered walls.

Paint shield

Glass scraper

Paint shield and scraper
There are various plastic and metal shields for protecting glass when window frames and glazing bars are being painted, and glass that does get spattered can be cleaned with a razor blade clipped in a special holder.

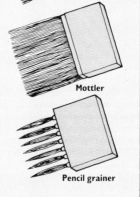

Stencil brush

Mottler

Pencil grainer

CLEANING BRUSHES

● **Emulsion paint**
As soon as you finish working with emulsion paint wash it from the brush with warm soapy water, flexing the bristles between your fingers to work all paint out of the roots, then rinse the brush in clean water and shake out the excess. Smooth the bristles and slip an elastic band round their tips to hold the shape of the filling while it is drying.

Holding the shape of a brush

● **Oil paint**
If you are using oil paint you can suspend the brush overnight in enough water to cover the bristles, blot it with kitchen paper next day and continue painting.
When you have finished, brush excess paint out on newspaper, then flex the bristles in a bowl of thinners. Some finishes need special thinners, so check for this on the container; otherwise use white spirit or a chemical brush cleaner. Wash the dirty thinners from the brush with hot soapy water, then rinse it.

Soaking a brush

● **Hardened paint**
If paint has hardened on a brush, soak its bristles in brush cleaner to soften the paint which will become water-soluble and will wash out easily with hot water. If the old paint is unusually stubborn dip the bristles in some paint stripper (◁).

STORING PAINTBRUSHES

For long-term storage fold soft paper over the filling and secure it with an elastic band round paper and ferrule.

PAINT PADS

Paint pads are a fairly recent development aimed at helping inexperienced painters to apply oil and emulsion paint quickly and evenly. They are not universally popular, but no one disputes their value in painting large flat areas. They cover quickly and are unlikely to drip paint if they are loaded properly.

Standard pads
There is a range of rectangular pads for painting walls, ceilings and flat woodwork. They have short mohair pile on their painting surfaces and handles on their backs.

Edging pad
To paint a straight edge—between a wall and a ceiling, for instance—use an edging pad with small wheels or rollers that guide it parallel to the adjacent surface.

Sash pad
A sash pad has a small mohair sole for painting glazing bars. Most sash pads have plastic guides on their backs to prevent them straying onto the glass.

PRESSURIZED PAINTING SYSTEM

With a pressurized painting system you can work continuously for as long as its reservoir contains paint. An ordinary soda-syphon bulb delivers the paint at a slow but steady pace, and a control button on the handle releases it to the painting head, which is detachable and can be a roller, a brush or a pad as required. You can carry the reservoir or clip it to your belt for greater freedom of movement.

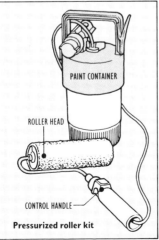

PAINT CONTAINER

ROLLER HEAD

CONTROL HANDLE

Pressurized roller kit

CLEANING PAINT PADS

Before dipping a new pad into paint, brush it with a clothes brush to remove any loose nylon filaments.

● When you finish painting, blot the pad on old newspaper, then wash it in the appropriate solvent—water for emulsion, white spirit or brush cleaner for oil paints, or any special thinners recommended by the paint manufacturer. Squeeze the foam and rub the pile with gloved fingertips, then wash the pad in hot soapy water and rinse it.

● Even after washing, a new pad may be stained by paint, but the colour will not contaminate the next batch of fresh paint.

Pad tray
Pads and trays are normally sold as sets, but if you buy a separate tray get one with a loading roller that distributes paint evenly onto the sole of a pad drawn across it.

PAINT ROLLERS

A paint roller is efficient for painting large areas quickly. On the better type the cylindrical sleeve that applies the paint slides onto a revolving sprung-wire cage on a cranked handle. The sleeves on this type of roller are easily changed. Don't buy one whose sleeve is held in place by a small nut and washer. Even if the nut doesn't get lost, corroded or paint-clogged it's much too fiddly.

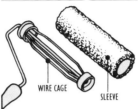

WIRE CAGE   SLEEVE

Sizes of roller sleeves
Sleeves for standard rollers range from 175mm (7in) to about 337mm (1ft 1½in) in length but there are smaller rollers for painting narrow strips of wall or woodwork.

Deep-pile sleeve

Short-pile mohair

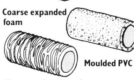

Coarse expanded foam

Moulded PVC

Types of roller sleeves
There are roller sleeves of various materials to suit different paints and surface textures. Most are of **sheepskin** or **synthetic fibre**, both of which suit emulsion paint and leave an even finely textured finish. Use a **deep-pile** sleeve to paint a heavily textured surface, a **medium-pile** one for smooth walls and ceilings.
Short-pile roller sleeves, usually of mohair, are made for use with oil paints.
The cheap **plastic-foam** sleeves are unsatisfactory both with oil and emulsion paints. They leave tiny air bubbles in the painted surface and the foam often distorts as it dries after washing. But they are cheap enough to be thrown away after use with finishes—like bituminous paint—which would be hard to remove even from a short-pile roller sleeve.

Use a **coarse expanded-foam** sleeve for applying textured coatings. There are also **moulded PVC** rollers with embossed surfaces to pattern all kinds of textured paints and coatings.

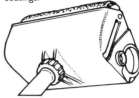

Extending a roller
If your roller has a hollow handle you can plug it onto a telescopic extension handle so as to reach a ceiling from the floor. Loading an extended roller can be tricky, but you can buy one with a built-in reservoir that keeps the roller charged and holds enough paint for a large area.

CLEANING A ROLLER

Remove most of the excess paint by running the roller back and forth across old newspaper. If you plan to use the roller next day apply a few drops of the appropriate thinners to the sleeve and wrap it in plastic. Otherwise clean, wash and rinse the sleeve before the paint can set.

● **Emulsion paint**
If you've been using emulsion paint flush most of it out under running water, then massage a little liquid detergent into the pile and flush it again.

● **Roller washer**
You can mechanize the job with a roller washer that stands in the sink, its hose attached to a tap. Lower the roller, complete with sleeve, into the washer and turn on the tap. The force of the water spins the roller head and flushes the paint from it out of the base of the washer into the drain. The roller is cleaned in about one or two minutes.

● **Oil paint**
To remove oil paint pour some thinners into the roller tray and slowly roll the sleeve back and forth in it. Squeeze the roller and agitate the pile with your fingertips. When the paint has all dissolved wash the sleeve in hot soapy water.

SEE ALSO
Details for: ▷

Using pads	68
Using rollers	68

1   2   3

1 Corner roller
You cannot paint into a corner with a standard roller, so unless there are to be different adjacent colours, paint the corner first with a shaped corner roller.
2 Pipe roller
A pipe roller has two narrow sleeves, mounted side by side, which locate over the cylindrical pipework to paint it.
3 Radiator roller
This is a thin roller on a long wire handle for painting behind radiators and pipes.

Roller tray
A paint roller is loaded from a sloping plastic or metal tray whose deep end acts as a paint reservoir. Load the roller by rolling paint from the deep end up and down the tray's ribbed slope once or twice so as to get even distribution on the sleeve.

● **Essential tools**
Standard pads
50 and 200mm
(2 and 8in)
Sash pad
Large roller and selection of sleeves
Roller tray

483

PAINTSPRAYING EQUIPMENT

Spraying is so fast and efficient that it's worth considering if you plan to paint the outside walls of a building. The equipment is expensive to buy but it can be hired from most tool-hire outlets. You can spray most exterior paints and finishes if they are thinned properly but tell the hire company which one you wish to use so that they can supply the right spray gun with the correct nozzle. Hire goggles and a facemask at the same time.

SEE ALSO

◁ Details for:
Wallbrush	**482**
Using a spray gun	66
Reinforced emulsion	67
Pasting wallcoverings	93
Hanging wallcoverings	94
Tyrolean finish	171

Preparation

As far as possible plan to work on a dry and windless day, and allow time to mask off windows, doors and pipework. Follow the setting-up and handling instructions supplied with the equipment, and if you are new to the work, practise a little beforehand on an inconspicuous section of wall.

Compressor-operated spray

With this equipment the paint is mixed with pressurized air to emerge as a fine spray. Some compressors deliver compressed air to an intermediate tank and top it up as air is drawn off by the spray gun, but most hired ones supply air directly to the gun. The trigger opens a valve to admit air, at the same time opening the paint outlet at the nozzle. The paint is drawn from a container, usually mounted below the gun, and mixes with compressed air at the tip. Most guns have air-delivery horns at the sides of the nozzle to produce a fan-shaped pattern.

Spraying textured paint
Hire a special gravity-fed spray gun to apply reinforced emulsions and 'tyrolean' finishes. The material is loaded into a hopper on top of the gun.

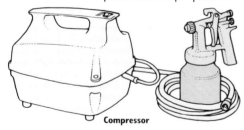

Compressor

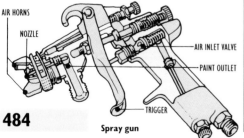

AIR HORNS
NOZZLE
AIR INLET VALVE
PAINT OUTLET
TRIGGER

484

Spray gun

Airless sprayer

In an airless sprayer an electric pump delivers the paint itself at high pressure to the spray gun. The paint is picked up through a tube inserted in the paint container and the pump forces it through a high-pressure hose to

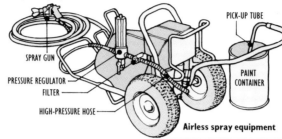

PICK-UP TUBE
SPRAY GUN
PRESSURE REGULATOR
FILTER
PAINT CONTAINER
HIGH-PRESSURE HOSE

Airless spray equipment

a filter and pressure regulator which is adjustable to produce required spray patterns. The paint leaves the nozzle at such high pressure that it can penetrate skin, so most such spray guns have safety shields on their nozzles.

USING SPRAYERS SAFELY

Follow any safety advice supplied with the sprayer but take the following precautions in any case:

- Wear goggles and a facemask when spraying.
- Don't spray indoors without proper extraction equipment.
- Atomised oil paint is highly flammable, so have no naked lights and do not smoke when you spray.
- Never leave the equipment unattended, especially where there are children or pets; if the gun has a safety lock, engage it while you are not actually spraying.
- Unplug the equipment and release the pressure in the hose before trying to clear a blocked nozzle.
- Never aim the gun at yourself or anyone else. If you accidentally spray your skin at close quarters with an airless gun seek medical advice at once.

CLEANING A SPRAY GUN

Empty out any paint left in the container and add some thinners. Spray the thinners until it emerges clear, then release the pressure and dismantle the spray nozzle. Clean the parts with a solvent-dampened rag and wipe out the container.

COMMON SPRAYING FAULTS

Streaked paintwork
An uneven streaked finish results if you don't overlap the passes of the gun.

Patchy paintwork
Coverage won't be consistent if you move the gun in an arc. Keep it pointing directly at the wall and moving parallel to it.

Orange-peel texture
A wrinkle paint film resembling the texture of orange peel is usually caused by spraying paint that is too thick, but if the paint seems to be of the right consistency you may be moving the spray gun too slowly.

Runs
Runs will occur if you apply too much paint, probably through holding the gun too close to the surface you're spraying.

Powdery finish
This is caused by paint drying before it reaches the wall. Hold the gun a little closer to the wall surface.

Spattering
Pressure that's too high will produce a speckled finish. Lower the pressure until the finish becomes satisfactory.

Spitting
A partly clogged nozzle will make the gun splutter. Clear the nozzle with a stiff bristle from a brush—never use wire—then wipe it with a rag dampened in thinners.

PAPERHANGERS' TOOLS

You can improvise some of the tools needed for paperhanging, but even purpose-made equipment is inexpensive so it's worth having a proper kit.

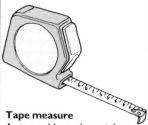

Tape measure
A retractable steel tape is best for measuring walls and ceilings to estimate the amount of wallcovering you'll need.

Plumb bob and line

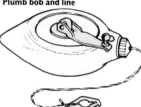

Retractable plumb line

Plumb line
Any small weight suspended on fine string can be used to mark the position of one edge of a strip of wallpaper. Hold the end of the line near the ceiling, allow the weight to come to rest, then mark the wall at points down the length of the line.

A purpose-made plumb line has a pointed metal weight called a plumb bob. In expensive versions the line retracts into a hollow plumb bob containing coloured chalk and is coated with chalk as it is withdrawn. When the line hangs vertically stretch it taut, then snap it against the wall like a bowstring to leave a chalked line.

Paste brush
Apply paste to the back of wallcovering with a wide wallbrush (◁). Alternatively use a short-pile mohair roller. Clean either tool by washing it in warm water.

PASTING TABLE

Though you can paste wallcoverings on any convenient flat surface a proper pasting table is ideal. It stands higher than the average dining table and is only 25mm (1in) wider than a standard roll of wallpaper, making it easier to apply paste without spreading onto the work surface. The underframe folds flat and the top is hinged, so the table can be carried from room to room and stowed in a small space.

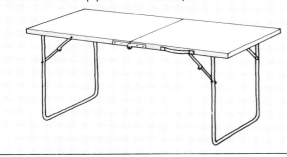

Paperhanger's brush
This is a brush used for smoothing wallcovering onto a surface. Its bristles should be soft, so as not to damage delicate paper, but springy enough to provide the pressure to squeeze excess paste and air bubbles from beneath the wallcovering. Wash the brush in warm water when you finish work to prevent paste hardening on the tips of the bristles.

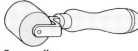

Seam roller
Use a hardwood or plastic seam roller to press down butted joints between adjacent strips of wallpaper, but not on embossed or delicate wallcoverings.

Rubber   Felt

Smoothing roller
There are rubber rollers for squeezing trapped air from under wallcoverings, but use a felt one on delicate and flocked wallpapers.

Paperhanger's scissors
Any fairly large scissors can be used for trimming wallpaper to length, but proper paperhanger's scissors have extra-long blades to achieve a straight cut.

Craft knife

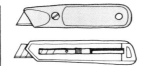

Use a knife to trim paper round light fittings and switches and to achieve perfect butt joints by cutting through overlapping edges of paper. The knife must be extremely sharp to avoid tearing the paper, so use one with disposable blades that you can change easily when one gets blunt. Some craft knives have short double-ended blades clamped in a metal or plastic handle. Others have long retractable blades that can be snapped off in short sections to leave a new sharp point.

TILING TOOLS

Most of the tools in a tiler's kit are for applying ceramic wall and floor tiles, but others are needed for laying soft tiles and vinyl sheeting.

Spirit level (▷)
You will need a spirit level for setting up temporary battens to align a field of tiles both horizontally and vertically.

Profile gauge
A profile gauge is for copying the shapes of pipework or door mouldings to provide a pattern for fitting soft floorcoverings. As you press the steel pins of the gauge against the object you wish to copy they slide back, mirroring the shape. When you want to copy another shape press the needles against a flat surface to reposition them in a straight line.

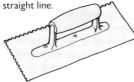

Serrated trowel
Make a ridged bed of adhesive for ceramic tiles by drawing the toothed edge of a plastic or steel tiler's trowel through the material.

Tile cutter
A tile cutter is a square-section rod of steel with a pointed tungsten-carbide tip. The tip is for scoring the glazed surface of a ceramic tile so that it will snap cleanly along the scored line. Other cutters have steel wheels like glass cutters (▷).

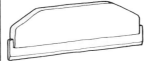

Saw file
A saw file has a bent metal frame that holds the thin wire rod under tension. The rod is coated with particles of tungsten-carbide hard enough to cut through ceramic tiles. Circular in section, the file will cut in any direction, so it can cut curved and straight lines with equal ease.

Squeegee
A squeegee has a blade of hard rubber mounted in a wooden handle. Use one for spreading grout into the gaps between ceramic tiles.

Nibblers
It is impossible to snap a very narrow strip off a ceramic tile. Instead score the line with a tile cutter, then break off the waste little by little with tile nibblers. They resemble pincers but have sharper jaws of tungsten-carbide that open automatically when you relax your grip on the spring-loaded handles.

TILE-CUTTING JIGS

A tile-cutting jig greatly simplifies the cutting and fitting of border tiles to fill the edges of a field of tiles. With the one tool you can measure the gap, score the tile and snap it along the scored line.

Using the jig
To measure the size of the tile to be cut slide the jig open until one pointer is against the adjacent wall and the other is against the edge of the last full tile (1). The jig automatically allows for grouting.

Fit the jig over the tile to be cut and with the tile cutter score the tile through the slot in the jig (2).

The cutter includes a pair of clippers with angled jaws for snapping the tile in two. Align the scored line with the pointer on the jaws and squeeze the handles until the tile breaks cleanly (3).

1 Measure the margin

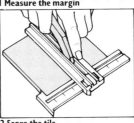

2 Score the tile

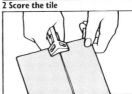

3 Snap the tile

Floor tile jig
Large cutting jigs for floor tiles can be hired or bought from good DIY stockists.

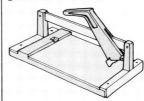

SEE ALSO

Details for: ▷

Spirit level	478
Glass cutters	480
Pasting wallcoverings	93
Hanging wallcoverings	94-97
Tiling	102-104, 110
Fixing ceiling tiles	112

Staple gun
A staple gun is used for fixing mineral-fibre tiles to battens attached to a ceiling. The hand-operated type has a trigger that works a spring-loaded striker, which drives two-pronged staples into the work. It can be tiring to use with an outstretched arm. An electronic tacker makes light work of the largest ceilings and is much more powerful than the hand-operated tool, though its force is adjustable to suit the various materials.

Hand-operated gun

Electronic tacker

● **Essential tools**
Steel tape measure
Plumb line
Paste brush
Paperhanger's brush
Seam roller
Scissors
Craft knife
Pasting table
Spirit level
Serrated trowel
Tile cutter and jig
Nibblers
Saw file
Squeegee

485

SEE ALSO

◁ Details for:
Tape measure 462
Try square 462
Clearing sinks 348
Clearing a WC 349
Clearing drains 350

PLUMBER'S AND METALWORKER'S TOOL KIT

The growing use of plastics in plumbing is likely to affect the trade considerably, and while plastics have been used for drainage for some years the advent of plastics suitable for mains pressure and hot water will have the greatest impact. But brass fittings and pipework of copper and other metals are still the most commonly used for domestic plumbing, so the plumber's tool kit is still basically a metalworker's one.

SINK AND DRAIN CLEANING EQUIPMENT

There's no need to hire a plumber to clear blocked appliances, pipes or even main drains. The necessary equipment can be bought or hired.

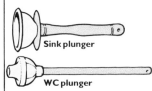

Sink plunger

WC plunger

Plunger
This is a simple but effective tool for clearing a blockage from the trap or WC pan. A pumping action on the rubber cap forces air and water along the pipe to disperse the blockage.

When you buy a plunger make sure that the cup is big enough to surround the waste outlet completely. The cup of a WC plunger may have a cone that makes a tight fit in the trap.

Compressed-air gun
A blocked wastepipe can be cleared with a compressed-air gun. A hand-operated pump compresses air in the gun's reservoir, to be released into the pipe by a trigger. The gun has three interchangeable nozzles to suit different outlets.

WC auger
The short coiled-wire WC auger, designed for clearing WC and gully traps, is rotated by a handle in a hollow rigid shaft. A vinyl guard prevents scratching of the WC pan.

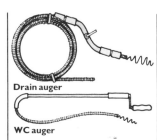

Drain auger

WC auger

Drain auger
A flexible drain auger of coiled wire will pass through small-diameter wastepipes to clear blockages. Pass the corkscrew-like head into the pipe until it reaches the blockage, clamp on the cranked handle and turn it to rotate the head and engage the blockage. Push and pull the auger until the pipe is clear.

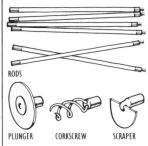

RODS

PLUNGER   CORKSCREW   SCRAPER

Drain rods
You can hire a complete set of rods and fittings for clearing main drains and inspection chambers. Traditionally the rods are of flexible cane and wire, but modern ones come in 1m (3ft 3in) lengths of polypropylene with threaded brass connectors. The clearing heads comprise a double-worm corkscrew fitting, a 100mm (4in) rubber plunger and a hinged scraper for clearing the open channels in inspection chambers.

MEASURING AND MARKING TOOLS

Tools for measuring and marking metal are very like those used for wood but are made and calibrated for greater accuracy because metal parts must fit with great precision.

Scriber
For precise work, mark lines and hole centres on metal with a pointed hardened-steel scriber—but use a pencil to mark the centre of a bend, as a scored line made with a scriber may open up when the metal is stretched on the outside of the bend.

Spring dividers
Spring dividers are like a pencil compass, but both legs have steel points. These are adjusted to the required spacing by a knurled nut on a threaded rod that links the legs.

Using spring dividers
Use dividers to step-off divisions along a line (1) or to scribe circles (2) . By running one point against the edge of a workpiece you can also scribe a line parallel with the edge (3).

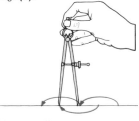

1 Stepping-off

2 Scribing a circle

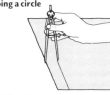

3 Parallel scribing

Centre punch
A centre punch is for marking the centres of holes to be drilled.

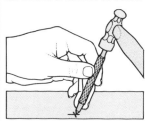

Correcting a centre mark

Using a centre punch
Place the punch's point on dead centre and strike it with a hammer. If the mark is not accurate, angle the punch toward the true centre, tap it to extend the mark in that direction, then mark the centre again.

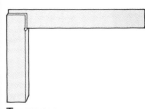

Steel rule
You'll need a long tape measure (◁) for estimating pipe runs and positioning appliances, but use a 300 or 600mm (1 or 2ft) steel rule for marking out components when absolute accuracy is important.

Try square
You can use a woodworker's try square (◁) to mark out or check right angles, but an all-metal engineer's try square is precision-made for metalwork. The small notch between blade and stock allows the tool to fit properly against a right-angled workpiece even when the corner is burred by filing. For general-purpose work, choose a 150mm (6in) try square.

METAL-CUTTING TOOLS

You can cut solid bar, sheet and tubular metal with a hacksaw, but special tools for cutting sheet metal and pipes will give you more accuracy and speed the work.

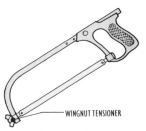

WINGNUT TENSIONER

General-purpose hacksaw
A modern hacksaw has a tubular steel frame with a light cast-metal handle. The frame is adjustable to blades of different lengths, which are tensioned by tightening a wingnut.

CHOOSING A HACKSAW BLADE

There are 200, 250 and 300mm (8in, 10in and 1ft) hacksaw blades. Try the different lengths until you find which suits you best. Choose the hardness and size of teeth according to the metal to be cut.

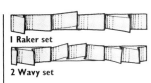

I Raker set

2 Wavy set

Size and set of teeth
There are fine and coarse hacksaw blades, graded by the number of teeth per 25mm (1in). A coarse blade has 14 to 18 teeth per 25mm (1in) and a fine one has 24 to 32. The teeth are set—bent sideways—to make a cut wider than the blade's thickness and prevent it jamming in the work. Coarse teeth are 'raker set' (**1**), with pairs of teeth bent in opposite directions and every third or fifth one left in line with the blade to clear the cut of metal waste. Fine teeth are too small to be raker set and the whole row is 'wavy set' (**2**).

Use a coarse blade for cutting soft metals like brass and aluminium, which would clog fine teeth, and a fine blade for thin sheet and the harder metals.

Hardness
A hacksaw blade must be harder than the metal it is cutting or its teeth will quickly blunt. A flexible blade with hardened teeth will cut most metals, but there are fully hardened blades that stay sharp longer and are less prone to losing teeth. Being rigid and brittle they break easily. High-speed steel blades for sawing very hard alloys are expensive and even more brittle than the fully hardened ones.

Fitting a hacksaw blade
Adjust the length of the saw frame and slip the blade onto the pins at its end, the teeth pointing away from the handle, then apply tension with the wingnut. If the new blade wanders off line when you work, tighten the wingnut.

If you have to fit a new blade after starting to cut a piece of metal it may jam in the cut because its set is wider than that of the old worn blade. Start a fresh cut on the other side of the workpiece and work back to the cut you began with.

Turning a blade
Sometimes it's easier to work with the blade at right angles to the frame. Rotate the square-section spigots a quarter turn before fitting the blade on the pins.

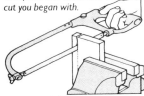

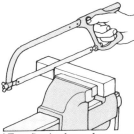

I Turn first kerf away from you

Sawing metal bar
*Hold the work in an engineer's vice, the marked cutting line as close to the jaws as possible. Start the cut on the waste side of the line with short strokes until it is about 1mm (1/16in) deep, then turn the bar 90 degrees in the vice, so that the cut faces away from you, and make a similar one in the new face (**1**). Continue in this way until the kerf (cut) runs right round the bar, then cut through the remainder with long steady strokes. Steady the end of the saw with your free hand and put a little light oil on the blade if necessary.*

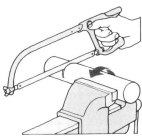

Sawing rod or pipe
As you cut a cylindrical rod or tube with a hacksaw rotate the work away from you until the kerf (cut) goes right round it, then cut through it.

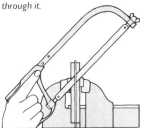

Sawing sheet metal
To saw a small piece of sheet metal, sandwich it between two strips of wood clamped in a vice. Adjust the metal to place the cutting line close to the strips, then saw down the waste side with steady strokes and the blade angled to the work.
Clamp thin sheet metal between two pieces of plywood and cut through all three layers at once.

Sawing a groove
To cut a slot or groove wider than a standard hacksaw blade fit two or more identical blades in the frame at the same time.

Junior hacksaw
Use a junior hacksaw for cutting small-bore tubing and thin metal rod. In most types the blade is held under tension by the spring steel frame.

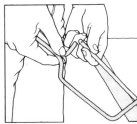

Fitting a new blade
To fit a blade, locate it in the slot at the front of the frame, then bow the frame against a workbench until the blade fits in the rear slot.

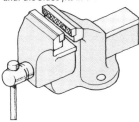

Engineer's vice
A large engineer's or metalworker's vice is bolted to the workbench, but small clamp-on ones are also available. Slip soft fibre liners over the jaws of a vice to protect workpieces held in it.

Cold chisel
Though plumbers use cold chisels to hack old pipework out of masonry they are also for cutting metal rod and slicing the heads off rivets. Keep the tip of yours sharpened on a bench grinder.

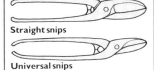

Straight snips

Universal snips

Tinsnips
Tinsnips are heavy-duty scissors for cutting sheet metal. Straight snips have wide blades for cutting straight edges, and if you try to cut curves with them the waste gets caught against the blades, though it's possible to cut a convex curve by removing small straight pieces of waste and working down to the marked line. Universal snips have thick narrow blades that will cut a curve in one pass and will also make straight cuts.

Using tinsnips
As you cut along the marked line let the waste curl away below the sheet. If the metal is too thick to be cut with one hand clamp one handle of the snips in a vice so that you can put your full weight on the other.

Try not to close the jaws completely each time, as it can cause a jagged edge on the metal. Wear thick work gloves when you are cutting sheet metal.

SHARPENING SNIPS

Clamp one handle in a vice and sharpen the edge with a smooth file; repeat with the other and finish by removing the burrs from the backs of the blades on an oiled slipstone (▷).

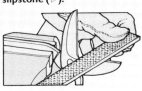

Sheet-metal cutter
Unlike tinsnips, which will distort a narrow waste strip on one side of the cutting line, a sheet-metal cutter removes a narrow strip as perfectly flat as the larger sheet. It is also suited to cutting rigid plastic sheet, which can crack if it is distorted by tinsnips.

Tube cutter
A tube cutter will cut the ends of pipes at exactly 90 degrees to their length. The pipe is clamped between the cutting wheel and an adjustable slide with two rollers, and is cut as the tool is revolved round it and the adjusting screw tightened before each turn. Keep the cutter lightly oiled when you use it.

Chain-link cutter
Cut large-diameter pipes with a chain-link cutter. Wrap the chain round the pipe, locate the end link in the clamp and tighten the adjuster until the cutter on each link bites into the metal. Work the handle back and forth to score the pipe and continue, tightening the adjuster intermittently to cut deeper, until the pipe is severed.

SEE ALSO
Details for: ▷

Slipstone	469
Cutting pipe	353, 361

Sheet-metal cutter

Tube cutter

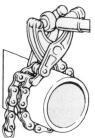

Chain-link cutter

● **Essential tools**
Junior hacksaw
Cold chisel
Tinsnips
Pipe cutter

487

SEE ALSO

◁ Details for:
Soldering pipes	353
Drill stand	472
Centre punch	486
Spring dividers	486
Bending pipes	355
Storage cistern	379

DRILLS AND PUNCHES

Special-quality steel bits are made for drilling holes in metal. Cut 12 to 25mm (¹/₂ to 1 in) holes in sheet metal with a punch.

Twist drills

Metal-cutting twist drills are very like those used for wood but are made from high-speed steel and with tips ground to a shallower angle. Use them in a power drill at slow speeds.

Mark the hole's centre with a centre punch (◁) to locate the drill point and clamp the work in a vice or to the bed of a drill stand (◁). Drill slowly and steadily and keep the bit oiled.

To drill a large hole make a pilot hole first with a small drill to guide the larger one.

When drilling sheet metal the bit may jam and produce a ragged hole as it exits on the far side of the work. To prevent this, clamp the work between pieces of plywood and drill through the three layers.

Hole punch

Use a hole punch to make large holes in sheet metal. Mark the circumference of the hole with spring dividers (◁), lay the metal on a piece of scrap softwood or plywood, place the punch's tip over the marked circle, tap it with a hammer, then check the alignment of the punched ring with the scribed circle. Reposition the punch and, with one sharp hammer blow, cut through the metal. If the wood gives and the metal is slightly distorted, tap it flat again with the hammer.

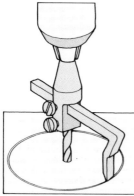

Tank cutter

Use a tank cutter to make holes for pipework in plastic or metal storage cisterns.

METAL BENDERS

Thick or hard metal must be heated before it can be bent successfully, but soft copper piping and sheet metal can be bent while cold.

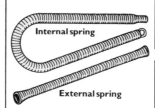
Internal spring

External spring

Bending springs

You can bend small-diameter pipes over your knee, but their walls must be supported with a coiled spring to prevent them buckling.

Push an internal-type spring inside the pipe or an external-type one over it. Either type of spring must fit the pipe exactly.

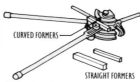
CURVED FORMERS

STRAIGHT FORMERS

Tube bender

In a tube bender, pipe is bent over one of two fixed curved formers that give the optimum radii for plumbing. Each has a matching straight former which is placed between the pipe and a steel roller on a movable lever. When this lever is moved towards the fixed one the pipe is bent over the curved former. The formers support the pipe walls during bending.

You can get extra leverage by clamping the fixed lever in a vice and using both hands on the movable one.

Soft mallet

Soft mallets have heads of coiled rawhide, hard rubber or plastic. They are used in bending strip or sheet metal, which would be damaged by a metal hammer.

To bend sheet metal at a right angle, clamp it between stout battens along the bending line. Start at one end and bend the metal over one of the battens by tapping it with the mallet. Don't attempt the full bend at once but work along the sheet, increasing the angle and keeping it constant along the length until the metal lies flat on the batten, then knock out any kinks.

TOOLS FOR JOINING METAL

You can make permanent watertight joints between metal components by using a molten alloy that acts like a glue when it cools and solidifies. Mechanical fixings like compression joints, rivets and nuts and bolts are also used for joining metal.

SOLDERS

Solders are special alloys for joining metals and are designed to melt at temperatures lower than the melting points of the metals to be joined. Soft solder, a tin-and-lead alloy, melts at 183 to 250°C. Brazing, a method of hard soldering involving a copper and zinc alloy, requires the even higher temperature of some 850 to 1000°C.

Solder is available as a coiled wire or a thick rod. Use soft solder for copper plumbing fittings.

FLUX

To be soldered, a joint must be perfectly clean and free of oxides. Even after cleaning with wire wool or emery, oxides will form immediately, preventing a positive bond between solder and metal. Flux forms a chemical barrier against oxidation. Corrosive, or 'active' flux, applied with a brush, actually dissolves oxides but must be washed from the surface with water as soon as the solder solidifies or it will go on corroding the metal. A 'passive' flux, in paste form, is used where it will be impossible to wash the work thoroughly. Though a passive flux will not dissolve oxide it will exclude it adequately for soldering copper plumbing joints and electrical connections.

Some wire solder contains flux in its hollow core. The flux flows fractionally before the solder melts.

Soldering irons

Successful soldering needs the work to be made hot enough to melt the solder and cause it to flow; otherwise the solder will solidify before it can completely penetrate the joint. The necessary heat is applied with a soldering iron.

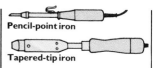
Pencil-point iron

Tapered-tip iron

There are simple irons that are heated in a fire, but an electric iron is much handier to use and its temperature is both controllable and constant. Use a low-powered pencil-point iron for soldering electrical connections and a larger one with a tapered tip to bring sheet metal up to working temperature.

Tinning a soldering iron

The tip of a soldering iron must be coated with solder to keep it oxide-free and maintain its performance. Clean the cool tip with a file, then heat it to working temperature, dip it in flux and apply a stick of solder to coat it evenly.

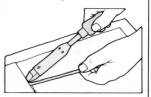

Using a soldering iron

Clean the mating surfaces of the joint to a bright finish and coat them with flux, then clamp the joint tightly between two wooden battens. Apply the hot iron along the joint to heat the metal thoroughly, then run its tip along the edge of the joint, following it with solder. Solder will flow immediately into a properly heated joint.

Gas torch

Even a large soldering iron cannot heat thick metal fast enough to compensate for heat loss away from the joint, and this is very much the situation when you solder pipework (◁). Though the copper unions have very thin walls the pipe on each side dissipates so much heat that an iron cannot get the joint itself hot enough to form a watertight soldered seal. Use a gas torch with an intensely hot flame that will heat the work quickly.

The torch runs on liquid gas contained under pressure in a disposable metal canister that screws onto the gas inlet. Open the control valve and light the gas released from the nozzle, then adjust the valve until the flame roars and is bright blue. Use the hottest part of the flame—about the middle of its length—to heat the joint.

Fibreglass mat
Buy a fireproof mat of fibreglass from a plumbers' merchant to protect flammable surfaces from the heat of a gas torch.

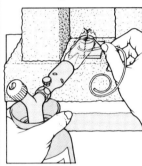

Hard-soldering and brazing
Use a gas torch to hard-solder or braze. Clean and flux the work – if possible with an active flux – then wire or clamp the parts together. Place the assembly on a fireproof mat or surround it with firebricks. Bring the joint to red heat with the torch, then dip a stick of the appropriate alloy in flux and apply it to the joint. When the joint is cool chip off hardened flux, wash the metal thoroughly in hot water and finish the joint with a file.

Hot air gun
Some hot air guns, designed for stripping old paintwork, can also be used for soft soldering. You can vary the temperature of an electronic gun from 100 to 600°C. A heat shield on the nozzle reflects the heat back onto the work.

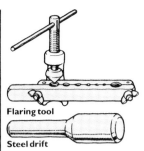

Flaring tool

Steel drift

Flaring tools
To make a non-manipulative joint (▷) in plumbing pipework the ends of the copper pipes are simply cut square and cleaned up to remove sharp edges. For a manipulative joint (▷) the pipe ends must be flared to lock into the joint.

The simplest way to flare a copper pipe is with a steel drift. First slip one joint cap-nut onto the pipe, then push the narrow shank of the drift into the pipe. Strike the tool with a heavy hammer to drive its conical part into the pipe, stretching the walls to the required shape.

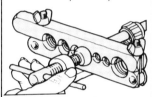

Using a flaring tool
A proper flaring tool will shape pipework more accurately. Again with the cap-nut in place, clamp the pipe in the matching hole in the die block, its end flush with the side of the block, then turn the screw of the flaring tool to drive its cone into the pipe.

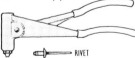

RIVET

Blind riveter
Join thin sheet metal with a blind riveter, a hand-operated tool with plier-like handles. The special rivets have long shanks that break off and leave slightly raised heads on both sides of the work.

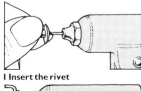

I Insert the rivet

2 Squeeze the handles

Using a riveter
Clamp the two sheets together and drill holes right through the metal, matching the diameter of the rivets and spaced regularly along the joint. Open the handles of the riveter and insert the rivet shank in the head (1). Push the rivet through a hole in the work and, while pressing the tool hard against the metal, squeeze the handles to compress the rivet head on the far side (2). When the rivet is fully expanded the shank will snap off in the tool.

SPANNERS AND WRENCHES

A plumber uses a great variety of spanners and wrenches on a wide range of fittings and fixings, but you can hire the ones that you need only occasionally.

Open-ended spanner
A set of the familiar open-ended spanners is essential to a plumber or metalworker. In most situations pipework runs into a fitting or accessory and it is not possible to use anything but a spanner with open jaws. Most spanners are double-ended, perhaps in a combination of metric and imperial sizes, and sizes are duplicated within a set for when two identical nuts have to be manipulated simultaneously, as on a compression joint, for instance.

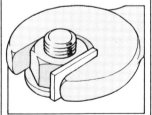

Achieving a tight fit
A spanner must be a good fit or it will round over the corners of the nut. You can pack out the jaws with a thin 'shim' of metal if a snug fit is otherwise not possible.

Ring spanner
Being a closed circle, the head of a ring spanner is stronger and fits better than that of an open-ended one. It is specially handy for loosening corroded nuts if it can be slipped onto them from above.

Square nut   **Hexagonal nut**

Choosing a ring spanner
Choose a 12-point spanner. It is fast to use and will fit both square and hexagonal nuts. You can buy combination spanners with rings at one end and open jaws at the other.

Box spanner
A box spanner is a steel tube with its ends shaped into hexagons – an excellent tool for reaching a nut in a confined space. Turning force is applied with a tommy bar slipped into a hole drilled through the spanner. Don't use a very long bar. Too much leverage may strip the thread of the fitting or distort the thin walls of the spanner.

Adjustable spanner
Having a movable jaw, an adjustable spanner is not as strong as an open-ended or ring spanner but is often the only tool that will fit a large or over-painted nut. Make sure the spanner fits the nut snugly by rocking it slightly as you tighten the jaws. Grip the nut with the roots of the jaws. If you use just the tips they can spring apart slightly under force and the spanner will slip.

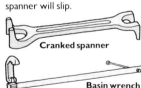

Cranked spanner

Basin wrench

Cranked spanner and basin wrench
A cranked spanner is a special double-ended wrench for use on tap connectors (▷).

A basin wrench, for the same job, has a pivoting jaw that can be set for either tightening or loosening a fitting.

Radiator spanner
Use a simple spanner of hexagonal-section steel rod to remove radiator blanking plugs (▷). One end is ground to fit plugs with square sockets.

SEE ALSO

Details for: ▷

Non-manipulative pipe joints	354
Manipulative pipe joints	354
Tap connectors	352, 365
Blanking plugs	401

● **Essential tools**
Blind riveter
Set of open-ended spanners
Small and large adjustable spanners

Stilson wrench

The adjustable toothed jaws of a stilson wrench are for gripping pipework. As force is applied the jaws tighten on the work.

SEE ALSO

◁ Details for:
| Sharpening bits | 471 |
| Disconnecting pipes | 354 |

Chain wrench

A chain wrench does the same job as a stilson wrench but it can be used on very large-diameter pipes and fittings. Wrap the chain tightly round the work and engage it with the hook at the end of the wrench, then lever the handle towards the toothed jaw to apply turning force.

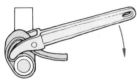

Strap wrench

With a strap wrench you can disconnect chromed pipework without damaging its surface. Wrap the smooth leather or canvas strap round the pipe, pass its end through the slot in the head of the tool and pull it tight. Leverage on the handle will rotate the pipe.

Plier wrench

A plier wrench locks onto the work. It will grip round stock or damaged nuts and is often used as a small cramp.

Using a plier wrench

Squeeze the handles to close the jaws while slowly turning the adjusting screw clockwise until they snap together (1). Release the tool's grip on the work by pulling the release lever (2).

● **Essential tools**
Plier wrench
Second-cut and smooth flat files
Second-cut and smooth half-round files

1 Adjusting the wrench

2 Releasing the wrench

FILES

Files are used for shaping and smoothing metal components and removing sharp edges.

CLASSIFYING FILES

The working faces of a file are composed of parallel ridges, or teeth, set at about 70 degrees to its edges. A file is classified according to the size and spacing of its teeth and whether it has one or two sets.

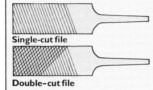

Single-cut file

Double-cut file

A single-cut file has one set of teeth virtually covering each face. **A double-cut file** has a second set of identical teeth crossing the first at a 45-degree angle. Some files are single-cut on one side and double-cut on the other.

The spacing of the teeth relates directly to their size: the finer the teeth the more closely packed they are. Degrees of coarseness are expressed in numbers of teeth per 25mm (1in). Use progressively finer files to shape a component and gradually to remove marks left by coarser ones.

File classification

Bastard file – Coarse grade (26 teeth per 25mm) – For initial shaping. *Second-cut file* – Medium grade (36 teeth per 25mm) – For preliminary smoothing. *Smooth file* – Fine grade (47 teeth per 25mm) – For final smoothing.

CLEANING A FILE

Soft metal clogs the teeth of files but can be removed by brushing along the teeth with a file card—a fine wire brush. Chalk rubbed on a clean file will reduce clogging.

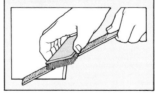

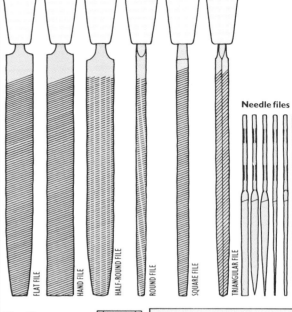

Needle files

FLAT FILE · HAND FILE · HALF-ROUND FILE · ROUND FILE · SQUARE FILE · TRIANGULAR FILE

Flat file

A flat file tapers from its pointed tang to its tip, both in width and thickness. Both faces and both edges are toothed.

Hand file

Hand files are parallel-sided but tapered in their thickness. Most of them have one smooth edge for filing up to a corner without damaging it.

Half-round file

This tool has one rounded face for shaping inside curves.

Round file

A round file is for shaping tight curves and enlarging holes.

Square file

This file is for cutting narrow slots and smoothing the edges of small rectangular holes.

Triangular file

The triangular file is for accurately shaping and smoothing undercut apertures of less than 90 degrees.

Needle files

Needle files are miniature versions of standard files and are all made in extra-fine grades. They are used for precise work and to sharpen brace bits (◁).

FILE SAFETY

Always fit a wooden or plastic handle on the tang of a file before using it.

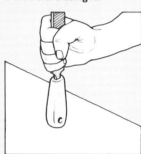

1 Fitting a file handle

2 Knock a handle from the tang

If an unprotected file catches on the work, the tang could be driven into the palm of your hand. Having fitted a handle, tap its end on a bench to tighten its grip (1).

To remove a handle, hold the file in one hand and strike the ferrule away from you with a piece of wood (2).

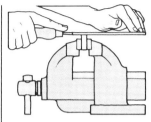

Using a file
When you use any file keep it flat on the work and avoid rocking it on the forward strokes. Hold it steady with the fingertips of one hand on its tip and make slow firm strokes with the full length of the tool.

To avoid vibration, or 'chatter', hold the work low in a vice or clamp it between two battens.

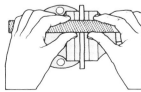

Draw filing
You can give metal a smooth finish by draw filing. With both hands, hold a smooth file at right angles to the work and slide it back and forth along the surface, then polish the work with emery cloth wrapped round the file.

PLIERS

Pliers are for improving your grip on small components and for bending and shaping metal rod and wire.

Engineer's pliers
For general-purpose work buy a sturdy pair of engineer's pliers. The toothed jaws have a curved section for gripping round stock and side cutters for cropping wire.

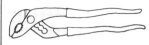

Slip-joint
or waterpump pliers
The special feature of slip-joint pliers is a movable pivot for enlarging the jaw spacing. The extra-long handles give a good grip on pipes and other fittings.

FINISHING METAL

Apart from its appearance metal must be clean and rust-free if it is to be painted or soldered.

Wire brush
Use a steel wire hand brush to clean rusty or corroded metal.

Wire wool
Wire wool is a mass of very thin steel filaments. It is used to remove file marks and to clean oxides and dirt from metals.

Emery cloth and paper
Emery is a natural black grit. Backed with paper or cloth for polishing metals, it is available in a range of grades from coarse to fine. For the best finish, work through the grades, using progressively finer abrasives as the work proceeds.

I **Glue paper to a board**

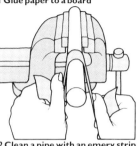

2 **Clean a pipe with an emery strip**

Using emery cloth and paper
To avoid rounding the crisp edges of a flat component, glue a sheet of emery paper to a board and rub the metal on it (1).

To finish round stock or pipes, loop a strip of emery cloth over the work and pull alternately on each end (2).

Buffing mop
Metals can be brought to a shine by hand, using liquid polish and a soft cloth, but for a really high gloss use a buffing mop in a bench-mounted power drill or grinder.

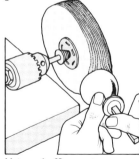

Using a buffing mop
Apply a stick of buffing compound—a fine abrasive with wax—to the revolving mop, then move the work from side to side against its lower half, keeping any edges facing down.

Reseating tool
When the seat of a tap is so worn that even a new washer will not make a perfect seal (▷) you can grind a new seat with a reseating tool. Removing the tap's headgear and jumper (▷) and screw the cone into the body of the tap. Lower the threaded section with the knurled adjuster, then turn the tommy bar to operate the cutter.

WOODWORKING TOOLS

A plumber needs basic woodworking tools (▷) to lift floorboards, notch joists for pipe runs and attach pipe clips.

SEE ALSO

Details for: ▷

Woodworking tools	462-474
Replacing washers	342
Dismantling taps	342
Preparing metal	60-61

● **Essential tools and materials**
Engineer's pliers
Wire brush
Wire wool
Emery cloth and paper

SEE ALSO

◁ Details for:
Double insulation	**288**
Supplementary bonding	**290**
Power drill	**471**
Using a tester	289
Stripping flex	293
Stripping cable	302
Running cable	303–305
Drilling joists	305

Torch
Keep a torch handy for checking your consumer unit when a fuse blows on a lighting circuit. You may also need artificial light when working on connections below floorboards or in a loft, and a torch that stands unsupported is very helpful.

Diagonal cutters

● **Essential tools**
Terminal screwdrivers
Wire cutters
Wire strippers
Power drill and bits
Electronic mains tester
Torch
General-purpose tools

492

ELECTRICIAN'S TOOL KIT
You need only a fairly limited range of tools to make electrical connections. The largest number is needed for making cable runs and fixing accessories and appliances to the house structure.

SCREWDRIVERS

Buy good screwdrivers for tightening electrical terminals. The cheap ones are practically useless, being made from such soft metal that the tips soon twist out of shape.

Terminal screwdriver
A terminal screwdriver has a long, slim cylindrical shaft ground to a flat tip. For work on the terminals in sockets and larger appliances buy one with a plastic handle and a plastic insulating sleeve on its shaft. Use a smaller driver with a very slim shaft to work on ceiling roses or to tighten plastic terminal blocks on small fittings.

Cabinet screwdriver
You will need a woodworking screwdriver to fix mounting boxes to walls.

SPANNER

A small spanner is needed for making the earth connections in some appliances and for supplementary earth bonding (◁).

WIRE CUTTERS

Use wire cutters for cropping cable and flex to length.

Electrician's pliers
These are engineer's pliers with insulating sleeves shrunk onto their handles. You'll need them to cut circuit conductors and to twist their ends together.

Diagonal cutters
Diagonal cutters will crop thick conductors more effectively than electrician's pliers. To cut meter leads you may need a junior hacksaw.

WIRE STRIPPERS

There are various tools for removing parts of the plastic insulation that covers cables and flexible cords.

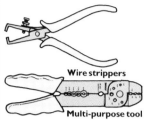

Wire strippers

Multi-purpose tool

Wire strippers
To remove the colour-coded insulation from cable and flex, use a pair of wire strippers with jaws shaped to cut through the plastic without damaging the wire core. There is a multi-purpose version that can both strip the insulation and crop the wires to length.

Sharp knife
Use a knife with sharp disposable blades for slitting and peeling the outer sheathing on conductors.

DRILLS

When you run circuit wiring you need a drill and several special-purpose bits for boring through wood and masonry.

Joist brace
A joist brace has a chuck that takes standard brace bits but its side-mounted handle and ratchet mechanism allow drilling in the restricted space between floor and ceiling joists.

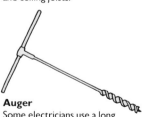

Auger
Some electricians use a long wood-boring auger to drill through the wall head plate and noggings when running a switch cable from an attic down to its mounting box, but it's hard to use such a long tool in the restricted roof space of a small modern house or apartment.

Power drill (◁)
A power drill is best for boring cable holes through timbers and making wall plug fixings for mounting boxes. As well as a standard masonry bit for wall fixings you will need a much longer version for boring through brick walls and clearing access channels behind skirting boards.

If you shorten the shaft of a wide-tipped spade bit you can use it in a power drill instead of hiring a special joist brace.

TESTERS

Even when you have turned off the power at the consumer unit use a tester to check that the circuit is 'dead'.

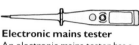

Electronic mains tester
An electronic mains tester has a light in its handle that glows when its screwdriver-like tip touches a 'live' wire or terminal. You have to place a fingertip on the tool's metal gap for the light to work but there is no danger of a shock. A small test button on the handle tells if the tool is in working order.

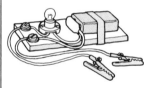

Continuity tester
A continuity tester will test whether a circuit is complete or an appliance is properly earthed. You can buy a tester or make one by connecting a 9-volt battery and a bulb via short lengths of flex and crocodile clips.

Using a continuity tester
Switch off the power at the consumer unit before making the test. To discover, for example, which are the two ends of a buried disconnected cable, twist the black and red conductors together at one end, then attach the crocodile clips to the same conductors at the other end (1). If the bulb lights up the two ends belong to the same length of cable.

To check that a plug-in appliance is safely earthed, attach one clip to the earth pin of the plug—the longest of the three—and touch the metal casing of the appliance with the other clip (2). If the earth connection is good the bulb will glow brightly; a dimly

glowing bulb indicates poor earthing, which should be checked professionally.

Don't use the appliance if the bulb lights up when you attach the clip to either of the other pins (3). It is dangerous and should be overhauled professionally. Make sure the plug fuse is working.

You cannot test a double-insulated appliance (◁) as it has no earth connection in the plug.

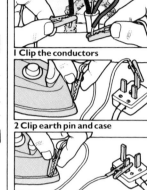

1 Clip the conductors

2 Clip earth pin and case

3 Clip one other pin and case

GENERAL-PURPOSE TOOLS

Every electrician needs tools for lifting and cutting floorboards, for fixing mounting boxes and for cutting cable runs through a building.

Claw hammer
For nailing cable clips to walls and timbers.
Club hammer
For use with a cold chisel.
Cold chisel
For cutting channels in plaster and brickwork so as to bury cable or mounting boxes.
Bolster chisel
For levering up floorboards.
Wood chisels
For notching floor joists.
Padsaw or power jigsaw
For cutting through floorboards close to skirtings.
Floorboard saw
A floorboard saw is best for cutting across a prised-up board, though a tenon saw is a reasonable substitute.
Spirit level
For checking that accessory mounting boxes are being fixed horizontally.
Plasterer's trowel or filling knife
Use either tool for covering concealed cable with plaster or other filler.

12

TIMBER AND BOARDS	494
ADHESIVES	495
FIXINGS	496
BLINDS AND CURTAIN RAILS	499
SHELVING	500
GLOSSARY OF TERMS	501
INDEX	504

REFERENCE & INDEX

SEE ALSO

◁ Details for:
T&G boards   87
Cross-cutting   463

TIMBER AND MAN-MADE BOARDS

Timber is classified in two main groups, softwood and hardwood, according to the type of tree it comes from. Softwoods are from the evergreen coniferous trees like firs and pines, hardwoods from the deciduous broad-leaved ones. Most softwoods are in fact softer than most hardwoods, but that is not invariably so.

SOFTWOODS

Softwood is usually referred to loosely as 'pine' or 'deal', whatever its origin. Most of the wood you see in a timber yard is softwood as it is by far the cheaper and more widely used for structural house timbers, floorboards, stairs and the simpler kinds of furniture.

Buying softwood

Most softwood is available in rough and smooth versions called, respectively, sawn and planed. The rough unplaned surface of sawn timber means that it is suitable only for jobs where it will be out of sight. Where appearance is important you need planed wood—that is, of course, sawn and planed—which has been through a planing machine and is relatively smooth. But here a confusion can arise. Planed timber, or 'PAR' (planed all round), is always slightly thinner and narrower than its nominal dimensions. Machine planing takes about 3 to 6mm (⅛ to ¼in) off the width and thickness, and the loss is not uniform and so the wood is always referred to in terms of its nominal size, the size before planing. You have to take this into account when you plan jobs involving softwood. Planed hardwoods are actually the size they are said to be.

Timber yards use the metric system but if you think and work in imperial measures, the men in the yards are experts at instant conversion.

Choosing softwood

A number of defects that can be found in softwood should be avoided, especially when a job's appearance is important. For this reason it is always best to go and pick out the wood yourself. Never simply order by phone.

Knots

Knots can look attractive in pine, but they must be 'live' knots, the glossy brown ones. 'Dead' knots, the black ones, will shrink and eventually drop out, leaving holes.

Warping

Is another common problem. Sight along the edges of each board to check that it is not bowed or twisted.

Shakes

Are cracks or splits in timber.

End shakes

These are splits in the ends of boards, and can be cut off, but the split section should not count in what you pay for.

Heart shakes

These are irregular cracks, usually accompanied by warping through the board's width.

Cup shakes

These can occur when a board comes from the centre of a tree. The small centre ring splits away along the board's length.

Surface checking

This is when many fine cracks appear on the timber's surface. Very fine ones may be removed by planing, or filled if the work is to be painted; wood with wider ones should be rejected.

Other defects

Watch out for rough patches that have escaped the planer, damage from workmen's boots and calculations in ball-pen left on boards by other customers.

Cutting to size

At extra cost, a timber yard with modern woodworking machinery can cut wood to size for you, but a busy yard worker with a handsaw won't produce an accurate result. It's best to buy a little over length and cut your own wood to size.

Most yards will cut a board to the length you want unless it leaves too small an offcut to be sold, in which case you have to buy the whole board.

Seasoning softwood

Softwood is not usually well seasoned and is often exposed to damp in the yard, so it's best to let it dry out indoors for a week or so before use, preferably in the room where it is to be used, and lying flat, not propped against a wall.

Standard sizes and sections

Planed softwood comes in a range of standard thicknesses and widths, from small sections of a nominal 12.5 by 12.5mm (½ by ½in) to planks 23mm (¹⁵/₁₆in) thick by 250mm (9¾in) wide. It can also be bought tongued and grooved for matchboarding and machined into a variety of sectional shapes known as mouldings for such uses as architraves, glazing bars, skirting boards and picture rails.

HARDWOODS

Hardwoods are much more expensive than softwoods and must usually be sought from specialist timber merchants. They are mainly used nowadays only to achieve a particular appearance or for special structural purposes.

Ordering hardwoods

Hardwoods – teak, mahogany, oak and many others—have to be ordered by their specific names.

Ramin

There is one relatively cheap hardwood called ramin, now used widely for the smaller mouldings—picture framing, dowelling, scotia, half-round, quadrant, edge lipping and so on—and also available in small-section strips and battens. Ramin is pale brown and seems almost grainless. It splits rather easily when being nailed.

Simulated hardwoods

The expensive hardwoods have been supplanted in many of their traditional applications by man-made boards veneered with hardwood.

MAN-MADE BOARDS

Four man-made boards are used widely by woodworkers—plywood, chipboard, blockboard and hardboard.

Plywood

Is a sheet material made by bonding a number of thin wood veneers together under high pressure. It is exceptionally strong and the better qualities are much used in furniture manufacture, while other grades are often for such exterior purposes as shuttering.

The veneers, or plies, in plywood always lie with their grain directions alternating and always come to an odd number so that the grains of the two outer ones run in the same direction.

Plywood surfaces

The outer veneers of plywood are usually of hardwood, commonly birch, but the material can also be obtained surfaced with quality hardwoods and melamine.

Plywood sizes

The normally available thicknesses are from 3 to 18mm (⅛ to ¾in) and there are several sheet sizes. Standard sheets measure 2440 by 1220mm (8 by 4ft), 1220 by 1220mm (4 by 4ft) and 1220 by 610mm (4 by 2ft).

Chipboard

Is made from small softwood chips bonded together under pressure. There are several grades, including a tough one for flooring and others for shuttering and roofing.

Chipboard surfaces

Standard chipboard is sanded smooth on both sides and can be simply filled and primed for painting. There are also several proprietary brands of the material with a timber or melamine veneer and others with a melamine surface specially for worktops.

Chipboard sizes

Standard chipboard sheets measure 2440 by 1220mm (8 by 4ft) and are available in 9, 12, 15 and 18mm (⅜, ½, ⁹/₁₆ and ¾in) thicknesses. The thickest one is by far the most commonly stocked. The melamine- and timber-finished chipboard is in the 15mm (⁹/₁₆in) thickness and comes as planks either 1820mm (6ft) or 2440mm (8ft) long. A wide range of widths is available – from 150mm (6in) up to 600mm (2ft).

Blockboard

Blockboard consists of a core of rectangular wood battens sandwiched between two softwood veneer surfaces by pressure bonding. It is usually sold in an 18mm (¾in) thickness but may also be had 12.5 and 25mm (½ and 1in) thick.

Blockboard is used where structural strength like that of plywood is needed but with more bulk and rigidity, as in a worktop with a long unsupported span. The outer veneers of blockboard need only final finishing, but the edges may need some filling. Where appearance is important exposed edges need to be covered with wood lipping.

Hardboard
Is compressed softwood pulp in sheets. It has less structural strength than other man-made boards but is very cheap and effective for many uses.

Types of hardboard
Standard hardboard is brown and 3.2mm (⅛in) thick, with one shiny side and one matt. Other types include *pegboard* – perforated hardboard; *screening hardboard* – with decorative piercing; *decorative hardboard* – with a decorative moulded surface; *medium hardboard* – a softer type; and *standard grade* – with a coloured enamel or printed woodgrain on one side.

Uses and sizes
Standard hardboard is light, easy to cut and ideal for small sliding doors, cabinet backs, drawer bottoms and underlay for floor covering. The standard sheet measures 2440 by 1220mm (8 by 4ft) but many suppliers sell subdivisions of this size.

ADHESIVES
Modern adhesives are greatly superior to the old glues they have supplanted and have very powerful bonding properties. Though there is no 'universal adhesive' that will stick anything to anything you can bond most materials to most others if you choose the right adhesive.

There is now an impressive range of adhesives for specific purposes; those discussed here relate to the procedures dealt with in this book.

Woodworking
To glue wood and man-made boards for use indoors, apply a polyvinyl acetate (PVA) woodworker's glue to one or both of the mating surfaces, cramp or weight the work and wipe off any excess glue squeezed from the joint with a damp cloth. The joint can be handled within 30 minutes and the bond is complete in 24 hours.

For outdoor work use a waterproof powdered synthetic-resin glue that you mix with water for use, or a two-part (resorcinal and urea) adhesive whose parts are applied separately to the faces being glued. The latter sets when the faces come together. Both these glues require the work to be cramped or weighted during the setting period.

For indoor work where cramping or weighting is not possible – fixing wall panels to a batten frame, for example – use a synthetic rubber-based contact adhesive. Apply it to both mating surfaces, allow it to become touch-dry, then press the surfaces together by hand. The bond is almost instantaneous.

An alternative for small non-cramping jobs is a two-part acrylic adhesive. The parts are not mixed for use; one is applied to each mating surface of the joint and bonding begins when they meet.

Fixing synthetic laminates
Contact adhesives were developed for fixing synthetic laminates to wood and other surfaces. No cramps or weights are needed, though some pressure improves the bond. The newer contact adhesives allow some repositioning of the mating surfaces; with the older ones the instant bond meant that laminates placed wrongly could not then be moved, so it's best to ensure that you choose a contact adhesive with what's called 'slideability'. Apply adhesive to both surfaces, let it become touch-dry, then press them firmly together.

Fixing floor coverings
Flooring adhesives must be versatile enough to fix a wide range of coverings – cork, vinyl, linoleum and many others – to such surfaces as floorboards, concrete, cement screed and hardboard underlays, to name only some. They must also be able to withstand regular floor washing and the spillage of various liquids. Such multi-purpose flooring adhesives are of two types: rubber-resin and latex. Either will stick virtually any covering to any floor surface. They are semi-flexible and will not crack or fail due to slight movement of the covering.

Fixing ceiling tiles
Expanded or foam-polystyrene ceiling tiles, and larger panels of that material, are fixed with a synthetic latex-based 'non-flamm' adhesive to plaster, cement, hardboard and timber surfaces. The thick adhesive has gap-filling properties that allow the material to be fixed effectively to quite uneven surfaces, and the tiles or panels to be adjusted after they are in place.

Fixing ceramic tiles
Ceramic tiles are fixed with a white adhesive that may be had ready-mixed or in powder form. Ordinary 'thin bed' adhesives are for tiling on fairly flat surfaces, and there are 'thick bed' ones for use on rough and uneven surfaces. There are water-resistant versions for use in kitchens and bathrooms and heat-resistant ones for tiling round cookers and fireplaces.

Ceramic floor tiles are now often laid with a sand-and-cement mortar to which a special builder's adhesive – PVA bonding agent – is added to improve adhesion, a method also used for sand-and-cement renderings and concrete repairs.

Gluing metals
Metals can be glued with epoxy-resin adhesives, which produce such a powerful bond as to have replaced welding and riveting in some industries. The adhesives are in two parts, a resin and a hardener, and most require their parts mixed together, then used within a certain time after mixing. Another type, acrylic-based, has two parts that are applied separately to the mating faces. These impose no time limit as they are dormant until the faces meet, when a chemical bonding reaction begins.

Epoxy-resin adhesives are also generally suitable for joining glass, ceramics, fibre glass and rigid plastic, though some products will not join all of these, so ensure that you get the right adhesive for the job.

Gluing stainless steel
Stainless-steel plumbing can be glued with a special adhesive and activator. Key the end of the tube and the inside of the fitting. Spray the activator onto both surfaces. After 30 seconds apply a ring of adhesive to the leading inside edge of the fitting and another to the end of the tube. Assemble the joint and leave it to harden for at least two minutes.

Cyanoacrylates
The cyanoacrylates, or 'super glues', come close to being the universal adhesives that will stick anything. They rapidly bond a great many materials – including human skin, which led to cases of fingers, even eyelids, being glued together inadvertently when they were introduced (See Adhesive Solvents, ▷).

Usually supplied in tubes with fine nozzles, super glues must be used sparingly. They are commonly employed in joining small objects of metal, glass, ceramic, glass fibre and rigid plastic.

Glue guns
An electric 'hot melt' glue gun is loaded with a rod of solid glue that melts under heat when the gun is activated and discharged as a liquid onto the work. The components are pressed or cramped together and the glue bonds as it cools. Glue guns are useful for accurate spot-gluing, and there is a choice of glue rods for use with various materials. The glues normally cool and set within 20 to 90 seconds.

Cold gun-applied adhesive for fixing wallboards and ceiling tiles is supplied in cartridges fitted with nozzles. When the gun's trigger is pressed a ram pushes on the base of the cartridge and forces out the glue.

SEE ALSO

Details for: ▷	
Levelling a floor	57
Ceramic tiles	99
Ceiling tiles	101
Cramps	473
Adhesive solvents	496

SEE ALSO

◁ Details for:
Fixing floorboards	178
Nail set	472
Nailing techniques	472-473
Adhesives	495

ADHESIVE SOLVENTS

When using an adhesive you will inevitably get some where you don't want it, usually on your hands, so have the right solvent handy for the glue in question and use it promptly, as the more the glue has set the harder it is to remove. Once a glue has set hard it might be impossible to dissolve it.

ADHESIVE	SOLVENT
PVA woodworking glue	Clean water
Synthetic-resin	Clean water
Resorcinal and urea	Clean water
Two-part acrylic	Methylated spirit
Rubber-based contact glue	Acetone
Rubber-resin	Petrol
Synthetic-latex	Clean water
Epoxy-resin	Acetone or methylated spirit: Liquid paint stripper if hard (not on skin)
Cyanoacrylates (Super glues)	Special manufacturer's solvent
PVA tile adhesive	Clean water

BRAND-NAME GUIDE TO ADHESIVES

Unless a manufacturer prints the type of glue on its container, it can be difficult to identify the adhesive you need. The brand names listed below are intended to help you recognize a type of glue. This is not necessarily a list of recommended products.

PVA Adhesives
Bostik 8 Woodworking
Brummer wood adhesive
Clam 7
Copydex Woodfix
Dunlop Woodworker
Evo-Stik wood adhesive
Evo-Bond building adhesive
Hermetite wood glue
Humbrol Extra Bond
Loctite Wood Bond Rapid
Unibond Universal PVA
Unibond Woodworker

Contact adhesives rubber-based
Bostik 3 Contact
Dunlop Powerfix
Dunlop Thixofix
Clam 3
Evo-Stik Impact
Evo-Stik Time-bond
Evo-Stik 528
Humbrol Superstik
Unibond Unistik

Epoxy-resin adhesives
Araldite (3 versions)
Bostik 7 Quick-set
Hermetite standard and fast
Humbrol Superfast Epoxy
Loctite Tough Bond

Synthetic-resin adhesives
Bostik 2 Weatherproof
Humbrol Carpenters' Wood Glue
Humbrol Cascamite
Humbrol Cascophen

Two-part acrylic adhesives
Bostik 10 Hyperbond
Loctite Multi-bond

Rubber-resin and synthetic-latex
Clam 9
Dunlop flooring adhesive
Evo-Stik 873 flooring adhesive
Evo-Stik 863 ceiling tile adhesive
Evo-Stik panel adhesive (Gun-O-Prene)
Evo-Stik Parkibond
Homeseal wall panel adhesive
Humbrol ceiling tile adhesive
Humbrol flooring adhesive
Unibond cork floor-tile adhesive
Unibond wallboard adhesive

Cyanoacrylates (Super glues)
Bostik 12 Superglue
Hermetite Super Glue Plus
Humbrol Wonderbond (3 versions)
Loctite Super Glue-3
Supergluematic
Super Glue Xtra

Resorcinal and urea
Cascophen

PVA tile adhesives
Evo-Stik wall tile adhesive
Humbrol ceramic tile adhesive
Dunlop PVA wall tile adhesive
Clam ceramic tile adhesive

Stainless-steel plumbing adhesive
Loctite 638 (Activator 'N')
Permabond A128 ('Speed' primer)

FIXINGS

An important part of any assembly or construction work is choosing the right fixing method. As well as the time-tested variety of nails and screws for woodwork, and the nuts, bolts and rivets for metal work, there are nowadays a number of patent devices that speed and simplify many jobs.

NAILS

Nails, used with or without glue, provide a cheap, quick and simple fixing method for woodworkers, and there are also many special types of nail for other purposes.

Round plain-head wire nail
Rough general carpentry. Bright steel or galvanized finish. Size: 20 to 150mm (¾ to 6in).

Round lost-head wire nail
Joinery. Head can be punched in and concealed. Bright steel finish. Size: 40 to 75mm (1½ to 3in).

Lath nail
Fixing laths and thin battens. Galvanized finish. Size: 25 to 40mm (1 to 1½in).

Ring-shank nail
Fixing man-made boards. Bright steel. 20 to 100mm (¾ to 4in).

Square twisted plain–head
General purpose. Twisted shank gives extra grip. Bright steel or sherardized. 20 to 100mm (¾ to 4in).

Cut clasp nail
Carpentry and fixing wood to masonry. Black iron. 20 to 30mm (¾ to 1¼in).

Cut floor brad
Nailing floorboards to joists. Black iron. 40 to 75mm (1½ to 3in).

Oval wire nail
Carpentry. Can be punched in and concealed. Bright steel. 25 to 150mm (1 to 6in).

KEY TO TYPES OF ADHESIVES
1 PVA woodworking glue
2 Synthetic-resin/ Resorcinal and urea
3 Rubber-based contact
4 Epoxy-resin
5 Rubber-resin
6 Synthetic-latex
7 Cyanoacrylates
8 Acrylic
9 PVA tile adhesive

Use this chart as a guide for gluing the materials on the left to those across the top.

	WOOD AND MAN-MADE BOARDS	MASONRY	PLASTER	METAL	STONE	GLASS	CERAMIC	RIGID PLASTIC/ FIBRE GLASS
WOOD/MAN-MADE BOARDS	1,2,3,7,8			8		8	8	8
METAL	8			4, 7, 8	4, 7	4, 7, 8	4, 7, 8	7, 8
SYNTHETIC LAMINATES	3	3	3		3			
FLOOR COVERINGS	5, 6	5, 6			5, 6			
CEILING TILES/PANELS	6	6	6		6			
CERAMIC	8, 9	9	9	8	9	8	4, 7, 8	8
STONE		4			4	4		
GLASS	3, 4, 8	4	4	4, 7, 8		4, 7, 8	4, 7, 8	8
RIGID PLASTICS/FIBRE GLASS	8			8		8	8	4, 7, 8

Oval lost-head
As oval brad, but smaller head gives neater finish. Bright steel. 25 to 150mm (1 to 6in).

Plasterboard nail
Fixing plasterboard to battens. Jagged shank for good grip. Bright steel, sherardized or galvanized. 30 to 40mm (1¼ to 1½in).

Panel pin
Cabinet work and fine joinery (with glue). Bright steel. 15 to 50mm (⅝ to 2in).

Veneer pin (moulding pin)
Applying veneers and small mouldings. Bright steel. 15 to 50mm (⅝ to 2in).

Hardboard panel pin
Fixing hardboard and light plywood. Diamond-shaped head goes in flush with board. Coppered. 20 to 40mm (¾ to 1½in).

Clout (slate) nail
Fixing slates and roofing materials. Galvanized or bright steel. 20 to 100mm (¾ to 4in).

Felt nail or large-head clout
Attaching roofing felt, webbing etc. Bright steel or galvanized. 12 to 25mm (½ to 1in).

Roofing nail or drive screw
Fixing corrugated sheet to timber. Spiral shank gives extra grip. Used with washers. Galvanized. 65 to 115mm (2½ to 4½in).

Twisted-shank spring-head nail
Fixing sheet materials and man-made boards. Galvanized. 65mm (2½in).

Masonry nail
Fixing wood to masonry. Hard steel, bright or blued. 15 to 100mm (⅝ to 4in).

Escutcheon pin
Fixing keyhole plates etc. Brass. 15 or 20mm (⅝ or ¾in).

Duplex-head or shuttering nail
For temporary fixing. Head extension used for pulling nail out. Bright steel. 45 to 100mm (1¾ to 4in).

Pipe nail
Chisel-tipped for holding down pipes to masonry. Galvanized. 75 to 100mm (3 to 4in).

Sprig or cut brad
Glazing, picture framing and fixing linoleum. Black iron. 12 to 20mm (½ to ¾in).

Corrugated fastener or wiggle nail
Making rough mitre and butt wood joints.

Timber connector
Making rough mitre and butt wood joints.

Staple
Rough carpentry and fixing fencing wire. Bright steel or galvanized. 10 to 40mm (⅜ to 1½in).

Wire dowel
Hidden fixing in woodwork, one point entering each component. Bright steel. 40 to 50mm (1½ to 2in).

Upholstery nail
Upholstering furniture. Domed decorative head. Brass, bronze, chromed or antique. 3 to 12mm (⅛ to ½in).

Drugget pin
Laying carpet. Large flat head antiqued. 15 and 25mm (⅝ and 1in).

Tack
Attaching fabric to wood; carpeting. Blued, galvanized or coppered. 6 to 30mm (¼ to 1¼in).

Insulated masonry nail
Securing electric cable and micro-bore pipe to masonry. Nail is driven through a plastic cable grip. Made in various shapes and sizes.

Screw nail
Pilot-pointed nail with an helical-threaded shank and countersunk head. Fixing hardboard, plywood and sheet materials. Bright steel. 12 to 50mm (½ to 2in).

SEE ALSO

Details for: ▷	
Fitting carpet	117
Fixing plasterboard	159
Fitting glass	202
Roof slates/tiles	226
Corrugated roofing	227
Roofing felt	228
Fixing cable	303
Chain link fencing	414

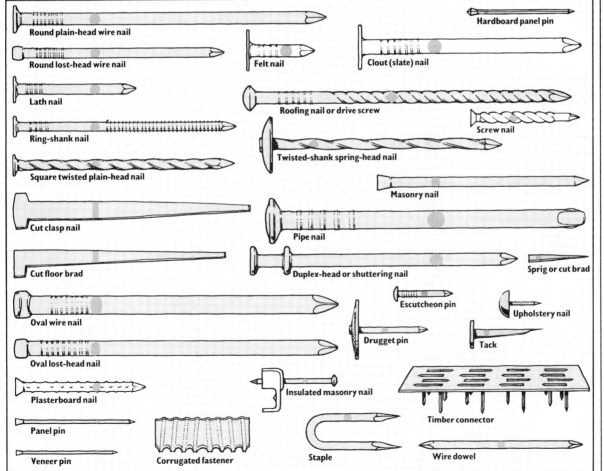

Key to diagram
Grey symbols superimposed on the nails and pins represent their cross section.

Preventing split wood
A blunt nail punches its way through timber instead of forcing the fibres apart. To avoid splitting, if that seems likely, blunt the point of a nail with a light hammer blow.

Removing a dent in wood
If you dent wood with a misplaced hammer blow put a few drops of hot water on the dent and let the wood swell. When it is dry smooth it with abrasive paper.

497

SEE ALSO

◁ Details for:
Thermal plasterboard	269
Countersink bits	472
Screwdrivers	473
Inserting screws	473
Drilling masonry	479

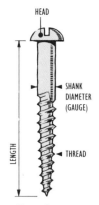

HEAD

SHANK
DIAMETER
(GAUGE)

LENGTH

THREAD

Parts of a screw
You will avoid confusion if you use the correct terminology when ordering screws.

SCREWS

Screws for woodworking and work partly involving wood come in a small range of head shapes suited to various purposes and in a choice of materials and finishes. Screws are ordinarily made of mild steel, but for corrosion-resistance and other special purposes you can also get brass, aluminium and stainless-steel screws as well as chromium-, zinc- and cadmium-plated and sherardized, bronzed and japanned ones.

Screwheads
There are four basic head shapes:

Countersunk head, for work where the screw must be recessed flush with the work surface or below it.

Roundhead, or *domed,* usually used with sheet material that is too thin for countersinking.

Raised head, a combination of domed and countersunk, often used for attaching metal items like door furniture to wood.

Mirror screws, countersunk screws with threaded centre holes for attaching decorative domes, are for holding up fixed wall mirrors and the like.

A further subdivision of all these screws is between those with traditional **slotted heads** and those with **cross-slotted** heads, which need special cross-section screwdrivers.

A 'new generation' of wood screws is case-hardened to give them torsional strength and 'abuse-proof' heads. They have narrow shanks and deep, sharp, widely spaced threads that are claimed to make them easier and quicker to use while giving a better fixing. These, too, have slotted or cross-slotted heads.

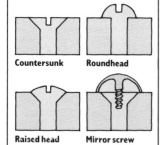

Countersunk	Roundhead
Raised head	Mirror screw

Slotted head · Cross-head

Sizes and gauges
All screws, whatever their type, are described in terms of their length, given in millimetres or inches, and their shank thickness, or gauge, expressed as a simple gauge number from 1 to 20. The length of a screw is the distance between its tip and the part of the head that will lie flush with the work surface. The thicker the screw the higher its gauge number. Gauges in most general use are 4,6,8 and 10.

Woodscrews are available in lengths from 6mm (¼in) to 150mm (6in), but not every length, head shape and material is made, let alone stocked, in every gauge. Generally the largest range of lengths, head shapes and head slot types is to be found in gauges 6 to 12.

Cups, sockets and caps
Countersunk and raised-head screws may be used with metal screw cups or sockets, which increase their grip, and sockets also make for a neat appearance. Countersunk screws can be concealed beneath brown or white plastic caps.

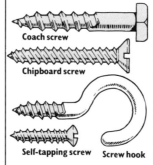

Coach screw

Chipboard screw

Self-tapping screw · **Screw hook**

Special screws
Coach screws, for heavy-duty application like building a work bench, have hexagonal or square heads which are turned into the work with a spanner. Large washers prevent the heads cutting into the timber.

Chipboard screws have a double spiral thread running throughout their length and only taper at the very end. These features enable them to get a strong grip in this relatively weak material.

Screw hooks and eyes in various styles and sizes are available for both light- and heavy-duty applications.

Self-tapping screws with slotted heads in all three styles are produced for fixing thin materials such as sheet metal or rigid plastic. They are so named because they cut their own threads as they are driven home.

WALL FIXINGS

To make secure fixings to any but solid wooden surfaces involves the use of various fixing aids. These range from the simple plug to take a woodscrew in a hole drilled in brick or masonry up to fairly elaborate heavy-duty devices complete with bolts. There are also special products for making fixings to hollow walls.

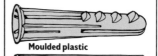

Moulded plastic

Extruded plastic

Fibre

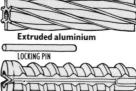

Extruded aluminium

LOCKING PIN

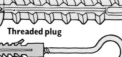

Threaded plug

Clothesline fixing

Wall plugs
There are light- to medium-duty **moulded plastic wall plugs** to take a range of wood screws, generally from No 4 gauge to No 14. Some are colour-coded for easy recognition. A wall plug is pushed into the drilled holes and the screw then driven into the plug, which expands to grip the sides of the hole tightly.

There are also **extruded plastic plugs,** simply straight tubes, which take only the thread of the screw and so must be shorter than the hole. These are cheaper than moulded plugs but less convenient, as are the **traditional fibre** ones which serve the same purpose.

Aluminium wall plugs, both the moulded and the extruded type, are used where heat might affect plastic ones, and there are **threaded plugs** for use in walls of crumbly material like aerated concrete. These plugs themselves are threaded outside and are screwed into the soft material to provide a socket for the screws.

A hole in masonry or brick too irregular to take a plug can be filled with **asbestos-substitute plugging compound,** which

moulds itself to the shape of the hole. Wet the material, ram it into the hole, then pierce a hole in it for the screw. Let it dry out a little before inserting the screw.

Heavy-duty nylon wall plugs are supplied with coach screws or with screw hooks for use as clothesline and similar attachments.

Expansion bolt

Expansion bolts
These are for making very rugged fixings. There are various designs, but all work on one basic principle: a bolt is screwed into a segmented metal shell and engages the thread of an expander. As the bolt is tightened the expander forces the segments apart to grip the sides of the hole. Some expansion bolts have built-in hooks and eyes.

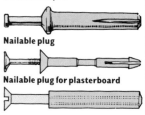

Nailable plug

Nailable plug for plasterboard

Hammer screw

Nailable plugs
These can be used to speed up jobs in which a great many fixings have to be made. There are two types: one is simply a flanged expansion sleeve with a masonry nail. The other consists of a ready-assembled wall plug and 'hammer screw'. Both are simply hammered in but the hammer screw of the second type has a thread and a slotted head, and can be removed with a screwdriver. Nailable plugs are often used for fixing battens and frames, wall linings, ducting and skirting boards.

Frame fixing

Frame fixings
These are designed to speed up screw fixing by eliminating the need to mark out and pre-drill the fixing holes. Position the item to be fixed and drill right through it into the wall, then insert the frame fixing, a long nylon plug with a plated screw, and tighten the screw. Typical uses for the device are fixing battens, wallplates, doors, window frames and fitted furniture to walls.

Fixings for hollow walls

There are many variations on each of several devices for making fixings to hollow walls of plasterboard on studs, lath and plaster and so on. All of them work on the principle of opening out behind the panel and gripping it in some way.

Special wall plugs, plastic toggles and *collapsible anchors* all have segments that open out or fold up against the inside of the panel. A rubber anchor comes complete with its own steel bolt which, when tightened, draws up an internal nut to make the rubber bulge out behind the panel.

Metal gravity toggles and *spring toggles* have arms that open out inside the cavity. A gravity toggle has a single arm, pivoted near one end so that its own weight causes it to drop. A spring toggle has two spring-loaded arms that fly open when they are clear of the hole and a bolt that draws them tight up against the panel.

A nylon strap toggle has an arm that is held firmly behind the panel while the screw is driven into its pilot hole.

The cheap special wall plugs and collapsible anchors remain in their holes if their screws have to be removed. Plastic toggles, nylon strap toggles and the more expensive gravity toggles and spring toggles are all lost in the cavity if their screws are taken out. The rubber anchor can be removed and used elsewhere.

None of these devices should be used for fixings meant to take a heavy load. Instead locate the timber studs and fix directly into these. Even for moderate loads the larger spring and gravity toggles should be used on lath and plaster walls rather than plug-type devices.

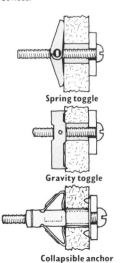

Spring toggle

Gravity toggle

Collapsible anchor

FIXING A ROLLER BLIND

Fitting a roller blind is fairly straightforward; many kits include manufacturer's instructions. A kit consists of a wooden roller with two plastic or metal end cups, one of them spring-loaded to work the blind; two support brackets; a narrow lath; a pull-cord with a knob. You buy the fabric separately and cut it to width and length.

Rollers come in several standard lengths. Unless you find that one of these fits your window exactly, get the next largest and cut it down to size.

Measuring up

The blind can hang within the window aperture or down the front of it. The former leaves the sill accessible when the blind is down; the latter gives better draught protection but means fitting the supports to the wall, not the window frame.

Inside hanging

Fit the supports to the top of the window frame as close to the sides as possible. Remove the right-hand end cap, the one with a round pin, from the roller, cut the roller to fit neatly between the supports and replace the cap.

Forward hanging

Measure the width of the frame, add 100mm (4in) and fit the supports that distance apart above and on either side of the window. If the frame is of the old-fashioned type that projects from the wall, fix wood blocks of that thickness to the wall, then fix the supports to them. Cut the roller to fit between the supports as above.

The fabric

This must be cut exactly rectangular or it will not run evenly on the roller. Cut the width to fit between the two end caps, and the length to cover the window plus an extra 200 to 300mm (8 to 12in). Make a bottom hem 6mm (1/4in) wide, then turn it up to form a sleeve for the lath. Glue and tack the other end of the fabric to the roller, taking care to align the top edge with the roller's axis. Fix the pull-cord to the lath.

Holding the roller with its flat spring-loaded peg on the left, roll the fabric up so that it hangs from the roller's far side. Place the roller in the supports and pull down the blind. Now make it return. If it returns sluggishly it needs more tension. Pull it halfway down, carefully lift it off the supports, roll it up fully by hand and replace it. If it now flies back too violently take the rolled up blind off the supports, unwind it a little by hand and replace it.

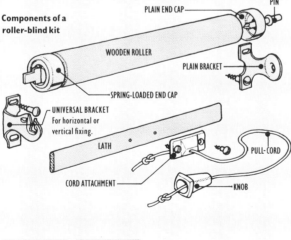

Components of a roller-blind kit

PLAIN END CAP

PIN

WOODEN ROLLER

PLAIN BRACKET

SPRING-LOADED END CAP

UNIVERSAL BRACKET
For horizontal or vertical fixing.

LATH

PULL-CORD

CORD ATTACHMENT

KNOB

Inside hanging
The roller blind covers the glass only.

Forward hanging
The blind covers the entire frame.

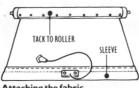

TACK TO ROLLER

SLEEVE

Attaching the fabric
Tack the blind to the roller and sew a sleeve for the lath.

FIXING CURTAIN RAILS

Modern plastic or aluminium curtain rails are easy to fit where there is a wooden window frame and only a little less so where there is not. In the latter case, use a wall fixing or screw a timber batten to the wall above the window, paint it to match the wall and fix the rail supports to it. A similar wall fixing is often preferred for a small alcove window so that the rail can be extra long and the curtains can be drawn clear of the aperture for maximum daylight.

Measure the length of rail you need, allowing a little for cutting, and be sure to get the right number of gliders, hooks and support brackets.

The curtain rail can be bent to follow the curves of a bow window, but any curve should have a rail support on either side of it, which may mean buying extra ones. In a rectangular bay window keep the curves gentle, as ones that are too tight will obstruct the gliders.

Simply screw the rail supports to the window frame with the screws supplied, using a spirit level to keep them level and properly aligned. Start with the two end supports, placing them so that they will be about 25mm (1in) from the ends of the rail, then distribute the rest evenly between them. Some support brackets are designed for both window and ceiling attachment, so be sure that yours are the right way up.

Fit an end stop to the rail, slide the gliders onto it, fit the other end stop and mount the rail on the brackets. Some rails slide onto the supports, some clip into them and some have to be screwed to them.

Where a curtain rail must be fitted to the ceiling the rail supports must be fixed to joists—though some builders install a special ceiling batten for the purpose—and longer screws may be needed. Check, of course, that the rail you buy is suitable for ceiling fixing.

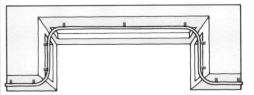

Supporting the rail
Fix a rail support on each side of any curve.

SEE ALSO

Details for: ▷

Stud partitions	121
Locating wall studs	137

Fixing to batten
Screw a straight curtain rail to a wall-fixed batten.

Alcove window
An extended rail allows curtain to be drawn clear.

Wall-fixed support bracket

Ceiling-fixed support bracket

499

SEE ALSO
◁ Details for:
Drilling masonry   479
Wall fixings   498

SHELVING

Depending on where it is and what it is to be used for, shelving can be anything from a set of planks on functional-looking brackets in a garage to elegant spans of teak or plate glass on apparently delicate supports of coloured light alloy.

Whatever its form or context shelving is the cheapest, simplest and most economical kind of storage.

Fixing shelves

Shelves must not only stay up, they must not sag under their load. A load cantilevered on brackets from a back wall will impose great stress on the fixing screws, especially the top ones. If they are too short or of too small a gauge, or if the wall plugs are inadequate, the fixings may be torn out. The wider the shelf the greater the danger of this. A shelf with its ends supported on battens within a brick or masonry alcove will not tear the screws out unless they are a great deal too small.

Shelf span

Sagging occurs when the span of a shelf between supports is too long in relation to its thickness or its load, or both. On this score solid timber, or blockboard with its core running lengthways, are best for sturdy shelving. Veneered chipboard, though popular because of its appearance, will eventually sag under relatively light loads, so it needs support at closer intervals than timber does. But any of these materials can be stiffened with a hardwood batten glued along the underside.

A 25mm (1in) thick timber shelf for a substantial load would need support about every 900mm (3ft) along its length, as would a blockboard one of the same thickness, whereas veneered chipboard of that gauge would have to be supported about every 750mm (2ft 6in).

Even a short shelf on two brackets should have them placed well in from its ends to avoid central sagging. For this reason alcove shelves resting on end battens must be quite thick in relation to their length.

Wall fixing

The type of wall involved has a bearing on all this. On solid brick or masonry, supports for a shelf may be fixed almost anywhere; on a stud partition they must be fixed to the studs unless you put up special cross battens for them between the studs.

For most ordinary shelving, brackets fixed to a back wall of brick or masonry with 50mm (2in) screws and proper wall plugs should be adequate. Wide shelves intended for a heavy load such as a television set and/or stacks of LP records may need more robust fixings, though enough brackets to prevent sagging will also share the weight more effectively. Drill into the wall with a masonry bit, insert plastic wall plugs and screw the brackets to the wall. Brackets must be big enough to support almost the whole width of the shelf.

To fix end battens into the sides of an alcove follow the same procedure, but remember to allow for the thickness of the battens when choosing screw lengths.

Fixing brackets to a stud partition involves simply making pilot holes for the screws in the studs, as does fixing them to cross battens, which are themselves fixed to the studs.

To install several shelves in an alcove a good idea is to fix a wooden 'ladder' on each of the alcove sides and rest the shelf ends on the 'rungs'. The ladder stands on the floor, and can be fixed to the brick or masonry with very few fixings.

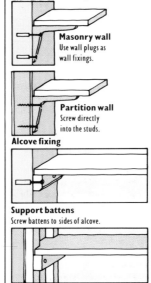

Straight-wall fixing

Masonry wall
Use wall plugs as wall fixings.

Partition wall
Screw directly into the studs.

Alcove fixing

Support battens
Screw battens to sides of alcove.

Timber ladder
Make a ladder for each side.

Patent shelving systems

There are many patent shelving systems on the market with brackets that slot or clip into metal upright supports which are screwed to the wall. In most of them the upright has holes or slots that take lugs on the rear of the bracket, and these are at close enough intervals to allow considerable choice in the level at which the shelves can be placed. In one system the upright has continuous slots over its whole length so that the brackets may be placed literally at any level.

One advantage of such systems is that the weight and stress of loaded shelves are distributed down the supporting uprights. Another is that once the uprights are in place further shelves may be added as the need arises with no necessity for more fixings. Yet another is that they allow shelving arrangements to be changed easily. Early versions of such systems were a little too 'industrial' for some tastes, but today's have colours and finishes quite in keeping with good modern decor and furnishings.

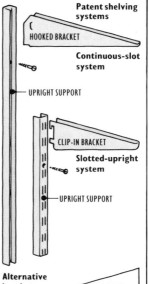

Patent shelving systems

HOOKED BRACKET

Continuous-slot system

UPRIGHT SUPPORT

CLIP-IN BRACKET

Slotted-upright system

UPRIGHT SUPPORT

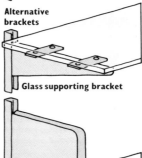

Alternative brackets

Glass supporting bracket

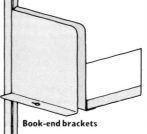

Book-end brackets

Fitting shelving systems

The support must be properly vertical, and the best way of ensuring this is to fix it at first lightly, but not too loosely, to the wall by its top screw, then hold it vertical with the aid of a spirit level and mark for the bottom screws (**1**). With the bottom screw in place you can check that the upright is vertical in its other plane, and not sloping outward because of a sloping wall. If it does slope you will have to place discreet packing behind it to correct it (**2**). Also put packing wherever the upright is away from the wall owing to random hollows. Where there are very marked hollows it may be necessary to use slightly extra-long screws.

Put a bracket on the upright, then one on the second upright while it is held against the wall. Get a helper to lay a shelf across the brackets, then use a spirit level to check that the shelf is horizontal. Mark the top hole of the second upright, then fix that upright as you did the first one.

1 Plumb the upright support
Use a spirit level to plumb the upright, then mark the bottom fixing hole on the wall.

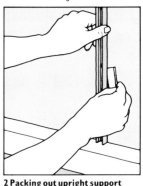

2 Packing out upright support
Push packing behind the upright if the wall is not vertical.

GLOSSARY OF TERMS

A

Accessory
An electrical component permanently connected to a circuit – a switch, socket outlet, connection unit etc.

Aggregate
Particles of sand or stone mixed with cement and water to make concrete, or added to paint to make a textured finish.

Airlock
A blockage in a pipe caused by a trapped bubble of air.

Appliance
A machine or device powered by electricity. or A functional piece of equipment connected to the plumbing – a basin, sink, bath etc.

Architrave
The moulding around a door or window

Arris
The sharp edge at the meeting of two surfaces.

B

Back-siphonage
The siphoning of part of a plumbing system caused by the failure of mains water pressure.

Balanced flue
A ducting system which allows a heating appliance, such as a boiler, to draw fresh air from, and discharge gases to, the outside of a building.

Ballast
Naturally occurring sand and gravel mix used as aggregate for making concrete.

Baluster
One of a set of posts supporting a stair handrail.

Balustrade
The protective barrier alongside a staircase or landing.

Banisters
See balustrade

Batt
A short cut length of glass- or mineral-fibre insulant.

Batten
A narrow strip of wood.

Batter
The slope of the face of a wall that leans backwards or tapers from bottom to top.

Blind
To cover with sand.

Blown
To have broken away, as when a layer of cement rendering has parted from a wall.

Bore
The hollow part of a pipe or tube. or To drill a hole.

Burr
The rough raised edge left on a workpiece after cutting or filing.

Buttercoat
The top layer of cement render.

C

Came
The grooved strip of lead which holds the glass in a leaded light or a stained-glass window.

Cap-nut
The nut used to tighten a fitting onto pipework.

Casing
The timber lining of a door opening.

Catenary wire
A length of wire cable suspended horizontally between two points.

Cavity wall
A wall of two separate masonry skins with an air-space between them.

Chamfer
A narrow flat surface on the edge of a piece of wood – it is normally at an angle of 45 degrees to adjacent surfaces. or To plane the angled surface.

Chase
A groove cut in masonry or plaster to accept pipework or an electrical cable. or To cut such grooves.

Circuit
A complete path through which an electric current can flow.

Concave
Curving inwards.

Conductor
A component, usually a length of wire, along which an electric current will pass.

Convex
Curving outwards.

Cornice
The continuous horizontal moulding between walls and ceiling.

Counter-bore
To cut a hole which allows the head of a bolt or screw to lie below a surface. or The hole itself.

Countersink
To cut a tapered recess which allows the head of a screw to lie flush with a surface. or The tapered recess itself.

Coving
A pre-fabricated moulding used to make a cornice.

Cup
To bend as a result of shrinkage – specifically across the width of a piece of wood.

D

Dado
The lower part of an interior wall – usually defined with a moulded rail. or In the USA – a housing.

Damp-proof course
A layer of impervious material which prevents moisture rising from the ground into the walls of a building.

Damp-proof membrane
A layer of impervious material which prevents moisture rising through a concrete floor.

Datum point
The point from which measurements are taken.

DPC
See damp-proof course.

DPM
See damp-proof membrane.

Drip groove
A groove cut or moulded in the underside of a door or windowsill to prevent rainwater running back to the wall.

Drop
A strip of wallpaper cut to length ready for pasting to a wall.

E

Earth
A connection between an electrical circuit and the earth (ground). or A terminal to which the connection is made.

Eaves
The edges of a roof that project beyond the walls.

Efflorescence
A white powdery deposit caused by soluble salts migrating to the surface of a wall or ceiling.

ELCB
Earth-leakage circuit breaker. See residual-current circuit breaker.

End grain
The surface of wood exposed after cutting across the fibres.

Ergonomics
The study of the physical relationship between the human body and its surroundings.

Extension
A length of electrical flex for temporarily connecting the short permanent flex of an appliance to a wall socket. or A room or rooms added to an existing building.

F

Face edge
In woodworking, the surface planed square to the face side.

Face side
In woodworking, the flat planed surface from which other dimensions and angles are measured.

Fall
A downward slope.

Fascia board
Strip of wood which covers the ends of rafters and to which external guttering is fixed.

Feather
To wear away or smooth an edge until it is undetectable.

Fence
An adjustable guide to keep the cutting edge of a tool a set distance from the edge of a workpiece.

Flashing
A weatherproof junction between a roof and a wall or chimney, or between one roof and another.

Flaunching
A mortared slope around a chimney pot or at the top of a fireback.

Flute
A rounded concave groove.

Footing
A narrow concrete foundation for a wall.

Frass
Powdered wood produced by the activity of woodworm.

Frog
The angled depression in one face of some housebricks.

Furring battens
See furring strips.

Furring strips
Parallel strips of wood fixed to a wall or ceiling to provide a framework for attaching panels.

Fuse board
Where the main electrical service cable is connected to the house circuitry. or The accumulation of consumer unit, meter etc.

G

Galvanized
Covered with a protective coating of zinc.

Gel
A substance with a thick jelly-like consistency.

Going
The horizontal measurement between the top and bottom risers of a stair or the depth of one tread.

Grain
The general direction of wood fibres. or The pattern produced on the surface of timber by cutting through the fibres. See also end grain and short grain.

Grommet
A ring of rubber or plastic lining a hole to protect electrical cable from chafing.

Groove
A long narrow channel cut in wood in the general direction of the grain. or To cut such channels.

Grounds
Strips of wood fixed to a wall to provide nail-fixing points for skirting boards and door casings. See also pallets.

Gullet
The notch formed between two saw teeth.

H

Hardcore
Broken bricks or stones used to form a sub-base below foundations, paving etc.

Hardwood
Timber cut from deciduous trees.

Head
The height of the surface of water above a specific point – used as a measurement of pressure; for example, a head of 2m. or The top horizontal member of a wooden frame.

Head plate
The top horizontal member of a stud partition.

Heave
An upward swelling of the ground caused by excess moisture.

Helical
Spiral shaped.

Hoggin
A fine ballast, usually with a clay content, used to form a sub-base for concrete pads or paving.

Hone
To finely sharpen a cutting edge.

Horns
Extended door or window stiles designed to protect the corners from damage while in storage.

Housing
A long narrow channel cut across the general direction of wood grain to form part of a joint.

I

Insulation
Materials used to reduce the transmission of heat or sound. or Nonconductive material surrounding electrical wires or connections to prevent the passage of electricity.

J

Jamb
The vertical side member of a door or window frame.

Joist
A horizontal wooden or metal beam used to support a structure like a floor, ceiling or wall.

K

Kerf
The groove cut by a saw.

Key
To abrade or incise a surface to provide a better grip when gluing something to it.

Knurled
Impressed with a series of fine grooves designed to improve the grip.

L

Lath and plaster
A method of finishing a timber-framed wall or ceiling. Narrow strips of wood are nailed to the studs or joists to provide a supporting framework for plaster.

Lead
A stepped section of brick- or blockwork built at each end of a wall to act as a guide to the height of the intermediate coursing.

Lintel
A horizontal beam used to support the wall over a door or window opening.

M

Marine plywood
Exterior-grade plywood.

Mastic
A non–setting compound used to seal joints.

Microporous
Used to describe a finish which allows timber to dry out while protecting it from rainwater.

Mitre
A joint formed between two pieces of wood by cutting bevels of equal angles at the ends of each piece. or To cut the joint.

Mole
A tallow-soaked felt pad used to smooth a soldered lead joint.

Mono-pitch roof
A roof which slopes in one direction only.

Mortise
A rectangular recess cut in timber to receive a matching tongue or tenon.

Mouse
A small weight used to pass a line through a narrow vertical gap.

Mullion
A vertical dividing member of a window frame.

Muntin
A central vertical member of a panel door.

N

Needle
A stout wooden beam used with props to support the section of a wall above an opening prior to the installation of an RSJ or lintel.

Neutral
The section of an electrical circuit which carries the flow of current back to source. or A terminal to which the connection is made. or A colour composed mainly of black and white.

Newel
The post at the top or bottom of a staircase that supports the handrail.

Nogging
A short horizontal wooden member between studs.

Nosing
The front edge of a stair tread.

O

Outer string
See string.

Oxidize
To form a layer of metal oxide as in rusting.

P

Pallet
A wooden plug built into masonry to provide a fixing point for a door casing.

Pare
To remove fine shavings from wood with a chisel.

Pargeting
The internal render of a chimney.

Party wall
The wall between two houses and over which each of the adjoining owners has equal rights.

Penetrating oil
A thin lubricant which will seep between corroded components.

Phase
The part of an electrical circuit which carries the flow of current to an appliance or accessory. Also known as live.

Pile
Raised fibres which stand out from a backing material as with a carpet.

Pilot hole
A small-diameter hole drilled prior to the insertion of a woodscrew to act as a guide for its thread.

Pinch rod
A wooden batten used to gauge the width of a door casing.

PME
See protective multiple earth.

Point load
The concentration of forces on a very small area.

Primer
The first coat of a paint system to protect the workpiece and reduce absorption of subsequent coats.

Profile
The outline or contour of an object.

Protective multiple earth
A system of electrical wiring in which the neutral part of the circuit is used to take earth-leakage current to earth.

PTFE
Polytetrafluorethylene – used to make tape for sealing threaded plumbing fittings.

Purlin
A horizontal beam that provides intermediate support for rafters or sheet roofing.

R

Rafter
One of a set of parallel sloping beams that form the main structural element of a roof.

Ratchet
A device that permits movement in one direction only by restricting the reversal of a toothed wheel or rack.

RCCB
See residual-current circuit breaker.

Rebate
A stepped recess along the edge of a workpiece, usually as part of a joint. or To cut such recesses.

Render
A thin layer of cement-based mortar applied to exterior walls to provide a protective finish. Sometimes fine stone aggregate is embedded in the mortar. *or* To apply the mortar.

Residual-current circuit breaker
A device which monitors the flow of electrical current through the live and neutral wires of a circuit. When it detects an imbalance caused by earth leakage, it cuts off the supply of electricity as a safety precaution.

Reveal
The vertical side of an opening in a wall.

Riser
The vertical part of a step.

Rising main
The pipe which supplies water under mains pressure, usually to a storage cistern in the roof.

Rolled steel joist
A steel beam usually with a cross section in the form of a letter I.

RSJ
See rolled steel joist.

Rub joint
Glued wood rubbed together and held by suction until set.

Rubber
A pad of cotton wool wrapped in soft cloth used to apply stain, shellac polish etc.

S

Sash
The openable part of a window.

Score
To scratch a line with a pointed tool. See also scribe.

Scratchcoat
The bottom layer of cement render.

Screed
A thin layer of mortar applied to give a smooth surface to concrete etc. *or* A shortened version of screed batten.

Screed batten
A thin strip of wood fixed to a surface to act as a guide to the thickness of an application of plaster or render.

Scribe
To copy the profile of a surface on the edge of sheet material which is to be butted against it: to mark a line with a pointed tool. See also score.

Set
A small rectangular paving block.

Sheathing
The outer layer of insulation surrounding an electrical cable or flex.

Short circuit
The accidental rerouting of electricity to earth which increases the flow of current and blows a fuse.

Short grain
When the general direction of wood fibres lies across a narrow section of timber.

Sill
The lowest horizontal member of a stud partition. *or* The lowest horizontal member of a door or window frame.

Sleeper wall
A low masonry wall used as an intermediate support for ground-floor joists.

Soakaway
A pit filled with rubble or gravel into which water is drained.

Soffit
The underside of a part of a building such as the eaves, archway etc.

Softwood
Timber cut from coniferous trees.

Sole plate
Another term for a stud partition sill. *or* A wooden member used as a base to level a timber-framed loadbearing wall.

Spalling
Flaking of the outer face of masonry caused by expanding moisture in icy conditions.

Spandrel
The triangular infill below the outer string of a staircase.

Staff bead
The innermost strip of timber holding a sliding sash in a window frame.

Stile
A vertical side member of a door or window sash.

Stopper
A wood filler which matches the colour of the timber.

String
A board, which runs from one floor level to another, into which staircase treads and risers are jointed. The one on the open side of a staircase is an outer string, the one against the wall is a wall string.

Stud partition
An interior timber-framed dividing wall.

Studs
The vertical members of a timber-framed wall.

Subsidence
A sinking of the ground caused by the shrinkage of excessively dry soil.

Supplementary bonding
The connecting to earth of exposed metal appliances and pipework in a bathroom or kitchen.

T

Tamp
To pack down firmly with repeated blows.

Template
A cut-out pattern to help shape something accurately.

Tenon
A projecting tongue on the end of a piece of wood which fits in a corresponding mortise.

Terminal
A connection for an electrical conductor.

Thinners
A solvent used to dilute paint or varnish.

Thixotropic
A property of some paints which have a jelly-like consistency until stirred or applied, at which point they become liquified.

Top coat
The outer layer of a paint system.

Torque
A rotational force.

Transom
A horizontal dividing member of a window frame.

Trap
A bent section of pipe below a bath, sink etc. It contains standing water to prevent the passage of gases.

Tread
The horizontal part of a step.

U

Undercoat
A layer of paint used to obliterate the colour of a primer and to build a protective body of paint prior to the application of a top coat.

V

Vapour barrier
A layer of impervious material which prevents the passage of moisture-laden air.

Vapour check
See vapour barrier.

W

Wall plate
A horizontal timber member placed along the top of a wall to support joists and to spread their load.

Wall string
See string.

Wall tie
A strip of metal or bent wire used to bind sections of masonry together.

Waney edge
A natural wavy edge on a plank. It might still be covered by tree bark.

Warp
To bend or twist as a result of damp or heat.

Water closet
A lavatory flushed by water.

Water hammer
A vibration in plumbing pipework produced by fluctuating water pressure.

WC
See water closet.

Weathered
Showing signs of exposure to the weather. *or* Sloped so as to shed rainwater.

Weep hole
A small hole at the base of a cavity wall to allow absorbed water to drain to the outside.

Workpiece
An object being shaped, produced or otherwise worked upon. Sometimes shortened to 'work'.

Page numbers in *italics* refer to photographs and illustrations.

A

abrasive papers 469, 481
abrasives 469, 481, 491
accessory 501
acid
 oxalic 54
 safety 62
acrylic adhesives 495, 496
acrylic double glazing 273
acrylic lacquers 86; *86*
adhesives 495–6
 acrylic 495, 496
 brand name guide 496
 contact 89, 101, 105, 109, 495; *89*
 epoxy resin 495, 496
 flooring 109, 118, 495, 496
 for carpets 117
 for tiles 103, 105, 106, 108, 112, 495, 496
 for wallboards 89, 97; *89*
 latex 97, 109, 117, 495
 PVA bonding agent 43, 47, 495, 496
 paste 55, 93, 97
 polystyrene 112
 rubber resin 495
 solvents 496
 super glues 495, 496
adjustable spanners 489; *489*
aggregates 65, 169, 438, 501
 storage 439; *439*
air conditioners 284; *284*
air locks 341, 501
airbricks 276, 385; *276*
alarm systems 238, 239, 243
alkali-resistant primer 43, 50
alloy nails 224
aluminium
 alloy nails 224
 corrosion 61
 gutters 234, 235; *235*
 spirit-based sealer 43, 50
 tape 233; *233*
 windows 197; *197*
 wood primer 43, 53
Anaglypta 90, 96; *90*
ants 247; *247*
apartments 13
 Building Regulations 19
 decorating schemes 36; *36*
 planning permission 19
appliances, electrical
 see electrical appliances
arches 132; *132*
archways, papering 95
architects 17, 20
architraves 88, 501
 fitting 125, 185; *125*
arris 501
artificial respiration 291; *291*
asbestos cement 48, 227
 cutting 226, 227
 gutters 234, 235
 paints 64
 primer 43, 48
 safety precautions 48, 227
 slates 224, 225, 226
attics
 insulating 267; *267*
 security 238, 239
 ventilating 277; *277*
 see also lofts
auger bits 471; *471*
augers 349, 486, 492 *349, 486, 492*

B

BCO
 see Building Control Officer
back siphonage 501
backsaws 463; *463*
balanced flues 276, 279, 393, 501
ballast 501
balusters 214, 501
 repairing 218, 219; *218, 219*
balustrades 214, 501
 Building Regulations 214, 218, 219
 repairing 218–20; *218–20*
banister brushes 66; *66*
banisters *see* balustrades
basements
 damp-proofing 258; *258*
 ventilation 276; *276*
basin wrenches 489; *489*
basins 363; *363*
 clearing blockages 348; *348*
 connecting to water supply 366; *366*
 fitting 363, 365–6; *363, 365–6*
 installing 139, 363, 365, 366; *139, 365*
 mounting 139; *139*
 plumbing 363–6; *363–6*
 sealant 103; *103*
 supplementary bonding 290
 types 363; *363*
bath paint 85, 367
bathrooms 15, 290, 370
 decorating schemes 35; *35*
 electrical safety 290
 extractor fans 279; *279*
 lighting planning 38; *38*
 room temperature 394
baths 367–9; *367–9*
 bath/shower mixers 370; *370*
 clearing blockages 348; *348*
 installing 367–9; *367–9*
 painting 367
 panelling 369; *369*
 plumbing 367–9; *367–9*
 removing 368
 renovating enamel 367
 sealant 103; *103*
 supplementary bonding 290; *290*
 types 367; *367*
bats 248; *248*
batt 501
battens 161, 221, 224, 501; *120, 121, 161*
 drip battens 230; *228*
 screed battens 503; *157*
batter 501
bay windows 210; *210*
beading 202, 204; *202, 204*
beam compass cutters 201, 480; *201, 480*
beams 128, 129, 131; *129, 131*
bedrooms 15
 decorating schemes 33; *33*
 planning lighting 38; *38*
bell pushes 322; *322*
bell wire 244, 322
belt sanders 470; *470*
bench grinding 467
bench hooks 463; *463*
bench planes 466; *466*
bending pipes 488; *488*
bending springs 488
BESA box 326, 331; *326*
bevel-edge chisels 468; *468*
bib taps 342
bidets 373; *373*

bits 471, 472; *471, 472*
bitumen base coat 47
bitumen latex emulsion 231, 258, 452; *231, 258, 452*
bituminous felts 224, 228, 2
bituminous paint
 for metalwork 85, 86
 primer 43
black lead 85–6; *86*
blanking plugs 401
bleach
 used on timber 54; *54*
 used on walls 44
bleed valves 399; *399*
blind riveters 489; *489*
blinds
 roller blinds 499; *499*
 roof windows 211; *211*
block planes 466; *466*
blockages 348–50; *348–50*
 air locks 341
 basins 348; *348*
 baths 348; *348*
 drains 350; *350*
 stacks 349; *349*
 WC pan 349; *349*
 wastepipes 348; *348*
blockboard 54, 494; *54*
blockwork *see* concrete blocks
blowtorches 58, 60, 481; *481*
boards 54, 494; *54*
 fixing 88; *88*
 floorboards 176–7; *176–7*
 plasterer's boards 478
 see also blockboard; chipboard; hardboard; plywood; softboard
bog gardens 459; *459*
boilers 392–3, 398; *392*
bolster chisels 304, 480, 492; *154, 304, 428, 480*
bolts 239, 240
bonding agents 151
bonding plasterboard 162; *162*
bonds and bonding 426, 431; *426, 431*
 new into old 127; *127*
 piers 432; *432*
bookshelves 500; *500*
 hanging on studs 139
bore 501
bow windows 210; *210*
box spanners 489; *489*
brace bits 471, 479; *471, 479*
braces 471, 492; *471, 492*
bracing floors 173; *173*
bracket and plate fixing 475; *475*
brass
 cleaning 61; *61*
 door furniture 189; *189*
 pipes 351
brazing 489
brick-cutting saws 130; *130*
brick tiles 100, 106; *100, 106*
brick trowels 478; *428, 478*
bricklayer's lines 479; *479*
bricklaying techniques 428–31, 449–50; *428–31, 449–50*
bricklaying tools 428, 478; *428, 478*
bricks and brickwork 252, 421–2, 428–31; *421–2, 428–31*
 bonding 127, 426, 431, 432; *127, 426, 431*
 cleaning 44
 colours 422; *422*
 control joints 433
 cracked 252; *46*
 efflorescence 44, 46, 258; *44*
 estimating 421
 fire surrounds 389
 laying 428–31, 449–50; *428–31, 449–50*
 lintels 124; *124*

 painted 48, 64, 67, 69
 paving 449–50; *449–50*
 piers 432; *432*
 pointing 430; *430*
 priming 43, 46, 48
 renewing old bricks 168
 spalling 46, 48; *46*
 stained 44; *44*
 storage 421
 texture 422; *422*
 types 421–2; *421–2*
bridged cavity walls 253–4; *254*
bridle joints 476; *476*
British Gas 393, 398
British Standard Code of Practice (BS)
 glass 200
 mortise locks 240
 plugs 295
 roofing felts 228
 shaver sockets 316
buffing mops 491; *491*
builders and sub-contractors 20
builder's squares 462, 478, 486; *462, 478, 486*
builder's tool kit 478–80
building blocks *see* concrete blocks
Building Control Officer (BCO) 18, 46, 121, 124, 126, 129, 182, 209
 applying for permission to 129
 see also Building Regulations
Building Regulations 17, 18, 19, 129, 135
 balustrades 214, 218, 219
 calculating lintel size 124
 conservatories 19
 converting floors 180
 converting a house 19
 converting loft 19
 damp-proof course 431
 demolition 19
 doors 19
 extensions 19
 fire-resisting doors 194
 floor joists 180
 footings 427
 garages 19
 garden walls and fences 19
 handrails 218, 219
 hedges 19
 insulation 269
 open-tread stairs 213, 215
 plumbing 19
 roof windows 211
 swimming pools 19
 treads 215
 ventilation 135, 277
 windows 19, 209, 211
burglar alarm systems 238, 239, 243
burglary 238, 239
business premises
 Building Regulations 19
 planning permission 19
butt hinges 186, 187; *186, 187*
butt joints 475; *475*
buttercoat 501
butyl liners 455
buzzers 322

CPO see Crime Prevention Officer
cabinet scrapers 470; *470*
cabinet screwdrivers 473, 480, 492; *473, 492*
cable connectors 333; *333*
cable running 139, 141, 303–5; *303–5*
cable stripping 302; *302*
cables 302–5; *302–5*
calcium plumbate primer 43
cames 203, 501; *203*
  cleaning 61
cap-nuts 501
carlite plaster 149, 151
carpenter's mallets 473; *473*
carpets 115–17; *116–17*
  adhesives 117
  choosing 116
  estimating 115
  fitting 117; *117*
  laying 57, 115, 117; *117*
carpet squares 115
carpet tiles 100; *100*
  laying 109; *109*
  setting out 107; *107*
casement windows 196; *196*
  locks 78, 86, 242
  painting 78; *78*
  rattling 204
  replacing 209; *209*
casing 501
cast ironwork 60
  blacking 86; *86*
  gutters 234, 235; *235*
catenary wire 501
caulking compound 233
cavity fixings 139
cavity ties 122; *122*
cavity trays 229, 276; *229, 276*
cavity walls 120, 122, 198, 229, 251, 435, 501; *122*
ceiling roses 69, 98, 324, 325; *69, 98, 324*
ceilings 142–7; *142, 144–6*
  ceiling roses 69, 98, 324, 325; *69, 98, 324*
  centre pieces 98, 155; *98, 155*
  loft access 147; *147*
  lowering 142–6; *144–6*
  painting 67, 69; *69*
  panelling 88
  papering 92, 98; *98*
  plasterboard 51, 154, 166; *154, 166*
  repairing 154; *154*
  slatted 143, 145; *144*
  stains 50
  supporting 130
  suspended 143, 145, 146; *145, 146*
  tiles 101, 102, 112, 495; *112*
cellars 16
  damp-proofing 258; *258*
  paints 67
  ventilation 276; *276*
cellular-core wallboards 123, 140–1; *123, 140–1*
  door openings 141; *141*
  fitting fixtures to 141; *141*
cellulose filler 53, 54
cement 168, 438
  asbestos 48, 227
  bandage 236
  mixer 170; *170*
  paints 43, 51, 64, 65, 67
  storage 169, 439
  waterproof coating 258

cement rendering 168
  paints 67
  primer 43
  types 168
central heating 19, 390–403; *390–5, 397–403*
  boilers 392–3, 398; *398*
  controls 395, 403; *395, 403*
  convectors 394; *394*
  draining 397; *397*
  problems 396
  pumps 402; *402*
  radiators 393, 399–401; *393, 399–401*
  running costs 391
  systems 390–1
  temperatures 394–5
centre pieces 98, 155; *98, 155*
centre pulls 189; *189*
centre punches 486; *486*
ceramic tiles 99; *99*
  adhesives 495, 496
  cutting 104, 110; *104, 110*
  fire surrounds 384, 389
  for floors 57, 62, 110
  for walls 62, 103
  hanging 103, 105; *103, 105*
  laying 110; *110*
  setting out 102; *102*
cesspools 350; *350*
chain link cutters 487; *487*
chain link fencing 410, 414; *410, 414*
  posts 412, 413, 414; *413, 414*
chain wrenches 490; *490*
chamfer 501
chase 501
chemical strippers 59
chimes 322; *322*
chimneys 382, 385
  capping 385; *385*
  fires 244
  flashing 232; *232*
  flaunching 501
  flue liners 48, 388–9; *388–9*
  maintenance 226
  stacks 12
  stained paint 48; *48*
  sweeping 382, 387; *382*
chipboard 54, 494; *54*
  flooring grade 175, 176; *175*
  laying flooring 179; *179*
  pre-felted 228
chippings 169, 452; *452*
chisels 468–9, 480, 487, 492; *468–9, 480, 487*
  sharpening 469; *469*
  storing 469; *469*
chromate primer 43
circuit fuses 289, 296, 306
  fuse carriers 299; *299*
  old fuse boards 297, 306; *297*
circuit breakers 289, 296, 299, 300; *299*
  MCBs 296, 300; *299, 300*
  RCCBs 297, 298, 332, 335, 503; *297, 332*
circuits, electrical
  see electrical circuits
circular saws 465, 479; *465, 479*
cisterns 344–6, 360–2, 379; *344–6, 360–2, 379*
clamp-on vices 474; *474*
clamping a jointed frame 474; *474*
clamping boards together 474; *474*
claw hammers 472, 479, 492; *472*
clay blocks 123; *123*
clay tiles 223, 224
clearing drains 348–50; *349–50*
clearing sinks 348; *348*
clearing WC pan 349; *349*
clipped-point knives 480; *480*

closeboard fencing 411, 415; *411, 415*
clothes
  on fire 244
  working 40
club hammers 479, 492; *428, 479*
coal chutes
  security 238, 239
cobblestones 451; *451*
cockroaches 247; *247*
cockspur handles 242; *242*
cold chisels 304, 480, 487, 492; *304, 480, 487*
cold cure lacquer 75, 84
cold water storage cisterns 340, 379; *340*
cold water taps and pipes 340
colour 24–31; *24–31*
  bathrooms 35; *35*
  bedrooms 33; *33*
  dining areas 34; *34*
  kitchens 34; *34*
  living rooms 32; *32*
  pattern 29; *29*
  schemes 25–7; *25–7*
  single rooms 36; *36*
  texture 28; *28*
combination planes 466–7; *466–7*
combination squares 462; *462*
compressed-air guns 348, 486; *348, 486*
compressor-operated spray 484; *484*
concrete 438–45; *439–40, 442–5*
  binding 49
  calculating 440–1
  cleaning 49
  cracks 49; *49*
  cutting 447; *447*
  dampness 49
  dry-packed 438
  ingredients 438
  laying 442–5; *442–5*
  lintels 124, 198; *124, 198*
  mixing 439; *439*
  paints 64, 65, 67, 69
  paving 440–43; *440–43*
  primer 43
  ready-mixed 439
  repairing 49; *49*
  roofing tiles 223, 224, 225
  sealing 49
  slabs 446, 453–4; *446, 453–4*
  solid floors 173, 182–3; *173, 183*
  spalling 49, 454; *49*
  steps 454; *454*
  surface finishes 445; *445*
  swimming pools 460
concrete blocks 123, 133, 150, 423, 424; *423, 424*
  building 434–5; *434–5*
  control joints 434; *434*
  decorative screens 435; *435*
  estimating 423
  storage 423
  types 423; *423*
condensation 231, 254, 267, 268; *254*
  causes 255, 275
  controlling 283; *283*
  in kitchens 279–80; *279–80*
conservation areas 17, 19, 209, 211
conservatories
  Building Regulations 19
  leaks 233
  PVC glazing 273
  planning permission 19
consumer units 296, 298, 306, 336; *298*
contact adhesives 89, 101, 105, 109, 495; *89*
continuity testers 492; *492*

convector heaters 394; *394*
converting one room to two 135, 138
converting two rooms to one 128
cooker hoods 281, 314; *281*
  installing 316
  running costs 287
cookers 16
  enamel paint 86
  running costs 287
  wiring 317–18; *317–18*
coping saws 464, 479; *464, 479*
copings 252, 429, 430; *429, 430*
copper
  cleaning 61
  nails 224
  pipes 351, 354, 355
corner blocks 475; *475*
corner rollers 485; *485*
cornice mouldings 501
  making a new length 156; *156*
  repairing 156; *156*
corrosion 60–1; *60–1*
  inhibitor 397
corrugated iron 61
corrugated sheet roofing 227
countersink 472, 473, 501; *472, 473*
countersink bits 472; *472*
coving 167, 501; *167*
cowls 385, 388; *385, 388*
cracks 409; *409*
  in concrete 49; *49*
  in plaster 50; *50*
  in render 47; *47*
  in walls 12, 46, 73; *46*
craft knives 485; *485*
cramp heads 473; *473*
cramps 473–4; *473–4*
cranked spanners 489; *489*
crazy paving 448; *448*
creosote 75
Crime Prevention Officer (CPO)
  advice from 238
cross-cut saws 463, 465; *463, 465*
cross-head screwdrivers 473, 480; *473*
cross-peen hammers 472; *472*
crowbars 480
cupboards 500
  fitting 139
curtain rails 499; *499*
cutters, pipes 487
cutting
  concrete 447; *447*
  glass 200–1; *200–1*
  metal 487; *487*
  pipes 353, 361, 487; *353, 361, 487*
  tiles 104, 106, 110, 485; *104*
  wood 463, 464, 465; *463, 464, 465*
cutting gauge 463; *463*
cutting list 144
cutting-in brushes 78, 482; *78, 482*
cyanoacrylates 495, 498
cylinder rim locks 240; *240*
  fitting 241; *241*
cylinders
  plumbing 380; *380*

DOBETA
  see Domestic Oil Burning Equipment Testing Association
DPC see damp-proof course
DPM see damp-proof membrane
dado 501
damp 12, 251–8; *251, 253, 254*
  causes 251–3

damp *continued*
curing 254–8; *254–8*
on masonry 44, 46, 48, 231
penetrating damp 251, 252–3, 270
rising damp 251, 253
testing concrete 49
using plaster on damp 149
see also efflorescence; spalled bricks; spalled concrete
damp-proof course (DPC) 44, 122, 173, 180, 258, 501
Building Regulations 431
as cause of damp 253
for parapets 229; *229*
in walls 251, 426, 431; *251*
injecting a chemical DPC 257; *257*
inserting 256; *256*
types 256
damp-proof membrane (DPM) 49, 173, 175, 182, 258, 501
as cause of damp 253
in floors 251, 258; *251*
damp-proofing
cellars 258; *258*
walls 254–8; *254–8*
datum point 501
deadlocking bolts 239, 240
deathwatch beetle 246; *246*
decorating 40–118; *40–118*
applying finishes 63–118; *63–118*
equipment 40–2; *40–2*
masonry 44–9, 64–6; *44–9, 65–6*
means of access 40–2
metalwork 60–1, 85–6; *60–1, 85–6*
paint 63–86; *63–74, 76–86*
panelling 87–9; *87–9*
plaster 50–1; *50–1*
preparation and priming 43–62; *44–62*
staining 81; *81*
tiling 62, 99–112; *62, 99–112*
wallcoverings 52, 90–8; *52, 90–1, 93–8*
woodwork 53–9, 74–84; *53–9, 74, 75–84*
see also under individual treatments and materials
decorating schemes 32–6; *32–6*
bathrooms 35; *35*
bedrooms 33; *33*
dining rooms 34; *34*
kitchens 34; *34*
living rooms 32; *32*
single rooms 36; *36*
decorator's tool kit 481–5; *481–5*
dehumidifiers 283
demolition
Building Regulations 19
diagonal cutters 492; *492*
dial meters 286
diaphragm valves 345; *345*
dining rooms 15
decorating schemes 34; *34*
lighting planning 38; *38*
room temperature 394
disc sanders 470; *470*
disconnecting pipes 354
dishwashers
drainage 377
plumbing 376; *376*
running costs 287
wiring 316
dismantling taps 342; *342*
distemper 51; *51*
primer 43
District Surveyor
see Building Control Officer
Domestic Oil Burning Equipment Testing Association (DOBETA) 393
door knockers 189; *189*
door viewers 239, 240; *240*
doorbells 322; *322*

doors 19, 184–95; *185–95*
battened doors 188; *188*
Building Regulations 19
casings 190; *190*
construction 184, 190; *184, 190*
dividing doors 192–3; *192–3*
draughtproofing 262–3; *262–3*
fire-check 184, 194, 244; *194*
fitting 186–7; *186–7*
flush doors 77, 184; *77, 184*
flush panelling 188
folding doors 192–3; *192–3*
frames and casings 185, 190–1; *185, 190–1*
furniture 189; *189*
garage doors 194–5; *194–5*
glazed doors 77; *77*
locks 240
painting 77; *77*
panel doors 77, 184; *77, 184*
papering around 95; *95*
repairs 188, 191; *188, 191*
security 238, 239; *240*
shortening 57
sills 191; *191*
sizes 184, 195
sliding doors 192–3; *192–3*
staining 81; *81*
sticking 188; *188*
weather stripping 263; *263*
see also French windows
doorways 126–7, 136, 141, 163; *126–7, 136, 163*
double glazing 204, 271–4; *204, 271–4*
acrylic 273
as security 239
insulation 260, 271–4
plastic materials 272–3; *272–3*
sealed units 271; *271*
secondary glazing 271–4; *271–4*
triple glazing 271; *271*
double insulation 288; *288*
dovetail nailing 472; *472*
dovetail saws 177, 463; *463*
dowel bits 472; *472*
dowel joints 472, 476–7; *476–7*
dowelling jigs 472; *472*
downpipes 234; *234*
as cause of damp 252
painting 66; *66, 86*
repairing 236; *236*
security 238, 239
drain augers 486; *486*
drain cleaning equipment 486; *486*
drain rods 486; *486*
drainage system 338, 347–50, 369; *347–50*
blockages 348–9; *348–9*
for ponds 457; *457*
roof 234; *234*
draincocks 379; *379*
draining central heating 397; *397*
drains
clearing 348–50; *348–50*
rodding 350
draught excluders 262
draughtproofing 260, 264
doors 262–3; *262–3*
draughts 262, 264
draw filing 491; *491*
drill and countersink bits 472; *472*
drill stands 472; *472*
drilling holes in glass 201; *201*
drilling joists 305
drilling masonry 479; *479*
drills 471, 479, 488, 492; *471, 488, 492*
power drills 471–2, 479, 492; *471–2*
safety 472
sharpening 471

drip battens 230; *228*
drip grooves 251, 253, 254, 501; *254*
drip moulding 254, 501; *254*
drips 230; *230*
drives 19, 408, 440, 444; *444*
brick paving 450
concrete 440
laying 19, 444; *444*
stone chippings 452; *452*
tarmac 452; *452*
drum sanders 55, 56; *55, 56*
dry lining 148; *148*
dry partition walls 140–1; *140–1*
dry rot 180, 249, 276; *249*
treatment 249
dry stone walls 436; *436*
drying time 43, 64, 69, 76, 85
dusting brush 481; *481*

E

earth clamps 290, 297; *290, 297*
earthing 288, 306, 501
earthing system 297
protective multiple earth 297, 502
see also circuit breakers
eaves 222, 225, 230, 501; *222, 225, 230*
gutter systems 234; *234*
ventilating 277; *277*
efflorescence 44, 46, 49, 501; *44*
on brickwork 44, 46, 258; *44*
on concrete 49
on new plaster 50
electric drills 471, 479
electric shock treatment 291; *291*
electrical appliances 16, 314–22, 501
running costs 287
wiring 316–21; *316–21*
see also under separate appliances
electrical circuits 288, 301, 311–13, 315–17, 320, 323, 335, 501; *301, 311–13, 315–17, 320, 335*
bell systems 322
cooker circuits 317; *317*
heat/light circuits 315; *315*
immersion heaters 319; *319*
kitchen circuits 316
lighting 301, 323–4; *301, 323*
new circuits 329–31; *329–31*
porch lights 332; *332*
power circuits 308–13; *308–13*
pump systems 333; *333*
radial circuits 301, 313; *301, 313*
ring circuits 301, 311; *301, 311, 313*
storage heaters 320
towel rail circuits 315; *315*
types 301; *301*
wall heater circuits 315; *315*
electrical systems assessment 306–7
electrician's pliers 492; *492*
electrician's tool kit 492; *492*
electricity 12, 286–336; *287–336*
adapting power circuits 311–13; *311–13*
basics 288
bathrooms 290, 370
cables 302–5, 306, 334, 335; *302–5, 334*
checklists 306–7
circuits 288, 289, 296, 301, 306, 323–4, 335–6; *301, 323–4, 335*
consumer units 296, 298, 306, 321, 336; *298, 313, 321*
cookers 287, 317–18; *317–18*
doorbells 322; *322*

earthing 288, 297, 306; *297*
economics 286–7, 391
exteriors 332–3; *332–3*
fixed appliances 314–22; *314–22*
fuse boards 296–7, 306; *296–7*
fuses 289, 299–300, 306, 314; *299–300, 314*
heaters 315, 318–21; *315, 318–21*
lighting 323–31, 336; *323–31, 336*
main switch equipment 296; *296*
measuring 289
mounting socket outlets 308–9; *308–9*
power circuits 308–13; *308–13*
repairs 292–5; *292–5*
resuscitation 291; *291*
rewiring 336
safety 69, 244, 280, 289–92, 294, 296; *289–91*
socket outlets 308–10; *308–10*
spurs 311; *311*
switches 327–8, 330; *327–8, 330*
Electricity Board 296, 297, 298, 319, 393
Economy 7 286, 318, 404
equipment supplied 320
testing 289, 306, 318, 335
electronic mains testers 289, 492; *289, 492*
electro-osmosis 256; *256*
emery boards 491; *491*
emery cloths 491; *491*
emulsion paints 63, 64, 65, 67, 75, 76
applying 69; *69*
exterior-grade 65
for metalwork 85, 86
reinforced emulsion 65, 67
solid 67
enamel
renovating 367
enamel paint 86
engineer's pliers 491; *491*
engineer's vice 487; *487*
Environmental Health Department 19, 135, 246, 248, 347
epoxy putty 236, 341; *341*
epoxy resin 495, 496
ergonomics 13–16, 501; *14–16*
estimates 20
expanded polystyrene 90, 97; *90*
expansion bolts 498; *498*
expansive bits 471; *471*
extension leads 294; *294*
extensions
Building Regulations 19
planning permission 19
External Wall Insulation Association 21, 270
extractors 279–81; *279–81*
installation 316
running costs 287

F

FPO *see* Fire Prevention Officer
fabric wallcoverings 91, 97; *97*
fanlights
security 243
ventilation 135
fans 279–81; *279–81*
fascia boards 222, 225, 501; *222, 225*
fat fires 244
Federation of Master Builders 20
felts 224
bonding 228

roofing 224, 228–31; *230*
types 229
fence 501
fences 410–17; *410–17*
erecting 414–17; *414–17*
posts 412–14; *412–14*
types 410–11; *410–11*
fibre tiles 62, 101, 112; *101*
fibreglass, adhesives 496
fibreglass mats 489; *489*
fibrous plaster 132
files 469, 490–1; *490–1*
cleaning 490; *490*
safety 490
fillers 53, 54, 149
cellulose 53, 54
filler board 150; *150*
grain 53, 80, 83; *53*
wood 53
filling knives 481, 492; *481*
finger plates 189; *189*
finishing sanders 470; *470*
fire-check doors 184, 194, 244; *194*
Building Regulations 194
fire prevention 244
blankets 244
extinguishers 244
fire-check doors 184, 194, 244; *194*
wired glass 199
Fire Prevention Officer (FPO)
advice from 143, 194, 238, 244
fire surrounds 60, 384, 386, 389; *384*
firebacks 382–3; *383*
cracked 382
installing 383; *383*
removing 383; *383*
sealing 383
fireplaces 383–6, 389; *383–6*
fitting 386; *386*
papering around 95
plastering over 153
removing 384–5; *384–5*
sealing 385; *385*
ventilation 264, 275; *275*
fires
chimneys 244
closed fires 386–9; *386–9*
fat 244
open fires 382–5; *382–5*
see also fire prevention
firmer chisels 468; *468*
fixings 496–500
flaky paintwork 48, 58, 60; *48, 58, 60*
flaring tools 489; *489*
flashings 211, 232–3, 501; *211, 232–3*
apron 232; *232*
as cause of damp 252
chimney 232; *232*
construction 232
repairs 233; *233*
flat files 490; *490*
flat roofs 228–31; *228–31*
abutments and parapets 229; *229*
coverings 228
felts 224, 228–31; *230*
insulating 265, 268; *268*
maintenance 230
renewing 230; *230*
repairs 231; *231*
flaunching 501
flex 292–4, 307; *293–4*
connecting 293, 294; *293*
extending 294; *294*
stripping 293; *293*
types 292
flies 247; *247*
float glass 199
floats 478; *478*
flock wallpaper 91, 97; *91*
floor tile jigs 485; *485*

floorboards 176–8, 304; *176–8*
cramps 178; *178*
fixing 178
saws 177, 479, 492; *177, 479*
floors and floorcoverings 107–11, 113–18, 120, 121, 172–83; *114, 118, 172–5, 177–83*
adhesives 109, 118, 495, 496
aligning 134; *134*
bracing 173; *173*
Building Regulations 180
ceramic tiles 57, 62, 110
construction 174; *174*
estimating 115
filling gaps 55, 133; *55, 133*
insulation 260, 264, 270; *270*
laying 178, 179; *178, 179*
levelling 57
lifting 177; *177*
paints 65, 75
parquet flooring 113–14; *113–14*
sanding 55–6; *55–6*
solid 173, 175; *173, 175*
staining 81
stone and slate 99
suspended 172; *172, 173*
types 176
varnishing 82; *82*
ventilation 276; *276*
woodworm treatment 246–7; *246*
flue boxes 386; *386*
flues 106
balanced flues 276, 279, 393, 501
fluorescent lights 325, 327; *325, 327*
foam drum sanders 470; *470*
foamed polyethylene coverings 91, 97; *91*
foil wallcoverings 91, 97; *91*
folding doors 192–3; *192–3*
footings 427, 432, 433, 501; *427*
Building Regulations 427
footlifters 159; *159*
foundations 120, 121; *120*
concrete mix 441–2
problems 121, 409
fountains 458
pump 458; *458*
frame cramps 126, 127, 473; *126, 127, 473*
frame fixings 498; *498*
framing anchors 174; *174*
freezers 16
running costs 287
French polish 75, 76, 83; *83*
French windows 238, 239, 243
painting 78
frenchman 45, 478; *45, 478*
fret saws 464; *464*
fridges 16
enamel paint 86
installing 316
running costs 287
frozen pipes 341; *341*
fungal growth
on masonry 44; *44*
on plaster 52; *52*
on steps 454
on wallpaper 52
fungicide 44
fused connection units 314; *314*
fuses 289, 296–7, 299–300, 306; *296–7, 299–300*
changing a fuse 300, 314; *300, 314*
fuse boards 296–7, 306, 501; *296–7*

G

G-cramps 473; *473*
galvanized metal 61
galvanized nails 224, 496–7; *497*
garages 16, 19
Building Regulations 19
cement paint 67
concrete paving 440
doors 194–5; *194–5*
planning permission 19
security 238, 239
garden rakes 480
gardens 406–46; *406–46*
bog gardens 459; *459*
Building Regulations 19
conservatories 19, 233, 273
drives 19, 440, 444; *440, 444*
fences 410–17; *410–17*
gates 418–19; *418–19*
gravel 451; *451*
lighting 333; *333*
paths 19, 440, 442, 444; *444*
patios 440; *438, 440*
paving 446–52; *446–52*
planning 19, 406–9; *406–9*
rockeries 459; *406, 459*
steps 453–4; *453–4*
swimming pools 19, 460
water gardens 455–9; *455–9*
garnet paper 469
gas heating
boilers 392, 398; *392*
running costs 391
gas torches 353, 488–9; *353*
gate valves 342
gates 418–19; *418–19*
hardware 419; *419*
posts 418; *418*
types 418, 419; *418, 419*
gauge sticks 102, 479
gauges 463, 479
gel 502
gel strippers 59, 501
gents saws 463; *463*
glass 199–201; *199–201*
adhesives 496
blocks 123; *123*
buying 200
cutting 200–1, 280; *200–1*
drilling holes 201; *201*
fire-resistant 199
fitting 202; *202*
removing 202, 205; *202*
repairing 202–3; *202–3*
security 238, 239
see also double glazing
glass cutters 200, 480; *200–1, 480*
glass drills 480; *480*
glass-fibre insulation material 87, 265
glass-fibre tape 51, 164
glass scrapers 482; *482*
glasspapers 469
glazier's tools 480
glazing 199–201; *200–1*
glazing bars 196; *196*
painting 77, 78
staining 81
gloves 480, 481; *481*
glue guns 495
going 212, 502
gouges 468–9; *469*
sharpening 469; *469*
grain filler 53, 80, 83; *53*
grainers 482; *482*
graining 71, 79; *71, 79*
granite fire surrounds 389

grants
for insulation 260
for roofing 226
grass cloth 91; *91*
grates 385; *385*
gravel 451; *451*
greenhouses 233
gripper strips 117; *109*
grommets 502
grooves 502
grounds 502
grouting 102, 110; *103*
gullets 502
gully, unblocking 349; *349*
gunmetal 351
guttering 60, 234–6; *234–6*
aluminium 234, 235; *235*
asbestos cement 48, 234, 235
as cause of damp 252
cast iron 234, 235; *235*
fitting 236; *236*
PVC plastic 234, 235; *235*
painting 86
maintenance 235; *235*
repairing 236; *236*
types 234; *234*
gypsum plaster 149, 151
finishing 152; *152*
loss of strength 152

H

hacking knives 480; *480*
hacksaws 479, 486–7; *479, 486–7*
half-round files 490; *490*
hallways 14
temperature 394
halving joints 475; *475*
hammers 472–3, 479, 492; *472–3, 479*
hand drills 471; *471*
hand files 490; *490*
hand routers 468; *468*
handbasins see basins
handrails 218–20; *218–20*
handsaws 463; *463*
hangers 174; *174*
hardboard 54, 495; *54*
as door panelling 188; *188*
as insulation 270
laying 57; *57*
hardcore 502
hardwoods 494, 502
hatchways 125
hatch doors 125; *125*
into lofts 147; *147*
hawk 152, 478; *478*
head plates 138, 502
heat exchangers 282–3, 284, 460; *282–3*
heated towel rails 315
heaters 315, 386–7, 394; *386–7*
convectors 394; *394*
fan-assisted 321
for swimming pools 460
immersion heaters 286, 318–19, 340; *318–19*
running costs 287
storage heaters 287, 296, 320–1, 390, 404; *390, 404*
water heaters 316, 380; *380*
heating 382–404; *382–404*
boiler maintenance 398; *398*
central heating 390–7; *390–7*
chimneys 388–9; *388–9*
circulating pumps 402; *402*
closed fires 386–9; *386–9*

heating *continued*
  control valves 403; *403*
  fireplaces 383–6; *383–6*
  open fires 382–5; *382–5*
  radiators 399–401; *399–401*
  solid fuel 386–7; *386–7*
  storage heaters 390, 404; *390, 404*
heave 121, 409, 502
hedges 19
hinge bolts 239
  fitting 241; *241*
hinges 186–7; *186–7*
hiring machinery 462
  cement mixers 170; *170*
hiring professionals 20–21, 128
hoggin 443, 502
holdfast 474; *474*
hole punches 488; *488*
hole saws 379, 465; *379, 465*
home security 12, 238–44; *238, 240–4*
  alarm systems 243
  doors 240–1; *240–1*
  fire protection 244; *244*
  guarding against intruders 239
  windows 242–3; *242–3*
honing 502
  blades 467; *467*
  flat tips 473
  gouges 469; *469*
  router cutters 468
honing guide 467; *467*
hook scrapers 55, 58, 470; *55, 470*
horns 186, 502; *186*
hot air guns 489; *489*
hot air strippers 59, 481; *59, 481*
hot water
  cylinders 261, 340, 380; *261, 380*
  heaters 380; *380*
  immersion heaters 318–19, 340; *318–19*
  insulation 260, 261, 319; *261*
  taps and pipes 340
house longhorn beetle 246; *246*
houses
  brick construction 120; *120*
  security 238, 239; *238*
  timber-frame construction 121; *121*
housing 502
housing joints 476; *476*

immersion heaters 318–19, 340; *318–19*
  running costs 287
  thermostats 286, 318, 395; *318, 395*
Incorporated Association of Architects and Surveyors 17
industrial strippers 59, 60
infestation 12, 246–8; *246–8*
  in roof timbers 222
Institution of Electrical Engineers 19, 288, 289, 370
insulation 12, 260–74, 286, 391, 502
  against sound 260, 271, 272
  Building Regulations 269
  cavity filling 268–9; *269*
  doors 262–3; *262–3*
  draughtproofing 260, 262–4; *264*
  floors 260, 264, 270; *270*
  grants 260
  plumbing 261, 266; *261, 266*
  roofs 260, 265–8; *266–8*
  specification 260
  types 265
  walls 87, 122, 268–70; *269*
  windows 264, 271–4; *264, 271*

insurance companies
  advice from 238
ironwork
  cast 60, 351
  corrugated 61
  wrought 60

jack planes 466, 480; *466*
jambs 502
Japanese gardens 407
jig
  dowelling 472; *472*
  tile cutting 104, 485; *104, 485*
jigsaws 304, 465, 492; *304, 465*
joinery 53
jointer planes 466; *466*
jointers 478; *478*
joints 140, 475–7; *140, 475–7*
  mortar 45, 430; *45, 430*
  nailed 472
  pipes 352–4, 356–9; *352–4, 356–9*
  step/string 213; *213*
  woodworking 475–7; *475–7*
joist braces 492; *492*
joist hangers 135, 174, 180, 221; *135, 174*
joists 172, 180, 502; *180*
  Building Regulations 180
  drilling 305
  fitting services 180
  hangers 135, 174, 180, 221; *135, 174*
  reinforcing 135, 173; *135*
  roofs 221, 228; *147, 228*
junction boxes 311, 324; *311, 324*

keyhole saws 464; *464*
keyholes
  sealing 263
kitchens 13, 16
  condensation 279–80; *279–80*
  decorating schemes 34; *34*
  equipment circuits 316; *316*
  extractor fans 279–80; *279–80*
  lighting planning 38; *38*
  room temperature 394
  safety 16
  supplementary bonding 290; *290*
  units 13
knee kickers 117; *117*

lacquer 75, 76, 84; *86*
ladders 40–2; *40, 41*
  accessories 40, 66; *40*
  how to use 41; *41*
  loft ladders 147; *147*
  safety 41, 225
  security 238, 239
  stepladders 40, 41; *40, 41*
  types 40
  working from 98
lagging 260, 261; *261*

laminated glass 199
lampholders 295; *295*
lap joints 475; *475*
lateral restraint straps 174; *174*
latex adhesive 97, 109, 117, 495
lath-and-plaster 50, 502; *123*
  ceilings 51, 154, 155; *154, 155*
  flush-mounting sockets 309; *309*
  patching 51, 154; *51, 154*
  repairing 154; *154*
  stud walls 123, 125, 126; *123*
  traditional techniques 148; *148*
  under stairs 214
lead 61
  flashing 232; *232*
  in paints 43
  painting 61
  patching 233
  pipes 351, 355; *355*
leaded lights 61, 203, 239, 271; *203, 271*
leaks
  patching 258, 341
  repairing taps 342; *342*
letter plates 189
letterboxes
  sealing 263
levelling furring battens 161; *161*
levels 478
light fittings 88, 325–7; *325–7*
  BESA box 326, 331; *326*
  fluorescents 327; *327*
  track lighting 326; *326*
  wall lights 331
lighting 323–30; *323–30*
  circuits 301, 323–4; *323–4*
  fittings 325–7; *325–7*
  in gardens 333; *333*
  installing 329–31, 332; *329–31, 332*
  planning 37–8; *37–8*
  switches 327–30; *327–30*
lime 168
lime-scale deposits 35, 378
limewash 51
  primer 43
Lincrusta 90, 96; *90*
liners 455–7; *455–7*
  flue liners 48, 388–9; *388–9*
  swimming pools 460
lining paper 50, 90, 94; *90, 94*
linseed oil 75
lintels 124, 198, 502; *124, 198*
  brick 124; *124*
  Building Regulations 124
  calculating size 124
  concrete 124, 198; *124, 198*
  fitting 128
  installing 126; *126*
  pressed steel box 129, 131; *129, 131*
liquid sanders 58; *58*
liquid strippers 59
listed buildings 209, 211
  planning permission 17, 19
living rooms 14
  decorating schemes 32; *32*
  lighting planning 37; *37*
  room temperature 394
locks 239, 240–3; *240–3*
  choice 240
  door locks 240–1; *240–1*
  fitting 241–3; *242–3*
  window locks 242–3; *242–3*
lofts 16, 19
  access hatch 147; *147*
  Building Regulations 19
  insulation 265, 266; *266*
  ladders 147; *147*
  running cables 304
  security 238, 239
  ventilation 265, 277; *277*
  see also attics
log-burning stoves 387; *387*

log pathways 451; *451*
louvre windows 197; *197*
  security 238, 239

MCBs *see* miniature circuit breakers
mallets 473, 479; *473*
man-made boards 494–5
marble fire surrounds 389
marbling 71; *71*
marine plywood 502
marking gauge 463, 479; *463*
marking knives 463; *463*
masking 72, 73; *72, 79*
masonry 44–9, 64–6, 420–37; *44–9, 64–6, 420–37*
  adhesives 496
  chalky surface 48; *48*
  cleaning 44–5; *45*
  drilling 479; *479*
  flaky paintwork 48; *48*
  mortar 169–70, 425, 434; *170, 425*
  mounting sockets to 308–9; *308–9*
  paints 64–6; *64–6*
  pointing 45, 430, 435; *45, 430*
  repairing 46
  waterproofing 46
  see also bricks and brickwork; concrete blocks; stones and stonework; walls
masonry saws 479; *479*
mastic 81, 502; *81, 254*
mastic asphalt 228
mastic guns 481; *481*
mattocks 480; *480*
metal detectors 280
metal pipe joints 352–5; *352–5*
metal tiles 101
  hanging 105; *105*
  setting out 102
metallic foils 91, 97; *91*
metallic inks 52
metallic paints 85, 86
metals and metalwork
  finishing 85–6, 491
  fire surrounds 389
  gluing 495, 496
  metal benders 488; *488*
  metal-cutting tools 486–7; *486–7*
  metal-joining tools 488–9; *488–9*
  preparation 60–1
  primer 43, 49, 60
  stripping 60
  varnishing 60, 85, 86
methylated spirits as thinners 76
mice 248; *248*
microporous stains (paints) 74–5; *74*
mineral-fibre tiles 112; *101*
miniature circuit breakers (MCBs) 296, 300; *299, 300*
mirror tiles *101*
  hanging 105; *105*
  setting out 102
mitre boxes 464; *464*
mitre cramps 473; *473*
mitre joints 477, 502; *477*
  for coving 167; *167*
moisture meters 49
moles 502
mortar 168, 425; *425*
  dyes 45
  for concrete blocks 435
  ingredients 425
  mixes 169–70, 425, 434; *170*
  pointing 45, 430; *45, 430*

mortar boards 150, 170, 478; *150, 478*
mortar joints 45, 46, 430, 435; *45, 430*
  brick tiles 106
  filling cracks 46, 47; *46, 47*
mortise 502
mortise and tenon joints 205, 477; *477*
mortise chisels 468; *468*
mortise gauges 463; *463*
mortise locks 239, 240; *240*
  fitting 241; *241*
mosaic tiles 99, 110; *99*
  hanging 105; *105*
  setting out 102
mould growth 52
  eradicating 52; *52*
  identifying 249
  on external masonry 44; *44*
moulding planes 466–7; *467*
mouldings 155–6; *155–6*
  around doors and windows *88*
  cutting 468; *468*
  making new lengths 156; *156*
  moulded ceilings 155; *155*
  plaster of Paris 51, 149
  repairing 156; *156*
  skirtings 181; *181*
  staining 81
  stripping 51, 58
moulds 44, 52; *44, 52*
mouse 502
mullions 502
multi-planes 467; *467*
muntins 502

nail sets 472; *472*
nail ties 126, 127; *126, 127*
nailable plugs 498; *159, 269*
nailed butt joints 475; *475*
nailed joints 472; *472*
nailing techniques 137, 472–3; *137, 472–3*
  for plasterboard 159, 166; *159*
  secret nailing *88; 88*
nails 496–8; *497*
  roofing 224
National Cavity Insulation Association 21, 269
Nature Conservancy Council 21, 248
needle files 490; *490*
needles 125, 126, 130, 131, 502; *126, 130, 131*
neighbours 408, 410
newel posts 502
nibblers 485; *485*
nicotine stains 50
noggings 137, 502; *137*
non-reflective glass 199
non-slip paint 85, 86
nosings 502
Novamura 91, 97

oil 75, 76, 84
  oil-fired boilers 392, 398; *392, 398*
  running costs 391

oil-based paint 63, 64, 67, 75, 76
  for metalwork 85, 86
oilstones 467
open-ended spanners 489; *489*
open fires 382–5; *382–5*
open-tread stairs 213, 215; *213*
oxalic acid 54

PME see protective multiple earthing
PVA admixture 438
PVA bonding agent 43, 47, 495, 496
PVC plastic 357
  double glazing 272–3; *272–3*
  gutters 234, 235; *235*
  pipes 357
  sheeting 227
pads 68, 69, 76, 80, 85, 162; *68, 80, 162*
  cleaning 483
padsaws 464, 479, 492; *464, 479*
paint kettles 482; *483*
paint rollers 64, 66, 68, 85, 483, 485; *68, 483*
paint scrapers 481; *481*
paint shields 78, 482; *482*
paint stripper 45, 58–60; *45, 58–60*
paintbrushes 66, 68, 69, 76, 78, 85, 482; *68, 80, 482*
  cleaning 482
  for varnishes 82
  storing 482
paints and painting 63–86; *63–86*
  basic system 63
  brickwork 48, 64, 67, 69
  brushes 66, 68, 69, 76, 78, 85, 482; *68, 80, 482*
  can holders on ladders 40
  decorative effects 70–3; *70–3*
  exterior masonry 64–6; *64–6*
  interior walls and ceilings 67–73; *68, 69*
  masonry paints 44, 64–5, 67
  metalwork paints 85–6; *85–6*
  non-slip paint 85, 86
  painting doors 77; *77*
  painting window frames 78; *78*
  painting woodwork 76–9; *76–9*
  preparing the paint 64
  priming 53–4
  rollers 64, 66, 68, 85, 483, 485; *68, 483*
  safety 64
  scrapers 481; *481*
  security paint 85, 86, 239
  shields 78, 482; *482*
  spraying 66, 484; *66, 484*
  stripper 45, 58–60; *45, 58–60*
  woodwork 76–9; *76–9*
pallets 502
panel doors 77, 184; *77, 184*
panel fencing 416; *416*
panel saws 463, 479; *463, 479*
panelling 87–9; *87–9*
  baths 369; *369*
  ceilings 88
  constructing framework *87*
  fixing *88*
  urethane panelling 89
  veneered timber 89
paper-backed fabrics 91; *91*
papering 90–8; *90–1, 93–8*
  ceilings 92, 98; *98*
  pasting 93; *93*
  problem areas 95–6; *95–6*
  special techniques 96–7; *96–7*

  tools 484–5; *484–5*
  walls 94–5; *94–5*
paperhanger's tools 484–5; *484–5*
papier mâché paste 55
parapet gutters 234; *234*
pargeting 48, 502
paring 468, 502; *468*
parking space
  brick paving 450
  concrete paving 440
parquet flooring 113–14; *113–14*
partition walls
  dry 140–1; *140–1*
  stud 135–9; *135–9*
paste 93, 97
  papier mâché 55
  stripper 59
paste brushes 484; *484*
pasting tables 485; *485*
pasting wallpapers 93; *93*
paths 19, 440, 442, 444; 444
  brick paving 449–50; *449–50*
  concrete paving 440, 441–3; *440, 441–3*
  laying 19, 444; *444*
  stone chippings 452; *452*
  tarmac 452; *452*
  wooden pathways 451; *451*
patios 440; *438, 440*
patterned glass 199
paving 446–52; *446–52*
  brick paving 449–50; *449–50*
  concrete paving 440, 441–3; *440, 441–3*
  crazy paving 448; *448*
  paving slabs 446–7; *446*
pebbledash 47
  paints 64
  patching 47; *47*
  rendering 171; *171*
penetrating damp 270
  causes 251, 252–3
pickaxes 480; *480*
piers 129, 131, 433, 435; *433*
  bonding 432; *432*
  brickwork 432; *432*
  reinforcing 433; *433*
pillar taps 342; *342*
pilot holes 502
pin hammer 472; *472*
pinch rods 502
pipe joints 352–4; *352–4*
pipe rollers 485; *485*
pipes 351–9, 363; *352–9, 363*
  bending 353, 361, 488; *353, 488*
  blocked 348; *348*
  concealing 363; *363*
  cutters 487
  cutting 353, 361, 487; *353, 361, 487*
  disconnecting 353, 354, 358, 359; *354, 359*
  draining central heating 397; *397*
  frozen 341; *341*
  installing 351
  insulation 260, 261, 266
  joining 352–5; *352–5, 366*
  metal 352–5; *352–5*
  painting behind 66, 85
  plastic 356–9; *356–9*
  soil 361–2, 366; *361–2, 366*
  steel 351, 354
  tiling around 104, 108, 109, 110, 114; *104, 108, 109, 110, 114*
  types 351
  wastepipes 348; *348*
  see also drainage system
pivot windows 197; *209*
planes 466–7, 480; *466–7*
  bench planes 466; *466*
  block planes 466; *466*
  combination and multi-planes 477; *477*
  jack planes 466; *466*

  jointer planes 466; *466*
  moulding planes 466, 467; *466, 467*
  plough planes 467; *467*
  power planes 466
  rebate planes 467; *467*
  sharpening 467; *467*
  shoulder planes 466; *466*
  smoothing planes 466; *466*
  spokeshave 466; *466*
  storing 466; *466*
planning 12–38; *12–38*
  assessing a property 12–16; *12–16*
  hiring professionals 17, 20–1, 128
  lighting 37–8; *37–8*
  planning regulations 18–19
  priorities 22–3
planning a conversion 128, 142, 143
  doing it yourself 22–3
  windows 209
planning permission 17, 18, 19
plans 18
planting 406–8
plaster and plasterwork 50–1, 148–71; *50–1, 148–71*
  adhesives 496
  applying 152, 157; *152, 157*
  buying and storing 148; *148*
  coving 167, 501; *167*
  cracks 50; *50*
  fibrous plaster 132
  finishes 51, 69
  making good 50; *51*
  mixing 151
  mouldings 51, 98, 149, 156; *156*
  plastering techniques 148–52, 157; *152, 157*
  preparing to decorate 50, 60
  primer 43
  repairing 51, 153–6; *51, 153*
  types 149, 151
  see also lath-and-plaster
plaster of Paris 149, 155; *155*
plasterboard 50, 148, 158–66; *123, 148*
  ceilings 154–5, 166; *154–5, 166*
  dry lining 148; *148*
  finishing 164–5; *164–5*
  fixing 159–63, 267, 268; *159–63, 268*
  flush-mounting sockets 309
  insulation 269; *269*
  making an arch 132; *132*
  patching 51, 154; *154*
  primer 43, 50
  sealing fireplaces 385
  stud walls 123, 125, 126, 137; *123, 137*
  types 158
plasterer's rule 152, 479
plasterer's tools 150, 478, 492; *150, 478*
plasterer's trowels 152, 171, 478, 492; *478*
plastering 148–71; *148–71*
plastic 357
  adhesives 496
  plumbing 356–9; *356–9*
  windows 197; *197*
plier wrenches 490; *490*
pliers 491; *491*
plough planes 467; *467*
plug cutters 472; *472*
plugging chisels 480; *480*
plugs 307
  nailable 498
  wall 479, 498–9; *479*
  wiring 295; *295*
plumb lines 478, 484; *478, 484*
plumber's tool kit 486–91; *486–91*
plumbing 19, 338–80; *338–80*
  access to 109
  baths 367–9; *367–9*

plumbing continued
bidets 373; *373*
cisterns 344–6, 360–2, 379; *344–6, 360–2, 379*
cylinders 380; *380*
dishwashers 376; *376*
drainage 347–50, 369; *347–50*
fitting in stud partitions 139
garden taps 378; *378*
regulations 19, 338
pipework 341, 351–9; *341, 352–9*
showers 369–72; *370–2*
sinks 374; *374*
taps 342–3; *342–3*
wash basins 363–6; *363–6*
washing machines 376–7; *376–7*
water softeners 378; *378*
plungers 486; *486*
plywood 54, 494; *54*
exterior-grade 176
laying 57; *57*
marine 502
panelling 89
pointing 45, 106, 430; *45, 430*
as cause of damp 252
mortar 45, 430, 435
pointing trays 478; *478*
pointing trowels 478; *478*
poisons 248
polishes 74, 75, 84; *74*
polycarbonate double glazing 273
polyester double glazing 273
polystyrene tiles 62; *101*
fixing 112
polythene vapour barrier 87
ponds 19, 455–9; *455–9*
construction 457; *457*
lighting 333; *333*
liners 455–7; *455–7*
planning 408, 456
raised-edge ponds 458; *458*
pools 460; *460*
porches 19, 322; *322*
leaks in glazing 233
security 238, 239
portable circular saws 465; *465*
portable jigsaws 465; *465*
Portsmouth pattern valves 345; *345*
post-and-rail fencing 417; *417*
post-hole augers 480; *480*
power circuits 308–13, 334, 336; *308–13*
adapting 311–13
junction box 311, 321
radial circuits 301, 313; *301, 313*
ring circuits 301, 312, 313; *301, 311, 313*
socket outlets 308–10; *308–10*
power drills 471–2, 479, 492; *471–2, 492*
bits 472; *472*
safety 472
power jigsaws 465, 479; *465, 479*
power planes 466; *466*
power routers 468; *468*
sharpening 468
power sanders 470; *470*
power saws 465, 479; *465, 479*
safety 248, 465
power tools 465, 471–2; *465, 471–2*
running costs 287
safety 465, 472
preparing wood 53
preparing metal 60–1
pressed steel box lintels 129, 131; *129, 131*
pressurized painting system 483; *483*
primers 43
alkali resistant 50
brick primer 46, 48
metal primer 43, 49, 60

wood primer 53–4
printed wallpapers 90; *90*
profile gauge 485; *485*
property assessment 14–16
props 125, 126, 130; *126, 130, 155*
protective multiple earthing 290, 297, 502
pump-action screwdrivers 473; *473*
pumps, circulating 402, 403; *402*
for fountains and waterfalls 458; *458*
purlins 502
putty 202, 204; *202*
epoxy 236, 341
replacing 81
putty knives 480; *480*

quarry tiles 62, 99; *99*
cleaning 62; *62*
cutting 111; *111*
setting out 111; *111*

R-values 260
RCCBs see residual-current circuit breakers
RSJs see rolled steel joists
rack bolts 239, 243
fitting 241, 242; *241*
radial circuits 301, 313; *301, 313*
radiator brushes 482; *482*
radiator rollers 485; *485*
radiator spanners 489; *489*
radiators 393–401; *393–5, 397, 399–401*
bleeding 399; *399*
enamel paint 85, 86
faults 396
insulation 260, 261; *261*
painting behind 68, 85
papering behind 95; *95*
removing 399; *399*
replacing 401; *401*
rafters 502
rag rolling 72; *72*
rag stippling 70; *70*
ramin 494
rasps 469; *469*
ratchet 502
ratchet screwdrivers 473; *473*
rats 248; *248*
rattling windows 204
ready-mixed concrete 439
rebate 502
rebate planes 467; *467*
rebated joints 476; *476*
reciprocating saws 465, 479; *465, 479*
red lead primer 43
red oxide 43, 60
refrigerators 16, 316
enamel paint 86
running costs 287
Regulations for Electrical Installations 289, 290
reinforced emulsion 65, 67
relief papers 90; *90*
render 168–71, 50.; *47, 170–1*
applying 171; *171*
as cause of damp 252

cracks 47; *47*
materials 168–9
mixing 170; *170*
pebbledash 47, 171; *47, 171*
repairing 47, 171; *47*
roughcast 171; *171*
techniques 168
texturing 171; *171*
repairs and improvements 120–236; *120–236*
replacing washers 342, 345; *342, 345*
reproduction panelling 89
reseating tools 491; *491*
residual-current circuit breakers (RCCBs) 297, 298, 332, 335, 503; *297, 332*
resuscitation 291; *291*
retaining walls 437; *437*
reveal 503
reverse pressure taps 342
rewiring 336
rim latches 240
ring circuits 301, 311; *301, 311, 313*
ring spanners 489; *489*
ripsaws 463; *463*
filing teeth 465; *465*
risers 214–15, 503; *214*
rising damp 251, 253
rising main 503
riveters 489; *489*
rockeries 459; *406, 459*
rodding blocked drains 350
rolled steel joists (RSJs) 128, 129, 131, 503; *129, 131*
roller blinds 499; *499*
roller trays 485; *485*
rollers 64, 66, 68, 85, 483, 485; *66, 68, 485*
cleaning 483; *483*
roof windows 197, 211; *211*
Building Regulations 211
fitting 211; *211*
roofs 12, 221–36; *221–36*
construction 120, 121, 221–5; *221–5*
coverings 223; *223*
drainage 234
flashings 232–3; *232–3*
flat roofs 228–31; *228–31*
guttering 234–6; *234–6*
infestation of timbers 222
inspection 226
insulation 260, 265–8; *266–8*
joists 221, 228; *147, 228*
maintenance 226; *226*
problems 222
roofing felts 224, 228–31
roofing materials 223
safety 225; *225*
sheeting 227
types 221, 223, 224; *221*
ventilation 277–8; *277–8*
rot 12, 180, 249–50
in roof timbers 222
preventative treatment 250
rotary sanders 55–6; *55–6*
roughcast render 171; *171*
routers 468; *468*
sharpening 468
Royal Institute of British Architects 17
Royal Institution of Chartered Surveyors 17
rubber resin 495
rubber tiles *101*
laying 109; *109*
setting out 107
rubbers 80, 83; *80, 83*
rust 47
removing stain 47
treatment 60

S

safety
acid 62
asbestos-cement sheets 227
concrete mixers 439
cutting concrete slabs 447
electricity 69, 244, 280, 289–92, 294, 296
files 490
glass 200, 202
kitchens 16
lacquer 84
ladders 41
painting 64, 484
poisons 248
power drills 472
power saws 248, 465
roofs 225
strippers 59
wood preservatives 250
safety glass 199
sample boards 31; *31*
sand 438
storage 169, 439; *439*
types 169
sanded plasters 149
finishing 152
sanders 55–6, 469–70; *55–6, 469–70*
liquid sanders 58
sanding a wooden floor 55–6; *55–6*
sanding by hand 469; *469*
sanding machines 55, 470; *55, 56, 470*
sanding wood 469; *469*
sandpapers 469
sash cramps 473; *473*
sash pads 483; *483*
sash windows 197; *196, 198*
painting 78; *78*
re-cording 207; *207*
sash rail 205; *205*
sealing 264
spiral balances 197, 208; *197, 208*
saw benches 465; *465*
saw files 485; *485*
saws 463–5, 479, 492; *463–5, 479*
backsaws 463; *463*
brick-cutting saw 130; *130*
frame saws 464; *464*
hacksaws 479, 486–7; *486–7*
handsaws 463; *463*
power saws 248, 465, 479; *465, 479*
sharpening 464–5; *464–5*
storing 263, 463; *463*
scaffold frames 40, 42, 388; *42*
scaffold towers 40, 42; *40, 42*
scarf joints 477; *477*
scissors 485; *485*
scrapers
paint 481; *58, 481*
wallpaper 481; *481*
wood 470; *470*
scratchcoat 503
screed 503
screed battens 503; *157*
screwdriver bits 472; *472*
screwdrivers 473, 480, 492; *473, 492*
screws 473, 498; *473, 498*
scribe 503
scribers 486; *486*
scribing hardboard 57; *57*
scribing plasterboard 160; *160*
sealants 103; *103*

sealers
 aluminium 43, 50
 on concrete 49
 preparation 43
 types 43
seam rollers 485; *485*
secret nailing 88; *88*
security 238–44; *238, 240–4*
 burglar alarm systems 243
 fitting locks 241; *241*
 guarding against intruders 239
 how a burglar gains entry 238; *238*
 protection against fire 244; *244*
 securing doors 240; *240–1*
 securing windows 242–3; *242–3*
security chain 239, 241; *241*
security paint 85, 86, 239
self-corbelling 124; *124*
self-levelling compound 49; *49*
septic tanks 350; *350*
serrated trowels 485; *485*
serving hatches 125
set 503
sharp knives 492; *492*
sharpening techniques
 bits 471; *471*
 cabinet scrapers 470; *470*
 chisels 469; *469*
 gouges 469; *469*
 planes 467; *467*
 power router bits 468; *468*
 saws 464–5; *464–5*
 snips 487; *487*
 twist drills 471; *471*
shavehooks 481; *481*
shaver sockets 316
sheathing 503
sheds
 concrete paving 440
 security 238, 239
sheet glass 199
sheet-metal cutters 487; *487*
sheet saws 479; *479*
shellac
 knotting 53; *53*
 polishing 83
shelves
 fixing 500; *500*
 hanging on studs 139; *139*
shelving 139, 500; *139, 500*
shingles 223
 nails 224
shiplap cladding 87, 89; *87*
shooting boards 466; *466*
short circuit 503
shoulder planes 466; *466*
shovels 480; *480*
showers 369–72; *370–2*
 choosing 369
 cubicle 371–2; *371–2*
 installing 372; *372*
 running costs 287
 sealant 103, 372; *103*
 trays 311; *311*
 units 370
 wiring 323; *323*
shrouded-head taps 342
silicon carbide paper 83, 469
sills 191, 206, 253, 254, 503; *191, 206, 254*
silverfish 247; *247*
single-coat plasters 148, 151, 153
sink-clearing equipment 486; *486*
sink plungers 486; *486*
sinks
 accessories 374
 clearing blockages 348; *348*
 installation 374–5; *375*
 kitchen 374–5; *374–5*
 types 374
Sirapite B 149, 151
size 50
skirting 177, 179, 181; *18 '*

mouldings 181; *181*
 painting 79
skylights
 security 238, 239
slate
 cutting 226; *226*
 fire surrounds 389
 flooring 99; *99*
 nails 224, 497
 roofing 223, 225, 226
slater's rippers 226, 480
slatted ceilings 143, 145; *144*
sledgehammers 479; *479*
sleeper walls 120, 172, 503; *120, 172*
sliding doors
 security 192–3, 243; *192–3*
slip-joint pliers 491; *491*
slipstone 469
smoke detectors 244; *244*
smoke stains 50
smoothing planes 466; *466*
smoothing rollers 485; *485*
soakaways 503
socket outlets 12, 88, 244, 306–7, 308–10, 311; *88, 307, 308–10*
soffits 503
soft-faced mallets 473; *473*
soft mallets 488; *488*
softboard 54; *54*
softwoods 494, 503
soil conditions 407
soil pipes 361–2, 366; *361–2, 366*
solar control glass 199
soldering 488–9; *488–9*
solders 353, 488
sole plates 503
Solid Fuel Advisory Service 21, 388, 393
solid-fuel fires 386–9; *386–9*
 boilers 392, 398; *393*
 running costs 391
Solid Smokeless Fuels Federation 393
solvents 496
spade bits 472; *472*
spades 480; *480*
spalled bricks 46, 48, 503; *46*
spalled concrete 49, 454; *49*
spandrel 503
spanners 489, 492; *489*
spattering 70; *70*
spearpoint knives 480; *480*
specialists 21
specifications 20
spiral balances 197, 208; *197, 208*
spirit levels 478, 485, 492; *428, 478, 485*
spokeshaves 466; *466*
sponge stippling 70; *70*
spontaneous combustion 84
spray guns 64, 66, 69, 76, 85; *66*
 cleaning 484
spraying 68
spraying equipment 484; *484*
spraying paint faults 484
spring dividers 486; *486*
spring-toggle fixings 139; *139*
spurs
 concrete 417; *417*
 electrical 311; 311
square files 490; *490*
squares 462, 478, 486; *462, 478, 486*
squeegees 103, 485; *103, 485*
stabilizing primer 43, 46, 47, 48, 49, 51
stacks
 clearing blockages 349; *349*
staff beads 503
stained glass windows 61
 security 239
staining 74, 75, 80–1; *80, 81*

stains
 on brick 48; *48*
 on ceilings 50
 on concrete 49
 rust stains 47
 smoke stains 50
 tar stains 48; *48*
stairs 212–20; *212–20*
 access to stairwell 42; *42*
 balustrades 214, 218–20; *218–20*
 Building Regulations 213, 215, 218, 219
 carpeting 117; *117*
 construction 213–14; *213–14*
 creaking 215; *215*
 lighting planning 38
 open-tread 213, 215; *213*
 painting staircase 79
 papering stairwell 96; *96*
 repairs 215–17; *215–17*
 types 212; *212*
standpipes 377; *377*
staple guns 485; *485*
steam strippers 52, 481; *52, 481*
steel
 lintels 124, 129, 131, 198; *124, 129, 131, 198*
 pipes 351, 354
stencilling 72; *72*
 stencil brush 482; *482*
steps 213; *213*
 garden 453–4; *453–4*
stiles 503
stilson wrenches 354, 490; *354, 490*
stippling 70; *70*
stone chippings 169, 452; *452*
stones and stonework 424, 436–7; *436–7*
 adhesives 496
 building 436–7; *436–7*
 chippings 169, 452; *452*
 cleaning 44
 crazy paving 448; *448*
 estimating 424
 fire surrounds 389
 flooring 99
 lintels 124, 198; *124, 198*
 paints 64, 67, 69
 primer 43
 tiles 99, 100, 106, 223; *99*
 types 424
 walls 436; *436*
 window sills 206; *206*
stopcocks 343
stoppers 53, 503
storage 16, 500
storage cisterns 340, 379; *340*
storage heaters 296, 320–1, 390, 404; *320, 390, 404*
 running costs 287
storing chisels 469; *469*
storing saws 463; *463*
straight knives 480; *480*
straightedges 479
strap wrenches 490; *490*
strings 213, 503
strippers
 chemical 59
 hot air 59, 481; *59, 481*
 industrial 59, 60
 liquid 59
 paste 59
 safety 59
 steam 52, 481; *52, 481*
stripping 58–60; *58–60*
 flex 293; *293*
 metal 60
 paint 58–60; *58–60*
 paper 52
 wood 58–9; *58–9*
structural repairs 120–236; *120–236*
structural survey 12, 17

stud-partition walls 121, 123, 135–9, 503; *123, 135–9*
 constructing 135–7, 138; *135–7, 138*
 cutting through 126, 128; *126*
 dismantling 133; *133*
 filling an opening 127; *127*
 fixing to 139; *139*
 making hatchway 125; *125*
studs 503
subsidence 409, 503
sugar soap 48, 50
Supaglypta 90, 96; *90*
super glues 495, 496
supplementary bonding 290, 503; *290*
supporting ceilings 130
Surform files 469; *469*
surveyors 17, 18
suspended ceilings 143, 145, 146; *145, 146*
suspended floors 172; *172, 173*
sweeping chimneys 382, 387; *382*
swimming pools 460; *460*
 Building Regulations 19
 heaters 460
 liners 460
 planning permission 19, 460
switches 327–30; *327–30*
synthetic laminates
 adhesives 495, 496
synthetic latex 496
synthetic resin 496

tacky rags 481
tank cutters 379, 488; *379, 488*
tanks
 insulating 266
tap connectors 352, 365
tape
 aluminium 233; *233*
 clear 233; *233*
 flashing 233
tape measures 462, 479, 484; *462, 479, 484*
taps 342–3; *342–3*
 connecting 366, 368
 dismantling 342
 garden 378; *378*
 kitchen 374; *374*
 leaking 342
 mixer 343, 364
 plumbing 342–3; *342–3*
 replacing 365; *365*
 selecting 364
 types 364, 374; *364, 374*
tar deposits 48; *48*
tarmac 452; *452*
templates 503
tenon saws 177, 463, 479; *177, 463, 479*
tenons 205, 503; *205*
terminal screwdrivers 492; *492*
terminals 293, 503; *293*
testers 289, 492; *289, 492*
textured coatings 65, 73; *73*
thermal plasterboard 269; *269*
thermostatic shower mixers 370; *370*
thermostats 286, 318, 395; *318, 395*
thinners 63, 64, 65, 69, 76, 85, 503
thistle plasters 149, 151
threshold draught excluders 262; *262*
tile cutters 485; *485*
tile-cutting jig 104, 485; *104, 485*

tiles and tiling 99–113; *99–113*
  adhesives 103, 105, 106, 108, 112, 495, 496
  ceilings 101, 102, 112; *112, 495*
  choosing 99–101; *99–101*
  cleaning 62; *62*
  cutting 104, 106, 111, 485; *104, 108, 111*
  dry laying 107
  hanging 103, 105; *103, 105*
  plastering 150; *150*
  preparation 62
  renovating 102
  replacing 226, 227, 384; *226, 227*
  roofing 223, 224, 225, 226, 252
  selecting 99–101
  setting out 102, 107, 110, 111; *102, 107, 111*
  see also under different types of tiles
tiling tools 485; *485*
timber connectors 135; *135*
timber-frame houses 121; *121*
tinsnips 51, 487; *51, 487*
tongued-and-grooved boards 87
tools and skills 462–92; *462–92*
  builder's 478–80; *478–80*
  decorator's 481–5; *481–5*
  electrician's 492
  metalworker's 486–91; *486–91*
  plumber's 486–91; *486–91*
  woodworker's 462–77; *462–77*
topping a saw 464; *464*
torches 492
toughened glass 199
track lighting 326; *326*
trailing sockets 294; *294*
traps 348, 350, 503; *348, 350*
treads 214–17, 503; *214*
trees 409; *409*
  planning permission 19
triangular files 490; *490*
trowels 478, 485; *478, 485*
try squares 462, 478, 486; *462, 486*
tube benders 488; *488*
tube cutters 353, 487; *353, 487*
tumble dryers
  running costs 287
turpentine as thinners 63
twist drills 471, 472, 488; *471, 472, 488*
Tyrolean finish 171; *171*

UV

U-values 260
unbacked fabrics 91, 95; *91*
undercoats 67, 503
underlays 116
  fixing 117
  roofing 224
universal saws 479; *479*
urethane
  in cellars 258
  panelling 89
valley flashings 232; *232*
valley gutters 234
valleys 222, 225; *222, 225*
vapour barriers 265, 267, 268, 503
vapour checks 143, 503
varnishes 74, 75, 76, 82, 86
varnishing
  metalwork 85, 86
  woodwork 82
veneered timber panelling 89
ventilation 265, 267, 275–84
  air conditioners 284; *284*
  Building Regulations 125, 277
  extractors 279–81; *279–81*

floors 276; *276*
  heat-exchanging ventilators 282–3; *282–3*
  open fires 382
  roofs 277–8; *277–8*
  walls 276; *276*
ventilators 275, 282–3; *275, 282–3*
  airbricks 276; *276*
  roof vents 277, 278; *277*
  window vents 275; *275*
verdigris 61
verges 222, 225, 230; *222, 225, 230*
vices 474; *474*
Vinaglypta 90; *90*
vinyl floorings 115, 118; *115, 118*
  laying 118; *118*
vinyl tiles 57, 62, 100, 102, 108; *100*
  gluing 108; *108*
  self-adhesive tiles 108
  setting out 107
vinyl wallcovering 52, 90, 91, 96
  blown vinyl 52
  peeling off 52

W-Z

WC 344–5; *344–5*
  augers 349, 486; *349, 486*
  blockages 349; *349*
  cisterns 340, 344–6, 360; *360*
  draining cisterns 340; *340*
  flap valves 344; *344*
  float valves 345, 346; *346*
  installing 362; *362*
  pans 360–1; *360–1*
  plungers 486; *486*
  removing 361; *361*
  small bore waste system 362; *362*
wall fixings 498–9; *498–9*
wall lights 331
wall plates 133, 134, 503
wall plugs 479, 498–9; *479*
wall studs 137
wall ties 122, 431, 432, 434, 435, 503; *122, 431, 432, 434*
wallboards 54, 87, 123; *54, 123*
  adhesives 89, 97; *89*
  pinning 89
  see also under different types of wallboards
wallbrush 482; *482*
wallcoverings 52, 90–8; *52, 90–1, 93–8*
  cutting 93; *93*
  estimating quantities 92
  pasting 93; *93*
  scrapers 481; *481*
  stripping 52, 481; *52*
  types 90–1; *90–1*
  washable 52, 91; *91*
walls 122–41; *122–7, 129–41*
  bonding 426; *426*
  brick 421–2, 426, 428–33
  building 429–31, 436; *429–31*
  cavity 120, 122, 198, 229, 435, 501; *122*
  closing 127; *127*
  concrete blocks 423–4, 434–5
  construction 121, 135–41
  copings 430; *430*
  cracks 12, 46, 73; *46*
  dividing 434
  external walls 122; *122*
  footings 426, 427
  formation 120
  insulation 87, 260, 268–70; *269*
  internal 123; *123*
  lining 94

lintels 124, 198; *124*
  openings 124–6; *124–6*
  painting 67–73; *68, 69*
  papering 94–5; *94–5*
  parapets 229; *229*
  partitions 135–41; *135–41*
  plaster 50–1, 148
  removing 128–34; *129–34*
  retaining 437; *437*
  spanning openings 124–6; *124–6*
  stability 426
  stone 424, 436; *436*
  structure 122–3; *122–3*
  textured coatings 73; *73*
  types 420; *420, 424*
  ventilation 276, 280
  waterproofing 254, 256–8; *256–7*
washbasins see basins
washers 342, 345; *342, 345*
washing machines
  drainage 377
  enamel paint 86
  installation 316
  plumbing 376–7; *376–7*
  running costs 287
wasps 247; *247*
waste disposal units 375; *375*
  installation 316, 375; *375*
wastepipes
  unblocking 348; *348*
water closet see WC
water gardens 455–9; *455–9*
  bog gardens 459; *459*
  pond liners 455–7; *455–7*
  pumps 458; *458*
  waterfalls 458, 459; *459*
water hammer 503
water heaters 316, 380; *380*
  running costs 287
water level 444, 478; *478*
water pressure 346, 369, 376
water softeners 378; *378*
waterfalls 459; *459*
  pumps 458; *458*
waterproofing walls 254, 256–8; *256–7*
wax polish 75, 76; *74*
  applying 84
  removing 84
weather bars 187; *187*
weatherboard moulding 187; *187*
weatherboarding 79; *79*
weatherproofing doors 187, 263; *187, 263*
web cramps 473; *473*
wet-and-dry paper 481
wet rot 180, 249; *249*
  treatment 249
wheelbarrows 480; *480*
wheelbrace 471; *471*
white spirit
  as thinners 63, 64, 65, 69, 76
  removing wax polish 84
window sills 206, 503; *206*
  causes of damp 253
  drip moulding 254; *254*
windows 19, 196–211, 238, 239, 242–3
  aluminium 197; *197*
  Building Regulations 19, 209, 211
  casement locks 78, 86, 242
  causes of damp 253
  construction 196–7; *196–7*
  fitting 198; *198*
  frames 205; *205*
  leaded lights 203; *203*
  lintels 198; *198*
  locks 78, 86, 242
  maintenance 205
  metal-framed 204
  painting 78, 86; *78*
  panelling around 88, 163; *88, 163*
  papering around 95

rattling 204
  ready-made 209; *209–10*
  re-cording 207; *207*
  repairs 202–8; *202–8*
  replacing 209–10; *209–10*
  sash locks 78, 242
  sealing 264; *264*
  security 238, 239; *242–3*
  sills 206; *206*
  spiral balances 197, 208; *197, 208*
  sticking 204
  tiling around 104, 106; *104*
  types 196–7; *196–7*
  ventilation 275, 280; *275*
  see also under different types of windows
wire brushes 481, 491; *481, 491*
wire cutters 492; *492*
wire strippers 492; *492*
wire wool 491; *491*
wired glass 199
wires 316–21
  earthing 288, 290, 297, 306, 501; *290, 297*
wiring 288–336
Wiring Regulations 288, 290, 326
wood and woodwork 74–84; *74, 76–84*
  adhesives 495, 496
  bleaching stains 54
  filler 53
  finishing 74–5; *74*
  fire surrounds 389
  French polishing 75, 83; *83*
  lacquering 75, 76, 84; *86*
  lintels 124
  oiling 84
  painting 76–9; *76–9*
  panelling 87–8; *88*
  preparing 53–9; *53–9*
  priming 53–4, 76; *53–4*
  staining 80–1; *80–1*
  tools 462–77; *462–77*
  treating new timber 53, 250
  varnishing 82; *82*
  waxing 84
  woodworm treatment 246–7; *246*
wood hardener 249
wood preservers 75, 76, 81
  types 250
wood primer 43, 53, 76
wood scrapers 470
  sharpening 470; *470*
wood stains 75, 76, 80, 81, 82
woodchip paper 90; *67, 90*
wooden floats 478; *478*
wooden pathways 451; *451*
woodscrews 473
woodworker's bench 474; *474*
woodworker's tool kit 462–77; *462–77*
woodworker's vice 474; *474*
woodworking joints 475–7; *475–7*
woodworm infestation 222, 246–7; *246*
  treatment 55, 246–7; *246*
work gloves 480, 481; *481*
work platforms 42, 46, 66, 131, 171, 225; *42, 96, 98, 171*
work sequence 22–3; *76*
working height 125
working outdoors 406–60; *406–60*
Workmate bench 474; *474*
workshops 16
  electrical circuits 335; *335*
  lighting planning 38
wrenches 490; *490*
wrought ironwork 60
  gates 419
yard gully 349; *349*
yellow flint paper 469
zinc flashing 232
zinc phosphate primer 43, 60